MELVILLE

Adam Ochs CHS
11/7/00

MELVILLE
A BIOGRAPHY

LAURIE ROBERTSON-LORANT

University of Massachusetts Press
Amherst

For my sons, Christopher and Mark,
whose "Go for it, Mom!" kept me going,
with all my love

First paperback edition published by the University of Massachusetts Press, 1998
Reprinted by arrangement with Clarkson N. Potter/Publishers
Printed in the United States of America
LC 98-4899
ISBN 1-55849-145-7

Library of Congress Cataloging-in-Publication Data

Robertson-Lorant, Laurie, 1940–
    Melville : a biography / Laurie Robertson-Lorant. — 1st pbk. ed.
        p.   cm.
    Originally published: New York : Clarkson/Potter Publishers,
c1996.
    Includes bibliographical references (p.   ) and index.
    ISBN 1-55849-145-7 (pbk. : alk. paper)
    1. Melville, Herman, 1819–1891–Biography.   2. Novelists,
American — 19th century — Biography.   I. Title.
PS2386.R635   1998
813'.3 — dc21
    [B]   98-4899
                                                        CIP

This book is published with the support and cooperation of the
University of Massachusetts, Boston.

British Library Cataloguing in Publication data are available.

"No species of writing seems more worthy of cultivation than biography since none can be more delightful or more useful; none can more certainly enchain the heart by irresistible interest, or more widely diffuse instruction to every diversity of condition."

Catherine Gansevoort Lansing

"He most improves who studies with delight
And learns sound Morals while he learns to write."

"Honor and Fame, with Diadems and Empires are the Arms of ambitious Men, but he that is Master of an excellent Pen, transcends them all."

"Great gains come daily to ingenious men
From that admired itinerant, the Pen."

Allan Melvill's copybook, Mr. Staniford's School, 1796

"I think we are very much in debt to the Phoenicians *for the invention of wrighting* [sic]. *I do not know what we should do without it."*

Julia Maria Melvill to Augusta Melville, 1834

"You must have plenty of sea-room to tell the Truth in, especially, when it seems to have an aspect of newness, as America did in 1492, though it was then just as old, and perhaps older than Asia, only those sagacious philosophers, the common sailors, had never seen it before; swearing it was all water and moonshine there."

Herman Melville, "Hawthorne and His Mosses" (1850)

Contents

List of Illustrations viii

Preface to the Paperback Edition xii

Preface to the First Edition xiv

Acknowledgments xviii

1. Lofty Origins 1

2. Snug Investments 17

3. Elegant Negligence 31

4. Tormented with an Itch for Things Remote 51

5. A Naturally Roving Disposition 73

6. The Wild, the Watery, the Unshored 87

7. The Floodgates of the Wonder-World 105

8. A Little Experience in the Art of Book-Craft 127

9. Fierce Cannibal Delight 151

10. Creating the Creative 175

11. The Man Who Lived Among the Cannibals 195

12. The Prince of Whales 217

13. The Ardent Virginian 239

14. A Sort of Sea-Feeling in the Country 257

15. One Grand Hooded Phantom 275

16. King of the Cannibals   299

17. Counter-friction to the Machine   321

18. Shadows Foreshadowing Deeper Shadows   341

19. What Sort of Bamboozling Story Is This?   361

20. Childe Herman's Pilgrimage   375

21. A Convulsed and Half-Dissolved Society   401

22. Fierce Battles and Civil Strife   425

23. A Time Rich in Catastrophes   457

24. A Survivor of the Civil War   479

25. A Time When Peace Had Horrors of Its Own   499

26. Agonies That Operate Unseen   519

27. Devilish Tantalization of the Gods   539

28. Confronting Sphinx and Angel   565

29. The Hellish Society of Men   583

30. The Rose Farmer in the Garden of Truant Eve   599

Afterword   617

Notes   621

Selected Bibliography   675

Illustration Credits   685

Index   687

LIST OF ILLUSTRATIONS

Page x: Genealogy

Page xxvi: Engraving of the landing of General Lafayette at Castle Garden, New York, on August 16, 1824.

Page 16: Portrait of Allan Melvill by John Rubens Smith, 1810.

Page 30: Major Thomas Melvill's house on Green Street in Boston.

Page 50: Melville's house in Lansingburgh, New York.

Page 72: Portrait of Herman Melville by Asa Twitchell, c. 1847.

Page 86: Whale stamps from the logbook of the 1840s whaling ship *William Baker.*

Page 104: Daguerreotype of Richard Tobias Greene, 1846.

Page 126: Miniature portrait of Gansevoort Melville, 1836.

Page 150: Daguerreotype of Elizabeth Shaw Melville, c. 1847.

Page 174: Photograph of Evert Duyckinck, c. 1847.

Page 194: Flogging as practiced on naval vessels in the 1840s.

Page 216: Portrait of Maria Gansevoort Melville, c. 1820.

Page 238: Photograph of Sarah Morewood, c. 1855.

Page 256: Engraving of Nathaniel Hawthorne by T. Phillibrown (after the portrait by Cephas G. Thompson).

Page 274: Drawing of a Marquesan native by Alfred T. Agate for the U.S. Exploring Expedition, 1838–1842.

Page 298: Photograph of Augusta Melville, c. 1855.

Page 320: The Halls of Justice, New York, also known as "The Tombs."

Page 340: Photograph of Lemuel Shaw, c. 1855.

Page 360: Photograph of the Melville children, from left to right, Stanwix, Frances, Malcolm, and Elizabeth, c. 1860.

Page 374: Watercolor of Mar Saba by Peter Toft, 1882.

Page 400: Melville's sketch of Arrowhead, 1860.

Page 424: Photograph of Herman Melville by Rodney H. Dewey, 1861.

Page 456: Photograph of Maria Gansevoort Melville, c. 1865.

Page 478: Photograph of Kate Gansevoort, c. 1864.

Page 498: Tintype of Malcolm Melville, c. 1865.

Page 518: Tintype of Herman Melville, 1868.

Page 538: Photograph of Peter Gansevoort, c. 1870.

Page 564: Manuscript of the opening stanzas of *The New Ancient of Days* (originally *The Old Boy of the Cave*).

Page 582: Photograph of Lizzie Melville, 1872.

Page 596: Drawing of a Marquesan Island scene by Alfred T. Agate for the U.S. Exploring Expedition, 1838–1842.

MELVILL[E]

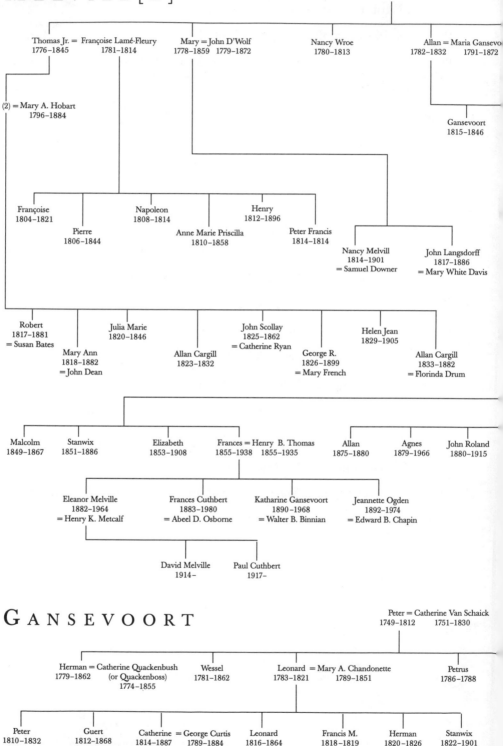

Thomas = Priscilla Scollay
1751–1832 1755–1833

Thomas Jr. = Françoise Lamé-Fleury
1776–1845   1781–1814

Mary = John D'Wolf
1778–1859 1779–1872

Nancy Wroe
1780–1813

Allan = Maria Gansevoort
1782–1832 1791–1872

(2) = Mary A. Hobart
1796–1884

Gansevoort
1815–1846

Françoise
1804–1821

Pierre
1806–1844

Napoleon
1808–1814

Anne Marie Priscilla
1810–1858

Henry
1812–1896

Peter Francis
1814–1814

Nancy Melvill
1814–1901
= Samuel Downer

John Langsdorff
1817–1886
= Mary White Davis

Robert
1817–1881
= Susan Bates

Mary Ann
1818–1882
= John Dean

Julia Marie
1820–1846

Allan Cargill
1823–1832

John Scollay
1825–1862
= Catherine Ryan

George R.
1826–1899
= Mary French

Helen Jean
1829–1905

Allan Cargill
1833–1882
= Florinda Drum

Malcolm
1849–1867

Stanwix
1851–1886

Elizabeth
1853–1908

Frances = Henry B. Thomas
1855–1938 1855–1935

Allan
1875–1880

Agnes
1879–1966

John Roland
1880–1915

Eleanor Melville
1882–1964
= Henry K. Metcalf

Frances Cuthbert
1883–1980
= Abeel D. Osborne

Katharine Gansevoort
1890–1968
= Walter B. Binnian

Jeannette Ogden
1892–1974
= Edward B. Chapin

David Melville
1914–

Paul Cuthbert
1917–

GANSEVOORT

Peter = Catherine Van Schaick
1749–1812 1751–1830

Herman = Catherine Quackenbush
1779–1862   (or Quackenboss)
1774–1855

Wessel
1781–1862

Leonard = Mary A. Chandonette
1783–1821   1789–1851

Petrus
1786–1788

Peter
1810–1832

Guert
1812–1868

Catherine = George Curtis
1814–1887   1789–1884

Leonard
1816–1864

Francis M.
1818–1819

Herman
1820–1826

Stanwix
1822–1901

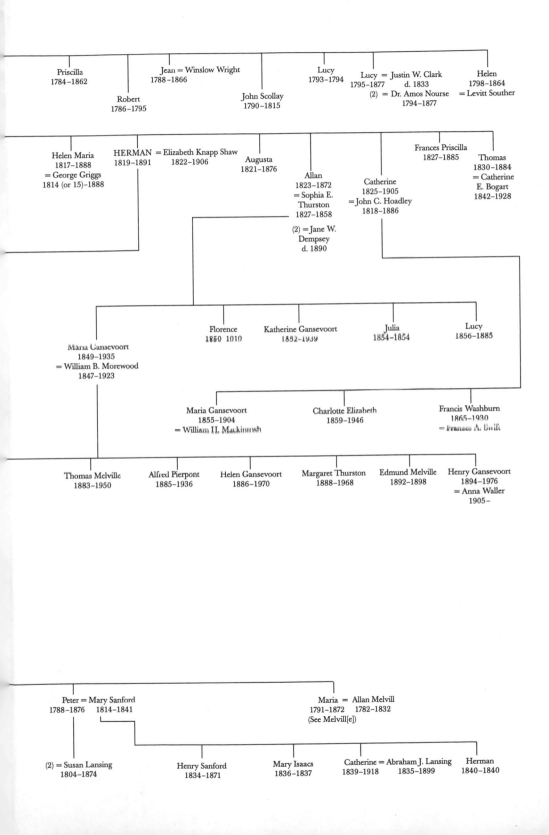

Priscilla
1784–1862

Robert
1786–1795

Jean = Winslow Wright
1788–1866

John Scollay
1790–1815

Lucy
1793–1794

Lucy = Justin W. Clark
1795–1877   d. 1833
(2) = Dr. Amos Nourse
1794–1877

Helen
1798–1864
= Levitt Souther

Helen Maria
1817–1888
= George Griggs
1814 (or 15)–1888

HERMAN = Elizabeth Knapp Shaw
1819–1891   1822–1906

Augusta
1821–1876

Allan
1823–1872
= Sophia E.
Thurston
1827–1858

(2) = Jane W.
Dempsey
d. 1890

Catherine
1825–1905
= John C. Hoadley
1818–1886

Frances Priscilla
1827–1885

Thomas
1830–1884
= Catherine
E. Bogart
1842–1928

Maria Gansevoort
1849–1935
= William B. Morewood
1847–1923

Florence
1860–1910

Katherine Gansevoort
1852–1939

Julia
1854–1854

Lucy
1856–1885

Maria Gansevoort
1855–1904
= William H. Mackintosh

Charlotte Elizabeth
1859–1946

Francis Washburn
1865–1930
= Frances A. Swift

Thomas Melville
1883–1950

Alfred Pierpont
1885–1936

Helen Gansevoort
1886–1970

Margaret Thurston
1888–1968

Edmund Melville
1892–1898

Henry Gansevoort
1894–1976
= Anna Waller
1905–

Peter = Mary Sanford
1788–1876   1814–1841

(2) = Susan Lansing
1804–1874

Maria = Allan Melvill
1791–1872   1782–1832
(See Melvill[e])

Henry Sanford
1834–1871

Mary Isaacs
1836–1837

Catherine = Abraham J. Lansing
1839–1918   1835–1899

Herman
1840–1840

PREFACE TO THE PAPERBACK EDITION

Since the first edition of this book appeared in June 1996, I have spent a year teaching in France. There I was happily removed from the debates over domestic violence in the Melville household that were swirling in the electronic air back home. Although I won't deny that during periods of heavy drinking, Melville may have struck out at Lizzie physically as well as verbally, I am not ready to label him a "wife-beater" or devalue his great literary art because of his character flaws.

Men who are egotistical and insecure can be charming to casual acquaintances and beastly to those they love and need the most, but a man can be abusive without stooping to battery. Although we know Melville often subjected his wife and children to hurtful remarks and emotional neglect, I find it hard to imagine him standing over Lizzie with a tire iron. Until further evidence emerges, I will continue to hope he channeled most of his anger into writing rather than inflicting it on his family.

Melville's sexuality, politics, and everyday behavior remain in many ways a mys-

tery. "If the acutest sage be often at his wits' end to understand living character, shall those who are not sages expect to run and read character in those mere phantoms which flit along a page, like shadows along a wall?" asks the narrator of *The Confidence-Man: His Masquerade*. What fascinates me about Melville's personality is his extraordinary resilience. He used humor to defend himself, and although he teetered on the edge of the abyss, he always managed to pull back in time. He read voraciously, seeking beauty in art and literature and wisdom in philosophy, and he wrote until the day he died.

Condemned to a painful psychological purgatory all his life, Melville returned obsessively to certain characters and themes; yet, at the same time, he strove toward new forms, new styles, new ways of looking at the world. In his later years, he seems to have made a kind of peace with himself and those around him, though he suffered and made others suffer along the way.

Most people, observed Margaret Fuller, live "mutilated lives." Although Ahab's fanatical pursuit of the white whale is blasphemous and doomed, the maimed captain's rage has its heroic side. Through Ahab, Melville expresses his anger and ours at the crippling compromises life forces us to make. Whatever is heroic in the human spirit surges through Melville's robust poetry and oceanic prose. Whatever in human beings yearns to explore new worlds, to share the pleasures of a sensual and spiritual paradise with a soulmate, lover, friend, lives on in Melville's prose and poetry. Whatever in the American character aspires to a true democracy whose strength is measured not by its acquisitions, but by its "all-hands-round" camaraderie with the rest of the world, lives on in Melville's relentless interrogation of the dangerous assumptions about race, class, and gender embedded in cultural constructions of our national identity.

At the first International Melville Society Conference in Volos, Greece, in July 1997, I was reminded how many devoted readers Melville has around the world. Many people know him primarily through *Moby-Dick,* an acknowledged masterpiece of world as well as American literature. I hope this new paperback edition will illuminate Melville's other writings and his turbulent life and times for an even larger audience. Finally, I want to thank the Melville fans who have pointed out the embarrassing slips of the pen that seem to creep into a book of this size. I hope I have corrected them all.

Southborough, Massachusetts
December 30, 1997

PREFACE TO THE FIRST EDITION

No American writer has been more puzzled over and written about, more lambasted and lion-ized, than Herman Melville. After achieving both fame and notoriety early in his career with Typee *and* Omoo, *which were based on his voyage to the South Seas, he published half a dozen more novels and a dozen or so short stories for popular magazines, then turned to poetry, publishing two major works that mark him as the first modernist poet in America. Although a small coterie of admirers in British universities passed dog-eared copies of* Moby-Dick *from hand to hand, and a number of young Americans became writers as a result of reading* Typee *and* Moby-Dick, *for decades the standard literary histories classified Melville as a minor travel writer and virtually ignored his novels, stories, and poems. Publication of Raymond Weaver's* Herman Melville, Mariner and Mystic *in 1921, Melville's posthumous* Billy Budd, Foretopman *in 1924, and Lewis Mumford's* Herman Melville: A Study of His Life and Vision *in 1929 sparked the Melville Revival, a reevaluation of his work by students of both literature and history.*

With the 1951 publication of Jay Leyda's monumental *The Melville Log: A Documentary Life of Herman Melville, 1819–1891* and the 1967 appearance of Leon Howard's *Herman Melville: A Biography*, which was based on the *Log*, Melville became firmly enshrined among America's canonical writers. Literary historians regard him as one of the greatest, if not the greatest of them all, and he has become the most written-about writer in America, though not the most widely appreciated or understood. Having gained a devoted readership both at home and abroad, he has been the subject of numerous dissertations, books, and articles, though few full-length biographies.[1]

Since I completed my dissertation on Melville and Race in 1972, much new material has come to light. In 1975, Walter D. Kring and Jonathan S. Carey published "Two Discoveries Concerning Herman Melville," and in 1983, a trunk containing five hundred Melville family letters and a manuscript draft of *Typee* was found in a barn in Gansevoort, New York. Even after the New York Public Library acquired these new Melville family papers in 1984, most scholars skimmed through the letters noting references to Melville and paying little attention to what the women in the family had to say.[2]

As a graduate student, I, too, paid little attention to Melville's private life and family. Following the lead of traditional Melvilleans who tended to see the women around Melville as mere appendages to the great man, I virtually ignored Melville's domestic life in deference to his literary career and his ideas. Ironically, I returned to family life as soon as I received my Ph.D. and dropped out of the Melville Society; during those years, I thought that if I ever returned to academic life, I would study nineteenth-century women writers, not pursue the Great White Male.

For about a decade now, Melville scholarship has been undergoing a sea change, with debates centering on Melville's sexuality, his relationship with his wife and children, and the degree of responsibility he bears for his older son's suicide. Paradoxically, whereas many of the great Melville scholars in the early years portrayed Melville as an *isolato*, many contemporary scholars feel Melville was actively engaged in his family and his culture, and highly sensitive to the ways in which injustices based on race, class, and gender differences kept America from living up to her own professed ideals.[3]

When I returned to Melville studies in 1987, I decided to start from scratch. Rereading his books and letters, digging through the voluminous family archives, and familiarizing myself with the latest scholarship gave me a new understanding of Melville, especially his later years, and I found the standard descriptions woefully inadequate.

Melville bristled with contradictions. Descended from Revolutionary War heroes on both sides of his family, he was an egalitarian Democrat who longed for a return to Republican ideals. A rover who traveled halfway around the world chasing whales and languishing in the Marquesas, he longed for emotional and financial security. Yearning for an intimacy he could neither define nor sustain, he married well but sought the company of men. He depended on the women in his life but resented his dependency. He doted on his children and grandchildren but often frightened them. Even when rejection, anger, and despair held him in thrall, he could amuse himself and others by telling apocryphal stories about the illegitimate children he had fathered in the South Seas.

Family members reportedly caught glimpses of the older Melville, in his red flannel sailor's shirt, standing or dancing in front of a mirror. Iconoclastic and irreverent, he belonged to an imperious clan that included seven siblings, innumerable cousins, aunts and uncles, a devoted and long-suffering wife, and four children, at least three of whom bore painful psychic scars. Although he wrote much cryptic fiction and abstruse poetry, he also wrote muscular poetry and oceanic prose that sends chills up and down the spines of readers whose linguistic ears are attuned to the cadences of Shakespeare and the King James Bible. Ideologically egalitarian but patrician to the core, he embodied the crippling contradictions inherent in American society. His writings reflect societal conflicts over slavery and imperialism, increased pressures on the family resulting from industrialization and Victorian sexual repression, and the crisis of faith precipitated by new scientific discoveries.

Melville was the troubled conscience of the age. His provocative, prophetic books compose a kind of underground history of America, and, not surprisingly, in an age of strident nationalism and expansionism, he was doomed to failure. As Vernon Parrington put it, "Such a man would not so much turn critic as embody criticism. His life laid upon America, was a yardstick to measure the shortcomings of a professed civilization." The lack of recognition and remuneration he received for his work exemplifies the plight of the visionary artist in a materialistic society. Although fame and neglect conspired equally to devour him, he survived the "Doom! Doom! Doom!" that D. H. Lawrence saw hovering "in the very dark trees of America." His books were lifeboats.[4]

I suppose it was my love of the sea and armchair adventure that initially attracted me to *Moby-Dick,* and Melville's "sperm-whale vision"—by which I mean his ability to entertain two (or more) contradictory ideas simultaneously—held me fast. Like Walt Whitman, he was "one of the roughs," a boisterous sailor who loved ribald jokes and racy stories, but he was also a shy, gentleman genius. He could pull off pranks one minute and probe metaphysical depths the next without skipping a beat. He drew on biblical and classical literature, European philosophy and Oriental wisdom, Puritan sermons and frontier tall tales, shipboard humor, popular novels, and the penny press to create literary masterpieces. Quintessentially American and thoroughly cosmopolitan, Melville contained multitudes.

Tragedy and comedy flowed with equal force through Melville's veins. Because he is larger than life in so many ways, I was reluctant to construct a biography that supports a single thesis rather than one that conveys what it might have felt like to live the life of this marvelous enigma, this ambiguity. I wanted not to reduce him to a psychological case study, but to show him as a living, breathing human being involved in a web of relation-ships, a complex and contradictory man who could be as insensitive to those around him as he was sensitive to the issues of his times.

Melville's struggle for personal fulfillment and literary greatness intersected with young America's struggles to forge a national identity. He believed America was losing her soul to slavery, imperialism, materialism, and greed, and his writings are a protest against injustice. Many modern readers, however, express disappointment that despite his abhorrence of slavery, he evidently did not involve himself in the antislavery move-ment or other political and social causes. While strong women such as Lydia Maria Child attacked slavery, Indian removal, and urban poverty head on, Melville concealed his crit-icisms of society amid tropes and symbols; yet, his writings were a protest against injus-tice. He saw himself as a citizen of a multiethnic Republic, an "Anarcharsis Clootz deputation from all the isles of the sea, and all the ends of the earth," as Ishmael put it, and I have tried to give readers of this book a sense of the cultural diversity of nineteenth-century America and Melville's awareness of that diversity.[5]

It might be said that the biographer works not with pen and paper, but with "smoke and mirrors." Biography is both a science and an art; it reminds us of the danger of con-fusing self with subject, fact with truth. Even though a biography must be solidly grounded in documentary evidence, intuition and empathy are intellectually respectable ways of knowing, too. Only fictional characters have to be consistent and their motives plausible, as Melville pointed out in *The Confidence-Man;* real people are unpredictable and para-doxical. Writing a biography is like doing a jigsaw puzzle with millions of pieces, many of them missing, and I am suspicious of biographies in which everything fits perfectly.

"Skeletons walk where questions begin," Eleanor Melville Metcalf remarked cryp-tically, speaking of Melville's brother Gansevoort. I think she meant that it is the unan-swered questions about a person that keep the spirit of inquiry alive. I have tried to convey essential *truths* about Herman Melville in such a way that a sensational new "fact" would enhance and complicate, but not invalidate, the portrait I have created here.[6]

Although I can't see Greylock from my window as I write this, in my mind's eye, I see "one grand hooded phantom," the ghost of Herman Melville, beckoning me over the edge of the next horizon, teasing me with tantalizing glimpses until I am forced to realize that "only in the heart of quickest perils; only in the eddyings of his angry flukes; only when in the profound unbounded sea, can the fully invested whale be truly and liv-ingly found out." The impossibility of grasping the "ungraspable phantom" ensures that the pursuit will never end, and in the last analysis, perhaps all anyone can say is what Pip says about the gold doubloon Ahab nailed to the *Pequod*'s mast: "I look, you look, he looks; we look, you look, they look."

ACKNOWLEDGMENTS

It's hard to imagine where Melville scholarship would be without the work of an earlier generation of Melvilleans that included Jay Leyda, Leon Howard, Charles Anderson, Merrel R. Davis, William H. Gilman, Wilson Heflin, Howard P. Vincent, and other pathfinders who showed us where and how to look, and why.

My re-entry into the Melville Society brought unexpected dividends, chief among them friendships with a new generation of Melville scholars. Joyce Adler's graciousness and generosity set the tone for many Melville gatherings; Marvin Fisher's passion for justice and dedication to excellent teaching helped me keep my two careers in balance; Carolyn Karcher's fierce commitment to scholarship inspired my efforts early in the game; and Lea Newman's irrepressible energy, enthusiasm, and encouragement spurred me on through the terrors of "Black Notch" and the "Mad Maid's Bellows-Pipe." Dominique Arnaud-Marçais's splendid hospitality made my 1992 sojourn in Paris unforgettable; Bruce Franklin's iconoclasm revitalized Melville studies; Bob Ryan's urbane wit and willingness to share information and ideas kept me on my toes; and Neal

Tolchin's awareness of the role grief played in Melville's early life made him a sensitive and intelligent critic of my *Pierre* chapter. Both Marvin Fisher and Lea Newman read much of the manuscript at one time or another, and their comments, criticism, and queries have been astute and wise. I am very grateful to both of them for their unfailing encouragement and support.

More recently, Melville scholars Wyn Kelley and Sheila Post-Lauria have been shipmates and midwives to the manuscript, and in the process, they have become fast friends. They have shared their knowledge freely, and they have taken precious time from their own work to make insightful comments on my manuscript. Our frequent telephone conversations, occasional luncheon meetings, trips to conferences, and marathon manuscript-swapping sessions kept me intellectually alive and sane. Their ideas are woven into the fabric of this book in myriad subtle ways as well as in the more obvious ones cited in the endnotes. Wyn read and reread the manuscript with keen intelligence, a sense of style, and a sharp eye. Her book on Melville's urban imagination gave me both theoretical and practical perspectives on what Manhattan meant to Melville. Sheila's ground-breaking study of antebellum literary culture greatly enriched my understanding of Melville's relationship to the marketplace.

Melvilleans Charlene Avallone, Hans Bergmann, Walter Bezanson, John Bryant, Gail Coffler, Hennig Cohen, Stanton Garner, Harrison Hayford, Tom Heffernan, Walt Herbert, Buford Jones, Joyce Kennedy, Kay Kier, Alma MacDougall, Merton Sealts, and Don Yannella have also been helpful and encouraging. Dr. Walter Donald Kring shared his views on the Melvilles' near-divorce with me and read the 1867 chapter of my manuscript critically. Distinguished Civil War historian William H. Freehling gave me a historian's perspective on my Civil War chapters, as did Hennig Cohen and Marvin Fisher, and naval historian William Fowler graciously sent me a copy of *Under Two Flags*.

Melville's great-grandson Paul Metcalf was most generous with his time and very supportive of my efforts to approach his family history with an open mind. Whenever I visited Paul and Nancy Metcalf's hilltop farm in Chester, they gave me a warm welcome. I am very grateful to Paul for his irreverent wit, his forthrightness, and his kind and supportive response to portions of the manuscript.

Without the courteous and knowledgeable people who work in museums and research libraries, scholars could not do their jobs, and without the Gansevoort-Lansing Collection, Melville studies would not exist. Mimi Bowling, Melanie Yolles, and Margaret Glover of the New York Public Library's Rare Books and Manuscripts Division, where the bulk of the Melville papers are housed, were unfailingly courteous, helpful, and efficient, as were staffers at the library's Berg Collection.

Robert G. Newman, a mainstay of Melville studies for many years, gave me shelter at the Berkshire Athenaeum, and both he and Ruth T. Degenhardt, Local History

Librarian at the Athenaeum, have been enormously helpful and fun to work with over the years. Denis Lesieur, Chief Librarian at the Lenox Library, opened Judge Julius Rockwell's unpublished papers and answered questions about the old courthouse and the Curtis Hotel, and the irrepressible Polly Pearce, curator of the Local History Room at the Stockbridge Public Library, shared her knowledge of Melville's contemporaries with me.

Eugene Taylor shared illuminating memories of working with Dr. Henry A. Murray, William A. Whittlesey III of Pittsfield described the "slave room" he had seen in the basement of Arrowhead when he was a child, and Grand Librarian Ward Williamson of Boston's Tremont Temple answered my questions about Major Thomas Melvill and Freemasonry. Lansingburgh historian Kathleen Tivnan showed me through the Spofford-Melville house in Lansingburgh and painted a vivid and attractive picture of the village in its heyday. Frances Broderick and Warren Broderick shared their vast knowledge of Lansingburgh history with me. John De Marco, owner of the Lyrical Ballad Bookstore in Saratoga Springs, New York, showed me his recent Melville acquisitions, including a bankbook belonging to Maria Melville. Walt Herbert, curator of the Osborne Collection at Southwestern Texas University, sent me material and responded to my queries, as did Duncan Osborne, a Melville descendant.

Susan Hand, Sally Linden, and other members of the staff of the Clapp Library at Wellesley College were unfailingly courteous and accommodating despite my sometimes importunate demands. At Harvard, Mike Raines and Harley Holden of the University Archives piloted me through the Murray Papers, and Dennison Beach and Melanie Wisner tirelessly fetched letters, books, and manuscripts from the bowels of the Houghton Library. Jean Ashton, May N. Stone, Diane Arecco, and Wendy Haynes of the perennially endangered New-York Historical Society; Leslie Nolan and Deborah Waters of the Museum of the City of New York; Winifred Collins and Virginia Smith of the Massachusetts Historical Society; Anne Caiger, curator of the Leyda Collection at UCLA; Gale Munro of the Naval Museum; and Chuck Haberlein of the Naval Historical Foundation all provided their assistance. Librarian W. Gregory Gallagher took me on a tour of the Century Club, and Jack Putnam shared his insights about Melville at the South Street Seaport.

At one time or another in the course of my research, I also visited, corresponded with, or telephoned the Albany Institutes of History and Art, the New York State Archives and Records Administration, the Boston Athenaeum, the Boston Public Library, the Schlesinger Library at Radcliffe, Widener Library, the Tozzer Library at Harvard's Peabody Museum of Ethnography, the Countway Library at the Harvard Medical School, the John Hay Library at Brown University, the American Antiquarian

Society in Worcester, Mystic Seaport, the New Bedford Whaling Museum, the Nantucket Whaling Museum, the Snug Harbor Cultural Center, the United States Naval Archives, and the Newberry Library in Chicago, and I am grateful for their assistance.

Well-preserved and well-catalogued manuscripts and letters—not Xeroxes, not microfilm, not typed synopses or transcripts—are indispensable to scholars. It is imperative that researchers be able to touch, smell, and see original documents, as sensory impressions, illuminating juxtapositions, and serendipitous discoveries occur often when scholars and students can handle original documents. Documents convey the spirit of their authors and inspire awe in even the most jaded and harried of researchers; moreover, archival research still yields unexpected discoveries, as when I came upon Dr. Titus Munson Coan's undiscovered notes of an 1892 conversation with Lizzie Melville that had been misfiled among the Coan Papers at the New-York Historical Society. This could never have happened had I not been able to consult the original documents.

Archives and private foundations that support teachers, scholars, writers, and artists are also absolutely vital to American education and culture. I am very grateful to the American Council of Learned Societies for awarding me a fellowship that enabled me to take a year's leave of absence from teaching and other school responsibilities to work on my book. Although the year off was not enough time to finish the project, without the year off, I could never have completed it. Having recently learned that ACLS supported teachers and artists who were blacklisted during the McCarthy reign of terror in the 1950s, I am doubly proud to have been a recipient of an ACLS fellowship and enormously grateful to Maud Chaplin, Jack Coogan, Marvin Fisher, and Lea Newman for taking the time and trouble to write letters of recommendation for me.

Three Heads of St. Mark's School and many of my colleagues supported or put up with my work on this book. Mark Barlow cheered me on at the outset, Chris Mabley supplemented the ACLS fellowship so I could take a year off and gave me a hug when I badly needed one, and Tony Hill has given the book his full support. Technology troubleshooters John Burwell, Dick Rader, and Ken Wells helped me become computer-literate and exorcised the micro-gremlins whenever they struck my Mac Plus or my Powerbook. Four English Department Chairs, Jack Coogan, Jay Engel, Craig Kerrick, and Sarah McMillan, supported my scholarly work wholeheartedly. Tom Edgar helped me sharpen the Afterword; Steve Lynch provided lifesaving transfusions of joie de vivre; Jana Porter brought her psychological insight and her writing skills to bear on several chapters; Barbara Putnam provided in-house solidarity with the world of working artists; Esther Ward added spice to whatever life dished out; and Aggy Belt, Andy and Lori Harris, Tom Wales, Rob Weedon, the school librarians, the business office, and other members of the St. Mark's community cheered me on. Weld Henshaw coached his son's tennis team for me one day so I could meet a publishing deadline, and Jerry Phillips kept me in touch with the real world. Last but not least, I am grateful to my students, especially Maria Raymond, Nabil Kassam, and Adam Schwartz, and to the late John Louden for establishing the travel fund that enabled me to fly to Europe several times.

When sitting hunched over the computer keyboard late into the night made me wonder if I would ever walk again, much less play tennis, I sometimes felt a flash of anger at my friend Cheeb Everitt for being the one to suggest that I write a Melville biography. While we were playing tennis one summer day in 1986, he proposed a short introduction to Melville, and although the book "grow'd like Topsy," I'm glad he started the ball rolling.

Tom Wallace somehow glimpsed the book's potential on the basis of what now seems to me an embarrassingly crude first draft, and I'm very grateful to him for taking it on and championing it all the way. I'm also grateful to Marc Jaffe for his enthusiasm for the book and for his excellent suggestions, to Bill Herrick and Paul Sherwin for their help, to Elaine Osio for putting me in touch with Patricia O'Toole and for her hospitality in California, and to Patty for putting me in touch with Shirley Wohl.

Many people at Clarkson Potter have contributed to the quality of the book, but my editor, Shirley Wohl, deserves my special thanks and my undying gratitude, as it was she who worked longest and most closely with me on the manuscript. Shirley is the kind of gifted, hardworking editor people say no longer exists, and I have been immensely fortunate to work with her. Her intelligence, enthusiasm, discernment, candor, personal warmth, and humor made her a valued collaborator.

Carol Southern challenged me with her great expectations for the book. Lauren Shakely, one of the few people I know who has actually read *Pierre,* has been staunchly supportive of my work. Roy Finamore has been sensitive to my wishes and my worries. He edited and cut the manuscript with great intelligence and imagination, and he has brought a fresh perspective to the design and visual layout of the book. Lenny Allen has been unfailingly accessible, patient, intelligent, reassuring, and affable. He has added humanity and humor to the editorial process and the selection of illustrations for the book. I'm also grateful to Andrea C. Peabbles for her assiduous work on both the text and the endnotes, which reached her at least one draft too early, and to David Smith for patient, thorough copyediting on a huge and complicated manuscript.

Having lived in Lenox, Massachusetts, for eighteen years or so, I am fortunate to have many friends in the Berkshires. Bill Shirer believed in the book almost before I did, and I wish he could be here to see the final product and to accept my heartfelt thanks. Inga Dean provided hospitality, humor, and good conversation, as did Elaine Steinert, a woman for all seasonings. Sally Begley has welcomed me to her sun-filled Stockbridge

Shangri-la many times over the years, regaling me with stories about nineteenth-century literary figures that are so vivid they sound like personal memories, and making trenchant comments about my manuscript. Valerie and Don Petersen gave me feedback on several chapters and provided stimulating dinner conversation, long Sunday-morning walks, and unforgettable adventures on cross-country skis. Michelle Gillett kept me in touch with the world of wit and poetry. Alice Wohl brought light into the mid-December darkness with her St. Lucy's dance, and Gloria McInerney, who sets a brisk pace climbing Monument Mountain and on the tennis courts behind the old Melvill house, gave me a comfy room not far from the Athenaeum and made discerning comments on portions of the manuscript. Susannah and Ira Marks gave me literal and figurative shelter from the storm in Old Chatham, New York, and Susannah's wisdom and humor relieved my anxiety and kept me from taking myself too seriously.

Monthly Thai lunches at Amarin with poets Wendy Mnookin and Julia Thorne kept me creatively crazy and connected me to worlds beyond Melville and St. Mark's, as did flying visits from my genius college roommate, Liia Vilms, whose computer handbook appeared while my book was taking shape. My dear friend Pinky Kruger provided me with a home-away-from-home in Manhattan, and New York will not seem the same without her hospitality, tough-mindedness, and charm. Muriel and Peter Bedrick shared their publishing experience and their spectacular view of Central Park, and Muriel has been a staunch friend and ally.

Polly and Bill Magenau have made a priceless contribution to this book by letting me use their cottage in South Wellfleet from time to time as a sanctuary. Their tranquil groves and gardens equidistant from the ocean and the bay have been an ideal place to work, rest, and play, and I'm enormously grateful for their generosity and friendship over the years. My good neighbors Leo and Lana Connors took care of my two cats whenever I was away from home; so did Christine Berryman and Bill Wiedergott.

In and around Southborough, I have been blessed with wonderfully supportive friends. Mary and Jack Coogan, my earliest friends here, have been through the worst with me. A formidable tennis player and ace proofreader, Mary read most of the manuscript, offering incisive criticism and corrections, and Jack's loving good humor, spiritual strength, and deep wisdom have helped the center hold. Diane and Jay Engel, who embody the principle that Art is Life and Living is an Art, have cheerfully put up with my crazy, unpredictable moods and my penchant for getting to places at the last minute. They have pried me away from my computer before rigor mortis could set in, by offering a marvelous array of temptations, including long walks, homemade bread and wine-tastings, concerts, operas, and plays. Gretchen and David Russell kept the spirit of misrule as green as the hills of Vermont, and the Framingham Friends kept the Inner Light burning.

Scholar-in-exile Alison Hambly rode shotgun on Herman and inspired me with her courage, and Peter Pease redeemed his ancestor Valentine Pease's tyrannical treatment of Melville by wining and dining me and dancing me away from the computer periodically. Adele Sobel made sure I put solid new foundations under the castles I was building in the air, and Checker Ives and Jan Sturgeon applied their healing arts to a body and spirit subjected to the brutality of a computer for long stretches of time.

Guido Röger contributed companionship, diversion, and delight during the final weeks of stressful summer editing. His sensitivity to language, objectivity, and precision significantly improved the preface. Bethany Wood's familiarity with Melville scholarship and her calm, cheerful, intelligent assistance made the final stages go smoothly under pressure of deadlines. I could not have finished on time without her help.

Without the support of my brothers Bill and Larry Robertson and the hospitality of the many friends who put me up in their homes, or just put up with me, I could not have written this book. I am blessed with wonderful colleagues, relatives, and friends, and I hope I haven't forgotten to thank anyone. Although quite a number of people read portions of the manuscript and offered suggestions, I alone am responsible for errors; I hope I will have a chance to correct them in subsequent editions of the book.

Thanks to Stefan Lorant, whom I met at Harvard, I enrolled in New York University's Graduate School of Arts & Sciences, where I was introduced to Melville. Sadly, the two NYU professors who inspired my first forays into scholarship have both passed away. Gay Wilson Allen's Whitman seminar introduced me to American Literature, and his Melville seminar opened the "floodgates of the wonder-world" to me, as I was a virtual Melville illiterate at that time. A gentle and good man and a great and humble teacher, Gay was an inspiring mentor, a steadfast friend, and a generous benefactor whose timely gift enabled me to buy my first computer. I am enormously grateful to him for his example and his help, and terribly saddened that he passed away while I was, quite literally, writing these acknowledgments. I hope this book lives up to his high expectations. William M. Gibson, a fine teacher and adviser, introduced me to Hawthorne and Emily Dickinson and encouraged me to break new ground with my dissertation. I think he would be pleased with this revisionist biography.

My son Chris has cheerfully put up with having to eat at a place mat–size space on a dining-room table piled high with books and papers. He has also had to put up with the strange moods, incomprehensible vagaries, distracted states, and alternating hyperactivity and fatigue of a mother who has been obsessively and irrationally pursuing a dead white male for the past eight or nine years—years during which we have both missed his brother, Mark, terribly.

Thanks, Chris, for taking all this in stride, for keeping your wonderful sense of humor, and for bringing me fresh flowers.

Mark, as Melville said in *Moby-Dick,* "deep memories yield no epitaphs."

Perhaps all writing is a kind of grief-work.

Laurie Robertson-Lorant

Southborough, Massachusetts

From the tip of Manhattan Island, five-year-old Herman Melvill could see the flotilla that greeted the Marquis de Lafayette as he sailed into New York Harbor in 1824.

LOFTY ORIGINS

Long before Herman Melville was born at the tip of Manhattan, the island was home to the Algonkians, who called it Manah-hatin, *"Island of the Hills." They hunted game amid the rolling meadows and lush woodlands, fished the freshwater ponds and streams, and harvested shellfish from the teeming waters of the bay. In 1524, Giovanni da Verrazano, a Florentine merchant who was searching for a passage to India, sailed through the narrows that would be named for him and claimed the island for the king of France, but the French did not establish an outpost there. It was not until the early 1600s, when Hendrik Hudson explored the river that now bears his name, and Dutch merchants established a trading post called Nieuw Amsterdam at the edge of the bay, that Europeans actually laid claim to the island.*

Eager to consolidate her trading empire in the New World, Britain took control of Nieuw Amsterdam in 1664, renaming it New York. To discourage rival nations from challenging its hegemony, the Crown commissioned privateers to harass foreign ships. New York remained an outlaw Tory port until 1783, when General Washington led his troops into the burned and ravaged city and ended the British occupation. The following year, the Empress of China *made* the voyage to Canton that opened the China trade to American vessels, ending England's domination of the seas.

Even after George Washington took the oath as President on the steps of Wall Street's Federal Hall, the British continued to regard the new nation as a colonial possession. In 1807, Parliament passed an Embargo Act designed to prevent American merchants from trading with Napoleonic France, and when those merchants refused to comply, the British navy blockaded the Atlantic ports in an attempt to cut off trade. Many American dry-goods importers, including two Boston merchants, Thomas Melvill and his son Allan, lost money when a ship in which they had invested was sunk by privateers. When the British began seizing American sailors and forcing them to serve on British vessels, the United States went to war.[1]

Herman Melville's grandfathers, Thomas Melvill of Boston and Peter Gansevoort of Albany, were both heroes of the American Revolution. They saw America grow from a fiercely pious seacoast colony whose political and religious beliefs were shaped by medieval and Renaissance traditions, to a modern nation pushing itself away from Old World influences toward New World autonomy and territorial expansion. These men never questioned their right to settle the New World, and they regaled their children and grandchildren with stories of their triumphs over the primitive, barbaric tribes who stood in the way of the "march of civilization" ordained by God. These were stories Herman Melville would grow up questioning.

Melville's paternal grandfather, Major Thomas Melvill, worked his way up in the mercantile world after early loss and hardship. His father, Allan, a native of Scoonie, Scotland, and his mother, Jean, both died when Thomas was ten, and he was sent to live in Newcastle, Maine, with his maternal grandmother, Mary Cargill, her five children, and Mary Whitten, an orphan whose parents had been killed by Indians. When he was old enough to enroll in the Boston Latin School, Thomas returned to Boston and boarded with his great-uncle James Cargill, a notorious Indian fighter who had earned the rank of colonel in the French and Indian Wars.[2]

After his graduation, Thomas enrolled in the College of New Jersey (Princeton) intending to study for the ministry, but after earning a bachelor's degree, he dropped out of the divinity course, allegedly for health reasons. It seems to have been something more than that, however—perhaps a spiritual crisis similar to the one that moved Ralph Waldo Emerson to renounce his ministry—because after traveling in Scotland, he settled in Boston, broke with Calvinism, and joined the Unitarian Church at Brattle Square.

As a young man, Thomas was active in the Massachusetts Lodge of Freemasonry and the Sons of Liberty. He was a close friend of Samuel Adams, whose portrait, painted by John Singleton Copley, hung in his home at 20 Green Street for many years. He became a local celebrity during the British occupation of the colonies, when he and the other members of his lodge slipped into the Green Dragon Tavern after dark, donned buckskin breeches, feather headdresses, and warpaint, and boarded three British ships. After dumping 342 chests of tea, valued at nine thousand pounds sterling, into Boston Harbor, the "Aboriginals," to use his son Allan's name for the patriot band, ran through the streets war-whooping, "Rally, Mohawks! Bring your axes, and tell King George we'll pay no taxes!" All of Boston poured out of doors and picked up the chant. Thomas kept the handful of tea leaves he claimed to have found in his boot the next morning to show his children and grandchildren, and when Allan, Herman Melville's father, had sons of his own, he never tired of admonishing them to live up to their grandsire's "daring chivalric deed."[3]

In 1774, with an honorary M.A. from Harvard, Thomas Melvill married Priscilla Scollay, whose forebears were Orkney Islanders. When the Revolution broke out, he became an artillery officer in the navy, distinguishing himself by fighting at Bunker Hill and firing the first battery at the retreating British fleet from an emplacement at Nantasket. After the war, he served as a state representative under the new national administration, and in 1796, George Washington appointed him Naval Officer for the Port of Boston. The War of 1812 brought Major Melvill back to active duty, and once the hostilities were over, he was given a lifelong position in the Boston Custom House. A well-respected citizen of Boston, he served as the local fire warden and as president of the Massachusetts Charitable Society.

Herman Melville's maternal grandfather, Colonel Peter Gansevoort, was also a hero of the Revolution, and like others of his generation, he owned slaves: a man named Sambo, a woman named Jude, and her two children. His first ancestor in the New World was Harmen Harmense Van Gansevoort, a master brewer who emigrated from the Netherlands around 1656 and settled in Fort Orange, later called Albany, where he opened a brewery and taproom. Harmen's son Leendert built the business up and passed it along to his son Harme, who in turn handed it over to his brother John to become a merchant, thus paving the way for the family to move from the plebeian sphere of their forefathers to the world of the patroons. By the mid–eighteenth century, the Gansevoorts were as much a part of the Hudson Valley aristocracy as the Van Rensselaers, Cuylers, Van Vechtens, Douws, Ten Eycks, and Frelinghuysens.[4]

It was Harme's son Peter who forged the family's alliance with history. During the Revolutionary War, Peter Gansevoort was given the command of Fort Schuyler (later known as Fort Stanwix), a strategic outpost overlooking the passage from the Hudson and Mohawk valleys to the Great Lakes. During their march to Fort Schuyler, Colonel Gansevoort's regiment was tracked so closely by the Mohawk sachem Joseph Brant that his Indian and Tory troops were able to roast venison on the still-smoldering campfires

of the Americans, but when Brant stormed the frontier fortress, the 750 defenders coun-
terattacked, driving the Indian and Tory forces back to Cherry Valley, where a massacre
ensued. White survivors testified that Brant, an Anglican convert who had translated the
Bible into the Mohawk language before renouncing white culture to become a member
of the tribe, had taken pains to protect women and children, wounded men, and prisoners from the slaughter; yet the official histories called him a "monster of cruelty."
Colonel Gansevoort, who torched native villages and destroyed the tribe's supplies of
food so they would starve to death, was commended for his valiant service and made
Commissioner of the Iroquois.[5]

An undated memoir written by Herman Melville's great-uncle Leonard Gansevoort
Jr. recounts a visit Joseph Brant made to the home of Colonel Henry Quackenboss, evidently a distant Gansevoort relative by marriage. When Brant saw the suite of rooms
reserved for him, he "gazed around at the furniture, pictures and bedstead with a surprised stare as if despising the ease and comfort," and when it was time to go to bed, he
rolled himself up in his tribal blanket and went to sleep on the carpeted floor.[6]

Many years later, on a sloop bound from New York City to Albany, Colonel
Quackenboss noticed a familiar figure "restlessly pacing the deck and peering over his
shoulder nervously." Recognizing "the stony expression of countenance and gleaming
eyes of the Sachem," he stole up behind him and hissed, "Cherry Valley! Cherry Valley!
Your conscience is troubled," in Brant's ear. Visibly moved, the old warrior replied,
"Never speak that name to me again. There was much blood! too much blood! Let us
say no more about it!"[7]

Colonel Gansevoort's staunch defense of Fort Schuyler prevented Brant and St.
Leger from linking up with Burgoyne's army at Saratoga, blunting the British drive
through New York State. His bravery made him a legend, and stories of the Revolution
provided Herman Melville's family with dinner-table conversation for years to come.
When Brant and Colonel Gansevoort happened to meet in Albany in 1797, they reminisced about the war like old comrades, so strong was the spell cast on them by that
heroic era.

After the war, Colonel Gansevoort received a large tract of land near Lake George
in recognition of his bravery. For a few years he operated the gristmill and sawmill on
the property himself, then leased the land to his oldest son, Herman, and returned to
Albany. Colonel Gansevoort was held in such esteem by his regiment and the city of
Albany that in 1809 he was promoted to brigadier general, and when he died in 1812,
he was buried with full military honors. His proud descendants treasured the drum he
had captured from the British, his portrait painted by Gilbert Stuart, and the badge of
the Order of the Cincinnati, an honorary society to which George Washington and other
revolutionary patriots belonged.[8]

His widow, Catherine Van Schaick Gansevoort, was left with a daughter, Maria, and four sons, Herman, Leonard, Wessel, and Peter. In 1813, Herman married Catherine Quackenboss and built a homestead not far from his mills. The town of Gansevoort grew up around the place, and Herman prospered, becoming a prominent citizen and a presidential elector in 1836. His brother Leonard H. stayed in Albany and ran a store until he died prematurely, leaving his widow to bring up five children. Wessel, a drunkard whose health was permanently damaged by venereal disease, ended up a shiftless ne'er-do-well.

Peter Gansevoort, the old colonel's namesake and the youngest and best educated of his four sons, attended the Dutch Church Academy, where he and James Fenimore Cooper became close friends. He went on to Williams College, but at the end of his first year he dropped out in disgust, complaining that Williams was a "sink of iniquity" where young men did nothing but drink and gamble. After finishing his studies at Princeton, he read law with Judge Tapping Reeve in Litchfield, Connecticut, then returned to Albany to clerk in the law office of Harmanus Bleecker. Rapidly moving up in the world, he became DeWitt Clinton's private secretary, and when Clinton became governor of New York, Peter Gansevoort was given a seat on the bench in the Court of Common Pleas. Later he served in the New York State Senate, but as a Democrat in a state controlled by Whigs, he never had much political clout or power.[9]

When Peter Gansevoort became the head of his family after his father's death, one of his chief duties was to make sure that his sister, Maria, found a suitable husband. Marriage was seen as a social and economic institution, not just as a means to personal fulfillment, and a daughter of the Albany Regency was expected to marry a member of the Dutch patrician class. The old Dutch families regarded wealth and power not as individual attainments, but as investments in the future of their families and communities, so marrying within the clan strengthened family ties and protected property from outsiders, especially from Yankees whose wealth was built on capital and speculation, not entrepreneurial industry and family ties.

Maria Gansevoort had been raised to conform to the highest standard of Dutch womanhood—a standard based less on either intelligence or beauty than on piety, moral rectitude, and family pride. She excelled at the womanly arts of sewing, cooking, needlework, choosing suitable wardrobes, and furnishing and managing an elegant household, and she also cultivated the social graces. As a child she had attended Mr. Merchant's Academy and the local dancing school, and she studied piano twice a week with J. C. Goldberg, a noted pedagogue who enjoyed playing the fine instrument that his young pupil's father had ordered from a prestigious London instrument maker.[10]

To mold Maria's character, her parents made sure she read religious tracts and didactic poetry, and during her adolescence, her brother Peter cautioned her not to read "too much fiction," as novels were thought to fill the heads of impressionable girls with dangerous romantic notions. While Peter's admonition did not entirely deter the spirited Maria from reading fiction, she kept two Bibles on her bedside table, one in English and one in Dutch, to protect herself from any heathenish ideas that might be lurking in the suspect texts. Thus, the woman who was to give birth to America's greatest literary genius was trained early to doubt the value of his art. Even after his first novel became a best-seller and Uncle Peter began calling him "Typee," his mother didn't feel comfortable with having a writer for a son.[11]

As a good Christian woman, Maria felt called to raise God-fearing children whose polished manners, fine penmanship, and unimpeachable integrity would attest to their superior upbringing and make them eligible to join the ranks of the Elect. Maria's mother had taught her that letter-writing was a woman's duty, so she became a prolific correspondent. Because Dutch was her mother tongue and English did not come naturally to her, she never quite mastered spelling and punctuation, but she wrote in a neat, ladylike hand and placed her letters in envelopes, as her brother had instructed her, so that they would not become wrinkled and soiled in transit. Throughout her life she wove an epistolary web designed to hold friends and family members together, as did her four daughters.

The Dutch gentry generally favored gatherings with family and close friends over lavish public entertainments, but an occasional ball was de rigueur for marriageable young women; thus, despite her father's death, Maria Gansevoort attended the ball honoring Admiral Oliver Hazard Perry in 1813. A coquettish and commanding young lady, Maria attracted the attention of several young officers from her grandfather's old regiment. None of them appealed to her as much as did Allan Melvill, who began visiting her brother around this time to explore the possibility of doing business in Albany.[12]

Unlike the typical Dutch swain, with his square jaw and ruddy cheeks, Allan Melvill had thin, aristocratic features. He wore his hair curled in the French style and, in his flyaway coat and tapered trousers, he cut a dashing figure on the dance floor. Scion of a fine old Boston family, Allan could trace his lineage to Sir Richard de Melvill and Sir John Melvill, Scots warriors of the thirteenth century who fought at Floden Field to defend Scotland's honor. His father brought him up on the maxims of Lord Chesterfield and sent him to the West Boston School, where he produced exemplary copybooks. He came to believe that his elegant penmanship, polished poetry, and pious sayings could guarantee success in the business world.[13]

One of eleven children, Allan had received a gentleman's education, which consisted of a Grand Tour of Europe, not college. While in Paris, he stayed with his older brother Thomas. Through Thomas, Allan made the acquaintance of such worthies as Joel Barlow and the Marquis de Lafayette, and, being fluent in French, he established a rapport with dry-goods suppliers in Paris and Lyon.

Compared with Paris, where, he dared say, he had made an international reputation for himself, Boston seemed stodgy and old-fashioned. Both he and his father, Thomas Melvill, a hero of the American Revolution, had been born in Boston, and for Allan, the old major's affectation of wearing the revolutionary tricorne hat and "small clothes" long after America had won her independence epitomized the backwardness of his hometown.

At some point, Allan entered into a kind of real estate partnership with his old school friend Lemuel Shaw, a Boston attorney, and Albany attorney Peter Gansevoort. Allan's father already owned land in Pittsfield, Massachusetts, and the three younger men hoped to acquire even more acreage in the Berkshire Hills and eastern New York State, for investment purposes and as a foundation for future trade. In those days, stagecoach travel between Albany and Boston through the Berkshires was quite efficient. The country was so small that Peter Gansevoort could hand a letter addressed "Lemuel Shaw, Boston" to the driver of the mail coach, and it would be delivered to Shaw in person the next day. Although they never created the trading empire of which Allan Melvill dreamed, the three men remained intimately connected all their lives. (Lemuel Shaw became engaged to Allan's sister Nancy, and although she died suddenly in 1813, Shaw carried her picture in his wallet through two happy marriages. Allan Melvill married Peter Gansevoort's sister, Maria, and his son Herman married Elizabeth Shaw, the daughter of his friend.)[14]

Allan's elegant manners and suave solicitude soon won Maria Gansevoort's heart, and his "lofty origins" and his noble pedigree eventually won him the approval of the Gansevoorts. Although marriage to a Boston merchant was a radical step for a daughter of the Regency to take, her brother Peter wanted her to be happy, so he gave his permission for Maria to marry Allan Melvill as soon as the two-year period of mourning for her father had ended.

Meanwhile, Allan was toying with the idea of settling in New York City once he was married. He was certain he could rise faster in the import trade by catering to social-climbing New Yorkers who followed European fashions rather than to conservative Bostonians, but every time he brought up the subject with Maria, she became anxious and defensive. She not only wanted to stay in Albany, near family and friends, but she had heard that New York was overrun with uncouth, tobacco-spitting Yankees busily cheating one another to get rich. When Major Melvill cautioned his son against a hasty move, and his business associate, Otis Swan, warned that New York had still not recovered completely from the effects of the British blockade, Allan decided to bide his time.[15]

On October 14, 1814, Allan Melvill and Maria Gansevoort were married in Albany's North Dutch Reformed Church. After a honeymoon trip to Boston to meet Allan's relatives, they returned to Albany, where they boarded with Maria's family, and Allan entered the wholesale dry-goods business. Now that he was a married man, it was hard for him not to be the head of his own household, and he could not have been happy about paying his in-laws $75 a month for himself, his wife, and a servant. Living with the Gansevoorts was not easy for this newly married young man; Maria adored her bachelor brother so passionately that Allan sometimes couldn't help feeling a twinge of jealousy, and "the old lady," as he called his wife's mother, ruled the roost.

A stern Calvinist, Catherine Van Schaick Gansevoort had sunk into such a deep depression after her husband's death that family and friends feared for her life. Eventually the strong-willed Caty pulled herself together and became so independent that she scandalized friends and family by violating the taboo against women traveling alone. She compromised by taking her slave Chris along as a companion, but her son Peter still did not approve.

Fortunately for the newlyweds, the pressures exerted on them did not interfere with the delights of conjugal love; and on December 6, 1815, the Melvills' first child was born. They christened him Gansevoort Melvill, a double-barreled name designed to secure him a place in Albany society and the greater mercantile world. At the same time, Allan Melvill still felt like an outsider in a city whose customs originated with the patroons.

New York State was so rich in timber and furs that some prognosticators believed that once western markets were opened up to eastern goods, Albany would eclipse Philadelphia, Boston, and even New York as a commercial capital. Some even talked of building a canal that would link the cities of the eastern seaboard to the Great Lakes and the prairies, opening the way to endless prosperity, but Allan Melvill was impatient. The economy still had not rebounded from the wartime depression, and by the spring of 1816 there were so many merchants competing for dwindling markets in Albany that Allan decided to return to Boston. Although Maria hated to leave her home, she was relieved to be moving to Boston, not New York. No sooner was little Gansevoort weaned than Maria became pregnant again, and in August 1817 the couple's first daughter, Helen Maria, was born. During the time he and Maria spent in Boston, Allan became restless. He wanted to rise quickly in the world, and it seemed to him that the energy for capital investment was shifting from the Boston Brahmins and the Dutch patricians to shrewd Yankee merchants. He felt certain that tidal waves of money would soon be flowing into the coffers of Manhattan's great mercantile houses and banks.

By New Year's Day of 1818, New York's trade with Europe and the Far East had outstripped that of both Boston and Philadelphia, and her port was generating one-quarter of the nation's revenues. "Almost every tide brought in or took out ships for foreign ports, and scarce a week passed that vessels did not arrive from, or sail for, all the different quarters of the world," James Fenimore Cooper wrote in his novel *Afloat and Ashore*. Men who imagined they could see flecks of gold flashing from the cobblestones circled the countinghouses like sharks, following the scent of money.

One of those men was Allan Melvill, who, after a year or so in Boston, had pretty much made up his mind to leave despite the objections of his family. Promising his father that he would remain in Boston if his French suppliers made a commitment not to shift their business to New York, he borrowed $6,500 from him for the purchase of fancy dry goods and made arrangements to go abroad. He included a trip to Scotland in his itinerary, as he hoped to establish his claim to a portion of his great-grandfather's £100,000 estate. He had no way of knowing that the Melvill estate was heavily entailed and would be worthless by the time the will was read.

After settling some legal wrangles over property in Pittsfield, Allan went to New York in March and booked passage for Liverpool aboard a fast-sailing packet named the *Triton*. Entrusting his "hearts best jewels" and the "idols of my bosom" to Peter Gansevoort, he asked his brother-in-law to "Give my hearts most tender & undivided love to my Maria, kiss *for me* as often as you please the chubby cheeks & ruby lips of my noble Boy & Cherubick Girl, but attempt not on your peril to supplant me in their affections, they may love *you* as much as they will, but they must love *me* more."[16]

A little over a month later the ship docked in Liverpool, a thriving port city whose population had ballooned from five thousand in 1700 to 100,000 in 1800, largely on the strength of the lucrative cotton trade with the American slave states. Noting that Liverpool was "a most wonderful place," second only to London, Allan went north by coach to Edinburgh, a city that appealed to him enormously. He pronounced it "the most desirable permanent abode in the British Dominion" from "physical, moral & intellectual points of view," as though he might have been toying with the idea of settling there someday.[17]

Carrying "a pair of fashionable dress Boots" for Maria and Helen Maria and "a highland cap ... fresh from Edinburgh" for Gansevoort, he journeyed on to Melvill House, the seat of the Earl of Melville and Leven, in Scoonie Parish. There, to his "infinite satisfaction," he saw "a Portrait of my Great Grandfather which evidently bears a resemblance to my own Father." Establishing family ties to the Scots nobility was as important to him as establishing financial ties to the French textile industry, as he unconsciously assumed that aristocratic blood made a man immune to the vicissitudes of the marketplace.[18]

The entire time Allan was abroad, he missed Maria. "My chief regret is that you are not with me," he wrote her, "as we are unhappily far asundered & cannot enjoy together that unspeakable interchange of sensation & sentiment which constitutes the bliss of wedded Love, & diffuses o'er the face of the creation the sunny warmth of kindred souls."

Signing himself "your fond, faithful & devoted friend & Husband until death," he pledged her the "constant fidelity, unchangeable love & undivided devotion of your husband & Lover," and in his next letter, he enclosed a "sprig of myrtle from Melville House" and sent kisses to "our lovely rose buds who reflect their Mothers brightness."[19]

Although such epistolary effusions were commonplace in the Victorian era, some scholars have speculated that Allan's flowery language was either a calculated cover-up for infidelity, or unconscious compensation for a guilty conscience. They speculate that because Herman Melville's 1852 novel *Pierre, or The Ambiguities* has autobiographical undertones, its main plot—Pierre Glendinning's discovery that his deceased father had abandoned an illegitimate daughter in France and that he has fatefully become incestuously attracted to her—must be autobiographical, too. Yet even scholars who are convinced that *Pierre* is based on fact believe Allan's alleged mistress was a well-known Boston milliner named Martha Bent, not a Frenchwoman. Illegitimacy and incest were commonplace themes in popular Victorian novels, and as far as we know, Allan had no children out of wedlock. Both Allan and his father had business connections with Mrs. Bent, and at least one scholar speculates that she was Thomas Melvill's paramour, not Allan's. In any event, there is little or no proof either way.[20]

When Allan arrived in Paris around the middle of June, he purchased "an elegant shawl for your ladyship" and met with his French suppliers, who very quickly confirmed his hunch that New York was the center of the mercantile world. "New York," he wrote his father, "is destined to become the Commercial Emporium of our Country; it is daily rising in wealth & splendour." Knowing that his father still hoped he would return to Boston and settle there, Allan assured him that "the sacrifice I make is painful in the extreme, for I had hoped to have pitched my tent at the side of my Father in my own natal soil, but duty to my Wife & Children wills it otherwise." Evidently, even those who had traded the harsh precepts of Calvinism for the softer counsels of Unitarianism had enough Puritan blood in their veins to assume that pain was inherently more virtuous than pleasure.[21]

While he was in France, Allan dined with the Marquis de Lafayette and the Fleurys, the family of Thomas Melvill Jr.'s late wife, Françoise. "France is still a delightful spot to visit, & many of the Inhabitants preserve their virtues inviolate," he assured Maria, but "Paris is a dangerous place for any Man for there the Gorgon's head of vice is concealed beneath the mask of beauty, & the artificial flowers of love bestrew the path of infamy, the force of bad example is ever in operation, & the temptation to evil bewilders the senses, folly usurps the place of reason, fashion tolerates infidelity, reflection is abashed by the arrogance of art, & the past & the future, time & eternity, are all lost in the [present] moment, & the gay and thoughtless multitudes who throng the avenues of Paris, pursue the phantom pleasure, with avidity." Like many other Protestant Americans, Allan was simultaneously attracted and repelled by Gallic sensuality.[22]

Maria, meanwhile, was bearing her husband's absence with her "characteristic fortitude" and keeping up the couple's social life. "I fully approve of your having generally accepted invitations," wrote Allan, "and that you have endeavoured to appear as cheerful as possible. This was precisely what I wished, truly becoming your Character as a Wife and Mother, and makes me more than ever proud of a woman, whose native good sense dictates the propriety of her conduct in every possible situation."[23]

His pedigree was of paramount importance. "It appears evident," he continued, "that I am sprung from a gentle & a royal line of ancestry on both sides through my Father & Mother—the founder of the Melvill family in Scotland being Brother to Queen Margarett wife of Malcolm Carnbee who came with her from Hungary in 1060—while tradition has it that the first of the Scollays of the Orkneys, from whom my good Mother is lineally descended … was Brother to a Queen of Norway—and it is not a little singular that while my Fathers arms are Crescents, my Mothers are stars—which seem to betoken the loftiness of their origin."[24]

By the middle of July, with money from his father, Allan purchased two sizable cargoes of goods, one to be shipped to his father in Boston aboard the brig *Eliza,* the other to be shipped to himself in New York aboard the *Adonis.* As he waited at Le Havre-de-Grâce for his ship to sail, he wrote Maria the kind of letter an apprehensive nineteenth-century husband might write before he crossed the sea: "Before committing myself & property to the mercy of the winds & waves, & the protection of Providence, I once more in the full tide of conjugal affection, address you these few lines to assure you of my love, & fidelity—should any unfortunate event retard our reunion, or separate us forever, do me the justice to cherish in the inmost orifices of your soft & constant heart, the recollection of our mutual attachment & affection, & never forget, that your Melvill has always been & will ever be [as] faithful & confiding as when he parted—embrace our little charmers for their tender & doting Father, & teach them to repeat his name in the accents of filial love."[25]

Allan habitually capitalized the entire name of GOD. When business was booming, GOD became his "Almighty Friend," and when business was lagging, he asked his father in Boston for another loan. Before long, he would make GOD a silent partner in the import trade.

Allan survived to regard his safe passage over the seas as a sign that Providence favored his latest enterprise. "Considering how much I have accomplished in 134 days," he wrote his father, "it seems almost a miracle." He saw himself as the hero of a cosmic drama, and having "travelled above 8000 miles which will average over 60 miles per day the whole time, without meeting with any difficulty or accident," he felt certain that he was destined for a stellar career.[26]

＊＊＊

In *Democracy in America* (1835), Alexis de Tocqueville wrote: "It is odd to watch with what feverish ardor the Americans pursue prosperity and how they are ever tormented by the shadowy suspicion that they may not have chosen the shortest route to get it. Americans cleave to the things of this world as if assured that they will never die, and yet are in such a rush to snatch any that come within their reach, as if expecting to stop living before they have relished them. They clutch everything but hold nothing fast, and so lose their grip as they hurry after some new delight."[27]

Cursed with great "restlessness of temper," Americans continually change direction "for fear of missing the shortest cut leading to happiness," de Tocqueville observed, and true to his prediction, many Americans of Allan's generation would abandon a culture based on land, family, and community to create a culture based on reckless speculation, crass opportunism, and shameless social climbing. The result would be a population afflicted with chronic restlessness and dissatisfaction and an economy that oscillated between boom and bust.[28]

Leaving the children with Maria's family in Albany, the Melvills took lodgings in Manhattan with Mrs. Margaret Bradish, who had turned the old Ludlow mansion on State Street, near the Battery, into a stylish, comfortable commercial residence. For eighteen dollars a week she provided a home to well-recommended travelers. While the Melvills were there, other guests included Mr. and Mrs. Bartley, the noted British acting couple, and their countryman Henry Fearon, and several American widowers and bachelors, among them Henry W. Brackenridge, author of a history of the War of 1812; Lewis Warrington of Virginia, recipient of a congressional medal for his role in capturing a British sloop; Captain Stephen Decatur, who had sunk the British frigate *Macedonian* in the War of 1812; and John Graham, Acting Secretary of State under James Monroe.[29]

Mrs. Bradish's establishment was far more elegant than the run-of-the-mill boardinghouse, but Allan and Maria were anxious to find a place of their own, as they missed their children. "It appears an age since I last saw my Dear little Children. I hope they are well, tell Mama I expected she would have sent me word if the Children had of [*sic*] been *too* noisy, as you have been so kind as not to complain, I presume they have behaved very well. There are several Children in the house belonging to Different Ladies but none in my opinion behave as well, by half, as my little Son & Daughter," wrote Maria in her usual pell-mell style.[30]

It was not easy to find decent, affordable lodgings in the city. Land was scarce, and people with money were building and building, and charging higher and higher rents for diminishing space. "I find it impossible," Allan wrote, "to procure a House in an eligible situation without paying an exorbitant rent say $800 to 1000 & even 1200, & the neighbourhood of my Business being essential, we may yet be compelled to board again this Winter which of all things I would wish to avoid, as it is time my little Family was permanently established, & to be at lodgings with Children is always inconvenient."[31]

Finally, the Melvills narrowed down their choices: "We have been looking at two houses, one in Walker St. is a handsome 3 story Brick house, fashionably finish'd, for $700 but too far from Mr. M——— ... the other is a New house next to Langs which you spoke off [sic] with a Basement, kitchen on the first floor, handsome Parlour, large Pantry in the Hall & a neat Pantry in the kitchen, & Deep in, fix'd in the Wall; first floor, two Elegant rooms connected by huge folding doors large Pantry between Black Italian Marble mantlepeices [sic] & between the folding doors a place for a Lamp." In addition to its "handsome" rooms, it afforded its occupants a "delightful" view of the Battery and a "Most genteel neighborhood in the City & a Healthy situation." They chose the latter house, situated on Pearl Street at the opposite end from Allan's office and store, near the Battery, and while Allan was signing the lease and arranging for the move, Maria went to Albany to fetch the children.[32]

By the time Allan Melvill arrived in 1818, Pearl Street was "the principal mercantile mart of the city." The Dutch had given the city's original waterfront the name *Perel Straet* because it was paved with oyster shells. After successive landfill operations extended the shoreline to South Street, Pearl Street was lengthened to accommodate the city's first free public school and the countless offices, taverns, shops, and warehouses deemed essential to the conduct of business in the port. Before crossing Broadway, Pearl intersected Wall Street, where the Tontine Coffee House, the Custom-House, and the great banking and exchange offices were located.[33]

The seaport's ceaseless bustle confirmed for Allan's addictive sensibility that great things were being done. He sent his father an official announcement that he had established himself "in this great commercial City for the regular importation of French goods," and asked him to send customers his way. He also notified the Earl of Leven, casually mentioning that New York was turning out to be very expensive for "even a small family," just in case his noble relative might remember him in his will. Leven died not long after, without even having mentioned his struggling American cousin, and Allan's dream that he would inherit ancestral lands in Scotland came to an end.

Eager to make the proper impression on his new business associates, Allan stocked his office with demijohns of port wine and Holland gin and humidors of fine imported cigars, and he joined the Societé Française de Bienfésance, where he made valuable commercial contacts. Walking the length of Pearl Street on the way home from work,

Allan occasionally stopped at historic Fraunces Tavern, the site of General Washington's eloquent farewell address to his officers. There, he and fellow merchants would swap shipping news and try to calculate how much more revenue the port could be expected to generate this year than the last, and when they were done, they would raise their glasses in a toast to the entrepreneurial spirit.[34]

In 1818, Herman Melville's "insular city of the Manhattoes, belted round by wharves as Indian isles by coral reefs" was a bustling seaport town, a labyrinth of streets and alleyways. A "forest of masts" towered above the warehouses and shops along its waterfront, and names like Canton, Guinea, Curaçao, Java, New Orleans, Papua, Calcutta, Maracaibo, and Marseilles rolled like poetry off the tongues of tattooed ruffians. From the docks, great wooden cities of sail set forth carrying cotton, tobacco, spirits, furs, lumber, whale oil, cheese, livestock, potash, and grains and flours to the farthest reaches of the globe and returned with sacks of sugar and casks of rum from the West Indies, spices and teas from India and Ceylon, crates of porcelain and bales of silk from China, boxes of Flemish lace and Belgian linens, bushels of cocoa beans, and slabs of rosewood, mahogany, and teak.[35]

Allan Melvill's principal imports were luxury items coveted by middle-class people who aspired to rise into the upper class. While he was in Paris, Allan had felt nothing but disdain for the "awkward appearance of women" and the "indecent & unbecoming exposure" of the "Belles [who] display ... the Boot when walking." Vulgar fashions affronted his sensibilities, and he vowed never to cater to the nouveaux riches, whose feelings of cultural inferiority led them to ape European manners and fashions in ways that struck visiting Europeans like Mrs. Frances Trollope, the mother of the British novelist, as quite ridiculous. Allan put notices in the shipping journals advertising everything from linen handkerchiefs, kid gloves, lace mantillas, and Leghorn hats to merino shawls, ostrich feathers, Morocco reticules, fine perfumes from Cologne, and taffeta and velvet ribbons. He approached the importation of fancy dry goods with a kind of missionary zeal, as though flounces, frills, and furbelows might bring refinement to the savage American consumer.[36]

Once the house was furnished to her liking, Maria realized that the mayor's wife had not yet called on her. "The Mayor's Lady Visits every Lady that comes to the City. She has Given half A dozen large Parties, all go, invitations to all except us ... I am worse than forgotten ... shunned by the inhabitants of this Selfish hateful Place," who "will not see merit" but "shut their Eyes against everything but wealth, Wealth is their reigning God & if you have not wealth, you must have patience to put up with every slight, & many mortifications."[37]

Maria was devastated at what she perceived to be a snub, but fortunately, just as she was "in a fair way of being a Misanthrope" through social neglect, the mayor's wife, Mrs. Cadwallader Colden, accompanied by her son and Governor Clinton's fiancée, Miss Kitty Jones, paid her the coveted welcome call. A visit from "Her Ladyship" was the signal for others to send invitations to the newcomers, and soon the Melvills were invited to a large party at the home of Smith Thompson, the new Secretary of the Navy. Though pregnant with her third child and suffering from morning sickness, Maria basked in her long-awaited acceptance into New York society.[38]

She passed the winter of 1818–19 caring for Gansevoort and Helen, doing needlework, and exchanging visits with the ladies of her social set. In the spring, she and Miss Adams, the governess, took the children to the Battery for daily outings, and in the evenings, she and Allan strolled arm in arm underneath the sycamores along the bay, greeting their neighbors and showing off their finery. With his lovely wife on his arm, Allan felt supremely confident that he was one of Heaven's favorite sons.[39]

As an upcoming citizen of the young Republics, Allan Melvill preferred Paris
fashions to the plain style of his Puritan forebears.

Two

SNUG INVESTMENTS

New York City in the summer of 1819 was an inferno. A wind from the south brought trop-
ical heat to the streets and alleyways, blistering the horses' hooves, and forcing even the most
fastidious businessmen to loosen their whalebone collars. The fine handkerchiefs they used as
towels were inadequate to absorb the perspiration that ran down their necks, saturating their
starched shirts. July bred epidemics of typhus, Asiatic cholera, and yellow fever with deadly
regularity, turning the city into a plague-stricken Thebes.

North of the seaport, between City Hall Park and Five Points, lay twenty thousand
Africans who had been buried by relatives with great ceremony and respect, some with coins
over their eyes, some with seashells placed lovingly beside their heads. The shipowners who had
brought them to the New World and merchants like Allan Melvill, of course, never ventured
uptown where freed slaves and poor laborers lived in frame houses or rundown shacks and
shanties. Nor did they explore the outskirts of the city to see Potter's Field, a site that would
later become Washington Square. There, where victims of pestilence lay buried, stood the gal-
lows. In July 1819 a crowd of men, women, and children gathered there in the oppressive heat

and humidity to see the hanging of Rose Butler, a Negress who had allegedly set fire to combustibles in a stairwell at her place of employment.[1]

All that sweltering summer, Allan Melvill worked overtime at his office, leaving Maria and the children in the care of Miss Adams, the nanny who doubled as maid and cook because he could not yet afford a full complement of servants. Fortunately, Allan's Pearl Street house, with its view of the harbor, and his store a few blocks east were two of the airiest places in town, and he had lived in the city long enough to know how to bait traps with molasses to catch the omnipresent and omnivorous cockroaches.[2]

The baby, due on the twentieth of July, had still not arrived by the last week of the month, and Maria was feeling fat and sluggish from the heat. With her husband working long hours and two small children to care for with a limited household staff, Maria welcomed her mother's arrival from Albany to wait out the long last weeks of pregnancy. Not the least pleasure of her company derived from speaking her mother tongue once more, which rekindled warm memories of her childhood.

Maria's mother still suffered episodes of depression, prompting Peter Gansevoort to exhort her not to dwell on "those evils which darken the gloom in which our path through life is shrouded," but to embrace "light and joy" in preparation for "the full radiance of a Christian's glory." Much less of a Calvinist than his mother, Peter advised her to go to Far Rockaway, where there was a chance the ocean breezes would blow away her somber mood: "You will find it better for body and soul than the composition and festering of factitious evils."[3]

As steamy July melted into August, Maria went into labor. She was attended by the tall, impeccably dressed Dr. Wright Post, who wore his powdered hair tied back in a queue. A prestigious senior staff surgeon at New York Hospital on Broadway, and a professor of anatomy and physiology at Columbia's College of Physicians and Surgeons, Dr. Post had recently won accolades for reattaching severed neck muscles and for perfecting a technique to block aneurysms by tying off the iliac artery. As senior warden of fashionable Grace Church at his death in 1828, he is memorialized on a stone in the church's vestibule as "judicious, skilful, and industrious in his deportment and in his religious principles a sincere, devout & humble Christian."[4]

The heat wave still had not broken when, at half past 11:00 P.M. on the muggy first of August, 1819, the new "little Stranger" entered "the babylonish brick-kiln of New York" with a lusty cry that testified to his sound lungs and rebellious spirit. As Dr. Post cut the umbilical cord, he assured the proud father that all his wife needed was a cool towel on her forehead, a change of linen, and a good night's sleep. Allan went to bed with "a grateful heart," pleased that "Our dear Maria displayed her accustomed fortitude in the hour of peril."[5]

The new baby was "a chopping Boy" who "sleeps well & feeds kindly," Allan told his friend Peter Gansevoort. With relentless heat still blanketing the air, it was nearly ten days before Maria felt strong enough to dine downstairs with her husband and the older children.[6]

Bringing a Christian soul into the wilderness of this world was a solemn responsibility. In an era when infant and maternal mortality were high, parents feared for the lives of their small children. "Deaths are always more frequent at this season," Allan wrote his brother-in-law, but "the City is as healthy as could reasonably be expected." Although Allan was a Unitarian, he consented to have his son baptized by a minister of the South Dutch Reformed Church to please Maria and her pious mother, who was a pillar of the Dutch Reformed Church in Albany.[7]

The day before the baby's christening, Caty sent out for citron, nutmeg, and four gallons each of Holland gin and rum to toast her grandson's entry into the Church and strengthen the resolve of the adults to keep the vows by which they promised to instruct this child "born in sin" in Christian doctrines. Dressed in an Irish linen christening gown as white as the robes of the redeemed, the rugged boy was christened Herman.[8]

In anticipation of slow summer sales and a sudden tightening of credit by the banks, Allan had worked hard from January to June, but the August recession was a dead low tide. "Business," he wrote two weeks after baby Herman's birth, "is absolutely stagnant, I am in fact doing nothing, & daily rejoice I have done no more, for those who have done little are the best off—we still have numerous failures and more anticipated. Those who have done more, suffer more; those who have done little, escape the worst failures." The American dream was beginning to show its nightmare side.[9]

The year of Herman Melville's birth was the year pauperism became a visible feature of American urban life. After the War of 1812, a new strident nationalism had replaced the classical republicanism of the Founding Fathers, ushering in an era of individualism that made commitment to the "common good" seem old-fashioned and naive.

America had emerged from the conflict proud and prosperous, but by 1819 the wings of economic expansionism had been clipped by a recession that led to a rash of bank failures and business foreclosures. Those who managed to hold on to capital profited from the misfortune of others by buying up property when values fell, and the gap between rich and poor widened dramatically. In New York City alone, twelve to thirteen thousand people went on relief, prompting John Quincy Adams to observe, "The multitudes are in deep distress."[10]

With yellow fever spreading from the docks and tenements all through the city, Maria Melvill packed up her three children—Gansevoort, who was three, Helen Maria, who was two, and Herman, who was now nearly six weeks old—and went upriver by steamer to wait out the epidemic at her family home in Albany. Allan stayed in the city taking the pulse of the economy and praying that "with the blessing of GOD, confidence will soon return & business revive again." Preoccupied with liquidating his assets to avoid foreclosure, he took a cavalier approach toward the fever that was driving his colleagues and competitors out of New York. Calling them alarmists who "cry mad Dog at the appearance of a puppy," he preferred to stay.[11]

Despite "irretrievable calamities," the young merchant remained optimistic. Like Maria in the throes of childbirth, Allan vowed fortitude. "Though Fortune has played me many a scurvy trick, I will not complain of the fickle Goddess, who may yet be inclined to smile graciously upon me." He assured his father that he would eventually earn Fortune's favors "by patience, resignation and perseverance." It would take him a decade to realize that the goddess Fortune was capricious as well as fickle, equally unimpressed by the Protestant work ethic and aristocratic pedigrees.[12]

American businessmen of Allan Melvill's generation believed in virtually limitless expansion and progress. They cut their teeth on the Bible, *Pilgrim's Progress*, and the writings of Benjamin Franklin. Franklin's *Autobiography* was the modern equivalent of the medieval exemplum or saint's life; *Poor Richard's Almanack* was a guidebook to moral and economic wealth. The example of Franklin's success imbued Allan Melvill with confidence that virtue and hard work would make him a success, if not actually a millionaire. Reminding himself that "riches and distinction ... are both insufficient to ensure happiness, or purchase health," he assured his father that all he wanted was to "provide for the rational wants of my beloved Wife & Children." Sadly, however, he spent no time reflecting on what those "rational wants" might be.[13]

In mid-November, Maria and the children returned from Albany. Fully restored to health by the cooler climate of the Hudson Valley and the ministrations of her family, she set to cleaning her "very dirty" house with a will. The precocious baby already had three tiny teeth, which made nursing a tricky affair. He was in so much pain that his mother, following the custom of the time, dipped her finger in a decanter and rubbed brandy on his gums. Years later, Melville would call teeth "a snug investment."[14]

After the New Year, Maria's friend Caroline Yates came to spend the winter with the Melvills. She doted on six-month-old Herman and kept Maria's spirits up by reading Dumas's *Louise de Vallière* aloud, first in French, then in English. With her friend visiting, Maria may not have noticed that her husband was growing more and more worried about his business.[15]

Allan had good reason to be anxious. By the end of the year, customers were too short of cash to purchase the cloth Allan's trained eye and hand had selected from the wares displayed by Parisian textilers. The new auction system was threatening to drive the Pearl Street merchants out of business. Prior to 1815, British manufacturers had sold their goods to exporters in Liverpool, who then sold them to importers in New York.

Each firm held title to the goods in its turn, relinquishing them only when they were sold to wholesalers. Once peace was concluded between the United States and England, however, British manufacturers could sell their goods directly to auction houses in New York, bypassing the older import-export firms and undercutting the price of exports from other countries, especially France. Fearing that the crisis would lead to the demise of small entrepreneurs, importers begged legislators to regulate the auction trade.[16]

Allan was caught between two increasingly incompatible worlds: the old economic order, in which personal integrity and quality goods and services guaranteed success, and the new economic order, in which bulk sales, bargains, and quick profits held sway. He borrowed heavily and indulged in some questionable practices, rationalizing as he went along. "I am proud to believe my reputation as a merchant firmly established throughout the City," he wrote his father, denying the extent to which he relied on others for financial support. Pulled deeper and deeper into debt, he promised his father that he would bring his "bad speculations" to a close and "dispose of them forever."[17]

He went on blindly, not seeing how far he had strayed from his original ideals; yet he could still write his father, "I doubt not of realising with time & patience under the blessing of Heaven all my rational expectations." The more irrationally he was behaving, the more often he used the word *rational* to describe himself. Despite his avowals of old-fashioned ethical standards and the revulsion he expressed at the underhanded practices of others, he would eventually be sucked into the vortex of moral compromise characteristic of the new market capitalism.[18]

Strolling at the Battery, the Melvills could always find a cool sea breeze and a canopy of leaves to shield them from the sun. Although their house opposite the Battery was convenient to Allan's place of business and quite adequate for their needs, Pearl Street in 1820 was not a fashionable residential address. The old town was becoming more crowded and commercial every day. Warehouses and countinghouses piled bales and boxes beside their doors, and stygian cellars yawned at pedestrians. With its open sewers, stagnant backyard wells, and garbage-choked gutters overrun by scavenging rats and snorting pigs with the mandatory nose-rings in their snouts, the commercial district had grown offensive to genteel sensibilities.[19]

Merchants who did business in this bustling, boisterous seaport were too busy going over shipping schedules and checking bills of lading to worry about the shoddy construction of tenements built to house recent immigrants. There was too much money to be made for them to worry about vile living conditions and the filth, or the noise of the clattering horseshoes and the rumbling wheels of carts and drays that made a man want to quit the office and stroll down to the Battery and let cooling sea breezes bathe his face and hair. A generation earlier, men swam naked at the Battery, but when proper citizens observed, or imagined, intimacy between men and complained, the city banned outdoor swimming and constructed two licensed indoor public baths that made decorous, healthful swimming available only to those who could afford the admission fee.[20]

Feeling "most uncomfortable" without his family, still in Albany, Allan kept busy house-hunting and moving the store to 134 Pearl Street. In the evenings he caught up on his reading. Of particular interest was Lemuel Shaw's article in the *North American Review*, about which Allan wrote: "Your Article on Slavery is a very forcible & argumentative view of a system alike repugnant to reason, justice & humanity, whose existence at the era of our independence was a national misfortune, but whose existence under our free & happy Constitution has become a national reproach, GOD grant it may not prove the ruin of our rising empire." Allan's concern for the future of the Republic was well-placed, as slavery would nearly destroy the Union in his children's lifetime; as with most other New York merchants, however, it didn't occur to him to examine the moral implications of the dry-goods business and the cotton trade.[21]

When Maria and the children returned from Albany in September, they moved right in to 55 Courtlandt Street. Baby Herman, who had celebrated his first birthday the month before, was now "entirely weaned." The new house was not far from the landing for the Hudson River Steamship Line at Gansevoort Street, near the whitewashed Fort Gansevoort, reinforced during the War of 1812 to cut off any British ship that happened to slip past patrol boats and gun emplacements at the Battery and Castle Clinton.[22]

The Courtlandt Street house was spacious enough to accommodate a decent household staff that now included a housekeeper, a cook, a nurse, and, soon, a waiter named John, whom Allan hired "to complete [our] domestic establishment." Shortly after the Melvills moved in, the city closed all the privies in the neighborhood for health and safety violations and ordered the owners to make the necessary repairs.[23]

Compounding the Melvills' discomfort was a winter so frigid that the East River, which almost never froze, was covered with a sheet of ice so thick that people had to skate between Brooklyn and Manhattan for lack of ferry service. The record cold kept the family shut in, incubating measles germs that left all three children suffering with "bad coughs, inflamed eyes, & virulent eruptions."[24]

While Allan was riding higher and higher waves of credit, his brother Thomas was being swamped by debt. In 1802, Thomas Melvill Jr. had been a successful banker "engaging in mercantile pursuits" in France, England, and Spain; he boasted that James Monroe, Joel Barlow, and the Marquis de Lafayette were among his intimates. He scandalized his family by marrying Françoise Raymonde Eulogie Marie des Douleurs Lamé Fleury, the adopted niece of Mme. Récamier's husband, without telling anyone beforehand. Thomas Melvill Sr. was "visibly impaired by anxiety" over his eldest son's elopement, and Allan and his sisters were "mortified."[25]

In 1811, Thomas returned to America bankrupt and settled in Pittsfield, Massachusetts. During the War of 1812 he was appointed to the post of commissary, earning the rank of major, and he served as an officer at the prison camp in Pittsfield. In 1814 his wife and baby and a six-year-old son took sick and died within days of one another, and a year later, he married the widowed Mary Ann Hobart. They raised a family that eventually included eight children of their own in addition to four children from Thomas's first marriage. In 1816, Thomas Melvill Sr. bought the old Van Schaick mansion in Pittsfield from a retired privateer, Elkanah Watson, the millionaire organizer of the Berkshire County Agricultural Fair, and he leased it to Thomas, who hoped the 246-acre property would sustain him and even turn a profit.

A struggling farmer who relied on bank loans to make ends meet, Thomas Melvill Jr. assumed his father would always stand behind him when crops failed and he fell into debt. However, the next time the notes came due, Major Melvill withheld payment and Thomas was jailed for debt in the spring of 1821. He was still in jail when his firstborn child, seventeen-year-old Françoise—Fanny—died.[26]

From his twelve-by-eighteen-foot cell in the county courthouse at Lenox, Massachusetts, Thomas wrote Allan asking for money and a pound of imported snuff. Having just borrowed two thousand dollars from his father to move and hire more servants, Allan did not even respond at first. After Thomas wrote again, asking him to sell an engraving to raise money, Allan did so and sent him a pound of snuff for his forty-fifth birthday with a terse note saying he was too busy to write. Wounded, Thomas replied that "if his worst enemy had written him he would not have *insulted him,* by a silent *envoy,*" adding sarcastically, "misfortune has not blunted my sensibilities."[27]

Although Allan also borrowed heavily from his father, he had no sympathy for his brother's plight; indeed, he seems to have been more worried that having a brother in jail might damage his own reputation than that Thomas and his family might be suffering. Allan's disapproval of his brother fed his grandiose opinion of himself. Thomas, by contrast, apparently held no grudge against Allan, perhaps because Maria was kind enough to visit his family while he was spending four long months in jail.

This unpleasantness persisted for a year, until the bank sued Major Melvill and Judge Shaw for reneging on their pledge to back the notes. They were defended against charges of collusion by Shaw's friend Daniel Webster, who managed to get the charges dropped, but the scandal nearly cost the old major his job in the custom house. Exhorting his father to "courage & resolution," Allan went to Washington in March to intercede for him and win his reappointment. In the end, Major Melvill bailed Thomas out, prompting Allan to comment pompously, "I highly approve of the immediate payment of the sums required to obtain the discharge of Thomas, who I trust will have gathered wisdom from experience, and enjoy the fruits of liberty in a rational manner." He evidently saw no connection between his brother's constant indebtedness and his own.[28]

Soon after weaning Herman, who was as "rugged as a Bear," Maria became pregnant with her fourth child. Baby Augusta arrived on August 24, 1821, and Maria suffered a postpartum depression that would last for many months.[29]

Toward the end of November, Allan persuaded his father to clear all his debts, leading him to believe that his financial situation had improved. In December, Maria's brother Leonard died, leaving his widow, Mary Anne, with five sons and a daughter to support. The burden of supporting Leonard's family fell to Peter Gansevoort, who was trying to keep the rapidly dwindling family fortune intact. He helped Leonard's family as best he could, and sent Maria a ticket for a $20,000 lottery as if to show he hadn't forgotten her. Her number never came up, and as she thought about her sister-in-aw's desperate situation, it must have occurred to her for a fleeting moment that the only thing keeping her family from a similar fate was the unpredictable grace of Almighty GOD.[30]

By New Year's Day of 1822, auction wholesaling was threatening Allan with ruin, and he despaired of a solution. The "evil" would continue until landlords and merchants reformed the system. Allan lamented the fact that "the People, I mean all the sober minded, well disposed Citizens, have much to suffer & more to fear before the mobocratical spirit which now reigns triumphant over this great State, shall submit to the genius of Wisdom," but, ironically, he himself succumbed to similar temptations. Believing he could compete by adopting a more aggressive method of merchandising, he advertised in the papers and began selling his silks, furs, and feathers directly to the highest bidder. So complete was his faith in his new scheme that he borrowed heavily from both his father and his brother-in-law to expand his business.[31]

When summer came, the first case of yellow fever was reported at Coffee House Slip. Between the epidemic and the business downturn, things were so bad by July that Allan decided to take a vacation with his family at the Melvills' house in Boston.

Their two-month summer sojourn gave the younger Melvills ample opportunity to tender condolences to their friend Lemuel Shaw, whose wife, Elizabeth, had died after giving birth to the couple's first daughter. The grieving widower named the baby Elizabeth after her mother, and she was cared for by her grandmother Susannah Shaw and Mrs. Sullivan, the Irish nurse. Maria, mindful of how perilous childbirth could be, realized before the summer ended that she was pregnant again.

After rambling across Massachusetts to Albany in a private carriage, visiting relatives along the way, the Melvills took the steamer to New York City in late autumn, in time to gird themselves against the inevitable onslaught of winter viruses. They went to the theater now and then, probably with business associates as often as with friends, as up-and-coming New Yorkers often mixed business with pleasure in the race to get ahead. Charles Mathews's performance of *Wild Oats* at the elegant Park Theatre just before Christmas so tickled Allan's fancy that he was "altogether unable to controul his risibility." Allan needed such moments of comic relief, as he was dangerously overextended financially.[32]

Maria's "condition" was so visible by New Year's that she joked about her rotundity, assuring her brother that it was fortunate she could not attend a certain dinner party because her "*imposing* presence" would be an inconvenience to the company, "considering the squeeze."

On April 4, 1823, "after displaying her usual fortitude," Maria gave birth to another "noble boy" after "hours of peril & anguish." She stayed in bed most of the next few weeks, and when she got on her feet again, she discovered that she had "increased in breadth most astonishingly."[33]

Allan pronounced the new baby "promising" and had him christened Allan Jr. by the Reverend Mathews of the South Dutch Church. The older children were "in ecstacies [*sic*] with the young Stranger" and tried to get him up "to play with them in the Garret" almost immediately. Three-year-old Herman, who evidently identified more closely with the new baby than with his priggish older brother, remarked, "Pa now got two ittle Boys." Gansevoort, who, according to his proud father, was already "given to ratiocination," asked where babies came from, and when his father replied that people got them at the market, Gansevoort retorted that "he had never heard of buying Children except for slaves."[34]

Precocious remarks such as this convinced the Melvills that their firstborn was exceptional. They had doted on Gansevoort from the moment of his birth, showing him off as though his every accomplishment confirmed their own greatness. Handsome, graceful, quick at his schoolwork, and the bearer of the Gansevoort name, he was clearly his mother's favorite, and with his father's aristocratic features and his facility for conversing with adults, he outshone his shy, stolid younger brother in every way.

As a child, Herman was slow to talk and even slower to read. Compared with the glib Gansevoort, he was inarticulate. With his apple cheeks, wavy brown hair, and soulful ultramarine eyes, Herman was a handsome little boy, but he lacked Gansevoort's refined looks and elegant deportment.

The unstable economy created constant tension in the household, and such an impressionable child as Herman was bound to sense the strain. Having money in the bank—even borrowed money—gave Allan a false sense of power, which made Maria feel hopeful and exhilarated. Being short of cash put Allan into a panic, but he refused to confront his anxieties openly or confide them to Maria. She suffered bouts of depression, and the sensitive Herman did the worrying for the family.

With autumn in the air, business improved, fanning the flames of Allan's confidence and Maria's lust for social status. She enrolled Gansevoort and Helen Maria, who was not yet six years old, in Mrs. Plucknett's dancing school and began to talk about moving to a better neighborhood. Allan's sister Priscilla was living with them now, and Allan promised to find a larger house next spring even though he still owed substantial sums to creditors. Their house felt so crowded they let John the waiter go, and Maria discovered that, with three women servants, there was really no need for a hired "Man" to do the work.[35]

Everyone in the family fell sick in October, and the "sickness & gloom" would persist into the following spring. Allan was laid up for five weeks, and Priscilla came down with a severe case of rheumatic fever that seemed almost worse than the typhus she had suffered several years before. She was confined to her third-story room for nearly three months and subjected to "Blisters, Leeches, & all the torture of Medicine" until the doctor said she was on the mend.[36]

By March, Maria was well enough to take the "fine air in Broadway" and enjoy a visit from her nephew Henry Gansevoort, who arrived with a bushel of crabs. The moment she felt strong enough, she berated her brother Peter for his apparent coldness and neglect: "It appears strange to me that circumstances should be allowed to change or weaken the attachment which I had every reason to suppose firmly seated on a Rock of Friendship, & supported by Pillars of consanguinaty [sic]. Peter I hope I am deceiv'd but their [sic] seems an indescribable something which whispers me I have lost that place in your heart & esteem which I had vainly hoped would have been mine through Life." She evidently had no idea her husband and her brother had been exchanging angry letters for the past few months.[37]

Gansevoort, who had a tendency to pulmonary weakness, had developed a cough that lasted all winter, and Herman, whose ruddy cheeks had been colorless since the fall, still looked "pale, thin, & dejected" when April came. "Our house has resembled a private Hospital," Allan told Peter Gansevoort. Ascribing the past winter's medical marathon to the river's dampness, he decided to move again. He took a four-year lease on a house at 33 Bleecker Street, halfway between Broadway and the Bowery, planning to move in by the first of May. Although the move meant he would have a slightly longer commute to the new office, it put him in the midst of that "Rialto of modern merchants," the auction rooms, "where I dare say even Shylock would be shy of making his appearance."[38]

From Bleecker Street, Allan and Maria could promenade up Broadway, the most fashionable thoroughfare in the Western hemisphere. Downtown, Broadway was a melee of locked carriage wheels and fierce horse fights that brought traffic to a snarling halt, and only the west side of the dirty, dangerous, dung-filled thoroughfare was suitable for the perambulations of respectable citizens. Drivers of lurching horsecars and thundering omnibuses placed bets on who could make the route in a faster time. Pedestrians had to have "an eye at each ear, in order to escape being run over or trampled down by the surging throng," a Swedish visitor reported. Living west of Broadway meant the Melvills never had to walk on the "shilling side."[39]

Maria was overjoyed with the move, as their handsome two-story house had a wide center hall, marble mantelpieces, a tearoom, a finished basement room for a nursery, "lofty ceilings" and large dormer windows on the second floor, and all the modern "conveniences" a lady could desire. In addition to Miss Adams, the governess, she had a housekeeper and a first-rate cook, and the house had a grassy yard where the children could play, and flower beds. Although the house "united the advantages of town and country" and seemed ideal in Allan's eyes, Maria's view of the "elegant white Marble Houses in Bond Street & also in Broadway" from her back window reminded her that she had still not reached her goal.[40]

Still, Bleecker's "open, dry & elevated location" was so much healthier than clammy Courtlandt that after Maria took the children to visit her family in May, the Melvills decided to spend the summer of 1824 in their new home. Fortunately the city was spared a major epidemic, and the Melvills were able to escape the heat by occasional excursions to places like Coney Island in hopes of relieving the "unpleasant fainting fits" that afflicted Maria.[41]

That summer, America celebrated the fiftieth anniversary of the beginning of the Revolution by inviting the Marquis de Lafayette over as "the nation's guest." New Yorkers threw flowers at him from their windows and balconies and treated him to a display of fireworks at the Battery and to numerous shows at Castle Garden, which, on one occasion, he entered dramatically on a white horse. Allan Melvill, however, declined to meet the marquis amid "countless throngs" of people, as "the mere ceremony of shaking hands with such a Man without the privilege of conversation had no charms for me." New York's governor DeWitt Clinton, a friend of Peter Gansevoort, welcomed Lafayette to Albany under the general's regimental flag, and the marquis paid his respects to several members of the Gansevoort family while he was there. When he was in Boston, he called on Major Melvill, who showed him the precious vial of British tea, but it's not clear whether Allan Melvill ever gained his hoped-for audience with the marquis.[42]

Conscious that he was the custodian of the family's patrician pride, Allan gave Herman's ten-year-old cousin Guert Gansevoort a royal send-off when he joined the

United States Navy in the fall. Guert signed on the USS *Constitution* for a three-year cruise, and stayed with the Melvills at Bleecker Street before launching himself "upon the great Ocean of life." Admonishing him to be "mindful of reputation as a Gentleman, & true to duty as an officer," Allan brought to bear the combined forces of GOD, Guert's widowed mother, Mary Anne, and the family honor as he enumerated the temptations Guert should avoid and the virtues he should cultivate so that "with Honour as a compass, & Glory for a watch word, you may in peace or war, become a brave & accomplished naval officer, defend 'the star spangled banner' of your country with courage and fidelity, & add lustre to a name distinguished in the Revolution by your paternal Grandfather."[43]

The advent of cool autumn weather boosted Maria's spirits and restored her health enough that with the help of the housekeeper, she was able to undertake an "alarming & formidable" Dutch housecleaning before Thanksgiving. Her brother Herman and his wife came for a visit, and when they left, five weeks later, Maria gave them five hundred of her pickled oysters to take to her mother and brother, explaining that despite their small size, they were "the same which some of our Stylish Neighbours in Bond Street gave at a large party of Fashionables."[44]

Herman was now in school, but, according to his mother, he did "not appear so fond of his Book as to injure his Health." His favorite pastime was teasing his older brother, and Gansevoort complained that he could not tolerate being "plagued with such a little Fellow." Herman and Augusta were making great progress in talking, and little Allan, who was as red-cheeked and hardy as Herman had been at his age, was teething.[45]

Maria was pregnant again, and this time she was experiencing rapid weight gain, shortness of breath, and frequent leg cramps and swelling. Feeling that fresh air would do her good, Allan insisted on taking her for a walk every morning before he left for work. The weather that Christmas was particularly "delightful," so Allan came home early and "induced by the enlivening rays of the setting Sun [they] strolled down the Bowery, & after an agreeable walk return'd home with renovated Spirits."[46]

At the end of February 1825, when Maria's brother Herman came to visit, he found all the Melvills "in excellent health & Spirits." In May, however, Maria went into a serious decline after the birth of her sixth child, Catherine. She badgered the servants until Allan ordered her to leave the domestic chores to the other women. All summer she voiced "serious fears" for her mind and body. She sent Gansevoort, who was not as "robust & hearty as formerly" because of a fever, to stay with her brother in Albany, and a month later she followed with the other children.[47]

Allan, meanwhile, had been planning to make a buying trip to France as soon as the baby came and Gansevoort was well again. It would be best to go in the spring, he thought, when the city would be widening Pearl Street, installing sewer lines, and straightening Coenties Slip, as business was bound to be disrupted then. He made several attempts to set up a meeting with the French firm of Grenot & Lefebre in hopes of renewing contacts with suppliers in Paris and Lyons, but the leisurely trips to France lay as far behind him as the Golden Age. He was still in the city that summer when the last vestige of the Dutch settlement, the old *Stadt Huys* on Pearl Street, was torn down.[48]

When Major Thomas Melvill died in 1832, Boston firefighters gathered outside his home to pay their respects to his widow, Priscilla Scollay.

THREE

ELEGANT NEGLIGENCE

"Let our age be the age of improvement," declared Daniel Webster as the first American went aloft in a hot-air balloon in July of 1825. From his vantage point above New York Harbor, balloonist Eugene Robertson could see crowds of men, women, and children waving flags and licking colored ices. In the other direction he could see the squadron of French ships that would take the Marquis de Lafayette home to France.[1]

When Lafayette returned to New York after riding "magnificent carousels of national hospitality," as Allan Melvill put it, New York gave him a rousing send-off. Allan probably took the older children to the Battery for the festivities while Maria rested from her latest childbirth. As soon as she felt up to it, she would gather her brood and go to Albany, returning to the city in time for the city's gala celebration of the opening of the Erie Canal.[2]

It was the year of the cotton boom, and New York's merchant princes were anticipating a new era of prosperity and expansion. To celebrate, a flotilla of ships led by Governor DeWitt Clinton aboard the Seneca Chief *sailed down the Hudson to the Battery, where they were greeted by a barrage of cannon fire.*

That September, Gansevoort and Herman entered the New-York Male High School on Crosby Street. This school, of which Allan was a stockholder and trustee, was set up according to the Lancastrian or monitorial system, a hierarchical pedagogy based on rote memorization, shame, and fear. Basic skills such as spelling, sentence parsing, and number recognition were inculcated by rapid-fire dictation, so that spelling and reading began with recognition of the alphabet, then moved on systematically to two-letter words, three-letter words, and so on, in a strictly mechanical sequence that paid no attention to either the etymology or the beauty of the words.

Students were flogged with questions, first by teachers, then by students who had mastered a given subject well enough to be appointed monitors. They were expected to instruct and quiz each younger student relentlessly until he made an error, at which point the next pupil would correct the error, then become the next target of the interrogation. Brothers often had to grill and be grilled by one another.

Boys who did accurate recitations were rewarded with prizes that ranged from bats, balls, and kites, to books, silver pens, and medals. Boys who failed were punished by devices designed to instill shame; some were forced to wear leg shackles, others had logs hung around their necks, and still others—the smaller boys, no doubt—were suspended from the ceiling in sacks or baskets. Six-year-old Herman, who by nature was a daydreamer and a poet, resented the school's rigid and unimaginative daily drill, but he feared humiliation more, so he probably complied as best he could. His ability to blend into the woodwork would serve him well in the navy, where he evidently managed to escape being one of the 163 men flogged during a single cruise.[3]

It's hard to imagine which was more harrowing for Herman—attending the Male High School or memorizing the Calvinist catechism at the Dutch Reformed Church on Broome Street. Its pastor, the Reverend Jacob Brodhead, a friend of the Melvills since his arrival at South Church in 1826, preached fiery sermons that emphasized God's ability to reclaim sinners who had fallen far below the reach of redeeming grace.

Brodhead, who later founded the Sabbath School Union to bring children out of their "moral darkness" into the light of strict orthodoxy, had no use for romantic notions about children imbibing "intimations of immortality" from clouds and flowers. He warned that without religious indoctrination, haphazard biblical education combined with secular pedagogy "would excite in the minds of children that self conceited, speculative, *free thinking* spirit, so subversive of all religious instruction." Exposed early to such stern doctrines, Herman approached religion with a mixture of anger, skepticism, and dread.[4]

This strict, often abusive educational regimen had a negative effect on the boy. He had trouble learning to read and write, and he never quite mastered handwriting and spelling. A shy, sensitive lad who felt great pressure to emulate his older brother, his anxiety over the competition for academic recognition and parental approval slowed him down. His parents clearly had lower expectations for him than for his brother, and he couldn't seem to break the vicious cycle. While the Melvills considered Gansevoort "a more than ordinary genius" and praised his slightest accomplishment, Herman was taken for granted even when he managed to do well. Taking refuge in *The Arabian Nights* and *The Travels of Marco Polo,* he developed a rich and secret inner life.[5]

In the spring of 1826, Herman, together with two of his sisters, contracted scarlet fever, which affected his eyes, interfering with his reading, and causing him to develop a visual weakness later on in life. At the same time, Maria was suffering from a breast lesion, rashes that stung like nettles, and an eye inflammation that confined her to her room.

Allan occasionally took the older boys to the store with him. As they walked, Herman would try to imagine what lay down the winding side streets with their "ranges of grim-looking warehouses, with rusty iron doors and shutters, and tiled roofs; and old anchors and chain-cable piled" out front, though his father always tugged his sleeve if he tried to wander off on his own. On the streetcorners, tough-looking boys his own age wearing slouch caps and coarse knickers hawked newspapers and handbills, and oyster vendors with gnarled fingers pried open the day's catch and served passersby succulent raw shellfish from their carts. Pearl Street was full of "old-fashioned coffeehouses" with "sunburnt sea-captains going in and out, smoking cigars, and talking about Havanna, London, and Calcutta." When the boys managed to persuade their father to walk all the way to the river, they saw the great shipyards, and from the docks, the heights of Brooklyn looming above the masts at the Navy Yard. These "shadowy reminiscences of wharves, and warehouses, and shipping" aroused an insatiable hunger in Herman's soul.[6]

Home, which was full of souvenirs of his father's trips abroad, also nurtured Herman's imagination. He liked to spend Sunday afternoons browsing through the two large green portfolios of French prints his father kept in the library; one of them showed whaleboats in pursuit of a whale stuck full of harpoons and pouring blood into the sea. Allan, who liked to quote Shakespeare, Cowper, Pope, and Young, had brought back from Europe furniture and exotic objets d'art, paintings and engravings depicting famous places, and three hundred books that included works by Corneille, Racine, Voltaire, and Rousseau. The library shelves were filled with the leather-bound volumes, whose spines were embossed with gold lettering, mostly French words Herman could not translate. When his father pronounced the words for him, their lilting music cast a spell.

Years later, Herman would remember with pleasure the rare occasions when his father would take time to draw a chair up beside the coal fire and tell the children stories about the "monstrous waves at sea, mountain high; of the masts bending like twigs; and all about Havre, and Liverpool, and about going up into the ball of St. Paul's in London." Listening to these stories, Herman "fell into long reveries about distant voyages and travels," imagining himself exploring "remote and barbarous countries" and returning with "dark and romantic sunburnt cheeks" to relate his adventures in Africa or New Zealand. An outwardly prosaic child, Herman lived a voluptuous inner life thanks to this early exposure to artworks and sea stories.[7]

Allan sent Herman to Albany in the summer of 1826. Recommending him to Peter Gansevoort as an "honest hearted double rooted Knickerbocker of the true Albany stamp" who "would do equal honor in due time to his ancestry, parentage & kindred," he cautioned his brother-in-law not to expect too much of the boy. "As far as he understands men & things [he is] both solid & profound, & of a docile & amiable disposition," but Herman was as well "very backward in speech & somewhat slow in comprehension." According to Allan, Herman needed to be kept away from "green Fruit & unseasonable exposure to the Sun & Heat," and he needed to be fitted for new shoes.[8]

Herman's visit to Albany exposed him to the Old World culture of the New World Dutch. The patroons who settled the Hudson River Valley with patents from the Dutch West India Company brought centuries-old customs with them from Holland. True believers in the Protestant ethic and adept practitioners of it, they consolidated their large family fortunes and bred in their children a sense of civic responsibility. Their penchant for hard work was balanced by their love of creature comforts and their generous hospitality. The older men whom Melville saw in his youth resembled the picturesque characters of Dutch folklore, even if they no longer wore the traditional knee breeches, silk stockings, and silver-buckled shoes. They enjoyed a relaxing pipe after dinner, and both men and women enjoyed hearty food and drink and liked to tell jokes and stories. Apple-cheeked women in their full-skirted, full-bodiced dresses and aprons, who resembled the women painted by artists like Frans Hals, kept a fire burning in the fireplace all winter and extended a warm welcome to visitors.

Houseguests joined members of the family padding up the stairs in their nightcaps and long stockings, carrying silver tankards and possets of hot spiced wine. The heavy oak sideboard in a Dutch home held a rack of clay pipes and a china dish of tobacco, and the servants kept it stocked with platters of cakes and crullers and carafes of wine, liqueurs, and ale. The colorful labels on the bottles lined up along the sideboard— Tenerife and Madeira wines, Jamaican rum, French cognac, and Holland gin—would conjure up for an imaginative boy like Herman Melville not so much the allure of alcohol as fantasies of voyages to faraway lands that lay beyond the sea.

In spite of Allan's nervousness about the impression his son would make, Uncle Peter found Herman quite delightful, and described him to Allan in "very flattering terms," commenting especially on the close friendship that was developing between Herman and his four-year-old cousin, the fatherless Stanwix Gansevoort. When he came home, his parents found him "much improved by his visits in mind person & estate, thanks to the guardian care of his dear Grandmother & Uncle for which he seems very grateful & for whom he displays a most affectionate attachment."[9]

Although he had to endure his parents' stern reminders that family visits were tests of character, Herman enjoyed being with relatives. He was a welcome visitor in the homes of his uncles and grandparents, and their eccentricities intrigued him. On his own, and not forced to compete with his conceited older brother, he blossomed.

Herman's sixteen-year-old cousin Priscilla came down from Pittsfield that fall to go to school in the city and help his mother with the younger children. Herman liked her because she never put on airs and she was a little mysterious at times. Sometimes, when he tried to imagine why his beautiful cousin looked so sad, he would remember that her mother was the French lady who had married his uncle and died before he was born.

With Priscilla helping out, Maria recovered from her illness sooner than expected, and before long she was pregnant again. Still oblivious of her husband's precarious financial situation and preoccupied with their budding social life, Maria concentrated on teaching her older children proper etiquette. She arranged visits with other mothers so that her older children could practice the social graces, and soon Helen and Gansevoort were receiving invitations to tea dances and parties.

The road to gentility was not paved with silk, however, as Gansevoort, who was nearly eleven, discovered when a plate of muffins dropped into his lap "in wild disorder" at a neighborhood tea. Although he was "frightened and the company screamed," he composed himself as a young gentleman was expected to do, and "after they were fairly on the plate again I took one."[10]

Gansevoort was the family celebrity. Looking ahead to the school declamations of prose and poetry, Allan and Maria promised him a party if he won a prize. Despite his weak lungs and his tendency to speak too rapidly, Gansevoort won the Crown as his parents had expected. He knelt on the dais like a squire being knighted while a "young miss" placed a wreath of mixed flowers and greens on his head and the Master of Ceremonies intoned that the Crown was the "Highest Civick Honor given by the Romans &c." Allan, who considered General Gansevoort "a model for the imitation of his offspring" and proudly wore his signet ring, hung the Crown from the general's portrait until after the holidays in honor of his eldest son's ascension to the family pantheon.[11]

Unfortunately, playing by the rules did not win Herman the recognition he craved from both his parents. When he earned a monitorship the following year, they did not seem particularly impressed. "Your little protégé Herman, although a Monitor at the High School, is rather indisposed this [evening]," Allan wrote Peter Gansevoort, subordinating Herman's achievement to his illness.[12]

Herman was now one of six children whose father, like most ambitious businessmen, was spending twelve hours a day at his office, trying to keep ahead of creditors.

His earlier confidence that the cotton boom was a harbinger of flusher times had caused him to pile up enormous debts. The pressure of supporting a growing family combined with his drive to secure social prominence left Allan increasingly self-delusive. In January 1827, apparently in an attempt to beat the auction system, he broke completely with the old ways of doing business and entered into "an entirely *confidential Connexion* with Persons combining every qualification but money."[13]

Taking advantage of what appeared to him to be a golden opportunity to reap a large profit with comparatively little effort, Allan became a silent partner in a jobbing firm that planned to buy up huge lots of imported goods and resell them at prices low enough to undercut the competition. He promised on the strength of his reputation to put $10,000 into the firm over the next three years, confident he would be able to meet his obligations. The creditors, however, put a squeeze on the jobbers sooner than they had anticipated, and when the jobbers in turn put the squeeze on Allan to come up with half of the money he had pledged, he had to admit that he had nothing.

While Allan was trying to figure out how to extricate himself from this dilemma and save face, Maria was planning an enormous Valentine's Day party. She invited forty neighborhood children, and despite a cold snap and a snowstorm so severe she was sure no one would venture out, twenty-five children came. She served "Lemonade Port Wine ... & Cakes of various kinds the sugar Plums, mottoes, Blomange [*sic*], preserves, Oranges & dried fruits," and although Maria, "never having so many Children together before," had no idea how much food she would need, "there was so much that the boys who found they could eat no more emptied with a great deal of ease their plates into their Breeches pockets."[14]

The guests considered "the best part of the evening's entertainment A Violin the man played admirably," and the Melvill children said "there never was a more delightful party given." Maria had to confess, however, that she was glad when it was over and would "ever after be cautious about promising another."[15]

While Maria was entertaining virtually the entire neighborhood, Allan was appealing to her brother to advance him money to meet his contractual obligations to his new partners. Now risking exposure as a fraud, in desperate tones he implored his brother-in-law to send him $5,000 at once, or the entire matter "will *explode* to my utter disgrace." Thoroughly fed up with Allan's irresponsibility, Peter refused.[16]

Putting moral scruples aside, Allan compounded one error with another, entering into an even shadier deal in hopes of extricating himself from the first: "My name will not appear in the firm, which will enable them to use my endorsement when necessary. The whole affair will take over *sub rosa*, and in entire confidence among all parties, and I have even now the best grounded assurance, that all is *safe* and *secret*, and with Heaven's blessing will remain so." He rationalized leaving the fine points to "Providence who sees the end from the beginning & reconciles partial evil with universal good." The conspiratorial tone of Allan's language distressed his scrupulous brother-in-law.[17]

Lost in his fantasies, Allan tried to convince Peter that his success in this dubious venture was divinely ordained; it would be a triumph "inspired by HIM who directs all mortal events … to HIM therefore, & to HIM alone, be ascribed all praise," but Peter Gansevoort knew better. He insisted that Allan sign a written agreement before entering into any more business deals, but Allan refused, saying gentlemen ought to take gentlemen at their word. He protested that drawing up legal documents evinced a lack of confidence in his business partners.[18]

He pleaded with his brother-in-law to give him the money, or "my Honour, dearer than life itself, will be forfeited." Becoming more hysterical with every letter, he cast all the blame on that "brace of harpies instigated by the spirit of gain" who had perpetrated this "crisis of my fate." Shamelessly he pleaded with Peter "as you esteem me, and *love our dear Maria*, do not I conjure you as a friend and Brother, disappoint me in the *utmost need.*" From the beginning, the transaction had gone against Peter's grain, but he had to rescue Allan if he wanted to protect his sister's husband from disgrace and ruin. On April Fools' Day, Peter advanced him $5,000 from the money Maria was to inherit from her mother, a decision that would cost her dearly later on.[19]

Against a backdrop of mounting disaster, Maria was gathering strength to bear a seventh child. Gansevoort was sent to his uncle's house in Albany, and Herman to his grandparents' in Boston. He liked the old major, who wore a cocked hat and funny clothes, and the old lady, who sat very straight in her chair when she did needlework because her rheumatism made her stiff. Their Green Street parlor contained such magical objects as a vial of tea leaves from the Boston Tea Party and a model ship made entirely of glass down to its fragile cannons and two rows of tiny sailors standing at attention on its dazzling deck. As Herman gazed at the miniature glass ship, whose prismatic hull, delicately furled crystal sails, and tiny spars and cables flashed rainbows on the wall, his mind filled with visions of unexplored lands across the seven seas. Imagining that the ship carried a mysterious cargo in her hold, Herman squinted and peered into her tiny portholes, but his eyes met only impenetrable darkness.

The baby came on August 26. They christened her Frances Priscilla after her paternal grandmother and the cousin whose willing assistance gave Maria a chance to rest fairly frequently in the first months of nursing yet another child.

While Herman was visiting his grandparents in Boston, Lemuel Shaw married Hope Savage, knowing she would be not only a loving wife, but also a loving mother to Elizabeth, who was now "a most amiable, intelligent, and engaging child." Shaw's judgment in domestic affairs proved very sound, as Hope was a generous and good woman whose stepdaughter called her "Mother" and made her a lifelong confidante.[20]

Shaw sent Elizabeth for tutoring to the school run by Mary Lamb at her home on Harvard Street, and he was very pleased with the results. During their courtship, he had bragged to Hope about his daughter's "considerable proficiency" at reading both "prose & poetry." Compared with the shy Melvill boy whose grandparents sometimes brought him by to play, Elizabeth was a literary prodigy, at least in the eyes of her adoring father, who readily admitted being "influenced by my partiality."[21]

While Elizabeth was dabbling in "ordinary" poetry at age five, nine-year-old Herman was still struggling to master cursive script. By the time he returned to school in the fall, he had gained enough confidence to write his aunt Lucy, "You asked me to write you a letter but I thought tht [sic] I could not write well enough before this." To his grandmother he wrote, "This is the third letter that I ever wrote so you must not think it will be very good. I now study Geography, Gramar [sic], Arithmetic, Writing, Speaking, Spelling, and read in the Scientific class book."[22]

Walking along the Battery from Corlears Hook to Coenties Slip, Herman lost himself in ocean reveries. He had grown into "a robust healthy boy with a robust healthy soul in him," a boy "crazy to go to sea." At the Battery, which had been widened in 1821 and planted with one hundred ornamental trees, children played hoops and ball, and adults promenaded arm in arm past the colorful booths and bandstands that drew city folk and tourists to the harbor on Sunday afternoons. From the shore of the "city of bays," Herman could see the "numberless masts of ships" that thronged the harbor, "the beautiful hills of Brooklyn," and the same seagulls soaring above the bay in "slow-wheeling circles," later described by his contemporary Walt Whitman in his poem "Crossing Brooklyn Ferry."[23]

Both Frances Trollope and John James Audubon were "incapable of conceiving anything more beautiful than the Harbor of New York," as Mrs. Trollope said. Audubon told the painter Thomas Sully he could stand at the Battery for hours to watch the tall ships "tossing over the foaming billow with the grace of wild swans." One day, Herman Melville would be a "quick-moving tar" like the one Audubon saw "hauling on a reef at the yard's end" as his ship caught the wind and sailed out of New York Harbor.[24]

A childhood spent watching sailing ships of all types and sizes gliding through their element like graceful seabirds, as actress Fanny Kemble later put it, gave Herman a hunger to follow in the wake of the great whales and explore the fabled islands of the Pacific Ocean. So too, exposure to the cosmopolitan tide that brought sailors of all races and nationalities into the bustling seaport gave him intimations of the myriad exotic worlds that lay beyond the Narrows.

Surrounded by a large and sometimes suffocating family, Herman often had trouble sorting out his thoughts and feelings, and he liked being alone. On Sundays, when the family made excursions to Flushing or Perth Amboy to escape the city's heat, or picnicked in Hoboken or on Staten Island, Herman longed to experience these places on his own without having to worry about his deportment. One spring day when he was almost ten, he got his chance to go off for the day to Hoboken, where he rode the "Pleasure Railway" at the Elysian Fields Resort in "high spirits."[25]

To boys Herman's age, such resorts held out the promise of forbidden pleasures. The writer Lydia Maria Child pointed out that "drink and cigars abound at Hoboken, and sounds are heard there, not at all resembling the worship of the heart in the stillness of nature," and Mrs. Trollope described "*reposoires,* which, as you pass them, blast the senses for a moment, by reeking forth the fumes of whiskey and tobacco ... there is one in particular, which has quite the air of a Grecian temple, and did they drink wine instead of whiskey, it might be inscribed to Bacchus."[26]

～༄

For over a year, Allan had been juggling secret transactions, all the while becoming more and more caught up in denial of their implications. Trapped in the fantasies he had woven for himself, he rationalized his behavior by appeals to a Creator whose assumed desire to see His creature get rich was rapidly becoming the strongest article of Allan Melvill's creed.

Nearly a year after his first shaky deal, with one dramatic failure and a rescue by his brother-in-law behind him, Allan was boasting that his *"confidential* connexion with the highly respectable general Commission House of Messrs L. P. De Luze & Co in the Dry Goods branch of their Business" afforded him "liberal compensation" for his services and "certain support" for his family. In the flush of anticipated success, he also leased a house situated on a lot two hundred feet deep at 675 Broadway, right up the street from the elegant Cable Building and Mercantile Exchange.[27]

The move to upper Broadway meant that the Astors and former mayor Philip Hone would be their neighbors, and that Allan would ride the horsecar to work with shipping magnates like John Aspinwall—unless, of course, those worthies preferred to take a private carriage. Confident that her family would soon be hobnobbing with the cream of New York society, Maria sent Gansevoort, Herman, and Augusta to Mrs. Whieldon's dancing school. Augusta, who at age five was practicing the cotillion for an upcoming ball, was pretty and light on her feet. At nine, Herman, despite his later facility at climbing ships' riggings like a "Jago's monkey," seemed incorrigibly clumsy compared to the agile Gansevoort, who had so much "native grace" that he sometimes didn't bother to learn the steps or move his feet correctly.[28]

Helen Maria did not attend dancing class owing to a disability that had left one of her legs shorter than the other. Although she was smart, she was "indolent," according to her father, perhaps because it depressed her not to be a "Sylph" like her sister Augusta. Herman, who was coming into his own as a scholar, surprised his father by earning a "best Speaker" commendation in the introductory department examinations at the high school.[29]

The Melvills moved into their new home on April 30, 1828, one day before the traditional May Day madness when every renter in New York who had not renewed a lease piled luggage and household effects at the edge of the gutter preparatory to moving to new lodgings. Maria waxed eloquent about the charms and virtues of her house, the openness of the surroundings, and the "pure air" it afforded the children for play. From the spacious center hall, the stairway led to bedrooms with fireplaces and marble mantelpieces. There was ample closet space, an attic for storage, and a "fine large vault for Vegetables & Meats, Butter &c in the Summer in the yard."[30]

It took the family a while to settle in, as the house had to be repainted. "Maria, myself & our 7 bairns have passed the last two nights in the same chamber, Gansevoort & Herman on one side of our Bed, & Helen Maria & Augusta on the other, all in elegant negligence on the floor—Allan & Catherine point to point at the two extremes of a cot in a snug corner, & Miss Frances Priscilla on the right flank in a cradle—surrounded on all sides by a maze of furniture," Allan wrote to Peter Gansevoort. His letter portrays a cozy if chaotic scene, charged with irony for those who, with hindsight, can see that the Melvills were poised on the edge of an abyss.[31]

As they would soon find out, prosperity was illusory. Overextending oneself had become a way of life in a country where, for some, a belief in upward mobility and unending prosperity had the force of revealed religion. Perhaps because the Melvills had established a rhythm for coping with reproductive and seasonal cycles, Allan had fallen into the trap of believing he could ride out economic ups and downs as well. With faith in Providence as his collateral, Allan had borrowed heavily from his father to finance the Broadway move, and by late fall he was on the skids again.

That summer, while Maria took the girls and the baby to Albany, and Gansevoort went to stay with his grandparents in Boston, Herman went to Bristol, Rhode Island, to the home of his aunt Mary Melvill and her husband, John D'Wolf, "an old sea-captain, with white hair" who "used to sail to a place called Archangel in Russia" and who was "the first sea captain I had ever seen," according to Herman. Captain D'Wolf, who had spent ten days in the Marquesas in 1804, had crossed Siberia by dogsled from the Sea of Okhotsk in Asia to St. Petersburg with Georg H. von Langsdorff, the naturalist who accompanied the A. J. Krusenstern expedition. D'Wolf named one of his children after Langsdorff, and while Herman was in Bristol, his uncle regaled him with stories that whetted the boy's already strong appetite to see the world.[32]

Herman was young enough to escape the hard realities of adult life through fantasy, but old enough and sensitive enough to feel the tension that lay just below the surface.

Between his father's bravado and his mother's affectations of gentility stretched oceans of anxiety. On the whole, the Melvills' attitude was fairly typical of the new middle class, for whom faith in the continued prosperity of America somehow took the form of faith in their own unlimited personal credit.

In an attempt to re-create the holiday conviviality of their ancestral homes, they celebrated Thanksgiving in the new house with a feast of turkey, plum pudding, assorted side dishes and pies, and cider by the barrel. Much to the children's delight and their parents' consternation, dinner was interrupted by unusual excitement. "We had just commenced eating when lo & behold a cry of fire directly under our windows to which we paid no attention untill the Cook run up stairs & said the chimney was burning at a great rate, which set us all in commotion filled the rooms & Pantries with an offensive smoke & quite cooled our dinner–not so our appetites, for after it was over we sat down but with less comfort finished our Meal," Maria wrote her mother. Indeed, figuratively speaking, the woods were burning.[33]

If America in the 1820s saw a shift away from old-fashioned, family-owned businesses toward new speculative forms of mercantile capitalism, so, too, it saw a shift from patrician politics to what some, including Allan Melvill, called "mobocracy." By July 4, 1826, when the nation celebrated the fiftieth anniversary of the signing of the Declaration of Independence, those two rival patriots, John Adams and Thomas Jefferson, had died. The America of the revolutionary generation was past.

In 1829 the incoming Jackson administration "cleansed the Augean stables" by handing out government jobs in return for political favors. Major Thomas Melvill, a "precious relic" of revolutionary days, was unceremoniously relieved of his post at the Boston Custom House. Despite appeals by Allan Melvill and Peter Gansevoort to both Martin Van Buren and Andrew Jackson on behalf of the "youthful disciple & confidential associate of John Hancock & Samuel Adams," the old patriot was forced into retirement.[34]

On May 6, Allan wrote his father that he was "proud & gratified to hear from various Persons, that you retired from the Custom House with the firmness & dignity of an old Roman." The letter bristles with resentment at "the rude injustice of your removal, & though as a Christian I may in time forgive, as a Son I will never forget the Man nor shall my Children while they remember you & me forget him who might & should have prevented it–I mean General Jackson, for I cannot consider him de facto President of my Country, who failing to exercise his just prerogatives & abusing his legitimate powers, has inflicted an offensive & unmerited injury upon my Father in defiance of his own professions respecting 'the surviving patriot Veterans of the Revolution'… the administration I fear will entail endless evils [to?] this Country, & having commenced in madness will terminate in ruin." In some ways Allan was right: the old major's removal presaged the emergence of the sharkish spoils system that led to widespread corruption of the civil service four decades later.[35]

In the midst of these sweeping changes, Allan Melvill held on to what gave him security: material evidence of the success he felt his good family deserved. After the move to Broadway, he enrolled Gansevoort in the prestigious Columbia Grammar School. Attached to Columbia College, which was near City Hall Park, the school boasted that its pupils were the children of New York's finest families.[36]

In July, Maria took some of the children to visit their Boston grandparents, parceling out the siblings to other relatives, and leaving Allan Jr. and Catherine home as "being the most rebellious & ungovernable." She asked her brother Herman Gansevoort if his nephew could spend the summer with him at his Saratoga County home, and when he replied that his wife was expecting relatives and they could not offer young Herman a bed, Maria was deeply offended and angry.[37]

For that unfilial rebuff, Maria denounced Herman Gansevoort as "unmanly" and too indulgent of his wife, whom she heartily disliked. "Nothing but fear of contagion could have induced me to refuse such a request," she complained to Peter. Herman ended up going to his grandparents' house in Boston, where Allan hoped he would be "a good obedient Boy," and Major Melvill reported that he was uncommonly good and "a great favorite with us all."[38]

That fall, Herman entered the Columbia Grammar School, and having two sons there fed the Melvills' dreams of one day entering high society. Gansevoort went on to distinguish himself as a classical scholar and English student, and Herman began to come into his own. By encouraging critical thinking and debate instead of rote memorization, the Columbia Grammar School gave the intellectually curious ten-year-old his first taste of the joy of learning. Allan reported that "Herman I think is making more progress than formerly, & without being a bright Scholar, he maintains respectable standing, & would proceed further, if he could be induced to study more—being a most amiable & innocent child, I cannot find it in my heart to coerce him, especially as he seems to have chosen Commerce as a favorite pursuit, whose practical activity can well dispense with much book knowledge." Herman's professed interest in commerce must have been a bid to gain his father's approval, as he showed little interest in it later.[39]

The Melvills began the next decade with the birth of their eighth and last child, Thomas, on January 24. Despite the arrival of another healthy baby, 1830 was a depressing year for the Melvills. Augusta was so ill that she had to be hospitalized, and Allan, who had recently established an office on Pine Street as an adjunct to his store, was forced to close it and work out of his home—something that simply wasn't *done* by residents of Broadway.

For Maria, this was a blow. She hated being within sight of the elegant marble mansions on Bond and Great Jones streets but unable to share in the glittering social life her wealthier neighbors appeared to be enjoying. Allan confided to his brother-in-law Peter that her "spirits are occasionally more than ever depressed, while the family requires extraordinary attention, & unless she soon obtains relief from mental excitement, by some favorable change in our condition & prospects, I fear that her health will suffer permanent injury—she is very desirous of removing to Albany, to enjoy once more the society of her connexions & friends."[40]

At the end of the summer, Maria got her wish to return to Albany, but not in the way she had imagined. Two and a half years after the move to Broadway, business took such a sharp downturn that Allan was forced to liquidate his business, cancel his lease, and flee New York to avoid public disgrace and ruin.

As Allan Melvill's fortunes were toppling, New Yorkers were celebrating the ascension to the throne of Louis-Philippe, the bourgeois French king. Writing to Peter Gansevoort, Allan extolled "the glorious revolution in France, & the triumph of the majesty of the People over the despotism of a Tyrant" and the appointment of their "admirable" friend Lemuel Shaw as Chief Justice of the Supreme Judicial Court of Massachusetts, a position he had been reluctant to hold until Daniel Webster urged him to accept it. The cavalier tone of Allan's letter suggests that his capacity for denial was nearly infinite.[41]

In all their years in New York, the Melvills never quite succeeded in moving up the slippery social ladder. Although it was certainly possible for an enterprising man to rise in the world, even in a metropolis as competitive as New York, Allan Melvill never attained the status of John Beekman, Henry Brevoort, John Aspinwall, or Philip Hone, nor did his success in the mercantile trade ever match that of the millionaires Alexander Stewart and Nathaniel Macy, or that of Luman Reed, whose brilliant career is a perfect foil to Allan's failure.

Reed, who had moved from upstate Coxsackie to Manhattan in 1815, very quickly made a fortune in the dry-goods business. Unlike the improvident Allan Melvill, Reed eventually would gain prosperity and prestige through prudent pursuit of mercantile endeavors. By living modestly, he was able to become a collector and later a patron of the arts, and after his death in 1844, a group of his friends would purchase his collection of paintings intact to create the New-York Gallery of the Fine Arts, the first permanent art collection in America.[42]

Reed perfectly epitomized John Adams's belief that the material success of one generation should pave the way for the cultural and artistic advancement of the next. In short, Luman Reed's career epitomizes the American dream at its best; Allan Melvill's career, by contrast, embodies the American nightmare of inflated hopes followed by a rapid rise and an equally rapid and disastrous fall.

By late September 1830, Allan was "deeply immersed in ... the agonies of packing up" and keeping "Bachelor Hall" with Herman, while Gansevoort accompanied his mother and sisters and the babies to Albany. "We shall probably have to winter with the old Lady until we find a suitable House in the neighborhood," he wrote John D'Wolf. He managed to save most of the household effects, but he had to sell most of his precious library to pay off debts. After they had sent the furniture and heavy luggage to Albany on the Ontario towboat, Allan and Herman went to Courtlandt Street to catch the steamer, but a violent storm delayed their departure until morning and forced them to spend the night in the terminal, dozing against their satchels like refugees.[43]

One hundred sixty miles upriver from the Port of New York, on the eastern edge of the wilderness, Albany, earlier called Fort Orange, became the hub of the country's bustling grain and fur trades and lumbering industry. Even before the opening of the Erie Canal in 1825, the north-south waterways and the east-west stagecoach lines converged there, and great fortunes were made by men like young John Jacob Astor, who amassed enough capital by bartering liquor for furs to establish the American Fur Company in 1808, and to conquer the Northwest Territory for eastern commerce.[44]

Even men of Allan's generation had made their fortunes in Albany. William James, for example, the grandfather of diarist Alice, philosopher William, and novelist Henry, started out there with a modest dry-goods and tobacco store and ended up owning his own savings bank. A founder of Union College and a member of the Erie Canal Commission, James left an estate worth $3 million when he died in 1832, making him the second richest man in America, after John Jacob Astor.[45]

Albany's economy expanded steadily after the Revolution. Merchants who settled in the city after the War of 1812 and built up their businesses slowly through hard work and careful reinvestment in their own firms, as well as in local civic organizations during the 1820s, were in a position to capitalize on the tremendous surge of prosperity that accompanied the opening of the canal.

It must have crossed Allan's mind that leaving Albany for New York in 1818 was a bad decision, as he was returning in a recession. Almost entirely dependent on Peter Gansevoort, he had to start over again as a clerk in the Denison Williams Company. The Melvills stayed with Maria's mother at first, but Allan had no desire to live with her for long. By October they were able to move into a house at 338 North Market, on the corner of tree-lined Steuben Street, one of the town's most desirable thoroughfares.

In flush times a decade earlier, Allan would have been accepted by the Albany establishment as virtually a native son because of his alliance with the Gansevoorts, but now he was an interloper with a blot on his escutcheon. Moreover, he had arrived at a time when even old established businesses in Albany were struggling, and there was no room for a newcomer to make his way. Hoping to have his own store before long, he borrowed heavily from his father.

Life in Albany was difficult for Allan Melvill, but for eleven-year-old Herman it was stimulating and fun. When the circus came to town, everyone turned out to see the acrobats, wild animals, and fireworks, and the city was full of parks where children could fly kites and play tag, or participate in organized games such as pitching horseshoes, tossing quoits, or bowling on the green. In the winter, Albany residents strapped metal blades to their boots and skated on the river, and in summer the boys—and perhaps even a few rebellious girls—shed their clothes and went swimming in one of the Hudson's many streams or tributaries, or thronged to the city's many ice-cream parlors.[46]

The city's earlier prosperity brought a cultural boom that saw the establishment of the Albany Institute of History and Art and various other museums, theaters, musical sodalities, and schools. Relieved not to have to worry about their children's education, the Melvills enrolled the girls in the Albany Female Academy, and in October 1830, Herman and Gansevoort joined their cousin Stanwix at Albany Academy, of which their uncle Peter was a trustee.[47]

Albany Academy's rigorous college preparatory curriculum and unconventional method of instruction required some adjustment on the parts of Herman and Gansevoort. The school's formidable principal, Dr. T. Romeyn Beck, ran "a God-fearing school," and, like Allan Melvill, did not hesitate to wield the righteous rod to instill discipline in his unruly charges. The boys soon learned Beck's rattan rules: "a switch for tardiness, a switch for inattention, two switches for disobedience." A distinguished scholar in the fields of geology, meterology, and medical jurisprudence, Dr. Beck was a supporter of the movement to guard the American language against the influx of vernacular expressions, slang words, and syntactical mutations brought in by immigrants. Herman, by contrast, loved both colloquial and classical locutions, and when he came to write, he created a "bold and nervous lofty language" in which he expressed the American experience more vigorously than did any other writer of his time.[48]

In 1821, at about the time Herman was learning to talk, Jean François Champollion was deciphering the hieroglyphics on the Rosetta stone, and other European scholars were learning to read Sanskrit. Unveiling the mysteries of the ancient world created a vogue for comparative religions in elite American schools and later inspired such American writers as Ralph Waldo Emerson, Henry David Thoreau, Walt Whitman, and Herman Melville to delve into Eastern thought as an alternative to the growing materialism of America. It may have been at Albany Academy that Herman first had an inkling that religion could involve poetry and spiritual yearning as well as obedience and dread, as the curriculum included "English grammar, Arithmetic, Geography, Reading & Spelling, Penmanship, Natural History, & Irving's Catechism of Universal, Grecian, Roman & English History, Classical Biography, and Jewish Antiquities." Although Herman would not stay long enough to take the more advanced courses, his exposure to the rich lore and literature of diverse cultures and world religions planted seeds that would blossom later in his life.

Despite what he later termed a "revulsion from the counting-room philosophy of [William] Paley," whose materialistic theories were in vogue at Harvard College and elite independent schools, Herman won "first best" in his class on the mathematics examination and received *The London Carcanet*, an anthology of Augustan prose and romantic poetry, as his prize. It ignited a spark of poetry in his soul and played the role of go-between in several adolescent flirtations.[49]

Just before the New Year, 1831, Catherine Van Schaick Gansevoort died in her seventy-ninth year. It was a great loss to Maria, who had looked forward to her mother's companionship now that she had come home; perhaps the turnout of four hundred people for the funeral offered a modicum of consolation.[50]

Shortly after Herman's twelfth birthday, Allan Melvill took his two oldest sons to Boston to see if he could persuade his father to help him out. On the way, they stopped over at Thomas Melvill Jr.'s farm in Pittsfield—a visit Herman never forgot. "Well do I remember the meeting," he wrote decades later. "It was in the larch-shaded porch of the mansion looking off, under urn-shaped road-side elms, across meadows to South Mountain. They embraced, and with the unaffectedness and warmth of boys—such boys as Van Dyck painted." Herman's highly idealized account of the meeting reflects either the end of the estrangement between the brothers, or rose-colored nostalgia on his part.[51]

While Augusta was lucky enough to be left in Pittsfield with the Melvill cousins, Herman stayed in South Hadley with his aunt Lucy and her stern husband, Justin Clark, a Calvinist who believed in predestination, usually of an unpalatable sort. When this joyless attorney died suddenly at the age of forty-one, Lucy Melvill married Dr. Amos Nourse, an old friend of Lemuel Shaw, and Shaw's daughter Elizabeth spent several happy summers with the Nourses.

By midsummer, Maria was grooming Gansevoort for Harvard. Although the interviewers "admired his intelligence," Gansevoort never did go to a university—probably for financial reasons. For Herman, apparently, neither parent entertained hopes of higher education, as most families sent only their firstborn son to college in those day.[52]

Both Herman and Gansevoort were acclimatized and successful at Albany Academy by the time eight-year-old Allan joined them there, but Herman had to be withdrawn the following October for reasons of health or finances, which interrupted his schooling once again.

The deep recession that Albany had suffered hit working people and the poor the hardest. The Alms House already had two hundred inmates, many of whom were imprisoned for owing far less money than Allan Melvill did, and Albany's mayor announced that owing to the large number of pauper children begging on the streets, a

"Soup House" would be set up in the basement of City Hall. Before long, soup kitchens were feeding six hundred people a day. Well-to-do citizens of Albany organized charities to meet the emergency, but they made none of the systemic changes that might have rendered such charities obsolete.[53]

With business stagnating and his father demanding repayment of his loans, Allan borrowed $2,000 from Peter Gansevoort to establish his own fur-and-cap store at 364 South Market Street. In December he went to New York to solicit customers for his wares, but as the name Melvill had a bad odor in Manhattan now, Allan's mission failed.

The trip was ill-fated from the start. Feeling defeated and anxious about money, Allan economized by booking a deck passage on the return steamer despite the obvious danger of exposing himself to subzero temperatures for twenty hours. To make matters worse, the ice on the Hudson was so thick above Poughkeepsie that the boat had to discharge its shivering passengers on the river's eastern shore. They were taken to Rhinebeck in an open wagon, then transferred to a covered sleigh that took them as far as Greenbush. Allan was forced to cross the frozen river on foot and trudge several miles through biting wind and numbing cold to reach his home. Nearly fifty years old and unaccustomed to such strenuous exercise at extreme temperatures, he arrived home exhausted, and deathly ill.[54]

Rather than remain in bed until he was fully recovered, he got up and went to work whenever he felt slightly better. His persistent cough soon turned into walking pneumonia, and the sicker he became, the more obsessive, frenzied, and unreasonable became his attempts to make up for his failure. Despite his illness, he worked twelve hours at a stretch, then came home feverish and couldn't fall asleep. Just after New Year's, he came home burning with fever and collapsed.

On January 5, 1832, he marked these lines from Psalm LV:

Attend unto me, and hear me: I mourn in my complaint, and make a noise.
My heart is sore pained within me: and the terrors of death are fallen upon me.
Fearfulness and trembling are come upon me and horror hath overcome me.

During the next few days, he slipped into a frightening delirium from which he never recovered, and on January 10, Peter Gansevoort notified Thomas Melvill Jr. that his brother's condition was now hopeless: "he was unwell, when he last wrote to you But persisting in giving attention to his business—He devoted himself so closely and assiduously as to produce a state of excitement, which in a great measure robbed him of his sleep. It is but a few days since he yielded to the wishes of his friends and remained at home. The excitement would not be allayed and yesterday he occasionally manifested an alienation of mind. Last night he became much worse—and today he presents the melancholy spectacle of a deranged man."[55]

Thomas rode over from Pittsfield to watch at Allan's bedside, and, shocked by his brother's appearance, wrote Lemuel Shaw, "I found him *very sick*–induced by a variety of causes–under great mental excitement–at times fierce, even *maniacal*." Thomas now prayed for a speedy end to his brother's sufferings, and peace: "Hope is no longer permitted of his recovery, in the opinion of the attending Physicians, and indeed–oh, how hard for a brother to say! I *ought not* to hope for it–for–in all human probability–he would live, *a Maniac!*"[56]

While his family prayed for him, Allan raved incoherently. On January 28, 1832, he made his final transaction with the business of this world, trading the clamor of sickness for the silence of death. In the margin of his Bible beside Psalm LV, Maria wrote: "This Chapter was mark'd a few days before my dear Allan by reason of severe suffering was depriv'd of his Intellect. God moves in a misterious way."[57]

As a Dutch Calvinist, Maria was expected to accept God's will, no matter how unfair and inscrutable it seemed. Thus, outwardly, she resigned herself to her husband's tragic death, numbly masking her true feelings before the children. Her stoicism must have seared Herman's heart. He was the dreamer, the one his parents had referred to as "innocent" and "amiable" and "shy," and the child in him still needed a mother to hold and comfort him.

Patriarchal Victorian families in England and America, however, thought kissing and hugging boys after they reached a certain age would make them "soft," so Allan had not hugged his son in years, and Maria had expressed her love by nagging him about his deportment and penmanship. Warmhearted and affectionate by nature, the boy experienced his mother's austere self-discipline as indifference, disdain, or even blame. He felt vaguely guilty toward his father and unloved by his mother, who buried her grief under layers of stoic depression as thick as the layers of black bombazine from which her elegant mourning dress was fashioned.

Now twelve years old, on the cusp of puberty, the boy was newly plagued by unfocused erotic dreams that left him aroused and agitated by mingled sensations of enormous masculine power and equally enormous shame. Having always resented his father's liberal use of the corrective rod, he now even more bitterly resented his father's abandonment of him and longed deep down for one manly and tender embrace.[58]

At times the entire house seemed to be spinning inside his head and stomach, and for a moment now and then, he would imagine that if he blinked his eyes and opened them, his father would be alive again. Having listened helplessly to his father's ravings, he had recurrent dreams from which he would awaken with a strangled sob. The nightmares lasted a long, long time, and always they were variations on related themes: a visceral longing for physical contact with a loving father, and a desperate desire to save himself from ruin by achieving something so great it would shake the very foundations of the world and make his parents love him more than Gansevoort.

Allan's sudden bankruptcy, illness, and violent death destroyed Herman's childhood world and made all his perceptions of reality and previous assumptions seem hollow. He felt as though he were being sucked into a maelstrom. Having experienced the unthinkable, young Herman Melville had crossed a great divide; from now on, the unthinkable became his constant companion, his tormentor, and his guide.

Melville wrote Typee *and* Omoo *in this rambling wood-frame house in Lansingburgh, New York, a thriving Dutch settlement at the confluence of the Hudson and Mohawk rivers.*

FOUR

TORMENTED WITH AN ITCH FOR THINGS REMOTE

An equalizer more effective than the Declaration of Independence, death threatened the pre-tensions to gentility of the rising middle class. As middle-class Americans struggled to estab-lish rituals to supply them with the security largely absent in their fluid, restlessly mobile society, the focus of funerals shifted away from the unpleasant fact of the human corpse itself to the behavior of the survivors. Death became sentimentalized, and mourning became a sec-ular cult divorced from religion, with "right feeling" replacing "right belief."

After the Great Awakening, most Protestant churches in America had abandoned the old Puritan obsession with the terrors of physical death and softened their theology. Preachers drew upon pastoral imagery to depict death as the Good Shepherd's final ingathering of His flock. The mourning manuals that proliferated in the mid–nineteenth century sentimentalized death, as did popular novels in which couples separated from each other and deceased infants sepa-rated from their parents were reunited in a "Heavenly Home" more domestic than divine.[1]

The grieving process was conceived to be linear, and recovery as progressive. There was no recognition that the pain of bereavement and loss recurred, that chance remarks and events could trigger flashbacks to the initial trauma and stop a mourner's heart. Mourners strove to curb their natural feelings or risk angering God, as this passage from a letter of Augusta Whipple Hunter to Augusta Melvill demonstrates: "[Since] Father's death I have not been able to forget myself in my excess of pleasure as I once did. Whenever I feel a little more gay than usual his dying bed seems before me, & I feel most powerfully that such gay & light thoughts ill become one who one day, perhaps not very distant must like him pass from earth—However cheerfulness is a different thing & a Christian duty—forgive me these thoughts."[2]

Mourners were held to a rigid code, from their style of dress to the gradually decreasing width of the black border on the indispensable calling card. Men returned to work after several days with a mourner's weed stuck in their hatbands, and women swathed themselves in layers of black bombazine, whose sooty appearance was meant to evoke the funereal phrase "ashes to ashes, and dust to dust." After a prescribed period, women were allowed to wear shiny black silk to signify the gradual abatement of their grief. Men stopped wearing black clothing and a mourning weed and had rings and watch fobs embossed with an urn and a willow tree, while women wore lockets, pendants, or brooches that held a lock of hair or a sketch of the deceased.[3]

New iconographies allowed people to express their sorrow in socially acceptable forms. Lithographers such as Nathaniel Currier sold mass-produced mourning pictures that featured the standard motif of a grieving girl standing under the drooping branches of a willow tree, or a tombstone on which the names and dates of the departed could be inscribed. Whenever a woman's private feelings clashed with these public attitudes, she could sublimate her sorrow by sewing a needlepoint mourning picture and teaching her daughters to do the same.[4]

Outwardly, the Melvills coped with Allan's death like proper Protestants. Maria assembled family members at her home for a funeral service characterized by dignity and emotional restraint. She kept her feelings to herself, sublimating them in socially acceptable gestures of mourning and turning to the Church for consolation. Maria Melvill's Calvinist upbringing had stressed resignation and submission to God's will; to question Fate was to question the Creator.

Sorrow and *resignation* were the words Maria knew for bereavement; she had no lexicon for the anger she felt toward her dead husband. She wanted to reprimand him for dying, for being so thoughtless, careless, and reckless with his health, but anger was one of the Seven Deadly Sins, and prolonged grieving indicated a rebellious heart and defiance of God's will. The one person to whom she might have turned to express her private feelings was her mother, but Caty lay buried in the family plot at Albany Rural Cemetery.

The 1830s saw the creation of rural cemeteries designed as gardens of repose for departed Christian souls. In these "cities of the dead," Death, once symbolized by the winged skull or death's head carved on gravestones in colonial churchyards, now came to be symbolized by smiling cherubs. With their winding walkways, gently rolling hills, and shaded knolls landscaped with trees and luxuriant shrubbery, these "gardens of death" provided a haven of pastoral beauty that denied the finality of death by evoking images of domesticity.

By providing the deceased with bucolic resting places far removed from the city and the marketplace, rural cemeteries reunited families torn apart not only by death, but also by the growing division between home and workplace. Allan Melvill was interred not far from the Gansevoort plot where Harme and his wife Maria Magdalena and old Peter Gansevoort and his wife Catherine Van Schaick lay at rest; later, Maria and several of their children would lie on the knoll beside him.[5]

Predictably, the marketing of burial plots soon became a profitable business. "We take stock in a graveyard as we do in banks and railways schemes," wrote Cornelius Mathews, the New York writer and editor who became a friend of Melville's. Entrepreneurs bought up land for the creation of richly ornamented cemeteries such as Mount Auburn in Cambridge, Massachusetts, which was established in 1831 so that those not yet departed could feel that their loved ones were in a place more tranquil and more beautiful than any they had known on Earth. A family's love for the dear departed began to be measured by the amount of money they spent on coffins, monuments, funeral services, and arrangements for perpetual care, and before people knew it, the laws of the marketplace had succeeded in transforming even death into a commodity.[6]

According to Calvinist doctrines, Allan's deathbed ravings made the salvation of his soul virtually impossible. At the prospect that her beloved husband might be consigned among the damned, Maria clung tightly to the Christian promise of eternal life rather than rejecting it. Seeking biblical assurances of God's mercy, she made a formal confession of her faith soon after her husband's death, and after "due examination," she was admitted into the First Dutch Reformed Church as a full communicant.

Thirty years later, in a letter to Kate Gansevoort, Maria expressed what she had been feeling then, though in a highly rhetorical, almost public style: "Oh the loneliness the emptiness of this world when a woman has buried the husband of her youth & is left alone to bring up their children, without a loved father's care & experience in the training them to fulfill life's duties & to point the way to heaven by his Christian example."[7]

Maria tried to bring her children up to be God-fearing, sober, dutiful young adults, encouraging the boys to go into the family business, and the girls to be agreeable. She added an *e* to the Melvill name, partly to enhance the aristocratic aura of the family name by adopting the Scottish spelling, and partly to give Gansevoort a fresh start by disassociating him from the aura of impropriety and failure surrounding his father's name. Gansevoort, who had run the shop at 364 South Market Street efficiently during his father's illness, withdrew from Albany Academy two months after his father's death to take over the fur-and-cap business.

Although Gansevoort was barely seventeen years old, his mother had great faith in his business acumen and expected him to step into his father's shoes. Uncle Peter advanced Gansevoort some money and witnessed Maria's endorsement of the transfer of the business from father to son: "This is to certify that my son Gansevoort Melvill, is carrying on the Fur, and Cap business in the City of Albany, on my account, and that I hold myself responsible for all debts contracted by said son, in the course of said business."[8]

At first it seemed that Gansevoort would make a go of the business. The opening of the Mohawk and Hudson Railroad had greatly increased shipments of lumber, grain, and furs through Albany, and money was flowing into the region, so the market for Moroccan and Circassian caps and buffalo sleigh robes was booming. On his first trip to New York as head of the business, Gansevoort discovered that the older merchants there had heard of him as "the young man who lately began the cap manufacture in Albany," not the son of the discredited Allan Melvill. Their recognition seemed an omen. In late September 1832, Maria noted that Gansevoort "says that in two years from this time he will make his Fur business worth a Net profit of $10,000 a year." He took every positive sign as a guarantee of future success, confident that he would soon be able to slough off the burden of his father's debts.[9]

After her husband's death, Maria was forced to live in a frugal, even austere, manner. Women in Victorian America had actually *lost* rights enjoyed by their colonial grandmothers; in New York State, for instance, they could not own property or manage assets. As a result, Maria had to ask her brother for every penny as though she had suddenly become his ward.[10]

Her attachment to him had always been strong—so strong, in fact, that "My dear Allan often use'd to say—'Maria you love Peter better than me or your Children,' & I can assure you his Death has not made me love you less—you are everything to me." She expected emotional as well as financial support from Peter, and when he fell in love with nineteen-year-old Mary Sanford and married her on August 4, 1833, Maria was more than a little jealous. She needn't have worried, however, because, unlike her brother Herman, Peter proved a generous if sometimes inconsistent benefactor to his sister's family right up until his death in 1876.[11]

While in some respects Maria's situation did not change dramatically after Allan's death, in other ways it changed drastically. Like other women in Victorian America, she had always been responsible for the running of the household while her husband tended to his business. Now, however, she had the responsibility of raising eight children but none of the comfort, companionship, and social status enjoyed by well-married women.

Bereft of physical and emotional closeness with her husband, she experienced feelings of abandonment and desolation that she tried to hide from her children.

Turning her anger inward, she suffered bouts of deep depression. Because her efforts at self-control and her attempts to be both a mother and a father to her brood often came across as rigidity and coldness, the children often experienced their mother as unaffectionate and stern. Somehow, Maria made her eight children sit motionless and silent by her bedside every afternoon while she took a nap—or so the family legend goes.[12]

While Maria repressed her grief by reverting to stern Calvinist doctrines and moving closer to her oldest son, Herman pushed his sorrow deep inside and kept his strongest feelings to himself, storing them inside and brooding on them secretly. He was taken out of school and put to work clerking in the New York State Bank, which his maternal grandfather had founded and of which his uncle Peter was a trustee. Not even thirteen years old and barely ready for long trousers and cravats, Herman may have welcomed the chance to enter the business world like his brother, partly because being more like Gansevoort might win him his mother's favor.

Years later he would write: "Talk not of the bitterness of middle-life and after life; a boy can feel all that, and much more, when upon his young soul the mildew has fallen; and the fruit, which with others is only blasted after ripeness, with him is nipped in the first blossom and bud. And never again can such blights be made good; they strike in too deep, and leave such a scar that the air of Paradise might not erase it."[13]

Walking to work along tree-lined State Street with businessmen wearing top hats probably made Herman feel important and grown-up at first, but before long he realized just how routine and monotonous bank work could be. His meager salary went straight into his mother's bank account, and he began to resent being forced to leave school just when he was beginning to enjoy studying. The loss of the opportunity to be a scholar turned him into a voracious reader and indefatigable autodidact.[14]

Because he was a second son who was neither the image of his father nor the apple of his mother's eye, young Herman's feelings were often overlooked, and for a time he actually believed he preferred it that way. Like Hamlet, the boy suffered in silence, adopting an ironic way of looking at the world as he confronted the tremendous cognitive dissonance between what he was feeling and what the adult world was telling him he ought to feel. Patriarchal culture, like Shakespeare's Claudius, tried to tell Herman that grief for his father was "unmanly" and showed "a will most incorrect to heaven," while the maternal world, like Gertrude, was silencing him with pious platitudes.[15]

"I must not think of those delightful days, before my father became a bankrupt, and died, and we removed from the city; for when I think of those days, something rises up in my throat and almost strangles me," he would write in *Redburn*, and later he would note in his copy of Shakespeare's plays, "Secret grief is the cannibal of its own heart."[16]

In the summer of 1832, an outbreak of cholera swept through Albany. Eleven hundred cases were reported, with four hundred people dead. Most of the city's 415 taverns were closed, and as residents lit tar pots to combat infection, Maria and her children fled to Pittsfield.

Maria had never felt comfortable with the rustic ways of her brother-in-law's family, but this time they were united by misfortune, and she appreciated their hospitality: "The family are very kind, the Children live on bread & milk, look brown & healthy— all have gain'd flesh, & my baby Tom is the picture of plenty & good nature. The air is delightful, we literally breathe sweets, the atmosphere is fill'd with fragrance from the new-mown hay, all around us, Gansevoort is employed, in raking & turning Hay, Fishing, rowing the Ladies across, & around a large pond back of the house, & in doing ample justice to the excellent Milk & delicious bread & Butter of the Farm we are happy here, but would wish to return to town as soon as would be prudent." Herman probably would have preferred to stay with his cousins on the farm, but he had to return to his job in Albany.[17]

From Pittsfield, Maria and Gansevoort went to Boston to ask Major Melvill not to saddle Gansevoort with his father's debts. With her mother's estate still locked up in litigation, and her husband having persuaded her to borrow against her inheritance, Maria had no money. The trip took its toll on her emotionally. Staying in her husband's boyhood home, where "every object served to remind me of him," made her feel lonely and sorrowful, and she needed all her fortitude to repress her feelings before strangers. "When I enter'd the old Mansion," she wrote Peter Gansevoort, "it was silent & dark as night, my feelings got the better of all restraint & I wept Hysterically for some time unable to controul them."[18]

It was unusual for Maria to let down her hair this way, and of course Herman was not there to witness it: "Herman I have not heard of since he left us at Pittsfield," she wrote her brother. "I hope he is with you, & made to occupy his time when out of the Bank in reading, & writing to me." Gansevoort added a postscript to her letter: "Give Ma's and my love to Herman, and please tell him that his mother desires him to be particularly careful of himself."[19]

Maria was very anxious about Herman's writing to her, and when she at last heard from him, she was delighted: "His last letter was much prais'd, for its superiority over the first, the hand writing particularly, he must practise often, & daily." Her sole thought was that Herman should perfect his penmanship to qualify for clerking or copying in a law office. "My best love to Herman, who I hope is a good Boy, & endeavours to make himself useful by writing &c," she wrote her brother as a postscript to one of Helen's letters. Years later, when he began to write fiction, he would write fast and furiously, as though he wanted to shake off the feeling that his mother was looking over his shoulder and criticizing everything he wrote.[20]

Maria's trip to Boston was fortuitously timed, because not long after she had talked with him, Major Melvill died suddenly. He had turned into an eccentric character who wore the "small clothes" of the revolutionary era long after they were out of fashion. As a neighborhood fire warden, the old patriot chased fire engines with the gusto of a small boy until he finally wore himself out fighting a fire in a brick building across the street from his house. He contracted a violent cold, followed by an attack of diarrhea that proved unresponsive to medicine, completely debilitating him.

Daniel Webster eulogized him as a symbol of America's heroic past, and Dr. Oliver Wendell Holmes, in his elegiac poem "The Last Leaf," painted an affectionate portrait of the old major trudging up Beacon Hill with the aid of a cane, wearing his "three-cornered hat," silk stockings, and knee breeches "all ... so queer." The death of Major Melvill, "the last Mohawk," symbolized the passing of the old order.[21]

The settling of his estate fell into the hands of Lemuel Shaw and John D'Wolf, who were still trying to make sense of Allan's account books and correspondence. Just before his death, Major Melvill had assured Maria that he would not entail Allan's debt on Gansevoort's business, but the probating of the will revealed that all his loans to Allan had been deducted from the estate. To fend off Allan's creditors, Judge Shaw brought suit on behalf of Allan's siblings, and they withdrew their sympathies from Maria partly out of embarrassment. She bitterly resented "the apparent utter desertion" of her children by their Melvill relatives.[22]

After the deaths of both Allan and his father, a long line of merchants and tradespeople to whom Allan had owed money approached the Melvills' door, among them milliner Martha Bent and her daughter, Anne Middleton Allen, two prominent Boston businesswomen. A vague letter from Thomas Melvill Jr. to Lemuel Shaw shows that the two women came to the door and made an unspecified "claim" on the estate, which in itself would hardly be noteworthy, except that a number of scholars, working backward from the text of Melville's *Pierre* (1852), a novel with a sensational incest plot, have concluded that the two women were Allan Melvill's mistress and illegitimate daughter. Despite exhaustive research, nothing has been found to prove that either of these women had a sexual relationship with either of the Melvills.[23]

Maria found herself having to appear in court frequently to straighten out her dead husband's affairs, and Judge Shaw, pledging himself a staunch ally of the family, gave Maria "strong assurances" that he would "at all times & under all circumstances, do all in my power, to promote ... the welfare of your children." While he lifted some of the burden from Maria's shoulders by representing her interests in settling Allan's estate, he refused to act as guardian of the children, recommending instead one of his associates in order to avoid a conflict of interest.[24]

Thomas Melvill Jr., who had known hard times himself, showed genuine sympathy for Maria's plight, although he could offer his sister-in-law little beyond a summer haven in the Berkshires. Still predominantly rural in character, Pittsfield pointed with pride to the 126-foot elm tree that towered over the town center, and the annual fall Cattle Show and Fair that drew entries from miles around. This two-day event featured a plowing contest and a parade as well as livestock judging, and Herman liked seeing the horses, cattle, oxen, sheep, swine, and other barnyard animals that filled the village green.

Earning his board and a small wage for doing farm chores provided Herman with an escape from his routine job at the bank and the rather formal social life of his mother's house at 3 Clinton Square in Albany. Working on the farm gave him a sense of physical well-being and wholeness, and he discovered that he liked being outdoors, working with his hands. His aunt and uncle and cousins lived much more informally than his mother and his siblings, and he enjoyed going on rambles with his country cousins. In early summer they went strawberrying in the fields down by the old limestone quarry, and in late summer they gathered blackberries and huckleberries up in the hills.

When he wasn't romping with his cousins, Herman enjoyed the company of his eccentric uncle, who had served as acting American consul in France at a time when James Monroe and Joel Barlow were frequent visitors to Paris. "Mild and kindly, with a faded brocade of old French breeding," as his nephew later described him, Thomas Melvill claimed he couldn't afford proper work clothes, and he wore his Sunday clothes to plow or hay the fields. "At the end of a swath, he would at times pause in the sun, and taking out his smooth-worn box of satin-wood, gracefully help himself to a pinch of snuff, partly leaning on the slanted rake, and making some little remark, quite naturally, and yet with a look, which—as I now recall it—presents him in the shadowy aspect of a courtier of Louis XVI, reduced as a refugee, to humble employment, in a region far from the gilded Versailles," Melville later wrote. He remembered his uncle sitting "by the late October fire on the great hearth of the capacious kitchen of the old farm-mansion ... gazing into the embers, his face plainly expressing to a sympathetic observer that his heart—thawed to the core under the influence of the genial flame—carried him far away over the ocean to the gay Boulevards."[25]

Thomas Melvill Jr., who won the annual plowing contest at the agricultural fair in 1818, became a prominent citizen of Berkshire County. He was elected president of the Berkshire County Agricultural Society in 1835, and the following year he was honored as the "first to introduce the Ruta Baga within the County." He also served on the Pittsfield school committee, taking an active role in trying to improve the local schools; it was undoubtedly as a result of his influence that Herman returned to Pittsfield to try schoolteaching a few years later. As Ben Austin, or "B.A.," Thomas wrote short editorials for the *Pittsfield Sun* that favored educational improvements and condemned the practice of imprisonment for debt, a subject about which he was an expert.[26]

Uncle Thomas was also an accomplished amateur artist, and he taught his nephew how to draw. Herman much preferred drawing pictures for his cousin Julia to struggling with his penmanship, and Julia Maria judged his sketches of seashells "very axceptable [*sic*] indeed." His uncle's erudition and entertaining affectations, as well as the companionship of his unaffected cousins and the lush beauty of the landscape, drew Herman back to the Berkshires later on.[27]

He was not able to come during the summer of 1834, however, as he had started work with his brother in the stores. Julia wrote in her breathless way, ending her letter with a charming non sequitur: "I was very much disappointed that Herman's buisnes [*sic*] would not allow him to visit Pittsfield this year but Gan said he could not let him becaus [*sic*] he was wanted in the store. I think we are very much in debt to the *Phoenicians* for the invention of wrighting [*sic*]. I do not know what we should do without it."[28]

Julia's letters, which were not discovered until 1983, provide glimpses of ordinary life on the farm and of Herman's siblings. From them we learn that Gansevoort was interested in a girl named Mary Warren; that Augusta had a pet bird and that Pittsfield people mistook her for a young widow when she was only fifteen because she wore spectacles and had a "sober" countenance. We also learn that Helen was so jealous of Gus's friendship with Julia that she made rude remarks about her; and that when nine-year-old Fanny spent a summer on the farm in 1836, she was such a hellion that Julia feared that "Aunt Maria will not own her when she goes home she has grown so wild & turned out dreadfully."[29]

Gansevoort, meanwhile, was boasting that he would make a $15,000 profit before the year was out. "To make money," he wrote in his journal, "it only requires a cool dispassionate disposition joined with talents even below mediocrity, and a determination to sacrifice every inclination and feeling that may come in contact with it." He worked such long hours that he often slept in the store, and in the little spare time he had, he either read novels, visited his club, or escorted young ladies to the theater.[30]

Settling into the role of the young man about town, Gansevoort enrolled in the Young Men's Association for Mutual Improvement, which gave him access to the club's library as well as several city libraries. For a $2 subscription, he could borrow the latest works of such popular authors as Lord Byron, Sir Walter Scott, and his uncle Peter's friend James Fenimore Cooper, and pass them along to Herman when he was done.

In May 1835, just when Gansevoort's fortunes were improving and it seemed that the family could get out of debt, the shop where the "Hair Seal Skins" were prepared burned to the ground, and there was not enough insurance to cover the whole loss. With his uncle's help, Gansevoort managed to set himself up again in business despite the fire.

Preparing furs for ladies' capes, men's hats, and sleigh robes as before, he counted and stacked hundreds of kangaroo and "Hair Seal" pelts, and as he became more familiar with the procedures, he experimented with faster ways of softening the skins, weighing by hand the alum and bran compounds used to treat them.

At times he hauled as many as five hundred muskrat pelts to the mill in a single load over country roads that were rutted and dusty, muddy, or icy depending on the season, and his friend Alexander Bradford sometimes accompanied him on his rounds. On one of his trips, Gansevoort ran across Herman, then a courier for the bank, drinking spirits at a tavern in Schenectady. Gansevoort was undoubtedly scandalized by his younger brother's misbehavior and gave him a stern temperance talk.[31]

Despite his resentment of Gansevoort, Herman patterned himself after his older brother in some ways. Gansevoort's path at this point was the conventional one for young men, and Herman's way of growing up was to follow in his footsteps. Thus, he enrolled in the Albany Classical School, which professed to "secure the two great ends of education: the cultivation of the intellect and the formation of character under the influence of the Christian religion." It also promised to prepare for business careers.[32]

This was a new era for education, as schools increasingly had to justify their existence by demonstrating that their graduates had marketable skills, not just erudition. Even the reformer Horace Mann reluctantly shifted the focus of his campaign to strengthen the public schools by stressing not so much the moral and intellectual value of an education as its market value.[33]

Ironically, while he was preparing for a practical career, Herman developed a "love of English composition" and his teacher, Charles E. West, praised his "deftness" at writing. Although he was "not distinguished in mathematics," according to West, he was "very much so in the writing of 'themes' or 'compositions,' and fond of doing it, while the great majority of pupils dreaded it as a task." During the course of that year, he decided to try his hand at teaching, but, realizing he would need Latin to qualify for a job, he returned to Albany Academy in the fall of 1836, staying until March 1837.[34]

Meanwhile, Helen Melville was attending the private boarding school run by Mrs. Charles Sedgwick, the sister-in-law of Catharine Maria Sedgwick, the celebrated novelist whose book *The Linwoods* struck Helen as her best so far. At Elizabeth Sedgwick's school in Lenox, Massachusetts, little girls studied Latin, and according to Helen, they could speak French like Parisians by the time they were ten. "By some sort of unknown alchymy [sic]," she wrote to Augusta, "Mrs. Charles," as the girls called her, "transforms all the common minds under her charge into geniuses: I cannot say that she has been equally successful with me, but certainly her other pupils are 'past the common,' as the Irish say. I hope to be of great assistance to you in your French, having in my own humble opinion improved very much under her care."[35]

Even so, Helen sometimes missed her family, and longed to return "to the shadow of the mother wing." She charged Augusta with the responsibility of being "the pattern girl" for their younger sisters, and she persuaded Gansevoort and Herman to drive over to Lenox on the weekends for tea.[36]

Gansevoort, meanwhile, had recovered sufficiently from the fire to expand the business. In September 1836 he advertised in the *Albany Argus* for "Twenty Hat Trimmers" and "Two Boys as apprentices to the hatting business," but the boom lasted no more than a year. Just as things were going better for the Melvilles, the bottom fell out of the economy.

~

"When will the bubble burst?" the poet William Cullen Bryant asked at the height of the land and money boom. Ever since President Andrew Jackson's attack on the Bank of the United States and the issuance of the Specie Circular, expansion of paper credits had gone on unchecked, to the delight of those who were making quick money at the expense of long-term economic stability. With inflation driving prices out of the reach of the lower classes, angry crowds surged through Manhattan's streets, waving placards that read, "BREAD, MEAT, RENT, AND FUEL! *Their prices must come down!*" In Boston, businessmen gathered at Faneuil Hall to protest the government's order requiring payment of specie at post offices, and the cotton baron Abbott Lawrence Lowell denounced the administration so vigorously that a newspaper rendered his words in capital letters: "THERE IS NO PEOPLE ON THE FACE OF GOD'S EARTH THAT IS SO ABUSED, CHEATED, PLUNDERED AND TRAMPLED BY THEIR RULERS, AS ARE THE PEOPLE OF THE UNITED STATES."[37]

All over the country there were calls for a complete separation between bank and state, and the volatile bank issue split the Democratic parties of New York and Massachusetts into conservative and radical wings. Labor blamed business for the crash, and business blamed the workers. Optimists believed the recession would bring about the reform of the paper-money system and the exclusion of organized-money power, or lobbies, from American politics; pessimists feared the depression would lead to the collapse of the Republic. The popular preacher Henry Ward Beecher described the debacle in apocalyptic terms: "The world looked upon a continent of inexhaustible fertility (whose harvest had glutted the markets, and rotted in disuse), filled with lamentation, and its inhabitants wandering like bereaved citizens among the ruins of an earthquake, mourning for children, for houses crushed, and property burned forever."[38]

The first major economic downturn for the new nation had come in 1819, the year of Melville's birth, but it was minor compared with the much more severe money crisis that led to the Panic of 1837. The Panic ruined those heavily in debt, as banks tightened credit drastically, plunging the country into a severe depression that lasted for five years. Numerous banks went under, nine-tenths of the nation's factories closed, and cities could not build almshouses and poorhouses fast enough to house the working-class families who found themselves jobless and out on the street. Despite the establishment of soup kitchens, people rioted, raiding food stores in desperation.[39]

With employers cutting back on hiring, it was not an auspicious moment for young men starting out on new careers, and even people with inherited wealth, such as Peter Gansevoort, saw their assets shrinking every day. Maria Melville tried to save the business by mortgaging some parcels of property she had inherited from her mother, but despite her best efforts, Gansevoort found himself unable to balance his credits and debits, and he had to dissolve the company.

Fifteen-year-old Allan was taken out of school owing eight dollars for tuition and twenty-five cents for pens, and placed in his uncle's Albany law office to save "the exchequer of the family," as he put it bitterly. According to Allan's journal, the same "family council" decided that Gansevoort should live with his friend Aly Bradford in New York and read law, and that Herman should spend the summer in Pittsfield helping tend his uncle's farm. The business went into receivership, and after witnessing his mother's bond for $50,000 at the New York State Bank, Herman returned to Pittsfield in the company of his cousin Robert Melvill, who had come to fetch him.[40]

As Thomas Melvill had discovered, being the "best farmer in Berkshire County" provided no insurance against the caprices of Nature. He lost six hundred bushels of Russian turnips to severe weather, and his livestock suffered a succession of illnesses, plunging him once again into debt at a time when credit was tight and banks were threatening to foreclose. In June 1837, he and his son John left for greener pastures in Galena, Illinois, planning to send for the rest of the family once they were settled.

With his uncle out West trying to make a new start on the prairies, Herman spent the summer in Pittsfield helping his aunt Mary with the chores and the haying. Maria must have had qualms about her son's spending so much time with ten cousins whom she considered untutored peasants, because in one of her letters, Julia made it a point to reassure her that Herman's conduct was exemplary: "...firstly you wish to know if he behaves himself with propriety next if he conducts himself with politeness. He is very good very polite. You need not feel uneasy about him we will try not to make him quite a savage while he resides in the country as you fear we shall." Being a savage, however, delighted Herman's heart.[41]

In the fall he went off to the hinterlands beyond Pittsfield to start a teaching job. Armed with his uncle Peter's gifts of *Self Teacher* (1834) and John O. Taylor's *The District School*, he took charge of thirty pupils at the Sykes District School, in a "remote & secluded part of the town about five miles from the village." He boarded with a man whom he considered the "perfect embodiment of the traits of Yankee character,—being shrewd & bold & independant [*sic*], carrying himself with a genuine republican swagger" and "perfectly free in the expression of his sentiments ... [he] would as soon call you a fool or a scoundrel, if he thought so—as button up his waistcoat.—He has reared a family of nine boys and three girls, 5 of whom are my pupils—and they all burrow together in the woods—like so many foxes."[42]

The house he lived in was "a mile and a half from any tenement whatever—being located on the summit of as savage and lonely a mountain as I ever ascended." Such lofty, desolate places appealed to Herman: "The scenery however is most splendid & unusual—embracing an extent of country in the form of an Amphitheatre sweeping around for many miles & encircling a portion of your state in its compass." All his life, Melville enjoyed brisk hikes and climbing, whether it was striding through the Berkshire Hills or scaling the rigging of a ship, the minarets of Turkey, or the campaniles of Italy.[43]

For Melville, teaching in a country school was a far cry from Mark Hopkins's ideal of a teacher and a student sitting on either end of a log, discussing great thoughts. Corporal punishment was considered an essential pedagogical tool, and schoolmasters were expected to rule their scholars with the rod. Like Walt Whitman, Henry David Thoreau, and other writers who tried schoolteaching in their youth, Melville found corporal punishment distasteful. Thanking his uncle for John Taylor's book, he wrote: "Intimatly [sic], am I acquainted with the prevalence of those evils which he alledges [sic] to exist in Common-Schools."[44]

Once he had "established a sistim [sic] in my mode of instruction" and made himself familiar "with the characters & dispositions of my schollars," he had "a few intervals of time ... which I improve by occasional writting [sic] & reading," and he thought he could stick it out. But trying to impart what Peter Gansevoort called "the bread of knowledge" to a gang of rowdies, some of whom were his own age and bigger physically, but lacking basic skills, was very frustrating. He had to fight off more than one challenge from a group of louts who threatened to "lick" him. By the end of the year he was so fed up with conditions at the school that he gave his notice and quit.[45]

Returning to Albany, Herman joined the Young Men's Association, determined to become involved in the city's intellectual life. He was just at the age when young men joined fraternal organizations and clubs, and, like Walt Whitman, he seems to have played the dandy around this time. He enrolled first in the Ciceronian Debating Society and then in the Philo Logos Society, a debating club that met in Stanwix Hall, a luxury hotel of blue Quincy granite built by Herman's maternal grandfather and great-uncle, who topped it with a shiny dome that wags called old Harme's brew kettle turned upside down.[46]

Fraternal organizations like the Odd Fellows, which met in local taverns, meeting rooms, lodges, and hotels like Stanwix Hall, gave young men a home away from home where they could read, smoke, drink, and discuss politics with one another out of earshot of the women. When the Industrial Revolution split home and workplace, giving women sway in the home and men increasing pressure to compete in the workplace, Masonic lodges and other fraternal societies sprang up to provide men with opportunities for noncompetitive association with other men.[47]

Soon after joining Philo Logos, Herman, who was the youngest member of the group, tried to unseat the club's president, Charles Van Loon, by calling a rump meeting and having his supporters declare him their leader. Naturally, Van Loon and his partisans fought back, and Melville found himself embroiled in a wrangle that was reported in the newspapers. *The Albany Microscope*, which proclaimed itself devoted to "popular tales, history, legends and adventures, anecdotes, poetry, satire, humour, sporting, and the drama," reported gossip with as much relish as the most sensationalistic modern tabloid. It featured exposés on the gambling dens and brothels that were springing up in the city, and warned that they were luring prominent citizens to vice and threatening to corrupt Albany's young men. The paper also printed the vitriolic exchange of letters between Melville and Van Loon.[48]

These letters reveal Melville's talent for satire and his love of puns. He clearly enjoyed attacking an opponent who could return his salvos with equal ferocity. He accused his rival of being a "silly and brainless *loon*" standing "in the *van*" of "narrow-minded and jealous" individuals. Van Loon, not to be outdone, fired back that Melville was "a moral Ethiopian" and a "*Ciceronian baboon*." In an attempt to regain the offensive, Melville dubbed his rival "a stranger to veracity," then quickly added that his "incoherent ravings" reminded him of "the croaking of a vulture when disappointed with its prey."[49]

Melville invoked the "peaceful spirit of the Gospel" to end the hostilities, and Van Loon, who was studying for the Baptist ministry, retaliated by calling Melville a "child of the devil, full of all subtility and all mischief." After supporters of each man began adding powder to the keg, a fellow member who signed himself "Americus" called for the combatants to declare a truce, and the furor died down. In the end, Melville became president of Philo Logos, and although he discovered how much fun it was to write satirical invective, he also learned that partisan debates divide even natural allies and polarize issues without resolving them.

Just as Herman and Gansevoort were beginning to establish themselves as leaders among the young men of Albany, Gansevoort became very ill and could no longer work, and Maria was forced to move the family to a less expensive neighborhood. In the first week of May 1838, with creditors demanding payment of the outstanding bills, the Melvilles relocated across the river ten miles north of Albany to Lansingburgh, an elegant village of about five hundred families, many of them prosperous merchants who had moved from Albany. According to Allan Melville Jr., "Economy was the object of this change of location, and the only one which influenced my mother to forsake the 'place of her heart,' her early companions and old friends. But what ties are so sacred as not to be broken."[50]

Maria's ties to her hometown were stretched, but by no means ruptured, by the move. The village boasted more than its share of Albanians, including Lansings and Quackenbushes, all of whom pursued an active social and community life. Maria's cousin Maria Peebles lived just down the street, and across the river in Waterford, which was connected to Lansingburgh by a covered toll bridge, lived the widowed Mary Anne Gansevoort, whose oldest sons, Leonard, Guert, and Stanwix, had gone to sea.

Lansingburgh prided itself on "the beauties of the adjacent scenery, the morality and strictly business character of the people, added to the sociality and intelligence of their every day intercourse—the freedom from sectarian interference in religious matters." By the time Maria Melville moved there, the town was fast "becoming the resort of many who prefer the quiet life of a country village to the noise and unhealthful atmosphere of a thronged city."[51]

Situated on the eastern shore of the Hudson River three miles north of the city of Troy and ten miles north of Albany, Lansingburgh was the creation of Abraham Jacob Lansing, a successful Albany merchant who in 1763 purchased a spacious home in Tascamsatick, or "Steen Arabia," as the Dutch settlers called the tract west of the Hudson opposite the middle branch of the Mohawk River. As soon as Lansing had the neighboring land surveyed, he deposited a map of the new town with the clerk of Albany County in 1771 and built several houses for himself and members of his family. He laid out broad streets and spacious lots around a village green and began selling building lots, and as early as 1786, the village had a newspaper as well as numerous churches, a music hall, a hotel, and thirty-five inns and lodges. It was incorporated in 1790.

During the 1830s and 1840s, thousands of tourists flocked to the village each year to see the exotic plants cultivated by Alexander Walsh, who was also a founder of county and state agricultural societies, and Lansingburgh became known as "The Garden of America." The town boasted several fine schools, including Lansingburgh Academy and the Female Seminary and one of the first free public schools in America. In the late 1840s, Lansingburgh would establish a school for free blacks.[52]

The Melvilles lived in a wood frame house built in 1786 that shared a wall with a brick house built by Abraham Van Vleck in 1772. The house faced River Street, and from its parlor windows, Herman could see the Hudson as it flowed between the middle and southern branches of the Mohawk River. Peach trees and willows lined the banks of the river across from Melville's study. The upstairs rooms were so fully exposed to the afternoon sun that Maria asked the landlord to provide her with window blinds. When he refused, she offered him half a year's rent in advance to install them, then asked her brother for one hundred dollars to cover the increased rent as well as firewood, charcoal, and other supplies.

Although he sent her the money, Peter chided her for her extravagance. "You might rather have done without the blinds, than give your landlord or your neighbors the false unfounded idea that you have means to pay rent in advance—I do not object to the thing itself, so much as to the effect upon your comfort & peace of mind, which such an impression may produce—Your creditors are becoming impatient ... if [they] hear that you are living handsomely at L, and particularly that you pay rent in advance, they will be inclined to annoy you by a sale of your furniture." The increasingly arch tone of his letters probably reflects his anxiety at having to assume the responsibility for his sister's large family in addition to his own.[53]

Having to adjust to modest circumstances went against everything for which Maria had been trained, everything she had grown up expecting life to be. To pay debts, she was forced to sell off some household effects, including a set of silverware, and she had not relished leaving her home in a fashionable Albany neighborhood to move to a smaller, more modest house. Still, at $125 a year, the wood-frame house was roomy and affordable, and Lansingburgh was a wonderful place for growing youngsters.[54]

Far from being a sleepy backwater in the 1830s and 1840s, Lansingburgh was a hub of trade and transportation. Village industries manufactured guns, scales, ink for United States currency, shirts and collars, furniture from imported mahogany, and the new oil-cloth linoleum that was becoming fashionable with working-class families who could not afford costly carpets.

Local potteries exported highly prized stoneware from the local kilns, and over two dozen brush factories imported boar bristles from China as well as tropical woods for brush-backs from Africa and South America. The largest of these, the McMurray Brush Factory, employed three hundred to five hundred men, women, and children, some of whom did fine inlay work and decorative painting on the backs of the more expensive hairbrushes—at no small risk to their eyesight. The town also boasted a brewery and several shipyards that produced close to three hundred ships between 1780 and 1830.[55]

Directly across from the house on River Street, Melville could see the shipyard where the great passenger packet *Royal Oak* had been built, and as he ambled along the riverbank, he could see oceangoing vessels in various stages of construction. Large cargo sloops and barges were tied up at the wharves, loading up on exports such as potatoes, coal, wheat, hops, lumber, lime, butter, cheese, and tobacco. When the dockmaster was not looking, Herman and his pals could explore the huge tunnels that had been built under the street for storage of goods during the winter before the spring rains raised the river enough to float larger vessels.

Living in a bustling river port whetted Herman's appetite for the sea. He barely had to leave his front yard to see the sleek, single-masted wooden sloops with their brightly painted green and white hulls gliding by on the river, and on the docks he could overhear sailors telling stories about places he had so far only read about in books. Right at the edge of his yard stood the little clapboard cottage of retired sea captain Abraham Baker, who had skippered several ships and was part owner of the *Wasp*, one of the largest and best known of the oceangoing schooners in the merchant trade. A master carpenter and an inventor, Baker had sold the improved gunlock he had designed to Lansingburgh's Caswell Gun Factory.[56]

In the summer of 1838, Melville again went to Pittsfield to help his aunt, Mary Melvill, through the haying season, returning to Lansingburgh after Robert Melvill's September 17 wedding to Susan Bates. Tired of working at stopgap jobs and disillusioned with teaching, he was eager to study for a reliable profession. Despite the still-depressed economy, the one profession that seemed to guarantee steady work and a living wage was engineering, particularly with the current upsurge in public works and the extensive renovation of the Erie Canal. At the suggestion of Peter Gansevoort, Herman enrolled in the engineering and surveying course at the Lansingburgh Academy, which pleased his mother no end. She was sure a certificate would guarantee employment.

Lansingburgh Academy, founded in 1795, was only a few blocks from the Melvilles' house. It boasted an extensive library and laboratories for the study of natural philosophy, chemistry, and astronomy. Its principal, Dr. Ebenezer Maltbie, a graduate of Andover Theological Seminary and former chaplain at Hamilton College, had a passion for zoological taxonomy. In 1858 he finished his comprehensive *Zoological Science, or Nature in Living Forms*, an illustrated and partially anecdotal classification of the animal kingdom begun decades earlier.[57]

When Herman received his certificate as a surveyor and engineer in November 1838, Peter Gansevoort introduced him to William Bouck, one of the five commissioners of the Erie Canal, assuming he would get a job. For some reason, however, even with a certificate signed by Dr. Maltbie and a letter from Peter Gansevoort recommending him as "a young man of talent and good education," Herman received no response to his application. Given the number of unsuccessful job searches to his credit, one wonders if he failed to make a good impression on the interviewer because he really didn't want to be tied down.[58]

What he really enjoyed was writing short pieces for the local papers on an old desk in the attic, whose high-peaked roof and four windows made it a perfect retreat for him. His "Fragments from a Writing Desk" appeared in the May 1839 issue of the *Democratic Press and Lansingburgh Advertiser* under the pseudonym "L.A.V." The first fragment expresses Melville's yearning for a male mentor, his romanticism and ambivalence toward women, and his scorn for the "beau," or dandy, who patterns himself after the British statesman and writer Lord Chesterfield, whose maxims Allan Melvill had seriously recommended to his sons. Gansevoort had taken them to heart, and even Herman had flirted with dandyism before rejecting such affectations, so the piece is to some extent a working-through of his relationship with his father and brother, as well as a way of laughing at himself. Its blend of melodrama and irony typifies the split between passionate commitment and self-mockery that would characterize Melville all his life.

In the second fragment, a melodramatic variation of the Lorelei myth, a mysterious woman excites the notice of the narrator and beckons him to her chamber, but refuses to speak. Frustrated by her silence, he embraces her and imprints "one long, long kiss upon her hot and glowing lips," then charges her to speak. Only when she moves her lips soundlessly does he realize in horror that she is "DUMB AND DEAF!" The "Fragments" foreshadow Melville's lifelong obsession with the idealistic vision that ends in despair and doom.[59]

This literary dalliance shows that a side of Melville was emerging that no one in his family could have predicted, or desired. From a boy slow to read and write, Melville was developing into a young man with literary aspirations.

Melville's early sketches created a fantasy world gleaned from romantic poetry and Oriental literature, perhaps in order to impress certain local girls. He courted several young ladies around this time, including Harriet Fly, the sister of his best friend, Eli James Murdock Fly, who was an apprentice in Peter Gansevoort's law office, and he seems to have fallen seriously in love with Mary Eleanor Parmelee, whose niece, Mary Louisa Parmalee, a great-granddaughter of Cornelius Lansing, wrote children's books under the pen name "Lynde Palmer." Melville read Tennyson's poems to her as they strolled along the banks of the Hudson, and several anonymous poems of his, addressed to her, appeared in the *Democratic Press and Lansingburgh Advertiser.* His literary flourishes apparently failed to impress Miss Parmelee, however; she eventually married the son of a local publisher-bookseller, Pelatiah Bliss, who later sold Melville's novels in his store.[60]

On May 23, 1839, Maria wrote a plaintive letter to her brother, begging for funds to pay the balance of the rent. "I have been under the painful necessity of again borrowing from Mrs. Peebles besides something owing the Shoemaker," she wrote. *"Can you send me a remittance this week.* I think some plan must be resolv'd upon, or something decided about my support untill my Sons can do for me & relieve my mind from an unsupportable weight of uncertainty—Hermen [sic] has gone out for a few days on foot to see what he can find to do—Gansevoort feels well enough to go about, & will leave for New York in a few days. My love to Mary—& the Children—Your only Sister Maria."[61]

The following day, when Herman returned "from his expedition, without success," he abandoned the search for employment, probably because deep down what he really wanted was to go to sea and soak up experiences for writing. Frustrated in two major areas of his life, employment and romance, he found the tension at home and the matchmaking by friends oppressive.[62]

A young man who had not yet left the nest risked being smothered by the maternal wing. Influenced by the prevailing cult of domesticity, which made mothers responsible for the moral and spiritual well-being of children while fathers toiled long hours in the marketplace, Maria molded her children into good Christians. She believed that attendance at Sunday school and flawless penmanship would both satisfy her daughters' emotional needs and guarantee their moral progress, and she tried to lift her sons from their "present state of depravity" by exerting her influence over them even when they were not living under her roof.[63]

Allan now worked in his uncle's law office and boarded "not in the most agreeable part of the city" with a distant cousin of his mother whom he considered "a very queer personage with a very suspicious disposition, and like all old maids very fond of gossiping." Whereas Allan feared he would perish from the overprotectiveness and meddling of Miss Wynkoop, his mother feared he would fall into vice and dissipation. "Obey your Mothers parting injunction," she advised, for "be assured my beloved Boy the future usefulness of a Man depends much upon the foundation laid in boyhood. The instruction you are receiving in our Sabbath School is very important, you are away from a Mothers care, under a comparatively strange roof—you need all the advice of a mother, were she with you *but love God* obey his commands & the religious & moral instruction."[64]

The dangers to young women were less drastic than the dangers to young men, provided they remained under the "mother wing" until they were married to husbands who would protect them from the evils of the world in exchange for the faithful execution of their duties as wives. Augusta, according to her mother, if she wished to be a success in life, had only to "Remember that an ardent desire to please can hardly fail of making you agreeable to those who wish your acquaintance."[65]

Allan was anything but agreeable. His combative temperament soon brought him into conflict with his uncle, and he lost his job: "I remained in my Uncle's office doing the business which generally falls to the lot of the youngest student until the latter part of May 1839, when my Uncle wishing to rid himself of all further expenses & responsibility on my account to obtain his object picked a quarrel with me, and my language (which he provoked) not being as he thought the most respectful towards him, he refused to notice me & when I afterwards begged his forgiveness *if* I had offended him he told me I must leave him."[66]

Worried about her brother's "nervous state," Augusta counseled him to avoid "gloomy introspections" and "would willingly have taken those feelings to myself to have restored you to your former cheerfulness." Allan, however, believed what he needed was to get away from home; he planned to try New York as soon as Gansevoort was well enough to return with him.[67]

Gansevoort had come home from his law studies in New York to recuperate from a mysterious affliction in one leg that so incapacitated him that at times he could not walk and had to be carried across the parlor to a chair by the fire. His disability sounds suspiciously psychosomatic, perhaps stemming from an unconscious conflict about "filling his father's shoes" and "standing on his own two feet."[68]

In the fall of 1839, Allan and Gansevoort went to New York together. Gansevoort lived with his friend Aly Bradford and worked in the law office with him, while Allan got a job with the law firm of Tenbroeck & French "on the miserable pitence [*sic*] of $5 a month." Never satisfied, Allan would move back to Albany to work in the law office of a friend or acquaintance named Dudley Burwell before moving back to New York to set up his own law firm.[69]

Mother Melville was understandably worried about her boys, especially Allan. The popular literature of the time assumed that to get ahead in the world, young men had to leave home to make their careers in the city, but the cities were depicted as dens of iniquity where young men would be dragged to perdition. This contradiction fostered a kind of social schizophrenia. Advice manuals stressing the dangers of life in the "wicked city" became a popular gift item as grandparents, parents, aunts, and uncles tried to extend the influence of the home to the workplace. If any of the sons of Allan Melvill actually read William Alcott's *The Young Man's Own Book*, which ran through twenty-one editions between 1834 and 1858, he must have taken to heart Alcott's remark that ambition and the pursuit of wealth, like masturbation, could cause insanity.[70]

More and more young men were leaving home to make their fortunes at a time when the traditional apprentice system, which guaranteed a boy room and board and training in a trade, was breaking down. Once they reached the city, sharpers and confidence men exploited their naiveté. In the face of these dangers to the morals of their sons, mothers invoked God and Motherhood, as when Maria admonished Allan to "*love God* obey his commands & the religious & moral instruction" and "remember your Mother with *deep enduring affection*" and "you will triumph over temptations."[71]

Herman, meanwhile, had decided that office work was claustrophobic drudgery. His cousin Leonard Gansevoort encouraged him to make a voyage to Liverpool, similar to the one he himself had made several years earlier, to test his vocation for the sea. Leonard's brother Guert, on the other hand, thought Herman should take care of his mother and sister, but if he insisted on going to sea, he ought to join the navy as a midshipman, which was at least a respectable position for a Gansevoort.[72]

But Herman had already made up his mind to follow Leonard's advice and make a short voyage as a cabin boy. Eager and excited, he soon gathered together his clothes and other supplies, ate his last home-cooked meal for many months, and said his goodbyes to the family. Anyone who secretly hoped that going to Liverpool would cure Herman of his wanderlust was to be proved wrong.

He went by steamer to New York, where he stayed with Alexander Bradford, who had connections in the shipping industry, and on June 4, 1839, he signed on as a cabin boy aboard the *St. Lawrence,* a small, three-masted, square-rigged merchant ship. He was wrongly listed on the crew roster as "Norman Melville, Aged 19, feet 5, inches 8½, complexion light, hair brown." After signing the ship's articles, he stocked his sea chest, and the next day he boarded the vessel, chose his bunk in the forecastle, and stowed his gear.[73]

All Melville knew about the ship was what the notice in the shipping columns said: "The ship *St. Lawrence,* Oliver P. Brown, master, will sail on Tuesday, and can take 50 or 100 bales of cotton, if offered immediately—Apply to Howland & Aspinwall, 55 South St." In addition to a cargo of cotton picked on southern plantations by slaves for shipment to the "dark Satanic mills" of Manchester, Birmingham, and Leeds, the ship would carry cabin and steerage passengers "handsomely accommodated at low rates."[74]

The day she was to sail, the ship was "in an uproar" as the crew checked the rigging and furled the canvas so the sails could be hoisted smoothly. With live pigs and chickens being carried on board along with salt beef, biscuits, and vegetables, the ship looked like a seagoing Gansevoort Market, as the open-air market on New York's West Side was called. Melville realized that sailing vessels were undemocratic when he saw casks of fresh water and spirits for the crew relegated to the hold, while wine and baskets of fruit went straight to the captain's cabin. The steerage passengers never mingled with the cabin passengers. Their bundles and boxes were shunted belowdecks, while the fine trunks of the more fortunate were carefully put away.

Once the vessel was trim, the harbor pilot came on board, and the ship weighed anchor and headed out to meet the tug that would shepherd her through the Narrows. As Herman stood on deck, he could see Fort Tompkins, which his father and Uncle John D'Wolf had taken him to visit when he was a child. Both men were with him in spirit during this first ocean crossing, especially his father, whose copy of *The Picture of Liverpool* was safely stowed in his sea chest. As the wind caught the sails, the ship "gave a sort of bound like a horse" and "went plunging along, shaking off the foam from her bows like the foam from a bridle-bit," and he found himself entering the "wide blank" of the Atlantic Ocean.[75]

Whatever anxiety and loneliness Melville may have felt as all sight of land dropped away and the ocean surrounded the small ship, his negative feelings were offset by the pleasure he felt as the ship surged under him: "Every mast and timber seemed to have a pulse in it that was beating with life and joy; and I felt a wild exulting in my own heart, and felt as if I would be glad to bound along so round the world."

Albany artist Asa W. Twitchell painted this portrait of the successful young author whose friends and relatives referred to him affectionately as "Typee."

A NATURALLY ROVING DISPOSITION

For the next four weeks, the 120-foot-long packet ship would be home, the sixteen crewmen and assorted passengers a new sort of family. Most of the crew members of the St. Lawrence *were white Americans, but the captain was a Swede, and the crew included an Irishman and a Greenlander; the cook and the steward were black. The oldest man on board after the captain was Robert Jackson, a thirty-one-year-old New Yorker whose name evoked the hated Andrew Jackson. In* Redburn, *his fictional account of the voyage, Melville would appropriate Jackson's name for a character who personified heartless evil.*

Melville was eager for raw experience, but uncertain about what the voyage held for him. As a new boy and a "lubber," he was assigned such unpleasant tasks as cleaning out the pig pens and chicken coops and swabbing the head, and such dangerous ones as scampering up the rigging to reef the sails in a storm. Hazing of younger and smaller men by seasoned tars took many forms, some as playful as tying their hammocks in a knot, others as sinister as sexual bullying. Whatever happened, enlisted men were expected to take everything in stride. As Richard Henry Dana Jr. wrote in Two Years Before the Mast, *"Whatever your feelings may* be, you must make a joke of everything at sea; and if you were to fall from aloft, and be caught in the belly of a sail, and thus saved from instant death, it would not do to look at all disturbed, or to treat it as a serious matter."[1]

At some point, Melville must have realized how little his life mattered to the strangers he was to live among for the duration of the cruise. What mattered to the captain and his mates were the ship, her cargo, and the safety of passengers whose relatives might sue. Sea captains, Melville discovered, were not fathers to their crew, so his success—indeed, his very survival—was up to him.

Once Melville recovered from the ravages of seasickness, adolescent fantasies about silent, seductive women gave way to the reality of gruff men, often intoxicated, barking orders that demanded instant obedience, or uttering foul oaths. As a greenhorn, he was the lowest of the low in a tough, hierarchical world that valued him less as an individual than as a cog in a bewildering machine:

> On board ship a sailor was expected to follow orders, not understand them, but jumping to execute commands was difficult when commands were issued in an almost entirely foreign language. What did I know, for instance, about *striking a top-gallant-mast*, and sending it down on deck in a gale of wind? Could I have *turned in a dead-eye*, or in the approved nautical style have *clapped a seizing on the main-stay*? What did I know of *passing a gammoning, reeving a Burton, strapping a shoe-black, clearing a foul hawse,* and innumerable other intricacies.

Loving the sounds of words, Melville learned quickly, and his vocabulary was the richer for the colorful expressions he heard all around him. Shipboard language had a robust pungency that was lacking in the self-conscious badinage of the Philo Logos Society, or in the sentimental rhetoric of genteel literature.[2]

Unusual words like *spanker boom, scuttle butt, jolly-boat, reef point, skysail, capstan, binnacle, holystone, belaying pin, scupper-hole, monkey-jacket, cloud-raker, flying jib, sou'wester, fife-rail,* and *shroud* tasted good on his tongue and sounded good to his ear even before he understood them. Once he had learned to use such unfamiliar tools as fids, serving-mallets, toggles, prickers, palms, and heavers, he could relax and enjoy the rush of oxygen to the lungs and muscles that comes from physical labor performed in the open air.

In addition to achieving shipboard literacy, he learned to perform tasks usually assigned to women back on land. In *Redburn,* he would write that a sailor

> must be a bit of an embroiderer, to work fanciful collars of hempen lace about the shrouds; he must be something of a weaver, to weave mats of rope-yarns for lashings to the boats; he must have a touch of millinery, so as to tie graceful bows and knots, such as *Matthew Walker's roses,* and *Turk's heads;* he must be a

bit of a musician, in order to sing out at the halyards; he must be a sort of jeweler, to set dead-eyes in the standing rigging; he must be a carpenter, to enable him to make a jury-mast out of a yard in case of emergency; he must be a sempstress, to darn and mend the sails; a ropemaker, to twist *marline* and *Spanish foxes;* a blacksmith, to make hooks and thimbles for the blocks; in short, he must be a sort of Jack of all trades, in order to master his own.[3]

In spite of the many shocks Melville received during his first voyage, he must have derived a great deal of satisfaction from being able to succeed at very demanding work. He had to master sleeping belowdecks in a swinging net of ropes called a hammock; climbing a rope ladder to the crosspiece of a wooden mast one hundred or more feet above a rolling deck; balancing on the rigging to knot reef points in a sail bellied with gusting winds; and staying awake during the "dog watch" from 4:00 to 8:00 A.M. In the rare moments when the weather was mild and his work was done, he could enjoy watching the "little fleeces of foam" that fringed the sea, and listening to the "strange, musical noise" the ship's bows made as they cut through the water.

Despite its hardships, a mariner's life offered beauty, novelty, and challenge. Melville liked feeling the sun on his face, the salt wind in his hair, and the rhythmic rocking of the hull beneath his feet, and on a fine day with a fair breeze and a clear blue sky, he could imagine that the stunsails billowing at the ends of the yards were "the wings of a great bird." About a month out of New York, the *St. Lawrence* docked at Liverpool.

Liverpool was the marvel of the maritime world and the hub of international commerce. Her docks could handle fifteen hundred vessels in a year, and at Prince's Dock, Melville could see "the noble New York packets, which at home are found at the foot of Wall Street," and "the Mobile and Savannah cotton ships and traders." He was well aware that Liverpool owed its prosperity to the "black gold" of Africa, and that New York was heavily invested in the cotton trade. His father had met abolitionist William Roscoe during his travels, and he "had often spoken to gentlemen visiting our house in New York, of the unhappiness that the discussion of the slave-trade had occasioned in Liverpool; and that the struggle between sordid interest and humanity had made sad havoc at the fire-sides of the merchants; estranged sons from sires; and even separated husband from wife." As the phenomenal success of *Uncle Tom's Cabin* would show so powerfully in 1852, most whites opposed slavery not because it denied rights to blacks, but because it destroyed the domestic happiness of families, both white and black.[4]

On shore, Melville found hopeless poverty and squalor "in almost endless vistas." Whole families were huddled in the streets; children were dying of disease and malnutrition. He saw "old women, rather mummies, drying up with slow starving and age; young girls, incurably sick, who ought to have been in the hospital; starving men, with the gallows in their eyes, and a whining lie in their mouths; young boys, hollow-eyed and decrepit; and puny mothers, holding puny babes." Next to the "dingy ware-houses" on the banks of the Mersey stood seedy bars and brothels, and along with the exotic array of cosmopolitan types that congregated in ports, pickpockets, cutpurses, and prostitutes lurked in alleyways, and starving beggars crouched against dock walls.[5]

Strolling through the city, Melville sought out attractions he had read about in his father's guidebook, such as the Moorish Arch in the railway station, which had been the subject of an etching in the *Penny Magazine.* He also saw the statue of Lord Nelson "expiring in the arms of Victory" that had four manacled Africans as its base, and it affected him so deeply that when he was writing *Redburn,* he transformed the monument into an icon of the sufferings inflicted by the slave trade.[6]

The gap between rich and poor in Liverpool seemed unbridgeable, and Melville must have wondered if America's economy was destined to produce such savage inequality in the future. Whereas British shipping magnates lived in opulent, new homes and worked in spacious, modern offices, more than a third of the city's population lived in filthy, rat-infested slums, where privies overflowed into the streets, causing typhus and consumption, and where some twenty thousand people, many in advanced stages of tuberculosis, lived in cellars. In Liverpool, all the evils of modern urban living observable in New York were magnified, and seemed irremediable.[7]

Being in another country gave Melville a new perspective on beliefs and customs he had taken for granted, as it does all thoughtful travelers. Black sailors walked arm-in-arm with fair-skinned Englishwomen, and clergymen walked by scenes of misery seemingly unmoved by the poverty and desperation of their fellow men. A skeptic by nature, Melville began to realize that social mores he had taken for granted back home were not universal truths, and he began to question the basic assumptions behind Christianity and Western economic institutions. Unprepared for the moral shock he experienced, he could not help wondering how the God who keeps His eye on the sparrow could be so blind to human suffering.

Many American businessmen felt that Adam Smith's *The Wealth of Nations* contained more revealed truth than the Holy Bible, and others, alluding to its July 4, 1776, publication date, called it the economic Declaration of Independence. Melville was among those who would question Smith's ideas, as Friedrich Engels, the son of a textile manufacturer in Manchester, was doing at about the time Melville was in Liverpool. In 1844, Engels's book *The Condition of the Working Man in England* appeared, and a few years later he and his collaborator, Karl Marx, would proclaim *The Communist Manifesto* (1848), denouncing laissez-faire capitalism as financially and morally bankrupt.[8]

During the month he spent in Liverpool, Melville was surprised by the number of

Africans he saw there, and probably just as surprised by the number of prostitutes. There were nearly three thousand of the latter in the city, most of whom congregated around the port, but Melville is largely silent about the behavior of sailors on shore leave in *Redburn*. While he freely admits that vice and iniquity are inevitable concomitants of a sailor's life, his fictional account of his exploits while ashore in Liverpool is artfully disguised, hinting at much, but revealing nothing.[9]

Shortly before the *St. Lawrence* was to sail for home, Melville wrote his mother that "he would give all the sights of Liverpool to see a corner of home." It was typical of him to miss his family when he was traveling, and to long to get away and travel when he was home. At first, it seemed the packet might return to New York by way of Charleston, so he was relieved when he heard that the ship would sail directly to New York. He told his mother that she could expect him home in late September, and she was so glad to hear from him that she wrote Allan, "I have just written Herman a few lines, his conduct delights me, he has shown himself to possess an independant [*sic*] spirit not deficiant [*sic*] in enterprise and willing to exert himself when necessary."[10]

The *St. Lawrence* docked at the Port of New York in late September, and as soon as Herman arrived back in Lansingburgh, he learned that his mother's creditors had lost their patience and that her landlord was threatening to cancel her lease. Panicked, she importuned her brother Peter to send her $50 a month for expenses, but he was able to send her only token amounts. Her brother Herman said he would like to help out, but his wife wouldn't let him. Allan, who was already earning more than he needed to cover expenses also promised to help his mother, but Gansevoort was too sick to work. In October the banks ordered Maria to sell her furniture to pay Gansevoort's back debts from the business—a humiliating blow to this proud woman.[11]

It was discouraging for Herman to find his mother and sisters no better off than when he had left them. His mother's complaints seemed shallow and self-indulgent after the real suffering he had witnessed in Liverpool. She lived in a handsome house in a pleasant village, surrounded by family and friends. She had a roof over her head, proper clothing, good food, and even a "woman of all work" named Rosey, who lived above the kitchen. So, while he sympathized with his mother's plight, he also realized her situation could not compare with the sufferings of the poor in Liverpool. He felt alienated from his own family, and restless to see the Pacific islands about which he had heard so much from other seafaring men.

At about this time, a sketch titled "The Death Craft," signed "Harry the Reefer," appeared in the *Democratic Press and Lansingburgh Advertiser*. As crude as it is, this quasi-Gothic sketch has some affinities with "Benito Cereno," a later Melville masterpiece. The narrator is accosted by a laughing first mate who points out to him the hideous "Death

Craft": "a blood-red flag streaming from her mast-head—at her jib-boom-end hanging suspended by its long, dark hair, a human head covered with congelated gore, and firmly gripping, between its teeth, a rusty cutlass! Her yards were painted black, and at each of their arms hung dangling a human skeleton, whiter than polished ivory and glistening in the fierce rays of the sun!" He awakens from this nightmare to find himself watched by two "lovely eyes" and realizes that "the fond young girl, whom twelve months ago, I had left a disconsolate bride [now] lay weeping in my arms!"[12]

Like the female figures in "Fragments from a Writing Desk," the "disconsolate bride" resembles the phantom women conjured up by Edgar Allan Poe, except that Poe's fantasy women are usually dead and Melville's are merely mute and mysterious, perhaps mirroring his mother's withholding behavior after her husband's death, or the frustration he felt at the coyness of young women. The exclamatory style was partly an affectation of the time, and partly a sign of Melville's inability to decide whether he wanted to write a serious bit of Gothic melodrama, or mock the genre.[13]

It wouldn't have taken Melville long to realize that he wouldn't support himself by writing ephemera for local newspapers, let alone help his mother with the household expenses, so he took a job teaching sixty pupils at the Greenbush & Schodack Academy in East Greenbush, New York—not far from Lansingburgh—a far more sophisticated school than Sykes. Once he'd bought clothing for his job from his sailor's pay and settled in at the new school, Melville was able to give his mother enough money to save their furniture from the auction block. Promising her $150 to $200 a year from his salary, he cut his expenses to the bone by walking the thirteen miles from home to work and back over the steep hills that doubled the distance between the two towns, rather than hopping the stagecoach to go home on weekends.

No one, at this point, could call Herman Melville an idler. "I feel cheered by Hermans prospects," Maria wrote Allan. "He appeared to be interested in his occupation—he has a great charge, & deep responsibility is attached to the education of 60 Scholars, which I understand is the number usual during the greater part of the year—I shall be most happy to see you & moreover will make every preparation in my power, to receive you on Christmas and Herman must endeavour to persuade his friend Fly to accompany him, which invitation I hope he will accept, & thereby enable Herman to return one of the many kindnesses which he has from time to time received from him."[14]

On the same page, after his mother had taken her last look at the letter, Herman wrote a few lines to Allan in a voice intended to sound "black":

> *My Dear Sergeant*
> *How is you? Am you very well? How has you been?—As to myself I haint been as well as husual. I has had a very cruel cold for this darnation long time, & I has had and*

does now have a werry bad want of appetisement—I seed Mrs. Peebles tother day and
she did say to me to not fail to tell you that she am well

No more at present
from you friend
T A W N E Y

"Tawney" was a common sobriquet for African-Americans, and Melville's jocular note must be a response to racist barbs about his suntan, darted at him by friends and relatives who, like most genteel Victorians, associated tanned skin with peasants, primitives, and slaves.[15]

His mimicry of the blackface lingo made popular by white minstrels is inept compared with the ventriloquism of a Joel Chandler Harris or a Mark Twain, perhaps because Melville spoke with accents and inflections typical of his class. His adult speaking voice probably sounded like a blend of Franklin Delano Roosevelt, John F. Kennedy, and Gore Vidal, and he appears to have had little ear for dialogue or slang. As much as he savored the words of workingmen, his own style was urbane and cultured, not colloquial, which makes the refreshing directness and informality of narrative voices like those of Tommo, Redburn, White-Jacket, and Ishmael even more of an achievement.[16]

Melville liked to shock family and friends by acting like a "savage," and he had let his hair get long and had grown a beard, of which he was quite proud. But his wild appearance was "a great source of anxiety" to Gansevoort, who admonished him to clean himself up and rejoiced when his brother finally got "his hair sheared & whiskers shaved" because he looked "more like a Christian than usual."[17]

Just as Melville was beginning to establish himself as a teacher at Greenbush & Schodack Academy and appreciate its superiority to the Sykes District School, the trustees informed him they could not pay him his wages because the school was facing bankruptcy, which Gansevoort considered "very singular conduct" on the board's part.[18]

With no guarantee that Herman would ever be paid, Maria was beside herself: "Hermans School is to be discontinued next week for want of funds until the winter—he thinks of going far-west, as nothing offers for him here—Oh that the Lord may strengthen me to bear all my troubles, & be pleased to sustain me under them.... I feel unusually depressed & troubled, and cannot throw it off. I feel as if my poverty & consequent dependance [*sic*], have robbed me of the affection of my dear brothers, at a time when true love & Friendship is alone to be tested, *in adversity*.... If you cannot possibly send me fifty, in mercy my dear Brother send me the amount of the rent."[19]

Feeling abandoned by her brother Peter, she asked Allan to act as a go-between: "I have written your Uncle Peter & desire you will hand him the letter & await his reading it, I am in trouble about the non payment of my quarters rent.... I have written your uncle Herman three times since I was last in Albany, he has not attended to the letters in act or deed—I know not what to do." Maria's asking him to deliver this begging letter to her brother must have enraged Allan, who wanted as little to do with his uncle as possible.[20]

After Greenbush Academy closed down, Herman did some substitute teaching in Brunswick Public School Number 7 on Gypsy Lane in the backwoods of Lansingburgh, but he made very little money. Eli Fly had recently turned down Peter Gansevoort's offer of a promotion to go west, and Melville decided to go with him and look for work out there. Failing other opportunities, he could always work with his cousin Robert, who had recently leased the Pittsfield farm and joined his father in Galena.[21]

The trip west was a new adventure for the "vagabond" Melville. Travel along the Erie Canal, a 363-mile-long boat-boulevard forty feet wide and four feet deep with an intricate system of locks and aqueducts, could be arduous and even dangerous. Drifters and con artists congregated in the mooring-towns and preyed on travelers, and the hard-drinking, tobacco-spitting young Canallers were often "wicked" men, although when Melville and Fly were set upon by an assailant, a Canaller who had "as stiff an arm to back a poor stranger in a strait, as to plunder a wealthy one" came to their defense.[22]

Too poor to buy tickets for passenger boats, Melville and his companion hiked the towpath alongside mules and horses or hitched rides on freighters, tramping through places that reminded Melville that his family's history was coeval with that of the nation. At Rome, New York, he passed the site of Fort Stanwix, which Colonel Peter Gansevoort had defended heroically from the British. The name *Rome* evoked associations with the Roman Republic and the Order of the Cincinnati formed by old revolutionaries such as George Washington and Melville's grandfather.

At the western terminus of the canal, Melville and Fly visited Buffalo, which was the quintessential frontier city. Strolling along its newly paved streets, they encountered Indians in blankets and buckskins, soldiers in uniforms with sword and sash, gentlemen in high hats and buttoned gloves, ladies wearing beribboned bonnets and carrying parasols, and immigrants from Ireland, Germany, France, and Norway.

By 1840, steam locomotives had been in operation for a decade, and the railroad was rapidly huffing and puffing its way into American folklore. To Emily Dickinson, the Iron Horse was a modern Pegasus, but to Henry David Thoreau it was a Trojan horse bearing treacherous gifts. He predicted that the railroad would only increase the "quiet desperation" which the mass of men felt as they confronted a rapidly changing world.[23]

The steam locomotive could not match a full-rigged sailing ship for grace and beauty, but it was a triumph of modern mechanical engineering. Coincidentally, the first steam locomotive run occurred the day Lemuel Shaw became a Massachusetts Supreme

Court justice, and it was Judge Shaw who introduced the concept of "public utility" and the principle of eminent domain that allowed the government to take private property deemed essential to the greater public good for construction of a continental railroad system. While many of Shaw's decisions favored large corporations, others sought to balance conflicting rights by helping the working man. In 1842, Shaw would pave the way for the formation of labor unions by striking down conspiracy laws that curtailed workingmen's freedom to organize.[24]

From Buffalo, steamships took travelers across the Great Lakes to Detroit and the newly chartered city of Chicago, touching at several towns, including Cleveland, along the way. Melville was struck by the pristine orderliness of western cities in contrast to the dirt and crowding in Albany and New York, not to mention Liverpool. The chance to catch a glimpse of these great western cities relieved the monotony of a voyage on which there was little for a former sailor to do but stand at the rail and stare at the water. When a fierce Lake Erie storm hit the ship, with "Borean and dismasting blasts as direful as any that lash the salted wave," afflicting seasoned travelers and horses with seasickness, Melville was in his element, and very glad he had "sea legs."

Along the shores of Lake Huron, Melville could see the wigwams of the Ojibways, Winnebagos, and Menominees, whose birchbark canoes kept pace with the white man's steamers. Beyond the "forest primeval," captured by Henry Wadsworth Longfellow in *Evangeline,* stretched the prairie where James Fenimore Cooper's legendary "Leatherstocking" had struggled to teach the new settlers to respect the old native ways.

Although it was fashionable back East to deplore the absence of romantic history and ruins, as he traveled westward, Melville could see many reminders of the young nation's storied past. Already, legendary fortresses of the Revolutionary War, such as Michigan's once-magnificent Fort Mackinac, which was razed by Chief Pontiac, seemed to be crumbling back into the soil.

By the time Melville saw the West, wild animals such as wolves had already fled deeper into the wilderness with every gunshot, leaving the buffalo herds, which had once "overspread by tens of thousands the prairies of Illinois and Missouri," to be decimated by greedy white settlers, who killed the great beasts for their hides—or sometimes for their tongues or simply for sport—and left the peeled carcasses to be stripped by scavenger birds, and rot. In *Moby-Dick,* he would conjure up visions of the "humped herds" that once "shook their iron manes and scowled with their thunder-clotted brows."[25]

Like the buffalo, the Native Americans who called the earth their "Great Mother" were being driven from their ancestral lands and resettled in uncongenial territories, usually on land unsuitable for farming. Under the Jackson administration's "pacification" policy, the Florida Seminoles had been nearly exterminated, and the survivors—mostly women, children, and old men—had been driven north to the Dakotas. In 1838, under

President Martin Van Buren, the Cherokee Nation was removed from its tribal home in the eastern woodlands and forced along the "Trail of Tears" to Oklahoma. As Melville stood "knee-deep among Tiger-lilies," gazing at the landscape unrolling before him, he sensed that the western prairies were haunted by the ghosts of the ancient peoples and their animals, much as Edgar Allan Poe imagined the woods and fountains of the eastern seaboard haunted by the spirits of the Hamadryads and gentle Naiads whom Science had "driven out."[26]

Melville and Fly either took a stagecoach to Galena or made all or part of the 170-mile journey on horseback, as the railroad did not reach the town until 1849. The Illinois prairies were in full bloom, spraying the countryside with bursts of red, yellow, and purple flowers. Later in the summer they would see fields of wheat and corn and rye stretching to the horizon. Both *Moby-Dick* and *The Confidence-Man* are imbued with the broad humor and boastfulness of the West, the raw energy and fluidity of the American frontier. In many frontier towns, boosters constructed enormous hotels before towns had residents and founded newspapers before there was any news. The idea was not to respond to demand, but to create demand, and American newspapers had no scruples about inventing news until real news came along. As one early editor explained, "We sometimes represented things that had not yet gone through the formality of taking place." When settlers did come to the western towns, they came fast, and they needed easy, affordable housing. In 1833 a Chicago firm developed the first balloon-frame house, which an unskilled man could build with little more than a hammer and a bucket of factory-made iron nails. These newfangled homes were built to be portable, as well, a feature European travelers cited as evidence that Americans were a tribe of restless, uncivilized nomads.[27]

Seeing his uncle Thomas again after several years, Melville was "struck by the contrast between the man and his environment." Still nostalgic for the boulevards of Paris, Thomas Melvill Jr. was no better off financially than he had been back east, and before long was dismissed by his employer for pilfering from the store where he worked. Once again the pursuit of success, material success, would lead a son of Major Thomas Melvill to disgrace and ruin.[28]

The depression that had slowed economic growth in the East had moved west just ahead of Melville and Fly, and if Herman had any thought of making a life for himself out West, he found few opportunities. At least one school in Galena had shut down for lack of money, and there were no teaching jobs available. Either he had no interest in writing for the local paper, or he applied and wasn't hired because "hard times" had hit the lead-mining town.[29]

Melville was just as happy to help his cousin with the haying; otherwise, he was content to drift and dream. Perhaps he was already hankering to go back to sea as he surveyed the land that opened before him like an inland sea. More than a year later, as he stood on the deck of a whaling ship, the miles of yellow plankton undulating on the surface of the sea like golden grain would evoke memories of the spectacular western landscape, linking the vastness of the ocean and the vastness of the prairies in his mind.

He soaked up as much spacious sky and spectacular countryside as he could that summer, taking trips such as the requisite excursion to the Falls of St. Anthony, where the mighty Mississippi originated as a small stream flowing out of majestic virgin forests from whence, as he later described it, it "winds evenly in between banks of flags or tracts of pine over marble sands." He watched "the cornetted elk & the deer" feeding "undisturbed" on its banks, unmolested by the "furred bear" that stood watching them in an almost human attitude.[30]

In a poem whose date of composition is unknown, Melville describes cornfields dwarfing regiments of cavalry, implying that Nature will outlive human violence:

> Files on files of prairie maize:
> On hosts of spears the morning plays!
> Aloft the rustling streamers show:
> The floss embrowned is rich below.[31]

Melville and Fly stayed with the Melvill family until the "fields of ripe and golden wheat" were harvested and the corn silks turned dry and brown, and then they left for home. They said their good-byes and took the steamboat from Galena to Cairo, passing the Mormon settlement at Nauvoo, one of the many communities created by Americans united by religious or utopian ideals.[32]

On their way east, Melville and Fly visited the Indian mounds at St. Louis and drifted downriver past towns with names like Herculaneum and Cape Girardeau, whose cliffs bore such ominous names as Devil's Oven and Devil's Anvil. Colorful place-names like these reflect both a shared history and American cultural diversity. In addition to the rich lexicon of Indian names (Minnetonka, Susquehanna), Spanish names (San Luis Obispo, Las Cruces), French names (Lac qui Parle, Bon Air), Dutch names (Watervliet), and German names (Kinderhook), new places were apt to have descriptive names (Long Island, Fairhaven), or take the name of a natural feature of the landscape (Big Timber, Silver Springs), a founder or prominent person (Jefferson City, Pinckneyville), a local incident (Council Bluffs, Wounded Knee), a lady love (Judith Basin, Elizabeth City), Old World cities (Heidelberg, Syracuse), and even reflect states of mind and moral qualities (New Hope, Fidelity, Independence).

Melville came home to a family oppressed by debt, disgrace, illness, and death. His mother evidently owed the New York State Bank nineteen thousand dollars she could not repay. Relations with her brother were strained until Peter's infant son, who was also named Herman, died in mid-October at the age of nine months, and the family had to pull together once again.[33]

After seeing how the rugged women of the western frontier managed in covered wagons, log cabins, and even sod houses on the open prairies, Melville had little tolerance for his mother's constant complaints about their cozy, comfortable home. He left Lansingburgh with his friend Fly to look for work in New York, where they found rooms at $2.50 a week. Fly soon found a job as a copyist in a local office—a position from which Melville's poor penmanship mercifully disqualified him, as he probably preferred not to take a job that would be routine copying. The two friends dined "in good health & tolerable spirits" with Gansevoort at Sweeney's every evening. Gansevoort was becoming as fussy and controlling as his mother, counseling his brother Allan to "Avoid all debt & pecuniary obligation of every kind as you would pestilence." He was right, of course, but coming from him, it sounded hypocritical and obnoxious.[34]

Melville was not one of those young men who wanted to be "pent up in lath and plaster—tied to counters, nailed to benches, clinched to desks," as he would phrase it in *Moby-Dick.* Rather than go job-hunting, he preferred reading James Fenimore Cooper's *The Red Rover*, whose pirate protagonist appealed to his rebellious nature, and Richard Henry Dana's best-seller *Two Years Before the Mast*. A great advance over the nautical narratives of the British author Captain Marryat, these books stirred the salt water in his blood, and Dana's account of his voyage to California rekindled his desire to sail to the South Pacific. To escape his mother's nagging, his older brother's officiousness, and the possibility that he might land a job he didn't want, he decided to go whaling.[35]

"Having little or no money in my purse, and nothing particular to interest me on shore, I thought I would sail about a little and see the watery part of the world," Ishmael would explain in *Moby-Dick*, surely speaking for the Melville of 1840 as he made up his mind to take the great voyage he had dreamed about since boyhood. Although members of the family were none too pleased about Herman's decision to go to sea as a common sailor, Gansevoort agreed to help him find a berth and make all the arrangements.[36]

To Melville, signing aboard a whaler meant at least four years' steady employment, not to mention an escape from the pieties of the parlor, but a four-year voyage halfway around the world in the company of hard-bitten sailors was no summer cruise to Liverpool. Despite the fact that young men who had started as common seamen aboard New England vessels had been known to rise to command their own ships, it was not a job about which a family like Melville's could really feel satisfied or proud, especially Mother Melville, who heartily wished her son would settle down and do something worthy of his paternity.

Melville, however, had developed an instinct for doing what he needed to do to survive psychologically, and being a sailor was infinitely easier than mastering the complex tasks of young adulthood. He looked to seafaring as a way of escaping not only his mother's nagging and the demoralizing search for jobs he didn't really want, but also the pangs of bourgeois courtship and the frustration of having to sublimate his sexual drives to narrow social forms and rituals. He longed to explore both the old worlds that beckoned from the other side of the globe and the new worlds that were stirring inside of him, and he knew that on a whaler he would either find himself or be lost forever amid the "unshored harborless immensities" of the world's oceans.[37]

Whalers used wooden stamps to record the day's catch in the ship's log.

THE WILD, THE WATERY, THE UNSHORED

As a small boy, Melville had envisioned himself as a voyager on far-flung seas, an explorer of strange lands. Hearing the liquid syllables of the French language spoken by his father and his uncle, as well as the polyglot tongues of sailors of every race and nationality who thronged Manhattan's wharves, and watching the oceangoing ships slide from the drydocks at Lansingburgh inspired in him an insatiable desire to go to sea. He longed to escape the provincial culture that constrained him, longed to discover the mythic paradise where body and soul could merge into one passionate organism powerful enough to leave all "ties and ballasts" behind and experience ecstatic union with the universe.[1]

Melville could easily have joined the navy or gone into the merchant trade, as would his youngest brother, Tom. Ever since the Empress of China *opened up trade with the Far East in 1784, many young sailors had aspired to skipper one of the great East Indiamen. Built in Maine or Massachusetts, these impressive ships, painted black to contrast with their billowing white sails, had a high, square stern that gave them a stately look on the water. Plying the seas between Sumatra and Singapore, Canton and Calcutta, they exchanged silks and sandalwood* for cottons and calicoes, and traded New England manufactures such as leather boots and shoes, clocks and watches, sewing machines, printing presses, plows, and parlor organs and other furniture, for Chinese porcelains and ivory fans, for coffee, tea, cinnamon, cloves, ginger, ginseng, and other exotic spices from the Indies, East and West. In 1833, thanks to the ingenuity of shipping magnate Frederic Tudor, the New England vessels had begun supplying ice to tropical climes and outposts of the British Empire such as Burma and India; it seemed there was nothing Yankee mariners could not do.[2]

Thomas Melville, who went whaling at age sixteen, eventually commanded merchant ships in the Pacific. Although Tom didn't marry until after he retired and became governor of the Sailors' Snug Harbor on Staten Island, most merchant captains were married, and some even took their wives and families to sea. Children aboard an ocean-going vessel tested the patience of both parents and crew. Some captains picked up exotic pets such as parrots, kangaroos, and monkeys on stops along the way, and kept them on board to amuse the children.[3]

Whalers' wives, too, often joined their husbands aboard the "blubber-hunters," cheerfully putting up with rolling, pitching decks soaked in blood and gore and oily dirt so thick that clothes had to be washed in salt water mixed with urine. Occasionally an unmarried woman disguised herself as a man to go whaling, often surviving several rigorous voyages before being detected. "Let them be sea captains," wrote the transcendentalist philosopher Margaret Fuller, thinking of women like Mary Russell, Augusta Penniman, and other intrepid wives who joined their husbands on whaling voyages.[4]

Given the deprivations and dangers they faced, the fact that they rarely made much money, and the disgusting living conditions aboard the whalers, it's a wonder that anyone other than fugitives from justice ever joined whaling crews. Some young men wanted the excitement of chasing and capturing the great leviathan, while others derived psychological satisfaction from being tough, daring, and rebellious. Still others sought to escape abusive relatives, pregnant girlfriends, tyrannical bosses, or angry creditors, and yet others sought the sexual freedom afforded by shipboard life and by shore leaves in foreign ports where women were not daughters of the Puritans, and men loved other men.

Warnings about the hazards of the sea did not deter Melville; in fact, they added to its attractiveness. Like most young men, he needed to test himself against the implacable forces of the universe. Whaling would give the reckless, rebellious side of his personality free rein, and at the same time the rough-and-ready sailor persona would camouflage the vulnerability to which his sensitivity and compassion exposed him. Like most adolescent risk-taking, Melville's decision to join the crew of a whaling ship was a reaction to emotional pain, as though, by placing himself in an extreme situation, he could objectify his fears and conquer them.

More consciously, his voyage to Liverpool had given him an appetite for the sea. He loved climbing the ship's rigging, feeling the wind in his hair, the sun on his back, and the stretch in the muscles of his arms and legs. He loved watching the play of sunlight and shadow on the surface of the sea, and hearing the sailors' chanteys and the strange tales they told. He longed to follow the great whales and experience the sexual adventures his cousins described when the women of the family were not present.

Seafaring was a respectable profession only for naval officers or merchant captains, not for whaling men. With rumors abounding among landlubbers about what motivated men to go to sea, sailors had to endure not only tyrannical captains, squalls, and whales, but also insinuations that they were all alcoholics, sexual deviants, and fugitives from justice. Many were. Whereas, in the 1830s and early 1840s, most Americans who joined whaling crews tended to be New England farm and village boys, by the mid-1840s more "packet rats"—rovers and drifters, drunkards and fugitives—signed on, and whalers soon became asylums for outcasts. Melville was fortunate in his shipmates, who were "much superior in morale and early advantages to the ordinary run of whaling crew," affording him "constant gratification."[5]

Almost all the Melville and Gansevoort men who went to sea went as commissioned naval officers, not as common seamen, and several had already met with misfortune or death. In July 1832, Herman's twenty-two-year-old cousin Peter L. Gansevoort, the oldest son of Leonard H. and Mary Anne Gansevoort, perished in the wreck of the schooner *Increase*. Three years later, however, Peter's brother Leonard signed on the whaler *Hercules* at New Bedford, and returned home safely in 1837 after a successful cruise to New Zealand.

Not everyone was as fortunate as Leonard. Mary Anne Gansevoort's other two sons, Guert and Stanwix, both naval officers and alcoholics, led troubled lives. Guert was twice disciplined for alcohol-related derelictions of duty, and Stanwix, who resigned his commission and became a near recluse, died of shock at the age of forty-two after falling from the roof of his house and breaking his ankle, an accident that sounds suspiciously alcohol-related, especially in the light of a letter his mother wrote in 1844: "In youth you left me; as I believe, *untainted by a vice*. After five years absence you return, to your Mothers longing heart—But oh how changed. You cannot drink without the most deleterious effects upon your character—from a gentleman, you descend to a querulous, profane, & unreasonable fellow."[6]

Shortly before Melville left for the Pacific in 1840, Midshipman Hun Gansevoort, the son of Peter and Mary Gansevoort, contracted a "venereal chancre" so "virulent and obstinate" that the fleet commander in Callao had relieved him of his duties on the USS *Constitution* and sent him home to recuperate. Hun would eventually go down with the *Grampus*, the brig that held the *Amistad* rebels captive during their trial in 1843.[7]

Pierre François Henry Thomas Wilson Melvill, born in Paris in 1806 to Herman's uncle Thomas and his French wife, was a romantic figure to his younger cousin. He sailed to the South Seas aboard the war sloop *Vincennes* in 1829, spending two weeks in the Marquesas while the ship took on fresh water and provisions before sailing to the Society Islands, Tahiti, and the Sandwich Islands, a route almost identical to the one Melville was about to follow. While Pierre was at sea, he came to a tragic end.[8]

Midshipman Melvill was court-martialed in 1832 for "yielding to paroxysms of passion" unbecoming an officer—namely, beating a shipmate viciously during a fight, no doubt under the influence of alcohol. Athough he was not dismissed from the navy, he received a strong reprimand, and shortly afterward he came down with a severe case of Asiatic cholera that nearly killed him. He died aboard a whaler in 1844 and was laid to rest six thousand miles from home.[9]

In 1840, with Hun Gansevoort aboard, the *Vincennes* was cruising the South Seas as the flagship of a fleet of six ships bound on a scientific and diplomatic junket known as the United States Naval Exploring Expedition, or the Wilkes Expedition, after its commander, Charles Wilkes. An avid amateur scientist who had an astronomical observatory at his home in Washington, D.C., Wilkes was convinced that Antarctica was a continent teeming with life, not a wasteland of ice floes and barren rocks, as everyone else assumed. After many frustrating delays and setbacks, he managed to assemble a crew that included, in addition to naval personnel, a number of distinguished scientists, artists, and cartographers, including Alfred T. Agate, James Dwight Dana, Charles Pickering, Titian Rembrandt Peale, and the philologist Horatio Hale, whose mother, Sarah Josepha Hale, edited *Godey's Lady's Book.*

The Wilkes Expedition left Hampton Roads, Virginia, in August 1838, for the unexplored South Polar region, circumnavigating the globe, taking soundings, and making observations that would prove beneficial to future naval operations and commercial shipping. During its four-year voyage, the expedition's cartographers surveyed 280 oceanic islands, mapping 180 of them; they also mapped the unexplored Oregon Territory of the Pacific Northwest, sailing past the sandbar at the mouth of the Columbia River to John Jacob Astor's famed Astoria, the jumping-off place for a lucrative Asian trade in sealskins as well as sea otter and beaver pelts. The zoological and botanical specimens gathered by the expedition's naturalists formed the nucleus of the National Museum of Natural History (now part of the Smithsonian Institution) first envisioned by John Quincy Adams and later championed by Martin Van Buren.

Although in part the purpose of the mission was to represent the United States as a benevolent and peaceful power, it failed in that respect, as the sailors would provoke fights with the natives from time to time. In the end, Wilkes's scientific contributions were undervalued by his contemporaries because of petty political jealousies and resentment of his overbearing ways. Even so, he received the Foundation Gold Medal from the Royal Geographical Society and later published a five-volume account of the expedition, which Melville read while he was writing *Omoo* in 1846.[10]

With exploration and discovery in the air, it's not surprising that after spending the Christmas of 1840 with his family in Lansingburgh, twenty-year-old Herman shouldered his duffel bag, exchanged final farewells with his family, and headed for the Pacific Ocean via New Bedford, Massachusetts.

Oddly enough, although Maria was a prodigious letter-writer, she did not inform the Pittsfield cousins that Herman had gone to sea; perhaps she was embarrassed, or ashamed. Melville's cousin Julia, who would undoubtedly have found the news exciting and would have wanted to share it with everyone, felt cheated: "We heard quite accidentally that Herman had gone to sea: the Melville family resemble the Jews in one particular, they are to be found in every part of the world."[11]

At the time of Herman's departure, Gansevoort was leaving for Boston to ask Judge Shaw for a loan so he could take a cruise to restore his health before embarking on a legal and political career. He accompanied Herman to New Bedford, where his brother signed on the *Acushnet*, the newest addition to America's six-hundred-vessel whaling fleet. The 359-ton square-rigged ship, with its two decks and three masts, each with a crow's nest where the man on the lookout for whales would stand, was so new it had not even been registered when Melville signed the papers. The ship's manifest shows that "Herman Melville: birthplace, New York; age, 21; height, 5 feet 9½ inches; complexion, dark; hair, brown" was given an $84 advance against his pay to equip himself with "necessaries" for a four-year voyage.[12]

Whalemen received a share in the profits from the voyage proportional to their rank. Melville's share, or "lay," for a first cruise barely covered necessities such as knives, soap, needles and thread, pen, paper, and ink, belts, shoes and socks, and pipes and tobacco. Sailors had to purchase these articles at marked-up prices from the captain's "slop chest," so they frequently netted as little as $200 from a four-year cruise, and if they were extremely unlucky, they could end up owing the ship's owner money. Some men signed on for the adventure and free room and board for a few years.[13]

With his customary solicitude, Gansevoort made sure his brother purchased practical, not frivolous, items for his voyage: an oilskin suit, red flannel shirt, and duck trousers; a straw tick, pillow, and blankets for his bunk; a sheath knife; a fork, a tin spoon, and a tin plate; needles, thread, and mending cotton; soap, a razor, and a ditty bag; and a large sea chest in which to store his belongings throughout the long voyage. Whatever private reservations Gansevoort had about his brother's decision to go whaling, he made sure Herman got a proper send-off and reported to their mother that he had never seen Herman "so completely happy as when he had determined upon a situation and all was settled."[14]

Once Herman was officially registered and properly supplied, Gansevoort went on to Boston, leaving his brother to explore the seaport on his own. Within a fortnight, Gansevoort would be bound for the West Indies aboard the schooner *Teazer,* confident that a few months of cruising the Caribbean and the Gulf of Mexico would cure his chronic pulmonary problems.[15]

On Sunday, Herman attended services at the Seaman's Bethel on Johnny Cake Hill, where the Reverend Enoch Mudge preached to sailors of all faiths or of no faith at all. Dedicated in 1832, the chapel looked down toward the harbor, as though the vigilance of God's minister could guarantee the safe return of the seaport's fleet. On the chapel wall hung, then as now, marble cenotaphs commemorating sailors lost at sea—some washed overboard and drowned, some attacked by maddened whales, others wrecked on remote reefs. To Melville, the white marble tablets, etched with stark black letters, were a "doleful" reminder of "the fate of whalemen who had gone before me."[16]

They were also a dare. "Danger always trails a deep-water sailor," people would say, and whalemen would answer, "For every drop of oil, at least one drop of blood." Whaling was more than strenuous and dirty; it was so hazardous that sailors liked to say the odds were two to one against a man's returning from a voyage. "Better dead than shipped aboard a blubber-hunter for a four-year cruise," men in the navy and the merchant service would say, but to someone of Melville's temperament, whaling was irresistible; it was the kind of job a man of his restless energy and intense feelings craved.[17]

New World whaling traced its origins to Captain John Smith, who obtained a permit from the British Crown to hunt whales as early as 1614. As the *Mayflower* approached its first landfall on the sandy spit of Cape Cod known today as the Province Lands, its weary passengers, entranced by the sight of porpoises and whales cavorting around the ship, decided to make their settlement on the mainland in the shelter of the bay. The first colonial whalers either waited for whales to wash up on shore or put out from land in small boats to chase the monsters as the natives did. Cape Codders soon discovered that the whales that came near shore were so full of oil that they floated when they were killed, and they called them "right whales," meaning they were the right ones to hunt.

The great boost for New England's whale fisheries came after 1650, when a dead whale washed ashore on Nantucket and people discovered that its enormous battering-ram of a head contained a rich lode of spermaceti, so called because medieval mariners believed this substance was cetacean seed.[18]

The sperm whale, or cachalot, was highly prized by New Englanders for its ivory teeth and for the hundreds of gallons of oil contained in its head and in the layer of blubber that kept it warm. A clear liquid, spermaceti turns white and waxy upon exposure to the air, which is ideal for candles or for soothing unguents (Shakespeare's "parmaceti for an inward bruise"). Although this whale eats approximately a ton of giant squid and octopus a day, it cannot digest the parrotlike beak of the squid, so it secretes a sticky substance known as ambergris to protect the lining of its bowels. This valuable substance is widely used as a base for fine perfumes.

Baleen whales are also valuable. Their toothless mouths open to reveal "scimitar-shaped slats" of stiff but pliable whalebone that resemble venetian blinds; this baleen, which is fringed with hair, strains out larger organisms so that only brit, or krill, a reddish, shrimp-shaped crustacean, can enter the tiny throat of the great whale. Baleen was used to make buggy whips, umbrella ribs, skirt hoops, collars, and corset stays, those "ridiculous affectations of gentility" that caused fashion-conscious women to move "like so many automatons," according to Melville. Thanks to whalebone corsets, their waists were pinched in so tightly that a rush of emotion caused them to faint, or suffer "the vapors," a frailty for which they were dubbed the "weaker sex."

Eager to hunt these magnificent creatures, the islanders invited Cape Codder Ichabod Paddock to Nantucket in 1690 to teach them offshore whaling, but these magnificent creatures rarely left the warm waters of the South Atlantic to venture to the cold waters off New England's shores. Then, in 1712, when Captain Christopher Hussey and his crew were blown out to sea and away from their usual fishing grounds by a storm, they spotted and harpooned a single-spouter that turned out to be the elusive sperm whale. Their catch set off a fever that infected the "fighting Quakers" of Nantucket with an unquenchable thirst for hunting whales on the open sea.

By the turn of the nineteenth century, shipyards were building larger and sturdier deep-water vessels capable of carrying half a dozen smaller whaleboats on their decks. At first these large whalers had to return to port frequently with their precious cargo, as the heavy ovens and vats for processing the oil remained on shore. In 1730, builders found a way to place the iron try-pots in a brick hearth on deck, providing insulation with a trough of water known as the "goose pen," or "duck pen." Once whalemen could process the oil on deck and store it in barrels in the hold, American vessels were able to hunt whales on the open sea for extended periods of time before making port to sell their cargo. Discoveries by Nantucketers of the "offshore Ground" near Chile and Peru in 1818, and the rich fishing grounds east of the islands of Japan a year later, inaugurated the "golden age" of New England whaling, which lasted from about 1825 to 1860. In those years the value of sperm oil doubled and then tripled, and the price of whalebone used for collars and corset stays rose fourfold.[19]

Despite the fluctuations of the market and the ups and downs of the major whaling ports—Nantucket, New Bedford, and Salem—it has been estimated that, by 1848, more than $70 million was invested in the industry, and seventy thousand persons derived their livelihoods from the slaughter. In 1857 alone, 329 vessels, valued at over $12 million and employing twelve thousand seamen, left New Bedford for the Pacific grounds. The impressive houses built by the affluent owners of these vessels attest to the success of the trade in its heyday, when it was said that if all New Bedford's ships were lined up, they would stretch for ten miles.[20]

The whaling trade, which was much more profitable than the equally savage sealing trade, survived almost until the outbreak of the Civil War, though it began to fall off after the discovery of gold in California in 1849 drew off manpower from New England crews. The financial panic of 1857 ruined investors, paving the way for the industry's demise. The discovery of cheaper, more accessible petroleum oil in Pennsylvania in 1859, followed by the invention of the incandescent lamp by Thomas Alva Edison in 1879, made whaling obsolete. By the time Edison pulled the switch on the electric pump generator he had installed at 257 Pearl Street in Manhattan and sent the first electricity pulsing through streetlamps in and around the neighborhood where Melville was born, steamships had taken the place of all but a handful of the old tall ships.

~~~

On January 3, 1841, in arctic cold, the *Acushnet,* under the command of Captain Valentine Pease II of Edgartown, cleared its mooring and "blindly plunged like fate into the lone Atlantic," leaving Fairhaven astern. Like most whalers, she was built for toughness and utility, not speed. Her stubby spars were shorter than those on clipper ships, so that when the crew was out hunting whales from longboats, the ship could be handled by a skeleton crew comprising the cooper, the cook, and the cabin boy, the only three men who did not join the chase.[21]

After the first flurry of "learning the ropes," which meant hauling canvas, bracing the yards, securing the halyards, and scurrying up icy masts while the mates barked orders from the deck, Melville had time to catch his breath and look around him. Nothing but ocean. When the horizon was an invisible line marking the boundary between a gray winter sky and the gray sea, the impossibility of perceiving the difference between Heaven and Earth came close to driving a man crazy. When the sun was out and the sea sparkled like stars in a bright blue sky, the synergy of eye and soul could make a man forget all thoughts of home. Now, in the dead of winter off New England's iron coast, with the rolling hills of Rensselaer and Berkshire counties and the green banks and gently pulsing waters of the Hudson and the Mohawk little more than a distant memory, Melville felt a profound sense of his isolation and smallness on the vast, watery globe. The loneliness that fastened its grip on him abated once he got to know his shipmates.

His twenty-six shipmates included four Portuguese, three black Americans, one Scotsman, one Englishman, and various white Americans of different nationalities. He would live and work in close quarters with these "mariners, renegades and castaways," sleeping on a straw-filled mattress in a narrow bunk belowdecks, where bilge oozed as the ship's 104-foot-long hull bucked and pitched on the crests and trenches of the deep.

The whaleman's job was dangerous and exhausting, and there were numerous drawbacks to being confined on a small wooden vessel with a group of men. Sexual harassment of younger seamen was common, and hygiene poor, as sailors, who were not very fastidious about their *toilettes* under the best of circumstances, shared inadequate facilities. The forecastle, usually pronounced *fo'c'sle,* and sometimes called the "Black Hole of Calcutta," was a cramped, dark, bug-infested space under the bows, reachable only by a ladder suspended from the small hatchway that was supposed to provide ventilation for the thirty or forty men who shared their sleeping quarters with rats and lice. At night, noxious smells wafted through the forecastle, mingling the odors of rancid oil and brine with a sickening mélange of tobacco, liquor, sweat, stomach gas, and sewage.[22]

Shipboard food consisted of "salt horse" (salted beef cut with pocket knives) and "scouse" (the Norwegian "lobscouse," a stew of hardtack and beans or potatoes sometimes mixed with salted beef or pork). Common vegetables such as raw carrots were considered great delicacies, and fruit was virtually nonexistent outside the captain's cabin except when the ship was cruising the South Seas. On Sundays the crew was treated to "plum duff," a paste of flour and water boiled with raisins and sweetened with molasses, though some captains were notoriously stingy with the raisins and molasses.

Sailors drank coffee or "longlick," a concoction of coffee, tea, and molasses. Rum was so strictly rationed by the mates that many sailors smuggled liquor aboard in their mess bags. The morning coffee took on strange flavors, sometimes tasting like lemonade, sometimes like herring, and sometimes like cheese, but in cold weather, sailors stopped caring how it tasted as long as it was boiling hot. Vile as it was, the coffee took the chill out of a man's bones. Hard sea biscuits could be immersed in it to soften them so a man could eat them without breaking a tooth; it would also flush out and drown the worms that infested this staple food of seagoing men. Unfortunately, if a man yearned for a mug of hot brew after reefing the maintop-yards on a stormy night or before taking the midnight watch, he was out of luck, as the cook had strict instructions to dole out coffee only at breakfast time. It was one of many annoying reminders of the limitations on a man's personal freedom when he was at sea.[23]

Conditions aboard whalers were so harsh that, to guard against desertions, captains would anchor their vessels far from land and allow the men shore leave only in ports known to harbor hostile natives or informers who would exchange a captured deserter for cold cash. Of the men who managed to jump ship successfully, most lingered to dally with the natives before shipping out on another vessel for the States; a few became beachcombers and never went home again.

For the first two months of the voyage, Melville felt needles of salt spray on his cheeks as he gazed out at the horizon, then down at the water knifing from the ship's black hull. When he was on deck in wintry weather, icicles formed on the whiskers he was regrowing after Gansevoort had forced him to shave off the beard he had raised on his voyage to Liverpool.

There was little life visible on the frigid North Atlantic, but as the ship cruised into the South Atlantic and neared the Tropic of Cancer early in March, Melville heard the first excited *"There she blows!"* that announced the presence of the mighty mammals who carried New England's economy on their backs, those creatures of myth and fable who baffled Job's attempts to fathom the mind of the Creator and swallowed up Jonah when he tried to flee God's call.[24]

In March 1841, somewhere off the coast of Brazil, Melville experienced the thrill of his first hunt. First he saw an undulating island of huge dark creatures half as long as the ship and nearly half as wide. Then a "gigantic Sperm Whale lay rolling in the water like the capsized hull of a frigate, his broad, glossy back, of an Ethiopian hue, glistening in the sun's rays like a mirror ... lazily undulating in the trough of the sea, and ever and anon tranquilly spouting his vapory jet ... like a portly burgher smoking his pipe of a warm afternoon."[25]

Suddenly the cry of "Whale-ho!" rang out, and the men lowered four or five thirty-foot-long whaleboats from the davits and deck by means of wooden pulleys, and scrambled for their seats. These lightweight, double-ended, clinker-built cedar boats allowed for quick changes of direction when panicked whales flailed with their flukes, or turned against the boat. The boat's crew consisted of a boatsteerer, four oarsmen wielding oars of varying lengths, and a harpooner, all barefoot so as not to scare the whales by the clumping of bootsoles on the boat's bottom. Ranged "like Ontario Indians on the gunwales of the boats," they raised the gaff to approach their quarry soundlessly by sail, or when the wind was not coming from the right quarter, they paddled or rowed with silent, feathered oars. If they were lucky, the unsuspecting whale would swim steadily and not dive, because once it went underwater, it might "mill," or accelerate its flight so rapidly that when it breached again and spouted, it might have gained more than a mile over its pursuers.

As soon as the whale was swimming steadily, the boatsteerer shouted, "There go flukes!" and the harpooner hurled his "long dart" into the tough muscles of the creature's hump. When the dart was thrown, the "magical, sometimes horrible whale-line" hissed out and shot past the necks of sailors who were rowing and trying to hold the boat on course, at the same time dousing water on the smoking fibers of the rope, heated by the friction of its passage around the loggerhead, and ducking to avoid being decapitated by the "horrible contortions" of the line.

Early whaling harpoons resembled the barbed spears used by the Eskimos, and although they were an improvement over the stone-headed spears and arrows used by the Indians, they tended to pull out as the whale bolted away. Not until 1848, when an African-American blacksmith from New Bedford named Lewis Temple designed the "toggle iron," whose blades opened out on impact and gripped the flesh of the struck whale, did whalemen begin to have an advantage over the creatures they pursued. In Melville's day, harpoons had a single hooked blade. Attached to the harpoon was the line, made of lightly tarred hemp in the early days, and of stronger, more pliable Manila rope in Melville's time. Before the harpoon was darted, the line lay coiled in a wooden tub (the newer boats carried two tubs), looking as harmless as a slumbering garden snake. Experienced whalers knew to coil the three-hundred-fathom-long line carefully, because "the least tangle or kink in the coiling would, in running out, infallibly take somebody's arm, leg, or entire body off."[26]

The men held their breath, for "to be seated then in the boat, is like being seated in the midst of the manifold whizzing of a steam engine in full play, when every flying beam, and shaft, and wheel, is grazing you." Finally the iron barb struck the flesh of the whale, and a geyser of blood shot into the sky and cascaded into the sea, attracting schools of sharks so inflamed with the thirst for blood that they tore one another apart and snapped mindlessly at their own entrails.

As soon as the whale felt the sting of the harpoon, it shot through the water, trying to throw off the pain, and the men braced themselves for the "Nantucket sleigh ride"—that wild career at speeds up to twenty-five knots over blistering waves, pulled by the maddened whale, when any man not secure in his balance and strong in his grip could be thrown from the boat and drowned. If the whale proved too strong, the tub oarsman had orders to cut the line with a hatchet and a sharp knife. During this commotion, the harpooner gingerly changed places with the boatsteerer so he could have the honor of dealing the death blow to the whale.

The men hung on for their lives as the whale charged frantically through the boiling sea, sometimes for many hours and sometimes pulling more than one longboat behind it. When at last, suffering from fear, exertion, and loss of blood, the doomed whale slackened its speed and gave a "flurry," its "tormented body rolled not in brine but in blood, which bubbled and seethed for furlongs behind in [its] wake," and its powerful flukes thrashed frighteningly close to the boat, threatening to dash it into the shark-infested waters.

Once the whale's energy was spent, the men hauled in the line and drew near their quarry by a maneuver known as "pitchpoling," so that the mate, who had moved to the bow of the boat, could pierce the creature's lungs with a sharp-bladed lance. Then "the whale once more rolled out into view; surging from side to side; spasmodically dilating and contracting his spout-hole, with sharp, cracked, agonized respirations," and "gush after gush of clotted red gore, as if it had been the purple lees of red wine, shot into the frighted air; and falling back again, ran dripping down his motionless flanks into the sea," which reddened and became viscous wih the dying creature's blood.

After the whale's great heart burst, the men marked their catch with a "waif pole" and went back after more whales. When the hunt was over, they towed each capture back and secured it to the ship. Working quickly in competition with rapacious sharks that were tearing gobbets of flesh from the floating whale, they took their places on a wooden platform suspended from the gunwales and fastened a huge hook to the whale's flank, peeling off strips of blubber and hoisting them to the deck with the aid of winches. With a ceremonial flourish, the mate severed the huge "head of Holofernes" from the creature's body and swung it over to the other side of the ship by means of a block and tackle. Then the jawbone was sawed out in one long piece, and the teeth were saved for scrimshaw.

The harpooner, lowered onto the back of the whale by a rope attached to a fellow sailor's waist, placed a hook in the animal's flank, and as the "prodigious blood-dripping mass" hung above the water by chains placed under its flukes, men armed with long-handled spades cut into the body, cranking the windlass and singing to keep their rhythm as they peeled off the eighteen-inch-wide "blanket-piece" of blubber. This operation caused the entire ship to lurch to one side as, trembling and quivering, she "nodded her frighted mast-heads to the sky."

After the skin and blubber were stripped from both head and body, the men concentrated on "baling the case" to scoop out its enormous quantity of spermaceti, a wax substance so valuable for making candles and unguents that they often lowered a small boy into the "great tun of Heidelberg" with a bucket and a spoon to make sure none of the precious substance went to waste.[27]

When at last all the blubber was spread out on the slippery deck, the men, barefoot and sliding around in "gurry," as they called the viscous mess of vomit, feces, oil, and blood, cut the large strips into square chunks called "horsepieces." That done, the mincer, using a two-handled cleaver, sliced the blubber into smaller pieces called "Bible-leaves" and tossed them into the try-pots—two iron cauldrons raised on bricks and heated by a wood fire. After all the oil was "tried out," the remaining "fritters" of blubber were tossed into the fire. The rolling of the ship, the sloshing of the blood and guts and blubber, the infernal heat and lurid light of the try-works' two iron cauldrons, and the oily smoke that blackened the sails and rigging as well as the men's faces and clothes, invested the whaleman's work with a diabolical allure. To Melville it seemed almost satanic to be "burning a corpse" as "with huge pronged poles [the men] pitched hissing masses of blubber into the scalding pots, or stirred up the fires beneath, till the snaky flames darted, curling out of the doors to catch them by the feet."

Only after they had finished trying out the blubber could the sailors wash off the crimson gore and sooty, oleaginous slime, swab the decks, coil the ropes, polish the brass, and hope they would have time for a rest, a smoke, a tot of grog, a chantey, and a coarse joke or two about the whale's immense genitalia before the next cry of "Whale-ho!" rang through the salt air.

The oil—anywhere from 80 to 160 barrels from a single sperm whale—was ladled into a cooling tank from which it would be funneled into huge wooden casks and stored in the vessel's hold. A prosperous cruise would yield about 2,000 barrels, or about 64,000 gallons, of the oil used to make candles and to fuel whale-oil lamps. If they were lucky, the men might also retrieve ambergris, or undigested fecal matter, which was used to spice wines and foods in the Near East. This precious excrement sold for $10 an ounce in Paris as a base for expensive perfumes, and for $643 an ounce in China, where it was considered an aphrodisiac.[28]

Tacking southward along the coast of South America, the *Acushnet* made a brief stop at Rio de Janeiro, where she transferred some two hundred barrels of sperm whale oil to the brig *Tweed* for shipment to Baltimore. Newly provisioned, she headed for Cape Horn, and on a squally day in early April she again encountered sperm whales. Off the Falklands, Melville saw his first albatross, "a regal, feathery thing of unspotted whiteness, and with a hooked, Roman bill sublime." This "goney-bird," as Melville and his ship-mates called the huge, ungainly creature, was that same "prodigy of plumage" whose wanton murder with a crossbow brought a curse on the ship in Coleridge's ballad *The Rime of the Ancient Mariner*.

By the middle of the month, a "fair, free wind" was "blowing steadily, through a bright translucent day, whose air was almost musical with the clear, glittering cold." As the ship neared Tierra del Fuego, the "land of fire," Melville could see the cliffs of Staten Land, the present Isla de los Estados, off the coast of Argentina, gleaming "in snow-white barrenness and solitude."[29]

Melville had formed his impressions of the voyage around the Horn from Richard Henry Dana Jr.'s *Two Years Before the Mast,* a book that had aroused in him "strange, congenial feelings" for its author. From Dana's graphic description of the icy sleet and spray that could lash a sailor's cheeks and eyes and bore through his bones as though he were not wearing a jacket or gloves, Melville must have expected the worst, but because it was summer in the southern hemisphere, the *Acushnet*'s passage around the Horn was not as bad as he had feared. Though winds and squalls from the enormous Antarctic continent buffeted her constantly, she made a safe passage around the tip of South America and squared her yards for the offshore cruising grounds.[30]

As the ship entered the South Pacific, she passed Diego Ramirez and Juan Fernandez, the mountainous island where Alexander Selkirk, the model for Defoe's Robinson Crusoe, had been marooned; in Melville's day, it was a Chilean prison colony. During the first few months of cruising, the *Acushnet* enjoyed "greasy luck," and Herman wrote Gansevoort that he was "in perfect health and not dissatisfied with his lot," as he had unusually congenial shipmates.[31]

By May, when the ship stopped at Callao for a 10-day respite, she had 200 barrels of sperm oil in her hold, and by August she had added another 350. October 1 was a record killing day, yielding 100 barrels of oil, and after their exhausting work was done, the men started betting on a short and prosperous cruise.

Soon afterward, however, their luck turned, and numerous sightings of whales yielded few captures, making the crew restive and irritable. Captain Pease responded by cracking down, and the crew's spirits fell. A seaman named David Smith deserted at Santa Harbor, but most of the men waited out the whale famine by writing letters home, sewing, and carving scrimshaw. They etched scenes of the sperm-whale fishery on whalebone, whale teeth, and even strips of baleen with a sailmaker's needle, bringing out their designs by darkening them with paint, tar, or ashes from the try-works. They also made ivory-headed canes, cribbage boards, and intricate scale models of whaling vessels for themselves, and for their wives and sweethearts they fashioned a variety of useful articles, including fans, letter openers, "jagging wheels," or pie crimpers, napkin rings, sewing baskets, spool racks, and "niddy-noddies," or "swifts," to hold yarn when they weren't home to hold it for their wives themselves. These intricate and delicate artifacts attest to the painstaking craftsmanship of many an otherwise uncouth tar. Because the whalemen of Melville's time usually spent three or four years at sea and sometimes had long waits between whale sightings, scrimshaw, originally called scrimshander, became the first art form created by white men on the American continent. Like folk art of all cultures, it was both decorative and practical.[32]

Discouraged at sailing around for months with no luck, the crew was near mutiny, so Captain Pease headed for the Galápagos to divert the men with a little tortoise-hunting. Six years earlier, Charles Darwin had visited these islands. He had published his observations of flora and fauna caught in an evolutionary time warp as the *Narrative of the Surveying Voyages of His Majesty's Ships* Adventure *and* Beagle. As the *Acushnet* sailed through "the enchanted isles" (so called by navigators because unpredictable currents made it seem as if they were constantly changing position), Melville was entranced by unusual sights such as Rock Rodondo, a tower of rock "like the famous Campanile or detached Bell-Tower of St. Mark." Jutting up "two hundred and forty feet high, rising straight from the sea ten miles from land," it seemed an image from Greek mythology.

Like the rock from which the Sirens serenaded Odysseus and his men, this strange mid-ocean outcropping streaked with guano sang an unearthly song. As the ship passed, Melville could hear the "demoniac din" of thousands of seafowl who made their nests in the rocky ledges, eave upon eave and nest upon nest, then circled overhead, "spreading themselves into a winged and continually shifting canopy." In "The Encantadas," Melville describes these volcanic islands six hundred miles off Peru as a Dantesque wilderness of rocks whose only audible sound was the hiss of snakes and lizards.[33]

The ship lay at anchor off Chatham's Isle for six days while the men went ashore in longboats to hunt huge sea turtles, called "tortoises" by the men, who captured three of these creatures and hauled them aboard the ship with the tackle designed to hold whale carcasses up out of reach of circling sharks. Gamy, succulent tortoise meat was a delicacy for protein-deprived men who made the shells into mirror backs, combs, and brushes, or strung them and played them like lutes and mandolins. The turtle hunt diverted the men momentarily from their disappointment over their failure to catch whales; it also provided Melville with images of man's slow progress in this life.

Early in December, Captain Pease, who was ill and treating the men badly, turned the ship toward the harbor of Tumbes to take in fresh fruit and water. The men gazed longingly at the grass huts and coconut palms that conjured visions of the tropical islands to the west and watched the tide go out, exposing the roots of willow trees to which clusters of oysters clung in an unusual form of symbiosis. The ship remained anchored outside the harbor for thirteen days, but in an attempt to assert the authority he had forfeited by his irrational behavior, Captain Pease refused to let the disgruntled crew go ashore for fear they might not come back again.[34]

During her months of cruising the Line, as sailors called the Equator, the *Acushnet* met a number of other vessels. These meetings, called "gams," were as elaborately choreographed as a woodcock's mating dance, beginning with the first manuever, known as "speaking a ship," which involved two ships showing their colors and tacking into precariously close proximity without touching so that the captains could exchange information about whale sightings. On such occasions, the captains frequently visited each other, feasting on delicacies not shared with their crews. While his oarsmen were rowing him to the other ship over the choppy waters between the two ships, the visiting captain stood bracing himself in the bow of the dory with his legs, not holding on to anything and trying not to sway or fall. When captains' wives and children were on board, entire families paid calls on each other. Women and children changed ships in a "gamming chair," a close relative of the breeches buoy, and the women usually tried to persuade their husbands to prolong the gam for several days because they were so starved for female company and the children were so desperate for playmates.[35]

Usually when ships met, they passed mail and news of home between them, but letters sent to or from oceangoing vessels had a poor chance of reaching their destinations. Six months was considered the average time for delivery, though one whaling wife complained that in three years her husband received only six of the hundred letters she had sent him. During gams, sailors also exchanged boasts and gossip. The captain of the *Rousseau* told of having his ship's hull pierced by a gigantic swordfish, but a story told by the *Acushnet*'s second mate, John Hall, fascinated Melville even more. Hall had served with Owen Chase, the first mate of the *Essex,* on another ship and heard firsthand his account of the ramming of the *Essex* by an angry sperm whale and the grisly tale of how the men were forced to resort to cannibalism to survive.

Chase had published his *Narrative of the Most Extraordinary and Distressing Shipwreck of the Whale-Ship* Essex in 1821, and since then, countless shipboard retellings had invested the *Essex* whale with supernatural qualities. Melville was eager to read Chase's narrative, but there were no copies in the ship's library. When the *Acushnet* gammed for several days with the Nantucket ship *Lima*, Melville's wish came true. By a coincidence that seems almost supernatural itself, he met Owen Chase's son, William Henry, who loaned him the copy of his father's narrative from his sea chest.[36]

Factual accounts such as Chase's narrative and J. N. Reynolds's "Mocha Dick: or the White Whale of the Pacific," which had appeared in the *Knickerbocker Magazine* in 1839, had ushered in a spate of tall tales featuring prodigious animals. The "penny press" that exploded onto American newsstands during the 1830s featured tall tales about monstrous creatures attacking humans. Exaggerated retellings of stories about a huge sea serpent that allegedly terrorized ships off the coast of Gloucester, Massachusetts, between 1817 and 1822 were followed by accounts of giant swordfish piercing hulls with their sharp bills and maddened sperm whales ramming vessels head-on and sinking them. One of the most daring and original of these stories was Eugene Batchelder's *A Romance of the Sea-Serpent, or The Ichthyosaurus,* which violated both the conventions of the new genre and the confines of verisimilitude by having its genial cetacean protagonist leave his watery home for the land to perform such preternatural feats as lecturing at Harvard and attending a Newport ball.[37]

By the time Melville wrote *Moby-Dick* in 1850, he was familiar with a number of these nautical narratives, among them Harry Halyard's *Wharton the Whale-Killer! or, the Pride of the Pacific,* a pulp novel featuring a whale that maliciously smashes a ship to bits. These sensationalistic adventure tales appealed to boys and young men far more than did the omnipresent temperance tracts and manuals of moral and hygienic advice given to them on birthdays by anxious parents and other relatives, most of which focused on dire warnings about the dangers of daydreaming, which was considered conducive to masturbation in the nineteenth century.

While older publications such as Donald Fraser's *American Magazine of Wonders* featured tales of monstrous animals, newer tabloids such as the *New York Herald*, the *Morning Post*, and the *Daily Sun* served up lurid accounts of sexual perversions and criminal acts to workingmen who were looking for vicarious thrills to distract them from the hardships and frustrations of their lives. Sailors slipped these cheap, lightweight pamphlets into their sea chests and swapped salacious stories with their mates during long ocean voyages, and as Melville remarks coyly in his 1850 novel *White-Jacket*, most sailors liked books that were "slightly physiological in their nature."[38]

Literary musings, however, were not in the forefront of Melville's mind while he was at sea. Long before he ever sailed for the South Pacific, the tropics had laid a moist, warm hand on him, pulling him beyond the boundaries of his "young inland imagination" to a garden of delights where he could experience that "one delirious throb at the center of the All." The Marquesas loomed in his mind's eye like an undiscovered planet, luring him on as the mysterious silver jet of vapor just over the horizon would lure the *Pequod* to her fateful rendezvous with Moby Dick.

*Richard Tobias ("Toby") Greene, who jumped ship with Melville, later corroborated
his friend's fictionalized account of their adventures in the Marquesas.*

SEVEN

THE FLOODGATES OF
THE WONDER-WORLD

Slightly over a year after setting off, Melville's ship turned westward toward the Marquesas. When the Acushnet *sailed into Taio Hae, or Anna Maria Bay, at Nuku Hiva, one of ten islands constituting the 230-mile-long Polynesian archipelago, the first thing Melville saw through the squally rain were the cones of two volcanoes whose fiery eruptions over the centuries had formed the peaks and valleys of the island. Through the mist he could see a 2,600-foot plateau from which rivers plunged over cliffs in the rainy season, forming spectacular waterfalls and flowing into narrow valleys planted with breadfruit and coconut.*

Beyond the sparkling white sand of the coastline rose steep hills covered with dense, tangled vines and tropical flowers so large and of such intense and vibrant hues that New Englanders and New Yorkers seeing them for the first time would close their eyes and open them again, as if to test the accuracy of their perceptions. Not far from the harbor stood the incongruous rectilinear buildings of missionary compounds, most notably the remains of a little wooden "city" established in 1833 by William Alexander and the vanguard of the American Board of Commissioners for Foreign Missions on the model of the Protestant mis-

sion in the Sandwich Islands. Somewhere deep in the interior, tribal villages nestled in the valleys, invisible to the invading eye.[1]

The awe and pleasure Melville felt as he surveyed the sweeping beaches and declivitous peaks that lay before him quickly turned to horror, however, as he caught sight of French warships lined up in the harbor with their six-inch cannons pointed "not at fortifications and redoubts, but at a handful of bamboo sheds, sheltered in a grove of cocoanuts!" Four thousand French troops, under the command of Rear Admiral Du Petit Thouars, had just occupied the island, and they were building a fort in preparation for establishing a colony. Was the paradise he had dreamed of all his life already lost?[2]

As the ship dropped anchor, Melville could see a flotilla of naked damsels swimming out to the ship holding garlands of flowers above their heads as gifts for the visiting sailors. Anticipating this reception, the sailors had already broken out the grog. Once the girls had dried themselves off and combed one another's hair, they began to dance—slowly, sensuously, making erotic gestures with their hips and hands, inflaming the passions of the men, who quickly turned the gracious welcome into a shameless orgy of unbridled lust, according to the account Melville gives in *Typee: A Peep at Polynesian Life*.[3]

But is this account true? Melville's arrival in the Marquesas brings us into a fictive realm where fantasy and dream coalesce, reaching back to retrieve an imaginary past, and reaching ahead to give birth to the artist. Whatever the facts were, the truth was that Polynesian maidens regarded the bestowal of sexual favors as an innocent form of hospitality, and Melville considered them more civilized than those hypocritical Christians who saw the islands as places to throw off all moral and religious restraints and to indulge their selfish passions.

Fed up with shipboard life under the tyrannical Captain Pease, who had fallen ill during the voyage and become increasingly bad-tempered and dictatorial, Melville decided to jump ship and explore the island. It was a wise decision not only for literary history, but also for his personal well-being. During the remainder of the *Acushnet*'s four-and-a-half-year maiden cruise, half of her crew would desert, one sailor would commit suicide, and two would die of venereal diseases. On the return voyage, her first and third mates jumped ship at Payta, Peru, leaving only eleven men on board when she arrived in port. In 1851, shortly after *Moby-Dick* was published, Melville learned that the *Acushnet* had run aground on St. Lawrence Island and broken up in heavy seas.

While the ship rode at anchor in the harbor, Melville persuaded his friend of "many pleasant moonlight watches," Richard Tobias Greene of Buffalo, New York, to desert with him. In preparation for their escape, Melville learned a few native words and gathered information about the island's geography. He and "Toby" stuffed a plug of tobacco, a few lumps of sea biscuit, and some cloth they hoped to use as barter into their ditty bags, and just as the ship was preparing to weigh anchor on July 9, under cover of a downpour they slipped over the side and made for shore.

To avoid capture, they headed into the jungle, and after a couple of hours of climbing hills overgrown with thick, twisted vines, they stood at the summit of a steep basalt cliff, half a mile above the harbor. Overhead, bright-winged birds flashed through the trees, and wild parrots squawked like monkeys in seeming mockery of man's claim to have ascended the evolutionary ladder. Below them in the harbor, they could see the ship, but the next day, when Captain Pease discovered their disappearance, he sailed the ship out beyond the harbor and dropped anchor, then stole back in a longboat to look for them. Short of hands, Pease attempted to recruit new crewmen, but his reputation had preceded him, so he was unsuccessful.

After climbing from peak to valley and valley to peak and valley once again, Herman and Toby reached a village whose inhabitants seemed friendly. European and American visitors generally allied themselves with one of the island's three warring tribes—the Taipis, the Teiis, or the Happars—and depicted the others as bloodthirsty cannibals, making it hard for outsiders to ascertain the truth. When Captain David Porter, fresh from his victories in the War of 1812, took possession of the Marquesas for the United States in 1813, he allied himself with the Teiis and laid waste the valley of their rival tribe, the Taipis, who were reputed to be cannibals, though they denied it. Twenty-two years later, when William Alexander came to Nuku Hiva to establish an American mission, he allied himself with the Taipis, accusing the Teiis of indulging in human sacrifices. Western travelers had disseminated such wildly contradictory stories about the islanders that it was difficult to tell whether they were vicious man-eaters or peace-loving "noble savages."[4]

Seeing how militant missionaries in the South Seas were destroying a peaceful, non-Christian culture radicalized Melville. He began to question who the "savages" were and who the "civilized." Reexamining his own society, he found the "examples of civilized barbarity, the vices, cruelties and enormities of every kind that spring up in the tainted atmosphere of a feverish civilization" to be far more abhorrent than the primitive rituals that, to the missionaries, marked the Oceanic peoples as "savages."[5]

Melville's reaction to Marquesan customs was very different from that of most other visitors. Charles S. Stewart, for example, who was chaplain aboard the USS *Vincennes,* considered the Polynesians naturally licentious, and blamed them for teaching visiting sailors wicked ways. While Melville was writing *Typee,* he consulted Stewart's book and peppered his manuscript with scenes and commentary designed to show another way of looking at the same material. Unlike Stewart, Melville saw the women as children of Nature debauched by invaders bent on raping "virgin" land.[6]

The natives turned out to be the Typees, a name that Melville teasingly translates as "lovers of human flesh." They welcomed Herman and Toby and treated them as guests, though from time to time the two men wondered if their hosts were cannibals. They remained in the village about four weeks, and like other Westerners who encountered Polynesians before the European and American invasion, Melville was especially struck by the physical beauty and dignified deportment of the men.

Bare-chested, muscular, and handsome, these Polynesian men wore earrings and other trinkets fashioned from sperm-whale teeth and leaves. Their long hair and androgynous style of dressing foregrounded masculine beauty in ways quite fascinating to nineteenth-century American males. They wrapped their loins in skirts of elegantly patterned tapa cloth that covered but did not compress their genitals, as trousers compressed the sex organs of Western men. It would not have taken Melville long to notice that when a man is wearing nothing but a loose skirt of thin cloth, his sex can become a prominent and provocative feature of his costume.

The women were less strikingly beautiful than the men, according to most accounts, though in *Typee,* Melville sensuously describes the pleasures of swimming nude with them. They were diminutive compared to American girls and had smooth olive skin and short dark hair. Like the men, they were bare-breasted and their dances were characterized by sinuous motions of the arms and suggestive undulations of the hips and pelvis that Victorian men would never have tolerated in their own women. Native men, some even dressed as women, also danced with the same provocative and alluring grace, arousing homoerotic feelings in sailors who had already experienced them, and in some who hadn't. For Melville, who was attracted to both men and women in ways he was still struggling to understand, this was a time of increased self-awareness, experimentation, and self-questioning.[7]

Polynesian courtship behavior was a far cry from the ethereal courtships conducted by young men who read poetry to Lansingburgh "belles" on the banks of the river. It resembled neither the restrained rituals prescribed by advice manuals written to prepare middle-class Americans for married life, nor the obscene perversions cooked up by the men who scribbled for the penny press. Marriage in Polynesia was based on a system of polyandry that allowed women two "husbands," or other officially sanctioned sexual partners. Their domestic arrangements usually involved a ménage à trois consisting of the wife, the husband, and a younger man, or boy, who might be available for sexual service to both the wife and husband. According to Melville, the Typees attained a high degree of "domestic felicity," a daring statement that would get him into trouble with readers who expected literature to reflect and uphold bourgeois moral values. At the same time, statements like these would also win him a cult following among men and women whose sexual passions were not proscribed by Victorian domestic ideology.

Melville's sojourn in the polymorphous paradise of Polynesia must have been both liberating and disturbing. South Sea islanders felt no self-consciousness about their bodies, and Westerners were continually startled by the sight of various types of couples fondling each other in public, or by young children casually fondling their own genitals while adults chatted among themselves, or looked on delightedly. Even an ordinary task like making fire by rubbing a hard stick against hibiscus wood was accompanied by erotic chants that made the act of starting a fire a mimetic form of sexual intercourse. He found it ironic that whereas Europeans needed only to strike one match to light a fire and Marquesans had to rub sticks together to get a spark, countless Europeans lived in abject poverty, lacking enough to eat, while people in the Typee Valley needed only to reach into the trees or turn over the fertile soil to find ample food.[8]

Melville saw the sexual differences between primitive and civilized societies as coeval with social and economic differences. His essential bisexuality, more conscious and less guilt-ridden, thanks to his sojourn in the South Seas, than that of the many repressed Victorians, would enable him to envision social organizations that would liberate human personality, not constrain it; yet he, too, was a child of his culture and his time, just as deeply wounded in his maleness as women were in their femaleness by a patriarchal culture that repressed the feminine in man and the masculine in woman and punished children for discovering an erotic universe in their own bodies.[9]

The sexual freedom of Polynesia was a refreshing change from timorous tête-à-têtes over Tennyson. Melville experienced the "mere buoyant sense of a healthful physical existence"–that pure sensual pleasure Jean-Jacques Rousseau thought only children and primitive peoples were capable of experiencing. It's safe to say that when a robust young man such as Herman Melville discovered there was more to sex than the "missionary position" described in marriage manuals, his Victorian notions of sexuality took a tumble.

Western visitors like Henry Adams and Paul Gauguin, who had never realized the degree to which their notions about gender were determined by fashion, were usually disoriented by the androgynous appearance of half-naked islanders. Until the missionaries came bearing cast-off trousers, corsets, and the loose, shapeless dresses known as "Mother Hubbards," gender boundaries between native men and women were often blurred. Both men and women bared their breasts above tapa skirts, wore feather earrings and pendants of polished shells, and bathed their skin with perfumed oils.[10]

In Oceanic languages, gender differentiation of pronouns was minimal despite the existence of many gender-related taboos *(tapu)*, and in many Oceanic cultures, androgynous individuals were thought to embody the ideal balance of male and female. Males, as the more privileged sex, frequently cross-dressed during religious observances to represent goddesses as well as the gods. Like the ancient Greeks, Marquesans idealized male beauty and eroticized male bonding, or *tayo*, which appealed to the fatherless Melville's longing for intimate relationships with men, supplying him with a sexualized metaphor for the brotherhood of man.[11]

In some parts of the Sandwich Islands and Tahiti, transvestites and feminized men were thought to possess heightened creativity and compassion, and they were chosen as the priests. Religious ceremonies were based on fertility rituals, so temples were built in the shape of the Earth Mother's spread thighs, idols such as the omnipresent *tiki* represented the erect phallus, and worshipers anointed their faces with semen after prolonged copulation inside the sanctuary.[12]

Tribal practices such as superincision of the penis and enlargement of the clitoris by massage and ligature emphasized the homologous nature of male and female genitals. Thus, in *Typee*, when Melville describes his alter ego Tommo defying the tribal taboo that forbade women to enter canoes by taking the "beauteous nymph" Fayaway canoeing with him on the lake, he slips in a naughty nautical joke designed to elude most genteel readers, including the women in his own family. As his "Typee dulcinea," to use Toby's phrase, stands facing him and holding her robe open to catch the wind, Tommo admires the helpful service she is performing by commenting, "We American sailors pride ourselves upon our straight clean spars, but a prettier little mast than Fayaway made was never shipped a-board of any craft." She is obviously naked, although Melville never says so explicitly, and only his fellow sailors would have known that in the local patois, the word *mast* referred to an enlarged clitoris, which resembled a penis.[13]

Melville managed to slip a great deal of bawdy humor past the pious critics and "soft, Cherubic" gentlewomen, as Emily Dickinson called them. In an era when religion, medical science, and new theories of industrialization were conspiring to repress all kinds of healthy sexual expression and punish transgressors, much fiction written exclusively for men pandered to their taste for the kind of sensational perversions and crimes that sprang from the dark side of the human psyche. In writing *Typee*, Melville hoped to attract not only women readers, but also men with broad sexual preferences who did not enjoy the violent perversions of the penny press.[14]

When Melville wrote *Typee* in 1846, he created a partially romanticized picture of native life as a foil to condemn the puritanical religious and sexual politics of Victorian America. Later ethnological literature, however, corroborates many of Melville's observations, from the importance of the festive "Feast of the Calabashes," to the probable practice of some ritual cannibalism in the sacred "Hoolah-Hollah ground," to the existence of a complex system of tribal *tapu* such as that which forbade women to board canoes or enter the "Ti" where the men held their meetings.[15]

Melville believed the Typees had a moral system based on "indwelling ... universally diffused perceptions of what is *just* and *noble*," and his sojourn among the Typees gave him "a higher estimate of human nature than [he] had ever before entertained."

Branding as self-serving hypocrites those Christian colonizers who believed western civilization was morally superior, Melville suggested that "four or five Marquesan Islanders sent to the United States as Missionaries might be quite as useful as an equal number of Americans despatched to the Islands in a similar capacity."[16]

Melville's sojourn in the Marquesas made him acutely aware of how culture imposes limitations on self-knowledge and self-expression by rigidly defining and determining gender, race, and class. He instinctively chafed at cultural codes and proscriptions against the expression of the many selves engendered in him by each new experience. Whereas his contemporary Walt Whitman would celebrate the phallus openly in his poetry, Melville expressed himself covertly through puns, jokes, and allegories. He embraced transgressive fiction to reclaim sexuality for serious literature, and when his own ambivalence, combined with heavy cultural and familial repressions, doomed his quest to failure, he went underground.

While he was in the Marquesas, Melville felt the pull of the sensual, easygoing life of the tropics, but however much he was attracted by its pleasures, he feared that if he stayed too long he would become so estranged from civilization that he could never return. Symbolized in *Typee* by the twin fears of being tattooed and being fattened up to be a feast for cannibals, his anxiety about allowing himself to remain in an infantilizing dependency more crippling than bourgeois domesticity, made four weeks in the Typee Valley enough for him, and he and Toby began to look for a way out.

On the pretext of going for medical help for Melville's infected leg, Toby left the village and returned to the port, where he found an Australian captain in desperate need of seasoned hands to man his ship for the voyage home. This captain, who had already heard there were two sailors living in the bush, had been hoping to find them and add them to his crew. Thus, in a much less dramatic fashion than he would describe later in *Typee*, Melville left Polynesia, carrying deep in his heart the vision of the Happy Valley that had opened his soul to an expanding universe.

～

During the second week of August 1842, Melville signed on an Australian whaler named the *Lucy Ann*. Once this fast-sailing bark left Nuku Hiva Bay for the Society Islands, he became conscious of a "contrast between the luxurious repose of the valley, and the wild noise and motion of a ship at sea." The contrast was so great "that at times my recent adventures had all the strangeness of a dream." The romanticizing process that would make *Typee* a synonym for "paradise" had begun.[17]

Badly run and badly neglected, the *Lucy Ann* had had an unlucky cruise, having taken only two whales since leaving Sydney. Twelve of the original thirty-two crewmen, including three mates and three harpooners, had deserted, and the men who were left were a dissipated lot. They drank heavily at all hours, and when they touched at the Coral Islands for water, they fired their muskets randomly at any natives who happened to be standing on the beach.

Captain Ventom was a petty tyrant whose nasty temper was exacerbated by ill health, and the first mate, John German, was a drunkard. Other than harpooner Benbow Byrne, whom Melville recasts as Bembo, the Maori who jumps on the back of a fleeing whale in *Omoo*, the only man for whom Melville appears to have had any respect or affection was John B. Troy, the ship's steward, whom he called "Dr. Long Ghost." This erudite and waggish "tower of bones" could quote Virgil, recite canto after canto of Samuel Butler's *Hudibras*, and debate the political ideas of Thomas Hobbes. A charming rogue whose sole medical qualification was his theft of pharmaceuticals from the ship's stores, John Troy was not above tying a line around a sleeping sailor's ankle and hauling him up the mast; naturally, he became Melville's chief companion.[18]

Losing control of his crew, Ventom headed for Tahiti, arriving in time to hear the French frigate *La Reine Blanche* firing two twenty-one-gun salutes to announce her arrival. Ventom was met by the consul and taken ashore for treatment of an abscess of the lungs. The authorities appointed the drunken first mate to skipper the ship, but since no sailor wants to serve on an unsafe ship, many of the men claimed they were too sick to work. Dr. Francis Johnstone, who was treating the captain's ailment, examined several crewmen and pronounced most of them fit to work, including Melville, who was still suffering from a leg injury incurred at Nuku Hiva.[19]

That night, most of the crew got drunk and rioted, and the following day, sailors armed with cutlasses and boarding-pistols arrived in cutters from the French frigate, boarded the *Lucy Ann*, and arrested the "mutineers," including Melville, who claimed that he and John Troy were part of a small group that had tried to dissuade the others from the mutiny. Confined for two days in "double irons," eating bad food and drinking watered wine, they were threatened with a trial that turned out to be a bluff on the consul's part.[20]

Melville was taken ashore in shackles with the other prisoners by a native escort, who marched them down Papeete's picturesque Broom Road, a gravel boulevard that had been built by convicts. Following the perimeter of the island, the road was "provided with narrow bridges of planks over the water courses and streamlets" that gave a fine view of the mountains on one side, and the ocean on the other. Having "escaped from the confined decks of the frigate," Melville savored the way "the air breathed spices" as the streams flowed and the green boughs swayed. "Far inland, all sunset flushed, the still, steep peaks of the island" rose "nine thousand feet above the level of the ocean."[21]

Melville, Troy, and the others were handed over to the British authorities, who locked them up in the "Calabooza Beretanee," a makeshift outdoor jail whose only furniture was the stocks, "a clumsy machine for keeping people in one place." Although he never got used to the feeling of "having one's foot *pinned*," Melville amused himself by observing his surroundings. Before long, he and Troy made friends with Warden Bob, who let them run loose all day, provided they agreed to return to the thatched jail for the night and to sit in the stocks, looking penitent, when the British or French authorities came to inspect the jail.[22]

Tahiti was more "advanced" in the "civilizing" process than the Marquesas had been; thus, Tahitians suffered not only from the bizarre tropical disease elephantiasis, which swells the extremities and stretches the skin until it hangs in baggy folds, but also from a host of "bodily afflictions ... unknown before the discovery of the islands by the whites." Chief among them, after smallpox, was syphilis, which nineteenth-century doctors cavalierly treated with toxic doses of mercury, resulting in numerous debilitating side effects.[23]

An influx of European diseases to which the islanders had no immunity had decimated the population. Of the 200,000 people that Captain James Cook had guessed lived on Tahiti in the 1770s, only nine thousand had survived into the mid–nineteenth century. Their once pristine dwellings were rundown and untidy, and many people seemed to be living in poverty. "The Tahitians are far worse off now than formerly," Melville concluded, and "their prospects are hopeless."[24]

The civil authorities in Tahiti had banned the manufacture of tapa cloth in order to force natives to buy textiles manufactured by whites abroad. When Melville had observed tapa manufacture in the Typee Valley, it struck him as an exemplar of labor in a utopian society, because it brought the entire Typee village together in a communal activity that made no separation between work and leisure as industrial societies tended to do. Villagers scraped and pounded mulberry leaves to a wearable thinness and decorated the softened cloth with geometric designs that complemented their tattoos. Imported textiles, by contrast, were expensive, and most natives found them uncomfortable and strange. Tahitians who couldn't afford imported cottons were forced to wear the constricting castoffs distributed by missionaries to enforce Western standards of decency, which gave them a "grotesque" and "deformed" appearance, reinforcing Western assumptions of the Tahitians' simplemindedness and cultural inferiority.

With British colonists trying to make the islands an extension of the factory system in places like Manchester and Leeds, the London Missionary Society had set up a cotton factory at Afrehitoo, which Melville later visited, ordering looms and spindles from London and sending a foreman out to recruit native workers and teach them how to card the cotton. At first, "the whiz of the wheels and spindles brought in volunteers from all quarters, who deemed it a privilege to be admitted to work, but within six months, not a boy could be hired; and the machinery was knocked down, and packed off to Sydney." To Melville, this was an object lesson in the absurdity of mercantile policies that made colonies send raw materials to rich nations for manufacture, then slapped tariffs on them and sold them back to the same poor nations at a profit, as the Crown had done when America was a British colony. It undoubtedly crossed Melville's mind that his paternal grandfather had committed an act of civil disobedience to protest similar exploitation of a colony by its mother country.[25]

As if the economic and social damage done by colonialism was not enough, the psychological and spiritual impact of colonialism was disastrous. The missionaries banned traditional religious ceremonies and passed stringent blue laws prohibiting tattooing and even such innocent pastimes as dancing, flute-playing, kite-flying, and singing the old ballads, on the grounds that these frivolous pursuits would make the natives indolent. Instead, the laws necessitated a force of constables, called "kannakippers," and, outlawing ancient agricultural festivals, like the Opio, or harvest-home of the breadfruit, fostered depression and lethargy.

Although Melville portrays himself as a madcap mariner, on a deeper level, he was an inquisitive observer, a budding artist, and a concerned social critic whose highly developed sense of decency and fair play gave him great sympathy for the natives whose sad fate he could not put out of his mind. He was outraged to see an ancient and beautiful culture destroyed by white invaders, and his early novels would bear witness to the injustices he saw inflicted on the islanders by representatives of the so-called civilized nations.

During the two weeks the mutineers spent under the jurisdiction of Warden Bob, a "corpulent giant, over six feet in height, and literally as round as a hogshead," John Troy managed to obtain laudanum and other drugs from Dr. Johnstone, instead of the paregoric he was dispensing to the other inmates. Fearing the consul might deport them to Sydney unless they sailed on the *Lucy Ann,* Troy and Melville escaped by canoe to the island of Imeeo, the present Moorea.

Attacked by mosquitoes, they worked as farmhands on a plantation in the valley of Martair, growing breadfruit, yams, and sweet potatoes, all of which produced enzymes to fight malaria. In their free time they hunted wild boars and wild cattle, and went spearfishing. They also visited villages that lay beyond the reach of the blue laws, enjoying the "generous hospitality" and "simple piety" of natives who wove tapa cloth and worshiped Oro. Melville gained a sense that life in precolonial Tahiti had been as idyllic as life in Polynesia, and he firmly believed that colonialism meant the destruction of the old island ways.

By November 1842, Melville was eager to get back on "the billows," and he made the rounds of Yankee whalers until he found one whose captain was "a sailor and no tyrant." Covering up their connection with the mutiny on the *Lucy Ann,* he and Troy signed on the *Charles & Henry,* which was owned by the Coffin brothers of Nantucket, but when the two men reported to the ship, the captain recognized John Troy as a Sydney "bird," or ex-prisoner, and kicked him off the ship. Melville had to say good-bye to his friend and leave Tahiti without his prankish sidekick; years later he heard that Long Ghost had ended up in California, hunting gold instead of whales.

The *Charles & Henry* was slightly smaller than the *Acushnet,* and much more crowded, but the inexperienced Captain Coleman treated his men decently. Unfortunately the voyage had not yielded a single barrel of whale oil after three months, so he changed course and, instead of turning back toward the Galápagos, he sailed for the Sandwich Islands, where he could stock up on pineapples and hogs and able-bodied men before cruising the whaling grounds off Japan. The ship docked at Lahaina, on the island of Maui, with five hundred barrels of oil, which was not an exceptionally lucrative cargo for twenty-eight months at sea, and Melville left the ship on May 2, 1843.[26]

The Sandwich Islands had changed dramatically since the first Polynesians landed on their shores and intermarried with the natives. Colonization was so far advanced that the towns were beginning to resemble villages in England and America. Lahaina, a favorite port for New England whalers, had as its centerpiece a stone church capable of holding eighteen hundred worshipers, and a seaman's chapel that could hold two hundred. Otherwise the town offered few diversions and no opportunities for employment, so Melville went to Honolulu. There he worked for a while setting up pins in a bowling alley, an occupation that won him some notoriety, as the missionaries did not consider bowling a respectable pastime. They boasted of having converted King Kamehameha from this vulgar sport to billiards, which was, in their eyes, a more appropriate recreation for a gentleman.

Honolulu was a thriving colony whose foreign population consisted of the families of sea captains as well as merchants, missionaries, and government officials. Although the wives of merchant captains generally accompanied their men to the exotic ports of the Far East, whalers' wives stayed safely in Honolulu while their husbands cruised the Pacific grounds. Most of the women enjoyed the time they spent in the island towns. They made friends with other wives and enjoyed a more casual social life than that of women on the mainland, though some, like Augusta Penniman, thought it "very cruel" to be separated from their husbands from May Day to Thanksgiving.[27]

Melville had arrived in the Sandwich Islands during a political crisis. The British had just sent Lord George Paulet of the British navy to Honolulu to seize the islands for Great Britain. Many of the islanders, and all the sojourning sailors and beachcombers, welcomed British rule as an antidote to the strict, moralistic regime of the American missionaries. American residents, however, were torn between resentment against the Crown and an even greater abhorrence of the French, who threatened to move in if the English failed to seize control.

Despite the unrest, Melville signed an indenture for a year with Isaac Montgomery, an educated English merchant three years his senior. Montgomery, who had come from Cumberland in 1838, was a supporter of Lord George Paulet and a vocal critic of American missionaries, and Melville liked him. On July 13, 1843, Melville began work as Montgomery's clerk-bookkeeper at an annual salary of $150 to be paid quarterly, plus free board, lodging, and laundry. His duties consisted of keeping the ledgers and doing inventory, measuring calico, and selling supplies to the store's customers.

Soon after he began working for Montgomery, riots and demonstrations broke out, and natives from surrounding islands swarmed into Honolulu and committed "deeds too atrocious to be mentioned." This melee convinced Melville that these "civilized" islanders were incapable of self-government at this point. His disillusionment with the natives and his contempt for the hypocrisy of the American missionaries, combined with his hatred of the French and his friendship with Isaac Montgomery, persuaded him to support a British takeover, which angered the American authorities even more than his hanging around bowling alleys denouncing colonialism.[28]

There was no love lost between Melville and the missionaries. An old man and a boy in cast-off clothes, harnessed to a cart like animals, pulling a missionary's wife dressed in starched white linen to Sunday services perfectly epitomized for Melville the underlying purpose of colonialization: enslavement and exploitation of the natives. "Not until I visited Honolulu," he would write, "was I aware of the fact that the small remnant of the natives had been civilised into draught horses and evangelised into beasts of burden. But so it is. They have been literally broken into the traces, and are harnessed to the vehicles of their spiritual instructors like many dumb brutes!"[29]

Civilization was so far "advanced" in the Sandwich Islands compared with Polynesia and Tahiti that the missionaries had built playgrounds for white children and then surrounded them with high fences, "the more effectually to exclude the wicked little Hawaiians." Because the whites did not allow children of different races to mingle, the younger natives and settlers, who might have grown up as friends, had no common life or mutual understanding on which to build a multiethnic community.[30]

Melville's very public denunciations of the colonial establishment aroused the ire of such local dignitaries as the famed medical missionary Dr. Gerrit P. Judd, who had been sent to Hawaii with his bride Laura Fish, a teacher. Melville was afraid Judd, whom he called a "sanctimonious apothecary-adventurer," would see him listed in the local shipping office as a deserter from the *Acushnet* and the *Lucy Ann* and turn him in, so he dissolved his contract with Montgomery and made plans to leave the island.[31]

On August 17, Melville joined the crew of the USS *United States,* a naval frigate bound for the port of Boston, enlisting as an ordinary seaman. Confident that wearing a uniform would protect him from the civil authorities, he signed on for three years or one cruise, which left him the option of quitting the navy when the ship returned to port.[32]

Melville could not have chosen a more rigidly hierarchical, oppressive, undemocratic world to enter than the world of a naval frigate. On a warship a man was not even allowed "to sing out, as in merchant vessels, when pulling ropes, or occupied at any other ship's duty." The gulf between officers and crew was wider than the gulf between Heaven and Hell. Although she was only three-quarters the size of the *Acushnet,* the *United States* was five times heavier, and nearly twenty times as many men were crowded onto her three decks. Each man had only eighteen inches in which to swing his hammock, and when the mates mustered all hands to attention, the men had barely enough room on the crowded decks to click their heels and salute. The skipper, Captain James Armstrong, was a tippler whose tendency to appear on the quarterdeck in various states of inebriation did not inspire confidence in his crew.

The daily drill gave the enlisted men little time to notice how cramped for space they were. At a shrill whistle from the boatswain's pipe and a shout of "All hammocks up!" the men hopped out of their canvas slings and threw clothes over their underwear, then rolled up their bedding and stowed it in the netting over the bulwarks, after which they clambered up the ladder, grabbed buckets and mops, and swabbed the decks.

By the time the cook doled out breakfast to each mess from the three copper cauldrons behind the mainmast on the gun deck, the men had worked up appetites that could not possibly be satisfied by coffee and dunderfunk, which was a mixture of "hard biscuit, hashed and pounded, mixed with beef fat, molasses, and water, and baked brown in a pan." Their other meals consisted of a "monotonous round of salt beef and pork" and hardtack, except when they could cajole the cook into diversifying the fare with "sea-rolls" and "Mediterranean pies." Each man was entitled to a "tot," or half-gill, of grog daily from the 4,840 gallons of whiskey stored in the hold.[33]

Naval regulations were strict and inflexible. Even when the men completed their seemingly endless chores efficiently enough to have a few minutes' rest, they were not allowed to unroll their hammocks and lie down. The lack of opportunity to sleep more than a four-hour shift, and the long time without food between the crew's early supper and sunrise the next day, struck Melville as a dangerous deprivation for men who had to be alert and ready for battle twenty-four hours a day. On mornings when Melville did not have cleanup duty after breakfast, he was free until the nine-o'clock inspection to read books from the ship's library, write letters, or climb the rigging in search of some privacy and solitude.

Most vessels, including whalers, and those whose captains brought their families aboard, were equipped with libraries. The library on the *United States* included mostly scientific and historical literature such as Darwin's *Narrative*, Bancroft's *History of the United States,* and Hough's *Military Law Authorities and Courts Martial,* as well as *Harper's Family Library*, which included a wide range of titles. Melville managed to steal time to read a dozen or more of these volumes in his fourteen months aboard the frigate.[34]

Among the ship's large crew, he found several men whose personalities and intellectual interests made them convivial companions, most notably John J. Chase, a "Briton, and a true-blue, tall and well-knit, with a clear open eye, a fine broad brow, and an abounding nut-brown beard." A "stickler for the Rights of Man and the liberties of the world," Chase had deserted a British ship in Callao to "draw a partisan blade in the civil commotions of Peru," then signed on the *United States* as an ordinary seaman. He spoke five languages and could recite long passages from Camoëns's *Lusiads* in the original Portuguese. Oddly enough, this man whom Melville most loved and admired harbored a career naval man's "unmitigated detestation" for whaling and called it "pig-killing," perhaps to get a rise out of Melville.

During night watches, Jack Chase sang "salt-sea ballads and ditties" in "his own free and noble style," directing the men's attention "to the moonlight on the waves, by fine snatches from his catalogue of poets." He had an "abounding air of good sense and good feeling about [him], that he who would not love him, would thereby pronounce himself a knave." Melville and the other members of his watch considered him a man whose superior intelligence and seamanship made him a natural leader, and within six weeks, Chase was appointed captain of the maintop.

Ephraim Curtis Hine, an aspiring young poet who went on to publish *The Haunted Barque and Other Poems* in Auburn, New York, in 1848, was another comrade of the maintop watch. Hine was undoubtedly the model for "Lemsford the poet" in *White-Jacket,* who hid his poems in a cannon barrel only to see his work blasted into the air, "every canto a twenty-four-pound shot," when gunners fired the piece for practice. This seemed an apt metaphor for the literary life when Melville was writing his fictional account of his naval experiences in 1849, just after critics had fired a "broadside" into *Mardi,* which he considered his masterpiece at that point in his career.

Melville also made friends with "a laughing philosopher" named Williams, a "thorough-going Yankee from Maine, who had been both a peddler and a pedagogue in his day," and Oliver Russ, a mysterious fellow who had enlisted under the name "Edward Norton." Williams told witty stories about "nice little country frolics," and Norton, whom Melville called "Nord," was "a reader of good books" who had "seized the right meaning of Montaigne." Nord was generally shy, but during one night watch, he and Melville "scoured all the prairies of reading; dived into the bosoms of authors, and tore out their hearts." Nord was so reserved that it wasn't until years later, when he told Melville he had named his first baby "Herman Melville Russ," that Melville realized how much their friendship had meant to his shipmate.[35]

The camaraderie of the maintop crew helped soften the sharp edges of naval discipline, as did the occasional peaceful moments aloft, when Melville could savor the crisp salt breeze and open sky, forgetting the compulsive activity and the sanctioned brutality of the officers. Less than a fortnight after the ship put out to sea, all hands came on deck for the monthly recitation of the Articles of War. These rules governed the conduct of naval personnel, and after reading each of them in the style of a litany, the clerk added the words "shall suffer death," intoning them with ominous solemnity to remind the five hundred members of the crew that their officers had absolute power over them and that they would be put in irons or flogged for the slightest deviation from naval regulations.

Whenever he was on deck, Melville could see the wooden hatch covers where sailors sentenced to flogging were roped to the grating at the ankles and wrists. Stripped to the waist, the miscreant would stand waiting for the "cat" to pounce at the least infraction of a rule. The cat-o'-nine-tails was a short-handled whip consisting of nine knotted leather thongs that were "laid on" a sailor's back by the boatswain's mate, who would grip the wooden handle and apply the allotted number of strokes to the victim's naked back. The sight of the bloody welts clawed by the "cat" sickened Melville, and he was determined never to risk such a punishment.

The mindless cruelty of navy discipline enraged him, and he began to see flogging as an apt metaphor for the relationship between tyrannical abuse of power and the rights of the common man. A sailor could be flogged for getting drunk, for talking back to an officer, for shirking a duty, and for myriad other infractions, some decided arbitrarily by the officer on duty. The floggings themselves usually seemed more severe than the crime warranted, and some officers all too obviously derived sexual pleasure from flogging other men. Most terrible of all in Melville's view was the practice of "flogging through the fleet," which meant that when his ship was in port, a poor condemned sailor, holding his bloody shirt in his trembling hands after a flogging on his own ship, could be transported from ship to ship and flogged aboard as many as a dozen vessels. For Melville, flogging symbolized man's inhumanity to his fellow man. Pondering the chaplain's role in this barbaric system, Melville wondered how "the religion of peace should flourish in an oaken castle of war."[36]

Despite his innate impulse to rebel when confronted by strict regimentation and mindless authority, Melville evidently managed to escape the lash by calling on his childhood skill at blending into the woodwork when he felt threatened. He mastered the monotonous daily routine of washing the hammocks, coiling the lines, polishing the brightwork, holystoning the decks, and scrubbing rust off the guns with a noxious, gritty powder so that he could almost perform these duties in his sleep. The entire time he was serving in the navy, a rebellion against naval discipline was raging inside him that would compel him to write *White-Jacket* at about the time Congress was hearing testimony by a number of prominent citizens who opposed the navy's practice of flogging.[37]

During his fourteen months in the navy, Melville stood at attention for 163 floggings, saw a man permanently crippled by a fall from the mizzen topsail yard, and witnessed five deaths and several close calls. The sight of a corpse in its white shroud, weighted with shot, sliding off the gangplank into the sea made even seasoned tars cast down their eyes and shudder. Perhaps because they actually had so little control over their own fates, sailors tended to be superstitious. Some were convinced that when a body was buried at sea, its spirit would rise and hover over the ship in the form of a bird or an eerie light, while others averred that taking a stitch through the nose of the deceased guaranteed that the body would rest peacefully on the bottom of the sea.[38]

After leaving the Sandwich Islands, the frigate headed toward the Marquesas, losing a man overboard on the way. When the ship anchored at Nuku Hiva on October 6, 1843, Melville could see that the French had imported gangs of convicts to build a fortress and stock its arsenal. The *United States* spent forty-eight hours in port with no shore leave for the crew, then set sail for Tahiti, where they stood at anchor some distance from shore to be inspected and provisioned. As the frigate passed Imeeo, Melville took a long last look at the South Seas.[39]

Brief stops in several South American ports provided Melville with some vivid images of ruined empires and decayed civilizations for his later fiction and poetry. Valparaiso, Chile, with its horseshoe-shaped bay and twenty rounded hills, was a pleasing sight from the water, but the town itself looked derelict with its rundown adobe huts and tattered thatched shacks. The whitewashed façade of Lima, Peru, masked an inner rot. The tile-roofed houses were crumbling from an earthquake fifteen years earlier, and buzzards swarmed over gutters clogged with human excrement and the rotting corpses of dead animals. At Callao, Melville saw the remains of a fortress and a city wall that conjured visions of Spanish imperial power, and, beneath the clear waters of the bay, the shimmering ruins of an entire city that had been destroyed by an earthquake and tidal wave. Strolling through once-elegant neighborhoods, Melville caught the eye of veiled women hanging clothes out on backstreet balconies, and in the arcades near the center of town, he watched mesmerized as women crocheted lace or twirled fried dough on sticks. On the outskirts, dogs and vultures scavenged bones from an open pit filled with human corpses.[40]

While the *United States* was anchored at Callao, Melville heard that three crewmen aboard the *Somers*, the navy's newest and fastest brig, had been accused of mutiny and summarily executed without a proper court-martial. Several other suspected conspirators were in irons. On the strength of a list of possible co-conspirators, scribbled in Greek by Midshipman Philip Spencer, the vessel's commander, Alexander Slidell Mackenzie, Commodore Perry's brother-in-law, had accused Spencer and two others of plotting to mutiny. With their natural antipathy toward officers, the enlisted men, most of whom were young recruits on this cruise, were saying that Mackenzie had trumped up the charges against the three sailors to shore up his own authority, instead of turning them over to a court-martial as naval regulations stipulated.[41]

The case received national publicity primarily because Midshipman Spencer, the alleged leader of the mutiny, was the son of President Tyler's Secretary of War, and members of the administration made political hay out of the event. Young Spencer was known to be a bad character who, as an undergraduate at Hobart College, had carried a copy of *The Pirate's Own Book* around the campus, boasting that he wanted to go into piracy after graduation. He never did graduate, however, as he was expelled for being drunk and disorderly, after which he joined the navy. Knowing that Spencer had already been disciplined by the corps several times, Mackenzie rejected him for his crew, but Commodore Perry overruled his decision for political reasons.[42]

When the *Somers* case was heard, the evidence showed that Spencer had conspired with Samuel Cromwell, who was known to have connections among pirates in Cuba, and that their accomplice Elisha Small had played a smaller role. Evidence showed that they had planned to solicit allies among the crew, then murder the officers and loyal sailors and take the fast-sailing brig to the Caribbean for an orgy of piracy, murder, rape, and enforced sexual slavery of any females they could capture. All three were executed.[43]

Mackenzie had asked Lieutenant Guert Gansevoort, who would later be commended for his exemplary conduct during the entire affair, to convene a drumhead court, and he and the other officers had recommended execution for Spencer, Cromwell, and their sidekick Small on the grounds that there was no room on the ship to house the malefactors—a judgment corroborated by architectural drawings of the ship. The ordinary jack-tar, who refused to believe that officers would suddenly have any qualms about holding prisoners belowdecks, no matter how cramped and uncomfortable the space, vilified Mackenzie, Guert, and the members of the drumhead court during every shipboard bull session for months.[44]

Even though Commander Mackenzie was an educated man and a writer of several books who was famous for his exceptional kindness to the younger apprentice seamen in his charge, resentment against abuses of power in the navy was so widespread that debate raged hotly in the press for months, and the subject continued to be discussed for years. Prominent friends of Mackenzie such as Henry Wadsworth Longfellow, Richard Henry Dana Jr., Senator Charles Sumner of Massachusetts, and Catharine Maria Sedgwick defended him vigorously, portraying him as a martyr to the political machinations of the Tyler administration and the shallowness of the uninformed public mind.

The punctilious James Fenimore Cooper pointed out that Mackenzie had followed a highly irregular procedure, but he was in the minority.[45]

While he was in Callao, Melville learned that his cousin Guert had presided over the rump trial that had recommended execution, and although he had ambivalent feelings toward Guert, to hear a close relative vilified by his shipmates was deeply disturbing. According to the scuttlebutt in Callao, Mackenzie regretted having acted on the recommendation of Guert and the other officers. Melville, who not long before had been jailed as a mutineer himself, was haunted by the story all his life; four decades later, it would undergo a sea change, resurfacing as *Billy Budd.*

~~~

Much to Melville's dismay, the *United States* was detained at Callao for two and a half months, and the men were denied shore leave. Their orders were to remain on the ship to run through the daily routines as the Commodore of the Fleet, Thomas ap Catesby Jones, was in the port for an official visit and inspection of the ships under his command. Twice a day, all hands were piped on deck for a formal ceremony, during which the first lieutenant ceremoniously raised and lowered his saber and touched the brim of his cap in salute to officers from Jones's ship, the *Constellation,* while Melville stood at rigid attention beside his gun on the quarterdeck. The only break in this tedious ten weeks came when the commodore was called home, and the captain of the *United States* was free to challenge both the *Constellation* and the British ship HMS *Vindictive* to a race out of the harbor. With Melville on the main royal yard, the "Old Waggon" won.[46]

Buoyed by the victory, the men felt sure their ship would be the next one ordered home. Instead, they were ordered to Mazatlán, Mexico, a month's cruise away, to pick up fifty thousand Mexican silver dollars for use by American vessels resupplying themselves in Latin American ports. Owing to some administrative snafu, the coins had not even been minted when they arrived, so the men had to wait almost three weeks for their cargo. When they finally turned over the moneybags at Callao, they were told they still did not have clearance to return to their home port.

When they finally weighed anchor for Boston, it was nearing midwinter in the southern latitudes. Strong headwinds sent huge waves crashing against the hull as the old ship plowed into the gale, "half burying herself at every plunge." It was so rough that a number of men checked into sick bay, leaving the rest of the crew to reef canvas and man the weather yards.

During the month it took for the *United States* to tack up the coast to Rio, Melville celebrated his twenty-fifth birthday. The frigate rode at anchor for a week in the "small Mediterranean" that lay in the shadow of Sugar Loaf Mountain, but again the men were not allowed shore leave, so Melville had to content himself with standing on deck inhaling the "languid and faint" breeze that "comes from the gardens of citrons and cloves, spiced with all the spices of the Tropic of Capricorn."[47]

While the *United States* was anchored off Rio, the supply ship *Erie* arrived in port to deliver 366 barrels of bread, fifty-seven barrels of butter, six boxes of tea, and two deserters. Apparently, Melville's cousin and childhood chum Stanwix Gansevoort was the officer of the deck that day, but because officers in uniform were not allowed to speak to enlisted men or even acknowledge their presence except to bark orders or reprimands, Stanwix ignored Herman. Had he been in his cousin's shoes, Melville would have considered it a point of honor to somehow circumvent naval regulations in order to greet a relative, and he was hurt and angry at his cousin for snubbing him. He took his revenge in *White-Jacket* by portraying midshipmen as spoiled, self-important tyrants who derived pleasure from ordering common sailors to be flogged, and in *Pierre* by modeling the arrogant, hypocritical Glendinning Stanly on Stanwix.[48]

Melville had developed a violent hatred of the entire officer class and built up enough resentment toward both Stanwix and Guert that when he was composing *Billy Budd*, he turned the *Somers* case inside out, endowing the common sailor with virtue and the officers with subtle and not-so-subtle malevolence—a point overlooked by critics who fail to contextualize the story historically. In any case, Melville's last significant experience in the navy was one that reinforced his perception of the institution as an undemocratic "man-of-war world."

On August 24, the *United States* challenged the French sloop *Coquette* to a race and won, before sailing "like a stately swan through the outlet" until she was "gradually rolled by the smooth, sliding billows, broad out upon the deep." Heartily sick of the navy, Melville couldn't wait to get home. He was relieved that he had not committed himself to more than one cruise, as he had concluded that naval frigates were "floating Hells," and that the *United States* was a "wooden-walled Gomorrah of the deep" where sodomy and "other sins for which the cities of the plain were overthrown" flourished.[49]

In *White-Jacket*, flogging and, more covertly, homosexual rape exemplified the way the privileged and powerful treated their less powerful fellow men. In Melville's view, the enlisted men made up a forecastle fraternity oppressed by tyrannical officers. Although Melville's narrator concludes that America "bears the Ark of the liberties of the world," Melville feared democracy would not survive the abuses of power sanctioned by militaristic colonialism.[50]

~⌒⌒~

Sailing around Race Point into Cape Cod Bay on October 2, Melville had his first taste in nearly four years of fresh cod from a Massachusetts fishing sloop. As the ship entered Boston Harbor, Melville saw the Bunker Hill Monument, a 221-foot-high Egyptian obelisk made of Quincy granite, high on a hill overlooking Charlestown. The monument had been dedicated by Daniel Webster the previous year, and John Quincy Adams had shocked many people by refusing to attend the ceremony, which he called Webster's "gull-trap for popularity." He confided to his diary that he considered Webster "a heartless traitor to the cause of human freedom" and President Tyler a "slave-breeder."[51]

The *United States* made port in time for the men to lower and furl the sails before the sun set over the Boston Navy Yard. Herman's cousin Guert Gansevoort was stationed aboard the *Ohio,* a floating office that never left the harbor. Although he had invited Helen Melville, her friend Elizabeth Shaw, and Miss Shaw's distinguished father to tour the ship, he would never again be the gay blade who had spent a shore leave in Boston in 1842 because Helen had told him the "ladies here are crazy after naval officers."[52]

The *Somers* mutiny changed Guert. He had arrived home in Waterford so ill and aged by the ordeal that his own mother hardly knew him. "He had a violent cold; coughing constantly; very hoarse his limbs so contracted; that he talked like an infirm man of seventy; his eyes were red & swollen, & his whole face very much bloated–his back and sides were so sore, from the strap & weight of the huge & heavy ships Pistols; that he would not raise himself erect–Having imprisoned so many of the crew; they were short of hands & he, poor fellow, did more than double duty–the eve of which I speak, his first visit to us; he had not had even his coat off in four days."[53]

Soon after his arrival home, Guert had been summoned to Washington to go before the court-martial trying Commander Mackenzie for his role in the *Somers* executions. Guert was well aware that if Mackenzie were convicted, he would be the next officer to be charged. His mother was horrified, and wrote her son Stanwix, "To have *Guert, honest & upright* as he is–keeping out of the way of Justice–and the idea of his being taken up, & lodged in prison under the charge of *murder*–was it not awful–my blood chills when I write it."[54]

Even after the court-martial exonerated both Captain Mackenzie and his lieutenant, Guert remained much "overshadowed" by his role in the affair and turned to alcohol for solace. For Herman, the *Somers* case would grow and change from a historical footnote to an epic story of the battle between good and evil, law and liberty, the head and the heart.

Four years at sea had given Melville an opportunity to explore many sides of himself, trying on several disguises and uniforms. When he later wrote the novel based on this voyage, he created for his fictional persona a quilted white canvas jacket as sturdy as a mainsail, but completely unsuited to wet weather, with pockets of all shapes and sizes where he could conceal his true emotions and safely stow his dreams. This fantas-

tic article of clothing gives his later book about his stint in the navy its title, and its protagonist a name. He later told Richard Henry Dana that the jacket "was a veritable garment—which I suppose is now somewhere at the bottom of the Charles river. I was a
great fool, or I should have brought such a remarkable fabric (as it really was, to behold)
home with me."[55]

On shipboard, Melville had found himself experiencing situations that presented
him with a profound disjunction between what he felt and what he was supposed to feel.
The exhilarating but bloodthirsty slaughter of the great whales, the alluring but disorienting sensuality of the islands, and the proud but sadistic discipline of the navy all
stretched him and challenged him enormously. Having no outlet for his sensitivity and
creativity, he rebelled, as he had at home. He returned from four years at sea ready to
proclaim himself "a savage, owing no allegiance but to the King of the Cannibals; and
ready at any moment to rebel against him."

After Melville returned to "snivelization," white paper became a means of both self-
concealment and self-expression, like the white jacket that nearly costs his eponymous
protagonist his life when he falls from the mainmast. By writing, Melville could fill the
white spaces with his own meanings. He could recapture and communicate his moments
of great insight, happiness, and fear: daydreaming and pondering the mysteries of
the universe from a perch high in the rigging, listening to songs and stories with the companions of his watch, dallying in the shade of a breadfruit tree with a beautiful native
girl, seeing blood spurt from welts cut in the backs of fellow sailors by the vicious "cat,"
and sighing with relief that, once more, he had managed to escape the lash.[56]

Writing would become his way of defending his personal freedom and unique
vision against both his domineering mother and the metaphorical "officers" of Victorian
culture—the rigidly prescribed rules of behavior and stifling moralistic piety that so often
masked hypocrisy. Having seen a "primitive" society in operation, he felt compelled to
ridicule both corrosive prejudices and bourgeois pretensions. He saw himself spreading
a gospel of justice and brotherhood that would transform the callous "man-of-war" world
of modern America into a parliament of brothers.

The young man who had left home a fatherless second son without prospects
returned home ready to throw open the floodgates of his imagination. Writing would
become his way of "lighting out for the Territory" where neither abusive captains nor
respectable widows could get their hands on him and "snivelize" him. Writing would be
his mutiny against the civilized cannibals who threatened to devour the inner man.

Gansevoort's thin, aristocratic features and graceful figure contrasted markedly with his brother Herman's ruddy Dutch complexion and robust physique.

EIGHT

A LITTLE EXPERIENCE IN THE ART OF BOOK-CRAFT

Melville arrived back in America the week the millennialists said the world would end. His voyage had taken him not only westward to the Pacific, but also back in time and deep into the primordial recesses of a self layered over by successive generations of familial and societal influences. In some respects, submerging himself in the sensuous ambiance of Polynesia had been a return to racial, cultural, and sexual infancy. Returning to his mother's house would put him in a curiously analogous but disquietingly different situation; it would be a return to childhood without the bliss, to a culture of individualistic striving and competition, a sojourn with a different breed of cannibal.

It was not difficult for one who had found the "fresh green breast of the new world" in the South Seas to envision the America that had "flowered once for Dutch sailors' eyes," and to lament its disappearance. Shedding his cultural biases with his clothes, he had approached Oceanic peoples with an open mind and come away with a "higher opinion of human nature" than he had previously entertained. Seeing colonialism in action had convinced him that the "white civilized man [is] the most ferocious animal on the face of the earth."

Melville remained in Boston for nearly two weeks because of "circumstances connected with the ship," and even before he was officially discharged from the navy, events on board made him acutely aware of the urgency of the slavery issue.[1]

Shortly before the *United States* reached port, the purser's servant, Robert Lucas, "a colored man somewhat advanced in years," of "good countenance, indicating a kind and benevolent disposition," asked to be allowed to remain in Massachusetts as a free man. A slave whose master had allowed him to enlist in the navy without releasing him from his bond, Lucas was, in effect, requesting political asylum. He was detained by the authorities until his case could be heard by Chief Justice Lemuel Shaw.[2]

Judge Shaw had already ruled on several cases involving slavery. In 1836 he had presided over the trial of the fugitive Med, who claimed that once her master had brought her to free soil, he had no right to hold her in bondage. Although Massachusetts had no statute on the books to overrule the Fugitive Slave Law of 1793, Judge Shaw was able to set Med free by applying principles of British common law. In 1842, however, the Supreme Court of the United States declared that states had an obligation to enforce property rights of citizens of other states, and Shaw was forced to return the fugitive slave George Latimer to his owner.[3]

The Latimer verdict outraged antislavery supporters. The abolitionist minister Wendell Phillips denounced the United States Constitution as "a covenant with death and an agreement with hell," and protestors took to the streets of Boston denouncing Judge Shaw. Incensed by the federal government's interference in the affairs of the commonwealth, the Massachusetts legislature enacted Personal Liberty Laws, which established the principle that no one could restrain the liberty of a person residing in Massachusetts, or claim that person as property in another state. Thus, from 1843 until the passage of the federal Fugitive Slave Law in 1850, Massachusetts was a haven for fugitives from "the peculiar institution."

While Melville was aboard the *Acushnet*, he must have heard that African captives had seized the slave ship *Creole*, which was bound for the slave markets of New Orleans; the captives intended to sail to Nassau, where British authorities would set them free. Most northern newspapers compared the Africans to patriots like Melville's grandfathers, and to Melville it was ironic that men bound for slavery in America had to look to England for their freedom.[4]

Much of the goodwill shown the *Creole* rebels by the northern press was the result of John Quincy Adams's stirring defense of the Africans who had seized the slaver *Amistad* two years before. The crusty old Adams took the case of the rebel Cinqué and his followers all the way to the Supreme Court, where he won their release and extradition to Senegal by arguing that they had seized the ship in self-defense against being kidnapped.[5]

As a sitting judge, Lemuel Shaw could not be partisan. Although he personally opposed slavery and assumed its abolition to be inevitable, he feared precipitous action would strengthen the resolve of slaveholders and lead to dissolution of the Union. The Personal Liberty Laws made it possible for him to argue that once a coasting vessel touched a Massachusetts port, no man could be held in bondage by the ship's commander or by any persons on board. Thus, he ruled that Melville's shipmate, Robert Lucas, should be set free—a decision that gave abolitionist forces a tremendous boost and sent a powerful signal to the slave states.

On October 14, 1844, a common seaman named Herman Melville, who was #572 on the muster roll of the USS *United States,* received his pay and the discharge papers that released him from the navy, that "asylum for the perverse, the home of the unfortunate" where "the sons of adversity meet the children of calamity" and "the children of calamity meet the offspring of sin," as he would say in *White-Jacket.*

Arriving in Boston after nearly four years at sea, Melville felt like a stranger in a strange land. Everyone he met was eager to hear about his adventures and to fill him in on what had happened while he was away. All four of his sisters had finished their schooling at the Albany Female Seminary, a noted progressive school, and Helen had been making long visits to Boston to see her friend Lizzie Shaw. Lizzie had made her debut in November 1841, at a ball in Faneuil Hall attended by the Prince of Joinville, Louis Philippe, and ever since, her social circle had included a number of eligible bachelors, most of whom were much more attractive to Helen than were the swains of Lansingburgh.

Under the watchful but lenient eye of Lizzie's warmhearted and generous stepmother, Helen escaped the role of deputy mother that Maria often tried to foist on her, and put herself in a position to meet eligible Bostonians. She thought she would like to spend the rest of her life in this quaint old town, even though its crooked streets and hills were so steep that during a sleet storm she and Lizzie had to grip the iron railing in front of the State House and "stoop like frogs" to climb the icy sidewalks to the Shaws' house on Beacon Hill.[6]

Boston offered Helen Melville many more social activities than Lansingburgh did. She could visit an artist's studio in the afternoon, eat an oyster supper at the home of Lizzie's cousin Jane Dow, and enjoy after-dinner *tableaux vivants* depicting the Pygmalion story or Abraham's banishment of Hagar and Ishmael. One evening the Shaws took her to see *Macbeth,* starring the celebrated British actor William Macready, and all she could think of the whole evening was how much Herman would have enjoyed the show, especially his favorite scene, where the witches stir "eye of newt and toe of frog" into a "thick gruel" while chanting spells over a "cauldron of Hell-broth."[7]

Herman had, of course, missed Charles Dickens's whirlwind tour of America, but Helen, who had been at the Shaws' when Dickens arrived in Boston, told him all about it. When the writer actually shook her hand, she vowed never to wash it or let another man hold it because the great "Boz" had touched it. As far as we know, she kept the latter part of this resolution until she met the Boston attorney George Griggs.[8]

Augusta, by contrast, found it hard to sustain interest in the young men she met in Albany and Bath, especially the one Helen called "the knight of the big head & constant grin"—although she enjoyed being escorted around Albany and Lansingburgh by Stephen Van Rensselaer, until it dawned on her that his reckless driving hinted at qualities undesirable in a marriage prospect.[9]

While the two older girls were concentrating on finding husbands, Gansevoort and Allan were focusing on establishing careers. In January 1842, with Judge Shaw's help, Gansevoort was sworn in as a member of the Court of Common Pleas. He soon discovered, however, that he preferred politics to litigation. As the elections approached, he went on the road as a stump speaker for the Democratic Party, and Allan stepped into his job as Examiner in Chancery. Whereas Gansevoort would avoid "any connection with the complex wire-pulling machinery" of Tammany Hall and concentrate on national politics, Allan would practice law all his life and involve himself in ward politics.[10]

During the turbulent party caucuses prior to the presidential election of 1844, allegiances were being reshuffled and old loyalties disavowed or reaffirmed. When warring factions could not unite behind Martin Van Buren, Gansevoort advanced the candidacy of James K. Polk. At about the time Herman was sailing from Rio de Janeiro to Boston, Gansevoort was on a campaign swing through western New York, Ohio, and Tennessee, visiting James Polk in Columbia, Tennessee, Henry Clay at Ashland, and Andrew Jackson at the Hermitage, where he discovered that southern hospitality meant plying guests with mint juleps served by immaculately groomed slaves in livery.[11]

Gansevoort must have known how much his father had hated Andrew Jackson for deposing John Quincy Adams, for instituting the egregiously self-serving spoils system, and for dismissing the old major from his job, but it didn't stop him from raising a hickory pole in Jackson's honor at a rally in Nashville attended by fifty thousand people. He campaigned vigorously for Jackson's protégé Polk and for the admission of Texas to the Union, dubbing Polk "Young Hickory" after Jackson, the old Indian-fighter whose "baptism of fire and blood at New Orleans" had won him the nickname "Old Hickory."

A charismatic orator long on style and short on substance, Gansevoort Melville roused audiences with hyperbolic rhetoric that ranged from the evangelical to the polemical, with subtle gradations of fustian and bombast in between. "My blood is up!" he crowed in Batavia, New York, launching into the kind of speech that Horace Greeley called "all gas and glory."[12]

On the stump, his inherited sense that he was the center of a cosmic drama served him well, as he drew "eager crowds." Most local commentators found him "eloquent and powerful," but former New York mayor Philip Hone called him "an itinerant spouter of nonsense, a sort of Anarcharsis Clootz, an orator of that part of 'the human race,' denominated Loco-focoes," and the popular Bowery politico and tabloid journalist Mike Walsh dubbed him "gander-brained Melville." Thomas Melvill Jr. feared he would find "that politics, are not *profitable*, & more than that,—that he has been made a tool, by party leaders & politicians, for the advancement of their own interests."[13]

Maria worried constantly about Gansevoort's poor health, as the southern cruise had not cured his chronic respiratory ailments. When he suffered a relapse of his illness, Maria asked Allan to "Be with your Brother as much as possible he is weak, very thin and at present he has no appetite—he is imprudent in exerting himself when he is unable to bear it, and in exposing himself to the changes of our variable climate without proper attention to his clothing."[14]

In charging Allan with the responsibility of watching out for his older brother, she was sending mixed messages. On the one hand, she warned Allan not to be "a slave of base passions and unrestrained desires" kindled by "the natural, depraved & consequently sinful propensities of your nature"; on the other, she admonished him to "cherish and cultivate an ardent warm attachment" to his brother as a defense against "the cold heartlessness of the world." It is hard to tell whether Maria's repeated fulminations against depravity and vice in her many letters to Allan express a concern based on knowledge of undesirable propensities, or whether she was merely conforming to cultural codes for maternal correspondence with a fatherless son who was his sire's namesake and a quick-tempered fellow.[15]

To impress upon Allan the importance of family cohesiveness, she related a parable about a man on his deathbed who calls in his sons and gives them each a small bundle of sticks, instructing them to break them. When they are unable to break them, the father unties the sticks and hands them out one at a time; naturally, the sons break them easily. "You will understand from the above illustration the great importance of unity & attachment between the eight of you," Maria wrote her son. It was a poignant plea from a woman who had suffered a traumatic loss and was on guard against another.[16]

With popular literature depicting cities as dens of iniquity, Maria kept up a barrage of letters designed to keep Allan on the straight and narrow, now that he was settled in New York. "Do not go out in the Evening with young men, but stay at home & study, go to bed early, be pure in mind, think finely, remember that from the 'heart proceeds all evil & learn to keep your heart with all diligence.'" Admonishing him to choose "respectability" over "an unrestrained indulgence of your unhallowed impulses & wicked passions," she reminded him that although he was far from a "Mother's anxious, loving & observing eye … there is a God above … who has promised to be a father to the Orphan." If he would "kneel before him in the solitude of your Chamber & ask his direction in time of trouble," she told him, he would *"be a happier Lad than you have ever been."* She was pulling out all the stops, not only drawing on the power of the cult of motherhood, but also implicitly forging an alliance between herself and God.[17]

It's difficult to know whether Maria's relationship with Allan is a fair sampling of what Herman would have experienced had he been home for the preceding four years, but it's safe to say Herman would not have had an easy time of it with Mother Melville and Father God in the ascendancy, and Gansevoort and Allan flanking him. Allan was acutely conscious of the social value of attending the right church, and he seems to have been impervious to the spiritual dimensions of religion, but Herman was fated to struggle with God, the devil, his absent father, and his mother. Although he harbored profoundly ambivalent feelings about religion all his life, Melville was a deeply religious man whose irreverence and skepticism sprang from a reservoir of spirituality that rejected the false gods of this world. Writing would become a way of exerting God-like power, not to control others, but to imagine, explore, experiment, and create.[18]

His mother believed that letters were meant not only to communicate, but to create a web of family relationships that time and distance could not break, and she taught her daughters that it was women's responsibility to knit families together. Herman and Allan, however, chafed against what they felt was an overly controlling intrusiveness. Like her brother Peter, Maria suffered episodes of depression or despondency, and occasionally threw what were described as "fits." One day while Helen was writing to Augusta, for instance, her mother "scanned the page with a critical eye, pronounced the chirography beneath contempt, and insisted upon my copying the document." When she protested this treatment, her mother "tore the unoffending sheet into a thousand pieces," inadvertently tearing Fanny's page as well. "The mood for composition is gone for the present, and if you consider its destruction a loss, you must lay the sin at Mama's door," she wrote her "nut-brown sister." Once Herman made up his mind to be a professional writer, he would make a conscious decision not to let the concern for how things might look to other people spoil his "mood for composition." Becoming a writer was Melville's way of telling his own truth.[19]

During much of 1843 and 1844, Helen, Kate, and Fanny were still living in Lansingburgh, and Augusta was living in Albany with her uncle Peter and teaching at the Sabbath Schools. Augusta's faith was a sober one, dedicated to charity and good works. She was, in fact, organizing drives to collect old Bibles and cast-off clothing for missionaries to distribute in heathen lands like the ones her brother had just visited. She was devoted to Herman and shared his love of literature, and when he returned from the Pacific, she rejoined the family in Lansingburgh and helped with the copying of his manuscripts. One wonders what she thought about her brother's criticisms of the missionaries."[20]

With Helen in Boston much of the time, concentrating on her social life, Augusta became the deputy mother, adopting their mother's tone in letters to Allan, who responded with sarcasm and irascibility to her long advicegiving epistles. When Augusta did write chatty letters about neighbors in Lansingburgh, Allan dismissed them as "all wind and sound signifying nothing," responding with a parody and two pages of squiggly lines. In Victorian families, the Christian belief that anger was a sin coalesced with the genteel secular conviction that emotional outbursts were *déclassé,* and open expressions of anger were taboo. It was Allan's role to express the family anger.[21]

The Melville women were not impressed by the various "enthusiastic" movements that raged like wildfire while Herman was at sea. The most influential was the millennialist preacher William Miller's tour of the "burnt-over district" of New York State, during which he predicted that the world would end in October 1843. His prophecy touched off an epidemic of suicides and murders, especially in isolated rural districts, and in Waterford, where Mary Anne Gansevoort lived, the town fathers closed shops, shut down schools, and turned public buildings into emergency prayer centers.[22]

Lydia Maria Child thought Millerite prophecies of "the burning of the world" were "done for waggery, or from that spirit of trade, which is ever willing to turn a penny on war, pestilence, or conflagration." Some people, like the owner of a Bowery dry-goods shop who put a placard in its window advertising "MUSLIN FOR ASCENSION ROBES!" did try to cash in on the hysteria, but not all merchants used the occasion to profit from people's fear. Some people simply panicked. In New York, a stove vendor closed his shop, and a shoemaker gave away all his shoes. Nerves were so frayed that when a group of boys set fire to a pile of wood shavings outside a window where a Mrs. Higgins was preaching and prophesying "with tempestuous zeal," many of her listeners screamed and fainted, taking it for a sign that Judgment Day had arrived. According to Miller's prophecy, "The Lord will certain leave the mercy seat on the 13th of this present October, and appear visibly in the clouds of heavens on the 22nd." Thus it was that Herman Melville returned from the Pacific just in time to greet the Judgment Day.[23]

"Until I was twenty-five, I had no development at all," Melville would tell Nathaniel Hawthorne in 1851. "From my twenty-fifth year I date my life. Three weeks have scarcely passed, at any time between then & now, that I have not unfolded within myself." Arriving home sunburned, bearded, and as rugged as a bear, Melville felt reborn. He had exciting stories to tell, and an audience eager to hear them, but he also had things to say that would shock his mother and sisters.[24]

After living by the Articles of War, Melville was glad to be back with family and friends in Lansingburgh, but returning to middle-class life could not have been easy for a young man who had sailed halfway around the world and lived for a month among "cannibals." He had to tone down his language and readjust to being treated like a child by a mother who couldn't help wondering when he would settle down and get a grown-up job. His mother was managing comfortably in modest circumstances, and his brothers and sisters seemed to be doing well, but other members of the family had not been so fortunate while he was away.

While Herman was at sea, Uncle Peter's wife Mary Sanford Gansevoort had passed away after a long illness, and by the time Herman returned home, his uncle had remarried Susan Lansing. In 1843, Hun Gansevoort, after recovering from syphilis, had gone down with the *Grampus,* and in 1844, Thomas Wilson Melvill had died of "inflammatory Rheumatism & Scurvy" aboard the whaler *Oregon,* and had been buried at Lahaina in the Sandwich Islands before his family even knew he was dead. The news stunned Melville's uncle Thomas, who had just reluctantly concluded that his son Henry was mentally impaired and would never be *"legally capable"* of affixing "his mark to a public act." Henry, who was paralyzed on his right side, had never learned to write or cipher, and despite his fondness for books, he could not remember anything he read.[25]

Melville became a celebrity of sorts in Lansingburgh. The more he told the story of his escape from the clutches of the cannibals, the more exciting it became. The numbers of savages grew with each rendition, and he embellished his accounts with such histrionics that his listeners imagined cannibals had burst into the room. It wasn't long before everyone was urging him to write his stories down, especially the "belles of Lansingburgh," who flocked around the suntanned sailor and sighed over his every syllable.[26]

Young Tom, who was only fourteen and a student at Lansingburgh Academy, idolized his older brother, and having a younger brother to look up to him and hang on his every word was a treat for Herman. Despite the decade between them, the two became close, and Tom would sign on a whaler at age sixteen at least partly as a result of his brother's stories. At seventeen, Fanny, too, looked up to her brother with uncritical admiration, but Kate, whom Herman was always attempting to cheer up by calling her his favorite and praising her for her wit, remains something of an enigma. With a large family to listen raptly to his tales, Herman felt like a returning hero, a good feeling after four years of being bossed around by autocratic sea captains and arrogant officers.[27]

He didn't need much prodding to pick up his pen. He not only had vivid tales to tell, but also wanted to express some strong political opinions. What he had seen of Western imperialism in the Pacific islands had shocked him. The "savages" he had met seemed much more civilized than the Americans and Europeans who were invading their lands. When he returned to find Democrats like his own brother supporting westward expansion in messianic terms, he knew he had found a debate into which he could pour his heart and soul.

As far as Herman was concerned, Gansevoort did not see the implications of unchecked imperialism. In fact, few Americans worried about the United States' policies abroad; with the economy not yet recovered from the depression of 1837, there were too many problems at home. In 1843 the price of corn and hogs had dropped to the level of 1822, and in 1844 the price of cotton hit an all-time low. A key Democratic strategy in the presidential campaign was to blame the Whig administration for the economic downturn and promise the voters reforms rather than to probe the connection between Whig trade policies and the nation's economic woes.

In attacking American expansion overseas, Melville was out of step with energetic young political hopefuls like Gansevoort, who believed it was the nation's "manifest destiny" to rule the world. Crying, "Yes, more, more, more! ... till our national destiny is fulfilled and ... the whole boundless continent is ours," John L. O'Sullivan, editor of the *Democratic Review*, called it "the fulfilment of our manifest destiny to overspread the continent allotted by Providence for the free development of our multiplying millions," and Young America took up the slogan. "The spirit of Young America will not be satisfied with what has been attained, but plumes its young wings for a higher and more glorious flight. The hopes of America, the hopes of Humanity must rest on this spirit," crowed the *Boston Times*, supporting the election of Polk and the annexation of Texas.[28]

To Melville, this jingoistic rant was obnoxious. Having retraced the steps of the so-called "march of civilization" by landing in unspoiled Polynesia, sailing from there to half-Westernized Tahiti, then spending some time in the "civilized" Sandwich Islands, Melville had come to believe colonization was a forced march to Hell that contradicted every principle on which America was founded. The "march of civilization" meant the destruction of native populations and the moral decay of the colonizers.

Maria must have breathed a sigh of relief to have her son home safe. His manners were no worse than before, and he did not appear to have been debauched by his long exposure to "all sorts and conditions of men." He was physically stronger and more self-assured, and although he looked too savage for Lansingburgh, he had not lost the slight shyness that distinguished him from other men his age and endeared him to friends and family members. Although he still lacked Gansevoort's polish and savoir faire, he was easier to get along with than the gruff and surly Allan. Maybe now he would settle down to earn a decent living.[29]

Melville, however, was marching to a different drummer. Perhaps by cloaking his attacks on Western imperialism in a travel narrative, he could influence public opinion without risking a breach with Gansevoort. Now that he had a little money in his pocket and his family seemed comparatively well off despite his mother's chronic dissatisfaction, he wanted to write a serious book about his travels instead of dreamy little sketches for local newspapers.[30]

Turning the spacious attic of his mother's house into a study, he consulted Charles

S. Stewart's *A Visit to the South Seas, in the U.S. Ship* Vincennes, *During the Years 1829 and 1830*, William Ellis's *Polynesian Researches*, Captain David Porter's *Journal of a Cruise Made in the Pacific Ocean in the U.S. Frigate* Essex, as well as Georg H. von Langsdorff's narrative of his voyage, and some other books that supplied him with background information about the islands. Within a few months he had transformed his four weeks in the Happy Valley into a rousing adventure story that combined elements of the travelogue and the picaresque novel. It was narrated in a colloquial conversational style and included a detailed but decorous description of native customs as well as attacks on colonialism and the missionary effort.

He submitted sample chapters of his finished manuscript to the Harper Brothers, who rejected the book on the grounds that it could not possibly be true, but fortunately, those "stage-managers, the Fates" were conspiring to expedite its publication. In July 1845, Gansevoort Melville was appointed secretary to the American legation in London by the victorious Polk administration, and a friend of his who worked for Harper's advised him to take a portion of the manuscript to London and show it to an English publisher. Because there were no international copyright restrictions, it was cheaper for American publishers to reprint English books than to publish new American authors, and prior publication in England helped guard against piracy by American publishing firms. Although the book was not finished, Herman seized the opportunity to give Gansevoort sample chapters to show to John Murray, the eminent publisher of the popular Home and Colonial Library.[31]

Gansevoort arrived in England in the fall, and even before he ordered his "uniform diplomatic coat & a pair of plain blue Saxony pants" and his ornamental sword, belt, and cocked hat, he placed Herman's draft in John Murray's hands. Although Murray thought the manuscript seemed too artful for a factual account, he liked what he read and asked Melville to send more. As soon as he finished a few chapters, Melville would send a batch to Gansevoort, who would proofread and correct them before delivering them to Murray. Even though Murray thought Melville was a "practised writer," not a sailor-author, by December 13 he had drawn up a contract for a two-volume edition of one thousand copies and an advance of one hundred pounds at half-profits.[32]

When Murray asked Melville to tighten up the text before publication, Melville did not know that Murray was so nervous about certain passages that he had hired one of his readers to go over the text and delete or change questionable passages. Melville's American publisher would have similar reservations, but no time to confer with Melville about their bowdlerization of the text, with the result that the American edition is even more corrupt than the English. The later revised edition deviates most from Melville's text, as many of the sexual references were drained of their pungency and humor, or entirely excised.[33]

Sometime between Thanksgiving and Christmas, Melville apparently went to Boston, either to visit the Shaws or to look for a job in the Custom House where his grandfather had worked, or both. Augusta's friend Millie Van Rensselaer had married Nathaniel Thayer the previous June, and the couple had taken up residence on Mt. Vernon Street, not far from the Shaws: "We were very sorry not to have seen more of Herman and were quite disappointed that he could not dine with us, as we had invited Mr. Prescott, Professor Jackson, & some of the distinguished & agreeable literary characters to meet him. When will the new book make its appearance? I am quite impatient to see it," wrote Mrs. Thayer.[34]

Her letter provides a rare glimpse of how close families and friends on the Albany-Boston axis were, how naturally Melville moved back and forth between the two worlds, how frequently he might have seen Elizabeth Shaw around this time, and how eagerly people were waiting to see the book he had written about the cannibals. Melville was in close touch with his sisters and their friends and well aware that the women closest to him represented the core of his potential audience, so he paid close attention to their reactions. Moreover, he was a well-brought-up young man, and well-brought-up young men were expected to be pillars of polite society, which required them to be unfailingly gallant to young ladies. Thus, when Augusta Melville's friend Augusta Whipple arrived early to attend church service with the Melvilles and the ladies were not ready, Herman was expected to do the honors: "Poor Herman," wrote Miss Whipple, "his countenance spoke his thoughts," as he contemplated "the task of 'making himself agreeable' to his sister's dull friend—I laugh at myself frequently when this picture rises But he succeeded admirably." He not only succeeded in entertaining the young lady; he also incorporated his memory of "some incidents" related to Miss Whipple that "*short* Sunday morn" into his next novel, *Omoo*.[35]

Just after the New Year, Washington Irving, who was the American minister in Madrid, arrived at the American legation in London to see Minister Louis McLane. McLane was away, however, which gave Gansevoort an opportunity to tell Irving about his brother's book. The following day, they breakfasted with John Murray, and after Murray left for his office, Gansevoort read portions of *Typee* aloud to Irving, who admired its "graphic" style and its "exquisite" descriptions. He advised Gansevoort to take the manuscript to George Palmer Putnam, Wiley & Putnam's London agent. Putnam became so engrossed in the manuscript that he missed church. Pronouncing Melville's narrative every bit as good as *Robinson Crusoe*, he sent it on to New York for Wiley & Putnam's Library of Choice Reading, and Melville joined the ranks of America's popular travel writers.

Melville's *Narrative of a Four Months' Residence among the Natives of a Valley of the Marquesas Islands,* dedicated "Affectionately" to Lemuel Shaw, appeared in England on

February 27, 1846, and within the month, the American edition entitled *Typee: A Peep at Polynesian Life* appeared at bookstores in New York. The dedication read: "To LEMUEL SHAW, Chief Justice of the Commonwealth of Massachusetts, This Little Work is Gratefully Inscribed by THE AUTHOR." When Gansevoort told his mother the book "had a fair chance for favor in the literary world," she told Augusta that Gansevoort "believed the book would have brilliant success."[36]

~~~

With the writing of *Typee*, Melville transformed a travel narrative into an artful tale of an American sailor's crossing cultural and sexual boundaries and becoming an artist and social critic. Before he reaches Nuku Hiva, Tommo's image of the South Seas replicates the stereotypes perpetuated by Anglo-American travel literature: "The Marquesas! What strange visions of outlandish things does the very name spirit up! Naked houris—cannibal banquets—groves of cocoa-nut—coral reefs—tattooed chiefs—and bamboo temples; sunny valleys planted with bread-fruit-trees—carved canoes dancing on the flashing blue waters—savage woodlands guarded by horrible idols—*heathenish rites and human sacrifices.*" After the fictional Tommo spends four months with the Typees, however, he comes to see himself and the world with new eyes.[37]

The transgressive nature of Melville's narrative becomes apparent the moment the fictional ship *Dolly* reaches Nuka Hiva. Usually, when ships docked in "civilized" ports, they were met by prostitutes, sometimes with bottles of liquor smuggled under their long skirts, but Tommo sees a laughing, chattering flotilla of "whihenies" emerging from the water, "dripping with brine and glowing from the bath, their jet-black tresses streaming over their shoulders, and half enveloping their otherwise naked forms." Watching them comb one another's hair and perfume their bodies with a "fragrant oil" from a "little round shell" they pass among themselves, before draping a "few loose folds of tappa" around their waists, Tommo exclaims, "What a sight for us bachelor sailors! how avoid so dire a temptation?" mocking the language of pious tracts designed for sailors, as Tommo obviously relishes this warm welcome.[38]

The mood changes quickly, however, as the presence of these uninhibited women excites the men to an orgy during which the ship is "wholly given up to every species of riot and debauchery" and "not the feeblest barrier was interposed between the unholy passions of the crew and their unlimited gratification. The grossest licentiousness and the most shameful inebriety prevailed." Tongue in cheek, Tommo reassures the reader that these indulgences with native women are the only thing that saves sailors from having to cruise around "Buggerry Island" and "the Devil's Tail-Peak," as less fortunate crews have been known to do, an allusion to homosexual shipboard practices that was cut from the American edition of *Typee*.[39]

The native women must submit to the "unholy passions" of the sailors: "Alas for the poor savages when exposed to the influence of these polluting examples! Unsophisticated and confiding, they are easily led into every vice, and humanity weeps over the ruin thus remorselessly inflicted upon them by their European civilisers. Thrice happy are they who, inhabiting some yet undiscovered island in the midst of the ocean, have never been brought into contaminating contact with the white man." Like Eve, these women, though sexually promiscuous, are essentially innocent; like Satan, the white man insinuates sin into this Polynesian paradise. By creating a subtext that undermines the surface text, Melville implies that imperialism is tantamount to rape.[40]

Soon after the ship anchors at Nuku Hiva, Tommo decides to jump ship with his chum Toby to escape further "servitude" to the "tyrannical usages" of Captain Vangs. After a harrowing hike that lasts several days, Tommo and Toby reach the outskirts of a settlement, where they see a young couple clad only in narrow girdles of tapa cloth, embracing underneath a breadfruit tree like Adam and Eve in Eden before the Fall. The two Americans soon realize that their hosts are the dread "Typees," reputed to be cannibals, but the natives give them such a warm welcome and treat Tommo's leg, which has become infected, so expertly with medicinal plants and unguents that their suspicions of cannibalism evaporate, and they settle down to enjoy life in "the Happy Valley."[41]

To Tommo, Marquesan warriors are "Nature's noblemen." The tall, "superb-looking" chief Mehevi walks with an erect and dignified bearing, wearing a headdress consisting of "long, drooping tail-feathers of a tropical bird," and around his neck he wears "several enormous necklaces of boars' tusks, polished like ivory." The olive complexions of the women make their teeth look like "the milk-white seeds of the 'arta,' a fruit of the valley."

Before long, he discovers the pleasures of skinny-dipping with bare-breasted girls. As the "amphibious young creatures" cavort around him "like a shoal of dolphins," seizing hold of him and tumbling him under the water for what is obviously sexual play, he hears "strange noises" ringing in his ears and sees "supernatural visions dancing before my eyes." This, he says, makes him feel as though he is "in the land of spirits," though he is clearly experiencing the ecstasy of the spirit through the ecstasy of the flesh.[42]

Tommo and Toby stay with old Marheyo and his wife, Tinor. Their son Kory-Kory, a combination valet, nurse, and *tayo*, or chum, cares for Tommo, carrying him around when a leg injury he sustained during the journey causes him pain, and pampering and petting him. Soon, Tommo grows suspicious of the motive behind the Typees' kindness and begins to wonder if they are treating him kindly to fatten him up for a stew. Melville's descriptions of Kory-Kory's ministrations are teasingly homoerotic, as though Melville wanted to leave his readers room to imagine as much or as little as they wanted.

Melville also throws a veil over Tommo's liaison with a maiden named Fayaway, beguiling his readers with tantalizingly discreet descriptions of their relationship. Years later, Melville devotees who visited the Marquesas were told authoritatively that an old lady named "Fa-a-wa" and a daughter sired by Melville were still living, and in middle age, Melville liked to tell people he had fathered a son there.[43]

Melville's Typee Valley is a utopia. The Typees exhibit a spirit of cooperation Tommo has rarely observed in "civilized" life, and their social relationships appear to be governed by an "inherent principle of honesty and charity toward each other." They make little practical distinction between family and friends, or work and play. Because they believe they hold "their broad valleys in fee simple from Nature herself" and "their goods in common," there is "not a padlock in the valley," and poverty and crime are unknown. Each islander reposes "beneath his own palmetto-thatching," or lies "under his own bread-fruit tree, with no one to molest or alarm him." There are "no cares, griefs, troubles, or vexations, in all Typee," and the "thousand sources of irritation that the ingenuity of civilized man has created to mar his own felicity" do not exist. Tommo sums it up "all in one word—no Money! That 'root of all evil' was not to be found in the valley."[44]

Tommo is tempted to remain in this paradise with Fayaway, but as soon as he starts to feel comfortable, the Typees insist on sending Karky, the tribal artist, to tattoo him. Then he begins to imagine that the "puarkee" his hosts are roasting may be human flesh, not pork, and the suspicion that his hosts may be pampering him in order to fatten him up for a feast sends his injured leg into a relapse and he knows he must leave, or lose himself completely.

While letting go of "civilized" inhibitions gave Melville great pleasure on one level, the loss of identity and control caused him tremendous stress. To a young man raised in a competitive culture, the complete absence of intellectual and economic striving proved more threatening than the cultural repressions of his own community.

As readers of pulp fiction would have known, cannibals were said to castrate male captives in order to fatten them up more quickly. Perhaps with this tidbit of information in mind, Tommo persuades Mehevi to send Toby back to the white settlement to fetch a doctor to attend to his leg, but when Toby does not return, Tommo decides he must escape on his own. Just then, Marnoo, a wanderer who is *tabu* among the tribes, arrives with a message that Tommo's friend has sent a ship to rescue him. Old Marheyo whispers the magic words "home" and "mother" knowingly in Tommo's ear, and Fayaway and Kory-Kory bid him a tearful farewell. He dashes toward the beach, pursued by a one-eyed warrior named Mow-Mow, whom he slashes with a boathook in order to break free.[45]

Tommo can no more remain in the Happy Valley than he can remain the man he was before he visited the islands. He must return home to tell his story and teach what he has learned: "Civilization does not engross all the virtues of humanity: she has not even her full share of them. They flourish in greater abundance and attain greater strength among any barbarous people. The hospitality of the wild Arab, the courage of the North American Indian, and the faithful friendships of some of the Polynesian nations, far surpass anything of a similar kind among the polished communities of Europe."[46]

As a result of his exposure to a primitive utopian society, Tommo comes to see relationships in "civilized" countries as cannibalistic. He questions whether "the mere eating of human flesh so very far exceeds in barbarity that custom which only a few years since was practised in enlightened England: –a convicted traitor, perhaps a man found guilty of honesty, patriotism, and suchlike heinous crimes, had his head lopped off with a huge axe, his bowels dragged out and thrown into a fire, while his body, carved into four quarters, was with his head exposed upon pikes, and permitted to rot and fester among the public haunts of man!" This passage foreshadows the punishment inflicted by Spanish courts on the African revolutionary Babo in the later story "Benito Cereno."[47]

Thus, for Melville, cannibalism was a metaphor for economic competition and social injustice. The new Solitary System, a penal reform inaugurated in Philadelphia in the 1780s, which Charles Dickens pronounced "cruel and wrong," is another example of the "remorseless cruelty" by which civilized society destroys "malefactors piece-meal, drying up in their veins, drop by drop, the blood we are too chicken-hearted to shed by a single blow which would at once put a period to their sufferings." Civilized man inflicts "horrors" on those wretches "whom we mason up in the cells of our prisons, and condemn to perpetual solitude in the very heart of our population," then has the audacity to force his way of life on defenseless savages to augment his own power.

Melville's experience gave him the "*point d'appui*," or leverage point, that Thoreau believed could lift the soul out of the mud so that the individual, and ultimately society, could be transformed. He became, in effect, a missionary from Oceania to the West. For Tommo, staying in the Happy Valley would have been more self-destructive than going home, but once he was home, the only way to survive was to go native in the inmost recesses of his soul.[48]

~~~

Typee: A Peep at Polynesian Life marks Melville's birth as an artist and signals his lifelong mutiny against injustice. In writing this novel, Melville transformed the materials of his personal experience into a picturesque but complex narrative. He lengthened the time of his stay in the Marquesas to give credibility to detailed descriptions of Marquesan culture, and he created symbols like Tommo's infected leg, which fluctuates with Tommo's alternating fear and longing, to signify the conflict between Tommo's dependency and his ability to stand on his own. These embellishments, combined with ribald humor and a limpid, poetic prose style, distinguish *Typee* from the prosaic factual travelogues so popular at the time.

It is difficult to know how much of what Melville describes in *Typee* is pure imagination, how much is wishful thinking, and how much is fact, but his description of a Happy Valley where money, poverty, and crime do not exist and sexual relationships are uncomplicated and free tapped buried memories of the Golden Age in readers. The essence of *Typee* is its mythic power, its ability to name a truth and bring it into being in the mind of readers, not merely to report it or reveal it. While many reviewers and even Melville's own publishers would express dismay at their own uncertainty about Tommo's veracity, most readers loved the book.

Even before *Typee* was on the stands, London's *Athenaeum* printed excerpts from it, and its influential reviewer Henry F. Chorley wrote laudatory accounts in two consecutive issues of the magazine. Chorley commended Melville's picturesque and poetic style, but he disputed the book's claim to be a completely factual account of the author's travels. The London *Times* reviewer praised the book for its "freshness and originality," which "cannot fail to exhilarate the most enervated and *blasé* of circulating library lounger" and gushed: "Enviable Herman! A happier dog it is impossible to imagine than Herman in the Typee Valley." *John Bull* compared *Typee* to *Robinson Crusoe* and praised Melville's "bewitching" style, and the *Examiner* alluded to doubts about the book's factuality, but brushed them aside as irrelevant.[49]

Thanks in part to Evert Duyckinck's orchestrating a "national" campaign for books in the Wiley & Putnam series, *Typee* garnered favorable notices from reviewers in Boston and New York, ranging from the popular writers Nathaniel P. Willis and William Gilmore Simms to the popular novelist Grace Greenwood (Sara Jane Lippincott), who professed "a solemn conviction of its truth," and wrote a good-natured parody of it for the *Saturday Evening Post*.[50]

Avid novel readers cared little whether a story was fact or fiction as long as it had strong characters and an exciting plot. *Typee* did more: it gave "a local habitation and name" to secret fantasies of boundless sensuality and freedom, and tapped the vein of social and economic idealism that had inspired the establishment of Fourierist communities like Brook Farm.

Duyckinck sent a review copy to Nathaniel Hawthorne, recommending it as "a lively and pleasant book, not over philosophical, perhaps." Hawthorne, who was now working in the Salem Customs House, reviewed it for the *Salem Advertiser*, saying he knew of "no work that gives a freer and more effective picture of barbarian life," though Melville tolerates "a code of morals" quite different from our own.[51]

Henry Wadsworth Longfellow noted Melville's "glowing descriptions of Life in the

Marquesas" in his journal, and the transcendental philosopher and pundit Bronson Alcott, the father of Louisa May Alcott, called it "a charming volume." Henry David Thoreau stuck a reminder to himself in the first draft of *Walden* to cite *Typee* as proof that elderly people in primitive societies are healthier than their civilized counterparts.[52]

Most American reviewers praised the book for its "easy, gossiping tone," its "fresh, graceful and animated style," and its "novel and striking" scenes and original observations, and ignored its political implications. The transcendentalist George Ripley advised readers to learn the "lesson which the leaders of this nineteenth century may learn from the Typee," and John L. O'Sullivan called it "a happy hit."[53]

Margaret Fuller, former editor of the transcendentalist magazine *The Dial* and a correspondent for the *New-York Daily Tribune*, called it "a very entertaining and pleasing narrative" that would amuse "the sewing societies of the country villages," while young Walter Whitman, a rookie editor on *The Brooklyn Eagle*, pronounced it "unsurpassed" as a book "to hold in one's hand and pore dreamily over of a summer day."[54]

The National Antislavery Standard initially called the book "curiously charming and charmingly instructive," but the following year, in its review of *Omoo*, the *Standard* treated *Typee* as a great contribution to the abolitionist movement: "The Typee," wrote the reviewer, "munches the muscles and tendons of his dead enemy between his molars, but inflicts no pain upon him; but with us the Calhoons [*sic*], Clays, and Polks feed daily upon the sweat, the tears, the groans, the despairing hearts, of living men and women; they do not eat the insensible flesh of their dead slaves, but they lacerate it when alive with whips and cauterize it with hot branding irons. We would advise our readers who are sick at heart, from reading the daily reports of the murders committed by our army in Mexico; or of the inhuman cruelties of our slaveholders in the South; or of the daily outrages upon the rights of humanity practiced by Christian judges, and lawyers in the Halls of Justice, to turn for relief to the amiable savages of Typee, whose greatest cruelty consists in devouring the body of an enemy who has been killed in a hand to hand scuffle." Two years later, in the Vivenza section of *Mardi*, a very explicit attack on slavery, Melville echoes the language of this review.[55]

In America, as in England, readers expected travel narratives to be factually accurate, not artfully romantic; to many people, Melville's story seemed exaggerated. Evert Duyckinck's brother George could not take it for "sober verity." He thought Melville's "exploits in descending the waterfalls beat Sam Patch and can you enlighten me as to how he gets down the last one. If I remember rightly, he is on top of a precipice at the end of one chapter and safe and sound at the bottom at the beginning of the next." His skepticism worried his brother Evert, who was especially sensitive to comments that reflected badly on the Wiley & Putnam's series. The literary rivalry between New York and Boston was so intense that when New Englander Nathaniel Hawthorne became a Wiley & Putnam's author, *Knickerbocker* editor Lewis Gaylord Clark accused Duyckinck of being a transcendentalist, which was the worst thing anyone could call a New Yorker.

By summer, more reviewers than not were questioning Melville's honesty and his intentions. Doubts about *Typee*'s authenticity added fuel to the fire ignited by religious magazines on both sides of the Atlantic, which attacked *Typee* as "racily-written" and questioned whether "such a volume should have been allowed a place in the Library of American Books." *The Christian Parlor Magazine* called Melville a "traducer of missions" and denounced *Typee* as the "apotheosis of barbarism! A panegyric on cannibal delights! An apostrophe to the spirit of savage felicity!" Especially embarrassing was their expression of incredulity that "such a press as Wiley & Putnam" would publish such an outlandish book and that the eminent Lemuel Shaw would allow his name to appear on such a lawless fiction.[56]

When the last group of reviews accused *Typee* of being a complete fabrication and refused to treat it as a legitimate travel book, Melville was so upset he wrote a letter to the *Albany Argus*: "The author desires to state to the public that TYPEE is a true narrative of events which actually occurred to him. Although there may be moving incidents and hairbreadth escapes, it is scarcely more strange than such as happen to those who make their home on the deep."[57]

Then, in response to a particularly "obnoxious" and "malicious" review in the *Morning Courier and New-York Enquirer* that called *Typee* a "monstrous exaggeration," Melville wrote a quasi-objective defense of the book and asked Alexander Bradford, who had recently published a book entitled *American Antiquity & the History of the Red Race,* to submit it to the paper under his name. He later admitted that planting a ghost-written article was "an awkward undertaking," written as if "by one who had read the book & beleived [*sic*] it–& moreover–had been as much pleased with it as most people who read it profess to be."[58]

The person least happy about the controversy *Typee* had created was Gansevoort's boss, Louis McLane, who disapproved of Melville's attacks on colonialism. He already considered Gansevoort the wrong choice for a London posting because the orator refused to tone down his support for Irish independence. Furthermore, America's dispute with Great Britain over the Oregon Territory was heating up, and Gansevoort, who had made many speeches denouncing British claims there, was much too outspoken for a diplomat. On more than one occasion he disgraced himself at receptions and dinner parties. It's not clear whether his behavior should be attributed to a kind of mania caused by his suddenly being thrust into prominence, a lack of inhibition caused by drinking too much on these occasions, or a behavioral aberration caused by a tubercular lesion growing on the brain. Whatever the reason, his propensity for making stump speeches at diplomatic dinners infuriated Minister McLane, who was suffering from a painful bladder stone and had little patience with a man who was giving him a pain elsewhere.

The "damp, foggy, dismal climate" of London aggravated Gansevoort's respiratory problems, making him pay "more attention to diet, exercise and regular hours. I never taste wine except at dinner, and then sparingly and brandy not at all. I find that malt liquor agrees with me better than anything else." Ceremonial appearances at the Court of St. James in the requisite "white casimere breeches, white silk stockings & pumps" bored him, and even attending the theater could not lift his spirits.[59]

On March 4, 1846, Gansevoort met with John Murray to discuss toning down *Typee*, and Murray warned him that "the genuineness of the Residence in the Marquesas is doubted, some thinking that it is an invention, & not a narrative." Returning to his apartment, Gansevoort lay stupefied on the sofa from late afternoon into the evening, until he finally dragged himself to bed at nine-thirty. The next morning he woke up with a severe headache and no vision in one eye; before long, the other eye would cloud over, too. His dentist extracted an abscessed tooth and recommended extraction of several others whose roots had died, but nothing seemed to help. On April 3 he wrote Herman that he was afraid he was "breaking up," and soon afterward he asked Minister McLane to relieve him of his duties at the embassy. He died in his lodgings on the twelfth of May, exhibiting symptoms of nervous derangement that might have been caused by tubercular meningitis.[60]

Although he was only thirty years old, his decline was as precipitous as his father's. News of his death did not reach the family in Lansingburgh until well after May 18; meanwhile, the embassy held a memorial service in Westminster Abbey, which was attended by "only 12 Americans or persons." Only in a negative sense had he fulfilled the family's unspoken expectation that he follow in his father's footsteps.[61]

On May 13, the day after Gansevoort's death, President Polk declared war on Mexico, claiming that Mexican forces had attacked American positions on the Rio Grande. Actually, the "invasion" was a fraud: American soldiers dressed in stolen Mexican uniforms had attacked their own garrison to give the administration an excuse to seize land that Mexico was refusing to cede to the United States. Texas was the crucible of Manifest Destiny, the testing ground for the nation's attitudes toward slavery, and, ultimately, the bellwether of its foreign policy.[62]

The war with Mexico was the first widely protested war in America's history. When word leaked out that the administration had staged the entire incident, massive protests led by prominent intellectuals and opposition politicians erupted all over New England. Most New Englanders were appalled at this betrayal of American ideals. Albert Gallatin, Secretary of the Treasury under Jefferson and the founder of New York University, denounced the war, as did Abraham Lincoln, the freshman congressman from Illinois, who gained national recognition by demanding that the administration be required to name the exact "spot" on which Mexico had invaded the United States. Debate on the issue reached fever pitch, spurring some people to want to learn more about their neighbor to the south. Thus, Allan Melville's fiancée, Sophia Thurston, one of Bond Street's most charming beauties, was home reading Prescott's *Conquest of Mexico* and Thompson's *Recollections of Mexico,* while Allan, who was running for state office on the Democratic ticket, was out counting precinct votes.[63]

Herman saw this opportunistic, fake war as a bad omen for America's future. He knew history well enough to recognize that the American republic was in danger of becoming a bloated empire, like ancient Rome. Unaware at this point that Gansevoort was dead, he wrote him a letter obliquely criticizing the jingoist faction that was supporting this degenerate version of Manifest Destiny: "Lord, the day is at hand, when we will be able to talk of our killed & wounded like some of the old Eastern conquerors reckoning them up by thousands;—when the Battle of Monmouth will be thought child's play—& canes made out of the Constitution's timbers be thought no more of than bamboos. —I am at the end of my sheet—God bless you My Dear Gansevoort & bring you to your feet again."[64]

Right after Melville wrote this letter on May 29, news of Gansevoort's death finally reached his family. Augusta poured out her grief to her cousin Catherine Van Schaick: "you know how I loved him, how I idolized him, how my very heart strings were entwined about him," and in the best sentimental style, she apostrophized the departed: "oh Gansevoort, my brother, my darling brother, how hard it is, to feel that I never, never can see you again."[65]

The shock and sorrow the family felt was sharpened by the knowledge that they could not afford to have Gansevoort's body shipped back home. Herman, now the head of the family, wrote directly to President Polk, Secretary of State James Buchanan, and Secretary of War William Marcy on behalf of his "mourning family, to whom Providence has brought unspeakable & peculiar sorrows," and asked for financial assistance "in view of the family's exceedingly embarrassed circumstances." Responding to Melville's request in respect of his brother's "universally acknowledged and signal services," Secretary Buchanan immediately authorized payment of all shipping costs and burial expenses.[66]

Maria, who had never wavered in her belief that her oldest son was destined for great things, was devastated: "My poor Gansevoort this early in life to die he was deeply belove'd [*sic*] by us, yes bound up in our very hearts.... His gigantic efforts to overcome more than ordinary obstacles, his too long and continued exertion both bodily & mental—I have no doubt occasioned his early & melancholy death," she wrote Lemuel Shaw.

"Time alone" can "bind up by its soothing influences my wounded heart, to raise from their present state of depression, my lost spirits."[67]

How the death of her oldest changed her relationship with Herman and how he responded to the change, we cannot know for sure, but later in life Melville allegedly told a grandniece that his mother "hated" him. One suspects Maria idealized Gansevoort even more after his death than before, perhaps making invidious comparisons between him and her other children in an attempt to make them live up to her expectations, as some parents have been known thoughtlessly to do. If so, Herman would have been wounded to the core.[68]

Melville traveled twenty hours by steamer to New York City to meet the ship that was bringing Gansevoort's body home. As he was waiting for the *Prince Albert* to dock, he wrote Peter Gansevoort that he would wait to write "until I can ascertain when the remains can be got ashore, & a day is fixed for removing them to Albany.... I believe that nothing can be done until the remains arrive." His clinical diction ("the remains") and neutral tone reflect the tight-lipped stoicism with which he defended himself against emotions too painful to acknowledge as he escorted his dead brother home aboard the *Henrik Hudson*.[69]

Gansevoort's death must have hit Herman hard, as there was much unfinished business between them. His feelings for his older brother had ranged from resentment and envy to friendship and gratitude for his assistance with the book. As fate would have it, Gansevoort's voice had been silenced just as his own was beginning to be heard.

Melville had barely begun to digest the reviews of *Typee* when Gansevoort died. The most annoying criticism of the book, from Melville's point of view, was not that it was too racy or too critical of the missionaries, but that it was not true, because, clearly, the reviewers' definition of "truth" was very different from his. He considered accuracy of detail in this type of book incidental to the deeper truths of head and heart. He was most troubled by the reaction of Duyckinck, who regarded the book with "a spice of civil skepticism." Books had become weapons in the literary battles that raged in New York in the 1840s, and doubts about Melville's veracity could undermine the credibility of the other volumes in Wiley & Putnam's Library of Choice Reading.[70]

Sensitive to charges that he was supporting "Munchausen" fantasy and romance in literature, Duyckinck backed off a bit from *Typee* the moment critics began accusing Melville of fabricating his adventures. An urbane high-church Episcopalian who had graduated from the Crosby Street School, Columbia College, and New York University, Duyckinck was the guiding spirit of the Tetractys Club, or "Knights of the Round Table," as Melville referred to the group who gathered at Duyckinck's Saturday-night suppers.

These writers, editors, and artists enjoyed erudite and witty conversation, and various magazines devoted to the advancement of American literary culture were born from the union of their brandy and cigars. In 1840, around the time Melville was leaving for the Pacific, Duyckinck and Cornelius Mathews, a pundit and sometime urban novelist, had founded *Arcturus*, a monthly magazine devoted to promoting American writers.[71]

Ironically, the *New York Evangelist*'s review calling Melville a liar ultimately worked in Melville's favor, because his old shipmate Richard Tobias Greene "chanced to see" that review and wrote a letter to the *Buffalo Commercial Advertiser* saying, "I am the true and veritable 'Toby,' yet living, and I am happy to testify to the entire accuracy of the work, so long as I was with Melville.... I request Melville to send me his address, if this should chance to meet his eye." Both the *Albany Argus* and the *Albany Evening Journal* reprinted Toby's letter, as did London's *Athenaeum*.[72]

Addressed to his "Friend 'Tommo,'" Greene's straightforward and painstakingly detailed account of what transpired after he left the Typee Valley to get help for Melville effectively countered his old shipmate's contention in chapter fourteen of *Typee* that Toby had "perfidiously" deserted him. Rejoicing at "this resurrection [sic] of Toby from the dead," Melville went to see his old shipmate, who was now a house and sign painter in Buffalo. He returned home with a daguerreotype of Greene and a lock of his hair, as if physical proof of Toby's existence could silence skeptics. To "the politely incredulous Mr. Duyckinck" he offered to write "an account of what befell him [Richard Tobias Greene] in escaping from the island—should the adventure be of sufficient interest."[73]

Much to Duyckinck's relief, Toby's letter had saved Melville's reputation as a truthful travel writer. Melville wrote John Murray proposing a revised edition of *Typee* with a sequel. "Indeed," Melville's letter argued, "the whole Typee adventure is now regarded as a sort of Romance of Real Life," and the addition of a sequel "containing a simple account of Toby's escape from the valley" would be "so convincing a proof of the truth of my narrative *as I sent it to London* that it can not be gainsaid." He also agreed to exclude passages that referred to the missionaries on the grounds that they interfered with the unity of the book, and were "altogether foreign to the adventure," whose interest "almost wholly consists in the *intrinsick merit of the narrative alone.*"[74]

He followed this with a delicately worded request for more money based on *Typee*'s "most flattering success," and a promise that the new book he was working on "embraces adventures in the South Seas (of a totally different character from 'Typee') and includes an eventful cruise in an English Colonial Whaleman (A Sydney Ship) and a comical residence on the island of Tahiti. The time is about four months, but I and my narrative are both on the move during that short period.... Permit me to assure Mr Murray that my new M. S. S. will be in a rather better shape for the press than the M. S. S. handed to him by my brother. A little experience in this art of book-craft has done wonders."[75]

Murray, however, was having second thoughts about publishing a new book by Melville, as the inevitable backlash against *Typee*'s runaway popularity was fueling a spate of negative reviews. On both sides of the Atlantic, *Typee* was being called the pipe dream of an overactive armchair imagination. John Wiley called Melville down to New York to discuss the cuts he wanted made, and John Murray reacted to the offer of a sequel by asking Melville to tone down the text for subsequent printings.

Although Melville resented having to expurgate his book, he did consent to a "*Revised* (Expurgated?–Odious word) Edition of *Typee*," rationalizing the changes as not really important–something the later Melville would never do. Murray agreed to pay Melville fifty pounds for "The Story of Toby," but instead of incorporating it in the new edition of *Typee*, as Melville assumed he would, Murray published it separately, in pamphlet form. Meanwhile, in America, the newspapers were bypassing Melville's version of Toby's story entirely, and reprinting the narrative directly from the *Buffalo Commercial Advertiser*.[76]

To add to Melville's aggravation, when he offered Murray a new manuscript, Murray hedged, saying he would make "as liberal an offer" as he could, and requesting "documentary evidences" of his stay in the Marquesas. Murray's "indescribably vexatious" request for further proof of his experiences irked Melville, even though Murray assured him that what he referred to as the "magic cabilistic [*sic*], *tabooistic* 'Typee'" would appear on the title page of future editions of the book, instead of the dry title originally chosen, to give the English edition an air of factual accuracy.[77]

In his letter, Melville blasted the "parcel of blockheads" who had questioned the authenticity of *Typee* as "senseless sceptics–men who go straight from their cradles to their graves & never dream of the queer things going on at the antipodes. I know not how to set about getting the evidence–How under Heaven am I to subpoena the skipper of the Dolly who by this time is the Lord only knows where, or Kory-Kory who I'll be bound is this blessed day taking his noon nap somewhere in the flowery vale of Typee, some leagues too from the Monument." In conclusion, "Typee must at last be beleived [*sic*] on its own account–they beleive it here now–a little touched up they say but *true*."[78]

How could he hope to be successful if he told the truth, when the truth as he saw it was not what others wanted him to see? By defending *Typee,* he was defending the integrity of his book as well as his own integrity, as family and friends had nicknamed him "Typee." Whether he liked it or not, he had become a product of the marketplace, a piece of public property to be shown off, then fattened up for the kill, just as Tommo had feared he might be in the Typee Valley.

The young man whose risqué account of his sojourn with the
"cannibals" had made him an overnight sensation married Elizabeth Shaw of Boston in 1847.

FIERCE CANNIBAL DELIGHT

When Melville returned home after four years at sea, one of the things he longed for, in addition to a meaningful vocation, and perhaps even a lucrative profession, was a soul mate, someone to whom he could open his heart and mind as he could to only a handful of close male friends. Ideally, this person would be a combination of Jack Chase and Fayaway: as frank and free as a maintopman, and as pliant and pretty as a native girl. At home, he was surrounded by a bevy of village girls who were attracted to him by Typee's aura of sensuality and danger and his instant celebrity, but none of these fair charmers stirred the deep waters of his soul. He began to wonder whether he was meant to be an "Omoo," or rover, all his life.

In his September 2, 1846, letter to John Murray, Melville admitted that he had not been able to work much on "the book on the stocks" that autumn, but he did not tell Murray that what kept him from his writing was not only the frustration of dealing with publishers and critics, but also the distracting presence of all those village "belles" vying for the celebrated young author's attention. He did not mention, either, that Helen's friend Elizabeth Shaw was spending eight weeks in Lansingburgh, and that as the oldest male in the family, he was expected to squire her around to dances and parties and that, somewhat unexpectedly perhaps, he found himself enjoying it.[1]

After four long years of living almost exclusively with men, many of them uneducated, he didn't really mind spending his evenings with Miss Shaw. She was more down-to-earth than the vivacious "belles of Lansingburgh," and less interested in impressing him than in having a meaningful conversation. She read poetry and novels and liked to look below the surface of things, perhaps because she, like him, had suffered great losses in her life. She wasn't somber, however; she had a sense of humor, and she was the only eligible girl who didn't seem to be pursuing him. He found it impossible to concentrate on his new book until she went back to Boston on the first of November.

Once Elizabeth was gone, Herman finished the manuscript quickly and took it to New York, where he left it with "a particular lady acquaintance of mine...[who] resides up town," then he went to Boston to visit the Shaws. The identity of this "particular lady" remains one of the many Melville mysteries, but whoever she was, her opinions carried enough weight with him that he threw out three chapters that criticized the South Sea missionaries.[2]

In late November, Melville went down to New York again to pick up his manuscript. He asked Duyckinck to read it "as a friend," not as a Wiley & Putnam editor, paying special attention to chapters that "refer more or less to the missions & the condition of the natives." Much to Melville's relief, even though his attacks on the missionaries were more pointed in this book than in *Typee*, Duyckinck liked the manuscript and remarked in a letter to his brother George that Melville "owes a sailor's grudge to the Missionaries & pays it off well at Tahiti. His account of the church building there is very much in the spirit of Dickens' humorous handling of sacred things in Italy."[3]

Put off by John Wiley's quibbles about the authenticity of *Typee*, Melville hoped he could persuade Harper's to publish his new book. "Melville is in town with new MSS agitating the conscience of John Wiley and tempting the pockets of the Harpers," Duyckinck informed his brother. When Melville reached Harper's, he handed the manuscript to Frederick Saunders, an editorial assistant. Although Mr. Harper was halfway out the door when Saunders asked if he would be interested in the latest book by Melville, Harper paused, then told him to take it sight unseen.[4]

With Allan as his agent, Melville signed a contract with Harper's on December 18, 1846, and within the fortnight he informed John Murray that Harper's would delay releasing the book until it had appeared in England—a move designed to prevent other British publishers from pirating it, as so often happened at a time when there were no international copyright laws. John Romeyn Brodhead, Gansevoort's successor at the American legation, would act as his agent for the book in England.

Feeling flush, Melville went to Boston to pay the Shaws a Christmas visit, bringing

Miss Shaw the lavishly illustrated *Floral Tableaux*. As the "language of flowers" was very much in vogue with young people, Lizzie and her friends all knew what each flower symbolized, and Herman learned from them. At the hefty price of six dollars, it cost a good deal more than a young author could afford, even one who had just signed a contract for a second novel, which suggests that he was getting serious about Miss Shaw and wanted to make a good impression on her and on her father.

Elizabeth Knapp Shaw was precious to her father. Her mother had died when she was born, leaving Lemuel Shaw a widower at forty-one. He named the baby Elizabeth after her mother, and doted on her. Lizzie was fortunate to have a loving father and grandmother and an Irish nurse to care for her. When she was five, her father married Hope Savage, an unaffected woman with a loving heart, whom Lizzie referred to as "my dear mother." Hope and Lemuel Shaw were devoted to each other and their four children: Lizzie and her older brother John, and the two boys they had together, Lemuel Jr. and Samuel.[5]

Lemuel Shaw brought his daughter up to be "kind, affectionate, obedient & good tempered," and by all accounts she lived up to his expectations of what a good girl should be. Everyone who knew her considered Lizzie very happy and very, very good. As a small child, she learned how to read and cipher from Mary Lamb, and how to play the piano, and she so impressed her father with how quickly she picked up reading and writing that when she was seven, he enrolled her in the Francis School, a monitorial school similar to the one Melville had attended. During her three years there, she received 155 merit marks, and only three demerits for "thoughtlessness." When she was nine, her father became Chief Justice of the Massachusetts Supreme Court, and the Shaws moved from Kneeland Street to 49 Mount Vernon on Beacon Hill. Elizabeth was sent to board at the Uxbridge Classical Academy, a girls' school, when she was ten, and from 1835 to 1841 she lived at home and attended the School for Young Ladies founded in 1832 by Ralph Waldo Emerson's second cousin George.[6]

George B. Emerson, past principal of Boston's all-male English Classical School, believed that young women deserved the same education as young men. In his opinion, it was not enough for them to be "good daughters and sisters, good neighbors, good wives, and good mothers." His school offered an academic curriculum consisting of English, Latin, arithmetic, science, and history that was the equivalent of the college preparatory course for young men. Graduates of Emerson's school could go on to either of the two colleges that took women in those days, the Mount Holyoke Female Seminary—Emily Dickinson's alma mater—or Oberlin College in Ohio, the first coeducational college in the United States.[7]

Lizzie chose not to attend either one, perhaps because few women went to college in those days or because she was in love with one, or two, young men. One was John

Nourse, a dear childhood friend who died in 1844, at just about the time both families expected them to get engaged. The other was Daniel McIlroy, a Harvard Law School graduate whom Judge Shaw ruled out as a romantic prospect because he was a Roman Catholic and an Irish nationalist.[8]

Lizzie's religious education was as informal as might be expected for a girl whose father had left the Congregational Church to become a Unitarian, and now saw nothing wrong with playing a few rubbers of whist on a Saturday night even after the Sabbath had begun. Lizzie knew the Bible well from Sunday school, and she showed off her knowledge of scripture, her love of parties, and her inventiveness on at least one occasion by composing a comical account of her cousin Jane Dow's party, which she called "the ninth chapter of III Chronicles," in mock-Biblical cadence and style. Had Melville seen this jeu d'esprit, he might well have been charmed by her wit and panache. If Lizzie had dreams of adventure and literary accomplishment without the self-confidence to realize them herself, as many young girls did, it would have been natural for her to be attracted to a man who was living out her fantasies.[9]

In January 1847, Evert Duyckinck, recently named chief editor of a new weekly called *The Literary World,* asked Melville's permission to run excerpts from *Omoo,* but Melville wanted to hold back until after the book was published. Instead, he offered to review J. Ross Browne's *Etchings of a Whaling Cruise,* and Captain Ringbolt's *Sailor's Life and Sailor's Yarns.* Both books were sad reminders that "the poetry of salt water is very much on the wane," and although he preferred Browne's "Voice from the Forecastle" over Ringbolt's view from the quarterdeck, he criticized Browne for presenting "unvarnished facts" with so little charm or romantic coloration. He brushed off Ringbolt's "little stories of the sea, simply and pleasantly told," and launched into his own vigorous description of the whaleman's adventures.[10]

Melville's review gives a clue to the direction he was going as he started writing his third book. The book he had promised fans of *Typee* and *Omoo* was to be a continuation of his two earlier books, a narrative of a whaling voyage in Japan and the South Pacific, but in keeping with his evolving aesthetic, he would, in effect, show writers like Browne and Ringbolt how to tell sea stories that would describe the sailor's experience of whaling in an erudite and poetic style.

On February 1, Melville shipped the proof sheets of *Omoo* off to his agent John Brodhead in London before attending a performance of Donizetti's opera *Lucia di Lammermoor* at Palmo's Opera House. He had no way of knowing that when the manuscript reached England, British customs officials in Liverpool would mistake it for a pirated book and seize it as contraband. When the manuscript finally reached London, John Murray offered Melville £150 in promissory notes contingent on sales, because *Typee* had not yet paid expenses.[11]

Melville was not making enough money to live comfortably on his own, much less support a wife, and at his uncle Peter's suggestion, he decided to apply for a government job so that he would not have to be dependent solely on his income as a writer. On February 4 he took the train to Washington to see his uncle's friend Senator John A. Dix and Secretary of War William L. Marcy, a former governor of New York whom Gansevoort had supported in the 1844 campaign. Both Peter Gansevoort and Maria Melville assumed the family's service to the nation would qualify Herman for one of the positions created in the Treasury Department by the new loan bill, but Melville had done nothing for the party, and the administration's debt to Gansevoort had been fully paid.[12]

Although he failed to gain a government appointment and a steady salary, Melville's trip was not fruitless. He attended a ball at the Russian embassy, where he spied the illustrious Admiral Thomas ap Catesby Jones and flirted a bit with "one of the sweetest of our Bond Street girls," as Catherine Dix, the senator's wife, described her. The "brief prospect of a closer tie" with a debutante who began pursuing him at the ball strengthened the inclination of his heart toward Elizabeth Shaw, and a visit to the Senate chamber while the Twenty-ninth Congress was in session sparked new ideas for the book he was working on.[13]

While Melville was in Washington, the £50 that John Murray had promised him for the sequel to *Typee* arrived, and after paying his debts and keeping $50 for spending money, he sent $40 to his sisters to show, as his mother put it, "his filial love of justice in paying his debts, his affection and gratitude to his Sisters, and his filial love to his Mother." Now that Herman was a famous writer, she urged him to accept invitations to lecture, and to have his portrait painted. Although he declined to lecture, he did agree to have his portrait painted by Asa W. Twitchell, an aspiring amateur who was making his living as a wheelwright in Lansingburgh, and who later made a career as an Albany portrait painter.[14]

Feeling confident that *Omoo* would seal his success as a writer, Melville went to Boston on March 9, apparently to ask Judge Shaw for his permission to announce his engagement to Elizabeth. Melville was undoubtedly aware of the sentimental reason behind Shaw's long-standing devotion to the Melvilles, and he knew that marrying Shaw's daughter would be like cementing an alliance between the two old families. Despite his reservations about Melville's solvency, Shaw was impressed by the young man's sincerity, intelligence, and ambition; however, he still was not ready to give him the go-ahead.[15]

Judge Shaw had nothing against novelists or poets—he had written poetry himself when he was young—but he didn't particularly want his only daughter to marry one. He must have worried that young Melville was the type to act on infatuation, and that even if the boy did settle down, he would not be able to take proper care of Elizabeth. The Dana boy had gotten the wanderlust out of his system after he graduated from Harvard by sailing to California, and he had written a very respectable account of his adventures before settling into a legal career. Young Melville, on the other hand, had no profession to fall back on, as far as Shaw could see. He liked the lad well enough—he seemed more levelheaded than his poor father—but few men could support a family on a writer's income. Still, Lizzie did look radiant when the handsome young sailor walked into the room, so Judge Shaw, who had a reputation for not making snap judgments on the bench, decided to keep an open mind.

The more time Herman Melville spent with Elizabeth, the more comfortable he felt with her. She was a solid, honest Yankee woman—practical, modest, thrifty, well educated, and capable of total loyalty. Lizzie loved hearing Melville expound on his reading and his ideas as much as she enjoyed hearing about his South Seas adventures. Like Desdemona, she loved him for the dangers he had passed, and like Othello, he loved her not only for her unaffected charm, but also for the image of himself that he saw reflected in her admiring eyes.

~

On March 27, 1847, *Omoo: A Narrative of Adventures in the South Seas; Being a Sequel to the "Residence in the Marquesas Islands"* was published in an edition of four thousand copies by John Murray, but the Harper edition, called *Omoo: A Narrative of Adventures in the South Seas,* did not appear until April 26. Melville had told John Murray that he intended his picaresque narrative to describe the "'man about town' sort of life, led, at the present day, by roving sailors in the Pacific," which probably accounts for his dedication of the book to his uncle Herman. It was pure Melville mischief, as Herman Gansevoort rarely left the tiny village that was named for him.[16]

The first printing of *Omoo* was sold out in a week. Although it found favor with the reading public and most mainstream critics, it provoked fierce attacks from the religious press, which found its enthusiastic endorsement of carefree island ways and its criticisms of soldiers and missionaries highly objectionable.[17]

Reactions to *Omoo* were even more widely divergent than reactions to *Typee.* On the positive side, *The Evening Mirror* praised its "brilliant and captivating style," its warmth... tropical luxuriance...genial flow of humor" and "happy enthusiasm," and *Godey's Lady's Book* said its "vivid descriptions of natural scenery" seemed "touched by the pencil of a painter." *Brooklyn Eagle* reviewer Walter Whitman praised it for its "richly good-natured style" and called it "thorough entertainment—not so light as to be tossed aside for its flippancy, nor so profound as to be tiresome."[18]

On the negative side, George Washington Peck called *Omoo* "venomous, and, indeed, venereous" and accused Melville of seeking to "excite unchaste desires" in his readers. Overstepping the bounds of good taste, Peck suggested that if Melville were truly virile, he would not have to boast about his exploits with native maidens. His remark that Melville was guilty of "cool, sneering wit" and a "perfect want of *heart*" hurt the sensitive ex-sailor more than his more slanderous insinuations, however, as Melville thought of himself as a man of good heart.[19]

Fortunately, Melville had the sense not to respond, so Jedediah B. Auld, a fellow member of the Duyckinck circle, came to his defense. Deploring Peck's "disgusting loathesomeness and personal blackguardism," Auld took it upon himself to speak for the "vast majority of readers here and abroad … [who read] Omoo with feelings of unmixed delight." He called Peck's review "spiteful," and accused him of "pandering to a depraved taste."[20]

Although *The National Antislavery Standard* applauded *Omoo* for its attacks on imperialism, *The English Review* complained that "the cloven foot is much too visible to be mistaken, despite the commonplace declarations of respect for religions and morals." Evert Duyckinck, however, labeled such comments "grossly abusive."[21]

The controversy over the book may have spurred sales, as two more editions followed on the heels of the first. W. E. Cramer, the editor of the *Daily Wisconsin*, editorialized, "We trust now that Mr. Melville will consider his life as fixed—that he will live and die an author. He has the genius to succeed, and by perseverance, he may carve his name as high in the Temple of Fame as an Irving or a Scott."[22]

Melville still was not making much money from his writing, however, and had Lemuel Shaw seen the financial statements from Melville's publishers, he would have known he had good reason to worry about his daughter's future. Despite the success of *Typee*, Wiley & Putnam's October statement showed a profit of only $172.52 from the sale of 1,286 paperbound copies and 428 cloth, and after this was divided between author and publisher, Melville made only $86.26, the equivalent of about $1,300 at current dollar values. Meanwhile, he had ordered so many books for himself and Allan that by the time Harper's deducted what he owed them, his net profits came to only $7.81.[23]

In the next quarter, the ledger showed that 797 paperbound copies and 382 clothbound copies had been sold. Subtracting expenses of $39.18 left a profit of $222.76, and Melville's share was only half of that. In the first two and a half years of its publication, *Typee* would garner only $1,465.49, and despite small reprintings and sales of foreign rights, the book netted him no more than $2,000 for the rest of his life, and *Omoo*'s sales did not make up for it. It seemed to Melville that an author received a very small percentage of the profit for his work, and he was beginning to suspect that writing was a charitable contribution to American culture, rather than a paid profession—a scary thought for a young man who was contemplating marriage.[24]

~

On May 4, Herman, Augusta, Allan, and Allan's fiancée, Sophia Thurston, went to see Thomas Cole's epic work *The Course of Empire,* originally commissioned by art patron Luman Reed. Reed's collection of old masters and American paintings formed the nucleus of the New-York Gallery of the Fine Arts, which was housed in a city-owned rotunda designed by the painter John Vanderlyn to resemble Oxford's Sheldonian Theatre. Melville, who was intrigued by the correspondences between visual aesthetics and literary style, found Cole's blending of the allegorical and the historical fascinating, and Cole's style influenced his next book, *Mardi and a Voyage Thyther.*[25]

Although he reveled in the stimulation New York afforded the senses and the mind, Melville found Lansingburgh more conducive to reading, studying, and writing. By the middle of May, his mother's attic was too hot to work in comfortably, so with the help of his sisters, Melville moved his desk, three mahogany chairs, and two trunks full of books into the sunny front room on the second floor. Once they had removed a bedstead, repainted the walls, put down a new carpet, hung new curtains to shield his eyes from the strong afternoon sun as the solstice approached, shelved his books, and set his favorite ship model on the desk, Melville was ready to write again.[26]

He made fitful attempts to work on his next book, which was supposed to pick up where *Omoo* left off, but he just could not get started. The books he had borrowed from Duyckinck's vast library had plunged him into metaphysical speculations, and he was beginning to want to write something more meaningful than a travelogue.

All spring, Melville immersed himself in his work—or tried to. He was feeling very unsettled and distracted, and it seemed impossible to concentrate. When he was reading or trying to write, he had the urge to leave his desk and go to Boston to see Lizzie, but being with her filled him with ideas and made him eager to get back to his writing. He was possessed by Poe's "imp of perversity," and to make things worse, he began noticing references to marriage in everything he read. The oxymoronic phrase "holy wedlock" probably did not describe what he had in mind, and he began to wonder whether marriage would resemble Heaven, the Happy Valley, or the Calabooza Beretanee, the British lockup in Papeete.

Noticing that Herman seemed "very restless and ill at ease and very lonely without his intended," Mother Melville wielded a "steering oar" behind the scenes to get the young couple to the altar. They had not yet announced their engagement, partly because of Judge Shaw's reservations and partly, it seems, because Lizzie was not eager to start her new life in another woman's house. She was a little afraid of Herman's mother, who was much less approachable than the gentle, sweet Hope Shaw, and she wasn't sure Mother Melville liked her, or approved of her Yankee ways.

Melville shuttled back and forth to Boston several times that spring, courting Lizzie and her father, until finally Judge Shaw agreed to the engagement. Herman hurried home to tell his family, and while he was busy in his mother's garden, hoeing "his favorite tomatoes," Helen was writing everyone she could think of, including her cousin Augustus Van Schaick, who was then in Rio de Janeiro. "Herman has returned from a visit to Boston, and has made arrangements to take upon himself the dignified character of a married man some time during the Summer.... I can scarcely realize the astounding truth!" Helen and her dear friend Lizzie would truly be sisters now.[27]

While Melville's sister bubbled with excitement, Maria was annoyed because no date had been set for the wedding: "I can see no reason why it should be postponed any longer, if Lizzie loves Herman as I think she does with her whole heart & soul why, she will consent to live here for the present, and she can be happy too—all the elements of happiness are thick around us if we only will hold them to us."[28]

Maria delegated Augusta, who was visiting the Shaws, to persuade Lizzie to set a date and Herman to agree to live in the Lansingburgh house until the couple could afford to be on their own. "If Lizzie loves [him] she can be as happy here as elsewhere, and you must tell her so, Herman is able to support her here now, and to wait for an uncertain future, which none of us can penetrate, would be unwise he is really unsettled and wont [sic] be able to attend to his Book if Lizzie does not reflect upon the uncertainty of the future, & consent to name some day say in July."[29]

Once Herman had decided that he and Lizzie would live with his mother, and the ever-prudent Judge Shaw had established a trust fund providing his daughter a yearly income, the wedding date, to Maria's great relief, was set for August 4, just three days after Melville's twenty-eighth birthday. Almost immediately, society columnists picked up the news: "Herman Melville, Esq., author of 'Typee' and 'Omoo,' we are happy to learn is likely to find more happiness in civilization than he ever enjoyed in the romantic Valley of the Marquesas. We expect to find the full particulars in a few days under the proper head, in some Boston paper." The tone of these notices suggests that few people expected Typee to settle down.[30]

Everyone had an opinion about Melville's intended. In Cambridge, Fanny Longfellow told her father, Nathan Appleton, that she thought Elizabeth Shaw "a peculiar choice" for the author of *Typee* "after his flirtations with South Sea beauties," because Lizzie struck her as a plain, almost homely, girl, and the abolitionist Edmund Quincy made the unchivalrous comment that Miss Shaw must have inherited her looks from her "distinguished father." Augusta's friends were very pleased, however. Millie Van

Rensselaer Thayer considered Lizzie "quite a pretty woman...gay, kindhearted," and Augusta Whipple Hunter praised "the expression of her countenance" and her "lovely and amiable" character.[31]

Friends of the Shaws were eager to meet the young man about whom they had heard so much; he sounded like quite an original, definitely not the Brahmin type. Ida Russell invited Melville to a tea at her home in Milton, to meet her cousin Richard Henry Dana, and shortly afterward she invited the Shaws to bring Melville to a dinner party that included as guests the Danas, Charles Sumner, and the Channings. After the ladies adjourned to the parlor, the men lit up cigars and filled their glasses, and it's safe to speculate that these ardent abolitionists talked about slavery and free soil, the two most burning issues of the day.[32]

With the pressures and uncertainties of courtship behind him, Melville went to New York in mid-July. Charles Fenno Hoffman had succeeded Evert Duyckinck as editor of *The Literary World*, and his chum Cornelius Mathews, a knight of the "Round Table," was editing *Yankee Doodle*, a humorous weekly popularly called "the American *Punch*." At Mathews's invitation, Melville tossed off a series of short satirical pieces called "Authentic Anecdotes of 'Old Zack,'" in which he lambasted Zachary Taylor, the Whig candidate for President.[33]

These sketches portray the hero of the Battle of Buena Vista as a vulgar, incompetent buffoon, but they are essentially cartoon caricature, not serious political satire. They owe a debt to frontier tall tales, urban tabloids, and posters advertising P. T. Barnum's American Museum, and they paved the way for Melville's last published novel, *The Confidence-Man*. Instead of attacking "Old Rough and Ready" as a slaveholder who slaughtered the Sac and Fox in the Black Hawk War, hunted down Seminoles in Florida, and became the hero of the imperialistic war with Mexico, Melville makes fun of him. Old Zack removes a Mexican mortar shell from his backside and lights his cigar with it, and gallops along with a tack sticking up from his saddle, never feeling it because he is so insensitive.

Melville's heart was obviously not in writing ephemera for the newspapers. As political commentary, these pieces seem sophomoric compared to incisive editorials like the one in the Concord, New Hampshire, *Independent Democrat* branding Taylor as "one of the greatest slaveholders in the United States" and accusing him of crimes against humanity: "He raises babies for the market and makes merchandize of his fellow men! He had a hundred mothers, with or without their babes for sale in the shambles. He furnishes creole virgins for the 'hells' of New Orleans, and riots on the ruins of souls for whom the Man of Sorrows died." Compared to this, Melville's sketches seem superficial, as though for some reason, he did not want to tackle slavery head-on.[34]

Prevailing *Knickerbocker* taste ran to genial satirical essays or dreamy, picturesque romances, and *Yankee Doodle* was intended primarily as entertainment. The "Old Zack" pieces, like his other short, topical pieces on events such as the sighting of a sea serpent at Nahant, the arrival of a Chinese junk in New York, and Barnum's latest moneymaking schemes, were not the kind of writing Melville aspired to do; he did not want to be remembered by posterity as a literary P. T. Barnum, much less as one of Barnum's freaks.[35]

At the same time, Melville knew that nothing made better copy than Barnum's "lean men, fat women, dwarfs, two-headed cows, amphibious sea-maidens, large-eyed owls, small-eyed mice, anacondas, bugs, monkeys, and mummies." Mass entertainment was the wave of the future, and Phineas Taylor Barnum, who had gotten his start in 1835 by purchasing the rights to exhibit Joice Heth, a former slave who claimed to be the 160-year-old ex-nurse of George Washington, knew how to ride the wave. He turned her trancelike memories of her life on Washington's plantation, her eerie renditions of old hymns and spirituals, and her mesmerizing sermons into a national gold mine.[36]

Draping the old Scudder's American Museum at Broadway and Ann Street with banners and huge advertising posters, Barnum created an attraction no visitor to, or resident of, New York would miss. With its revolving Drummond light and its unusual exhibits, Barnum's Museum was more entertaining than the theater, and it made traditional museums like Peale's in Philadelphia seem hopelessly old-fashioned. Whereas Peale's would show its bizarre freaks of nature only to scientists who were doing serious research, Barnum cashed in on the public's taste for sensationalistic novelties, even taking some exhibits to Europe. Everything he touched seemed to turn to gold. Once, having discovered a band of Indians encamped in Manhattan's dwindling woodland, he sent them to England to shoot pennies with bows and arrows for Victoria's amusement, and pocketed the profits.

Life was all a publicity stunt to Barnum. Lydia Maria Child called him "a genuine Yankee, for contrivance and perseverance," who "will circumnavigate the globe, to catch a monstrosity of any kind for his museum. . . . Giants, dwarfs, double-headed calves, no matter what, so that it be something out of nature. He would mount Phaeton's car to catch the comet with seven tails, plunge into Symmes's Hole for a dog with two heads, and go down the Maelstrom for a sea-serpent." Barnum was America's first urban tall-tale hero and the founding father of American showbiz.[37]

The great attractions at the American Museum in the 1840s were a mermaid and a midget whom Barnum called "General Tom Thumb." Tom Thumb became an international celebrity when Barnum took him on what was to be a triumphant tour of Europe. Unfortunately for the painter Benjamin Robert Haydon, a close friend of John Keats, Tom Thumb's arrival in London coincided with the unveiling of the work he considered his masterpiece: a series of huge historical canvases intended to make him the Gibbon or Macaulay of the visual arts. Preoccupied with Barnum's midget, so few people turned out for Haydon's opening that he killed himself in a fit of despondency, proving once more that it was the artist's fate always to be sacrificed to the spirit of the age.[38]

On July 30, 1847, Evert Duyckinck treated Melville to dinner at the Astor House Hotel, later noting in his diary that Melville was "to be married next Wednesday." Adding that he was "cheerful company," he noted that his writing was modeled "a great deal on Washington Irving." The following evening, Melville's friends threw him a bachelor party, and the day he turned twenty-eight years old, he went to Boston to become a married man.[39]

Although Lizzie "at first had some idea of being married in church," she decided to be married at home because "if it were to get about previously that 'Typee' was to be seen on such a day, a great crowd might rush out of mere curiosity to see 'the author,' making it very unpleasant for us both." Just before the ceremony, Lizzie took communion, and Melville found a four-leaf clover that Lizzie pressed between the pages of the great leather-bound, gilt-edged family Bible given as a wedding present by her aunt Lucy Nourse. This gave rise to a romantic family legend that on each anniversary thereafter, Herman would find a four-leaf clover and present it to Lizzie in memory of their wedding day—a legend created, or at least sustained, by Melville himself, perhaps as an antidote to the poisonous marital problems of their middle years, perhaps because he wished that it were true.

The ceremony was conducted "as privately as possible," with "only our relatives, and a very few intimate friends—about twenty-five people in all—and no bridesmaids. Dr. Alexander Young of New South Unitarian officiating." Everyone told Lizzie that she "went through the ceremony with the utmost calmness and composure," but her memory of the event was "all dreamy and indistinct…a vision of Herman by my side, a confused crowd of rustling dresses, a row of boots, and Mr. Young in full canonicals standing before me, giving utterance to the solemn words of obligation."[40]

For Hope Shaw, it was "a very pleasant day," and for Mother Melville it was a triumph, as she took full credit for piloting the happy couple into the safe harbor of Christian marriage. At fifteen, Lem Jr. had outgrown the childhood infatuation that led him to make Lizzie promise to marry him "when he was a *man*," and weddings were nothing more than a source of potential annoyance and embarrassment to him, with all the kissing and crying and carrying on before the refreshments came. He was relieved that Lizzie "behaved very well—did not cry, or anything of that sort." Thirteen-year-old Sam, who was equally apprehensive, had "solemn" memories of having to wear a blue jacket, and of "how disgusting the wedding cake got to be!"[41]

At around eleven that night, the sky over Boston was lit by a brilliant display of northern lights, and early the following evening the city was hit by a thunderstorm that blew down an observatory in Jamaica Plain and damaged several ships. By then, however, the newlyweds were having supper in "lovely and romantic" Center Harbor on the shores of Lake Winnipesaukee.[42]

By the time the *New-York Daily Tribune* printed a coy notice that a certain Fayaway was suing "Mr. Herman Typee Omoo Melville" for breach of promise for marrying "a young lady of Boston," Lizzie was writing her first letter to her mother as a married woman and signing it, "believe me as ever, your affectionate daughter–Elizabeth–even though I add to it–Melville–for the first time."[43]

Lizzie reported regularly on their leisurely trip by train, stage, and canal boat through the White Mountains of New Hampshire and eastern Canada, always leaving room for Herman to add a few words at the bottom of her page. "I trust in the course of some 2 weeks to bring Lizzie to Lansingburgh, quite refreshed & invigorated from her rambles," he wrote Judge Shaw. Lizzie reported that Quebec's fortress was "too savage & soldier-like" for her taste, but that she greatly enjoyed Montreal, a comment not to be underestimated as an expression of a vivacious personality.[44]

They returned through the mountains of Vermont and crossed Lake Champlain overnight aboard a canal boat so jammed with passengers and luggage that, even in the "ladies' saloon," women and children had to sleep on trunks and boxes. Having been "fully forewarned of the inconvenience we might expect" in spending the night on a canal boat, Lizzie was "fully determined to meet [it] bravely."[45]

Narrow shelves were set up for as many women as possible to "stow" their babies for the night, and Lizzie was asked to take an upper shelf:

> Of course I complied, and after failing in several awkward attempts, I managed to climb and crawl into this narrow aperture like a bug forcing its way through the boards of the fence. Sweltering and smothering I watched the weary night hours pass away, for to *sleep* in such an atmosphere was impossible. I rose at three o'clock, thinking it was five, spent a couple of hours curled upon the floor, and was right glad when Herman came for me, with the joyful intelligence that we were actually approaching Whitehall–the place of our destination. He also passed a weary night, though his sufferings were of the opposite order–for while I was suffering with the heat and the bad atmosphere, he was on deck, chilled and half-frozen with the fog and penetrating dampness, for the gentlemen's apartment was even more crowded than the ladies'–so much so that they did not attempt to hang any "shelves" for them to lie upon. All these [men] could do was to sit bolt upright firmly wedged in and if one of them pre-

sumed to *lean* at all or even to *nod* out of the perpendicular, it was thought a great infringement of right, and he was immediately called to order—so Herman preferred to remain on deck all night to being in this crowd.[46]

Lizzie's adventurous spirit and abundant energy come across well in this letter to her mother, suggesting that her pluck and good humor might have been what attracted Melville to her, and vice versa. She was willing to take new experiences in her stride, and she was a skilled writer, as most young people from good families in nineteenth-century America were expected to be able to express themselves neatly and artfully for the amusement and edification of family and friends.

Soon after the couple arrived back in Lansingburgh, they went to New York for Allan's wedding at the fashionable Church of the Ascension. Sophia looked beautiful as she walked down the aisle wearing a white glacé gown cut in the latest fashion. Augusta Melville was one of the bridesmaids, and Herman looked very debonair in his worked satin vest.[47]

Melville's cousin Priscilla thought Allan and Sophia looked "like Divinities." She asked Augusta whether she thought their love was "so ethereal (like *Herman's* & *Lizzie's*) that it bore them *upward* towards a *heavenly* paradise—or did they seek one among the lovely beauties of earth?" To call a newly married couple "ethereal" was the highest form of praise in genteel circles, where it was proper to speak of married love not as the sensual congress of two bodies, but as the spiritual communion of two souls. Everyone agreed that both couples seemed perfectly matched to each other, and eminently suited for lifelong bliss.[48]

The young Melvilles and their friends were all reaching marriageable age, and now that Herman and Lizzie were married, people assumed Augusta would be next: "I suppose that your turn comes next to lay your *heart*, a willing sacrifice upon the hymeneal altar—yet *another* [triply underlined] victim to the mischievous arts of the little gods," her cousin Priscilla wrote. That September, in fact, Augusta became engaged to Anthony Augustus Peebles, the son of her mother's cousin Maria Van Schaick Peebles, but by the following spring, the engagement had been called off. Gus's friend Augusta Whipple Hunter seems not to have been surprised at the broken engagement. She wrote Augusta, "so my dear, you are not to be married this spring to Augustus Peebles? Why Gus I am afraid you will disappoint some of your friends. *Perhaps* it would be an act of charity in you to confirm the *wisdom* of your acquaintances, by shaking Madam Rumor by the hand as for once a truth-telling dame." Her close friends seemed to have understood that Augusta would never marry, partly because she was so strongly attached to Herman, and partly because she evidently found friendships with women more satisfying than relationships with men.[49]

Sophia Thurston Melville read temperance tracts and recited a litany of warnings to her husband about the active poisons lurking in alcohol. It's not clear whether Allan's behavior prompted these warnings, but given the anxious missives Mother Melville had sent him after he first went on his own, Sophia's efforts to steer Allan clear of the alcohol abuse that seems to have been endemic among the men in the family were well advised. More serious-minded than many socialites from wealthy New York families, Sophia also kept up with current affairs and read serious novels such as Dickens's *Dombey and Son*; she not only read *Omoo*, but also the fourteen-page critique of it that appeared in *Blackwood's Edinburgh Magazine*.[50]

Allan found the "very amusing and highly complimentary" review "exceedingly flattering to the author." Although the *Blackwood's* reviewer took Melville to task for "glaring inconsistencies" in both tone and content, and accused him of inventing both his own name and the name Herman Gansevoort, he praised the book for its humor and its delightfully genial style. Even so, the book was a bit "too romantic" for him, but he thought its author must be "exceedingly good company."[51]

Melville could, of course, be good company, but at times, as he worked in seclusion on his ever-more-ambitious books, he could also be irritable and self-centered. Unlike most men, he worked at home all day, so the family had to tailor their schedule to his needs. Lizzie was immediately faced with the difficult job of adjusting to her husband's routine while sharing living quarters with her in-laws, especially Mother Melville, who ruled the roost. "I'm afraid no place will ever seem to me like dear old crooked Boston," she wrote Hope Shaw, but in those halcyon days of early married life, she was sure that "with Herman with me always, I can be happy and contented anywhere."[52]

Lizzie sometimes had to pinch herself to remember that she was a married woman. Marriage was what young girls lived for, but when it came, it took some getting used to:

> I can hardly realise the change myself—It seems sometimes exactly as if I were
> here for a *visit*. The illusion is quite dispelled however when Herman stalks
> into my room without even the ceremony of knocking, bringing me perhaps
> a button to sew on, or some such equally romantic occupation. Just imagine "a
> bride" (as the girls jokingly call me altogether) mending an old black coat or
> a pair of stockings—What a picture! But the romance of life must sometimes
> give place to the realities, unless we can be etherial [*sic*] and dispense with food
> and raiment.

She was beginning to think married life might not always be as "ethereal" as people wanted her to believe.[53]

It wasn't long before life in Lansingburgh became too confining for Melville. Now that he was a well-known author, conversant with New York writers and artists, a contributor to magazines, and an avid reader of esoteric books not available in village libraries, he wanted to be near the pulse of things. Allan, too, was thinking of finding a larger place now that he was married, so the brothers pooled their resources and bought a brownstone in New York at 103 Fourth Avenue, "between 11th and 12th Streets—rear of Grace Church." In October they moved not only their wives, but also their mother and sisters, to the city.[54]

For Melville, it was a chance to be right in the thick of urban life. Evert Duyckinck lived only a few blocks away, at 20 Clinton Place (the present-day 8th Street), and nearby Broadway offered many attractions. Melville could walk to Barnum's Museum, the new opera house, and the grand Astor House Hotel, which had two antiquarian bookshops in the lobby. Lizzie missed Boston and thought New York too fast, too noisy, too dirty, and too drab. Its nearly uniform, dull brown buildings facing gridlike streets, like so many soldiers standing at attention, had none of the charm of Boston's red brick Federal houses and hilly, winding streets. For Maria Melville, however, the move meant she had finally made it to a fashionable neighborhood.

~

New York was an exciting city in the 1840s. From Brooklyn Heights, journalist Walt Whitman could see the "countless masts, the white shore-steamers, the lighters, the ferryboats, the black sea-steamers" pulled up at piers on the East River. At that distance, New York became the magnificent "City of hurried and sparkling water! city of spires and masts! / City nested in bays! my city!" that Walt Whitman would celebrate in *Leaves of Grass*.[55]

Close up, however, lower Manhattan was a dirty, noisy, frenetic rabbit warren that little resembled the picturesque seaport town Melville had known as a boy growing up in the 1820s. Near the docks stood the offices of merchants and money brokers and dingy jobbers' warehouses. Carts hauling goods clattered by on the cobblestones, and rats slunk up from the wharves to take refuge in cellars already overrun with starving families. Fifteen to twenty thousand immigrants poured into the city every week and crowded into neighborhoods offering subhuman housing and "low, unsatisfactory, and demoralizing" amusements.[56]

Although observers such as Lydia Maria Child and Herman Melville appreciated the city's energy and diversity, they also recognized the dangers inherent in the new commercialism. Mrs. Child thought the men and boys "perambulating the thoroughfares" wearing placards had turned themselves into "walking advertisements," and from their own window the Melvilles could hear vendors "screaming in every variety of cracked voices." The "money-making rage" had taken over, Mrs. Child reported in her *Letters from New York.*[57]

New York was a maze of violent, disorienting contrasts. On Broadway, carriages and omnibuses clattered up and down at breakneck speeds as drivers whipped their horses, racing the rival vehicles to see who would establish the day's record time. Pedestrians stood at the curb, choking on explosions of dirt and dried horse manure, waiting sometimes for half an hour before a lull in this mayhem let them cross safely. At certain major intersections, coaches and carts locked wheels, and drivers yelled oaths and epithets at one another, until someone backed up to let the others pass.[58]

In some parts of the city, pedestrians strolled along tree-lined boulevards enjoying the elegant shops and galleries displaying antique furniture and objets d'art or through the small parks whose bowling greens provided recreation for workingmen on Sundays. At Battery Park, "if the sun is setting brilliantly, rainbows dodge about on the spray, as if playing bo-peep with the happy little ones," wrote Mrs. Child. In the spring and summer, children jumped rope and rolled hoops around the fountain in Union Park, making "as merry as birds."[59]

Although she characterized herself as "deeply enamored of nature," Lydia Child loved New York. "Why need I sigh for green fields? Does not Broadway superabound with beauty?" she asked her readers. "If I must live in a city, the fountains alone would determine my choice in favour of New-York."[60]

With most of the old freshwater ponds filled in for building lots, the city had built the Croton Reservoir at Forty-second Street, which looked like a low-walled fort. Its three large fountains were decorated with dolphins, nymphs, and tritons. Most of the city north of the slums enjoyed clean Croton water, but there were no free public baths. At one time, people could swim at the Battery, but, as noted earlier, genteel promenaders began complaining about young men who were in the habit of stripping off their clothes to bathe there. When the practice seemed to have taken on disagreeable overtones, the city fathers closed the harbor to swimmers and built indoor salt baths, which Allan Melville, for one, found very therapeutic.[61]

Mrs. Child and others were quick to point out that the prohibition of outdoor swimming unfairly penalized the poorer classes. "The wealthy can introduce water in their chambers, or float on the bosom of the tide, in the pleasant baths at the Battery," Mrs. Child opined, "but for the innumerable poor, this is a luxury that can seldom, if ever, be enjoyed.... the labouring man has to walk three or four miles to obtain a privilege so necessary to health. If the city would provide a huge covered basin, with a sprinkling fountain in the centre, for a shower-bath, it would be a notable donation to the poor."[62]

Generally, the city's cultural institutions catered to the well-to-do. Although a few seamen's institutions and mechanics' halls had reading rooms for their members, there were few community centers or libraries for workers in the congested slums downtown. Uptown, wealthy merchants established private subscription libraries, art galleries, and musical societies, but tickets for "patrician" entertainments such as the Italian opera and the four annual Philharmonic concerts were too expensive for the Melvilles to purchase on a regular basis. Some popular amusements were of dubious taste and character as far as the middle class was concerned, and few families could afford tickets to the brass-band concerts at Castle Garden, the Battery's elegant floating amphitheater. Vauxhall Gardens provided decent, affordable entertainment, and Niblo's Garden offered orchestral recitals amid orientalist-inspired shrubbery lit by illuminated fountains.

The large population of European working families were used to communal public spaces in cities, which made Sundays in New York very different from Sundays in Boston. "There is universal loco-motion on Sundays," wrote Mrs. Child. "Being the only leisure day with labourers, the temptation is strong to take their families into the country, for fresh air, and a sight of green fields," as they did in the Old Country. Huge double-decker Harlem omnibuses that looked like steamboats would be packed to overflowing with working-class families. "It is a cheerful sight to see them returning at sunset, with green boughs and bouquets of flowers." Not everyone welcomed foreigners as heartily as did Mrs. Child; some people resented their unfamiliar languages and their "funny" clothes.[63]

Steamer excursions along the Hudson, usually with music, helped relieve the "oppressiveness of summer" for those who could afford the passage. Sometimes children from public schools and orphanages were treated to boat rides, which Lydia Child applauded as evidence that society was beginning to realize that "her children need something more than food and raiment."[64]

Whereas interaction among classes, races, and nationalities had been fairly fluid when Melville was a boy, by the late 1840s, real-estate practices had created rigid class demarcations, and distinct ethnic groups had clustered together in isolated neighborhoods, setting housing patterns for many years to come. Guidebooks steered visitors away from neighborhoods deemed "dangerous," a word that meant (and often still means) different, foreign, and lower-class. Greedy landlords such as Trinity Church and the Astor family were gobbling up the land and herding the working poor and new immigrants into tenements. By the late forties, the housing market had made class divisions ineradicable, with workers and craftsmen having no stock in the city's resources— nothing but low wages and high rents. "Property reigns so supreme in the social compact, that the growth of souls is trampled like a weed under its feet, and human life is considered of far less importance," warned Mrs. Child.[65]

Areas such as Five Points were awash in crime, and on Wall Street, gangs of ruffians accosted brokers, and prostitutes plied their trade amid the "restless whirlpool of ever-striving selfishness." Lurid descriptions of urban life by opportunistic journalists like George "Gaslight" Foster and Ned Buntline fed on and reinforced class and race prejudice. To counteract New York's increasingly negative image, Mrs. Child assured her readers that most people in the city were of a "disposition to be good-natured and obliging."[66]

New York boasted twelve noble avenues, and in "spacious and airy" neighborhoods uptown, large, handsome houses were shooting up on vacant lots cleared "as if by the magic of Aladdin's lamp." Astor Place and Union Square, not far from the Melvilles' residence, had become elegant open spaces surrounded by brownstone houses, retail stores, eating establishments, and cultural landmarks. The new Astor Place Theatre, the old Astor House Hotel, and fashionable Delmonico's restaurant flanked Barnum's Museum, and new art galleries were opening next to phrenological cabinets and mesmeric parlors. Although much urban literature written for middle-class readers portrayed lower Manhattan in a lurid light, as far as Mrs. Child was concerned, New York was "not a Sodom."[67]

Shortly after the Melvilles settled into their new house, Evert Duyckinck took Melville to the opening of the American Art-Union, which featured works by Thomas Cole, Edward Hicks, and Thomas Sully, whose bathing nymph "suggested Fayaway" to Duyckinck. The opening included a display of *tableaux vivants* re-creating well-known works of art, and Melville met the poet William Cullen Bryant and the genre painter William Sydney Mount. A splendid successor to the Apollo Association, the Art-Union was the first and only subscription museum for the fine arts in the United States, charging $5 a year.[68]

Duyckinck considered Melville a "right pleasant man to pass an evening with," and thought his family situation was idyllic: "Melville has got into a happier valley than the Happar not far from here and the wife and I have looked in at the Ti—two very pretty parlors odorous of taste and domestic felicity."[69]

Once Melville had established a daily routine that allowed him to work uninterruptedly on his current book, Lizzie's main job was attending to household chores and being available when her husband needed her. "We breakfast at 8 o'clock," she wrote her mother,

> then Herman goes to walk, and I fly up to put his room to rights, so that he can sit down to his desk immediately on his return. Then I bid him good bye with many charges to be an industrious boy, and not upset the inkstand, and then flourish the duster, make the bed, &c in my own room...then ding-ding goes the bell for luncheon. This is half past 12 o'clock—by this time we must expect

callers, and so must be dressed immediately after lunch. Then Herman insists upon my taking a walk every day of an hours length at least.... By the time I come home it is two o'clock and after, and then I must make myself look as be-witchingly as possible to meet Herman at dinner.... At four we dine, and after dinner is over, Herman and I come up to our room, and enjoy a cosy chat for an hour or so—or he reads me some of the chapters he has been writing in the day. Then he goes down town for a walk, looks at the papers in the reading-room &c, and returns about half past seven or eight. Then my work or my book is laid aside, and as he does not use his eyes but very little by candle light, I either read to him, or take a hand at whist for his amusement, or he listens to our reading or conversation, as best pleases him. For we all collect in the parlor in the evening, and generally one of us reads aloud for the benefit of the whole. Then we retire very early—at 10 o'clock we are all dispersed—indeed we think that quite a late hour to be up.[70]

Clearly, Lizzie doted on her husband. She darned his stockings and replaced the drawstrings he had a habit of pulling out every time he removed his drawers. She picked up and folded his clothes, tidied his room, filled his inkwell, preened his quill pen, lis-tened to what he had written during the day, and made the fair copies of his nearly illeg-ible drafts to be sent to the publisher. She was proud of her husband's work and happy to be a part of what he was doing as long as he treated her as a valued partner, and not as a maid.[71]

As a girl, Lizzie had been an avid horseback rider, and she greatly enjoyed danc-ing. Early in her marriage, she must have imagined that life with "Typee" would mean travel and theater and concerts, but she would eventually have to conform to the expec-tations of a moody, unpredictable husband and a demanding, critical mother-in-law. Like a plant transplanted to a pot that is too small, she would have little room to spread her roots and grow in the cramped garden supervised by Mother Melville.

Lizzie enjoyed days focused on her domestic routine and her husband's writing more than days when she had to "go and make calls" on Herman and Allan's friends and "Mrs M's old acquaintances," who were "*so* polite" that she was "fairly sick and tired of return-ing calls." Only to her mother did she dare confess: "You know ceremonious calls were always my abomination, and where they are all utter strangers and we have to send in our cards to show who we are, it is so much the worse. Excepting calls, I have scarcely visited at all. Herman is not fond of parties, and I don't care anything about them here."[72]

On Christmas Eve of 1847, Herman and Lizzie took Fanny to the Astor Place Theatre—"the first place of public amusement I have attended since I have been here," Lizzie told her mother. When Lem Jr. came to town for a respite from his studies at the end of January, they took him up into the steeple of Trinity Church to see the view, and to the Astor Place Theatre for a performance of Donizetti's *Lucrezia Borgia,* and to a party at the Thurstons'.[73]

Melville loved music, but he often preferred staying home to putting on a stiff collar and a tie to meet people who felt that because he was an *Author,* they could ask intrusive questions and make inane remarks. Sometimes he needed quiet evenings at home to be ready for the next day's work.

The women of the house treated Melville like a pasha, and he, like *Mardi*'s Donjalolo in his harem, enjoyed being pampered and indulged in his whims. If he sounded brusque or irritable or seemed preoccupied when he was working, they took it as a sign of genius and humored him, as they were flattered to think their "Typee" might one day be as famous as the great "Boz."

〜〜

Melville's genius was unfolding daily. In the solitude of his study, he was discovering whole new continents within his own imagination. The company of a wife who molded herself to her husband's moods gave him the emotional anchor he had never had; their relationship was the safe harbor from which he could risk venturing into forbidden territory, knowing he had somewhere to return. Unlike Lizzie, who could not escape family pressures by fleeing to her room to write a book or paint a picture, Melville had a sanctioned retreat and creative work to do.

Traveling into the depths of the self was the most dangerous journey and the hardest work of all. In that labyrinth lurked the monster contradiction, the monster paradox. Sometimes it was when he was in the bosom of his family that he felt most alone, and it was when he was alone that he most longed for company. Sometimes when Lizzie reached out to him, he withdrew as though he were resentful of her for loving him, as though he instinctively felt she had no right to love him if his own mother didn't love him, no right to love him until he could love himself. Meanwhile, some part of him always seemed to be in rebellion, always crying out with "a fierce, a cannibal delight, in the grief that shrieks to multiply itself," always ready to jump ship and return to the flesh-lovers of Typee.

Like many people, Melville had ambivalent feelings about marriage. The literature of the day provided him with hackneyed references to henpecked husbands and nagging wives, and he drew on these stock characters for comic relief in the early chapters of *Mardi,* his sequel to *Omoo.* Sometimes loving and flirtatious, sometimes edgy and aggressive, Melville designed these passages to get a rise out of Lizzie and his sisters as he read aloud to them each night what he had written during the day. To please Lizzie, he wove references to the "flower language" of courtship into the narrative, which further suggests that *Mardi* was written with his new bride and other women readers in mind as well as educated men.

Although some have seen the termagant Annatoo and similar characters as evidence of Melville's misogyny, more than likely he was twitting his wife and sisters, as well as catering to male readers who enjoyed jokes at the expense of women. While Lizzie and Melville's sisters were copying his manuscripts for the printers, female novelists were doing the cultural work of exposing masculine oppression and subverting negative stereotypes of women in texts that tens of thousands of American women were reading every day.[74]

Meanwhile, Melville was reading voraciously, borrowing from Duyckinck's enormous library of approximately sixteen thousand books, and from the New York Society Library, which he joined soon after moving to the city. When he was not reading, writing, or playing cards with his family, he was debating literature, philosophy, and art over brandy and cigars or punch with the Knights of the Round Table, a male version of a ladies' sewing circle, which, nonetheless, produced nothing as useful as mended trousers or newly fashioned garments for the family. These conversations and his reading stirred Melville to metaphysical and cosmic questioning, and before he knew it, his book was taking on a strange new life of its own.

As 1848 drew to a close, Melville was ready to sign a contract for *Mardi*, even though he had recently told John Murray that he was disappointed in the "pecuniary value" put on *Omoo*. For his part, Murray was still convinced that the success of Melville's next book would be jeopardized by readers' doubts about the authenticity of the first two: "I wish some means could be taken to convince the English Public that your Books are not fictions, imitations of Robinson Crusoe—'Tis this Feeling of being tricked which impedes their Circulation here."[75]

In his reply, Melville ignored Murray's objections, preferring to reassure his publisher that the earlier books had not exhausted his material and that his sequels would not be "barren of novelty." The new book, he explained, "clothes the whole subject in new attractions & constant in one cluster all that is romantic, whimsical & poetic in Polynusia [*sic*]." He further alluded to the "rather bold aim" he had for his narrative, without saying what he had in mind. It undoubtedly annoyed him to have to defend his book to his own publisher after the first two had proved so popular with readers.[76]

Melville asked Murray for double the agreed-upon advance to carry him through until he could finish the manuscript, but the British publisher refused, insisting again on receiving some concrete proof of Melville's experiences. Exasperated by Murray's continual harping on the subject, Melville put the letter aside and did not answer it, probably because he was now writing furiously and didn't want to upset himself.

He wrote on, driven from his "sportive sail" by a "blast resistless," knowing he had left the safe world of factual narratives like Dr. Frederick Debell Bennett's *Narrative of a Whaling Voyage Round the Globe* (London, 1840) and the "old ontologies" of the classical philosophers for the world of Baron Munchausen, the Arabian Nights, medieval fabulists, and Oriental travelers, as well as Spenser, Swift, Rabelais, Burton, Coleridge, Lamb, Emerson, Carlyle, and the "crack'd Archangel," Sir Thomas Browne. These worthies had "stepped forward and given me their hands," which left him no choice but to follow his "crowned and sceptered instinct," renouncing the "good graces of those nymphs" the Unities, and embracing the "expanding soul" of a new book that was straining to break the bonds of conventional narrative.

As he sat hunched in his third-floor study, working on *Mardi,* wrapped in blankets against the cold, Melville knew the risks he was taking by allowing himself to soar into the metaphysical stratosphere. Anticipating the carping of critics, he has one of his characters ask why the writer Lombardo would "choose a vehicle so crazy?" To this, the philosopher Babbalanja replies, "It was his nature, I suppose."[77]

Evert Duyckinck, editor of The Literary World, *helped launch Melville's career and became his close friend.*

TEN

CREATING THE CREATIVE

On February 14, 1849, Mr. and Mrs. Herman Melville attended the poet Anne Charlotte Lynch's annual Valentine party. At this gathering they had an opportunity to meet New York artists and members of the "author-tribe," as Miss Lynch's list included, among other luminaries, Fitz-Greene Halleck, Nathaniel Parker Willis, Bayard Taylor, Charles Fenno Hoffman, Parke Godwin, Henry T. Tuckerman, Felix Darley, Asher Durand, G. P. A. Healy, Seba Smith, Caroline Kirkland, Grace Greenwood, William Cullen Bryant, Catharine Maria Sedgwick, and the celebrated preacher Dr. Orville Dewey.[1]

It was customary at this party for guests to compose and read Valentines to one another. Bayard Taylor, a poet whose popular travel book Views A-foot; or, Europe Seen with Knapsack and Staff *had been published by Wiley & Putnam in 1846, saluted "Typee" as the "bright painter of these tropic isles / That stud the blue waves, far apart." Wishing him "summer smiles / And fadeless foliage of the heart," Taylor, whose poem "The Persian Boy" was a celebration of "manly love...as tender and true as love of woman," invoked the "guardian genius" of the Happy Valley to "taboo" Melville's path from every ill. The follow-*

ing day, N. P. Willis published in the *Home Journal* the forty-eight verses that were read at the party.[2]

Lizzie had a marvelous time at the party. "I passed off for *Miss* Melville and as such was quite a belle!" she wrote her mother. Much as she enjoyed these occasions, however, she knew late nights were "very injurious" to Herman's writing. Whenever he ate a big supper, drank heavily, and stayed out late, he didn't "feel bright for writing the next day." Finally she decided—in the way some women have of revising their desires to match those of their husbands—that she, too, felt "very dissipated" after such parties and that she was content "to stay at home as long as he will stay with me."[3]

In Lizzie's day, respectable women either went out escorted by their husbands, remained home to receive callers, or returned calls in the company of female relatives. Respectable women did not attend evening entertainments with women friends, and they certainly never ventured out alone. Men, by contrast, felt entitled to have a night or two out a week with other men at private clubs, restaurants that had private rooms, or homes large enough to accommodate parties not attended by the wives. These all-male gatherings were considered a key to successful business dealings in the modern world. Home was supposed to be a haven from the competitive pressures of the marketplace, a sanctuary whose lamps were lit and tended by those vestals known as wives.

Evert Duyckinck's famous "cellar," where artists and writers gathered to discuss literature, politics, and philosophy over brandy and cigars, had almost as much cachet as an alcove at Delmonico's. Melville frequently attended Duyckinck's punch parties and Saturday-night suppers and sought Duyckinck's opinion on manuscripts. "Melville the other night brought me a few chapters of his new book which in the poetry and wildness of the things will be ahead of Typee & Omoo," Duyckinck told his brother George.[4]

"Wild" was how Melville felt while he was writing *Mardi*. He could feel dark undercurrents tugging at his soul as he searched for a way to express what had gone unsaid in the two travelogues for which he was famous. Voyaging had given him visions of self and society quite different from those instilled by family, church, and school. At times he felt the kind of terror Tommo experienced when he sensed that crossing boundaries might put him beyond the possibility of return. The power that surged through him felt like demonic possession or religious ecstasy. "All men are possessed by devils," says old Bardianna in *Mardi*: "Devils are divers; —strong devils, and weak devils, knowing devils, and silly devils; mad devils, and mild devils; devils, merely devils; devils themselves bedeviled; devils, doubly bedeviled." The trick was to go under but not let the Devil hold you there.[5]

At times Melville felt he had struck a Faustian bargain:

> No mailed hand lifted up against a traveler in woods can so appall, as we ourselves. We are full of ghosts and spirits; we are as graveyards full of buried

dead, that start to life before us. And all our dead sires, verily, are in us; *that* is their immortality. From sire to son, we go on multiplying corpses in ourselves; for all of which, are resurrections. Every thought's a soul of some past poet, hero, sage. We are fuller than a city. Woe is it, that reveals these things. He knows himself, and all that's in him, who knows adversity. To scale great heights, we must come out of lowermost depths. The way to heaven is through hell. We need fiery baptisms in the fiercest flames of our own bosoms. We must feel our hearts hot—hissing in us. And ere their fire is revealed, it must burn its way out of us; though it consume us and itself.[6]

As he wrote, he emerged from the ashes like the phoenix, experiencing the "play of freedom & invention known only to the Romancer & poet," a creative billowing of his imagination. Like the genius Lombardo whom he describes in *Mardi*, he felt his book galloping away with him as he "wrote right on; and so doing, got deeper and deeper into himself" until he plunged through "baffling woods" and at last came out "into a serene, sunny, ravishing region: full of sweet scents, singing birds, wild plaints, roguish laughs, prophetic voices," exclaiming "I have created the creative." These two passages reveal what may be the greatest secret of Melville's genius: his ability to heal himself by writing.[7]

By March 25, Melville was in such high spirits about what was flowing from his pen that he almost defiantly told John Murray he would not furnish the requested "documentary evidence" of the authenticity of *Typee* and *Omoo*, and that, furthermore, this book would be a departure from the earlier ones: "To be blunt: the work I shall next publish will in downright earnest [be] a 'Romance of Polynisian [*sic*] Adventure'—But why this? The truth is, Sir, that the reiterated imputation of being a romancer in disguise has at last pricked me into a resolution to show those who may take any interest in the matter, that a *real* romance of mine is no Typee or Omoo, & is made of different stuff altogether."[8]

He told Murray he had started out to write a "bona-fide narrative of my adventures in the Pacific," but "proceeding in my narrative of *facts* I began to feel an invincible distaste for the same; & a longing to plume my pinions for a flight, & felt irked, cramped & fettered by plodding along with dull common places,—So suddenly abandoning the thing alltogether [*sic*], I went to work heart & soul at a romance.... It is something new I assure you, & original if nothing more.... It opens like a true narrative—like Omoo for example, on shipboard—& the romance & poetry of the thing thence grow continuously, till it becomes a story wild enough I assure you & with a meaning too."[9]

Fearing that John Murray would bring it out in a "dish-water" format designed to please "the circulating Library," he had asked Murray not to put the usual "by the author of 'Typee' and 'Omoo'" on the title page, so as "to separate *Mardi* as much as possible from those books" and not predispose readers to expect more of the same. Having opened his long letter by accusing Murray of selling his soul to parley "with a ghost," or "imposter shade," he closed it by arguing that if Murray did not stand in the way of his creating a romance, it would be a real "literary achievement," and he would produce a book that "by sheer force of contrast" would convince skeptics of "the truth of Typee & Omoo." Murray's repeated request for "documentary evidence" of his having been in the South Seas exasperated Melville: "Bless my soul, sir, will you Britons not credit that an American can be a gentleman, & have read the Waverly Novels, tho every digit may have been in the tar-bucket?—You make miracles of what are commonplaces to us.—I will give no evidence—Truth is mighty & will prevail—& shall & must."[10]

Most readers could be satisfied with a few little truths, however, as long as they were entertaining as well as edifying. They looked for strong plots and characters with whom they could identify, either negatively or positively, and they looked for insight into their lives and the lives of others. Melville's obsession with discovering "Truth" and revealing it to readers of his novels was bound to strike most people as excessive.

Educated Americans tended to be eclectic in their reading tastes, and letters written by Melville family members and their friends show that during the 1840s and 1850s, they read *Dombey and Son, Vanity Fair, The Newcombes, Henry Esmond, Villette, Jane Eyre, The Scarlet Letter, The Blithedale Romance,* and *The Linwoods* by Catharine Maria Sedgwick. Gus's friend Augusta Whipple Hunter casually mentions reading Goethe's autobiography, and Mary Blatchford confessed to preferring Ik Marvel's *Reveries of a Bachelor* to *David Copperfield.* When *Typee* appeared and Gus discovered that Mary Blatchford had not read it right away, her friend explained that she was being "kept company" by Aeschylus, Sophocles, Virgil, and Dante just when Herman's book appeared; she planned to read *Typee* for relaxation after she had finished Grote's *History of Greece,* the work that capped her study of the classics.[11]

Obviously the Melvilles and their friends read many more books than are mentioned in their letters. None of them, for example, mentions reading Harriet Beecher Stowe's *Uncle Tom's Cabin,* either when it was serialized by *The National Era,* or when the book appeared in 1852 and sold a record 300,000 copies during its first year. Yet it seems impossible that Melville and members of his circle would not have read a book that everyone in America was reading and discussing.[12]

Reading aloud in the parlor in the evening, sharing the latest story, was a primary source of entertainment for most readers, and in genteel households, men and women knew many of the same books and often read the same periodicals. With readers like these, Melville was optimistic about expanding his audience by bridging the growing gap between popular fiction and serious literature.[13]

It was Melville's nature to turn a good idea into a mission, a pragmatic goal into an all-absorbing, passionate crusade. He wanted each book he wrote to be a breakthrough of some kind, to take him beyond the simple creation of a text to a new place, and *Mardi* was opening the floodgates. Approaching his twenty-ninth birthday, newly married, the oldest living son of a proud family, and a celebrity of sorts, Melville was experiencing a sense of his own power, and it was exhilarating.

The manic intensity with which he worked worried those who had to live with him, however. He was so possessed by *Mardi* that Lizzie began to fear for his health, and sometimes his sanity. He would sequester himself in his room for hours without moving or eating or drinking anything, then emerge with a "frequent exclamation" such as "Oh Lizzy! the book!–the book–what *will* become of the *Book*!" When this demon, whom he personified in *Mardi* as Azzageddi, took hold of him, it scared those who did not understand that the pleasure of creation can often involve pain.[14]

With Melville in this kind of compositional frenzy, Lizzie was looking forward to a visit from her cousin, Samuel Hay Savage, in May, as his company would provide her with an escort and a chance for some diversion. She wrote him a long letter, and to make sure he would not change his mind, she assured him, "Notwithstanding our family is so large, we have *two* unoccupied bedrooms, and each of us plenty of rooms besides. We are looking for Tom home some time this spring to add to our colony."[15]

Lizzie was delighted when Herman announced he would take a short break from his work, even though he went to Pittsfield without her, apparently on family business. While he was there, he missed "the idol of his heart," and the April weather gave him such an unpleasantly "cold reception" that he was forced to admit "the country is not *always* beautiful," according to Priscilla Melvill, who passed along the news to Augusta from Canandaigua, New York, where she was teaching school.[16]

With her husband away, Lizzie had time to reflect on her new life. Having married relatively late, after losing one beau to early death and the other to religious differences, she had fewer illusions about marriage than did many brides: "I think both men and women miss it who marry at an early age because they only anticipate the happiness which would be just the same to them after enjoying years of pleasure and freedom from care, which otherwise they lose–I am very, very happy now, more so than ever before, but still I'm very glad I waited as long as I did before entering into the 'married matrimonial state'–for I feel as young now as ever I did, whereas if I'd 'done it' at 18 or 20 years old, as some girls do, why I might have been quite an elderly matron now, and looked back to my school days as something that happened before the flood."[17]

In late April the shipping journals carried a notice that the whaler *Theophilus Chase* was homeward bound, and Maria started "watching and counting the days with great anxiety for [Tom] is the baby of the family and his mothers pet." Tom arrived home safely after a successful cruise, announcing his intention to go to sea again right away, this time on a merchant vessel, as he had decided on a maritime career. Herman took time out from his writing to help Tom secure a berth that would prepare him for future advancement, and Tom apparently navigated the shoals of young manhood safely by spending those years unmarried and away at sea.[18]

On May 5, a harried Lizzie jotted a note to Hope Shaw, saying "the book is done now," but this was wishful thinking on her part. Apologizing for not writing a longer letter, Lizzie explained that while she was copying the "final" sheets of her husband's book, she had accidentally torn up her longer letter, thinking it was her copy sheet for Herman's manuscript. Asking her mother to excuse her careless punctuation, Lizzie explained that Herman asked her not to punctuate the fair copies of his manuscripts so he could supply the punctuation himself. This new self-deprecating tone suggests that Mother Melville's obsession about other people's writing was having an effect on Lizzie, as her punctuation (her spelling, too, for that matter) was far superior to that of anyone in the Melville family, including Herman. The sudden tension in her letter to her mother suggests that the Melvilles were undermining the confidence built up by twenty-five years of careful nurturing by her parents and teachers.

When Lizzie's "rose cold," as she called it, began to bother her in early June, Herman urged her to leave the "warm dry atmosphere" of New York for the "salt air" of Boston as soon as the copying was finished. Lizzie, however, didn't think she would "feel at ease enough to enjoy my visit without him," and besides, she told her mother gaily, she was "afraid to trust him to finish up the book without me!"[19]

Melville's March 25 letter hinting at changes in the direction of the book did not please John Murray. He had no desire to publish a "romance," Polynesian or otherwise; he wanted a factual account of whaling in the Pacific. Faced with new restrictions on international copyright, he may have been looking for an excuse to dissolve the firm's connection with Melville, as on May 20, he apparently refused Melville's request for money and again demanded "original documents" to prove *Typee*'s authenticity.[20]

Melville was determined to resist these attempts to intimidate him: "In spite of the Antarctic tenor of your epistle," he replied, "I still adhere to my first resolution of submitting the sheets of my new work to your experienced eye.–I fear you abhor romances; But fancy nevertheless that possibly you may for once relent." He told Murray he had changed his mind about furnishing proof of his adventures, because one or two original documents had recently come to hand that he had planned to enclose, but he had mislaid one of them, so he would wait to send anything until the missing document turned up. Of course the missing document was never found, and undoubtedly Murray was not fooled.[21]

It wouldn't have mattered, anyway, what Melville told his publisher at this point, because circumstances were about to propel him into a new stage of composition that would make *Mardi* outrageously different from the book Murray wanted him to write. In June he purchased a copy of the Reverend Henry Francis Cary's translation of *The Divine Comedy*, and as he read, he discovered an epic landscape that corresponded to the "dark wood" through which he had been wandering in his imagination. Inspired by Dante, he took off on a new tack that would take him many thousands of miles into allegory before his "chartless" voyage came to an end.[22]

~~~

Eighteen forty-eight was a year of revolutions. In February the constitutional monarchy of Louis-Philippe, the "citizen King" of France, fell, sparking revolutions all over Europe. Austrians were demanding an autonomous government within the Austro-Hungarian monarchy, and Magyars led by Lajos Kossuth were demanding complete independence and dissolution of the Empire. Horace Greeley sent Margaret Fuller, an avid supporter of Garibaldi and Mazzini, to cover the revolution in Rome for the *New-York Daily Tribune*, and her dispatches, along with appeals by Kossuth and other leaders who looked to the one successful revolutionary nation in the world for support in their efforts to overthrow repressive regimes, kept Americans informed about events in Europe.[23]

In England, Karl Marx and Friedrich Engels had finished their economic research in the British Museum, and published a manifesto declaring that industrial capitalism was about to collapse from inner rot and that only an idealistic communist government could save mankind. Their book was not translated into English for two decades; meanwhile, the Chartists, who were calling for such modest reforms as universal male suffrage and the secret ballot, could not get their reforms through Parliament. American newspapers reported, rather gloatingly, that England was staggering under a huge debt and that dissension over Queen Victoria's policies would lead to the dissolution of Parliament.

The United States was in the throes of a presidential campaign, with the battle lines being drawn for a congressional debate over David Wilmot's proposal to forbid the extension of slavery into territories seized from Mexico. Debate over the Wilmot Proviso split the two major political parties, with New York State's antislavery Democrats voting to hold their own convention. They were known as "Barnburners" because they advocated shutting the door on slavery before "the horse" of liberty could get away, and the Democrats who went to the party convention were known as "Hunkers" because they voted to "hunker down" to save the Union at all costs.

Antislavery women had been furious ever since the World Anti-Slavery Convention in 1840 had excluded women on the grounds that they could not vote, so Lucretia Mott and Elizabeth Cady Stanton decided to organize their own convention. On June 22, 1848, in Seneca Falls, New York, the women proclaimed a "Declaration of Sentiments" that likened male rule to British tyranny and women's rights to the liberties for which patriots such as Melville's grandfathers had fought.

Lizzie Melville probably had little time or energy to worry about free soil and women's rights, as by now she knew that she was pregnant. Herman must have been overjoyed to learn that his first child was on the way, but also worried about Lizzie, knowing that her mother had died giving birth to her. In an era when childbed mortality for both mothers and babies was high, nine months could seem like an eternity.

Allan and Sophia, who was also pregnant, were planning to take Fanny with them on a short vacation to Black River, New Jersey. Herman was promising to take Lizzie to the Berkshires in August, after he had finished writing, and after they had paid a visit to the Shaws. Allan was running as the Hunker candidate for the New York Assembly against both a Whig and a Free Soiler, and although Herman would dedicate *Mardi* to Allan in gratitude for his assistance with contract negotiations, he made mockery of Tammany Hall in his new book.

Guert Gansevoort returned home that summer with a rehabilitated reputation, thanks to his heroic service with General Winfield Scott's army at Vera Cruz, spurring Melville to satirize imperialistic policies. As always, Herman's views ran counter to those of other members of his family.[24]

While Herman and Lizzie were in Boston in July, the Shaws gave a dinner party in their honor that included among its thirty guests Richard Henry Dana Jr., who had since Melville had last seen him been instrumental in the formation of the Free Soil Party. Several nights later, Dana invited Melville to a party he had arranged at the Parker House, where Melville met many of Boston's leading abolitionists, most of whom were considered dangerous radicals by New Yorkers, whose city's economy was heavily dependent on the cotton trade.[25]

In August, Herman took Lizzie to Pittsfield to rusticate at Melvill House as promised. His aunt Mary had moved back from Galena after her husband's death, and she and Robert and his "very quiet, timid, little wife," as Fanny Appleton Longfellow described her, had turned the old homestead into an inn. Charles Sumner had been a guest there, as had Henry Wadsworth Longfellow and his wife Fanny, a former summer resident of Pittsfield.[26]

After their vacation, Herman took Lizzie back to her parents' home to wait for the baby, then returned to New York to finish his book. He was still adding chapters to *Mardi* when the new year began, and he was reading Thackeray's *Vanity Fair* for recreation. Once Augusta finished making the fair copy of the manuscript, Herman delivered it to his publisher, and while they waited for the proof sheets, Gus went back to researching baby names.[27]

In the way of most old-fashioned fathers, Melville assumed that the vigorous kicker would be a boy, and he wanted to give him a name that would link him to his forebears as well as distinguish him from the Peters and Hermans and Thomases and Allans of the family. When Lizzie wrote from Boston suggesting Malcolm, a fine old Highland name, Augusta checked a genealogical tree and gave her enthusiastic approval to the choice: "Malcolm Melville!—What a beautiful name. There is something noble in its very sound. *Kind Lizzie* . . . You know the name comes from Grandma Melville's side of the house— the Scollay family." Repeating the name "Malcolm" over and over again for its musical sound, she could see a vision of Malcolm "in his plaided [*sic*] kilt, with his soft blue eyes, and his long flaxen curls."[28]

Everyone wanted the book to be printed and bound before the baby came. "The last proof sheets are through. 'Mardi's' a book!—Ah my own Koztanza!" Augusta exclaimed, thoroughly imbued by this time with the language and spirit of Lombardo's fictitious masterpiece. "Child of many prayers. Oro's blessing on thee."[29]

At the end of January 1849, Melville shipped a set of proofs of *Mardi* to John Murray with a request for two hundred guineas. He also repeated his earlier request that references to his two previous books not appear on the title page, as he wanted to differentiate the new book from them. Murray refused to meet his terms, but the manuscript was subsequently accepted by Richard Bentley, who agreed to pay Melville the princely two hundred guineas he had failed to obtain from Murray against the "moiety of the profits." Bentley was very enthusiastic about publishing *Mardi* and proposed a handsome three-volume set bound in forest green cloth embossed with gold.[30]

Melville then rejoined Lizzie in Boston, where he was able to walk to the Boston Athenaeum every day to borrow books on Judge Shaw's card. He also attended lectures, including one by Ralph Waldo Emerson. Although Emerson was reputed by New Yorkers to be "full of transcendentalisms, myths & oracular gibberish," Melville found the Concord Sage "quite intelligible." His favorable comments about Emerson prompted Evert Duyckinck to worry that Melville was turning into a transcendentalist. "Nay," Melville responded, "I do not oscillate in Emerson's rainbow, but prefer rather to hang myself in mine own halter than swing in any other man's swing."[31]

Flattering Duyckinck, whose Dutch name meant "diving duck," Melville wrote: "I love men who dive. Any fish can swim near the surface, but it takes a great whale to go down stairs five miles or more; & if he dont attain the bottom, why, all the lead in Galena can't fashion the plummet that will. I'm not talking of Mr. Emerson now—but of the whole corps of thought-divers, that have been diving & coming up again with blood-shot eyes since the world began."[32]

Melville also attended readings by the celebrated British actress Fanny Kemble, who had recently returned to the stage. Kemble, a niece of another noted actress, Sarah Siddons, had retired from the stage in 1832 to marry Pierce Butler, a Pennsylvania businessman. When he inherited a large plantation in Georgia, they moved there, and she was exposed to the horrors of chattel slavery and aspects of her husband's character that repulsed her. She took the unheard-of step of leaving him and suing for divorce, whereupon he sued for desertion, embroiling the couple and their children in a scandalous legal battle. Kemble was fortunate enough to be defended by the eminent Rufus Choate, and to be able to support herself by giving dramatic readings and through her writing.[33]

Although Melville complained that Kemble read Desdemona's part in *Othello* "like a boarding school miss," he thought she made "a glorious Lady Macbeth" despite being "so unfemininely masculine that had she not, on unimpeachable authority, borne children, I should be curious to learn the result of a surgical examination of her person in private." It was an uncharacteristically crude remark.[34]

⁓

At seven o'clock on the morning of February 16, 1849, Malcolm Melville was born in Boston, and two days later in New York, the first of Allan and Sophia's five daughters arrived. They named the baby Maria Gansevoort Melville, soon to be called "Milie" by her admiring family and friends.

Thrilled to see his new little son, Melville turned a congratulatory note to Allan into an extravagant rhapsody on his own child. This letter—so extraordinary that it deserves to be quoted in full—makes Malcolm sound like Paul Bunyan, Lancelot, Charlemagne, and one of P. T. Barnum's star attractions all rolled into one bouncing baby boy. The letter begins: "I have yours of yesterday. I am rejoiced that Sophia is well after her happy delivery," and continues in a torrent of hyperbole:

> Lizzie is doing well, also the phenomenon, which weighs I know not how many pennyweights,—I would say hundred-weights.—We desired much to have him weighed, but it was thought that no hay-scales in town were strong enough. It takes three nurses to dress him; and he is as valiant as Julius Cesear [*sic*].— He's a perfect prodigy. —If the worst comes to the worst, I shall let him out by the month to Barnum; and take the tour of Europe with him. I think of calling him Barbarossa-Adolphus-Ferdinand-Otho-Grandissimo Hercules-Sampson-Bonaparte-Lambert. —If you can suggest any thing better or more characteris-

tic, pray, inform me of it by the next post. —There was a terrible commotion here at the time of the event. —I had men stationed at all the church bells, 24 hours before hand; & when the Electric Telegraph informed them of the fact— such a ding-donging you never heard. —All the engines came out, thinking the State-House was on fire.

Of course the news was sent on by telegraph to Washington & New Orleans. —When Old Zack heard of it—he is reported to have said—"Mark me: that boy will be President of the United States before he dies." —In New Orleans, the excitement was prodigious. Stocks rose & brandy fell. —I have not yet heard from Europe & Pekin. But doubtless, ere this, they must have placed props against the Great-Wall. —The harbor here is empty: —all the ships, brigs, schooners & smacks have scattered in all directions with the news for foreign parts. —The crowd has not yet left the streets, gossiping of the event. —The number of calls at 49 Mt. Vernon Street is incalculable. Ten porters suffice not to receive the cards; and Canning the waiter, dropped down dead last night thro' pure exhaustion. —Who would have thought that the birth of one little man, when ten thousand of other little men, & little horses, & little guinea-pigs & little roosters, & the Lord only knows what, are being born—that the birth of one such a little phenomenon, should create such a panic thro' the world: —nay, even in heaven; for last night I dreampt [*sic*] that his good angel had secured a seat for him above; & that the Devel [*sic*] roared terribly bethinking him of the lusty foe to sin born into this sinful world.[35]

Signed, "H. Melville," the letter is addressed to "The Reverend Father in Wedlock, Allan Melville," with commas between his and Allan's names so the honorific appears to refer to both of them.

Lizzie's doctor was George Hayward, a cousin of Lemuel Shaw's who had distinguished himself by being the first physician to use anesthesia during an operation, but even with her beloved family physician in attendance, Lizzie had difficulty giving birth to the *wunderkind*. Two weeks after the delivery, Judge Shaw told Peter Gansevoort she was "recovering gradually but slowly, from the severe trial, which however she sustained remarkably well."[36]

During the two months the new parents stayed in Boston, it rained almost constantly. Melville spent much of his time reading Emerson's essays, Seneca's moral philosophy, and essays by Eastlake and Hazlitt on modern painting techniques and aesthetic theories, which influenced Melville's later work.[37]

The most exciting discovery Herman made during this period was Shakespeare, whose works he had avoided reading because the small print in all the editions he had seen thus far strained his weak eyes. When he came across a seven-volume edition of the plays printed "in glorious great type, every letter whereof is a soldier, & the top of every 't' like a musket barrel," he dove into it with a will. "Dolt & ass that I am I have lived more than 29 years, & until a few days ago, never made close acquaintance with the divine William," he wrote Evert Duyckinck. "Ah, he's full of sermons-on-the-mount, and, gentle, aye, almost as Jesus. I take such men to be inspired…if another Messiah ever comes twill be in Shakespeare's person."[38]

Having grown up hearing the King James version of the Bible, he delighted in Shakespeare's sonorous, supple poetry, dazzling metaphors, deep knowledge of human nature, complex characterizations, and genius for capturing the universal truth in a specific situation. He was so impressed at how brilliantly Shakespeare captured the essence of politics in *Julius Caesar* that in the margin beside Casca's description of the "rabblement" hooting and clapping for Caesar with their sweaty hands, he jotted, "Tammany Hall."[39]

Despite his love for Shakespeare, Melville claimed not to be one of those "*snobs* who burn their tuns of rancid fat at his shrine" and treat the Bard with pedantic solemnity. "I would to God," he wrote Duyckinck, "Shakspeare [*sic*] had lived later, & promenaded in Broadway. Not that I might have had the pleasure of leaving my card for him at the Astor, or made merry with him over a bowl of fine Duyckinck punch; but that the muzzle which all men wore on their souls in the Elizabethan day, might not have intercepted Shakspere's [*sic*] full articulations. For I hold it a verity, that even Shakspeare, [*sic*] was not a frank man to the uttermost. And, indeed, who in this intolerant Universe is, or can be? But the Declaration of Independence makes a difference."[40]

Duyckinck was a little worried that Melville's tendency to write books that defied popular taste would hurt both Melville's reputation and his own. He tried to establish Melville as a national writer who embraced both New England and New York by asking him to review Francis Parkman's *The California and Oregon Trail* and James Fenimore Cooper's *The Sea Lions* for *The Literary World.* Melville "warmly" recommended Cooper's last novel as "one of the happiest" productions of "our National Novelist," and in "Mr. Parkman's Tour," he called Parkman's account of his adventures among the Indians "very entertaining" and "obviously truthful," with a "true wild-game flavor." He criticized Parkman, however, for the common fault of "civilized beings sojourning among savages" to regard primitive cultures "with disdain & contempt," calling it "wholly wrong."[41]

Melville had composed *Mardi* in a state of highly charged intellectual and emotional energy, and he was facing the letdown that inevitably follows such a monumental undertaking. As he awaited publication of *Mardi*, Melville was acutely conscious that an artist who wanted to break new ground, rise to new heights, plunge to new depths, and weave together factual information, fictional invention, philosophical speculation, and social commentary risked being misunderstood by readers and reviewers, but as Emerson had said in his essay "Self-Reliance," "To be great is to be misunderstood." By expressing in *Mardi* the kind of cosmic consciousness he had experienced, Melville hoped to point the way to a type of fiction as expansive and diverse as the American continent. The effect on Walt Whitman, whom he never met, was profound.

Shortly before he left Boston, Melville learned that Charles Fenno Hoffman, Duyckinck's successor for a time at *The Literary World*, had suffered a psychotic breakdown and was in an asylum:

> This going mad of a friend or acquaintance comes straight home to every man who feels his soul in him,—which few men do. For in all of us lodges the same fuel to light the same fire. And he who had never felt, momentarily, what madness is has but a mouthful of brains. What sort of sensation permanent madness is may be very well imagined—just as we imagine how we felt when we were infants, tho' we can not recall it. In both conditions we are irresponsible & riot like gods without fear of fate. —It is the climax of a mad night of revelry when the blood has been transmuted into brandy—But if we prate much of this thing we shall be illustrating our own propositions.[42]

By portraying himself as a mad "scribbler," Melville was acknowledging the Dionysian wildness that impelled him to mix epic, satire, and poetry with nautical adventure. The enormous bursts of creativity he experienced, plus the never-forgotten horror of his father's derangement, constantly made him wonder how deep a "thought-diver" could go without falling into the abyss.

⌒

The Melvilles brought Malcolm and his nurse, Ellen Sullivan, home in early April. Lizzie was feeling strong again, and Augusta, who considered Malcolm her special pet, was on hand to push the royal carriage through the park.

Mardi: and a Voyage Thither was published in England on March 16, but it did not appear in New York until mid-April. This great, sprawling saga reflects a number of influences on its author beyond his travels in the South Seas: his voracious reading of romances, poetry, and philosophy; the esoteric gabfests of the Duyckinck circle; his study of mythology and Oriental lore; religious speculations; the political and social upheavals of the period; astrological arcana and astronomical references stimulated by the discovery of a new comet by the Nantucket astronomer Maria Mitchell in December

1847; the lectures of the botanist Louis Agassiz in 1848; and the language of flowers that Melville had learned from Lizzie. The book's energy and extravagance reflect his eclectic reading, intellectual curiosity, vigorous imagination, and newly married state.[43]

The opening chapters of *Mardi* hold to Melville's original intention of producing a narrative of the whale fishery in the South Seas. The narrator, who is as yet unnamed, jumps ship with his crewmate Jarl the Viking, and they drift on the open ocean in a small boat until they meet a wrecked brigantine with two survivors, the half-breed Samoa and his shrewish wife, Annatoo. Their Punch-and-Judy marriage is a burlesque of domestic ideology. Annatoo is anything but the "angel in the household" so dear to Victorians; she is a she-devil who physically abuses Samoa, whose smashed arm has to be amputated. The narrator and Jarl rescue this combative couple, and they all set out together in a small boat called a "chamois" because of the way it leaps "from watery cliff to watery cliff."[44]

After Annatoo falls overboard and drowns, they encounter a thirty-foot-long catamaran under the command of a sinister priest who warns them away from a curious tent that looks "as if it contained their Eleusinian mysteries." The narrator cannot resist sneaking into this sanctuary, where he discovers a "beautiful maiden" named Yillah, who is to be sacrificed to the gods of Tedaidee. Falling in love with the golden-haired, white-skinned princess at first sight, he kills the priest and rescues her.

Together they flee to the island of Odo, whose subjects, believing the narrator is their sun-god, call him "Taji." On Odo, ruled by King Media, Taji and Yillah enjoy a blissful idyll until they discover that this "land of pleasure unalloyed and plenty without pause" exists only for the king and his nobles. Most of his subjects live "in secret places . . . noisome caves, lairs for beasts, not human homes." Suddenly, three maidens appear and throw cryptic flower-messages at the lovers, and when their dark queen, called Hautia, appears, Yillah disappears.[45]

Taji, Jarl, and Samoa set out to find Yillah with their new companions, the repentant King Media of Odo; the philosopher Babbalanja; the historian Mohi, or "Braid Beard"; and the poet Yoomy. Pursued by the three sons of Aleema the priest and the enigmatic Queen Hautia, they explore the Mardian archipelago, whose islands epitomize human follies and vice, or represent the nations of the world. Naturally they cannot locate Yillah on absolutist, undemocratic islands such as Dominora (England), Franko (France), and Porpheero (Europe), or on Maramma (the Vatican), which puts authoritarian orthodoxy before the simple truths of the human heart.

The poet Yoomy urges his companions to seek Yillah in the "springland Vivenza," but King Media doubts that Yillah would find Vivenza a congenial place to stay because he has heard that Vivenza is "braggadocio in Mardi" whose citizens resemble "an army of spurred and crested roosters" crowing "at the resplendent rising of their sun," which suggests Gansevoort Melville and Young America.[46]

Even so, they sail to Vivenza, and their canoes pass beneath a majestic arch with immense hieroglyphics that read: "In-this-republican-land-all-men-are-born-free-and-equal." As they approach the arch, however, their "Champollion" Mohi notices a tiny qualifier chiseled in an angle of the arch, which says, "Except-the-tribe-of-Hamo," an allusion to the southern argument that the African is a descendant of Noah's third son, Ham, who was cursed by God for his disrespect to his father As Frederick Douglass said when asked to explain the southern rationale for slavery, "God cursed Ham, and therefore American slavery is right."[47]

Landing in Vivenza, they meet a citizen who proudly offers to lead them to the "great Temple of Freedom," but the first thing they see there is "a man with a collar round his neck" raising a "tappa standard" whose red stripes correspond to the "red marks of stripes" on the backs of the "collared menials" who serve the Temple chieftains. Drawing on his 1847 visits to Congress, Melville portrays these "dusky chiefs" as loutish men who pick their teeth, clean their ears, and spit tobacco during the Grand Council meetings, unmistakably burlesquing Daniel Webster, John Van Buren, James K. Polk, and Senator William Allan of Ohio. When the travelers see posters advertising rewards for the return of fugitives, they conclude that Yillah cannot be found on an island whose central temple has been built by slaves, so they head for Vivenza's milder southern shores.[48]

There they find men shackled together, toiling in the noonday sun to harvest plants for brutish masters who whip them savagely. When the travelers protest, the captives' overseer, Nulli, "a cadaverous, ghost-like man" with steel-gray hair and eyes like corposant-balls—obviously modeled on John C. Calhoun—argues that the slaves have no souls. When the visitors express shock, Nulli accuses them of hypocrisy, pointing out that the northern mill workers are also "slaves" because of their long hours and inhuman treatment. Southern apologists for slavery argued that chattel slavery was more humane than wage slavery, as they referred to the factory system, because factory owners in the North had no investment in their workers and simply replaced the sick or injured, whereas plantation owners had a financial stake in the welfare of their chattels and would feed, clothe, and house them properly, and take care of them if they became disabled.[49]

King Media pronounces slavery "a sin" that tears families apart, and when Yoomy raises the possibility that the slaves may someday revolt, the historian Mohi prophesies, "These South savannas may yet prove battlefields." Babbalanja brands slavery "a blot, foul as the crater-pool of hell," and, certain that Yillah cannot be found here, they flee.[50]

The only island that does not exemplify the vices and follies of mankind is Serenia, a land with no government. It is the home of Alma (Christ), whose "precepts rebuke the arrogance of place and power." Babbalanja decides to stay on Serenia, where peace, love, and harmony flourish forever, but even in a Christian utopia where people live by pure love and enjoy complete happiness, Yillah cannot be found.[51]

Love cannot be whole if its dark side is not acknowledged and confronted, so Taji must enter the bower of the temptress Hautia, who shows him Yillah's rose pearl as a token and a vision of Yillah's drowned face under the water offering him sexual pleasure and eternal youth. Uncertain to the end whether this means that Hautia and Yillah are one, or that Hautia has murdered Yillah and stolen the pearl, Taji paddles off alone, whether toward oblivion or a reunion with his beloved, no one knows.

Writing *Mardi* gave Melville a taste of Dionysian creativity that far surpassed the satisfactions of writing *Typee* and *Omoo*. Plunging into the "polysensuum" of *Mardi*, he experienced a wholeness that was comparable to the sense of fulfillment that comes from losing one's separateness in mutual ecstasy with a loved partner. But that kind of writing, like that kind of sex, was taboo.[52]

Protestant Christianity associated sex with sin and promulgated the notion that women had a duty to "save" men from their bestial natures. Thus, the image of women was split between whores and virgins—dark temptresses and fair angels like Hautia and Yillah. On some level, a man's passion for another man—as long as it found no direct sexual expression—was nobler than passion for a woman, even one's own wife. Official medical and religious ideologies of marriage concurred in divorcing sex from pleasure and making sexual reproduction the solemn duty of a Christian couple.

"Experts" like Sylvester Graham and Dr. Augustus Kinsley Gardner, whom Melville had met at one of Duyckinck's suppers, counseled men that husbanding their sperm would produce healthier babies. In their view, good women had no sexual urges, and for a man to feel lust, even for his own wife, was dangerous. So was masturbation, which depleted man's vital force and led to insanity and allegedly made women nymphomaniacs. "Spermatic economy" became the rationale for marital abstinence, prohibitions on autoeroticism, and opposition to all forms of birth control.

Augustus Gardner was a gynophobic surgeon who specialized in obstetrics and lunacy, a combination that explains why so many women suffered from debilitating diseases. After writing his Harvard thesis on syphilis, Gardner studied medicine in Paris, where he examined prostitutes in hospitals and morgues for venereal diseases and other afflictions of the female reproductive system. He gave Melville a copy of his book *Old Wine in New Bottles*, an account of his medical residency that has prurient undertones, but we have no record of what Melville thought of it. In *Conjugal Sins* and other books, Gardner treated sexuality as an aberration, warning readers that frequent intercourse even between legally married couples can be just as harmful as masturbation, nympho-mania, bestiality, and sodomy. He opposed all forms of birth control and advocated a puritanical program of abstinence and self-denial for both sexes.[53]

Men and women suffered equally from these notions, but in different ways. Without birth control, women who had active sex lives faced being constantly pregnant and nurs-ing. Even women with robust constitutions, such as Maria Melville, could be worn out by childbearing. Exhausted from regular pregnancies, many women found it difficult to relax and enjoy intercourse, especially with husbands who were told by doctors that women had no sexual desires and that their own desires were wicked and unnatural. It was not an atmosphere that fostered leisurely lovemaking, and sex often went under-ground.[54]

Given the inner conflicts Melville had inherited from his parents and the repres-sions Victorian culture imposed on sexuality, a former sailor who had undoubtedly experienced some form of homosexual activity at sea, and had languished on tropic islands with bare-breasted men and maidens, was bound to have trouble adjusting to a conventional marriage. If genteel Victorians experienced sexual pleasure, they kept it a secret or couched it in religious rhetoric, because official ideology branded carnal plea-sures as evidence of natural depravity. Writing was a safe form of sexual sublimation, a kind of metaphysical onanism by which Melville had the pleasure of losing himself in the "supersensuousness" of artistic discovery and creation.

In *Mardi,* Melville turned himself inside out, exposing myriad selves. Writing *Mardi* allowed Melville to enter into many characters and speak with multiple voices, not a sin gle narrative voice, and in Taji and his companions we hear the various voices inside Melville clamoring for expression. The philosopher Babbalanja and his alter ego Azzageddi often seem stronger spokesmen for Melville than the hero Taji. Babbalanja's wisdom serves as compass, keel, and rudder for Taji's romantic quest. While Babbalanja chooses to remain in his celibate Serenia, the Byronic Taji commits himself to follow Yillah to the ends of the earth, no matter what the cost. He refuses to compromise, and vows to pursue Yillah even if it spells his doom: "'Now, I am my own soul's emperor; and my first act is abdication! Hail! realm of shades!'" he proclaims, a rebel to the bit-ter end.[55]

Having purged himself of his doubts and despair by consigning them to his alter ego, Melville could now sit down to dinner with his family and perhaps even play a few rubbers of whist for relaxation, as Evert Duyckinck described: "I played the longest rub-ber of whist last night at his house I ever encountered. It was like his calm at sea—in the new book. What a punishment for a gambler in the next world—an interminable game of whist."[56]

Mardi is an ambitious, exasperating, marvelous book, full of topical references, literary allusions, comic interludes, metaphysical speculations, satire, allegory, Platonic dialogues and symposia, and some of the most poetic and exquisite descriptions of the sea and sea creatures in the English language. It also contains some of Melville's worst writing: a kind of self-indulgent, melodramatic rant that made readers dizzy, angry, and, finally, disgusted with Melville's incomprehensible lack of control.

A tour de force, but fatally flawed, the book completely overwhelmed readers who had enjoyed *Typee* and *Omoo,* and baffled critics. England's Henry Chorley, who had liked Melville's first two books, was put off by "the affectation of its style, in which are mingled many madnesses." Melville's intention seemed "foggy" to him, and he complained that "as a romance, it fails from tediousness...as a prose-poem, it is chargeable with puerility." *The London Examiner* called it "a transcendental *Gulliver,* or *Robinson Crusoe* run mad" while praising its "sly hits at mortal absurdities" and "thoughtful" philosophical digressions. *The Critic* recommended it to the "refined and thoughtful reader," not "the mere seeker after amusement," as "a production of extraordinary talent," but the reviewer for *Blackwood's Edinburgh Magazine,* who had loved *Omoo,* called *Mardi* "a rubbishing rhapsody" and pronounced it so much "trash"–a comment Melville almost seemed to have anticipated when he had Babbalanja declare, "Genius is full of trash."[57]

Some American reviewers called Melville a genius, while others thought him mad. Evert Duyckinck called *Mardi* not only a "very happy, genial production, in the best mood of luxurious invention, but a book of thought, curious thought and reflection." George Ripley, by contrast, dismissed the book as "a tissue of conceits...expressed in language that is equally intolerable for its affectation and its obscurity." *Graham's Magazine* struck a balance of sorts by acknowledging *Mardi*'s "defects," but also praising Melville for "a range of learning, a fluency of fancy, and an originality of thought and diction."[58]

The United States Magazine and Democratic Review extolled its "majesty poetry, which reminds us of the Hebrew," and Nathaniel Parker Willis found it "an exquisite book, full of all oriental delights." *The Southern Literary Messenger,* however, pronounced it "a failure" despite its engaging style, and the reviewer for the *Boston Post* called it "a mass of downright nonsense," which Melville attributed to pure spite because the reviewer's brother, the last man in America to be jailed for blasphemy, had been sentenced by Judge Lemuel Shaw.[59]

Mardi was much longer than Melville's two earlier books, as well as more complicated and much more unconventional in form and style, and Lizzie and Augusta feared it would not appeal to many readers. Lizzie thought her mother's reaction would be indicative of that of most readers, and mocking Henry Chorley's comment that *Mardi* was "foggy," she wrote, "I suppose by this time you are deep in the 'fogs' of Mardi—if the mist ever does clear away, I should like to know what it reveals to *you*—there seems to be much diversity of opinion about 'Mardi' as might be supposed. Has father read it? When you hear any individual express an opinion with regard to it, I wish you would tell me—whatever it is—good or bad—without fear of offence—merely by way of curiosity."[60]

Whether Hope Shaw liked it or not, the book did not sell. For every reader who found *Mardi* original and refreshing, there were two who found it wearisome, pedantic, and grotesque. Ironically, some of the negative reviews came closest to capturing *Mardi*'s spirit. *Saroni*'s reviewer, for example, complained that Melville plunged his readers "into the fathomless sea of Allegory...with monstrous Types, Myths, Symbols and such like fantastic weeds tangled in our vestments and hair," but that was precisely what Melville had tried to do. His visionary aesthetic, drawing from the deepest recesses of mind and soul, challenged conventional notions of narrative and pitted Truth against reality.[61]

Mardi had taken Melville nearly over the edge of the literary world. The storms inside him had driven him far from civilization, and, like a buccaneer, he had run before the wind through open ocean, displaying the skull and crossbones. But running recklessly with full canvas spread had nearly capsized him, and now, with negative reviews howling at him, it was time to reef sail, haul down the pirate ensign, and head for a quiet cove where he could stash his treasures and recoup for another voyage.

With enough faith in his own genius to believe he would find readers in the future, if not in the present day, he assured Lemuel Shaw that "Time, which is the solver of all riddles will solve *Mardi*."[62]

*Flogging, which Melville regarded as the perfect symbol of man's inhumanity to man,
was a common practice on naval vessels and cotton plantations.*

ELEVEN

THE MAN WHO LIVED
AMONG THE CANNIBALS

*Only in New York City could the simultaneous appearance of two Shakespearean actors ignite
the passions of partisans for whom politics and the arts went together like kerosene and fire.*

*On May 7, 1849, a mob gathered before the opera house at Astor Place to protest the
British actor William Macready's performance of* Macbeth *because they felt it competed with
a performance by the popular American actor Edwin Forrest, an outspoken nationalist. Forty-
seven New Yorkers, including Herman Melville, Washington Irving, Evert Duyckinck, and
Cornelius Mathews, signed a petition supporting Macready's right to perform, and the show
went on despite threats of violence.*

*Three nights later, Forrest's supporters stormed the theater with bottles, stones, and other
objects, determined to drive Macready back to England. Bystanders joined in, and the violence
escalated to such a fever pitch that the militia had to be called out. The mob then attacked the
soldiers, who fired into the crowd of twenty-five thousand, killing twenty-two people and critically wounding more than three dozen others. Before it was over, a hundred more people had
been injured, and eighty-six men, mostly craftsmen and laborers, were in jail.[1]*

The riot was an alarming outbreak of nativist bigotry, a harbinger of the politicizing of the arts and the split between "high" and "low" culture that developed at mid-century. The mob violence shocked well-to-do New Yorkers who were oblivious of the class and ethnic hatreds smoldering just below the surface of their city, and Melville wondered if citizens of a democracy would ever be able to exercise their power without degenerating into a hydra-headed mob. Although he was an egalitarian democrat who was keenly aware of economic injustices, Melville nonetheless sided with the patricians because he believed in artistic freedom and abhorred mob violence.

He also deplored the cynical opportunism of people like Ned Buntline, a self-proclaimed leader of the working class, who, in *The Misteries and Miseries of New York* and several other quasi-documentary books on New York, blamed the city's problems on the influx of European immigrants. These nativist attacks on foreigners dangerously widened existing divisions within the working class.

The Astor Place Riot was a reminder of how opinionated and fickle Americans could be about the arts, and a harbinger of how classism would fragment the American public and hurt artists who hoped for a large and diverse audience for their work. Well-educated Americans like the Melvilles, the Gansevoorts, and the Shaws read serious fiction and nonfiction, but as the pace of life quickened, most Americans preferred lighter fare. Readers of fiction looked for excitement and escape. They liked picturesque descriptions, strong characters, and dramatic plots, and they generally found theological speculations offensive and philosophical disputations just plain boring.

With *Mardi*, a book full of erudite allusions and abstruse metaphysical arguments, Melville was swimming against the cultural tide. Even to most educated readers, *Mardi*'s tedious digressions and reckless violations of narrative convention were disorienting and disturbing, and the author's bursts of melodramatic language were annoying. His narrator, Taji, was radically unstable, one minute an active participant, the next a fly on the wall. At times he even seemed to disappear and the author's voice intruded. Most readers considered these lapses of narrative control, combined with the rapid shifts from serious to comic tone, to be fatal defects.

Readers were very adept at reading between the lines and very sophisticated about distinguishing between an author's and a character's point of view, but destabilizing narrative authority was like dethroning God. Melville had broken the covenant between the writer and his readers, and as a result they rejected *Mardi*. It took seven years for the Harper's edition of three thousand copies to sell out, and only five hundred more copies were printed during the rest of the century.

Opining that the publisher had sabotaged it by sending out review copies accompanied by inane "puffs" and canned advertising blurbs that reviewers could reproduce without even opening the book, Melville blamed Harper's for the book's poor showing in America. Reviewers for major urban newspapers did read *Mardi*, however, and although Melville had to admit that the salvos they fired were "not unexpected," he was hurt by the personal attacks launched by some of them.

He knew American readers would have trouble accepting *Mardi*, but he expected British readers to be receptive to it because of its affinities with works of Robert Burton and Sir Thomas Browne. Thus, when London critics fired a "broadside" at his book, Melville blamed Richard Bentley for publishing it "in the ordinary novel form," which signaled readers that it was only "meant to entertain." He thought British readers "would have been better pleased with it, perhaps, had they taken it up in the first place for what it really is....–the peculiar thoughts & fancies of a Yankee upon politics & other matters."[2]

Acknowledging that those "who read simply for amusement" might have been repelled by the "metaphysical ingredients," and that their reaction was "not altogether unexpected," Melville told Bentley that, although it might have been "unwise" or "indiscreet" to write "a work of that kind," he had to do it. "Some of us scribblers, My Dear Sir, always have a certain something unmanageable in us, that bids us do this or that and be done it must–hit or miss."[3]

Melville had gambled with *Mardi*, and lost. He was in debt to his publishers, and his readers felt betrayed. Taji had voiced Melville's disobedience to the laws of the marketplace when he vowed to follow his heart. These "fiery yearnings their own phantom-future make," so "if after all these fearful, fainting trances the verdict be, the golden haven was not gained; –yet, in bold quest thereof, better to sink in boundless deeps, than float on vulgar shoals; and give me, ye gods, an utter wreck, if wreck I do." It no longer mattered that the quest was doomed to fail, as questing itself had become the goal.[4]

In fiction a man could follow impossible dreams, but in real life he had to pay the bills. Melville had the fantasy every serious writer has at one time or another of writing the book that will earn him enough money so he can go back to writing the kind of book he really wants to write and not have to worry about publicity and sales.

Richard Bentley had published a sumptuous edition of *Mardi*, and he, too, was disappointed with the book's reception. "As you observe the English critics have fired quite a broadside into 'Mardi.' This I cannot help thinking, has arisen in a great measure from the nature of the work: the first volume was eagerly devoured, the second was read–the third was not perhaps altogether adapted to the class of readers whom 'Omoo' and 'Typee' and the First Volume of 'Mardi' gratified. The effect somehow or other has been decidedly to check, nay I may almost say, to stop the sale of the book."[5]

A little testily, he implied that Melville was fortunate to be published at all because of the copyright situation. American publishers had refused to endorse international copyright regulations, so in the 1840s an American book could be copyrighted in England only if its American publisher would agree to simultaneous, or prior, publication there. While many British firms continued to deal honorably with American authors, others pirated American editions, and still others used the situation as a convenient excuse not to publish American books at all. The absence of international copyright agreements encouraged "wholesale thieving." Quite a few American publishers, notably Harper & Brothers, owed their initial successes to book piracy, and in retaliation, many English publishers stopped buying American books.[6]

Melville knew that if he intended to continue as a professional author, he had to contend with the copyright situation as well as the vagaries of the marketplace. He had to hope Congress would put an end to what Richard Bentley had called the "drivelling absurdity" of operating without copyright laws. In 1852, Melville would join Washington Irving, William Cullen Bryant, and a number of other writers in petitioning Congress to enact reciprocal international publishing agreements, but the bill was not passed until 1891, the year of Melville's death.[7]

Eager to recover his audience and write a book that would sell, he promised Richard Bentley that his next endeavor would be "a plain, straightforward, amusing narrative of personal experience—the son of a gentleman on his first voyage to sea as a sailor—no metaphysics, no conic-sections, nothing but cakes & ale. I have shifted my ground from the South Seas to a different quarter of the globe—nearer home."[8]

Having lost money on *Mardi*, Bentley could no longer afford to treat Melville as a "guinea author," to be paid in gold coin of the realm. He offered him only one hundred pounds for his next book, plus half of the profits—exactly the terms he had offered for *Typee* when Melville was an unknown author. Melville accepted Bentley's terms, grateful that Harper & Brothers had already advanced him $300.[9]

The lot of a professional author in Melville's America was quite different from that in Shakespeare's England, where wealthy patrons supported theaters, and plays were performed, not published in book form. In a nation where ninety percent of adult whites could read, American writers theoretically had an entire continent of potential readers, but with transportation and sources of capital still limited, book publishing was concentrated mainly in Philadelphia and New York. Boston did not emerge as a publishing town until the mid-1850s, when the founding of *The Atlantic Monthly* and the expansion of the railroad system made it possible for enterprising publishers like William D. Ticknor and James T. Fields to distribute books more easily to other parts of the country and, thus, attract established authors to their Boston firm.[10]

Costs of book production and transportation were high, with authors often having to bow to publishers' discount policies if they wanted to see their work in print at all. Although Matthew Carey had established the American Company of Booksellers in 1801 to regulate the book trade, in the 1820s an auction system, similar to the wholesaling binge that had discombobulated the import-export trade in Allan Melvill's day, broke out in the book market, allowing publishers to unload slow-moving books by selling them to retailers at cut rates, rather like today's remainders.[11]

In a sprawling democracy that stressed literacy as the stepping-stone to success, the potential readership for books was large, but it was also much more diverse than the English audience and much harder to reach. Many educated upper-class readers were staunch Anglophiles who preferred novels by Dickens, Thackeray, and Scott to historical romances such as James Fenimore Cooper's *The Last of the Mohicans*, Catharine Sedgwick's *Hope Leslie*, and Lydia Maria Child's *Hobomok*. Almost a thousand novels were published during the 1840s—nearly a tenfold increase since Melville's childhood—and much new fiction by American writers appeared in the thriving periodicals of the day. In fact, many of the women writers who would become best-selling novelists in the 1850s got their start in popular publications such as *Godey's Lady's Book*, which was read by both men and women, including Lizzie Melville.[12]

The growth of the working class created new readers who wanted books that would grab their attention and whisk them away from the daily drudgery of their lives. Most working-class women, if they had time to read at all, looked for novels that portrayed families happier than their own, while most working-class men preferred action-packed adventures set in exotic locales, or crime novels with urban settings. George Lippard's *The Quaker City*, for example, which pandered to male readers' taste for violence and sexual perversity, sold very well.

Not until the next decade—when women writers like Catharine Maria Sedgwick, Lydia Maria Child, Mrs. E. D. E. N. Southworth, Fanny Fern (Sara Payson Willis Parton), Grace Greenwood (Sara Jane Clarke Lippincott), Caroline Kirkland, Maria S. Cummins, Susan Warner, and Harriet Beecher Stowe would dominate the marketplace—did serious literature reach a diverse audience. These women writers attained celebrity status in the eyes of their devoted fans, and any one of their novels outsold all the major works of Emerson, Thoreau, Hawthorne, and Melville combined.

In the early days of settlement, most popular fiction was written anonymously by women whom newspaper publishers paid a flat fee to turn out romances for a distaff audience. This gave female writers modest support for their work and created something like a community of readers, as copies of these books were passed from hand to hand. None of the revolutionary generation who aspired to be professional authors—Susannah Rowson, Joel Barlow, Thomas Paine, Joseph Dennie, and Charles Brockden Brown—managed to make a living by the pen. In the next generation, only James Fenimore Cooper, who produced novels one after the other without revising them, and Washington Irving, who made $10,000 dollars in two years from his *Sketch Book*, managed to support themselves by writing. Countless others were either forced to abandon their literary aspirations for other professions, or take government jobs and write in their spare time.[13]

Between 1832 and 1860, the year that saw the publication of Hawthorne's last published novel, *The Marble Faun*, America became a nation of novel-readers, but the audience for fiction became so fragmented and so stratified that one spoke of "markets" for fiction, not a single market. Elitist publications such as *The Literary World*, which spoke out against the "floods" of popular fiction that threatened to drown the public's taste for serious literature, served only to help create a gap between "high" and "low" culture that Melville was trying hard to bridge in hopes that he could create a larger and more discriminating audience.[14]

Voyaging "chartless" through the archipelagoes of *Mardi* had convinced Melville that fiction captured the truth of human experience better than "unvarnished facts" did. In financial straits, however, he decided to dash off a fictional account of his 1839 voyage to Liverpool that would incorporate enough elements of popular literature to appeal to a broad audience of male and female readers. This was at a time when he thought he had already gained a new level of recognition as a professional writer, and consequently he felt that he was backtracking, losing ground.[15]

As he wrote about his first voyage, calling his autobiographical narrator/protagonist Wellingborough Redburn, he realized it would be painfully easy to follow the formula established by such writers of nautical adventures and picaresque novels as Captain Marryat and Charles F. Briggs—so much so, in fact, that his own youthful experiences began to seem fictive and clichéd to him. He began to toy with the idea that life imitated art, not the other way around, and as a result, although he considered *Redburn* an inferior production of his pen, it turned out to be a much more artful, fascinating book than he intended, or possibly even realized. Much to Melville's disgust, the book he called his "little nursery tale" would also turn out to be much more popular with readers and reviewers than *Mardi*, the book he considered his masterpiece.[16]

The reading public had Melville pigeonholed. They saw the author of *Typee* and *Omoo* as a sailor who wrote travel books, not as a professional author who was the satirist and Shakespearean poet-seer Melville aspired to be. To them, he was a common sailor who was erudite enough that they could feel smart for reading him, but not so much so as to make them feel ignorant by comparison. Melville thought that with *Mardi* he had made a breakthrough, but publishers and readers persisted in seeing him as the "man who lived among the cannibals." It made him feel like one of Barnum's freaks.[17]

∿

Having worked through the winter nearly frozen to his desk to finish *Mardi*, Melville was now writing furiously through sweltering summer heat and a cholera epidemic. Fortunately, the family survived both the fever and the two teething babies, and Melville managed to produce not just one, but two, books in rapid succession.

Daily walks gave him enough of a break in the middle of the day to keep him energized for writing, and cozy chats with Lizzie and a chance to relax and play with little "Barney," as he called the baby, who was a great source of entertainment as P. T. Barnum, gave him a feeling of connection to other people. Outdoor exercise and a large, active family provided a healthy balance to the solitary, sedentary labor of writing. In the evenings the family would play rubbers of whist or backgammon, or read the latest novels aloud. Sometimes Melville read portions of his manuscript to Lizzie and his sisters to see if it would pass muster with women readers. Now that Lizzie was busy with the baby, Helen was copying for Herman, and with her assistance he finished the first of the two books in time to celebrate his second wedding anniversary with Lizzie. Well before *The Literary World* announced in August that Harper's was about to publish another book by the author of *Typee* and *Omoo*, Melville had written Richard Bentley that his new book would "readily make two volumes got up in your style."[18]

In Wellingborough Redburn, the "son-of-a-gentleman" who has "a naturally roving disposition," Melville created a protagonist of great psychological complexity. Having grown up in a "hard-hearted world," young Redburn has "learned to think much and bitterly before my time." Forced by his father's tragic death and the poverty of his once-illustrious family to give up his "mounting dreams of glory" at an early age, he leaves his home in upstate New York and goes to sea, clearly suffering from emotional and spiritual poverty as well as economic deprivation: "There is no misanthrope like a boy disappointed; and such was I, with the warm soul of me flogged out by adversity."[19]

Melville's narrator engages the reader's sympathy at once; early biographers assumed the novel was autobiographical because of its psychological intensity and emotional authenticity, and in some ways, of course, it is. Yet, Melville's imagination plays with reality in a magical way, transforming the glass ship in his grandfather's parlor, "among whose mazes of spun-glass I used to rove in imagination," into a symbol of Redburn's hunger for both adventure and material security. "When I was very little, I made no doubt, that if I could but one day open the hull, and break the glass all to pieces, I would infallibly light upon something wonderful, perhaps some gold guineas, of which I have always been in want, ever since I could remember"—probably a little dig at Richard Bentley, who had paid him in paper pound notes instead of the coveted gold guineas.[20]

Looking into the miniature ship's hold stirs up "certain shadowy reminiscences of wharves and warehouses, and shipping, with which a residence in a seaport during early childhood had supplied me," and reminds him of his father's stories and of the seascapes and engravings of foreign landscapes that his father had brought back from his European travels. These "long reveries about distant voyages and travels" lead Redburn to think "how fine it would be, to be able to talk about remote and barbarous countries."[21]

Choking back "strangled sobs" and ill-equipped for the voyage he is about to undertake, he leaves home wearing a shooting jacket and carrying a fowling piece his older brother has given him to sell for passage money. His anger and insecurity make him hostile, and suspicious of other people he meets. When a short, fat man gawks at him, he points his gun straight at the man's left eye and almost pulls the trigger before "several persons starting to their feet, exclaimed that I must be crazy. So I was at that time; for otherwise I know not how to account for my demoniac feelings." Redburn's near-fatal rage suggests that even the most innocent and well-meaning person is capable of murder, but Redburn spends little time reflecting on his experiences. He tends to see evil as something external, not as an intrinsic impulse of the human heart.[22]

Cut loose from the moorings of home, Redburn is adrift in a sea of melancholy, and his first few days on the *Highlander* are miserable. The mates give him the dirtiest jobs, and he battles seasickness. As soon as he gets his sea legs, he decides to pay a social call on the captain. Because he is a gentleman's son, and because he has heard that sea captains often act "like fathers" to their crews, Redburn naively assumes that the captain will invite him into his cabin and treat him like a guest. The captain, however, ignores him, and his shipmates make fun of him, which strikes him as unaccountably rude. Redburn's ability to confront one new experience after another, without learning a single thing about himself or the world, makes the novel refreshingly nondidactic and more profoundly moral than conventional novels that show the hero progressing infallibly from innocence to experience.[23]

Melville holds this bumpkin's pretensions up to ridicule, as if self-satire could erase the memory of his own blighted hopes, and the narrative voice shifts from the disarmingly innocent and occasionally stupid narrator to the older Redburn, then to the author's voice breaking through to mock his struggling hero. These inconsistencies, however disconcerting, enhance the ambiguity of a text that does a "double-shuffle" with the reader by blatantly cannibalizing stock plots and characters, then deconstructing them.[24]

Apart from his red sailor shirt, Redburn's clothes are completely inappropriate for the sea. He wears new leather riding boots, a leaky tarpaulin hat, a "very genteel pair" of pantaloons "made in the height of the sporting fashion," and a fashionable moleskin hunting jacket. This incongruous and impractical garment flares open in the front, flashing his sexual vulnerability at the other sailors, who nickname him "Buttons" and make ribald jokes he doesn't understand. He becomes a "sort of Ishmael in the ship, without a single friend or companion" until his foolish aristocratic jacket finally shrinks and falls to tatters, releasing him to find an identity not preordained by declining family power, prestige, and privilege, or circumscribed by community and church.[25]

Melville models some of Redburn's shipmates on the men he sailed with in 1839, though his portraits are otherwise entirely fictitious. The "infernal" Jackson, who is slowly wasting away from the ravages of venereal disease, is thoroughly malevolent, like Shakespeare's Iago or Timon of Athens. He is drunk and profane not in the way of most sailors, but in a fiendish way, reveling in the evil and depravity he has both seen and perpetrated, quite unlike his prototype Robert Jackson, whose only "crime" seems to have been to bear the name of the hated Andrew Jackson, whose administration was a travesty of democracy as far as Melville was concerned.

Worst of all is Jackson's attitude toward slavery. "He had served in Portuguese slavers off the coast of Africa; and with a diabolical relish used to tell of the middle-passage, where the slaves were stowed, heel and point, like logs, and the suffocated and dead were unmanacled and weeded out from the living every morning, before washing down the decks." Jackson terrifies Redburn because he sees in him an image of what he might become if he gives in to evil impulses. He fears the hatred he feels toward the shipmates who have abused him will "master my heart completely, and so make a fiend of me, something like Jackson."[26]

Jackson's attitude toward slavery evokes Redburn's moral revulsion, and he finds a positive counterbalance to Jackson's racism in the pious black cook, who reads the Bible over and over again, trying to understand how Solomon could be considered so wise when his Temple was built by armies of slaves, and in Lavender, the *Highlander*'s black steward, who struts along Liverpool's docks "dressed very handsomely, and walking arm in arm with a good looking English woman."[27]

Noticing that Lavender walks at "a prouder pace" in Liverpool than in New York, where "such a couple would have been mobbed in three minutes, and the steward would have been lucky to escape with whole limbs," Redburn concludes that America leaves to other nations the "carrying out of the principle that stands at the head of our Declaration of Independence." Naively unaware that the woman is a prostitute, Redburn proclaims heartily that the steward is exercising "his claims to humanity and moral equality." Daring to draw a parallel between the "pursuit of happiness" and miscegenation, Melville reinterprets one of America's most sacred texts satirically, and, in the process, pokes fun at Redburn's naiveté.[28]

Skeptical about religious and political dogma, Melville also questioned economic dogma. He doubted that America's newest religion, laissez-faire capitalism, could save mankind. Thus his description of Redburn finding a copy of *The Wealth of Nations* in the *Highlander*'s library is a comic *reductio ad absurdum* of the theories of Adam Smith: "I read on and on about 'wages and profits of labor,' without getting any profits for my pains," says Redburn in the deadpan voice Melville reserves for his narrator's most incisive observations.[29]

Given several days' shore leave, Redburn finds a room in a boardinghouse and tours the city, carrying with him his father's old copy of *The Picture of Liverpool*, which directs him to landmarks no longer there, while providing no guidance through the moral maze that is the modern city. In Launcelott's-Hey, Redburn hears a "dismal sound . . . the low, hopeless, endless wail of some one forever lost" coming from a cellar fifteen feet beneath a crumbling old cotton warehouse. Approaching the pitiful sounds, he finds "crouching in nameless squalor, with her head bowed over . . . the figure of what had been a woman . . . her blue arms folded to her livid bosom two shrunken things like children, that leaned toward her, one on each side," all "dumb and next to dead with want."[30]

Wondering how "any body in the wide world" could "smile and be glad when sights like this were to be seen," Redburn tries to get help, but people seem hardened to the family's fate. His landlady refuses to give him extra food, and the policeman he meets when he is bringing them water tells him that particular alley is not on his beat. Finally he asks a woman from the neighborhood to help him relieve the family's suffering, but she merely shrugs and says, "she desarves it. Was she ever married?" tell me that."[31]

On the second day, he finds a way to smuggle bread and cheese from his landlady's table, dropping bits of it to the two starving girls and lowering a cup of water into the cellar so they can take a few feeble sips. Feeling better, he returns the next day to find the woman clutching a dead baby, half buried by rags and refusing nourishment. At this point he ponders doing them "the last mercy" but refrains, still convinced there must be a way to save the two older children. On the symbolic third day, however, "the vault is empty" and "in place of the woman and children, a heap of quick-lime was glistening."[32]

Redburn realizes that his well-meaning impulse to help these sufferers has merely prolonged their misery. The urban Madonna with her babe at her breast is thrice denied by society, just as Christ was thrice denied by Simon Peter. Allusions to "the empty vault" and to Jesus raising Lazarus from the dead express Melville's profound disillusionment with Christianity.

To escape the city's horrid sights and his own inadequacy as an agent of social change, Redburn hikes into the countryside, his head filled with storybook versions of English pastoral, but the first thing he sees is a sign that says, "MAN-TRAPS AND SPRING-GUNS!" Redburn realizes that the English countryside has become a "forbidden Eden," off limits to hikers and nature-lovers, and he fights off an impulse to "test his traps." He strolls on until he comes to a fairytale cottage whose owner is "confidentially communing with his pipe." Three "ravishing charmers" take him in and feed him, and he falls asleep "dreaming of red cheeks and roses."[33]

The next morning he awakes to find, standing over him, not a rosy-cheeked maiden as readers might have expected, but a boy about his own age who is "one of those small, but perfectly formed beings, with curling hair, and silken muscles, who seem to have been born in cocoons." With his "mantling brunette" complexion, "feminine as a girl's," small feet, white hands, "large, black, womanly" eyes, and a voice that sounds like a harp, this effeminate youth, who is an orphan from Bury St. Edmunds named Harry Bolton, becomes Redburn's "bosom friend."[34]

In a bizarre sequence most contemporary reviewers dismissed as an inexcusable digression, or damned as further evidence of Melville's lunacy, Harry, wearing false whiskers and a mustache to avoid detection, spirits Redburn away to London. In the city, they pass mincing dandies whom Redburn takes for noblemen, not the male prostitutes they are. They reach a "place of opulent entertainment" that Redburn calls Aladdin's Palace because it reminds him of the Arabian Nights. He sees "knots of gentlemanly men, with cut decanters and taper-waisted glasses, journals and cigars, before them" sitting at "numerous Moorish-looking tables, supported by Caryatides of turbaned slaves." While "obsequious waiters" serve them, the men reminisce about colonial campaigns in India, as smug and self-important as the clubmen Melville would caricature years later in his magazine sketch "The Paradise of Bachelors," and a good deal more explicitly epicene.[35]

When Harry orders "a pale yellow wine" with "a curious foreign name," Redburn exclaims, "What would my brother have said? What would Tom Legare, the treasurer of the Juvenile Temperance Society have thought?" Of course the reader knows very well what they would have said, but Redburn goes right ahead and drinks anyway, as he has already tried his first cigarette to "be one of the men." By showing in these two instances that Redburn "falls" when tempted, Melville implies that his visit to "the lowest and most squalid haunts of sailor iniquity in Liverpool" included his sexual initiation. The "ugly thoughts" that Harry's provocative "wink" stirred in Redburn turn out to be prescient, as their trip to London introduces the young American to the sexual underground frequented by aristocrats and gentlemen.[36]

Redburn holds on to "foolish golden visions" of being introduced to royal personages by his "Bury blade," as he punningly calls Harry, but instead, Harry suddenly drags him down a corridor "whose tesselated floors echo as if all the Paris catacombs were underneath," and leaves him alone in an inner room. The room is furnished with "Laocoon-like chairs," plush Persian carpets, "oriental ottomans, whose cunning warp and woof were wrought into plaited serpents, undulating beneath beds of leaves," and "mythological oil-paintings" depicting sexually explicit scenes, including one showing homosexual fellatio.[37]

While Redburn is gazing around the room in bewilderment, Harry reappears and thrusts a sealed letter into his hands, ordering him in desperate, fateful tones not to leave the premises, but to guard the letter and post it for him if he hasn't returned by morning. Redburn tries to hold Harry back, but, like Hamlet pulling his sword on Horatio when he tries to stop him from following his father's ghost, Harry brandishes a knife and bolts away.[38]

To Redburn, the whole establishment now seems "infected," as if "some eastern plague had been imported," and he feels "a terrible revulsion." He finds himself "mysteriously alive to a dreadful feeling, which I had never before felt, except when penetrating the lowest and most squalid haunts of sailor iniquity in Liverpool. All the mirrors and marbles around me seemed crawling over with lizards; and I thought to myself, that though gilded and golden, the serpent of vice is a serpent still." Despite misgivings about his safety, Redburn falls into a fitful sleep.[39]

Suddenly he wakes up to find Harry, as pale as death, standing over him, laughing deliriously and commanding Redburn to keep his little dagger for him so he won't be tempted to kill himself. Exclaiming, "it's an invitation to hang myself," Harry tears the bell rope from the wall, and when Redburn asks what ails him, he replies, "Nothing, oh nothing," and assumes "a treacherous, tropical calmness" that belies his suicidal bent. Making Redburn swear never to speak of the episode again, he flings down his purse and impales it on the table with his dirk.

This melodramatic episode ends as enigmatically as it began, with Redburn still unaware that Harry is caught in a vicious cycle of gambling, debt, prostitution, more gambling, and more debt. The two sit up all night, Harry with his hat on, drinking brandy, and Redburn dozing and dreaming fitfully, "like a somnambulist," a signal to antebellum readers that they, too, should stop and imagine what the character might be thinking.[40]

Not once does Redburn realize the tragic truth about Harry Bolton's life—he has squandered his fortune in gambling dens and has to repay his debts by prostitution—but Melville expected his readers to see that the underworld's trade in sex and other illicit commodities darkly mirrored the business world's hellish exploitation of human beings, black and white, who had a dollar value put on their bodies but no value put on their souls. The Dantean circles of gambling, debt, and prostitution in which Harry Bolton is trapped seem an apt, though savage, metaphor for Allan Melvill's sad career, and Redburn's ambivalence toward his brotherly intimacy with Harry Bolton seems an attempt to come to terms with sexuality, or perhaps even an attempt to come to terms with something only he knew about his older brother. Does Harry represent something troubling about Gansevoort?

Although they are worlds apart in terms of sexual experience, both Harry Bolton and Redburn are sexual outsiders who embody personal as well as cultural anxieties for Melville. Redburn's encounter with Harry Bolton seems to express Melville's anxieties about being a man in a family whose male members were prone to self-indulgent delusions and violent early deaths—a story he would tell with a vengeance in *Pierre*. In

Redburn, Melville explores a young man's emotional life as he passes from innocence through experience to impotence rather than empowerment.

As far as we know, Melville never actually went to London during his 1839 visit to England, and this lurid episode seems to have been written to titillate readers who enjoyed sensational underground literature. It resembles the rest of *Redburn* less than it resembles Melville's later novel *Pierre.* Redburn is one of Melville's "bachelors," a man whose limited exposure to real life and privileged position in society blind him to the moral complexities of life; Pierre is an older Redburn with an agonized and agonizing consciousness of the dark truths and painful realities to which Redburn remains oblivious and largely immune despite his early sorrow.

The *Highlander* sails for America with Harry and Redburn aboard, and during an otherwise dismal voyage home, Redburn's greatest pleasure is listening to the angelic singing of Carlo, a beautiful Italian youth whose eyes shine "with a soft and spiritual radiance" and whose "thick clusters of tendril curls" resemble "Falerian foliage." Melville's description of Carlo playing his hand organ has unmistakably autoerotic undertones, and it implies that artistic creativity springs from the homoerotic union of Orpheus and Pan.[41]

Redburn had grown from a straightforward account of Melville's maiden voyage to a tale that took on the classic mythic pattern of initiation, separation, and return, but Wellingborough Redburn, as his farcical name suggests, is no epic hero destined to slay the dragon and free the princess, nor is he a Bunyanesque pilgrim destined to conquer the Seven Deadly Sins and reach the Celestial City. He seems fated to return from Liverpool and London, the modern equivalents of Sodom and Gomorrah, shell-shocked and desensitized, his faith in the power of the individual to alleviate human suffering severely shaken.

When the ship reaches port in America and lowers its "old anchor, fathoms down into free and independent Yankee mud," the captain finds an excuse not to pay Harry the wages he owes him. Although Harry faces life in a new country with no money, Redburn coldly gives him a letter of introduction to an older acquaintance named Goodwell who clerks in "a forwarding-house," then heads home up the Hudson after piously assuring the jobless immigrant that if he keeps "a stout heart" and never despairs, "all will be well." It never once occurs to Redburn that Harry might have to prostitute himself to survive, because all along he has remained in complete denial about the realities of his friend's life. Later, Redburn learns that Harry's "melancholy" brought him "to the insanity of throwing himself away in a whaler," and that he died jammed between the ship's hull and a whale.[42]

Redburn's moral compass has been knocked askew, and his belief in his own goodness has gone fathoms down with the orphaned boy he has abandoned. When the old salt who has told him the tragic news of Harry's death asks, "Was Harry Bolton not your brother?" Redburn remains silent. The fatherless boy who left home a victim has come home an executioner. The "red burn" is the mark of Cain, who, when God confronted him with the murder of Abel, asked, "Am I my brother's keeper?" Yes, Melville unequivocally implies.

Harry is Redburn's psychological double, the repressed feminine side of himself that must be nurtured if he is to achieve full manhood, a precursor of Isabel in *Pierre*. Terrified, however, by Harry's ambiguous sexuality and the compromises he has made to survive in a world that cannibalizes the weak and vulnerable, Redburn sheds Harry more easily than he sheds his uncomfortable jacket, refusing, like Cain, to be his brother's keeper. Redburn returns to the safety of his village, with its temperance societies and charitable enterprises, having learned nothing at all, a precursor of Amasa Delano, the obtuse protagonist of Melville's masterfully subtle magazine story "Benito Cereno."

It's not surprising that Melville hated *Redburn* so much. Probing the wounds to masculinity was painful, especially when it brought Melville face to face with the fugitive self that swam below culture in a twilight world where those who did not conform to strictly delineated gender roles were defined as deviants. Perhaps the emergence of so much repressed material in *Redburn*, with its foretaste of the passions that would be unleashed in *Pierre*, indicates that Melville first became aware of his bisexuality during his cruise to Liverpool. Was Harry Bolton, who is set adrift by his only friend in what Larry the whaleman sarcastically calls "free Americky," Wellingborough Redburn's "secret sharer"?[43]

In some ways, *Redburn* is a literary joke. Melville modeled each episode almost systematically on every genre that was popular with some group of antebellum readers, as if to say, *Here's a little something for everybody; buy me.* It combines elements of *Pilgrim's Progess* with the picaresque novel, the travelogue, the nautical adventure, the sentimental novel, the sensational French romance, the gothic thriller, temperance tracts, urban reform literature, and the English pastoral.

Melville incorporated stock episodes from the melodramatic pulp fiction of the day, including the sailor with wives on both sides of the Atlantic who always has clean laundry, the drunkard who explodes from spontaneous combustion, the delirious suicide who throws himself into the sea, the plague-stricken immigrants, the sailor with an evil glint in his eye, the mysterious chum and the trip to a den of iniquity, and the hero's return home as a sadder but wiser lad, except that Wellingborough Redburn returns home no wiser and much less compassionate than before, a cynical reversal.

In the hands of Melville, whose own family amply illustrates many of the pathologies that troubled Victorian Americans, these stock situations expressed the collective anxieties of the young men of his generation. Alcoholism, insanity, disease, sexual tension, poverty, and sudden death gnawed at the edges of Melville's mind like rats in the corners of a ship's dark hold, making *Redburn* a far better book than he seems to have realized.

Melville dedicated *Redburn: His First Voyage, Being the Sailor-Boy Confessions and Reminiscences of the Son-of-a-Gentleman, in the Merchant Service* to "My Younger Brother, Thomas Melville, Now a Sailor on a Voyage to China," perhaps because when *Redburn* was published, Tom was the age Herman had been when he sailed to Liverpool.

The moment he finished *Redburn*, he started writing *White-Jacket, or The World in a Man-of-War*, which is based on his stint in the navy. In a digression that evokes the actual conditions under which he was working, Melville nods in the direction of domesticity:

> of all the chamber-furniture in the world best calculated to cure a bad temper, and breed a pleasant one, is the sight of a lovely wife. If you have children ... that are teething, the nursery should be a good way upstairs; at sea, it ought to be in the mizzen-top. Indeed, teething children play the very deuce with a husband's temper. I have known three promising young husbands completely spoil on their wives' hands by reason of a teething child, whose worrisomeness happened to be aggravated at the time by a summer complaint. With a breaking heart, and my handkerchief to my eyes, I followed those three hapless young husbands, one after the other, to their premature graves.[44]

An amusing burlesque of the sentimental style, this passage serves as a reminder that nothing could be more sentimental than the songs and stories of the men who followed the sea and those who waited for them to return—the narratives of Dana and Melville being notable exceptions.

If modern readers coming upon this passage assume that Melville is likening wives to the "furniture" of a man's abode, they would be both missing Melville's humorous intention and overlooking Lizzie's probable enjoyment of domestic satire. In any case, when little Malcolm and his cousin Milie got so cranky that they disturbed Melville at his work, Mrs. Sullivan could always take them out for an airing in their carriage.

Melville transformed his actual stint in the navy into a more subtly allegorical voyage than that depicted in *Mardi*, and one with far more sinister and far-reaching implications, given the navy's recent history. The theme of the entire novel is White-Jacket's struggle to escape being eaten alive in a civilized world that is every bit as cannibalistic as the Typee Valley.[45]

White-Jacket depicts abuses of power in the United States Navy as a microcosm of the modern political world. Melville's narrator identifies himself with the ill-fitting white canvas jacket he fashions for himself because he cannot afford a peacoat or proper sailor's surtout. Ill-suited to seafaring, this "strange-looking coat" of white duck has "a Quakerish amplitude about the skirts" that signifies pacifism and sexual ambiguity, both of which are dangerous to naval men. In addition to its skirts, White-Jacket's garment has "an infirm, tumble-down collar" and "a clumsy fullness about the wristbands," and is as "white as a shroud." Like Redburn's shooting jacket, this garment offers no protection to the wearer and interferes with the performance of his shipboard duties, even endangering his life. The white jacket makes its wearer vulnerable in a man-of-war world, as it connotes peacefulness and femininity; it also represents the outsider's need to wear disguises and play multiple roles in order to survive.[46]

Both Redburn's and White-Jacket's "frocks" symbolize their attempts to escape the straitjacket of Victorian masculinity. White-Jacket sews innumerable pockets both outside and inside his garment to protect himself from the cruelty and injustice of the "man-of-war world" where tipsy, tyrannical captains order enlisted men flogged unmercifully, goad black sailors into fighting one another for "fun," and force sailors to cut off their beards. Yet the jacket nearly costs him his life, too. At various points he is mistaken for an albatross, a ghost, and, finally, a shark.

The *Neversink* is no Serenia. The captain lords it over his crew, and the officers persecute the enlisted men. They are assigned the most dangerous jobs, while the officers, "safely standing on deck themselves, scruple not to sacrifice an immortal man or two, in order to show off the excelling discipline of the ship." Out of sight of the officers, the men drink smuggled whiskey and rum, and steal from one another with no compunction at all. They are so addicted to alcohol that when the ship's supply of grog runs dry, they mix eau de cologne and brown sugar with a drop of tar and drink it.[47]

Aboard the *Neversink,* flogging is the central metaphor for human relationships in the military. It is an "unendurable torture" during which "you see a human being, stripped like a slave; scourged worse than a hound. And for what? For things not essentially criminal, but only made so by arbitrary laws." The physical pain is enhanced by psychological indignity, as "in a sudden outburst of passion, perhaps inflamed by brandy, or smarting under the sense of being disliked or hated by the seaman," corrupt lieutenants can "order a whole watch of two hundred and fifty men, at dead of night, to undergo the indignity of the 'colt,'" which is the bit of rope most junior officers wear coiled around their hands for ready application to the nearest part of a sailor's anatomy.[48]

White-Jacket's most horrific scenes depict various forms of abuse and mutilation: flogging, amputation, racist bullying, and emasculation, or symbolic castration. With alarming frequency, such blatant abuses of authority, which often had sexual undertones, went unpunished, as officers usually took care of their own. White-Jacket escapes a flogging only because Colbrook, a remarkably handsome lady's man—who later becomes a legislator—intercedes for him while Jack Chase, curiously enough, stands on the sidelines and does not intervene.[49]

Even the chaplain takes the inhumanity of naval life for granted. This "transcendental divine stand[s] behind a gun-carriage on the main deck," as though about to sacrifice the "five hundred salt-sea sinners" whom he is lecturing on "the psychological phenomena of the soul, and the ontological necessity of every sailor's saving it at all hazards" on a gunpowder altar of God. In his Bible, Melville underscored Exodus 15:3, which asserts, "The Lord is a man of war," a chillingly militaristic line.[50]

In true military fashion, attendance at divine services is required, even though, as White-Jacket reminds us, this practice violates the constitutional guarantee that government will neither abridge religious freedom nor dictate belief and practice. This, he comments sardonically, "is only one of several things in which the Articles of War are opposed to the Constitution."[51]

Along with religion and law, medicine comes in for scathing criticism in *White-Jacket.* Captain Cadwallader Cuticle, the ship's sadistic surgeon and a connoisseur of "Morbid Anatomy," collects cancers and deformed limbs. Each night he thoughtlessly hangs his hat on the plaster cast of a former patient, a woman born with "a hideous, crumpled horn, like that of a ram, downward growing out from the forehead, and partly shadowing the face." White-Jacket, by contrast, pities the poor woman for her "gnawing sorrow" and grieves to think of anyone "leading a life of agonized penitence without hope." The thought of the suffering she must have endured makes his "whole heart burst with sorrow."[52]

Cadwallader Cuticle, as his name suggests, is modeled on Tobias Smollett's callous bonesetters. In a scene that seems to blend Hogarthian horror and Dickensian grotesqueness, a maintopman is brought to the sick bay with a ball of shot through his right thigh. Instead of tending to the patient right away, Cuticle consults with surgeons from neighboring ships about whether or not to amputate the leg, and they all advise him that it's unnecessary, but he goes ahead with it anyway: "They say he can drop a leg in one minute and ten seconds from the moment the knife touches it," an admiring colleague says. Predictably, the operation is a terrific success, but the patient dies surrounded by doctors telling ghoulish jokes.[53]

Aboard the *Neversink,* efficiency is the paramount value, not compassion. Baffled by man's capacity for evil, Melville portrays the "surgeon of the fleet" as a moral monster whose "apparent heartlessness must have been of a purely scientific origin," and his "man-of-war world" is uncannily prophetic of twentieth-century totalitarianism.[54]

The *Neversink* is a savagely racist and classist institution. In one scene, the sadistic

Captain Claret forces Rose-Water, "a slender and rather handsome mulatto," into a head-bumping contest with May Day, a "full-blooded '*bull-negro*' . . . with a skull like an iron tea-kettle." Claret watches their "gladiatorial" contest with glee, and after Rose-Water has nearly beaten May Day to a pulp, he orders the master-at-arms to arrest them for fighting on shipboard and flogs "both culprits" unmercifully, "in the most impartial manner," as White-Jacket puts it sarcastically.[55]

On the homeward voyage, Captain Claret suddenly decides that the sailors look like "savages" and that people in America will "think them all catamounts and Turks." This last mutilation, the "massacre of the beards," portrays the symbolic castration of the sailors by the officers. The men vow to resist the captain's tyrannical order, but naval discipline prevails, and even "Mad Jack" yields to the barber's scissors as the men are lined up and forced to submit to the humiliation of being shaved and shorn by order of the imperious officers.

Only old Ushant, "the Nestor of the crew," stands firm and keeps his beard. After enduring twelve lashes and spending the remainder of the voyage in the brig, he is set free on American soil, proclaiming triumphantly, "At home, with my beard!" Remembering his brother's order to have his whiskers sheared, Melville strikes back with the pen against both the aggressions of "severe and chastising fathers" and the repressions of "Home" and "Mother."[56]

Melville's adolescence had been complicated not only by the absence of his father during those crucial years, but also by his mother's having to play the roles of both mother and father to her children after her husband's death. In the fatherless Melville household, Mother Melville ruled with a "sense of duty [that] overc[ame] the sense of love." His father's early death cheated him of a chance to work through the natural rivalry that pits sons against fathers until he could achieve the generational reconciliation that would allow him to enter fatherhood unburdened by patricidal fantasies.

Having taken a scalpel to the United States Navy, Melville attempts to bandage the sensibilities of his readers by admitting in the last few chapters of *White-Jacket* that, although the *Neversink* has no room for "a seaman who exhibits traits of moral sensitiveness," other vessels are "blessed with patriarchal, intellectual Captains, gentlemanly and brotherly officers, and docile and Christianized crews." Somehow, though, his eleventh-hour assurances that not all frigates are like the *Neversink* and that "the American Navy needs no eulogist but History" do not offset the devastating effect of all that has gone before.[57]

As the *Neversink* approaches port, she leaves a "tranquil wake" that belies the hellish events of the cruise she has completed. White-Jacket takes his place in the maintop beside Jack Chase and his watchmates, looking to the "glorious Future" as he delivers a valediction to his shipmates:

We main-top men are all aloft in the top; and round our mast we circle, a brother-band, hand in hand all spliced together. We have reefed the last top-sail; trained the last gun; blown the last match; bowed to the last blast; been tranced in the last calm.... We have seen our last man scourged at the gang-way; our last man gasp out the ghost in the stifling sick-bay; our last man tossed to the sharks. Our last death-denouncing Article of War has been read; and far inland, in that blessed clime whitherward our frigate now glides, the last wrong in our frigate will be remembered no more.[58]

As the men rock hand in hand in their "Pisgah top," the "ever-noble Jack Chase, the matchless and unmatchable Jack Chase," sings out some lines of the Portuguese poet Camoëns, letting song and poetry have the penultimate word. The United States becomes the "world-frigate, of which God was the shipwright" and which "is but one craft in a Milky-Way fleet," sailing through the air "under sealed orders" from the "Lord High Admiral"—a troubling image of God's universe as a totalitarian dystopia flying blind.

Shortly before the *Neversink* reaches port, White-Jacket symbolically dies and is reborn. In a reverie, he falls from the mainmast, then hears a "thunder-boom" in his ear, and a "bloody film" passes before his eyes "through which, ghost-like, passed and repassed my father, mother, and sisters." His lungs collapse as he approaches "the cen-tre of the terraqueous globe," and he realizes this is Death, "the speechless profound of the sea." Struggling free of his cumbersome jacket, he propels himself to the surface and rips off the "shroud . . . as if I were ripping open myself." He swims away from the jacket just in time, as his shipmates mistake the white object for a marauding shark and dart their harpoons into it, missing him by inches.[59]

Like Ahab and, later, the reckless Pierre, Melville had to fling himself into the jaws of death to feel fully alive. It was as though he needed to risk his life again and again, fig-uratively speaking, to test whether the cruel, faceless universe cared if he survived. The ripping off of the white "shroud" signals his liberation from the self-imposed mutilation that service to the Articles of War implies, freeing him to be a writer. For Melville, fill-ing white paper with his ideas and visions, hiding them in pockets, and in pockets within pockets, allowed him to create texts that defied the "heartless immensities" that threat-ened to engulf and annihilate the soul.

～⁓

Redburn's popularity prompted Harper's to advance Melville $500 for "White-Jacket &c," and in September, Melville decided to take the manuscript to England him-self and sell it directly to Richard Bentley rather than sending it to him via his agent

John Brodhead. Thus he could travel and enjoy a much-needed rest before going to work on another book. He had made up his mind to ask Bentley for £200 plus an advance, and if Bentley would not meet this figure, he would offer the manuscript to other publishers.

Melville asked Evert Duyckinck, who had made his own Grand Tour of Europe a decade earlier, to accompany him, as Duyckinck would be the ideal guide through the art galleries of London and the Continent. In a letter to his brother George, Duyckinck wrote: "Melville put me all in a flutter the other evening by proposing that I should go to Europe with him on a cheap adventurous flying tour of eight months, compassing Rome! He sets out in a London packet in a few weeks carrying the proof of his new book." Duyckinck wasn't able to join Melville, but he loaned Melville four guidebooks, all of which would prove more helpful to Melville than *The Picture of Liverpool* had been to Redburn.[60]

Judge Shaw, who always had the welfare of his daughter and her family at heart, loaned Herman the money for his trip, but it was probably too costly for them both to go, and even if Judge Shaw were to give Lizzie money for the trip, it would be difficult to travel with the baby, and unthinkable to leave the little one behind.[61]

At first, Lizzie was "inconsolable" at the thought of Herman's being away for such a long time. In the end, however, she realized that the trip was a chance for her husband to recuperate from the strain he had been under since writing *Mardi*. He had produced three full-length novels in less than two years—one of them really three books in one. Lizzie hoped that he could negotiate an advantageous contract in London and that a change of scene would help him regain his strength and equilibrium.

With *White-Jacket* behind them, the Melvilles could again concentrate on domestic matters such as having Malcolm baptized. Lizzie had recently become a pew-renter at All Soul's Unitarian Church, so they called on the new pastor, Dr. Henry Whitney Bellows, to officiate at a service in their home. Then they made plans for Lizzie and Malcolm and the nurse to spend the time while Herman was in Europe with Lizzie's parents in Boston. "Lizzie is becoming reconciled to the idea of my departure," Melville wrote Judge Shaw, "especially as she will have Malcolm for company during my absence. And I have no doubt, that when she finds herself surrounded by her old friends in Boston, she will bear the temporary separation with more philosophy than she has anticipated. At any rate, she will be ministered to by the best of freinds [sic]."[62]

He was relieved to know she would be with her parents, as he wasn't sure how long he would be gone. If he could collect the one hundred pounds Bentley owed him for *Redburn* and get a large advance for *White-Jacket*, he planned to tour Italy and the Levant, but as he told Judge Shaw, he knew his travels would have to be "bounded by my purse & by prudential considerations," and he vowed that economy would be his "mottoe."[63]

Shortly before he left for England, Melville picked up a pamphlet called *The Life and Remarkable Adventures of Israel R. Potter (A Native of Cranston, Rhode Island), Who Was a Soldier in the American Revolution* from a downtown bookstall. It was the story of how one poor farmer who fought in the Revolution lost everything, was taken to England, and spent half a lifetime trying to get back to an America that had no place for him. Something in Potter's pathetic story struck a chord in the grandson of two heroes of the Revolution, so he tucked the pamphlet away for future use.

He also wrote Richard Henry Dana a "confidential" letter about *White-Jacket*: "This man-of-war book, My Dear Sir, is in some parts rather man-of-*warish* in style—rather aggressive, I fear.—But you, who like myself, have experienced in person the usages to which a sailor is subjected, will not wonder, perhaps, at any thing in the book. Would to God, that every man who shall read it, had been before the mast in an armed ship, that he might know something himself of what he shall only read of." Signing himself "fraternally yours—a sea-brother," he added a postscript to make sure Dana wouldn't confuse the two books: "A little nursery tale of mine . . . called 'Redburn' is not the book to which I refer above." *Redburn* was no "little nursery tale."[64]

Melville told Judge Shaw that he expected *White-Jacket* to "be attacked in some quarters" because of its graphic exposé of abuses by naval officers. He anticipated "no particular reception of any kind" for *Redburn*, however. "It may be deemed a book of tolerable entertainment;—& may be accounted dull." He felt *Mardi* was a work of genius and that *Redburn* and *White-Jacket* were "two *jobs*, which I have done for money—being forced to it, as other men are to sawing wood," but he was selling himself short, as despite their popularity in their day, they are fine, enduring books.[65]

"In writing these two books," he went on, "I have not repressed myself much—so far as *they* are concerned; but have spoken pretty much as I feel." Yet, "being books, written in this way, my only desire for their 'success' (as it is called) springs from my pocket, & not from my heart. So far as I am individually concerned, & independent of my pocket, it is my earnest desire to write those sorts of books which are said to 'fail.' —Pardon this egotism."[66]

Maria Gansevoort Melville raised eight children after her husband's death and remained a strong force in their lives.

TWELVE

THE PRINCE OF WHALES

On a wet and blustery October 11, 1849, his brother Allan and George Duyckinck saw Melville off for England and the Continent. The Southampton, a three-decker sailing packet, was piloted through the Narrows by a "large, beefy-looking fellow" who looked more like an oysterman than a sailor. Once the ship reached open water, she squared her yards and "dashed on, under double-reefed topsails" in "half a gale."[1]

For his first ocean crossing as a passenger, Melville had a "spacious berth" with a large washstand, a sofa, and a mirror, and he was "the only person on board" to be "honored" with a private stateroom. "I have plenty of light, & a little thick glass window in the side, which in fine weather I may open to the air. I have looked out upon the sea from it, often, though not yet 24 hours on board," he wrote in his journal.[2]

The first morning out dawned clear, and he climbed the rigging "by way of gymnastics" before breakfast. "The ocean looked the same as ever," and he relished "the old emotions of being at the masthead." By 10:00 A.M., gale winds and rain had forced most of the passengers below the decks to suffer the agonies of seasickness. As the others weathered their first storm at sea, it was hard for a seasoned tar like Melville not to feel smug.[3]

The ship's passengers included an Englishman who carried moose antlers with him as "trophies of his prowess in the woods of Maine" and "a middle-aged woman who sturdily walks the deck, & prides herself upon her sea legs, & being an old tar." But Melville also found some congenial companions, foremost among them George Duyckinck's friend George J. Adler, a native of Leipzig who taught German philology at the University of the City of New York (renamed New York University in 1896). Dr. Adler, who had recently finished compiling "a formidable lexicon (German & English)" which made him "almost crazy, he tells me, for a time," was traveling abroad for his health.[4]

Melville and Professor Adler spent hours discussing "Fixed Fate, Free Will, foreknowledge absolute," and when they weren't debating the relative merits of the philosophies of Kant, Swedenborg, and Schlegel, they were consulting Dr. Franklin Taylor, a cousin of "the pedestrian traveller" Bayard Taylor, about "a plan for going down the Danube from Vienna to Constantinople; thence to Athens in the steamer; to Beyroot [sic] & Jerusalem–Alexandria & the Pyramids." The two philosophers were eager to travel with Dr. Taylor, as he had "a good deal of experience in cheap European travel" and knew German, which Melville thought would be helpful in Austria and Turkey: "I am full (just now) of this glorious Eastern jaunt. Think of it!"[5]

For the next few days, squalls buffeted the "rolling & pitching" ship, and everyone except Melville was deathly sick. Seasickness could drive people to desperation, and one evening when he went out on the deserted deck to escape the "nausea noise" below, Melville spied "a man in the water, his head completely lifted above the waves." "Man overboard!" he shouted, grabbing a rope and tossing it to the drowning man, but to his horror, the man refused help from several seamen who had swung out over him on chains and lowered ropes. He allowed himself to drift out of reach until, expelling a few bubbles, he sank out of sight. "I was struck by the expression of his face in the water," Melville wrote. "It was merry."[6]

The captain, unruffled by the incident, told Melville that the poor chap had threatened to jump earlier, holding his child in his arms, and that four or five passengers threw themselves overboard during every transatlantic crossing. Once a man had hurled himself into the sea with his wife standing right beside him, and as her husband went down for the third time, the woman shrugged her shoulders and said there were "plenty more men to be had." Encounters with other passengers who were harboring strange delusions led Melville to observe that "mad feelings found something congenial in the riot of the raging sea."[7]

In his solitary moments, Melville enjoyed the voyage as only a trained seaman who has none of the customary duties or restrictions can: "Fine moonlight night, & we rushed on through snow-banks of foam," he wrote after one of his voluntary watches in the maintop. One night the captain drew him aside to show him corposants on the yardarm. These flaming balls of electrical energy, resembling "large, dim stars in the sky," the first Melville had ever seen, reappear in *Moby-Dick*.[8]

October 14 was a "regular blue devel [*sic*] day," but despite the strong swells, Melville stretched his legs on rolling, slippery decks that sent other passengers into fits of prayer. Although reading was difficult in such rough seas, Melville managed to settle down with the copy of Caroline Kirkland's *Holidays Abroad; or, Europe from the West* that he had borrowed from George Duyckinck. A "spirited, sensible, fine woman," Mrs. Kirkland had written a lively account of her experiences on the Michigan frontier as well as this vivid account of her European tour.[9]

Melville was especially taken by her opening description of Samuel Rogers, the eighty-seven-year-old "Nestor of English poets," as he was carrying a letter of introduction to Rogers from Judge Shaw's friend Edward Everett, editor of the *North American Review*. An erudite, acerbic bachelor and a banker by profession, Rogers had written and published poetry in his youth, and two of his poems appeared in Melville's well-thumbed *London Carcanet*. It was considered a great honor to dine from gold-plated dishes in Rogers's spacious breakfast room, which housed one of the finest private art collections in Europe. A breakfast with Rogers, Mrs. Kirkland had written, was "among the much-coveted and long-remembered pleasures of the traveller."[10]

Once the storm blew off and the weather turned "beautiful," the landlubbers groped their way up on deck, pronouncing Melville "a hero, proof against wind & weather" because he had managed both to read and to walk upright during the big blow. Melville, who thoroughly enjoyed his shipboard celebrity, was so pleased to see a woman reading *Omoo* on deck that he showed off a bit by doing "feats in the rigging," which the others considered "a species of tight-rope dancing." His daring ascent of the polished spars impressed them mightily, as did his calling each sail by its proper name.[11]

Suddenly the brisk following wind changed quarter, and as the ship pushed against headwinds under sunny skies, Melville felt enervated. He even found it hard to read: "The sea has produced a temporary effect upon me which makes me for the time incapable of anything but vegetating." Feeling vulnerable and "homesick from the start," he scrawled, "What's little Barney about?" and "Where's Orianna?" in his journal, using two of his pet names for his child and wife.[12]

Melville spent most of his time promenading on deck, occasionally "with some of the ladies," or playing shuffleboard. In the evenings he played chess or a rubber of whist in the salon. Not wanting to strain his eyes after months of intense work, he avoided heavy reading, but when "Newfoundland weather—foggy, rainy, &c." enshrouded the ship, he stayed in his cabin skimming over Murray's guidebook to Venice, which he had borrowed from Evert Duyckinck.[13]

On some evenings, Melville went on deck with Taylor and Adler to see the "splendid spectacle" of moon-spangled water from the bow; on other evenings, the three philosophers discussed Kant and Hegel over champagne, mulled wine, or whiskey punch in the bar. Eating and drinking with so little physical labor to do put weight on Melville, even though he ran "about aloft a good deal."[14]

Melville and Taylor, who was "full of fun," organized high jinks to amuse themselves and their fellow passengers. One day, Melville put Taylor up to playing "a rare joke" on "a sickly youth" named McCurdy. Borrowing a cloak, Taylor passed himself off as Miss Wilbur, an earnest young woman who prided herself on "winning souls to Christ," and made "advances" on the neurasthenic young man.[15]

A favorite shipboard entertainment on ocean cruises was the mock trial, which may have been a gentler version of King Neptune's Court, the rite of passage sailors had to undergo when they first "crossed the Line." One afternoon, Melville and Taylor arraigned Adler before the captain on a mock criminal charge, and the same evening they "put the Captain in the Chair, & argued the question 'which was best, a Monarchy or a republic?' "[16]

Three weeks from New York, the *Southampton* passed the Scilly Isles, and Melville sighted land birds. Although the newer steamships could make the crossing in a week and a half or two weeks, Melville had chosen the slower vessel to economize. Eager to see HMS *Victory,* which lay in drydock at Portsmouth after returning from Trafalgar with Lord Horatio Nelson's body, Melville was disappointed when they sailed past the harbor without stopping.

For two days the ship tacked up the Channel against the wind, and just as Melville could see plowed fields on the Isle of Wight, the wind "fell flat calm." They sat in irons for hours until a wind blew up from the west and the crew "squared the yards & struck away for Dover," about sixty miles away.[17]

Melville was beginning to doubt that the ship would make land "next week—or next year." He felt so bloated from lack of exercise that he persuaded Adler and Taylor that the three of them should leave the ship at Dover and walk most of the way to London via Canterbury. As he retired to his stateroom to pack the carpetbag he had borrowed from Adler, someone dropped "a mysterious hint" about his "green coat." He marked his luggage to be sent on separately by boat to London, and wrote in his journal: "This time tomorrow, I shall be on land, & press English earth after the lapse of ten years—*then* a sailor, *now* H. M. author of 'Peedee,' 'Hullabaloo' & 'Pog-Dog.' For the last time I lay aside my '*log*,' to add a line or two to Lizzie's letter—the last I shall write onboard."

"('Where dat old man'–'Where books?'),," he added parenthetically, hearing little Malcolm's voice with memory's ear.[18]

The ship docked at Deal instead of Dover at 5:00 A.M., and as Melville set foot on the very spot where Julius Caesar had commenced his conquest of Britain centuries earlier, he imagined conquering Richard Bentley with his man-of-war narrative. Reaching Sandwich after a brisk walk, he and his friends breakfasted in "a tumbledown old inn" and "finished with ale & pipes." They visited "Richboro Castle," a Roman fortification with a spectacular view of the sea, and ambled around the town, then took the train to Canterbury, whose cathedral was "on many accounts the most remarkable in England. Henry II, his wife, & the Black Prince are here–& Becket. Ugly place where they killed him. Fine Cloisters." That evening they ate supper at the Falstaff Inn and went to a play that had "more people on the stage than in the boxes. Ineffably funny, the whole affair."[19]

The next morning, after downing a "glass of ale," Melville and his friends boarded the train, and by the time they reached London they were so famished that they stopped at the first chop house they saw, and ate a huge meal before booking three rooms near the Strand. As they walked from 25 Craven Street to Queen's Hotel to find their "ship friends," Melville noticed that, as predicted, people were looking askance at his green coat.[20]

The other travelers were already out sightseeing, so Melville, Adler, and Taylor went to Julien's Promenade Concerts in Drury Lane, where "great crowds" of people gathered to hear music. In the concert hall's well-stocked reading room, Melville read reviews of *Redburn* in *Bentley's Miscellany* and *Blackwood's* that struck him as "very comical" for "treating the thing as real." Although he claimed to have written *Redburn* "to buy some tobacco with," and thought it ridiculous for critics to "waste so many pages upon a thing, which I, the author, know to be trash," he was not above checking to see whether copies of the book were available in stores along Paternoster Row.[21]

The following day, Melville went to Richard Bentley's office at 8 New Burlington Street, only to learn that his publisher had gone to Brighton for the weekend. Bentley's assistant gave him more reviews of *Redburn*, which he found "laughable" in the extreme. Leaving Bentley's, he walked to 50 Albemarle Street, but he managed to miss John Murray, too.[22]

Disappointed, he went on to the National Gallery, where he saw masterworks by Guido Reni, Salvator Rosa, Raphael, Hogarth, Teniers, Claude Lorrain, and others that were familiar to him from prints and books in Evert Duyckinck's collection. He also saw paintings by a number of modern British artists, most notably the iconoclastic J. M. W. Turner, whom art critic John Ruskin had praised in his book *Modern Painters*.[23]

That evening, Melville and his companions took "a dark ramble" through Chancery

Lane and Lincoln's Inn Fields, winding up at the Princess Theatre on Oxford Street, where they saw several short pieces in the "half price" pit. The next day, Melville went to Cheapside alone to see the parade of ships and bands and banners celebrating the Lord Mayor's election—a display of pageantry that struck him as "a most bloated pomp, to be sure." Strolling back along the embankment of the Thames, he paused before a cast-iron statue of the old Duke of Wellington, and as he crossed a bridge over the dark river, he mused that London might be described as "a city of Dis (Dante's) clouds of smoke—the damned &c—coal barges—coaly [sic] waters."[24]

Receiving a note from Richard Bentley offering to come up from Brighton at the author's convenience, Melville responded that he would be at Bentley's office Monday morning.

Melville "lounged away the day—sauntering thro' the Temple courts & gardens" and "down Holborn Hill, thro' Cock Lane," reputedly the haunt of ghosts, though they were ghosts soundly disbelieved in by Dr. Johnson. As he wandered around Smithfield Market, the site of Bartholomew Fair, then past Charter House and through the Barbican Gate, near John Milton's home, a helpful fire officer took him to see the birthplace of Dick Whittington and showed him the way to the old Guildhall, where "a crowd of beggars were going to receive the broken meats & pies" from the "great civic feast & festivities" he had observed the day before.[25]

The grotesque contrast between the two events furnished Melville material for a satirical sketch called "Poor Man's Pudding and Rich Man's Crumbs." As he wrote later, the scene "within the hall" was comical. "Under the flaming banners & devices, were old broken tables set out with heaps of fowls hams &c&c pastry in profusion." As London's starving poor lined up to be served the leftovers from the Lord Mayor's feast by uniformed lackeys, "foreign ministers & many of the nobility" looked on like "gilded dunces."[26]

After viewing the headsman's block on Tower Hill, whose "very plain" axe-marks were grisly reminders of the executions of Kilmarnock and the Scottish Lords, Melville visited the Temple Church, which featured stone effigies of the Knights Templar, several of whom were depicted with crossed legs to indicate that they had been on a Crusade. A secret society dedicated to the highest ideals of holiness and honor, the Templars were forced to disband their brotherhood when their leaders, charged with heresy and sexual misconduct, were executed. Melville was fascinated by the Templars, who seemed emblematic of vice and corruption masquerading as virtue and purity.[27]

Although most guidebooks steered tourists away from the unlicensed theaters known as "gaffs," Melville talked Adler into attending a "Penny Theatre." Located in the overcrowded, dangerous slum districts, these establishments were considered "infamous nuisances, loathsome receptacles and holes of iniquity" by "respectable" Londoners.

Patrons gained access to the gallery by climbing rough ladders up to rickety seats so crowded together that fistfights were continually breaking out. Melville found the spectacle rather "comical," but Adler was "afraid."[28]

On Monday morning, Melville met with Richard Bentley. Bentley, who prided himself both on his taste and on his generosity to writers, immediately gave Melville the hundred pounds owed for *Redburn,* and after perusing *White-Jacket*'s table of contents, he offered "£200 for a first 1000 copies of the book (the privilege of publishing that number). And as we might afterwards arrange, concerning subsequent editions." A liberal offer. But he could make "no advance." Citing the "vexatious & uncertain state of the Copyright matter" as his reason for not giving Melville a cash advance, Bentley refrained from reminding Melville that the firm had lost money on *Mardi.*[29]

Needing cash for further travels, Melville took the manuscript straight to John Murray's office on Albemarle Street, but the publisher was out of town. Frustrated and disappointed, he walked to St. Paul's Cathedral, where he sat for over an hour listening to the choir and feeling "homesick & sentimentally unhappy."[30]

In 1849, England still held public executions. The crowd that gathered before dawn on November 13 to see Maria and George Manning go to the gallows was unusually large, as it was rare for a married couple to be hanged together. The Mannings had not only conspired in the brutal murder of a friend, but they were unrepentant and vindictive, turning against each other during their trial.[31]

Melville and Adler paid half a crown each "for a stand on the roof of a house adjoining," which put them on the level of the jail roof on which the gallows had been erected. From this vantage point they could see "an inimitable crowd in all the streets. Police by the hundreds. Men & women fainting. . . . The mob was brutish." As Melville watched the couple being "hung side by side—still unreconciled to each other," he could not help thinking that it was a striking "change from the time they stood up to be married, together! All in all, a most wonderful, horrible, & unspeakable scene."[32]

Unbeknownst to Melville, Charles Dickens was among the crowd of thirty thousand "screeching, and laughing, and yelling" onlookers, and he shared Melville's revulsion at the barbarism he witnessed: "I believe that a sight so inconceivably awful as the wickedness and levity of the immense crowd collected at the execution could be imagined by no man, and could be presented in no heathen land under the sun. . . . When the two miserable creatures . . . were turned quivering into the air, there was no more emotion, no more pity, no more thought that two immortal souls had gone to judgment, no more restraint in any of the previous obscenities than if the name of Christ had never been heard."[33]

Although this ghastly spectacle did not ruin their appetite for breakfast, Melville and Adler spent the remainder of that "dreary & rainy day" in Regent's Park, enjoying the comparative sanity of the animals in the Zoological Garden. Melville, perhaps in an attempt to blot out the image of the Mannings dangling from the nooses around their necks, stood for a long while watching the "fine giraffes."[34]

The next day, wearing his "*green* jacket" with defiant pride despite disapproving stares from passersby, Melville called on the august John Murray, who had asked him for a set of the proofs. While Murray read the manuscript, Melville and Adler saw Taylor and McCurdy off for the Near East, then tramped around St. John's Wood and Primrose Hill, from which Melville saw "a curious view." Toward Hampstead Heath, "the open country looked green, & the air was pretty clear; but cityward it was like a view of hell from Abraham's bosom. Clouds of smoke, as though you looked down at Mt. Washington in a mist"—an image no doubt remembered from his honeymoon.[35]

Melville went by himself to the afternoon service at Westminster Abbey, which was so crowded he was forced to stand, and later he and Adler ate supper at "The Edinburgh Castle," Melville's "beau ideal of a tavern—dark-walled, & like a beefsteak in color, polite waiters, &c" in detail. At this pub, which was noted for "its fine Scotch ale, the best I ever drank," he "had a glorious chop & a pancake, a pint & a half of ale, a cigar & a pipe, & talked high German metaphysics" with the professor.[36]

Oddly enough, Melville describes the pubs, especially those with literary associations, more fully than the great ecclesiastical and cultural institutions. His journal entry on a morning visit to the British Museum is telegraphic: "big arm & foot—Rosetta stone—Ninevah [*sic*] sculptures—&c." From the museum he walked to Albemarle Street to hear John Murray's verdict on *White-Jacket*. When Murray said that publishing the book "would not be in his line," Melville took the proofs to Henry Colburn, the publisher of Marryat, Bulwer-Lytton, and G. P. R. James.[37]

That evening, Melville met Adler at the Mitre Court Tavern, Fleet Street, where Samuel Johnson had dined regularly. They ate a very fine "stewed rump steak," bread, cheese, and ale, then went across the street to the rival "Dr. Johnson Tavern," the "darkest" of them all, where Melville smoked a cigar and drank another bumper of ale. Afterward, they saw a performance of Colley Cibber's comedy *She Would and She Would Not,* then paid a visit to Tennyson's "Cock Tavern," where they ordered two glasses of the stout "for which the place is famous" (it "sells no ales"), and smoked their pipes before retiring for the night.[38]

Based on his almost nightly inventory of what he ate and drank while he was in London, it's not surprising that Melville had to buy a new pair of "pantaloons" so he could leave his tight trousers with a tailor to be let out. He ate heavy, meaty meals and drank prodigious amounts of various types of alcoholic beverages. After a dinner party in East Sheen on November 24, for example, he noted in his journal that he came back to his room at midnight with "an indefinite quantity of Champaigne [*sic*] Sherry, Old Port, Hock, Madeira, & Claret in me."[39]

On Saturday, November 17, "Adler proposed a visit to the Dulwich Gallery," which was situated in "a most sequestered, quiet, charming spot indeed." This "gallery full of gems" owned Guido Reni's *St. John in the Wilderness,* Nicolas Poussin's *Assumption of the Virgin,* Murillo's paintings of peasant boys, portraits by Sir Joshua Reynolds, works of Titian, Salvator Rosa, and Claude Lorrain, and many Dutch and Flemish genre paintings, which were to influence Melville's later work. Melville and Adler were so impressed by the collection that they strolled through "green meadows & woodlands steeped in haze" to savor the "profound calm."[40]

When Melville returned to his lodging, he was greeted by a message from Henry Colburn, rejecting his manuscript on the grounds that "the cursed state of the copyright matter" forced him to turn it down. Dejected, Melville realized he might have more trouble selling the book than he had anticipated: "Bad news enough–I shall not see Rome–I'm floored–appetite unimpaired however–so down to the Edinburgh Castle & paid my compliments to a chop."[41]

During the next couple of days, Melville attended a performance of *Othello* that featured William Charles Macready, who "panted hideously," and a "very pretty Desdemona." He also listened to music at the Temple Church and Westminster Abbey, and during evensong at St. Bride's he "blushed a good deal, what with Stout, jam, heat, & modesty" and "excited a vast deal of gazing," either because he was wearing his green coat, or because he was so obviously inebriated.[42]

After seeing George Adler off for Paris, Melville mapped out his strategy for selling *White-Jacket.* First he presented his letters of introduction from Evert Duyckinck to the bookseller Thomas Delf and former Wiley & Putnam agent David Davidson, a friend of Duyckinck's, who later took Melville to dinner and to the American Bowling Saloon, where Melville "rolled one game & beat him."[43]

The following day, Melville took the proofs of *White-Jacket* to Edward Moxon, who had published the English edition of *Two Years Before the Mast.* He was "ushered into one of those jealous, guarded sanctums, in which these London publishers retreat from the vulgar gaze. It was a small, dim, religious looking room" which reminded him of "that Greenland whaler discovered near the Pole, adrift & silent in a calm, with the frozen form of a man seated at a desk in the cabin before an ink-stand of icy ink. Just so sat Mr. Moxon in that tranced cabin of his. I bowed to the spectre, & received such a galvanic return, that I thought something of running out for some officer of the Humane Society, & getting a supply of hot water & blankets to resuscitate this melancholy corpse."[44]

Although he had been a poet in his youth, Moxon was as "stiff, cold, clammy, &

clumsy" as a block of Arctic ice, and Melville's attempts to warm him up with "clever speeches" failed until he happened to mention having "dived into a volume of Charles Lamb's prose during the crossing." At the mention of that "rare humorist & excellent hearted man," much loved by Americans as a "charming punster," Mr. Moxon "brightened up—grew cordial—hearty." He told Melville that Lamb was "the best fellow in the world to 'get drunk with'" and that he had "many a time put him to bed." Despite this hard-won camaraderie, Moxon, too, declined to meet Melville's terms because of the copyright question.[45]

John Murray, like Richard Bentley, was hospitable to Melville while he was in London, showing him through the "gallery of literary portraits" in his office and inviting him to dinner with John Lockhart, editor of the *Edinburgh Review* and biographer of Sir Walter Scott. Melville found Murray's lodgings sepulchral and Lockhart "a thorough going Tory & fish-blooded Churchman & conservative" who wore "a prodigious white cravat (made from Walter Scott's shroud, I suppose)" and stalked about "like a half galvanized ghost." The other diners were "fifth rate looking varlets—& four lean women" whose "stiffness, formality, & coldness" Melville abhorred to the point that he "felt like knocking all their heads together." He survived the evening by conversing with a woman who had been in China, and with Queen Victoria's physician, Dr. Henry Holland, the son-in-law of the critic Sydney Smith, who had written *Travels in the Ionian Isles* (1815). Before turning in that night, Melville scrawled in his journal, "Oh Conventionalism, what a ninny, thou art, to be sure."[46]

By contrast to the austere Murray, Richard Bentley had a warm and gracious manner that grew on Melville, and he passed several relaxed evenings at Bentley's home, where he dined informally with the publisher's family and several travel writers. His greatest pleasure, however, was stopping by Bentley's office for his mail and finding a letter from home: "All well, thank God—& Barney a bouncer," he told his journal.[47]

Everywhere Melville went, he was conscious of the tremendous gap between rich and poor. During a tour of Greenwich Hospital, he was shocked to see wretched "crowds of pensioners" and wounded war veterans huddled together in bleak wards while tourists browsed through the "Painted Hall" of heroes, admiring the "sea-pieces & portraits of naval officers, coats of Nelson in glass cases." He talked with an old pensioner who told him an inside story about "sanctioned irregularities" in Lord Nelson's navy, and he saw an American, a "Negro," who had been impressed aboard a British frigate and was now in forced exile from his home.[48]

The next day, at Windsor Castle, Melville saw the mast of the *Victory* and a commemorative bust of Lord Nelson, as well as a Cellini shield and a Gobelin tapestry, and on leaving the tower he caught a glimpse of Queen Victoria "coming from visiting the sick Queen Dowager." Noting that she looked like an "amiable domestic woman" in need of complexion creams, he watched her drive off with Prince Albert in a carriage and four, flanked by outriders. Melville, who was certainly no monarchist, was charmed by the royal couple as they waved, noting in his journal, "God bless her, say I, and long live the prince of whales," one of the more amusing examples of Melville's idiosyncratic orthography.[49]

Melville got to know many "fine fellows, and hearts of bloods" in London, notably Henry Stevens, whom he "in some sort loved" because "he had been acquainted with 'my wife,' that is to say with Dolly." Stevens was a bookseller and dealer in antiquities whose clients included the Library of Congress, the Smithsonian Institution, and James Lenox of New York, for whom he had arranged the purchase of a Gutenberg Bible. Stevens took Melville to the British Museum for a private showing of manuscripts and "many rareities" [sic] including the Magna Carta, a Bible that had belonged to Charlemagne, and Shakespeare's autograph in a volume of Montaigne's *Essais*.[50]

Melville also met several people who had known Gansevoort during his brief tenure at the American legation. At one dinner party he had a long conversation with a friend of Gansevoort's who had seen him "not long before his end" and who spoke of him "with much feeling." By the time Melville returned to his room, the ghost had been conjured. Noting in his journal that he had seen a copy of *Typee* in his host's parlor, he mused, "No doubt, two years ago, or three, Gansevoort was writing here in London, about the same hour as this—alone in his chamber, in profound silence—as I am now. This silence is a strange thing. No wonder the old Greeks deemed it the vestibule to the higher mysteries."[51]

This entry reveals how closely Melville guarded the secrets of his heart. Whereas his journal usually records impressions for later use in his fiction, and contains evidence of frequent yearnings for his wife and child, rather than profound reflections on what his experiences meant to him, this entry expresses Melville's deep feelings for his dead brother. Perhaps the slightly intoxicated state in which Melville seems to have spent much of his first fortnight in London masks complicated and powerful emotions about Gansevoort. After recording his feelings about his brother, he "passed a most extraordinary night," suffering "one continuous nightmare till daylight." Oddly enough, writing in his journal the next morning, he attributed his disturbed sleep to the "cup of prodigiously strong coffee & another of tea" he had consumed the previous evening, rather than to the effects of grief.[52]

By November 27, Melville was ready to leave London. He threw a few clothes and other necessaries in the little portmanteau he had purchased for his jaunt to the

Continent and took the Channel steamer *Emerald* for Boulogne, glad that he would at least see something of the European continent, if not Italy and the Near East.

He arrived in Paris by train in the late afternoon. After checking into the Meurice and savoring some of the hotel's splendid cuisine, he went to Galignani's Reading Room to look for a message from his friend Adler, but he found none there. Realizing he could not afford to stay on the elegant Rue de Rivoli, he crossed to the Left Bank the following morning to find the *pension* Augustus Gardner had recommended. He engaged a sixth-floor room at Mme. Capelle's, "across the Pont (within a biscuit's toss of the Morgue)," then visited the Bourse, where stock traders formed "a mystic circle" before the altars of finance, and the Palais Royal.[53]

From Mme. Capelle's, he walked down to the Seine and explored that "noble old pile," the Cathedral of Notre Dame, then strolled through the Marais all the way to the Place de la Bastille before taking an omnibus back to the Louvre, where he spent three hours looking at "Heaps of treasures of art of all sorts. Admirable collection of antique statuary. Beats the British Museum," he wrote laconically.[54]

Repairing to Galignani's after dinner to read the newspapers from America, he discovered that gold had just been discovered in California and that "the thing called 'Redburn' had just been published" in New York. *The Literary World,* calling him "the De Foe of the ocean," was praising his least favorite book for "its strong relishing style" and "fidelity to nature." Before he could get too upset over the reviews, however, a note arrived from Adler, giving him "great joy."[55]

At the appointed hour, he went to Adler's lodgings, but his friend was "not in—so sat & jabbered as well as I could with Madam till he arrived. Was rejoiced to see him— we went together to his room—he brought out tobacco & we related our mutual experiences." When Melville got back to his room, he made a fire, but he could not get comfortable. It was "not home &—but no repinings," he wrote. The room gave him an uneasy feeling: "I don't like that mystic door (tapestry) leading out of the closet."[56]

The next morning he and Adler went by omnibus to Père-Lachaise Cemetery, where they saw the tomb of Abelard and Héloïse, and after strolling among the monuments, they tramped back through the city, crossing and recrossing the Seine, never tiring of the grand panorama visible from every bridge. After supper they stood in line at the Comédie Française hoping to see the celebrated Rachel, but they "were cut off." When they tried a second time to see Rachel and failed, they settled for the Opéra Comique and an "exquisite" cup of hot chocolate at the elegant Café de Fory.

On Sunday, Melville and Adler attended services at L'Eglise St.-Roch and a concert at the "Madeleine," the huge Church of St. Mary Magdelene, which was built in the style of a Greek temple to honor the armies of Napoleon. Melville visited other places in Paris that were either beautiful or bizarre, including the city morgue and the Musée

Dupreyten, which featured the "Pathological. Rows of cracked skulls. Skeletons and things without a name," the Palais Luxembourg, where he saw modern French paintings, and the Bibliothéque Royale, which featured stunning Dürer prints and Holbein etchings. Although he pronounced Versailles "a most magnificent & incredible affair altogether," the Hotel de Cluny, a medieval museum built over the ruins of Roman thermal baths, struck him as "just the house I should like to live."[57]

Adler tried to persuade Melville to remain in Paris for further "peregrinations," but Melville had his heart set on a cruise along the Rhine. "I regretted his departure very much," Adler wrote George Duyckinck, "but all I could do to check and fix his restless mind for a while at least was of no avail. His loyalty to his friends at home and the instinctive impulse of his imagination to assimilate and perhaps to work up into some beautiful chimaeras . . . the materials he has already gathered in his travels, would not allow him to prolong his stay."[58]

Unencumbered by even a portmanteau to avoid high luggage fares, Melville boarded a train that took him through Brussels, Liège, and Aix-la-Chapelle (Aachen) to the Rhine. At Cologne he attended Sunday services in the cathedral and went to St. Peter's Church to see Peter Paul Rubens's *Descent from the Cross*. He also saw "some odd old paintings; & one splendid one (a sinking ship, with the Captain at the mast-head — defying his foe)." The unfinished Dom, with the "everlasting crane" on its tower, would become a metaphor for Ishmael's never-to-be-completed cetological system, a trope for Melville's desire to achieve transcendent sublimity with his art. Repository of the treasure of the Magi, the Dom with its soaring High Gothic arches lifted his soul.[59]

His noon meal included "innumerable courses" with "an apple-pudding served between the courses of meat & poultry." Lingering over his last sip of yellow Rhenish wine, he gazed out at the great river, then "sallied out & roamed around the town–going into churches, buying cigars of pretty cigar girls, & stopping people in the streets to light my cigar. I drank in the very spirit & soul of old Charlemagne, as I turned the quaint old corners of this quaint old town. Crossed the bridge of boats, & visited the fortifications on the thither side. At dusk stopped at a beer shop–& took a glass of *black ale* in a comical flagon of glass.... I feel homesick for sure–being all alone with not a soul to talk to– but then the Rhine, is before me, & I must on. The sky is overcast, but it harmonizes with the spirit of the place."[60]

His bunk on the steamer to Coblenz was too cold for sleep, so he went on deck just in time to find "the boat gliding between tall black cliffs." When he reached the confluence of the Rhine and the Moselle, he scaled the fortress of Ehrenbreitstein: "The view from the summit superb. Far away winds the Rhine between its castellated mountains." In this country of Prince Metternich, full of "curious old churches, Gothic, half Italian," he ate midday dinner at "The Giant" and "drank nothing but Moselle wine–thus keeping the counsel of the 'governor of Coney Island' whose maxim it is 'to drink the wine of the country in which you may be travelling.' " At dusk he stood "in the silence at the point where the two storied old rivers meet" and looking up at the "frowning fortress," it occurred to him that "some 4000 miles [away was] America and Lizzie.–Tomorrow, I am *homeward-bound*. Hurrah & three cheers!"[61]

Aboard the Düsseldorf boat he decided that, despite the glorious ruins, "the river Rhine is not the Hudson." In Brussels he retrieved some shirts from the laundry and embarked on a "long dreary cold ride to Ostend on the coast," during which he was seized "with a fit of the nightmare." After surviving an execrable Channel crossing without getting sick, Melville arrived back in London the next day.[62]

As soon as he had shed his "villain's garb" and washed and shaved, he went to Bentley's office to check for mail. Along with some letters from home, he found an invitation from the poet and art collector Samuel Rogers and a note from the Duke of Rutland, inviting him to visit Belvoir Castle in January. How perverse fate could be! The coveted invitation from the duke had arrived too late, and the date specified for his visit was three weeks away. With Malcolm "growing all the time," he was missing out on the spectacular events of his son's babyhood. Letters from Lizzie and Allan made him feel "the blues most terribly–Felt like chartering a small-boat & starting down the Thames instanter for New York."[63]

Afraid he might not be able to sell *White-Jacket* before leaving England, Melville decided that his "green coat plays the devil with my respectability here" and bought himself "a Paletot in the Strand so as to look decent." He also "bought a pair of pantaloons for one pound five" and had a barber cut his hair, which was "as long as a wild Indian's."[64]

The following day, he purchased a "much desired copy of Rousseau's Confessions" on Holywell Street, where both prostitutes and booksellers peddled their wares, and, determined "to do something about that 'pesky' book," he called on Richard Bentley. Not finding the publisher in the office, Melville spent the next few hours shopping and wishing he had more cash to spend. "I very much doubt whether Gabriel enters the portals of Heaven without a fee to Peter the porter–so impossible is it to travel without money."[65]

When Melville returned to Bentley's office the following afternoon, the publisher, "a very fine frank off-handed old gentleman" whom he had grown to like, offered him two hundred pounds at six months for the first one thousand copies, with the book to be published on the first of March. Having "succeeded most admirably in his business here," as David Davidson reported to his friend George Duyckinck, Melville was elated; he could now go home.[66]

As usual, Melville wanted to do two incompatible things simultaneously: to visit Belvoir Castle to see how the English aristocracy really lived, and to go home as soon as possible, so he had put off answering the Duke of Rutland's invitation. Resolving to make up his mind in the afternoon, he went to church to hear "my famed namesake (almost) The Reverend H Melvill" of St. Thomas, Goswell Street, preach. The Reverend Melvill was as popular in London as Henry Ward Beecher was in Brooklyn, and Melville thought his sermon on charity was "admirable" if one granted the premises of "an 'orthodox' divine."[67]

He returned from church in a meditative mood, and found himself overwhelmed by homesickness: "It is now 3 P.M. I have had a fire made & am smoking a cigar. Would that One I know were here. Would that the Little One too were here," he pined. "I am in a very painful state of uncertainty. I am all eagerness to get home . . . yet here I have before me a style of life, which in all probability I shall never have again. I should much like to know what the highest English aristocracy really & practically is." Was it worth delaying his departure? "Three weeks!" he exclaimed in his journal. "If I could but get over *them*!"[68]

Although Allan would call him "a ninny" for not going to Belvoir, and he would kick himself later "for neglecting such an opportunity of procuring 'material,'" he felt it would be "intolerable" to spend another three weeks away from Lizzie and his bouncing Barney, so the next day he booked passage on the *Independence*.[69]

Before Melville left London, he attended a gentlemen's dinner "up in the 5th story" of Elm Court hosted by John Murray's cousin and partner, Robert Francis Cooke, who had wandered among gypsies in his youth. Dinner in this "Paradise of Batchelors [*sic*]" provided Melville with material for a later story, and the next morning, Melville had a late breakfast alone with Samuel Rogers, a "rather remarkable-looking old man," whose breakfast-room was full of "Superb paintings" hung gallery-style from floor to ceiling. These private treasures included oils painted by almost every great European master from Michelangelo, Raphael, and Rembrandt to Titian, Velázquez, Tintoretto, and J. M. W. Turner, whose "boggy, squitchy" seascapes fascinated Melville.[70]

Melville had hardly a moment's respite during his last week in London, as several acquaintances invited him to dinner at their clubs. He met Charles Knight, the publisher of the *Penny Cyclopaedia,* one of his favorite reference books, and John Tenniel, who would later become famous for his illustrations to *Alice in Wonderland* and *Through the Looking-Glass.*[71]

Before leaving, he purchased several books and a London map labeled "(A.D.

1766)," which would come in handy "in case I serve up the Revolutionary narrative of a beggar."[72]

Right after Christmas, Melville went to Portsmouth to see Lord Nelson's *Victory* and boarded the *Independence* for America. As a brisk breeze sped the ship toward Land's End, he closed his journal with a terse "No events happen—& therefore I shall keep no further diary." Happy to be "pointing for home," he couldn't wait to dive into the books he had purchased.[73]

He had done very little reading on the voyage out; games, parties, and talks with Adler and Taylor had afforded his eyes and overworked brain a much-needed rest after the intense activity of the past few years. On the voyage home, however, he was already beginning the great ingathering that preceded the composition of a new book. He read Beaumont and Fletcher's *Fifty Comedies & Tragedies* and a dozen more volumes, underscoring, annotating, and writing marginal comments.[74]

As soon as the *Independence* docked in New York on January 31, Melville rushed home to see his wife and baby. Sam Shaw, who had accompanied Lizzie and Malcolm down from Boston, stayed with the Melvilles for a few days before returning home laden with gifts from Herman, who was especially proud of the "university bread trencher" he had brought back for Hope Shaw, as this type of enormous serving tray, modeled on those used in university dining halls since medieval times, had become very fashionable in British homes of late. He had already sent Judge Shaw a broadside from London announcing the Mannings' execution.

Among Melville's gifts for his immediate family were matching kid gloves and shoes from Paris for Lizzie and a silver fork for little Malcolm. He presented Evert Duyckinck with a specially bound three-volume edition of *Mardi* and a fine edition of Samuel Butler's *Hudibras,* and gave Evert's brother George a bronze medal "from a mountainous defile of a narrow street in the Latin Quarter of Paris, where I disinterred it from an old antiquary's cellar."[75]

With his gift of *Mardi* for Duyckinck, Melville enclosed a florid "apology" for giving him a book with uncut leaves for his "choice conservatory of exotics & other rare things in literature," assuring him that, nonetheless, a book with uncut leaves "may possibly—by some miracle that is—flower like the aloe, a hundred years hence—or not flower at all, which is more likely by far, for some aloes never flower." What he meant was that if he could not achieve recognition for *Mardi* in his own time, he was certain that posterity would award it immortality. His words were more prophetic than he knew.[76]

～

Much as she'd missed Herman while he was abroad, Lizzie had surprised herself by having a good time. It was fun to be "single" again after two years of married life. A bride who had moved away from her hometown had little opportunity to see her closest friends. The Shaws had "much young company" while Lizzie was home, and she enjoyed seeing her women friends and relatives as much as her husband enjoyed the company of Allan, the Duyckincks, and other men. She especially loved showing Malcolm off and reminiscing with Jane Dow and others about their girlhood escapades and what had transpired for them since they were last together.

She was used to the way her father expressed his love for her through affectionate gestures and words. Her husband, by contrast, oscillated between playful teasing, extravagant gallantry, and painful needling, keeping Lizzie off balance with his unpredictable behavior and moods. Instead of daring to say what she needed for fear he would react defensively or with sharp sarcasm, she kept her feelings to herself. Having an overly critical mother-in-law made things worse; almost before she realized what was happening, her confidence in herself had been diminished. A few months with her family in Boston had done her a world of good. Still, as much as she savored the return to girlhood freedom allowed by her husband's absence, she was overjoyed when she learned that her "darling husband," as Augusta referred to Herman, would be home soon.[77]

Although Melville had longed to be with his family while he was away, soon after the greetings, the gifts, the shared stories, and the bursts of play and silliness with Malcolm, he went back to work again. When Evert Duyckinck offered him concert tickets right after his arrival, he turned them down, later remarking, "I should have gone—as I love music—were it not that having been shut up all day, I could not stand being shut up all the evening—so I mounted my *green* jacket & strolled down to the Battery to study the stars." Tracing the white wake of the Milky Way across the black reaches of outer space was far more appealing to Melville than sitting inside a concert hall after a day of writing.[78]

About a month after Melville returned to America, *White-Jacket* was released and reviewed in England. *John Bull*'s reviewer grudgingly granted that Melville was "an improving and a vastly improved writer," and speculated that the "rattling youngster" must have been transformed into "a thoughtful man" either by "the influence of time," the "salutary castigation of criticism," the "chastening experience of life," or "the severe conflict of a better principle within." He went on to attack Melville's "freedom in touching upon sacred subjects," complaining that "deeper and more dangerous still, there is running through the whole of his views a philosophy which ill accords with the truth of revelation."[79]

The *Athenaeum* reprinted several excerpts from the book and extolled Melville's "poetry of the Ship," but made no mention of the chapters exposing naval abuses. For its reviewer, Henry F. Chorley, *White-Jacket* was proof that, despite "a thousand faults," Melville's work had "more vivacity, fancy, colour and energy than ninety-nine out of the

hundred who undertake to poeticize or to prate about 'sea-monsters or land monsters.'"
Chorley, who had compared *Mardi* unfavorably to Turner's "foggy" canvases, now compared Melville favorably to genre painters like Van Der Velde. To Melville, who considered Turner a genius and *Mardi* superior to all his other books including the latest, this was a painful irony.[80]

While some reviewers pointed out every flaw they could find in *White-Jacket*, the critic for *The Spectator* commented that Melville had skillfully woven a series of "disquisitions" into his narrative, but took issue with his views on naval discipline. *The Atlas* was relieved to note that Melville thought conditions in the British Navy superior to those in the American, while *Britannia* asked how "the monstrous abuses and horrible tyranny he relates could have arisen under the jealous eye of Republican rule."[81]

Bentley's Miscellany, which had an obvious interest in promoting sales of the book, compared Melville favorably to other nautical writers, singling him out as one who "bathes the scene in the hues of a fanciful and reflective spirit, which gives it the interest of a creation of genius." With this rather inaccurate description of its style, the review called *White-Jacket* Melville's finest production. This was sincere praise, as in the same issue two other books published by Bentley received unfavorable notices.[82]

American publication of *White-Jacket* came in early spring, heralded by publication of excerpts from the book in *The Albion* and *The Literary World*. Anticipating strong sales from a book that was not only well written and carefully constructed, but topical as well, Harper's printed more than five thousand copies of *White-Jacket*, half in paper, half in cloth, but by the end of the first year, sales had slowed to a trickle.[83]

In an unsigned review of the book, Evert Duyckinck cited Melville's narratives for their "union of culture and experience, of thought and observation, that sharp breeze of the forecastle alternating with the mellow stillness of the library, books and work imparting to each other mutual life, which distinguishes the narratives of the author of *Typee* from all other productions of their class." The second part of the review focused on the alleged abuses of discipline in the navy, deeming the book "thoroughly American and democratic" and supporting Melville's right to "blow out" on the matter.[84]

The Albion's reviewer considered Melville reckless in condemning flogging itself rather than abuses of the practice, and Herrman S. Saroni, in *Saroni's Musical Times*, though he supported the absolute truthfulness of Melville's account based on his own "long and grievous penance in a man-of-war," felt that total abolition of flogging was ill-advised until steam power could replace manpower. Still, he suggested placing a copy of *White-Jacket* in every library to awaken "adventurous youth from their day-dreams of 'spicy islands' and 'moonlit waters.'"[85]

The most negative comments came, predictably enough, from the *Boston Post*, which advised Melville to stick to writing romances and not dabble in subjects such as "the administration of terrestrial affairs," on which he was not qualified to give opinions, "whether of religion or government, of ships or armies," and from *The United States Magazine and Democratic Review*, which accused Melville of making all his heroes British because English publishers paid better than their American counterparts. Noting that Melville had been "threatened by a rope's-end in the service," this reviewer commented snidely that he now seemed to be "approaching the end of his rope."[86]

Most American reviewers were won over by Melville's paean to Americans as "the peculiar, chosen people–the Israel of our time; [who] bear the ark of the liberties of the world" and praised him for his courage in attacking naval abuses. The book even redeemed him somewhat in the eyes of the religious press. *New-York Daily Tribune* reviewer George Ripley thought Melville had "performed an excellent service in revealing the secrets of his prison-house, and calling the public attention to the indescribable abominations of the naval life, reeking with the rankest corruption, cruelty, and blood."[87]

Melville undoubtedly knew that hearings had already been held in Washington concerning alleged abuses in the navy when he prefaced *White-Jacket* with the question, "Who knows that this humble narrative may not hereafter prove the history of an obsolete barbarism?" He clearly intended the book to serve as propaganda as much as art, in hopes of ending the oppressive practice of flogging that "is utterly repugnant to the spirit of our democratic institutions" and "involves a lingering trait of the worst times of a barbarous feudal aristocracy; in a word, we denounce it as religiously, morally, and immutably wrong."[88]

While his denunciation of flogging drew kudos from Nathaniel P. Willis, who called for reform in all military services, naval authorities such as Rear Admiral Thomas O. Selfridge Jr. attacked Melville's "many misnomers, misstatements & inconsistencies" in an attempt to discredit the book. The admiral's father, Thomas O. Selfridge, a prominent Federalist lawyer, had shot dead the eighteen-year-old son of a political opponent in downtown Boston. Claiming that he had acted in self-defense and in defense of his honor because the youth had attacked him with a hickory cane, he had taken refuge in jail "to elude *the fury of democracy*." He was acquitted partly because both Thomas Melvill Sr. and Lemuel Shaw testified on his behalf, another irony of history.[89]

How much influence *White-Jacket* actually had on subsequent reforms has never been determined. Rear Admiral Samuel Franklin, who, at the height of the controversy, advocated putting Melville's "eloquent appeal to the humane sentiment of the country ... on the desk of every member of Congress," claimed *White-Jacket* had "more influence in abolishing corporal punishment in the Navy than anything else." He later wrote that as a result of Melville's exposé, "a law was passed soon after the book appeared abolishing flogging in the Navy absolutely, without substituting any other mode of punishment in its stead." Most historians, however, feel it merely caught the wave of reform. Whether or not *White-Jacket* influenced the debates, when Congress finally outlawed flogging in the navy, Melville offered up "devout jubilations."[90]

～⁀

Pirates and confidence men were legion in the new nation, whose secret motto seemed to be "get rich quick" instead of "liberty and justice for all." In the expanding cities and rapidly proliferating new towns, an unscrupulous operator could swindle gullible customers out of their money and move on to a new town and change his name before the fraud could even be detected. They often adopted aliases and multiple identities, though some were notorious enough to rate coverage by the newspapers; such publicity gave them a kind of romantic immunity, as Americans have always admired frontier desperadoes and city slickers who know how to beat the system. Because the laws of the new market economy seemed to follow not so much enduring economic principles as the shrewd tactics of a sleazy poker game—bluffing, cheating, stacking the deck, and raking in the chips—the confidence man became a national archetype.[91]

Even the art world had its schemers and sharpers. One such literary confidence man was Thomas Powell, who had fled England to escape a charge of forgery. His main claim to fame when he arrived in New York was that he was English, which gave him instant cachet with culturally insecure Americans. This "bluff, hearty, lively Englishman, fond of genial companionship, good beer and conversation," soon joined the regulars at Pfaff's Restaurant, the literary hangout at 653 Broadway where journalist Walt Whitman held court at a corner table.

Powell had managed to ingratiate himself with Evert Duyckinck by giving him a copy of Tennyson's poems, allegedly annotated by the author, and showering him with phony anecdotes about British writers and politicians he pretended to know well. Duyckinck had loaned him sums of money that were never repaid, and Melville, before his departure for England, gave him a copy of *Mardi*, which Powell reciprocated with advice not to drink an alcoholic beverage in London without first asking its price. He also assured Melville that in England he would find "no low press or publishers to abuse him, & no respectable persons to believe him if they did," an allusion to Powell's being arrested in New York on charges he managed to evade by blatant lying.[92]

Duyckinck had sent the "Powell Papers" to Melville in London, and Melville's initial reaction was to feel sympathetic to the "Poor fellow—poor devel [*sic*]—poor Powell!" By December 17, 1849, however, "certain persons had called upon him denouncing Powell as a rogue." They had obviously seen Powell's *Living Authors of England*, a book not of criticism and biography, but full of scurrilous gossip, which had come out the month before. In it, Powell attacked Charles Dickens, who responded with an open letter to Lewis Gaylord Clark at the *Knickerbocker* calling Powell a "scoundrel" who had been a forger, a thief, an attempted suicide, and a lunatic in his home country. Clark, who had never had much use for Duyckinck or Cornelius Mathews, jumped at the chance to lambaste Duyckinck's "Mutual Admiration Society."[93]

Nathaniel Parker Willis wrote an editorial crediting Melville with being "one of the first and most signal realizers of the effect of the recent English repudiation of copyright," to which Powell retaliated with an unsigned diatribe to the *New York Herald* that charged "the flippant, kaleidoscopic, polka-dancing Melville" with being able "to line his pockets pretty substantially by the revenues accruing from his English editions." In the same piece he accused Washington Irving of plagiarism, so by the time Powell's *Living Authors of America* appeared in 1850, labeling Irving and Melville "the worst enemies of the national mind," everyone in New York was fed up with Powell and had decided he was beneath their notice.[94]

It was difficult for Melville to concentrate on serious writing when he was constantly being barraged by gossip and trivia, and when Charles F. Briggs in *Holden's Dollar Magazine* lumped him and Joel T. Headley together as "the two most popular writers among us, just now," Melville must have been annoyed. Headley was primarily a travel writer and military historian, not a serious fiction writer, and Melville did not want to be called a travel writer, or a sailor-novelist like Captain Marryat.[95]

These petty squabbles distracted Melville and soured him on New York soon after he returned from his trip. With Lizzie expecting another child and a new book incubating, he couldn't escape to sea again, but he could unfurl the sails of his imagination in his new book on the sperm whale fishery.

In March 1850 Melville reviewed James Fenimore Cooper's *The Red Rover* for *The Literary World*. Melville was fascinated by the "Red Rover," an enigmatic character through whom Cooper explores mysteries of identity that Melville, too, was pondering. Oddly, his review focused so much more on the way the volume was designed than on the text that it was published as "A Thought on Book-Binding," a Melvillean joke. By writing about the book's binding, which is a kind of costume or disguise, and a surface identity, Melville implied the ultimate unknowability of the text, and the mystery of the text beyond the text, both of the book and of the universe.[96]

Melville's next book would develop motifs Cooper borrowed from popular fiction, among them the ship's captain whose strange behavior convinces his crew that he is possessed by the devil. A stock character borrowed from novels featuring criminal protagonists on dark errands, bug-eyed corpses, and monstrous sperm whales ramming ships and sinking them to the bottom of the sea, the demonic captain becomes the main antagonist to Ishmael, the teacher-sailor-artist-narrator of *Moby-Dick*. Whirlpools of memory and desire churned through Melville's mind as he was about to set forth on what might be called his Berkshire voyage.

The Melvilles' neighbor Sarah Morewood, an indefatigable
arranger of picnics and parties, managed to stand still long enough for
Pittsfield photographer Rodney Dewey to take her picture.

THIRTEEN

THE ARDENT VIRGINIAN

Until now, living in the crowded town house had not slowed Melville's phenomenal rate of production, and with the women taking turns preparing the fair copy from his nearly illegible scrawl, he had completed five novels since returning from the Pacific. At age thirty-one, he was a well-known but controversial author who wrote at breakneck speed partly because he was bursting with turbulent emotions and raw creative energy, and partly because he could never make enough money from writing to pay his bills. Forced to rely on frequent subsidies from his father-in-law, he was always hoping the next book would be the one to make him financially independent.

Lizzie was finding life in the house "trying" now that the two toddlers were tearing around and Sophia was pregnant again. Tired of the "noise and city dirt," and "dreading the warm weather" that brought on her "rose cold," she was also eager to put some distance between herself and her meddlesome mother-in-law, something she kept to herself.[1]

Herman couldn't face a summer of writing in a hot, stuffy third-floor room, and worse, health authorities were predicting especially virulent epidemics that season. Pleasant memories of the Berkshires made him eager to introduce little "Barney" to the sights, sounds, smells, and rhythms of summer in the countryside he had loved so deeply as a boy. With his cousin talking about selling the old place, he wondered how many more chances he and Lizzie would have to visit his "first love," the Melvill farm, or "Banian Hall," as he called it, after the banyan tree in *Mardi*: "it seems the old original Hall of all this neighborhood—besides, it is a wide-spreading house, and the various outhouses seem shoots from it, that have taken root all round."[2]

Reviews of *White-Jacket* were still appearing when Melville wrote his "sea-brother," Richard Henry Dana Jr., to thank him for his good words about the book and about *Redburn*. Feeling bound to his fellow "blubber-hunter" by "a sort of Siamese link of affectionate sympathy," he wrote: "About the 'whaling voyage'—I am half way in the work, & am very glad that your suggestion so jumps with mine. It will be a strange sort of a book, tho', I fear; blubber is blubber you know; tho' you may get oil out of it, the poetry runs as hard as sap from a frozen maple tree;—& to cook the thing up, one must needs throw in a little fancy, which from the nature of the thing, must be ungainly as the gambols of the whales themselves. Yet I mean to give the truth of the thing, spite of this."[3]

Since 1847, when Melville had reviewed J. Ross Browne's *Etchings of a Whaling Cruise* for *The Literary World*, a number of whaling stories had been swirling through his mind. On April 29 he renewed his membership in the New York Society Library, and to jog his memory, he read or reread a half-dozen whaling narratives and Charles Wilkes's book on the United States exploring expedition. He also consulted Bayle's historical *Dictionary*, Kitto's *Cyclopaedia of Biblical Literature*, and Charles Knight's *Penny Cyclopaedia of Useful Knowledge*, which supplied him with the factual information about cetaceans that he needed to satisfy the demands of publishers for a narrative grounded in fact, not fantasy.[4]

In 1850 the novel was still not considered an elevated literary form by many educated Americans, especially those raised in religious households where fiction was thought to be frivolous, if not downright immoral. French novels were deemed indecent and risqué, and hybrid forms were even more suspect than novels and romances. Even Nathaniel Hawthorne had built an elaborate historical scaffolding around *The Scarlet Letter* to deflect criticism from his near-scandalous romance about Puritan New England.

For Melville, who had cut his teeth on the King James Bible, Shakespeare, Rabelais, Cervantes, Dante, Milton, Sterne, Burton, and Browne, no subject matter was off limits, and traditional literary forms were straitjackets. He much preferred to write organic, mixed-genre works that gave a sense of the narrator's mind probing, questioning, reflecting, shaping, and composing, but that meant challenging conventional notions of narrative, as he had done with the ill-favored *Mardi*, and risking oblivion.

Needing money to move the family to the Berkshires for the summer, Melville wrote to Richard Bentley toward the end of June to tell him that he expected to have ready for publication in the fall "a romance of adventure founded upon certain wild legends in the Southern Sperm Whale Fisheries, and illustrated by the author's own personal experience, for two years & more, as a harpooner."[5]

These "wild legends" included not only stories he had heard on shipboard, but such tales as J. N. Reynolds's story of the legendary Mocha Dick, published in the *Knickerbocker* in 1839, and Owen Chase's account of the ramming of the *Essex* by an eighty-foot-long sperm whale. "The reading of this wondrous story upon the landless sea, & close to the very latitude of the shipwreck had a surprising effect upon me," he noted in his copy of Chase's *Narrative*.[6]

In Thomas Beale's *The Natural History of the Sperm Whale*, Melville marked a passage describing a whale sinking horizontally under the water, leaving a whirlpool where his huge body had once floated, and in the margin, he wrote, "white & green vortex in the blue—as when a ship sinks." He also underlined Beale's description of a sinking ship making "horrid sounds of thunder, terrible in the extreme, *causing a sickening of the very soul,*" and on the title page he jotted, "Turner's pictures of whalers were suggested by this book." Turner's "aesthetic of the indistinct," his flouting of salon rules by using color to blur boundaries and dissolve conventional notions of form, struck a chord with him.[7]

Promising Richard Bentley that the new book would be worth more than his previous books because of its "great novelty," he requested an advance of two hundred pounds, the sum he had received for *White-Jacket*. Despite Melville's prediction that he would have the manuscript ready by the fall, the new book was fathoms away from being done. By the time Melville got in touch with Bentley again the following year, his manuscript had undergone a sea change into something rich and strange.

In July, Herman, Lizzie, Sophia, and the children left Allan practicing law in Manhattan and moved to Pittsfield for the summer. To familiarize himself with Berkshire history, Melville invested seventy-five cents in a *History of the County of Berkshire, Massachusetts by Gentlemen in the County, Clergymen and Laymen* (1829), edited by the Reverend David Dudley Field, rector of the Congregational Church in Stockbridge. This book contained such curiosities as the story of bugs that miraculously ate their way out of a table made from an apple tree in which their eggs had been deposited six to eight decades earlier. Henry David Thoreau would retell this story at the end of *Walden*, and Melville would base a magazine story on the tale.[8]

As a welcoming gift, Aunt Mary gave Herman a copy of Nathaniel Hawthorne's *Mosses from an Old Manse*, whose title sketch contained dreamy references to *Typee*, and made sure he knew the Hawthornes had moved to nearby Lenox. Melville hardly had time to glance at the book before his cousin invited him on a "rambling expedition" through South County. Robert was chairman of the "Viewing Committee" of the Berkshire County Agricultural Society, of which his father had been three times president, and he was hoping that if Herman came with him on his annual inspection of the crops, he might be able to inveigle him into writing the report.[9]

They drove south through Lenox and over the mountain to Richmond, where they stayed the night at old Captain Caleb Smith's pondside inn during a severe thunderstorm. The next morning they drove through Stockbridge and across the Housatonic "plains" to Great Barrington, Egremont, and Sheffield.[10]

A few months later, a report on the inspection tour that gave absolutely no information about the state of Berkshire agriculture appeared in the *Culturist and Gazette* under Robert's name. In mock-heroic style, the writer extols the efforts of farmers to exterminate ancient tribes of insects and reptiles, exhorting them to appreciate the benefits of manure and make special efforts to conserve it. The author of the report, who sounds suspiciously like the author of the chapter on ambergris in *Moby-Dick*, makes the wry suggestion that philosophers, naturalists, and farmers should take great pleasure "in contemplating that benign process by which ingredients the most offensive to the human senses are converted into articles that gratify the most delicate taste, and pamper the most luxurious appetite." The report occasioned a less skillful parody, the "Bunkum Agricultural Society...Report of the Committee on Crops," by "Z. Q. Factminus, Esq. Chairman."[11]

Melville usually wrote in the mornings and took his family for carriage rides in the late afternoon, after the midday meal. Among their favorite outings were visits to the Shaker settlement on Mount Lebanon. Founded in England by Mother Anne Lee before she emigrated to America, the "Shaking Quakers" believed in a deity with male and female characteristics—which may have recalled for Melville the holy hermaphrodites of Oceania—and, like the Typees, they lived and worked and worshiped communally. The men, predominantly farmers and craftsmen, created beautiful furniture and fashioned useful wooden objects such as rakes, clothespins, flat straw brooms, pegboards, clothes hangers, and straight-backed rocking chairs. The women sewed, quilted, cared for livestock, tended gardens of medicinal and healing herbs, and created nourishing new dishes from native foods.

Eschewing fleshly appetites, Shakers took a vow of celibacy. Even couples who had been married before joining the community took the vow and slept in sex-segregated dormitories. They increased their numbers by adopting orphans, who were sent out into the world at a certain age and allowed to choose freely whether to leave the community, or return. Unlike Charles Dickens, who found the Shakers "grim" and quipped that their women were so ugly he could understand why the men were celibate, Melville was charmed by their simple handcrafted inventions, their singing, their dancing, and their nondoctrinal practice of religion. Eager to learn more about their unusual beliefs and practices, he bought a copy of *A Summary View of the Millennial Church, or United Society of Believers, Commonly Called Shakers* (1848).[12]

At the end of July, Melville went to New York to bring his mother and sisters to Pittsfield, and, while there, invited Evert Duyckinck and Cornelius Mathews, the latter a former editor of *Yankee Doodle* and the author of *Little Abel & the Big Manhattan* and *Behemoth: A Legend of the Mound-Builders,* to join him for a week at Melvill House. Duyckinck had arranged for the reissue of Hawthorne's *Mosses from an Old Manse* in Wiley & Putnam's Library of America in 1846, and he was probably looking forward to talking with Hawthorne, as his new novel, *The Scarlet Letter,* was a great success. Given the rivalry between New York and New England, Duyckinck may have thought he would woo Hawthorne away from Ticknor & Fields, a Boston publisher.[13]

On "the cars" between New York and Stockbridge, either by coincidence or pre-arrangement, Duyckinck and Mathews met David Dudley Field Jr., a jurist and legal scholar who would be revered by some as an "American Cicero," and vilified by others for defending New York's "Boss" Tweed. Field had grown up in Stockbridge and was the oldest son of the Congregationalist pastor who had written the history of Berkshire County that Melville had just purchased. His brother Cyrus would invent the trans-atlantic cable, and his niece (?) Rachel would become a popular novelist.

Now that the railroad linked Berkshire County and New York, men like attorney Field and Melville's neighbor John Rowland Morewood, a summer resident of Pittsfield and owner of a hardware factory in Manhattan, could commute to the city on a weekly basis. By the end of the summer, Morewood and his wife, Sarah, who enlivened Pittsfield's social life with her imaginative picnics and parties, would settle there.[14]

The time had come to establish a strong national literary culture in America; yet, writers in New England and New York could argue as fiercely over literary style as chefs in Boston and Manhattan could argue over chowder. Dudley Field, who had roots in New England and professional ties to New York, found the rivalry between writers in New England and New York ridiculous. Inviting the New Yorkers to stay overnight, Field proposed a New York–New England summit meeting to introduce Melville to Nathaniel Hawthorne and a number of other local literary lights.[15]

Following his arrival at Melvill House, Duyckinck wrote his wife, Margaret, who remained "encased in hot bricks in New York" taking care of their children, that it was "a rare old place—an old family mansion, wainscoted and stately, with large halls & chimneys—quite a piece of mouldering rural grandeur." From the house, Duyckinck could see "a broken plain surrounded by mountains" and "dark lakes set in the hollows or the murmuring brooks of the meadows, whose cool pebbly sound is only surpassed by the breezes in the tree tops above them." To the north he could see Mount Greylock, the highest mountain in Massachusetts: "From the spot where I am looking over the spires of pleasant Pittsfield the cleft two humped Saddleback is the hugest wonder."[16]

Knowing Melville only as an urban cosmopolite, Duyckinck was particularly impressed by his sympathetic identification with the rural landscape: "Melville knows every stone & tree & will probably make a book of its features."[17]

The following day, their neighbor, the irrepressible party-giver Sarah Morewood, whirled the Melville party away for an afternoon excursion on Pontoosuc Lake. Mrs. Morewood, whom Cornelius Mathews dubbed "the Princess of Pic Nic," was suitably garbed "in linen sack" and "armed with a bait box and fishing rod for the finny sport," while Lizzie, who was not yet outfitted for rusticity, appeared in "a great flopping straw hat tied under the chin, floating about with the zephyrs in blue, pink or lilac."[18]

From August 4–the Melvilles' third wedding anniversary–to August 12, when Duyckinck and Mathews left, Melville and his family and friends were continually on the go. Like most great artists, Melville could operate on two planes simultaneously. While outwardly he was enjoying madcap summer days filled with parties, picnics, dinners, rambles, hikes, and even a fancy-dress ball, inwardly he was ruminating over the book he was writing, taking in every conversation and every experience and reflection on experience. The concatenation of New Yorkers and Bostonians would spark one of his greatest essays, and his meeting with Nathaniel Hawthorne would transform his saga of the sperm whale fisheries into one of the greatest expressions of the American mind.

On a misty August 5, Melville, Duyckinck, and Mathews awoke to the sounds of small birds singing "sweeter than the Sunday newsboys or the demented milk man" of Manhattan and went to the railway station, where they met Dr. Oliver Wendell Holmes, novelist, poet, professor of anatomy, and dean of the Harvard Medical School. Holmes owned a summer house at Canoe Meadows in Pittsfield, not far from Melvill House, and he, too, had been pulled in by the "lion lasso" of Dudley Field. After a ride that took them "down by the cars fifteen miles or so" to Stockbridge, they came to a "lower level in a Chinese painted green saucer, with water, trees and verandahs, edged by blue mountains." They were met by Field at the Stockbridge station and taken to his estate, Eden Hill, designed by Frederick Law Olmsted, the future architect of New York's Central Park and Boston's Emerald Necklace.[19]

Alighting from the carriage, Melville and his companions ran up a nearby hill "by way of a rehearsal, for the grand climb" up Monument Mountain while they waited for Nathaniel Hawthorne and the others to arrive. Hawthorne, who had left his wife Sophia home to mind the children, arrived in a "sumptuous" carriage driven by his publisher, James T. Fields, just as young Harry Sedgwick showed up on horseback to pilot everyone in three wagons over the rutted roads.[20]

When the procession reached the base of "the scarred & blasted peak," Duyckinck and Hawthorne walked ahead of the others, while Cornelius Mathews, or "Humble Self," as he called himself, made up nicknames for his fellow hikers. Evert Duyckinck became "Silver Pen," Melville "New Neptune," Hawthorne "Mr. Noble Melancholy," and Dr. Holmes, *The Atlantic Monthly*'s "Autocrat of the Breakfast Table," was dubbed "Mr. Town Wit." James Fields and his wife Eliza, who were both dressed for the boulevards, not the hills—he sporting black patent-leather pumps, she wearing a blue silk dress more suitable for a Beacon Hill tea dance than a Berkshire ramble—became "Mr. Greenfield" and "The Violet of the Season." Young Sedgwick was called "Harry Gallant, a twig of a celebrated Stockbridge tree," and David Dudley Field "Our Stately Inviter." His daughter, Jeanie Lucinda, was simply called Jenny, and Joel T. Headley, author of *Napoleon and his Marshals*, the "most talked about" writer of the group at that moment in history, either had no nickname, or no one bothered to record it.[21]

As they trooped up the mountain, "a black thunder cloud from the south dragged its ragged skirts towards us—the thunder rolling in the distance," and a sudden shower drove the climbers under an overhanging rock. The portly Dr. Holmes, who had received a fair amount of ribbing for toting along his "glazed India-rubber bag," playfully "cut three branches for an umbrella" to protect the ladies. Then the waggish doctor uncorked the bottles of chilled champagne he had been carrying, poured the bubbly into silver mugs, and passed it to his thirsty friends.[22]

While they waited for the storm to blow past them up the valley, Melville had a chance to talk with Hawthorne, and by the time the weather cleared two hours later, Melville was eager to climb to the top. Puffing their way up the last hundred yards, climbing ledges of rock chiseled into the mountain like giant steps, the hikers emerged breathless into the hot sun and clambered to the summit over boulders of granite that looked as though a race of Titans had piled them there to build a temple, then abandoned them. From the mountain's masthead, sixteen hundred feet above sea level, Melville, the only one who wasn't winded, could look out over the wide green valley of the Housatonic to the massive hump of Mount Greylock looming beyond the plain. Looking over the edge, he could see crags studded with pines plunging toward the base of the mountain and, in the canyon of sky below him, a red-shouldered hawk circling lazily in the sky.[23]

While the others were prancing along the ridges, the rambunctious Melville dashed out onto a peaked rock that jutted into thin air like the bowsprit of a ship. Legs braced, he hauled "imaginary ropes" for the "delectation" of his companions. His recklessness frightened the others, and Dr. Holmes protested that it affected him "like ipecac." Duyckinck, however, pronounced Melville "the boldest of all," noting with amusement that when Hawthorne "looked mildly around for the great Carbuncle," he resembled a character in one of his own stories.[24]

After the festivities, the merrymakers rode back to Field's house for a "Feast of Quidnuncs," an enormous midday dinner of "turkeys and beeves" well moistened with appropriate wines, brandies, and champagnes and finished off sweetly with huge dollops of homemade ice cream. James Fields was surprised that the normally shy

Hawthorne "rayed out in a sparkling and unwonted manner." Saying he had never seen "Hawthorne in better spirits," Fields declared it "a happy day throughout."[25]

During the three-hour-long repast, the men fell to discussing Melville's comment in *White-Jacket* that British sailors were physically stronger than their American counterparts. Before long, they found themselves in a heated debate about American and British authors. Holmes laid down "several propositions of the superiority of Englishmen," and while Melville "attacked him vigorously," Hawthorne just "looked on."[26]

Such heady talk was grist for Melville's mill. Holmes's defense of the superiority of English writers over American ones thoroughly galled Melville. He had always believed American democracy ought to produce national writers as great as Shakespeare, or even greater, and he was beginning to think that in Nathaniel Hawthorne, America might at last have a native genius to rival "the divine William."

After the literary lions had devoured their feast, the women sat on the verandah drinking cool drinks and chatting, and the men roared through Ice Glen. Scrambling over gigantic glacial boulders in this glen cool enough to keep iced punches chilled, they cavorted around, sliding through tunnels and over boulders until someone noticed that Hawthorne and Melville were nowhere to be seen. Fearing an accident, they searched the area and found the two men deep in conversation. From then on, Hawthorne, who thought Ice Glen looked "as if the Devil had torn his way through a rock & left it all jagged behind," proved to be "among the most enterprising of the merrymakers."[27]

Later, they were joined by Catharine Maria Sedgwick, the first lady of American letters, who lived in Lenox with her brother. Charles Sedgwick was clerk of the Berkshire Court where Chief Justice Shaw presided during his official visitations, and his wife Elizabeth ran the school Helen Melville had attended. Miss Sedgwick, *grande dame* of the noble Sedgwick family of Stockbridge, had published a number of novels that paved the way for Hawthorne's historical romances, including *A New England Tale* (1822), an attack on religious hypocrisy and intolerance, and the popular *Hope Leslie* (1827), a story of the frontier. Her portrayal of the heroic Magawisca's bond with Hope Leslie, a daughter of the Puritans whose sister was married to an Indian brave, broke new ground.[28]

When Miss Sedgwick, whose books Helen Melville knew, asked Melville what he was working on, he told her he had "a new book mostly done—a romantic, fanciful & literal & most enjoyable presentment of the whale fishery,—something quite new." Evert Duyckinck reported to his brother George that "a cross examination on Hope Leslie and Magawisca" revealed that Melville was woefully ignorant of her work, but she invited them all to tea the following day.[29]

Although we have no direct evidence that Melville read Sedgwick's work, several of his writings show her influence. The relationship of Ishmael and Queequeg, for example, probably owes more of a literary debt to the blood sisterhood of Hope Leslie and

Magawisca than to the stilted friendships between Indians and settlers in James Fenimore Cooper's novels of the frontier. The opening chapters of *Pierre* (1852) evoke the style and historical consciousness of both Sedgwick and Lydia Child's *Hobomok*, and Melville's story "Poor Man's Pudding and Rich Man's Crumbs" gives the nod to Sedgwick's *The Poor Rich Man and the Rich Poor Man* (1836).

When Allan arrived from the city, Melville hitched a pair of horses to a light carriage and drove his brother and their guests up to Lebanon to see the Shakers. An old Shaker woman showed them a bedroom in the women's quarters and told them that the "curious camel's hump raised in the middle of the bed, lengthwise," was "a kind of Berkshire mountain range where two sisters slept together–that they should not roll on one another." Seeing a long-handled brush on a bedstead in the men's quarters, Melville asked what it was used for, and, in the "plain Saxon" characteristic of the Shakers, their guide said, "Why, I guess it's for him to scratch himself with when he itches." Given Melville's sense of humor, it's easy to imagine that this tour of Shaker dormitories influenced the comical descriptions of Ishmael and Queequeg sharing a bed at the Spouter-Inn.[30]

The following day, Melville and his guests, still in a rollicking humor, rode over to call on Hawthorne, who, since May, had been renting a cottage–the "red shanty," as Hawthorne called it–on the Lenox estate of William Aspinwall Tappan. "Popping the corks in his nervous way," Hawthorne greeted his visitors by opening a bottle of Heidsieck that an aspiring poet named Mansfield had given him to toast the "next genius" he met. Whether Hawthorne realized it or not, Herman Melville was that genius.[31]

Sophia Hawthorne found Melville fascinating: "Mr Typee is interesting in his aspect–quite–I see Fayaway in his face," she wrote her sister, Elizabeth Peabody, who, as editor of *Aesthetic Papers,* had published Henry David Thoreau's "Resistance to Civil Government" the previous year.[32]

Hawthorne tended to be shy and defensive with new acquaintances, but he liked Melville "uncommonly well," and invited him to return for a longer visit. "I liked Melville so much," he wrote his close friend Horatio Bridge, author of *Journal of an African Cruiser,* "that I have asked him to spend a few days with me"–a surprising declaration, as Hawthorne had the reputation of discouraging overnight guests so he could concentrate on his work.[33]

Friday, August 9, dawned rainy and overcast, so Melville had the whole morning to himself to work on a review of *Mosses from an Old Manse* for *The Literary World.* While he sat in "a papered chamber" in the "fine old farmhouse–a mile from any other dwelling, and dipped to the eaves in foliage–surrounded by mountains, old woods, and Indian ponds," pouring out his admiration of "the Man of Mosses," Lizzie and the other women "ransacked" old wardrobes and trunks to make costumes for the masquerade party Sarah Morewood was giving that evening. Gathering "green goggles, yellow stuff for breeches, antique hats, long-tail coats, brought down from garrets; heavy boots, of a past fashion, fished up from cellars," they worked feverishly all afternoon.[34]

Later in the day, Melville and Duyckinck rode over to the Pittsfield depot, hoping to "capture" their friend William Allen Butler, editor of the American Art-Union's *Bulletin*, for the ball before he and his wife boarded the New York train. The high-spirited Melville, luxuriantly bearded and riding "a black pony of questionable build, gait and behavior," created quite a sensation by whisking Mrs. Butler from the platform and carrying her off, while her husband and Evert Duyckinck chased after them "in a most serpentine and erratic manner." After spending the morning composing a piece on Hawthorne that turned into a tour de force of self-discovery and self-disclosure, Melville was feeling elated and energized.[35]

That evening, "Fairy Belt," as Mathews called Sarah Morewood, threw open her house for a magnificent costume ball to which Lizzie came dressed as a flower girl, and Herman came as a Turk in robes and turban. Cornelius Mathews disguised himself as a Down East Yankee with three hanks of flax for a wig; Evert Duyckinck, dressed up as a waiter, served sherry cobblers; and the sophisticated Sophia Melville wore a black dress with a long train and an old-fashioned hat that made her look like a duchess. It was a gala affair, with dining and dancing in spacious, candlelit rooms.[36]

August 10 dawned cloudy, giving the revelers an excuse to sleep a little later than usual and Melville a chance to finish the review so that Duyckinck could take it back to New York in time for the next issue of *The Literary World*. At around noon, the inexhaustible Sarah Morewood, who had mastered "the art of making a toil of pleasure," burst in on them with the news that the roads were now passable despite the rain. She had even prepared a picnic, so they could make no excuses for staying home. They piled into one long wagon, "stowed fourteen deep," and, "like a flight of Cossacks in the desert," rode north to take in the view from Constitution Hill in Lanesborough.[37]

Allan and Sophia, who was eight months pregnant, came in a separate conveyance in case Sophia tired before the others, and several of the party took turns riding one of two saddle horses. As the procession came to a halt at the foot of the hill, the horse pulling Allan and Sophia's wagon bumped into the horse Lizzie was riding, and she was thrown to the ground. Lizzie was wearing a shorter-than-usual skirt, and when Melville saw her fall, he hurled himself from the horse he was riding in a burst of chivalry, attempting to save his wife from immodesty as well as bodily harm. When Sophia saw Herman and Lizzie rolling over on the grass, she started screaming, which so angered Melville that he barked at Allan to take her home, even though she had pulled herself together once she realized Lizzie was unharmed. Amid "bad feelings," Sophia and Allan drove back to Pittsfield.[38]

Once the commotion was over, Sarah Morewood, followed by a coachman carrying a wicker hamper of food, led the picnickers to the summit, where they lay about sunning themselves "like so many shepherds and shepherdesses on the mountain-top" until they got hungry and decided to head back. About halfway down the mountain, they came to a ledge where they found a cloth "magically spread" and heaped with a lavish luncheon prepared and served by unobtrusive servants.[39]

The next day, Sunday, Duyckinck proposed visiting Lebanon to observe the Shakers "at their spasms," but just as they arrived, the elders called a private conference and closed the meeting house to visitors, so they were not able to see the dancing as they had hoped. As they were leaving with a few small gifts they had purchased, Sarah Morewood pulled up in her barouche and suggested they stop at Hancock Shaker Village on the way back, to see the great round barn. This unusual stone structure, measuring 270 feet in diameter, contained enough large stalls to accommodate "a span of horses and 52 horned cattle." They all enjoyed a "fine race" around the barn except for Sophia, who was so far along in her pregnancy that she was "afraid of being mistaken for a cow or an elephant."[40]

Later that afternoon, Melville probably showed Duyckinck his finished article on Hawthorne before giving it to Lizzie to make the fair copy. Wanting to rise above the New York–New England rivalry and appear totally objective in his attacks on the establishments of both cities, Melville had signed the review "By a Virginian Spending July in Vermont," to avoid identification with either Boston or New York.[41]

The review was a call to arms against Boston critics who saw Hawthorne as "a pleasant writer, with a pleasant style,–a sequestered, harmless man, from whom any deep and weighty thing would hardly be anticipated–a man who means no meanings." It was a slap at New York critics, too; the "Virginian" dismissed Washington Irving as "a very popular and amiable writer" who, despite being "good, and self-reliant in many things, perhaps owes his chief reputation to the self-acknowledged imitation of a foreign model, and to the studied avoidance of all topics but smooth ones." Calling Irving a writer with the soul of "a grasshopper," the "Virginian" opined that a great writer should not have to bend to fit into a literary circle or swim in a particular "school." Thus, Melville attacked both the innocuous pleasantries of the Knickerbocker School and the "literary flunkeyism" of Bostonian Anglophiles.[42]

Melville cited Shakespeare's extraordinary popularity in American towns from the eastern seaboard to the western frontier as evidence that "lofty" literature could be popular with democratic audiences. Because Hawthorne was similarly lofty and popular as well as being a son of the New World, Melville saw him as the new American Bard, greater than Shakespeare himself. Duyckinck, who had once almost lost his editorship of the magazine in these literary wars, thought Melville had gone a little overboard by elevating Hawthorne above the "Swan of Avon"; so, to forestall a spate of cancellations by offended Anglophiles and to save the credibility of *The Literary World*, which reached the largest and most critical audience of any periodical in America, he evidently persuaded Melville to tone down the comparison by suggesting that Hawthorne was not an American Shakespeare, but rather the writer who was paving the way for a future Bard who would establish a great national literature on American soil.

According to Melville, most Americans knew Shakespeare not from the printed page, but from "the tricky stage," where he was "forced" to pander to "mere mob renown" with "Richard-the-Third humps, and Macbeth daggers." Hawthorne, by contrast, "refrains from all the popularizing noise and show of broad farce, and blood-besmeared tragedy; content with the still, rich utterances of a great intellect in repose." What makes Shakespeare great, Melville contends, is that "through the mouths of the dark characters of Hamlet, Timon, Lear, and Iago, he craftily says, or sometimes insinuates the things, which we feel to be so terrifically true, that it were all but madness for any good man, in his own proper character, to utter, or even hint of them."[43]

Ironically, to the modern reader, Melville seems much more Shakespearean than Hawthorne because his range of subjects and locales is wider and his characters more varied, and because he is more comical and free-spirited. Melville relished Shakespeare's bawdy, ribald humor as much as he savored the high tragedy, but he felt that Hawthorne was the one American writer who had the deeply felt tragic sense America needed in order to reach cultural maturity. "You may be witched by his sun light,—transported by the bright gildings in the skies he builds over you;—but there is the blackness of darkness beyond," Melville would write in his essay "Hawthorne and His Mosses."[44]

Despite its contradictions and occasionally muddled thinking, Melville's essay is a kind of literary Declaration of Independence for American writers. Falling into the great tradition of Emerson's "The American Scholar" and "The Poet," and Whitman's 1855 preface to *Leaves of Grass*, it articulates his vision of the kind of writer he wanted to be and his struggle to reconcile democratic values with high literary standards.

Because of the popularity of *The Scarlet Letter*, Melville imagined that Hawthorne was able both to write what he wanted and to support himself by his writing; yet, although *The Scarlet Letter* sold five thousand copies within two months of its publication, it sold only one thousand more in the next two years. Even at his peak, Hawthorne could expect to sell no more than five or six thousand copies of a book, and Melville less, while best-selling novels by Hawthorne's "damned mob of scribbling women" often sold tens of thousands of copies and enjoyed steady sales for many years.[45]

These women writers like Sedgwick, Child, Warner, Cummins, Fern, Stowe, and others, who were trying to push the novel toward serious themes and social criticism, chafed against convention, but they knew they had to work within accepted forms to reach large audiences. Male writers such as Hawthorne and Melville, who wanted to stake a claim for American fiction as a serious literature that equaled or surpassed the finest products of the British pen, aspired to write literature that would sell well and be read long after they were gone; they were competing, however, not only with established British authors, but also with women who were writing highly provocative and successful domestic and sentimental novels, and with men who were writing thrillers.[46]

One way for writers to gain a broader audience was to write short fiction for periodicals read by both men and women. When Louis Antoine Godey invited Melville to contribute to *Godey's Lady's Book*, which had seventy thousand readers, Melville evidently agreed, as his name appeared on a list of future contributors. He never followed through, however, probably because he was busy writing *Moby-Dick*, then *Pierre*.[47]

Once Lizzie had finished making the fair copy of "Hawthorne and His Mosses," Melville supplied the punctuation just in time for Duyckinck to take the manuscript back with him, and by the time he and Mathews reached New York, Melville was working on his whaling book again. Rummaging around in the corn loft of the carriage house, he found an old desk whitened with the guano of pigeons who had laid their eggs in the pocky wood, and, hauling it to the "garrett-way" of the house, he placed it at a "little embrasure of a window . . . which commands a noble view of Saddleback," away from the household commotion.[48]

Melville considered himself fortunate to be away from Manhattan during the summer, and he couldn't resist rubbing Duyckinck's nose in it: "What are you doing there, My Beloved, among the bricks & cobble-stone *boulders*? Are you making mortar? Surely, My Beloved, you are not carrying a hod?" Alluding to the repaving of Broadway between Clinton Place and Union Square, Melville reminded his friend that "chemically speaking, mortar was the precipitate of the Fall; & with a brickbat, or a cobble-stone *boulder*, Cain killed Abel."[49]

Duyckinck's next letter was accompanied by a wicker basket bearing a dozen bottles of Heidsieck and an "Oriental-looking" box of cigars that had "an Antilles smell," or, as Melville described them, "twelve beautiful babies" of "uncommon intelligence ... full of animation and hilarity," and the "bundles" of cigars "all harmonizing together like the Iroquois." Duyckinck also enclosed a package for Melville to give to Hawthorne, without telling him it contained his three latest books, which Hawthorne had not seen, and Melville passed it on without knowing what was in it.[50]

After reading the books Duyckinck had sent him "on the new hay in the barn," Hawthorne wrote that he had read Melville's works "with a progressive appreciation of their author." He liked *Redburn* and *White-Jacket* for their "unflinching" realism, and he considered *Mardi* "a rich book, with depths here and there that compel a man to swim for his life," though he wished Melville had "brooded" on it longer, so as to make it even better. He had guessed correctly that Melville wrote at a white heat, like Azzageddi when the fit was on him.[51]

"Hawthorne and His Mosses" appeared in two installments in *The Literary World* on August 17 and August 24, 1850, and when Sophia Hawthorne read it, she wrote an appreciative letter to Duyckinck calling the "ardent Virginian" the "first person who has ever in *print* apprehended Mr Hawthorne," a critic of "generous, noble enthusiasm" who "surrounds himself with glory" while bringing out the glory of his subject. Whoever the author of these "inspired utterances" might be, he had spoken her "secret mind."[52]

Sophia felt the reviewer evinced "Great Heart & Grand Intellect combined" by comparing her husband to "the Swan of Avon," and she told her sister she must read the review by the marvelous Virginian immediately: "The freshness of primeval nature is in that man, & the true Promethean fire is in him. Who can he be, so fearless, so rich in heart, of such fine intuition? Is his name altogether hidden?"[53]

Reading *Mosses from an Old Manse* was a catalytic event for Melville, comparable to John Keats's discovery of Chapman's Homer. He had sensed from the stories that Hawthorne was a kindred spirit, and meeting and talking with him had confirmed his intuition. In this man "immeasurably deeper than the plummet of the mere critic," Melville recognized a universal genius. His portrait of Hawthorne as a writer who "hoodwinks" his readers and whose fictions conceal dark, subversive truths is clearly a projection of his own complex relationship to his texts, his family, and his audience.

To Melville, Hawthorne's unique power came from the combination of his closeness to nature and his tragic sense of life. Although he expressed "ruddy thoughts" and imbued the landscapes of his stories with a "perennial green," like the transcendentalists, his writings were suffused with the "great power of blackness" that came from that "Calvinistic sense of Innate Depravity and Original Sin, from whose visitations, in some shape or other, no deeply thinking mind is always and wholly free."[54]

A man of violent contradictions himself, Melville recognized both the "soft ravishments" of that "omnipresent love" which imbued Hawthorne's writings with a "mystical depth of meaning" and his pervasive "blackness, ten times black." By Melville's logic, Hawthorne's insight into the dark mysteries of the human soul was quintessentially American as well as Shakespearean, because Hawthorne's "wild, witch voice" spoke "the sane madness of vital truth" in "a world of lies" where "Truth is forced to fly like a scared white doe in the woodlands; and only by cunning glimpses will she reveal herself, as in Shakespeare and other masters of the great Art of Telling Truth,—even though it be covertly, and by snatches."[55]

We have no direct evidence that Melville had read *The Scarlet Letter* before he wrote "Hawthorne and His Mosses," but it is hard to believe that he had not, because certain images of sunlight and darkness in the review are so suggestive of the forest scenes in

Hawthorne's great romance. *Pierre*, furthermore, seems consciously conversant with Hawthorne's masterpiece, and both books center on triangles of forbidden love.

When Melville visited the red cottage on September 3 in response to Hawthorne's invitation, neither Nathaniel nor Sophia had any idea that he had written "Hawthorne and His Mosses." Now that he was alone with them, however, he could not keep the secret for long, as the article was all they talked about. After he revealed to Sophia that he was the "Virginian" and said he had "dashed off" the entire piece before meeting Hawthorne at the picnic, they had "some delightful conversations . . . about the 'sweetest Man of Mosses.'" Sophia found Melville "very agreeable and entertaining," describing him in glowing terms: "A man with a true warm heart & a soul & an intellect—with life to his finger-tips—earnest, sincere & reverent, very tender & *modest.*"[56]

Sophia was mesmerized by Melville's languid, seductive eyes—eyes that Nathaniel Parker Willis called "Spanish." Describing Melville to her sister, she wrote, "I am not sure that I *do not think him* a very great man. He has very keen perceptive power, but what astonishes me is, that his eyes are not large & deep —He seems to see every thing very accurately, & how he can do so with his small eyes, I cannot tell. They are not keen eyes, either, but quite undistinguished in any way. His nose is straight & rather handsome, his mouth expressive of sensibility & emotion—He is tall & erect with an air free, brave, & manly. When conversing, he is full of gesture & force, & loses himself in his subject—There is no grace nor polish—once in a while, his animation gives place to a singularly quiet expression out of those eyes, to which I have objected—an indrawn, dim look, but which at the same time makes you feel—that he is at that instant taking deepest note of what is before him—It is a strange, lazy glance, but with a power in it quite unique—It does not seem to penetrate through you, but to take you into himself."[57]

Sitting out on the verandah of the red cottage overlooking Stockbridge Bowl "in the golden light of evening twilight, when the lake was like glass of a rose tint," Melville told Sophia that "Hawthorne was the first person whose physical being appeared to him wholly in harmony with the intellectual & spiritual" and the "sunny haze & pensiveness, the symmetry of his face, the depth of eyes, the gleam—the shadow—& the peace supreme all were in exact response to the high calm intellect, the glowing, deep heart—the purity of actual & spiritual life."[58]

Mutual adoration of Hawthorne became their bond, and Melville's endearing combination of boyish enthusiasm and sensuality appealed to Sophia:

> Mr. Melville is a person of great ardor & simplicity . . . all on fire with the subject that interests him. It rings through his frame like a cathedral bell. His truth & honesty shine out at every point. At the same time he sees things artistically, as you perceive in his books. I have just read again Typee. It is a *true history,* yet

how poetically told—the divine beauty of the scene, the lovely faces & forms—the peace & good will—& all this golden splendor & enchantment glowing before the dark refrain constantly brought as a background—the fear of being killed & eaten—the cannibalism in the olive tinted Apollos around him—the unfathomable mystery of their treatment of him.[59]

Hawthorne aroused in Melville an intellectual and spiritual passion that paralleled his intense involvement with his art. He was the most beautiful man Melville or any of his contemporaries had seen. "Handsomer than Lord Byron!" Elizabeth Peabody once exclaimed. It's no wonder that Melville found this gentle, older man attractive; in him, Melville had discovered a soul mate, a father, a brother, and a friend.[60]

Theirs was a friendship based on shared tragedy as well as artistic affinity, as both of them had experienced early sorrow. Hawthorne had lost his father when he was four, and only a year before Melville met him, his mother had died after a painful illness during which the grief-stricken Nathaniel had remained at her bedside so obsessively that Sophia feared for his health.

Hawthorne's forebears came from iron Puritan stock. His grandfather Nathaniel Hathorne and his father, Daniel Hathorne, were both sea captains. Daniel, who had a tendency toward moodiness and depression, was said to have been "the sternest man that ever walked a deck," and after he died in Suriname, Dutch Guiana, Hawthorne's uncle, Robert Manning, became guardian and surrogate father to the boy.[61]

Manning, whose ancestor Nicholas had been convicted by Puritan magistrates of incest with his sisters, for some reason insisted on having his young nephew sleep in the same bed with him until he was about fifteen years old, although there was plenty of room in his chamber for a second bed. There is no evidence that Robert Manning molested Nathaniel sexually, and it was fairly common for people to share beds in the unheated houses of the nineteenth century; however, Manning evidently transgressed boundaries in ways that disturbed Nathaniel, as he was on guard against physically demonstrative men for the rest of his life.[62]

Hawthorne's mother and sisters, worried that his health was delicate, "petted" (pampered) him. When he was nine, he injured his foot playing ball at school, and they coddled him unmercifully, treating him almost as an invalid. As a consequence, he remained lame until he was twelve, reading widely and deeply and becoming more and more introspective as he matured.

All his life, Hawthorne struggled to exorcise demons of Puritanism far stronger than those that occasionally sank their claws into Melville. His first ancestor in the New World, William Hathorne, had ordered Anne Coleman, a Quaker woman suspected of witchcraft, whipped to the outskirts of town, and his great-great-great-grandfather, the unrelenting Judge John Hathorne, had condemned a number of Salem women to death for the same reason. When he was a child, Hawthorne learned that one of the accused witches had pronounced a curse on all of Judge Hathorne's descendants before she was hanged, and it haunted him so much that he added a *w* to his name to distinguish himself from them. In writing *The Scarlet Letter*, Nathaniel had tried to liberate the dark, sensuous woman buried within his soul only to have his male ancestors reach out and yank her back before the grave. It was as if Hawthorne's Puritan forebears had invoked the family curse to make the boy behave, as if at times he heard the witch's laugh.

Sophia, who was devoted to her husband, loved Melville for loving him. Although she was a very private person who struck some people as prudish, she warmed up to people once she knew them, and she and Melville evidently enjoyed an innocent and safe flirtation. In any case, their friendship aroused something in each of them. Lizzie seems never to have accompanied Herman on his visits to the red cottage, and from what we know of Melville, the similarity between his relationship to the Hawthornes and the three-way marriages he had observed in the Marquesas probably amused him.

In the review of *Mosses,* the "Virginian" pays a great tribute to Hawthorne in sentences highly charged with erotic imagery: "I feel that this Hawthorne has dropped germinous seeds into my soul. He expands and deepens down, the more I contemplate him; and further, and further, shoots his strong New England roots into the hot soil of my Southern soul." Although this was a common trope, in Melville's hands it becomes one of the two most erotically charged passages in nineteenth-century American literature.

Even so, neither Evert Duyckinck, a conservative Episcopalian, nor Sophia Hawthorne, who bowdlerized her husband's letters and journals after his death (especially his references to drinking), found Melville's language in the least controversial, and when Sophia's aunt Rawlins, a typical reader of the time, complained about the review, it was not because she found the language sexually suggestive, but because she thought it irresponsible and excessive of Melville to compare Hawthorne to Shakespeare: "No man of common sense would seriously name Mr. H, deserving as he is of respect and admiration, in the same day with Shakespeare!"[63]

"Hawthorne and His Mosses" reveals as much about Melville's aspirations as it does about Hawthorne's peculiar gifts. When Melville exhorts readers to "confess" Hawthorne as though he were a personal savior, and "[em]brace the whole brotherhood" of literary men, he is expressing his hope that readers will embrace Herman Melville as well, "for genius, all over the world, stands hand in hand, and one shock of recognition runs the whole circle round."[64]

Melville passionately admired Nathaniel Hawthorne for probing the "blackness of darkness" below the surface of American life.

FOURTEEN

A SORT OF SEA-FEELING IN THE COUNTRY

As fall approached, Melville couldn't bear to leave the Berkshires. His friendship with Hawthorne stimulated him intellectually, and his domestic life gave him more security and pleasure than he had ever experienced before. In Augusta's view, Herman and Lizzie were "two such happy hearts" that they made the world seem a much less scary place.[1]

In mid-September, with a three-thousand-dollar loan from Judge Shaw, Melville bought a 160-acre farm abutting the old Melvill property from Dr. John Brewster, who was moving nearer to town. Situated about two and a half miles from Pittsfield, the farm included a "quaint old house, built in the early days of the settlement of the town, by Capt. David Bush," according to the Pittsfield Sun. *Although Melville told the Hawthornes he intended to build a "real towered house" on the property, in the thirteen years he lived in Pittsfield, he never had enough money to build a house to suit him.*[2]

Early in October the Pittsfield Sun *reported that the Morewoods had decided to become permanent residents of Pittsfield, and that Melville had bought a farm not far from the summer residence of Dr. Oliver Wendell Holmes. The* Boston Daily Times *picked it up and* announced: "Herman Melville, the popular young author, has purchased a farm in Berkshire county Mass., about thirty miles from Albany, where he intends to raise poultry, turnips, babies, and other vegetables." Melville did raise corn, turnips, potatoes, and pumpkins, and he and Lizzie produced three more children while they lived in Pittsfield.[3]

The Melvilles moved into their "mountain home" during the "glowing & Byzantine" days of Indian summer. The sky remained cloudless for ten days, treating them to the spectacle of scarlet maples aflame amid the "changing light and shade upon the forest slope."[4]

After a Sunday spent "*Jacquesizing* in the woods," Melville wrote Duyckinck that "the heavens themselves look so ripe & ruddy, that it must be harvest-time with the angels.... You should see the maples—you should see the young perennial pines—the red blazings of the one contrasting with the painted green of the others, and the wide flushings of the autumn air harmonizing both. I tell you that sunrises & sunsets grow side by side in these woods, & momentarily moult in the falling leaves." Amid such "wild sublimity," Melville felt entirely at home.[5]

He loved the farm. Every time he turned over a clod of the rich soil, he found Indian artifacts, so he called the place "Arrowhead." When he first moved there, he stayed "in the open air all day, except when assisting in lifting a bedstead or a bureau." Needing exercise to relieve the physical and mental stress of writing six to eight hours a day, he chopped wood, did farm work, and rode into town every day to get a newspaper and discuss politics with such local sages as Joseph Edward Adams Smith, a newspaper editor, poet, pundit, and local historian who became his friend.[6]

The main house, a large farmhouse, had been built in 1780 "after that peculiarly quaint style of architecture which places the chimney—the hugest in proportions—immediately in the centre, & the rooms around it" so that each room had a flue leading from the central chimney to its fireplace. This impressive structure had nine rooms facing off it, none of which had locks or bolts, and although they were cozy and comfortable, Augusta found the arrangement "totally void of grace & beauty." She also wanted locks installed on all the doors, so during the Melvilles' first two weeks in the new house, locksmiths were called in, as well as carpenters to build cabinets. Melville, who was not very handy with tools, judging from his reference to a hammer "that so cruelly bruised the very finger that guides my pen," did manage to put casters on the bed without professional assistance.[7]

The pride of the parlor was the corner cupboard, which the Melvilles used as an étagère, a set of shelves commonly used in Victorian homes for displaying knickknacks. Among the first admirers of the new house were Lizzie's parents, who doted on their grandson. An affectionate father who had looked forward to grandchildren, Lemuel Shaw had no inhibitions about being silly around children. When the Shaws were in town, visitors to Arrowhead were treated to the sight of the Chief Justice, whose "lynx-eye and compressed lip" terrified all who approached the federal bench, down on all fours playing with the baby. Shaw barely winced when plump little Malcolm grabbed his hair and pulled it to make "the horsey" go. The sight of Shaw frolicking with Malcolm and his cousin Milie elicited from Shaw's fellow jurist Ebenezer Hoar the quip "If Barnum could have secured the group he would make his fortune."[8]

During the Shaws' visit, Melville had an opportunity to discuss with his father-in-law the legal ramifications of the latest legislative debates in Washington. He had just received from Evert Duyckinck a newspaper report on the Senate's decision to outlaw flogging in the United States Navy–a reform for which Melville thought he could take some credit. The courts were also debating the passage of stricter copyright laws in response to a petition filed by the publishers of Irving, Melville, and a number of other writers against international piracy of literary works.[9]

After months of debate, Congress had put limits on the spread of the "peculiar institution" to placate the North, while adopting a federal Fugitive Slave Law to appease the South. The Great Compromise of 1850 required federal judges to subordinate their consciences to the federal statute by ordering escaped slaves returned to their masters, putting Lemuel Shaw in an awkward position. He could either resign his position or uphold the law and work for change; he chose the latter, and found himself at odds with some of his closest associates and friends.

Even before passage of the Fugitive Slave Law, the Garrisonians had wanted "no union with slaveholders," charging that in the interests of sectional harmony, moderates had become unwitting instruments of the close commercial affiliation that had sprung up between "the cotton spinners of the North and the cotton producers of the South"–or, as Charles Sumner put it, between the "lords of the loom, and the lords of the lash." Boston magnates feared that the abolition of slavery would cause the collapse of the carefully balanced mercantile alliance between the North and the South, and when ships carrying cotton to the mills also began to carry black stowaways, the precarious balance between the two sections of the country began to totter.[10]

In Pittsfield, slavery had a human face, as two escaped slaves who claimed to be African princes lived there. Another former slave, Samuel Harrison, an educated man, became chaplain of the Second Congregational Church the year the Melvilles moved to Pittsfield. Moderates saw the peaceful evolution of African-Americans into full citizens as the goal of the antislavery movement, but they also vowed that southern claims to extend slavery were to be "met, resisted and prevented at all hazard ... come what may," to quote U.S. Representative Julius Rockwell of Berkshire County.[11]

On October 4, 1850, the former slave Frederick Douglass spoke at Faneuil Hall, prompting Boston abolitionists to form the Boston Vigilance Committee, with Richard

Henry Dana Jr. as its head, and before the month was out, there were more than eighty members pledged to rescue fugitives. Passage of the law divided northerners into factions that either cited William H. Seward's doctrine of the "Higher Law" as a basis for civil disobedience, or supported the "Union-saving" defense of the Constitution, as espoused by Daniel Webster and Lemuel Shaw.[12]

The new statute inflamed abolitionists in Massachusetts. Henry David Thoreau compared Daniel Webster's support for the Great Compromise to "a dung-beetle pushing its ball," and William Lloyd Garrison burned a facsimile of the United States Constitution.[13]

The inflammatory rhetoric of the Garrisonians disturbed even Lydia Maria Child, an outspoken and dedicated abolitionist herself, and in Melville's view, extremist talk was no substitute for intelligent, progressive action. From his friend Joseph Smith, a radical antislavery man, and his brother-in-law Richard Lathers, a South Carolinian who had freed his slaves before moving to the North, Melville had ample opportunity to hear opposing views on slavery and abolition, which made him realize that while morally there were not two sides to the slavery question, politically the problem had no simple solution. It was no longer a matter of whether slavery should exist or not, but of how to eradicate an entrenched institution by which both North and South were bound together in a commercial alliance. Like many others, Melville feared that exacerbating sectional hatred and racial bitterness would engulf blacks and whites alike in a tidal wave of blood.

By November the Melvilles and their three household servants were completely settled into their house. Helen had left to visit friends, but, unlike her sister, Augusta did not "sigh for the dry pavements and bright lights of Broadway." She was looking forward to presiding over the Thanksgiving feast at Arrowhead, as Mother Melville had gone to Albany, and Lizzie was planning to take Malcolm and his nurse to Boston for the traditional Shaw festivities. She hated to go without Herman, but he was too busy working on his book to take a break. "These 'New England girls,'" Augusta observed to Mary Blatchford, "can't think of Thanksgiving anywhere but under their father's roof–their peace of mind for years depends upon it, even if they have to travel miles to do it."[14]

Augusta invited Mary Melvill and her family to hitch up Old Jenny and come over for the holiday dinner, and with "steps flying" around the kitchen and pantry, she and the cook set about the tasks of raisin-storing, citron-cutting, and egg-beating. With ten people to be seated, Herman's library was pressed into service as an extension of the dining room.[15]

Thanksgiving Day in Boston was so stormy that guests, swathed in cloaks and bundled in buffalo robes, pulled up at the Shaws' in an old lumber wagon. Blue-eyed Malcolm, "beautiful & lovely, almost too superior for this earth," was such a hit with the Shaws that they brought him into the dining room with the dessert and placed him on the table in front of a basket of apples and grapes, whereupon he cried out at the top of his voice, "bamdiddle, bamdiddle." Unfortunately, if his mother managed to translate this Orphic saying for the prodigy's admirers, it is lost in the mists of history.[16]

In mid-December, with snowdrifts piling up to the first-floor windowsills, Melville sat writing at his desk in the north-facing room on the second floor. Whenever he paused for a moment to look out the window, he could see the "gigantic shape of Greylock" looming on the horizon like a whale. "I have a sort of sea-feeling here in the country, now that the ground is all covered with snow," he wrote Evert Duyckinck. Nights when he would "wake up & hear the wind shrieking," he imagined the farmhouse was a whaling ship: "I almost fancy there is too much sail on the house, & I had better go on the roof & rig in the chimney."[17]

He also described the routine he followed while his family was away:

> I rise at eight—thereabouts—& go to my barn—say good-morning to the horse, & give him his breakfast. (It goes to my heart to give him a cold one, but it can't be helped). Then, pay a visit to my cow—cut up a pumpkin or two for her, & stand by to see her eat it—for its [sic] a pleasant sight to see a cow move her jaws—she does it so mildly & with such a sanctity. —My own breakfast over, I go to my work-room light my fire—then spread my M.S.S. on the table—take one business squint at it, & fall to with a will. At 2½ p.m. I hear a preconcerted knock at my door, which (by request) serves to wean me effectively from my writing, however interested I may be. My friends the horse & cow now demand their dinner—& I go and give it them. My dinner over, I rig my sleigh & with my mother or sisters start off for the village.... My evenings I spend in a sort of mesmeric state in my room—not being able to read [by candlelight]—only now and then skimming over some large-printed book.

His letter closes with a jocular request for "fifty fast-writing youths" to help him finish the "Whale" and all his future books.[18]

Writing *Moby-Dick* was a Herculean task, a feat worthy of Shakespeare, Sir Thomas Browne, Rabelais, and Paul Bunyan combined. At times Melville felt that no mortal pen could possibly transcribe the thoughts that were teeming and tumbling through his brain. A man "must have plenty of sea-room to tell the Truth in," he had written in "Hawthorne and His Mosses," and now his own imagination was at flood tide.[19]

How could it be, Melville wondered as he was writing, that "for six thousand years—and no one knows how many millions of ages before—the great whales should have been spouting all over the sea, and sprinkling and mistifying the gardens of the deep, as with so many sprinkling or mistifying pots; and that for some centuries back, thousands of hunters should have been close by the fountain of the whale, watching these sprinklings and spoutings—that all this should be, and yet, that down to this blessed minute (fifteen and a quarter minutes past one o'clock P.M. of this sixteenth day of December, A.D. 1850), it should still remain a problem, whether these spoutings are, after all, really water, or nothing but vapor—this is surely a noteworthy thing."[20]

As he wrote, his narrative seemed to carve new channels, sound greater depths, raise new questions, and suggest more mysteries to be explored. As his thoughts fed on themselves, nourishing new reflections and engendering new ideas, the manuscript grew longer and longer and seemed farther and farther away from being done with every passing day. How could a book that had seemed almost finished before he left New York, suddenly seem so far from completion? Sometimes he feared he would never be able to bring the work to a satisfactory conclusion, and in the darkest moments he feared that he would finish it only to discover it was all "sound and fury, signifying nothing." Despite these chimeras, Melville wrote on so furiously during Lizzie's absence that right before Christmas he had to drive to the paper mill in Lee, Massachusetts, to buy more paper, and Augusta wrote Helen that she did not need to rush home to help with copying, as it would be a while before the manuscript was ready.[21]

Something seemed to be drawing him toward ever-expanding horizons, like the spout of a phantom whale. His story unfolded before his eyes until it became not merely his voyage, or the voyage of any whaleman he had ever known, but an epic journey. It was the *Iliad* and the *Odyssey* in one: a war story and a spiritual voyage. As he added chapters, characters, strange events, and abundant whaling lore, "facts" about whaling took on mythic resonance. While at times he felt he was on a wonderful voyage of discovery, at other times he felt he was lashed to the back of a sounding whale, with harpoon lines wrapped around his neck, being dragged through the seas by a monster that would not let him go.

By New Year's, Melville was so impatient for Lizzie to return that he "could not endure her absence with Malcolm any longer." He missed his son's "winning ways" so fiercely that Augusta wrote Helen, "As for Malcolm—I almost tremble for him. Herman will fairly devour him"—an ominous metaphor, in retrospect. Much to Melville's delight, Lizzie finally returned the week after New Year's. Malcolm's "bright intelligent little face" and "sparkling eyes" charmed everyone until he resumed his normal toddler terrorism and Melville had to "pitch in" to "His Babyship" to show him who was boss.[22]

As Melville worked on his ever-expanding manuscript under what Lizzie later called "unfavorable circumstances," the women structured their busy lives around his schedule. While he wrote, they took turns preparing the midday meal, doing household chores, writing letters, and copying his manuscripts. When he was finished, he drove the ladies around the countryside or to Mrs. Chapman's sewing circle. Evert Duyckinck called Melville a "Blue-Beard who has hidden away five agreeable ladies in an icy glen," which amused Melville so much that he showed them the letter. But does Duyckinck's trope also suggest a dark side to life with Melville?[23]

During the long winter evenings, the Melvilles would eat a simple supper of buttered toast and tea at around seven, after which they would sometimes play whist or backgammon, but mostly they would gather beside the chimney hearth and read aloud. This winter they were reading *David Copperfield* and Schiller's *Ghost Tale,* which caused Augusta to dream something "too strangely sad, too wildly sorrowful" to be shared even with her dear friend Mary Blatchford.[24]

In mid-January, fresh powder snow brought such excellent sleighing weather that Augusta couldn't stand being cooped up any longer. Since it would be nearly dark by the time Herman would emerge from his study, Augusta and her mother made up their minds to learn to drive the rig themselves. "All the ladies drive themselves here," Gus told Mary Blatchford, "it is decidedly the fashion. And a most convenient one, as well as a delightful one." When Mother Melville pointed out that, unlike their more refined sisters in Albany and Lansingburgh, Berkshire women had been driving teams of horses all their lives, her stubborn son finally agreed to teach the women how to drive.[25]

Persuaded that his horse Charlie was so gentle "even a woman" could manage him, Melville allowed his mother and sister to make an experimental run to Robert Melvill's house. When Herman walked over to join them later for a cup of tea, they announced triumphantly that they had driven the four miles without difficulty. "Now we shall be quite independent," Augusta told Helen. "As you may imagine we are all highly delighted at the idea of being able to drive off whenever we have an inclination to taste the fresh air."[26]

Melville liked to take a walk or a drive every afternoon, even "in defiance of wintry elements." When no one else would venture out, he and Augusta would "brave piercing winds & penetrate trackless wastes in search of adventure," coming home refreshed and exhilarated.[27]

One day, Melville impulsively drove through the snow to pay the visit to Hawthorne that he had been putting off for so long. He found Hawthorne "buried in snow" as though "all wrapped up & tucked away under a napkin," hard at work finishing *The House of the Seven Gables.* Although Hawthorne was not in the mood for company, Sophia gave Melville the "warmest of welcomes" and served him a supper of cold chicken. She also gave him a copy of *The Grandfather's Chair* for Malcolm, and when Hawthorne appeared for supper, he presented him with a copy of his *Twice-Told Tales.* Melville, who knew only "A Rill from the Town Pump," found these stories even more subtle than the "Mosses," although they were "an earlier vintage from his vine."[28]

Melville invited the Hawthornes, whom he described to Augusta as "the loveliest family he ever met with, or anyone can imagine," to come for a few days' visit at Arrowhead within the next fortnight, and when Sophia agreed, he was pleased, as he was looking forward to "getting [Hawthorne] up in my snug room here, & discussing the Universe with a bottle of brandy & cigars." Gus was so nervous at the prospect of meeting Hawthorne face to face that she urged Helen to come home immediately and lend her superior "powers of entertainment" to the occasion.[29]

Several days later, Sophia Hawthorne sent word that they would be able to visit only for a day, as her husband couldn't tear himself away from his new book for long. Disappointed, Melville wrote Hawthorne a mock-protest against this "side-blow," accusing Sophia of keeping him home by means of her "syrenisms," and reissuing his invitation: "Your bed is already made, & the wood marked for your fire." Two fowls had been marked out as "destined victims for the table. I keep the word 'Welcome' all the time in my mouth, so as to be ready on the instant when you cross the threshold.... Do not think you are coming to any prim nonsensical house—that is nonsensical in the ordinary way. You won't be much bored with punctilos [sic]. You may do what you please—say or say not what you please." Who could have failed to be charmed by an invitation to a house that was not "nonsensical in the ordinary way"?[30]

While Melville waited for the Hawthornes' reply, he had plenty of opportunity for recreation, as it was perfect sleighing weather. One afternoon he took his mother, Lizzie, and Augusta to Lenox, but fearing they might be "precipitated down a steep hill," they all got out of the sleigh and walked the rest of the way to the village. Gus "respectfully suggested" taking the longer road on the return trip, to avoid the hill, and as they passed Charles and Elizabeth Sedgwick's house, they spied them at tea through the dining-room window and made an impromptu call. Mary Dewey, the wife of the Unitarian minister Orville Dewey, was there, but Catharine was in New York visiting her nephew Robert, whose son had a broken arm. Charles said his sister would be sorry to have missed the Melvilles, and sent his love to Helen, whom he remembered from her days at his wife's school.[31]

Few such glimpses of serendipitous socializing could be found in the various Melville archives before 1983, when five hundred family letters were discovered in a barn. As a result, much early scholarly literature about Melville portrayed him as an "isolato" and almost perversely found ways to show that Melville and his family were abnormal or deviant, rather than seeing their complexities and contradictions as typical of normal human beings who were living sometimes ordinary, and often extraordinary, lives.

In 1851, Evert Duyckinck, who had been made editor of *Holden's Dollar Magazine,* wanted to republish Hawthorne's "Ethan Brand," and he wrote to him asking for a photograph. Despite his distaste for sticking his "damnable phiz" before the public eye,

Hawthorne sent Duyckinck the requested daguerreotype without a fuss. Melville, by contrast, was insulted when Duyckinck asked him to send a photograph along with "a light nautical tale" for publication. Offended by what he felt was trivialization of his work, Melville shot back, "'A dash of salt spray'!—where am I to get salt spray here in inland Pittsfield? I shall have to import it from foreign parts." He was not "in the humor" to "write the thing you want," and he had no desire to have his "mug" engraved, because everyone's "mug" could be seen in magazines these days. As far as Melville was concerned, having one's picture in a magazine was "presumptive evidence" of being "a nobody," and he emphatically did not want to be "*oblivioned* by a Daguerrotype."[32]

When Duyckinck suggested that Melville might prefer to have his portrait painted the next time he came to town, Melville's mother began nagging him to sit for "a first-rate artist," or risk appearing "very strangely stiff," so he backed down and sent Duyckinck the requested photograph.[33]

Melville's relationship with his mother was complicated; his feelings toward her were ambivalent at best. Except for his four years at sea, the weeks he and Lizzie had been away on their honeymoon, and the brief period when he and Lizzie had stayed at Melvill House before moving to Arrowhead, he and his mother had always lived in the same house. Like many mothers of adult sons, she wanted him to be independent, but also to do things the way she thought he should. It was hard for her not to treat him like a child one minute and a surrogate husband the next. Like many young men, Melville longed for maternal nurturing but resented his mother's attempts to control him, and he often took out his frustrations by being irritable with his wife.

Relationships among members of the Melville clan tended to be less physically close but more emotionally suffocating than relationships among members of the Shaw family, which was hard on Lizzie. Her family tended to be more relaxed than Herman's, and her father had always been demonstrably affectionate with her in small but important ways. Her husband, by contrast, was a man of large and contradictory gestures, and few of what she would describe as normal, ordinary moods or tranquil domestic graces. If he could be charming and affectionate at times, he could also be gruff, or given to ignoring her completely.

Sharing her house with her formidable mother-in-law was a delicate balancing act for Lizzie. Mother Melville had rigid expectations of how people should behave, and she was not one to keep them to herself. Sometimes Herman would join his mother in needling Lizzie, and sometimes he would use Lizzie as a buffer against his mother. Either way, Lizzie had to be constantly on her guard and alert to her husband's unpredictable behavior.

The pressure to emulate her mother-in-law was demoralizing, especially since, in Mother Melville's eyes, no Yankee girl could ever live up to Dutch standards of housekeeping. A nineteenth-century country household such as Arrowhead provided myriad chores for everyone in the family. Tending the animals, plowing and planting the fields, harvesting the crops, and haying kept the men busy; cooking, baking, churning butter, and tending children kept the women occupied. In the spring, women undertook the great cleaning, which involved airing out and storing woolens, hanging carpets on a line and beating them, washing curtains, bedspreads, and windows. They planted flowers and herbs and vegetables, and in the autumn they put up preserves, dipped and molded candles, and caught up on the sewing, mending, and darning while the smoke from the great fireplaces that heated their homes blackened curtains, furniture, and floors with a film of soot.[34]

Although Lizzie regarded housekeeping as an important job and took pride in her work, it was not a sacred calling to her, as it was to her mother-in-law. She liked well enough to cook and bake—especially gingerbread and pies—and she kept the house reasonably neat and clean despite having less household help than the Gansevoorts ever had, but Mother Melville never gave her credit for anything she did. It seemed that no matter how hard she worked, she was perpetually "stowing down & clearing up," only to begin the process again a few hours later.[35]

Lizzie also had a more relaxed attitude toward child-rearing than did either the Melvilles or the Gansevoorts. Whereas Maria, who had been brought up by her Calvinist parents to believe in the natural depravity of Man, demanded that children be obedient and dutiful from an early age, Lizzie had learned from her Enlightenment parents that children were innately good, and thought to bind them to right conduct with silken cords, not chains. The first years of Lizzie's married life were dominated by a mother-in-law who could be utterly charming and even coquettish with friends, but intimidating and insensitive at home. Even something as simple and pleasurable as playing the piano in the parlor could become a battleground in a war Lizzie was bound to lose, as she could not play without subjecting herself to criticism from Maria.[36]

Melville's resentment of his mother's controlling ways was manifested in childish ways that did nothing to change the family pattern of avoiding direct confrontation and negotiation. In early March, for example, he dropped his mother at the Pittsfield depot and left her to wait for the train alone. The minute she got to Allan's place in New York, she let Augusta know how "ungallant" Herman had been, "dumping me & my trunks out so unceremoniously at the Depot. Although we were there more than an hour before the time, he hurried off as though his life depended upon his speed." Probably Melville's "life" did depend on getting back to his work as quickly as possible so he would not lose momentum while he was working on the complex and demanding *Moby-Dick,* and he evidently was in no mood to explain the exigencies of a writer's life to his mother.[37]

Two days later, Melville rode over to the Hawthornes' at dusk, and Sophia served a light supper of champagne foam with buttered bread and cheese. Melville urged Hawthorne to come for a visit as soon as possible, and Hawthorne surprised him by driving over to Arrowhead with his daughter Una the next day, despite deep spring snow. The handsome Hawthorne made quite an impression on the Melville women, especially Augusta, who was a great fan of his books. Her description of her meeting with him prompted Mary Blatchford to refer to Hawthorne ever after as "Gus's beau ideal."[38]

The two men spent most of that day in Melville's great barn, "smoking and talking metaphysics," with Hawthorne lounging on the carpenter's bench and Melville sprawled out on the hay. Their "ontological heroics"–lubricated by liberal doses of gin, champagne, or brandy–afforded Melville the kind of intense intellectual stimulation he needed, and Hawthorne proposed publishing their conversations as "A Week on a Work-Bench in a Barn"–a takeoff on Henry David Thoreau's *A Week on the Concord and Merrimack Rivers*–in which they would make fun of what Hawthorne called the moon-calf idealism of the transcendentalists.[39]

Before Hawthorne left, he gave Melville the four-volume *Mariner's Chronicle* that his uncle had given him, thinking these accounts of shipwrecks, fires, and famines at sea might provide Melville with material for a whaling story that was turning into, so Melville had told him, a narrative with apocalyptic overtones.[40]

Clearly, Melville was infatuated with Hawthorne's intellect, captivated by his artistry, and charmed by his elusive personality. Although the two men were drawn together in an undeniable sympathy of soul and intellect, the friendship meant something different to each of them, and they expressed their feelings in very different ways. Whereas Melville would have thought nothing of exchanging a hearty hug with a male friend, Hawthorne avoided casual physical contact. Sophia once observed that "he hates to be touched more than anyone I ever knew," which seems a curious comment from the mother of his children, especially in light of the passionate letters he wrote Sophia while he was courting her.[41]

Although they were fifteen years apart in age and temperamentally quite different, Melville and Hawthorne were natural allies and friends. Whether talking about child-rearing or debating philosophy, their time together seemed so short and so precious that Melville found himself talking excitedly, pouring out the strangled yearnings of his soul. Hawthorne found Melville's manic intensity exhausting at times, and Melville longed to remedy Hawthorne's lack of "plump sphericity" with a serving of "roast-beef, done rare."[42]

Both wounded men, Hawthorne and Melville dealt with their pain quite differently, Hawthorne by repression and reserve, Melville by active struggle. Although the deaths of his parents had shaken his faith in Providence, much as the death of Melville's father had shaken his, Hawthorne coped with his doubts by repressing them. Melville, by contrast, confronted his doubts and fought fiercely to test the universe and hold God accountable. Every meeting between the two men was an intricate dance, an intellectual courtship.

Melville's feelings for Nathaniel Hawthorne defy the categorization so fashionable in today's discussions of gender politics. In Victorian America, passionate same-sex friendships provided, as they do today, a salutary balance in the lives of single adults of both sexes. Melville, an ex-sailor who may have experienced some forms of physical intimacy with other men, sought male friends partly to compensate for losing his father so early and partly because his relationships with Lizzie and the other women in his family did not supply the kind of comradeship he enjoyed with men—smoking, drinking, and swapping bawdy stories, perhaps re-creating the camaraderie of the forecastle, without fear of a reprimand from the ladies.

Passionate friendships between two men or between two women—the latter were called "Boston marriages"—were a Victorian institution, as were close relationships between a couple and a friend of either sex, usually an unmarried man or woman. Catharine Sedgwick described such friendships in a letter to her niece: "I am not transcendental, as you know, but it seems to me that where there is a true, a spiritual friendship, there is a spiritual body formed by a delicate distillation from the events of mutual concernment, and that whatever we feel and act together adds to the vigor and beauty of that body."[43]

The comparative strictness of social forms and greater formality protected people from unsanctioned intimacy, and although some same-sex friends were sexually intimate, most found security in platonic friendships involving hugging and other nonsexual forms of touching.[44]

Ralph Waldo Emerson, who referred to love as "the passion that rebuilds the world for youth" and fosters "the progress of the soul" toward "increasing virtue and wisdom," praised the Greek ideal of male-male friendship as a paradigm for all human relationships, and at one point in his life he fell in love with a young man named Martin Gay. According to Emerson, same-sex relationships left behind "the touch and clawing," the "rash" intrusion into another's soul that stands in the way of that "deep peace between two spirits" that treats its object as "a god." Nathaniel Hawthorne, by contrast, felt palpable anxiety about intimacy between men, and he relied more heavily on Sophia as a companion than Melville, who was surrounded by women, relied on Lizzie at this point.[45]

Much to the Melvilles' disappointment, when the day for the Hawthornes' visit finally came, Hawthorne sent his regrets "owing to sickness in his family,—or else, he's up to the lips in the *Universe* again," Melville joked, offering to "send Constables" to fetch him. Despite Melville's promise to serve "excellent Montado sherry" and a "most potent

Port," to season "mulled wine with wisdom, & buttered toast with story-telling," and to "crack jokes & bottles from morning till night," Hawthorne postponed his visit.[46]

Soul mates in some ways, they were opposites in others. Melville's art was Dionysian, passionate, impulsive, and organic. He would strip himself of all defenses, reaching out to others in hopes of changing their hearts and minds. Hawthorne's art, by contrast, was Apollonian, cool, structured, and controlled. Hawthorne was Daedalus, artfully constructing a protective labyrinth around the hurt and angry inner child. Melville was Icarus, soaring recklessly toward the sun.

⁓

Whatever the precise nature of their social intercourse that afternoon and on subsequent occasions, Hawthorne was impressed by Melville's ability to make people feel "snug and comfortable" at Arrowhead. Yet, like Duyckinck, he may have sensed "a little lower layer" in Melville's volatile personality. Interestingly, Melville especially admired Hawthorne's "Fire-Worship," in which appears a passage describing the potential of an ordinary hearth fire to escape and "run riot" through a house, leaving nothing but the family's "whitened bones." In his review of *Mosses*, Melville had singled out the sentence "The possibility of mad destruction only made his domestic kindness the more beautiful and touching," calling it "exquisite," which seems fitting, as it seems an apt description of the volcanic Melville.

Sometime during March 1851, Melville received word that his old friend Eli James Murdock Fly, worn down by poverty and a series of dead-end jobs, had become an invalid. Fly had married a woman from Hingham, but at some point Melville became a kind of guardian to him. Taking time out from his book, Melville escorted Fly from Greenbush to Springfield, Massachusetts, where he got on a train for Brattleboro, Vermont, to take the "water-cure."[47]

Work on the book was slowed for a few weeks by Fly's illness and by a "twilight of the eyes" so severe that Melville had to steal about "like an owl." Wishing he "had more day-time to spend out *in the day,*" when the first break came in the weather, he hired a couple of men to build a porch on the northern side of the house so he could sit outdoors and read away from direct sunlight that might hurt his eyes. This and other renovations and additions made the house more comfortable and increased its assessed value by twenty-five percent, so Melville was very pleased with his investment.[48]

Melville was still adding whole new chapters to his nearly completed "Whale" on March 27, when Hawthorne wrote asking him to check when he went into town whether a large box of clothes had arrived at the railroad depot in Pittsfield. He also asked Melville to buy a wooden clock for $1.50 and have the expressman forward it with the clothes. In a postscript, Sophia asked him to deliver a message to the cabinetmaker who was fashioning a new bedstead for them. While this may sound trivial, it is the only extant letter from Hawthorne to Melville, and it suggests that Hawthorne and Melville enjoyed a much more mundane, everyday relationship than some biographers have led people to believe.[49]

When Melville delivered the clock and bedstead to the red cottage in person on April 11, Hawthorne gave him a copy of *The House of the Seven Gables,* which had just been published. Although Hawthorne had given the book a sunny ending in response to criticisms that *The Scarlet Letter* was too gloomy to appeal to a mass audience, Melville sensed Hawthorne's grasp of the "tragicalness of human thought in its own unbiased, native, and profounder workings." He admired Hawthorne for his unflinching apprehension of "the absolute condition of present things as they strike the eye of the man who fears them not, though they do their worst to him."[50]

Melville wrote his comments to Hawthorne in the form of a review of *The House of the Seven Gables* that–like "Hawthorne and His Mosses"–reveals as much about Melville himself as it does about its subject: "There is the grand truth about Nathaniel Hawthorne. He says NO! in thunder; but the Devil himself cannot make him say *yes.* For all men who say *yes,* lie; and all men who say *no,*–why they are in the happy condition of judicious, unencumbered travellers in Europe; they cross the frontiers into Eternity with nothing but a carpet-bag,–that is to say, the Ego. Whereas those *yes*-gentry, they travel with heaps of baggage, and, damn them! they will never get through the Custom House." In retrospect, these images seem uncannily prophetic of Melville's last meeting with Hawthorne in Liverpool, when Melville was on his way to the Holy Land.[51]

When Sophia Hawthorne read Melville's letter, she was delighted. Quoting a passage from it to her sister Elizabeth, she wrote: "The fresh, sincere, glowing mind that utters it is in a state of 'fluid consciousness,' & to Mr. Hawthorne speaks his innermost mind about GOD, the Devil & Life if so be he can get at the Truth–for he is a boy in opinion–having settled nothing as yet … it would betray him to make public his confessions & his efforts to grasp–because they would be considered perhaps impious, if one did not take in the whole scope of the case." It had always amazed her to hear people open up to her shy husband as if he were their "innermost Father Confessor," and it especially pleased her "to hear this growing man dash his tumultuous waves of thought up against Mr. Hawthorne's great, genial, comprehending silences … such a love & reverence & admiration for Mr. Hawthorne as is really beautiful to witness."[52]

Hawthorne's understanding and encouragement, whether partially a figment of Melville's own imagination or a rare relaxation of his habitual reserve, freed Melville to "write the other way," diving to a "little lower layer" of metaphysical speculation that would make his whaling book a masterpiece, not just of American literature, but of world literature.

With "The Whale" taking longer to harpoon than he had anticipated, and Lizzie expecting the couple's second child, Melville was very worried about money. At the end of April he asked Harper's for an advance, but they refused, saying they had "to make an extensive and expensive addition to our establishment" and enclosing a bill for outstanding charges of nearly $700, which was a huge debt on top of the money he was spending on the house. Fortunately, he was able to borrow $2,050 at 9 percent interest for 5 years from Tertullus D. Stewart, an old Lansingburgh friend who had settled in the Berkshires.[53]

Lack of support from his publisher and anxiety about money left Melville feeling drained and discouraged just when he was hoping to finish his book before summer so that he could relax and socialize. Fortunately, he had a large and attentive family, an active social life, and farm chores that forced him "out of doors," or he might have caved in completely to physical ailments as a reaction to the mental and emotional strain of writing. At times, only his faith in the greatness of his book kept him going.

Farm work, however, was not much more relaxing than working at a desk, and it was even harder on the joints. Stiff and sore with blisters from "building and patching and tinkering away in all directions," and suffering from eyestrain, writer's cramp, and a bad backache, Melville had to put off seeing Hawthorne again because he couldn't face "the long jolting" of the journey to Hawthorne's house and back. He had to save himself for planting his crops and finishing his book.[54]

At the end of May, after the corn and potatoes had been planted, Melville made a quick trip to New York to deliver the bulk of his manuscript to Harper's so they could make plates and print proof sheets. Within twenty-four hours, he was back in the Berkshires and cooped up indoors because of heavy rain, writing a long letter that expressed his almost messianic sense of his own literary mission and his fear that he might be doomed to failure: "Though I wrote the Gospels in this century, I should die in the gutter," he told Hawthorne.[55]

"Try to get a living by the Truth," he wrote, "and go to the Soup Societies.... Truth is ridiculous to men.... What I feel most moved to write, that is banned,—it will not pay. Yet, altogether, write the *other* way I cannot. So the product is a final hash, and all my books are botches." Feeling "cheerly disposed" but "a little bluely," he exclaimed, "Would the Gin were here!" Melville spun an elaborate fantasy about smuggling bottles of champagne into Paradise ("I won't believe in a Temperance Heaven") so that he and Hawthorne could put the cares of this world behind them and "strike our glasses and our heads together, till both musically ring in concert."[56]

Melville believed no artist should have to worry about money, fame, and reputation. "All fame is patronage. Let me be infamous: there is no patronage in that. What 'reputation' H.M. has is horrible. Think of it! To go down to posterity is bad enough, any way, but to go down as a 'man who lived among the cannibals'!" he exclaimed, mocking his reputation as a travel writer.[57]

If only a man could "live in the All" as Goethe had advised, he wrote Hawthorne. There was "some truth" in this "all" feeling: "You must have felt it, lying on the grass on the warm summer's day. Your legs seem to send out shoots into the earth. Your hair feels like leaves upon your head." For a man who liked to say he was not a transcendentalist, Melville sounds suspiciously like Emerson and Whitman.[58]

By the middle of June, while Augusta and Helen were taking turns with the fair copy, Melville was still adding "shanties of chapters and essays" to the book that matched the new "shanties of houses" the workmen were adding to his house. He took Augusta back with him to New York to finish the copying, as there were revisions to be done while the plates were being made and the first sheets were coming off the press. Helen stayed to help take care of Malcolm, as Lizzie was suffering from a "rose cold" so severe she had to keep a wet towel over her face so she could breathe.[59]

Staying with Allan and Sophia at Thirty-first Street and Lexington Avenue, Melville read proofs and made corrections in a small, hot, third-story room, rewriting the closing pages while the opening pages were being printed. Before the "Whale" was even "half through the press," he returned home, unable to tolerate "the heat and dust of the babylonish brick-kiln."[60]

"The Whale" went to press with enough summer left for enjoyment of the usual outings and parties, visits to Hawthorne at "Tanglewood," and visits from the Shaws. Lizzie, gravid in the summer heat and humidity and taking second place in Herman's thoughts to the "grand hooded phantom," welcomed the company of her parents, who always anchored her emotionally. Unlike the hypercritical Mother Melville, Hope Shaw gave Lizzie the unconditional love and steady support that Herman could not always supply, as he was increasingly subject to sudden mood swings.

On June 29 he offered to send Hawthorne a "fin of the *Whale* by way of a specimen mouthful," and warned him that the book was broiled in "hell-fire. It has as its motto (the secret one), *Ego non baptiso te in nomine* –but make out the rest yourself," he wrote, probably aware that Hawthorne considered *The Scarlet Letter* a "positively hell-fired story."[61]

Before the "tail" of the book was quite "cooked," Richard Bentley offered to buy the English rights for £150, less than Melville was expecting. He wrote back that English publishers ought to honor international copyright laws, as American publishers had no interest in looking after the rights of authors: "This country & nearly all its affairs are governed by sturdy backwoodsmen–noble fellows enough, but not at all literary, & who care not a fig for any authors except those who write those most saleable of all books nowadays–i e–the newspapers, & magazines. And tho' the number of cultivated catholic men, who may be supposed to feel an interest in a national literature, is large & every day growing larger; yet they are nothing in comparison with the overwhelming majority who care nothing about it." It seemed scandalous to Melville that "this country is at present engaged in furnishing material for future authors; not in encouraging its living ones."[62]

While waiting for Harper's to send a batch of finished books, Melville received an "easy-flowing long letter" from Hawthorne that "refreshed all [his] meadows," and he responded by proposing a "little bit of vagabondism before Autumn comes. Graylock we must go and vagabondize there. But ere we start we must dig a deep hole and bury all the Blue Devils, there to abide till the Last Day." He signed the letter, "Goodbye, his X mark," as though for a moment he had become Queequeg, the *Pequod*'s cannibal harpooner, to Hawthorne's Ishmael.[63]

"I am tormented with an everlasting itch for things remote. I love to sail forbidden seas, and land on barbarous coasts," Ishmael proclaims in Moby-Dick.

FIFTEEN

ONE GRAND HOODED PHANTOM

On August 1, 1851, his thirty-second birthday, Melville, sporting a broad-brimmed hat, rode over to Lenox to pay a surprise visit to the Hawthornes. On the way, he came upon Nathaniel and son Julian in a grove, where Hawthorne was reading his mail after a walk to the post office. Melville greeted them in Spanish, and as soon as Hawthorne realized the "cavalier on horseback" was his friend, he invited him home. Melville lifted Julian onto his horse, and the boy rode back to the red cottage "with the freedom and fearlessness of an old equestrian" as the two men walked alongside and chatted. Later he told his father "that he loved Mr. Melville" as much as he loved his papa, his mama, and Una.[1]

That evening, Hawthorne and Melville "had a talk about time and eternity, things of this world and of the next, and books, and publishers, and all possible and impossible matters, that lasted pretty deep into the night." Sophia had taken Una and baby Rose to visit her sister in West Newton, and the two men, "if the truth be told, smoked cigars even within the sacred precincts of the sitting room."[2]

Hawthorne and Julian came to Arrowhead the following week, while George and Evert

Duyckinck were visiting, and for the next few days they were all whirled about by that "maelstrom of hospitality," Sarah Morewood, who had planned several excursions. The first was a picnic at Berry Pond in Pittsfield's State Forest, followed by a trek to Balance Rock. As a surprise, Mrs. Morewood had hidden a music box beneath the poised boulder, and as she led Melville and the others to the picnic spot, they could hear "mysterious and enchanting music" emanating from the boulder. Melville named the stone "Memnon" after the Egyptian statue that sang by the Nile each dawn, and he toasted the ancient mysteries with champagne; the stone would play a role in his next novel.

The following day, Melville, the Duyckincks, and Hawthorne visited the Hancock Shakers. Evert Duyckinck thought the "glass eyed preacher" looked "like an escaped maniac" and that their religious services were "ghastly." Hawthorne was so discomfited by the way the women and girls scrutinized him, and so disturbed to learn that two men slept together in a narrow bed, that he pronounced the Shakers a "filthy set" in his notebooks. Melville certainly did not share Hawthorne's squeamishness, as the opening chapters of *Moby-Dick* include hilarious descriptions of Ishmael and Queequeg sharing a honeymoon bed at Peter Coffin's Spouter-Inn.[3]

The "grand excursion of the week" was the ascent of Saddleback, as Mount Greylock was known locally, by a party of eleven that included Herman, Augusta, Allan and Sophia, the Duyckinck brothers, Sarah Morewood, and some of her women friends, but apparently not Lizzie. Laden with "an indefinite supply" of cold meats and champagne, the intrepid band went to North Adams on the train. They climbed the 3,491-foot mountain, hiked three miles to a wind observatory owned by Williams College, and set up camp under an enormous moon. Melville clambered up a tall tree "with the agility of a well trained sailor," and hacked down branches with his axe to make a fire, then fanned the flames while Sarah Morewood laughed at his jokes and stories.[4]

Essentially finished with his "whale," Melville remained in high spirits through the month of August. When Sam Shaw and Sam Savage came to visit, he raced them up and down the hills until they begged for mercy. After their "rambles," they tapped a "cask of 'London dock'" and played a game of kickball, or soccer, inspiring a bit of ribald philosophizing on Melville's part in a subsequent letter to Savage: "We are all foot-balls, more or less. It is important, however, that our balls be covered with a leather, good & tough, that will stand banging & all 'the slings and arrows of outrageous fortune.'" Whatever "happens to a man in this life is only by way of a joke, especially his misfortunes," he wrote, sounding very much like his racy narrator Ishmael, for whom the universe seemed to be a "vast practical joke" at times.[5]

By mid-September, when Melville went to New York to sign the Harper's contract for *Moby-Dick, or The Whale* and *The Literary World* announced its forthcoming publication, he was already mulling over ideas for his next book. Sarah Morewood had sent him two popular novels, Edward Bulwer-Lytton's *Zanoni* and Harriet Martineau's *The Hour and the Man*, but he was too busy writing to read them right away: "The Fates have plunged me into silly thoughts and wayward speculations," he wrote Mrs. Morewood, "which will prevent me, for a time, from falling into the reveries of these books—for a fine book is a sort of revery to us—is it not?" These "silly thoughts and wayward speculations" were undoubtedly the first inklings of *Pierre*.[6]

Allan had already shipped a set of corrected proof sheets of *Moby-Dick* to the British publisher, and on October 18, three luxurious volumes entitled *The Whale* appeared in London bookstalls. Not only did Bentley forget to change the title to *Moby-Dick* as Melville had requested, but each volume had a right whale embossed on its spine instead of a sperm whale. The text of the English edition was badly mutilated, too. Being cautious, Richard Bentley had hired a special editor to go over the manuscript and delete anything that could remotely be construed as blasphemous, sexually suggestive, or unsympathetic to the monarchy, and this editor had butchered the text by creating more than seven hundred discrepancies between the English and American editions, moving the "Extracts of a Sub-Sub-Librarian" to the end of the book, and chopping off the "Epilogue" completely. This amputation opened Melville to ridicule for writing an "impossible" story whose narrator "appears to have drowned with the rest."[7]

Unfortunately, one of the earliest and most widely-circulated reviews of *Moby-Dick* was written by Henry Chorley, the extremely conservative critic for London's *Athenaeum*, whose disapproval of mixed-genre works had caused him to denounce *Mardi*. Chorley's description of *Moby-Dick* as "an ill-compounded mixture of romance and matter-of-fact" that resembled "so much trash belonging to the worst school of Bedlam literature" was picked up by other reviewers, who accused Melville of a "fatal facility for the writing of rhapsodies." For some reason, many American newspapers reprinted Chorley's review, but few, if any, reported that London's *Morning Advertiser* had extolled Melville's vast knowledge and his "dramatic ability for producing a prose poem," or that the paper's reviewer found no book "more honourable to American literature" than *Moby-Dick*.[8]

—〰—

"To produce a mighty book, you must choose a mighty theme," Ishmael exclaims as he grapples with the greatest whaling story of all time. A great American epic on the order of *Gilgamesh* or the *Odyssey*, the story of the hunt for the white whale resonates with the power of ancient myth.[9]

Drawing on many sources, conscious and unconscious, *Moby-Dick* touches the mind on many levels. It combines American tall tales and hunting stories with echoes of *Macbeth* and *King Lear*, combines biblical allusions with Rabelaisian humor, Shandyean scatology with sublime poetry, sailor yarns and chanteys with Oriental mythology, and detailed, accurate descriptions of whaling with sermons and homilies, philosophical meditations and supernatural prophecies. Except for some portions of Captain Ahab's stagy soliloquies, its "bold and nervous lofty language" almost entirely escapes bombast. Melville's words are wind and water, his sentences are sails, his paragraphs the brain cells, nerves, and ligaments of the great creature who brushes continents with his flanks, sounding the depths where the keel of the universe was laid, cruising beyond the reach of Job's questions, Jehovah's answers, or Jonah's prayers.[10]

With the instinct of a born storyteller, Melville sounds a dramatic opening chord with "Call me Ishmael." The informal, imperative voice establishes a radical intimacy that disarms the reader while commanding immediate attention. By introducing himself as Ishmael, the narrator identifies with the disinherited son of Abraham by the bondswoman Hagar. He is an outcast, a dispossessed, discontented landsman whose purse is empty and who has a "damp, drizzly November in [his] soul." Abominating "all honorable respectable toils, trials, and tribulations of every kind," he rejects privilege based on skin color, money, or patrician ancestry, and identifying with the "meanest mariners and renegades and castaways" on the world's oceans, he prefers to go to sea a a common sailor, shipping out "as a simple sailor, right before the mast, plumb down into the forecastle, aloft there to the royal masthead."[11]

Wandering through New Bedford's "blocks of blackness" in search of a place to stay, Ishmael stumbles into an African church, then finds a room at the Spouter-Inn, where he must share a bed with a sailor, who turns out to be a tattooed Polynesian harpooner. Although he terrifies Ishmael by jumping into bed with a tomahawk between his teeth, by morning, after this strange bedfellow has rolled over in his sleep and hugged him tightly, Ishmael has to admit that he has slept soundly in Queequeg's "bridegroom clasp."[12]

Melville's description of the relationship between Ishmael and Queequeg provides an exuberantly comical, iconoclastic vision of brotherly love and cross-cultural harmony. Queequeg carries embalmed human heads on his belt, wears a Native American wampum belt, smokes a tomahawk peace pipe, prays to an African idol named Yojo, and observes the Muslim fast of Ramadan, and he looks like "George Washington cannibalistically developed." In the motherly-fatherly embrace of this cosmopolitan cannibal, the spiritually orphaned Ishmael experiences a "melting" of his stiff "Presbyterian" prejudices and deliverance from misanthropy and despair: "No more my splintered heart and maddened hand were turned against the wolfish world," Ishmael explains retrospectively. "This soothing savage had redeemed it."[13]

After sharing a smoke of the tomahawk pipe with Ishmael, Queequeg presses his forehead against Ishmael's forehead, clasps him around the waist, and declares that they are "married; meaning, in his country's phrase, that we were bosom friends; he would gladly die for me, if needs should be." Invoking the Golden Rule, Ishmael argues that it's all right for him to "turn idolator" to please a friend, so he makes offerings of sea biscuits to Yojo, the little idol, and prays with Queequeg before they go to bed. Chatting like an old married couple in their "hearts' honeymoon," they sleep as peacefully as a "cosy, loving pair."[14]

In the morning, they sign on the whaler *Pequod* together, even though a crazy old man who calls himself Elijah prophesies that they are doomed if they agree to serve with "Old Thunder," as he calls Captain Ahab. Eventually, they will find out that Ahab has lost a leg to a white whale named Moby Dick, and that ever since he was "dismasted" and unmanned by it, Ahab has been vengefully hunting the white whale. Ahab's voyage is not a quest but a vendetta, a demonic holy war. He sees the whale as a symbol of everything that is unfathomable and unconquerable in the universe. His fanatical determination to "strike through the mask" and deal a death blow to the white whale contrasts dramatically with Ishmael's receptivity to many truths, not merely one exclusive Truth.[15]

The hunt for the white whale provides a metaphor for man's search for meaning in a world of deceptive appearances and fatal delusions. Unlike Ahab's murderous pursuit of Moby Dick, Ishmael's "Cetology" blends Puritan sermons and scientific anatomies, describing the tools and tasks of whaling realistically and symbolically as Ishmael explicates the texts of whaling, then demonstrates their moral and spiritual application to human life. His taxonomy of whales demonstrates the limitations of scientific knowledge and the impossibility of achieving certainty, and the biblical echoes and analogies supply the theological resonance for his attempt to perceive the eternal truths that lie beyond religious faith. After a detailed description of every type of whale known to man, he reduces his scientific knowledge to the childlike perception that the whale is *"a spouting fish with a horizontal tail."*[16]

Ishmael and Ahab embody antithetical attitudes toward life. Whereas Ahab lusts to revenge himself on the white whale, Ishmael is drawn to the open ocean by "the overwhelming idea of the great whale himself." He simply wants to follow the "portentous and mysterious monster" through the "floodgates of the wonder-world" to explore "wild and distant seas" where he can experience "all the attending marvels of a thousand Patagonian sights and sounds." He looks to Nature and the heart of man for intimations of Truth, gaining reverence for the whale and learning to savor moments of peace and transcendence rather than searching obsessively for fixed belief. Ahab's dogmatic rigidity, symbolized by the "iron way" of the railroad to which he likens himself, dooms his ship to destruction, as a sea captain does not sail along a fixed track, but must know how to work with the wind, tacking or running, letting out the sail or reefing to reach his destination. Although for a time Ishmael becomes caught up in Ahab's monomania, in the end he breaks free to achieve a polypositional stance that takes him from Puritanism to a kind of pantheism, from suicidal despair to spiritual rebirth.[17]

Both Ishmael and Ahab are set adrift in an existential void to make their own meanings, as Melville was following his father's death. Taken together, the two characters dramatize Melville's dialogic struggles with family, culture, history, and self. Rejecting both his mother's oppressive Calvinism and his father's utilitarian Unitarianism, Melville sought his own truth, but he could never quite shake off the strangling cords that bound him to the monster Deity who hid His face from the spiritually orphaned Melville, only to turn and make a devastating reckoning just when he thought he could break away. By killing Ahab, not the whale, Melville killed off the bleak "November in his soul" and bobbed up from the maelstrom that swallows up the "last chip" of the *Pequod,* whole, proclaiming: "I myself am a savage, owing no allegiance but to the King of the Cannibals, and ready at any moment to rebel against him."

Through Ishmael, who lives to tell his story, the whale becomes *The Whale,* affirming the power of the artist to triumph over death by conferring immortality. Moby Dick's survival affirms the existence of spiritual forces in Nature that man should treat with reverence, not contempt. Melville's prodigious white whale takes away the sinners of the world and lets the Ishmaels of the world—the teachers, the poets, the artists, the shamans—live.

Moby-Dick draws from a deep reservoir of Native American folklore and myth. It is a vision quest, a narrative sweat lodge or purification ritual, and a Ghost Dance mourning the closing of ancient spiritual frontiers. It is Melville's lament for the extermination of the Indians by white settlers and the importation of Africans as slaves, both of which sowed seeds of sin and death in the New World Garden. It is an apocalyptic vision of industrialization and imperialism, an elegy for the medicine man supplanted by the gunslinger.

Just as whaling was both brutal and heroic, New England's "errand into the wilderness" was both civilized and savage. King Philip's War decimated the indigenous tribes of southern New England, and when Captain Benjamin Church, the renowned Indianfighter, killed the great chieftain Metacomet, whom the colonists called "King Philip," or "the great leviathan," the Puritans quartered his body and left it for the wolves, sending his hands to Boston, and sticking his head on a pike in Plymouth. Cotton Mather called it "divine retribution," and before the bleached skull was put on display in Boston, Increase Mather took the jawbone of the "blasphemous leviathan" home with him as a souvenir.[18]

The *Pequod* sports ghoulish trophies of whale hunts, and her name evokes the Pequot War, in which about five hundred men, women, and children of the Pequot tribe were exterminated. She is "a cannibal of a craft, tricking herself forth in the chased bones of her enemies." Her tiller is fashioned from the jawbone of a whale, and her owners interview prospective crew members in a makeshift office that looks like a wigwam. Such associations make it plain that *Moby-Dick* serves as Melville's attempt to redeem America's blood-guilt by writing New World history "the other way"—a way that conflicts with Puritan histories like Cotton Mather's *Magnalia Christi Americana*, with the heroic legends about Melville's own grandfathers, with the jingoistic stump speeches his brother Gansevoort made for the Democratic Party in 1844, and with the racist legal system Judge Shaw was forced to uphold after the Compromise of 1850.[19]

Swimming against the racist tide of most popular fiction, Melville invested the *Pequod*'s three nonwhite harpooners with the dignity of priests, kings, and princes, and relegated the three white mates, Starbuck, Stubb, and Flask, to the status of cowards, knaves, and fools, substituting a hierarchy of merit for the hierarchy of privilege that puts whites in command of people of color. Queequeg, the Polynesian prince, Tashtego, the Wampanoag warrior, and Daggoo, the coal-black African who might have been a king in his own land, are Nature's aristocrats, while the white mates are vulgar savages. Whereas the cannibal Queequeg casually saves the lives of three men during the voyage, the Quaker Starbuck fails to stop Ahab from pursuing his blasphemous quest, even though he knows the ship and crew are doomed otherwise.

Tashtego retains the dignity of "those proud warrior hunters" who treated the animals they killed with respect and reverence, while Stubb cuts a steak from the "small" of the whale and eats it while taunting the old black cook, Fleece. The unlettered but eloquent Fleece ignores Stubb but preaches a sermon to the sharks that concludes, "Wish, by gor! whale eat him, 'stead of him eat whale. I'm bressed if he ain't more of a shark dan Massa Shark hisself." Like many of Melville's black characters, Fleece is compliant and obedient on the surface, but covertly rebellious against white tyranny.[20]

The third harpooner, Daggoo, is "a gigantic, coal-black negro-savage with a lion-like tread [who] retained all his barbaric virtues." Standing before him, the third mate, Flask, "seems a white flag come to beg truce of a fortress." Whereas Daggoo conducts himself with dignity and self-restraint, the crude little Flask maliciously darts his harpoon into an ulcerated sore on the flank of a blind, old, crippled whale, and after "more than sufferable anguish," the wounded animal turns up "the white secrets of his belly" and dies.[21]

Even Pip, the black cabin boy whom the white sailors order to play the tambourine in "Midnight, Forecastle," is woven round "with tragic graces." The smallest and least significant member of the crew, Pip feels fear and awe when that "anaconda of an old man," Captain Ahab, swears to hunt the white whale at all costs, and he nearly dies of a cracked brain and a broken heart when Stubb abandons him in mid-ocean. A native of Tolland County, Connecticut, who "had once enlivened many a fiddler's frolic on the green," Pip loves life, so he has a healthy respect for the perils of the chase. When he jumps in terror from the whaleboat into the sea, Stubb warns him not to do it again, saying the next time they won't come back for him. "We can't afford to lose whales by the likes of you," he says, "a whale would sell for thirty times what you would, Pip, in Alabama." Then Pip jumps again in fright and is not rescued for many hours, during which he is "carried down alive to wondrous depths, where strange shapes of the unwarped primal world glided to and fro," and "among the joyous, heartless, ever-juvenile eternities, Pip saw the multitudinous, God-omnipresent, coral insects, that out of the firmament of waters heaved the colossal orbs. He saw God's foot upon the treadle of the loom, and spoke it; and therefore his ship mates called him mad." In a later scene, he comes upon his shipmates staring at the gold doubloon Ahab has nailed to the mast as a reward for sighting Moby Dick. While their interpretations of the symbols carved on the coin are completely subjective, Pip sums up the essential ontological mystery: "I look, you look, he looks; we look, ye look, they look."[22]

In Melville's world, "man's insanity is heaven's sense," so Pip returns to the ship as wise as King Lear's Fool. Ahab recognizes that Pip speaks the truth, but he is fated to ignore the promptings of his heart and unable to turn back from disaster. Even when his wife and child appear to his mind's eye to call him home, Ahab does not reverse the helm as Ishmael did when he realized that his moral compass had been turned around by staring into the infernal try-works that was "burning a corpse" to transform blubber into marketable oil.

Always conscious that the economy of America's shipping industry was inextricably bound up with slavery, Melville explores American attitudes toward Nature and civilization, slavery and freedom, sexuality and power, much more subtly in *Moby-Dick* than in *Mardi.* He conjures the totem whale to counteract the Founding Fathers' support for genocide and slavery. By telling the truth about the disastrous course the Ship of State was following, Melville risked alienating moderates like Nathaniel Hawthorne and Lemuel Shaw.

While Melville was composing *Moby-Dick,* history was coming to a boil in Boston, and Lemuel Shaw was facing the most serious challenge of his career. In April 1851 the case of Thomas Sims, a fugitive from a Georgia plantation, came before the Massachusetts Supreme Judicial Court, and under the new federal Fugitive Slave Law, Judge Shaw would have to rule that Sims must be returned to his owner. Shaw, who, in 1849, had infuriated abolitionists by upholding the right of city schools to choose to be racially segregated, now became the target of protestors who filled the streets around the courthouse demanding the release of Sims.[23]

All during the Sims trial, Boston was a city under siege. With mobs of whites and free Negroes gathered outside the courthouse, federal marshals cordoned off the building with chains and set up an armed guard to prevent abolitionists from rescuing Sims, as the Unitarian minister Thomas Wentworth Higginson and his cohorts had rescued the fugitive Shadrach not long before. When Shaw decided to place Sims in the custody of federal marshals for extradition to Savannah, New England writers and intellectuals were outraged. Henry Wadsworth Longfellow proclaimed it a "Shame that the great Republic, the 'refuge of the oppressed,' should stoop so low as to become the Hunter of Slaves." In Longfellow's opinion, Boston had become "a city without a soul."[24]

Almost all of the participants in the case had close ties to Melville, including Sims's attorney Richard Henry Dana Jr., who was the first president of the Boston Vigilance Committee, an activist organization pledged to harbor fugitives and abolish slavery. After the decision, the exasperated Dana wrote in his journal, "Our temple of justice is a slave pen!" Dana considered the Fugitive Slave Law "a tyrannical statute" and Shaw a "weak judge" for upholding it, and he considered it a disgrace to Boston and an affront to the United States Constitution that a federal judge would pick up the skirts of his judicial robe to climb over chains in order to reach the bench in order to uphold an immoral law. Thus, when Melville's Father Mapple, whom Ishmael hears preaching in the Whaleman's Chapel, exhorts his congregation to root out sin whenever and wherever they find it, even in the highest councils of the land, saying, "Delight is to him, who gives no quarter in the truth, and kills, burns, and destroys all sin though he pluck it from under the robes of Senators and Judges," we hear the voices of abolitionists like Melville's friend Dana.[25]

Dana's journal captures the electric atmosphere surrounding the courthouse during the trial: the strained nerves and explosive tempers of police and protestors, the tense watchfulness of the free northern Negroes, the incipient violence. Dana used the image "black squall" for the dark, somber faces that became more numerous and foreboding as crowds gathered outside the federal courthouse to wait for the verdict, and it may be no coincidence that in chapter 40 of *Moby-Dick*, when white sailors taunt Pip and Daggoo, and Daggoo reaches for his knife, saying "White skin, white liver!", a sudden white squall intervenes to avert racial violence. By exploring the conventional Western color symbolism that links blackness with evil and whiteness with purity, as he does in the chapter "The Whiteness of the Whale," Melville invites the reader to question laws and moral judgments based on skin color and racial classifications.[26]

Ishmael, who started his voyage by asking cynically, "Who ain't a slave?" ends the voyage wondering whether man is a "money-making animal" willing to enslave his fellows and kill other creatures for profit, or a demigod capable of love and mercy. Cradled by Queequeg's coffin life buoy, he bobs above the whirlpool with his sense of wonder intact, his embrace of the dark "other" having buoyed him above the wreck.[27]

~~~~~

Even before he finished "trying-out" his "Whale," Melville knew he had composed a masterpiece. It must have seemed that a lifetime had passed since he started to write a factual account of sperm whaling, solidly grounded in accurate descriptions of shipboard life and cetological information, and with no allegorical superstructure. In the end he had woven a complex tapestry of metaphysics and naturalism, secular sermons and philosophical meditations, bawdy jokes, tall tales, and sailor yarns.[28]

He had written "a wicked book," as he told Hawthorne, not only because he had deconstructed cherished myths about American history, but also because he had made fun of the official sexual ideology of Victorian America, especially those ideologies that linked the conquest of America's "virgin land" to the "Manifest Destiny" of the human sperm, as entrepreneurs determined to open new markets across the vast continent regularly did.[29]

Popular medical mythology, which was still strongly Puritanical in its biases, advocated "spermatic economy," or the husbanding of the male's reproductive fluids by abstinence from intercourse more frequent than once a month, even within the confines of marriage. To conserve their energy for the conquest of the continent and the procreation of manly pioneers, men were supposed to husband their vital seminal fluid, treating it as an investment in the future, rather like stocks and bonds, as medical experts were saying that the longer spermatozoa were stored in the body, the more potent and vigorous a man's offspring would be.[30]

Most doctors and ministers condemned fornication, homosexual behavior (which they called "sodomy"), and masturbation, which was thought to deplete the life force in men and cause nymphomania in women, and they opposed contraception and abortion as inimical to the production of future citizens of the Republic. Physicians such as Evert Duyckinck's friend Augustus Kinsley Gardner, and clergymen, including the Reverend John Todd, the pastor of the Second Congregational Church in Pittsfield, condemned all sexual activity not directed toward procreation, extending their prohibition even to the intercourse of married couples. Dr. Todd, a self-appointed sexual prophet, was the author of *A Student's Manual,* an advice book for young men, which Allan Melville acquired in 1839 and which Herman probably read.[31]

With the Industrial Revolution driving a wedge between home and workplace, Christianity driving a wedge between body and soul, and the medical profession driving a wedge between men and women, sexual energies were savagely repressed. While men found outlets for their frustrations through the institutionalized aggression of the business world and the lawless violence of the frontier, women kept busy doing household chores and good works for their communities. Caught between the Scylla of serial pregnancy and the Charybdis of abstinence, genteel men and women suffered from neurasthenia and various other chronic complaints, and some couples practiced companionate marriage or cultivated same-sex friendships to fill the void.[32]

As a sailor, and as a sojourner in the South Seas, Melville undoubtedly experienced sexual behavior unmentionable in Victorian drawing rooms and genteel novels. When his preconceptions and prejudices about sexuality were challenged by these experiences, he explored new definitions of masculinity in his books, and channeled his anxiety into bursts of bawdry and burlesque. In *Moby-Dick,* the language itself conflated seafaring with sex, so puns on *semen* and *seaman, sperm* and *spermaceti,* came naturally to wordsmith Melville. It must have amused him mightily that the economy of New England, the bedrock of American Puritanism, rested on a slippery substance with a double meaning. It made whaling the ultimate form of "spermatic economy."[33]

In "A Squeeze of the Hand," Melville daringly transforms a description of whalemen "squeezing case" into a vision of men working not in competition with one another, but in cooperative homosocial bliss that completely defies the official sexual ideology:

> Squeeze! squeeze! squeeze! all the morning long; I squeezed that sperm till I myself almost melted into it; I squeezed that sperm till a strange sort of insanity came over me; and I found myself unwittingly squeezing my co-laborers' hands in it, mistaking their hands for the gentle globules. Such an abounding, affectionate, friendly, loving feeling did this vocation beget; that at last I was continually squeezing their hands, and looking up into their eyes sentimentally; as much as to say... Come; let us squeeze hands all round; nay let us squeeze ourselves into each other; let us squeeze ourselves universally into the very milk and sperm of kindness.

By abbreviating the word *spermaceti* to *sperm,* Melville conflates the waxy substance taken from the head of the sperm whale with the image of men dreamily squeezing one another's hands, which clearly signify their sex organs. In *Moby-Dick* he created a language in which he could write about male sexuality in a witty and iconoclastic manner, elevating masculine homoerotics from perversity to a kind of poetry.[34]

Like "the great camerado" Walt Whitman, Melville envisioned the egalitarian social order as a noncompetitive, nonhierarchical fraternity of men who were shipmates and brothers. "A Squeeze of the Hand" is as much a "language experiment" as Whitman's paean to the "winds whose soft-tickling genitals rub against me." Both men were trying to create new ways of writing about sex, and although we have no evidence that Whitman read *Moby-Dick*, he certainly knew *Typee* and *Omoo*, and he probably read *Mardi* as well. It would not be far-fetched to speculate that it was reading Melville's sexually adventurous whaling story, along with Emerson's essay on "The Poet," that transformed a journalist and minor temperance novel–writer named Walter Whitman into the great American bard whose *Leaves of Grass* unfolded in 1855.

Melville's ribald description of sailors squeezing sperm not only subverts the pronouncements of preachers and ministers, it also deconstructs bourgeois ideas of masculinity and dissolves gender boundaries, as Ishmael and his shipmates squeeze sperm until it turns into the milk of human kindness. Quite unexpectedly, Ishmael segues from homoeroticism into domesticity and marriage; as fraternal love joins seamlessly with a vision of domesticity as Ishmael kneads the "gentle globules" of sperm into the stuff of cozy wedded life:

> Would that I could keep squeezing that sperm for ever! For now, since my many prolonged, repeated experiences I have perceived that in all cases man must eventually lower, or at least shift, his conceit of attainable felicity; not placing it anywhere in the intellect or the fancy; but in the wife, the heart, the bed, the table, the saddle, the fire-side, the country.

This seems both an autobiographical confession and a view of sexuality that transcends gender categories.[35]

If the subtext of "A Squeeze of the Hand" is the whaleman's penis and testicles, the more obvious subtext of "The Cassock" is the whale's "grandissimus," an "unaccountable cone,–longer than a Kentuckian is tall, nigh a foot in diameter at the base, and jet-black as Yojo, the ebony idol of Queequeg." After removing the "dark pelt" from this unnamed mysterious object, the mincer cuts arm-holes in it and slips it on. Thus "invested in the full canonicals of his calling," the skin of the whale's penis, he becomes "a candidate for an archbishoprick," and the whale's huge phallus becomes a religious totem, like Queequeg's black pagod. By stripping Christianity down to seminal pagan rituals, Ishmael reaffirms the ancient connection between spirituality and sexuality and declares his independence from conventional restraints. Not surprisingly, Ahab and all of the crew except Ishmael die in the sacrilegious attempt to destroy the grand and god-like Moby Dick. The potent whale kills the Puritan preacher and anoints the American Artist with spermaceti, blood, and brine.[36]

Melville playfully warned Sarah Morewood to avoid *Moby-Dick*: "Dont you buy it– dont you read it, when it does come out, because it is by no means the sort of book for you. It is not a peice [sic] of fine feminine Spitalfields silk—but is of the horrible texture of a fabric that should be woven of ships cables & hausers [sic]. A Polar wind blows through it, & birds of prey hover over it. Warn all gentle fastidious people from so much as peeping into the book—on risk of a lumbago & sciatics."[37]

Although Melville claimed that *Moby-Dick* was not a book for ladies, many passages affirm values traditionally regarded as feminine in Western thought. It is as though Melville intuitively sensed, perhaps in the deepest recesses of his own heart, an inner mother—not the haughty, controlling Victorian matriarch, but the great goddess whose nurturing presence antedated the angry God of the Hebrews and the Puritans. In "A Bower in the Arsacides," for instance, Ishmael strolls through a temple made from the skeleton of a beached whale and senses the subtle presence of a "weaver-god" who seems to metamorphose into an androgynous old crone plying her shuttle through the loom of the "message-carrying air." Interestingly, the goddess and her pagan priestess appear in poems written during the last decade of Melville's life.

When Queequeg plunges into the severed head of the sperm whale to deliver Tashtego from an oily death, Ishmael concludes that "Midwifery should be taught in the same course with fencing and boxing, riding and rowing." The pagan Queequeg is midwife to the Christian Ishmael's soul, teaching him that only by a kind of spiritual midwifery can a man give birth to himself, and only by embracing the darker brother and the inner feminine side of himself can the American, the "new man," attain a kind of cosmic consciousness, a sense that the universe is overflowing with love and delight, not rage and competition.[38]

Beneath the churning sea of Melville's prose, an ancient wisdom rocks these all-too-vulnerable voyagers on its maternal bosom. In "The Grand Armada," Nature becomes a maternal force that can transform the ocean into "an enchanted calm" that has the power to make men stop killing, at least momentarily. Fleeing pirates off the Java coast, the *Pequod* glides between two whales into "the innermost heart of the shoal," where the whalemen are granted a beatific vision of "young Leviathan amours," pregnant whales of "enormous girth," and nursing mothers with their suckling calves. Transfigured by this vision of "dalliance and delight," the whalemen lower their harpoons for a few precious moments. All too soon, however, they take to their whaleboats to hunt the great bulls who guard these "submarine bridal-chambers and nurseries."[39]

Horrified by the orgy of murder that ensues, Ishmael watches a harpooned whale "churning through the water" in agony as he tries to shake loose the cutting-spade and throw off the hemp that entangles him. "Tormented to madness," the whale flails about in the water, endangering his fellow creatures as well as the excited men, who gain only one "killed and waifed" whale for all the carnage. Horrified by the violence of the men and the cruelty of the whaling industry, which turns Job's leviathan into a commodity to be sold to the highest bidder, Ishmael expresses sorrow over the ruthless slaughter of the gentle creatures, infusing the narrative with a compassionate moral vision.[40]

After the *Pequod* sinks, Ishmael survives to tell his harrowing story. Protected by "unharming sharks" and "savage sea-hawks sail[ing] with sheathed beaks," he floats above the whirlpool until he is rescued by the *Rachel,* a whaler searching for her captain's son, who has been swept overboard. The lost boy is twelve years old, the same age Herman Melville was when his father died. When the "devious-cruising" *Rachel* rescues Ishmael from the sea, it is as though the lost boy has been reborn.

On October 22, 1851, Lizzie gave birth to the couple's second child, whom they named Stanwix in honor of Colonel Peter Gansevoort's great victory at Fort Stanwix. Melville was so flustered that he failed to notice that on the birth certificate beside "Maiden Name of Mother" the clerk had mistakenly written "Maria G. Melville, birthplace, Albany." The scribe's error was never corrected, and many post-Freudian scholars and biographers, seizing on what they assumed was a revealing slip of the pen by Melville himself, used it as the basis of some wildly wrongheaded speculations, particularly those writing about Melville's next novel, *Pierre.*[41]

Fatigued and weak after a difficult delivery, Lizzie ran a high fever and began hallucinating. When the wallpaper designs started gyrating wildly, nearly driving her insane, the women of the household draped the walls with sheets. Even after the fever subsided, she suffered from a breast infection that made nursing painful. At first it seemed the baby might not thrive, but by November 5, Grandmother Melville was expressing relief for everyone: "Stanwix is small & thin, but a bright little thing, his dark eyes looking about so wise, he is also little trouble, sleeping a good deal & having a famous appetite, he will soon be plump."[42]

During this crisis, *Moby-Dick, or The Whale* was officially published in New York on November 1, 1851. The dedication of the volume reads:

IN TOKEN

OF MY ADMIRATION FOR HIS GENIUS

THIS BOOK IS INSCRIBED

TO

NATHANIEL HAWTHORNE

Harper's had printed 2,915 copies and bound them in cloth embossed with a gilt life preserver, but several reviewers complained that at $1.50 apiece, Melville's book was prohibitively expensive.[43]

A few days later, probably before Melville had copies of his book in hand, the Melville clan, except for Lizzie, who was still too weak to go out, left for Charles and

Elizabeth Sedgwick's house to attend a party to which the British novelist G. P. R. James had been invited. Maria, Kate, and Helen had wrapped themselves in fur muffs and buffalo robes for the sleigh ride through moon-spangled snow to Lenox. Herman, who loved driving, was in "excellent spirits" when they arrived. After greeting his host and hostess, he found Hawthorne, who told him that Sophia was at home with the children and that they had to take turns going out, as "they could not be spared together."[44]

Mrs. James arrived explaining that her husband was unable to attend because he had just "commenced a new book" that day, a rather suspicious excuse that prompted Mr. Sedgwick to whisper to Mrs. Melville that he was just as glad James hadn't showed up, because he "snuff[ed] so much" that his clothes were always covered with dust and no one who spoke to him could avoid inhaling it.[45]

Conversation centered on the death of a ten-thousand-pound circus elephant, named Columbus, that had fallen through the new bridge at North Adams. Miss Catharine Sedgwick, who had happened to see the accident, described how members of the traveling menagerie laid the poor creature in a clearing and built a hut over him. Before long, she said, the "sublimely dreary carcass" looked "dreamily around, his proboscis curled up, without struggle or movement, seeming to express the submission of the mightiest thing on earth to a stern, inexorable, omnipotent Fate," and died as nobly as "The Dying Gladiator." When she finished her story, someone said that the owners had demanded $15,000 in damages from the town, and Mrs. Melville called it "another job for the lawyers."[46]

It was the season for the kind of animal drama that kept the penny press in business, as that same week Evert Duyckinck sent Melville a newspaper clipping about the sinking of the *Ann Alexander* by a harpooned whale, to which Melville responded with characteristic hyperbole: "Your letter received last night had a sort of stunning effect on me. For some days past being engaged in the woods with axe, wedge, and beetle, the Whale had almost completely slipped me for the time (& I was the merrier for it) when Crash! comes Moby Dick himself (as you justly say) & reminds me of what I have been about for the past year or two. It is really & truly a surprising coincidence—to say the least. I make no doubt it *is* Moby Dick himself, for there is no account of his capture after the sad fate of the Pequod about fourteen years ago. Ye Gods! What a Commentator is this Ann Alexander whale. What he has to say is short & pithy & very much to the point. I wonder if my evil art has raised this monster." The hint of self-destructiveness peeping through Melville's demiurgic conceit may well reflect his feelings about the botched publication of his masterpiece.[47]

By this time, many more reviews of the book had appeared. British critics who recognized the influence of their own metaphysical writers—Browne, Burton, Lamb, Carlyle, Coleridge, Sterne, and De Quincey—praised *The Whale. John Bull* was delighted to discover "philosophy in whales" and "poetry in blubber"; the *Morning Chronicle* praised Melville's "originality" and "abounding vigour"; and the *Illustrated London News* called the book "remarkable for fairness, good temper, and good humour." In a metaphor that must have delighted Melville, *The Leader* characterized *Moby-Dick* as "a strange wild work with the tangled overgrowth and luxuriant vegetation of American forests, not the trim orderliness of an English park." The *Morning Post* called *Moby-Dick* "a book of extraordinary merit ... one of the cleverest, wittiest, and most amusing of modern books."[48]

American reviewers who actually read *Moby-Dick* found much to praise. The *Morning Courier and New-York Enquirer* wrote that "The author writes with the gusto of true genius, and it must be a torpid spirit indeed that is not enlivened with the raciness of his humor and the redolence of his imagination." Horace Greeley admired Melville's "subtle mysticism," and the transcendentalist George Ripley paid tribute to the book's "richness and variety of incident, originality of conception, and splendor of description," adding, "Beneath the whole story, the subtle and imaginative reader may perhaps find a pregnant allegory, intended to illustrate the mystery of human life." These were not the kinds of comments, however, to turn a book into a popular best-seller.[49]

Conservative American reviewers did not like *Moby-Dick*. Evert Duyckinck's friend William Allen Butler wrote in the *National Intelligencer* that, despite the book's "literary excellencies," he felt obligated to register a "decided protest against the querulous and cavilling innuendoes" and its "irreverent wit." Boston's *Daily Evening Traveller*, while conceding that the book exhibited "much tact, talent and genius," took Melville to task for occasional "indelicacies" and "profaneness," and the reviewer for the *Boston Post* called the book "a crazy sort of affair," definitely not worth its price.[50]

Most upsetting to Melville was the first installment of *The Literary World*'s two-part review. For the first two-thirds of the review, the writer, presumably Evert Duyckinck, summarized the *Ann Alexander* incident, and when he finally got around to mentioning *Moby-Dick*, he wrote, "To the popular mind this book of Herman Melville, touching the Leviathan of the deep, is as much of a discovery in Natural History as was the revelation of America by Christopher Columbus in geography." Only those who read to the end learned that *Moby-Dick* described "some very strange, romantic, and withal, highly humorous adventures at New Bedford and Nantucket" told in "Herman Melville's best manner," which, of course, meant in the style of *Typee* and *Omoo*.[51]

Duyckinck had recently begun to lean toward the more conservative side in the debate over literary form, which was unfortunate for Melville, as *Moby-Dick* was a triumph of mixed form and metaphysics skillfully blended with spellbinding narrative. Thus, when Nathaniel Hawthorne, whom the literary establishment considered a model craftsman, wrote Melville a letter praising the book, Melville was ecstatic, as he undoubtedly believed that whatever his friend wrote about the book would counteract the effect of Duyckinck's mixed review. Yet, Melville evidently read much more into Hawthorne's letter than Hawthorne intended, as nothing Hawthorne wrote shows that he was as excited about *Moby-Dick* as Melville thought he was.[52]

Melville was starved for full-blooded, unconditional recognition from a father or a true literary mentor, and Hawthorne's response to *Moby-Dick* gave the man whom Sophia Hawthorne had called a "boy" the kind of validation no parent had ever given him. An older man whose handsome features matched the standards of ideal masculine beauty Melville had invested in characters such as Marnoo, Jack Chase, and Harry Bolton, Nathaniel Hawthorne played the paternal role for Melville as his own father never had.

Thanking Hawthorne for his "joy-giving and exultation-breeding" letter, he called it "the good goddess's bonus over and above what was stipulated" for the "ditcher's work" he had done on *Moby-Dick*. Hawthorne's appreciative letter made Melville feel "pantheistic," as though he and Hawthorne were co-communicants in a religion of literature: "A sense of unspeakable security is in me this moment, on account of your having understood the book. I have written a wicked book, and feel spotless as the lamb," Melville declared. "Whence come you Hawthorne? By what right do you drink from my flagon of life? And when I put it to my lips—lo, they are yours, not mine. I feel that the Godhead is broken up like the bread at the Supper, and that we are the pieces. Hence this infinite fraternity of feeling."[53]

Fearing that Hawthorne would think him mad to write such a long, emotional letter, Melville explained that the "truth is ever incoherent, and when the big hearts strike together, the concussion is a little stunning." In closing, he said he would understand Hawthorne's not answering such a long letter, and in any case, if he addressed his reply to "Herman Melville," he would "missend it—for the very fingers that now guide this pen are not precisely the same that just took it up and put it on this paper." Although he apologized for responding to Hawthorne's "plain, bluff letter" with such "gibberish," he could not stop himself from pouring out his gratitude and imagined himself with a paper mill at one end of the house and an "endless riband of foolscap rolling in upon my desk; and upon that endless riband I should write a thousand—a million—billion thoughts, all under the form of a letter to you. The divine magnet is on you, and my magnet responds. Which is the biggest? A foolish question—they are *One*."[54]

Melville must have assumed that Hawthorne would write a review of *Moby-Dick*, perhaps a rebuttal for *The Literary World*. Not wanting to ask him directly, Melville hinted at it by reminding him that "Hawthorne and His Mosses" had been a "paltry" piece for which he did not expect Hawthorne to reciprocate: "Don't write a word about the book," he wrote, hinting to Hawthorne in a backhanded way. "That would be robbing me of my miserly delight." Hawthorne, unfortunately, took him at his word. A laudatory review from Hawthorne might have boosted sales of *Moby-Dick* considerably, as Hawthorne's audience was larger than Melville's, and after Melville's "Hawthorne and His Mosses" appeared in *The Literary World*, advance orders for *Mosses from an Old Manse* skyrocketed. Hawthorne, however, never wrote a public word about *Moby-Dick*, perhaps because he did not want to abandon the conservative line on the issue of mixed-form novels, or perhaps simply because he was too self-centered and self-absorbed to think how much it would have meant to Melville.[55]

To be sure, Hawthorne was preoccupied with his own affairs, as he and Sophia had decided it was time to leave Lenox. Hawthorne had always detested the Berkshire climate, and he could not face another winter surrounded by snowbanks and cooped up in tight quarters far from the center of town. The red cottage had no room for guests, or for live-in help, which, with three growing children, meant that he and Sophia could never go out together.[56]

Their landlady, Caroline Sturgis Tappan, delivered the coup de grace when she accused the Hawthornes' hired girl, Mary Beekman, of conspiring with Mrs. Peters, their black cook, to plunder the estate's orchard of apples to bake pies. When Hawthorne asserted his family's right to enjoy the fruits of Nature, Mrs. Tappan asserted her sovereignty over the trees, and the argument escalated to absurdity. For Nathaniel, this foolishness was the last straw. On a snowy, sleety day in late November, the Hawthornes fled their blighted Berkshire Eden.

In mid-November, after receiving bound copies of *Moby-Dick*, Melville had evidently invited Hawthorne to lunch at the Curtis Hotel in Lenox to give him an inscribed copy of the novel and see his reaction to its laudatory dedication. Hawthorne, whose admiration for Melville had grown since their first meeting, must have been thrilled. In his *A Wonder-Book*, which was published a few weeks earlier, he describes Herman Melville "shaping out the gigantic conception of his 'White Whale,' while the gigantic shape of Graylock [*sic*] looms upon him from his study-window." It may have been their last meeting before the Hawthornes left the red house overlooking Stockbridge Bowl.[57]

Hawthorne left the Berkshires before he and Melville could climb Greylock and explore New York together as they had planned. The loss of the one man to whom he could open his deepest heart and mind stirred up grief for the loss of his father long buried in his soul. Although Hawthorne was neither a surrogate father nor a bear-hugging Queequeg, Melville had grown to rely on the intellectual and spiritual sustenance he drew from their relationship, and his friend's departure left a kind of void.

The day the Hawthornes left Lenox, Lizzie took Stanwix and the nurse and went to Boston to see her family doctor, as she was still weakened by the fevers she had suffered after giving birth, and was troubled by a lump in her left breast. Dr. Hayward allowed her to continue nursing, but before long her right breast became clogged and the nipple cracked, causing her a great deal of pain. When the affliction persisted despite poulticing, he advised her to stop nursing. Underweight at birth and weaned too early, Stanwix did not build up the immunities that mother's milk normally supplies.[58]

The next day, the second installment of *The Literary World*'s review of *Moby-Dick* appeared. In it, Duyckinck called the book "a most remarkable sea-dish, an intellectual chowder of romance, philosophy, natural history, good feeling, bad sayings ... exhibited in vivid narrations," but he added the unaccountable comment that all this had occurred in spite of the author, not because of him. Acknowledging that Melville "wrestles" with "very strong powers," Duyckinck faulted him for mixing romance with "statements of fact" and cloaking his satire with "a more or less opaque allegorical veil." He concluded by saying he could not tell which fault of Melville's was the worst, "the piratical running down of creeds and opinions, the conceited indifferentism of Emerson, or the run-a-muck style of Carlyle."[59]

The barbs thrust by *The Literary World* cut deep, especially the implication that *Moby-Dick* was sacrilegious. Melville was wounded by such treatment from a friend who ought to have known him well enough to understand that it was not religion he hated, but dogmatism and hypocrisy, and that he had intended to satirize narrow-minded fanaticism, not to deny the power of spiritual ideas or to ridicule belief. Hawthorne wrote Duyckinck directly to complain about *The Literary World*'s poor treatment of *Moby-Dick*. "What a book Melville has written!" he exclaimed. "It gives me an idea of much greater power than his preceding ones. It hardly seemed to me that the review of it, in the Literary World, did justice to its best points." Yet he still did not write a review of his friend's book.[60]

Melville must have felt as though both Hawthorne and Duyckinck had thrown him to the cannibals. He probably never knew that Hawthorne had objected to Duyckinck's negative review; he was too busy wrestling with his own feelings. His infatuation with Hawthorne was based on an illusion, like the image of Narcissus in the pool.

Perhaps writing a great book about love would bring him some success. He envisioned a hero who would sacrifice his worldly possessions and conventional happiness for a love that makes great ethical and spiritual demands on him, then forces him to question whether love and virtue are merely cruel illusions. There was the rub. For the book to be popular, he would have to bring his hero out of the valley onto a mountaintop of blazing affirmation, but as he looked back on his life, all he saw were relationships that forced him to adjust his expectations and make compromises.

He remembered how proud he had been of his patriot grandfathers, and how disillusioned he had been when he found out that the Founding Fathers were slaveholding hypocrites and humbugs as well as great architects of liberty. He remembered how much as a child he had admired his father, and how frightened and guilty his father's bankruptcy and degrading death had made him feel. He thought of how closely he and Lizzie had worked on *Mardi* when they were first married, and of how hard it had been for him to accept her love and support wholeheartedly because he always suspected that she loved her own idealized image of him, not the flawed man he knew himself to be. Sometimes when Lizzie reached out to him, he reacted with an irrational anger that seemed to stem from resentment against his mother for not loving him unconditionally when he was a child. She had hardly noticed him in the shadow cast by Gansevoort, and as he got older, he began to suspect that his older brother's polished manners had been a façade and his life a masquerade.

Sometimes it must have seemed as though his mother expected him to fail. He thought of his own inner conviction that he was destined to achieve greatness, and how time and time again, like a ship battling a howling storm at sea, he had been dashed against the lee. He wondered if she could possibly be right. With *Moby-Dick* he had succeeded in accomplishing what he had set out to do; yet it had made no difference to either his reputation or his bank account. Why had he told Hawthorne he did not care about literary recognition, when, in fact, he cherished the hope that he would one day be numbered among America's greatest literary men?

The world seemed to be closing in on Melville, and the early darkness and iron cold of late November sent him into a deep depression. Most evenings he just sat in his rocker puffing his meerschaum pipe and watching the great fireplace "swallow down cords of wood as a whale does boats." The intensity of his feelings for Hawthorne confused and troubled him, and he had lost touch with Lizzie during her pregnancy and illness. Two childbirths and the daily business of living in a large family sapped Lizzie's strength and dimmed the glow of their early married life, especially since at times Herman seemed to treat her as much like a servant as his mother did. Before he realized what was happening, the harmony they had enjoyed in their early married days had eroded, and it would take years for the wounds to heal.[61]

Hawthorne's departure threw Melville's emotional compass off course at an extremely vulnerable time; he felt like a bastard child deprived of his true patrimony. As he tried to write his way through this emotional thicket with his new book, he found himself rushing headlong and blind, crashing through the underbrush not knowing what he might discover, plunging deeper and deeper into the forest, finding himself in places so dense and dark they could be perceived only with an inner eye.

By December, Melville had buried himself so deeply in his work that Sarah Morewood worried openly about him. He did not "leave his room till quite dark in the evening—when he for the first time during the whole day partakes of solid food—he must therefore write under a state of morbid excitement which must injure his health." To lure him out, she hastily arranged a party for the Melvilles and a few of her close friends. Maria Melville pettishly pronounced the invitation "too informal" for her notice and the weather too wild for travel even around the corner, but Herman, who chafed at his mother's snobbishness and relished going out in violent weather, accepted for them all.[62]

Mrs. Morewood had concocted an old-fashioned English Christmas party, with holly and mistletoe and apple-bobbing, but Melville wasn't his usual convivial self when he arrived. He was clearly preoccupied, even obsessed, with the book he was working on, and when Mrs. Morewood remarked that his reclusive life caused his city friends to think he was insane, Melville replied gloomily that he had long ago come to the same conclusion. It took several holiday potations to restore his sociability, but later in the evening, he propped a balsam wreath on his head and pranced around the room like a merry Saint Nicholas dancing a hornpipe on the deck of a ship far out at sea.[63]

Although Melville could be a difficult and moody character at home, he was usually high-spirited with friends, especially when he was the center of attention, and Sarah Morewood enjoyed his company. When he was in a flirtatious mood, he "courted" her playfully, calling her his "goddess" and her home a "paradise," and she flirted back in the same language of flowers he and Lizzie had employed during their courting days. Her husband, Rowland, a rather conservative businessman, had a much harder time warming up to Melville than she did, and she wrote that "he dislikes many of Mr Hermans [sic] opinions and religious views," thinking it "a pity" that "Mr. Melville so often in conversation uses irreverent language," because "he will not be popular in society here on that account."[64]

Melville relished the role of *enfant terrible*, and Mrs. Morewood misjudged him when she wrote George Duyckinck, "I think he cares very little as to what others may think of him or his books so long as they sell well." He wanted to write the kind of popular romance that Mrs. Morewood and other intelligent ladies would buy and read, and he also wanted to cultivate a broad audience. He resented being constantly misrepresented by the critics.[65]

Late reviews of *Moby-Dick* appeared to scuttle Melville's hopes that any book of his could be both great and popular. Among those reviews were a number of nasty personal attacks as well as condemnations of the book's ideas and style, and reading them left him feeling battered and vulnerable. Predictably, sectarian reviewers attacked him for his irreverence, but a number of mainstream periodicals joined *The Literary World* in denouncing Melville for his attacks on Christianity. Even New York's *Commercial*

Advertiser chastised Melville for "sneering at the truths of revealed religion." The *Southern Quarterly Review* objected to Melville's politics and what it called his "ravings," and called *Moby-Dick* a "monstrous bore." The *United States Magazine & Democratic Review* accused him of "trying to ascertain how far the public will consent to be imposed upon ... gauging, at once, our gullibility and our patience" by producing "increasingly exaggerated and increasingly dull" books. "Mr. Melville never writes naturally. His sentiment is forced, his wit is forced, and his enthusiasm is forced." The review accused Melville of "morbid self-esteem" and attacked "all his rhetorical contortions, all his declamatory abuse of society, all his inflated sentiment, and all his insinuating licentiousness."[66]

By the time the mass-circulation monthly *Godey's Lady's Book* had informed its more than seventy thousand readers that *Moby-Dick* ought to secure a worldwide reputation for its author, the damage had been done. *Moby-Dick* sold only 1,500 copies during its first month on the stands, 2,300 copies more in the next year and a half, and 5,500 in the next half century. With half of his royalties earmarked by Harper's to pay back debts, Melville made just $556.37, less than for any of his previous books. His lifetime earnings from *Moby-Dick* would amount to $1,260, with another $81.06 in royalties being paid to Lizzie between the time of Melville's death in 1891 and her own death fifteen years later.[67]

Attributing Melville's growing moodiness to his literary exertions, his mother and other members of the family pressured him to stop writing, but he had no desire to be dependent on Peter Gansevoort and Lemuel Shaw. Although he certainly wanted to make money from his writing, he wrote primarily as a means of exploring the universe, and as a necessity of spirit. Writing was as natural to him as breathing.

When Melville turned from sea stories to write a domestic novel, he found himself staring for the first time into the abyss that women writers confronted daily as they tried to reconcile the conflicting demands their culture made on them. Women, traditionally assigned to the home, were allowed to write domestic fiction, which feminized novel-writing and gave it a lower status than was accorded to such male pursuits as business, medicine, the law, or the writing of history. Ironically, because they were marginalized, both as women and as artists, most female novelists were spared being called "idlers." As "scribblers" rather than "professional" authors like the men, they had popularity with little recognition, but at least they did not have to prove that they were New World Shakespeares.

The risk inherent in being a male novelist in America in the 1850s was tremendous, especially for Hawthorne and Melville, who admired Shakespeare but wanted to emulate the financial success and status of Washington Irving and James Fenimore Cooper, albeit without their provincialism. Their relationship to a profession dominated by women, whose rebellion against conventional sexual roles was as deftly disguised as egg whites folded into a soufflé, was complicated by their ambivalence toward both women and themselves.

Being an American Shakespeare seemed an impossible dream in a nation whose leveling tendencies and marketplace ethics more often rewarded mediocrity and sensationalism than originality, complexity, and robust artistry. After years of pitting his tremendous ambition against the limitations of his audience, Melville felt perilously close to the worst fate of unrecognized genius: rejection, self-doubt, and madness.[68]

*Melville's sister Augusta, who professed a "literary thirst," made fair copies of her
brother's manuscripts and preserved the family correspondence.*

SIXTEEN

KING OF THE CANNIBALS

Shortly before New Year's Day, 1852, Melville received a letter from Sophia Hawthorne prais-
ing Moby-Dick, *especially the bewitching "Spirit-Spout." Having wrongly assumed that
"women have small taste for the sea," he was "really amazed" by her insight into "the part &
parcel allegoricalness of the whole." Although he knew "some* men" *liked the book, the "only
woman" who liked it, as far as he knew, was Sophia. Claiming that he hadn't realized that
Moby-Dick was "susceptible of an allegoric construction" before reading her letter, he com-
plimented her discernment: "You, with your spiritualizing nature, see more things than other
people," but even so, "My dear Lady, I shall not again send you a bowl of salt water. The next
chalice I commend, will be a rural bowl of milk." [1]*

*Soon after this, Melville went to New York, taking Augusta with him to prepare the fair
copy of his new manuscript, which he considered finished. The trip was not a pleasant one, as
Melville was unable to persuade Harper's to meet his contract demands, and he and Evert
Duyckinck evidently had a falling-out. After thanking Duyckinck for the "very curious and
duly valued" gift of some "nutcrackers," Melville estranged himself from his old friend for*

several years. Although scholars have generally assumed the word *nutcrackers* literally refers to a New Year's gift, it seems more likely that Melville was thanking Duyckinck for his "ball-busting" two-part negative review of *Moby-Dick*, because soon after, Melville canceled two subscriptions to *The Literary World*: his own and one he had given his old friend Eli Fly.[2]

Although the modest sales of *Moby-Dick* had somewhat reduced Herman's debt to Harper's, Allan was not able to negotiate a favorable contract for *Pierre*. Under the scaled-down terms that Harper's offered, Melville could not collect royalties until 1,190 copies had been sold to pay for the plates. Of the $500 he was to receive when he signed the contract, only $300 constituted an advance against future royalties, while the balance represented royalties already earned by his previous books. In addition, Harper's offered a flat royalty of 20 cents per copy after expenses, instead of the usual half-profits, and told Melville that he would have to buy review copies and send them out himself. These terms were a slap in the face to Melville, who longed to be free of the economic worries that kept him dependent on the generosity of others. He resented publishers for treating even "the greatest lettered celebrities of the time," the "full graduates in the University of Fame," as "legal minors forced to go to their mammas for pennies wherewith to keep them in peanuts."[3]

It seems incredible that Melville plunged into the writing of another book so soon, as while he was writing *Moby-Dick*, he had told Hawthorne of his "presentiment" that he would "at last be worn out and perish, like an old nutmeg-grater, grated to pieces by the wood, that is, the nutmeg." He had written six novels between 1846 and 1851, hurrying each book into print more impatiently than the last. Whatever the psychological reasons for this frenetic rate of production, the practical reasons for it were clear: he was determined to write a novel that would sell.[4]

Conscious of the popularity of women writers like Angela Marsh-Caldwell, Sarah Ellis, Grace Aguilar, and Elizabeth Sewell with Sarah Morewood and the women in his immediate family, Melville set out to write a domestic best-seller. He drew on *Hamlet, Romeo and Juliet,* Mary Shelley's *Frankenstein,* Mme. De Stael's *Corinne,* Dante's *Inferno,* the mixed-genre novels of Edward Bulwer-Lytton, German romantic novels such as Schiller's *Ghost Tale,* and the French sensational romances of Eugène Sue, as well as *The Scarlet Letter* and *The House of the Seven Gables,* all of which reflected widespread *angst* about science, religion, sexuality, politics, and death. The French sensational romance, a genre designed to subvert social hypocrisy and political hegemony, dished out illicit passions in endless combinations, with incest and adultery being the most common themes. They featured mysterious revenants and other paranormal phenomena, as did German romantic novels like Goethe's *Elective Affinities,* which Americans avidly read in translation. The bizarre plot of this novel concerns "adulterous" lovers who fantasize about each other while making love to their respective spouses; when the woman gives birth, the baby resembles her lover, not her husband. In his typically omnivorous fashion, when Melville composed *Pierre, or the Ambiguities*, he combined elements of all of these popular American and European novels rather than confining himself to one model, reflecting through the instability of his text the instability of moral values.[5]

Melville's protagonist, Pierre Glendinning, renounces his mother, his fiancée, and his patrician inheritance in a high-minded gesture of Christian altruism that turns out to be rationalized sexual desire for a dark-haired girl who claims to be his long-lost half sister—or, as some gay scholars have argued, unresolved homoerotic oedipal desire for the adored father whom the mysterious girl so closely resembles. Perhaps because Americans equated all things French with sensual pleasures not sanctioned by the Calvinist catechism, Melville made the girl's mother a Frenchwoman uprooted by the French Revolution and her father an American merchant who resembles Allan Melvill.[6]

Melville was sensitive to the ways in which familial and social patterns layer the lives of individuals, and it seems logical that having experienced family relationships as suffocating at times, he chose incest as his theme. Despite his promise to Sophia Hawthorne that he would be nice, not naughty, Melville modeled most of the characters in the novel on friends and family members and made the central crisis in his hero's young life the discovery that his father had sired an illegitimate daughter and never acknowledged her existence.

If ever readers needed Melvillean double vision—the sperm whale's two eyes, one on either side of its head, focused simultaneously on two distinct but equally credible realities—they need it with *Pierre*. The novel obviously deals with "family matters," as Willie Morewood delicately put it, but which ones? Many readers have assumed that Pierre is a thinly disguised Melville and that the other characters in the story all literally represent members of his family. Recently, many have assumed that the novel's hysterical style reflects Melville's discovery that his father had an illegitimate daughter, and gay scholars, calling incest a code word for the one topic that remained taboo with respectable publishers, have argued that *Pierre* reveals Melville's homosexuality.[7]

Whatever secrets Melville may or may not have intended to reveal with *Pierre*, incest, especially between fathers and daughters, held a special fascination for Victorians, as it unconsciously replicated for them the power imbalance between men and women in a patriarchal society. Parlor walls in many Victorian homes, including Arrowhead and the red cottage, displayed reproductions of Guido Reni's *Beatrice Cenci*, whose subject killed her sexually abusive father with a dagger, and in 1860 the portrait would play a prominent role in *The Marble Faun*, Hawthorne's last finished novel, and the one that most openly expresses his sexual ambivalence. The incest theme allowed

Melville to explore the transgressive nature of sexuality as well as the intricacies of passionate friendships and family relationships.[8]

The scandalous love affair between Lord Byron and his half sister Augusta titillated cultivated Americans, and Augusta Melville's friends teased her that she would never find a husband because no man could ever measure up to her adored brother. The only man attractive enough to displace Herman temporarily as Augusta's "beau ideal" was Nathaniel Hawthorne, who was safely unavailable, and to an objective observer it seems clear that Augusta's feelings were most deeply engaged by women friends rather than by men. Given the complicated relationships among those in Melville's circle, it is no wonder that he chose incest as the subject of a sensational novel designed to appeal to a broad audience.[9]

While Melville may have started out to write a novel designed to appeal to the general reader, *Pierre* rapidly turned into a burlesque of popular fiction and, ultimately, a parody of itself, as though Melville had tried to write a serious novel drawing on popular themes and employing popular conventions, only to reach the point where he found he could no longer restrain himself from switching to satire and making his narrator an antagonist, not an ally, to his protagonist. Burlesquing several popular genres, Melville out-emotes the most sentimental novels of the period and takes satire and melodrama over the edge to create a kind of bourgeois tragedy requiring the ritual sacrifice of a hero who is the finest flower of Republican manhood and the perfect product of Victorian sexual ideology.[10]

Despite its flaws, *Pierre* marks a significant advance in Melville's artistry. Whereas, in his earlier books, allusions tend to bob on the surface of the narrative stream, in *Pierre* he successfully internalizes the archetypal patterns underlying the great works on which he draws most heavily. Literary echoes flow through the narrative like the currents of an underground river.

Writing to Richard Bentley about *Pierre*, Melville took an aggressive tack, arguing that he was entitled to more than "half profits" with no advance because he had written a book in the popular vein, but the British publisher turned him down in a letter that made a cutting reference to the "too rapid succession" with which Melville produced books. He also enclosed—perhaps accidentally, as he apologized for it later—some penciled calculations of how much money the company had lost so far on Melville's books.[11]

Hurt and offended, Melville did not contact Bentley again until he sent him a set of corrected proofs of the American edition with a long cover letter acknowledging that his earlier books had not done as well as he had hoped, but assuring the British publisher that the latest book was designed to *sell.* He described the new work as "possessing unquestionable novelty" and "very much more calculated for popularity than anything you have yet published of mine—being a regular romance, with a mysterious plot to it,

& stirring passions at work, and withall, representing a new & elevated aspect of American life." Asking Bentley to let "bygones be bygones," he requested an advance of one hundred pounds, which was only half of what Bentley had given him for *White-Jacket.* He also asked Bentley to publish the novel in a cheap, mass-circulation format under a pen name, perhaps "By a Vermonter," or "By Guy Winthrop," to differentiate it from his "sailor-narratives" and to appeal to working-class as well as genteel readers.[12]

Bentley responded with a pointed reminder that despite Melville's "genius," his earlier books had all been "failures," except for *Typee* and *Omoo,* because they were not "written in a style to be understood by the great mass of readers." When he pointed out that the author had "offended the feelings of many sensitive readers," and proposed having "a judicious literary friend" make "such alterations as are absolutely necessary," Melville cut off communication for several months.[13]

At the end of May, Bentley formally rejected *Pierre,* falling back on the copyright problem as an excuse, but Lemuel Shaw Jr., who was in London at the time, claimed to know the other side: "I was told," he wrote his parents, "what I knew before, that he is losing the prestige of his name which he gained by his first books, by writing so many books that nobody can read. I wish very much he could be persuaded to leave off writing books for a few years, & that is what his friends here say."[14]

The frustrations generated by *Pierre* seemed endless. Every time Melville tried to detach himself emotionally from the book and just finish it in the superficial manner he thought would ensure its success, he found himself drawn deeper into his story. It seemed to change tone and direction as he wrote, shaping and reshaping itself in kaleidoscopic permutations. Instead of carrying him to new heights as the "chartless" *Mardi* had done, the "ambiguities" of *Pierre* were dragging him down into the depths like the "unearthly, formless, chance-like apparition of life" he had described in *Moby-Dick.* "Leviathan is not the biggest fish," he wrote Hawthorne, "I have heard of Krakens."[15]

The lack of support from Duyckinck, Bentley, and most of his family embittered Melville and inspired self-flagellating additions to the novel. Writing to satiate the ravenous demons who were gorging themselves on the marrow of his soul, he lashed out at the literary establishment and mocked his own dream of writing a truly great and important book, adding 150 pages that turned *Pierre* into a savage attack on middle-class morality, the literary establishment, his family, and himself.

In some ways, Melville seems to have been giving himself the flogging he had avoided aboard the *United States.* Perhaps, on some unconscious level, he felt that he deserved punishment because his father's violent death, which coincided with the onset of his puberty, seemed the fulfillment of a "hideous and intolerable" oedipal fantasy that replayed itself in the death of his older brother. Thus, in the early chapters, Pierre resembles Gansevoort Melville, and in the second half of the novel, which focuses on Pierre as a writer, he clearly resembles Herman, making *Pierre* one of the first great modern psychological novels in Western literature.[16]

No writer ever created a language more volcanic than Melville did in *Moby-Dick*. "Give me a condor's quill! Give me Vesuvius' crater for an inkstand!" Ishmael cried as he grappled with *The Whale*. No one had written about both love and whaling in the language of Shakespeare, the Bible, and *The Divine Comedy* as brilliantly as Melville had, and few dared loosen the stiff collars and stays of Victorian convention to attempt the elevation of the sentimental and the sensational to high art as he did in *Pierre*. Having created a "bold and lofty nervous language" for his whaling saga, Melville created a language that merged ideas and emotions seamlessly for his dark romance of domesticity.[17]

His dedication of *Pierre* not to a family member, but "To Greylock's Most Excellent Majesty" suggests the anger he felt at his family and at Hawthorne's Olympian insensitivity. Perhaps it was just as well that he dedicated the book to the mountain he had hoped to climb with Hawthorne, as only a mountain could have withstood the shock of a novel that dragged its author, his family, and his friends into a maelstrom of passion, adultery, incest, murder, and suicide.

⌇

Pierre reads like a narrative nervous breakdown. It is the most difficult of Melville's books to write about because relationships and roles overlap and the boundaries within and between people are liminal, permeable, and unstable. Exploring the multiple roles people play in one another's lives—how the roles of sister, mother, daughter, wife, brother, father, son, husband, lover, and friend interweave and overlap and interpenetrate—Melville mingles fact and fiction until good and evil, truth and falsehood, tragedy and comedy, intertwine inextricably and ambiguously.

Probably the funniest tragedy ever written, and certainly the greatest potboiler of all time, *Pierre* is, among other things, an antiheroic epic whose patrician hero is striving to achieve ideal Republican manhood, but fails.

After a virtuosic opening paragraph that demonstrates what a brilliant conventional romance he could have written had he stuck to his original plan, Melville loads every rift with golden irony. The opening chapters of *Pierre* echo the historical romances of Catharine Sedgwick and Nathaniel Hawthorne, but like a hologram whose depths contain ghostly images, Melville's descriptions draw the reader to "a little lower layer." His Saddle Meadows combines features of Arrowhead, Broadhall, and Herman Gansevoort's estate in Saratoga County, and descriptions of the countryside merge such Berkshire landmarks as Mount Greylock ("the Mount of the Titans") and Balance Rock ("the Memnon Stone") with the landscape of the upper Hudson Valley. Unlike Thomas

Cole and other painters of the Hudson River School, who saw the grandeur and sublimity of the land as the staging-ground for a civilization to be characterized by "plenty, virtue, and refinement," Melville saw America as a lost paradise haunted by the sorrowful spirits of the dispossessed, a widowed land.[18]

The novel's young hero, Pierre Glendinning, enjoys a pampered, pastoral existence. Nurtured by the combined "poetical and philosophical" influences of the country and forays into "the deep recesses of his father's fastidiously picked and decorous library," young Pierre is one of Melville's bachelors. A thoroughbred who wears the blinders of wealth and privilege, he is outwardly a noble greyhound, and inwardly a moral mutt. He basks in the reflected glory of his slaveholding grandfathers, both heroes of the Revolutionary War, proud of his claim to "a monopoly of glory in capping the fame-column, whose tall shaft had been erected by his noble sires." Pierre's grandfather is clearly modeled on Colonel Peter Gansevoort, and particular objects venerated by Pierre—the captured banners, the drum, and the General's phaeton—correspond to actual family relics. While on the surface the Glendinnings seem the apotheosis of the Revolutionary generation, below the surface they resemble the doomed dynastics of Poe and Hawthorne—the Ushers, the Pyncheons, and the Maules.[19]

The "long uninterrupted possession by his race" of Saddle Meadows turns out to be a lie. Three Indian kings had been "the aboriginal and only conveyancers of those noble woods and plains," and the Glendinning deeds, though "full of pride to Pierre," are bloody deeds. Pierre's paternal grandfather, a six-foot-four-inch slaveholder who once dined with "the gentlemanly, but murderous half-breed, Brandt," had "annihilated two Indian savages by making reciprocal bludgeons of their heads." The narrator's ironic statement that "all this was done by the mildest hearted, and most blue-eyed gentleman in the world" establishes General Glendinning—and, by extension, Melville's maternal grandfather—as the prototype for the Indian-hater of *The Confidence-Man*.[20]

The history of the Glendinning family evokes the anti-rent wars of New York State, which pitted patricians like James Fenimore Cooper and Peter Gansevoort against the tenant farmers who were virtual serfs on their land. Since 1629, Kiliaen Van Rensselaer and the patroons had perpetuated feudalism in the New World with their "haughty rent-deeds," until finally desperate tenant farmers facing foreclosures declared war on the "land sharks." Dressed in calico costumes and feather headdresses, they raided the great estates and demanded the right to purchase "freeholds" from these "worldly princes."[21]

Melville's Orientalist imagery links the Dutch settlements to Eastern despotisms. Saddle Meadows is not bathed with the clear light of egalitarian democracy, but suffused with a "Hindooish haze" behind which an "eastern patriarchalness sways its mild crooks over pastures whose tenant flocks there shall feed, long as their own grass grows, long as their own water shall run." These echoes of Jackson's 1829 treaty with the Cherokees link the tenant system with the colonial dispossession of the Indians from their lands, implying that the "fame-column" erected by Pierre's sires stands on blood-drenched soil.[22]

Dubbing the anti-rent wars "A Great Revolution," balladeers compared the landowners to "feudal lords" and the farmers in calico to the "Mohawks" of the Boston Tea Party: "Our feudal lords in coaches ride / Puffed up with vanity and pride / Their boasted wealth they do forget / Was purchased by the tenant's sweat." Driving his grandfather's phaeton, which was built to "draw forth old Pierre, as the Chinese draw their fat god Josh," young Pierre reins his steeds as "grand old Pierre had reined [his] before." This carriage, which resembles old Peter Gansevoort's prized calèche, is "fit for a vast General," but the "plumed hearse" has outlived its "noble load."[23]

By associating the Dutch aristocracy with the British monarchy and the tenants with Boston's revolutionary patriots, Melville implicitly pits his Melville grandsire against the Gansevoorts. Furthermore, when Pierre rebels against his Glendinning heritage to champion two women marginalized by society for their sexual transgressions, Melville forges a link between egalitarian democracy and transgressive sexuality that recalls Redburn's acceptance of interracial relationships and Ishmael's "matrimonial embrace" of a tattooed cannibal. Torn between his aristocratic pedigree and the promptings of his democratic heart, Pierre is destined to become "a thorough-going Democrat in time; perhaps a little too Radical altogether to your fancy."[24]

An only child and the last to bear the Glendinning surname, Pierre is the coddled son of the beautiful but imperious widow Mary Glendinning, who delights in the fact that "in the clear-cut lineaments and noble air of her son" she could see "her own graces strangely translated into the opposite sex." She demands that her son be a perfect gentleman like the gallant father whom he enshrines in his heart, and at age sixteen, "girded with Religion's silken sash," he partakes of the sacraments with his mother and promises to be a Christian gentleman like his dear departed father.[25]

Mary Glendinning resembles Maria Melville in many respects, as both were proud and domineering women who had a flirtatious side. Pierre's relationship with his mother early in the novel resembles that of Gansevoort Melville with Maria Melville more than it does Herman's relationship with her; curiously, it also resembles Hawthorne's relationship with his mother. Victorian matriarchs exercised iron control in sanctioned female ways, which tended to be passive-aggressive and highly manipulative. According to Melville's granddaughter Eleanor, Mother Melville made her eight children sit silent and motionless by her bedside while she took her afternoon nap, and later in life, she tended to treat Herman like a child and Lizzie like a servant. Like Ahab, Mary Glendinning is not a specific person, but a cultural archetype. She is the Victorian matriarch bound to the patriarchal repressions of American Protestantism, which held women responsible for children, morality, and religion, and men responsible for money, politics, and power. Widowed by the ruthless marketplace, she embodies the sundering of the male and female realms from each other and the suppression of the feminine.[26]

An oedipal Adam and Eve in an incestuous Eden, Pierre and Mrs. Glendinning express their "romantic filial love" by cooing to each other, and they compare themselves to Romeo and Juliet. Mrs. Glendinning adores her son for his "sweet docilities," but his hearty appetite for breakfast disgusts her because it makes him seem so lower-class, and this puts Pierre in a double bind so painful he cannot allow himself to acknowledge it consciously. Fondling her father's regimental baton, the "symbol of command," her "Infinite Haughtiness" implicitly holds her son's masculinity in her hand. Although Pierre has the makings of a robust soul, the hand of destiny will crush him.[27]

Pierre is ignorant of the world beyond the "dear park" presided over by his mother, and the only flaw in the "sweetly-writ manuscript" of his life is that "a sister had been omitted from the text." Disappointed that "so delicious a feeling as fraternal love had been denied him," he often wishes that his father had brought "a daughter!!" into the world. Pierre's primal longing for a sister expresses the desire of Victorian men to recover the androgynous natural self that had to be ruthlessly repressed in order for men to rise in a fiercely competitive hierarchy. Figuratively speaking, all men had secret sisters, but the culture had locked them up and thrown away the key.[28]

Pierre attempts to create the missing sibling bond with his coquettish mother, but she treats him more like a *cavaliere servante* than either a brother or a son. Calling her "sister Mary" as he stoops to tie her slipper lace or tie a bow in her hair ribbon, Pierre treats her like an empress, or a queen, verbally cross-dressing and becoming a kind of court eunuch by referring to himself as the "First Lady in Waiting to the Dowager Duchess Glendinning." This exaggerated gallantry seems at once a venting of Melville's old resentments against Gansevoort, a way of talking back to his mother, and a parody of Victorian conduct manuals.[29]

Pierre transfers his impulse to "love, and protect and fight for" a sister to Lucy Tartan, a childhood playmate who is the daughter of a cherished friend of his dead father's and practically a sister, as Elizabeth Shaw was when Herman courted her. Pierre's relationship with Lucy mimics what the nineteenth-century courtship manuals called "sparking," carefully choreographed courtship rituals designed to keep smoldering sexual passions from bursting into flames.

Like Baudelaire, who sought to subvert bourgeois morality, and Mallarmé, who wanted to "purify the language of the tribe," Melville sought to push sentimental excess to such extremes that it would burst of its own flatulence. Pierre and Lucy bill and coo in a self-consciously florid style so artificial that it sounds like a defense against sexual passion rather than an expression of it: "'Smell I the flowers, or thee?'" cried Pierre. 'See I lakes, or eyes?' cried Lucy, her own gazing down into his soul, as two stars gaze down into a tarn." Replete with archaic diction and hysterical exclamations, *Pierre* mocks the affectations of its central characters, dragging them out of the genteel world of parlor Christianity and the sentimental pastoral romance, where cows are "kine," into the sordid underworld of the French sensational novel and the quasi-realistic urban literature of New York.[30]

Both mothers steer their children toward marriage, the only acceptable expression of sexuality. Mrs. Glendinning wants Pierre to marry Lucy because she "will not estrange him from me; for she too is docile." Mrs. Tartan furnishes her parlor with objects designed to make Pierre think of matrimony when he visits Lucy. Although he is aware of the artifice, Pierre is not offended, as he is willing to be bound by the silken cords as long as his "angel" Lucy holds them. However, he is terrified of his sexual feelings. When Lucy sends him to her room to fetch her easel, he sees her virginal white bed and feels momentarily paralyzed. Staring at "the snow-white bed reflected in the toilet-glass," he sees two beds, "an unbidden, most miserable presentiment." Lucy observes that he seems flustered, and he tells her he has "just peeped in at paradise," instinctively translating his sexual anxiety into religious metaphors as characters in sentimental novels are wont to do.[31]

As Pierre is returning home that night, a mysterious female face bearing "mortal lineaments of mournfulness" peers out at him from the trees. Just as the face seems about to reveal "glimpses of some fearful gospel" to him, it disappears. The next day, Pierre escorts his mother to her sewing circle as usual, but this time, when he enters the room and his name is announced, one of the girls utters a "sudden, long-drawn, girlish, unearthly shriek." Pierre assumes she has pricked her finger with a needle until he recognizes her face as the one that appeared to him through the trees.[32]

His encounter with this apparition plunges him into "infernal catacombs of thought." Assaulted by "bannered armies of hooded phantoms," he tries to break the spell of the mysterious girl's "weird inscrutableness" by conjuring the image of his beloved Lucy, but he cannot.[33]

Reading his odd mood as a lover's restlessness, his mother urges him to set an early date for his wedding, but having internalized the Victorian notion that men are beasts in need of domestication by pure women, Pierre imagines that his "fleecy" bride-to-be is "of Airy light" while he is "of heavy earth," and fears that marriage between them would be "an impious thing!"[34]

One evening a hooded stranger hands him a letter from the mysterious girl, who claims to be his half sister, Isabel. At this, Pierre remembers that on his deathbed, his father had called out for a daughter in his delirium, and that his aunt Dorothea had told him that before his father married his mother, he had been in love with a French girl who might have been a royal refugee from the French Revolution. Seeking a key to these mysteries, Pierre takes from its hiding place in his closet a cherished portrait of his father, and as he stands before it in a reverie, he tries to imagine what his father was like in his younger days.[35]

Like Allan Melvill, Pierre's father lived in France, amassed a collection of prints and engravings and a library of domestic and foreign books, and died when his son was twelve. Pierre cherishes the portrait of his father, which shows him as "a fine-looking, gay-hearted, youthful gentleman," lounging in a chair with an air of "bladish" dalliance. This "chair-portrait," which Pierre's mother hates, is clearly modeled on the 1810 painting of Allan Melvill that shows him seated in a chair, his hip inclined toward the viewer in a provocative pose resembling the posture of an odalisque. Hair tousled, mouth half open as if about to speak, eyes catching the eyes of the viewer, as if a little startled to be observed, Allan sits with his left arm resting languidly across his lap, fingering his watch fob with his left hand, as his right hand closes around the arm of the chair, the index finger casually tilted upward toward subtle contours in his trouser-front that seem to invite the wanderings of a hand. As Pierre stands before the painting of his father, he hears him whispering, "Youth is hot, and temptation strong, Pierre," and suddenly his image of his father as an ideal figure "without blemish, unclouded, snow-white, and serene" crumbles.[36]

The next morning, while he is debating whether or not to tell his mother about Isabel, Pierre goes down to breakfast and finds that the Reverend Falsgrave has come to inform Mrs. Glendinning that Delly Ulver, the daughter of one of the farmers on her estate, has become pregnant by a married tenant. When she decrees that Delly be banished from the parish, Pierre protests, pointing out that Jesus forgave the adulteress, but Falsgrave replies in a condescending tone that the Bible cannot always be taken literally. Offended by such moral casuistry, Pierre demands to know whether the commandment to "honor thy Father and thy Mother" should be followed in every circumstance. When Falsgrave says it must, Pierre asks angrily, "Should I honour my father, if I knew him to be a seducer?" whereupon Mrs. Glendinning abruptly puts an end to the conversation.[37]

Determined to "follow the endless, winding way" no matter how devastating the truth may be, Pierre rides out that night through the "owl-haunted" darkness to the red cottage where the orphaned Isabel now lives alone after a childhood spent in a series of foster homes. Relating her tragic history to Pierre, she claims to be the by-blow of a love affair between the French mother she never knew and a tall gentleman who visited her when she was a little girl, kissed her on the cheek, and whispered the word *Father* before disappearing from her life. As she speaks, Pierre notices, or imagines, a resemblance between her face and the face of his father in his cherished portrait, and he is convinced that her story must be true. The next morning he behaves so strangely that his mother assumes he has quarreled with Lucy and badgers him until he runs away to the huge balanced rock he calls "the Memnon Stone" and lies beneath it, daring it to fall on him.

When the "Terror Stone" fails to crush him with its "Mute Massiveness," he takes it as an omen that he must hear the remainder of Isabel's story.[38]

At their next meeting, Isabel tells him that the man who called himself "Father" had given her a fine linen handkerchief, and that she was able to decipher the name "Glendinning" embroidered on its border. When Pierre asks to see it, she tells him it is lost and instead shows him a guitar she bought from a peddler who told her that it came from a great estate. Somehow she knew intuitively that the estate was Saddle Meadows and that the guitar had once belonged to her mother. She holds the instrument up to the light so Pierre can see the name "Isabel" written inside it, then plays it for him. Mesmerized by her mournful music and the perfume of her dark flowing hair, which spills over him as she plays, Pierre vows that if she is indeed his father's daughter, he will take care of her as a Christian brother should. While the reader suspects that Isabel may have been conjured up by Pierre's own narcissistic fantasies, he sees her appearance as a challenge to his determination to live according to ethical imperatives derived from the heart rather than from arbitrary social norms.[39]

Resemblances between Isabel and Nathaniel Hawthorne have led some readers to see the novel as Melville's declaration of love for the "Man of Mosses." Isabel lives in a "little red farm-house, three miles from the village, on the slope toward the lake," and her surname "Banford" echoes Melville's telling Hawthorne that what he really wanted to write was "banned." More to the point, the image of Isabel's long, dark hair enveloping Pierre evokes the passionate moment in *The Scarlet Letter* when Hester Prynne meets her lover Arthur Dimmesdale in the forest after seven years have passed. As she takes off the prim cap that covers her long, dark hair, and lets it fall over her shoulders, she tells the tormented young minister that their adulterous love had "a consecration of its own" and persuades him to run away with her. Curiously, despite the many attempts to prove that *Pierre* is at least in part a *roman à clef*, no one has suggested that Isabel could represent Sophia Hawthorne as well as her husband, since Sophia and Herman appear to have enjoyed a harmless flirtation. Clearly, both men were fascinated by romantic triangles and dangerous love affairs in 1852.[40]

While Melville was writing *Pierre*, Hawthorne was writing *The Blithedale Romance*, a novel inspired by his sojourn at Brook Farm, the transcendentalist utopia founded by George Ripley. In this novel, Hawthorne attempts to endow his feminine side with erotic power. The Pierre-Lucy-Isabel triangle, like the Coverdale-Hollingsworth-Priscilla triangle in *The Blithedale Romance*, stands the Hester-Dimmesdale-Chillingworth triangle on its head. Whereas Hester lived out her life with dignity and some sense of spiritual fulfillment despite being thwarted in her quest for sexual liberation, the passionate bluestocking Zenobia, who has been identified as a composite of Margaret Fuller and Sophia Hawthorne's sister, Elizabeth Peabody, is doomed to die at Blithedale, while men and women less courageous than she go on to lead half-lives, sublimating their sexual energy in housework or reformist zeal.

Pierre holds Hawthorne's successful romances up to a dark, distorting mirror that transforms their features into monstrous ones, which suggests that Melville's novel is less a love letter to Hawthorne than an angry attack on the friend who had let him down. Whereas Hester quietly transforms sin and suffering into a kind of sainthood, Pierre noisily transforms potential sainthood into a snake pit of sin and suffering. It is as though he has come to feel that his love for Isabel has not a consecration, but a desecration, of its own.

Echoing Margaret Fuller's *Woman in the Nineteenth Century* (1845), Hawthorne had suggested in *The Scarlet Letter* that one day men and women would enjoy a new relationship, and that Hester Prynne might be the "destined prophetess" of the new order, but he had been unable to conceive a destiny for Hester that transformed relationships between the sexes. Although her daughter, Pearl, escapes by inheriting great wealth and marrying an English lord, thus realizing every middle-class American girl's romantic dream, Hester, bound to the men in her life long after they are gone, remains in Boston as midwife and minister to the women in her community.[41]

Victorian women were expected to save men from their baser drives to ensure the stability of the family, so those with obvious sexual desires, like Hester Prynne, were considered witches, whores, and nymphomaniacs. Women—at least the kind respectable men married—were seen as asexual "angels in the household," while men were viewed as "beasts" whose sexual urges had to be channeled into reproduction, sublimated in work, or relieved by prostitutes.[42]

Many scholars have speculated that the triangulated relationships in the novels Melville and Hawthorne wrote in 1851 and 1852 reveal homoerotic feelings that the two men were dealing with in very different ways. Hawthorne and Melville were especially sensitive to the marginalization of sexuality, because as artists who in very different ways transgressed gender boundaries and questioned sexual roles in their novels, they were doubly marginalized. Emerson once wrote of homoerotic friendships that "men have sometimes exchanged names with their friend, as if they would signify that in their friend each loved his own soul." While Melville and Hawthorne did not exchange "names," their novels cross-fertilized each other, and at times they almost seem to be carrying on dialogues in their novels. In fact, they seem almost to have swapped narrative strategies in writing *Pierre* and *The Blithedale Romance.* Melville, who had always written from a first-person point of view, adopted an omniscient but highly unstable third-person narrative voice, while Hawthorne made his narrator, Miles Coverdale, a sexually ambivalent observer-participant. It almost seems as though, in one of their excited conversations, they might have conspired to experiment with writing each other's books.[43]

Oddly, neither *Pierre* nor *The Blithedale Romance* was very popular with readers, perhaps because they were uncomfortable when confronted with the repressed material of their own lives. Yet Hawthorne and Melville both tried to loosen—at least fictionally—the stranglehold that Victorian sexual ideology had on them. If *The Blithedale Romance* is about searching for paradise in New England and discovering that it does not exist because sex always creeps in to corrupt paradise, *Pierre* is about discovering that a utopia without sex is no utopia at all.

~~~~

Pierre is a minefield for anyone attempting a biography of Melville. At times it almost seems that Melville wrote it purposely to torture scholars, tease psychologists, and send biographers rummaging through family closets in search of skeletons. The hundreds of articles and books about *Pierre* attest to its being a virtually inexhaustible source of apparent clues to the "dark, mad mystery" of Melville's life and art. For decades, even though Melville and Morewood descendants told Melville's earliest biographer that they remembered seeing Melville throw letters and manuscripts into the great fireplace at Arrowhead, Melville scholars and biographers have argued over *Pierre* and prayed that a new letter or diary entry would be found to shed light on this provocative and perplexing text.[44]

The second half of the book is recklessly self-punishing, as though Melville were flagellating himself, not only with the pain of early losses and the frustrations and disappointments of his relationship with Nathaniel Hawthorne, but also with his failure to win a large and loyal audience for his fiction or sustain the early promise of married life. A tragicomic view of Victorian sexual ideology and an orgy of Dionysian dismemberment, *Pierre* was ultimately, for its author, a healing journey through a psychosexual labyrinth.

Although Pierre is haunted by images from Dante's *Inferno* and *Hamlet* and afraid that evil forces may be tempting him toward the verge of Hell, he gradually convinces himself that Isabel is his sister and that he is responding to "the unmistakable cry of the godhead through her soul." Returning to the red cottage, he tells her of his decision to take care of her and of the disgraced Delly, who, since losing her baby, has been provided for by Isabel. Planting "burning kisses" on Isabel's brow, he pronounces himself "infallibly her brother" and says they must pretend to be man and wife to make their relationship acceptable to the world.[45]

Hoping to lighten the blow by keeping Isabel's claim to sisterhood a secret, Pierre tells his mother that he and Isabel are married, even though he knows the "fictitious alliance" will break Lucy's heart. Indeed, she falls into a swoon on hearing the news, and takes to her bed, deathly ill. With that, Mrs. Glendinning, whose "reserved strength and masculineness" Pierre has come to dread, banishes her "vile boy" forever. "Twice disinherited," and fated to "do his own self-will," not the will of his family, he cries, "Henceforth, cast-out Pierre hath no paternity, and no past" and turns his back on Saddle Meadows forever. Moving into the Black Swan Inn, he throws his father's portrait and his childhood memorabilia into the "crackling, clamorous flames" of the fireplace.[46]

"Driven out an infant Ishmael into the desert," Pierre takes Isabel and Delly to New York. During their journey, he reaches under the seat of their coach and finds a "sleazy" pamphlet condemning Christianity as an unworkable religion that causes the human race nothing but misery. The author, philosopher Plotinus Plinlimmon, posits a dichotomy between heavenly and earthly morality that allows him to argue that God expects nothing more from man than a kind of "virtuous expediency," or enlightened self-interest. Easily swayed, Pierre begins to wonder if there is any moral basis to Christianity.[47]

Although Pierre has written his cousin, Glendinning Stanly, about his coming to town, when the coach pulls up before Glen's mansion, the place is completely dark. Dismayed, Pierre orders the coachman to drive them to the watch-house of the ward, somewhat irrationally leaving Isabel and Delly with the police and "a base congregation" of "frantic, diseased-looking men and women of all colors" while he returns to Glen's house. Now finding lights blazing and a party in full swing, he storms past the butler and confronts his cousin, who denounces him as an intruder and calls his resemblance to Pierre Glendinning "a remarkable case of imposture and insanity," then has him thrown out of the house.[48]

Shocked by his boyhood playmate's "heartless neglect" of him, Pierre fetches the women from the precinct house and goes to look for Charlie Millthorpe, the son of an impoverished farmer from Saddle Meadows who supports himself, his widowed mother, and his sisters by working in a law office. The decent, hardworking Charlie, who aspires to be a poet, immediately finds lodgings for the three exiles in the abandoned Church of the Apostles, a colony of "strange nondescript adventurers and artists" that includes "all sorts of poets, painters, paupers and philosophers."[49]

Pierre, who has already published several volumes of sentimental verse and some moral essays, now detests these juvenile writings and uses his sonnets to light cigars and stoke the hearth fire. Denouncing publishers for their commercialism, materialism, and superficiality, he accuses magazine editors of treating authors as "public property." Pierre's attack on "Young America" and the editor of the *Captain Kidd Monthly* expresses Melville's anger at Evert Duyckinck for his reviews of *Moby-Dick* and at all publishers for the genteel paternalism that masked the cannibalistic nature of a relationship in which the writer contributed his brains and energy and time and talent to produce a book in return for a pitifully small percentage of the profits.[50]

Aspiring to produce something truly great, Pierre writes ferociously all day, and every evening, Isabel strums her guitar for him. Through its mystic music he discovers the erotic origins of his art. One night as they sit with their arms around each other, Isabel leans her head on his breast, and in response to their mutual "throbbings," Pierre forbids her to call him "brother" ever again. The tantalizingly ambiguous language hints at consummated incest, as does Pierre's horrified reaction. Convinced that his high-mindedness was simply disguised lust, he exclaims, "Virtue and Vice are trash!" Vowing to "gospelize the world anew, and show them deeper secrets than the Apocalypse!" he confines himself to "a beggarly room in the rear-building of the Apostles" and labors feverishly over his masterpiece in a solipsistic trance. From Isabel's mesmerizing instrument, Pierre feels "chapter after chapter born of its wondrous suggestiveness; but alas! eternally incapable of being translated into words; for where the deepest words end, there music begins its supersensuous and all-confounding intimations."[51]

Pierre toils over his manuscript in the solitude of his room, while Isabel listens outside the door for the "long lonely scratch of his pen" and wonders whether Pierre's work is "creation, or destruction." To punish himself for his sexual transgression, he adopts the stoical rituals of "those forlorn fellows, the Apostles." He bathes outdoors in ice-cold water in December to mortify his flesh, then sits hunched over his writing desk, swaddled in his grandfather's old blue army cloak. Instead of the rich estate to which he once was the proud heir, he has only "a rickety chair, two hollow barrels, a plank, paper, pens, and infernally black ink, four leprously dingy white walls, no carpet, a cup of water, and a dry biscuit or two."[52]

When he learns that his mother has died and left Saddle Meadows to his "soul-alien," Glen Stanly, who wants to marry Lucy, he feels as though he is entangled in a "snake's nest." He curses himself as a "heartless villain, as the murderer of his mother," and an "idiot fool" who has "resigned his noble birthright to a noble kinsman for a mess of pottage, which now proved all but ashes in his mouth." He imagines the "blue-eyed, mystic-mild" philosopher Plotinus Plinlimmon watching him from a tower window with a "malicious leer," shouting "Vain! Fool! Quit!" and hissing "*Ass! Ass! Ass!*"[53]

Sensing the impossibility of telling the whole truth about human life, he feels he is writing two books, "of which the world shall only see one, and that the bungled one." The book taking shape in his head and heart exists for himself alone. "The larger book, and the infinitely better, is for Pierre's own private shelf. That it is, whose unfathomable cravings drink his blood; the other only demands his ink. But circumstances have so decreed, that the one can not be composed on the paper, but only as the other is writ down in his soul."[54]

Barring the door to his study with a dagger, he works compulsively, and although Isabel and Delly remain devoted to him, he shamelessly neglects them. He feeds voraciously on those he loves while his book revolves in his aching head like "a vast lumbering planet, threatening to destroy his health, his eyesight, and his sanity." A prisoner of his purgatorial routine, Pierre cannot eat or sleep: "Morning comes: again the dropped sash, the icy water, the flesh-brush, the breakfast, the hot bricks, the ink, the pen, the from-eight-o'-clock-to-half-past-four, and the whole inclusive hell."[55]

The descriptions of Pierre composing his masterpiece capture the physical agony and emotional ecstasy Melville experienced while writing *Moby-Dick*: the straight wooden chair hard as an Inquisitor's stool, the spine a rusty harpoon, the wrist a splintered whalebone, the arm and hand cramped from holding a quill pen, the neck and shoulders tightening like a capstan spike, the eyes like swollen barrels pushing against their metal bands, the nerves in the legs numb and tingling, hungry to walk, to run, to climb—and always, the thoughts that sparkle and dart like silver fish, the doubts gaping like sharks' jaws, the phrases that roll like surf and dissolve like sand, until all at once, whole paragraphs come crashing against a sun-drenched shore, achieving a metalinguistic resonance that is closer to poetry than to prose.[56]

Melville achieved something extraordinary with *Pierre*. He pushed back boundaries to render a wide range of emotions with savage intensity, scaling heights and plumbing depths rarely attempted by the fiction writers of his day. Each day he tunneled through the "heart's recesses deep" until he stood with Dante in the "perilous wide waste" of Hell. Gazing up "the lonely steep" he had to climb, with an inferno boiling beneath him and paradise many valleys and mountains away, he struggled with the terror of "our mortal life."[57]

As Pierre is wrestling with his manuscript, Lucy, now recovered from a nervous breakdown, unexpectedly arrives with her easel. Having come to feel that Pierre's revolt against family and class was a noble undertaking, she is determined to live with Pierre as a sister and support herself by painting. Her mother, convinced that Pierre is a villain, pursues her and tries to persuade her to marry Glen Stanly and live at Saddle Meadows, but Lucy insists on staying with Pierre. Denouncing Pierre's "incredible folly and depravity," Mrs. Tartan calls down God's judgment on him and casts her daughter off. Soon, Lucy becomes Pierre's "Good Angel," and the resentful Isabel, who tries to prevent Pierre from writing, quickly becomes his "Bad Angel." By splitting the image of woman into light and dark archetypes—the virginal Lucy and the sensual Isabel—Pierre fails to integrate sex and sanity.[58]

Unable to resolve his feelings for the two women, he dreams that he is wandering through fields of catnip and amaranth—symbolizing the struggle between "man's earthly household peace and the ever-encroaching appetite for God." Dreaming of the Mount of the Titans, where he rambled as a child, he sees his own face superimposed on the body of the mutilated and half-buried Titan, the "leaden demi-god—piled with costly rocks." He imagines that he is "an American Enceladus … the son and grandson of an incest," entombed in earth and rock and paralyzed from the waist down.[59]

Pierre wakes up from his dream breathless and exhausted, feeling the presence of "doubly incestuous Enceladus within him," an allusion to the double legacy of Melville's grandfathers. Although his "union" with Isabel has released in him a tremendous flood of creative energy by putting him in touch with the repressed feminine side of himself, he can never "regain his paternal birthright." His conflicting erotic energies render him impotent, and his art becomes solipsistic and self-referential.[60]

The novel's climax comes when Pierre and the women go on a "family outing" to a nearby art gallery. On the wall opposite a portrait of Beatrice Cenci he sees the portrait of an unnamed European aristocrat who bears an uncanny resemblance to Isabel. The mute dialogue between the two paintings stirs "the most latent secrecies of his soul," and he realizes that he has no proof his father ever had a bastard daughter, and that even if he did, there is no proof that Isabel "rather than any other living being, *was that daughter*" because Isabel looks as much like the stranger in the painting as she looks like Pierre's father. Asking himself "how did he *know* that Isabel was his sister?" he realizes that his willingness to believe her story with so little evidence masked ulterior motives that were base and foul.[61]

Branding himself a moral monster, the "Enthusiast to Duty" brings his book to a nihilistic conclusion and submits it as "a regular romance," but his publisher rejects it with a caustic letter: "Sir:—You are a swindler. Upon the pretence of writing a popular novel for us, you have been receiving cash advances from us, while passing through our press the sheets of a blasphemous rhapsody, filched from the vile Atheists, Lucian and Voltaire." The letter echoes the negative reviews of *Mardi* and *Moby-Dick*, at the same time anticipating the devastating reviews of *Pierre* with uncanny accuracy.[62]

Melville ends his novel with a *Hamlet*-like catastrophe when Glen Stanly and Lucy's brother Frederic arrive to rescue her from Pierre's degenerate clutches. Brandishing two pistols, Pierre wounds Frederic and kills Glen, whereupon he is tried for murder and imprisoned. When Isabel and Lucy visit him, Pierre tells Lucy his secret, and she dies of a broken heart. Seizing a vial of poison Isabel has hidden in her bosom, the fated boy drinks it and slumps to the floor dead. Isabel then finishes the poison and falls across his body, her head on his heart, "her long hair" arboring him like "ebon vines." Her last words, "All's o'er, and ye knew him not," echo Horatio's tribute to the dead Prince.[63]

Pierre must die, not because he has overreached himself as Ahab did and must be punished for his impiety, but because his rebellion was, in the end, so distressingly bourgeois. Pierre may have left Saddle Meadows, but Saddle Meadows has never left Pierre. His journey has taken him through a dark night of the soul that led not to enlightenment and bliss, but to existential nothingness and despair. "The fool of Truth, the fool of Virtue, the fool of Fate," Pierre is not a survivor like Ishmael, whom the sea buoys up so he can tell his story, but a wounded pilgrim on a harrowing inner journey that ends at an empty tomb: "By vast pains we mine into the pyramid; by horrible gropings we come to the central room; with joy we espy the sarcophagus; but we lift the lid—and nobody is there!—appallingly vacant as vast is the soul of man!"[64]

Pierre ends in darkness: "Deep, deep, and still deep and deeper must we go, if we would find out the heart of a man; descending into which is as descending a spiral stair in a shaft, without any end, and where that endlessness is only concealed by the spiralness of the stair, and the blackness of the shaft." In this abyss, there is no God to say, "Let there be light." These waters are whaleless waters where the chase turns inward, where the hunter harpoons himself because there is no whale, only the hunter, the harpoon, and the elusive jet of an imaginary whale.[65]

∾

Writing about *Pierre* is like tap-dancing in quicksand, or swimming through the kelp-choked Sargasso Sea. Melville's text has been known to hold those who tried to fathom it underwater until they nearly drowned. Swimming toward the glint of sunken treasure buried in the sand, scholars have glimpsed a diabolical *roman à clef*, a sublime epistemological odyssey, a coy homosexual disclosure, an attack on patriarchy and the literary establishment, or a satirical exposure of the paralyzing domestic ideology of antebellum America. Although one or two critics have called it Melville's greatest novel, most have dismissed it as an abysmal failure, a self-indulgent embarrassment.

Cultivated readers and reviewers were revolted by the nihilism to which its hero eventually descended. The publication of *Pierre* opened Melville to a firestorm of criticism that made even the worst of the negative reviews of *Mardi* and *Moby-Dick* seem tame. It was one thing to question the universe as he had done in *Moby-Dick*, but when he turned a basilisk eye on the landlocked world of domesticity and revealed how inextricably tied together love and hate can be, all hell broke loose. Friends and family members reacted to the caustic criticism of Herman's novel with stunned silence. The book did not even enjoy a *succès de scandale*. It turned out to be Melville's most abysmal failure, with positive comment on *Pierre* having to wait for the era of Freud and Jung, when Melville's characters were seen as aspects of their creator's troubled psyche and he was praised for his psychological acuity. Although *Moby-Dick* made readers uneasy by raising the specter of devil-worship and blasphemy, Melville's whaling story took place far enough offshore to keep most readers from realizing how subversive his vision really was.[66]

Pierre is *Moby-Dick* turned inside out, and even wickeder. It is that "most dangerous game," a hunt with a human quarry, a quest that leads through the dark corridors of the human heart into the prison of the self. Yet, by identifying with the divided Pierre, Melville created a protagonist who was both subject and object, externalizing self as both narrator and text. By merging Pierre the character with *Pierre* the book, and sacrificing his protagonist to purge the anger and disgust he felt at almost everything about his life and his career, Melville ultimately escaped the psychological disintegration that threatened him in 1852.[67]

Melville breaks with the first-person narratives that reached their apotheosis in *Moby-Dick* to tell his story through an omniscient narrator. This narrator, however, is not a benevolent, God-like demiurge whose concern for the fate of his characters creates a coherent moral universe and reassures the reader that justice and love will ultimately triumph over villainy and greed. Instead, this narrator becomes increasingly critical of the protagonist, intruding sarcastically, scourging the hero, or antihero, with mockery and ridicule, and ultimately deconstructing the fictive universe he has created. Like the malevolent dwarf or gremlin of fairy tales, or Poe's "imp of the perverse," the intrusive narrator jeers at the highest aspirations and ideals of the hero, deriding Pierre in a voice that seems to be Melville's one minute and Pierre's the next. It is this peculiar ventriloquism that makes the novel so unstable and erratic.

Pierre destroyed Melville's credibility almost completely; it ruined his reputation with the elite critical establishment and alienated cultivated readers. Melville had tried to write a novel that would appeal to the growing readership of women as well as to working-class readers who wanted sensational plots and who relished seeing "their betters" taken down a peg or two, but instead of including the novel in its cheaper line of fiction, which was reaching a mass audience, Harper's priced it at $1.50, making it affordable only to the very people Melville was attacking in the book. Working-class readers who would have savored Melville's satire of the Hudson River aristocrats were put off by its price and its florid style, and middle-class readers objected to Melville's heretical notions.[68]

Readers of serious literature in Melville's day had a tacit understanding that novels would uphold the normative values of civilization in the New World, which were Christian and as patriarchal as the papacy. Novelists could question these values and bring them into conflict with others as long as mainstream middle-class values were reaffirmed by the structure of the plot and as long as the face of a loving, omniscient deity remained discernible behind the narrative mask. Melville, however, saw the self as essentially unknowable and the universe as a conundrum, full of teasing ambiguities, which made his readers extremely uncomfortable. He portrayed closed worlds devoid of divine order or social coherence, and allowed them to crush the weak and the strong with equal ferocity.

Most antebellum authors made a kind of covenant with their readers that human destiny ultimately lay in the hands of a benevolent and just God who would punish wickedness and reward goodness. Harriet Beecher Stowe, for instance, constantly reassured her readers that the sufferings of her characters had meaning, and that even if human beings were being brutally enslaved or murdered in this world, salvation would surely come to them in the next. Violating this covenant, Melville abandons Pierre and the other characters in the novel to malevolent forces and takes away their hope of future redemption.

Pierre did not fare well in the marketplace. Although reviewers in popular magazines generally compared the novel favorably with more conventional sensational romances, the American and British editions together sold only 1,423 copies. Melville earned just $58.25 from his half-share of the profits, and he ended up owing Harper's nearly $300. Like the doomed Enceladus, the author of *Pierre* was a mutilated giant half-entombed in the black earth and immured in the rock of rejection and debt, his arms upraised in the "reckless, sky-assaulting mood" that had energized his greatest writing.[69]

On their way to "The Tombs" in Manhattan, condemned prisoners were led to their cells beneath an arch that bore Dante's legend, "Abandon Hope, All Ye Who Enter Here."

SEVENTEEN

COUNTER-FRICTION TO
THE MACHINE

With Pierre *behind him, Melville was free to putter around the farm. Hiring a boy named David to help plant the crops and prune the orchards, he fell happily into a rustic rhythm of chores in the morning and outings in the afternoon. Lizzie was well enough to enjoy long drives again, so she and Herman and various members of the family made half a dozen excursions through the Berkshire Hills, stopping for tea with Sarah Morewood. They paid a visit to the Shakers and had lunch in "the old-fashioned town of Hancock," and Melville showed Gus and Fanny the Sykes District School and the "magnificent view" from Constitution Hill. In June, after Tom arrived home from the Pacific, Herman took Lizzie, Helen, Tom, and Fanny to camp out on Greylock for two nights while his mother and Augusta took care of the children.*[1]

On July 1, after a family reunion at Arrowhead, Melville went to Nantucket with Judge Shaw, who wanted him to introduce him to "some of the gents at New Bedford & Nantucket." The two men took the train to New Bedford, where they met John Clifford, the attorney general who had successfully prosecuted Harvard professor John Webster for the grisly murder of his colleague, George Parkman. Shaw had sentenced Webster to hang, and although he and Clifford must have reminisced about the gruesome case in Melville's presence, Melville made no literary use of the case.[2]

Once Melville and Shaw reached Nantucket, the windswept outpost of heather, sand, and sea from which the "fighting Quakers" had set forth in pursuit of whales, Melville became curious about the lives of the women who governed the island and ran its businesses while their menfolk were away at sea.[3]

"One night we were talking," he later told Hawthorne, "of the great patience, & endurance, & resignedness of the women of the island in submitting so uncomplainingly to the long, long absences of their sailor husbands, when, by way of anecdote, this lawyer gave me a leaf from his professional experience."[4]

Clifford's story concerned Agatha Hatch, the daughter of a Falmouth lighthouse keeper, who saved a sailor named James Robertson (called "Robinson" by Melville) from drowning in a shipwreck and later married him. They moved out to Nantucket, but when Agatha was pregnant, James went to sea again. Years passed without even a letter from him. Then suddenly, when their daughter was seventeen, Robertson showed up. He gave Agatha a small sum of money, then disappeared again. This time, however, he kept in touch with his daughter, and on the eve of her wedding, he appeared with a gold watch for the bridegroom and three shawls for the bride. Noticing that the shawls had been worn, Agatha found out that Robertson had married a second time, but she refrained from prosecuting him for bigamy because she did not want to disgrace the family name. Robertson was so touched by her forbearance that he asked Agatha and the newlyweds to move to Missouri with him, and when they refused, he went west alone and there married a third time without divorcing the first two wives. Clifford told Agatha's story with such "unaffected sympathy" that Melville could not get it out of his mind.[5]

While he was on Nantucket, Melville met two men he had mentioned in *Moby-Dick*: Captain George Pollard, the "most impressive, tho' wholly unassuming, even humble" master of the whale ship *Essex*, whose crew had to resort to cannibalism to survive when their ship was sunk by an angry sperm whale, and Thomas Macy, who gave Melville a copy of Obed Macy's *The History of Nantucket*. He also met William Mitchell, the astronomer he had mentioned in his *Yankee Doodle* piece "The New Planet," and Mitchell's "celebrated daughter [Maria], the discoverer of comets."[6]

This brilliant woman, who was a year younger than Melville, had helped her father chart a solar eclipse when she was twelve years old, and at fourteen, she knew how to rate chronometers. When she was eighteen and working at the Nantucket Athenaeum, Maria Mitchell read every available book on astronomy. Her self-study of scientific literature made her so skeptical about the Bible that at age twenty-five she was read out of

Quaker meeting for "questioning." In 1847, Mitchell discovered a comet while looking through her father's telescope on the roof of their house. For her achievement, the King of Denmark, an astronomy buff, awarded her a gold medal, and the American Academy of Arts and Sciences granted her membership. In 1850 she became a member of the American Association for the Advancement of Science, and from 1865 to 1888 she was a professor of astronomy at Vassar College. Several years later, while traveling from Paris to Rome with the Hawthornes, Maria gave the Hawthorne children astronomy lessons through the window of their train compartment.[7]

Women did not usually make major scientific discoveries from roof-walks, which in seafaring towns were designed not as astronomical observatories, but as safe places from which women could watch for the return of the tall ships that would bring their men home from the sea. So many whalemen lost their lives—as Melville noted when he put a double check beside "Widows, 202" in his copy of Macy's history—that these rooftop porches came to be known as "widows' walks," symbolizing female devotion and fatalistic stoicism, not intellectual adventure.[8]

Melville's visit to the rugged island from which America's first whalemen had put out to sea influenced both "The Encantadas" and his poem "After the Pleasure-Party." From Nantucket, he and Shaw went to Martha's Vineyard and the Elizabeth Islands, then to Falmouth and Sandwich, before returning to Boston. According to Judge Shaw, Melville proved a sociable companion who saw "many things & met with many people, whom he was extremely glad to see."[9]

Back in Boston everyone was talking about Hawthorne's latest novel, and when Melville overheard a woman telling her husband proudly that she had brought him "*Hawthorne's* new book," he wrote his friend the good news. Hawthorne replied with an invitation to Concord, but by the time the letter reached Melville, he was back at Arrowhead. He had to decline the invitation because he had just "returned from a two weeks' absence; and for the last three months & more I have been an utter idler and a savage—out of doors all the time," and he was ready to get back to work. Besides, he was eager to read *The Blithedale Romance* himself, as Ticknor & Fields had just sent him a copy of Hawthorne's account of his Brook Farm "daydream" at the author's request.[10]

The Blithedale Romance seethes with erotic undercurrents reminiscent of those in *Pierre,* but Hawthorne subordinates emotions to ideas. Whereas the Dionysian Melville, dauntless braver of ferocious winter storms, gave the dark horses of his imagination their heads, the Apollonian Hawthorne kept his tightly reined in, fearful that they might gallop away with him.

While he was reading *The Blithedale Romance,* Melville received from John Clifford a transcript of the "Agatha story" that excited his "most lively interest." Although the Agatha character appealed to Melville, he initially believed the story was better suited to Hawthorne's genius than his own. He sent the transcript to Hawthorne with an inscribed copy of *Pierre* and a detailed letter in which he acknowledged that "perhaps this great interest of mine may have been largely helped by some accidental circumstance or other; so that, possibly, to you the story may not seem to possess so much of pathos, & so much of depth. But you will see how it is."[11]

After describing exactly how he thought the material should be handled, Melville apologized for his "strange impertinent officiousness," concluding: "You have a skeleton of actual reality to build about with fulness & veins & beauty. And if I thought I could do it as well as you, why, I should not let you have it." If Melville hoped to reestablish his former intimacy with Hawthorne by offering him the story, he was bound to be disappointed, as Hawthorne was busy writing a presidential campaign biography for Franklin Pierce; besides, Hawthorne thought the material was much more in Melville's line.[12]

Meanwhile, 150 copies of *Pierre* had reached the newspapers, and while reviewers in working-class and mass-market periodicals loved the mix of satire and sensation, critics who considered themselves arbiters of taste and guardians of culture damned the book. Many of these "cultivated" critics joked in print that Melville had lost his mind and that his friends were trying to send him to an asylum. Reacting violently against *Pierre*'s hysterical style and nihilistic immorality, they compared it to a French sensational romance and warned readers not to read it lest they find themselves utterly debauched.[13]

The Literary World led off with an attack on the book's specious morality, written by either George or Evert Duyckinck: "The most immoral moral of the story, if it has any moral at all, seems to be the impracticability of virtue; a leering demoniacal spectre of an idea seems to be peering at us through the dim obscure of this dark book, and mocking us with this dismal falsehood." The review included an enormous list of archaisms and grotesque words coined by Melville, who had deliberately created these pretentious locutions to satirize social climbers but he affected aristocratic manners.[14]

Melville's old nemesis at the *Boston Post* announced that "the amount of trash" in *Pierre* was "almost infinite—trash of conception, execution, dialogue and sentiment," and *The Albion* pronounced it a "crazy rigamarole" and a "dead failure." The reviewer for the *Springfield Daily Republican* felt that whatever this "new Melville" had gained in the way of greater "subtlety of thought, more elaborateness of manner (or mannerism), and a higher range of imagination" had been gained "at a sad sacrifice of simplicity and popular appreciation." In the same vein, the New York *Day Book* blazoned the headline HERMAN MELVILLE CRAZY, and the *New York Herald* called Melville's novel "one long brain-muddling, soul-bewildering ambiguity," attributing its flatulent diction to "a distempered stomach disordered by a hasty supper of half-cooked pork chops."[15]

In late September, Lizzie's parents had a "very agreeable visit" with the Melvilles, during which Hope Shaw found Lizzie "in health & the two children very promising," and she reported that the "old lady," as she called Mother Melville, had taken over the training of David, the hired boy, and that under his tutelage Malcolm had picked "three barrels of potatoes." Mrs. Shaw's wish that the farm might "yet flourish" may have been a polite way of saying she hoped Herman would find another way to make a living, as *Pierre* was an embarrassment to the family. Oakes Shaw told Lem that "Herman has published another book some *high faluting* romance which is spoken of with anything but praise at least so far as I have heard."[16]

All that fall, reviewers were smacking their lips over the excesses of *Pierre*. Newspapers and magazines ran plot summaries that made it sound absurd, quoted passages of Melville's purplest prose out of context, and featured parodies of passages that had been parodies themselves. *Godey's Magazine and Lady's Book*, for example, advised Melville to return to "his native element, the ocean" to cool off.[17]

Many critics complained that *Pierre* was not "American," and when they conducted mock searches for the father of this bastard novel, he always turned out to be a Frenchman. They considered *Pierre* prima facie evidence of the decadence that was afflicting America. *Graham's*, for instance, praised the book's "force and subtlety of thinking and unity of purpose" and the "great splendour and vigor" of many of its scenes, but deplored its "intolerably unhealthy" spirit, blaming its degenerate tendencies on "the peculiarities of Poe and Hawthorne," two writers who had already been accused of succumbing to the seductions of the French.[18]

Opinions about *Pierre* were divided along class lines, with negative reviews in elite newspapers and magazines resembling those of other sensational novels, especially those by European authors. Alexandre Dumas was denounced for his clumsy plots, Eugène Sue for his prurience, and Edward Bulwer-Lytton for mixing genres. George Sand's romances were so popular with female readers that critics resorted to *ad feminém* attacks on her for her liaison with Frédéric Chopin and her habit of occasionally wearing male attire. Even Hawthorne was not exempt from criticism. New York's Methodist *National Magazine* cited both "the late miserable abortion of Melville" and Hawthorne's "morbid propensity for morbid characters" as evidence that American literature was irrecoverably diseased.[19]

One or two journals attempted to give Melville the benefit of the doubt by suggesting that *Pierre* might have been intended to be satirical, but most reviewers could not find language strong enough to condemn the book and vilify its author. George Washington Peck called *Pierre* a "repulsive, unnatural and indecent" novel whose author "dares to outrage every principle of virtue," striking "with an impious, though, happily, weak hand, at the very foundations of society," and the *Southern Literary Messenger* accused Melville of having "deviated from the legitimate line of novelist." As far as most critics were concerned, Melville had violated the unwritten rule that novelists must uphold middle-class Christian values.[20]

Years later, Lizzie reported that Herman thought the reception of *Pierre* something of "a joke," and that it had nothing at all to do with his leading "a recluse life." She claimed that although "it might have affected his literary reputation, it concerned him personally but very little." While on the one hand Melville felt a certain perverse satisfaction at being branded a literary outlaw by purists and snobs, on the other hand he needed to build a larger audience if he wanted to make a living as a writer. It is hard to believe Melville was quite as sanguine about the attacks on *Pierre* as Lizzie later claimed, as these fulminations of critics hurt his reputation with readers of his own class, and family members who thought he was losing his mind urged him to stop writing altogether.[21]

Separated from Hawthorne and estranged from Evert Duyckinck during these years, Melville apparently did not reach out to other writers. He turned down an invitation to contribute to an anthology of Berkshire writers called *Taghconic; or Letters and Legends about Our Summer Home,* which Joseph Smith edited under the pseudonym "Godfrey Greylock." Smith included poems by Sarah Morewood and John Hoadley, a Pittsfield engineer, and although he mentioned Melville in the introduction, Melville's pride evidently kept him from appearing with amateurs. To please Peter Gansevoort, he attended the Albany poet Alfred Street's reading at the Pittsfield Young Ladies Institute, but when he failed to pay Street "a call or the least attention," his uncle called him a "sorry boy" and exclaimed, "Oh Herman, Herman, Herman, truly thou art an 'Ambiguity.' "[22]

With Malcolm an active three-year-old, and Stanwix now crawling, Maria thought Herman and Lizzie should leave the children in her care and go off to Europe, but this was forgotten when Lizzie discovered she was pregnant again. She and Herman took the children to Boston to spend Thanksgiving with the Shaws, and Melville used the opportunity to visit the Hawthornes in Concord. He tried to persuade Hawthorne to write the Agatha story, but his friend wouldn't budge. Instead, he offered Melville notes he had made about the Isles of Shoals during a two-week vacation, and suggested setting the story there. Soon after Melville returned to Arrowhead with the family, he wrote Hawthorne that he had changed his mind and wished he "had come to his determination at Concord, for then we might have more fully and closely talked over the story, and so struck out new light." What they did talk about during Melville's visit to Concord remains a mystery, but Melville's statement that "I greatly enjoyed my visit to you, and hope that you reaped some corresponding pleasure" sounds quite formal in comparison with his earlier letters to his friend. Seeing Hawthorne again evidently broke the spell.[23]

Around New Year's, New York critic Fitz-James O'Brien gave a book-by-book evaluation of Melville's literary career for a series called "Our Young Authors" that appeared in *Putnam's Magazine* in February 1853, perversely ignoring *Moby-Dick* for *Pierre*. Summing up Melville's career, O'Brien concluded that Melville "does not improve with time" and that "his later books are a decided falling off, and his last scarcely deserves naming." As a curative to Melville's "poisoned" thought, "drunken and reeling" language, "antipodical" style, and "bad" morals, O'Brien offered "A little wholesome advice [that] may save him a hundred future follies . . . Let him diet himself for a year or two on Addison, and avoid Sir Thomas Browne, and there is little doubt that he will make a notch on the American Pine."[24]

The hopes of friends and relatives that Melville would at last write a successful novel were savagely dashed by the reception of *Pierre*. In the process of trying to write a novel that would *sell*, he had uncovered a family nightmare that was paradigmatic for Victorians. He had also exposed his own family to indecent fantasies, and they were mortified. Their concern for his mental health was a projection of their shock and outrage at the distorted image of family and behavior patterns that Melville found stultifying. As though they were in the presence of a dangerous lunatic, family members avoided talking about the book, concentrating instead on trying to wean Melville away from the pen.

Melville never allowed much time to elapse between finishing one project and starting another, for fear of facing that dreaded state in which a writer looks at blank paper and sees the existential void. During the winter of 1853, Melville worked on a novella called "The Isle of the Cross," based on the Agatha story. By April 1, when Sam Savage noted that Stannie could "stand, as gay & as light as a wick, & as firm as the wax which surrounds it," Melville was deep into his new work and awaiting the birth of his third child. He was convinced he could make money with his writing; moreover, for Melville, writing was as natural as breathing.[25]

His mother was determined to get him away from his writing desk in order "to materially renew, & strengthen both his body & mind," and now that Nathaniel Hawthorne had been named United States Consul in Liverpool by Franklin Pierce, she thought the administration ought to give Herman a position, too. She urged Allan to ask Hawthorne to "speak to the President" on Herman's behalf and to do "all in his power" to find him a diplomatic post, and she asked her brother Peter to use his influence in Washington as well. "Constant indoor confinement with little intermission to which Herman's occupation as author compels him, does not agree with him," she wrote. "This constant working of the brain, & excitement of the imagination, is wearing Herman out, & you will my dear Peter be doing him a lasting benefit if by your added exersions [*sic*] you can procure for him a foreign consulship."[26]

Judge Shaw and other politically connected friends, unaware of the notoriety

Melville had gained while he was in Honolulu, thought he would be the perfect person for the Hawaiian post; moreover, the climate would be beneficial to his health. Richard Henry Dana wrote of the "great importance of having a consul at the Sandwich Islands who knows the wants of our vast Pacific Marine," and commending Melville's maritime experience and his integrity, he asserted that his friend would not serve "owners & masters" at the expense of common seamen. The post was awarded to a party hack from upstate New York, who, ironically, was also counting on the warm climate to restore his health.[27]

Proclaiming that "the name of Melville was associated with early republicanism & Jeffersonian doctrines," Melville's Pittsfield supporters lobbied for the lucrative Antwerp post, but they could not name anything he had done to help the Democratic Party. Even though James Van Buren wrote President Pierce that Melville's family "have been from time out of mind almost without exception, honest men, sound Democrats & patriotic citizens," Melville was passed over because he was not an active participant in party politics and because so many of his recommenders stressed the benefit of the posting to Melville rather than to American foreign policy. After Antwerp was awarded to a party member, Melville was offered Rome, but the post paid so little that a man had to be independently wealthy to accept an appointment there.[28]

Melville, who was not a Pierce supporter, took this flurry of job-hunting less seriously than his family and friends did. Although he liked the idea of being paid to live abroad, he didn't want to leave his family, and with a third child on the way, he really couldn't think of transplanting his large household to a foreign country. He also had no intention of giving up writing, even if it put him under constant pressure and subjected him to rejection and obscurity. With characteristic understatement, Lizzie noted, "We all felt anxious about the strain on his health in the spring of 1853."[29]

Melville finished "The Isle of the Cross" just in time for the birth of the new baby. Lizzie fared "very well, compared with her situation on the last similar occasion," her father reported happily. That same day, Priscilla Melvill, who was eagerly looking forward to the appearance of a new Melville book, wrote Augusta that she was "constantly looking in the journals & magazines that come in my way, for notices of it." When she learned that the baby had arrived on May 22, Priscilla suggested that as the new story was "almost a twin sister of the little one," Herman and Lizzie ought to name their first daughter "for the heroine if there *is* such a personage." They named her Elizabeth, and called her Bessie to distinguish her from her mother.[30]

Lizzie's parents were planning to go to London that summer, and before they left, Judge Shaw made a last attempt to secure a consular post for his son-in-law and wrote out a will leaving one-fifth of his estate, minus the $5,000 he had loaned Herman, to Lizzie.

In early June, Melville went to New York to show his manuscript to Harper's and to see Peter and Susan Gansevoort off for England, giving them letters of introduction to Robert Cooke and other London friends, as well as a list of things to see. He brought Malcolm with him, and he and Allan and Sophia took the older children to the Hippodrome. Sophia, an avid reader who had plenty of household help and leisure time, was reading Thackeray's *Henry Esmond* in preparation for the British novelist's lecture tour—another indication that members of the Melville clan kept up with the latest British fiction—and undoubtedly would have loved to see Herman join the exalted ranks of Dickens, Thackeray, and Trollope.[31]

A few days later they went by train to New Rochelle to visit Sophia's sister Abby and her family at "Winyah." Abby's husband, Richard Lathers, was a South Carolinian who had freed his slaves before moving to New York City to go into the insurance business. Lathers raised sheep at his castlelike estate, and a decade or so later he would purchase a dairy farm right across the street from Arrowhead and build a magnificent house called "Abby Lodge" in honor of his wife. Melville was impressed by Lathers's extensive library, his knowledge of history, and the complexity of his political views, and Lathers, a southern gentleman of the old school and a Burkean conservative, found Melville's "highly individual views of society & politics" stimulating.[32]

Melville returned home with Malcolm in time to attend Pittsfield's Fourth of July celebration. He had turned down an invitation to be the main speaker, but he heard Julius Rockwell praise Major Thomas Melvill for his patriotic service to the country, and Herman Melville for the "entertainment and instruction" he had given to the world.[33]

~⌒

Back in 1851, Richard Bentley had asked Melville to contribute something original to *Bentley's Miscellany;* although Melville acknowledged that newspapers and magazines were "the most saleable of all books nowadays," he apparently did not send any stories to British publications. At that time he was immersed in novel-writing; he may also have been reluctant to write for magazines, as the short pieces he had written for *Yankee Doodle* and other popular periodicals seemed ephemeral compared with books. He loved the heft of books, the smell of calfskin, the bright colors of cloth bindings, the flash of gold letters on the spine. Books were written to last for centuries, magazines to satisfy the curiosity of an hour.[34]

When *Harper's New Monthly Magazine,* which had published "The Town-Ho's Story" and other excerpts from his novels, asked Melville to write for them, he changed his mind. Writing short fiction was more manageable than tackling another novel, and magazine publication offered Melville the haven of anonymity he had once sought for *Pierre.* By sugaring satire over with genial rhetoric, he could address deeply disturbing social, political, and economic issues, and if he wrote for a popular mainstream publication, he could reach a larger audience than he had with the novels he had written, and make decent money, too.

With new presses that could print twelve thousand pages an hour, *Harper's* was able to produce an inexpensive magazine that reached 100,000 readers. Although it featured a mix of stories, poems, informative articles, and serialized novels, *Harper's* was resented by a number of writers for reprinting British novels such as Dickens's *Bleak House* and Thackeray's *The Newcombes* instead of publishing original works by American authors. In response to these complaints, Charles F. Briggs, George W. Curtis, and Parke Godwin persuaded George Palmer Putnam to start a magazine devoted to the work of Americans. Putnam, a cousin of Allan's wife Sophia, invited seventy writers to contribute, and during its first year the magazine received 980 submissions.[35]

While *Harper's New Monthly Magazine* aimed at a large cross-section of American readers, *Putnam's* cultivated a well-educated, politically liberal audience that numbered from two thousand to twenty thousand at various times during its short existence. *Putnam's* authors included Melville, Thoreau, Cooper, Longfellow, Lowell, Charles Eliot Norton, Charles A. Dana, Horace Greeley, George Ripley, and Bayard Taylor. Richard Henry Dana Jr. was one of its editors, and although conservatives denounced *Putnam's* as the mouthpiece of the "Black Republicans" because of its strong antislavery bias, William Makepeace Thackeray called it "much the best magazine in the world ... better than Blackwood's is or ever was!"[36]

Melville was "admirably paid" for the stories he wrote between 1853 and 1856, receiving $5 a page from *Putnam's* and as much as $100 from *Harper's* for a group of stories. Sometime that spring or summer, he wrote "Cock-a-Doodle-Doo! or the Crowing of the Noble Cock Beneventano," "The Fiddler," and "The Happy Failure: A Story of the River Hudson," all of which appeared in *Harper's*. He also wrote the more substantial "Bartleby the Scrivener: a Story of Wall Street," which was published in installments in the October, November, and December issues of *Putnam's Magazine.*[37]

While Melville's *Harper's* stories tend to be short, quasi-sentimental sketches, those he wrote for *Putnam's* are inclined to be densely textured political allegories. Placing readers on a knife-edge between illusion and reality, as Hawthorne does in "Young Goodman Brown" and "The Minister's Black Veil," Melville invites multiple interpretations. His narrators tend to be smug, upper-middle-class, churchgoing white men confronted by situations that challenge their assumptions. By making the narrator's personality and prejudices the real subject of the story, Melville forces complacent readers to question the role that race, social class, and gender plays in shaping their opinions and their lives.[38]

In two short pieces published by *Harper's*—"The Happy Failure" and "The

Fiddler"—Melville satirizes American attitudes toward success. "The Happy Failure" is a boy's story of how his uncle, an inventor, learns humility when his invention, the "Great Hydraulic-Hydrostatic Apparatus for draining swamps and marshes and converting them at the rate of one acre the hour into fields more fertile than those of the Genessee," fails to work. The inventor, his black servant Yorpy, and the narrator take the contraption, a tangle of metal pipes resembling a "huge nest of anacondas and adders," ten miles upriver in their skiff to test it. When the device falls on Yorpy's foot, the inventor lashes out at the "dunderheaded old black" and orders him to "Take your black hoof from under the box!" When the apparatus fails to work, the inventor kicks it so hard that he breaks it, but after a moment of despair, he mellows and says to his nephew, "Boy, take my advice, and never try to invent anything but—happiness." He gives Yorpy the twisted metal so he can sell it for scrap and make some tobacco money, and Yorpy thanks Providence that his old "massa" is himself again. "Boy, I'm glad I've failed," the inventor tells his nephew. "I say, boy, failure has made a good old man of me." Years later the inventor dies, and the boy imagines that his last words were, "Praise be to God for the failure!" By ending with the moralistic epiphany that was typical of *Harper's* stories, Melville may have been trying to win back readers who had been scandalized by *Pierre*.[39]

"The Fiddler" takes an ironic look at the fate of the artist in America. The narrator, Helmstone, is a poet whose masterpiece has been "damned" by the critics. Seeing him nearly crushed by rejection, his friend Standard points out to him that the violinist Hautboy, despite his fall from fame, exudes "extraordinary cheerfulness." Helmstone, who considers himself a genius, assumes the fiddler is a mediocre artist who deserves his fate, until he hears Hautboy play exquisitely. Standard explains that Hautboy was a famous child prodigy at age twelve, but later gave it up to teach the instrument: "*With* genius and *without* fame, he is happier than a king. More a prodigy now than ever." When Standard whispers Hautboy's real name to the poet, Helmstone tears up all his manuscripts, buys a violin, and signs up for lessons with him.[40]

For "Cock-a-Doodle-Doo," Melville created a narrator who is convinced that the "great improvements of the age," such as the locomotive and the steamship, facilitate "death and murder" rather than progress. Suddenly, a cockcrow that sounds like "Glory be to God in the highest!" lifts him out of the "doleful dumps." He decides he must have the wondrous creature, but he cannot find the bird. Stopping to pay his woodcutter the back wages he owes him, he discovers the rooster there. He offers to buy the bird from the woodcutter, Merrymusk, who refuses to part with him because, although he is poor and his wife is dying and his four children are starving to death, whenever the cock crows, he feels happy. The narrator returns to the shanty determined to force Merrymusk to sell, but when he arrives, the woodcutter and his entire family are dying.

One by one, with each cockcrow, they die, and when they are gone, the cock shakes the "sparkles from his golden plumage" and expires "in a rapture of benevolent delight." The narrator buries the bodies and carves the rooster's image on the grave-stone, and then he walks off, chortling a hearty "COCK-A-DOODLE-DOO!–OO!– OO!–OO!–OO!"[41]

The story pokes fun at addictive optimism. In 1853, for example, the great orator Edward Everett announced confidently, "The United States has solved all the major problems of mankind." This was a curious observation to make about a nation whose citizens were grinding the bones of hundreds of thousands of the continent's original inhabitants under their wagon wheels as they rolled westward, and holding four million Africans as slaves. Still, expansionists crowed triumphantly when the government purchased land on the Mexican boundary of the Rio Grande that had been bloodily contested in the Mexican War. This transaction, known as the Gadsden Purchase, established the southern borders of the nation and opened the way for construction of a railroad line from the cotton states clear through to the Pacific. While plantation owners reveled in their victory, abolitionists denounced the projected rail corridor as another link in the chain binding Americans to chattel slavery.

As Melville well knew, wage slavery in northern factories and housing patterns in cities like New York caused as much suffering as chattel slavery. "Bartleby the Scrivener: A Story of Wall Street," a longer and more complex work than the three *Harper's* stories, is a starkly symbolic rendering of the working world and the struggle for physical and psychic space within the modern city. It anticipates the work of Franz Kafka and other twentieth-century allegorists of alienation and absurdity.

Characterizing himself as a "rather elderly" Wall Street lawyer who has always believed "that the easiest way of life is the best," the narrator boasts that he is "an eminently *safe* man" who does "a snug business among rich men's bonds and mortgages and title-deeds," that he is "one of those unambitious lawyers who never addresses a jury, or in any way draws down public applause," and that in his "pleasantly remunerative" job as a Master in Chancery, he "seldom [had to] indulge in dangerous indignation at wrongs and outrages." He was "not unemployed" by "the late John Jacob Astor." The double negatives establish the lawyer as an unreliable narrator whose voice is not the voice of his creator.

By the time John Jacob Astor died, in 1848, he was the wealthiest landlord in New York City, far outstripping Trinity Episcopal Church. Astor made his fortune first by trading whiskey and rifles to Indians for skins and furs, then by stripping all the sandalwood from the Hawaiian Islands and smuggling opium from Smyrna to Canton. During the Panic of 1837 he bought up foreclosed properties in Manhattan, subdividing the land and dividing older brick homes into small apartments, or building rickety wooden tenements for working people and newly arrived immigrants. By 1850, Manhattan was virtually a private empire controlled by the Astor family, who collected as much as $100,000 a year in rents.[42]

The narrator's worshipful invocation of John Jacob Astor, "a name which, I admit, I love to repeat, for it hath a rounded orbicular sound to it, and rings like unto bullion," marks him as a materialist. Thus, when the "pallidly neat, pitiably respectable, incurably forlorn" Bartleby comes to work as his copyist, he seems almost to have been conjured up out of the narrator's subconscious mind. Like the specters that haunt Dickens's Ebenezer Scrooge, Bartleby is the ghost of social conscience haunting the precincts of the ruling class.[43]

Melville's Wall Street, like Hamlet's Denmark, is a prison. The law office is utterly sealed off from the life being lived outside its "high, blank walls." None of the men in the story has a visible family or a home, and the workplace is dysfunctional. When Bartleby shows up and asks the lawyer for a job, the lawyer stations him behind a green folding screen so he can call him when he needs him and ignore him when he doesn't. Bartleby's cubicle faces a dead, blind wall that symbolizes the moral blindness of the law and the invisibility of the underclass on whose labor prosperity depends. Except for the chambermaid who lives in the attic and cleans the lawyer's office, the world of Wall Street is a world without women, a closed world where relationships are defined by their utility alone. The lawyer's three employees, scriveners Turkey, Nippers, and Ginger-Nut, are ridiculously inefficient, but he adjusts to their eccentricities because he pays them only four cents per hundred words, and they are docile, obedient, and hardworking, willingly doing a job the lawyer himself finds a "very dull, wearisome, and lethargic affair ... to some sanguine temperaments ... altogether intolerable."[44]

Even John Jacob Astor, "a personage little given to poetic enthusiasm," would refuse to do such mindless work, according to the lawyer, who finds it equally inconceivable that "the mettlesome poet Byron would have contentedly sat down with Bartleby to examine a law document of, say five hundred pages, closely written in a crimpy hand." Thus, according to the narrator's own description, legal copying is blinding, cramping, uncreative work.[45]

Bartleby does his work quietly and efficiently until one day the lawyer asks him to proofread, and he responds blandly, "I would prefer not to," which shocks and baffles his employer. By voicing a personal preference, Bartleby throws a monkey wrench into the whole system; it is almost as though Melville created Bartleby to embody Thoreau's idea that a person who resists oppression acts as "a counter-friction to the machine" that crushes initiative and creativity. As the story develops, it becomes clear that for the average worker, the office is a cell.[46]

Bartleby refuses to copy and perform the other tasks for which he has been hired, always with the same polite, calm taciturnity, which the lawyer finds completely exasperating. "Nothing so aggravates an earnest person as a passive resistance," the lawyer remarks; this seems an echo of Henry David Thoreau's "Resistance to Civil Government," which was first published in Elizabeth Peabody's *Aesthetic Papers* in 1849. This essay, also called "On the Duty of Civil Disobedience," inspired Mahatma Gandhi to overthrow the British colonial rule and Martin Luther King Jr. to launch the civil rights movement in America. While we have no concrete evidence that Melville read Thoreau's great protest against the Mexican War and slavery, it is hard to imagine that he did not have Thoreau's essay in mind when he wrote this story.[47]

Ironically, the lawyer is as reluctant to throw out Bartleby as to throw out his plaster bust of Cicero, but when he and the other copyists begin to use the word *prefer* compulsively, the lawyer's colleagues look askance at the behavior of the scrivener, and the lawyer fears for his reputation with his peers. The lawyer pleads with Bartleby to leave, arguing forcefully that any reasonable man would quit the premises, but Bartleby replies, "At present I would prefer not to be a little reasonable," whereupon the lawyer gives him his wages and orders him to leave by morning. Assuming that Bartleby will vacate the premises, he is completely astounded to find him there the next day, and in his frustration, he has a sudden impulse to murder the scrivener.[48]

One Sunday, while walking through the deserted canyons of Wall Street on his way to Trinity Church "to hear a celebrated preacher," the lawyer stops at his office and discovers that Bartleby is actually living there. Although initially he feels sympathy for the scrivener's "miserable friendlessness and loneliness," his pity soon turns to hostility, and he feels "disqualified" from churchgoing that day, though he hardly knows why. He never reflects on the absurdity of a civilization that allows huge amounts of livable space to be set aside for banks and office buildings when so many families live in tenements or on the city streets. Wall Street's emptiness on Sunday mornings and throughout most of the night mirrors the emptiness of a civilization that takes better care of objects than people.[49]

Rather than having Bartleby arrested for vagrancy, the lawyer moves his entire office. When the new landlord finds Bartleby living on his premises, he holds the lawyer responsible, so the lawyer invites Bartleby to come home with him, but Bartleby adamantly refuses. Desperate, the narrator drives out into the suburbs in his "rockaway," an allusion to the flight of the moneyed classes from the city, which was changing the composition of the population.[50]

The new landlord, who subscribes to competitive marketplace ethics rather than the old social contract, has no qualms about exercising his right to have Bartleby arrested for vagrancy and imprisoned in the Halls of Justice, also known as the Tombs. In Melville's day, this massive Egyptian-style municipal jail constructed by the City of New

York on the site of Collect Pond—formerly a source of clean drinking water for city residents—bore the legend from Dante's *Inferno*, "Abandon Hope, All Ye Who Enter Here," over its main entrance. It was an apt symbol of the fate of the urban poor, as debtors imprisoned in the Tombs had little chance of paying their bills and going free.

Still trying to do his Christian duty, the lawyer visits Bartleby and pays the grubman extra to see that Bartleby gets special food, but Bartleby turns his back on him. The next time the lawyer visits, he finds Bartleby curled up against a stone wall in the prison courtyard, lying not on the grass but on the concrete, having starved himself to death.

The lawyer is a man of assumptions, while Bartleby, like Melville, is a man of preferences. The lawyer's frustrated attempts to understand and control Bartleby parallel the reader's frustration at not getting from Melville the usual information about the scrivener's background and a possible motivation for his strange behavior. Just as Bartleby refuses to tell his story, Melville refuses to use narrative to reinforce accepted views of either fiction or ethics, preferring to force readers to question their own assumptions in hopes of deepening their moral vision.

Melville was fascinated by paradox and impatient with stories that sought to reassure readers that the world was just. Even as he was writing the most successful fiction of his career, he rebelled against fiction's inability to reveal the deepest truths or counteract the shallowest of lies. In an epilogue, the lawyer reports that Bartleby once worked in the Dead Letter Office in Washington, as though that bit of information could help us understand the scrivener. "Dead letters!" he exclaims. "Does it not sound like dead men?" Was Melville identifying with Bartleby's alienation from the city and the world of work? Was he criticizing the legal profession and his brother Allan, who was a ward politician and a member of the Sons of Tammany?[51]

On one level, Bartleby may represent the writer who is forced to produce books easily classified and marketed by publishers, as well as the writer whose family is trying to force him to give up writing for a secure government job. If Melville landed a diplomatic post, he would have to do something he preferred not to do: carry out or "copy" policies that were moral "dead letters" as far as he was concerned. Antislavery readers of *Putnam's Magazine* would have picked up on Melville's pointed association of "dead letters" with Washington, D.C., as it was their view that recent compromises with the slave power were, in effect, making "dead letters" of the Declaration of Independence and the Constitution. On one level, the narrator's closing exclamation, "Ah Bartleby! Ah humanity!" appears to mock the typical sentimental *Harper's* ending; on another, it expresses the tragic recognition that a person without food, shelter, and creative work might as well be in jail.[52]

"Too long a sacrifice/Can make a stone of the heart," writes W. B. Yeats, and when the stone cannot be rolled away, resurrection is impossible. Like the implacable stones in *Pierre*, the walls of the lawyer's office represent the social and economic barriers erected against advancement in a world that seems designed to keep workers subservient to the ruling class. In this world of "dead, blank walls," Bartleby is a petrified Pierre.[53]

If *Pierre* reflected a crack-up of sorts, the stories and sketches were Melville's attempt to salvage and reassemble a shattered kaleidoscope of myriad selves by focusing not on inner psychodrama, but on the outer world. Working within the conventions of narrative fiction while quietly showing how individuals were crippled by the economic and social order, Melville brought material that had run away with him in *Pierre* under control. The heroes of his short fiction are the antagonists to his smug protagonists. They are the rebels, the artists, and the working poor, the disappointed and disillusioned dreamers of a downsized dream.

~⁓

In August, Malcolm became a "scholar at the white school-house" down the road, going off every morning "with his pail of dinner in one hand and his primer in the other," while Stanwix, who was not quite three, was talking away despite suffering from whooping cough. With Lizzie nursing infant Bessie, and Sarah Morewood too preoccupied with a sick child to organize one of her incomparable picnics, Melville and Sarah's husband, Rowland, climbed Mount Greylock, and on another occasion, Melville hiked the Taconic Dome with "a party of gentlemen." He was no longer identified by locals as "the fellow who bought Doc Brewster's farm"; he had become a local celebrity. As he drove around in "an old brown lumber wagon, propelled by a horse whose apparent age and humble bearing ought to command respect," the "unassuming, but very popular" thirty-four-year-old author struck the locals as "a stalwart, earnest, resolute looking man."[54]

That September, Melville's sister Kate married John Chipman Hoadley in a small family ceremony at St. Stephen's Episcopal Church in Pittsfield. A founder of the Berkshire Athenaeum and a trustee of the Massachusetts Institute of Technology, Hoadley worked for a locomotive and textile-loom manufacturer in Pittsfield. Although Melville had tried to discourage the match because Hoadley was a widower, he grew to like him and decided he was a "man of worth" who showed "much cultivation of mind." Hoadley was also an amateur poet, so Melville gave him a volume of Thomas Chatterton's poems inscribed "To My Brother," and a copy of the London edition of *The Whale* inscribed "from his friend Herman Melville." On the flyleaf he wrote: "All life (says Oken) is from the sea; none from the continent. Man also is a child of the warm and shallow parts of the sea in the neighborhood of the land." The newlyweds moved to Lawrence, Massachusetts, where Hoadley made a modest fortune by inventing the Hoadley portable engine.[55]

In October, Melville received a letter from Evert Duyckinck informing him that his old companion George Adler had been committed to the Bloomingdale Asylum for manifesting what today would be called paranoid delusions. Adler had signed his letter, "G. F. Adler, insane man at this hospital, reading, rolling ninepins, eating (what he can get) and sleeping with a better appetite than usual." Melville must have felt a *frisson* when he learned of his old friend's condition, as the spirited metaphysical speculations he and Adler loved to indulge in constituted the very habit of mind for which Melville himself had been pronounced crazy by reviewers, relatives, and friends.[56]

That fall, Helen Melville became officially engaged to a Boston attorney, George Griggs, and Melville's cousin Priscilla quit her teaching job in Canandaigua and moved to Arrowhead. At twenty-six, with no prospect of marriage, Priscilla had decided to move to Pittsfield and become a seamstress. She stayed with the Melvilles until the following spring, after which she moved into town to be nearer to her customers.

For some reason, Melville was "prevented" from publishing "The Isle of the Cross," but Harper's paid him $300 in advance to write a nonfiction book about tortoise-hunting in the Galápagos. Unfortunately, Harper's soon had to suspend its operations for a while, owing to a warehouse fire in which 2,300 copies of Melville's books, worth about $1,000, were destroyed.[57]

Helen and George Griggs married in January 1854, celebrating with a week-long house party. When Mother Melville visited them in the early part of February, she enlisted Helen's help in persuading Herman to take up lecturing, and wrote her son: "*One Lecture* ... can be repeated seventy times with success. All the lecturers now prepare one lecture & travel the country with this one for the whole season", they "are feasted made much of & seldom less than fifty dollars are given to the lecturer.... Know my dear darling Herman all your friends, relatives & admirers, say that you are the very man to carry an audience, to create a conversation, to do wonders. To close this subject I will only request you to think over this *not* new subject when in a happy hopeful state of mind, and there is a chance of your coming to the wise conclusion, to do that thing, which at once, and by the same agreeable act, will bring us fame & fortune." Melville, however, had no desire to display himself before an audience like one of Barnum's freaks.[58]

On February 20, 1854, Melville promised Harper's that his "proverbially slow Tortoises" would soon be "ready to crawl into market," but neither "The Isle of the Cross" nor the tortoise-hunting book was ever published. Instead, he reworked material from both into a series of sketches called "The Encantadas, or The Enchanted Islands." Almost as soon as it appeared in *Putnam's Magazine* under the pseudonym Salvator R. Tarnmoor—a name that evokes the painter Salvator Rosa and the romantic atmosphere of the words *tarn* and *moor*—readers recognized the allusive, allegorical style as Melville's.[59]

Although the ten sketches are unified by their setting, Melville's Galápagos is a state of mind, a monochromatic, purgatorial world forgotten by time and stricken by a curse. Leaving out the colorful flowers and birds and the diverse life-forms that inhabit the islands, he creates a bleak and tragic view of human destiny, a projection of the darkness and despair that engulfed him from time to time as he realized that America was not an earthly paradise after all.[60]

Although on the surface "The Encantadas" form a barren wasteland bearing little obvious resemblance to New York, Liverpool, or London, the "belittered" landscape resembles a postapocalyptic metropolis. The spirit of Dante broods over these bleak islands. Originally discovered by buccaneers looking for remote havens in which to stash their loot, they seem to lie under a "special curse." In this wasteland, Nature seems to be devolving rather than evolving. "Like split Syrian gourds left withering in the sun ... cracked by an everlasting drought beneath a torrid sky," they are so rainless and dry that they seem to be crying out for Lazarus to dip his finger in water to cool their tongues and resurrect them. [61]

Cursed with a compulsion to drag around their heavy shells and beat their heads against obstacles, the great tortoises cannot escape "their drudging impulse to straight-forwardness in a belittered world." The tortoises, with their black shells and white under-bellies, exemplify man's precarious place in the universe and his torturously slow, uncertain evolution. These ancient, armor-plated creatures are no match for marauding sailors who make "a merry repast from tortoise steaks and tortoise stews," then turn their shells into soup tureens and their breastplates into serving platters. Thus, in the Darwinian struggle to survive, some species start out hopelessly behind.[62]

From "Rock Rodondo," the narrator surveys the topography of the islands and tries to understand what kind of men the buccaneers who once hid among these islands were. On Barrington Isle, their main hiding place, he finds "seats which might have served Brahmins and presidents of peace societies," even sofas of stone and turf. Concluding that even "cut-throats" are not "unmitigated monsters," he asks, "Could it be possible, that they robbed and murdered one day, revelled the next, and rested themselves by turning meditative philosophers, rural poets, and seat-builders on the third?"[63]

With the contrasting stories of Hunilla, the Chola Widow who survives heart-breaking loss and unspeakable cruelty to become a kind of saint, and Oberlus, the hermit who reverts to diabolical tyranny, Melville explores the moral extremes of human behavior. This sketch seems to incorporate both the Agatha story and "The Isle of the Cross." "Norfolk Isle and the Chola Widow" tells the sad story of Hunilla, a woman shipwrecked on a desolate island and deserted by "faithless" Heaven after losing her husband and brother to the sea. After she suffers years of unspeakable abuse from passing sailors, the narrator and his shipmates take pity on her. They give her safe conduct to

Peru and enough silver to help her get on her feet. When the narrator last sees her, she is riding into Payta town on a small gray donkey with an "armorial cross" on its shoulder. Her face "set in a stern dusky calm," the Chola Widow resembles Jesus entering Jerusalem on Palm Sunday. Melville leaves her story unfinished, perhaps because the story of Christ's being hailed as the Messiah one week and crucified the next is not a cheerful enough story for a popular magazine.[64]

Melville raises a woman of color to heroic stature while portraying colonialism as an earthly hell. In "Hood's Isle and the Hermit Oberlus," the hermit Oberlus is modeled on Shakespeare's Caliban as well as on a renegade described in Porter's *Voyage to the Pacific.* Instead of turning Hood's Isle into a garden spot of Western civilization, the "wild white creature" Oberlus captures passing sailors and makes slaves of them "out of mere delight in tyranny and cruelty." He brings into "this savage region qualities more diabolical than are to be found among any of the surrounding cannibals." When this "most incredible of tyrants" tries to enslave a lone Negro (an obvious allusion to Robinson Crusoe's "benign" enslavement of his man Friday), the Negro overpowers Oberlus and hands him over to an English smuggler who confiscates all his property. However, somehow Oberlus escapes and gathers a small army of slaves who join him in marauding along the coast of South America. When he tries to set fire to a ship in Payta, the authorities catch him and throw him in jail, where "for a long time Oberlus was seen; the central figure of a mongrel and assassin band; a creature whom it is religion to detest, since it is philanthropy to hate a misanthrope."[65]

Melville reached a pinnacle of stylistic brilliance in "The Encantadas." His tragic vision buoyed up by wonderfully poetic prose, at times he seems to be cresting on the blank-verse line of English epic, as when he writes that these godforsaken islands know "neither the change of seasons nor of sorrows." At other times he surges toward a longer, looser prose line that anticipates the free-verse line of Walt Whitman, as when he writes, "The great full moon burnt in the low west like a half-spent beacon, casting a soft mellow tinge upon the sea." J. E. A. Smith praised the sketches for "the simplicity of diction, vividness of description and power of narrative which made *Omoo* and *Typee* two of the most charming books ever written." Charm was not all that Melville had in mind, however, when he wrote "The Encantadas." He knew that both enchantment and danger lurk beneath the surface of the sea.[66]

In court, the great Massachusetts jurist Lemuel Shaw intimidated witnesses and attorneys, but at home he was a playful, loving father and grandfather.

EIGHTEEN

SHADOWS FORESHADOWING DEEPER SHADOWS

In the Berkshires in late March of 1854, fierce storms buffeted the farmhouse and frigid winds kept everyone indoors. Maria and Fanny stayed in New York, leaving the inmates of Arrowhead to fight cabin fever. "We–that is–Lizzie, Augusta, Herman, the little folks, & myself are driven to the necessity of being very *amiable, and obliged to play the agreeable for mutual entertainment–within doors–for the weather continues very severe, gales, and snowstorms prevail,* even *yet, with* no *promise of Spring and we are becoming rather weary of winter quarters," Priscilla Melvill wrote Lemuel Shaw. Even so, "Lizzie's little ones have made* wonderful *advances physically and mentally during the winter."*[1]

With Gus as his copyist, Melville worked on a new batch of stories that, like diptychs on church altars, consisted of paired contrasting sketches, after the fashion of the popular magazine writer Mary Jane McIntosh and the novelist Catharine Maria Sedgwick, whose novel The Poor Rich Man and the Rich Poor Man *was similarly constructed to dramatize the widening gap between male and female, good and evil, rich and poor.*[2]

In "Poor Man's Pudding and Rich Man's Crumbs," which appeared in Harper's New

Monthly Magazine in June 1854, Melville draws on cooking metaphors from Mrs. Pullan's *The Modern Housewife's Receipt Book: A Guide to All Matters Connected with Household Economy* (London, 1854), a book on domestic management, which he had given Lizzie as a present. In the first half of the story, a man who has a tendency to romanticize poverty encounters a poor family that subsists on "bitter and mouldy" pudding made of "damaged" rice and rank salt pork "from last year's barrel." Not one to romanticize poverty, Melville implies that the poor do not feast on the "just desserts" of the America dream; instead, they starve on the "practical misery and infamy of poverty."[3]

In the second sketch, the narrator observes the annual Guildhall banquet in London, where liveried servants toss out the remnants of the royal feast to a starving, bedraggled mob that scrambles for the scraps from the rich man's table. His clothes so torn and tattered that he resembles a beggar himself, the narrator flees this spectacle in horror. Unlike the typical *Harper's* story, both of these sketches end pessimistically.

The provocative diptych called "The Paradise of Bachelors and the Tartarus of Maids" draws on Berkshire scenes and London experiences, as well as on such literary sources as Dante and Boccaccio, to expose the link between privilege and oppression. In "The Paradise of Bachelors," the narrator visits the Temple Bar, a London club where men eat, drink, smoke, and talk dispassionately about esoteric subjects. Like the other "bachelors" Melville portrays in his fiction, these glib debaters in their "snug cells" appear to have no connection to the world of women, work, and children. They see the world through a haze of tobacco and alcohol typical of urbane gentlemen's clubs whose conviviality often seemed superficial to a man familiar with the life-and-death friendships forged in the forecastle.[4]

"The Paradise of Bachelors" gives "a local habitation and a name" to Emerson's fatuous dictum "The nonchalance of boys who are sure of a dinner…is the healthy attitude of human nature." Whereas Emerson held up "the charming irresponsibility of boys" as the proper attitude of the self-reliant man, Melville portrays these privileged "bachelors" as morally stunted, selfish parasites. Pampered and spoiled by the chief barrister of the Inns of Court, who entertains them royally, these nine "gentlemen" are as insulated from the common man and woman as the nine founders of the Knights Templar or the nine justices of the Supreme Court. They remain blissfully unaware of the link between their sybaritic ease and the miserable drudgery of those who toil in frigid factories that turn their buttonless, worn-out shirts into fine letter paper so expensive that the "maids" who manufacture it cannot afford to purchase it themselves.[5]

"The Tartarus of Maids," its companion piece, is an elaborate allegory that begins as the narrator, a "seedsman" on his way to procure inexpensive seed packets, is riding his black horse sixty miles through a hollow called "the Devil's Dungeon" into the "Black Notch" along "Blood River," until, blown by chill winds from "Mad Maid's Bellows'-

Pipe," he arrives at a "large whitewashed" paper factory at the base of "Woedolor Mountain." A boy named Cupid takes the narrator on a tour of the building, which is managed by a strange character called Old Bach, or Bachelor, and in the rag-room he sees pale young women, who are always referred to by the foreman of the factory as "girls," choking on lint as they tear apart old shirts that look as though they had been "gathered from the dormitories of the Paradise of Bachelors." The maids toss the rags into huge vats that boil them to an eggy pulp, and nine minutes later they emerge as sheets of white paper. As a huge, phallic piston embosses each sheet with a wreath of roses, "rows of blank-looking girls, with blank, white folders in their blank hands, all blankly folding blank paper," work beside a sharp erect sword blade, which reminds them of "their fatal sentence." The narrator notices that the maids are so drained of life by the frigid temperature in the factory and the mechanical drudgery of their labor that the rose of youth no longer blooms on their "sheet-white" cheeks.[6]

Based in part on Melville's visits to Carson's "Old Red Mill" and the Crane Paper Company, which manufactured the paper used by the Treasury Department for the nation's currency, this complex story cunningly conflates the paper manufacturing process, childbirth, and writing, exposing the link between economic and biological bondage in an era without reliable birth control. Exploitation of female factory workers was common. They worked twelve to thirteen hours a day for a weekly wage of $2.50, which was often paid not in cash, but in scrip redeemable only at the company store. They lived in crowded dormitories and had little or no medical care unless they worked for one of the companies that had an infirmary for its workers. While Edward Everett was comparing these fairy princesses of capitalism with the *houris* of the Arabian Nights, and Nathaniel Hawthorne was calling the Dover girls the "Sapphos of the Age" because they put out a literary magazine, the mill girls were referring to themselves as "slaves" and praying they wouldn't lose a hand to the whirling spindles. If they became disabled, they lost their jobs, their meager wages, their shelter, and, more often than not, their marriageability. "The working woman has no rights," George Foster wrote in *New York in Slices*. "She can be oppressed, cheated, and trampled upon."[7]

By 1854, when Melville wrote "The Tartarus of Maids," the lifeblood of female operatives was flowing downstream, taking the reproductive capacity and creative energy of these young women with it. The quality of life in these "seats of creative industry," as Edward Everett had called them, had deteriorated to the point that "mill girls" writing for such publications as the *Lowell Offering* were likening their longing to revisit Nature's "still and lovely scenes" to the desperate thirst of a traveler in the desert for an oasis.[8]

By linking the rags used in the manufacture of paper and books to the rags women used to stanch the flow of menstrual blood, Melville suggests a link between paper manufacturing, writing, and human reproduction. He takes a dark view of industrialization's power to cripple both men and women by cutting them off from natural sources of power. It had taken him the equivalent of two pregnancies to write *Moby-Dick,* and while he was working on *Pierre,* Lizzie had suffered through a difficult pregnancy with Stanwix. Male writers such as Melville were having less success with the books they produced than were women writers like Mrs. Stowe, who brought both babies and successful books into the world with what, to Melville, appeared to be great ease.[9]

As far as we know, only one of Melville's stories was rejected: "The Two Temples," a diptych that draws an invidious comparison between an Anglican church and a London theater. His fictional parish combines features of Trinity Episcopal Church and Grace Church, the most fashionable church in New York. Its rector, Dr. Tyng, a renowned preacher, baptized Allan and Sophia's children, and the eminent Dr. Wright Post was senior warden of its vestry. In Melville's fictional church, the snobbish parishioners doze off as an old windbag preaches at them, and they treat the narrator with coldness and hostility; in the theater, by contrast, the audience is "gladdened" by the performance, and they treat the narrator with joy and charity.[10]

Not surprisingly, *Putnam's* editor Charles F. Briggs, who recognized particular individuals as targets of Melville's satire, wrote him that he was "very loth [*sic*] to reject" the story because it contained "some exquisitely fine description, and some pungent satire, but my editorial experience compels me to be very cautious in offending the religious sensibilities of the public." George Palmer Putnam, who was worried that "some of our church readers might be disturbed by the *point* of your sketch," asked Melville to revise the story and resubmit it, but Melville refused, so "The Two Temples" remained unpublished in his lifetime.[11]

Ironically, because of the skewed laws of the literary marketplace, Melville enjoyed greater success as a magazine writer than as a novelist. By April 1854, when he went to New York to celebrate Allan's birthday, he had made over $500 from his stories, and he was working up the story of Israel Potter, the Revolutionary War veteran who ended up an impoverished mender of old chairs. Hearing about her brother's latest project, Helen Griggs wrote from Brookline: "I shall be quite wild to make the acquaintance of 'Israel Potter,' and to have the Fourth of July come. I shall make George procure me my Independence namely—a new novel, & a paper of candy."[12]

When Melville had completed sixty pages of the projected three-hundred-page manuscript, he sent them to George Palmer Putnam with a request for serial publication in *Putnam's Magazine.* He asked $5 a page for the magazine rights and an advance of $100 on eventual publication in book form, as well as retention of the copyright, promising at least ten printed pages an issue and assuring Putnam that his text would "contain nothing of any sort to shock the fastidious" and "very little reflective writing. ..nothing weighty. It is adventure."[13]

Melville's Israel Potter traces his roots back to American prehistory, when the continent was "a wilderness abounding with wild beasts," and in some ways he resembles Pierre Glendinning. Unlike Pierre, who was a member of the gentry, Israel is a poor landless farmer who dreams of owning his own land, and when his father's opposition to his courtship of a neighbor's daughter forces him to leave home, he resorts to hunting and trapping and trading with the Indians, then goes to sea, first on a merchant ship, then on a whaler. Weary of wandering, he comes home and enlists in the Continental Army. After the Revolution, his money is worthless, and he cannot purchase land.[14]

Israel spends the next half century in exile in London as a prisoner, spy, bondsman, bricklayer, and itinerant chair-mender. In the course of numerous adventures during which he is shunted back and forth between England and America by circumstances beyond his control, Potter manages to meet Benjamin Franklin, Ethan Allen, and John Paul Jones, all of whom Melville extols as representative American types before subjecting them to ruthless caricature. Franklin is portrayed as a penny-pinching hypocrite and secret libertine, Allen as a physically strong but intellectually impotent mountain man, and Jones as a freebooting American imperialist: "Intrepid, unprincipled, reckless, predatory, with boundless ambition, civilized in externals but a savage at heart, America is, or may be, the Paul Jones of nations."[15]

Although Melville intended his satirical adaptation of Israel Potter's story to be an indictment of America's failure to live up to its professed ideals, readers and reviewers praised its "half-comic, half-patriotic" tone, its "manly and direct" style, and its charm, ignoring its political implications. Only *The Albion* picked up the anti-imperialist tenor in Melville's portrait of John Paul Jones as a soldier of fortune who epitomized an America "civilized in externals but a savage at heart." *The Albion's* reviewer drew a parallel between the predatory Jones and the notorious Ostend Manifesto, whereby America proclaimed its intention to seize Cuba if Spain refused to sell the island to the United States. The reviewer for *The National Magazine* thought he detected "a tinge of obscure sarcasm" in the book's dedication, but no reviewer commented on the book's ironic concluding scene. Israel comes back to his native land an old man, arriving in Boston just in time for the Fourth of July parade, and while he is standing in front of Faneuil Hall, a "patriotic triumphal car" plows into him and nearly kills him, symbolizing history's callous disregard for the common man.[16]

Melville dedicated *Israel Potter* "To His Highness, the Bunker-Hill Monument" because for him, the history of the ruined patriot Israel Potter epitomized America's betrayal of her Revolution. The novel was serialized in *Putnam's Magazine* and later published in book form by G. P. Putnam & Company as *Israel Potter: His Fifty Years of Exile.* Melville received a total of $421.50 for the 75-cent book, which sold just short of three thousand copies in its first six months at a twelve-and-one-half-percent royalty. Although it is one of the most accessible and entertaining of Melville's novels, it has been largely ignored in modern times.[17]

In *Pierre,* Melville had turned on his clannish, elitist family, devouring them with sharkish glee; in *Israel Potter*, he deals with the betrayal of the American dream in a less personal way. The link between *Pierre* and the narrative of "the revolutionary beggar" was forged by Melville's reflections on the patrician families whom Melville saw "rise and burst like bubbles in a vat," as he expressed it in *Pierre*. If that novel is a secret history of the "Founding Fathers" of the Gansevoort-Melville clan, *Israel Potter* and the short fiction are American history written "the other way."[18]

～

In the early summer of 1854, Lizzie became pregnant with the couple's fourth child. In an effort to reduce the stress that was wearing Herman out, Lizzie took over the bookkeeping and kept track of the titles and dates of his stories. Her handwritten memos, which have proved invaluable to scholars trying to determine dates of composition, show that Melville was working on "The Lightning-Rod Man," "Jimmy Rose," and "The 'Gees," three tales that satirize religion, sentimental rhetoric, and scientific racism.[19]

A literary folktale with biblical overtones, "The Lightning-Rod Man" implies that while science has become the new religion, religion has become a form of insurance for individuals who want to feel safe, as well as for clergy who want to corner the market on faith so they can keep their followers in line and themselves in business.

For many of Melville's contemporaries, optimism was a kind of secular religion. The protagonist of the eponymous "Jimmy Rose," a wealthy and popular New York bon vivant, resembles both Melville's uncle Thomas and old Major Melvill. When he loses his fortune and his friends abandon him to the "last dregs of poverty," Jimmy holds on to his illusions, even though he is "as poor as any rat." Sentimental to a fault, the narrator imagines that this "ruined man" will "immortally survive" in the soil of the grave, a conclusion that mocks sentimental stories that encourage readers to cling to their illusions.[20]

"The 'Gees" has generated a great deal of controversy because, read "straight," it gives the impression that Melville was a racist, which is impossible to conceive in the light of his other work. The grossly stereotypical description of the 'Gees, as these Cape Verdean offspring of African women and Portuguese convicts are called, echoes the pseudoscientific racialist theories of George R. Gliddon and Josiah Nott, who claimed to have scientific proof of white supremacy. As the narrator explains, whites feel "innate disdain" for the 'Gees and consider them subhuman, so sea captains have no compunction about kidnapping them and forcing them to work on their ships. In fact, they prefer 'Gees as crewmen because they will work for biscuits and don't need to be paid real money. Even though the 'Gees tend to be clumsy and untrained for sea duty, most captains "provide for all contingencies" by grabbing twice as many as they need, so that if one falls overboard and drowns, another can step in and do his work. The narrator's matter-of-fact tone, so shockingly inappropriate to the immoral situation he is describing, characterizes him as an unreliable person whose racist assumptions Melville is holding up to scorn and ridicule.[21]

According to the narrator, some Nantucket Quakers have been talking about "sending five comely 'Gees, aged sixteen, to Dartmouth College; that venerable institution, as is well known, having been originally founded partly with the object of finishing off wild Indians in the classics and higher mathematics," but again, his remarks cannot be taken at face value, as the phrase "finishing off" has sinister connotations. Perhaps Melville was familiar with Benjamin Franklin's story about the Indian who complained about the effect of white colleges on the young men of his tribe. According to Franklin's native informant, "When they came back to us, they were bad runners, ignorant of every means of living in the woods, unable to bear either cold or hunger, knew neither how to build a cabin, take a deer, or kill an enemy, spoke our language imperfectly, were therefore neither fit for hunters, warriors, nor counselors; they were totally good for nothing." In other words, they had been "finished off" by white schools.[22]

The narrator's comment that the 'Gee is especially qualified for "intellectual training" because of his "docility," "excellent memory," and "still more excellent credulity" implies that authoritarian pedagogy fosters racism and oppression. Once the 'Gees are "finished off" at white schools, the narrator tells us, they are "liable to be taken for naturalized citizens badly sunburnt," a wry statement that implies racial differences are no more than skin deep.[23]

In 1840 a Frenchman named Cyrus Macaire came to America to make his fortune as a portrait photographer in the southern states, but his prints were so underexposed that white customers refused to buy them because they made them "look like Negroes." Not one to lose money, the resourceful Frenchman sold them to black customers whose self-image was so weak they could be persuaded to recognize themselves in the features of their masters. Macaire's absurd scheme succeeded because the virus of racism blinded both whites and blacks.

When Herman Melville signed himself "Tawney" at the age of nine, it was in a spirit of rebellion, as only "wild Indians," sailors, and members of "the lower orders" had sunburned skins. Whites associated dark skin with peasants, savages, and slaves, and before long, blacks with lighter skins and European features were granted greater social status and prestige by those African-Americans who had internalized the racism of their oppressors.

Putnam's serialization of *Israel Potter* gave Melville a steady monthly income that allowed him to relax over the coming holidays. In November, Maria returned to Pittsfield from a visit with her brother Peter in Albany, and Herman met her at the depot in Housatonic and marched her to his carriage around puddles of water with exaggerated gallantry, holding a lantern in one hand and her arm in the other. A few days later the Melvilles set off for Boston, where they spent the holidays visiting the Shaws, the Griggses, and the Hoadleys.[24]

In February 1855, Melville was seriously incapacitated by an attack of sciatica, and Mackey, who liked to dress up and play-act and often took parts in plays at school, tried to entertain his father by impersonating storybook characters. The boy's favorite role seems to have been Jack the Giant-Killer, perhaps because as the son of a formidable father, he identified with the little boy who was brave enough to challenge and outwit the scary giant.

In March, Lizzie delivered the couple's fourth child, Frances, who was called Fanny. Fortunately, the delivery was comparatively easy, as Lizzie had to take care of a husband who was "helpless" during much of that spring. He could not keep up with the monthly mortgage payments, and when Tertullus D. Stewart demanded full repayment of his loan, Melville's rheumatism flared up at just about the time the spring plowing and planting had to be done. Unhandy with tools and unable to take care of a large property without hired help, Melville made up his mind that he would have to sell the farm.[25]

Even after the rheumatic inflammation subsided, he found it difficult to move, and even more difficult to sit at his writing desk for long periods. These physical ailments and the inevitable stresses and sorrows of family life sapped Melville's energies and plunged him into a depression that only deepened when his sister Helen, who had been expecting "an infant Hercules, or a goddess Diana," took sick during the late stages of her pregnancy and prematurely delivered a stillborn boy. Kate Hoadley, by contrast, suffered through a difficult and scary pregnancy, but gave birth to a healthy baby, named Maria Gansevoort Hoadley.[26]

That spring, Melville learned that *Putnam's Magazine* was going to be sold, which threatened to cut off his best source of income, as the bulk of the $1,329.50 he had earned from publication in both *Harper's* and *Putnam's* magazines came from the longer *Putnam's* stories. His mother, deeply distressed by what she saw as his physical and psychological disintegration, again tried to steer him toward a political career. For Melville, however, writing *was* a political career, because he confronted the social and political issues of the day in his stories and sketches. Although he relied on writing for psychological survival, deep down he still believed art had the capacity to change the way Americans perceived reality, and he still imagined he could influence the course of history with his pen.

During the winter and spring of 1855, Melville composed "Benito Cereno," an indictment of "benign" racism that is one of the masterpieces of his career. His brilliant adaptation of the "ghastly & interesting" *Narrative of Voyages and Travels in the Northern and Southern Hemispheres*, published in 1817 by Captain Amasa Delano, an ancestor of Franklin D. Roosevelt, opens as the captain of an American sealer discerns a mysterious ship that, from afar, resembles a floating monastery. When the Yankee captain boards the ship, he discovers that the strange vessel is a Spanish slaver and that the dark figures who resemble cowled Black Friars, or Dominicans, are actually enslaved Africans. The slaver's captain, a young Spaniard named Don Benito Cereno, tells Delano that most of his crew were wiped out by a plague that also killed the ship's owner, his friend Don Alexandro Aranda, so the Africans have to help with the running of the ship. As Don Benito tells his story to Delano, he faints repeatedly, and his faithful black servant, Babo, supports him with his arm. The "liberal" Delano, a "Massachusetts man" who assumes that Africans are jolly primitives who love bright colors and have a special talent for waiting on white people, constantly compares the "fun-loving" Africans to animals. Boasting that he takes to Negroes "not philanthropically, but genially, just as other men to Newfoundland dogs," he offers to buy Babo from Don Benito by way of complimenting the black for being such an excellent body servant. Despite misgivings prompted by the provocative behavior of several of the remaining Spanish sailors and various other unsettling events, Delano cannot fathom what is really going on aboard the ship.[27]

Melville builds suspense by limiting his third-person narrative to Delano's point of view until the point where Delano himself realizes with a shock that the Africans have taken over the ship and slaughtered most of the whites, and that Babo has woven an elaborate web of deception from the American's own prejudices. By the end of the story, Melville has drawn readers who adopt Delano's view of the *San Dominick* into the same entangling web.

Melville's version of Delano's story differs from the original narrative in a number of ways. He changed the date, and he changed the names of the two ships from the actual *Perseverance* and *Tryal* to the symbolic *Bachelor's Delight* and *San Dominick*. He also invented a number of significant symbols for his fictional adaptation of Delano's narrative: the somnambulistic white noddy, or albatross, in the rigging, a trope for Delano, the white man sleepwalking through history; the ship's shrouded figurehead, covered by a cloth on which someone has scrawled the cryptic words "follow your leader"; the stern-piece showing a "dark satyr in a mask" holding his foot on the neck of a prostrate figure, also masked; the ship's flawed bell, which evokes the cracked Liberty Bell in

Philadelphia; the majestic Atufal, who was a king in Africa, and who appears before the Spanish captain in chains and a padlock each time the bell tolls, to beg his freedom; the straight razor with which Babo shaves Don Benito Cereno, and the flag of Spain with which he wipes the Spaniard's blood from the razor; and, finally, the "Gordian knot" that Captain Delano cannot undo.[28]

In this tough-minded story, Melville indicts slavery without sentimentalizing either the blacks or the whites. He makes it clear that Don Alexandro Aranda's having allowed the Africans to move around the decks unfettered does not change the fact that he considered them his property and planned to reshackle and sell them as soon as the ship reached port. Aranda's leniency in keeping his "cargo" on deck, where fresh air and water would ensure a higher survival rate, can be seen as purely self-serving, since better health meant fewer deaths, and fewer deaths meant more profit for the slaveowner. Moreover, freedom within the confines of a slave ship did not protect the women against rape and sexual abuse; in fact, cleaning them up and letting them roam the deck instead of leaving them crammed in a filthy hold made them more accessible to the lustful crew. After Aranda's death, the women, whom Delano imagines to be as docile and sweet as does with their fawns, shave Aranda's bones clean with their hatchets, then hang his skeleton over the carved figurehead of Cristobal Colón as a warning to the surviving Spaniards, covering it with a cloth when another ship draws near.[29]

Melville deconstructs "niceness" as a moral category at the end of the story; when the Americans board the ship, they restrain themselves from maiming or killing the Africans, not because they are kind, but because they plan to claim the "cargo" and want it to be undamaged. The willingness of the American captain to continue the slave trade parallels the willingness of the "enlightened" Founding Fathers to bring the slavery of the Old World into the New.[30]

After Delano and his men overpower the Africans and take control of the ship, the narrative switches to a legal deposition that purports to establish the "facts" of the case—which, of course, means the Spanish point of view. Failing to grasp Melville's reason for including a dry legal document, *Putnam's* editor George William Curtis assumed that the placing of the deposition at the end of the story was laziness on Melville's part, and he complained that Melville did everything "too hurriedly." The deposition, however, actually frames the story to form a mutilated triptych, with the implied third panel being the "voiceless" Babo's version of the story. The legalistic language obscures the moral issues and nullifies the Africans' point of view, as history written by the colonizers always does.[31]

Ironically, Delano's blindness nearly costs him his life and the life of Don Benito, yet, he learns nothing from his experience or the Spanish captain's ordeal, and less about the sufferings of the blacks. In a coda following the conclusion of the trial, Delano blithely suggests that Don Benito can forget his harrowing ordeal, but the Spaniard remains haunted by the shadow of "the Negro." Like Charles V, the Holy Roman Emperor who ordered the first Africans shipped to Santo Domingo to replace the Indians who had been worked to death by Columbus and his men, Don Benito retires to a monastery. In the end, Babo's point of view comes across wordlessly and lingers in the reader's mind. The story closes with the haunting image of Babo's head, "that hive of subtlety," impaled on a pole in the Plaza by the "civilized" Spaniards. The "unabashed gaze" of Babo stares down the long corridors of history in accusation and defiance, a challenge to a nation heading inexorably toward civil war.[32]

Melville knew the scriptural warning, "Those who sow the wind shall reap the whirlwind." He changed the date of the events described in the story from 1805 to 1799 to evoke memories of the revolution in Santo Domingo and altered the description of Babo so that the Senegalese mastermind resembled Haitian patriot Toussaint-Louverture, president of the first black republic in the New World. *Putnam's,* in fact, had just published a lengthy article about Toussaint that was a slap in the face to southerners for whom the words Santo Domingo conjured memories of the slave rebellions and massacres perpetrated by Nat Turner, Denmark Vesey, and Gabriel Prosser in the 1830s.

By suggesting that the rebel Africans were as patriotic as his own grandfathers, Melville echoes a point made by John Quincy Adams in his defense of the *Amistad* mutineers. In words reminiscent of the Declaration of Independence, the narrator implies that the slaves' objective—to commandeer the ship and sail to Senegal, where they could be free—was morally justified. They had to revolt and kill their owner and most of the Spanish sailors, except those whom they needed to navigate the ship, or they had no hope of regaining the freedom that was their natural right. Thus, Melville's version of Amasa Delano's *Narrative* turns colonial history on its head and reflects the legal dramas of the times.[33]

In May 1854, the case of Anthony Burns nearly tore Boston apart, as it had three years earlier. While Lemuel Shaw was hearing arguments in the Burns case, a great throng assembled outside of Faneuil Hall to hear Wendell Phillips and Theodore Parker urge civil disobedience to force the bailiffs to free the fugitive. The abolitionist editor Thomas Wentworth Higginson and his supporters stormed the jail to release Burns, but the attempt failed for lack of numbers, and a volunteer deputy was shot and killed in the skirmish. Parker, Phillips, and Higginson were all charged with "obstruction of justice," but the case was thrown out on a technicality. When Chief Justice Shaw ordered Burns remanded to the custody of his owner, William Lloyd Garrison burned facsimiles of the United States Constitution, the Fugitive Slave Law, and the court decision.[34]

Like Daniel Webster in 1850, Lemuel Shaw considered preservation of the Union more important than the abolition of slavery because he felt that, despite its flaws, the

Constitution was mankind's best hope for liberty and justice for all, and that slavery would wither away of its own accord. The scorn heaped on Shaw for upholding the wicked statute put Melville in an awkward position. Not wanting to risk a rift with his father-in-law, he expressed his dissent allegorically instead of openly.[35]

Richard Henry Dana was an editor for *Putnam's* around the time "Benito Cereno" was published, and his Boston Vigilance Committee owned a vessel named the *Moby Dick* that was used to transport fugitives from slavery to freedom, so it's not surprising that Melville's stories reflect the controversy over slavery.

"The Bell-Tower," which was written during the summer of 1855, opens with two epigraphs on slavery. This baroque tale with an Italian setting implies that even the most nobly conceived edifice can be destroyed by a fatal flaw, just as the Union could be destroyed by slavery. John Hoadley, who read the story by a dim lamp, found it "wild, mysterious," and "strangely fascinating," and despite his wife's urging him not to spoil his eyes, he refused to put the story aside until he had finished reading it.[36]

Around the time he finished writing "The Bell-Tower," Melville suffered another attack of sciatica, and, according to Lizzie, Dr. Oliver Wendell Holmes came over from neighboring Canoe Meadows and "prescribed for him." The textbooks of the period traced some sciatica attacks to syphilitic infection and recommended as treatment a compound containing arsenic, morphine, opium, ammonia, turpentine, iodide of potassium, tincture of aconite, and belladonna. Like so many popular remedies of the era—for instance, calomel pills, or "blue pills," which were known to contain dangerous amounts of mercury—such remedies often produced side effects more harmful than the disease.[37]

In "I and My Chimney," personal pain becomes an apt metaphor for the agonizing pains that were racking the body politic. This "thoroughly magazinish tale" dramatizes the conflict between an old-fashioned fellow who enjoys sitting by his "huge, corpulent old Harry VIII" of a chimney, and his modern wife, who wants to remove the great central chimney so the house can be remodeled.[38]

Melville's narrator defends his physical space and his psychological integrity by clinging to such mundane manly recreations as smoking his pipe and drinking the prized cordials that he keeps in a closet in the chimney against the intrusions of his energetic wife, his two daughters, and a master mason whom they hire to figure out how to demolish the chimney without toppling the whole house. When the "bustling wife" proposes tearing out the "backbone" of the house to open a passageway, the narrator resists, vowing that "I and My Chimney will never surrender."[39]

Melville's "Chimney" has an intricate political architecture. The story's conflict between the innovative wife and the conservative husband over making internal improvements to their house recalls the internecine warfare between the Democratic "Hunkers" and "Barnburners" over public works in New York State—a dress rehearsal for the devastating battle over the question of extending slavery to the western territories. Melville may well have disguised these topical references to avoid confrontation with his brother Allan, who owed his nomination to the New York State Assembly in 1848 to the Hunker faction.

The old house in the story has features of both Broadhall and Arrowhead; its twelve-by-twelve-foot chimney resembles the huge fireplace at Arrowhead, while the "secret closet" may well have been the apple and potato bins in the cellar of Broadhall, where runaway slaves were supposedly hidden until they could be safely transported to freedom. Locally, to the present day, the cellar at Arrowhead is said to have contained a "slave room," an idea that is not so far-fetched if one considers that the East Street home of Dr. John Brewster, the previous owner of Arrowhead, became an underground railroad station after he moved there. Melville may well have known of such activities through his friend Joseph Smith, who was considered such a radical abolitionist that shortly after hiring him as an editor in 1853, the publishers of the *Pittsfield Sun* forbade him to write political editorials.[40]

In a memoir of Melville published in Pittsfield's *Evening Journal* in 1891, Joseph Smith compared Melville's back troubles to similar ailments suffered by Charles Sumner, perhaps with an image from Sumner's electrifying keynote speech at the Free Soil Convention in mind. Calling for the immediate overthrow of the slave power, Sumner had exhorted the delegates to select a candidate who would meet three requirements: "the first is *back-bone*; the second is *back-bone*; and the third is *back-bone*," a trope for moral conviction and personal integrity also implied by Melville's narrator. For some unknown reason, Lizzie deleted comparisons of Melville with Sumner from a copy of Smith's memoir before passing it on to a young journalist named Arthur Stedman who was contemplating writing a biography of Melville.[41]

Sumner, an ardent abolitionist, had stayed at Melvill House in 1844 while recuperating from an illness, and the authors of the WPA guide to the Berkshires have drawn connections between Sumner's visit and rumors that the house was a safe haven for fugitives. Sumner had little use for temporizers like Judge Shaw, and Shaw considered Sumner brash and tactless, as did many moderates. In 1845, Sumner had riled Shaw by using the traditionally nonpolitical Fourth of July Peace Oration to launch into a tirade against slavery, the Mexican War, and the annexation of Texas and Oregon, so when Sumner applied for a professorship at the Harvard Law School soon afterward, Shaw blackballed him. In 1849, Sumner had represented Benjamin Roberts, a black father who sued the Boston School Board for refusing to allow him to send his daughter to the nearest public school, but he lost the case when Judge Shaw refused to order the school to admit the girl on the grounds that racial differences led to "natural" discrimination and that "natural discrimination" could not be overcome by legislation.[42]

Shaw's ruling in the case of *Roberts v. the Boston Public Schools* paved the way for the Supreme Court's legalization of segregation in 1896, when the Court's ruling in the case of *Plessy v. Ferguson* mandated "separate but equal" schools and public accommodations for black Americans. How Melville, who had criticized segregated schools in *Omoo,* felt about the ruling can only be guessed, but it seems possible that he wrote this somewhat cryptic, multilayered story to express an allegiance to abolition that would have horrified Judge Shaw and many of Melville's relatives on both sides of the debate.[43]

At the height of the agitation over the Sims case in 1851, Richard Henry Dana wrote: "The conduct of the Ch. Justice, his evident disinclinations to act, the frivolous nature of his objections, & his insulting manner to me, have troubled me more than any other manifestation. It shows how deeply seated, so as to effect, unconsciously, I doubt not, good men like him, is this selfish hunkerism of the property interest on the Slave question." Could Meville's narrator represent Judge Shaw?[44]

Readers who mistakenly identify the narrator of "I and My Chimney" with Meville misread his tone and assume the story reveals his dissatisfaction with his marriage rather than with the political factionalism that was paralyzing the nation. In a marginal note on a copy of the manuscript, Lizzie noted that the narrator's wife was based on "his mother— who was very vigorous and energetic—about the farm &c." Obviously, her self-serving notation is no proof of Melville's intention, but it seems perverse to reject her statement out of hand with no evidence to the contrary and equally perverse to treat the story merely as the domestic complaint of a hen-pecked husband. While on one level, the narrator's defense of his "Grand Seigneur" may reflect Melville's attempts to defend his writing from intrusions by oversolicitous family members, especially his mother, on the other hand, it is clearly an allegorical rendering of the crippling sectional conflicts that threatened to plunge the nation into civil war.[45]

In 1851, Richard Henry Dana had feared the United States might intervene in foreign wars or start a phony war to "furnish a pretext for the conquest of Cuba," as the federal government seemed ready to allow American business to turn the entire Caribbean region into a plantation. Even though the slave trade was illegal, between 1845 and 1854, increased demands for slaves to work in the cane fields made clandestine operations highly profitable. Abolitionists protested that workers rarely survived more than five years in these forced labor camps, and Walt Whitman wrote a series of articles listing the names of ships engaged in the illegal trade and calling for congressional action, but nothing was done to put an end to it.[46]

Worse, in 1854, three proslavery Democrats—James Buchanan, John Y. Mason, and Pierre Soulé—were dispatched to Ostend, Belgium, by Secretary of State William Marcy to draw up a secret agreement allowing the United States to take Cuba by force if Spain refused to sell it. When details of the manifesto became public, the press denounced it as a conspiracy to turn Cuba into an American sugar plantation. In 1855, with Franklin Pierce in office, the slaveowners and the jingoes were clamoring for the annexation of Cuba and the extension of slavery into the Caribbean. To Melville, it all seemed like a dangerous replay of the Mexican War, and in "I and My Chimney" he personifies imperialism as a stranger stumbling around in a darkened house and getting lost. The beau of the narrator's daughter leaves the dining room by the wrong door and ends up on the back stairway. He opens another door and finds himself gazing into a yawning cellar, then backs into "a dark pantry." Finally, as he gropes for a way out, he thrusts his "white kids into an open drawer of Havana sugar"—a reference to the Ostend Manifesto and the recent entry of Melville's creditor Tertullus Stewart into the sugar business in New York.[47]

Although the narrator manages to foil his wife's attempts "to abolish the chimney in toto," he ends up a prisoner of the chimney, which was constructed by a kinsman who was a "Borneo pirate." As he thinks of him, "vague flashings of ingots united in my mind with vague gleamings of skulls," linking slavery with piracy and alluding to the retired privateer Elkanah Watson, from whom Melville's grandfather purchased Melvill House in 1816. The narrator cannot leave the house for fear of its destruction, even though "hunkering down" to defend his "Bunker Hill Monument" will not ensure its survival. When he finally does venture out one day, "three savages in blue jeans" throw brickbats at him and drive him back indoors.[48]

Melville's complex symbolism is never merely self-referential. While the emotional energy for the story undoubtedly came from both his physical ailments and his staunch efforts to defend his writing against the assaults of his family, especially his mother, the intellectual energy came from the conflation of his own physical and emotional agony with the nation's agony, especially the bitter controversies over slavery. The narrator's house, with its double flues and warring factions, suggests a "house divided," a common metaphor for sectional conflict even before Abraham Lincoln made the phrase memorable. As the historian Henry Adams wrote when he looked back on this period, the air "reeked" of civil war.[49]

In August 1855, when artist and illustrator Felix Darley and Treasury Department employee Maunsell Field drove up from Stockbridge to call on Melville and Holmes, they found Melville in a mellow mood. As he walked his visitors around the yard, Melville proudly pointed to his "superb trees" and told them "he spent much time there *patting them upon the back.*" Together, they strolled over to Holmesdale, where he and

Dr. Holmes launched into a discussion of "East India religions and mythologies" conducted with such "skill and brilliancy on both sides" that Darley and Field lost track of the time and forgot to go to dinner.[50]

Like many well-read New Englanders of his day, Melville was attracted to Eastern religions. Although he rejected both his mother's Calvinism and his father's Unitarianism, he was a deeply spiritual man. He attended church voluntarily on occasion, and he lamented the collapse of a central core of religious faith as much as he dreaded religious fanaticism and repressive orthodoxy. Despite his quarrels with organized religion, Melville feared that democracy could not survive in a society devoid of moral and spiritual values. The determination and drive that made America a dynamic, progressive nation had a dark side, as the rise in violent crimes in the cities and on the raw edges of the frontier was destroying people's trust in one another and their confidence in the very idea of community.

In "The Apple-Tree Table: or, Original Spiritual Manifestations," Melville pokes fun at spiritualism and other fads that purport to provide material evidence of religious truths. The story is a comical adaptation of the anecdote about the bugs hatching from the old table, which Melville had read when he first moved to the Berkshires and which Thoreau had retold in *Walden*. The narrator clings to the worm-eaten old table on which he keeps a copy of Cotton Mather's *Magnalia Christi Americana*, representing the old Puritan religion, and his wife and daughters berate him for believing religious superstitions. One day, however, eggs that had lain dormant for 150 years suddenly hatch, and insects emerge from the pockmarked wood, forcing the skeptical women to believe in the Resurrection.[51]

The story was written at an odd time in Melville's life. He was not feeling well, and although he was enjoying success as a magazine writer, he was beginning to feel he was reaching a dead end creatively. In August 1855, the state Insane Asylum Commission sent a delegation to the Berkshires to locate a site for a new asylum, and they chose Arrowhead as one of the prospective sites, which must have amused Melville. Their visit came at an opportune time, because he was more determined than ever to sell the farm, so, as he took the commissioners on a tour of the grounds, he was hopeful they might choose Arrowhead. Disappointed by their choice of another site, he began making notes for a novel designed to satirize the absurd and venal aspects of American society.[52]

When Sarah Morewood invited the Melvilles to a September costume ball, Herman was still too stiff and sore from the effects of sciatica to feel like dressing up and dancing, but he couldn't resist escorting the women and children to the party. Mrs. Morewood's sister, Mrs. Ellen Brittain, came dressed as a squaw, and Lizzie wore a "costume of cyphers," which won her the prize for the most imaginative costume and prompted "Uncle Joe" Smith, who was robed as a "Friar in orders grey," to pun that her costume "did nothing well." Armed with sword and buckler, and bearing on his belt the inscription "I am the gallant Cornishman/Who slew the giant Cormogan," young Malcolm marched around impersonating Jack the Giant-Killer. As Melville stood undisguised on the sidelines watching the costumed dancers whirl around the floor, he was gathering images and ideas for future books. "Life is a pic-nic *en costume.* One must take a part, assume a character, stand ready in a sensible way to play the fool. To come in plain clothes, with a long face, as a wiseacre, only makes one a discomfort to himself, and a blot on the scene," he would later write of his wallflower status.[53]

A few days later, Melville took his mother on "a few days jaunt" to Saratoga and Glens Falls, visiting Herman Gansevoort, whose wife was critically ill, on the way back. Herman left his mother at her brother's house and returned to Arrowhead. When Catherine Gansevoort passed away at the end of October, Herman took Augusta and Fanny back to Gansevoort for the funeral and left them there to help their mother while he went home. Meanwhile, the Shaws were visiting Lizzie. Lemuel and Hope Shaw doted on their "bright & noisy" grandchildren, and when the judge began making a kite for Malcolm, his wife predicted that it "would be larger than Lizzy & her four children all together."[54]

That fall, winter arrived early. On September 24, Melville drove through fierce snow squalls to visit his cousin Priscilla, who had established herself in Pittsfield as an expert on "EMBROIDERY and the making of the nicer articles pertaining to Ladies', Gentlemen's, or Children's wardrobes." Although sewing was a perfectly respectable job, it was not an easy one, as a seamstress worked fifteen to eighteen hours a day to make one fine linen shirt and received only 25 cents for it or, on average, $1.50 a week, and Melville was very protective of his unmarried cousin.[55]

At around this time, Melville was writing a novel satirizing the go-getting spirit of the age, and he wrote publisher Joshua Dix about it, asking for an advance. Dix turned him down because his partner George Curtis had told him to "decline any novel from Melville that is not extremely good," but when Melville suggested a collection of his *Putnam's* stories in book form, Curtis agreed. "I don't think Melville's book will sell a great deal, but he is a good name upon your list," he told Dix. "He has lost his prestige,— & I don't believe the Putnam stories will bring it up. But I suppose you can't lose by it. *I* like the Encantadas, and Bartleby, very much."[56]

Melville sent both stories, along with "Benito Cereno," "The Bell-Tower," and "The Lightning-Rod Man," to Dix & Edwards along with a new title story, and in May 1856, *The Piazza Tales* was published in America and, soon afterward, in England. Plagued by financial troubles, Melville hoped that readers who had enjoyed the stories in *Putnam's* would want to purchase the collection and that those who had missed their chance to read them in the magazine would buy them in book form.[57]

"The Piazza," an introductory sketch to the volume, started out as a genial ramble around his house, on the order of Hawthorne's "The Old Manse." Dissatisfied with his lot, the story's protagonist imagines that the tantalizing "spot of radiance" on a neighboring mountain emanates from the home of a radiant person, and longing to meet this glamorous individual, he hikes to the cottage, where he finds a lonely, unhappy girl named Marianna living in a bare room littered with dead wasps. She has one wish: to descend and see the happy person who lives in the shimmering "white" house at which she gazes through her fly-specked window. When the narrator realizes that he and his rundown farmhouse have been the objects of Marianna's fantasies just as much as she has been the object of his own, he takes his leave, chastened by the realization that all idealism is an illusion.

The Piazza Tales garnered three dozen notices, many of which echo the early reviews of *Typee* and *Omoo*. They all emphasize Melville's "peculiar richness of language, descriptive vitality, and splendidly sombre imagination," as well as his customary "boldness of invention, brilliancy of imagination, and quaintness of expression," rather than his subtle social commentary. *Godey's Lady's Book*, to which Lizzie subscribed, criticized Melville's style for "an affectation of quaintness, which renders it, to us, very confused and wearisome," but other reviewers saw the stories as a sign that Melville had recovered "much of his former freshness and vivacity" after his "unfortunate" performance in *Pierre*. When *The Piazza Tales* appeared in book form, his old shipmate Richard Tobias Greene wrote from Sandusky, New York, to say that "The Encantadas" had "called up reminiscences of days gone by" and that his two-year-old son "glories in the name of 'Herman Melville.'"[58]

Despite its favorable reception, *The Piazza Tales* did not sell well. Even though the *American Publisher's Circular* reported that the stories Melville had published in *Putnam's* "were, in no small degree, instrumental in raising that journal to its present proud position—the best of all American monthlies," Melville's name alone did not have the drawing power of *Putnam's Magazine*. Thus, once again, he found himself looking into the triple gulf fixed between the quality of his writing, its reception by the public, and the publisher's balance sheet. Books needed larger audiences than magazines did to make a profit, and Melville's volume recouped only $628.20 of the $1,048.62 spent to produce 2,500 copies. Melville had also lost his best venue for short fiction, as *Putnam's* was now in receivership.[59]

All through June and into the month of July 1856, Melville worked on a novel that family members referred to as "Herman's new book." Lem Shaw apparently did not even know its title when he wrote his brother Sam, "I believe [Herman] is now preparing another book for the press; of which Augusta is making the fair copy for the printer & which will be published before long. I know nothing about it; but I have no great confidence in the success of his productions." Ironically, the next novel Melville wrote was called *The Confidence-Man: His Masquerade*, and it was so difficult to follow and so cynical that its annihilation in the marketplace was virtually guaranteed.[60]

The Herman Melville children, from left to right, Stanwix, Frances, Malcolm, and Elizabeth,
grew up on a farm in the Berkshire hills of Massachusetts.

NINETEEN

WHAT SORT OF BAMBOOZLING STORY IS THIS?

In late April of 1855, several eastern newspapers, including the Albany Evening Journal, *reported that the notorious "William Thompson" was up to his tricks again. If Melville happened to see the story, he probably remembered "Thompson" as the fellow who had used half a dozen aliases to swindle hundreds of people before he was arrested in New York in April 1849, and incarcerated in the Tombs. When a local journalist referred to Thompson as a "confidence-man," the phrase entered common parlance. Four months later the* New York Tribune *identified one "Julius Alexander Byron" as "The Confidence Man No. 2," and Burton's Theatre on Chambers Street celebrated the emergence of this new folk hero by presenting a farce entitled "The Confidence Man."*[1]

All over America, cynical opportunists pushing "free enterprise" to the limit were hustling their gullible countrymen with ingenious get-rich-quick schemes. The burgeoning towns and cities provided these sharpers with anonymity, and on the ever-changing frontier, they could cheat their neighbors and move on. While preachers and pundits pontificated that the exploits of the confidence man "Thompson" were evidence of America's moral decline and his capture proof that good always triumphs over evil, Evert Duyckinck surprised his friends by commenting that it was "not the worst thing that can be said of a country that it gives birth to a confidence man."[2]

In a fluid, acquisitive society, it was hard to tell the difference between legitimate business practices and America's national pastime: the confidence game. As many commentators pointed out, the most common confidence schemes mirrored the daily dealings of powerful businessmen and politicians, who could get away with major crimes while petty criminals had the book thrown at them. Implying that the righteous indignation of the establishment was hypocritical and self-serving, George Houston, the congressional reporter for the *Knickerbocker News*, brought his article on William Thompson to a sarcastic close: "Let him rot then in the 'Tombs,' while the Confidence Man on a large scale fattens, in his palace, on the blood and sweat of the green ones of the land!... Long life to the real 'Confidence Man'–the 'Confidence Man' of Wall Street–the 'Confidence Man' of the palace up town–the 'Confidence Man' who battens and fattens on the plunder coming from the poor man and the man of moderate means! As for the 'Confidence Man' of the Tombs, he is a cheat, a humbug, a delusion, a sham, a mockery! Let him rot!"[3]

It wasn't long before analogies between domestic criminality and foreign adventurism were commonplace, especially given America's growing involvement in hemispheric politics. In 1856, New York's *Weekly Times* denounced the Pierce administration for recognizing the phony regime of William Walker, an American soldier of fortune who invaded Nicaragua with a small army of mercenaries and declared himself that country's president. Branding Walker's coup as an attempt to turn Nicaragua into an American plantation, the paper's editor pointed out that Walker had tried to take Baja California and Sonora from Mexico two years earlier.[4]

With newspapers full of stories about slick operators like Thompson and Walker, it's not surprising that Melville would write a novel whose protagonist turns out to be a shape-shifting sharper on a Mississippi River steamboat traveling from the Missouri Territory toward the southern states. *The Confidence-Man: His Masquerade* owes its genesis to the merging of an unpublished manuscript fragment based on Melville's western trip with a group of stories intended for serialization in *Putnam's Magazine*. As these very different works merged into a connected narrative, Melville shifted away from the original western travelogue to urban dialogues and stories, borrowing humorous chapter headings such as "Chapter 14: Worth the consideration of those to whom it may prove worth considering" from his friend Nathaniel Parker Willis's series of sketches on New York life entitled *Hurry-Graphs*.

The magisterial tone of the fragment known as "The River" indicates that Melville may have intended to write an epic of the Mississippi that would rival his great epic of the sea. He describes how, as the Mississippi journeys from the "wild rice lakes" of Minnesota through the "beautiful prairies" of Missouri and Illinois, it imparts a "feeling of sublimity" to the observer, and Melville joins painters such as Thomas Cole and Asher Durand in praising the American landscape for its spiritual grandeur. By the time he wrote *The Confidence-Man*, however, America seemed more an "unweeded garden" than an earthly paradise; the pastoral vision of America survived more in picture postcards and stereoscopic pictures than in actuality.[5]

More grotesque than picturesque, this dark, satirical novel takes readers into the "heart of darkness" that beats in the jungles of America. The novel's setting is the steamboat *Fidèle,* whose "great white bulk" resembles "some whitewashed fort on a floating isle," perhaps Fort Gansevoort, the old "white fort" in New York Harbor that became obsolete after the War of 1812. Like Lima, Peru, the "whitewashed" city of corruption in *Moby-Dick,* the world of *The Confidence-Man* is a world of "whited sepulchres"—that is, people whose virtuous appearances conceal a rotten core, and institutions whose benevolent intentions cover up their malevolent practices. Like the slaver *San Dominick,* the *Fidèle's* appearance is deceptive, and like the frigate *Neversink,* she is a floating city with passengers as diverse as "Chaucer's Canterbury pilgrims, or those oriental ones crossing the Red Sea towards Mecca in the festival month."[6]

As the *Fidèle* steams away from the dock, the natural landscape recedes, and a motley crew of human beings takes center stage, plunging the reader into a disorienting world of shifting identities. They are "a piebald parliament, an Anarcharsis Cloots congress of all kinds of that multiform pilgrim species, man" whose "Tartar-like picturesqueness; a sort of pagan abandonment and assurance," represents "the dashing and all-fusing spirit of the West, whose type is the Mississippi itself, which, uniting the streams of the most distant and opposite zones, pours them along, helter-skelter, in one cosmopolitan and confident tide." These "natives of all sorts and foreigners; men of business and men of pleasure; parlor men and backwoodsmen" are all hunters: "farm-hunters and fame-hunters; heiress-hunters, gold-hunters, buffalo-hunters, bee-hunters, happiness-hunters, truth-hunters, and still keener hunters after all these hunters." They are the avatars of a materialistic society that turns human beings into commodities, and virtues and vices into counters in a cynical bunco game.[7]

The novel's action commences abruptly at sunrise on April Fool's Day, when "there appeared, suddenly as Manco Capac at the Lake Titicaca, a man in cream colors, at the water-side in the city of St. Louis." This mysterious stranger, who is "preternaturally white, from his fair cheek, downy chin and flaxen hair to his white fur hat with long fleecy nap," boards the riverboat "unaccompanied by friends" and carrying "neither trunk, valise, carpet-bag, nor parcel." He stations himself on deck just below a placard offering a reward for the capture of "a mysterious imposter, supposed to have recently arrived from the East." This "lamb-like man," who may or may not be the impostor mentioned in the poster, takes out a small slate and writes, "Charity . . . thinketh no evil . . . suffereth long, and is kind . . . endureth all things . . . believeth all things . . . never faileth," erasing each phrase and adding another after the key word *Charity*. Nearby, the ship's barber, William Cream, can be seen posting a sign that reads "NO TRUST" outside his shop.[8]

In this topsy-turvy world, crooks have more credibility than prophets. After the white mute mysteriously disappears, a "grotesque negro cripple, in tow-cloth attire" just as mysteriously appears and kneels on the deck, his mouth open wide so passersby will toss coins into it as they might toss balls or beanbags into the mouth of a cardboard cutout in an amusement park. He identifies himself as "Black Guinea," a "dog without massa," and while a few people accuse him of being a white man in disguise, most distrust him because of his skin color. They all bully and mistreat him, and, after announcing a list that includes some, but not all, of the various confidence men who follow him, he shuffles away, leaving them to debate his identity.[9]

Melville was acutely aware that skin color determined a person's destiny in America. In 1856, the "land of the free" contained within its constantly expanding, constantly contested borders both Indians who had been driven from their ancestral lands and a captive nation of four million enslaved and one-half million free Africans. While shipping companies and cotton barons called this infamous business "free enterprise," abolitionists called it kidnapping and piracy. On these semantic differences hung the lives of millions of human beings and the integrity of the federal Union.[10]

Most of the patriots of the revolutionary generation, from George Washington and Thomas Jefferson to Melville's great-uncle and his maternal grandfather, were slaveholders. The "hero of Fort Stanwix" owned several slaves, including one named "Sambo," and a "Negro wench" named Jude, with "her two children." On May 30, 1793, Leonard Gansevoort bought from one Simon Ridder a mulatto slave named Tom, and in 1796 he sold to Abraham A. Lansing a Negro man named Peter, who was about twenty-two years old, and bought a Negro slave named Caesar. In 1812 he manumitted his faithful slave Chloe, a woman under fifty whom he deemed capable of caring for herself if she were freed. If even the Founding Fathers were involved in the buying and selling of human beings, it seemed evident to Melville that racism and greed had swindled Americans out of rights promised by the Declaration of Independence.[11]

In 1835, Alexis de Tocqueville observed that

> All the Indian tribes who once inhabited the territory of New England—the
> Narragansetts, the Mohicans, the Pequots—now live only in men's memories;
> the Lenapes, who received Penn one hundred and fifty years ago on the banks

of the Delaware, have now vanished. I have met the last of the Iroquois; they were begging. All of the nations I have just named once reached to the shores of the ocean; now one must go more than a hundred leagues inland to meet an Indian. These savages have not just drawn back, they have been destroyed.

That same year, United States troops destroyed the highly developed Seminole civilization in Florida, massacring the men and boys and driving the surviving old men and the women and small children from their sacred ancestral lands to "reservations" located on remote, inhospitable, barren land far to the north. Shortly afterward, the United States Army drove the surviving members of the Cherokee Nation from their homes and forced them to undertake a long march to the Indian Territory (now Oklahoma) that came to be known as the "Trail of Tears." Four thousand people died of diphtheria, measles, whooping cough, and grief along the way, but President Martin Van Buren assured Congress that the "happiest effects" had been produced by giving the Cherokees "new homes" west of the Mississippi.[12]

In a chapter of *The Confidence-Man* titled "The Metaphysics of Indian-Hating," Melville turns James Hall's influential *Sketches of History, Life, and Manners, in the West* (Philadelphia, 1835) inside out, deliberately contradicting Hall's portrait of Colonel John Moredock. Melville portrays Moredock, the sole survivor of an Indian massacre, not as a hero, but as a righteous avenger hell-bent on exterminating the red "gangs of Cain" who murdered his wife and children. Like the modern Rambo, the Indian-hater is a true believer and a perfect patriot; he is also a merciless killer and a cold-blooded racist like Davy Crockett, who, in some versions of the tall tale, shot stray Indians and Mexicans for target practice. Melville shows that the glamorization of Indian-fighting leads logically to genocide.[13]

Everyone on Melville's riverboat is trying to sell something: shares in a comprehensive "World Charity," stock in the "Black Rapids Coal Company," lots in a real-estate development called "The New Jerusalem," patent medicines and elixirs like the "Omni-Balsamic Reinvigorator" and the "Samaritan Pain Dissuader," and miraculous inventions such as the "Protean easy-chair." Altruists raise money for Christian missions and charities such as the "Seminole Widows and Orphans Society," and a man with a brass plate, who claims to be an agent for the "Philosophical Intelligence Office," persuades a backwoods bachelor from Missouri to buy a rehabilitated juvenile delinquent to help him with his chores, even though the backwoodsman dislikes and distrusts boys and will undoubtedly abuse them.

Stories within stories, schemes within schemes, *The Confidence-Man* is a funhouse whose mirrors reveal human character as inconsistent, unscrupulous, and unreliable. Interpolated tales like the story of the harpy Goneril, Charlemont's story of the gentleman-madman, and Charlie Arnold Noble's story of China Aster, a poor maker of sper-maceti candles, whose life and the lives of his wife and children are ruined by a loan from his friend Orchis, who has won the lottery, dramatize the ways by which people are corrupted by the love of money. Melville's caustic satire spares no one, from Methodist ministers and charitable ladies to herb doctors and bonesetters who try to convince everyone that their competitors are quacks and humbugs.

In the world of *The Confidence-Man*, nothing is certain, nothing is unequivocally true; everything is ambiguous and confusing. Is the Confidence-Man one or many? Are the "man in cream colors" and Black Guinea manifestations of a single confidence man, or are they annunciatory figures like the angel Gabriel and John the Baptist? How does anyone know which strangers can be trusted, which cannot? P. T. Barnum once exhibited a man who claimed he had changed himself from Negro to Caucasian by chewing on a certain medicinal weed. Barnum's outrageous flummery richly exemplifies the spirit of a time when clowns and criminals could be easily confused. Like Allan Melvill, Barnum died declaring bankruptcy, his hoaxes a funhouse mirror of the business and political world.

The Confidence-Man is a tour de force of topical satire and teleological razzle-dazzle; its convoluted scenes are as intricately choreographed as a minuet or a saraband. Fiercely dialogic, sharply cerebral, sardonic, and controlled, it is the least personal and least emotionally accessible of Melville's books. Scholars have variously identified the book's characters with contemporary figures ranging from Henry Ward Beecher, Horace Greeley, Thomas Hart Benton, and Fanny Kemble to Emerson, Thoreau, Hawthorne, and Poe, not to mention Melville himself. His great achievement lay in his ability to subsume topical satire in a work of literature that would endure after the public figures who inspired the characters and caricatures were long gone. Blurring the distinctions between reformers and swindlers, crooks and congressmen, he exposes the underlying similarity of their methods.

After 1837, when poverty became a persistent problem in the "land of plenty," reform movements began springing up all over the country. Churchgoing wives of wealthy businessmen threw themselves wholeheartedly into charitable projects designed to relieve the suffering of people whom their husbands had reduced to penury by perfectly legitimate business practices. European visitors, such as Charles Dickens, who satirized hypocritical do-gooders in his *American Notes* and in his novel *Martin Chuzzlewit,* found this strange alliance among business, religion, and the reforming spirit to be peculiarly American.

While Melville was growing up in New York, orphans and children abandoned by parents too poor or too drunk to care for them roamed the streets in gangs, begging and stealing to buy alcohol and food. Vagrant youth became so numerous in lower

Manhattan in 1825 that the same men who had organized the Free School Society of New York to provide "for the education of poor children, who do not belong to or are not provided for by any religious society" also established The New York House of Refuge, the first reform school in America. Both schools followed a Lancastrian model that was even more strict than the regime followed by the New-York Male High School, which Herman and Gansevoort Melville attended in the 1820s. After being subjected to militaristic regimentation for about a year and a half, children at the House of Refuge were pronounced reformed and returned to family and friends, sent out as indentured sailors or tradesmen, or put to work as hired hands on western farms.[14]

The reform movement had its undeniable dark side. Orators congratulated the nation on the growing number of hospitals, temperance societies, prisons, insane asylums, homes for the aged, and reform schools, but failed to notice that America was spawning more and more invalids, alcoholics, lunatics, unwanted children, homeless people, and desperate criminals. To Melville, every new charitable institution was proof that poverty and injustice were on the rise.[15]

When Herman Melville's home state was the western boundary of "civilized" America and everything beyond it was a state of mind known as "the frontier," the fur trade flourished. By enlisting the help of native trappers like the Mohawks and Iroquois, who had been driven into the wilderness by the incursions of the white man, the French, who could trade goods worth one *livre* in Paris for pelts worth two hundred *livres*, built an enormous trading empire in the New World before 1715. Whites often defied local ordinances to give the Indians guns, ostensibly to protect themselves against rival tribes, but actually in order to secure their allegiance in driving out interlopers from other "civilized" nations who were trying to displace them.[16]

Fort Orange, the Dutch settlement that became Albany, was the hub of the bustling fur trade and lumbering industry because of its location on the eastern edge of the wilderness, upriver from the Port of New York. Unlike the French, who sought political empire, the Dutch sought economic control. They believed peaceful coexistence with the Indians was sound business policy, and in the early days, settlers like Henry Quackenboss entertained trappers and traders such as the great Sachem Hendrick in their homes.

European colonialization radically transformed North America. Europeans called the continent "unpeopled" and seized it for themselves. From the Puritan point of view, America was the battleground for a preordained Holy War between Christian civilization and Satanic savagery. The settlers saw New England as a "desolate and howling wilderness" whose inhabitants were "vultures of hell." Believing they were the "people of God" sent into "the Devil's territories," the settlers made war on the natives, treating them as subhuman unless they converted to Christianity and agreed to be baptized. King Philip's War in 1676 virtually wiped out tribes that had lived in the eastern woodlands for generations, and by 1700 the estimated 70,000–100,000 Indians living in the northeastern corner of the continent in 1600 had, in effect, been replaced by Europeans. By 1751, the year of Thomas Melvill's birth, only 1,681 of the aboriginal inhabitants of Massachusetts remained alive, 37 of them in Boston proper. Few tribal artisans ventured into the city anymore to sell their wares, as most local tribespeople had either been exterminated or driven deep into the forest.[17]

Once the colonists had stripped the Indians of their natural rights and their ancient tribal lands, they began the process of appropriating to themselves the signs and symbols of the people whom they had destroyed. They used guerrilla warfare against the British and put images of Indians and bison on everything from cornmeal sacks to coins. Thus, Thomas Melvill and his patriot band disguised themselves as "Mohawks," and Peter Gansevoort claimed that the drum his father had captured from the British beat "in unison with the war-whoop and yell of the merciless savage."[18]

For a portion of his youth, Thomas Melvill lived with his great-uncle James Cargill, who became a confirmed Indian-hater when the family of his cousin Mary Whitten was slaughtered by Indians right before her eyes. Famous for the unusual ferocity with which he fought the "savages" during the French and Indian Wars, Cargill boasted about the number of scalps he had taken during his career. Melville's grandfather lived with a real Indian-hater for a while when he was a boy, and his father knew a survivor of frontier violence firsthand when Mary Whitten, or "Aunt Polly" as she came to be called, joined the Melvill family circle in Boston during Allan Melvill's youth.[19]

While Melville was writing *The Confidence-Man*, Guert Gansevoort was given the command of the U.S. sloop-of-war *Decatur*, even though he had a propensity to drink on duty. His mission was to defend the Seattle territory against the "incursions" of its two thousand native inhabitants, and before he was relieved of his command for being intoxicated while on duty later in the year, he managed to earn a commendation from the Secretary of the Navy for his role in clearing the Indians out of the Northwest. All this was enough to make a thinking person such as Melville suspect that the "march of civilization" was not a noble humanitarian enterprise, but a cynical confidence game.[20]

～

"What does it profit a man to gain the world," the Holy Scripture asks, "if he loses his immortal soul?" Melville, for whom the Shakespearean language of the King James Bible was a second pulse, did not confuse Adam Smith with Jesus Christ. No man could serve both God and Mammon, although poor Allan Melvill had tried. Melville probably saw his father's letters at some point in his life, as it was the custom for widows to inspire their sons to live up to the example of their fathers by sharing the paternal Word with them. Read in the light of his eventual downfall and disgrace, Allan Melvill's litany of confidence in himself, his business, and his GOD has sinister undertones. Ironies that escaped Maria Melville, however, were troubling to her son. His father had turned mercantilism into a religion, and his betrayal of his ideals was horrifying. Had his death come as a punishment for his sins?[21]

Allan Melvill was the incarnation of the spirit of the age ushered in by Benjamin Franklin, the wily prophet of the secular religion known as capitalism. Writers of advice manuals, guides to success, mercantile journals, and biographies of businessmen conflated moral principles with sound business practice. William Alcott, for example, the author of *The Young Man's Guide*, espoused trust in one's fellow man as essential to success, while Freeman Hunt, the editor of a merchants' magazine and author of two guides to mercantile philosophy, regarded commerce as "the offspring of God." Contemporary exponents of capitalism, whether essayists or writers of sentimental parables, wanted to convince their readers that hard work and sacrifice would pay off in both this world and the next.[22]

To Melville it seemed that the nation's moral fiber was unraveling and that the body politic had contracted a degenerative disease, so it's not surprising that *The Confidence-Man*, the last work of prose fiction he published in his lifetime, ends in disillusionment and despair. In the novel's last scene, the "parti-hued" Cosmopolitan, Frank Goodman, enters his stateroom and finds an old man, dressed in flowing robes, squatting on a stool; he is holding a Bible and mumbling "apocrypha" and "apocalypse" to himself as a lamp revolves above him, casting eerie shadows on a horned altar. Goodman asks him how he knows that what the Bible says is true, and the old man assures him that his "Counterfeit Detector" warns him against false prophecies and frauds, but when Goodman reminds him that the Bible says "Jehovah shall be thy confidence," the old man discards his lie detector and leaves the room holding on to his money belt and his chamber pot, which the Cosmopolitan has managed to make him believe is a life preserver. As he extinguishes the lamp, the flames of the altar glow halolike on his wrinkled brow. The cryptic conclusion, "Something further may follow of this Masquerade," has led many to believe that Melville intended to write a sequel to, or continuation of, this narrative, but he never did.[23]

Originally "Dedicated to victims of Auto da Fé"—alluding to the Inquistion's burning of heretics at the stake—the novel plays with heretical ideas about politics, religion, and the art of fiction. The Cosmopolitan has been identified with God, with Vishnu, and with Buddha, P. T. Barnum, Uncle Sam, and Satan. He has been compared to the Deity worshiped by the Orphite sect of Gnostic Christians. The God of *The Confidence-Man* is a cousin of Emily Dickinson's "Mighty Merchant" and Mark Twain's "Mysterious Stranger," a precursor of modern tricksters like Ralph Ellison's Rinehart and John

Fowles's magus. Could God be one of Satan's disguises, or could God and the Devil be two faces of one capricious Deity?[24]

Unlike the "revolving Drummond light" in Barnum's American Museum that "ray[s] away from itself all round it" until "everything is lit by it," *The Confidence-Man* casts shadows everywhere. Balancing his narrative on the knife-edge between reality and appearance, Melville explored what he called "the mystery of human subjectivity" and the nature of fiction itself. The characters in *The Confidence-Man* are not the fictively believable people created by novelists and playwrights to satisfy the demands of readers and critics; they are "such inconsistent characters as nature herself" creates. Challenging popular notions of the novelist's art, the narrator asks, "Is it not a fact that, in real life, a consistent character is a rara avis?"[25]

Melville, like the Confidence-Man, was "quite an original." On the one hand, he was a creative genius whose vision transcended the purely personal; on the other, he was still an orphaned son who longed for his father's approval and his mother's unconditional love and affection. At times, self-doubt and insecurity interfered with his efforts to love himself and others; at other times he erupted with the unquenchable anger of a child, venting his frustrations on those who loved him most and were most vulnerable, Lizzie and the children.[26]

Torn between the authoritarianism of his father's generation and the new generation's belief that loving guidance produced cheerful obedience, Melville was dangerously inconsistent with his children. When they were entertaining and did not challenge his authority, he could be affectionate and indulgent, but when they made demands or asserted their own wills, he could be emotionally withholding and tyrannical. Prone to baffling contradictions and dramatic mood swings, he could be sociable and high-spirited in public, then moody and irascible at home.[27]

When Melville was cooped up in his study writing, or trying to relax with his family after hours spent at his desk, he often could not let go of tension, and the stress tightened his muscles painfully. When he was socializing with men friends who drank right along with him, the pain subsided. At the height of his sciatica attacks in the early winter of 1855, for example, he attended a literary party in honor of William Makepeace Thackeray in Evert Duyckinck's famous "cellar," and apparently no one at this convivial gathering noticed that he was not well.

Some family members blamed Herman's moodiness and poor health on his writing, which was a convenient way of denying his growing dependence on alcohol. Although at this remove and with so little evidence, it's difficult to determine how much Melville drank, it seems certain that during the mid-1850s he came to rely on alcohol for relief of his physical pain and emotional distress. In our day he would almost certainly be diagnosed as manic-depressive and put on medication. His use of alcohol as a muscle relaxant and painkiller probably increased his propensity to indulge, thus exacerbating the highs and lows to which he was subject, and deepening his depression. As Melville's drinking grew worse, his moods became more unpredictable and dangerous, and even if Lizzie and his mother and sisters did not nag him openly, he must have sensed their anxiety and resented it.[28]

The family lived comfortably and had some household help, but Melville never felt secure because he was not self-supporting and had to rely on the generosity of Lemuel Shaw, who put Arrowhead in trust for Lizzie. Some records show that the Melvilles had approximately $8,000 in the bank at around this time, including a nest egg of $1,000 and stocks worth over $5,000, but early loss had instilled in Herman a fear of losing everything suddenly, creating a sense of powerlessness that made him feel impoverished regardless of his actual material assets. In any case, money was tight in 1856, and the Melvilles were feeling the pinch. Although magazine earnings erased most of his publishing debt, Melville's royalty statement from Dix & Edwards showed that *The Piazza Tales* had not yet made expenses, which did not bode well for his new book.[29]

On his thirty-seventh birthday, Melville went to Gansevoort, taking a copy of *The Piazza Tales* with him. While he was there, he and Allan made an "excursion of pleasure" to Lake George with Allan's former law partner, Daniel Shepherd, whose new novel, *Saratoga, a Tale of 1787*, included a stirring description of the defense of Fort Schuyler by Melville's grandfather. After spending time with his uncle and mother, Melville went home through Albany so he could pay a call on Peter Gansevoort, who urged him to bring the family back the following week for a meeting of the American Association for the Advancement of Science. Melville became so preoccupied with his own affairs once he arrived home that he promptly forgot about the invitation, and his uncle, who had "reserved the whole house for you, Lizzie & the children," was miffed.[30]

Melville had his mind on finishing *The Confidence-Man* so he could take it with him to New York. Augusta was preparing one copy of the manuscript for Dix & Edwards, and another for Melville to take to England, and he was so busy proofreading and making corrections that he declined the "kind invitation" from "the ever-excellent & beautiful Lady of Paradise—slip of the pen—of Broadhall, I mean" to attend her second costume ball. Augusta, however, put down her copyist's quill to adorn herself in a fanciful gown of flowers, and Bessie went to the party as a three-year-old Bo-Peep. Lizzie, who fashioned a dress of leaves and put nests in her hair to impersonate "the Genius of Greylock," drew praise from the *Berkshire County Eagle* for her "original and unique" costume.[31]

The strain of trying to finish his book took a great deal out of Melville, and he was prone to what Sam Savage, in a letter to his aunt and uncle from Guatemala, called "ugly attacks." Sam wrote sympathetically that "Lizzy no doubt alone has had many of life's real trials to conflict with, but she's one of those who bear up well, & it shows her character—Herman I hope has had no more of those ugly attacks. Kind remembrances to them." The attacks Sam mentions may well refer to the bouts of rheumatism and sciatica that plagued Melville, but if the persistent rumors that he occasionally lost control of his temper and struck Lizzie are true, the phrase may have had a double meaning that was understood only within the family.[32]

Whatever the case, by the end of August, Lizzie feared Herman was on the verge of a nervous collapse. Family and friends were urging him to move to New York or Brooklyn, and Judge Shaw was concerned. "I suppose you have been informed by some of the family," he wrote Sam, "how very ill Herman has been. It is manifest to me from Elizabeth's letters, that she has felt great anxiety about him. When he is deeply engaged in one of his literary works, he confines him[self] to hard study many hours in the day, with little or no exercise, & this specially in winter for a great many days together. He probably thus overworks himself & brings on severe nervous affections." Shaw, perhaps realizing it was futile for Lizzie to try to reason with her husband when he was in such a state, advanced him $1,500 from Lizzie's inheritance so he could spend "four or five months" traveling in Europe and the Holy Land.[33]

On September 27, Melville said good-bye to Lizzie and Malcolm and the girls and took Stanwix to Gansevoort to stay with his grandmother and his aunts, Fanny and Kate, then went to New York to hammer out an agreement with Dix & Edwards. While he was in the city, he met with Evert Duyckinck, who noted in his diary that Melville had blown in "fresh from his mountain charged to the muzzle with his sailor metaphysics and jargon of things unknowable." They spent a "good stirring evening" together, "ploughing deep and bringing to the surface some rich fruits of thought and experience" over brandy and cigars, and once again Duyckinck was treated to a glimpse of Melville's amazing erudition and freewheeling mind. Now that his breach with Duyckinck was healed, he could relax and enjoy the literary gossip, racy stories, and political debates that were standard fare at Clinton Place. Their conversation ranged from admiring references to Robert Burton's atheistical ironies to pungent retellings of a tale from the *Decameron* and an anecdote about a judge who spied on a prayer meeting of female convicts at Sing-Sing and reported that it was "an orgie of blasphemy and indecency."[34]

Meanwhile, Lizzie and Augusta were busy closing up Arrowhead. Cousin Priscilla came over to lend a hand and found Lizzie "up to her eyes in business, hastening, as much as possible, the preparations for her departure—her *out-of-door* affairs detain her now." Once the housework was done, Lizzie took the girls to stay with her parents in Boston, leaving Malcolm at Longwood with the Griggses, while Augusta went to Gansevoort to take care of Stanwix.[35]

Shortly before his ship was scheduled to depart, Melville signed a contract and turned his manuscript over to Dix & Edwards, leaving Allan to oversee the printing. He wrote Peter Gansevoort that he would soon be "sailing for the other side of the ocean," and his uncle responded by sending him "best wishes & sincere prayers for a pleasant & safe voyage & the restoration of your health on your return to your family & friends."[36]

Knowing that Herman had been talking about going abroad for over a year, Maria told her brother she hoped Herman would "feel content to remain away for six months at least for he has sadly overworked his strength–& requires recreation, freedom from care, from writing, & the little petty cares, & annoyances, of the farm which are ever recurring & are so distasteful to him."[37]

Rumors have persisted that Melville pushed Lizzie down the back stairs in a fit of anger, and that his in-laws were hoping he would not return from the Holy Land, but no documentary evidence for either accusation exists, so no one knows for certain what forms their various interactions took. While we know that Melville burned letters and personal papers from time to time, we have no way of knowing whether he was destroying sensitive documents or simply getting rid of papers too trivial to save. Even if we had these lost documents, they would not tell us the whole truth about Herman Melville, as documentary evidence itself can be misleading. Melville's passport, for example, described him as thirty-seven years old, five feet eight and three-quarters inches tall, with dark brown hair, an oval face, a fair complexion, blue eyes, a "medium" mouth and forehead, a straight nose, and a round chin. Yet he actually seems to have stood around five feet ten inches, and many people who knew him personally thought of him as taller, perhaps because of his charismatic intensity, his stalwart bearing, and his erect, almost military posture.[38]

How does one take the measure of a man? By his achievements, his failures, his nightmares, or his dreams? In *The Confidence-Man*, Melville wrote that "if the acutest sage be often at his wits' end to understand living character, shall those who are not sages expect to run and read character in those mere phantoms which flit along a page, like shadows along a wall?" If, as Melville says, human beings are inconsistent, ever-changing, constantly evolving, and ultimately unknowable creatures, what is any novelist or biographer but a trickster and confidence man?[39]

Watercolorist Peter Toft painted The Holy Palm of Mar Saba *for Melville in appreciation of* Clarel: A Poem and Pilgrimage in the Holy Land.

TWENTY

CHILDE HERMAN'S PILGRIMAGE

On October 11, 1856, seven years to the day after his trip to London and the Continent, a "right hearty" Melville boarded the Glasgow, a new screw propeller–driven steamer that could shave about a week off the 1849 crossing time.[1]

Most of the passengers on the ship were Scottish and English commercial travelers, or salesmen, "who did little but drink and gamble the whole way over," and Melville avoided them. The only American was Henry Willard, a Princeton Theological Seminary graduate who was "very uninteresting but better than nobody" until Melville became acquainted with Colonel George Campbell Rankin, a retired British officer who had commanded native troops in the Punjab. Rankin had written an attack on Christianity called What is Truth?, or Revelation Its Own Nemesis (1854), and he and Melville "had many long talks" on "fixed fate &c." They managed "to kill time" even during a gale that kept passengers belowdecks for thirty-six hours and forced the ship to "lay to" for about eighteen hours.[2]

Only fifteen days after leaving New York Harbor, the ship reached Rathlin Isle, north of Ireland, and Melville saw Arran Ailsa Crag looming through the mist. As the ship docked at

Greenoch, Melville suffered a temporarily disfiguring mishap: "A sailor was lowering a boat by one of the tackles," he wrote, "the rope got foul; I jumped to clear it for him, when suddenly the tackle started, and a coil of the rope (new Manilla) flew up in my face with great violence, and for the moment, I thought my nose was ruined for life."[3]

In Scotland, Melville began keeping a journal. Although many of his entries are mere fragments, some paint vivid pictures of the places he visited in the six months he was abroad. The entries do not always indicate whether he was alone or with others while sightseeing, but the journals on the whole portray him as gregarious and sociable. He may have been thinking of writing a continuation of *The Confidence-Man* with Oriental characters, or a popular travel book that would reap financial rewards for him, as it had for George Curtis and Bayard Taylor. In the end, however, the fruits of his travel would be his journal, some brilliant narrative and lyric poems, and an epic based on his pilgrimage in the Holy Land.

"Much pleased" with Edinburgh, he stayed there five days, making a side trip to see Abbottsford, the home of Sir Walter Scott. He half wanted to visit Scoonie parish, where his great-great-grandfather had served as minister for many years, but no one seemed to have heard of it.[4]

From Scotland he took "parliamentary trains," the cheapest class, to Liverpool, where he checked into the White Bear, whose proprietors pressed drinks on pub patrons as though they were hosting a private dinner party, then rendered an unexpected bill. Melville found it a "comical affectation" even though he was on a tight budget, and avoided the hostelry's pub from then on.[5]

For Melville, Liverpool was full of memories. He moseyed around the waterfront inspecting the Mediterranean steamers and exploring the new docks, and contemplated Nelson's statue "with peculiar emotion, mindful of 20 years ago," then tried to locate Nathaniel Hawthorne in Rock Ferry. The Hawthornes had moved, he was told, so the following day he went to Hawthorne's office.[6]

"Herman Melville," Hawthorne noted, "came to see me at the Consulate, looking much as he used to do (a little paler, and perhaps a little sadder), in a rough outside coat, and with his characteristic gravity and reserve of manner." Hawthorne found his old friend's condition disturbing: "Melville has not been well, of late; he has been affected with neuralgic complaints in his head and limbs, and no doubt has suffered from too constant literary occupation, pursued without much success, latterly; and his writings, for a long while past, have indicated a morbid state of mind."[7]

Although Hawthorne felt a little uncomfortable at first because of his "ineffectual attempt to get him a consular appointment," he invited Melville to Southport, a seaside village "20 miles distant on the sea-shore, a watering place," where they arrived in time to find "Mrs. Hawthorne & the rest awaiting tea for us." Melville brought only "the least little bit of a bundle, which, he told me, contained a night-shirt and a tooth-brush," Hawthorne observed. "He is a person of very gentlemanly instincts in every respect, save that he is a little heterodox in the matter of clean linen."[8]

The two men conversed "on pretty much our former terms of sociability and confidence," and Hawthorne took the next day off so he could spend it with his friend. They took a long walk on the beach and sat down "in a hollow among the sand hills (sheltering ourselves from the high, cool wind) and smoked a cigar," and in his notebook, Hawthorne gave a perceptive description of Melville's spiritual state:

> Melville, as he always does, began to reason of Providence and futurity, and of everything that lies beyond human ken, and informed me that he had "pretty much made up his mind to be annihilated"; but still he does not seem to rest in that anticipation; and, I think, will never rest until he gets hold of a definite belief. It is strange how he persists—and has persisted ever since I knew him, and probably long before—in wandering to and fro over these deserts, as dismal and monotonous as the sand hills amid which we were sitting. He can neither believe, nor be comfortable in his unbelief; and he is too honest and courageous not to try to do one or the other. If he were a religious man, he would be one of the most truly religious and reverential; he has a very high and noble nature, and better worth immortality than most of us.[9]

Melville's journal entry is terse by comparison, like a deft Japanese brush stroke, imbuing a seemingly empty landscape with forceful simplicity: "An agreeable day. Took a long walk by the sea. Sand & grass. Wild & desolate. A strong wind. A good talk." That evening the men enjoyed the pleasures of "hearth and home," drinking stout and playing fox and geese with Hawthorne's children.[10]

The differences between the two are striking. Taciturn in his letters to Melville, Hawthorne reveals a keen intuitive awareness of his friend's tumultuous spiritual life in this century. Melville, effusive in his letters to Hawthorne by contrast, records their meeting in a laconic entry whose staccato rhythm suggests emotional restraint. Hawthorne was witch and wizard; Melville was magus, maze, and minotaur.

The following afternoon the men returned to Liverpool so that Hawthorne could catch up on his office work and Melville could make final arrangements for his Mediterranean voyage and write some letters to family members, who, so far, had not heard a word from him. Melville secured a visa from the Turkish consulate, and Hawthorne endorsed his passport: "Good for Constantinople (via Malta & Gibraltar) Egypt & tour about the Continent."[11]

At week's end, on a half-rainy Saturday, Hawthorne took Melville by omnibus to

Chester, the "only place within easy reach of Liverpool, which possesses any old English interest," as Hawthorne put it. After partaking of veal pies and damson tarts at a confectioner's, they visited Chester Cathedral, returning to the snuggery at the Yacht Inn for a pint of stout and a smoke. As they chatted with the landlord, they were mindful that Jonathan Swift had been a guest of the inn while he was Dean of St. Patrick's Cathedral in Dublin.[12]

When Melville saw Hawthorne again on Monday, he told him "he already felt much better than in America; but observed that he did not anticipate much pleasure in his rambles, for that the spirit of adventure is gone out of him." Before he left, he assigned Hawthorne power of attorney to sign the agreement for British publication of *The Confidence-Man*, and Hawthorne noted, "He is certainly much overshadowed since I saw him last; but I hope he will brighten as he goes onward."[13]

On November 18, Melville boarded the screw-steamer *Egyptian*, carrying only "a carpet-bag to hold all his travelling gear," which struck Hawthorne as "the next best thing to going naked." He noted in his journal that Melville "wears his beard and mustache, and so needs no dressing-case—nothing but a tooth-brush—I do not know a more independent personage. He learned his travelling habits by drifting about, all over the South Sea, with no other clothes or equipage than a red flannel shirt and a pair of duck trowsers. Yet we seldom see men of less criticizable manners than he."[14]

Melville knew he would "miss much" by making the tour during the winter. "June is so much better. But that can't be helped," so he was pleasantly surprised when the weather turned as "warm as May" as soon as the ship passed through the Straits of Gibraltar. As the ship steamed along the Spanish coast, the mate came on deck in a straw hat and shirtsleeves, and Melville threw open his coat, pronouncing the Mediterranean a "paradise."[15]

As the sun rose on the twenty-sixth of November, he could see snow-crested mountains on the coast of Africa, "wild-looking" Algerian villages, and "piratical" coves and bays. He enjoyed glorious weather during the passage from the Pillars of Hercules to Malta, and while the ship lay at anchor all day to take in provisions, he and the other passengers explored the fortress city, hewn of sea-worn rocks, until the ship's whistle called them back. That night, unpredictable Aeolus blew with such ferocity that Melville had to secure himself in his berth so he would not roll out.[16]

The first stop was Syra (Syros), "the depot for the Archipelago." Xebecs, "trim and light" three-masted vessels with both square and triangular sails, used by Arab corsairs, flitted around the harbor like sea birds, and Melville could see "lighters" wearing tasseled Phrygian caps and loose blue drawers "weighing bales, counting codfish," and stacking "bales of tobacco, jars of oil," and "goat skins, filled, not with the flesh of goats, but the blood of the grape," on the quay. Everywhere, men with big black mustaches wearing loose trousers, embroidered jackets, and long-tasseled red fezzes that made them look like "flamingos" were smoking and talking in tavernas, or "sauntering" on the docks, while others were sitting in boats, or "picking up rags, carrying water casks, &c."[17]

Leaving Syra, the *Egyptian* passed Pelion and Ossa and steamed toward Thessaloniki. At daybreak, "Captain Tate" (Robert Taitt) called Melville out on deck to see snow-capped Olympus and conical Mount Athos looming on either side of the ship. Taitt told Melville a story about arms stored in the hold of a ship throwing off its compass and causing it to be wrecked, which he would later rework in three poems. The "most conspicuous objects" he could see as they entered the harbor were minarets and cypresses, and he speculated that Turkish architects had tapered the minaret to mimic the cypress tree. The "mingling of the dark tree with the bright spire," he wrote, was "expressive of the intermingling of life & death."[18]

Thessaloniki, a walled town originally fortified by the Genoese, was now guarded by Turkish warships on one side and by Olympus, towering "in plain sight," on the other. Thessaloniki's "filthy" marketplace and winding, crowded streets overlaid on the ruins of successive empires reminded Melville "of Five Points." It seemed that while the poor were "all struggling for huge bales and bundles of rags," wealthy residents and tourists were treating the place like a private playground. When an Englishman named Duckworth told Melville that he had done "a day's shooting in the Vale of Tempe," Melville was scandalized by the fellow's callous attitude toward the history of the place: "Ye Gods!" he wrote, "whortleberrying on Olympus." This trigger-happy Englishman became the model for the boorish Glaucon in *Clarel*.[19]

Carrying a letter of introduction from a clerk in the shipping office, Melville rode into the hills to visit the estate of Djékis Abbot, a member of the local ruling class who was so powerful that even the Sultan treated him with deference. Abbot's villa, "Little Paradise" (Urendjick), named for its formal gardens and rare trees, was enclosed by a high stone wall and guarded by armed soldiers, but Melville was given a tour and invited to tea by Abbot himself. Descended from the Anglo-Greek family that had brought the British Levant Company to Thessaloniki, Abbot was both a hedonist and a hardheaded businessman, and after savoring "sweetmeats & liqueurs & coffee," Melville left this Shangri-la pondering the ease with which Eastern men accepted the contradictions of life and their own personalities, and he later modeled the Greek merchant in *Clarel* on his host.[20]

Waiting for the *Egyptian*'s boilers to be fired, Melville stood at the railing watching the deck passengers file on board–Turkish women, veiled Negroes, two "beys effendi in long, furred robes of yellow, looking like Tom cats," and some "very pretty women of the harem." In response to false rumors that Louis-Napoléon had been assassinated, many of the men were carrying guns, which crewmen confiscated and discharged on the dock before storing them in the hold. When the loud report of firearms almost touched off a civil disorder, Melville wondered how the gods could remain indifferent to the fate of humanity: "Upon this uproar at the landing Olympus looked from afar cold & snowy. Surprising the Gods took no interest in the thing. Might at least have moved their sympathy."[21]

~~~

Steaming through the Dardanelles, the *Egyptian* entered the Sea of Marmara and groped the last three miles to Constantinople through dense fog and cold so penetrating that Melville thought it must be "very miserable for the Turks & their harems" after they had been "doused out by the deck-washing." In the distance Melville could hear the muffled clanging of ships' bells sounding warnings through the raw air, and as night fell and the ship sat shrouded by fog, a boy tied his caïque to their ship and went to sleep, impressing Melville with his "easy ways."[22]

Two days later a breeze blew up, and as the fog slowly evaporated, Constantinople appeared like "magic." Melville could see the cathedral of St. Sophia gradually emerging from the mist with a "coy disclosure, a kind of coquetting."[23]

Melville took rooms at the Hotel du Globe in the suburb of Pera. Inside the city, he felt entombed. There were no parks or open spaces where the soul could breathe, and at night it was too dangerous to go out, "owing to footpads & assassins." Even by day, all he could see were "cemeteries, where they dumped garbage" and a man sawing wood over a tomb. He found himself going in circles, "just like getting lost in a wood. No plan to streets... Perfect labyrinth. Narrow. Close, shut. If one could but get *up* aloft, it would be easy to see one's way out. If you could get up into tree. Soar out of the maze. But no."[24]

Constantinople was a cornucopia of contrasts. At this unique conjunction of water, land, and sky, Europe and Asia met and exchanged raucous sounds and pungent odors. Melville visited St. Sophia, the Column of Constantine, the six-towered mosque of Sultan Achmet, the Hippodrome, which was modeled after the Circus Maximus of ancient Rome, and the Great Bazaar where he felt suffocated by "immense crowds." A "wilderness of traffic" surrounded him: "Furniture, arms, silks, confectionery, shoes, saddles—everything.... You lose yourself, & are bewildered & confounded with the labyrinth, the din, the barbaric confusion of the whole." Looking down into the Cistern of 1,001 Columns was like looking into a "palatial sort of Tartarus." Crypts, tunnels, and even natural caves terrified him, as though they might draw him into their depths and swallow him up forever.[25]

As he crossed and recrossed the bridges linking the city's precincts, Melville could see the "splendid barges of the Pashas darting under the arches." Climbing a watchtower "of vast girth & height [constructed] in the Saracenic style," he found himself gazing out on a scene that took his breath away: "My God, what a view! Surpasses everything." The bays swept "round in great amphitheatres," and spread below him was an "indescribable" prospect that took in "The Propontis, the Bosporus, the Golden Horn, the domes, the minarets, the bridges, the men of war," as well as Nature's columns, the cypress trees. Europe and Asia seemed to be Life and Death yearning to embrace across the "cleaving Bosporus."[26]

Visiting the Pigeon Mosque and the mosque of Suleiman, Melville decided that the Moslem practice of removing one's shoes before entering the sacred precincts was more sensible than the Western practice of removing one's hat before entering a church. "Muddy shoes, but never muddy heads," he thought as he entered a domed room covered with mats and "beautiful rugs of great size & square." Seeing portmanteaus, chests, and bags belonging to the many Turks who had come to bow their heads and chant their prayers in harmonies exotic to the Western ear, Melville thought of Christ's injunction against laying up "treasures where moth & rust do corrupt, &c."[27]

Strolling under a deep blue cloudless sky, he reached a pontoon bridge and stopped to savor the "delightful elastic atmosphere" of the Golden Horn. Although it was December, it felt like "a kind of English June cooled & tempered sherbet–like with an American October; the serenity & beauty of summer without the heat." In "the vast suburbs of Galata," he saw "great crowds of all nations–money changers–coins of all nation circulate." Listening to the babel of languages spoken in the streets, Melville felt that the "great curse" of travel was "not being able to talk to a fellow being." Noting that his guide kept his hands firmly in his pockets to guard against the omnipresent thieves, he toured the town warily. Every alleyway had a "horrible grimy tragic air," and the "rotten & wicked looking houses" looked "as if a suicide hung from every rafter." In this city of Cain, adherents of three religions struggled for the undivided attention of the Deity, celebrating "three Sundays"–"Friday, Turks; Sat, Jews; Sunday, Romanists, Greeks, & Armenians."[28]

Everywhere, past and present coexisted and interpenetrated; everywhere, life and death cohabited and commingled in a terrifying embrace. As Melville was watching jugglers and chanting priests, he was swept up by an Armenian funeral procession on its way to the cemetery. He was shocked to see a woman lying "over a new grave–no grass on it yet," ululating and calling to her newly buried relative. "Such abandonment of misery!" he thought, as he watched her put her head down as close to the grave as possible and beg her loved one to utter just one word. "This woman and her cries," Melville wrote later, "haunt me horribly." By the end of the day he felt "utterly used up . . . broken on the wheel."[29]

After two more days of sightseeing, Melville hired a caïque to ferry him across the channel to Asia Minor, the jumping-off point for voyages to Egypt and Northern Africa. The caïque, a "sort of carved trencher or tray," proved unexpectedly luxurious, and he felt like a potentate. "Cushioned like [an] ottoman. You lie in the boat's bottom. Body beneath the surface. A boat bed." From his vantage point on the water, he could see a fleet of fishermen drawing in their nets as the sun set over Seraglio Point, bathing the Sultan's palaces in golden light and setting the hills aglow "like sapphire."[30]

In Scutari, the most Oriental of Constantinople's suburbs, Melville boarded the *Acadia* bound for Alexandria, crossing the Sea of Marmara and sailing through the Dardanelles at daybreak. After an early-morning rain, the plain of Troy, with Mount Ida in the background, and Sappho's Lesbos, "a large & lovely island, covered with olive trees," nestled near the Turkish coast, came into view. The ship docked overnight at Mytilene, and although the island looked an inviting "dark rich bronzy green, in marked contrast with the yellow & parched aspect of most other isles of the Archipelago," Melville did not go ashore.[31]

When the ship stopped at Smyrna, the sight of that "most ungainly creature," the camel, brought out the child in Melville, rousing him to whimsical humor:

> From his long curved and crane-like neck (which he carries stiffly like a clergy-man in a stiff cravat), his feathery-looking forelegs & his long lank hind ones, he seems a cross between an ostrich & a gigantic grasshopper. His hoof is spongy, & covered with hair to the ground, so that walking through these muddy lanes, he seems [stilting] along on four mops.[32]

Leaving Smyrna, the ship passed near Mykonos and Tinos, but strangely enough, although in a later poem he waxed lyrical about sublime "aureolas" rolling from a "god-like group" of "sunned Greek seas and skies," Melville seems to have had no desire to explore those fabled kingdoms where gods and goddesses once dallied with mortal men and women, loving them and leaving them forever changed.[33]

Compared with Pacific islands still "fresh as at their first creation," the Greek islands in winter seemed "sterile & dry" to him. Even Delos, the sacred birthplace of Apollo where "flowers rose by miracle in the sea," struck Melville as "a barren moor," and when he looked upon "the bleak yellow of Patmos," he wondered "who would ever think that a god had been there." Both islands seemed to him to have "lost their virginity"; they were "disenchanting."[34]

Of Greece, Henry Miller wrote in *The Colossus of Maroussi*: "Here the light penetrates directly to the soul, opens the doors and windows of the heart, makes one go naked, exposed, isolated in a metaphysical bliss which makes everything clear without being known. No analysis can go on in this light: here the neurotic is either instantly healed or goes mad." Had Melville been able to travel through Greece in June, he might have been able to slough off the Victorian soul-sickness that afflicted him. Neither Puritan New England nor materialistic New York could satisfy the hunger of a pilgrim longing to embrace a faith that could burn away dogma and purify the soul, and Melville does not seem to have experienced the healing fusion of body and soul that Greece bestows on those who surrender to its exquisite sensuality.[35]

When the *Acadia* docked at Syra, immigration officials kept her in quarantine for twenty-four hours, even though the passengers showed no signs of disease. Melville noted that the houses in this hilly town seemed to be "clinging round its top, as if desperate for security, like shipwrecked men about a rock beaten by billows." When the quarantine was lifted before noon on Christmas Day, he went ashore "to renew [his] impressions of the previous visit." The brightly dyed tassels worn by Oriental men seemed incongruous in the mechanized modern world. He decided the Greek man of any class was "a natural dandy" and that the native costume was so impractical for work that it "must have been devised in some Golden Age."[36]

Once the ship was under way for Alexandria, the captain "mildly celebrated" Christmas "with a glass of champagne." On December 28, after plowing through seas so rough that most of the passengers were sick, the *Acadia* came within sight of Cleopatra's Needle and Pompey's Pillar, which to Melville looked like "a long stick of candy, well sucked."[37]

Before leaving for Cairo, Melville picked up his passport at the American consulate, where he met several officers of the USS *Constellation*, among them naval surgeon John Alexander Lockwood, who had written a pamphlet denouncing flogging around the time *White-Jacket* was published. Together, he and Melville traveled the 130 miles to Cairo along the Nile on the newly opened railroad line, which impressed Melville so much that he wrote a poem describing it: "Plump thro' tomb and catacomb/Rolls the Engine ripping." Afraid that the engine's "gust" would dislodge "Egypt's ancient dust" and erode the Pyramids, Melville asks, "What glory left to Isis/Mid loud acclaim to Watts his name?"– a pun that even the master punster of Walden Pond, who also used the railroad as a symbol of the machine's intrusion into the New World Garden, might have envied.[38]

As soon as Melville and Dr. Lockwood arrived in Cairo–the gateway to the Valley of the Kings–they checked into Shepherd's Hotel, then sallied out to see the city. It seemed to Melville that Cairo was "one booth and Bartholomew Fair–a grand masquerade of mortality." A city of four hundred mosques, its prosperous sections were very animated, with lighthearted people of all ages thronging the streets, many of them leading animals. While turbaned men drove camels or chatted about business, veiled women wearing black silk caftans adorned with jewels bobbed along on donkeys, their elbows held out for balance and control.[39]

To Melville's great dismay, the public squares were infested with "multitudes of blind men" who had "flies on the eyes at noon" and "Children opthalmick" because there was "Too much light & no defence against it," also because there was not adequate sanitation and the people touched their eyes with unclean hands. Melville was especially sensitive to the strong sunlight of the treeless desert regions, and if there was one saving grace of traveling in the winter months, it was that his weak eyes were not exposed to the intense ultraviolet rays of summer.[40]

In an extraordinary poem titled "In the Desert," Melville identifies the intense light with the effulgent radiance of the Godhead known as the Shekhinah, the feminine and indwelling aspect of the Deity extolled in the Zohar, a Jewish mystical text that became a sacred part of later Kabbalistic tradition. According to Jewish lore, the Shekhinah is the angelic light that descends from the cloud of glory that rests between the cherubim on the Almighty's mercy-seat to become a loving, mourning mother sharing the exile of the people of Israel. Melville's Shekhinah routs the armies of Napoleon and becomes a symbol of the transience of Empire in the last two stanzas:

> Battling with the Emirs fierce
> Napoleon a great victory won,
> Through and through his sword did pierce;
> But bayonetted by this sun
> His gunners drop beneath the gun.
>
> Holy, holy, holy Light!
> Immaterial incandescence,
> Of God the effluence of essence,
> Shekhinah intolerably bright!

Melville's poem is a sunburst, an epiphany that demonstrates Melville's knowledge of Gnostic and cabalistic literature as well as of orthodox Judeo-Christian scriptures.[41]

From the Citadel built by Saladin in 1166 to repel the Crusaders, Melville saw Cairo, the "dust-colored city" covered with "the dust of ages," two hundred feet below, "nipped between two deserts–the one leading to Suez & the Red Sea, the other the Libyan Desert." The pillars of the mosque inside the Citadel were made of "Alabaster. Could make brooches of them." Only an old whaleman used to turning leviathan teeth and bones into scrimshaw would think of that. Well, perhaps a woman might, or a jeweler.[42]

Like Walt Whitman and many other antebellum Americans, Melville could read about Egyptian religion and Near Eastern goddess cults in popular magazines and books like the *Penny Cyclopaedia*, and he was fascinated by occult lore and such secret societies as the Knights Templar and the Freemasons. Novels such as Schiller's *Ghost Tale*, or "Ghost-Seer," which centers around a Jesuit conspiracy, were very popular in pre–Civil War America, especially after the anti-Masonic controversy in the 1830s, and when Melville imagined briefly that someone was following him in Constantinople, he thought of the Schiller novel Augusta had read to the family in the winter of 1851.[43]

Freemasons apotheosized the Great Pyramid as a symbol of the afterlife, and initiates were forced to undergo ritual burial and resurrection as part of their induction into the order. Melville's maternal grandfather was a member of the revolutionary Order of the Cincinnati, a quasi-Masonic society to which Washington and many of the Founding Fathers belonged; his paternal grandfather belonged to the Green Street Lodge, and his father had belonged to the Society of St. Andrew's, an order of Scottish Freemasons. The Masonic symbol of a pyramid crowned by God's all-seeing eye appears on American currency, perhaps because the first president and his secretary of the treasury, Alexander Hamilton, were Masons.

Melville's references to Freemasonry always express skepticism, as when Pierre delves into the pyramid and finds the sarcophagus empty, or when he wrote to Nathaniel Hawthorne, "We incline to think that the Problem of the Universe is like the Freemason's mighty secret, so terrible to all children. It turns out, at last to consist in a triangle, a mallet, and an apron–nothing more!"[44]

On New Year's Eve, 1856, Melville and Dr. Lockwood mounted donkeys, driven by barefoot boys who prodded their charges with sticks, and rode toward the Valley of the Nile. Confiding to his journal that he knew how it felt to be "thrown by donkeys," Melville professed a "great love" for these "Hacks."[45]

Purple as mountains seen from a distance, on closer inspection the pyramids appeared to hover slightly above the sand, like triangular hot-air balloons. Close up, they were all angles, broken cliffs of sand, "zig-zag" ledges two to five feet high with paths up stone steps that reminded Melville of trails cut through the Alps by generations of hikers and Roman legionnaires. None of the engravings Melville had seen in magazines and books had prepared him for the vastness of the desert and the nearly obliterated traces of a sophisticated agricultural civilization whose artisans had once built well over a hundred pyramids along the Nile. As he stood marveling at the ghostly survivors that loomed before him, the vapors lifted, and around the apex he could see kites soaring, sweeping the air with their bat-black wings. "Nothing in Nature gives such an idea of vastness. A balloon to ascend them." They were like vast strata of geologic time petrified and upheaved from the ocean's floor to rest in the desert as a monument to Earth's antiquity.[46]

As he and Lockwood scaled the Pyramid of Cheops, Melville could see Arab guides in flowing white mantles ascending effortlessly, as though angels were spiriting them up to Heaven. His journal reads as though written during the climb. At first the entries reflect his leisurely pace, but soon they become breathless, frantic, terse: "Resting. Pain in the chest. Exhaustion. Must hurry. None but the phlegmatic go deliberately."[47]

An old man with the "spirits of youth," who has waited for this chance all his life, faints halfway up and has to be carried down. When the guides revive him, he tries to go into the interior through an opening that resembles a "shoot for coal or timber," but again he faints and has to be brought out. Defeated, he leans "against the pyramid by the entrance—pale as death."[48]

Melville concludes that the old man is "oppressed by the massiveness & mystery of the pyramids." A pause, then Melville admits frankly, "I myself too. A feeling of awe & terror came over me. Dread of the Arabs. Offering to lead me into a side-hole. The Dust. Long arched way,—then down as in a coal shaft.... Then as in mines, under the sea. The stooping & doubling." It occurs to Melville that this would be a "horrible place for assassination," which means, of course, that he is thinking how perfect it would be.[49]

Melville's entry describing the actual ascent is so full of ambiguous referents that a cursory reading can give the impression that it was Melville who fainted in an attempt to scale the Pyramid. But no. Melville, only thirty-seven years old and an avid climber, makes it to the summit: "When I was at top, thought it not so high—sat down on edge, looked below—gradual nervousness & final giddiness & terror." When he looks down, he feels the inevitability of the Fall. Vertigo dances with claustrophobia: "I shudder at the idea of the ancient Egyptians. It was in these pyramids that was conceived the idea of Jehovah. Terrible mixture of the cunning and awful. Moses learned in all the lore of the Egyptians. The idea of Jehovah was born here."[50]

The pyramids are not arranged in line, and the space between them makes Melville think of Crawford Notch, the "Notch of White Mountains," as Thomas Cole had painted it and as he remembered the passage from his honeymoon. Oddly enough, Melville has little to say about the brooding monster whose riddle was solved by Oedipus: *"The Sphynx:* back to desert & face to verdure. Solid rock." That was all.[51]

The entries in his journal begin to expand backward, describing the ride to the pyramids—past villages, through gates, over bridges, alongside aqueducts, through groves of palms and long avenues of acacias in the suburbs of Cairo, until he is back in Cairo, where the climate in winter "is the reign of spring upon earth, summer in the air, and tranquility in the heat." Savoring the "soft luxurious splendor of mornings. Dewy. Paradise melted & poured into the air," he knows why "these people never drink wine."[52]

Years and years ago, in what must have seemed like another life, he had written to Hawthorne, "I am like one of those seeds taken out of the Egyptian Pyramids, which, after being three thousand years a seed and nothing but a seed, being planted in English soil, it developed itself, grew to greenness, and then fell to mould." Did Hawthorne ever confide to Melville over brandy that he and Horatio Bridge believed there was a parallel world of beings like ourselves on this planet whom we could not perceive and with whom we could not communicate?[53]

"Never shall forget this day," Melville wrote in his journal after he returned from the Valley of the Kings. How could all this have happened within a single day? There is something unreal about measuring time with machines, he reflects. It seems he has read this idea somewhere, or experienced a feeling that, for a split second, a fissure has opened into another world, and through that fissure he has glimpsed something that seems both familiar and disconcertingly strange, something indefinable that materialized in a blink of consciousness, then vanished beyond the corner of his eye.[54]

～

On New Year's Day of 1857, Melville said good-bye to Dr. Lockwood and returned to Alexandria to book passage for the Holy Land. He was dismayed to learn that he would have to wait two days, "which might have been spent more delightfully in Cairo." He did little or no sightseeing, using the delay to write in his journal and read a "book on Palestine" without making note of its name.[55]

Instead of writing about Alexandria, he kept doubling back to write about the pyramids, adding paragraphs and revising, crossing out phrases and changing words. He couldn't get the Pyramid out of his mind: "Its simplicity confounds you." He wonders who designed it and how and why it was made. He tries to describe it precisely, the way an engineer or an architect might, thinking that way he might be able to grasp its meaning, but it defies scientific analysis and makes objectivity seem a paltry thing. Everything he writes about the Pyramid becomes infused with the spiritual resonance of metaphor, and eventually he will compose a poem asking the Pyramid if exploration of its "caves and labyrinths" will yield evidence of a "Cosmic Artisan." It seems this "dead calm of masonry" has as little to do with Nature as with Man, and Melville decides that the Pyramid was conceived by "that supernatural creature, the priest" so that he "could rear the transcendent conception of a God." In any case, Melville concludes, "for no holy purpose was the pyramid founded."[56]

Melville crossed the eastern Mediterranean by steamer, grateful for the warm weather, needing nothing to fan his thirst for Jerusalem. After bucking a dangerous rolling swell, the ship landed at Jaffa on January 6, and he immediately hired a Jewish dragoman to take him to the Holy City. After a "delightful ride" across the Plain of Sharon in sight of the mountains of Ephraim amid fields of red poppies, they reached Ramla. Dinner at the "alleged" hotel was dreadful: cold meat on broken crockery, circled by flies and mosquitoes. Unable to sleep in this wretched place, Melville roused the guide at 2:00 A.M. and they set out across the desert by moonlight, stalked by "three shadows" for a good portion of their journey.[57]

The moon set before dawn, and they rode through the dark until morning spilled its "pale olive light" into the valley as they were "just entering the mountains." They breakfasted in a cave by a ruined mosque in "withered & desert country" before making the "hot & wearisome ride over the arid hills" in sunlight that adversely affected his eyes for the rest of the afternoon. In Jerusalem, Melville found lodgings at the Mediterranean Hotel, and from his balcony he could look out over the Pool of Hezekiah, the Church of the Holy Sepulchre, and the ruins of a Roman Catholic convent destroyed long ago in a forgotten war, all of which he would describe in his epic poem *Clarel*.[58]

The next day, exploring the hills with his guide, he met a party from Boston whose dragoman was a Druse named Abdallah, the model for the guide Djalea in *Clarel*. Combining forces, these pilgrims set out together for Judea and Bethlehem across the Plain of Jericho, whose orchards bore only the bitter apples of Sodom. Melville climbed the Mount of Temptation, the "black, arid" promontory from which Satan pointed out the kingdoms of the world to Jesus, tempting Him to renounce His ministry and accept a terrestrial throne, and below him, the Dead Sea looked surprisingly like Lake George. The mouth of Kedron looked to Melville like the "Gate of Hell," and the few sheiks smoking outside their tents seemed to be a "charmed circle, keeping off the curse." After viewing Masada, the peak from which one thousand Jews jumped to their deaths to evade capture by the Romans, Melville and his companions bedded down in the mountains of Moab amid rain and distant rumbles of thunder. A crack of lightning, followed by cries of jackals and howls of wolves, drove them to break up their camp and ride out onto the "mouldy plain" where nothing grew "but wiry, prickly bush."[59]

In the morning, they were met by Arabs who greeted them with "native dignity" and warned them to be alert for bands of brigands, but despite this alarming news, Melville's party rode down to the Dead Sea. On closer inspection, the edge of this sunken sea resembled no shore he had ever seen: "foam on beach & pebbles like slaver of mad dog—smarting bitter of the water—carried the bitter in my mouth all day—bitterness of life—thought of all bitter things—Bitter is it to be poor & bitter, to be reviled, & Oh bitter are these waters of Death, thought I." The sudden appearance of a rainbow over the Dead Sea seemed a sign that "heaven, after all, has no malice against it," but may simply be indifferent to Man: "Must bring your own provisions, as well, too, for mind as body."[60]

Nothing could have prepared Melville for the barrenness of Judea. A landscape devoid of verdure, moisture, grace, Judea was the skeleton of the world. "You see the anatomy—compares with other regions as skeleton with living & rosy man." There was "no moss as in other ruins—no grace of decay—no ivy—The unleavened nakedness of desolation—whitish ashes—lime-kilns." The plains bore traces of the slime of snails, the flea-bitten sheep and goats looked wretched, and the venerable monastery of St. Saba had to be approached through a "sepulchral ravine, smoked as by fire, caves & cells."[61]

The Great Laura of Mar Saba was an enigma of rock, a honeycomb of mysterious passages. Even though it was a hostel that offered travelers a comfortable night's sleep on the way to Bethlehem, monks peered out at visitors through tiny portals in immense iron doors before admitting them. Outside, on the crags overlooking the monastery, gaunt hermits slept in caves. In the morning, Melville went to chapel, then he and his companions rode over the hills to Bethlehem to see the supposed birthplace of Jesus, which turned out to be accessible only by crawling into a dank hole lit by olive oil lamps. Feeling cheated, they raced rain showers back to Jerusalem, and when their guide pointed out the first view of the city in the distance, Melville realized he would not have recognized it, as it resembled "arid rocks."[62]

"No country," Melville wrote, "will more quickly dissipate romantic expectations than Palestine—particularly Jerusalem." To some the disappointment is "heart sickening." The village of lepers was a hellish place: "houses facing the wall . . . their park, a dung-heap. They sit by the gates asking alms,—their whine." He could respond only by "avoidance of them & horror." Even the names of surrounding places had a ghostly sound: "Jehosophat, Hinnom, &c." On the Via Dolorosa he saw "women panting under burdens—men with melancholy faces," and wandered among tombs "till I began to think myself one of the possessed with devels [sic]."[63]

The Church of the Holy Sepulchre lay at the end of an alley full of "an accumulation of the last & least nameable filth of a city." With its "broken dome" and its "painted mildewed wall," it had a "plague-stricken splendor." Entering it plunged him into claustrophobic gloom, and after being "wedged" into the tomb to view "the anointing-stone of Christ, which veined with streaks of a mouldy red looks like a butcher's slab," he was "glad to escape as from the heat & jam of a show-box. All is glitter & nothing gold." It was another "sickening cheat."[64]

Even at the "Beautiful, or Golden Gate" through which Christ went to Bethany and later came back to cheering crowds waving palms, Melville found it hard to picture Jesus as a real person, and it was even harder to grasp "such a thing as to realize on Mt. Olivet that from there Christ rose." He longed to "saturate" his mind with the atmosphere of Jerusalem, "offering myself up as a passive subject, and no unwilling one, to its weird impressions," and to that end, he "always rose at dawn & walked without the walls," where he found "clusters of townspeople reposing along the arches near the Jaffa Gate where it looks down into the vale of Gihon, and the groups always haunting the neighboring fountains, vales & hills." They, too, seemed to feel the insalubriousness of "so small a city pent in by lofty walls obstructing ventilation, postponing the morning & hasting the unwholesome twilight."[65]

A city "besieged by [an] army of the dead," Jerusalem was so crowded and had so many "cemeteries all round" that homeless people lived among the tombs, which was a shock to someone familiar with America's paradisiacal rural cemeteries.

Melville left Jerusalem on January 18 with a question: "Is the desolation of the land the result of the fatal embrace of the Deity?" If so, "Hapless are the favorites of Heaven." Violent weather forced him to wait six days in Jaffa before the steamer to Europe could leave. There he met several people who would figure in *Clarel*: a Seventh-Day Adventist couple named Saunders who were trying to found an agricultural school for the Jews; "an old Connecticut man wandering about with tracts" designed to convert Moslems and Jews to Christianity; an elderly English teacher named Mrs. Williams; and a fanatical deacon named Walter Dickson. Melville, who thought it was "against the will of God that the East should be Christianized," thought these missionaries were all misguided, if not downright daft.[66]

Jaffa was "a port before the Flood," and although he did take "a bath in the Mediterranean," Melville experienced profound loneliness and depression: "I am the only traveller sojourning in Joppa. I am emphatically alone, & begin to feel like Jonah. The wind is rising, the swell of the sea increasing, & dashing in breakers upon the reef of rocks within a biscuit's toss of the sea-wall. The surf shows a great sheet of yeast along the beach."[67]

When the fierce squalls abated, Melville took a steamer to Lebanon, from whence he departed for Smyrna by way of Cyprus aboard an Austrian vessel, the *Smirne*. Exhausted from four nights of sleeplessness due to an "affliction of bugs & fleas & mosquitoes," he didn't go ashore in Larnaca. "One finds that, after all, the most noted localities are made up of common elements of earth, air, & water," he wrote wearily.[68]

On February 5, after passing Rhodes, the *Smirne* steamed "among the Sporades all night" under a bright moon. As the ship passed Samos and Patmos, Melville imagined Venus rising from the sea, but soon he "was here again afflicted with the great curse of modern travel–skepticism. Could no more realize that St. John had ever had revelations here, than when off Juan Fernandez, could believe in Robinson Crusoe according to DeFoe. When my eye rested on arid height, spirit partook of the barrenness.–Heartily wish Niebuhr & Strauss to the dogs. –The deuce take their penetration & acumen. They have robbed us of the bloom."[69]

In his *Roman History*, the German scholar Barthold G. Niebuhr separated verifiable facts about Roman history from accretions of myth and legend, and in *Das Leben Jesu* and *Christliche Dogmatik*, his compatriot David Friedrich Strauss presented arguments that the

Gospel accounts of Jesus' life and ministry were largely fictions concocted from wishful thinking based on messianic prophecies. By challenging the belief that the Scriptures were the direct Word of God revealed by priests and prophets, practitioners of the "higher criticism" cast doubt on the authenticity of the Bible. Melville's reaction to the dissection of biblical stories was mild compared with the outrage expressed by orthodox theologians and believers. Melville's is not a believer's indignation, but an agnostic's wistful longing for a compelling belief not dependent on books and priests for its validity or power.

By the time the ship docked in Smyrna, Melville had a raging neuralgic headache from five nights of "utter sleeplessness." He switched to a paddlewheel steamer and stayed in bed during the "tempestuous, cold passage" to Piraeus, the port city of mainland Greece. As he rode to Athens in the moonlight, the Acropolis, looking like "cakes of snow" frozen together, with no seams, glowed eerily in the distance, and the Parthenon's "blocks of marble [looked] like sticks of Wenham ice," and the "contrast of rugged rock with polished temple" seemed "strange."[70]

Melville checked in at the Hotel d'Angleterre, which was listed in Murray's guidebook as one of the three best hostelries in the city, and then spent the rest of that day and the next exploring Athens on foot. He was fascinated by the way the Parthenon would appear and disappear and suddenly reappear unexpectedly as he rounded a corner, a breath-stopping apparition from every vantage point. An embodiment of human aspiration toward the Divine, the Temple of Athena inspired a quatrain in which he defined the classical spirit as "Not magnitude, not lavishness / But Form—the Site; / Not innovating wilfulness, / But reverence for the Archetype."[71]

Melville kept the Acropolis "in sight nearly all the way" back to Piraeus, where he boarded a steamer for Messina, Sicily. After a day spent walking through seaside villages, he embarked for Naples.

Traveling second class, he had an uncomfortable berth, and his wakefulness kept him on deck as the ship steamed by Mount Etna. At daybreak on February 18, the ship left Capri in its wake and entered the Bay of Naples. It was close to Carnival time, and although Naples seemed "the gayest city in the world," Melville sensed sinister forces at work behind the mask. "Corpses dressed for a ball" observed at the Temple of Venus seemed a fitting symbol for a city that was virtually a police state.[72]

Naples was ruled by a Bourbon regime that feared a recurrence of the civil disorders of 1848, and so held the reins of power tightly, arresting dissenters and keeping an eye on foreigners who might foment rebellion. The police kept scrupulous track of all those who entered and left the Kingdom of the Two Sicilies, granting only limited visas to aliens and requiring detailed information about their whereabouts and plans. Without notifying the authorities, Melville changed hotels, so three days after he arrived in

Naples, he received a visit from the police commissioner, "a jabbering man with a document" who demanded to know why his papers were not in order. Melville paid the concierge a napoleon to handle the paperwork for him. Used to breathing the free air of America, Melville felt stifled in a city so bent on repression and control, and in his narrative poem "Naples in the Time of Bomba," he denounces the "dire tyranny" represented by "the overlording flag." Already, sporadic rebellions in the provinces were presaging the revolution that would topple the regime in four years.[73]

While he was in "gyved Naples," he and two companions rode horseback to Pompeii, which he said was "better than Paris." There he saw Vesuvius, the smoking volcano that was his "inkstand" while he was writing *Moby-Dick*: "Red & Yellow. Bellowing. Bellows, flare of flame. Went into crater. Frozen licorice." He "came down with a rush" and made the "cold ride" back to the hotel without a coat, arriving about midnight. The next morning he bought a "good coat for $9."[74]

Vesuvius commanded the center of the Bay of Naples, a crescent-shaped sweep of coastline dotted with grottoes, caves, castles, and shrines that evoked "the variety of old religions (Sybil's cave) and yet the Romish superstition," too. Seeing the oracle's cave, Melville exclaimed: "What in God's name were such places made for, & why? Surely man is a strange animal. Diving into the bowels of the earth rather than building up towards the sky. How clear an indication that he sought darkness rather than light."[75]

The museums of Naples, with their bronze utensils from Pompeii and Herculaneum, paintings by Domenichino and Correggio, and "a touchingly maternal" Madonna of Raphael, whetted Melville's appetite for Rome. After enduring the inevitable paperwork and delays, he started for Rome by stagecoach, arriving at 10:00 A.M. and checking into the Hotel de Minerve, where he found his first letter from home, then he headed right for the Capitol Tower to take in the famed panoramic view. Because he had been up for hours, however, the Imperial City "fell flat . . . oppressively flat" on him. The Tiber looked like "a ditch, yellow as saffron," and though the interior of St. Peter's came "up to expectations," its dome was "not so wonderful as St. Sophia's." He was so exhausted by three in the afternoon that he ate supper at 6:00 P.M. and went to bed early, and the next morning, after checking for a message from Sam Shaw, he went to the Capitol and to the Colosseum, which rose like a "great hollow among hills," reminding him of the "Hopper of Greylock." The Hall of Emperors in the Capitol Museum sickened him, but he lingered before the statue of Hadrian's favorite, Antinoüs, and the poignant statue of the Dying Gladiator, which seemed to him proof that "humanity existed amid the barbarousness of the Roman time, as it now [exists] among Christian barbarousness."[76]

After a walk to the Pincian Hill, he stopped in at the Caffe Greco, a *poste restante* where travelers could leave and pick up mail, and a favorite haunt of Anglo-American expatriate artists, like the "sculptor with dirty hands" seated at a table in the corner amid dense smoke. Browsing through print shops, Melville bought a reproduction of Guido Reni's beguiling portrait of Beatrice Cenci, the original of which he had marveled at when he visited the Palazzo Barberini.[77]

The Cenci story, a lurid melodrama combining patriarchal tyranny, female victimization, sexual perversity, and religious hysteria, aroused in Victorians deeply repressed sexual and familial anxieties. Count Francesco Cenci, a Roman aristocrat convicted of sodomy, repeatedly beat and raped his wife and his daughter Beatrice, telling the frightened girl that incest was a sacrament because it had produced saints. Beatrice endured his rages and perverse sex acts until she was old enough to hire assassins to kill her father. She was beheaded for the crime, but mourners followed her body to the grave, praising her as a martyr and a saint. Father-daughter incest encoded the anxious, convoluted sexual politics of the Victorian era, and Guido's rendition of the tragic Beatrice became a cultural icon for Victorians. Pitying the poor girl became a way of exorcising the guilt induced by the culture's pervasive misogyny.

After visiting the Baths of Caracalla, Melville wandered among the ruins, over "natural bridges of thousands of arches" and through "glades, & thickets among the ruins." Suddenly a "Thought of Shelley" popped into his head, and he went off without a guide to find the Protestant Cemetery. When he reached the gates, he headed for the grave of John Keats to read the epitaph that Joseph Severn had engraved on his friend's tombstone: "Here lies one whose name is writ in water." Popular legend held that Keats was killed by critics, and Melville, who knew how it felt to be flogged by reviewers, empathized.[78]

During his three and a half weeks in Rome, driven by the relentless instructions in Murray's *Handbook* and his own fully matured love of the fine arts, Melville dove into museums, galleries, churches, villas, and gardens until he nearly drowned in the flood of history and art. He felt a special affinity for Piazza di Spagna #66, where Byron had begun writing "Childe Harold's Pilgrimage" in 1817. After seeing the Baths, Monte Cavallo, St. Peter's, Santa Maria Maggiore, the basilica of St. John Lateran, innumerable arches, gardens, and tombs, and the "Loggie of Raphael & Sistine Chapel," he had to sit a long time by an obelisk to recover "from the stunning effect of a first visit to the Vatican." He evidently fell victim to "Stendhal's syndrome," acute exhaustion and psychic disorientation brought on by sensory overload and changes in diet during travel. He pushed himself so hard that he also suffered a painful and frightening relapse of his eye trouble.[79]

Feeling that there was "no place where [a] lonely man will feel more lonely than in Rome," Melville invited two Americans he had met in Naples—Peter Rousse, a lawyer from New Jersey, and his sister Anna—to join him for sightseeing. They saw everything, from the revolting Cloaca Maxima, a "gloomy hole—trailing ruins into the sewer" and a "tomb with olive trees on it—sown in corruption, raised in olives," to the sublime *Pietà* of Michelangelo. In the Vatican Museum's "Hall of Animals," a fatigued Melville lingered before bronze beasts that seemed "Wordsworthian" because they expressed "the gentle in Nature."[80]

Melville particularly admired paintings by Raphael, Titian, Salvator Rosa, and Claude Lorrain, and sculptures by Bernini, Praxiteles, and Michelangelo. The sensuality of Italian painting was a revelation to him. American painters shied away from nudity and subjects considered scandalous by American critics and genteel gallery-goers, and many American artists had fled to Italy to escape the Puritan constraints of their native land. The availability of male and female models of all ages, the affordability of spacious lodgings, the accessibility of fine marble, and the presence of trained artisans who could help with the strenuous work of carving and polishing statuary made Rome a mecca for neoclassical sculptors, and the Eternal City became virtually an Anglo-American artists' colony.

Public hours for viewing artists' studios were listed in all the guidebooks, and Melville sought out the American sculptors Edward Bartholomew and William Page and toured the studio of the renowned English sculptor John Gibson. A charismatic figure, Gibson scandalized the art world by coloring his figures with vivid washes in the authentic manner of the Greeks. Moderns who associated marble bleached by centuries of wind and sunlight with the classical ideal found Gibson's work at best tasteless and at worst obscene. After seeing Gibson's *Colored Venus* and talking with the artist, Melville envisioned "repeopling" the Colosseum with the colorful statues that had originally graced the stadium's niches in ancient times.[81]

Just before he was to leave for Florence, Melville finally connected with Sam Shaw, who brought him a letter from home. Young Sam, now twenty-two years old, had hoped to meet up with him earlier so they could travel together at least part of the time, but Melville, not wanting to be tied to rigid timetables and knowing he would be subject to erratic steamship schedules, had not been able to supply Sam with an exact itinerary. Unfortunately, as Melville had little more than an hour before he left, they "met to part." Sam, relieved to see that despite the execrable Roman climate, Melville's health was "much improved," reported, "He is considerably sunburnt and is stout as usual." Lizzie must have been grateful to have news of her husband, as he was apparently so preoccupied with seeing and recording what he saw that he did not write home frequently.[82]

In Florence, with guidebook in hand, Melville visited the Pitti Palace and the Uffizi Gallery, and although he wrote that it would be "idle to enumerate" its treasures, he noted that Cellini's head of Perseus, the astonishing bronze *Wrestlers,* and Titian's Venus impressed him more than the Venus de Medici. As in Rome, he tried to see everything there was to see, and as he was rambling through the back streets, he suddenly found himself in front of the Campanile and the Duomo designed by Brunelleschi and decorated by Vasari. He was "amazed at their magnificence," and though he couldn't enter, he bought "fine mosaics" as a souvenir.[83]

During the next few days, Melville visited the Boboli Gardens and Dante's tomb at Santa Croce, and saw the frescoes of Andrea del Sarto and the delicate Giottos that seemed to have inspired Perugino and Raphael. Not all tourist attractions in Florence were beautiful, however. The Museum of Natural History featured "terrible cases & wildernesses of rooms" containing anatomical specimens and also hideous representations of plague victims by a Sicilian artist who sculpted lifelike miniatures out of wax. "In a cavernous ruin. Superb mausoleum like Pope's, lid removed shows skeleton & putridity. Roman sarcophagus–joyous triumphal procession–putrid corpse thrown over it–grating–rats, vampires–insects . . . slime & ooze of corruption. Moralist, this Sicilian."[84]

While Melville was in Florence, he also paid a call on the American sculptor Hiram Powers, an "open, plain man . . . fine specimen of an American," in Melville's view, though considered by others blunt, garrulous, and eccentric because he wore an apron and a fez. When Powers's statue *The Greek Slave* (1843) was shown at the Great Exhibition in New York in 1851, it raised a storm of protest because it depicted a nude woman completely undraped except for manacles and chains. The statue offended both those who disapproved of nudity and those who objected to the idea that the nude female form might be acceptable if depicted as a victim or a slave. In his journal, Melville mentions meeting Powers and seeing *America, Il Penseroso,* and *The Fisher Boy,* but he makes no further comment on his visit to the artist's studio.[85]

After an excursion to Fiesole to see Boccaccio's villa, the villa of the Medicis, and a Franciscan convent, Melville packed his carpetbag for an early departure to Bologna. "On the principle that at Rome you first go to St. Peter's," the minute he reached Bologna, he tried the famous sausage, and toured the oldest university in the Western world. From there he went on to Ferrara and crossed the river Po to Padua, where he ate at the "famous caffe of Pedrocci" and saw Giotto's Chapel.[86]

On April 1, 1857, the day *The Confidence-Man* was officially published in New York and a week before Longman's brought the book out in England as *Melville's Confidence Man,* Melville arrived in Venice, which Byron had called "the revel of the earth, the masque of Italy." From the train station, he went by gondola to the Hotel Luna, and the next morning after breakfast at Florian's, he threaded his way past scaffolding and entered the "oily looking interior" of St. Mark's Cathedral. Despite this first impression, when he saw the cathedral a day or so later at sunset, he was struck by the "holyday" aspect of its "gilt mosaics" and pinnacles and later by the gaiety of the throngs who congregated all night in the Piazza San Marco to eat, drink, dance, talk, and flirt. Like Lord Byron, Melville found Venice "the pleasant place of all festivity."[87]

A "sea Cybele fresh from ocean," as Byron described it in *Childe Harold's Pilgrimage,* "Venice rises as from the stroke of the enchanter's wand." To Melville it seemed to rise from "Pantheist energy of will" as from a "Coral Sea . . . in reefs of palaces" that prove "Pan's might." As he strolled out along the Lido, a desolate strip of sand between the lagoon and the Adriatic, he was reminded of Battery Park as he had known it in his childhood, before Castle Garden became the entry point for thousands of European immigrants each day.[88]

He toured the Ducal Palace, where he met a young man named Antonio and engaged him as a guide. Antonio, who had lost all his money in the 1848 revolution, entertained Melville with anecdotes about Byron's romantic exploits, which included midnight swims across the Grand Canal to visit a lady friend. Antonio's pidgin-English philosophizing appealed to Melville; he recorded snatches of it, noting parenthetically, "for Con. Man," which strongly suggests that he had not given up the notion of writing a sequel to that book.[89]

Antonio took Melville through the Venetian gold-chain and glass-bead manufactories, as well as to the Foscari Palace, the Palazzo Moro, supposed home of the model for Shakespeare's Othello, and the Galleria dell'Accademia, where he saw Titian's *Assumption of the Virgin* and other masterworks. Titian's voluptuous women, "drawn from nature," their skin a "clear, rich, golden brown," their features as clear cut as a cameo, appealed to the sensualist in Melville.[90]

The city's vibrant street life charmed him as well, and from time to time, like all visitors to Venice, he enjoyed lounging at a café near St. Mark's or in a chair by the arcade on the Rialto, watching "well-dressed Venetians float[ing] about in full bloom like pond lilies." He rode in gondolas through the "mirage-like" city to the steps of the Ducal Palace under the Bridge of Sighs, lingering to watch "the tumblers & comic actors in the open space near Rialto," especially "the expression of the women Tumblers," as he walked by moonlight through the Piazza San Marco. "Rather be in Venice on rainy day, than in other capital on fine one," he jotted during his four-day sojourn there.[91]

Leaving Venice at dawn on April 6, he went via Verona to Milan, where he enjoyed "noble views of Lago di Garda with Mount Baldus in distance." Milan Cathedral, with its "burning window at the end of the aisle," struck him as more glorious than St. Peter's, and the view from its summit was so enthralling that he thought he might "write a book of travel" upon the "glorious" cathedral's tower. In the church of Santa Maria delle Grazia he saw Leonardo's *The Last Supper,* but it was so water-stained, faded, and torn that a photographic copy of it had to be displayed beside the original. The masterpiece sparked reflection on how "the joys of the banquet" had so soon given way to Judas's betrayal, and Melville reflected philosophically that "The glow of sociability is so evanescent, selfishness so lasting."[92]

From Milan he went to Turin and Genoa, then caught the steamer for Arona on Lago Maggiore. He rode past cascades and through numerous small villages, making frequent stops along the way and running into both John Lockwood and Dr. Henry Abbott, the noted Egyptologist. Abbott was storming around complaining about his travel arrangements until Melville calmed him down enough to engage him in a "discussion of the gods &c." and persuaded him to take a ramble through the hills around Lucerne.[93]

Abbott, who always wore a red tasseled fez and "full and exact Turkish costume," was the kind of eccentric Melville loved. Born in England in 1812, Henry Abbott married an Armenian woman and moved to Cairo, practicing medicine and amassing a collection of Egyptian antiquities valued at $100,000 during his two decades there. In need of funds, he decided to sell his collection in New York, but, finding no buyer, he opened a gallery on "the gayest and most crowded part of Broadway" instead. Around the walls of Abbott's museum were "slabs of limestone" with "chiseled hieroglyphics" depicting a variety of animals and insects, whom the Egyptians believed had souls. The museum began losing money around 1855, and Abbott threatened to take the collection back to Cairo. Walt Whitman, who revered the Egyptians for their "vast and profound religion," was among the "lovers of antiquity" who worked to keep these treasures in New York and open to the public—a goal reached in 1860, when the New-York Historical Society purchased the collection. Melville's journal gives no indication whether he had visited the gallery before meeting Abbott in Milan, but he may well have done so.[94]

Following an excursion to Lake Lucerne, Melville caught the coach to Bern. After thrilling views of the Bernese Alps and the Jura range, the rustic simplicity and neatness of Swiss cottages soothed his overloaded senses. Either before or after leaving Basel, he met Henry A. Smythe, a New York merchant and banker who would later help him secure a post in the New York Custom-House. Smythe and Melville traveled together by train and boat from Strasbourg to Kiel and Heidelberg, where they toured Germany's oldest university.[95]

Arriving in Frankfurt with Smythe, Melville walked to Goethe Platz and saw "Faust's Statue," then "Luther's preaching place" as well as the Judengasse and the Rothschilds' countinghouse, and in the evening he had dinner and rode around town with Smythe and Abbott. From Frankfurt through Mainz, Cologne, Düsseldorf, and Utrecht, Melville apparently traveled with a party that at one time or another included Smythe, Abbott, Abbott's daughter, and Theodore Sedgwick Fay, a friend of Nathaniel Parker Willis, who had been the first American resident minister in Switzerland.[96]

Melville's main objective in Holland was Amsterdam's Trippenhuis Gallery, where he engaged a guide so he could study the Dutch masters thoroughly in the limited time he had. He especially admired Rembrandt's *Syndics* and *Night Watch* and reveled in "Dutch convivial scenes" by genre painters such as Hals, Teniers, and Breughel. He made very specific notes on the paintings he saw, and later wrote "At the Hostelry" and several shorter poems based on his visits to Dutch museums and galleries. After seeing the house in Rotterdam where Erasmus wrote *In Praise of Folly*, he left for London.

On a dreary Sunday at the end of April, Melville checked into the Tavistock Hotel in London, then ambled through Hyde Park and Kensington Gardens. During the next two days, he went to Madame Tussaud's wax museum, and visited the Crystal Palace, a huge building constructed of iron, wood, and glass for the Great Exhibition of 1851. All Souls' pastor Henry Whitney Bellows, who had praised the Great Exhibition for its "noble & unmistakable tendency to unite man with God," dubbed the Crystal Palace "the digest of the universe," but to Melville it seemed "a vast toy," much "overdone."[97]

At the Vernon & Turner Galleries in the National Gallery, Melville saw the paintings Turner had bequeathed to the nation in 1851, one of which, *The Fighting Temeraire*, inspired an elegy that Melville included among his Civil War poems, published in 1866. Turner's turbulent dark storms and shipwrecks had influenced the composition of *Moby-Dick*. After touring Greece and Italy, Melville found himself looking with new eyes at Turner's sun-flooded Venetian scenes and his paintings of ships sailing under skies suffused with golden light.[98]

After a tour of Oxford and brief stops at Stratford and Warwick, Melville went on to Liverpool, where he booked passage on the *City of Manchester* and called at the consulate. If he had hoped to have time to tell Hawthorne about his trip, he must have been very disappointed, because his old friend was too busy to stop and chat or have a smoke with him. "Saw Hawthorne. Called on Mr Bright. Got presents. Trunk. Packed," he wrote in his journal. His entries are rushed and fragmentary, perhaps because he was tired and impatient to be heading home.[99]

Melville left for home on May 5, more dispirited about the modern world than ever, but more knowledgeable and excited than ever before about classical and European art. "We sham, we shuffle while faith declines," he declares in his poem "The Age of the Antonines." In comparison with modern civilization, ancient times seemed to have been a Golden Age that Melville rather romantically pictured as the "Solstice of Man," the "summit of fate . . . [and] zenith of time / When a pagan gentleman reigned, / And the olive was nailed to the inn of the world / Nor the peace of the just was feigned." He was beginning to realize that if even sites sacred to the great religions of the West were debased by materialism, perhaps it was human nature, not society, that led to the degeneration of the race. If this was so, what hope was there for humanity?[100]

Though his quest for religious certainty had foundered on the rocky shoals of the Holy Land, his search for aesthetic transcendence had been revitalized by the splendid architecture, paintings, and sculpture he saw in Europe and the Near East. The classical synthesis he imagined the ancients had achieved was shattered, but although the marble columns lay in ruins, that grand and glorious expression of the human spirit and lofty classical ideals, the Parthenon, still rose and floated into his inmost soul like a snow hill in the air.

Homesick for his family while at sea in 1860, Melville drew this sketch of Arrowhead, which made him "feel as if I were there, almost—such is the magic power of the fine Artist."

TWENTY-ONE

A CONVULSED AND HALF-DISSOLVED SOCIETY

Just about the time Melville was standing atop Milan Cathedral contemplating the "host of heaven," Augusta was imploring Peter Gansevoort to find him a steady job. Despite her avowed "literary thirst," Gus was convinced that if Melville returned to "the sedentary life" of "an author writing for his support," he "would risk the loss of all the benefit to his health which he has gained by his tour, & possibly become a confirmed invalid. Of this his physicians have warned him." Assuring her uncle that "Mamma's … heart echoes all I have said about Herman," Augusta thought they might be able "to induce him to lay aside his pen" if they could greet him at the dock with the news that a position at the Custom-House was a fait accompli. "To be sure, Herman has never been a politician, but he belongs to a Democratic family, & one which has done much for its party, & received little from it," she wrote. He "is just one of those persons who should be considered in filling these places, for he has done honor to, & reflected credit upon his country."[1]

The English reviews of The Confidence-Man *were largely favorable.* The Athenaeum *called the book "invariably graphic, fresh, and entertaining," and* The Leader *praised the* "almost rhythmic" narrative for its "cordial, bright American touches." The "dry vein of sarcastic humor" running through the narrative struck one critic as "a very deep one indeed." *The Westminster and Foreign Quarterly Review*'s book critic found Melville a "bitter observer" whose "view of human nature is severe and sombre," but he pronounced *The Confidence-Man* "a remarkable work [which] will add to [Melville's] reputation" and said he was looking "forward with pleasure to his promised continuation of the masquerade." Even *The Saturday Review*, which took issue with the "irreverent use of Scriptural passages," applauded Melville's attack on the "money-getting spirit which appears to pervade every class of men in the States, almost like a monomania ... the most dangerous and most debasing tendency of the age."[2]

Shortly before *The Confidence-Man* was published in America, Fitz-James O'Brien set the tone for its reception with a retrospective of Melville's career. Writing in the April 1853 issue of *Putnam's Magazine,* O'Brien pronounced the novel "thoroughly American" and credited Melville with having "all the metaphysical tendencies which belong so eminently to the American's mind—the love of antic and extravagant speculation, the fearlessness of intellectual consequences, and the passion for intellectual legislation, which distinguish the cleverest of our people," but he also accused Melville of having thrown his talent away on a morbidity that "has perverted his fine mind from its healthy productive tendencies."[3]

Many critics faulted Melville for abandoning picturesque narratives to indulge in metaphysical speculations. The reviewer for *Mrs. Stephens' Illustrated New Monthly* charged that despite his "more individualized—more striking, original, sinewy, compact; more reflective and philosophical" style, Melville seemed to be "bent upon obliterating his early successes" by writing a novel that made as much sense read backward as forward; and Philadelphia's *North American* complained that Melville's readers were "choked off at the end of the book like the audience of a Turkish story teller, without getting the end of the story."[4]

Although some readers thought *The Confidence-Man* represented "nineteenth century notions" accurately, others were "mystified by this latest of Melville's strange vagaries." The *Berkshire County Eagle* declared that "as a picture of American society," the book was "*slightly* distorted," and Lizzie's half brother Lem told their brother Sam that Melville's new book belonged to "that horribly uninteresting class of nonsensical books he is given to writing—where there are pages of crude theory & speculation to every line of narrative—& interspersed with strained & ineffectual attempts to be humorous." Notices calling *The Confidence-Man* "bitter, profane and exaggerated" rubbed salt in the wounds of family members and friends who had been stung by the public's reception of *Pierre.*[5]

As soon as his ship docked in New York on May 20, Melville went straight to Boston. Lizzie was encouraged by his "much improved health," but Mother Melville, who seemed "to have renewed her youth and to have quaffed the elixier [*sic*] of life," was not pleased with her son's condition. Her putting pressure on him to become a lecturer must have made him moody around her, because male friends found him sociable and eager to talk about his trip. Lem Shaw Jr. invited Judge Shaw, Mr. Dana, Dr. Holmes, and Melville to a "sumptuous repast" consisting of "First Course Salmon in French style, Mock Turtle soup, Spring chicken, squabs, broiled turkey, mutton chop sweetbread, Canvass back duck and too many other things to enumerate" plus "every kind of dessert" and libations of burgundy, hock, claret, Madeira, Heidsieck, sherry, and anisette. Melville spoke with such animation that someone said he ought to consider lecturing, whereupon Dr. Holmes quipped that a lecturer was "a literary strumpet subject for a greater than whore's fee to prostitute himself."[6]

Melville had little enthusiasm for public speaking. Lem Shaw told his brother Sam that "Herman says he is not going to write any more at present & wishes to get a place in the N. Y. Custom House," but to be considered for the post, he would have to be a New York resident. Friends of Lizzie's urged them to move to Brooklyn instead of Manhattan, and in July, Melville signed an agreement to purchase a house one block from the Flatbush Avenue streetcar stop in Brooklyn.[7]

By the time the Melvilles arrived back in Pittsfield, it was too late to plant turnips, potatoes, buckwheat, and corn. With no prospect of earning money from the farm that year, Herman advertised Arrowhead in the *Eagle* and the *Sun*:

> FOR SALE. THE PLACE now occupied by the subscriber (two miles and a half
> from Pittsfield village by the east road to Lenox), being about seventy acres,
> embracing meadow, pasture, wood, and orchard, with a roomy and comfort-
> able house. For situation and prospect, this place is among the pleasantest
> in Berkshire, and has other natural advantages desirable in a country residence.
> H. Melville.

The ad ran for several weeks, but had no takers. When Melville could not come up with the down payment of $2,200, he was forced to back out of his contract and give up the Brooklyn house.[8]

Balance sheets for *The Confidence-Man* showed Melville owing money to both publishers. Less than half of the one thousand copies printed in England were sold, and shortly after the book appeared, Dix & Edwards folded. Melville had asked George William Curtis to save the plates of both *The Piazza Tales* and *The Confidence-Man* for future editions, but Curtis was still paying back debts owed by *Putnam's Magazine*, so he was in no position to reissue books. When the company's founders liquidated their assets, they auctioned off the plates of Melville's books and merged with a printing company that issued a cheap reprint of *Israel Potter* and paid no royalties.

In August, Melville received an invitation to contribute to a new magazine called *The Atlantic Monthly*, and he replied that he would be happy to contribute to this "laudable enterprise," but did not know when he could have an article ready. Although the first issue of the magazine listed Melville as one of the "literary persons interested in [this] enterprise," he apparently never submitted anything, which is puzzling, given his success as a writer of short fiction.[9]

Family members and literary friends stepped up their efforts to persuade Melville to undertake a lecture tour. George Curtis pointed out that lecture fees, unlike book royalties, were paid promptly, and by September, Curtis was able to tell Allan that Herman "thinks well of lecturing, and wants to be hung for the whole sheep, and go the entire swine. His animal tastes can be easily gratified, I presume." When Curtis pressured him to decide on a topic, he responded that he had "been trying to scratch my brains for a Lecture," but had not yet found an edifying text. "What is a good, earnest subject?" he asked Curtis, quickly answering his own question: "Daily progress of man towards a state of intellectual & moral perfection, as evidenced in the history of 5th Avenue & 5 Points" he proposed sarcastically.[10]

To Charles Dickens and countless visitors to New York, Fifth Avenue and Five Points epitomized the unbridgeable gap between the rich and the poor. Merchants and shipping magnates who had made their fortunes from real estate or the lucrative cotton trade were building marble mansions uptown, away from the commercial districts, and Fifth Avenue was becoming a haven of wealth and privilege. Five Points was a "corrupt district" at the intersection of Worth, Park, and Baxter. Known as New York's "Hell," its sleazy gambling dens, saloons, and brothels flourished on land owned by wealthy individuals and fashionable churches.

Melville's sarcasm reflects his sensitivity to the profound economic and social crisis America was facing in 1857. The gold rush, the frenzied speculation in land and railroads, sudden reductions in import duties that favored southern planters over northern mill owners, and the grain glut caused by overproduction for the Crimean War all combined to create runaway inflation, and the bottom fell out of the economy that autumn. Several of the nation's largest banks suspended operations, sending Wall Street into hysteria and Boston into a "financial derangement" that banker Amos A. Lawrence feared would "spread ruin over every interest." As business after business went bankrupt in New York, unemployed workers took to the streets with huge signs demanding "BREAD OR DEATH!"[11]

The precipitous growth in unemployment and homelessness in northern cities was driving a dangerous wedge between upper and lower classes. In New York, Republican newspapers supported the business community's view that poverty and unemployment should be taken care of by private charities. When Mayor Fernando Wood proposed using public funds to hire the unemployed to do public works, Republican columnists called him a communist, and when he demanded equality between "the rich who produce nothing and have everything and the poor who produce everything and have nothing," they denounced him as a demagogue.[12]

Widespread joblessness caused anger and frustration, and nativists exploited people's fear of foreigners and the lower class by blaming them for the increase in street crimes. Although most thought it "a very bad practice" to carry a revolver, many "respectable" citizens felt they were not safe without a gun. Faced with an inadequate police force to deal with outbreaks of violence, Mayor Wood allowed street gangs such as the "Dead Rabbits" and the "Bowery Boys" to help the metropolitan police keep order, but as soon as these hobnail-booted ruffians were given power, they abused it by terrorizing blacks and "foreigners." Branding City Hall "a sink of corruption," attorney David Dudley Field asked the governor to restore order. The state police were sent in to break up the alliance between the metropolitan police and Irish toughs, throwing the city into a "stage of siege."[13]

Meanwhile, the western states were embroiled in territorial disputes. The passage of the Kansas-Nebraska Act in 1854 and the Lecompton Convention's attempt to adopt a constitution that legalized slavery in Kansas without submitting it to the voters for ratification exacerbated sectional animosities. As the proslavery forces gained strength, and talk of slave rebellions in the South increased, the western states were reluctant to adopt state constitutions outlawing slavery for fear thousands of blacks would seek refuge within their borders. Northern politicians were so afraid of antagonizing wealthy cotton planters that William Walker, the white supremacist puppet president of Nicaragua who had been installed by American businessmen, received a hero's welcome when he returned to New York after his ouster by Nicaraguan nationals.[14]

Industrialization and the abundance of "free" land in the West made land grants, real estate, railroad stocks, and corporate bonds lucrative sources of income for enterprising investors, all of whom claimed to be spreading the "blessings of civilization" throughout the nation while they were getting rich. While men of civic vision such as the architect Frederick Olmsted and the clergymen Henry Whitney Bellows and Wendell Phillips were warning of the deleterious effects of unchecked materialism, many of the nation's elected representatives were going along with the new economic manifest destiny espoused by merchants like William B. Astor, August Belmont, William Aspinwall, and Allan Melville's brother-in-law Richard Lathers, who formed the Democratic Vigilant Association in 1859 to protect northern investments in the South.[15]

Large companies sent operatives to Washington to pressure Congress to pass legislation favorable to them, and as these lobbyists swarmed into the nation's capital, politicians with their eyes on their stock portfolios rather than on the Constitution became servants of the special interests rather than of the people. Congressmen accepted campaign contributions from land speculators, government contractors, and seekers of bank charters and railroad franchises, and as news of election frauds, conflicts of interest, and bribes filled the newspapers, citizens became disillusioned. Even the once-revered Daniel Webster was not free of the taint of political corruption; while arguing legislation favorable to the banking industry in the Senate, he remained on the payroll of the Bank of the United States. Ralph Waldo Emerson confided to his journal that he was fed up with that "class of privileged thieves who infest our politics," those "well dressed well-bred fellows ... who get into government and rob without stint and without disgrace." *Harper's Weekly* charged that the heads of city departments in New York were "as lawless as eastern pashas" and challenged educated men to fix things. The *New York Herald,* identifying money as "the overshadowing evil at Washington" and the money power in politics as "a rapacious monster," called lobbyists "the third estate in government."[16]

The Dred Scott case had been decided while Melville was in the Holy Land, and repercussions were still being felt throughout the country. Scott, a slave who had been taken by his owner from Missouri to the free territories of Illinois and Wisconsin, sued to avoid being taken back to Missouri. When Scott claimed that his residence in free territories made his re-enslavement unconstitutional, three justices of the Supreme Court argued that slaves could not institute legal action of any kind because they were not citizens, and he was ordered to return to the plantation.

The decision enraged abolitionists and disappointed moderates who had assumed that slavery would wither away of its own accord, while southern apologists for slavery felt emboldened to step up their attacks on the antislavery North. "Ye hypocrites, reform yourself, before you preach to us!" cried one Kentucky editor. Frederick Douglass urged "abolitionists and colored people" to meet this new injustice in a "cheerful spirit," as he believed that "unlooked for and monstrous as it appears," the decision would prove to be a "necessary link in the chain of events preparatory to the complete overthrow of the whole slave system."[17]

~~~

Against this backdrop of mounting social, political, and economic conflict, Melville decided to reconsider lecturing. His literary reputation, his travels to exotic lands, and his cultural and artistic interests were appropriate qualifications for joining the most prominent program of platform presenters in the country. Even if a speaking tour probably would not boost his literary reputation, frequent changes of scene would be far more beneficial to his health than hunkering down again to write fiction that was destined to fail in the marketplace.

In 1826, businessman Josiah Holbrook, a graduate of Yale, had proposed a series of lectures for towns and villages that were not close to universities or cities, and the American Lyceum Movement was born. It was founded to improve the conversation of ordinary citizens who would, in turn, support libraries, museums, and public schools. By 1834, lecturing had become the rage. Americans avid for intellectual stimulation had set up three thousand lyceums around the country, and writers and reformers were mounting the podium in droves. During the winter of 1837–38 alone, the twenty-six programs sponsored by the Boston Lyceum under its president, Daniel Webster, were attended by thirteen thousand people. By the mid-1850s, the Lyceum, named for the school in Athens where Aristotle taught philosophy, had become "a fixed American institution," according to *Harper's Weekly*. Celebrities such as poet-philosopher Ralph Waldo Emerson, educator Horace Mann, abolitionist Wendell Phillips, feminists Lucy Stone and Elizabeth Cady Stanton, and travel writer Bayard Taylor drew large crowds.[18]

By late October 1857, Melville had secured a number of bookings, and Mary Melvill was hopeful that Herman's tour would bring him as far west as Galena, where they would "rejoice" to see him. John Hoadley, who had moved to Lawrence, Massachusetts, and set up his own company to manufacture and market the portable engine he had invented, arranged for Melville to make his debut at a benefit for the Lawrence Provident Association on November 23. Despite a devilish echo in the hall, Melville warmed to the occasion because it was his initial delivery of the talk and because friends and family were in the audience. He was as animated in Lawrence as he would ever be on the lecture platform, and the day after he spoke, the Lawrence *Courier* praised his "keen insight, honest independence, bold originality, and great justness of vision," describing his delivery as "nervous and vigorous, yet easy and flowing, and falling constantly into the most melodious cadences." Unfortunately, a severe thunderstorm reduced the turnout and limited the proceeds to little more than thirty dollars.[19]

Melville chose Roman statuary as the subject best suited to the articulation of his philosophy of art and least likely to involve him in controversy and debate. Describing masterpieces a traveler sees as he enters the world's grandest outdoor museum, he warned that the modern emphasis on industry and science was threatening to destroy the reverence for the arts that had flourished during the classical period. He argued that noble ideals and images, not military conquests, make a civilization great, and he faulted Christianity for robbing Western culture of its "heroic tone" by destroying the mythology of the ancient world. Contrasting the invention of the printing press with the nobility of the "best thought" of the ancients in "law, physics, or philosophy," he asserted that science is "beneath art" because its standards are practical, not aesthetic.[20]

According to Melville, art is intrinsically moral because it is the "incarnation of grandeur and of beauty." Its value lies in its power to enlarge human experience through empathic imagination. Describing the statue *The Dying Gladiator,* he remarked that, to appreciate it, the viewer must rebuild the Colosseum in imagination and repeople it "with the terrific games of the gladiators, with the frantic leaps and dismal howls of the wild, bounding beasts, with the shrieks and cries of the excited spectators."[21]

If great works are to live again for each new generation, they must have great audiences:

> These marbles, the works of the dreamers and idealists of old, live on, leading and pointing to good. They are the works of visionaries and dreamers, but they are realizations of soul, the representations of the ideal. They are grand, beautiful, and true, and they speak with a voice that echoes through the ages. Governments have changed, empires have fallen; nations have passed away; but these mute marbles remain—the oracles of time, the perfection of art. They were formed by those who had yearnings for something better, and strove to attain it by embodiments in cold stone.[22]

More reviewers than not criticized Melville for choosing an esoteric subject rather than something easier to comprehend. While one reviewer praised him for the "striking and beautiful thought" he had introduced "when speaking of the equestrian statues of Rome, and the expression of untamed docility, rather than conquered obedience which their artists have given to the horse," another took him to task for his "monotonous description of such 'dead heads' as Demosthenes, Julius Caesar, Seneca, Plato, Tiberius and Apollo."[23]

Once word got out through the *New-York Daily Tribune*'s announcement of the winter lecture season, Melville received invitations for "numerous engagements ... in Boston and its vicinity." When Henry Gansevoort heard Melville speak at Boston's Tremont Temple, he compared him to Icarus: "When he essays philosophy he seeks to ascend by waxen wings from his proper sphere only to find his mind dazzled, his wings melted, and his fall mortifying." Reviewers noted that the talk went on too long and had a tepid but polite reception, and Henry thought his cousin ought to stick to "wild, bold word painting" rather than indulging in "metaphysical disquisitions." Offstage, Melville "was in a fine flow of humor," which Henry "enjoyed exceedingly. There is doubtless positive originality in him. Brilliancy but misanthropy. Genius but less judgement. He evidently mistakes his sphere. He has dropped the pen of candid narration for that of captious criticism. He does the latter well but he can do the former much better."[24]

Unlike the mesmerizing Emerson and the histrionic Bayard Taylor, who spoke without any notes, Melville read his lectures. As a result, his delivery was accounted "dull," "unobtrusive," "subdued," "sing-song," "monotonous," and "ministerially solemn." Despite his "rich and mellow" voice, he failed to breathe life into his ideas, and they remained abstractions. The Auburn, New York, *Daily Advertiser* pronounced his performance "the most complete case of infanticide we ever heard of," as he had "literally strangled his own child."[25]

In the midst of the tour, he managed to spend Christmas in Gansevoort with his mother, Uncle Herman, and Augusta, stopping at Arrowhead before going on to lecture in New Haven. Unfortunately, his lecture did not spark the enthusiasm of his auditors. By the time his tour ended in New Bedford, on February 23, 1858, he had barely earned enough money to make the effort worthwhile. For fourteen paid appearances in cities as far-ranging as Ithaca, Montreal, Cleveland, Rochester, Cincinnati, Chillicothe, Sandusky, and Clarksville (Tennessee), he grossed $645, and twice he lectured gratis. After traveling expenses of $221.30, he was left with a net profit of only $423.70, disappointing but more than he had ever made for three months' work.[26]

On his way home to Pittsfield, Melville stopped in Gansevoort to see his mother, and found himself laid up with a "severe crick in the back" that kept him at his uncle's place longer than he had planned. Although Lizzie later claimed that "he never regained his former vigor & strength," by the end of the summer he was strong enough to take a "tramp in woods" with Sam Shaw, and Evert and George Duyckinck found their friend's "offhand hearty sailor grace" and energy unabated. Driving the brothers up the Mohawk Trail to see the new Hoosac Tunnel, he set a fast pace "through the mud to the end of the excavation, a little over a thousand feet."[27]

When Lemuel Shaw visited Arrowhead in September, he found Melville "as well as I have seen him for years." Elizabeth was tending to her household chores "with great care and satisfaction," and the children were "greatly improved, in appearance and conduct." Sadly, however, after being "kept alive for months by an egg and a small glass of whiskey," Allan's wife, Sophia, a "very gentle, sweet woman" only thirty-one years old, died from tuberculosis that October, leaving her husband with five children, four girls and a boy.[28]

Three weeks later, Priscilla Melvill died, and as the days grew shorter and the early darkness more profound, Melville was feeling low. His eyes were bothering him so much that when George Duyckinck sent him a five-volume set of Chapman's Homer, he cut the pages but could not read the text. When he declined an invitation to go to Boston for the Thanksgiving holiday, Judge Shaw sent him a check for one hundred dollars to help with "family supplies for the approaching winter," and invited him to visit whenever his lecturing brought him to Boston.[29]

Taking a cue from reviewers who urged him to talk about adventures, not ideas, Melville decided to lecture on "The South Seas," using the topic as a springboard for critical reflections on the modern world, as he had done in his first lecture. Recommending a sojourn in those "unviolated wastes ... those far-off archipelagoes from the heat and dust of civilization" as a tonic for "jaded tourists to whom even Europe has become hackneyed, and who look upon the Parthenon and the Pyramids with a yawn," he threw out a cautionary word: "The natives of these islands are naturally of a kindly and hospitable temper, but there has been planted among them an almost instinctive hate of the white man." Those in the audience who recalled the shock Tommo felt when he saw French sailors taking potshots at the natives who lined up to welcome them would have heard the sarcasm in Melville's rhetorical question "Who has ever heard of a vessel sustaining the honor of a Christian flag and the spirit of the Christian Gospel by opening its batteries in indiscriminate massacre upon some poor little village on the seaside—splattering the torn bamboo huts with blood and brains of women and children, defenseless and innocent?"[30]

He blamed Christian imperialists for turning "an earthly paradise into a pandemonium" and, concluding with a hope "that adventurers from our soil and from the lands of Europe will abstain from those brutal and cruel vices which disgust even savages with our manners," he suggested that Christians might forbear from contact with native cultures until they had created "a civilization morally, mentally, and physically higher than one which has culminated in almshouses, prisons, and hospitals." Despite Melville's blunt remarks, this lecture was well received, especially in Pittsfield, where it was described as "redolent of the spicy odors of the South Seas, and sparkling with original thoughts." After the enthusiastic reception he received in Burbank Hall, he felt "ready to lecture in Labrador, or on the Isle of Desolation off Patagonia," provided they would "pay expenses and give a reasonable fee."[31]

Melville's tour took him to Yonkers, Baltimore, Lynn, Quincy, Rockford, and Chicago, as well as Pittsfield, Boston, and New York. When he spoke at Boston's Tremont Temple on January 31, 1859, his brother Tom was in the audience, and as soon as Herman had a break in his schedule, they went to Gansevoort to see their mother. Shortly afterward, he spoke at the New-York Historical Society, where an audience of "highly respectable" and "eminent *literati* … evinced their gratification by applause and attention," according to Henry Gansevoort, although the hall was only "about half filled owing to the want of proper advertising." Henry, who had disliked "Statues in Rome," pronounced Herman "emphatically himself" and the lecture "a treat long to be remembered."[32]

In Milwaukee, the westernmost point on his tour, Melville fulfilled expectations held by fans of *Typee*, as "soft, voluptuous ease" and "drowsy enchantment" were his "predominant characteristic." A Rockford, Illinois, reviewer, however, found him a slightly bilious chap for one of such "good physique," and his lecture seemed a "painful infliction" of facts readily available "on the shelves of almost any library."[33]

Lyceum speakers had to appeal to a broad, eclectic audience, but Melville had no knack for communicating passion for his subject to large audiences. The more lectures he gave, the more his delivery deteriorated. Large lecture halls lacked the intimacy of the Lansingburgh sitting room, the sociability of Evert Duyckinck's cellar, or the coziness of the Hawthornes' parlor where Melville had spun his tales of the Typee Valley. Public auditoriums were often cavernous and cold, and auditors thought nothing of chewing tobacco and spitting the juice indiscriminately, taking swigs from pocket flasks, rattling newspapers, and whispering to their neighbors during a speech. Melville was too proud and too self-absorbed to entertain such boorish audiences, and he soon grew aloof and stale. Moreover, when his insecurity about public speaking surfaced, he mumbled over his notes, hardly daring to raise his eyes from the text. Repeating himself night after night was not his style; his active, protean mind needed to be constantly grappling with new ideas and finding new ways of expressing them.

～

At home, life went on while Melville was on tour. In December 1858, Kate Hoadley gave birth to a second daughter, Charlotte, and the following February his old shipmate Oliver Russ named his newborn boy Herman Melville Russ. Malcolm was studying "arithmetic, with cyphering, geography, spelling, and reading," and every Friday he had "to speak a piece" in school. Proud possessor of the fastest clipper sled in the Berkshires, Malcolm beat all the boys in the neighborhood at sledding races that cold, snowy February, and one afternoon, after skating for hours, he built a snow house "big enough for 15 boys to go into."[34]

Melville's tour, which lasted until March, grossed only $518.50, a paltry sum compared with the large fees commanded by some speakers. When Titus Munson Coan and John Thomas Gulick, two students who had been born and raised in the Hawaiian Islands by American missionary fathers, drove down from Williams College to visit him one April morning, they found him rocking on his piazza, absorbed in philosophical meditations, while he was awaiting Lizzie's return from Boston with little Bessie. Coan, who had had "quite enough of Greek philosophy at Williams College," wanted to "hear of Typee and those Paradise islands," but Melville "preferred to pour forth his philosophy and his theories of life" until "the shade of Aristotle arose like a cold mist between myself and Fayaway."[35]

Even so, the young man couldn't help being favorably impressed by his host's erudition: "Melville is transformed from a Marquesan to a gypsy student, the gypsy element still remaining strong in him. And this contradiction gives him the air of one who has suffered from opposition, both literary and social. With his liberal views he is apparently considered by the good people of Pittsfield as little better than a cannibal or a beach-comber. His attitude seemed to me something like that of an Ishmael; but perhaps I judged hastily.

I managed to draw him out very freely on everything but the Marquesan Islands, and when I left him he was in full tide of discourse on all things sacred and profane."[36]

John Gulick left a fairly detailed description of Melville: He "stands erect and moves with firm and manly grace. His conversation and manner, as well as the engravings on his walls, betray little of the sailor. His head is of moderate size with black hair, dark eyes, a smooth pleasant forehead and rough heavy beard and mustache. His countenance is slightly flushed with whiskey drinking, but not without expression. When in conversation his keen eyes glance from over his aquiline nose."[37]

Despite his drinker's complexion, Melville "possessed a mind of an aspiring, ambitious order, full of elastic energy and illumined with the rich colors of a poetic fancy." Yet he seemed "a disappointed man, soured by criticism and disgusted with the civilized world and with our Christendom in general and in particular." He escaped the barbarism of the modern age by immersing himself in the study of classical civilization, and as Gulick observed, "the ancient dignity of Homeric times afforded the only state of humanity, individual or social, to which he could turn with any complacency."[38]

A polymath who could warm to any topic if his interlocutors showed interest, Melville enjoyed the opportunity to impress these young men with the force of his personality and the depth of his erudition. Unable to tear themselves away, after lunch the students kept Melville company when he took the "wagon to the next village where he was expecting to meet his lady on the arrival of the next train," grateful for whatever time he gave them.[39]

Melville did not tell Coan and Gulick that he was reading and writing poetry. He had acquired Francis James Child's collection of English and Scottish border ballads, as well as volumes of verse by Robert Herrick, George Herbert, and Andrew Marvell, and although he told Evert Duyckinck he was "doing nothing," he apparently sent one or two little "Pieces" to a magazine that spring.[40]

In July he sent Allan's law partner Daniel Shepherd, the "Wall Street scholar," an invitation to Arrowhead written in the style of Marlowe's "The Passionate Shepherd to His Love."

> Come, Shepherd, come and visit me:
> Come, we'll make it Arcady:
> Come, if but for charity.
> Sure, with such a pastoral name,
> Thee the city should not claim.
> Come, then, Shepherd, come away,
> Thy sheep in bordering pastures stray.

He concludes with a promise to serve stronger stuff than Shepherd's favorite ruby claret:

> —Of bourbon that is rather new
> I brag a fat black bottle or two.—
> Shepherd, is this such Mountain-Dew
> As one might fitly offer you?[41]

On August 1, 1859, Melville celebrated his fortieth birthday, and Sam Shaw brought him Emerson's collected poems as a gift. Inside the volume, Melville jotted Anacreon's paean to the grasshopper: "Happy thing!" that "seem'st to me / Almost a little god to be!" Melville may have wished he could fiddle and chirp with no thought of the morrow, as at this juncture he was a man whose successes all seemed to be behind him, a man whose health was unreliable and troublesome. Unlike Allan, who had a good income and some lucrative investments, Melville was largely dependent on his wife's family for financial support. After clearing up some questions about the deeds, he sold eighty acres of pastureland to George Willis in order to discharge a debt of $5,500 to his father-in-law, then transferred the title on the property to Judge Shaw, who signed it over to Lizzie as "an estate of inheritance." Herman tried to console himself with the knowledge that the great artists of the past had relied on patrons for support. In America, however, men were expected to be the breadwinners; like Enceladus, he was half free from his cultural conditioning and half bound by it.[42]

That fall, taking a cue from reviews that faulted him for not talking about his voyages, Melville composed a third lecture, "Traveling: Its Pleasures, Pains, and Profits," and delivered it in Flushing, New York. After a rather dreamy opener, he enumerated the predictable advantages and disadvantages of travel instead of recounting personal experiences, but he made such obvious advantages as leaving home to experience new sensations and returning to the comfort of the "old hearthstone" sound much less exciting than "the persecutions and extortions of guides" and the omnipresence of bedbugs and fleas. Roman fleas evidently intrigued American travelers abroad; when Kate Gansevoort made the Grand Tour with her family in 1860, she thought the creatures so remarkable that she wrapped several of them in paper packets and brought them home. They now reside in the New York Public Library's Gansevoort-Lansing Collection.[43]

Unfortunately, Melville's lecture lacked drama, originality, and wit, especially when compared with a performance by Bayard Taylor, "the armchair traveller." Melville's rather long-winded pronouncement that travel teaches "personal humility, while it enlarges the sphere of comprehensive benevolence till it includes the whole human race" said little more than his statement that the first benefit of travel was that "you get rid of a *few* prejudices. . . . the stock-broker goes to Thessalonica and finds infidels more honest than Christians; the teetotaller finds a country in France where all drink and no one gets drunk; the prejudiced against color finds several hundred millions of people of all shades of color, and all degrees of intellect, rank, and social worth, generals, judges, priests, and kings, and learns to give up his foolish prejudices." In the Levant, he pointed out, people who would be regarded as ignorant peasants by educated Westerners often speak half a dozen languages fluently, while the Western traveler often does not speak any language beside his own. "The sight of novel objects, the acquirement of novel ideas, the breaking up of old prejudices, the enlargement of heart and mind," he concluded, "are the proper fruit of rightly undertaken travel."[44]

Feeling unwell after this engagement, Melville spent a week in Manhattan reading Vasari's *Lives of the Painters* and visiting art galleries and museums. When he returned to Arrowhead toward the end of November, he was sick and demoralized. "Herman Melville is not well," Sarah Morewood told George Duyckinck, "do not call him moody, he is ill."[45]

He secured only two more speaking engagements, both in Massachusetts, and this truncated tour yielded a scant $110. The three lecture tours together earned only $1,273.50, minus expenses. Few could touch the success of the charismatic Reverend Henry Ward Beecher, whose voice was "the bell of the soul ... the iron and crashing of the anvil ... a magician's wand, full of incantation and witchery," and who was said to have made $30,000 a year in his heyday. Ralph Waldo Emerson, whom Melville had dubbed "a Plato who talks through his nose," made $1,700 lecturing in 1856, and Bayard Taylor could count on around $5,000 per season.[46]

Despite his strong opinions about contemporary culture, Melville eschewed political and social commentary, as most audiences favored entertainment, quick, painless wisdom, practical advice, or current events over philosophical ruminations. When John Brown and his abolitionist cohorts raided the federal arsenal at Harpers Ferry in October 1859, Henry David Thoreau and other New Englanders made public pleas for clemency during the trial. After his execution, they called the self-appointed liberator of the slaves a God-inspired martyr whose desperate act foreshadowed the violence to come, but Melville did not comment publicly on Brown until 1866, when he apotheosized him in a poem.[47]

By the beginning of 1860, Melville had given up lecturing completely. He was back home in early February, stocking up on books like a squirrel hoarding nuts for winter. While he was in New York at the end of January, he had purchased *The Poetical Works of Andrew Marvell.* Impelled by an inner necessity most of his family could not comprehend, Melville turned to reading and writing poetry, keeping it a "profound secret" between himself and Lizzie.[48]

Once again, what Melville wanted to do would not pay. Only one American—Henry

Wadsworth Longfellow—had ever come close to making a living by writing poetry, and Melville could not have been confident that the type of poetry he wanted to write would bring him either artistic recognition or remuneration. The most popular poets of the day were writing primarily didactic and sentimental verse, but Melville's idols were not poetasters like Farquahar, Tupper, and Hemans. They were the great masters such as Homer, Dante, Shakespeare, and John Milton.

On February 25, 1860, Illinois congressman Abraham Lincoln stepped off the ferry at the Courtlandt Street pier in New York City, not far from one of Melville's childhood homes. He was scheduled to give an address at the Cooper Union. Despite blizzard conditions, 1,500 citizens showed up to see the gangly prairie lawyer who had held his own against Stephen A. Douglas, the "little giant" of the recent senatorial debates, though he had failed to win a Senate seat. After being escorted to the podium by David Dudley Field and William Cullen Bryant, Lincoln delivered a closely reasoned, richly cadenced defense of the federal Union and promised to stop the extension of slavery into new territories. His arguments against slavery and his vision of America as a "house" tragically "divided" against itself paved the way for his nomination as the Republican Party's candidate for the presidency and put New York bankers and merchants on their guard.[49]

Melville was hibernating with his books when Allan's announcement that he planned to remarry jolted the entire clan awake. Friends and family considered Allan's fiancée, Jane Louisa Dempsey, a spoiled, selfish spendthrift. "I am so sad to hear of Allan Melville's engagement to be married so soon," wrote Sarah Morewood. "God help his dear little family. I am disappointed in Allan Melville—he is now only an acquaintance of the past." Allan, however, was not the sort of man to be swayed by the opinions of others. He could be opinionated, surly, and combative, and although these qualities were well suited to the rough-and-tumble political world of Tammany Hall, friends and family members were annoyed. Despite the fact that she had rubbed everyone the wrong way, Allan married "Madam Jane," as Helen called her, that April in Philadelphia.

When Tom arrived home at the end of April and found Herman dejected and seemingly at loose ends, he invited him to keep him company on his upcoming voyage. Much to the family's relief, Herman jumped at the chance to see San Francisco and Shanghai. Judge Shaw told him the trip would afford "a fair prospect of being a permanent benefit to your health," and offered to "do anything in my power to aid your preparation, and make the voyage most agreeable and beneficial to you." Melville's tactful and generous father-in-law may have had an ulterior motive for wanting him to get away. While he genuinely wanted Herman to be well, he probably also thought Lizzie needed a vacation from her demanding and difficult husband.[50]

Planning to be away an entire year, Melville spent the month before Tom's ship, the *Meteor,* was scheduled to sail trying to get a volume of poems ready for publication. Feeling rushed and uncertain as to how his poems would be received, he left the manuscript with Lizzie to copy. "Anything not perfectly plain in the M.S.S." was to be referred to Lizzie, who was to proofread the final sheets before they were bound to "detect any gross errors consequent upon misconstruing the M.S.S." Evert Duyckinck was to oversee "the launching of this craft–the committing of it to the elements," and Allan was to negotiate the contract and guide it through the press. Giving Allan explicit instructions to offer the poems to Appleton and Scribner, not Harper's, and to be willing to accept half-profits after expenses, Herman advised him to confer with Evert Duyckinck before signing anything. He wanted Allan to pressure the publisher to produce the volume as quickly as possible, and not "For God's sake to have *By the author of 'Typee,' 'Piddledee' &c* on the title page, and not to allow any clap-trap announcements or 'sensation' puffs, but to let the title-page be simply Poems by Herman Melville." He did not expect to make money on the book, as "of all human events, perhaps, the publication of a first volume of verses is the most insignificant."[51]

Sharing the secret of his writing poetry and preparation of the volume brought Herman and Lizzie closer for a time. He looked to her for help because she had quietly supported his turn to poetry instead of joining the chorus urging him to quit writing. Treating Lizzie as a partner instead of sniping at her fulfilled the earliest wish she had shared with her mother as a married woman, and it sowed the seeds of the intimacy that would blossom in the last decades of their lives, after terrible turmoil and tragedy burned away the cankers that had attacked the roots of their married life.

At the end of May, Melville stowed his gear on the *Meteor,* and while he and Tom were waiting for the cargo and provisions to be loaded, they posed for an ambrotype that made them look like twin grizzly bears. Melville's reading for the long voyage comprised some periodicals, which he called "lazy reading for lazy latitudes," and a small library that included editions of the poems of Homer, Dante, Milton, Wordsworth, and Schiller, a volume combining the New Testament and the Psalms, and Nathaniel Hawthorne's *The Marble Faun,* which Sarah Morewood had given him. The Hawthornes were returning to Concord from Italy just about the time Melville was boarding the *Meteor*, and Hawthorne's latest novel revealed an attraction to classical sculpture and a fascination with the story of Beatrice Cenci as intense as Melville's.[52]

Soon after Melville's departure, Lizzie sent his manuscript and instructions to Allan off to Evert Duyckinck. In a postscript she explained that in his haste, Herman had forgotten to say that the book "should be plainly bound, that is, not over-gilt," adding that "to 'bluc and gold' I know he has a decided aversion." She asked Duyckinck to check the manuscript for inaccuracies because Herman had prepared it so hastily and to give his opinion of the poems: "you need not be afraid to say *exactly* what you think."[53]

Around the time Melville was watching the Southern Cross from the deck of the *Meteor,* Charles Scribner was returning his poems to Evert Duyckinck. Although Scribner had "no doubt they are excellent," he had recently published volumes of poetry by Edmund Clarence Stedman and George P. Morris, and he had no desire to commit himself to "another venture in that line," as "the prospect is that neither of them will pay."[54]

Lizzie was indignant at the rejection. In a feisty letter that would have delighted Herman, she thanked Evert Duyckinck for his "kind endeavors about the manuscript, regretting that its course does not run smoothly, thus far." She did "not consider its rejection by the publishers as any test of its mint in a literary point of view—well knowing, as Herman does also, that *poetry* is a comparatively uncalled-for article in the publishing market—I suppose that if John Milton were to offer 'Paradise Lost' to the Harpers tomorrow, it would be promptly rejected as 'unsuitable' not to say, denounced as dull."[55]

The voyage on the *Meteor* proved not to be the relaxing vacation cruise Tom had promised Herman. During the first week out, the ship encountered such foggy, rainy weather that Melville suffered terribly from seasickness. Even after the sky cleared and his appetite started to come back, he felt queasy. With a leather cap pulled down over his ears and forehead to protect him from the wind, he sat on deck reading, writing in his journal, or watching flying fish and Portuguese men-of-war. Several weeks later, the *Meteor* was sideswiped by an English brig whose captain had fallen asleep, leaving a half-blind mate at the helm. Only Tom's quick thinking saved his ship from complete destruction as the brig "blundered down across our bow, & was locked with us for a time, ripping & tearing her sails" and damaging the ship's foreyard and main.[56]

In the evenings, he and Tom played chess or chatted over brandy and cigars, and as soon as the weather turned pleasant, Melville rallied. Even though his stomach was "not yet completely settled," he scampered out on the flying-jib boom to take in the "glorious view of the ship." The good weather didn't last long, however, and by late June the ship lay motionless in the "Doleful Doldrums—The whole ship's crew given up to melancholy, and meditating darkly on the mysteries of Providence."[57]

Rounding the Horn in winter was every bit as horrible as Richard Henry Dana's description of it. The *Meteor* was tossed by icy gales and battered by hail and sleet that froze to the deck and made the footing extremely dangerous. Several men were washed from their posts and one sailor seriously injured. As the ship passed through the "Strait of Le Maire," Melville shuddered. Its "Horrible snowy mountains—black, thunder-cloud woods—gorges" resembled a "hell-landscape." Nearby Staten Land, an island "all covered with snow," struck him as uninhabitable forever, it was "so barren, cold, and desolate." By contrast, Tierra del Fuego, the "land of fire," was inhabited by "wild people" who must have been taking refuge in their caves, as August was the dead of winter in the southern hemisphere. The *Meteor's* passage around Cape Horn was much more arduous than the *Acushnet's*, especially for a middle-aged mariner who was much less well equipped to withstand both the physical and emotional strains than the young sailor of twenty years ago.[58]

On August 9, with a fierce gale pelting the ship with snow and sleet and hail, a young Nantucketer named Benjamin Ray "fell from the Main topsail yard to the deck, & striking his head foremost upon one of the spars was instantly killed." Traumatized by Ray's death and the "harrowing spectacle" of seeing the lad's chum Macey Fisher crying over the body, Melville described the scene in almost obsessive detail: "'I have lost my best friend,' said he; and then 'His mother will go crazy—she did not want to let him go, she feared something might happen.'"[59]

His journal entry indicates how deeply he was disturbed by this calamity:

> Ray's fate … belongs to that order of human events, which staggers those whom the Primal Philosophy hath not confirmed. —But little sorrow to the crew—all goes on as usual—I, too, read & think, & walk & eat & talk, as if nothing had happened—as if I did not know that death is indeed the King of Terrors—when thus happening; when thus heart-breaking to a fond mother—the King of Terrors, not to the dying or the dead, but to the mourner—the mother. Not so easily will his fate be washed out of her heart, as his blood from the deck.[60]

When Melville described the same event in a letter to Malcolm, however, he did not express his emotions or describe the shock felt by Ray's shipmates. Influenced by Victorian models of paternal letter-writing, he recounted the event coldly and ended with some harsh, ominous advice:

> Well, all at once, Uncle Tom saw something falling through the air, and then heard a thump, and then—looking before him, saw a poor sailor lying dead on the deck. He had fallen from the yard, and was killed instantly. —His shipmates picked him up, and carried him under cover. By and by, when time could be spared, the sailmaker sewed up the body in a piece of sailcloth, putting some iron balls—cannon balls—at the foot of it. And, when all was ready, the body was put on a plank, and carried to the ship's side in the presence of all hands. Then Uncle Tom, as Captain, read a prayer out of the prayer-book, and at a given word, the sailors who held the plank tipped it up, and immediately the body slipped into the stormy ocean, and we saw it no more. —Such is the way a

poor sailor is buried at sea. This sailor's name was Ray. He had a friend among the crew; they were both going to California, and thought of living there; but you see what happened.[61]

Evidently, the father who found no lesson in Benjamin Ray's meaningless death expected his eleven-year-old son to learn a lesson from his account of the tragedy. He seems to have been using Ray's death to warn Malcolm that a young man who left home and set off on his own risked danger, even death, which must have struck the oldest son of an author known for his youthful adventures as typical parental hypocrisy.

Melville apparently felt he had to be increasingly stern with Malcolm as he got older, and by underestimating the boy's capacity for empathy and compassion, he missed an opportunity to foster Malcolm's emotional growth and forge a bond with him by sharing his own thoughts and feelings. He wrote Malcolm frequently, on some occasions telling him about sighting a whaling ship, on others admonishing him to obey his mother:

> I hope that you have called to mind what I said to you about your behaviour previous to my going away. I hope that you have been obedient to your mother, and helped her all you could, & saved her trouble. Now is the time to show what you are—whether you are a good, honorable boy, or a good-for-nothing one. Any boy, of your age, who disobeys his mother, or worries her, or is disrespectful to her—such a boy is a poor shabby fellow; and if you know any such boys, you ought to cut their acquaintance.[62]

This stern letter implies that a boy's character is essentially fixed, with no middle ground, no shades of gray, no room for human frailty or error. It could be a page from a Calvinist book on child-rearing.

Melville clearly missed his children during this trip; yet, as the children grew older, he tended to take the stern, admonitory tone that Victorian fathers were expected to have with their sons, forgetting that boys, too, need love and nurturing in order to grow:

> Now my dear Malcolm, I must finish my letter to you. I think of you, and Stanwix & Bessie and Fanny very often; and often long to be with you. But it can not be, at present. The picture which I have of you & the rest, I look at sometimes, till the faces seem almost real.

Although Melville mentions Stanwix, he seems not to have written him a letter. In general, Stannie appears to have been the forgotten second son, as Herman was during his own early childhood. Melville fathers for several generations practiced an emotional primogeniture that took a heavy toll on younger sons, so perhaps it was not surprising that even as an adult, Stanwix never settled down.

Fatherless during his adolescent years, Melville as a father himself had trouble balancing consistent discipline and guidance with friendship and affection, especially when it came to raising sons. He was much more affectionate and playful with the girls, who, of course, were younger, too. In a letter to Bessie meant to be read aloud by "Mamma," he wrote about sea birds following the ship as he fed them crumbs: "They never see any orchards, and have a taste of the apples & cherries like your gay little friend in Pittsfield Robin Red Breast Esq." At the bottom of the page, he printed in big block letters designed to be read by a seven-year-old, "I hope you take good care of little FANNY and that when you go on the hill, you go this way." Under a pencil sketch of two little girls walking uphill, he wrote, "That is to say, hand in hand," signing it, "By-By/Papa."[63]

On a separate sheet, he drew a pencil sketch of Arrowhead that shows Lizzie and the girls standing with open arms as he arrives back home. This drawing, which made him "feel as if I was there, almost—Such is the magic power of a fine Artist," shows surprising skill at rendering mood and details: "Be it known I pride myself particularly upon 'Charlie' & the driver—It is to be supposed that I am in the carriage; & the figures are welcoming me." By the time the *Meteor* sailed into San Francisco Bay, Melville was feeling very homesick.[64]

On October 12, a light western wind blew the *Meteor* into the magnificent harbor Sir Francis Drake had discovered. From the Vallejo Street wharf, Melville could see the Mission Dolores, established by Spanish missionaries and traders on the site of an Indian village. The sights, sounds, and smells of San Francisco were very different from those of New York and Boston, but Melville did not record his impressions of the West Coast in his journal. He stopped writing after the death of seaman Ray.

Melville had a a letter of introduction to Thomas Starr King, a protégé of Henry Whitney Bellows who had become pastor of the Unitarian church in San Francisco. A dynamic preacher who did droll imitations of Ralph Waldo Emerson, King took Melville to dinner at the spectacular bayside home of Colonel John Frémont and his wife, Jessie, who ran the most celebrated literary salon in the West. She had married the dashing Colonel Frémont in 1841 despite intense opposition from her father, Missouri senator Thomas Hart Benton, and it happened to be the nineteenth anniversary of their elopement, so in all probability she treated her guests to some pungent anecdotes about how Washington socialites had reacted to her scandalous elopement.[65]

Newspaper reports of Melville's arrival in San Francisco prompted several groups to invite him to lecture, but he declined, as he had decided to curtail his trip. Herman was so homesick that when Tom learned he might have to carry cargo to England instead of the Far East, he decided to tour the city and go home. He booked passage on the *Cortez*, which took him to Manzanillo, Acapulco, and Panama City via the Isthmus of Panama, avoiding the harrowing trip around the Horn. After crossing the isthmus on a railroad purchased with Vanderbilt money and the lives of five thousand workers, Melville reached Aspinwall, New Grenada, named for the shipping magnate William Henry Aspinwall. At this squalid settlement, which Richard Henry Dana Jr. called a "Dismal place. Swamp, torrid marsh, hot, damp … the worst place I ever saw," Melville boarded the Vanderbilt Steamship Company's *North Star,* a fast sailer that had once been the commodore's private yacht. Now it was an overcrowded commercial vessel noted for its shabby service, filthy accommodations, disgusting food, clogged toilets, and scarcity of lifeboats. Melville met these discomforts by burying himself in a volume of Schiller's poems, barely raising his eyes from the book except when the ship made a brief stop at picturesque St. Augustine, Florida.[66]

Herman's letter announcing his imminent arrival in New York surprised his family. Mother Melville immediately assumed that his health had not improved: "I feel so much disappointed, I had fondly hoped that a Voyage to India under kind Tom's care would have quite brought Herman back to health." When he arrived in New York on November 12, Allan broke the news that the poems he had left with Lizzie had not found a publisher. He probably also told Herman how disturbed the Sons of Tammany had been by the Republican victory in the previous week's elections. South Carolina had threatened to secede if Lincoln was elected, and talk of open rebellion by the cotton states had Gotham's businessmen and bankers extremely worried. While Melville's feelings about the election are not recorded, it's safe to say that Allan's involvement in Tammany put Melville in an awkward position, as most New York Democrats were southern sympathizers.[67]

In 1860, Melville's birthplace boasted a population of 813,699, of whom twelve thousand were free blacks, as slavery had been abolished by the state constitution in 1827. New York was heavily dependent on the cotton trade, which brought in $200 million a year, as well as on western wheat. With seventy-five percent of the nation's imports coming through the Port of New York, the city was enjoying unprecedented prosperity that year. Gazaway Bugg Lamar, the president of the Bank of the Republic, never tired of pointing out that it would be disastrous if a Republican victory pushed the South to secede and southern planters defaulted on the huge loans New York's major banking institutions had extended to them.[68]

As fierce debates raged among Unionists, abolitionists, and Copperheads, New York's merchants sided with the southern planters. Democratic politicians like New York's governor Horatio Seymour and Manhattan's mayor Fernando Wood made no secret of their southern sympathies. Wood, an avowed Copperhead whom attorney-diarist George Templeton Strong called a "limb of Satan," wanted New York to secede from the Union and declare itself a neutral city, free to profit from equal trade with all sections of the country, as further defections by the cotton states threatened to cripple commerce in the thriving port.[69]

The first Sunday Melville was back in New York, he escorted Kate Gansevoort to services at Grace Church, paid calls on the poet Anne Lynch and the essayist Henry T. Tuckerman, and joined Evert Duyckinck for a few rounds of brandy and cigars in the late evening. He went to Boston to spend Thanksgiving with Lizzie and the children at the Shaws', then home "to get matters in readiness for them–putting up the stoves, airing the bedding–warming the house, and getting up a grand domestic banquet." Sarah Morewood had offered the Melvilles the hospitality of her house until they could move into Arrowhead, but Herman had declined. Lizzie told her "the order of things is completely reversed, since Herman is going on to Pittsfield to get the house ready for *me*–that is, to get Mr. Clark to put the stoves up, and get it *warm* for me to go to work in–A new proverb should be added 'Wives propose–husbands dispose'–don't you think so?"[70]

As soon as Lizzie and the children returned and everyone had settled back into the domestic routine, Melville began to miss being at sea with Tom. In a lyric titled "To the Master of the *Meteor*," Melville alluded in mannered word and tone to the loneliness sailors feel in the midst of the vast ocean:

> Lonesome on earth's loneliest deep,
> Sailor! who dost vigil keep–
> Off the Cape of Storms dost musing sweep
> Over monstrous waves that curl and comb;
> Of thee we think when here from brink
> We blow the mead in bubbling foam....
> > Of thee we think,
> > To thee we drink,
> And drain the glass, my gallant Tom![71]

Although his first attempt to publish a book of poems had failed, Melville did not give up writing poetry. He concentrated on occasional poems, written in emulation of poets he was studying, and on poems based on his travels. Vignettes such as "A Rail Road Cutting near Alexandria in 1855" draw on his travels, while verses like "Falstaff's Lament over Prince Hal Become Henry V" reflect his reading. Poems that captured memorable moments created bulwarks against aging and inevitable death.

He also wrote a number of short poems on domestic subjects, many of which take their inspiration from the genre paintings he had seen in the homes of his Dutch relatives and in museums such as the Trippenhuis in Amsterdam. It's not known whether poems such as "In a Pauper's Turnip-Field" and "Field Asters," which describe life on the farm, or poems such as "A Dutch Christmas up the Hudson in the Time of Patroons" and "Stockings in the Farm-House Chimney," which evoke the hearty spirit of holidays "in the house of the sickle and the home of the plough," were written for this volume, or much later. Nostalgic poems about life at Arrowhead may have been written well after Melville moved back to Manhattan.[72]

Although Melville abandoned the *Frescoes of Travel* once he returned from the Holy Land, his trinity of poet, painter, and scholar—outlined on the flyleaf of his journal—foreshadows the complex identities of the mature Melville. He was a poet bent on transmuting his impressions of travel into metaphysical explorations, a connoisseur intent on transforming his growing appreciation of classical sculpture and European painting into a mature philosophy of art grounded in an ethical sensibility, and a student of history bent on understanding the rise and fall of civilizations past and present, including his own increasingly imperiled nation. What Melville needed was another Leviathan, another "mighty theme."

Shortly before Christmas, while the Melvilles were preparing for the long Berkshire winter, South Carolina seceded from the Union. Mississippi, Florida, Alabama, Georgia, Louisiana, and Texas subsequently seized all federal property within their borders and joined with South Carolina to form the Confederacy. Clio, the Muse of history, was about to provide Melville with a theme worthy of an American Homer: the Civil War.

This handsome portrait of Melville was taken by Pittsfield photographer Rodney H. Dewey in 1861, the year America erupted in civil war.

TWENTY-TWO

FIERCE BATTLES AND CIVIL STRIFE

American politics was taking an ugly turn. With the formation of the Confederacy under Jefferson Davis, rumors were flying that the President-elect would be assassinated before he reached Washington. Melville's friend Richard Tobias Greene was confident Lincoln would take "the oath of office on the Capitol Steps in spite of all fire eating bragadocios [sic]," but others were not so sure.[1]

With most Manhattan merchants and shipping magnates heavily invested in the cotton trade, bankers feared that southern plantation owners would renege on their debts, so in December 1860, Richard Lathers called the Democratic Vigilant Association, a group of lawyers and businessmen, to his Pine Street office to draft an appeal to the South. Although he had freed his own slaves before moving from South Carolina to New York, Lathers opposed immediate abolition by government decree; he favored educating the slaves and training them in democratic leadership, then freeing them and sending them back to Africa. A pro-Union southerner, Lathers wanted to avoid a war that would bring Great Britain in to protect the cotton trade.[2]

Treading a fine line between conservatism and self-interest, the men who participated in the Pine Street meeting drafted a series of resolutions censuring former governor William H. Seward and the radical abolitionists for calling the conflict between North and South "irrepressible," and imploring southern leaders not to rush into civil war. Lathers and Millard Fillmore were to present New York's resolutions to Jefferson Davis, but Fillmore took sick at the last minute, so Richard and Abby Lathers went alone. Everywhere they went, they heard southerners threatening to seize federal property within their borders in retaliation for the insults being heaped upon them by abolitionists and northern newspapers. They also saw what looked like preparations for war.

The growing belligerence of the South frightened Lincoln's supporters, and when South Carolina demanded the withdrawal of federal troops from Charleston Harbor, tensions mounted. Many saw it as a prelude to armed conflict, and in January 1861, when New York's *Star of the West,* carrying two hundred men to Fort Sumter, was driven back by a bombardment from batteries on Charleston's Morris Island, even pro-slavery New Yorkers were outraged.[3]

On February 18, the day Jefferson Davis was inaugurated as President of the Confederacy, U.S. President-elect Lincoln and his wife Mary Todd arrived at the Hudson River Railroad depot in New York amid rumors of a southern conspiracy to prevent him from taking the oath of office. As "the illustrious cortege mov[ed] slowly down to the Astor House with its escort of mounted policemen and a torrent of rag-tag and bobtail rushing and hooraying behind," diarist George Templeton Strong noted that "the great rail-splitter's face ... seemed a keen, clear, honest face, not so ugly as his portraits." When the procession reached the Astor House Hotel, across from Barnum's American Museum, Walt Whitman thought there was "a dash of comedy, almost farce, such as Shakespere [*sic*] puts in his blackest tragedies" in the spectacle of the tall figure stretching his arms and legs as he alighted from his open barouche and exchanged mutually curious glances with "the sea of faces" around him.[4]

Well aware that prominent Manhattan businessmen and politicians had helped finance the campaign of his Democratic rival, Stephen Douglas, Lincoln spent his first day in the city mending fences. The following day, the President, the First Lady, and their three sons visited Barnum's Museum, whose feature attraction was the *What-is-it?,* which was advertised as "a cross between a nigger and a baboon." As Melville had shown in "Benito Cereno" and "The 'Gees," many people considered Africans subhuman, and this chimpanzeelike creature was said to be proof that Africans practiced bestiality. George Templeton Strong thought he was simply "an idiotic negro dwarf" whose "fearfully simian" anatomical features made him "a great fact for Darwin," but Kate Gansevoort pronounced the poor chap "disgusting."[5]

Despite Walt Whitman's worry that "many an assassin's knife and pistol lurked in hip or breast-pocket," Lincoln survived his visit to New York. His "perfect composure and coolness" favorably impressed all but the most die-hard Copperheads, and his statesmanlike composure quelled some of the suspicion city people harbored toward the homely fellow who was widely caricatured as a country bumpkin.[6]

In the South, hatred of Lincoln and the North had reached a fever pitch. When detective Allan Pinkerton learned of an assassination plot whereby the presidential train was to be derailed and thrown down an embankment somewhere between Harrisburg and Baltimore, he insisted that the President-elect disguise himself and "steal a march" through Baltimore on the night train to avoid detection. The ruse opened Lincoln to ridicule from newspaper cartoonists, but it worked. Two weeks after leaving Springfield, Illinois, he arrived safely in the nation's capital with his entourage, and a week later he became the sixteenth President of the no-longer-United States.[7]

As office-seekers flocked to the capital for the inauguration, Lincoln and his Cabinet worked overtime to set up a government capable of holding the Union together. If Virginia and Maryland were to join the Confederacy, the capital would be surrounded by rebel states, and war would be unavoidable. Considering the amount of dissension and bitterness Lincoln's election had caused, the new administration could ill afford to squander its patronage; every appointment had in some way to bind factions, regions, and clashing constituencies together.

Now that Melville was home from the Barbary Coast and San Francisco, his family worried less about the impending national crisis than about what Herman would do. When Allan advised him to apply for the consulship in Florence, Herman asked his Republican brothers-in-law John Hoadley and George Griggs for help in contacting the right people in Washington. Allan asked Lemuel Shaw to use his influence as well, and despite his being seriously ill, the judge graciously agreed. "I am as deeply impressed as you possibly can be of the necessity of Herman's getting away from Pitts," he wrote Allan. "He is there solitary, without society, without exercise or occupation except that which is very likely to be injurious to him in over-straining his mind." Knowing that Melville's chances of landing a plum diplomatic post like Florence were slim, he advised Allan to "take some measures if the consulship cant [sic] be obtained, to get an office in the N. Y. Custom House," where he could do "the moderate daily labor required there, & thus be enabled to live in N. Y. & remove him from Pittsfield."[8]

It was unrealistic for Melville's family and friends to believe he could obtain a consulship. Unlike his two brothers, who were active Democrats, and Nathaniel Hawthorne, who had written the campaign biography of Franklin Pierce, Melville had never involved himself in politics, and his party affiliation remains unknown. To Melville, politics seemed alienating and perverse. Ideologically a Jeffersonian Democratic-Republican of old patrician stock, Melville thought the nation needed leaders who were men of education, taste, and culture, not rough-and-tumble Manhattan ward heelers. Lincoln's greatness was not evident in 1861; for all Melville knew, "Old Abe" had been chosen by backroom politicians making deals around a brass spittoon.

Friends and family members were hopeful that the lack of involvement in Democratic politics that had hurt Melville's chances in 1853 would help him now. Two of his close relatives were Republican legislators. His obstetrician uncle, Amos Nourse, had served out the last month of Vice President Hannibal Hamlin's Senate term when he became the governor of Maine, and his brother-in-law John Hoadley, an abolitionist friend of Charles Sumner, had been elected to the Massachusetts legislature in 1858. Hoadley wrote Sumner that Melville's "appointment, as a literary man, would be thought a graceful act by men of all classes and parties, and would add to the popularity and support of the Administration." Alexander Bradford persuaded David Dudley Field and several other prominent attorneys to endorse Melville's character, intellect, and patriotic spirit, and John Hoadley submitted directly to the President a petition signed by several Lawrence businessmen.[9]

After asking Thurlow Weed to approach Governor Seward on his behalf, Melville turned for help to Richard Henry Dana Jr. and Berkshire County Superior Court judge Julius Rockwell, a Republican who had served in the Senate with Charles Sumner. Dana abandoned his policy of never writing recommendations for anyone to write several letters to Sumner mentioning Melville favorably, and Judge Rockwell submitted to the President a petition signed by a number of Pittsfield's business leaders. In a personal note to Sumner on behalf of his "neighbor & friend," he wrote that Melville's "genius–his imperfect health–his 'res augusti domi'–his noble wife, and four children" ought to speak "trumpet tongues" for him.[10]

Melville arrived in Washington on March 12 in time to attend Lincoln's second levee, or reception, at the White House with the Nourses. "There was a great crowd, & a brilliant scene," he wrote Lizzie. "Ladies in full dress by the hundred. A steady stream of two-&-twos wound thro' the apartments shaking hands with 'Old Abe' ... without cessation for an hour & a half. Of course I was one of the shakers. Old Abe is much better looking [than] I expected & younger looking. He shook hands like a good fellow–working hard at it like a man sawing wood at so much per cord. Mrs. Lincoln is rather good-looking I thought. The scene was very fine altogether. Superb furniture–flood of light–magnificent flowers–full band of music &c." Later that evening, Melville went to dinner at the Nourses' and met Hannibal Hamlin, whose wife reminded him of Lizzie.[11]

The nation's capital was tense with the transition. Melville, who didn't much like cooling his heels in office corridors, spent more time strolling around the unfinished city than standing in line outside Senator Sumner's office door, and on one of his walks, he came upon the unfinished Washington Monument: "huge Tower some 160 feet high of white marble," he wrote Lizzie, "could not get inside. Nothing been done to it for long time." The monument's stub jutted up from the stagnant marsh where, thirty years before, John Quincy Adams had taken early-morning swims in clean, clear water. To Melville, the stunted monument symbolized the nation's failure to reach the lofty heights to which the Founding Fathers had aspired. In 1861 much of Washington was a swamp, so pestilent in summer that George Templeton Strong said that "of all detestable places, Washington is the first."[12]

The Capitol, too, was unfinished at this time. Architects who submitted bids for the building's expansion found it impossible to extend the new wings outward on an axis with the existing building without leveling the hill on either side, and when that turned out to be prohibitively expensive, they drew up plans to place the two wings at right angles and the massive new dome slightly off center on the eastern portico. When the cornerstone for the addition was laid, the wood-and-brick Bulfinch dome that had crowned the magnificent neoclassical edifice since 1825 had to be removed, leaving a gaping hole. This decapitated citadel of representative government formed a backdrop to the inauguration ceremonies of several presidents, including Lincoln, before the new dome was finished in 1863. In the volume of poems he published after the Civil War, Melville uses the iron dome as a symbol of the Republic.[13]

Getting in to see government officials was not as easy as he had hoped, and his next few letters to Lizzie from Washington reflect both discouragement and homesickness. He spent an entire Sunday morning soaking up sun on a bench in Lafayette Park, across Pennsylvania Avenue from the White House, and writing a letter expressing his doubts that anything would come of his efforts besides "a good trip" south in pleasant weather. The next morning he added a brief but loving note to his letter before mailing it: "Dearest Lizzie: Feel rather overdone this morning—overwalked yesterday. But the trip will do me good. Kisses to the children. Hope to get a letter from you today. Thine, My Dearest Lizzie, Herman."[14]

Melville received no encouragement from Sumner about the Florence post, so he decided to try for a consulship at Glasgow. Although Sumner sent a memo to the State Department recommending Melville for the Glasgow post or a consulship in Geneva or Manchester, nothing came of it. Timothy Bigelow Lawrence, son of the Massachusetts "Cotton Whig" Abbott Lawrence, was appointed consul to Florence, and William Dean Howells, the young printer-journalist from Ohio who had written Lincoln's campaign biography, was sent to Venice.[15]

Before Melville could get in to see Sumner again, he was called home by a letter from Lizzie saying that her father was critically ill and not expected to recover. A few days before, after riding aimlessly through Boston in his carriage until about midnight, Judge Shaw had come home restless and thirsty, talking obsessively and incoherently about "bondages, corporations, and business of all kinds." Then, suddenly, he could neither talk nor breathe, and he had to be put to bed. Before Lizzie and Herman could reach her father's bedside, he was dead, evidently the victim of a stroke. After an Easter funeral service at the South Meeting House, presided over by Dr. Orville Dewey, Melville went home to look after Fanny and Bessie, leaving Lizzie and her mother to mourn the passing of a loving husband and father, and Boston to mourn the passing of a great constitutional jurist rooted in New England federalism.[16]

Like Judge Shaw, Melville had no doubts about the rightness of the antislavery cause, but he believed that slavery should be abolished gradually, without bloodshed if possible. He seems never to have involved himself directly in the antislavery controversy, perhaps because the rhetoric on both sides was so inflammatory that negotiation and compromise seemed impossible, and he feared that armed conflict between the slaveholding South and the free North would destroy the Union. Unlike Nathaniel Hawthorne, who thought it might be just as well if the South seceded, Melville was a steadfast Union man.

The crisis came to a head when, despite President Lincoln's efforts to mollify those who regarded the presence of even a skeleton force of one hundred men at the mouth of a key southern seaport as a provocation, South Carolinians began taking potshots at federal troops and the fort's defenders began shooting back. The attackers bombarded Fort Sumter for thirty-six hours, and although no lives were lost, Old Glory came down, and the flag of the Confederacy flew over Charleston Harbor.

When the firing started, Richard Lathers was in Mobile, Alabama. He was branded an "alien enemy" by the press and advised by the mayor of New Orleans to cancel his trip and leave the South, or risk being lynched by angry mobs. Returning to New York, Lathers was denounced as a traitor by the Republican press, and death threats began appearing in his mail. The threats ceased as soon as war broke out, but although Lathers donated substantial sums of money to the Union Army and gave generous paid leave to employees of his who enlisted, he never received any recognition for his attempts at peacemaking.[17]

Just after midnight on April 13, 1861, as Walt Whitman was walking down Broadway toward the Brooklyn ferry after an evening at the opera, he heard "the loud cries of newsboys who came tearing and yelling up the street, rushing from side to side more furiously than usual" with the news that Fort Sumter had been attacked. New York's crack Seventh Regiment, which was known for its college-educated, upper-class recruits and its precision drilling, immediately attracted new members, including

Melville's cousin Henry Sanford Gansevoort, and his friend Sanford Robinson Gifford of Gansevoort, New York, a landscape painter who had studied with Albert Bierstadt.[18]

The next morning, President Lincoln issued a call for state militias to send 75,000 men to protect the nation's capital. Four days later, Virginia joined the Confederacy, and when Lincoln ordered a blockade of southern ports, Arkansas, North Carolina, and Tennessee followed suit. With eleven states now part of the Confederacy, a "police action" obviously could not keep the South in line. Pittsfield's Allen Guard was among the first units to mobilize. Massachusetts had already sent its Eighth Regiment to Philadelphia and its Sixth Regiment to Baltimore to guard federal forts and arsenals, so when the call went out from President Lincoln to Governor Andrew of Massachusetts, Pittsfield mobilized even more quickly than New York. On April 19, as the Sixth Regiment was being set upon by street gangs wielding clubs and throwing paving stones, killing sixteen people, Pittsfield gave its first contingent of guardsmen a hearty send-off. The men boarded the train for Fort McHenry promising their loved ones that they would put the rebellion down swiftly and come right home.[19]

In Boston, Ralph Waldo Emerson felt a "whirlwind of patriotism ... magnetize all discordant masses under its terrific unity." In New York, even Copperheads like ex-mayor Fernando Wood rallied around the flag. Red, white, and blue bunting fluttered from the Lord & Taylor store and A. T. Stewart's "marble palace," and half a million people turned out for a mass rally in Union Square to show their devotion to the northern cause. While the staff of New York Hospital prepared for casualties, surgeons and residents at Bellevue, including Dr. Titus Munson Coan, made plans to expand the hospital's emergency facilities and to redesign medical school courses to train interns in military medicine. While Coan stayed in New York, Allan's brother-in-law, Dr. Henry Thurston, a surgeon with New York's Twelfth Regiment, went south.[20]

Although they were no longer able to brook the defiance of the rebels, many New York businessmen did not believe the North could win the war, but the city's ministers assumed that God was on their side. The rector of Trinity Church enlisted the help of ships' riggers to fly an enormous "Stars and Stripes" from the church's spire, and All Souls' minister Henry Whitney Bellows preached a sermon in which he called preservation of the Union a righteous cause, implying that Lincoln had a mandate from Heaven and that the North could not be vanquished. Apotheosizing the government, he declared, "The State is indeed divine," hubristic language that would have made Sophocles' Theban prophet Tiresias recoil in horror.[21]

Both North and South considered the conflict a holy war. Clergymen in New York, hopeful that the war would purge the North of its materialism as well as end slavery, rallied behind the President and the Union. Brooklyn pastor Henry Ward Beecher, Harriet

Beecher Stowe's brother, and others were saying that only war could lead to peace, but Melville had "Misgivings," which he expressed later in a poem:

When ocean-clouds over inland hills
Sweep storming in late autumn brown,
And horror the sodden valley fills,
And the spire falls crashing in the town,
I muse upon my country's ills—
The tempest bursting from the waste of Time
On the world's fairest hope linked with man's foulest crime.
Nature's dark side is heeded now—
Ah! optimist-cheer disheartened flown—
A child may read the moody brow
Of yon black mountain lone.
With shouts the torrents down the gorges go,
And storms are formed behind the storm we feel:
The hemlock shakes in the rafter, the oak in the driving keel.

With its echoes of Protestant hymn motifs, the last line puts the impending conflict into a biblical context that undergirds all the poems Melville wrote about the war.[22]

Soon the Battery and other parks around lower Manhattan were dotted with recruiting booths and tents, but conditions in the training camps were deteriorating. Hastily sewn, ill-fitting uniforms, sold by department store magnates A. T. Stewart and Rowland Macy, were splitting at the seams, guns were misfiring, much of the food was rancid, and so few of the men had access to fresh water or toilets that infectious diseases were spreading rapidly. Mothers, sisters, wives, and sweethearts wondered what would become of the men when battle injuries were added to their suffering.

Dr. Elizabeth Blackwell, the first woman physician in the United States, had founded the New York Infirmary and College for Women to provide care for female prisoners and to create a workplace free of the harassment and intimidation she had encountered as a woman doctor in hospitals run by men. A friend of Florence Nightingale, Blackwell was determined to avoid the horrors of the Crimea, where more men had died from poor medical care than from battle wounds. She gathered together a hundred prominent women, including Mrs. William Cullen Bryant, Mrs. Peter Cooper, Mrs. Henry Whitney Bellows, Mrs. Henry Raymond, and Louisa Lee Schuyler, a great-granddaughter of Alexander Hamilton, to form the Women's Central Relief Association. Juliette Raymond asked her husband to run a notice in his newspaper, *The New York Times,* and in response, four thousand women showed up at the Cooper Union and organized an "army of volunteers." Henry Whitney Bellows went to Washington to ask the

President for official recognition, and Lincoln appointed him president of the United States Sanitary Commission in the East.[23]

Before long, Eliza Bellows had turned the Sunday-school room in All Souls' rectory into a workroom where wives of prominent parishioners prepared bandages and compresses and made up packages of foodstuffs and such amenities as soap, towels, sheets, stationery, pens, pillowcases, nightgowns, socks, underwear, and slippers for the soldiers in the field. Soon, churches and synagogues all over the Northeast were working to provide the comforts of home to men on the battlefields.[24]

The women of Berkshire County, led by Mrs. Curtis T. Fenn, Sarah Morewood, and Lucy Rockwell, also formed a ladies' auxiliary to supply the soldiers with articles that would make army camps more homelike, and they made banners for public buildings and silk flags for every regiment. Sarah Morewood added a special touch by giving each man a pillow stuffed with milkweed floss and a small flag he could carry into battle, inspiring one western regiment to name its camp for her. "Nothing," wrote Catharine Maria Sedgwick, "pleases me better than the zeal among our young women in working for the hospitals. We hear no gossip but the more rational talk about hospital gowns, comfortable socks, and mittens. Our whole community from Mrs. Kemble down to some of our Irish servants, are knitting." Some Berkshire women, caught up in the first flush of excitement and confident that the insurrection would be put down in short order, made blackberry wine to send the men off in good spirits, but when the survivors of the first disastrous battles returned a few months later, broken in body and haunted by the carnage they had seen, these women knew they were in for a long, hard war.[25]

In mid-May, around the time Queen Victoria declared Britain's intention to stay out of the American war, Herman was preparing to join Lizzie and Malcolm in Boston. Sister Fanny came to Arrowhead to look after Bessie and little Fanny, bringing Stanwix and Allan's daughter Lucy with her. Stannie built a little house for the girls and played catch with them, and another time, the children all gathered flowers and made "little round curls of the dandelion stems."[26]

By June, Herman was back in New York City. He and Evert Duyckinck went with Allan and his family to see Guert Gansevoort, who had been assigned to shore duty at the Brooklyn Navy Yard after being found drunk aboard the *Decatur* following the siege of Seattle in 1856. While they were there, they saw Captain James Ward, the first naval casualty of the war at sea, lying in state "with lighted candles at the feet and head." For Evert Duyckinck, Ward's death symbolized the "iniquity of this rebellion" perfectly. Guert showed them the new breech-loading Dahlgren naval gun and gave them a tour of the black-hulled *Savannah*, a captured Confederate privateer that was drawing huge crowds of sightseers to the docks. New Yorkers were appalled that an enemy vessel had come so near their shores, and Democratic politicians pointed out that the government had done nothing since the Army Corps of Engineers had warned the city two years before that its old forts were in serious disrepair. David Opdyke, the Republican mayor, suggested sinking coal barges at the Narrows to prevent an attack on the city, but because no one could figure out how to keep Confederate marauders from entering the harbor without interfering with commercial shipping, the harbor remained open, and vulnerable to attack.[27]

Burdened by thoughts of war, Herman went to New Rochelle with Allan and the Duyckinck brothers to spend an afternoon at Winyah Park, Richard Lathers's "truly magnificent house, eighty feet front, with a deep piazza running the whole length, which is enclosed as a Conservatory & filled with handsome flowers." An avid collector of European art, Lathers had furnished his Tuscan villa with paintings, engravings, fine furniture, and marble and terra-cotta sculptures. Strolling through the ornate, high-ceilinged rooms, drinking blackberry wine and gazing at the sparkling blue waters of Long Island Sound during what Lathers called "high strawberry time," gave them all some relief from "the war agitations of the times." The appearance of a comet, "a brilliant apparition in the north near the Great Bear," for several days struck Melville as a fitting symbol of the cataclysm. In his poem "The Conflict of Convictions," he would write: "The terrors of truth and dart of death / To faith alike are vain / Though comets, gone a thousand years, / Return again." The war was "man's latter fall"—not a crusade, but a curse that "heaps Time's strand with wrecks" and destroys all hope of human progress.[28]

Melville returned to Pittsfield around the time the Pollock Guard began training on the old cattle showgrounds where Thomas Melvill Jr. had once presided over the agricultural fair and drove Stannie out to the parade grounds to watch the soldiers drill. No sooner had the maneuvers begun than smoke began billowing from the Pittsfield Woolen Mills, and as most militia companies were formed from volunteer fire brigades, the men had to drop their rifles, grab leather buckets, fill them with water, and run to put out the fire, so Herman and Stanwix did not see the drill. Unlike Malcolm, Stannie never developed an obsession with guns and uniforms, and spending time with his father probably meant more to him than watching soldiers march and practice loading rifles.[29]

Although Stanwix wasn't as enamored with war as Malcolm was, he was delighted when his mother sent firecrackers from Boston. On the Fourth of July Stannie took charge of setting off the Roman candles and torpedoes, which greatly impressed the other children, and the booming of the cannons and the ringing of church bells from town kept him awake all night. Stanwix was an unusually sensitive boy. During a visit to Leonard Gansevoort's lumber mill in Glens Falls later that summer, as he was watching the "splendid waterfall" turn a huge wheel that had six more mahogany hoppers than Granduncle Herman's wheel, Stannie saw "two little girls picking up chips to burn" after the boards were sawed, and he felt sorry for them, "they were both [so] poor."[30]

The first skirmishes went badly for the Union. After Thomas "Stonewall" Jackson and the Confederates routed the Yankees at Bull Run on July 21, 1861, the swashbuckling General Robert E. Lee foiled Major General George B. McClellan's drive through the Virginia peninsula by feigning a retreat into Richmond that drew 100,000 Union troops into a deadly trap. In a burst of hyperbole, a Georgia secessionist called First Manassas (as the Confederates called Bull Run) "one of the decisive battles of the world" because "it secured our independence," and realist George Templeton Strong called it "Black Monday," exclaiming, "We are utterly and disgracefully routed, beaten, whipped by secessionists."[31]

Melville was horrified to see the nation sacrificing its young men to the cannibal god of war. In his poem "The March into Virginia, Ending in the First Manassas," he describes Yankee recruits blithely "chatting left and laughing right" in "Bacchic glee," going to war as to a "berry-party, pleasure wooed." The macabre pun of "berry-party" is intentional, as they perished blindly, "enlightened" only by the "vollied glare" of rebel artillery. "All wars are boyish, and are fought by boys," but the young soldiers who dashed onto the battlefields as though they were going to a ballgame, a fire, or a Sunday-school picnic grew up fast once they saw the bleeding bodies of their comrades lying in the dust, their skulls and bones crushed by cannonballs, their once-shining eyes staring sightlessly at the indifferent sun.[32]

Hourly, the death toll mounted. Bloody beyond anything Americans had ever experienced, the war came home to noncombatants in the North in condolence letters to wives and mothers from Secretary of War Edwin Stanton and in columns of maimed and mutilated men streaming into makeshift hospitals set up in cow pastures, baseball lots, and public parks. When survivors of Bull Run who did not need hospitalization reached Washington, they drowned their grief in alcohol and smothered their fear in desperate sexual encounters. The Union Army's respite from Hell turned into an orgy, and the war-torn capital resembled Pandemonium.

Although 4,500 men were killed, wounded, or captured at Bull Run, most northerners were excited by their patriotism and courage. Lydia Maria Child thought the North only "needed defeats and reverses to come up manfully to the work of freedom," so that the rebellion could be put down swiftly. When the next few battles, "with all their terrible incidents," made her downright "sick at the thought of those poor soldiers stabbed after they were wounded, shot after they dropped down from fatigue," she wrote ruefully, "My heart bleeds for the mothers of those sons."[33]

The first great fallen hero on the northern side was Melville's neighbor Nathaniel Lyon, a general who lost his life that August while trying to defend Missouri from the

Confederates. Although Lyon was cheerily eulogized by countless poetasters, Melville portrays him as a poignant symbol of those "hearts … of deeper sort, / Prophetic, sad" who fight bravely for their cause despite "Known death." He imagines this seasoned officer writing his will by candlelight and leaving "his all / To Her for whom 'twas not enough to fall" before going into battle. To his men, Lyon was the epitome of a great officer; despite being wounded by "a sheet of balls," he rallied his men by fighting to the death heroically. Melville's imaginary corpsman remembers how "We fought on the grass, we bled in the corn- / Fate seemed malign," but Lyon never retreated; "his only flight / Was up to Zion / Where prophets now and armies greet brave Lyon."[34]

Given his age, his weak eyes, and his history of back trouble, Melville could not participate in the war; his name, however, was kept on the militia rolls. Melville was as ambivalent about the war as he was about everything. In letters to serious soldiers like his cousin Henry and some of the officers he met later in the war, Melville adopts an admiring tone, but on a newspaper notice about "The Charge of the Light Brigade," he wrote "Stuff by a swell man," and drew a hand pointing off the page, then stuck the clipping in his two-volume set of Tennyson. He had enough of the blood of his grandfathers in his veins to admire the heroism of both officers and common soldiers and to feel proud of friends and relatives who were fighting, but he hated the brutality of war.[35]

In August, Melville went to Boston to bring Lizzie home, leaving the girls with Helen and George while they paid a visit to Gansevoort with Malcolm, whom Stannie had been asking to see all summer. They reached Albany too late to see Uncle Peter and Aunt Susan before they went for a vacation at the Pavilion at Far Rockaway, taking Allan's daughter Kitty with them. Herman wrote that he wished they might "roll night and morning in the surf" to keep their "clear cheeks and sparkling eyes." At Gansevoort he found the family well except for Uncle Herman, who was feeble but free of pain and able to eat and sleep comfortably.[36]

Restless even after he settled back at Arrowhead, Melville found it hard to concentrate. As the afternoon shadows grew longer and darker, he sat on his piazza watching the goldfinches dipping and bobbing above the meadow and the swallows and swifts wheeling and darting in and out of the old barn. Seeing that "certain slant of light" and feeling the premonitory chill of a long Berkshire winter in his bones, he began to dread the coming winter. Now that Lizzie's stipend from her father made maintenance of two households feasible, Herman decided to spend the winter in New York; he leased a place at 150 East Eighteenth Street, not far from his friend Evert Duyckinck.

He spent Christmas and New Year's in Boston with the family, then returned to New York to meet Tom, who had sold the *Meteor* in Calcutta. After taking Tom to Boston to visit the Griggses and the Hoadleys, Herman returned to New York with a copy of Uncle

John D'Wolf's *A Voyage to the North Pacific and a Journey through Siberia More than Half a Century Ago*, which had just been published by a Cambridge press.[37]

No sooner had he settled into the new quarters than he was felled by a severe attack of rheumatism, and Lizzie rushed to his side. "Rheumatism-bound" most of the winter, he finished his uncle's book and invited Duyckinck for a visit: "Mrs Melville and I will be glad to see you & your brother any evening. If you have nothing better to do, come round tomorrow [Sunday] evening, and we will brew some whiskey punch and settle the affairs of the universe over it—which affairs sadly need it, some say." He asked Duyckinck to loan him works by Elizabethan dramatists, "except Marlowe, whom I have read," and he pored over the plays of John Webster and Thomas Dekker and the poetry of Thomas Hood, James Clarence Mangan, Thomas Moore, Robert Fergusson, and Matthew Arnold.[38]

Marginalia from this period reveal Melville's attempts to resign himself to the melancholy fact that the world rewards artistic achievement with indifference, if not ridicule, and that no amount of success can stave off sickness or death. Too incapacitated to take his customary neighborhood strolls, he cultivated the solitude that "opens discoveries and kindles meditations" in the man of genius, revealing the world to be a "magical garden of Armida," in the words of Isaac Disraeli. Marking Hood's wry quatrain, "What is a modern poet's fate? / To write his thoughts upon a slate;– / The Critic spits on what is done,– / Gives it a wipe, and all is gone," he underscored a biographer's observation that when the poet Thomas Hood kept writing despite a serious illness, his "poetical vigour seemed to advance *just in proportion as his physical health declined.*"[39]

As Melville sat nursing his aches and pains, tens of thousands of men were dying to the south, and tens of thousands more were losing eyes and limbs. Legs and arms shattered by large-caliber soft lead bullets fired at low velocity or crushed by cannonballs could not be rebuilt; they had to be sawed off. Exhausted surgeons performed amputations under unsanitary conditions, going from one sufferer to the next with little more than the wipe of a blade on soiled and sweaty trousers. Although ether was available in a few large cities, field surgeons had to use whiskey for both anesthesia and disinfectant during amputations.[40]

Unburied corpses and amputated legs, feet, arms, and hands were piling up on every battlefield, and the nation's municipal, state, and national treasuries were hemorrhaging with debt. In New York City alone, the war debt came to more than $600 million, and bank reserves sank below $30 million. War casualties received preferential treatment over civilians at city hospitals, and wounded soldiers for whom hospitals had no room stayed at camps like the one situated where the Crystal Palace had stood (in present-day Bryant Park) before it burned down in 1858.

At one time or another, as many as fifty thousand men lay wounded or dying a stone's throw from the halls of Congress, in hospitals where both Walt Whitman and Louisa May Alcott served as nurses. Whitman, who decided to become a nurse while he was walking past piles of amputated limbs searching for his brother at Fredericksburg, visited most of the six hundred or so hospitals in and around Washington. Unembarrassed by emotional intimacy or physical proximity to men, he proved such a loving, charismatic healer that wounded and recuperating soldiers called him "Father" and compared him to Jesus Christ. Although both he and Alcott wrote graphic and moving books about the war, Whitman believed "The real war will never get in the books."[41]

Despite their supposed fragility, middle-class women proved to have as much stamina as men, once they left their corsets and plush Victorian parlors behind. *Harper's Weekly* devoted a double centerfold to "that exquisite type of angelic womanhood, the Sister of Charity," pointing out that the war had produced "scores of Florence Nightingales, whose names no one knows, but whose reward in the soldier's gratitude, and Heaven's approval, is the highest guerdon woman ever won." After the surrender, the magazine recommended extending civil rights to women and allowing them to vote.[42]

Victorian clothing for men seemed designed to sever mind from body, while women's clothing seemed designed to transform sexuality into a beautiful artifact, or object. Genteel women wore corsets that literally deformed them; they often had ribs removed to achieve the waspish waist that appeased the twin idols of fashion and femininity, so naturally they fainted whenever a slight shock or surprise altered their blood pressure. Men wore collars of whalebone, stiff paper, and later steel that literally choked off their breath, and Walt Whitman noticed that male visitors to the field hospitals who happened to glance toward the "probing" of an "awful wound at an unguarded moment" often fainted. Men who worked in hospitals wore soft-collared shirts, and women wore looser dresses than their civilian sisters ever wore in public. Women who felt healthier and stronger doing backbreaking, emotionally draining hospital work than making and returning routine social calls resented their petticoat prisons after the war.[43]

With naval warfare undergoing a revolution, Melville wrote a number of poems commemorating and lamenting the fortunes of those who fought at sea. In November 1861, sixteen old whalers had been loaded with stones and sunk at the mouth of Charleston Harbor to prevent Confederate frigates from breaking the Union blockade, and although none of them was a ship on which Melville had sailed, he saw the destruction of these "worn and ancient one[s], / With great bluff bows, and broad in the beam" as a "pirate deed" that would be avenged by "ghosts in gales," a phrase that has the flavor of Native American prophecy.[44]

The one vessel of that vintage that was still afloat was his old ship the *United States,* which now flew a Confederate ensign; it was an ignoble end for this proud warrior. In 1861, *Harper's Weekly* had featured an illustrated report on Europe's full-rigged "Shot-proof iron steamships," and Senator Stephen Mallory, who was now the Confederate Secretary of the Navy, had told the chairman of the House Committee on Naval Affairs that "not a moment should be lost" in constructing ironclads. Not long after the Union's first ironclad ship, the *Monitor,* slid from its drydock into the East River and destroyed a Confederate vessel that was making its way up the coast; New Yorkers were jubilant.[45]

Two months later, the Confederacy's ironclad *Virginia* rammed and sank the *Cumberland* and the *Congress* in an attempt to break the blockade of Chesapeake Bay, and nearly half the crew of the *Cumberland* perished. Although Melville the mariner had portrayed naval frigates as floating hells, Melville the poet chanted the name *Cumberland* to conjure up the Golden Age of seafaring:

> Noble name as ere was sung,
> Slowly roll it on the tongue—
> Cumberland! Cumberland!
> Long as hearts shall share the flame
> Which burned in that brave crew,
> Her fame shall live—outlive the victor's name;
> For this is due.
> Your flag and flag-staff shall in story stand—Cumberland!

The next day, the *Monitor* arrived at Hampton Roads, Virginia, to avenge the attack, only to be met by the equally formidable *Virginia.* Their duel epitomized the antiheroic nature of modern warfare. Although the *Monitor* succeeded in saving the Union fleet from destruction, the historic confrontation between the two seagoing fortresses ended in a draw.[46]

For Melville, the advent of ironclads designed to ram frigates and troopships rather than engaging them in a fair fight meant the passing of those wooden monarchs of the sea whose billowing sails and rolling decks kept a man in close touch with water, wind, and sky. As the ironclads plow through "wind and wave that keep the rites of glory," those old "hearts-of-oak," the "great historic wooden warships," either sink to watery graves, or survive long enough to be towed to drydock, like "The Fighting *Temeraire.*" Inspired by J. M. W. Turner's elegiac painting, Melville described the noble ship, "Dismantled of [her] guns and spars, / And sweeping wings of war," being towed to her berth by a "pigmy steam-tug" as the last rays of the setting sun fade into the horizon.[47]

Melville wrote several poems about naval warfare from diverse points of view. The speaker in his poem "A Utilitarian View of the Monitor's Fight" extols the practical value of the new iron ships in a harsh, percussive style anticipating that of such modernists as Hart Crane and Ezra Pound. Banging "rhyme's barbaric cymbal," the utilitarian narrator spits out fricatives to emphasize how modern warriors measure this battle where "all went by crank, / Pivot, and screw, / And calculations of caloric" as a success. To the new breed of sailor, mechanical images such as "The ringing of those plates on plates ... the clangor of the blacksmith's fray ... the anvil-din" place war "Where war belongs–Among the trades and artisans." To the poet, however, this cacophonous metallic music makes modern warfare "less grand than Peace." Melville hoped the "plain mechanic power" of these ungainly metal arks would strip warfare of its glamour and render it extinct.[48]

On land, the fortunes of the North began to improve when Grant's "grim-faced boys," their ranks "riven" by dug-in Confederate sharpshooters, took Tennessee's Fort Henry and Fort Donelson "under a sunless sky of lead" in February of 1862. Repulsed by the defenders of Fort Donelson, exhausted Union troops attacked, until with "one grand surge along the line," they stormed the hill and replaced the rebel ensign with Old Glory–an event that *Harper's Weekly* captured in a dramatic cover illustration. Despite a "death-list" that flowed "like a river," this battle gave Union morale a boost and helped turn the bloody tide in the Union's favor. "The spirit of old defeat is broke / The habit of victory begun; / Grant strikes the war's first sounding-note / At Donelson."[49]

In addition to praising the heroic Union troops, Melville paid tribute to the southern soldiers who came to the aid of their wounded enemies in his poem "Donelson":

> Some of the wounded in the wood
> > Were cared for by the foe last night,
> Though he could do them little needed good,
> > Himself being all in shivering plight.
> The rebel is wrong, but human yet;
> He's got a heart, and thrusts a bayonet.
> He gives us battle with wondrous will–
> This bluff's a perverted Bunker Hill.

To Melville, the compassion shown by men who had fought on opposite sides in this bitter battle foreshadowed the reconciliation that needed to occur before the nation's wounds could heal. In this long poem, the diverse voices of people waiting for news of the war alternate with newspaper headlines and telegraph messages to give a sense of urgent modernity, as when a bald-headed man posts a placard on a door that reads: "GLORIOUS VICTORY OF THE FLEET! / FRIDAY'S GREAT EVENT! / THE ENEMY'S WATER-BATTERIES BEAT! / WE SILENCED EVERY GUN! / THE OLD COMMODORE'S COMPLIMENTS SENT PLUMP / INTO DONELSON!"[50]

With McClellan's army bogged down on the Virginia peninsula, and Kentucky still in the Union, Congress abolished slavery in the District of Columbia, and at the end of April, 100,000 troops, including Toby Greene, massed on the Tennessee-Mississippi border to fight a deadly battle. In two days, more than twenty thousand men lost their lives, and tens of thousands sustained brutal wounds, intensifying hatred on both sides.

In "Shiloh," a melodious elegy for the men who were killed in their fierce battles, Melville implies that Nature will embrace their souls, and the Old and New Testament connotations join sacrament and sacrifice in scenes of contemporary crucifixion:

> Skimming lightly, wheeling still,
>   The swallows fly low
> Over the field in clouded days,
>   The forest-field of Shiloh—
> Over the field where April rain
> Solaced the parched ones stretched in pain
> Through the pause of night
> That followed the Sunday fight
>   Around the church of Shiloh—
> The church so lone, the long-built one,
> That echoed to many a parting groan
>   And natural prayer
> Of dying foemen mingled there—
> Foemen at morn, but friends at eve—
> Fame or country least their care:
> (What like a bullet can undeceive!)
>   But now they lie low;
>   While over them the swallows skim.
>   And all is hushed at Shiloh.[51]

In tones of subdued irony, he acknowledges the irreparable human cost of the conflict. Not long after this sad skirmish, the North achieved a stunning victory at New Orleans when Admiral David Farragut lashed himself to the rigging and drove his ship through a line of floating hulks that were chained together at the entrance of the harbor. Herman's cousin Ned Curtis participated in Farragut's bold attack, which caught the Confederate defenders by surprise. With the loss of only one federal ship and taking the city without firing a shot, Farragut destroyed the opposing fleet. "New Orleans gone—and with it the Confederacy?" cried the South Carolina diarist Mary Chesnut. "Are we not cut in two?"[52]

Evoking Exodus, the speaker of Melville's poem "The Battle for the Mississippi" exclaims, "The Lord is a man of war!" as he describes the naval battle in vigorous staccato phrases:

> The shock of ships, the jar of walls,
>   The rush through thick and thin—
> The flaring fire-rafts, glare and gloom—
>   Eddies, and shells that spin—
> The boom-chain burst, the hulks dislodged,
>   The jam of gun-boats driven,
>   Or fired, or sunk…

The closing image of "the captains and the conquering crews / Humbl[ing] their pride in prayer" puts a human face on Heaven's decree, and as the men "mourn their slain," the poem's speaker concludes that "There must be other, nobler worlds for them / Who nobly yield their lives in this."[53]

The war was never far from the minds of Melville and his family, as they and everyone they knew had friends and relatives fighting or doing war-related work. Sarah Morewood surmounted ill health and gave of herself so selflessly that "her library table was strewn with the photographs and grateful letters of soldiers who had been strangers to her till the war began." The wives of doctors, ministers, and merchants in New York pitched in, too. Eliza Bellows, for example, overcame near-invalidism to serve on a floating hospital near Fortress Monroe. Lizzie brought beef tea to soldiers in the makeshift hospitals that were springing up all over town, and later she sewed twice a week at the Ladies' Soldiers' Relief Association. In Albany, Kate Gansevoort knitted stockings and made up gift parcels for the soldiers, and in New Rochelle, Allan's daughter Kitty and the Lathers children rolled bandages. When Kate Gansevoort sent Aunt Melville some diagrams for "army socks & army mittens," she promised to work on them as soon as Fanny returned from Boston to help her with the housework, as she was "much disposed to knit for our good Soldiers."[54]

Among the men who fought or aided the war effort were cousins Henry and Guert Gansevoort, Dr. Henry Thurston, Ned Curtis, several Hobart cousins, and Robert Melvill, who enlisted his boat in the civilian auxiliary fleet on the Mississippi and may have known the young Mark Twain. Toby Greene saw combat, as did John Hoadley's nephew Henry Pease. Hoadley moved his family from Lawrence to New Bedford to take charge of a copper-rolling mill, and in 1863 he was made assistant quartermaster and a captain in the Massachusetts state militia.[55]

Melville followed the progress of the war via firsthand reports from participants, telegraph dispatches, and such publications as *The Rebellion Record* and *Harper's Weekly*, which published aerial views and battlefield scenes rendered by artists Theodore Davis, Alfred Waud, and Thomas Nast. In 1862, with men being fed to the insatiable war machine by the hundreds of thousands, mainstream periodicals in the North were publishing graphic evidence of Confederate atrocities that included ghoulish illustrations of torture implements found on plantations and "secesh souvenirs" such as necklaces of human teeth and drinking bowls made of human skulls.[56]

Melville had been too ill to attend Herman Gansevoort's funeral in March or visit the gravesite until he went to Gansevoort to bring Stanwix home to Pittsfield in April. Melville's mother and sisters were virtually bringing the boy up, and Stannie idolized Augusta. She supervised his education and made it her special responsibility to mold his character. Like her mother, she felt that women bore a special responsibility for knitting the family together and bringing children up to be pious Christians and good citizens. She took the moral and spiritual guidance of her niece and nephews seriously, and from Arrowhead, Stannie wrote that he missed her Sunday school, and he promised "to speak the *truth*, to *obey* Mamma, and Papa, and say my *prayers*."[57]

A dedicated Sunday-school teacher, Augusta gave gifts of food and money to the indigent who came begging at her door, and regularly contributed money for the purchase of Bibles to be sent to "heathens" in far-off lands. Although Herman may have scoffed inwardly at Augusta's missionary zeal, he probably kept his feelings to himself. He was all too glad to have his unmarried sisters take an active role in the training of his children, because Lizzie had more than enough to do in running the household and meeting the needs of the various members of her family. In an era when boundaries between home and school were relatively fluid, older relatives, especially mothers, grandmothers, and aunts, tutored boys and girls at home to supplement their education.[58]

Lizzie had received a scare when her mother accidentally set her cap on fire and burned herself, though not seriously, and although she returned home in time for spring cleaning, she was unwell. The house was turned "upside down" and everything was "topsy-turvy," according to Stannie, who came in from the pasture to show his mother a bird's nest and found her unable to "walk around the house all over," which must have frightened him. Lizzie never had enough household help, partly because money was tight, especially during the war, and partly because cooks resented the way Herman badgered them about the strength of his coffee and the consistency of his oatmeal. They quit fairly frequently, so inserting a desperate appeal for a new cook in the local papers, Melville offered "HIGHEST wages." By the middle of the month, Lizzie was able to put on her dress and "crawl round again," and by the end of May she was strong enough to take the new horse out for a short ride.[59]

Malcolm rode the horse almost every day. He was making friends and doing well at his Newton school, having passed at least one of his examinations with a performance topped only by a boy who was four years older than he. Like Gansevoort Melville, Malcolm seems to have received more attention for his achievements than his younger brother did, even though Stanwix was just as studious. Melville liked to hear him conjugating verbs and declining Latin pronouns: "'Hic-haec-hoc'—'horum, horum, horum,' he goes it every night," Melville boasted to Tom, who was on the other side of the world in command of a new ship, the *Bengal Tiger*.[60]

Although it felt good to be back in the Berkshires, Melville was determined to sell Arrowhead and move to New York permanently. These days, whenever he did farm chores or split firewood, he ended up with back spasms and blisters, and with most of Berkshire County's able-bodied men and boys in uniform, it was difficult to find farmhands. On the twenty-second of May, he hitched up his old wagon and rode into town to place another ad in the *Berkshire County Eagle*. Although the ad ran through August 14, the economy was so depressed there were no takers.[61]

Melville had enough of his mother's Calvinism in his blood to believe in the existence of evil, but despite his pessimistic inclinations and his deep insight into the evil that lurked in his own heart and the hearts of his fellow men, he had not lost either his idealism or his sociability. For a writer who was struggling much of the day to master the difficult craft of writing poetry, banter and persiflage served as recreation, as his rambling response to Tom's letter from Pernambuco illustrates. Tom wrote that he was having some trouble with a lazy crew member whom he "uncivilly stigmatise[d] as a jackass," and Herman replied teasingly that the sort of fellow who "improves his opportunities in the way of sleeping, eating and other commendable customs" was just the sort of fellow he would want in his crew. "For my part," he wrote, "I love sleepy fellows, and the more ignorant the better. Damn your wide-awake and knowing chaps. As for sleepiness, it is one of the noblest qualities of humanity."[62]

In typical Melville fashion, he then thought of the millions of sociable fellows who were under the sod enjoying the long, friendly snooze of death, so he threw in some quotations from "the Bible," as he called Byron's *Don Juan*, and he recommended the strap as the most effective means of administering correction to slackers. He joked that he had sold his "doggerel" to a trunk-maker, who "took the whole stock off my hands at ten cents the pound" to line his trunks, calling the transaction "a great bargain," and he advised Tom, "when you buy a new trunk again, just peep at the lining & perhaps you may be rewarded by some glorious stanza stareing [*sic*] you in the face & claiming admiration."[63]

Shifting abruptly to a more serious topic, he assured Tom that "the rascals" were on the run everywhere, and he implied that with Guert, who was as "brave as a lion, a good seaman, and a natural-born officer," at the helm of the *Adirondack*, "a fine new sloop of war," there was still time for him to "turn out the hero of a brilliant victory" that would end the war. Melville's hyperbole notwithstanding, when Guert was recommended for this new commission, a junior officer objected that his "habitual drunkenness" made him unfit for command, but Samuel F. DuPont, who considered Guert "one of those who cannot be temperate and to be safe must be abstinent," pushed the appointment through.[64]

When Uncle Peter heard about Guert's promotion, he reminded him that twelve bottles of fine old Madeira had been stored in the family wine cellar for thirty years to celebrate just such an occasion. He seems to have forgotten both Guert's earlier flawed command and his problems with alcohol. The *Adirondack* was ready to sail in mid-July, and a month later, Guert ran the ship into a rock in the Bahamas. He was charged with negligence, although he was eventually cleared by a court-martial. The more he drank, the more disasters he caused, and the more he drank, the more unlikely his recovery became.[65]

~~~

The first week of July 1862 found McClellan's artillery grappling with the Confederates for seven days to hold Malvern Hill. It was Second Lieutenant Henry Gansevoort's first battle, and Union forces, with "haggard beards of blood," suffered far greater casualties than the attackers. When the newspaper accounts of "that fearful seven days battle before Richmond" appeared, "gloom and sorrow filled every loyal American heart." The Fourth of July turned out to be "a bright beautiful day in nature" that year, but no one "dared to celebrate," according to Sarah Morewood, because of the "news of a partial defeat and a terrible loss of life among our troops." To make matters worse, "several men from our little village were shot down by their own shells as our Company were obliged to fire over their men's heads in order to reach the enemy. . . . July was a sad month in the history of this war," wrote Mrs. Morewood, "not because we had a slight defeat, but because so many homes were made desolate by death—'killed' is so fearful to read when we know the friends of the killed."[66]

Despite the war, life at Arrowhead was busy and serene that summer, and the fall was an unusually sunny, pleasant one. Melville took the children on a hunt for wild wintergreen, and they rode horseback every day. The boys chased wild rabbits and caught sunfish, while the girls tended the garden, picked berries, collected glass beads, sewed pincushions, mended clothes, pressed flowers, read the latest popular books, and helped with the household chores. On rainy days the boys played ball or marbles, and the girls decorated their dollhouses and crocheted dresses for their dolls. While Malcolm was practicing Latin, Stanwix was studying geography, grammar, and spelling; both boys practiced composition and public speaking at home to prepare for school.[67]

Every afternoon, Melville drove into town to get the mail and checked the telegraph office for the latest dispatches, sometimes swapping war news with Uncle Joe Smith and other local journalists. As regiment after regiment went to the slaughter, the armchair generals in the North were working overtime, and few agreed with Lincoln's conduct of the war. In the evenings, family members took turns reading aloud, usually from British novels pirated by American publishers, while others scraped the lint from old linen to make surgical dressings for wounded soldiers.

Toward the end of August, when Sam Shaw came for a visit, he and Melville rode to Cheshire and climbed Saddleback. "There was no more ardent and indefatigable excursionist among [the] hills and valleys of Berkshire County than Herman Melville," Joseph Smith would write, as Melville's ailments never kept him from tramping the hills.[68]

When he wasn't keeping tabs on troop movements, riding, hiking, or taking the children to gather chestnuts at Lulu Falls, Herman was reading the poetry of Heinrich Heine and making extensive marginal comments in his copy of Emerson's *Essays,* Second Series. Although he admired Emerson's vision of the underlying unity of Nature and Art, he took issue with many of Emerson's statements because they seemed disconnected from social concerns and devoid of compassion. A passionate egalitarian despite traces of patrician pride, Melville believed Emerson's smug elitism and "self-conceit" fostered "illusions" and led him to make "gross and astonishing errors," and he blamed Emerson's "errors, or rather blindness" on "a defect in the region of the heart."[69]

In September, McClellan halted Lee's ill-conceived drive to the north through Maryland, which gave the Union forces a tremendous boost. Actually three simultaneous battles, the fierce fighting around Sharpsburg sealed the success of the peninsular campaign. After the shooting stopped, this "most lovely" country "reeked with the stench of death," and according to George Strong, the "horrible congregation of wounded men" resembled "Gustave Doré's pictures embodied in shivering, agonizing, suppurating flesh and blood."[70]

More than twice as many Americans fell in the final day of fighting at Antietam as fell during the War of 1812, the Mexican War, and the Spanish-American War combined. Young William Dwight Sedgwick, the son of Melville's Lenox neighbors Charles and Elizabeth Sedgwick, was killed, and Henry Gansevoort and young Oliver Wendell Holmes Jr. were wounded. Searching for his son, Dr. Holmes was appalled to find dead and wounded men lying in dried blood days after the actual fighting had ceased. The battlefield was "a pitiable sight, truly pitiable, yet so vast, so far beyond possibility of relief that many single sorrows of small dimension have wrought upon my feelings more than the sight of this caravan of maimed pilgrims." When Mathew Brady exhibited in his Broadway gallery a series of battlefield photographs called "The Dead at Antietam," New Yorkers filed through in shocked and reverent silence.[71]

In his poem "The Victor of Antietam," Melville praises McClellan as the powerful "stormer" who "manned the wall" and "propped the Dome," thereby "atoning" for the

Union defeat in the battle of Bull Run. Although Antietam was only a partial victory, the overall success of the peninsular campaign prompted Lincoln to announce that he would issue a proclamation freeing all slaves held within rebel territories within ninety days. Many northerners hoped that once the slaves were free, they would join the badly mauled Union army and help it defeat the Confederacy.[72]

As soon as the weather began to turn cold that autumn, Melville leased a "square old-fashioned house on South Street in the rear of Backus block" in Pittsfield, near a livery stable and far away from country roads that would soon be blocked by snow. While Lizzie struggled to fit her old window shades to the new fixtures, Melville and his helpers hauled wagonload after wagonload of household effects and knickknacks to the new house. Unfortunately, he suffered a serious accident one day while he was riding back to Arrowhead in Joe Smith's box wagon to pick up a few last items. One of the iron struts gave way, and the young horse pulling the wagon got so frightened that he bolted, flinging the two men to the ground. Smith, though landing on his head, was only stunned and bruised, not seriously injured, but Melville fell "with his back in the hollow of the frozen road," breaking his left shoulder blade and tearing muscles.[73]

For many weeks he felt vulnerable and fragile, and Lizzie, convinced that the jarring of a horse or wagon would aggravate his inflamed spine, urged him to take walks for exercise instead, which proved beneficial to his health. Joseph Smith felt the incident had a lasting effect on Melville. The "prolonged agony and the confinement and interruption of work which it entailed, affected him strangely," he wrote later. Although before the war, Melville had always been "a driver daring to the point of recklessness," after the accident, "he not only abandoned the rides of which he had been so fond, but for a time shrank from entering a carriage." According to Smith, "it was long before the shock which his system had received was overcome; and it is doubtful it ever was completely." However, after the shock wore off, Melville drove fast again.[74]

In December, with his arm still in a sling, Melville wrote Sam Shaw that his neuralgia was still giving him "a love-pinch in the cheek now and then," but that he was "in a fair way of being completely restored to what I was before the accident." He claimed that recovery was flattering to his vanity because it allowed him to "indulge in the pleasing idea that my life must needs be of some value."[75]

The accident made Melville all the more conscious of his mortality. "I once, like other spoonies, cherished a loose notion that I did not care to live very long," he told Sam Shaw, "but I will frankly own that I have now no serious, no insuperable objections to a respectable longevity. I dont [sic] like the idea of being left out night after night in a cold church-yard." Alongside a crude drawing of a skull and crossbones, he added, "Pretty topics for a friendly note, you say. (By the way, Death, in my skull, seems to tip a knowing sort of wink out of his left eye. What does that mean, I wonder?)" He concluded by reporting that Lizzie, though "jaded by her manifold cares" of settling into the new house, was well and the children were flourishing.[76]

The Melvilles celebrated Christmas in the South Street house. As the Gansevoorts and Melvilles had a habit of exchanging useful or edifying gifts, Augusta gave Stanwix a copy of a book called *Learning to Think*, a gift undoubtedly less than perfectly delightful to a boy of eleven. In his thank-you note, Stannie reported, "I hung up my stocking and got a pocket comb, a chain, two cents, and a paper of candy." Malcolm had made stilts for himself and his brother, while Stanwix had made a collar for the little gray and white puppy who had recently adopted him. Herman gave nine-year-old Bessie *The Poetical Works of Mrs. Felicia Hemans*, perhaps as much to see what made the poems of this British rhymester so popular as to please his growing daughter.[77]

That winter, while the younger children and their cousins were happily skating on cold, snowless Silver Lake or the Housatonic River, thirteen-year-old Malcolm preferred to act grown-up. A budding actor since early childhood, he was preparing for his debut in a school production, and as he strolled "upstreet" unaccompanied by parents and pesky siblings, he affected the manner of a laureate of the stage in anticipation of acting at West's Theatre, where traveling theater troupes and local performers appeared. No account of Malcolm's debut has come down to us, but Stanwix described the minstrel show they saw at West's the following March: "One of the darkies would talk just like a white man, the other one would talk like a black man, they were all white men, but painted black." Stannie told Aunt Augusta they were "real funny," especially their patter about a dog who knew arithmetic.[78]

Minstrel shows were among the most popular forms of entertainment in Melville's day, though Oliver Wendell Holmes and others found them revolting. Surely the man who wrote "Benito Cereno," a story so sensitive to the subtle relationship between role-playing and oppression, found blackface comedy disturbing, too. The stereotyping of African-Americans as childlike Sambos too ignorant to understand citizenship, much less share political power with whites, created insidious and lasting prejudice.[79]

In this atmosphere, Lincoln's proclamation emancipating the slaves held "in rebel territories" was gunpowder thrown into an open fire. While free blacks eager to don uniforms to fight for freedom and full citizenship welcomed the proclamation, southerners denounced the President as a tyrant, a dictator, and a hypocrite for tolerating wage slavery in the North. Northerners who were fighting for the Union and didn't "give a fig" about the blacks felt betrayed and deserted in large numbers. Abolitionists faulted Lincoln for freeing only those slaves held in southern states and accused him of freeing them simply so the males would join the army. When Emerson, Longfellow, Whittier, and other New Englanders heard the proclamation read in the Boston Music Hall, they greeted it with cautious celebration. Lydia Maria Child attacked it as a cynical "war measure" and complained that "no recognition of principle of justice or humanity surrounded the political act with a halo of moral glory."[80]

Despite his abhorrence of slavery, Lincoln could not envision Negro equality any more easily than most whites could, and unlike Frederick Douglass and other black leaders, he was unwilling to set slaves free without a plan. For the throngs of blacks who gathered outside the Cooper Union in New York, however, the day the proclamation was read was a day of uninhibited jubilee. The proclamation took effect on January 1, 1863, and as refugees from cotton plantations and tobacco fields streamed into Union encampments in large numbers, *Harper's Weekly* printed a story on freed Negroes marching north.[81]

The issuing of the Emancipation Proclamation in the middle of the war not only failed to bring an end to the hostilities, but may actually have prolonged them by sharpening the North's already bitter debate about the true aims of the war, dividing the West, and stiffening the South's resistance. When apologists for the Confederacy cited the Declaration of Independence as the justification for what they called the Second American Revolution, conservative Unionists like Orestes Brownson rashly suggested doing away with the "Jacobin" document. It was a harbinger of how little common ground would be left to stand on when the smoke of battle cleared.[82]

By the first week of February 1863, when Melville could dress himself and take long walks without a twinge of pain, he went to New York for two weeks. He felt spry enough to walk the distance between Allan's office on Pine Street and his house on Thirty-fifth Street, stopping along the way to buy Bessie the special drawing paper she had requested. Bessie, who also liked to sew, was making Malcolm "a worsted pincushion with a green border shaded down and MM is in the middle of it and filled up with scarlet red" for his birthday. Sadly, not much more than a decade later, she became so crippled by arthritis that she could no longer draw or sew.[83]

While he was in the city, Melville had a chance to see his cousin Henry, who was recuperating from typhoid fever after fighting in the second battle of Bull Run and being wounded at Antietam. "The other day, be it known unto you, Incomparable Kate," he wrote his cousin, "I went with Allan and his wife to Fort Hamilton, where we saw Lieutenant Henry Gansevoort of the U. S. Artillery. He politely led us to the ramparts, pointing out all objects of interest. He looked well and warlike, cheerfully embarked in the career of immortality." In Henry's honor, Kate had photographs of the portraits of General Gansevoort and his wife made for various family members, and when Melville thanked her, he commented that while his grandmother's portrait was "clear and admirable," the "Hero of Fort Stanwix" appeared to be "under a net of eclipse, emblematic perhaps of the gloom his spirit may feel in looking down upon this dishonorable epoch."[84]

At home, Lizzie and the children were "grumbling at the want of sleighing" in the Berkshires, so Helen tried to lure them to Boston, where there was more than enough snow. Lizzie hesitated to interrupt the girls' education by taking them away from Miss Sperry's School, but Helen insisted that if the girls brought along their schoolbooks, she would teach them. "You shall have no more care or anxiety about them and they shall lose none of their new-found erudition," Helen wrote. "I consider myself competent, with suitable elementary books as aids, to infuse into two youthful minds the very first principles of science, & George can exercise their mathematical faculties."[85]

Before Lizzie could get away, a heavy March snowstorm hit the Berkshires, blanketing South Street and keeping everyone in the family housebound except Herman and Malcolm, who hitched up the wagon and ventured out to church. Malcolm, who was now fourteen, took the reins to save his father's arm.

Lizzie had another reason for hesitating to go away. Malcolm and Stanwix could be little hellions, and Melville was too preoccupied and too inconsistent to deal with them effectively. She had unpleasant memories of the "goings-on" that had occurred the last time she left the boys at home with Herman and the maid while she went to Boston. Helen, however, wouldn't take no for an answer: "As to the boys, if with Herman for authority, & restraint, & wholesome correction (if needed)—and your household treasure, for the care of their bodies and stomachs, their outer & inner man or *boy*—they cannot keep said souls & bodies together for a few weeks, without any startling outbreak of boyish outlawry, you had better send said boys to the House of Correction." In the end, Lizzie decided to take Stanwix and the girls to Boston, and Augusta agreed to look after Herman and Malcolm at Arrowhead.[86]

Once this was settled, Lizzie could relax and enjoy Helen's lively description of the latest Boston styles. "It is the fashion now to comb back the hair over a high cushion, powder it freely with gold, silver, or *diamond* powder, and then ornament it with whole birds, butterflies, & insects of all descriptions. A lady at the opera wore a good-sized *nest* with *eggs* in it, on her head, held on by a wreath of hummingbirds. Even *caterpillars* are worn." Lizzie probably found the latest fashions amusing.[87]

As soon as Lizzie and the children reached Boston, Helen wrote Augusta a quick note: "The little girls are as good as kittens, & happy as larks, tell Herman." Both she and Lizzie took Herman's helplessness for granted, as she told Augusta that her "presence there must be a great solace to Herman in the absence of wife, and girl-bairns." Stannie looked "rather 'peaked' after his hooping-cough [*sic*]; but was in most uproarious spirits." He and Lizzie's nephew Oakes Shaw went for a ramble along the waterfront without telling anyone, which gave Lizzie and Helen both gray hairs, and when they joined forces with Helen's nephew Willie Griggs, "the three male juveniles together were entirely too much for our middle-aged nerves," according to Helen, who was "thankful they could amuse themselves out of doors" until they ambushed her husband George and knocked off his hat with snowballs. George fired back a good-natured but well-aimed barrage designed to discourage such attacks. While these northern noncombatants were enjoying snowball fights, hundreds of women were storming through the business district of Richmond, Virginia, smashing windows and looting shops and markets because prices in the war-ravaged South had become so inflated that middle-class families could not meet their basic needs.[88]

Lizzie stayed in Boston until shortly after the anniversary of her father's death on March 30, but only after a rather tense epistolary power struggle with Augusta. Gus wanted her to return two days earlier than she had planned, perhaps because she was tired of ministering to Herman's needs while Mary, the maid, watched "Miss Gusty" work and complained, or perhaps because at times she liked to lord it over Lizzie. When Lizzie and the three younger children arrived back in Pittsfield, they looked so rested that Herman couldn't help noticing how much they had profited by their trip. The children had thoroughly enjoyed their visit, and as always, being with her mother had done Lizzie enormous good, not to mention the comfort her daughter's presence must have been to the bereaved Hope Shaw.[89]

With the snow gone and the weather unusually warm and dry that April, the Melvilles threw open all the windows to give the house a much-needed airing, but Mary took sick and insisted on closing them. She lolled around in bed, claiming she was ready to "give up" completely until Lizzie's "daily dose of 'Bourbon & Bitters' ... so propped her up, that she [felt] 'quite smart again.'" Herman took her malingering as one more sign that it was time to move back to the city, where better household help would be available. In Glens Falls, Melville's cousin Mary Curtis, too, was complaining that she had no cook or servant "excepting a little contraband [a northern word for a freed slave] in the kitchen to wash up pots and kettles."[90]

Allan and Jane had been thinking of buying a country place, so in mid-April, Herman went to New York for two weeks, and he and his brother came to an agreement whereby Allan would buy Arrowhead for three-fourths of its assessed value of $4,000 and Herman would buy Allan's New York house for $7,750, with Mrs. Thurston continuing to hold the $2,000 mortgage on it. Because the Pittsfield property was in her name, Lizzie used the $3,000 legacy she had received from her family physician, Dr. George Hayward, to pay off the mortgage, and Sam Shaw assisted Allan with the legalities of the transaction. Herman could use the $900 left to him by his aunt Priscilla on her death the previous November for much-needed repairs on the New York house. "Herman seems to be much pleased with the prospect. He has always liked New York, & is not the first man who has been beguiled into the country, & found out by experience that it was not the place for him," wrote Mother Melville. They would move back to the city in the fall.[91]

When Allan came up alone to look over the property in May, the weather was so gorgeous that he sent for the rest of the family right away. The boys had made a pen for two pet rabbits, and the girls were helping Lizzie in the garden. Mackey was riding Charlie, and Stannie a horse named Kate. On Sundays, Stannie and the girls studied the catechism their mother had given them to prepare for their baptism that fall. It seemed a perfect place for raising children.[92]

After a family excursion to the Shaker community and a grand picnic on the trailing arbutus ground, "Madam Jane" announced that she didn't want to leave the Berkshires. "How long do you predict that Madam will be satisfied & contented in such a quiet corner of the earth?" Helen asked. Jennie was used to having four servants at her beck and call, so she simply assumed someone would watch her five children while she went shopping. Lizzie was irritated, and Mary, the maid, grumbled that there were enough children around to "shingle a house."[93]

In June, Allan had their furniture, kitchen utensils, cookstove, and servants shipped up from the city. Jennie had decided it was too chilly for her summer wardrobe, so she and Milie, who at fourteen was beginning to tower over her mother, went back to New York to get warmer clothes, leaving the rest of her children "out in the cold," as Lizzie put it. While Lizzie was girding herself for the "rose cold" that laid her low each summer, Bessie was suffering from such severe headaches that Lizzie kept her home from school. Although Bessie was one of the best scholars in her class, Lizzie said she would rather have her "grow up a perfect dunce than have her health suffer."[94]

❦

To the south, the Union's strength and resolve were being sapped by defeats in the field. "Unless we can awake a new spirit among our people, disaster must sooner or later come," Judge David Davis told Julius Rockwell. Henry Gansevoort and Ned Curtis joined the ranks of the many men who dropped out either permanently or temporarily because of illness and battle fatigue, and Toby Greene was listed as a deserter until he reappeared. Even though the army had to offer bounties to encourage white soldiers to enlist, efforts to train and equip black soldiers were being met with resistance from white northerners. Judge Davis advised Rockwell not to let his son William command a black regiment, but to wait for a commission "in the regular army." *Harper's Weekly*, however, was trying to drum up support for the new Negro regiments by running illustrations of "southern chivalry," as they called the grisly evidence of southern atrocities.[95]

Soon after the Confederates scored a resounding victory at Chancellorsville, the tide began to turn in favor of the Union. First, Lee's ablest officer, General Stonewall Jackson, was killed, then Lee took the disastrous step of crossing the Potomac to follow the retreating Union army into Pennsylvania. Finally, on a moonless night, Admiral

David Porter, "a brave man's son," ran his flotilla of eleven boats downstream past the Confederate batteries on the Mississippi and joined forces with General Grant to take Vicksburg. Both Robert Melvill and Toby Greene had a hand in the success of this daring raid, which Melville later commemorated in his poem "Running the Batteries."[96]

With Grant victorious at the Mississippi, with Meade's army massing just north of the Potomac, and with the Horatio Seymour Guards organized by Henry Gansevoort guarding his rear flank at Gettysburg, Pennsylvania, Lee found himself encircled. In a desperate move, he ordered General George E. Pickett to charge the Union lines, and during three days of fierce fighting, 6,500 men were killed or captured amid "shrieks of shells- / Aerial screamings, taunts and yells." Pickett, whose army was decimated, never forgave Lee for ordering this suicidal assault.[97]

One-third of the 150,000 men who fought at the battle of Gettysburg were killed, including fifteen regimental commanders, two dozen other officers, and an entire brigade from the University of Mississippi. On the Fourth of July, 1863, with 28,000 of his own men and almost as many Union soldiers dead, Lee withdrew. Most observers believed one last military thrust would bring the Confederacy to its knees, but with regular battalions, fleets and squadrons held back to put down the riots in New York, Lee was able to pull back unpursued. David Davis thought "letting Lee escape was one of the great disasters & humiliations of the war.... If Lee had been prevented from crossing the Potomac & thoroughly whipped by Meade — this rebellion w[oul]d have been virtually ended."[98]

Thirsting to deliver the coup de grace, the federal government instituted conscription to replenish weakened Union forces, but many northerners rebelled. New York was shaken by the most violent civil disturbance in its history, and Rowland Morewood and other friends of Melville's witnessed the fury of the mob. Although Melville remained out of range of the volcano that erupted over the announcement of a draft lottery, he later wrote a complex and controversial poem about the riots.[99]

Far away from the smoke of the battlefields, the Melvilles were enjoying their last summer in the Berkshires. Kate and John Hoadley and their little girls came for a "popping, flashing" Fourth of July. Charlotte and Minnie had recovered from illnesses that had drained their mother's strength, and it was an unusually good season for berries. Fanny and Helen picked fourteen quarts of raspberries and made eighteen quarts of raspberry and currant jam one day. During the last week of July, it rained so hard that even the piazza windows had to be closed. Roads turned into rivers, and bales of hay floated across the pasture.[100]

The second week of August, Lizzie and Herman left the children with Jennie and drove off together on a trip that was both a farewell to the Berkshires and a second honeymoon. Their week-long excursion took them to romantic Bash-Bish Falls and to Mount Everett, Copake, Great Barrington, Monterey, and the hill towns of Becket,

Savoy, and Cummington. Despite the excessive heat, Lizzie thoroughly enjoyed the trip. "We passed through some of the wildest and most enchanting scenery, both mountain and valley and I cannot sufficiently congratulate myself that I have seen it before leaving Berkshire." As it was their last summer in the Berkshires, they may have reminisced about their life at Arrowhead, perhaps conscious for a few hours of the deep contentment known to couples who share a common history of pain and pleasure.[101]

At the end of the month, Pittsfield's Forty-ninth Volunteer Infantry returned from a nine months' tour of duty in Louisiana and "a great deal of hard fighting." Six hundred survivors, two-thirds of the regiment, had traveled from Baton Rouge to Cairo, Illinois, via Mississippi steamer, then by rail to Pittsfield and a depot thronged with cheering crowds. Homes and businesses were decorated with "flags and festoons," and brass bands from schools and musical sodalities played as the regiment marched to the public park under evergreen arches and banners with "appropriate [patriotic] mottoes."[102]

In the evening, the Melvilles attended Sarah Morewood's soirée honoring Colonel William Francis Bartlett, the organizer of the Berkshire regiment, who was now about to take command of the Massachusetts Fifty-seventh. A Harvard graduate who had lost a leg in the war, he was something of a legend for leading troops into combat carrying a velvet-padded crutch balanced on his saddlebow. Once, when new recruits proved inept at mastering their drills, he removed his cork leg and performed the sequence rapidly for them on his good leg until they could do it, too. For Melville, Bartlett exemplified the stoic endurance the human race needed to survive its terrible history. In his poem "The College Colonel," Melville would write that he had "lived a thousand years / Compressed in battle's pains and prayers, / Marches and watches slow."[103]

Sarah Morewood's party ended with a dazzling fireworks display, her swan song, as she was very far gone with consumption. Unable to make her customary visits to sanitaria down South, she was growing weaker every day. Before Malcolm returned to school in Newton, and Stannie went back to Gansevoort, Lizzie had Stannie, Fanny, and Bessie baptized by the Reverend Orville Dewey, and in early October, Herman went to New York to enroll Fanny and Bessie in the Stuyvesant Square Quaker School.[104]

While Melville was in the city, Sarah Morewood died "peacefully" at the tender age of thirty-nine, having "suffered much pain." Her last words as she gazed out the window were "How heavenly!" Lizzie, who had watched by her bedside the entire day and helped dress the body for burial, was profoundly moved: "It has been a very solemn and eventful day for me, for it is the first death I ever witnessed—And I feel that I have lost a very dear and much attached friend—for thirteen years we have been on the most intimate terms without the least shadow of a break in our friendship." Lizzie remained close friends with Sarah's sister, Ellen Brittain, all her life.[105]

Mrs. Morewood's death had come so suddenly that her body had to be placed in a vault until the Pittsfield Cemetery could get the plot ready for burial. Although Melville was asked to be a pallbearer, he did not return from New York in time for the service at the Episcopal church, so he sent a small white wreath for the coffin in his stead. Allan and Jennie sent a cross of flowers, and Lizzie asked Sam to send a wreath from Boston so that she would have something "appropriate" for her dear friend. Herman arrived in Pittsfield in time to attend the interment, bringing a big basket of peaches for the family.[106]

To both Herman and Lizzie, it seemed an era had come to an end. They were no longer Pittsfield residents, and the friend and neighbor whose boundless energy and creativity had epitomized Berkshire summer hospitality was gone as well. Aunt Priscilla, Uncle Wessel, and Aunt Mary Melvill's son John had all died recently, Henry Thurston's wife Elizabeth had died giving birth to the couple's third child, and George Duyckinck had died in March. The Melvilles' circle was a "diminished thing," to borrow a phrase from Robert Frost.

Winter hit early that year, and with the carpets rolled away, the floors were freezing cold. Lizzie was so out of patience "living in this forlorn uncomfortable condition—carpets up, window shades down, & everything in boxes" that she couldn't wait to move. Herman had neither the time nor the energy to describe "the thousand and one botherations incident to a removal of one's household a hundred & sixty miles, the fitting up & furnishing of a house &c &c," but he did note that it cost as much to transport their household effects from the freight depot in Manhattan to the house on Twenty-sixth Street as it had cost to ship them from Pittsfield to the city.[107]

Sometime before leaving Arrowhead, Lizzie gave a bust of her late father to the Lenox Courthouse (now the Lenox Library), and Melville packed his books and sorted through old papers, trying to decide what to take with him. At some point he burned letters in the big fireplace, perhaps including those he had received from Nathaniel Hawthorne while he was writing *Moby-Dick*, as years later, he told Julian Hawthorne that it was his "vile habit to destroy nearly all my letters." In his memoirs, Julian portrayed Melville as a tormented soul who had consigned unspeakable secrets to the flames.[108]

To Melville, burning old documents in the great fireplace must have seemed insignificant compared with the fires smoldering in the nation's heartland. In the autumn of 1863, American farmers were in uniform, harvesting death amid "immense charred solitudes" that were "once farms," and Melville's imagination was haunted by the "chimney-stacks that reign / War-burnt upon the houseless plain / Of hearthstones without neighborhoods." At a time when he badly needed a burst of creative energy and renewed purpose, the war was convincing him of the impermanence of everything.[109]

Maria Gansevoort Melville attained the age of eighty in good health, her coquetry undimmed.

TWENTY-THREE

A TIME RICH IN CATASTROPHES

The Melvilles' new neighborhood echoed with the clang of iron-shod hooves against cobble-stones as horses drew steam cars from the tandem terminals of the New York & New Haven and the New York & Harlem railroads to equipment sheds and stables a few blocks to the east. Halfway down the block and cattycorner from the market on Fourth Avenue stood a modest three-story brownstone registered in the name of Elizabeth S. Melville, who would never have let outsiders know the deed was in her name, not her husband's.[1]

The house at 104 East Twenty-sixth Street was just the place for an aspiring author to live and work, but Melville had already passed the midpoint of his life after publishing nine novels and sixteen magazine stories and sketches. He was much too well known and too pro-lific to be considered an aspiring author, and too out of favor with the critics and the reading public to be considered a grand old man of American letters. Despite his inclusion in Evert Duyckinck's 1855 Cyclopaedia of American Literature, *Melville was an ex-celebrity, a travel writer who had lost his way. Few remembered much about him except that there had been some notoriety or impropriety connected with his books, and even they could not recall the details.*

While a few kept the idealistic young adventurer's vision of the Happy Valley in their hearts as they watched the land they loved being blown apart by civil war, most people thought of him as a flash in the pan, a failure.

Fourth Avenue was *déclassé* but decent, and Twenty-sixth Street was quite respectable. It was well uptown from the port, the commercial district, Wall Street, Five Points, and the teeming slums. When Melville walked east along Twenty-sixth Street toward the river, he passed a carriage factory at Lexington and an ironworks on First Avenue before reaching Bellevue Hospital, and later, the Eclectic Medical College. When he walked west on the street, he came to Madison Square Garden and the new Union League Club. Formed by Frederick Law Olmsted, Henry Whitney Bellows, and others who broke away from the Union Club when it accepted southern sympathizers as members, the Union League saw itself as an association of Christian patriots pledged to fight for the preservation of the Union and the education of freedmen so they could assume the responsibilities of citizenship after the war.[2]

On West Twenty-fifth Street, the poet Anne Lynch, whom Melville had met in 1848, was writing her comprehensive *Handbook of Universal Literature.* Two blocks north, on West Twenty-seventh Street, men could be seen alighting from private carriages after dark before the "Seven Sisters," the city's largest and most elegant bordello. Mutely tolerated by long-suffering wives and sweethearts, these high-toned brothels advertised their charms in such publications as the lavishly illustrated *Guide to the Seraglios of New York,* available at newsstands.[3]

For those who preferred outdoor recreation, the city provided oases of greenery such as Madison Square Park at Fifth Avenue and Twenty-third Street. During the 1830s, when Madison Cottage, a stagecoach stop and post tavern, stood at the junction of Twenty-third Street, Broadway, and Fifth Avenue, the park was the city's unofficial social center. Mayor James Harper, whose motto was "Trust in God, pay your bills, and keep your bowels open," turned the park into a parade-ground in the 1840s. Madison Cottage was torn down in 1853 to make way for Franconi's Hippodrome, New York's version of the Roman Colosseum, and in 1863, the park was an army camp.[4]

Melville would live at 104 East Twenty-sixth Street for the rest of his life. He was a great walker who enjoyed fresh air and exercise as well as the medley of sights, sounds, and smells that reward the man who strolls a great city's streets conscious of history, alert to new sensations, and inquisitive about human diversity. If he walked up Fifth Avenue toward Central Park, Melville would pass the Croton Reservoir, a *faux*–Egyptian tomb that occupied the site of the old Crystal Palace. Two blocks farther north, at Forty-fourth Street, he would come to the charred shell of the Colored Orphan Asylum, which had been burned to the ground during the draft riots. A hike to the hinterlands a short distance away would take him past the construction site at Fifty-second Street where workmen were building a five-story brownstone for Madame Restell, the notorious "female physician" and "professor of midwifery." Having made a fortune with her "Celebrated Preventative Powders for Married Ladies," Restell moved uptown to flaunt her success. She built a mansion and, to antagonize the church officials who had tried for years to close her business down, had liveried coachmen drive her past the new cathedral and archdiocesan headquarters every afternoon on her way to Central Park. While the wealthy merchants who later erected grand mansions at a safe distance from hers complained sniffishly that her presence lowered property values, this skilled abortionist was plying her trade comfortably "amid velvets and buhl, satin and rosewood, mirrors and bronzes."[5]

In the three decades Melville lived there, Twenty-sixth Street would see many changes. In 1871, Commodore Vanderbilt would lease the old railroad sheds to P. T. Barnum, who stabled Jumbo the elephant and other large animals brought from Africa for his circus right down the street from the homes of Herman Melville, Theodore Roosevelt, and Jenny Jerome, the future mother of British prime minister Winston Churchill. In 1876, Lorenzo Delmonico would follow his wealthy clientele uptown to Fifth Avenue and West Twenty-sixth Street, filling the whole block with the most elegant and expensive restaurant in New York.[6]

In 1889, Stanford White's new Madison Square Garden, crowned by a graceful, open-columned Venetian tower, would rise at the far corner of Twenty-sixth Street in place of the old railroad depots, but Melville would not live to see Augustus Saint-Gaudens's controversial thirteen-foot-high statue of Diana take her place atop the building. This nude golden goddess, balancing on one delicately arched foot while nocking an arrow on the string of her golden bow, caused almost as much of a sensation in 1892 as Hiram Powers's statue *The Greek Slave* had caused in 1852 when it was exhibited at New York's Crystal Palace. Evidently, Americans believed bare-breasted women, even goddesses of bronze or marble, belonged in Polynesia, not New York.[7]

New York had grown dramatically since the Melvilles' departure in 1850, and the gap between rich and poor had widened precipitously. As immigrants flooded into the city, the well-to-do blazed a trail northward, putting ever-increasing distances between themselves and the masses of people who huddled in the dank cellars and rickety tenements of Hell's Kitchen. Leaving such seamy entertainments as Tommy Norris's rat-baiting dogs and topless female boxers to the workingman, the city's richest men—A. T. Stewart, William B. Astor, August Belmont, Dr. Samuel P. "Sarsaparilla" Townsend, and others—gobbled up open land uptown and built estates that they furnished with masterpieces of European art. By 1863, Fifth Avenue had eclipsed Broadway as the city's most fashionable thoroughfare.[8]

Dubbed "the most radical city in America" by Walt Whitman in 1855, New York was a city in crisis in 1863. The war was bleeding the wounded nation dry. "War prices, high tariff, reign of shoddy," Edmund Clarence Stedman, stockbroker, poet, and book reviewer, complained in his diary. The top one percent of the populace controlled sixty-one percent of the city's wealth, and although prices had risen forty-three percent, wages had risen only twelve percent. A Workingmen's Protective Union had been formed to improve the lot of laborers, but working women still earned only a small fraction of the wages earned by men for equivalent work. Many resorted to prostitution to feed their children, or hired themselves out as wet nurses to make extra money. Advertisements offering "a good fresh breast of milk" for sale appeared in James Gordon Bennett's *New York Herald* alongside reports that the city planned to spend $10,000 on a grand ball and banquet catered by Delmonico's to welcome the Russian fleet that fall.[9]

Just prior to Melville's return to the city, several sensational events occurred besides the visit of the Russian fleet: the extravagant wedding of P. T. Barnum's Tom Thumb and his bride brought the cream of New York society to Grace Church with expensive gifts for the tiny couple; the Great Rally for Democracy at Cooper Union, organized by women, gave a boost to the flagging war effort; and the draft riots, the most violent civil disturbance in New York's history, plunged the city into an orgy of barbarism.[10]

The immediate cause of the riots was the announcement that the names of thirty thousand New Yorkers had been put into a draft lottery, but the underlying causes were complex. Opposition to conscription was symptomatic of racial tensions and class conflict, as well as war exhaustion, which made it difficult to replenish the depleted Union ranks. Almost all whites considered forced conscription an infringement of their freedom. Middle- and working-class whites who would have enlisted anyway considered the draft an insult to their patriotism, while others resented having to fight for slaves already set free by presidential edict. Moneyed men had always been able to evade the draft by rationalizing that they were needed at home to defend the economy. Thus, Andrew Carnegie, J. P. Morgan, Chester A. Arthur, Grover Cleveland, George Templeton Strong, and the fathers of two future presidents–Theodore and Franklin Roosevelt–all hired working-class substitutes. George Strong, for example, paid $1,100 for a "big Dutch boy of twenty or thereabouts" to go to war for him.[11]

For blacks who were willing to fight and die to free their enslaved brothers and sisters in the South, the drafting of white men exclusively was one more reminder that they were being denied the rights and responsibilities of citizenship. New York was more racially polarized in 1863 than it had been in 1855. Between 1825 and 1845, the city's black population had grown as a result of the state's abolition of slavery in 1827, but by 1860 it had decreased, partly because the mortality rate among blacks had risen dramatically, and partly because many black families had relocated to escape mounting harassment and job discrimination. Most streetcars had lately become segregated, and for a decade or more, the wards nearest the port had become economic battlegrounds between free Negroes descended from slaves owned by the men of the revolutionary generation and the more recent immigrants from Europe, who were overwhelmingly of Irish origin.

Thanks to Tammany's unlimited supply of whiskey and lack of scruples, Irish immigrants became citizens and voters almost the moment they cleared customs at Castle Garden. Black men who had established solid homes, churches, and schools in the port a generation or two earlier than the Irish were often pushed out of decent housing and jobs and outnumbered at the polls, and they had to show assets of at least $250 before they were allowed to vote. Even conservative George Templeton Strong deemed such prejudicial restrictions unreasonable because Negroes "behave like Christians, bear no malice, and commit no outrages."[12]

Racial and ethnic antipathies that had been smoldering for years reached the flash point during the draft riots. The announced start of the draft lottery, Saturday, July 11, 1863, went smoothly, but the next day, when the names of the conscripts were published in the newspapers, people took to the streets to protest the tyranny of the federal government. Whites who marched up Broadway with huge banners that read "NO DRAFT!" were joined by rowdies whose rage was fueled by alcohol, and a march that started out as a peaceful demonstration very quickly turned into an all-out race and class war as the predominantly Irish gangs rampaged through lower Manhattan, throwing paving stones through windows, tearing down telegraph wires, and ripping up railroad tracks. After attacking Superintendent of Police Kennedy and several patrolmen on the beat, the mob stomped a captain of the national guard to death with their hobnailed boots and viciously assaulted blacks and interracial couples. Women beat up prostitutes, then looted shops of soap, starch, and other goods rendered scarce by the prolongation of the war.[13]

After ransacking an arms factory owned by Mayor Opdyke, the rioters stormed uptown to burn the draft offices at Forty-sixth Street. On their way, they terrorized residents of Murray Hill and pillaged valuable furniture and works of art. At Forty-fourth Street, they broke down the picket fence surrounding the Colored Orphan Asylum and torched the wooden building, trapping many of the children inside and scaring neighborhood residents, including the human-rights activist Elizabeth Cady Stanton, her husband Henry, and their tenant Susan B. Anthony, half to death. After the draft offices went up in flames, the mob surged back downtown to sack the *Tribune* office. Rumors flew that the riot was "an organized insurrection in the interest of the rebellion" led by Jefferson Davis himself.[14]

Gangs like the ones who had turned the anti-abolitionist riots of 1835 into a bloodbath committed such vicious atrocities against black citizens that even George

Templeton Strong, who had scorned abolitionists before the war, was forced to admit that "this infernal slavery system has corrupted our blood, North as well as South!" As angry mobs surged through the streets, Strong joined with John Jay, and other prominent citizens in urging the mayor to declare martial law, but Opdyke, fearing that drastic action would lead to all-out war, refused. With fires flaring all over the city, Strong and several other prominent citizens took it upon themselves to telegraph the President to send in federal troops. Only when rioters attacked the mayor's home and threatened the nearby homes of Colonel Frank E. Howe and David Dudley Field did Mayor Opdyke call for help, and on July 14, General Wool brought in 800 troops from the harbor forts, the Brooklyn Navy Yard, and West Point.[15]

Career civil servant Maunsell Field, who in happier days had watched Melville lovingly pat the trees at Arrowhead, recalled that when rioters threatened to pull down the Custom-House and sack the Treasury, "arms were distributed to all the employes [sic], and hand-grenades and carboys of vitriol were placed at every window. There was a military guard of raw troops about the building nearly all the time, but we apprehended more danger from it than from the rioters. We kept a loaded *mitrailleuse* facing the Pine Street Entrance, and we had two field-pieces worked by gunners from the Brooklyn Navy Yard." Thus, Allan Melville, whose office was at 37 Pine, had to pass through a war zone to get to work.[16]

Governor Horatio Seymour issued a proclamation demanding an end to the mayhem, but it had no effect. Finally, when rumors started flying that the rioters planned to cut water and gas mains, he ordered two thousand policemen into the streets. Although most midtown omnibuses and horsecars were back in service on the morning of July 16, pockets of rioters still controlled the city's extreme eastern and western wards from behind makeshift barricades. Early the next morning, the Seventh Regiment, the vanguard of an occupying army soon to come, arrived from the front. From his office window, George Templeton Strong could see "a gunboat at the foot of Wall Street, the Custom-House and Treasury full of soldiers and live shells, and the howitzers in position to rake Nassau Street from Wall to Fulton." After a pitched battle at Gramercy Park late that night, order was restored.[17]

The price of peace was military occupation. Every Union regiment in the East, save one, converged on the city to prevent a recurrence of rioting, and their commander, General John A. Dix, suspended habeas corpus and set up a secret police force to keep a close watch on "suspicious" citizens. One of those kept under surveillance was Richard Lathers, whose pastor, the Reverend Morgan A. Dix of Trinity Church, was General Dix's son.[18]

The draft riots, in the words of Walt Whitman, were "the Devil's work." They lasted four days and left 119 people dead, 306 wounded, and 450 men and women under arrest, of whom sixty-seven were eventually tried and convicted of specific crimes. Private property losses came to around $5 million, and the cleanup cost the city around $1.5 million. The riots did have some positive effects. The city earmarked $2.5 million for the relief of destitute women and children, some prominent businessmen formed an anti-Tammany Citizens' Association to work for housing reforms, and Jim Crow streetcars were abolished, but not before most of the black middle class had fled to neighboring communities.[19]

With an estimated 50,000 to 75,000 people caught up in the violence, newspapers all across the country had carried the story. Writing from Illinois, David Davis compared the New York mob to "an old fashioned European mob," and asserted that "The conscript law must be enforced in that city, otherwise there will be trouble in other cities." The draft lottery resumed in August under heavy military guard with a blindfolded man drawing names from a revolving drum.[20]

As Melville well knew from accounts of the 1835 anti-abolitionist riots and the Astor Place melee, riots had become regular occurrences in his city. Still, the levels of savagery to which thousands of white New Yorkers had regressed in their attacks on law-abiding blacks shocked even those who would never have socialized with blacks and had moved uptown to avoid contact with the "lower orders" of the white population. Patricians like Henry Gansevoort and Henry Whitney Bellows believed that only Draconian measures could keep the base passions of the "lower orders" in check.[21]

In "The House-top: A Night Piece (July, 1863)," Melville adopts the point of view of a man watching the draft riots from his roof. The poem's powerful opening lines evoke the baleful, claustrophobic atmosphere of a city suffering under a midsummer heat wave: "No sleep. The sultriness pervades the air / And binds the brain—a dense oppression, such / As tawny tigers feel in matted shades, / Vexing their blood and making apt for ravage." The intense heat arouses ferocious passions as the unleashed Tammany tigers surge through the steamy streets setting fires and plunging the city into chaos. "Beneath the stars the roof desert spreads / Vacant as Libya," violence engulfs the city as the speaker of the poem watches in horror, and the "Atheist roar of riot" drowns out the voice of God.[22]

Under "parching Sirius," the dogs of race and class war are loosed, and amid the baleful glare of "red Arson," the "Town is taken by its rats—ship-rats / And rats of the wharves." No longer "held in awe" by "civil charms / And priestly spells ... a better sway / Than sway of self," the city's largest Roman Catholic minority "rebounds whole aeons back in nature" to a state of savagery. In response, "Wise Draco comes, deep in the midnight roll / Of black artillery" to put down the rebellion and to impose martial law, "in code corroborating Calvin's creed / And cynic tyrannies of honest kings." The "dull and dead" rumble of advancing troops led by General John A. Dix sounds the death knell of democracy and the advent of the kind of militaristic government against which the Founders had warned, one which rests on the assumption that man is essentially evil. It constitutes a "grimy slur on the Republic's faith" that "Man is naturally good / And—more—is Nature's Roman, never to be scourged." Melville's observer takes the tragic view. While great armies clash on the nation's battlefields, in the heart of the city, poverty, class conflict, race hatred, and the inevitable authoritarian crackdown threaten to destroy the "Founders' Dream."[23]

The speaker of the poem indicts white mobs for their brutality and laments the imposition of martial law, portraying the blacks as helpless victims swept up in a "blood-dimmed tide" of anarchy. His use of bestial images such as "tigers" and "rats" to denote the whites, not the blacks, recalls the reversals Melville achieved in "Benito Cereno." From the "house-top," which represents the long-range view, the historical perspective, and not the limited perspective of the "man in the street," regardless of his class, Melville's narrator sees the barbarism of the white mobs and the cynicism of their leaders as harbingers of political and moral chaos.

The draft riots forced the Union League Club to make good on its promise to sponsor the first Negro regiment in New York State. Though paternalistic in their attitudes toward blacks, the founders of the Union League believed the economy of the North could not prosper unless businessmen made a commitment "to deal justly and mercifully with the colored people in [their] midst," as Olmsted put it. Henry Whitney Bellows argued that formation of a Negro regiment was a first and necessary step toward the eventual enfranchisement of the former slaves, and *Harper's Weekly* supported the idea.[24]

Abolitionists had always argued in favor of training blacks to fight alongside whites. "Will the *slave* fight?" Wendell Phillips had asked. "If any man asks you, tell him No. But if anyone asks you will a *Negro* fight, tell him Yes!" Naval crews had been racially mixed for a long time, and blacks had fought valiantly in the sea war of 1812, so when the Union gained a beachhead at Port Royal, South Carolina, in 1862, President Lincoln had ordered the formation of the first Negro regiment, the South Carolina Volunteers. Its commander, Colonel Thomas Wentworth Higginson, the noted Unitarian minister and stalwart abolitionist, later wrote a memoir called *Army Life in a Black Regiment,* in which he asserted: "'Til the blacks were armed, there was no guaranty of their freedom."[25]

Massachusetts followed suit soon after, commissioning that state's first Negro regiment, the Fifty-fourth Infantry, with Boston Brahmin Robert Gould Shaw as its commander. Young Shaw had balked at leading Negro soldiers until his abolitionist parents, concerned that their son had no direction to his life, pressured him to do it. While he was training the troops, he became so impressed by their gallantry and their loyalty to the Union that when his regiment was sent to soften up the defenses at Fort Wagner so that white troops could take the fort without suffering too many casualties, he marched proudly at the head of the ranks, right into a barrage of enemy fire. Colonel Shaw and one hundred of his men were slaughtered in this "ill-planned and murderously bungled" assault, and he was buried in a mass grave with them. Those who looked back on his brief and tragic career either called Shaw a traitor to his race, or eulogized him as a hero.[26]

The massacre of the Fifty-fourth Massachusetts in July 1863 did not deter black New Yorkers from enlisting, as they were only too eager to prove themselves in battle. Even though Negro regiments were segregated units led by white officers who thought of themselves as "the best culture" and compared colored soldiers to the sepoys of British-ruled India, military service did provide a way out of mental and emotional slavery for the blacks who managed to survive the bloody battles yet to come.[27]

The following winter, as a drawing by Thomas Nast shows, the Grand Review of the Army brought troops marching ten abreast, in seemingly endless columns, through the streets of Washington. Nast's drawing does not show how exhausted the men were, or how many soldiers had deserted. Whites who resented the emancipation and the presence of Negro troops were becoming so reluctant to fight that the government had to offer them bounties to enlist, and before long, bounties had to be paid to black soldiers, who were demoralized by the way they were being treated by the army. When they weren't stuck in the front lines to serve as cannon fodder, they were made to dig graves and bury bodies. As a result, casualties among black soldiers were proportionately much higher than among whites, from wounds and from diseases.[28]

In the spring and summer of 1863, tens of thousands of men died at Chancellorsville, Vicksburg, and Gettysburg. Melville's friend Toby Greene, who was on leave from his position near Vicksburg, thought the war was far from over; others feared the Union might not win. "*How sad this War*," Melville's cousin Helen Melville Souther wrote to Augusta. "Would that brethren might live together in unity!"[29]

At Lookout Mountain, Tennessee, General Grant's "armies in the valley . . . fortified in right" were climbing the "torrent-torn" heights amid "thunders, / And terrors, and a blight." As armies struggled "like ghosts" in the "grayish mist" for control of Chattanooga, the crags resounded with "the clangor / Of the war of Wrong and Right" as Union troops repulsed "swarms of rebels" to reach "the sunlit steeps" of victory. Toby Greene survived, but "some who gained the envied Alp / ... Dropped into death's wide-open arms, / Quelled on the wing like eagles struck in air."[30]

Their sightless eyes fixed on cold stars, the ardent young warriors who fell at Chattanooga under Grant's "solicitude" gain immortality through Melville's artistry and vision:

> Forever they slumber young and fair,
> The smile upon them as they died;
> Their end attained, that end a height:
> Life was to these a dream fulfilled,
> And death a starry night.[31]

Herman and Lizzie celebrated the arrival of 1864 with a party to which they invited Allan, Jennie, Evert Duyckinck, Sarah Morewood's sister Ellen Brittain, and several other close friends and relatives who could be counted on to "come early, stay sociably & go early," as Lizzie put it. Reminiscent of her earlier observation that Herman felt "used-up" for writing if he stayed out too late in the evenings indulging in food, drink, or entertainment, her comment suggests that Herman was trying to adhere to a regular regimen of reading, ruminating, and writing poetry.[32]

In February, Melville paid off the last $200 he owed Harper's, but no sooner was one small worry off his mind than a larger one intruded. His mother fell ill, and he hurried to Gansevoort, "bringing with him many delicacies to tempt her appetite." He probably feared the worst; several weeks earlier, his cousin Helen Souther had died at her home in Hingham. With the older generation slipping away, Herman worried that his mother, to whom he had grown closer with every passing year, might be the next to go. Maria recovered quickly, however, and when he stopped in Albany to have lunch and attend an art exhibit with Peter and Susan Gansevoort, he was able to reassure them that she was on the mend. Only a year earlier, Kate Curtis had written her cousin Kate Gansevoort, "I think she is one of the most remarkable persons I ever knew—I look at her with wonder, and astonishment and can not realise, she is over *seventy*—How active she is; and youthful in her feelings—I must say; she is a splendid old lady."[33]

Melville arrived back in the city in time to see New York's Twentieth Colored Regiment go off to war. Despite fears that a public display of Negro soldiers sporting white gloves and gaiters, shiny boots, and polished rifles would "loose hell again," these black men paraded proudly behind a brass band from the Twenty-sixth Street wharf on the East River to Union Square, perhaps right past the Melvilles' house, as thousands of New Yorkers cheered. At Union Square they heard a proclamation of support from more than a hundred "Mothers, Wives and Sisters of the members of the New York Union League Club," including Mrs. John Jacob Astor, Mrs. William Cullen Bryant, several Roosevelts, and Mrs. Robert Gould Shaw, the young colonel's widow.[34]

After receiving regimental colors dedicated to "God and Liberty!" from the women, the troops marched downtown to board the ships that would take them to New Orleans. They were escorted by about 250 members of the Union League Club. As the procession entered precincts that had been hotbeds of anti-black violence during the draft riots, some of the band's musicians wanted to turn back, so the Union Leaguers broke into a chorus of "John Brown's Body." When onlookers joined in, the band rallied, and New York's first Negro regiment was sent off to war with a rousing fanfare.[35]

In some respects, New York had come a long way since 1860, when Mayor Fernando Wood had felt free to boast openly that he had no intention of "dying for a lot of niggers." By the time ten thousand Union soldiers, led by General Dix and including twenty-seven military bands, marched through New York on April 4, 1864, to herald the opening of the Metropolitan Fair, all New York was swept up in the tide of pro-Union patriotism. Organized to raise money for the Union Army, the great Metropolitan Fair featured hundreds of booths staffed by women wearing crisp uniform dresses accented by satin sashes. Tables held historical souvenirs and other curios, and Indians performed tribal dances while society women costumed as Dutch dames and black women pretending to be household slaves enacted scenes representing the first Dutch settlement.[36]

Melville contributed his poem "Inscription for the Slain at Fredericksburg" to a commemorative volume titled *Autograph Leaves of our Country's Authors*, to be auctioned off at the fair. In his cover letter he wrote: "The Sanitary Fairs to be held in several of the larger cities will do an immense service to our soldiers. God prosper them, and those who work for them, and the great Cause which they are intended to subserve." Melville's opinion was not shared by Walt Whitman, however, who thought the Sanitary Commission's bureaucratic regulations were interfering with the kind of personal care he and other nurses in field hospitals wanted to provide for wounded men. Despite the "disgusting state of fashionable excitement" that brought diamond-bedecked women out in broad daylight and threatened to spoil the event for Harriet Woolsey, Henry Bellows felt confident the fair would rekindle "the latent patriotism of this vast metropolis" and unify "its fragmentary and disjointed population."[37]

Melville was restless that spring. He felt so well that he began to wish he could observe "the strife in the pines" firsthand, so when Allan's law partner, George Brewster, received a commission as a captain in Company K and was told to report to Henry Gansevoort's regiment in Vienna, Virginia, Herman convinced Allan that they ought to go along. Jennie insisted on coming, too, and bringing their oldest daughter, Milie, but Allan persuaded her to stay home and wait until they could be sure of getting passes to visit Henry's camp. The first week of April, the three men took the train to Washington, where they checked into the Ebbitt House, an unpretentious boardinghouse on "newspaper row" across from the opulent Willard Hotel.[38]

The following day, Brewster went on alone, leaving Herman and Allan to apply for passes and wait for a break in the weather as well. Torrential rains had been inundating the city and the surrounding countryside for days, swelling the Potomac beyond its banks, washing out the railroad bridge to Harpers Ferry, and making the roads impassable just as General Grant was gearing up for an offensive.[39]

Allan telegraphed Richard Lathers requesting that he ask Secretary Stanton for permission, and Herman wrote directly to Charles Sumner. Although Sumner was busy steering a constitutional amendment abolishing slavery through the Senate, he gave Melville a note from the floor recommending him to the provost marshal as "a loyal citizen & my friend." Before Lathers had time to reply to Allan's cable, they received permission to visit the front. They may also have visited Guert Gansevoort at Fortress Monroe, where the masts of the *Cumberland* could be seen protruding eerily from the dark waters of Hampton Roads.[40]

Meanwhile, Allan's headstrong wife, Jennie, had packed up Milie and taken the overnight train for Washington, and when they couldn't find Allan and Herman at the Ebbitt House, she checked into the Willard Hotel. Nathaniel Hawthorne, who had stayed there in 1862, thought the Willard's bustling lobby could "much more justly be called the center of Washington and the Union than either the Capitol, the White House, or the State Department." Stuck in the fashionable hotel without a male escort, Jennie had to content herself with watching celebrities such as General Ulysses S. Grant come and go.[41]

Assuming that Allan and Herman had left for Virginia without her, Jennie wrote Henry a note begging him to let her and Milie visit: "Don't worry. We can endure more than Allan & will think anything nice," she wrote, but Henry was already on his way back to Washington to investigate discrepancies in an ordnance report. When Herman and Allan returned to town from their visit to Guert, they found a note Jennie had left for them at the Ebbitt House. Just as they were joining her at the Willard, Henry checked into the Ebbitt House, so they missed each other.[42]

Either the War Department would not grant the women passes to Henry's camp, or the two men persuaded them not to make the trip, as Herman and Allan went alone, unaware that Henry was in Washington. The only way to reach the camp was to hitch a ride on a freight car loaded with supplies, then ride eight miles from Fairfax Station to Vienna over bumpy, muddy "corduroy roads" made of logs laid crosswise in the dirt. Despite his bad back, Herman did not mind the rough ride; in fact, it whetted his appetite for further adventures.

Herman and Allan entered the camp unchallenged and wandered around for a while, probably noticing how much bleaker it looked than the artists' renditions of camps they had seen in *Harper's Weekly*. Instead of neat rows of smart white tents pitched amid lush meadows, the grass on "the slope / Of what was late a vernal hill" had been chewed up by soldiers' boots and horseshoes, and the trees had been burned as firewood months before. Still muddy from the rain, the ground dissolved every time the two men took a step.[43]

When they finally walked into brigade headquarters and introduced themselves, the men on duty were startled and embarrassed, especially the camp's commander, Colonel Charles Russell Lowell of the Second Massachusetts Cavalry. The regiment was stationed "south of the Potomac in Virginia and within a gallop of the Long Bridge at Washington" for the purpose of keeping supply lines open and to protect the capital against the infamous Forty-third Virginia Partisan Rangers, known as Mosby's Raiders. These guerrillas blew up bridges, robbed trains, stole livestock, food, and ammunition, and harassed Union pickets with impunity, so tight security was imperative. Mosby's men had slipped in and stolen horses and mules right from under the noses of pickets at Henry's camp a few months earlier, and they had ambushed a patrol from a neighboring regiment, killing the commanding officer and half the men. As a result, when Colonel Lowell realized that Herman and Allan had slipped in unobserved, he drew up strict new guidelines to protect the camp.[44]

Once the initial shock and embarrassment of Herman and Allan's invasion of the camp wore off, Colonel Lowell and the other officers welcomed them. A nephew of *Atlantic* editor James Russell Lowell and an acquaintance of Ralph Waldo Emerson, the Harvard-educated "college colonel" Charles Lowell swore oaths by Plato and knew the works of Melville's favorite authors well enough to discuss them in depth with Melville while he was there. Lowell had recently married Josephine Shaw, the bright and witty sister of the late Robert Gould Shaw and a sister-in-law of George W. Curtis. Called "Josey" by her friends and "Effy" by her husband, she was pregnant when Melville met her, and with a baby on the way, she had chosen to join her husband in his bivouac rather than be separated from him. An energetic, fearless young woman who spoke three languages and rode horseback like a man, she tended sick and wounded soldiers in the camp hospital and probably showed Herman and Allan through the wards while they were there. With Henry away on company business, the Lowells entertained the Melville brothers at the small frame house the army had commandeered for them.[45]

Several officers of the three regiments stationed at Vienna were college graduates, and Melville knew the brigade's surgeon, Dr. Oscar C. DeWolf of Pittsfield, and adjutant Edwin Y. Lansing, whose brother Abraham later married Henry's sister Kate, and he and Henry had a grand old time talking. One topic of conversation would have stirred memories of the *Somers* mutiny in Melville's mind. One of the men had defected to join Mosby's commandos, and while roaring drunk, he had attacked a patrol, wounding several former buddies before he was caught. A drumhead court convened by Colonel

Lowell condemned him to death; according to adjutant Lansing, this had a sobering effect on a brigade made skittish by constant rebel raids.[46]

Lately the raiders had taken advantage of the flooded river and the curtailment of rail service occasioned by the recent storms to disrupt supply lines, seizing grain and corn meant for Union larders and redirecting it to Confederate troops. When the Partisan Rangers began harassing civilian travelers, Union commanders decided the time had come to flush them out, and just as Herman and Allan arrived at Henry's camp, five hundred men were preparing to ride out in search of Mosby's hidden headquarters, determined to put an end to the reign of terror that had gripped the region.

Herman and Allan were "the antipodes." When Herman announced his intention to join the scouting party, Allan decided to rejoin his wife and daughter in Washington. Obtaining permission from Colonel Lowell to go along, Melville borrowed a horse, a red flannel shirt, and some warm outer clothing from George Brewster—or Bruce, as he was called—who had been ordered to stay behind to guard the camp with the other new recruits. Young Bruce, who admired Melville, was only too happy to oblige, and Melville kept his shirt as a souvenir. At the end of the year, Bruce was captured by Mosby and sent to Libby Prison near Richmond, but he and several other inmates escaped. Black families disguised him as one of their own and conducted him to freedom along the Underground Railroad, and eventually he found his way home safely. In honor of Bruce and other prisoners of war, Melville later wrote the poignant poem "In the Prison Pen."[47]

On the morning of April 18, Melville mounted Bruce's horse and fell in with the cavalry. Colonel Lowell, wearing a dashing crimson sash to inspire his men to bravery, led the long column, comprising 240 soldiers, a civilian guide with a personal score to settle with Mosby, a regimental chaplain clad in black clerical garb, Dr. Benjamin Rush Taylor, wearing his green medical corps sash, a surgeon, a burly hospital steward, a horse-drawn ambulance, and a nearsighted literary man named Herman Melville who was probably unarmed.[48]

Cantering along in this manly company, Melville apparently forgot about his physical ailments, even while sleeping on the cold, damp ground. The main character in his poem "The Scout Toward Aldie" is invigorated by the ride. He enjoys the tingling in the muscles of his thighs and feels as fit as the hospital steward, a "healthy man," and as "alive as Mosby in mountain air." In Melville's poem, the soldiers ride into the "forest deep," their horses splashing as "they cross the freshet-flood" and straining as they climb "the muddy bank," showing no colors and holding their sabers so they won't rattle or ring and alert the rangers to their approach. In fact, Mosby and his men kept the entire force under surveillance as it wound through the countryside toward Aldie on the Little River. Unfortunately, the dozen or so rangers Lowell's brigade captured along the way turned out to be green recruits, "sophomores from the glen / Of Mosby," not veterans.[49]

On the basis of rumors that one of Mosby's men was to be married in Leesburg after nightfall, and that Mosby himself might attend the festivities, Lowell sent seventy-five foot soldiers to storm the ranger wedding. Arriving too late to ascertain whether their quarry had been there or not, Lowell's men drew fire, and in the ensuing skirmish, one of their number was killed and several others wounded. The men returned to camp believing the casualties had been caused by their own troops until the examining physician verified that their wounds had been inflicted by the enemy. All in all, it was an ignominious defeat.[50]

When Melville arrived back at the camp, he found Henry there, sporting his broad-brimmed cavalry hat and ready to spend an evening chatting before Herman left for the headquarters of the Army of the Potomac to meet General Grant. Grant had run a leather shop in Galena, Illinois, with his brother in 1859, so he undoubtedly knew Robert Melvill and his family. Before the week was out, Herman was back in New York, adding his stories to the tales Allan, Jennie, and Milie were telling about their trip.[51]

The scouting party's failure to accomplish its objective emboldened Mosby. Confident that well-trained guerrillas on home territory could outmaneuver and outfight a much larger conventional force, the audacious Mosby sent Lincoln a lock of hair and a note threatening to personally cut a hank of hair from the President's head. Although Mosby never succeeded in infiltrating the capital during the war, his commandos managed to draw off troops from the front and keep Union tacticians off balance for the remainder of the war. Many of Mosby's men kept fighting even after the surrender.

Mosby survived the war to father eight children while practicing law and working for the government. An opportunist to the end, he switched to the Republican Party well after it had abandoned the idealism of its antislavery founders to become the party of patronage and privilege. He became a supporter, then a close friend, of Ulysses S. Grant, who appointed him U.S. consul in Hong Kong and, later, an assistant attorney in the Justice Department.[52]

Participation in the scout gave Melville material for a long narrative poem, the only one of his *Battle-Pieces* based on firsthand experience of the war. In "The Scout Toward Aldie," Melville describes a world of chivalry shattered by Mosby's ruthlessness. The scouting party rides out of camp toward the territory where "Mosby's men ... dare to prowl," leaving the "Capitol Dome–hazy–sublime– / A vision breaking on a dream" behind them. As the long cavalry column curves gracefully southward through the misty sunlight of the April morning, hospital patients who were once "as bold, and gay" as their healthy comrades salute them with "Bandage, and crutch, and cane, and sling."[53]

As the Yankee soldiers enter woods "where once tobacco grew / Drowsily in the hazy air," they intrude on a pastoral landscape which is about to be "ravaged." Orchards "in pleasant lowlands" bear fruit in peace, and cows feed undisturbed in their presence, and "the valley-folk [are] only good / To Mosby, and his wandering brood." Mosby's men are perfectly at home here; they are "moccasin-snakes ... [who] kill and vanish; through grass they glide."[54]

The freshness of Melville's stanza, a dissonant, truncated variant of rhyme royal, makes the poem, like so many of his *Battle-Pieces*, as fine an example of poetic innovation at midcentury as Whitman's sprawling free-verse line or Dickinson's tightly constructed, irreverent, gnomic poems. With its echoes of Cervantes and Chaucer, the poem evokes a world where "love in a tent is a queenly thing" and where "the prayer and sob" of parting are conducted in private, unseen even by the poet's eye. The fictional colonel is a romantic figure loosely modeled on Charles Lowell, and at the end of the poem, the brave young warrior lies dead "amid wilding roses that shed their balm." Buried in a "green-wood graveyard hid from ken, / Where sweet-fern flings an odor nigh," he leaves his bereaved bride to "dream of Mosby and his men" for her remaining "threescore and ten" years. The colonel's early death epitomizes the futility of war, and his grieving widow embodies the sorrow of an entire nation, especially women without husbands, and children without fathers.[55]

Although his poems about the war are somber and reflective, Melville's letters to former comrades in the field are full of military posturing and male bravado. When he heard that Brigadier General Robert O. Tyler had sustained a wound in his ankle, he congratulated him on gaining a scar that would not only prove his patriotism, but also appeal to "the sweet eyes of the sympathetic ladies, who, you know, have a natural weakness for heroes." In fact, the wound crippled Tyler for life and wore down his constitution.[56]

As soon as he had recovered from the "acute attack of neuralgia in the eyes" caused by his exposure to the dampness, the spartan accommodations, and the rough ride, Melville wrote a long letter to his cousin Henry. In it he dwells fondly on his visit and asks to be remembered to the men he met in camp, and especially to his friend Bruce: "Say to him that I hear the neigh of his war-horse in my dreams, likewise that I have a flannel shirt of his in my keeping."[57]

His letter ends with the mock-heroic, "And now, Col. Gansevoort of the 13th N. Y. Cavalry, conceive me to be standing some paces from you, in an erect attitude and with manly bearing, giving you the military salute. Farewell. May two small but choice constellations of stars alight on your shoulders. May your sword be a Lesson to the despicable foe & your name in after ages be used by Southern Matrons to frighten their children by. And after death (which God long avert, & bring about after great battles, quickly, and in a comfortable bed, with wife & children around) may that same name be transferred to heaven—bestowed upon some new planet or cluster of stars of the first magnitude. Farewell, my hero & God bless you."[58]

Henry was never much of a hero, however. Restless and moody, he had attended Harvard Law School only to please his exacting, authoritarian father, as he yearned to emulate his grandfather's illustrious military career. Peter Gansevoort, whom the people of Albany called "the general" even though he had never worn a uniform, drew up legalistic contracts to keep his son in line, and he insisted that Henry apprentice himself to an attorney in New York. During a family tour of Europe, Henry had flirted with the notion of joining Garibaldi's Red Shirts, but he knew that if he stayed in Italy, his father would cut him off.[59]

Once Henry got back to New York, he signed up to drill with the crack Seventh Regiment, and the minute the call to arms was sounded in 1861, he quit his job and enlisted in the army as a private, claiming that he was not made "for continuous confinement," but for "open air work and practical, adventurous and romantic life" that balanced "mental activity with physical activity." Although his sister Kate cautioned him not to "throw away all the advantages" he had received, she promised that the family would stand behind him if he emulated his grandfather's "gallant conduct" by putting on the "mantle of courage, bravery and patriotism." After a month of service in the ranks, he asked his father to use his influence to get him a commission as a second lieutenant.[60]

His finest hour came during the peninsular campaign, when he showed bravery under fire, and after being wounded at Antietam, he was promoted to lieutenant colonel. Unfortunately, he contracted malarial fever while guarding Meade's rear flank with the Thirteenth Cavalry in Pennsylvania, and had to be sent to a New York hospital for treatment. Greatly weakened by the disease, he never regained his former strength and vigor, partly because he also suffered from chronic venereal disease. After nearly nine months in New York, he returned to the front; before long, however, his men were charging that his poor health, his habit of making frequent trips to Washington to visit houses of ill repute, and his arrogance in commandeering a private residence for his own quarters made him unsuitable for a command post. When attempts were made to remove him, political influence was brought to bear; the charges would be dropped, and his principal accuser would be transferred to another regiment. On one occasion, Henry flogged a black servant for stealing a pair of pistols, and he was ostracized by most members of the regiment. He finally left the regiment unofficially and stayed home recuperating for an indefinite length of time, thereby joining the many men who fled combat without permission before the long, cruel war was over.[61]

Although Henry was almost married to the military, he did entertain thoughts of marrying Allan's beautiful friend Rachel Turner, a southern belle whom George Brewster also courted unsuccessfully. Herman wrote the charming poem "Iris" to honor "her eyes, her mouth— / Magnolias in their languor / And sorcery of the South." Finally, Henry returned to his regiment, where he was a frequent target of ethical inquiries and a frequent victim of fevers and other illnesses. After his death from tuberculosis in 1871, his family had his journals and letters printed and bound to give to relatives, friends, and selected libraries, notably the Harvard College Library and the Berkshire Athenaeum. Unfortunately, Henry's observations tend to be less interesting and less attractive than the volume's deckled edges and handsome leather binding.[62]

～⌐

Toward the end of May 1864, Melville received the news of Nathaniel Hawthorne's death. He had not seen his old friend since the Hawthornes had returned from Rome and settled into "The Wayside" in Concord, Massachusetts. Hawthorne had tried but been unable to finish any of the strange Gothic manuscripts he had begun since publication of *The Marble Faun.* Just prior to the opening of the Metropolitan Fair, Hawthorne and his publisher William D. Ticknor had checked into the Astor House on an excursion to Washington that was designed to restore Hawthorne's health. The chances are that even if Melville had met them on the street, he would barely have recognized the stooped, gray-haired man accompanying Ticknor as his handsome friend. Shunned by New Englanders because of his support of Franklin Pierce, handicapped by deafness, and plagued by other physical infirmities, Hawthorne had aged dramatically. He began to feel better when they reached Philadelphia, but the younger, stronger Ticknor had caught a cold. Despite, or perhaps because of, the ministrations of a doctor, Ticknor's malady rapidly turned into pneumonia, and he died on April 10. Hawthorne, convinced that Death had taken the wrong man, sat beside the body like a stone, waiting for the terrible mistake to be rectified, and it took several people to pry him away.[63]

After that, a mysterious malady seemed to eat away at Hawthorne. When Sophia urged him to see a doctor, he refused, saying doctors had killed his friend. Franklin Pierce, whose wife had died the previous year, invited Hawthorne to accompany him on a trip through New Hampshire, and Sophia sent them off with her blessing, certain it would restore her husband to good health. As the two men were touring the countryside, Pierce noticed that Hawthorne was having trouble walking and using his hands. He failed to appear for breakfast on the morning of May 19, and when Pierce went into his room, he found him dead.

Melvilles and Gansevoorts generally kept their emotions under wraps, but Herman could not hide his feelings from his wife: "We have just received a letter from Lizzie," Maria wrote to her brother Peter. "She writes that Herman was much shocked at hearing of Mr. Hawthornes sudden death. Herman was much attached to him & will mourn his loss." Although Melville had not seen his old friend for what seemed many years, Hawthorne's death severed a link to the old dreams of literary greatness that had burned in him during the writing of *Moby-Dick.* The novels both men wrote after 1851, especially

Pierre, The Blithedale Romance, and *The Marble Faun,* resonate with echoes of their intensely complicated and painfully daedalian relationship.[64]

After Hawthorne's death, Melville reread *Mosses from an Old Manse* in an attempt to commune with the spirit of his departed friend, perhaps hoping to catch from those dark stories a wind as strong as the one that had filled his sails during the composition of *Moby-Dick.* He marked several passages in Hawthorne's "Monsieur du Miroir" with remarks such as "He will pass to the dark realm of Nothingness, but will not find me there," and next to it, "This trenches upon the uncertain and the terrible."[65]

⁓

Meanwhile, the war raged on. With both the North and the South sick and tired of all the killing, leaders on both sides tried to negotiate a peace. "Our bleeding, bankrupt, almost dying country longs for peace, shudders at the prospect of further wholesale devastation, of new rivers of human blood," Horace Greeley said just before he and John Hay were leaving to meet the Confederate commissioners in Niagara Falls, Canada, to try to negotiate an end to the war.[66]

Increasing numbers of people turned to religion to make some sense of all the suffering. Spiritualism, millennialism, and various evangelical movements were sweeping the country, camp meetings and revivals enjoyed a popularity not seen since the 1840s, and new churches were being founded every day. Many people were convinced that 1864 was the millennium predicted by the prophets.[67]

Maria, Malcolm, Kate, and Helen attended a revival meeting in Gansevoort around this time, probably out of curiosity; camp meetings to them were more a form of entertainment than a spiritual experience, as the emotionalism of evangelical Christianity seemed excessive to the Gansevoorts. Maria wrote to Henry: "The short time I was there, a woman it was said 'got religion' she lay on her back in front of the Pulpit with hands upraised & screaming with all her might. I did not see because of the crowd but Malcolm struggled through and saw her, six very respectable looking men dressed in black sat in the place for preaching behind the desk, they occasionally stept [sic] forward & said something to the crowd which I could not hear. We were all standing on the stout plank seats, an immense crowd standing between the seats & the pulpit. Then one of the six rose & with a stentorian voice ordered every one on their knees–for prayers."[68]

Before leaving early with Malcolm, the "stern" and "uncompromising" Maria, who disdained homemade clothes and made fun of the dresses Lizzie sewed for her daughters, made note of the congregation's finery: "More than 1000 persons were said to be there yesterday afternoon. Helen & Kate were astonished to see the fashionable dresses. Waterfalls, & Cataracts, their muslin spencers, long, very long dresses, many stylish looking ladies, handsome equipages were on the grounds." These chic outfits may not have been biblical prerequisites for the salvation of the soul, but as the war ground on, those who were comparatively well off sought in material things the spiritual solace that was eluding them.[69]

In late August, Admiral Farragut sank the Confederate ironclad *Tennessee* and took Mobile Bay, and in October, General Philip Sheridan routed Jubal Early's men at Cedar Creek. In that battle, Charles Russell Lowell sustained multiple wounds, but he fought bravely to the death. A month later, his widow gave birth to Carlotta, the daughter she had been carrying when Melville met her at the Virginia camp. Many who mourned the young cavalry officer felt he would have made a great President of the United States.

In the fall, Guert Gansevoort and Thomas Melville both arrived home from the sea, but under very different circumstances. Tom, the successful captain of a merchant vessel, sailed home on the *Bengal Tiger* after completing his seventh voyage. Guert had been reprimanded for his poor management of the *Adirondack* and sent home to Glens Falls. While he was there, his brother Leonard died. Family and friends soon noticed that Guert was behaving "strangely," which was hardly surprising, as he was grieving both for his brother and for his own career. He had been told he could either return to his old ship, the *Roanoke*, as a member of the crew, or retain his officer's stripes by taking a desk job at the Brooklyn Navy Yard. Although he would have preferred to go to sea again, he was too proud to accept demotion, so he held a desk job until severe neuralgia of the spine forced him to retire.[70]

Eighteen sixty-four was an election year, and although Amos Nourse, John Hoadley, and George Griggs were all Republicans, most members of the Gansevoort-Melville clan were Democrats who supported General George B. McClellan. The party's platform, however, called for a swift end to the war, which left Henry Gansevoort and every other soldier who had seen his comrades die or sustain wounds on the battlefield feeling betrayed. When a great many Democrats rebelled against the platform, McClellan declared that he could not support it and promised to win the war for the Union before making peace with the Confederates. Satisfied, Henry not only voted for McClellan, but apparently pressured members of his regiment to support McClellan, too, quite against army regulations. A court of inquiry reprimanded him, and the men in the regiment began calling him a Copperhead.[71]

So many Republicans refused to support Lincoln's renomination that most Democrats assumed McClellan would win easily. *Tribune* editor Horace Greeley told the Republican convention he would support anyone but Lincoln, and although William Lloyd Garrison supported the President, Wendell Phillips and Orestes Brownson wanted to run Frémont, which split the old antislavery coalition. Despite great disagreement over which man had the best chance to beat McClellan, the Republicans nominated the President on the first ballot.

Not surprisingly, the campaign was a dirty one. McClellan's supporters called Lincoln a filthy storyteller, an "Old Ignoramus," a liar, a thief, a buffoon, a usurper, a monster, a robber, a fiend, a butcher, a tyrant, a despot, an old scoundrel, a land-pirate, a braggart, and a "long, lean, lank, lantern-jawed, high-cheek-boned, spavined, rail-splitting Stallion." Even so, Lincoln won by "enormous and universal majorities in almost all the states." Voters were evidently swayed by Lincoln's pointing out that it was "best not to swap horses while crossing a river." He was reelected, and abolitionists were ecstatic. "I give you joy of the election," Ralph Waldo Emerson exulted to a friend. "Seldom in history was so much staked on a popular vote. I suppose never in history."[72]

While it's not known how Melville voted in November, or whether he voted at all, his views on the war, slavery, and postwar peace seem closer to Lincoln's views than to those of any other candidate. If he was at all influenced by his abolitionist brother-in-law John Chipman Hoadley, or his Republican uncle Amos Nourse, he may even have voted for the President. Although Melville and Lincoln had met only briefly and superficially before the war, the two men shared a love of literature and a philosophy of history formed by Shakespeare, the Bible, and the Greek and Roman classics, and the rivers of tragedy ran deep enough to break their hearts.[73]

While men like Henry Gansevoort were serving at the battlefront, women like his sister Kate (center) were serving valiantly on the homefront.

TWENTY-FOUR

A SURVIVOR OF THE CIVIL WAR

The Melvilles had much to be thankful for in 1864. Confederate sympathizers in New York had stopped torching nearby public buildings such as the St. Nicholas Hotel, and thousands of slaves and prisoners of war, including Colonel Frank Bartlett, had been liberated by the advancing Union Army. "United We Stand!" crowed Harper's Weekly *in its patriotic Thanksgiving double spread. Tom was home from the Pacific, but he had to remain aboard his ship at night, so Mother Melville came to New York for a family reunion that included four of her sons and sons-in-law and eight of her grandchildren. She was in such good health that the rest of the family couldn't keep up with her zealous sleigh-riding and tireless socializing.[1]*

With General William Tecumseh Sherman's drive through the Carolinas and Georgia that autumn, a Union victory seemed assured. As Sherman's army marched toward the sea, they freed slaves from plantations and broke open the prisons. They were appalled by what they found. Confederate troops had been shooting black prisoners of war on sight and starving white prisoners to death in hellish dungeons. Southerners held in prisons like the one set up in New York's City Hall Park received rations not much worse than what Union infantrymen received, but in the South, food was so scarce that there was nothing to feed the northern prisoners. They were so starved they got down on their hands and knees at latrines and grubbed through feces for undigested beans and corn. Seeing survivors from Belle Isle, Walt Whitman asked whether "those little livid brown, ash streaked, monkey-looking dwarfs" were not really "mummied, dwindled corpses." A southern woman who observed surviving federal prisoners being moved from Richmond to Andersonville was horrified to see men with untreated gangrenous sores, and most of them so emaciated they were little more than walking skeletons. "My heart aches for those poor wretches, Yankees though they are," she wrote, "and I am afraid God will suffer some terrible retribution to fall upon us for letting such things happen. If the Yankees should ever come to southwest Georgia and go to Anderson and see the graves there, God have mercy on the land!"[2]

Many Union soldiers vowed revenge. Sherman's triumphant march turned into an orgy of violence as Union soldiers laid waste to Atlanta and looted and pillaged and burned their way across Georgia to the sea. By the time Sherman wired the President on Christmas Day that he had taken Savannah, many northerners felt that Sherman's army had disgraced the Union cause by its barbaric conduct, and southern newspapers were spreading rumors that Sherman's real mission was to claim slaves as war booty so he could re-enslave them in northern factories.[3]

The new year dawned on a nation utterly changed by years of war. On January 31, 1865, thanks to the efforts of men such as Charles Sumner, the United States Congress voted 119 to 65 to pass the Thirteenth Amendment, which abolished slavery throughout the land. Two days later, John Rock, a black attorney and physician from Boston, was admitted to practice before the Massachusetts Supreme Judicial Court, and four days later, General Robert E. Lee was given total command over the ruined armies of the Confederacy. Specie issued by the Davis government was worthless, and food was so scarce in the devastated cities that people began devouring pets and wild animals and exchanging valuables for food. When revulsion at eating rats that had been crawling over corpses proved stronger than the craving for fresh meat, people ate gloves and boots to stave off stomach pains. "The deep waters are closing over us," wrote South Carolina diarist Mary Chesnut.[4]

Despite a slide in the stock market that had investors worried, the upper classes in New York remained insulated from the worst effects of the war. Profiteers made money selling arms and whiskey, and their wives flaunted elaborate new styles of clothing. "People's consciences have suffered the same depreciation as the paper dollar," Henry Bellows complained. "What kind of sentiments are to have power with the new time and the new civilization?" It was the same question Melville was asking, though in another way.[5]

Toward the end of February, Bayard Taylor invited Melville to join "The

Travellers," a club dedicated to talk, cigars, and "frugal refreshments." Its members included Henry Whitney Bellows, the inventor Cyrus Field, the composer Louis Gottschalk, and the painters Felix Darley, Albert Bierstadt, and Frederic Church, many of them acquaintances of Melville's who belonged to the Century and other clubs. Melville was probably a guest from time to time at both the Authors' Club and the Century, which Allan had joined in 1859, but he was not a member of any of New York's exclusive clubs, as he could ill afford the dues and dinner fees, and doubtless felt he could not spare the time from writing. To Melville, clubs, even literary and artistic ones, probably closely resembled the "paradise" of self-indulgent "bachelors" he had skewered in *Putnam's*, and he certainly knew himself well enough to realize that becoming a club-man-author would not satisfy his soul's hunger for immortality.[6]

If Melville needed a reminder of how precarious literary celebrity could be, he received one when T. B. Peterson & Brothers of Philadelphia, the firm that had purchased the plates of *Israel Potter* from Putnam's, began running advertisements for "THE REFUGEE by Herman Melville, Author of 'Typee,' 'Omoo,' 'The Two Captains,' 'The Man of the World,' etc. etc." Incensed at the change of title and the inaccuracy of the attributions to his name, he wrote an indignant letter to *The World*, although he must have known it was futile to protest.[7]

No longer "the man who lived among the cannibals," had he become the "author of 'Typee,' 'Piddledee &c'"? Was he doomed to be one of those little-known authors whose books could be found moldering on the shelves of the downtown bookshops in which he liked to browse? It seemed he would always be classified as a travel writer whose more ambitious and profound books were destined to be considered aberrations by readers and reviewers. In fact, for two generations, writers of standard literary histories grouped Melville with writers of travelogues, not with writers like Poe, Hawthorne, Emerson, or Stowe.

On March 3, 1865, Abraham Lincoln took the oath of office for the second time under the newly completed dome of the enlarged Capitol Building. He exhorted Americans to "bind up the nation's wounds; to care for him who shall have borne the battle, and for his widow, and his orphan—to do all which may achieve and cherish a just and lasting peace, among ourselves, and with all nations." Lincoln's eloquence melted Melville's heart, but could it melt the heart of a nation hardened by civil war?[8]

The speaker of Melville's poem "The Conflicts of Convictions" prays that the Capitol's iron dome will turn out to be "Stronger for stress and strain." If not, he predicts that "Power unanointed" will usher in a dark age, and "the Founders' dream shall flee." The speaker of the poem puts no faith in the power of good to overcome evil, and death's "silent negative" seems the only certainty in a universe where God seems entirely unmoved by human suffering:

YEA AND NAY—
EACH HATH HIS SAY;
BUT GOD HE KEEPS THE MIDDLE WAY.
NONE WAS BY
WHEN HE SPREAD THE SKY;
WISDOM IS VAIN, AND PROPHESY.

Melville is saying that Man cannot rely on God to change human history. The burden of shaping history falls squarely on Man, whose vision and power are tragically limited.[9]

In April 1865, four years after the attack on Fort Sumter, Richmond fell, and the "weary years and woeful wars / And armies in the grave" came to an end. For James Russell Lowell, the fall of the Confederate capital was news "from Heaven." It was closely followed by the surrender at Appomattox, which saw "the warring eagles fold the wing," but while northerners felt relieved and vindicated by the victory, southerners felt alienated and betrayed.[10]

One week after Grant and Lee put their signatures on the proclamation of surrender, the actor John Wilkes Booth sneaked into the president's box at Ford's Theatre in Washington and shot Lincoln just behind the ear. The assassination of the leader who had pledged to "bind up the nation's wounds" and restore peace to the shattered republic plunged much of the nation into inconsolable grief. Lincoln's funeral cortege paused in New York on it way across the country to the family burial plot in Springfield, Illinois. As sixteen gray horses drew the enormous canopied catafalque past 500,000 mourners to the rotunda at City Hall Park, the streets were noticeably hushed, the people stunned. Public and privately owned buildings alike were draped with heavy black crepe banners, giving the city the appearance of a "vast mausoleum." When Richard Lathers tried to buy black bombazine for the Great Western Insurance Company at A. T. Stewart's store, he was told the fabric was in such demand it was being rationed. During the days the slain President's body lay in state, with thousands of mourners paying their respects to "The Great Emancipator," the Metropolitan Police reported a precipitous drop in the number of arrests for drunkenness, robbery, and murder in a city that was rapidly becoming known for its skyrocketing crime rate.[11]

Richard Lathers delivered a eulogy at Tammany Hall, and Melville expressed the nation's grief in an elegy called "The Martyr."

> Good Friday was the day
> Of the prodigy and crime,

When they killed him in his pity,
    When they killed him in his prime
Of clemency and calm—
    When with yearning he was filled
    To redeem the evil-willed,
And, though conqueror, be kind;
    But they killed him in his kindness,
    In their madness and their blindness,
And they killed him from behind....
    There is sobbing of the strong,
        And a pall upon the land;
    But the People in their weeping
        Bare the iron hand:
    Beware the People weeping
        When they bare the iron hand.

As the above excerpts from the poem suggest, Melville feared that the cycle of violence set in motion by the war would not come to an end without concerted efforts at peacemaking by both sides.[12]

With their "Father Abraham" dead, the people in Melville's poem "America" look to their "lorn Mother," whose painful progress from the innocence of "young Maternity" to speechless horror "at the fury of her brood" results in "power dedicate and hope grown wise." Like the great statues by Thomas Crawford and Hiram Powers that Melville had seen during his trip to Rome, Melville's America stands firm with "Law on her brow and empire in her eyes," ready to meet the future "with graver air and lifted flag."[13]

That April, Melville attended the National Academy of Design's annual exhibition to see the work of his cousin Henry's comrade Sanford Robinson Gifford and that of other artists whom he knew and admired. Gifford's *The Coming Storm,* a striking depiction of dark thunderclouds bearing down on the Catskill Mountains, stirred in Melville memories of Hawthorne's "blackness" and Shakespeare's tragedies, particularly since the painting was owned by the actor Edwin Booth, brother of the President's assassin. Calling the actor "Shakespeare's pensive child," for whom "all feeling hearts must feel," he imagined that Booth must have been "fixed and fascinated" by "dim inklings from the shadowy sphere" when he bought the painting. "No utter surprise can come to him / Who reaches Shakespeare's core," wrote Melville, as "That which we seek and shun is there– / Man's final lore."[14]

During the third week of May, the Army of the Potomac marched through the nation's capital twenty-five abreast, wearing clean, pressed uniforms and flying the colorful banners of myriad regiments; the Negro regiments marched behind the white regiments carrying not the rifles they had been issued to help win the war, but picks and shovels. For Melville, the Grand Review of the Army was an "Abrahamic river," a "Patriarch of floods" that would "muster into union– / Eastern warriors, Western braves," mingling the "streams of ocean" from "Europe's marge" with "rills from Kansas." In his poem about "The Dissolution of Armies at the Peace," the "steely play" and the "Splendor and Terror" of the "Aurora-Borealis" are replaced by the "pale, meek Dawn" of peace.[15]

Besides destroying the economy of the South, the war badly disrupted the economy of the North. In upper New York State, so few men and boys were available to work that Augusta surprised Herman and Lizzie by coming to New York City at the end of June to look for help, and she hired a German couple almost before their feet touched the shore. Northern businessmen and entrepreneurs went south, where cheap labor was plentiful, to buy or build factories. Allan Melville resumed the business dealings in Savannah and New Orleans he had begun before the war, while Tom Melville and John Hoadley, who had recently been appointed a trustee of the Massachusetts Institute of Technology, bought up land in West Virginia and speculated in petroleum. Although they were all "making money very rapidly," Herman was too broke and too preoccupied with writing to become a venture capitalist. His primary investments were his books, his primary capital his rich imagination.[16]

While one half of the nation mourned its now-revered former leader and the other half tried to recover from the ruin of its economy and the destruction of its way of life, Melville worked on his poems. The war now had a definite beginning, middle, and end, and he began composing his American *Iliad*, not as a continuous narrative, but as a sequence of interrelated elegies, documentary narratives, and reflective interludes commemorating the hundreds of thousands of people who had died or been wounded in the war. Along with telegraph dispatches, firsthand accounts from relatives and friends, and written summaries in *The Rebellion Record*, he consulted the superb illustrations in *Harper's Weekly* for help visualizing battle scenes and recapturing the emotional tone of those dreadful years. Like the web of correspondence spun by his female relatives to hold their family life together, Melville's poems were a way of holding the fragile strands of America's national life together.

In the summer of 1865, Melville took frequent breaks from writing to clear his head and exercise his body. Henry had returned to Albany, and Guert was at home in Glens Falls, so Herman undoubtedly saw them. While he was in Gansevoort in August, he helped Augusta dole out "a grand supply of iced cakes, sugar-plums, peaches nuts, biscuits &c" to the fifteen hundred Christian souls who attended the annual gathering of the Sabbath schools. When a thunderstorm drove everyone to shelter before they could devour the last of the home-baked goods, the leftovers, like the surplus food in "Poor Man's Pudding and Rich Man's Crumbs," were given to charity.[17]

Melville seemed "unusually well," probably because work on his poems was progressing, and because he felt that his writing was contributing something positive to the nation's recovery from the war. Kate and John Hoadley had their first boy, Francis, in October, and the Melvilles spent Thanksgiving in Boston, then returned to New York for Christmas. Melville gave each member of the family one of the bound volumes of *Harper's Weekly* he had ordered in October as a gift. Following the family tradition of exchanging edifying gifts, Malcolm gave his sister Fanny a book called *Ethel's Story: Illustrating the Advantages of Cheerfulness, by the Child's Friend.*[18]

The Melville women spent the long evenings that winter reading aloud from *Faith Gartney's Childhood* and *The Gayworthys* by Adeline Whitney, a writer of children's books who had been a classmate of Lizzie's at George Emerson's school, and also from *The Clever Woman of the Family*, the latest book by the popular British novelist Charlotte Mary Yonge, a book Helen had given them for Christmas.[19]

Melville was solitary much of the time, owing to the normal demands of a writer's life, but he was not nearly as reclusive as some biographers have made him out to be; he went out whenever he needed to take a break from writing. Although he turned down an invitation from Susan Gansevoort to a party in Albany to celebrate Uncle Peter's recovery from a small stroke, he made at least one appearance at the home of Alice and Phoebe Cary. The Cary sisters, writers of didactic poetry and short stories, had moved to Manhattan from the Midwest, and their Sunday-evening salons were very popular with the New York literati. When the editor Charles Hemstreet met Melville at one of these literary evenings, he thought he told stories "far better than he had ever written anything." In his memoir, Hemstreet described, but did not date, the event:

> He began at the beginning, telling of his boyhood in New York, of his shipping as a common sailor, and of his youthful wanderings in London and Liverpool. In true sailor fashion, and with picturesque detail, he spun the tale of his eighteen months cruise to the sperm fisheries in the Pacific, and held his hearers' close attention while he related the coarse brutality of his captain, who had forced him to desert at the Marquesas Islands. Then he traced his wanderings with his one companion through the trackless forest of Nukahiva and his capture by the Typee cannibals. He related how there was little hope in his heart that he could ever escape, but that he still held tight to life and his courage did not desert him; how with the thought of death before him by night and by day

he yet hourly studied the strange life about him and garnered those facts and fancies which he afterwards used to such advantage in his successful *Typee*. It was a thrilling tale to listen to.

Obviously, Melville could muster his old charm and skill at spinning lively yarns when he was in the mood. He may even have enjoyed playing "the man who lived among the cannibals" for an evening, as it made him feel like a young celebrity again.[20]

Lizzie was busy copying several poems so that Herman could send them out to magazines, and when "The March to the Sea" appeared in the February issue of *Harper's New Monthly Magazine*, Kate Gansevoort was pleasantly surprised. "I have never read any of his poetry before," she wrote Henry. "*This piece* is very inspiring & describes Sherman's Grand March." Tom thought his brother's poem "splendid," and Frances Priscilla Melville thought it "grand." Four more of Melville's poems were published anonymously in *Harper's New Monthly Magazine* before *Battle-Pieces* appeared, but he never received payment for any of them.[21]

He needed another book to make some money from his writing and to regain as much of his reputation as was possible. The idea of writing another novel had evaporated during his trip to the Holy Land, when he gave up the idea of composing a sequel to *The Confidence-Man*, and although the volume of poetry he had left with Lizzie before his 1860 cruise had not been accepted for publication, he thought a book of poems about the war was certain to appeal to readers. Book-length poems, especially those by British writers, had been selling well before the war. Along with Elizabeth Barrett Browning's *Aurora Leigh* and Alfred Tennyson's *Idylls of the King*, long narrative poems by Henry Wadsworth Longfellow and James Russell Lowell enjoyed healthy sales in America, where ninety-one percent of the adult white population could read. In Melville's mind, a book of poems about the Civil War was sure to sell, and for a man whose income had been $851 the past year, that was a happy prospect.[22]

Melville knew that the poems he was writing were far superior to anything currently appearing in newspapers and magazines. Popular poetry was characterized by traditional quatrains, metronomic regularity, and perfect, often predictable, rhymes. The *Rebellion Record*, for example, always followed its digests of the war with dozens of rousing patriotic verses designed to cheer the men on to ever greater heights of bravery and to reassure the families of the dead and wounded that battle deaths had meaning. Even the poems by such well-known writers as Longfellow and Bryant that appeared in these volumes made no effort to render realistically either the tedium or the horror of the war. When Melville thought about putting his vision of the nation's future before the American people, he felt a burst of missionary fervor, a surge of the old feeling that perhaps something he wrote could change history.

Melville's experimentation with new verse forms and conflicting voices in his poems creates a richness and complexity unequaled by any poetry of the war, including Walt Whitman's *Drum-Taps*, which appeared in May 1865. No record of Melville's having read these poems exists, and they are very different from his own. Whitman's war poems are purely personal and impressionistic; unlike Whitman and the more conventional versifiers, Melville looks at events from different points of view. He chronicles battles that were significant both historically and personally, and memorializes battles in which friends and family members participated, placing the war in the context of humanity's endless struggle to evolve beyond barbarism.

Melville intended the seventy-odd poems in *Battle-Pieces and Aspects of the War* to mourn the nation's dead, to commemorate the heroism of both sides, and to set the tone for postwar rebuilding. Thus, he exhorts his victorious brethren in the North to listen to "the better angels of their nature" and work for reconciliation with the defeated South. In the prefatory note to *Battle-Pieces*, Melville claimed that the fall of Richmond had inspired him to start writing the book and that to compose the volume, he had "but placed a harp in a window, and noted the contrasted airs which wayward winds have played upon the strings," a disingenuous disclaimer of his conscious craft and his political agenda. More than likely, however, he wrote some of the poems during the war years and others later, adding this note to forestall attacks on them by critics.[23]

In March, while Allan and Jennie were traveling in Egypt and the Near East, Mother Melville became ill while visiting New York, and Gus rushed down to help take care of her. A visit from Uncle John D'Wolf at the end of the month perked everyone up, and sometime during the late spring or early summer of 1866, Melville wrote the prose supplement and notes to his *Battle-Pieces*. After he had gone over the final proofs and made corrections, Lizzie recorded his instructions for the printer: "New fly leaves may be put on here—and two added at the end—Muslin on Boards [?] in [on?] binding—Edges to be trimmed." The job done, Melville and John Hoadley went to Gansevoort to see Tom and the family, while Lizzie took the children to Boston. Although he arrived at his mother's house in Gansevoort "looking thin & miserable," by the time of his forty-seventh birthday, Melville felt rested and relaxed. While Augusta looked on admiringly from a hammock, he played a fierce game of croquet, proving himself "quite a hand," according to his sister.[24]

Full of energy after a fortnight of recreation, he went to Lake George for the day with Tom, whose sea stories always entertained him, then he headed back to New York via Albany, stopping for dinner with Peter and Susan Gansevoort. He arrived in New York the next day at about the same moment Lizzie, Malcolm, and the girls arrived from Boston, leaving Stanwix and Lem Shaw to go to Arrowhead. Once the Melvilles were home, Malcolm went back to work. After turning seventeen in February, he had taken a job as a clerk in Richard Lathers's Great Western Marine Insurance Company at a salary of $200 a year.

Melville shepherded his book through production, eagerly awaiting the first printed copy, and on August 17, 1866, *Battle-Pieces and Aspects of the War* appeared. It was published by Harper & Brothers and dedicated to "the memory of the three hundred thousand who in the war for the maintenance of the Union fell devotedly under the flag of their fathers," with no mention of the equal number of Confederates who had died. In its "Book World" column, the *New York Herald* listed it as one of Harper's new titles, adding, in a parenthetical note after Melville's name, "For ten years the public has wondered what has become of Melville."[25]

The poems draw on such classical works as the *Iliad*, the Bible, John Milton's *Paradise Lost*, Plutarch's *Roman Lives*, the plays of Shakespeare, and *The Divine Comedy*, as well as on contemporary sources. To match the dissonance of his poems to the cacophony of the war, he created ragged margins and used subtle enjambment and caesura more skillfully than most of his contemporaries. Despite their occasional rough edges and frequent Latinate abstractions, the poems are moving and profound. Ranging from traditional ballads to poems with passages inspired by newspaper headlines and P. T. Barnum's placards, this poetic sequence establishes Melville as the first modernist poet in America. As he wrote in "The Armies of the Wilderness," his "entangled rhyme / But hints at the maze of war."[26]

Battle-Pieces opens with "The Portent," an eerie and impressionistic portrayal of "Weird John Brown," not as a crazy terrorist swinging from the gallows, but as a prophet in whose "streaming beard is shown... The meteor of the war." The sequence progresses dramatically from intimations of cosmic upheaval to sketches that capture the moods and viewpoints of combatants on both sides of the conflict.

Time and again, Melville stresses the youthful innocence of the men engaged in "this strife of brothers" and the kinship between "the zealots of the Wrong" and the "enthusiasts for the right." In "The Armies of the Wilderness," for example, Union soldiers watching through field glasses as Confederates chase a baseball realize that "they could have have joined them in their sport / But for the vale's deep rent." They feel not comradeship and confidence, but a "presentiment" of death and a deep "mistrust" that any "final good" can come from a conflict that separates man from man.[27]

In this epic poem, Melville transcends politics by a metaphysical yoking of images of sublime human aspiration and tragic human failure to suggest Man's tenuous place in a universe of forces that will outlast the human race:

> A path down the mountain winds to the glade
> > Where the dead of the Moonlight Fight lie low;

A hand reaches out of the thin-laid mould
    As begging help which none can bestow.
But the field mouse small and busy ant
    Heap their hillocks, to hide if they may the woe:
By the bubbling spring lies the rusted canteen,
And the drum which the drummer-boy dying let go.
    Dust to dust, and blood for blood—
      Passion and pangs! Has Time
    Gone back? or is this the Age
      Of the world's great Prime?[28]

Echoing Milton and the Bible, Melville juxtaposes images of war in Heaven and war on Earth with naturalistic touches: "The wagon mired and cannon dragged / Have trenched their scar; the plain / Tramped like the cindery beach of the damned— / A site for the city of Cain." Man and Nature regress as all "is ravage and range, / And gardens are left to weeds." The garden of intellect and statecraft cultivated by Virginians James Madison and Thomas Jefferson is choked with weeds, and the wisdom that once reposed in "Virginian gentlemen's libraries old— / Books which only the scholar heeds" have been "flung to his kennel" by their degenerate descendants.[29]

If man were wise enough to leave war "to the red and black ants" of Thoreau's mock-heroic *Iliad* in *Walden*, this "happy world" might at last "disarm." Instead:

    The fight for the city is fought
      In Nature's old domain;
    Man goes out to the wilds,
      And Orpheus' charm is vain.
In glades they meet skull after skull
    Where pine-cones lay—the rusted gun,
Green shoes full of bones, the mouldering coat
    And cuddled-up skeleton....[30]

A war that started out as a Christian crusade has become a pagan saturnalia of inhuman brutality that leaves crippled men holding "a ragged barked stick for a crutch" as they "limp to some elfin dell" and "hobble from the sight of dead faces—white / As pebbles in a well." Like sightless Oedipus, the boys who rush blindly into battle become ghosts blown by night winds roaring "at the height of their madness" through "gloomed shades." The war drags Heaven down to Hell and blasts the finest flower of Christendom to Hades, where "plume and sash" decking "the pall of the dead" are mere "vanities now."[31]

The *Battle-Pieces* are sober, dark meditations on human history that portray war as the ultimate form of cannibalism. Depicting the war as an incalculable waste rather than, more conventionally, as the triumph of good over evil, he attempts to put the deaths of the "nameless brave" into some broader, more universal perspective until war itself, not other people, becomes the enemy.

Two-thirds of the way through the volume, in a series of short poems titled "Verses Inscriptive and Memorial," Melville creates a literary Gettysburg Cemetery by composing epitaphs for the men who rest in wilderness graves. Perhaps written initially for inclusion in condolence letters to families who had lost their loved ones, these poems memorialize the slain Union soldiers in a compressed style that anticipates Edgar Lee Masters's *Spoon River Anthology*. Melville wrote some of the "Verses Inscriptive and Memorial" for friends and relatives who had lost loved ones in the war—George W. Curtis, for instance, whose half brother Joseph was killed at Fredericksburg in December 1862. The discrepancy between the war's lofty aims and the grisly reality was disheartening, but in the poems written after the war ended, he concentrates more on what the war revealed about the nation's values and future direction than on realistic descriptions of the war itself.[32]

Melville's poems about the war explore his own feelings about the conflict, but they also chronicle the events of those bloody years, putting them in historical perspective. He portrays the arrogant northerner bloated with victory and the proud southerner embittered by defeat in order to provide differing perspectives on the war. This use of different personae was a risky innovation for a writer whose themes were certain to rouse volatile passions in his audience.

With future reconciliation in mind, he wrote two poems about Sherman's march: one from the northern point of view, and one from the southern. "The March to the Sea" starts out as a lyrical celebration of the "glorious glad marching" of "Sherman's miles of men" to "charred Atlanta" and the sea:

> All nature felt their coming,
> 　　The birds like couriers flew,
> And the banners brightly blooming
> 　　The slaves by thousands drew.
> And they marched beside the drumming,
> 　　And they joined the armies blue.

Sherman's men are heroic liberators who march "till their broad laughter" meets "the laughter of the sea," but soon, flushed with conquest, these "plumed fighters and campaigners" become "foragers" who "help themselves from farm-lands." In the end, the "trampling of the Takers" brings famine to the land and a "stern decree" of indelible hatred that jeopardizes any hope of future peace and reconciliation: "For behind they left a wailing, / A terror and a ban, / And blazing cinders sailing, / And houseless households wan, / Wide zones of counties paling, / And towns where maniacs ran." The poem never breaks stride, but the imagery darkens steadily, and the word *remember* takes on an increasingly ominous, sarcastic tone: "Was it Treason's retribution– / Necessity the plea? / They will long remember Sherman / And his streaming columns free / They will long remember Sherman / Marching to the sea."[33]

Sherman's vindictiveness aroused vengeful passions in the vanquished which spoiled the Union victory and jeopardized the work of Reconstruction. Going against the grain of most northern intellectuals of his day–most notably Lizzie's pastor, Henry Whitney Bellows–Melville feared that not only had the war not redeemed the sin of slavery, but also that a bad peace would damn the nation to cycles of unending violence and retribution.

In "The Frenzy in the Wake," Melville voices the southern point of view. In an image reminiscent of the *San Dominick*'s stern-piece, he imagines humiliated southerners who resent "the Oppressor's knee / That grinds upon the neck" vowing eternal war on their conquerors. As Union regiments from "frozen Maine" and "far Minnesota" advance "in a whelming sea," the ghosts of slain southerners beg to be avenged on both the "African–the imp!" who "gibbers, imputing shame," and "the flag we hate, the flag whose stars / Like planets strike us through." The speaker of the poem, who sees southern skies turned to "brass" by burning woods, and cities reduced to "pillars of dust," vows that "even despair / Shall never our hate rescind."[34]

Because he took an enormous risk in *Battle-Pieces* by criticizing Sherman's conduct so soon after the war, in a note explaining that the piece was written while reports of Sherman's return from Savannah were coming back to the North, Melville made sure his readers understood that the speaker of the poem was not the poet himself, but a persona. He clearly disassociates himself from the southern view in order to urge the North not to enact punitive measures against the former foe. Knowing he could not influence the South and that his responsibility lay in influencing northern attitudes, he writes not as a partisan, but as a student of the past and a steward of the future who remembers how "the promise of the first French Revolution" was violated by the Terror, which threw supporters of the Revolution "into doubts and misgivings."[35]

In "The Fall of Richmond," Melville parodies the jog-trot rhythms and stock images of patriotic poetry to expose it as jingoistic bombast. The Yankees exult in the victory of "Grant the brave" over "The helmed dilated Lucifer," clearly implying that the North is godly and the South Satanic. Their hubristic chant, "God is in Heaven, and Grant in the Town / Right through might is Law–*God's way adore*," ironically echoes Robert

Browning's "God's in his heaven / All's right with the world!" The victors twist the Christian ethic of love into a code of conquest, gloating over a military triumph and failing to be merciful to the vanquished foe, thereby jeopardizing future peace and harmony.[36]

Like other postwar guardians of democracy such as Mark Twain and Henry Adams, Melville sensed a danger for the nation in northern "braggadocio," and in "Lee in the Capitol," he depicts the Confederate general as a noble foe, saying, "Who looks at Lee must think of Washington," cautioning that to crush the South would be "to copy Europe in her worst estate ... tyranny you reprobate." The soundest "fruit" that the blasted tree could produce, Lee tells his interrogators, would be "re-established law," by which Melville means a marriage of natural and divine law that would ensure moral rightness, justice, and harmony. Not everyone felt so kindly disposed toward Lee, however. Lydia Maria Child, for example, did not feel "blood-thirsty toward any of the rebels," but she felt no "especial tenderness for Lee" because he had put the honor of Virginia before the integrity of the Union even though he claimed he believed the rebellion was wrong.[37]

Melville's closing "Meditation" echoes his initial "Misgivings"–misgivings born of the sense that the waste of war far outweighed any gains won on the battlefield and that the legacy of sectional bitterness would poison national life for generations to come. The speaker of the poem is a northerner attending the funeral of two kinsmen slain in the last battles of the war–brothers who had served in opposing armies. Without compromising his loyalty to the northern cause–abolition of slavery and the preservation of the Union– the mourner pleads for the North to put the war behind it and forgive the defeated South:

> If men for new agreement yearn
> > The old upbraiding best forbear;
> *"The South's the sinner!"* Well, so let it be;
> But shall the North sin worse, and stand the Pharisee?

The final image of the poem suggests the restraint and compassion that Melville considered the key to the future survival of the nation: "When Vicksburg fell, and the moody files marched out, / Silent the victors stood, scorning to raise a shout," he writes, calling on the North to adhere to the chivalric code. His hope for the future is that humility will save "the flushed North from her own victory," and that the code of honor that the "manful soldier-view" exalts should become the model for the nation's Reconstruction.[38]

After he had completed the writing and arranging of the poems, Melville added a prose "Supplement" to the volume in which he exhorted white Americans to support policies that would ensure racial justice and eventual social and political harmony.

Speaking as "one who never was a blind adherent," Melville argued that "the work of Reconstruction, if admitted to be feasible at all, demands little but common sense and Christian charity." Pleading with his northern brethren not to demand abject, hypocritical contrition from the South, he asserts that the South has been "taught by the terrors of civil war to feel that Secession, like Slavery, is against Destiny; that both now lie buried in one grave; that her fate is linked with ours; and that together we comprise the Nation."[39]

Melville saw himself as a national, not a regional, poet. When he pleaded with northerners to "be Christians toward our fellow-whites, as well as philanthropists toward the blacks, our fellow men," he was trying to be just and fair. He wrote the Supplement to persuade the North not to deal punitively with the vanquished South, as he did not believe one section of the country could prosper at the expense of another. He believed the nation needed a free, revitalized agricultural South stripped of slavery to provide a healthy counterbalance to the rapidly industrializing North.

His friendship with Richard Lathers made it impossible for him to demonize southerners. From Lathers, Melville knew that many great works of art held in private collections in Georgetown had been destroyed during the war by marauding Union soldiers, and from Allan and Evert Duyckinck, he knew that even educated southern moderates like their friend New Orleans attorney Charles Gayarre had been ruined by the war. Eager to bring North and South together, Richard and Abby Lathers invited prominent political and military leaders to a grand ball that brought together the granddaughters of Generals Grant and Lee, one of many such attempts by Lathers to affect reconciliation and heal the nation's wounds.[40]

Having seen firsthand how harmful it was for a society to consign to itself all goodness and to another society all evil, Melville was acutely aware that projecting evil outward onto the "enemy" and believing that by vanquishing the foe one can eradicate one's problems posed a danger to society. Melville had warned frequently of the moral dangers white Christians faced if they demonized the "heathens" rather than confronted their own savagery, and in *Moby-Dick*, he had shown how vengeful demonizing and scapegoating of an enemy led to the revenger's ruin. The scapegoating of the Indians by the Puritans and the projection by southern slaveholders of their own dark fantasies onto a captive African workforce had eaten away at the soul of America.

The Supplement to *Battle-Pieces* poses problems for readers who wonder why Melville did not include strong African-Americans among the characters or champion their cause as strongly as he supported compassion for the defeated South. Melville believed that slavery was "against destiny," and that northerners had a responsibility to exercise both "paternal guardianship" of the freed slaves and "kindliness to communities which stand nearer to us in nature." Even outspoken abolitionists like Wendell

Phillips believed whites would have to shelter the "victim race by patronage, by protection, by privilege, by recognizing its claim to an equal manhood" before former slaves could stand on their own feet. Many African-Americans did not agree. In an 1862 address to the Boston Emancipation Association titled "Free the Slaves, Then Leave Them Alone," Frederick Douglass argued that what the Negro needed first and foremost was immediate and unconditional liberation from white rule, benevolent or otherwise.[41]

Ironically, many educated southern whites trusted Negroes more than they did Yankees. Charles Gayarre, an attorney who served in the Louisiana State Senate after the war, wrote Evert Duyckinck that he would rather have "the blackest negro in the state" for a senate colleague than a "Yankee aristocrat—some baron of codfish, or marquis of nutmeg," especially since it would give him "infinite delight to witness the amazement of Sumner or Wilson, on their seeing my sable friend out Hotspurring the Hotspurs of the South." Gayarre, a friend of Richard Lathers with whom Allan Melville, in his capacity as legal advisor to the Great Western Insurance Company, did business, was completely ruined by the war. His letters to Evert Duyckinck, written in broad strokes of black ink of unusual boldness and elegance, paint a poignant picture of the aftermath of the war: "The Southern people think that it is now no longer a disgrace to submit to conditions which are forced upon them at the point of the bayonet, when the whole world sees that they are powerless to resist." In answer to invitations to come north, he wrote that he was too poor to travel: "If I thought it would pay, I would write books, and occasionally go North to publish them," but "in our country Literature cannot support decently an honest fellow," even though "some trashy writers of novels or other pulmonary or apoplectic compositions" are said to have "reached an income of ten thousand a year."[42]

Just as in his earlier writings, Melville had attempted to liberate blacks from white stereotypes; he includes two poems in *Battle-Pieces* that give strong images of black strength. The first is "The Swamp Angel," the great Parrott gun that bombarded Charleston from Morris Island on August 22, 1863, until Union ironclads could steam in and seize control. Threatened by the "coal-black Angel / With a thick Afric lip," who "dooms with far decree," the city's inhabitants "live in a sleepless spell / That wizens, and withers, and whitens." As they flee "their crumbling walls," they call on their patron, St. Michael, to deliver them from the powerful gun, but their cries prove useless; "the white man's seraph ... has fled from his tower / To the Angel over the sea," and the "coal-black Angel" rules. Although the narrator recognizes that the city must fall to the black avenger, he prays that "Christ, the Forgiver" will convert the mind of whoever "joys at her wild despairing."[43]

In "Formerly a Slave. An Idealized Portrait, by E. Vedder, in the Spring Exhibition of the National Academy, 1865," Melville transforms Elihu Vedder's Jane Jackson, an African-American Broadway peanut vendor whose son was fighting with the Union Army, into a Sibyl, or Madonna. Vedder's painting shows Jane Jackson in a "reverie" expressive of "the sufferance of her race" and their "retrospect of life." Although a "now too late deliverance dawns upon" her race, "she is not at strife," because she "takes prophetic cheer" from her calm faith that "Her children's children [they] shall know / The good withheld from her." The long-suffering black woman looks "far down the depth of a thousand years," her "dusky face lit with sober light," her expression "sybilline, yet benign."[44]

Although in these two poems, Melville presents strong images of black power that complement each other, readers seeking robust, heroic portraits of African-Americans as rebels, abolitionists, leaders of the Underground Railroad, and soldiers in Union regiments are disappointed by *Battle-Pieces* because Melville did not create vivid characters like Tawney, Daggoo, and Babo for these poems, but personifications of heroic qualities. Insofar as Melville failed to create a new, heroic vision of free African-Americans in his poems, some feel *Battle-Pieces* is a failure, even though Melville condemned slavery as a great wrong: Fearing that the North would remain blindly self-righteous and fail to work for broader social and economic justice, Melville believed the North must transform itself from within before it could hope to make the "Founders' Dream" a reality. Hatred and retribution would only betray the noble aims for which the war was fought and perpetuate the cycle of Old World inequality and suffering which America had promised to end.

With an audience of exultant northerners and embittered southerners in mind, Melville portrays the war as a "tragic action" that has not produced the desired catharsis. Thus, he ends the Supplement on a solemn note: "Let us pray that the terrible historic tragedy of our time may not have been enacted without instructing our whole beloved country through terror and pity; and may fulfillment verify in the end those expectations which kindle the bards of Progress and Humanity."[45]

Arguing for an "effective benignity" that "is not narrow in its bounty," because "true policy is always broad," Melville cautions that even if "those of us who always abhorred slavery as an atheistical iniquity" exult in its "downfall," the North must "forbear from measures of dubious constitutional rightfulness toward our white countrymen," as "rightly will more forbearance be required from the North than the South, for the North is victor . . . The years of the war tried our devotion to the Union; the time of peace may test the sincerity of our faith in democracy." Unfortunately, this was not what war-ravaged people wanted to hear, and on August 27, 1866, Melville was accused of "treasonous language" by the *New York Times*.[46]

By September 1866, reviews of *Battle-Pieces* began appearing. While a few critics emphasized the strengths of the poems over their defects, and defended the patriotism of the Supplement, saying it completed the symmetry of the book, several prestigious critics attacked the Supplement and harped on the all-too-obvious weaknesses of the poems. Others tried to avoid politics and strike a balance. The *American Literary Gazette and Publishers' Circular,* for instance, wrote that Melville "has abundant force and fire," and that "his words will kindle afresh the patriotic flame. But he has written too rapidly to avoid great crudities. His poetry runs into the epileptic. His rhymes are fearful." Similarly, Charles Eliot Norton observed in *The Nation* that, although the volume contains "the rough ore of poetry," it was obvious that "Nature did not make [Melville] a poet."[47]

Harper's New Monthly Magazine gave the poems high praise as "among the most stirring lyrics of the war," but William Dean Howells wrote a caustic review in *The Atlantic Monthly* charging that the poems resembled "no poetry you have read … no life you have known," and asking whether it is possible "that there has really been a great war, with battles fought by men and bewailed by women: Or is it only that Mr. Melville's inner consciousness has been perturbed, filled with the phantasms of enlistments, marches, fights in the air, parenthetic bulletin-boards, and tortured humanity shedding, not words and blood, but words alone?"[48]

Melville gave copies of the book to members of his family, but like Kate Gansevoort, who enjoyed "The March to the Sea" but found the other poems "too deep" for her comprehension, most of his family found reading an entire book of war poetry oppressive. Henry Gansevoort thought the volume had "some beautiful things in it" despite "so much of Emerson & transcendentalism in his writing that it never [would] really touch the common heart," and though he concluded that "this work shows him to be a poet of high order & certainly of originality," Henry was no more aware than most other commentators of what it was that made *Battle-Pieces* so original. Few people really cared about the intricacies of prosody. In the excitement of working on the poems and feeling confident of their success, Melville had forgotten to consider that, like Amasa Delano, most people wanted to forget the shadow the war had cast on them.[49]

Clear in his vision of how the nation might better realize the dreams of its founders, Melville must have hoped as he worked on the book that his readers would somehow be inspired by his words to forge a lasting peace, but like Reconstruction, *Battle-Pieces* was a failure. Of an edition of 1,260 copies, more than 300 were given to reviewers, and two years following its publication, only 486 copies had been sold. For Melville, who had cast himself in the lofty role of biblical prophet and Shelleyean poet-statesman, the response to *Battle-Pieces* was disheartening, if not crushing. He lost $400 on the venture, and the book sank into oblivion. Misunderstood and neglected despite his extraordinary powers of witness and prophecy, Melville the epic poet seems in his way as much a martyr to the base and bitter spirit of the times as the slain President.[50]

As 1866 drew to a close, Melville looked ahead and saw a void. After nearly ten years out of the public eye, his heroic bid to reestablish himself as a major literary figure had failed. Harper's was keeping seven of his earlier books in print, but they were not selling fast enough to pay for the books he had purchased from the firm. He still had no means of supporting his family, and even though their financial situation had improved owing to Lizzie's recent inheritance of a bit of money, Herman was a virtual dependent. He had no marketable skills and no way to make a living wage.

Without waiting for family and friends to hound him again about getting a government job, Melville wrote to Henry A. Smythe, the banker whom he had met in Switzerland in 1857, to ask about working at the Custom-House, as Smythe had recently been appointed Collector of Customs for the Port of New York. Although it's doubtful that Melville went out of his way to impress government officials of his fitness to inspect cargoes and fill out routine forms, he probably realized that publishing a volume of "patriotic verses" would finally make him eligible for a government appointment. Thus, ironically, being a poet turned out to have some practical value after all.

Clerking in an insurance office by necessity, not personal preference,
Malcolm Melville joined a volunteer regiment in hopes that he might someday
lead the adventurous life of a soldier.

TWENTY-FIVE

A TIME WHEN PEACE HAD
HORRORS OF ITS OWN

For Melville, the postwar period began with two suicides. In June 1865, Edmund Ruffin, the
"unhappy Secessionist ... who with impious alacrity" fired "the first shot of the Civil War at
Sumter ... fired the last one into his own heart at Richmond" rather than let himself be ruled
by the United States government. Or so Melville wrote in the Supplement to Battle-Pieces;
in fact, the veteran of Charleston's Palmetto Guard blew the top of his head off. Several months
later, Melville's Pittsfield neighbor, Dr. Timothy Childs, a professor of anatomy at Bellevue
Hospital in New York, took a large quantity of morphine to a hotel room and died with his
hand on a Bible, leaving a note for his wife, the contents of which were not revealed. Lizzie,
Maria, and Augusta had been part of Mrs. Childs's sewing circle in the mid-1850s and one
of them saved Dr. Childs's obituary along with other newspaper clippings that included an
article on the stormy domestic life of Abraham and Mary Lincoln.[1]

    Punitive measures against the South increased sectional and racial hatreds, bringing the
nation close to a second civil war. The Fourteenth Amendment to the Constitution guaranteed
the civil rights of all born or naturalized United States citizens, and the voting rights of all

males twenty-one and over who had not committed a crime or participated in the late rebellion. It also prevented those who had "engaged in insurrection or rebellion against the United States, or given aid or comfort to the enemies thereof" from holding federal office. Thus, when, on December 5, 1866, Herman Melville took the oath as District Inspector of the United States Customs Service, he was required to swear that he had "never voluntarily borne arms against the United States." Only after he had signed an affidavit promising that he would "support the Constitution of the United States" was he given a numbered tin badge to be worn on his lapel, plus "a set of government locks, a record book or two, forms and stationery."[2]

Melville worked as a customs inspector on the docks six days a week, with national holidays and two weeks off a year. At $4 a day, his annual "pittance," as John Hoadley called it, amounted to about $1,200, which was what Hawthorne had been paid by the Salem Custom-House in 1846. By comparison, a jailkeeper in a state prison earned about $2,000 a year and a minister earned about $5,000, and was provided with housing. Regardless of their political affiliation, Custom-House employees were forced to give two percent of their salary to the Republican State Committee.[3]

Every weekday morning, Melville reported to an office near Gansevoort Pier on the North River, which he shared with Colonel Henry L. Potter, a severely wounded veteran who wore "the offending bullet" on his watch chain. District inspectors were required to provide their own offices, either by lease or loan from friends, so they tended to move frequently. Melville and Potter moved around the corner to 62 Harrison Street the following year, and in 1869, Melville moved to an office near Gansevoort Street, closer to home. If he had to go to a funeral or meet a train, he was allowed to leave his partner in charge and in slack times he could take an hour or so off to stroll or sit on a park bench reading or working on a poem. Nevertheless, Melville must have hated having to conform to a rigid schedule after years of self-directed, self-paced writing.[4]

His primary job was checking the docking certificates and bills of lading of all incoming vessels and inspecting all cargoes for prohibited imports such as illegal animal hides, wines and spirits whose strengths or quantities violated existing regulations, cigars illegally packaged, contraceptive devices, and obscene materials. He also checked and itemized all provisions before they were loaded onto departing vessels, filling out countless forms and reports on all incoming ships for the Barge Office. If he found a ship's papers in order, he gave the cartmen waiting on the pier a sign that they could unload the vessel. If a ship didn't have proper papers or was found to be carrying contraband, he locked the gangway until the authorities arrived. It was mindless, routine work for a man of Melville's restless energy and genius—quite a comedown from serving in a foreign embassy, or sailing the metaphysical seas of *Moby-Dick* and *Mardi*. After exploring several continents and voyaging through the vast oceans of the mind, he had joined the landlocked drones.[5]

Melville was not the first great writer to become a civil servant in order to pay his bills. Geoffrey Chaucer, Robert Burns, Nathaniel Hawthorne, and other literary men had all held similar positions, though none of them served as long as Melville did. Edgar Allan Poe had tried and failed to secure an appointment. Walt Whitman had worked as a clerk in the Interior Department's Office of Indian Affairs until his boss found the page proofs of his homoerotic *Calamus* poems in his desk drawer and fired him.[6]

Distinguished relatives and friends of Melville's had also held civil-service jobs. Major Thomas Melvill had been a collector in the Boston Custom-House, and both Leonard Gansevoort and George Duyckinck had served as customs officers in New York State. But times had changed. After four years of war, corruption permeated public life; graft, bribery, and embezzlement riddled the civil service. The spoils system, originally designed to "cleanse the Augean stables" when the Jackson administration took office, had rapidly degenerated into a cynical power-grab by partisans who appointed their friends to inside jobs. Unscrupulous politicians used their wealth to influence legislators, and many appointees were either incompetent or corrupt. Some appointees, like Cornelius Vanderbilt and George Law, could not write or spell correctly; others loafed and drank to intoxication on the job. Employees secured their positions not through merit, but through "intrigues, solicitations or coercions." Even Melville, it must be said, had received his position through a personal favor; he had no particular qualifications for the job.[7]

Despite the unsavory reputation of the civil service, several other writers—among them Charles F. Briggs, Richard Henry Stoddard, Barry Gray, and Richard Grant White—worked for the Customs Service concurrently with Melville, though at other venues. In fact, the prevalence of literary men in the service prompted the *Springfield Republican* to question "whether such positions leave them entirely free to write independent political articles, or criticisms on American life." Stoddard, who knew Melville only "casually and officially," thought he seemed "as reserved as a man of genius had a right to be" on the job, and later called him an "American mystic" and "one of our greatest unrecognized poets." Melville wrote nothing about his job, and nothing explicit about the Custom-House. His silence, like Bartleby's, speaks volumes.[8]

Melville probably did not find many congenial fellow workers in the Custom-House. Stoddard described his fellow employees as "incapable 'fogies' of all ages—the mentally lame, halt, and blind." Except for Henry Potter, who came from a literary family, most of the men Melville worked with did not share his love of literature and philosophical speculation. On days when he felt tired of his job, he may have thought of Nathaniel Hawthorne's comment on his stint as a surveyor in Salem: "I endeavored to calculate how much longer I could stay in the Custom-House, and yet go forth a man....

A dreary look-forward this, for a man who felt it to be the best definition of happiness to live throughout the whole range of his faculties and sensibilities!" Although it was impossible for Melville while working in the "asylum of nonentities" that was the New York Custom-House to recapture the "All-feeling" he had talked about in an 1851 letter to Hawthorne, he would create an ambitious poem reflective of the moral and spiritual crisis of which the scandals of the Grant and Johnson administrations were only symptoms.[9]

When Melville began working at the Custom-House, his sponsor, Henry A. Smythe, the first merchant to hold the post, had been Collector of Customs for about a year, and already his integrity was being questioned. Originally praised by the *Evening Post* as "a man of unimpeachable personal integrity and of diligent habits," and endorsed by *Harper's Weekly* for his "business tact and energy of character, as well as his executive ability," Smythe was now being denounced as a "schemer and a Republican partisan" for removing 830 out of 903 Custom-House officials "at the rate of three decapitations every four days of his term, including Sundays!"[10]

After a congressional committee found the management of the Custom-House "a disgrace" and Smythe's "rigid integrity" a sham, there were calls for his removal and a sweeping program of reform, and he was eventually convicted of stealing millions of dollars from the city. By 1877, so many appointees were cheating and embezzling money that the state attorney general's office launched an investigation and dismissed two hundred employees for incompetence, dishonesty, and neglect of duty. Many operatives routinely stole from warehouses, extorted money from merchants, and took bribes, which prompted E. L. Godkin to write in *The Nation* that the prime qualification for working in the Custom-House was to be a thief. To be sure, in Melville's district, weighers and measurers, as well as guards who patrolled the wharves at night to prevent smuggling, had ample opportunity to make money on the side, but Godkin's remark must have stung Melville. He survived this purge and several others by performing his duties with unimpeachable integrity, keeping his job through cutbacks and purges for twenty years without ever receiving a pay raise.[11]

Working for the organization that epitomized the political corruption of the postwar era, Melville brushed up daily against the slimy underbelly of the establishment. Editor George W. Curtis, a crusader for civil-service reform, would have been impressed by Melville's ability to remain uncorrupted in a hotbed of corruption. To Curtis, politicians were "vampires who suck the moral lifeblood of the nation," and the spoils system was "a monster only less threatening than slavery." Melville, however, was used to marching to his own drummer; now he was using what he had learned about self-camouflage in the navy to good advantage.[12]

On the positive side, the constant exposure to seagoing vessels carrying exotic spices, Oriental carpets, porcelains, statues, and other works of art kept Melville's memories of his youth on the high seas alive, and he used his situation to advantage by filling the pockets of his blue inspector's jacket with small yellow squares of paper, on which he jotted notes and drafts of poems, instead of payoff money.

Glad to be earning his own money, he may have preferred hiding behind the customs inspector's badge to being in the public eye. Authorship had come to be more satisfying for him when it was a private activity engaged in almost secretly. To go before the public as a once-popular writer would subject him to a greater sense of alienation than he experienced when he was alone, reading and working on his poetry. He wore the role of author, as his society defined it, like an ill-fitting, conspicuous jacket.

In one of his poems he contrasts the Custom-House with the "authentic Edens" that existed in a happier era:

> My jacket old, with narrow seam—
> When the dull day's work is done
> I dust it, and of Asia dream,
> Old Asia of the sun!
> There other garbs prevail;
> Yea, lingering there, free robe and vest
> Edenic Leisure's age attest
> Ere Work, alack, came in with Wail.

Like Ishmael, Melville was "tormented with an everlasting itch for things remote," for the myriad diverse worlds that lay just over the horizon.[13]

To family members who had once feared for his sanity, Melville's having a job was a relief. When Maria, Fanny, and Augusta stayed with the Melvilles in February and March, they found Herman "quite well," as did Kate Gansevoort, who thought his getting out every day was doing him a world of good: "His intercourse with his fellow creatures seems to have had a beneficial effect," she wrote Henry, since "he is less of a misanthrope."[14]

With Herman out of the house most of the day, Lizzie's job of household management became much easier. Some of the disorder her in-laws attributed to slovenly housekeeping stemmed from the unpredictability of her husband's demands and his habit of nervously interfering in domestic matters whenever his writing was not going well. Even now he badgered her about his morning coffee, often changing his preferences from day to day but not telling her until she had prepared it, and he took it upon himself to give every cook he hired exact instructions as to how to prepare his oatmeal.[15]

Melville apparently compensated for feelings of powerlessness in his professional life by bullying his servants, wife, and children. Much as the children loved their father, they too were glad of a respite from his intense, unpredictable moods. Even when he was in a good mood, the force of his personality and his need to be the center of attention put enormous demands on others, and when he was in a bad mood, he could be a terror. Like the tyrannical captains he had portrayed in his novels, Melville probably provoked rebellious feelings in his "crew" by the capricious way he ruled the home, especially when he was drinking. Such feelings, however, could never be openly acknowledged, not even in the inmost recesses of the heart. Yet, Melville remained dependent on his wife to manage things, and if at times he accepted the situation gracefully, at other times he took out his frustrations by "challenging Lizzie," as their niece Milie later put it delicately. Tensions between Herman and Lizzie put an added strain on Malcolm.[16]

During the early 1850s, Melville had been able to exorcise his demons by writing them out. Before the war, he had underscored in his copy of the *Odyssey* the words of Odysseus to Nausicaa: "Nought beneath the sky / More sweet, more worthy is, than firm consent / Of man and wife in household government. / It joys their wishers well, their enemies wounds, / But to themselves the special good redounds." Subsequently, however, the physical pain and nervous exhaustion from which he suffered left him short-tempered, and his drinking grew worse.[17]

An unsympathetic person might characterize Melville as a failed writer who held a low-level government job, drank too much, heckled his wife unmercifully about the housework, beat her occasionally, and drove the children to distraction with his unpredictable behavior. A sympathetic observer might characterize him as an unappreciated genius, a visionary, an iconoclastic thinker, a sensitive, orphaned American idealist, and a victim of a crude, materialistic society that ate artists and visionaries alive and spat out their bones. He was both, and more.

~~~

When the Melvilles moved back to New York in 1863, they found themselves within walking distance of the new home of their old parish, the Church of the Divine Unity, now All Souls' Church, at Fourth Avenue and Twentieth Street. The congregation had built itself a striking Byzantine basilica whose alternate stripes of light yellow Italian Caen stone and red Philadelphia brick prompted wags to call it "the Beefsteak Church," or "the Church of the Holy Zebra." In this fashionable Unitarian church, the eminent Dr. Henry Whitney Bellows preached to a congregation that included William Cullen Bryant, Catharine Maria Sedgwick, and any number of prominent New Yorkers. Mrs. E. S. Melville rented a modest pew in the back gallery of the church for herself, attending with her daughters and sometimes with other relatives and friends. On occasion, her husband, the novelist Herman Melville, attended services with his family, too.[18]

A passionate advocate of moral and spiritual reform, Henry Bellows served as president of the New York Association at a time when that organization was attacking the spoils system and spearheading a movement to reform the civil service. Bellows considered capitalism "somewhat antagonistic" to Christianity and took the nation to task for its addiction to "comfort and luxury," its "indolent self-indulgence," and its "vicious materialism" in his sermon "The Mission of America." Like Melville, Bellows was a patrician with a social conscience, but there's no evidence that the two men were friends or had a personal relationship of any kind. Bellows may have taken himself and his religion a bit too seriously for Melville, and Melville's irreverent humor may have offended the morally earnest minister.[19]

In May 1867, Henry Bellows was drawn into the vortex of the Melvilles' life when Sam Shaw, who was handling some property for the minister, wrote asking for help with his "sister's case," which "has been a cause of anxiety to all of us for years past." Because existing laws made it almost impossible for a wife to leave even the most abusive of husbands without forfeiting all claims to property and children, Bellows suggested kidnapping Lizzie and taking her to Boston, where Melville could be prevented from seeing her and ordering her to return.[20]

Sam considered this desperate scheme unwise; he also doubted Lizzie's willingness to go along with it.

> She will tell you that all the reasons set forth in your letter have been urged over and over again by me as a ground for separation, that we have offered to assist her to the best of our ability and that the Melvilles also, though not till quite recently, have expressed a willingness to lend their assistance. The whole family understands the case and the thing has resolved itself into the mere question of my sister's willingness to say the word. Of course we should not act against what we believed to be her *real* wishes and we must base our claim to act on what *she* knows and not on what *we* know. If I understand your letter it is proposed to make a sudden interference and carry her off, she protesting that she does not wish to go and that it is none of her doing. But I think this would only obscure the real merits of the case in the eyes of the world, of which she has a most exaggerated dread. I see no way in which she can throw off the responsibility of deciding for herself in this matter, and if it is her own act I do not see why she should wish it to appear to be the act of others, unauthorized by her.[21]

Spousal abuse is notoriously difficult to detect, especially in cultures that grant men full authority over wives and children. Although rumors that Herman threw Lizzie down the back stairs on at least one occasion surfaced decades later, no conclusive evidence of marital abuse exists, which is not surprising, given the reticence of those involved. Yet two recently discovered letters—Sam Shaw's letter asking Henry Bellows for advice about his "sister's case" and Lizzie's letter thanking her pastor for his "active interest," wise "counsel," and "encouraging words"—have survived, and they suggest that Lizzie's family considered her plight dire.[22]

A woman who left her husband put herself in extreme jeopardy. Not only were scandal and social ostracism inevitable, but in 1867, a woman who sought a divorce or separation also risked complete financial ruin. In 1848, New York's legislature had passed the Married Woman's Property Act, which gave women more control of personal property than they had previously enjoyed, but a married woman who failed to prove her case for separation or divorce could still be forced to surrender her claim to property held jointly with her husband or registered in her own name. Thus, if Lizzie left Herman without sufficient grounds or sued without ample proof of her husband's culpability, she could lose everything.[23]

As soon as a married woman took her husband's name, she ceased to exist as an individual. According to the principle of *couverture* enunciated in *Blackstone's Commentaries,* man and wife were one flesh, which meant that a married woman's rights derived not from the Constitution, but from her husband's rights. Although the concept of middle-class marriage was changing in the 1860s to give married women more rights and more autonomy in cases where husbands violated the marriage bond, wives found it difficult to obtain protection or redress. Between 1867 and 1906, more than a quarter of a million American women sought divorces from their husbands, over eighty percent of them on grounds of either physical or mental cruelty, but only wives who were submissive, virtuous, and pious stood any chance of winning settlements.[24]

The prevalence of domestic violence in America and the lack of legal redress for women against abusive husbands prompted suffragist Elizabeth Cady Stanton to call marriage "legalized slavery." Invoking the ideals of "Republican womanhood," Stanton tried in 1861 to get the New York legislature to consider making wife-beating grounds for a woman to gain a divorce, but the bill did not pass. Thus, New York remained one of only six states that did not allow a divorce or separation on grounds of cruelty. In 1867, a married woman was still legally under her husband's protection, even if he abused her, and she could not commence a lawsuit on her own. Either her husband or a *"prochain ami"* had to bring the suit on her behalf, which relegated her to the status of a child and meant that every woman suing for a divorce or separation had to mount her campaign from within the home, under the roof of the very man who was abusing her. If a judge concluded that she had provoked her husband's conduct by her behavior or words, or by neglect of her household duties, he would send her back to him with a strong reprimand and an admonition to try harder to make the marriage work.[25]

When a marriage failed, judges tended to assume that the "angel of the household" had somehow "fallen." It was very difficult for a woman to obtain a separation and nearly impossible for her to divorce her husband even if he abused her, because a woman was expected to use her moral superiority to reform a man who fell into sinful ways. If, by contrast, a man could prove that his wife had committed adultery or deserted him, he could cast her off with no alimony, no custodial rights, and no means of support, as such actions violated the Victorian ideal of womanhood and undermined the sacred Home. A false accusation of adultery by a husband against a wife was considered the ultimate form of marital abuse and subject to severe judicial censure, and a woman could seek a divorce for adultery or desertion. However, even if her petition was successful, she was often granted only a separation and ordered to remain celibate for life.

Sam Shaw knew Lizzie would balk at Dr. Bellows's melodramatic scheme, so he made a counterproposal. He would bring Lizzie to Boston for a visit, during which her "friends" would inform Herman of her intention to seek a separation and warn him not to try to see her. Sam planned to ask Dr. Augustus Kinsley Gardner to testify in court that a separation was essential to Lizzie's health, but he knew that once she took the initiative to leave, she put herself in great jeopardy. Even a physician's affidavit might not persuade a judge to grant her a separation, because her leaving could be used to prove that she was "acquiescing in the separation" at her family's request.[26]

Sam realized that Lizzie had no chance of obtaining a divorce unless she brought charges against Melville herself; otherwise "It may well be said Here is a case of mischief making where the wife's relations have created all the trouble." Sam feared that if Lizzie were asked in court why she had not left of her own volition before being abducted by her relatives, "her very patience and fortitude [could] be turned into arguments against her belief in the insanity of her husband." She might not even be granted a separation if the court thought she had allowed her relatives to talk her into "thinking herself a much injured woman" against her will. If Lizzie lost the case and was not granted a separation, future relations with her husband would be intolerable, and if she won, he could countersue and most likely be awarded all their property, even property in Lizzie's name.

For all these reasons, Sam thought "the safest course [was] to let her real position become apparent from the first, namely that of a wife, who, being convinced that her husband is insane *acts* as if she were so convinced and applies for aid and assistance to her friends and acts *with* them." Concluding that Lizzie would have left her husband sooner "if not for imaginary and groundless apprehensions of the censure of the world upon her conduct," he asked Bellows to help allay Lizzie's fears for her reputation and to support a less drastic plan of action "by which the present lamentable state of things can be ended."[27]

The Shaws might well have wondered what marriage to Herman Melville had to offer Lizzie beyond the wifely status that defined the respectable Victorian woman. She owned the house and now had sufficient assets to carry on without her husband, who had demonstrably failed as a protector and provider. Lizzie clearly had ambivalent feelings about leaving her husband, and Sam's comment to Bellows that "the thing has resolved itself into the mere question of my sister's willingness to say the word" suggests that she was less eager to leave Herman than her family realized. Undoubtedly, Lizzie feared a scandal and, deep down, believed women did have a special duty toward their husbands. She had proven her devotion by sewing buttons back on his clothes without complaint when he carelessly ripped them off, by structuring her day around her husband's writing schedule, and by copying and proofreading his manuscripts late at night by lamplight when he was too irritable to speak a civil word. Subordinating her own needs to her husband's without expecting appreciation or gratitude, she conformed to the wifely ideal upheld by Protestant Christianity and sentimental fiction. Every force imaginable—from sermons and lithographs in popular magazines to domestic novels, didactic poetry, and handbooks on domestic economy—taught women that they had a sacred obligation to raise their families in a virtuous home by being "the perfect pattern of a wife," to use her uncle Amos Nourse's characterization of her.[28]

While reformers like Sara Jane Lippincott, who wrote under the pseudonym "Grace Greenwood," derided the "true feminine genius" of 1850 as "timid, doubtful, and clingingly dependent; a perpetual childhood," the cultural icon of woman was the passionless martyr who stood by her man, no matter how low he fell. As Phoebe Cary had written in her "Psalm of Marriage," woman belonged in "the bivouac of life" where she could "be a heroine—a wife!"[29]

Not only did powerful cultural influences and legal strictures combine to dissuade Lizzie from going through with the proposed separation, but her family's attitude toward the man she had loved—and doubtless still loved on some level—may also have sounded so extreme to her, and their denunciations of him so violent, that she actually began to feel protective of him. If, in championing her cause, the Shaws let fly all the criticisms of Melville they had been storing up for years while Lizzie was still emotionally attached to Herman, their strategy might have backfired. The more vehemently they denounced her husband and threatened to have him declared insane, the more sympathetic she might have felt toward him, and the more guilty about asserting her power or demanding her own rights.

After a series of private interviews with Bellows, Lizzie wrote to thank him for "calling in the busy moments" before his departure for Europe, and for his "active interest" in her welfare. "I do so now—most sincerely—and whatever further trial may be before me, I shall feel that your counsel is a strong help to sustain, more perhaps than any earthly counsel could," she wrote. "I lay to heart your encouraging words, and pray for submission and faith to *realize* the sustaining power of the Master's love, and to approach his Table in the very spirit of his last command." Women were generally rewarded for knitting relationships together and punished for asserting their autonomy, so with her self-image and her self-esteem hanging in the balance, Lizzie chose to stay and make peace with her situation.[30]

Soon after this, in an edition of poems by the Portuguese writer Luis de Camoëns, Melville underscored the line "Woman was to him as a ministering angel, and for the little joy which he tasted in life, he was indebted to her." He also marked these lines from a sonnet by Camoëns: "My senses lost, misjudging men declare, / And Reason banish'd from her mental throne, / Because I shun the crowd, and dwell alone." Yet it was not his reclusiveness that troubled his friends and family, but his excessive drinking and his unpredictable, volcanic temper.[31]

If genius is close to madness, Melville was close to madness from time to time. Madness was never far from his mind or the minds of those closest to him; the way in which his father had died haunted him. Other people did not necessarily agree on when he seemed mad and when he seemed quite sane. While, on the one hand, he might have been grateful for the way the down-to-earth Lizzie balanced his erratic moods, he might, on the other, have unconsciously resented her passivity at times, as a woman's goodness often makes a man feel all the more guilty for his abusive behavior. Lizzie's docility may even have sparked some of her husband's outbursts and reinforced unhealthy repressions that adversely affected their four children. At the same time, her forbearance held the marriage together, making eventual renegotiation and reconciliation possible.

Once Lizzie made her decision to remain in the marriage, she stuck by it, but she and Herman went their separate ways that summer. Herman and Malcolm, both of whom had two weeks off from their jobs in August, visited Arrowhead and Gansevoort, where they met Stanwix, while Lizzie went to Boston with the girls. By early September the Melvilles were back together in New York, and outward signs of strain in the household were no longer visible. Herman went off to the Custom-House each morning, and Malcolm went to the insurance office. Unfortunately, as the relationship between Herman and Lizzie improved, Melville's anger began to shift from his wife to his older son.

The anger Melville had directed at God when he was a younger man seems to have refocused itself after the war. Rather than God, he now blamed Man and his imperfect societies for the evils of the world. As God seemed more and more powerless to control his wayward creatures, Melville began to feel that God was not an omnipotent Creator, but an incompetent father whose children had gone astray.

～

In the eighteenth century, the Holy Bible, John Bunyan's *Pilgrim's Progress*, and Daniel Defoe's *Robinson Crusoe* were considered indispensable guidebooks for life in the "moral wilderness" that was America. Between 1828 and 1860, however, as the locus of American society shifted toward the cities, books offering practical advice to young men about everything from hygiene and deportment at social functions to rules for sexual behavior and success in the marketplace suddenly flooded the bookstalls of America. To warn young men, whose passions were like "keg[s] of powder uncovered amid the sparks of a blazing furnace," against the dangers and temptations of cities where "savages" lurked, "not in gloomy forests, but under the strength of gaslight," these writers painted both urban life and young men's propensities to dissipation in the most lurid colors. The proliferation of such books suggests that the anxiety caused by the demands of an increasingly competitive urban marketplace had swelled to a kind of panic.[32]

Cotton Mather's *Essays to Do Good*, Benjamin Franklin's *Dogood Papers*, *Poor Richard's Almanack*, and *The Way to Wealth* all assumed that virtue was essential to a man's success. Franklin's secularized moral accounting led logically to Henry Clay's concept of the "self-made man." Emersonian self-reliance took the American boy's fantasies of absolute freedom from social constraints a step further by divorcing individualism from Christian morality. In an era when enterprising men were leaving farms and villages for the city, Emerson's vision seemed hopelessly romantic, not practical. In the 1840s and 1850s, T. S. Arthur's moralistic urban novels had a much greater influence on the popular mind than did the works of Emerson, and by the late 1860s, when the Reverend Horatio Alger Jr., who decided to become a writer after reading *Moby-Dick*, penned his one hundred best-selling novels that made "rags to riches" a popular slogan, self-improvement was construed in almost completely practical and materialistic terms. No matter that "Holy Horatio" Alger was dismissed from a parish in Brooklyn for molesting boys, a young man embarking on "the voyage of life" was supposed to follow Alger's formula of "pluck and luck" to get ahead. A man who loafed and "invited his soul" like Walt Whitman would get nowhere.[33]

Although popular literature showed boys making good by a combination of upright conduct and hard work, more often than not, boys like Malcolm Melville depended on relatives and friends to find them jobs. Thus, now that he had finished school, Malcolm went to work for Richard Lathers at the Great Western Marine Insurance Company. As the older son, he felt the burden of parental expectations most heavily. His childhood forays into acting showed that he shared his father's histrionic streak, but if he harbored fantasies about a stage career, he evidently received no encouragement either at home or at boarding school. Malcolm may have considered clerking in an insurance agency little more than a stepping-stone to a future career, but Grandmother Melville considered it an ideal situation: "He is but 17 years old gets a salary of $200 a year," she wrote. "They all have a fine lunch at the office equal to a dinner, & if kept in after six in the evening have a regular supper. Mr Lathers who is President, is an active industrious man—Prompt, energetic, & just the Man for Malcolm or any other boy."[34]

To Malcolm, working full time meant he was an adult, and as most young people do when they begin to earn a little money of their own, he assumed he could spend his wages as he liked and go out with his friends without asking his parents for permission or being subjected to a curfew. Like most parents of grown children, Herman and Lizzie found the adjustment difficult. Their older son, whom they still considered a dependent and a child, was now a workingman with friends and acquaintances they might never meet, and habits about which they were completely ignorant. Despite Malcolm's newfound independence, as long as he was still living under their roof, his parents wanted to protect him from the temptations and dangers that lurked in the big city.

Growing up during the war, Malcolm imbibed romantic fantasies about soldiering from the family's patriotic talk about the glories of military service, and shortly after his eighteenth birthday, he joined the New York State National Guard. When Melvilles and Gansevoorts talked about the Civil War in public, they tended to stress the glory and the heroism over the pain and sorrow. The adults in the family probably realized that Malcolm's surface bravado masked deep feelings of despair, but to an adolescent male whose great-grandfathers had been heroes of the Revolution, military service must have seemed far more attractive than a desk job. And Malcolm's prized possession was a gun.

The war had brought violence into almost every home, and if muskets and rifles were considered a necessity in western frontier homes, pistols were fast becoming a household appliance for eastern city dwellers. Due to a great increase in crime, revolvers had become so fashionable that every week *Harper's Weekly* carried several advertisements for various models, including one dainty enough to be tucked into a lady's evening bag. The magazine *Our Young Friend* featured instructions for children on how to pretend-shoot a gun without injuring themselves or others. A shy boy who, since his earliest childhood, had identified with Jack the Giant-Killer, Malcolm made home an imaginary battleground. Indulging the passion for theatricals that his family had found so entertaining when he was a child, he strutted around the house in his uniform, brandishing his service revolver until his sisters ran off squealing into the next room. One wonders how the adults in the household responded to this scary game. Did Lizzie admonish Malcolm and exhort him to behave? Did Herman ignore him, reprimand him, or laugh and walk away?[35]

Being only twelve when his father died, Melville had never learned the steps of the intricate dance between a maturing son feeling his oats and a father so threatened by the waning of his strength that he cannot gracefully let go. He had profoundly ambivalent feelings about Gansevoort, who had lorded it over him during their adolescence, and the sudden death of the older brother, who was both role model and focus of resentment for Herman, deprived him of the chance to work through yet another crucial and complicated relationship with an older male relative.

As the older son, Malcolm had to bear the brunt of his father's inexperience both at being a grown-up son and having one. He also had to navigate the Scylla and Charybdis of mixed messages from his parents. Whereas Lizzie tended to be indulgent with the children, acting as a buffer between them and her temperamental husband, Herman could be as stern and uncompromising as the most autocratic captain. Allan Melvill had alternately coddled Herman, of whom he expected little, and punished him with a few switches of the corrective rod in the dispassionate manner expected of well-bred fathers.

Like many creative, controlling, egocentric men, Melville was unpredictable and inconsistent with his children. At times he was relaxed and playful; at other times he was irascible and tense. To some extent he saw his children more as extensions of himself than as separate individuals. When they were small, he could amuse them with dramatic stories or childish banter and show them off to visitors, but as they got older, his self-conscious, even self-serving, efforts to show off to others merely embarrassed and annoyed them.

Melville's ironic sense of humor often had a cutting edge. He used humor both as a defense mechanism and as a mask to conceal an anger he feared unleashing, but he was too self-centered to realize when he was carrying a joke too far or entertaining himself at the expense of others' feelings, especially with regard to his children. On one occasion his daughter Fanny asked him what "property" was, and he teased her unmercifully, making fun of her ignorance by calling her "Miss Property" over and over again in an aggressive manner until she was reduced to tears. Lizzie's attempts to assuage the children's hurt feelings by saying, "Papa doesn't mean anything, run along to school," could not drown out their father's disconcertingly loud laughter.[36]

To compensate for being seriously out of control in some ways, Melville needed to feel he was lord and master of the house. The older and more independent the children became, the less he was able to relate to their complex needs, and the more inconsistent and unreasonable he became. Lizzie, by contrast, was even-tempered and supportive in her dealings with the children, but unassertive. In conflicts between the children and their father, she knew better than to try to change the ways of her strong-minded husband, or to cross him in any way. When Malcolm began testing limits he himself had perhaps not thoroughly established, Melville, unable to process his anxieties about his son's safety and talk it through with him, established rules that must have seemed to Malcolm arbitrary and unfair.

Now that Malcolm was earning his own money and wanted to go out at night with his friends, his father, a risk-taker himself as a young man, worried that these late-night forays would expose him to the manifold dangers and temptations that lay in wait for unwary youths in the taverns and back alleys of New York. Lizzie worried for her son's health and safety, and Melville felt he could not slacken the reins without relinquishing control, so one or both of them would sit up anxiously until he came home.

Testing the limits, Malcolm began staying out later and later, until finally his father took away his house key and told him the door would be locked promptly at 11:00 P.M. Such vigilance apparently stemmed from anxiety about Malcolm's drinking or gambling, not to mention his exposing himself to thieves and prostitutes, and to Malcolm, the crackdown proved that his parents considered him a child.

On Tuesday, September 10, 1867, Malcolm stayed out until 3:00 A.M., and Lizzie waited up for him. "When he came home," Sam Shaw told his mother, "he said he had been at an entertainment in Yorkville given by some friends." They probably went to Niblo's Gardens, a popular nightclub that had recently moved uptown to Yorkville, a residential working-class neighborhood on the Upper East Side that was populated mostly by Germans and Eastern Europeans. Niblo's, which featured musical comedies with girls who "wore no clothes to speak of," attracted men about town like Tom Melville and John Hoadley, who occasionally attended shows.[37]

According to Lizzie, Malcolm showed no signs of having had any liquor, so she chided him for his lack of consideration, but did not scold him "in the least." Then he kissed her good night and went up to bed. As Kate Gansevoort told her brother Henry, Lizzie did not remonstrate with Malcolm and "cannot blame herself for having induced him from despair at her fault-finding, to put an end to his life."[38]

The next morning, Malcolm did not appear downstairs at the usual time, so one of the girls went up to make sure he was awake. He responded but still did not come down to breakfast. When Lizzie started upstairs to see what was wrong, Herman gruffly ordered her "to let him sleep, be late at the office & take the consequences as a sort of punishment." Melville left for the office, and Lizzie tried several times to awaken Malcolm, but his door was locked and he did not respond. Perhaps because this was "not an unusual thing," Lizzie decided to wait for Herman to come home to deal with the situation, but for some reason he did not arrive home until "unusually late." Finding Malcolm's door still locked, he broke into the room and saw the son whom he had called "a perfect prodigy, as valiant as Julius Caesar," lying in bed in his nightclothes. He was curled up on his left side in a semi-fetal position, a pistol in his right hand and a bullet hole in his right temple.[39]

Melville summoned Augustus Gardner, who called the coroner. After subjecting the family to "the distressing ordeal of having an inquest at the house," the coroner's jury reached the verdict that "the said Child came to his death by Suicide by shooting himself in the head with a pistol at said place while laboring under temporary insanity of Mind." They sent the Melvilles a copy of the report and a bill for $11.31.[40]

To Sam Shaw, the circumstances of Malcolm's death seemed "very mysterious." Despite Malcolm's recent habit of staying out late at night, Herman and Lizzie assured Sam that "there was nothing in his dissipation more than a fondness for social frolicking with his young friends, and acquaintances that he made down town. They know he had *no* vices." The Melvilles continued to make a great point of denying that Malcolm ever drank when he went out with his friends, which seems hard to believe, given the family history and cultural links between drinking and masculinity.[41]

Questions abound. When did Malcolm fire the fatal shot? Did he wait until he was alone in the house to point the gun at his head and squeeze the trigger? Did no one in the family hear the shot, or did someone hear it and not register the awful truth? Did Lizzie wait in terror for Herman to come home, and why did he come home so late that night?[42]

Neither Herman nor Lizzie cried during the funeral, which was held at the Melville home on Saturday, September 14, at eight-thirty in the morning. Lizzie, exhausted and suffering from shock, seemed oddly unaware of the finality of what had happened, and Herman appeared "quite composed." Stanwix, by contrast, cried uncontrollably, causing Augusta to fear his heart was broken beyond repair.[43]

With Henry Bellows touring Europe, Dr. Samuel Osgood of the Church of the Messiah read 1 Corinthians XV from the Episcopal burial service, delivered a homily, and offered a prayer from the King's Chapel prayer book. Then six of Malcolm's friends from the volunteer company walked past the bier and paused for a last look at their comrade before placing four wreaths and several crosses made of white flowers on the coffin, raising the coffin to their shoulders, and bearing it down the steps and out into the street to the Harlem Railroad car that Allan had hired for the journey to Woodlawn Cemetery in the Bronx, where Malcolm was buried in his regimental uniform.

The reactions of the family to the trauma ranged from the unnaturally controlled to the hysterical. Sixteen-year-old Stanwix had known that Malcolm took his pistol to work with him to show it off, and that he slept with it under his pillow every night, but he had said nothing, so he was inconsolable. Augusta reacted in her characteristically moralizing tone: "Poor Mackies death is a lesson to all who place pistols under their pillows he must have been handling the pistol, for it was found in his hand." Kate Gansevoort rather irrationally warned Henry, who had survived Antietam and several other battles, to "beware of carelessness with your pistols."[44]

Herman and Lizzie's stoic demeanor was somewhat disturbing to other adults, so it must have been a frightening thing for Stanwix and the girls. "I pity the poor parents— both Cousin Herman & Lizzie are of such nervous temperaments I should fear for *their peace of mind,*" Kate Gansevoort wrote Henry. Wondering "if poor Malcolm really committed the act or was it an accident," Kate cast around for reasons, but all she could come up with was the observation that "Cousin Herman is I think a very strict parent & Cousin Lizzie thoroughly good but inefficient." Although she considered suicide a "cowardly act," she did not deny that Malcolm had taken his own life, and she was glad suicide was not a crime in New York State.[45]

Now that Malcolm was gone, he could do no wrong; Melville idealized him and inadvertently pushed Stanwix away. Two days after finding his son dead, he wrote a letter to John Hoadley in which he created an image of Malcolm reminiscent of the sentimental "mourning pictures" so fashionable during the Victorian period: "I wish you could have seen him as he lay in his last attitude, the ease of a gentle nature. Mackie never gave me a disrespectful word in his life, nor in any way ever failed in filialness." The degree of denial seems staggering.[46]

He mythologized his relationship with Malcolm to the point that he seems almost to have imagined that his son had died fighting in the war. To his niece Milie he wrote, "We have been getting new photographs made from two tintypes—one representing him in his ordinary dress, and the other in the regimental one." A week after the funeral, Melville presented a tinted photograph of Malcolm in his uniform to his volunteer company, and Lizzie chose an inscription for Malcolm's gravestone from a book of hymns given to her by her friend Ellen Brittain: "So good, so young, / So gentle, so sincere, / So loved, so early lost, / May claim a tear."[47]

Newspaper accounts on the thirteenth of September of Malcolm's death reported that it was intentional, with one paper calling it "a strange case of suicide" caused by "a temporary aberration of mind." Within three days, John Hoadley had persuaded the coroner's jury to modify its verdict. "To correct any erroneous impressions drawn from their verdict of 'suicide,'" the five jurors explained in the *Evening Post* that they had learned since the inquest of Malcolm's "boyish whim" of sleeping with a pistol under his pillow: "We believe that his death was caused by his own hand, but not that the act was by premeditation or consciously done [which] goes to clear the reputation of the deceased young man from the imputation of suicide." Along with this notice, the *Post* printed a statement from Dr. Osgood attesting that Malcolm had been known to handle his gun "sometimes too freely, and with something of the boyish recklessness of a newly-made soldier," but that he was a "cheerful, upright, affectionate youth," whose face in death was entirely "placid and free from mark or passion or despair."[48]

Anxious to absolve Malcolm of charges of insanity and suicide, John Hoadley sent these two items to Boston newspapers along with a long eulogy asserting that "suicide, voluntary self-destruction, was in his case impossible" because he was a "manly, engaging" youth of unfailing sweetness and gentleness who enjoyed "bright business prospects, good social position, [and] the love of all who knew him, not one of whom even suspected him of a wrong action or evil thought."[49]

John Hoadley's account of Malcolm's last hours took on a more sentimental coloration than Sam Shaw's earlier report: "He was out until three o'clock in the morning of the night before his death; but he had never been in the slightest degree under the influence of liquor; and his manner as he kissed his mother, who was sitting up for him, sat down by her side, put his arm round her neck, begged her pardon for keeping her up so long, promised not to do so again, and told her all about the manner in which he had spent his evening, must have proved to her his innocence, his purity, and his truth, and must give assurance to her wounded heart that her darling boy never harboured a single thought prompting to self-destruction." But an uncle's consolations cannot erase the pain a mother feels when she outlives her child, or wash away the guilt of a father whose last words to his son were harsh reprimands.[50]

At the end of the month, Herman and Lizzie went to Arrowhead to visit Allan. "They feel poor Mackie's loss deeply," their friends and relatives agreed. Hoping a trip would distract them from their grief, Allan invited Herman and Lizzie to spend ten days at Arrowhead, and Richard Lathers gave them a tour of Abby Lodge, the lavish estate he was building right across the road. Revisiting the Berkshires, which were full of memories of Malcolm's childhood, was painful for the Melvilles.[51]

As often happens in the case of a sudden, violent death, those closest to the deceased go into shock, and the death seems a nightmare from which they will awaken any moment. In the days and weeks closely following the event, Herman and Lizzie appeared reasonably composed. When Kate Gansevoort visited the Melvilles before Thanksgiving, she reported that "they all feel Malcolm's death but the knowledge of its not being a crime mitigates their grief."[52]

Death was never far from their minds. Bad dreams alternated with fleeting fantasies that Malcolm might return, that his death might somehow be a terrible mistake or misunderstanding, a cruel joke, or a bid for their attention that would soon be explained away. The shock, bewilderment, and sorrow never left them; they simply buried them deeper in their hearts.

For the rest of his life, Melville would brood over the sins of omission and commission that had led up to Malcolm's death, trying to imagine what he could have done differently, but no matter how hard he tried, he could not imagine how to change the outcome of that fateful evening. However he turned it over in his mind, it always ended tragically. His poem "The Apparition," which was written in response to an explosion that killed numerous Union soldiers and almost killed Pittsfield's hero Frank Bartlett, seems the perfect epitaph for this *annus horribilis*:

> So, then, solidity's a crust—
> > The core of fire below;
> All may go well for many year,
> But who can think without a fear
> > Of horrors that happen so.[53]

In this haunting tintype dated 1868, Melville's eyes mirror the tragedies of the 1860s.

AGONIES THAT OPERATE UNSEEN

Melville may have believed superficially that his son had been devoured by the nameless hor-
ror that lurked in the labyrinth of the city, but deep down he feared that the monster wore his
own face. Repressed grief and denial took their toll on members of the family. Herman was
laid up until Christmas with a "Kink in his back," Lizzie began to suffer intermittent ner-
vous spells and neuralgia, and Stanwix, as though to drown out the imagined pistol shot and
the inner voices accusing him of contributing to his brother's death, began to suffer from the
deafness that would plague him for the rest of his life.[1]

On the surface, life returned to normal after Malcolm's death. In November, Thomas
Melville was appointed governor of the Sailors' Snug Harbor, a retirement home for seamen
comprising dormitories, an elegant Seaman's Chapel, a domed Renaissance Memorial Church
and Music Hall, and the "Front Five," a row of Greek Revival buildings designed by the architect Minard LaFever. Originally established in the Bowery by the ex-privateer Robert Randall
in 1831, Snug Harbor had moved to the north shore of Staten Island, overlooking Kill Van
Kull. An inexpensive ferry ride from the Battery, Staten Island, dotted with farms, boasted a

diverse population that ranged from a thriving colony of free blacks who harvested oysters from rich offshore beds to wealthy merchants from Manhattan who had built weekend homes in fashionable New Brighton.[2]

With its impressive classical buildings, stately trees, broad lawns, and lush formal gardens, Snug Harbor was a "nice berth" for a retired merchant captain. As governor, Tom was provided with a commodious mansion and received a salary of $2,000 a year, which he was told might soon be doubled by the trustees. When he invited his mother and sisters to move to Staten Island and keep house for him, Augusta accepted, but Maria declined, saying that at "threescore & ten & over," she preferred to "remain snug at home through the cold winter months" and that she had just turned down a "very earnest" invitation from Herman and Lizzie to move to Twenty-sixth Street.[3]

The Melvilles now had quite an orbit in which to travel: New York and Staten Island, Albany and Gansevoort, Boston and Pittsfield. Across Holmes Road from Arrowhead, where Allan and his family lived, Richard Lathers's Abby Lodge was "even grander than Winyah, with many balconies and bay windows, a music room, a picture gallery, and a solarium-greenhouse where grapes could be grown."[4]

Shortly after Tom had assumed the governorship of Snug Harbor, he began courting Catherine Bogart, the daughter of New York's chief medical examiner, and on June 6, 1868, they were married. With the aid of "strengthening cordials" sent by Herman and Tom, Mother Melville, who had been under the weather all spring, rallied in time to attend the wedding. After the ceremony, the party of thirty traveled via carriages and ferry to a reception held at Winyah, where they celebrated with claret punch and cake and danced to "the famous Orchestrian," a popular twenty-two-piece musical ensemble.[5]

Malcolm's absence was painfully apparent at family gatherings, but Herman and Lizzie were also constantly beset by other reminders of their loss. It was an era when Alice Cary, Elizabeth Stuart Phelps, and others were creating a happy literature of death, which portrayed deceased infants and children living in cozy houses and tending pretty gardens in Heaven while they waited for their loved ones to join them there. Every newspaper and magazine was publishing these sentimental poems, and Lizzie clipped one titled "The Fount of Bitterness" from the *Boston Evening Transcript* to file with her collection of newspaper verses. According to this poem, the mourner who was nursing the "heart of bitterness that craves relief in overflow" might find solace in imagining the dear departed fishing in "Eden's glorious streams." Lizzie became intrigued with spiritualism, but there is no evidence she ever attempted to establish contact with the son she mourned.[6]

On July 15, 1868, Guert Gansevoort died, and soon afterward, Melville's old friend George Adler died in the Bloomingdale Asylum, a victim of a mental disorder. Adler was buried in the graveyard beside Trinity Church, and Guert was buried in the family plot at Albany Rural Cemetery. Augusta and Tom had recently had the remains of their father and their brother Gansevoort moved nearer to their uncle Herman's grave, and Kate and Herman visited the plot to see about having a monument erected. Kate sent Melville a photograph of an ornate mausoleum a few weeks later, and he wrote a flirtatious reply, comparing her to a rose and pretending to be worried that Lizzie might catch him writing to her—an indication that he had not lost all his mirth despite the settled sorrow in his heart.[7]

In the beginning of September, Lizzie took Bessie and Fanny to Boston for a visit, while Stanwix, who was suffering from a bad cold, stayed in New York, where he was still working as a clerk in Allan's office. Hope Shaw was worried about Lizzie, but the exact nature of her concern is not clear: "Mrs Helen Griggs called here and I had a full and plain discourse with her about not writing to Mrs Melville, & giving her sympathy for her distress relating to her husband when all Mrs M asks [is] a little sympathy from her friends." It is hard to tell whether her reference to Lizzie's difficulties relates to Herman's health or his bad treatment of her.[8]

The year 1868 drew to a festive close when nine Melvilles and eight Bogarts converged for Christmas dinner at Snug Harbor. Maria, who had recently made a whirlwind tour to see her seven children and six of her seven grandchildren, reported that Snug Harbor seemed to be "a very social place little family whist parties, private Billiard tables, or I should say perhaps Billiard tables in private houses—are very general." Herman and Lizzie stayed the night, returning to the city on December 26 to give a party for Lizzie's nephew Oakes Shaw, who bore an uncanny resemblance to Malcolm.[9]

In some ways, Mother Melville kept the family going after Malcolm's death. She saw herself as the quintessential mater familias who, like the sun, controlled the orbits of her satellites, and her regular visits to Manhattan, Staten Island, Albany, and Pittsfield drew the family circle tighter. To Herman and Lizzie, whose hearts were scarred by grief and conflict, Maria's fierce energy, which had once seemed so intrusive, may well have felt supportive at this point. Maria, moreover, was aging gracefully, and now that her children and grandchildren were old enough to be responsible for themselves, her old playfulness and coquetry re-emerged, making her much more fun to be around.

Outwardly, Melville followed his normal routine of going to the Custom-House each day, reading and writing poetry when he could steal some time from office drudgery. In the evenings he read, or played backgammon with Lizzie, or went over to Evert Duyckinck's place for brandy and conversation. Inwardly he was brooding on moral and spiritual questions that would find expression in *Clarel* and *Billy Budd*. He read Jeremy Taylor's *The Rule and Exercises of Holy Dying*, in which he underscored a vivid description of the tortures a troubled conscience can inflict on a man, and noted that it was much nobler to be driven to despair by guilt than to be "a careless merry sinner."[10]

At the end of the winter, Stanwix decided to go to sea. After working as a clerk in Allan's office, he had apprenticed himself to a dentist whose son was a friend of his, but his recurrent deafness made working in a dentist's office difficult. Although Herman and Lizzie were not pleased at the idea of sending their surviving son off around the world, they gave their consent because they were certain that "*one* voyage to China [would] cure him of the fancy." Tom recommended the *Yokohama*, and on March 31 a flotilla of anxious Melville women descended on the vessel. Captain Paul, who was nothing like the sadistic sea captains described by Herman in his early books, promised that Stanny would share a room with three other gentlemen's sons who had signed on for the voyage, and Lizzie and Augusta decided they liked the old skipper. Saying good-bye to her only living son cannot have been easy for Lizzie when, on April 4, he sailed for the Far East.[11]

Almost two years to the day after the conversation with Dr. Bellows that sent her back to Herman determined to hold their marriage together, Lizzie was so moved by one of Bellows's Sunday sermons that she wrote a verse commentary on his chosen text:

> II Timothy, 4th chap. 7th verse
> "Hold on," my soul, with courage for the "fight"
> "Hold out" my feet, the weary "course" to run
> "Hold fast" my faith, bring patience to the "rack"–
> Oh God, thou knowest each hour of need! look down,
> Give thine own help for courage, strength and faith,
> Or never may we win the victor's waiting crown.

The urgency of her prayer suggests that keeping faith with the Church's teachings was important to Lizzie, but not always easy.[12]

In June 1869, Kate and Henry Gansevoort joined the Melvilles on Staten Island to celebrate Lizzie's forty-seventh birthday, and less than a week later, Herman, Allan, Richard Lathers, and Evert Duyckinck rejoined Tom for the annual trustees' dinner. Tom's life at Snug Harbor was comfortable and pleasant. He liked to show off his lavish hospitality, as did Catherine her exemplary Dutch housekeeping. Maria, who visited Snug Harbor frequently, enjoyed the beautifully landscaped grounds and the elegant guest rooms in the governor's mansion.

As soon as Lizzie felt her "rose cold" coming on, she went to Boston. Herman stayed in New York with Augusta to help look after the girls, leaving her in charge of the household in August while he vacationed in the Berkshires. He stayed at the Curtis Hotel, a stately *grande dame* of a brick building adjacent to the old county courthouse and jail in Lenox where Thomas Melvill Jr. had once been incarcerated for debt. Perhaps he chose not to stay at Arrowhead because it brought back bittersweet memories of Malcolm. At any rate, attending a picnic "at which nearly all Pittsfield was present" made him conscious of the tremendous emotional distance he had traveled since leaving Arrowhead. At fifty, he realized that the halcyon Berkshire summers were past, and he saw himself reflected in William Wordsworth's haunting image: "The marble index of a mind forever / Voyaging through strange seas of Thought, alone."[13]

The Civil War, that "sad arch between contrasted eras," was a watershed. George Ticknor of Harvard felt America had changed so drastically during the war years that "it does not seem to be as if I were living in the country in which I was born." As material progress took the place of spiritual progress, the nation seemed to be moving further away from its ideals, rather than closer. In the America of the 1870s, the quest for utopia took many forms, as myriad religious, political, social, economic, and cultural movements vied to set the moral direction of the country for the remainder of the century and possibly for the century to come.[14]

Despite their dramatic entry into public life during the war, women had made little genuine progress toward full citizenship since the Seneca Falls Convention of 1848 rewrote the Declaration of Independence to include women. In 1867, Elizabeth Cady Stanton had called for an end to "all discrimination on account of sex or race," so that "our government may be republican in fact as well as in form: a government by the people, and the whole people; for the people, and the whole people." But prejudice against women's participation in public life was too deeply ingrained in American society for Stanton's words to be taken seriously by men, and men were still the only ones who could change a system based on their own entrenched privilege and power.[15]

Soon after the war ended, Andrew Carnegie, John D. Rockefeller, and other captains of industry had begun to create a managerial utopia of unbridled corporate profits based on high prices, low wages, and aggressive international trade designed to provide markets for domestic manufactures. To protect themselves, working-class men formed organizations such as the National Labor Union in 1866 and the Knights of Labor in 1869, to put labor's economic and social vision on the national agenda. In his campaign for an eight-hour workday, the labor leader William H. Sylvis claimed that only "the virtue, the intelligence, and the independence of the working classes" could ensure "the success of our republican institutions." Advocating "equal pay for equal work," he called for the admission of women and blacks to the National Labor Union, and the Knights of Labor followed suit, demanding government ownership of communications and transportation facilities and an end to monopolistic takeovers that crushed small businesses and destroyed the democratic dream.[16]

The unholy alliance of politics and big business threatened to turn John Winthrop's City on a Hill into a bloated Babylon or Rome. One of the most dramatic of the many scandals of this era was the 1867 scheme whereby a group of insiders at Crédit Mobilier, a railroad construction company, set up a dummy company and paid themselves $50,000 a mile to build a railroad line that cost $30,000 a mile. When some members of Congress learned that Crédit Mobilier's director had declared dividends of 348 percent in a single year, they launched an investigation, at which point Crédit Mobilier sold shares of valuable stock under the table to key congressmen, and the inquiry was halted.

An equally dramatic scandal occurred in 1869, during the presidency of Ulysses S. Grant, when Jim Fisk and Jay Gould conspired to corner the New York gold market. They bribed the President's brother-in-law to put a freeze on the Treasury's gold bullion, thus driving the price of gold upward and allowing Fisk and Gould to rake in huge profits hourly. Dozens of investors were ruined before the Treasury released its gold to stabilize the market. The President managed to escape censure by claiming he had been duped by his associates, who appointed their friends to office so that there was little oversight of their unscrupulous machinations. Pundits quipped that both major political parties shared the motto "What's the Constitution among friends?"[17]

The city government of New York had the worst reputation of any in the country for corruption. "To be a citizen of New York is a disgrace," George Templeton Strong wrote in 1868. "Boss" Tweed and the "bloodsuckers" of Tammany, as Henry Bellows called them, allegedly swindled the city of anywhere from $50 million to $200 million and silenced honest citizens by threatening to raise their tax assessments if they spoke up against corruption. Relentlessly hounded by *Harper's* cartoonist Thomas Nast and the editorial staff of the *Times*, the 240-pound William Marcy Tweed was indicted on 220 criminal charges. His attorney, David Dudley Field, had successfully defended the notorious Jim Fisk, but nonetheless, Tweed was convicted on 204 of the charges.[18]

In the late 1860s and early '70s, citizens hopeful of cleansing the city of its myriad social and economic evils formed neighborhood-improvement organizations such as the West Side and East River associations, and established philanthropic institutions such as Louisa Lee Schuyler's New York State Charities Aid Association, which was designed to improve the working and living conditions of the lower classes. When Mark Twain visited the city in 1867, he was shocked to discover that 100,000 people were living in cellars and that tenements built for eight families "swarmed with two or three hundred persons." The perilous state of the city's multiplying millions was graphically depicted in such realistic fictions as Junius Browne's *The Great Metropolis* and Matthew Hale

Smith's *Sunshine and Shadow in New York*, which added reformist overtones to the urban novel so popular in the 1840s.[19]

City planners saw public works as a means of improving the moral climate of the city. Broadway was widened, and an elevated railway was constructed to relieve the notoriously congested traffic on the streets and to enable more people to avail themselves of the incomparable attractions of the great Central Park that the poet William Cullen Bryant had originally proposed to serve as the "health-breathing lungs of a great city." Frederick Law Olmsted, co-designer of the park with Calvert Vaux, envisioned it as an urban pastoral utopia, a "simple open space of greensward" surrounded by a "depth of wood" where people could assemble with "evident glee in the prospect of coming together, all classes largely represented, with a common purpose not at all intellectual, competitive with none ... all helping to the great happiness of each."[20]

Before long, however, upper-class New Yorkers grew tired of being driven through the park's ten miles of fashionable carriage drives every afternoon to avoid meeting members of "the lower orders," and they began describing Olmsted's Eden in terms reminiscent of William Bradford's "howling wilderness." To them, the park was not a place of refuge for countless numbers of homeless people, most of them law-abiding and nonviolent, but a dark forest haunted by savages who preyed on middle- and upper-class New Yorkers. To make the area around the park more inviting to cultivated people, the city fathers proposed flanking the park with two spectacular museums, the American Museum of Natural History and the Metropolitan Museum of Art. When the opening of the museums in the mid-1880s failed to stop the accelerating flight to the suburbs, Olmsted's noble dream, to turn New York into a cultured but democratic city instead of a mere nerve center of commerce and capital, appeared to be doomed.

Melville knew the Celestial City could come into being only through the alchemy of art. He was composing a poem that would take him on a spiritual quest that led eastward toward Jerusalem, the birthplace of the Western world's three great religions.

Books were Melville's spiritual refuge from what Matthew Arnold called, in his poem "Empedocles at Etna," that "root of suffering in himself, / Some secret and unfollowed vein of woe, / Which makes the time look black and sad to him." Arnold's tragic hero appealed to Melville. To be serving his country in one of the least heroic jobs imaginable was a strange fate for a man who aspired to be an epic poet. He was a genius surrounded by mediocrity, whose job kept him financially afloat. Still, there were times when he enjoyed working at the waterfront. He liked watching the ships glide into the harbor against the backdrop of the majestic Palisades, listening to the rough lingo of the seamen and the many languages spoken by sailors from around the world, and swapping stories with men whose adventures reminded him of his own youth at sea. Amid the bustle of the docks, Melville did what he had always done; he found his own "insular Tahiti" and moored there for psychic and artistic survival, transcending the daily tedium of his life through the energy of his imagination.[21]

Melville often found mental dialogues with fellow writers more stimulating and more satisfactory than actual conversations, and Matthew Arnold's words often echoed his own thoughts. "There is more power and beauty in the well-kept secret of one's self and one's thoughts, than in the display of a whole heaven that one may have inside one," Arnold wrote in his *Essays in Criticism*. When he confessed that "the literary career seems to me unreal, both in its essence and in the rewards which one seeks from it, and there fatally marred by a secret absurdity," Melville noted: "This is the finest verbal statement of a truth which every one who thinks in these days must have felt." Arnold's observation that talented temperaments who seek perfection can be productive even when a "mysterious malady" makes work "the most intolerable of tortures" also hit home, and in the margin, Melville jotted, "So is every one influenced—the robust, the weak—all constitutions—by the very fibre of the flesh, & chalk of the bone. We are what we were made."[22]

In September of 1869, the "neuralgia & weakness" that had overtaken Lizzie soon after Malcolm's death flared up again. Although she was considerably cheered up by Stanny's letter from Shanghai saying that he felt well and liked the sea "even better than he thought he would," she was not well enough to entertain Peter and Susan Gansevoort when they visited New York in October. Lizzie was never too sick not to worry about Herman, however, and prior to the arrival of the Gansevoorts, she cautioned Susan not to "tell him that I said he was *not well*—but if you think he looks well, I hope you will tell him." Her spirits were low when Mother Melville arrived for the holidays, partly because she missed her own mother, but she rallied and enjoyed the turkey her brothers had sent down from Boston.[23]

The Melvilles spent a quiet Christmas and New Year's worrying about Stanny, who had not written since September. It was not until February, when he sent them a newspaper clipping about himself from London, that they learned he had jumped ship in England. "Poor Cousin Lizzie," wrote Kate Gansevoort. "She will be almost broken hearted. Such is life & if boys are not boys in their childhood they will run away & explore for themselves when they should be preparing themselves for the duties of life."[24]

With both sons gone and their daughters suddenly turning into young ladies, Herman and Lizzie felt their lives were flying by. Bessie was now seventeen, and on March 2, Fanny turned fifteen. As a birthday present, Melville gave her *The Buried Cities of Campania: or, Pompeii and Herculaneum* by W. H. Davenport, a volume he found in an antiquarian bookshop while he was stocking up on philosophy, poetry, and travel books about the Near East.[25]

One day on his way to the office, Melville strolled into the Gansevoort Hotel at the corner of Little Twelfth and West streets to buy tobacco, and on a whim he asked the salesclerk what the word *Gansevoort* meant. When the young man replied that he had no idea, a bystander answered, "This hotel and the street of the same name are called by a very rich family who in old times owned a great deal of property hereabouts." Their ignorance of the hero of Fort Stanwix "aroused such an indignation in [Melville's] breast" that he could not respond, and, in "the philosophic privacy" of the District Office, he moralized "upon the instability of human glory and the evanescence of—many other things."[26]

Perhaps aware that Melville was feeling the transitoriness of human existence, John Hoadley arranged for him to have his portrait painted by Joseph Eaton. The family treated Melville's sitting for the portrait as a great event, and when it was done, Allan and Jane threw a party in Herman's honor and displayed the handsome painting on their piano for the guests to admire. It was eventually hung in the Melvilles' back parlor, where it peered from the shadows of the room and frightened their granddaughter Fanny so much when she was a child that she ran past the doorway without daring to look in.[27]

Stanwix arrived unexpectedly in Boston in mid-July, the day before Lizzie was scheduled to arrive there, and stayed with the Griggses. He looked robust, much taller and stouter than before, and everyone was pleased to see that the seafaring life had matured him. Herman remained in New York until mid-August, when he and Lizzie took the train to North Conway, New Hampshire, a place they remembered fondly from their honeymoon. After a week's vacation together, Lizzie went back to Boston, and Herman returned to New York via Gansevoort and Albany. The following weekend he made a quick trip to Boston to see Stanny while Lizzie and her brother Sam were sojourning in Saco, Maine. By the time Stanny arrived in Gansevoort to visit his grandmother, he was talking about going to work for John Hoadley's firm in Lawrence, as he felt he had "a decided taste for machinery."[28]

Melville, who already suspected that machinery was the snake in the New World Garden, was back in New York running up a bill for books designed to help him escape the machine age. He bought *The Literary Works of Joshua Reynolds,* half a dozen of Nathaniel Hawthorne's books, several more volumes of poetry (including the works of Shakespeare and Tennyson), and several books on Near Eastern antiquities. For Christmas that year, he gave Lizzie *Walks about the City and Environs of Jerusalem,* but instead of giving the girls books he needed for his research, he gave Bessie Mrs. Anna Jameson's *Characteristics of Women,* and Fanny *The Holy Grail,* by Alfred Tennyson.[29]

As he passed the age of fifty, Melville enjoyed reading diaries and memoirs as well as philosophy. In his copy of the *Diary Reminiscences and Correspondence of Henry Crabb Robinson,* he double-underscored a passage objecting to the term "self-murder," undoubt-edly because the question of whether Malcolm had killed himself accidentally or intentionally still haunted him. He also carried on a running dialogue with Ralph Waldo Emerson in the margins of his copy of *The Conduct of Life*. On the one hand, he objected to Emerson's fatuous optimism and his disdain for traveling; on the other, he applauded the sage's assertion that the "simple virtues" are the "foundation of friendship, religion, poetry and art," writing a hearty "True & admirable! Bravo!" in the margin.[30]

~~~

An average woman of her time, Lizzie had no art of her own through which to work out her inner struggles, other than that of making a home from which men and children went off to lead their own lives. To keep her mind from dwelling on Malcolm's suicide, she made frequent jaunts to the mountains or seashore, and visited friends and relatives as often as possible. While Fanny helped her mother with the household chores, Bessie was becoming increasingly crippled by arthritis in her hands. Lizzie took care of Bessie and catered to Herman's needs, but she often missed her Boston friends, who liked to read and discuss the latest books, unlike New York matrons, whose favorite topic of conversation was clothes, or Herman, who was prone to bandying about abstruse philosophical concepts and aesthetic theories. She worried about Stannie constantly, especially since he had changed his mind about settling into a man-ufacturing job with John Hoadley's firm and gone west, to try his fortunes in Sedgwick, Kansas.[31]

In April 1871, Henry Gansevoort died during a recuperative voyage to Nassau, and Kate, who had gone down to nurse him back to health, had to bring his body home. She sent Henry's overcoat to Herman, but he preferred to wear his comfortable old coat on his daily walks in Central Park, so Henry's coat hung in a closet until Lizzie asked Kate if she could pass it along to Stanwix, who couldn't afford to buy one for himself.[32]

Herman and Lizzie went to New Hampshire again that summer for their vacation, and in the fall, Lizzie's brothers went to Paris to bring back for burial the body of their friend William Rounseville Alger, because Alger, who had died incurably insane, had no family. Melville purchased and read Alger's book *The Solitudes of Nature and of Man, or The Loneliness of Human Life*, making particular note of passages that linked solitude to the intellectual life.[33]

At a time when Melville was brooding on the great unsolved mysteries of life and death and concentrating all his creative energy on producing another major piece of writing, the words of Beethoven's "Heiligenstadt Testament" had special resonance for him: "I was nigh taking my life with my own hands," the great composer had written, "but Art held me back. I could not leave the world until I had revealed what lay within me." As long as Melville was writing, he had a reason for living and a way of holding on to the separateness and autonomy he valued so much.[34]

Despite his need for solitude, Melville came out of his isolation to celebrate Christmas with the family at Snug Harbor. Mother Melville, that "most remarkable old lady," looked "well and bright," but Lizzie, on whom Malcolm's death weighed more heavily than usual during the holidays, felt "as much of sadness as gladness, and the places left vacant by the dear ones who have 'gone up higher' seem more empty still." Tom served up a "bountiful and luxurious banquet" at "a big table, belted round by big appetites and bigger hearts," the largest of which belonged to the host, who took great delight in seeing family members enjoying themselves so heartily. Unfortunately, Tom's extravagant parties brought him a reprimand from Snug Harbor's trustees when a clerk accused him of misappropriating food from the corporate larder for his personal use. Although the ensuing investigation revealed no evidence of intentional dishonesty, the trustees adopted new accounting procedures to guard against such lapses.[35]

The year 1872 brought Melville new sorrows. In February, Allan, who had been battling tuberculosis for some time, suffered a collapsed lung and died in great agony, leaving his wife and children heartbroken and their household without its "rudder." As he passed into "the unknown world of spirits," Allan looked "so young & so fair" that no one could quite believe he was really dead. For Herman, the death of his churlish but devoted younger brother meant the loss of the man who had been his partner in everything from negotiating book contracts and arguing over politics to visiting the front in the middle of the war and attending Saturday suppers at the Century Club.

Weakened by grief, Maria fell ill after Allan's funeral. Shortly after this, Captain John D'Wolf died at ninety two, and on April 1, Maria, who had seemed so full of life a year earlier, died in her eighty-second year. True to form, she had left detailed instructions for her funeral, and everyone had to agree that her choosing to be laid out in a white alpaca dress and tulle cap was a stroke of genius. Kate Gansevoort's weary question "How many more of those I love must I see buried?" spoke for the entire family. Herman, whose relationship with his mother had been a source of much hurt and anger in the past, but one of much warmth and affection in recent years, was deeply affected by her death, especially coming as it did so soon after the others.[36]

Lizzie, meanwhile, had been trying to recover the tinted photograph that Herman had presented to Malcolm's regiment after his death. Although the company had been disbanded years earlier and its effects sold or stored in Albany, Herman managed to trace the portrait to the home of a newly married couple who had purchased it in a secondhand shop to place among various knickknacks expressive of the families' collective identity. It was the fashion for middle-class Victorians to display stereopticons featuring views of natural monuments, city landmarks, and Civil War battlefields alongside family photographs, reproductions of artworks, personal mementos, and photographs of men in uniform. As the young couple had no relatives in the war, they had placed an unknown soldier's picture on their mantel to symbolize their patriotism, so they readily accepted Herman's offer to exchange it for a more valuable, handsomely framed watercolor showing another unknown young soldier.[37]

The search for Macky's photograph, which was made even more meaningful by its seeming absurdity to outsiders, drew Herman and Lizzie together. For his fifty-third birthday, Lizzie gave him a copy of Nathaniel Hawthorne's novel *Septimius Felton; or The Elixir of Life*, which Una and the poet Robert Browning, who had become a friend of the Hawthornes during their sojourn in Rome, had transcribed for posthumous publication, and taking the two girls with them, they celebrated their silver wedding anniversary with Allan's grieving family in Pittsfield.[38]

When Herman returned to work, Lizzie went to Boston to see her mother, then to Quebec for a brief holiday with her brother Sam, who could not get over his shock at seeing "how generally feeble she is, and prematurely old." The excursion somewhat relieved the respiratory ailment from which Lizzie was suffering, and by November, when the weather grew cold and the pollen disappeared from the air, she was feeling strong enough to withstand the news that she had lost $5,000 worth of property in a Boston fire. To offset Lizzie's loss of the $500 in annual income from the property, Kate Gansevoort sent her a check for that amount, along with a belated anniversary gift, a silver soup ladle. The gifts reached Herman in New York while Lizzie was away, but he was so ill with an influenza virus that attacked his eyes that he had to ask Bessie to write a thank-you note for him. When Lizzie came home a week later, she thanked Kate and told her she was frustrated by Herman's being so absorbed in his work that "all the *financial* management" fell on her. With Christmas approaching, she was sliding into her annual holiday depression; she wrote Kate that "the losses in our family circle come home forcibly at these anniversary times."[39]

In 1872, with the economy in recession, Melville was afraid he would be transferred or even dismissed from his job, even though so far he had survived periodic purges because of his unimpeachable honesty. John Hoadley offered to put in a word for him with commissioner George Boutwell, and his letter is a well-deserved tribute to Melville:

> Proud, shy, sensitively honorable, –he had much to overcome, and has much
> to endure; but he strives earnestly to so perform his duties as to make the
> slightest censure, reprimand, or even reminder,–impossible from any superior–
> Surrounded by low venality, he puts it all quietly aside, –quietly declining of-
> fers of money for special services, –quietly returning money which has been
> thrust into his pockets behind his back, avoiding offence alike to the corrupting
> merchants and their clerks and runners, who think that all men can be bought,

and to the corrupt swarms who shamelessly seek their price; –quietly, stead-fastly doing his duty, and happy in retaining his own self-respect.

He ended with a plea, not for "advancement or promotion [Melville] does not seek," but for security against removal, especially now that Mrs. Melville's property had been destroyed in the Boston fire.[40]

In February 1873, about the time his parents feared they would never hear from him again, Stanwix returned home after wandering through Arkansas and Mississippi to New Orleans before boarding a steamer bound for Havana. From Cuba he had gone to Costa Rica and, with two fellows he had met along the way, trekked through Nicaragua until they all contracted fever and one of the young men died. Stanwix and his remaining companion buried him on the beach, wondering which of them would be next. Eager to leave Central America, Stanwix joined a naval surveying expedition, but the schooner on which he shipped to Aspinwall was wrecked in a heavy gale just as it reached port, and he lost everything, including all his clothes. He ended up in the hospital, and as soon as he recovered, he came home.[41]

Intending to stay in New York "forever," Stanny resolved to give dentistry another try. He apprenticed himself to a Dr. Read, but after little more than a month on the job, he realized he had become too nearsighted for a career in dentistry, and his deafness had returned to plague him. "Fate is against me," he wrote Grandmother Shaw just before he went to California.[42]

Melville, meanwhile, had been laid up with a "sudden & severe illness" for almost two months, and Lizzie had exhausted herself taking care of him. Afflicted with her own recurrent nervous condition and resigned to the fact that Stanny was possessed by "a demon of *restlessness*," she sublimated her sadness in elaborate preparations for Oakes Shaw's graduation from Harvard, joining Bessie and Fanny in "dressmaking with all our might" to drive down her own demons.[43]

By late May, Herman had completely recovered and gone back to work. While he was at the office and the girls were at school, Lizzie was alone most of the day, and she looked forward to visits from Kate Gansevoort, who often came to the city to shop. "When Herman is gone all day, or the largest part of it, the house seems utterly deso-late–it is quite a new sensation for me to have the days seem so *long*–We are counting the days for going to Pittsfield and think with longings of the refreshing breezes from the hill-tops," she wrote her cousin.[44]

In the years since their near-divorce, the Melvilles had apparently mellowed toward each other. It's quite possible that in 1867 Lizzie had delivered the kind of ultimatum that the temperance literature of the day recommended, and that her brother Sam, of whom Herman had always been very fond, by appealing to Melville's considerable pride, had succeeded in negotiating some kind of agreement with him on Lizzie's behalf. Whatever passed between the various parties during the crisis, it seems that after Lizzie decided to give Herman a second chance, he tried to be a decent husband. As Melville grew to prefer the companionship of the woman with whom he shared unfathomable sorrow to the false consolations of the bottle, the *Sturm und Drang* of 1867 faded, becoming little more than a hellish memory.

~

The year 1873 was a bleak one for the country economically, with a stock market panic forcing some six thousand small businesses to close and thousands of people to take to the streets to look for work or beg for food money. Despite the deepening depression, Herman and Lizzie had "a *delightful* visit" at Arrowhead in August, "walking, or driving, or sitting out doors . . . as if we could not get enough of the reviving air, after being nearly suffocated in the heat and *smell* of New York."[45]

The fall even brought vicarious romance to the Melvilles, as their niece Milie became engaged to Willie Morewood, and Kate Gansevoort announced that she and her longtime beau, Abraham Lansing, were finally going to be married. However, the Melvilles could not attend the wedding, as Herman was unable to "leave his post at this very pressing time of business."[46]

Kate and Abe, who had known each other all their lives, had been engaged on and off since 1862. Abe was a businessman of solid Dutch stock of whom Kate's father approved, and he relished the "incomparable Kate's" eccentricities as much as Herman did. Melville, having always been a little smitten with his tart-tongued but good-hearted cousin, welcomed Abe as a potential ally in teasing her, but Kate was not intimidated by them. "Poor fellow," she teased Abe, "even Cousin Herman says if you are not happy it will be *my fault*–how cruel always to blame we poor women!!!" Married when she was in her forties, Kate suffered a series of miscarriages and did not have children. She showered Bessie and Fanny with gifts of clothes and jewelry, and listened impartially to confidences from both Herman and Lizzie.[47]

A force to be reckoned with in Albany, Kate was known not only for her wealth and power, but also for her generosity to local charities. In her later years she developed a few eccentricities. When electric trolleys replaced horse-drawn cars and the motormen no longer stopped right in front of her house but sped right by to the stop on the corner, she planted herself in the middle of the track and forced the car to come to a halt. Once inside, she refused to pay the fare because the newfangled vehicles were shaking plaster from the walls of her house, forcing her to pay for repairs. She was such a charming character, however, that friends even put up with her bizarre habit of setting a place at her table for departed relatives.[48]

In March 1874, Herman and Lizzie received word that with George Nourse's help, Stanwix had found a job on a sheep ranch in California and was making $25 a month. In June, young Maria Gansevoort Melville and Willie Morewood were married at Snug Harbor, where the wedding guests were treated to a feast of "salads & tongue sandwiches Strawberryies [*sic*] & Cream, Champagnes &c." Kate Lansing remarked that everyone "looked well as they always do," and that "the Melville Clan was strong powerful & very defensive." Such joyous occasions sharpened their grief and aroused anxiety for their surviving children.[49]

In October, Susan Gansevoort died, and in accordance with her wishes, Kate Lansing sent Fanny and Bessie one hundred dollars each to buy a black silk dress for the funeral. Lizzie wore her black mourning dress constantly these days, but in her later years she would not allow her granddaughters to wear black ribbons in their hair, and insisted on bright colors. Almost immediately after his wife's death, Peter Gansevoort's health began to deteriorate, but before he reached his ninetieth birthday, he gave his nephew $1,200 to help defray the cost of publication of his new book.[50]

Shortly before Christmas, Stanwix, who had been in California seeing "more of the ways of the world" for the past eighteen months, wrote Hope Shaw that he wanted to come home again, but he was reluctant to return with so little to show for his efforts. Lizzie followed up by urging Stanny to put aside his "compunctions about coming home no better off in fortunes than when he left." He did not stay for long, however. By the end of 1875 he had moved to San Francisco.[51]

That Christmas, Augusta gave a party for eighty Sunday-school children in Gansevoort. In her description of it for Kate and Abe Lansing, her excitement bubbled over:

> Sleigh after sleigh drives up, until a party of eighty fills the rooms which look charming in the Xmas green. The whole lower part of the house is hung with wreathes [*sic*], & garlands, & holly (pepper pods) for the mistletoe. From the north parlor steals out the sweet carolling of the children. The lights burn brightly, the chandelier throws down a glow upon the "Colored Paris Views" on the opera porte folio, with its huge stereoscope. . . . A bell sounds! & the *three* hall doors open as if with one hand. The glories of the Gansevoort S. S. Xmas Tree burst open the dazzled eyes of the little ones! (The little candles twinkled like stars) with its golden balls, & bright reflectors; its waving flags & gorgeous cornucopias; its beautiful bon-bon boxes & its lovely chromos; its colored picture books & its loaded boughs! The children stand spellbound!

A perfect Victorian Christmas, it would be her last.[52]

Gus's letter reveals her "buoyant and cheerful enthusiasm." Although according to Abe Lansing, Augusta "took counsel of her conscience and her God and nothing swerved her from her sense of right and duty," even her religious faith could not turn her "strong, energetic & self reliant will & character" into dogmatism. She loved literature as well as the Holy Bible, and Herman may have gotten the title for his lyric poem "Hearts-of-Gold," which celebrates good-fellowship, from Augusta, as, in a letter to the Lansings, she called the Magi "*hearts* of gold" whose gifts symbolize the priceless life and ministry of Jesus.[53]

Written accounts of the Melvilles' doings become sparser and sparser as the family circle diminished during the remaining decades of Herman's life. Despite the absence of written accounts suggesting that he and Lizzie enjoyed an active social life, Melville was not entirely forgotten during these years, and he and Lizzie may have had more of a social life than we can document. A chance account of the Melvilles dining with the music publisher Gustav Schirmer and his wife in the Dakota apartments on West Seventy-second Street suggests that other such gatherings went unrecorded and that Melville was not as much of a confirmed recluse or misanthropic hermit as some biographers have claimed.[54]

During the winter of 1875–76, Melville worked feverishly on his enormous poem about the Holy Land, and while he was at the office, Lizzie made the fair copy. "Herman is pretty well and very busy," she told her mother, "pray do not mention to *any one* that he is writing poetry—you know how such things spread and he would be very angry if he knew I had spoken of it—and of course I have not, except in confidence to you and the family—We have been in much fear lest his pay should be reduced, as so many others have, but it has not been, so far—it is hard enough to get along at all." Melville evidently was worried that if word got out that he was writing again, especially during office hours, he might not be able to hold on to his job.[55]

Under great pressure at work and impatient to finish his poem, Melville made unreasonable demands on his family. Fanny recalled "the rhythm with which her father would recite, while pacing the floor, certain verses he had written, looking for approbation, she thought, from his wife and daughters." When Lizzie fell behind with the copying, he made Fanny copy and proofread sections of *Clarel,* and years later she complained that her father had roused her out of bed at 2:00 A.M. and thrust printed galleys at her, ordering her to look them over immediately. Having to proofread such a long and difficult poem must have been torture for a twenty-year-old girl whose main interest in life was getting her "beauty sleep."[56]

In a letter to Kate Gansevoort, Lizzie wrote, "The book is going through the press, and every minute of Herman's time and mine is devoted to it—the mere mechanical work of reading proof &c is so great and absorbing. . . . Just as soon as the stress is over, I will let you know & then hope you will come down and make us a good visit." In a "secret" note written after Herman had perused the initial letter, Lizzie describes the strain they all endured:

> The fact is, that Herman, poor fellow, is in such a frightfully nervous state, & particularly now with such an added strain on his mind, that I am actually *afraid* to have any one here for fear that he will be upset entirely, & not be able to go on with the printing–He was not willing to have his own sisters here, and I had to write Augusta before she left Albany to that effect–that was the reason she changed her plan, and went to Tom's–If ever this dreadful *incubus* of a *book* (I call it so because it has undermined all our happiness) gets off Herman's shoulders I do hope he may be in better mental health–but at present I have reasons to feel the gravest concern & anxiety about it–to put it in mild phrase– please do not speak of it–you know how such things are exaggerated–& I will tell you more when I see you.[57]

Augusta's postponed visit never occurred. In late March, she suffered an internal hemorrhage, and when Herman rushed to Snug Harbor and found her lying near death, he could hardly control his grief. On April 4, Augusta, the sister who had poured all her energy into taking care of the family and doing good works for her parish, who was an avid reader of novels and a willing amanuensis for her brother, died. Three days later, while Melville was taking Augusta's body by boat to Albany for interment in the family plot, as he had taken his brother Gansevoort's body some thirty years before, Evert Duyckinck's friend Augustus Gardner died, and Melville was unable to attend his funeral.

Melville was fortunate to have received Peter Gansevoort's support for his book when he did, as shortly after New Year's Day, 1876, in one of her last letters to her brother, Augusta had informed him that their uncle was not expected to live much longer. By a strange stroke of fate, Melville's benefactor died on January 4, the very day Melville signed a contract with G. P. Putnam & Sons for publication of *Clarel*, a poem permeated with images of death, decay, and disillusionment.

These latest losses drove Melville deeper into his work. By the end of April, a greatly relieved Lizzie announced in a letter to Kate Lansing that the book was "at last" set in type and ready to be plated. Although he wanted to remain anonymous, his publisher urged him to put his name on the title page, and Melville agreed. "I shall be so thankful when it is all finished and off of his mind," Lizzie wrote, "and cannot help hoping that his health will improve when he is released from this long continued mental strain."[58]

On June 3, 1876, one month after the Centennial Exhibition of the Declaration of Independence in Philadelphia, *Clarel: A Poem and Pilgrimage in the Holy Land* appeared with this dedication:

By

A SPONTANEOUS ACT

NOT VERY LONG AGO,

MY KINSMAN, THE LATE

PETER GANSEVOORT

OF ALBANY, N. Y.

IN A PERSONAL INTERVIEW PROVIDED FOR THE PUBLICATION
OF THIS POEM, KNOWN TO HIM BY REPORT,
AS EXISTING IN MANUSCRIPT.

JUSTLY AND AFFECTIONATELY THE PRINTED BOOK IS
inscribed with his name.

Augusta would have been thrilled to hold this impressive two-volume set in her hand. Each book was bound in fine-ribbed cloth embossed with a gilt Jerusalem cross cradled by palm trees and crested with three crowns beneath a star stamped on its cover, a handsome variation on the Jerusalem "ensign"–the "palms, cross, diadems, / And star– *the Sign!"* (IV, ii, 68-69) which Agath, the woeful mariner of the poem, has tattooed on his forearm along with drops of blood symbolizing the Crucifixion.[59]

In celebration of *Clarel*'s completion, Lizzie adopted a kitten, and Herman inscribed a set of books for her: "This copy is specially presented to my wife, without whose assistance in manifold ways I hardly know how I could have got the book (under the circumstances) into shape, and finally through the press. Herman Melville June 6, 1876, New York, 104 East 26th St."

Necessarily self-absorbed during the composition and production of *Clarel*, Melville probably never realized what the creation of this monumental work had cost them all. Yet his recognition of her contribution evidently made it worthwhile for Lizzie in the end. Almost single-handedly she would keep her husband's reputation alive until a new generation of readers better attuned to his sensibility discovered him.[60]

In 1864, the poet and travel writer Charles Warren Stoddard, an admirer of Melville and a friend of Bret Harte and Mark Twain, had visited Hawaii looking for evidence of Melville's sojourn there, but he could find nothing. In 1867 he had sent Melville a volume of his poems and a request for information about his Pacific voyages, for inclusion in his *South Sea Idylls*. Thanking him for the poems, Melville answered his question with the terse reply "I do not wonder that you found no traces of me at the Hawaiian Islands," offering no further explanation.[61]

When Mark Twain visited New York in 1868, he called it a "splendid desert" and complained that the pace of life in the city was destructive for the nerves: "There is something in this ceaseless buzz, and hurry, and hustle, that keeps a stranger in a state of unwholesome excitement all the time, and makes him restless and weary." Melville may not have left traces of himself on the sands of Waikiki, but he did want to leave his footprints on the sands of Time. Failing that, he hoped to leave at least one large footprint in the "splendid desert" of New York.[62]

Melville's uncle Peter Gansevoort could easily be mistaken for a grizzled old New England sea captain.

TWENTY-SEVEN

DEVILISH TANTALIZATION
OF THE GODS

"Though I wrote the Gospels in this century, I should die in the gutter," Melville wrote Hawthorne in 1851. Five years later, on the verge of a nervous breakdown, Melville journeyed to the Holy Land in search of spiritual healing as well as physical and mental health. His travels through the labyrinth of biblical history convinced him that Man could not build the City of God on this earth; he must find the Promised Land in his own heart. Clarel: A Poem and Pilgrimage in the Holy Land *springs from Melville's profound disillusionment with the era of Darwin and Marx, of Social Darwinism and the Robber Barons—an era when new scientific discoveries challenged Christian teachings and when many Americans exchanged their faith in God for faith in the almighty dollar.*

Biblical historiography and exegesis underwent a revolution in the middle of the nineteenth century. The French scholar Joseph Ernest Renan had portrayed Jesus as a purely historical figure, not as the incarnate Son of God, and German practitioners of the "Higher Criticism" as David Friedrich Strauss and Barthold Niebuhr interpreted the Scriptures not as the one true Word of God, but as a mosaic whose myriad pieces revealed tantalizing glimpses of the Truth. At the same time, archaeological discoveries in the Near East forced scholars to re-evaluate the place of Judaism and Christianity among the world's religions. When the opening of the tombs of the Pharaohs during the Napoleonic campaigns proved that the ancient Egyptians worshiped one God and believed in an afterlife, students of comparative religions established links between Christian sacraments and pagan rites, challenging the assumption that monotheism was a uniquely Judeo-Christian revelation.[1]

New scientific theories that entered mainstream American thinking after the Civil War exacerbated the religious crisis. Sir Charles Lyell's *Principles of Geology* (1830–33) and Charles Darwin's *On the Origin of Species* (1859), followed by *The Descent of Man* (1871), directly refuted the biblical Creation story. After Lyell's discovery of the stratification of rocks made the opening chapters of the Book of Genesis seem metaphorical, Darwin traced Man's descent from primates, making the belief that God created Man in His own image a ludicrous idea. Evidence that the earth had evolved over eons of time and that humans had evolved by natural selection shook Christendom to the core.

This theological and scientific revisionism had profound implications for both religious and social thought. Matthew Arnold, the English poet and critic, whose *Culture and Anarchy* (1867) was among the works Melville read closely and annotated around this time, warned of the imminent collapse of Western culture. To many, it seemed that everything worth preserving and passing down to future generations would be swept away in a tide of political, social, and religious revolution.

Cut loose from the moral moorings to which the Founders had tied their ship of state, America seemed to be drifting toward moral anarchy. Before the war, religious and social reformers had tried to provide a "counter-friction to the machine" by creating transcendentalist communes, Fourierist Phalanxes, and socialist utopias. Even factory towns such as Lowell and Lawrence were originally designed to be like villages, with time for cultural pursuits and opportunities for operatives to learn new skills, but after the war, as free blacks and successive waves of European immigrants flowed into the overcrowded cities of the Northeast, mill owners realized that they could replace their present labor force with people willing to work longer hours for lower wages in factories that were increasingly unsanitary and unsafe. The model factory towns of New England became William Blake's "dark, satanic mills," where workers were simply cogs in a machine. The Chautauqua Assembly, founded in 1874 by Sunday-school teachers to foster intellectual and cultural enrichment, tapped this earlier utopian spirit, eventually sponsoring settlements in Palestine.

It was not surprising that utopianism found fertile soil in America. Even before 1516, when Sir Thomas More located his *Utopia* in the unexplored western lands, Europeans had been projecting their utopian dreams onto a mythical New World. John Winthrop's

City on a Hill merged smoothly into Jefferson's divinely ordained secular Democratic Republic. As the Puritan commonwealth of true believers was to be the City of God in the Devil's territories, the Enlightenment City of Man was to be a beacon of liberty to the enslaved Old World. Despite stark differences, both visions of America's unique historical mission had messianic overtones that persuaded the drafters of the Constitution to mandate the separation of church and state. Even so, for many Americans, political ideology came to have the force of revealed religion.[2]

As though words could guarantee the spiritual and emotional health of the new nation, the Founding Fathers drafted documents intended to secure hard-won freedoms and shape the way Americans perceived themselves. Thus, when Jefferson wrote the Declaration of Independence, he changed John Locke's "life, liberty, and property" to "life, liberty, and the pursuit of happiness"—a less materialistic but much more nebulous goal. To workingmen, decent housing, food, and clothing for themselves and their families seemed a prerequisite for happiness, but there were no constitutional guarantees that a person could meet basic needs even by working. Despite Jefferson's idealism, material possessions came to be regarded as a sign of individual worth, and those who did not own property were relegated to the lower class and disenfranchised.

In 1868, the British philosopher Herbert Spencer's phrase "survival of the fittest" entered the jargon of American intellectuals, and before long, American sociologists such as William Graham Sumner had married Darwin's theory of natural selection to laissez-faire capitalism and spawned the bastard known as "Social Darwinism." This pseudoscientific theory made it possible to justify class stratification and savage economic inequalities, all but obliterating the Social Contract. If, for example, the 259,000 European immigrants who came through Castle Garden in 1869 failed to find jobs and decent housing, it was obviously not the system's fault, according to Social Darwinists, but the fault of the immigrants themselves.[3]

Privileges based on inherited wealth and American citizenship were taken for granted by those whose money guaranteed them a place in the power structure and access to lobbyists and legislators. During the 1870s and 1880s, while the federal government was giving land grants to the railroads and handing out subsidies to large corporations, monopolies were destroying small companies, and leaders of business and industry were calling their success the "survival of the fittest." Cutthroat competition became a divinely ordained feature of economic life, with the growing gap between rich and poor now seen as natural, inevitable, and, ultimately, right.

The Idea of Progress, which in an individualistic frontier society meant bigness, newness, and profitability rather than moral, cultural, and spiritual advancement, became an article of quasi-religious faith in America. As the culture became more materialistic, increasing numbers of people turned to evangelical sects for direct religious experience and emotional catharsis. Mesmerism and spiritualism, which Melville satirized in "The Apple-Tree Table," enjoyed a resurgence, with table-rapping and séances gaining renewed currency among the hundreds of thousands of people who had lost loved ones to the war.

The postwar era abounded in cruel ironies. Jobless veterans and amputees who resorted to hawking handwritten, crudely bound copies of their personal reminiscences of the war on streetcorners rarely earned enough for food and lodging, while noncombatants such as Evert Duyckinck and Horace Greeley, with access to the means of publication, could make money on lavishly illustrated magazines commemorating the Civil War. The men who were to become the next generation's millionaires—Andrew Carnegie, Cornelius Vanderbilt, Jim Fisk, and J. P. Morgan—got their start by selling obsolete ships, defective rifles and ammunition, shoddy uniforms, and other discarded equipment to the Union Army. As Wall Street operator Daniel Drew put it, there's "good fishing in troubled waters," and Social Darwinism became the angler's creed.[4]

The racial implications of Social Darwinism were as pernicious as its class and gender implications. In 1869 a French visitor, Georges Clemenceau, called Reconstruction "Darwinian" because whites branded as unfit blacks who were unable to thrive in the postwar order. The Ku Klux Klan was waging a counterrevolution in the South by terrorizing black homesteaders and free laborers; some people excused their depredations as "survival of the fittest." *The Atlantic Monthly* announced archly that it was "tired of the Negro question," and by 1876 the Supreme Court had overturned key provisions of the civil rights bills of 1870 and 1871, thereby removing legal protections for black voters. Social Darwinism enabled whites to absolve themselves of responsibility for attacking the endemic racism that ensured that black Americans would remain second-class citizens clinging to the lowest rung of the slippery ladder of wage slavery.[5]

The war destroyed the economy of the South. In the late 1860s, while once-affluent southerners like Charles Gayarre were "starving," northerners like Allan Melville went south to survey the damage and assess the chances of investing in new industries such as petroleum. Out west, meanwhile, with the help of Lemuel Shaw's doctrine of eminent domain and outright gifts from the federal government of millions of acres of land formerly settled by Indians, railroads were gobbling up land, and Congress was making decisions that affected farmers and ranchers for generations to come.[6]

A generation before the German economist and sociologist Max Weber exposed the unholy alliance between the Protestant ethic and the spirit of capitalism, Mark Twain and others were denouncing the crass spirit of the age and the pervasive political corruption at every level of government. Twain's "Revised Catechism," a satirical attack on Boss Tweed that appeared in the *New-York Daily Tribune* in 1871, begins:

Q. What is the chief end of man?

A. To get rich.

Q. In what way?

A. Dishonestly, if we can, honestly if we must.

Q. Who is God, the only one and true?

A. Money is God. Gold and greenbacks and stocks–father, son and the ghost of the same–three persons in one: these are the true and only God....[7]

With big money in power, the politics of the postwar era were vicious and low. The line between lobbying and bribes had become nearly invisible, and political corruption was rampant. The nation's motto seemed no longer to be "In God We Trust," but "Every man for himself, and the Devil take the hindmost." By 1872 the administration was wallowing in so many scandals that no one believed Grant could possibly be re-elected. An unusually large number of qualified people announced their candidacy for Grant's office, among them labor's champion, Horace Greeley, and Victoria Woodhull, the first woman to run for president, with Frederick Douglass as her running mate. Woodhull and her sister, Tennessee Claflin, edited a journal espousing women's suffrage, free love, and socialism, and they were the first to publish *The Communist Manifesto* in the United States. Right before the election, Grant made a public apology for the misdeeds of his administration and promised to clean house, and he won a second term. His re-election prompted the historian Henry Adams to observe, "The progress of evolution from President Washington to President Grant, was alone evidence enough to upset Darwin."[8]

~~~

"Damn fools!" Melville sputtered as he read the newspapers. As his daughter Fanny said years later, he "railed at conditions in the country at large, to anyone who would listen, with much heat and oratory." Clearly, Melville despaired of reversing the drastic changes that swept the nation after the war; instead, he would create a literary witness to the social and political disintegration all around him.[9]

In the early nineteenth century, as smoke blackened the skies over Manchester and Leeds, William Blake had asked whether "Jerusalem"–meaning God's city, not Mammon's–could be built in "England's green and pleasant land." When Melville visited the Near East in 1856, he realized that Blake's "Jerusalem" did not exist in the Holy Land either. In *Clarel: A Poem and Pilgrimage in the Holy Land,* Melville projects his doubts, his skepticism, and his yearning to find a settled faith on the vast canvas of ancient and modern history, composing both a spiritual autobiography and a spiritual biography of

Anglo-American man in the nineteenth century. Half seeker, half cynic, modern man is an Ishmael wandering in the deserts of faith without a guide.

The poem's protagonist is a young American theological student who is searching for love and religious faith in an age of doubt and disillusionment. Open-minded, eager to learn about the world and other people and hungry for belief, Clarel has strong affinities with such characters as Tommo, Redburn, White-Jacket, and Ishmael. Advised by a countryman to temper his "New World's worldly wit" with the "Semitic reverent mood" by encountering "Asia old," Clarel comes to Jerusalem to plunge into "the expanse of time's vast sea." Covered with the dust of travel and weighed down by the conundrums of theology, he arrives at a hostel, eager to purge his soul of "bookish vapors." As he scans the "walled and battlemented" town, Jerusalem's "blank, blank towers," he feels trapped, so he retreats to his room. There he imagines he has boarded a ship that will take him on a dangerous voyage, but he decides he must take the risk, because "To avoid the deep saves not from storm."[10]

In a prayerful mood, Clarel goes to the Church of the Holy Sepulchre and immediately falls under the spell of its "shadowy spaces" and the "haze of mystery" that pervades "the vast nave's azure night," where pilgrims kneel with "small lamps, dispersed, with glow-worm light." This sanctuary provides him with a refuge from the "pedlars of vaunted tricks / Venders [sic] of charm or crucifix" who surround the "miracle-play of haunted stone." Charmed by the "costumes strange" and the "polyglot" of Asian tongues, he stands at the city gate watching a great "human wave" flow into Jerusalem for Easter Week.[11]

As he walks through the crowded, winding streets, wishing the living Christ would appear to him, an elderly man riding a donkey and carrying a Bible introduces himself as "the sinner Nehemiah." An American who has come to the Holy Land from "Narragansett's marge," Nehemiah seems to be "upheld invisibly by faith serene." Clarel hopes he will be the spiritual guide for whom he has prayed, but this "flitting tract-dispensing man" who gives out handbills announcing the Second Coming of Christ and the founding of the New Jerusalem turns out to be more a salesman than a man of faith.[12]

Clarel and Nehemiah "rove the storied ground" together, but Clarel cannot find traces of the Living God in a land where the "Garden of King Solomon" has become "a cauliflower-bed / To serve the kitchens of the town." His tour of the city is not a linear journey, but a succession of forays in and out of alleyways and holy sites, descents into catacombs, ascents to parapets and walls, all of which serve as reminders that history is a heap of ruined empires.[13]

As Clarel roams the city with Nehemiah, he has two wordless encounters with a hunchback whose "responsive look" holds out hope that "minds which from poles adverse have come" can meet. Clarel soon learns that the boy is an orphaned Italian named Celio, who longs to find his "Bice," or Beatrice, but despairs of finding love because of his deformity. He accuses God of standing aside during eighteen hundred years of "enigma and evasion," then renounces his faith and dies mysteriously. When Clarel obtains the boy's journal, he is shocked by the depth of his "negation," and he mourns Celio as a brother and "second self" who asked questions he has never dared to ask.[14]

At the Wailing Wall, Clarel senses that, beneath his feet, the elders sleep their "silent sleep" of centuries in "chambered wells and walls." The precinct of the Temple is "a spot with ruin all bestrown," a "cloaca" through which Clarel must pass to prepare himself for his soul's journey. At the "blind wall" where Jewish women are performing the "Friday rites," he sees a maiden whose eyes seem to "promise Paradise." She is Ruth, the daughter of an American expatriate named Nathan, whom Nehemiah knows. From the start, Clarel is smitten with her "Eve-like face / And Nereid eyes with virgin spell," and after a series of meetings, they become engaged.[15]

Clarel still cannot achieve peace of mind, however. Whenever he thinks of Ruth, the image of the beautiful but deformed Celio clouds his vision, "haunting the air and in the heart." The young Italian's humped back encodes Clarel's sexual ambivalence and his fear that carnal love will turn to lust, making the spiritual union he hopes to achieve in marriage impossible.[16]

Ill at ease, he tours the crumbling city with Nehemiah, encountering many people, including those who will accompany him on his pilgrimage. One of these is a mysterious American named Vine, an artist of unspecified "gifts unique." From the moment he sees Vine, Clarel feels there is "a bond" between them, and many commentators have pointed out that Vine resembles Nathaniel Hawthorne. Vine isolates himself from Clarel and the other pilgrims, either standing off to one side, observing them with "ambiguous elfishness," or absentmindedly stripping bark off twigs or throwing stones on his shadow in a ravine until they form a cairn.[17]

Clarel approaches Vine, yearning for "communion true," but when he hints at the "feminine" and "passionate mood" that makes him want to call Vine "brother," a shadow falls across the shy man's face. Troubled by his "sick" feelings, Clarel berates himself for finding a place in his heart for "such solicitudes apart / From Ruth."[18]

Clarel's ambivalent attraction to Celio and Vine as well as Ruth reflects his longing to break through sexual boundaries to create an inclusive community where male and female, Jew and Gentile, Old World and New, can come together. His marriage to Ruth would bring the orphaned American into a Jewish family, ending the spiritual exile begun by Ruth's grandfather, but sadly, Ruth's father and grandfather have brought a curse on their descendants.

When her father, Nathan, was a child, his father left New Hampshire and traveled west with the pioneers, who left "legacies of farms behind." When he reached Illinois and saw "three Indian mounds / Against the horizon's level bounds," which from a distance resembled the Pyramids, he decided to stay there. Instead of coexisting peacefully with the Indians, Nathan's father drove them from their land, a primal crime that turned farming into an act of rape, not regeneration. In retaliation, "our Mother Earth" vomited rocks down the mountain without warning and killed him. Knowing deep down that the rockslide was caused by the avenging spirits of tribes massacred years earlier, Nathan suffers recurrent nightmares in which he is haunted by an Indian skull peering at him from amid falling boulders.[19]

Even after he shakes off the nightmares, Nathan feels cursed. He embraces deism, then pantheism, but he finds no home in any philosophy or faith. Resigning himself to the penitential toil of tilling "an altered earth," like Adam, he farms to support himself and his widowed mother. When she dies, he finds himself "Alone, and at Doubt's freezing pole," wrestling "with the pristine forms / Like the first man."[20]

Just when he can see no way out of this purgatorial cycle, Nathan meets Agar, a Jewess whose name links her with Ishmael's mother, Hagar, at a grain market and falls in love. He converts to Judaism so they can marry, then sells his land and goes into business and has two children, but he does not feel fulfilled. Nathan has a vision of "the crag of Sinai" behind the wall of "crumbling faith," and he decides "with seed and tillage [to] help renew" and "reinstate the Holy Land" by joining the Zionist movement.[21]

Nathan's story reverses the Puritan myth that cast New Englanders in the role of God's Chosen People in the Promised Land. He is not the unfallen Adam tilling the soil of the New World Garden, but a cursed son whose work has become a constant re-enactment of the Fall. Securing a tract of land on Sharon's plain, Nathan and Agar find themselves neighbors of hostile Arabs who are determined to drive Jewish settlers out of Palestine. Nathan, whose "sires in Pequod's wilds" regarded the Indians as "foes pestilent to God," treats the Arab tribesmen as "slaves meriting the rod," and shortly after Clarel and Ruth become engaged, Arab raiders ambush Nathan and kill him.[22]

The moment he learns of Nathan's death, Clarel goes to Ruth and her mother, planning "to grieve with them and lend his aid," but Talmudic law forbids Ruth to see a Gentile while she and her mother are in mourning. Leaving his ring as a betrothal pledge, he departs disconsolate and walks the streets in a trance. A funeral procession passes him, the pale young woman lying on her flower-strewn bier appearing like a bride decked out to be married to "that Blue-Beard, cruel Death." Frightened by this ominous vision, Clarel joins a band of pilgrims bound for Jesus' birthplace at Bethlehem, hoping that his forced separation from Ruth will at least enable him to resolve his doubts. As Clarel turns his back to the city and heads into the desert, the omniscient narrator stands aloof, like God.

Although Melville initially modeled Book Two of *Clarel* on *The Canterbury Tales*, it differs from Chaucer's poem in that Melville's pilgrims recite their personal stories, not *contes* and *fabliaux*, and much of the poem consists of debates and arguments between the pilgrims and those whom they meet along the way. By juxtaposing characters who voice contrasting attitudes toward life, then introducing a character who strikes a balance between them, Melville gives dramatic form to a kind of Hegelian thesis, antithesis, and synthesis. In creating Clarel and the various pilgrims he meets on his journey, Melville turned himself inside out, exposing myriad selves through the various characters and working dialectically to bring these disparate voices into harmony.[23]

The pilgrim band includes Nehemiah, an insufferably cheerful Anglican priest named Derwent, an embittered Swedish revolutionary named Mortmain, an American adventurer named Rolfe, the reclusive Vine, and a number of interesting minor characters whom they have met along the way. Their guide, Djalea, a Druze from Lebanon, wears a dashing striped dark woolen cloak with a white sash, a white turban, and spurless boots that signify his gentle control of Zar, his mare. His six Bedouin bodyguards manifest such "sacerdotal chivalry" that Djalea is praised by Derwent as a model for the leaders of the world's warring nations.[24]

Of all the pilgrims, the American adventurer Rolfe most appeals to Clarel. Blue-eyed and speaking with Hawthorne's "wizard chord / And forks of esoteric fire" as well as Melville's "illogical wild range / Of brain and heart's compulsive interchange," the tawny-complexioned Rolfe rides "in saddle pommelled high ... Indian-like, in pliant way / As if he were an Osage scout / Or gaucho of Paraguay." An erstwhile mariner, like Melville, Rolfe has sojourned in the South Pacific, where the "curse of poverty is unknown" and people feel a "cordial joy in Nature's sway." After living in the islands, he has become a self-exiled wanderer, unable to readjust to civilization.[25]

To Clarel, Rolfe is like "Rama, whom the Indian sung– / A god he was, but knew it not," because he so successfully balances "Hellenic cheer and Hebraic grief," a "genial heart" and "brain austere," and doubt and belief, while most of the pilgrims and the characters they encounter represent dangerous extremes. Derwent, the Anglican priest, and Mortmain, the Swedish revolutionary, for example, stand at opposite poles in terms of attitude and belief.[26]

Mortmain, who fought in the European revolutions of 1848, saw his idealism betrayed as the revolutionaries adopted the tactics of their oppressors and became tyrants like the ones they had overthrown. Having lost his faith in religion and political systems based on the perfectability of Man, he has become a monarchist. He believes human beings are inherently "vicious" and must have a "king," or "severer" ruler. With his sinister name (*mortmain,* or "dead hand," is a legal term signifying lifelong bondage to a church or corporation), his black skullcap, and his "vehemence too mad to stem,"

Mortmain casts a shadow on the cavalcade. He curses the ocean and the stars—recurrent symbols of transcendence in the poem—for allowing the "black slaver" to cross the seas in service of "Mammon's hate," chants blasphemous hymns to Sodom and Mars, calling the red star "Wormwood," and sips the waters of the Dead Sea, which taste like gall.[27]

Derwent identifies with the playful dolphins he once observed throwing rainbows from their tails; he does not trouble himself with tough theological questions. Mindful that Christ had to be crucified before He could rise again, Clarel finds Derwent's refusal to grapple with the painful imperatives of sacrifice and sorrow irresponsible. As he thinks of Ruth, trapped behind "the ramparts of despair," Clarel finds himself leaning toward Mortmain's bitter pessimism because Derwent's blithe optimism seems so shallow.

Named for William Wordsworth's soft-flowing river Derwent, the genial cleric believes in the beauty of Nature, the benevolence of God, and the essential goodness of Man, but he does not believe in the existence of evil. He skims the surface of things, dangerously blind to the endless struggle between good and evil, which exhausts humanity. By remaining optimistic that man can control the institutions he has devised and shape them for progressive ends, he cannot truly minister to man. Rolfe, by contrast, has come to feel that even the most enlightened, progressive institutions are doomed to fail, and that time is running out for the human race. Neither "Eden nor Athens shall come back: / And what's become of Arcady?" Rolfe asks.[28]

As the pilgrims cross the desert, "Sands immense / Impart the oceanic sense: / The flying grit like scud is made / Pillars of sand which whirl about / True kin be to the waterspout."[29]

In Judea, a "caked, depopulated hell" whose stones are reminders of Cain's murder of Abel, they encounter the geologist Margoth, an apostate Jew and "Hegelized" convert to science who collects and analyzes rocks and shatters the "old theologic myth." Margoth has no reverence for the holy places and scorns the sentimental nostalgia that prevents his companions from envisioning the practical uses to which this vast, undeveloped desert might be put.[30]

Margoth's hammer symbolizes the shattering of religious certainty by new scientific discoveries. His hostility to religion troubles Rolfe, who tells Derwent that Margoth "stuns, and would exterminate / Your creeds as dragons." Like one of Hawthorne's mad scientists, Margoth is a monomaniac. When Mortmain draws a slanted cross and a rock, Margoth scrawls his own defiant message: *"I Science, I whose gain's thy loss, I slanted thee, thou Slanting Cross."* Rolfe warns Margoth that in death he may discover mysteries that science cannot measure, and the narrator observes that the sun and rain and wind will soon obliterate their blasphemous graffiti.[31]

Book Two ends with the melancholy Vine finding Nehemiah's lifeless body washed up on the shore after following his delusory dream of the New Jerusalem straight into the poisoned waters of the Dead Sea. Although Clarel has come to see Nehemiah as a deluded old fanatic, the death of that "friendliest mind / Unfriended" saddens him. As the pilgrims bury Nehemiah, an avalanche of rock sends up a shower of dust, and as a "fogbow" fades from the sky, it takes with it Clarel's hope of finding someone to guide him along the spiritual path.

~~~~~

Book Three opens as the pilgrims are approaching the monastery of Mar Saba through the high desert. The abbey itself is perched high on a mountain, so they must climb sideways "betwixt the wall / And flanked abyss" hearing "the fall / Of stone, hoof-loosened, down the crags." In this austere place, inhabited by an army of solemn monks, they meet a Cypriot wine merchant whose "gay Hellene lightheartedness" cheers the pilgrims up, and a merchant from Mytilene, who tells them that whenever he has to deliver supplies to this gloomy place, he sings this little ditty to himself:

> "Life is not by square and line:
> Wisdom's stupid without folly:
> Sherbet to-day, to-morrow wine—
> Feather in cap and the world is jolly!"

While Clarel half wishes he could be so carefree, he wants more from life than pleasure and jollity.[32]

While they are at the monastery, the pilgrims encounter a number of others, foremost among them the "wretched Agath," whose "weird and weather-beaten face" bears evidence of the ordeal he suffered when he was the pilot of a cursed ship. The lone survivor of a fatal wreck, the misanthropic "Timoneer" has a "bleeding tree" resembling a Crucifix tattooed on his arm, and his terrible story convinces Clarel that true faith depends on "discipline and grief." While Clarel retires to his room thinking of Ruth, the other pilgrims stand before the huge palm tree in the courtyard of the monastery, meditating on Agath's dramatic description of the shipwreck he survived.[33]

As Book Four opens, the pilgrims are joined by the "self-exiled" Ungar, son of a "wigwam maid" and a Maryland Catholic, a Civil War veteran who is fighting as a mercenary with the Turks. With his "high-boned" cheeks and his "long hair, much like a Cherokee's," Ungar cuts an impressive figure. His "brown eyes" reflect the "sad woods" of his native land, "where wild things sleep," and the livid saber slash and blue powder burn on his face symbolize the deep scars inflicted on America by the Civil War.[34]

Possessed of an "Anglo brain" and an "Indian heart," Ungar is a deeply divided man, doubly divided by the Civil War. Although he spoke out against the "Iniquity" of holding slaves "spite the prejudice of kin / And custom," he fought as an officer for the Confederacy, and he rues "the evil day" when brothers fought from "bias" and "bitterness." Under cover of the larger conflict, Union troops pushed westward and took more Indian land than at any other time in the nation's history, wiping out whole tribes in Utah and Colorado in the process, making the Civil War an extension of the fratricidal war waged by the white man against the native peoples since the first settlers landed.[35]

Objecting to Ungar's denunciation of the barbarities of the Anglo-Saxon race, Derwent cites the proliferation of charitable institutions as evidence that the industrialists of the North have good Christian consciences, and Ungar scoffs, "Your alms-box, smaller than your till / And poor-house won't absolve your mill." When Ungar denounces democracy as the "Arch strumpet of an impious age" in whose name the North wrecked the economy of the South, Rolfe argues that America still has enough room to nurture democratic institutions. The "waste-weirs which the New World yields / To inland freshets" and her "vast reserves—the untried fields" will "keep off and delay / The class-war, rich-and-poor-man fray / Of History." Ungar responds by warning that from this class warfare "alone / Can serious trouble spring."[36]

Don Hannibal, a Mexican soldier who lost a leg and an arm in his homeland's fight against United States aggression, shares Ungar's disillusionment. Passing through Palestine in search of a country where he can feel at home, he tells Clarel and the others that the Old World has become a "blest asylum from the New," and says he is going to the East: "Asia for me, Asia will do."[37]

In a prescient passage, Ungar warns that Western industrialism will transform man into "A skilled destroyer" whose power will eclipse that of God, enabling a "new Hun" to growl his imprecations. During the Franco-Prussian War, a well-organized, aggressive Prussian army inflicted a brutal war on France to solidify the German empire. When the Paris Commune, offspring of the French Republic of 1848, was crushed in 1871, militarism triumphed, ushering in a new era in not only European politics but all world history.[38]

When Rolfe asks whether Ungar believes America is doomed, Ungar answers that the "impieties" of America make her "corruption" inevitable. He sees the New World as a debased, fallen Eden, glutted with "material arts" and shrunken to the "dead level of rank commonplace." Ungar predicts that America's "slumberous combustibles" will eventually rebel at being "debased into equality" and rise to plunge America into anarchy. Rolfe argues that without the myth of perfection to kindle "hope's advance," civilization will have "squandered" its "last inheritance." With the "strange look / Of one enlisted for sad fight / Upon some desperate dark shore," Ungar leaves.[39]

At Bethlehem's Church of the Star, Clarel meets a pleasure-loving French Jew from Lyona who has come to Bethlehem because the town has a reputation for pretty girls.

The carefree Lyonese tries to convince Clarel to romp "unabashed in Shushan's bowers" by reciting to him the most erotic passages from the Song of Solomon, but in seminary, Clarel was taught that the Song of Solomon was an allegory of Christ's courtship of the soul, not a love poem. When he tries to rebut the Lyonese by quoting from the commentaries of Saint Bernard, the Frenchman laughs at such pedantry and launches into a paean to the charms of Jewish women. Too shy to tell his companion that he is betrothed to a woman as beautiful as the women he is describing, Clarel tries to steer the conversation away from flesh-and-blood women to a discussion of the aesthetics of feminine beauty, an almost humorous debate in which Melville shows how intellectuality acts as a defense against emotional intimacy.[40]

That night, Clarel shares a room with the Lyonese, whose "rich, tumbled, chestnut hood of curls" is like "a Polynesian's girl's," and he dreams that he is standing at a crossroads between two kingdoms, one ruled by the young sensualist, the other by a "pure pale monk," and that he must choose between them. As he leans slightly toward the spiritual kingdom, "clasping arms" that could belong either to Ruth or to the young French Jew reach out to "detain / His heart from such ascetic range," and he wakes up. As a result of this intentionally ambiguous dream, Clarel concludes that love for men and love for women spring from the same source and are perfectly compatible.[41]

Realizing that erotic pleasures, too, are part of life, Clarel feels ready to embrace sexual love wholeheartedly. Tragically, however, he is fated never to consummate the love he has struggled so hard to accept and enjoy. By forcing the lovers apart, patriarchal religion exacts a cruel sacrifice, doubly orphaning and widowing poor Clarel before he can reach the promised Paradise of woman's love and sexual wholeness.

In a tragic *dénouement* reminiscent of Act Five of *Hamlet*, the surviving pilgrims return to Jerusalem through a graveyard. Noticing some freshly turned soil, Clarel approaches and stands over "two narrow pits," looking at the "twin figures on the ground ... / Folded in cloaks," and is shocked to see the embroidered scarf he had given Ruth as a gift in the grave. The elders inform him that Ruth died of "fever–grief: / 'Twere hard to tell; was no relief," and that soon after, the doubly bereaved Agar died, "babbling of gulls and ocean wide– / Out of her mind."[42]

Clarel curses the elders for parting him from Ruth, and blasts the "blind, blind barren universe" that has blasted him. Then he jumps into Ruth's grave and kisses her lifeless hand. He keeps watch until night's damp chill jars him from his meditation, whereupon he returns to the Holy City in time to see the gray dawn of Ash Wednesday appear over Olivet.[43]

Grief-stricken, Clarel goes through Passion Week numb and unmoved. The "cheerful choral strain" of the Palm Sunday celebration serves only to remind him that Christ will be crucified. On Good Friday he sees in his mind's eye a procession of all those who have died since he arrived in Jerusalem: Celio "in a dampened mirror glassed," Nehemiah "with charnel beard," Mortmain "pallid as a wolf-bone," Nathan "sullen" with "Hades in his eyes," Agar "with such wandering mien / As in her last blank hour was seen," and Ruth so "estranged in face" that he barely recognizes her.[44]

Despite an outpouring of Easter hymns that sounds like a great "hallelujah after pain," Ruth does not "burst the prison" of Death as Jesus did. Whitsuntide brings Clarel no comfort, either, and he follows the Way of the Cross amid a "sluggish" stream of "strangers and exiles," thinking how absurd it is that Man can "wire the world" and talk through cables "far under the sea"—as President Buchanan and Queen Victoria did in 1858—while he receives no "message from beneath the stone" that covers Ruth.[45]

Clarel feels condemned to continue life's journey alone, and in the Epilogue, the poet wonders what can sustain the young man now that his love lies in the grave. If God does not exist, "Science the feud can only aggravate." All that remains is the hope that "death may prove unreal at the last, / And stoics be astounded into heaven."[46]

In a conclusion that seems almost tacked on, the poet—who, unlike the narrator of *Pierre*, has seemed intensely sympathetic to the plight of his characters throughout the poem—points to spring as Nature's evidence of the soul's resurrection:

> Then keep thy heart, though yet but ill-resigned—
> Clarel, thy heart, the issues there but mind;
> That like the crocus budding through the snow—
> That like a swimmer rising from the deep—
> That like a burning secret which doth go
> Even from the bosom that would hoard and keep;
> Emerge thou mayst from the last whelming sea,
> And prove that death but routs life into victory.

Following thousands of lines of knotty tetrameter and intense dialogue, the sudden switch to end-stopped, metronomically regular lines of iambic pentameter sounds insincere.[47]

Most readers preferred platitudes to *Clarel*'s "deep diving," however, and Melville knew his audience. His own mother had once chided him for not being a "Christian" writer like Martin Farquhar Tupper, the British poet whose conventional verses on such abstract topics as Death, Beauty, Friendship, Sorrow, and Love were immensely popular with genteel readers because the glib order they imposed on the chaos of experience reaffirmed their faith. Melville may well have expected to be read one way by pious readers, and "the other way" by those perceptive enough to appreciate rough meter and changes in voice.

Melville handles the tetrameter line with greater flexibility in *Clarel* than he had in "Lee in the Capitol." The shortened epic lines emphasize the constriction of the human spirit in a world governed by science and technology rather than by faith and art, but he enjambs lines with much greater frequency than most poets of his time, and he employs the caesura, or breath pause, skillfully at various points in the line, giving his verse much more variety of phrasing than other long narratives of this period. Even the awkward inversions that many readers find off-putting can be seen as reflective of the hard-fought struggle between faith and reason, God and Satan.

Like Emily Dickinson, Melville deliberately employs slant, or off-rhymes, such as "hearth" and "mirth," "proved" and "loved," "turns" and "Thorns," "search" and "porch," "Word" and "abroad," to convey the dissonance of the times, and his rhyming of words with antithetical meanings, such as "doubt" and "devout" or "malign" and "divine," emphasizes the clash between modern culture and age-old beliefs. His prodigious vocabulary ranges from archaisms to colloquialisms, from the language of religion, historical allusion, and pastoral poetry to the neologisms of science, commerce, and industry, and like Whitman he creates metaphors and epic similes that yoke opposites such as past and present, east and west, nature and city, land and sea, man and God.

As Melville knew, a poem of eighteen thousand lines divided into 150 cantos was "eminently adapted for unpopularity." Despite its many brilliant descriptive passages, sharp characterizations, and provocative ideas, *Clarel* is little read because of its length and complexity, its abstruse references, tortured syntax, and often stilted style. Yet it is a marvelously ambitious poem, indisputably great in its own way.[48]

Few copies of *Clarel* circulated in England, because no British publisher would risk a separate edition of a long, esoteric poem by an unpopular American writer; copies had to be requested from whatever stock Putnam's had on hand. Those who did read the book had mixed reactions. The London *Academy*'s reviewer found it "a book of very great interest, and poetry of no mean order." Noting that the "rugged inattention to niceties of rhyme and metre here and there seems rather deliberate than careless," he advised readers "to study this interesting poem, which deserves more attention than we fear it is likely to gain in an age which craves for smooth, short, lyric song, and is impatient for the most part of what is philosophic or didactic." Another critic, however, complained that he could "not understand a single word" of *Clarel*.[49]

Even American reviewers who were friends and lifelong admirers of Melville's work found *Clarel* bewildering. Edmund Clarence Stedman called the poem "something of a puzzle, both in design and execution," with "no plot" and a style that flows "with a smooth, agreeable current," then "seems to foam and chafe against unmanageable words like a brook in a stony glen." Franklyn B. Sanborn, praising Melville's early novels for their "masculinity," "rich imagination," and "singular picturesqueness," considered

Clarel an unfortunate comedown, and *The World*'s anonymous reviewer—possibly Richard Henry Stoddard, now retired from the Custom-House to pursue a full-time literary career—complained that even the few "bold, clear, and judicious" lines were "lost in the overwhelming tide of mediocrity."[50]

John Hoadley, himself an accomplished versifier, pronounced *The World*'s review "very flippant and foolish in the extreme." By far Melville's most appreciative reader during this period of his life, Hoadley believed *Clarel* would put Melville "on a higher plane than anything he has before written" and fervently wished it would "make him at once rich, famous and happy!" Although *Clarel* was "not easy reading," Hoadley felt it would "grow on thoughtful reading." Unfortunately, however, few readers were willing to stick with *Clarel* as long as Melville's brother-in-law. Tom Melville's query to Kate Lansing, "Have you seen Hermans Book yet & what do you think of it?" expresses the bewilderment of almost everyone who tried to read the poem.[51]

Even though long narrative poems such as Tennyson's *In Memoriam* and *Idylls of the King,* Longfellow's *Evangeline,* and Whittier's *Snow-Bound* were very popular, *Clarel* did not sell because it was ponderous in places and not easy to read. Three years after its publication, Melville would sign a form authorizing the sale of 224 copies of the handsome two-volume edition of *Clarel*—the first and only one—to a paper mill that could pulp books and turn them into something useful. Thus, *Clarel* remains one of the great unread poems of American literature.[52]

By now, Melville did not expect recognition or remuneration for his work. Having written *Clarel* to confront the great spiritual conundrums of the age and to extend his range, Melville would continue to write poetry and one last great work of prose. Having a work in progress is what keeps a writer alive.

Peter Gansevoort's gift of $1,200 did not, as it turned out, even cover publication costs. When Harper's sent Melville a bill for an additional $100 for advertising expenses and distribution of review copies, he wrote Kate Lansing to inquire whether the additional sum came "within the scope of Uncle Peter's design or not," and his cousin sent him a personal check for $100 with her heartiest good wishes for the book's success. Embarrassed to be the object of his cousin's charity, he returned the check to her, but his "Lady Bountiful" was so offended that she sent him another one. Despite receiving an additional bill from Harper's for $84.12 for books he had purchased during the writing of *Clarel,* he held on to the check, then donated the sum to the New York Society for the Relief of the Ruptured and Crippled, most of whom were mutilated veterans of the Civil War.[53]

Since June, Lizzie had been making plans to leave the city to escape the effects of her "rose cold." With a gift from her brother Lem, she arranged a protracted holiday in the White Mountains with the girls, finding "comfortable quarters for Herman during our absence, so as to shut up the house." At the home of the Misses Harnett, who served meals and took in boarders, Melville could dine in company with other people and even entertain friends by prior arrangement. "I think the change will benefit him also—take him out of himself," Lizzie told Kate Lansing.[54]

In August, Melville joined Lizzie and the girls in the mountains, and toward the end of his two-week vacation, they all went to Boston to visit the Griggses and the Shaws. Then Melville returned to his duties in New York, leaving Lizzie and the girls at her parents' house. "Lizzie & the girls are jolly" and "I myself am ever hilarious, & pray sincerely that you & your Abraham may likewise ever be so," he told his cousin Kate.[55]

The Lansings now owned Stanwix Hall, which had closed down when the Panic of 1873 plunged the country into a depression. Now that the economy was improving, Abe wanted to reopen it, and he wanted Melville's suggestion about the name. Melville had strong feelings on the matter, as Stanwix Hall had been built by Peter Gansevoort on the site of Harme Gansevoort's combination home, brewery, and store a year after it burned in 1832. A large commercial hotel that included a restaurant, a ballroom, shops, offices, and a meeting room, Stanwix Hall was so named by Peter in honor of his father's Revolutionary War triumph. Local wags, however, called it "old Harme Gansevoort's brew kettle turned upside down" because of its shiny neoclassical dome.[56]

Melville's nostalgia for past glories increased in proportion to the social and cultural disintegration taking place all around him. He told Abe Lansing he thought the name "Stanwix Hall" sounded too "indefinite" and suggested calling it *Fort Stanwix Hotel*. That is genuine, historic, natural, and purely American. It avoids the snobbish imitation of English names [so common?] to our N. Y. hotels. It sets a good example. It is the thing." However much Melville saw his ancestors, especially the Gansevoorts, as pirates because of their patrician power and privilege, in "real life" he took pride in being a member of a family whose history was coeval with the nation's. It is one of the many contradictions of this complex and contradictory man.[57]

⌇

"The American people love to be humbugged," P. T. Barnum once said. After moving to the Hippotheatron at Fourteenth Street in 1872, Barnum created a Travelling World's Fair in 1873, and built a colossal Hippodrome right up the block from where the Melvilles lived, on land belonging to the Harlem Railroad. Barnum exhibited two white whales, probably belugas, at the International Centennial Exposition in Philadelphia commemorating American independence, but whether Melville saw them or not is anybody's guess. "It is immense," he told Kate Lansing of the Exposition, "a sort of tremendous Vanity Fair."[58]

Between May 10, 1876, when the Liberty Bell and the city's church chimes announced the opening, and November, when the fair closed down, almost ten million people visited the Exposition. Fairgoers ogled George Washington's false teeth and admired the artistry of Edmonia Lewis, the first African-American sculptor to achieve recognition. Many saw for the first time the sacred dances of the Plains Indians and myriad artifacts purloined from the vanishing tribes that were displayed as examples of "a primitive stage of civilization." With all these wonders on exhibit, few noticed when guards attempted to prevent Frederick Douglass from entering the 450-acre fairground. Fortunately, the leonine ex-slave who edited the abolitionist newspaper *North Star* was able to prove his identity and gain admittance without further harassment.[59]

Visitors to the Exposition rode the first monorails and outdoor elevators in America, and marveled at the dazzling array of gadgets and machines, the most formidable of which was the thirty-foot-tall, 1,500-horsepower Corliss Double Walking-Beam Steam Engine. During the opening ceremonies, President Grant and Brazilian president Dom Pedro threw the switch amid much fanfare, setting seventy-five miles of belts and shafts in motion. As William Dean Howells watched it drive row after row of lathes, saws, drills, looms, pumps, and presses, the thought crossed his mind that this colossus had the power to crush humanity.[60]

Nowhere was the truth of Emerson's observation that "Things are in the saddle, and ride mankind" more evident than at the Exposition. According to manufacturers, the latest products of American invention and industry, such as reed parlor organs, sewing machines, kitchen ranges, ready-made shoes, linoleum floor coverings, and canned foods, would spread wealth and leisure and civic virtue throughout the land. Two of the most popular inventions were Alexander Graham Bell's telephone and Philo Remington and Christopher B. Sholes's typewriter, the machine that in a generation would replace scriveners like Bartleby with female secretaries.

With women running the telegraph system, printing presses, and sewing looms, most people thought such inventions as the typewriter would do more to usher in a new era of independence than would the 1848 "Women's Declaration of Independence," which Susan B. Anthony and Elizabeth Cady Stanton read at a counter-centennial in downtown Philadelphia on the Fourth of July. Few women at this point were stopping to ask how machines could "emancipate" them when the workforce was full of men who were struggling to feed their families, and even though women made up twenty percent of the workforce in 1876, they had no hope of higher wages, benefits, or better jobs until they won the right to vote.

Insofar as the inalienable Rights of Man were remembered at all, most people interpreted "Man" as white males and "Rights" not as ends in themselves, but as means to the commercial and economic success that would give the nation prominence in world affairs. Mark Twain chose the centennial year to personify America as a small town where regular boys triumphed over evildoers and never had to worry about reaching puberty. Twain's Christmas present to America in December 1876 was a story about a beguiling scamp named Tom Sawyer and his pal Huckleberry Finn, a fitting gift to a nation that was changing so rapidly and moving ahead with so little sense of common purpose and direction that many people resisted growing up.

Twenty-five-year-old Stanwix Melville was having trouble just holding down a job and making ends meet, and it seemed he would never establish himself in a satisfying career or be able to support a family. He had bought shares in a San Francisco whole-sale house after the owner promised to make him a partner, but when the man re-neged on the deal, Stanwix lost all his money. Desperate, he wrote Lem Shaw Jr., asking for a $60 loan so he could move to the Black Hills: "I have made up my mind, this is a chance, & I may be lucky there, at any rate I can get miners wages which is more than I can make here; and I am going this winter if I die of starvation or get frozen to death on the road ... do not let any one know of my intentions." Lem sent him $75, and Stanwix told his parents he was working in an "iron & steel firm," which sounded better than a mine shaft, because working as a miner was tantamount to suicide for someone with his history of pulmonary weakness. Predictably, Stanwix did not thrive in the rough-and-tumble atmosphere of a mining camp, as exposure to the underground dampness and cold, and to the fumes of noxious kerosene lamps, turned his respiratory weakness into full-blown tuberculosis, forcing him to return to California.[61]

Herman Melville's future in 1877 was uncertain. With rumors of corruption and incompetence at the Custom-House on the increase, employees were being closely scrutinized. Each of the three top employees made more money than the President of the United States, while Melville earned only $1,200 a year. The previous autumn, an order had come down to cut the pay of customs officers, but it had since been re-scinded, and in this strained atmosphere, many influential people were calling for re-form. George W. Curtis, a past chairman of the Republican Party in New York State, called the spoils system "a monster only less threatening than slavery," and denounced politicians as "vampires who suck the moral lifeblood of the nation." In 1880, Curtis would succeed Henry Whitney Bellows as president of the New York Association, a group of civic leaders who advocated reforming the civil service by establishing a merit system.[62]

Melville somehow managed to keep aloof from the turmoil all around him. His old habit of blending into the woodwork, quietly doing his job, and taking refuge in his own thoughts had served him well in a job he sometimes enjoyed, sometimes toler-ated, but more often barely endured. Now that he had finished *Clarel,* he was in one of those troughs that often follow completion of a major work. Mentally tired, and fearful that he might never be able to get started on a new project, he was tense and irritable, which upset Lizzie.

It bothered her that he was still squabbling with his cousin Kate, who was Lizzie's friend, but Herman's match for pride. When Kate, who had taken umbrage when her cousin refused her gift of $100, came to New York on a shopping trip without calling on the Melvilles, Lizzie, fearing their tiff would jeopardize her friendship with Kate, tried to heal the breach between Herman and her. "I want you *always* to mention Herman's name in your letters," she wrote, "especially if it is to say anything about coming down—*I* know your feeling is always right to him, and so does everyone else, but he is *morbidly* sensitive, poor fellow, and I always try (though I can't succeed to my sorrow) to smooth fancied rough edges to him wherever I can—so I know you will understand why I mention it." Lizzie must have worked on her husband, too, as Herman's following letter to Kate was gracious to a fault. He was very anxious that she not think for a moment that he was "prompted by the remotest thought of wounding you, or any absurd idea of setting up for myself a spurious dignity."[63]

Even without family squabbles, 1877 was a distressing year. The hotly contested election of 1876 had gone to Rutherford B. Hayes by one electoral vote after Republicans traded Reconstruction for the presidency and southern Democrats sold out their candidate, Samuel J. Tilden, by agreeing to support Hayes if federal troops were withdrawn from the South. With the Compromise of 1877, the federal government abandoned the freedmen to the terrorism of the Klan, paving the way for legalized segregation in the mid-1890s.[64]

"How about President Hayes?" Melville had asked his cousin Kate rhetorically in his letter of apology to her. "What's the use? life is short, and Hayes' term is four years, each of 365 days." At this stage of his life, Melville preferred to study philosophy and work through the unresolved personal issues that troubled him than to get worked up over contemporary issues such as the bloody railroad strikes that broke out when owners cut wages with no warning and ended when President Hayes sent in federal troops, leaving hundreds of workers dead and millions of dollars' worth of property destroyed.[65]

Melville must have felt that he had outlived the times. He had poured the enormous labor of a decade into a monumental poem that struck his family as an eccentric indulgence and made absolutely no impression on the reading public. The few favorable comments by readers such as Edward Sanford, a friend of Kate Lansing's who said he liked the book very much and wondered how Melville knew so much about the Jews, served only to remind him how unappreciated he was by other people.[66]

Only John Hoadley, with whom he was occasionally exchanging poems, seemed to understand and appreciate his work. Hoadley, who had recently been experimenting with free verse, became his confidant, though Melville was an irregular correspondent. Apologizing for not answering a letter sooner, Melville promised to buy "a hair-shirt and a scourge" to use on himself for a week or so as penance for his remissness: "I am verging upon three-score, and at times a certain lassitude steals over one—in fact, a disinclination for doing anything except the indispensable. At such moments the problem of the universe seems a humbug, and epistolary obligations mere moonshine, and the—well, nepenthe seems all-in-all."[67]

Before sending the letter, he added: "Just looked over the accompanying letter which I wrote this morning. It is a queer sort of an absurd scribble, but if it evidences good fellowship and good feeling, it serves the purpose. You are young (as I said before) but I aint; and at my years, and with my disposition, or rather constitution, one gets to care less and less for everything except downright good feeling. Life is so short, and so ridiculous and irrational (from a certain point of view) that one knows not what to make of it, unless—well, finish the sentence for yourself." He signed the letter, "Thine in these inexplicable fleshly bonds H. M.," boldly adding, "N. B. *I aint crazy.*"[68]

Like many creative people, Melville was subject to mood swings. Passionate by nature, but reserved with people he did not know, when Melville felt comfortable with someone, he let down his guard and expressed himself without inhibition, as though being slightly out of control was a way of testing relationships, as well as a strategy for psychological survival. His active imagination and intellectual energy conflicted with the limitations of the marketplace, and his restive physical energy warred against his sedentary occupation and the ravages of time. When he was younger, he drank in response to anger and depression, or to take the edge off the tremendous energy and drive that had no safe outlet in his domestic environment. At times he lost control, and his drinking led to outbursts of temper, possibly including physical abuse of Lizzie, if the rumors can be believed. His drinking appears to have tapered off in later years, possibly because, as his energy waned, he had less need to anesthetize himself, and partly because he was making a concerted effort to cultivate what William Wordsworth called "the philosophic mind." Drinking less, he could take things a bit more in his stride. Although his tendency to oscillate between depression and elation became less pronounced as he grew older, the old undertow could still pull him down.

As the Melvilles grew older, habit and their common history of joys and sorrows kept them together. Melville put fewer demands on the family now that *Clarel* was behind him, and Lizzie no longer had a houseful of opinionated in-laws to contend with. Melville was paying evening visits to Evert Duyckinck again, and he made frequent calls on Tom and Catherine at Snug Harbor, where "old salts" told yarns he could weave into his poetry. Lizzie, too, must have had more time for her own activities and friends, though she seems to have spent most of it caring for Herman and Bessie.

Lizzie's uncle, Amos Nourse, died in April, and with Helen living in Brookline, Kate Hoadley back in Lawrence, Stanwix out in California, and Malcolm, Maria, Allan, and Augusta gone to their maker, the immediate family was much diminished. As Herman mellowed, Lizzie put the pain that had driven her to seek a separation behind her, and her old feelings of protectiveness toward her husband returned. Melville received his bequest of $500 from the estate of Peter Gansevoort, and Lizzie told Kate Lansing she hoped it would "make him really happier to have something to call his own—poor fellow he has so much mental suffering to undergo (and oh how *all* unnecessary) I am rejoiced when anything comes into his life to give him even a moment's relief." Lizzie had something to be concerned about, because by June, rumors that the Custom-House staff would be cut had reached the newspapers. For weeks, Melville worried that he would lose his job, and although he was relieved to learn at the end of the month that he had survived the latest "pruning" of two hundred employees, he was not pleased when he learned that he would have to work longer hours.[69]

Lizzie, meanwhile, received a gift of some money from her brother Lem to take Bessie to the mountains. Looking forward to "the general relaxation from care & anxiety, and the real benefit which we all experience," she wanted to spend six weeks in Jefferson, New Hampshire, but she didn't feel she could leave "Herman alone so long, in his state of mental health, with a free conscience," so she made arrangements for him to dine out at the Misses Harnetts' again. While the women were gone, Kate Lansing sent Herman one of Peter Gansevoort's sleeve buttons as a memento, and he thanked her heartily. This time, when she came to the city, he took her to see the new Lenox Library, a "superb" collection that would one day merge with the Astor Library to form the nucleus of the great New York Public Library.[70]

Melville spent the first week of his August vacation with his sister Frances Priscilla in Gansevoort before joining Lizzie and the girls in New Hampshire. The vacation went by quickly, and once he was back in New York, he found it "decidedly lonely in the house" without the women. In a letter to Kate Lansing, he launched into a thorough-going denunciation of work: "Whoever is not in the possession of leisure can hardly be said to possess independence. They talk of the *dignity of work*. Bosh. True Work is the *necessity* of poor humanity's earthly condition. The dignity is in leisure. Besides, 99 hundredths of all the *work* done in the world is either foolish and unnecessary, or harmful and wicked."[71]

He was not trying to amuse his cousin when he wrote those lines. His office had moved uptown, and his hours at the Custom-House had just been increased, but even though he had a longer day and a more arduous commute, Melville was not given a salary raise. He was two years away from turning sixty, and he was just plain tired.

In August 1877, Fanny Melville, an attractive, impatient twenty-two-year-old who had suffered an unnamed crisis remediable only by "Divine Help" the previous year, was sitting on the railing of the porch at Plaisted House swinging her legs–or rather, swinging her long skirt, as legs were meant to be invisible in public places. She was wondering how she would ever meet an interesting young man in Jefferson, New Hampshire. Although she had met some eligible young men at balls and parties in New York, she did not have a beau. As she stared out across the lawn at the mountains, her eyes met those of a young gentleman who was embarrassed to be caught staring back at her.[72]

He was Henry B. Thomas, a mustachioed Philadelphian who fell in love with Fanny at first sight. Once they had been properly introduced, he learned that the gentleman he had noticed crossing the lobby of the hotel "with a certain air" to purchase a cigar, the bearded man whose "erect bearing and squared shoulders" gave him "a dignity that seemed to add to his height," was Miss Melville's father, and he was pleased. Many people, including Henry Thomas and Melville's niece Charlotte Hoadley, thought Melville stood at least six feet tall, although he was actually only five feet nine or ten.[73]

"A simple, straightforward, practical young man from a rather conventional Philadelphia family," Henry Thomas had a "quiet & gentlemanly" manner that endeared him to everyone, even Herman, who was very hard to please. When Lizzie came home with Bessie and the radiant Fanny that fall, she bought some new furniture, spruced up the front parlor, and had the house painted, as it was about to be the scene of a serious courtship. Then she went to Boston for Thanksgiving and returned to celebrate Christmas at Snug Harbor with the clan.[74]

Melville's end-of-year royalty statement from Harper's reported that the combined sales of *Omoo, Redburn, White-Jacket,* and *Moby-Dick* for that year had totaled 192 copies, which gave him $64.38, most of which he spent on books and prints. At New Year's, Melville suffered the first of several attacks of erysipelas, an acute inflammation of the subcutaneous tissue caused by a streptococcus virus. Sometimes called "Saint Anthony's fire" because the saint was said to have been afflicted by it, this disease often began with an irritation of the skin around the throat caused by a stiff collar. The attack left him with a temporary paralysis of both hands and such discomfort in his joints that it was impossible for him to write.[75]

Although Henry Thomas was not as wealthy as the man of her dreams, Fanny "surrendered the citadel" at the end of April 1878, and became engaged to the steadfast suitor who had won her heart. The Melvilles celebrated the happy occasion by inviting Henry to a crab dinner that turned out to be quite a spectacle, with Melville standing over a platter of crabs with a hammer and cracking them noisily on a wooden board while he reeled off anecdotes and made extravagant toasts. After all these years, Melville's appetite still amazed his family. Years later, his granddaughter Eleanor liked to tell people about the enormous number of jacket-potatoes he once devoured, and how she wished she had kept count so she could tell the world.[76]

The Melvilles celebrated the Fourth of July together at Snug Harbor, after which Lizzie and Fanny went to Boston and Bessie to Pittsfield. The following week, the women went to the mountains together, and Melville stayed in the city working, except for a weekend he spent in Albany with the Lansings. Henry liked riding the ferry as much as Herman did, so while Lizzie and the girls were in New Hampshire, Melville took him to Snug Harbor. Several family members thought Henry had won Melville over by being the only member of the family who didn't object to the way Melville constantly shifted his seat and moved around on the ferry to get the best possible view.

In mid-August, Evert Duyckinck died, with Melville the last man to see him alive. Stanwix had not written for a long time, so when news came that he was hospitalized in Sacramento, his parents were almost relieved; at least they knew he was still alive. Lizzie was anxious about Stannie's health and welfare; she had already lost one son, and dreaded losing another. It must have been hard on her to have Stannie so far away during his illness, but while she might have been able to afford a trip out west, she was not well enough to travel alone to California, and she was needed at home. Herman had to work, and Bessie's arthritis had flared up so painfully that she was unable to dress herself or eat without assistance.

Kate Lansing, a frequent guest in the house, thought the Melvilles lived an unnecessarily spartan life. Having felt the cold drafts that came through the cracks in the floor of Herman's room, she sent him a handsome carpet, but he passed it along to Bessie for her room. Lizzie explained that "He is so enamored of a *floor* without a 'stuffy carpet' that he does not want to have it covered at all but only have a mat here & there—I fear it will be cold for him in the winter, but as all the cracks have been filled up, he thinks not." Melville probably thought the warmth would alleviate Bessie's symptoms, and Kate, fortunately, was not offended by his not making use of her gift.[77]

With romance in the air, Lizzie spent the "special legacy" of $100 she received from Aunt Lucy Nourse to fix up the back parlor so the lovebirds could sit and spoon without being subjected to Herman's well-meaning but blundering intrusions. Tickled as he was to see the young couple together, he sometimes forgot that Henry had come to be with Fanny, not to chat with him. Once, when he walked through the front parlor late at night and found Henry still talking to Fanny later than he thought proper, Herman asked a little too sarcastically whether the young man wanted oatmeal or mush for break-fast. Although her father often aggravated her, Fanny was delighted when he invited Henry to a "little Thanksgiving affair" while Lizzie was in Boston.[78]

The last year of the decade saw a number of illnesses and deaths in the family, and one birth. Shortly after New Year's Day, 1879, when Kate Lansing came to town, she found Herman well but Lizzie suffering one of her "run down," or "prostrated turns." She could not walk across the room without staggering. At the same time, Bessie's fingers had to be bound in splints to straighten them. By the time Milie Morewood gave birth to a daughter, whom she and Willie named Agnes, Lizzie was completely recovered from her illness, but Bessie, who was only twenty-six years old, needed constant care, so Lizzie took her to the Catskills for the better part of the summer. Melville, who was feeling well again, went to New Jersey to see his new grandniece, and in mid-August he joined his family in the mountains, presumably celebrating his sixtieth birthday quietly.[79]

The deaths of close relatives brought the Melvilles a measure of bittersweet finan-cial security, as it was paid for with great sadness when Hope Shaw, Lizzie's beloved mother, confidante, and friend, died at the end of the summer. Her sons arranged a bequest of $2,000 for each of Lizzie's children and made Lizzie a legatee of their mother's $300,000 estate, and Lizzie's aunt Martha Bird Marett and her daughter Ellen both remembered her and the children in their wills. Reflecting that money gained not through work, or even luck, but through the deaths of loved ones, was a bitter boon, Melville must have thought back ambivalently to the Happy Valley, where that "root of all evil," money, did not exist.[80]

In *Clarel*, he had tried to create a vision of an earthly Paradise, only to be reminded that Paradise does not exist on this earth. No Paradise exists outside the Mind of God, which, for Melville, was tantamount to the artist's imagination, and no utopia exists out-side the human heart. As Melville saw the empires he had fancied crumbling along with the empires of antiquity, the philosophy of history expressed in *Clarel* became a philos-ophy of life. Faced with the insults of aging and the inevitability of death, he would attempt to create island paradises reminiscent of Greece and Polynesia by writing lyric poems. These lines from the masque of the Wandering Jew in Book Three of *Clarel* announce the theme of Melville's entry into his seventh decade:

> Go mad I cannot: I maintain
> The perilous outpost of the sane.[81]

*Melville's lifelong interest in science and his irreverent wit coalesce
in* The New Ancient of Days *(first called* The Old Boy of the Cave*), a poem
comparing the latest archaelogical discoveries to a "Barnum-show."*

CONFRONTING SPHINX AND ANGEL

On the wall beside his desk, Melville kept a piece of paper that bore Schiller's motto "Keep true to the dreams of thy youth." How far away the Pacific Islands must have seemed to him. Life in the city, bouts of illness, and the ravages of grief had taken the edge off his restless energies, and the idyllic world of sensual pleasure without guilt that he had envisioned while writing Typee *was only a memory.[1]*

The 1880s began with Fanny's marriage to Henry Thomas at All Souls' Church. The ceremony was a simple one, as Lizzie's ill health prevented her from making elaborate preparations, and though rainy, it was a happy day. The newlyweds made their home in Orange, New Jersey. That fall, while Lizzie was in Boston for Thanksgiving, Herman enjoyed occasional visits from his cousin Kate and twice saw Sarah Bernhardt perform, but he felt like too much of "an old fogy" to go all the way to Albany just for a weekend when Abe Lansing invited him. Making flourishes of the pen that were unusual for him, he wrote his sister that he was learning "high Dutch penmanship," probably because he didn't want to have to depend on the sometimes ailing, sometimes absent Lizzie to copy his poems. Bessie's hands were so stiff and sore from rheumatoid arthritis that she could hardly hold a pen.[2]

Although the 1880s brought much sorrow to the Melvilles, they also brought great joy. Herman and Lizzie became grandparents when Fanny and Henry's first child, Eleanor, was born on February 24, 1882. In April, Lizzie went down to help Fanny "break in the 'babby' [*sic*] to going without its nurse," and while she was away, Herman and Bessie entertained Melville's nephew, Francis Hoadley, who escorted Bessie to the zoo. P. T. Barnum happened to be there that day, and Lieutenant Hoadley shook his hand.[3]

Lizzie and Bessie spent much of the summer of 1882 at the Overlook Mountain House in Woodstock, New York, and Herman joined them for a week. Stanwix wrote home "constantly" that summer, but Lizzie's happiness at hearing from him was tempered by news that he could not shake his chronic cough. He was now in the early stages of tuberculosis.[4]

That fall, the founders of the Authors Club invited Melville to join, but he evidently decided not to, after attending one meeting. One member, Charles De Kay, surmised that "He had become too much of a hermit," and that "his nerves could no longer stand large gatherings." Future Columbia University professor Brander Matthews found him "shy and elusive," an "unobstrusive personality, with a vague air of being somehow out of place in our changing and chattering groups." Although Melville went to The Century Club with Allan now and then, and may even have attended an event at the Authors Club on occasion, modern literary societies, with their stuffy bylaws and their expensive dues, made him nostalgic for the days when wits and "deep divers" gathered informally in Evert Duyckinck's cellar to exchange ideas over brandy and cigars.[5]

Despite his distaste for club life, Melville enjoyed the company of men who shared his intellectual interests and literary tastes, and during his last decade, old and new admirers gravitated toward him. Titus Munson Coan, a physician who was now a writer and literary agent as well, and a member of both the Authors Club and The Century, stopped by frequently and brought Melville any gossip worth repeating. A favorite anecdote was Bayard Taylor's story about trying to carry on a conversation with a camel at the Jardin des Plantes. Taylor first addressed the camel in English, but it did not respond, so he tried French, with the same result. Only when he spoke to the camel in Arabic did the beast respond, reclining its head against Taylor's portly chest.[6]

A Melville admirer since his college days, Coan reveled in the company of the "man who had lived among the cannibals." For Coan and others of his generation, Melville's fictionalized adventures showed the way to personal liberation and cultural transformation; however idealistic and impractical it might prove in postindustrial America, the myth of the Happy Valley made the dreams of their youth the treasured memories of their old age. In his *Life in Hawaii, an Autobiographical Sketch of Mission Life & Labors*, published in 1882, Coan observed that during "four months of romantic captivity, the gifted author of 'Typee' and 'Omoo' was only four or five miles distance from the harbor whence he had fled." Coan's assertion could almost be a metaphor for Melville's life, because, despite his rovings, Melville was more of a homebody than were most men of his generation.[7]

When Walt Whitman told Coan he thought "American artists of all classes are doddered with theories, they read and think too much, they see and feel too little," he could not have been thinking of Melville, as Melville could expound on any subject with tremendous erudition and no trace of affectation or pretentiousness: "What stores of reading, what reaches of philosophy were his!" exulted Coan. "He took the attitude of absolute independence toward the world. He said, 'My books will speak for themselves, and all the better if I avoid the rattling egotism by which so many win a certain vogue for a certain time.'"[8]

Not everyone, however, had as easy a time as Coan in drawing Melville out. When Julian Hawthorne came to interview him for a family memoir in the summer of 1883, he found Melville "looking pale, sombre, nervous, but little touched by age." Distracted and apparently ill at ease, Melville hopped up every few minutes to open or close the courtyard window before being able to relax enough to focus on the interview. When Julian asked to see his father's letters, Melville said they had all been destroyed, "as if implying that the less said or preserved, the better!" He appeared a little incoherent on some subjects, and grew quite agitated at being asked to remember "the red-cottage days."[9]

Melville's behavior may have had something to do with Julian's demeanor, as the mustachioed young man was no longer the winsome boy who had adored "Mr. Omoo" and loved riding his big, black Newfoundland dog. A failed speculator and a would-be writer, Julian had turned into a rather stiff and self-important fellow, with none of the charm and sensitivity of his parents. He also had an ax to grind, as he was determined to ferret out dark secrets, which understandably put Melville on his guard. Above all, his presence was a painful reminder that both Nathaniel and Malcolm, who had been three years younger than Julian, were gone.

Despite the "sad interview," Julian described Melville kindly in *Hawthorne and His Circle:* "He conceived the highest admiration for my father's genius, and a deep affection for him personally; but he told me during our talk, that he was convinced that there was some secret in my father's life which had never been revealed, and which accounted for the gloomy passages in his books. It was characteristic in him to imagine so; there were many secrets untold in his own career. But there were few honester or more lovable men than Herman Melville."[10]

Although Julian wrote two books of memoirs and several articles about Melville, he never said what he thought these "many secrets" were, but his insinuations disturbed Mary Louisa Parmalee, who married Augusta's old beau Anthony Augustus Peebles. She wrote Abe Lansing: "I have been reading Hawthorne's Life and find it very entertaining, principally because it is so indiscreet. It does not chloroform the poor little literary butterflies in its collection, but just sticks a pin through them, and calls you to look. I wonder if Herman Melville was consulted about the appearance of his name? I should think some of the allusions would be very trying to a person of his sensitive nature."

Melville may have wanted people to think of him as a brooding genius with secrets to keep, like the Great Pyramid, one of his favorite icons of the Self, perhaps because he thought a reputation for being aloof and cantankerous might discourage importunate busybodies from requesting interviews.[11]

Not that Melville couldn't be aloof and cantankerous, but in the last decade of his life he became reclusive more through necessity than by inclination, as his circle of family and friends narrowed steadily. He and Lizzie and Bessie were plagued by physical ailments, and he was constantly reminded of his own mortality. His cousin Robert died in December 1883, and his brother Tom died of a heart attack in March 1884, which was quite a shock. Two months later, Lemuel Shaw Jr. died of apoplexy, and in July, Melville's aunt Mary died. Tom's funeral at Snug Harbor was "a sad sad sight" as the "old sailors with bared heads, & tearful eyes" said farewell "to their devoted friend & Governor." Melville was so grief-stricken by the loss of his only surviving brother and the youngest of his siblings that he came down with "a kind of rheumatic gout." Tom's death broke Melville's last link with the old salts at Snug Harbor, whose yarns and chanteys recalled the good-fellowship of his seafaring days. Part of Melville would always be with Tom on the high seas, and part of Tom would live on in *John Marr and Other Sailors.*[12]

Death was not the only visitor during these years, however. Fanny's second daughter, Frances Cuthbert, had been born before Christmas, and when Lizzie took Bessie to Orange for three weeks to help with the baby, Eleanor was learning to talk. "Little Eleanor is much delighted with her 'tunnin little baby sister,'" Lizzie wrote Kate Lansing, "and is always begging to 'kiss her'—she is as good as a child can be, but is very active and needs constant watching . . . you would laugh to hear her talk—which she does from morning till night in a most entertaining way." Eleanor developed into a bright, outgoing little girl whose antics provided a welcome distraction from the seemingly endless procession of losses the family suffered during the 1880s, and on a deeper level, the existence of grandchildren served to remind Melville that future generations brought new life.[13]

In some ways, Melville had been old before his time, both physically and intellectually. In his youth he was driven by boundless physical energy and a desperate emotional need to create, create, create. The breakneck composition of seven novels in eight years had taken its toll early in life, and the sting of seeing *Putnam's* fold and his ambitious war poetry go unappreciated had taken their toll in midlife. Emotional stress, eyestrain, and sciatica impelled him to drink and smoke heavily, setting in motion a vicious cycle whereby alcohol both alleviated his physical complaints and aggravated the psychological ones, but through it all, his survival instincts and core resiliency kept him afloat. Although periodically he battled illness and depression, in later life he seems to have cut down his drinking to an occasional snifter of brandy for "solace." Despite the depredations of advancing age, Melville was neither excessively misanthropic nor embittered, and at times his old energy came out in flashes of wit and sallies of storytelling.[14]

Midway into his seventh decade, Melville had to take stock and make some choices about how he would live the rest of his life. As a writer, a husband, a father, and a public figure, he had to come to terms with tragedy and failure before he could move on. His lifelong mutiny against family, self, society, and God had given birth to a brilliant and tempestuous, if uneven, body of work, but he had failed to support his family by writing. He had not achieved either the wide audience he wanted for his work or recognition from the literary establishment. He had wounded his wife and children, and had seen many of his own dreams die. He had also failed to exorcise his demons or change the course of history.

"Cruelly disenchanted with politics," Melville brooded over a civilization more divided and directionless than ever. With rapid industrialization, the floods of immigrants lured to America by glittering promises were not able to find decent homes and jobs, and hard-core poverty in New York increased dramatically. While rich industrialists built marble châteaux and furnished them with European paintings and antiques, residents of shantytowns huddled in makeshift dwellings thrown together from salvaged scraps. In 1880, the *Daily Graphic*, the first illustrated daily newspaper in the world, ran photographs that showed the proximity of upper Fifth Avenue's squalid Shantytown to the mansions of the Astors, Aspinwalls, and Vanderbilts. Instead of regulating corporate profits and creating jobs, power brokers shifted the burden of relieving human suffering to private philanthropic institutions. Influenced by Social Darwinists who claimed that charity would "emasculate" the lower classes, Charles Russell Lowell's widow, Effy, founded the Charity Organization of New York in 1882 with the promise that she would encourage the poor to do public service, not give them handouts.[15]

Middle-class businessmen and merchants who hoped to become rich were great believers in Carnegie's "gospel of wealth," and the more they competed for profits, the more hectic life became. "Immense injury is done by this high-pressure life," Herbert Spencer warned, "it is time to preach the gospel of relaxation." When Oscar Wilde toured America in 1882, it seemed to him that everyone in America was "in a hurry to catch a train." Although Americans prided themselves on their burgeoning transportation system, at least one visitor to New York considered the new elevated railway "an ever-active volcano over the heads of responsible citizens." In 1882, Thomas Alva Edison leased a power station at 257 Pearl Street and brought electricity to eighty-five businesses and dwellings in several of Manhattan's oldest wards, and the following year, Mrs. Cornelius Vanderbilt appeared at one of her costume balls as an incandescent bulb.[16]

Visitors from Europe were both fascinated and repelled by the fast pace of life, the brash manners, the emphasis on money, and the rampant commercialism that assaulted them in New York. While wealthy music-lovers eager to attract the best European singers to New York were raising money to build the Metropolitan Opera House, social climbers with more money than taste were squandering money on ostentatious parties. The city had no harmony of design, no sense of proportion, restraint, or modesty. P. T. Barnum was advertising Jumbo, the world's largest elephant, as though he were a patent medicine, and the omnipresence of garish advertising prompted the French composer Jacques Offenbach to call New York "Castoria," a play on words linking the Astors to castor oil, a common all-purpose remedy that was hard to swallow.[17]

When the Brooklyn Bridge opened amid much fanfare and festivity in 1883, few remembered how many immigrant workers had been crushed by cement blocks or drowned by fallen pilings while working on the project; immigrant laborers were plentiful enough to be expendable. By the mid-1880s, forty-five percent of all industrial workers made less than $500 a year, and forty percent lived in slums with no running water or electricity. By the end of the decade, eleven million of the twelve million families in America lived on less than $1,200 a year–Melville's annual salary. So stark were the inequities that when Cornelius Vanderbilt died in 1885, he left an estate of $200 million; yet when workers went on strike the following year to obtain decent wages and minimal safety standards in the workplace, the Chicago police gunned them down in Haymarket Square. In 1886, New York celebrated the completion of the Statue of Liberty with the greatest nautical parade since Lafayette's visit in 1825. The Melvilles had probably seen the gigantic bronze arm and torch at close range, when it was on display in Madison Square Park prior to the statue's installation on Bedloe's Island.[18]

The excesses of the Gilded Age turned even the conservative Midwesterner William Dean Howells into an anarchist sympathizer, and inspired journalist Edward Bellamy to write his utopian novel *Looking Backward, 2000–1887,* in which he imagined a benevolent system of industrial socialism. Less sanguine than Bellamy about America's future, Mark Twain launched a satirical attack against scientific materialism in *A Connecticut Yankee in King Arthur's Court.*

As for Melville, however astute his insights into the ways race and class deprived Americans of their God-given rights, however sharp his attacks on aristocratic pretension and Christian hypocrisy, however caustic his attacks on the Wall Street spirit, his words did not have the power to end cruelty or injustice. Words did not have the power to put roses in the pallid cheeks of factory workers or to restore classical standards of beauty to a world where trinkets and gadgets were prized above masterpieces of sculpture, poetry, and painting.

So much, like the unspoiled innocence of verdant tropic isles and the ordered beauty of the classical world, seemed irrevocably lost. His dreams of love and happiness and literary greatness, as well as his dream that postrevolutionary America would usher in a new era of liberty and justice, remained unfulfilled. Once an idealistic young man who had fancied that the written word could influence people to work for a better world, at age sixty-five Melville was content to cultivate his own garden, both literally and metaphorically.

For his birthday, Lizzie gave him Samuel Hole's *A Book About Roses*. She had recently learned that the springtime allergies she had always referred to as her "rose cold" were in fact hay fever, and with her encouragement, Melville dug up the small yard behind their house and planted a rose garden. He loved growing roses. He dried the petals and enclosed them in letters and gifts for relatives and friends, and his last book of poems, *Weeds and Wildings Chiefly: With a Rose or Two,* became a kind of bouquet for Lizzie.[19]

As he grew older, Melville reevaluated the relationship that had sustained itself through so many shocks and sorrows and learned to appreciate the woman who had shared his life. "Grown wise by experience," Melville had written in *Mardi*, describing the tempestuous marriage of Samoa and Annatoo, "they neither loved overkeenly nor hated, but took things as they were; found themselves joined without hope of a sundering, and did what they could to make a match of the mate." If friction existed in the Melville household during these years, it must have been over such trivialities as Herman's insistence on wearing his "Constantinople" pajamas around the house even when they had company, or Lizzie's allowing Eleanor and her cousin Agnes Morewood to jump on her bed and shriek delightedly when he was trying to work in the next room. Herman understandably preferred loose, comfortable clothing to street clothes when he didn't have to go out to the office, and Lizzie was loath to break up a game that brought her granddaughters such pleasure. Perhaps by this time they had learned to compromise.[20]

Through the writing of *Clarel*, Melville had thrown off the stranglehold of organized religion and turned inward to focus on his own spiritual growth, or what Schopenhauer called "the necessity of transforming the self." Sometime prior to January 1, 1884, he had formally become a member of All Souls' Church, perhaps because he simply liked the new minister, Theodore Chickering Williams, better than he had liked Dr. Bellows, or perhaps because Williams was a poet whose sermons were more mystical and less moralistic than those of Bellows. Melville's becoming a communicant had less to do with his having resolved the conflict between belief and unbelief than with his realization that there were few moorings left for a weary mariner who needed a safe place to anchor his wandering soul. A believer in the "intersympathy of creeds," as he had expressed it in *Clarel*, he studied Oriental philosophies as well as Western theology, reading such works as Thomas Maurice's seven-volume *History of Hindostan* (London, 1797) and his *Indian Antiquities* (London, 1800) and also books about Buddhism, Zoroastrianism, and world mythologies.[21]

Around Thanksgiving of 1884, Bessie became so ill with "muscular rheumatism" that Lizzie had to hire a nurse from a nearby training school to help her. With Bessie sick and Tom gone, Christmas was a melancholy time. Frances Priscilla spoke for all the Melvilles when she said that "ever since Tom's marriage he has been the center, the warm-hearted centre, of all the family joys and pleasures at . . . [Christmas] and the day can never be again to any of us, what it has been in years past." Tom's widow, Catherine, spent the holiday with Fanny and Henry and their two little girls, all much subdued by the absence of their beloved Captain Tom.[22]

Sorrows multiplied in 1885. The treatment for Bessie's illness was so severe that right after the New Year, her beautiful long hair had to be cut off and her head completely shaved. An invalid at thirty-two, Bessie remained a spinster all her life. In May, Melville's aunt Lucy died in Bloomingdale Asylum after long hospitalization for a "hopeless" mental illness, and two months later his sister Frances Priscilla died at age sixty-eight, leaving fewer than half of Maria and Allan Melvill's eight children still alive.[23]

Melville's "The Admiral of the White," dedicated to Tom, was published in May 1885, in both the *New-York Daily Tribune* and the *Boston Herald*. The poem retells the story he had heard in Thessaloniki in 1856, about a ship's compass being thrown off by a concealed cache of arms.[24]

Later expanded and renamed "The Haglets" for Melville's privately published *John Marr and Other Sailors* (1888), the poem surges through more than forty stanzas composed of five lines of iambic tetrameter and a sixth line of iambic pentameter, after the fashion of a Spenserian *canzone*. It opens with the narrator imagining the "recumbent effigy" of the Admiral of the White describing his last voyage home. As the "eddying waters whirl astern, the ship plunges" through the waves "with bellying sails and buckling spars," and the Admiral fails to notice that the frigate has been drawn off course by hidden "blades whose secret thrill / Perverts overhead the magnet's Polar will." Fancying himself an "advancing conqueror . . . whose dream of power no tremors jar," he ignores the circling sharks and the three haglets, or kittiwakes, who fly above the ship like "shuttles hurrying in the looms." Doomed by her commanding officer's arrogance, the vessel hits a reef and sinks to the bottom of the sea, where the drowned sailors rest in "Unfathomable sleep" amid the rusting cannons. The poem ends as the narrator imagines the arrogant Admiral asking, "Must victors drown?—Perish, even as the vanquished did?" Man stands between "the abysm and the star," the narrator concludes, and he must not presume to know the mind of God.[25]

Even though poems in this vein might well have appealed to contemporary readers, Melville evidently did not submit more poems to newspapers and magazines. With *Clarel* behind him, he was beginning to enjoy writing sea narratives and short lyrics, but he had little interest in commercial publishing. At this point, most of the family income came from money Lizzie had inherited, rather than from Melville's writing or his job. Whereas he received a royalty check from Harper's for $223.72 from the small but steady sale of his books, Lizzie received over $33,000 from her brother Lem's estate, out of which she gave Herman a monthly allowance of $25 to buy books and prints.[26]

Lizzie spent most of the summer of 1885 worrying about Stanwix, who had been forced by his illness to move to San Rafael for its drier climate. He seemed destined to be a vagabond, never able to take hold and make a happy life for himself, and now he was chronically ill besides. She also worried about Herman because, once again, employees were about to be dismissed from the Custom-House. Through Kate, she asked Abe Lansing to put in a word for him, "as apart from everything else, the *occupation* is a great thing for him—and he could not take any other post that required head work, & sitting at a desk."[27]

Melville, however, was eager to retire. In his poem "Montaigne and His Kitten," he compares the kitten's carefree life to human life, where "poor dizzards strain and strive / Rave and slave, drudge and drive / Chasing ever, to and fro, / After ends that seldom gain / Scant exemption from life's pain." Believing life should be a perpetual kittenhood, Melville's Montaigne invites his kitten Blanche to "frisk to-night" with him: "Gambol, skip, and frolic, play," he tells her. "Wise ones fool it while they may!" A variation on the *carpe diem* theme, this lighthearted lyric portrays work as purgatorial drudgery and play as a way of attaining paradise.[28]

In the copy of Edgar Evertson Saltus's book on Balzac that Lizzie had given him for his sixty-sixth birthday that August, Melville underscored the French writer's statement that the great secret of strong and creative lives "is to forget life's misfortunes." As he struggled to meet life's blows during these years, the specters of his father's violent death and Malcolm's suicide loomed menacingly before him, but he was determined not to let life break him in the end.[29]

In late August, Melville spent a few days at the Homestead Inn in Pittsfield while Lizzie and Bessie went to Jefferson, New Hampshire, so that Lizzie could escape "the enemy," as she called her hay fever. During Melville's visit to the Berkshires, which would be his last, his old friend Joseph E. A. Smith found him sociable and in good spirits: "He did not evince the slightest aversion to society but appeared to enjoy the hearty welcome which it gave him; time having enhanced instead of diminishing the local pride in and regard for him," and there was no trace of anything "morbid in his nature." According to Smith, though Melville was ever conscious of his patrician lineage and quiet "in general society," he "bore nothing of the appearance of a man disappointed in life, but rather had an air of perfect contentment, and his conversation had much of his jovial, let-the-world-go-as-it-will spirit."[30]

That fall, Melville sent a copy of "Montaigne and His Kitten" to Lizzie's cousin Ellen Marett Gifford and she asked him for his photograph, so he sent her one, replying playfully, "What the deuse [*sic*] makes him look so serious, I wonder. I thought he was of a gay and frolicsome nature, judging from a little rhyme of his about a Kitten, which you once showed me. But is this the same man? Pray, explain the inconsistency, or I shall begin to suspect your venerable friend of being a two-faced old fellow and not to be trusted." He kept up an extensive correspondence with Ellen, who was "a sensitive, delicate creature, an amateur artist," and "a loyal, generous friend," according to her friend Wendell Phillips. He enclosed poems and rose petals in his letters, as sharing poems with a few appreciative friends and relatives can sometimes be a more satisfying form of publication than putting them before an unresponsive, faceless audience.[31]

❧

In the mid-1880s a whole new generation of British writers discovered Melville. The Scottish critic Robert Buchanan came to America in the summer of 1884 to meet both Melville and Walt Whitman, and easily found Whitman at his home in Camden, New Jersey, but for some reason he could not locate Melville: "I sought everywhere for this Triton, who is still living somewhere in New York. No one seemed to know anything of the one great imaginative writer fit to stand shoulder to shoulder with Whitman on that continent." In a poetic tribute to the two authors, Buchanan called it scandalous that "Melville, whose magic drew Typee, / Radiant as Venus, from the sea, / Sits all forgotten or ignored, / While haberdashers are adored!" He apparently didn't think to consult the city directory for the address of the "sea-compelling man, / Before whose wand Leviathan / Rose hoary white upon the Deep / With awful sounds that stirred its sleep."[32]

The maritime novelist and historian W. Clark Russell, who considered Melville first among "the poets of the deep" and "the greatest genius" in America, wrote an article for

The Contemporary Review of London, in which he called *Moby-Dick* "a medley of noble impassioned thoughts ... madly fantastic in places, full of extraordinary thoughts, yet gloriously coherent." Assuring Melville that his reputation in England was "very great" and that discriminating readers thought him the equal of "many renowned English writers," Russell struck up a correspondence and dedicated his novel *An Ocean Tragedy* to Melville.[33]

James Billson, an ardent admirer of *Mardi*, sent Melville his articles on the "pessimist poet" James Thomson and several of Thomson's books. Melville greatly admired Thomson's "massive and mighty" poem *The City of Dreadful Night*, which he read more than once. "Its gloom is its sublimity," he wrote after the first reading, and later he exclaimed, "The confronting Sphinx and Angel, where shall we go to match them?" Although he claimed to be "neither pessimist nor optomist [*sic*] myself," Melville found Thomson's pessimism refreshing "if for nothing else than as a counterpoise to the exorbitant hopefulness, juvenile and shallow, that makes such a bluster in these days–at least, in some quarters." To Melville, Thomson was one of those "certain men of genius who remain always obscure because they are all genius, having no vulgar profitable talents." His relative obscurity, like Melville's, demonstrated that "the further our civilization advances upon its present lines so much the cheaper sort of thing does 'fame' become, especially of the literary sort." It also pleased him to learn that Thomson was interested in William Blake, as Melville was attracted to Blake's mysticism.[34]

Other British fans included J. W. Barrs, a friend of Billson's who was a great admirer of *Pierre*, and Henry S. Salt, a Fabian socialist and biographer of James Thomson. Salt planned to edit a new edition of *Typee* for John Murray's Camelot Series, but his plans fell through when the British publisher turned him down.

In America, Melville was referred to by newspaper columnists as "A 'Buried' Author," and the literary historians of the time generally lumped him with William Starbuck Mayo, author of *Kaloolah*, as a minor travel writer. J. W. Carroll, a professor at New York College, considered Melville a prime example of "the transiency of literary reputation" because he was "generally supposed to be dead" after being "buried in a government office." Characterizing Melville as "a genial, pleasant fellow, who, after all his wanderings, loves to stay at home . . . and indulge in reverie and reminiscence," Carroll paid homage to him as one "whose song has been of Nature's heart and Man's."[35]

Among those who knew that Melville was alive and well were librarians and booksellers and their patrons who recognized the "handsome and vigorous, if elderly" man who steadied himself with a heavy bamboo cane while browsing for books and prints. When a writer for *The Literary World* spotted Melville in a bookstore, he reported that the gray-haired author's "eyes are still bright and his movements quick." Remembering how Melville's romances of the South Seas had delighted his youthful imagination, he concluded, "Had [Melville] possessed as much literary skill as wild imagination his works might have secured for him a permanent place in American Literature."[36]

During a visit to New York in 1886, the Danish artist Peter Toft, a friend of Clark Russell's, met Melville and found him "a delightful talker when in the mood," though "abnormal, as most geniuses are . . . [having] to be handled with care." Toft presented Melville with two watercolors he had done, one of Rock Rodondo and the other commemorating the battle between the *Bonhomme Richard* and the *Serapis,* but Melville parried Toft's attempts to discuss his books by claiming that he had forgotten them. Not realizing that Melville would have preferred discussing painting rather than his own writing, Toft concluded that Melville "seemed to hold his work in small esteem."[37]

Melville had held on to his post as customs inspector partly through economic necessity and partly because he needed something to anchor him emotionally, but now, with his salary no longer required to pay bills and his having been transferred to Simonson's lumberyard on the East River at Seventy-ninth Street, a tedious and time-consuming commute, he decided to retire at the end of the year and devote his time to writing.[38]

Having asked Abe to intercede for Herman at the Custom-House, Lizzie felt she had to account for the decision:

> For a year or so past he has found the duties too onerous for a man of his years, and at times of exhaustion, both mental and physical, he has been on the point of giving it up, but recovering a little, had held on, very naturally anxious to do so, for many reasons.–This month was a good turning point, completing 19 years of faithful service during which there has not been a single complaint against him–So he retires honorably of his own accord–He has a great deal of unfinished work at his desk which will give him occupation, which together with his love of books will prevent time from hanging heavy on his hands–and I hope he will get into a more quiet frame of mind, exempt from the daily invitation of over work.[39]

The year 1886 brought another tragedy. Stanwix was hospitalized in Sacramento, and before the end of February he was dead, at the age of thirty-five. Herman and Lizzie did not visit him when he was dying, and the written record has an elliptical, evasive quality that gives the impression that Melville was indifferent to the fate of his second son and that only Lizzie agonized over Stannie's unsettled life and illness. Had Melville written his son off, or driven him away? Had Stanwix disappointed or disobeyed his father, as Malcolm had?[40]

Although Melville received the news of Stannie's death with outward stoicism, Lizzie's grief was so profound that Helen Griggs worried about her: "I am so sorry for Lizzie! It is sad indeed to have had Stannie die away from home. But it seems he had a friend, who did all he could to make him comfortable, and there was money enough to procure all that was necessary for his comfort. It is sad enough; but it might have been worse, since there is so much consolation for his poor mother. Ah me. The sorrows that lie round our paths as we grow older!" Helen visited Lizzie in May and found her inconsolable: "She is in great trouble; and seems unable to find solace for her grief. It was *so* hard,–the sickness and death so far away!"[41]

Lizzie sublimated her sorrow in caring for Bessie, but it took a toll on her physically and emotionally. Herman wrote poetry and took time to help Kate Lansing and Helen clean out the house in Gansevoort before putting it up for auction. He decided to keep a huge sideboard for the house on Twenty-sixth Street, where, as space was at a premium, it would have to be squeezed into the back parlor. He had no desire, at this stage of his life, to be reminded of the "flight of hours" by the "high clear-toned strike" of the English grandfather clock, so he gave it to Fanny.[42]

From Gansevoort, Melville went to Glens Falls to visit the Curtises, stopping on the way at his favorite barbershop, where he made an indelible impression on an eleven-year-old boy named Ferris Greenslet, who later became an editor at Houghton Mifflin:

> Soon after I was installed in the chair a buggy drove up and made a dashing stop, and after hitching the horse the driver came into the shop to have his whiskers trimmed, announcing that he had driven up from Gansevoort, some eight or nine miles, in a flat hour. Clad in a blue double-breasted suit of a seagoing flavor, he was seventy-ish, with a lot of hair and a beard well grizzled, a vigorous body, "plump sphericity," a well tanned countenance, a bright and roving eye, all making up a singularly vital and impressive personality. I remember no one that I have met in the fifty odd years since more vividly.[43]

Soon, Melville was regaling the barber and his customers with "joyous" tales of his adventures in the South Seas, and according to Greenslet, when the barber asked whether there were "any girls down there," Melville responded enthusiastically.

> "My God!" said the whiskerando, "I'll say there were! I went back to the island a couple of years after I left there on board a man-of-war and the first thing I saw when I went ashore was my own little son about a year and a half old running around naked in the sun on the beach."

"How did you know it was your son?" asked the barber.

"He had to be," said the storyteller. "He carried his bowsprit to starboard."

Greenslet's memoir, like other accounts we have of Melville in his last decade, testifies to what Greenslet called his "central *joie de vivre*."[44]

Melville loved to shock people, and in the company of men where he didn't have to watch his language or censor himself to please feminine standards of gentility, the old tar unbuttoned his ribald wit happily. He was amused and flattered by persistent rumors that he had fathered a child in Polynesia, so he kept them going just enough so that Melvilleans encountering blue-eyed boys in the South Seas would wonder.

~~~

It might be said that each of the Melville children acted out the pathology of his or her father in some way. With Malcolm having killed himself, and Stanwix having wandered off to die outside of the bosom of the family with a male companion at his side, it seemed the two boys had been sacrificed to the harsh gods of Victorian paternity. The girls, figuratively speaking, divided their parents' good health and ill health unevenly between them, with Bessie replicating her father's physical ailments on her virgin body like stigmata, and Fanny exorcising the demons of patriarchy by marrying and giving birth to four daughters and no sons but blaming her father for all her later troubles.[45]

When John Hoadley died, in October 1886, Melville lost not only a brother-in-law and friend, but also a fellow poet and one of his most sympathetic readers. Increasingly now, his world was inhabited by ghosts, so granddaughters were a blessing. While Henry Thomas was in the Berkshires bicycling with a friend that August, four-year-old Eleanor dictated to her mother a letter that must have melted Melville's heart:

> My dear Grandpa, Frances and I have got a new doll, my dolly's name is Dinah and Frances' dolly's name is Susie and you haven't seen them. When I was just getting into bed, I saw a 'ittle fly in the water, and I took him out with my hand and put him on the floor. We went out to take a walk with Mamma and we saw the biggest rooster he ever saw in his life. And we saw the pigs and they were going to sleep, and we gave them some grass to eat. And we saw a picture of a circus, and a horse was sitting up a table with a bib on eating his dinner and two waitress. And there was a horse going on a bicycle. . . . Mamma lets me have corn for dinner if I eat my meat. We had 'ittle tiny kitties and they runned away. I send a kiss to Grandpa. Goodbye from Eleanor M. Thomas.

Eleanor inherited some of her grandfather's literary sensibility, eventually writing a full-length family memoir and editing Melville's journals for publication. She also donated a valuable collection of family papers and books to the Harvard College Library.[46]

Whenever the girls visited Twenty-sixth Street, Lizzie would give them each a penny for each gill of pebbles they removed from the garden. As they did their chores, they could hear their grandfather pacing in his study, "walking off energy instead of turning to writing as a safety valve for smoldering fires." According to Eleanor, he would stand on the inside balcony and point with a light bamboo cane at things he wanted the girls to notice. Bessie often read stories aloud to them in Lizzie's room while they cut out paper dolls, and once she took Fanny to the theater and to a French church.[47]

Melville liked to sit on the narrow iron porch on the second floor, smoking the small meerschaum pipe he had bought on his wedding journey, and the girls would set up canvas folding chairs beside him, eager for the predictable moment when he would point his cane at the match holder and tell them to make sure the red and blue china butterfly on the cover had not flown away. Fanny especially enjoyed listening to the plaintive music of the Aeolian harp on the windowsill, because she fancied that it reminded her grandfather of the wind in the rigging at sea. Reading *White-Jacket* years later, she discovered that even then he had recommended keeping an Aeolian harp "as a cure for the blues."[48]

As soon as the girls were old enough to walk with him, Melville took them to Central Park, "the Mecca of most of our pilgrimages." They could barely keep up with his long strides, or understand the long words he used, but they were proud of their grandfather, who cut "a brave and striking figure as he walked erect, head thrown back, cane in hand, inconspicuously dressed in a dark blue suit and a soft black felt hat." Eleanor would skip "gaily along beside him, anticipating the long jogging ride in the horse cars . . . and the broad walks of the park, where the joy of all existence was best expressed by running down the hills, head back, skirts flying in the wind. He would follow more slowly calling, 'Look out, or the cop may catch you!' I always thought he used funny words: 'cop' was surely a jollier word than policeman."[49]

Eleanor enjoyed the unusual words and droll expressions Melville used. His pet name for her was "Tittery-Eye," after a nautical nickname in *White-Jacket*. Once when they came back into the house after an outing, he stopped in front of the colored engraving of the Bay of Naples hanging in the front hall, and said, "See the little boats sailing hither and thither," a comical phrase she had never heard before. She refused to finish her oatmeal every morning, just so she could hear Melville say, with a "warning whisper," "Jack Smoke will come down the chimney and take what you leave."[50]

Fanny remembered Melville as a "tall man who towered over my head, wore a most amazing beard, and took such long strides when we went walking that it needed all my fast trotting to keep abreast of him." She held tight to his hand at the zoo so she wouldn't be eaten by lions and tigers, and when they went for rides around the lake on a swan boat, she would think what an "absurd contrast" there was between those tame cruises and her grandfather's "long voyages in pursuit of the monstrous whale, on stormy seas in rugged ships." Once, Melville took Fanny to see the chamber of horrors at the Eden Musée on Fourteenth Street, and the life-size wax gorilla carrying a pale maiden in his huge, hairy arms so terrified her that she made him promise never to take her there again.[51]

Although Fanny was younger and shier than Eleanor, and more timid, she was not afraid of her grandfather, as she was never "the victim of his moods and occasional uncertain tempers." She spent more time with her grandparents than did Eleanor, who "being older, was more easily left at home when domestic upheavals necessitated sending away one of the little girls for safekeeping." Like so many other ambiguous words and phrases in the family letters, the word *upheavals* has never been explained.[52]

Eleanor was not afraid of her grandfather, but some of his treasured possessions looked pretty spooky to a little girl. The bloody whaling scene by Garneray, hanging in the stairway leading to Fanny's third-story room, scared Eleanor, and the plaster cast of Antinoüs that stood "on a tall white pedestal in the corner of the front parlor, draped with a long white net veil to keep the city dust from settling on the beautiful features and curly hair of the young Roman," frightened Fanny. Eleanor cringed at the "strange plaster heads . . . searching blindly with sightless balls" from atop the bookcase, and the Eaton portrait exercised a "potent fascination" over her.[53]

Melville's study, on the other hand, was full of delightful toys. His huge mahogany desk held intriguing objects such as "a rolling ruler decorated with different varieties of green ferns, a large velvet pincushion mounted on an iron stand, and a little black metal candlestick for sealing wax." For a worktable, Melville had rigged up an "inclined plane" and covered it with pebbled green paper. It had "no cavity for inkwell, no groove for pen and pencil, no drawer for papers," and it stood in an alcove with manuscripts and books, which the girls were forbidden to touch, piled all over it. The walls of the study were lined with shelves that held colorful, gold-lettered books, and Melville allowed the girls to use them as building blocks as long as they were careful not to soil the bindings or tear the pages.[54]

Sadly, Melville feared his grandchildren would turn against him as they grew older, but they thought of him with "nothing but a remembrance of glorious fun, mixed with a childish awe, as of someone who knew far and strange things." Every afternoon, Melville would sit in the comfortable chair in Lizzie's room to read, and Eleanor would clamber into his lap and hold on to his whiskers to steady herself while he spun tales of fabulous adventures in exotic lands. His was "no soft silken beard, but tight curled like the horse hair breaking out of old upholstered chairs, firm and wiry to the grasp, and squarely chopped," and he didn't object to her squeezing it during the most exciting of his "wild tales of cannibals and tropic isles." Only years later did she realize that her grandfather had been the hero of these adventures, and that every time he told them, "he was reliving his own past."[55]

A surprising number of people remembered those South Seas stories with great affection, and just when it seemed Melville was doomed to obscurity, a new generation of readers discovered the books that had delighted their parents in their youth. To those who had read *Typee* and *Omoo* in the mid-1840s, Melville was a romantic adventurer who acted out their fantasies of escape from cultural constrictions on sexual and artistic freedom. For the artist John La Farge and the historian Henry Adams, Melville's island sojourns conjured the myth of American innocence and reestablished a fictive antebellum Golden Age, and they used *Omoo* as their guidebook in Tahiti. Young Jack London discovered *Typee* and for "many long hours dreamed over its pages," resolving one day to visit the Happy Valley. Lafcadio Hearn discovered Melville via Charles Stoddard's *South Sea Idylls* around the time he encountered Louis-Marie-Julien Viaud's "new Gnosticism of nature-feeling and nature-religion," but Robert Louis Stevenson, who, at Stoddard's suggestion, read *Typee* and *Omoo* on his way to the Pacific, carped about Melville's "bad ear" for transliterating native words, and called him "a howling cheese."[56]

Unfortunately, Melville profited little from the devotion of even these die-hard fans. When Harper's sent its twenty-seventh and last statement to him on March 4, 1887, along with a check for a mere $50.02, he was reminded that as long as the values of the marketplace ruled, the artist was doomed to be a castaway.[57]

At age fifty, Lizzie Melville seems to have regained some of the self-confidence and pluck she displayed before she married into the formidable Melville family.

Twenty-nine

The Hellish Society of Men

Shortly after New Year's, 1888, Melville received a bequest of $3,000 from his sister Frances Priscilla that made it possible for him to take a cruise to Bermuda in March, and to have several volumes of poetry privately printed. According to his granddaughter Fanny, Melville sailed for the South Atlantic aboard the Trinidad, *clad in "a heavy coat and plush cap" and carrying a "bundle called a shawlstrap in one hand and the inevitable cane in the other." On the return leg of the voyage, other sources suggest, the ship ran into the storm that was pummeling the eastern seaboard with hurricane-force winds and rain, so between St. Augustine, Florida, and Cape Hatteras, North Carolina, the passengers and crew had to crawl around the deck on their hands and knees. Melville arrived home in a downpour, and the temperature dropped so fast overnight that by the next morning, two feet of snow had fallen, burying New York. Telegraph poles snapped, electrical wires lay in tangles atop three- and four-foot-high drifts, and from the front parlor window, Melville and little Fanny could see policemen digging horses out of snowdrifts.*[1]

The Blizzard of '88 was the biggest snowstorm in the nation's history, so when spring finally came, it seemed miraculous. Wearing funny rectangular sunglasses with cut-off corners, Melville took four-year-old Fanny to Madison Square to see the tulips. While she romped through the flower beds, he sat on a park bench "off in some distant land or on a rolling ship at sea with nothing to distract his thoughts," becoming so lost in his reverie that he forgot about her and walked home alone. Bessie opened the door expecting to untie the bow she had made in Fanny's cap strings with her crippled fingers, and when she saw her father without the child, she was horrified. They dashed out, Melville in the lead and Bessie hobbling along behind.[2]

In the meantime, Fanny had discovered that her grandfather "had vanished just like the mysterious person I had always imagined him to be," and dodging the traffic, she had made her way safely to Twenty-sixth Street. She was toddling along, trying to spot the Melvilles' tawny cat on the fence in front of the look-alike brownstones, when she saw her grandfather and her aunt racing toward her, Herman looking terror-stricken and contrite, and Bessie moving more quickly than anyone thought possible.

The preceding paragraphs make a good story, but it's not certain that the events happened precisely as described. Undated references to Melville's bundling up to go to sea, to the big snow, and to the tulips in the park appear in Fanny's adult recollections, but Fanny may have conflated events of two years into one. From a biographer's point of view, 1887 is virtually a lost year of Melville's life, and references to the Bermuda cruise are fragmentary and somewhat contradictory. We do know that Melville sent Lizzie a wooden book rack from Bermuda in March 1888; that he stood at the window with Fanny after a big snow; and that when she was about four years old, he absentmindedly walked home from the park without her. By weaving these facts together, it is possible to compose a narrative that rings true, although its factual accuracy cannot be proven. As German critic Wolfgang Iser has written, "no tale can be told in its entirety."[3]

Art and politics continued to preoccupy Melville long after the completion of *Clarel*, as the poems and short prose pieces that came to be known as "the Burgundy Club sketches" show. In "At the Hostelry," a verse symposium, thirty great European painters discuss the social and aesthetic meaning of the picturesque, and in "Naples in the Time of Bomba," Melville adopts the persona of Major Jack Gentian, a patrician democrat whose conservatism makes him protective of America's hard-won liberties and a foe of monarchy, to attack the repressive, counterrevolutionary regime of the Bourbons that he had encountered during his 1857 visit to Italy. Like *Billy Budd*, "Naples in the Time of Bomba" expresses Melville's disillusionment with a world that seemed to have substituted the reactionary rationalism of Edmund Burke for the common sense of Thomas Paine.[4]

Writing with no concern for the marketplace was deeply satisfying to Melville, and he began grouping his poems for private printing. In general, they fell into several categories: reminiscences of old seafaring days, vignettes of life at Arrowhead, reflections on history and art inspired by his travels, philosophical and religious meditations, and explorations of mythology.[5]

One of the nautical poems originally intended for inclusion in a volume of "sea-pieces" was a sentimental ballad called "Billy in the Darbies," the prison reverie of an old mutineer waiting to be executed. After he had written a prose preface to the ballad, he decided to hold it in reserve, and after the addition of much new material, "Billy in the Darbies" grew into *Billy Budd*, a novella loosely based on the *Somers* mutiny of 1843.[6]

The case had haunted both Melville and the United States Navy for almost half a century. In his *Autobiography* (1883), Thurlow Weed described a conversation in which Hun Gansevoort had told him that his cousin Guert had complained about being railroaded into agreeing to the execution of Philip Spencer, and in May 1888, *The American Magazine* published an article in which Lieutenant H. D. Smith tried to exonerate the officers who had sentenced the mutineers to death. Given that the continued controversy had driven Guert deeper into depression and more heavily into drink than even his hereditary predispositions might have driven him, it's possible that Melville began writing *Billy Budd* as a way of imagining his cousin's untold story and began to imagine an "inside narrative" that went far beyond anything Guert could have told him. As Kenzaburō Ōe, winner of the 1994 Nobel Prize for Literature, said recently, "We cannot write true nonfiction. We always write fiction, but through writing fiction, sometimes we are able to arrive at the truth."[7]

By the spring of 1888, Melville had drafted seventy manuscript leaves, altering the focus of the original ballad substantially. The old mutineer had metamorphosed into a naive young sailor prone to stutter under stress, and an antagonist had emerged in the person of John Claggart, the malevolent master-at-arms who falsely accuses Billy Budd of fomenting mutiny. The novella is not "about" the *Somers* mutiny, however. It springs from profound meditations on moral and philosophical issues occasioned by historical events. Its main characters are nothing like the actual participants in the incident; they are representative figures in the struggle between good and evil, which Melville has given "a local habitation and a name."

⁓

When George Griggs died in May, Herman and Lizzie feared that Helen, who was battling cancer, would succumb to her illness quickly now that he was gone. Herman was not feeling very well himself, so before taking Lizzie and Bessie to Fire Island for a weekend, he wrote: "I, Herman Melville, declare this to be my will. Any property, of whatever kind, I may die possessed of, including money in banks, and my share in the as yet undivided real estate at Gansevoort, I bequeathe to my wife. I do this because I have confidence that through her our children and grand-children will get their proportion of any benefit that may accrue. —I appoint my wife executrix of this will. —In witness whereof I have hereunto set my hand and seal this 11th day of June 1888."[8]

Melville wanted to publish as many of his poems and prose sketches as he could while he had the time and energy. In September, *John Marr and Other Sailors with Some Sea-Pieces* was privately printed by Theodore L. De Vinne & Company in a limited edition of twenty-five copies, dedicated to British novelist W. Clark Russell. The book bore no author's name on the title page, as it was intended for distribution to relatives and friends. The title character, John Marr, a "lone-hearted mariner" who is disabled by a "crippling wound," moves west, and after losing his young wife and infant child to fever, he leases his log house to a newcomer and lives in it as a tenant.[9]

In an elegiac reverie, Marr mourns not only the end of the great age of sail and his personal losses, but also the disappearance of America's aboriginal prairies. The whites have all but exterminated the Indians, and the thirteen million bison that once streamed "countless in processional herds" have dwindled. The march of civilization has pushed the frontier westward until "America can today hardly be said to have any western bound but the ocean that washes Asia."[10]

Marr has nothing of value except his memories, and although his shipmates "could not all have departed life, yet as subjects of meditation they were like phantoms of the dead." Three of the "shadowy fellowship" of mariners whom Marr evokes are "Bridegroom Dick," "Tom Deadlight," and "Jack Roy," a king among men, modeled on Melville's old shipmate Jack Chase. Jack Roy's "watchmates of times long ago," with their "tattooings, ear-rings, love-locks curled," epitomize those "barbarians of man's simpler nature" who are precursors of the "upright barbarian" Billy Budd.[11]

As "Tom Deadlight," an old sailor who has "received orders to sail for the Deadman," bids farewell to his messmates and the "ladies of Spain," he takes his messmates' "flipper" in his own and makes a last request: "don't sew me up without *baccy* in mouth, boys / And don't blubber like lubbers when I turn up my keel." The use of sailor lingo expresses Melville's affection for his old shipmates and the old salts rusticating at Snug Harbor, as well as for his brother Tom, who, ironically enough, was reputed to be very hard on the pensioners in his charge.[12]

Two sections of "Bridegroom Dick" shed light on Melville's preoccupations during the writing of *Billy Budd*. With tears in his eyes, the sentimental old salt tells his "old lassie" the story of a noble Finn who showed such "racked self-control" while waiting to be flogged that the ship's captain spared him, saying he "hadn't any heart" to "degrade that tall fellow." Describing the "compassionate abasement" sailors feel when one of their shipmates is flogged, Dick pays tribute to the magnanimous Captain Turret for sparing a common sailor when many another commander would have flogged him, bringing a tear to his wife's eye, too. In another section of the poem, Dick praises "Guert Gan" for his victory at Vera Cruz, and in yet another section of the poem, he depicts him as "Tom Tight," a lieutenant who remains silent about the *Somers* case even when friends ply him with liquor: "Gentlemen, the more I tipple, the tighter do I get," Tom Tight declares, his reticence keeping him "true to himself and loyal to his clan."[13]

In addition to chanteylike lyrics and longer narratives such as "The Haglets," *John Marr and Other Sailors* includes the epigrammatic "Pebbles," dark meditations on Nature's indifference to the fate of Man such as "The Berg" and "The Maldive Shark," and romantic evocations of "The Enviable Isles" of the Pacific. Melville's old shipmates long to revisit "Pantheistic ports: / Marquesas and glenned isles," those "Authentic Edens in a Pagan sea" that hold out hope "here and hereafter" that Man will be able to "touch a Paradise" once more. But Man, the orphaned child of the universe, cannot touch Paradise either on Earth or in Heaven—at least not for more than a moment, ephemeral or fleeting—so he must create it imaginatively through Art. Thus, "The Aeolian Harp at the Surf Inn" wails "Thoughts that tongue can tell no word of!" echoing "man's strain—The hope of his heart, the dream in his brain."[14]

In "The Figure-Head," a sentimental poem about the carved statues on the prow of the *Charles-and-Emma*, Melville pays tribute to a married couple who have stuck together through a lifetime of storms. Once a "lad and lassie gay," they have been buffeted by "iron-rust and alum sprays / And chafing gear, and sun and dew" until they have nothing but the "tears in their eyes, salt tears not few." Bravely they cling to the prow of the ship until their hug relaxes "with the failing glue," and they fall to their deaths one dismal night. It's hard to read this poem without imagining that the pair are Herman and Lizzie, two ailing oldsters whose marriage had weathered many storms. Although as a young man Melville had felt that his relationship with Lizzie never quite matched the intensity of his relationships with men like Toby, Jack Chase, and Nathaniel Hawthorne, he evidently realized as he grew older that nothing could match the companionship of an understanding wife and the emotional resonance of shared family history.[15]

A modern reader encountering Melville's vigorous sea poems can't help thinking they might have found an audience in their own time, had they been published. Friends to whom Melville had sent copies of *John Marr* responded very favorably. From Deal, England, dedicatee Clark Russell called "The Figure-Head" the "gem of the collection" and "Tom Deadlight" "profoundly good . . . profoundly maritime." Richard Henry Stoddard, who had made a name for himself as a poet and critic after his stint in the New York Custom-House, wrote that despite "all his defects" and his "untrained imagination," Melville was "a man of unquestionable talent, and of considerable genius."[16]

Meanwhile, Melville was working steadily on *Billy Budd*, and by November the manuscript had more than doubled in size, filling 150 pages. He added a preface that placed the story in its historical context, and composed an eloquent tribute to Admiral Nelson, who had always epitomized for Melville the gallant heroism of the great age of sail. In December, after "long years of suffering from something like internal cancer in the stomach & liver," Helen died, leaving Herman and Lizzie bereft. Lizzie missed her "affectionate letters," her "bright sunny disposition," and her "ever-ready sympathy." Of the eight Melville siblings, only two were still alive, Herman and his sister Kate.

With so many friends and relatives dying, it's not surprising that many of Melville's late poems are meditations about death. In "Pontoosuce," for example, he implies that although Man cannot envision the afterlife, he can see intimations of immortality in Nature. In this poem, a female spirit kisses the narrator with "her warm lips" and brushes his brow with her "cold chaplet," then vanishes, leaving him with a mystical vision of a universe where nothing ever dies. In this poem, as in many of the poems Melville was writing concurrently with *Billy Budd*, the emergence of a female spirit, or goddess, provides the male narrator with a vision of transcendence and immortality through the integration of masculine and feminine forces of the soul. These poems provide an intriguing counterpoint to the dark vision of the political world portrayed in *Billy Budd*.[17]

All winter Melville worked on the novella, writing additional scenes on the backs of discarded drafts of poems in order to save paper. Inspired by Robert Southey's *Life of Nelson* (New York, 1855) and the six-volume *Naval History of Great Britain* (London, 1860) by William James, Melville pondered the qualities that had made Lord Horatio Nelson one of the great naval commanders of all time. He revised "Billy in the Darbies," making the sailor a young man innocent of mutiny rather than an old mutineer, and he developed the character of the ship's commander, who was originally intended to resemble Admiral Nelson. The more Melville worked on his story, however, and the more the character of Captain Vere evolved, the less he resembled Admiral Nelson and the more he resembled Edmund Burke, the eloquent critic of the French Revolution.[18]

By March 1889 the manuscript numbered 350 leaves, with the story taking a tack Melville had not originally foreseen: Despite his intuitive knowledge that the young sailor is innocent, Captain Vere orders Billy hanged for mutiny, and his fellow officers question his motives and his sanity. Melville set the historical preface aside; he also greatly expanded the role of Billy's would-be protector, the old Dansker. In June, when *Cosmopolitan* magazine ran a three-part series by Gail Hamilton (Abigail R. Dodge) called "The Murder of Philip Spencer," Melville was still adding scenes and characters. By deepening the role of Captain Vere and complicating the story's narrative point of view, Melville created perplexing moral ambiguities. The story became a political passion play, a language experiment, and, ultimately, a personal confession and catharsis, as Captain Vere comes ultimately to represent the generation of the fathers in its willingness to sacrifice its sons to authoritarian patriarchal power.[19]

The story is set in 1797, between the French and Haitian revolutions, when it was so difficult for the British navy to recruit men that they were impressing convicts and fugitives and seizing merchant sailors and forcing them to serve on naval frigates. Many British officers were so paranoid about the allegiance of their men that "lieutenants assigned to batteries felt it incumbent on them, in some instances, to stand with drawn swords behind the men working the guns"; service aboard a warship was tantamount to legalized kidnapping and slavery. At no time did Melville forget that the impressment of American sailors by British warships helped bring about the War of 1812, which convinced the English that America would never again be a British colony.[20]

As the story opens, Billy is serving aboard the British merchant ship the *Rights-of-Man* when he is impressed and forced to serve aboard the HMS *Bellipotent* (called the *Indomitable* through several revisions). Captain Graveling watches helplessly as Billy packs his bag and says good-bye to his comrades and "good-bye to you, too, old *Rights-of-Man.*"

According to the narrator, Billy resembles the legendary "Handsome Sailor," a "superior figure" who sports a gay silk handkerchief, ear hoops of gold, and a Highland tartan bonnet, earning the "spontaneous homage" of his shipmates. In a late addition to the manuscript, the narrator compares him to a "common sailor so intensely black that he must needs have been a native African of the unadulterate blood of Ham." Before the racialist debates over slavery polarized and paralyzed nineteenth-century Americans, many historians had argued that civilization had first arisen in the Valley of the Nile and that Adam, the first man, was an African. By midcentury, however, this theory had gone underground, as had the notion that there were once black Buddhas, a belief advanced by some mythologists. Melville knew a sailor named William Budd, but even more intriguing, "Budd" is the core syllable of "Buddha," and Melville clearly associates Billy with both Jesus and the Buddha, as well as with that "black pagod of a fellow," the Handsome Sailor.[21]

Billy Budd, whose shipmates call him "Baby Budd," is a foundling whose only flaw is a speech impediment that causes him to stammer under pressure. He is entirely without self-consciousness or guile. He is described as a "peacemaker," a "young Adam before the Fall," an "Apollo," and an "upright barbarian." Like Queequeg, Tashtego, and Daggoo, he has all the "barbaric virtues" with which nature can endow a man.

By mingling races and religions to characterize Billy, much as he had with Queequeg, Melville linked the innocent young sailor with tribal peoples of color who have been victims of the "march of civilization," endowing him with archetypal power and historical resonance. Thus, when the "urbane" master-at-arms, John Claggart, sets Billy up for a fall, and the "civilized" Captain Vere, the "white forecastle magnate," condemns him to die on the gallows, Billy represents not only the common sailor unjustly sacrificed to the exigencies of war, but also the "noble savage" slaughtered and enslaved by whites, the "darker brother" murdered by the precursor of "citified man," Cain.[22]

Aboard the British frigate, the young foretopman does his job without grumbling, especially after he sees a man flogged for missing an order, and the sight of his shipmate's naked back "gridironed with red welts and worse" makes him determined never to merit punishment or correction. Billy leads a charmed life until the master-at-arms, John Claggart, develops a "spontaneous and profound" antipathy toward him because his "masculine beauty" excites the admiration and envy of the other sailors.[23]

Like Shakespeare's Iago, Claggart is afflicted with "a depravity according to nature." It "folds itself in the mantle of respectability" and "partakes nothing of the sordid or sensual"; instead, it is "serious, but free of acerbity," according to the narrator. One day, when Billy accidentally spills his soup in the mess, Claggart, acting on the mingled sexual attraction and murderous envy that Billy's "significant personal beauty" and "heroic" demeanor incite in him, taps him suggestively on the backside with his rattan cane, saying, "Handsomely done, my lad! and handsome is as handsome did it, too!" Claggart's subsequent behavior contradicts the narrator's assessment of him, as it is "sordid and sensual" enough to cause the downfall of another man, and it is certainly not "free of acerbity."[24]

Despite warnings from the old Dansker, who likes Billy and distrusts Claggart, Billy refuses to believe that "Jemmy Legs" is "down on him," which makes him vulnerable to entrapment by the cunning officer. One day an afterguardsman tries to talk Billy into joining a mutiny, and even though Billy refuses, the malicious master-at-arms accuses him of mutiny. Billy's radical innocence makes it impossible for him to survive in a man-of-war world.

When Captain Vere summons Billy to his cabin to confront his accuser, he cannot speak. "Gagged" by helpless rage, Billy lashes out and strikes Claggart on the temple, accidentally killing him, and Vere immediately responds, "Fated boy, what have you done?" As the captain stands over Claggart's snakelike body, trying to get his bearings, "the father in him, manifested toward Billy thus far in the scene, was replaced by the military disciplinarian." In a manner that strikes the other officers as somewhat hysterical, Vere cries out, "Struck dead by an angel of God! Yet the angel must hang!" and convenes a drumhead court, justifying his unconventional response as necessary to deter future mutinies.[25]

The Honorable Edward Fairfax Vere is a forty-year-old bachelor whose bookish daydreaming has earned him the appellation "Starry Vere." According to the narrator, he is connected to the "higher nobility," and the narrator hints that he may even be Billy's natural father. A martinet and a closed-minded reactionary dead set against "novel opinion," he has earned his advancement by unquestioning devotion to discipline and duty, not by any devotion to his men or heroism.[26]

Throughout the proceeding against Billy, Vere argues for the death penalty, and when the other officers object, he argues rhetorically, "How can we adjudge to summary and shameful death a fellow creature innocent before God, and whom we feel to be so? It is Nature. But do these buttons that we wear attest that our allegiance is to Nature? No, to the King." For Vere, martial law takes precedence over natural or divine law, over mercy and compassion:

> "[Let] not warm hearts betray heads that should be cool. Ashore in a criminal case, will an upright judge allow himself off the bench to be waylaid by some tender kinswoman of the accused seeking to touch him with her tearful plea? Well, the heart here, sometimes the feminine in man, is as that piteous woman, and hard though it be, she must here be ruled out."

Vere associates decisiveness with manliness and clemency with womanly weakness, and he is willing to sentence an innocent young man to death rather than allow the feminine heart to rule the masculine head. When the officer of the marines urges clemency, or at least mitigation of the sentence, Vere invokes the Mutiny Act, arguing that "private conscience" must yield to "that imperial one formulated in the code under which alone we officially operate."[27]

By conforming to military law, Vere perpetrates a monstrous injustice. His sending an innocent young man for whom he has "fatherly" feelings to the gallows is "a matter for psychologic theologians to discuss," a "mystery of iniquity" much subtler than Claggart's bold-faced malignity. To salve his conscience, Vere conducts a private interview with Billy. The narrator speculates that "the austere devotee of military duty, letting himself melt back into what remains primeval in our formalized humanity, may in the end have caught Billy to his heart, even as Abraham may have caught young Isaac on the brink of resolutely offering him up in obedience to the exacting behest," but he offers no evidence for this view, and the reader never learns what actually transpires between them.

The reference to Abraham and Isaac functions more to alert the reader to the narrator's rationalizing than to describe an actual occurrence. The narrator's assertion that when "two of great Nature's nobler order embrace," it is a sacramental exchange, a kind of communion, the quasi-liturgical language is recognizable to the reader as a particularly offensive kind of moral casuistry. The reality behind this pompous prose is that a man who has power over another man has decided, for reasons not clearly understood by his peers, to be cruel instead of compassionate, merciless instead of merciful, and to scapegoat an innocent victim in order to gain power. Thus, Captain Vere resembles neither the noble Admiral Nelson nor the compassionate Captain Turret of "Bridegroom Dick," but a manipulative, self-serving Machiavel.[28]

Vere tells the crew "that the master-at-arms was dead, that he who had killed him had been already tried by a summary court and condemned to death, and the execution would take place in the early morning watch. The word 'mutiny' was not named in what he said." Meanwhile, Billy lies in a trance until the ship's chaplain arrives and tries "to bring home to him the thought of salvation and a Savior." Billy listens "out of politeness," with about as much interest or understanding as "a Tahitian, say, of Captain Cook's time or shortly after." Seeing that his efforts are in vain, the chaplain kisses Billy on the cheek as Judas Iscariot kissed Jesus, then leaves him to his fate.[29]

The hidden analogues of the kind of perverted patriarchal power that flourishes on the *Bellipotent* are rape and child abuse–the sins for which the Order of the Knights Templar was ultimately disbanded by the Church. Like the Templars, who were accused of sodomy as well as burning their own illegitimate babies to avoid detection, each of the main characters in *Billy Budd* is a bachelor in a world of motherless men, and each is crippled in some way. Billy's stammer signifies his helplessness in the face of unspeakable injustice, Claggart's rattan cane represents his twisted sexual aggression, and Vere's brass buttons symbolize his determination to remain buttoned up against the promptings of the heart.[30]

The next morning, with Vere standing as stiff as a ramrod to one side, Billy is brought on deck, and with the hemp around his neck, he delivers the conventional felons' benediction, "God bless Captain Vere!" As Billy is hanged from the yardarm, "a vapory fleece hanging low in the East was shot through with a soft glory as of the fleece of the Lamb of God," but the story ends not with the image of "rosy dawn," but with a number of brief scenes that undercut the religious symbolism. When murmurs of protest well up from the men, the boatswain extinguishes them with a shrill whistle, and the sailmaker's mates wrap Billy in his canvas hammock, place the body on a plank, and slide it into the sea, to the accompaniment of a "croaked requiem" of seabird cries.[31]

Several additional scenes offer conflicting interpretations of the event. First, the purser comments on the absence of the customary ejaculatory spasm during the hanging, remarking that Billy's death seemed more a case of "euthanasia" than execution, then the ship's surgeon expresses strong doubts about Vere's sanity, and the fleet newspaper erroneously reports that Billy Budd, the ringleader of a planned mutiny, had "vindictively stabbed" John Claggart and been duly hanged. Not long after Billy's death, the *Bellipotent* and the French ship *Athée* (*Atheist*) engage in battle, and Captain Vere is wounded. Heavily drugged, he is taken to Gibraltar, where he dies calling for "Billy Budd, Billy Budd!" in his delirium as Allan Melvill evidently never called out for his son Herman from his deathbed.[32]

Billy becomes a folk hero to the other sailors, who treat a chip of the yardarm from which he was hanged "as a piece of the Cross," and the narrative closes with the sentimental ballad "Billy in the Darbies," in which the condemned prisoner says good-bye to "Bristol Molly" and "Taff the Welshman" before he goes to his rest "fathoms down." Even though the ballad cannot begin to express the tragic complexity of Billy's fate, it evokes the reader's sympathy, and in so doing affirms that justice is a higher good than political expediency. What remains to give meaning to human suffering is art, and all that is left to celebrate the mystery of sin and sorrow is a sailor's simple song.[33]

After Melville's death in 1891, Lizzie put the manuscripts of *Billy Budd* into a tin breadbox for safekeeping, and after her death, in 1906, Eleanor and Fanny became custodians of their grandfather's papers. Since 1924, when *Billy Budd* was first published posthumously, various versions of the novella have appeared, giving rise to diametrically opposed interpretations of the story. Forming "testament of acceptance" and "testament of resistance" factions, some scholars have seen the tale as evidence of Melville's neoconservative defense of the old order against the rising tide of revolution, while others have seen it as clear evidence of Melville's lifelong antimilitarism and growing pessimism about the future of democracy and human rights in a machine age. Still others have provided an ironic reading of the tale as an indictment of Christianity, a destabilizing of legal authority, or a protodeconstructionist assault on history as a subspecies of fiction. Like a maze, the story leads readers into one ethical cul de sac, or moral dead end, after the other. *Billy Budd,* however, ensnares its readers much more subtly and insidiously than Melville's more aggressively tricky text, *The Confidence-Man,* because here it is the narrator himself, not any of the slippery characters he has created, who is the ultimate confidence man.[34]

Although some commentators argue that if Melville had lived to finish *Billy Budd,* he would have corrected the many factual errors and inconsistencies in it, others attribute them to old age, and still others believe he purposely sprinkled them throughout the text to cast doubt on the narrator's veracity. Judging from such obvious examples as "Bartleby," "Benito Cereno," and *The Confidence-Man,* Melville was quite capable of making the instability of the text a symptom of an "inside" narrator's inability to perceive and report the truth. The frequency of such contrasts between preconception and reality is made explicit by the false newspaper account that Melville added to the narrative, strongly suggesting that he intended the reader to realize that although the narrator has "inside" knowledge of military procedures, he has no common sense and no compassion. As the narrator's story becomes increasingly convoluted, the moral issues become more complex, casting doubt on the historical record.

No other text of Melville's is as protean, as unstable, as this late unfinished masterpiece. Paradoxically, too, no other Melville text exists in manuscripts so revealing of its extraordinary evolution and expansion (over what were to be the last five years of its author's life), no other work of Melville's has been printed and published in so many different forms, no other Melville text has been so canonized as the apotheosis of its creator's finest art (even though he never finished it), and no other text has given rise to so many conflicting interpretations as *Billy Budd*. The painstakingly researched and reconstructed "genetic text" of *Billy Budd, Sailor (An Inside Narrative)* prepared by Harrison Hayford and Merton M. Sealts Jr. in 1962 reveals Melville's own uncertainty about what he was writing. The so-called genetic text reproduces, analyzes, and attempts to date all of Melville's drafts, excisions, additions, penciled jottings, and revisions. Thus, although it is one of his best-known and most studied stories, *Billy Budd* continually rewrites itself, causing the reader's idea of the text to disintegrate.[35]

With apologies to the reader, it is difficult to write about *Billy Budd* without falling naturally into the convoluted, hair-splitting, overly self-conscious style of the novella's narrator. Snakelike, the double negatives, the conditional and subjunctive verbs, the abstract nouns and cautious qualifiers, insinuate themselves into the consciousness, predisposing the reader to expect an impeccably reliable narrator—a historian, or perhaps a keeper of meticulous naval records—a man of unimpeachable authority and objectivity capable of reporting facts in an unbiased and unemotional manner.[36]

Through quasi-legalistic jargon and pseudo-logical hair-splitting, the narrator tries to make the reader understand and accept the reasons behind Billy's sentencing and execution. The cognitive dissonance created by the narrator alerts the reader to counterintuitive abstractions, implicitly challenging the reader to find out ethical directions by indirection. In a man-of-war world, the voice of the people is strangled by propaganda, which is violence transformed into a bloodless art.

The *Bellipotent* resembles a twentieth-century totalitarian state where government officials invoke "national security" to cover politically expedient violations of civil rights, and where military necessity dictates that perversions of language are acceptable political weapons, and justice as civilians know it does not exist. In *Moby-Dick*, Ahab bends the crew to his insane will by incantatory language and brilliantly orchestrated ritual. With its intentional inaccuracies and syntactical twists and turns, *Billy Budd* anticipates George Orwell's *1984*.

Yet the voiced narrator is not the only teller of the tale; there is a silent narrator, too, perhaps a voice that spoke to Melville in a deeper register as he worked on later versions of the story and his characterization of Captain Vere evolved. At first, Melville intended Vere to be a sympathetic character, but gradually he became more and more condemnatory. It is as though Melville heard two voices, one defending Vere's decision to execute Billy, the other accusing him of murder, and he saw an opportunity to experiment with voiced and unvoiced narrators. Readers of "Benito Cereno" were deceived along with Amasa Delano until Melville turned the tables on them both, and in *Billy Budd* he created a text that told two different stories, the official story and the "inside" narrative of the story. Refining the technique he had mastered in the short fiction of the 1850s, Melville created his most diabolical narrator, an heir of Satan who speaks with a forked tongue, and the first practitioner of Orwellian doublespeak.

Billy Budd is a vision of the political world as "wise Solomon's hell," a place where institutionalized violence infinitely more civilized and subtle, and hence more dangerous, than the physical brutality of the *Neversink* shapes the thoughts and actions of those in power and ultimately enters the bloodstream of the Law. A bitter exposure of hegemonic historiography as cynical political expediency, the story implies that the relationship between the ruling elite and those whom they dominate is a sanctioned spiritual rape. In a paragraph replete with equivocal conditional verbs and biblical allusion, the narrator describes a putative postsentencing interview between Captain Vere and Billy: "The austere devotee of military duty, letting himself melt back into what remains primeval in our formalized humanity, may in the end have caught Billy to his heart even as Abraham may have caught young Isaac on the brink of resolutely offering him up in obedience to the exacting behest." After the enactment of this "sacrament," as the narrator calls it, Vere, Billy's judge and executioner, consigns Billy to "holy oblivion." The implication that Vere is a father secretly embracing his "natural" son before sending him to his death invidiously compares the relationship between officers and men to the relationship between a sexual abuser and his victim, underscoring the cannibalistic nature of patriarchal power.[37]

Billy Budd is a strangled cry from a child abandoned by his father, not only ritual enactment of the perversions of patriarchy, with Billy's unsexed body the altar on which the blood of the Lamb is split, and a confession of guilt by a father whose "abandonment" of his own son led to that son's suicide. It is Melville's "inside narrative" of Malcolm's death, and perhaps an acknowledgment that he had driven away Stanwix, too. Like Vere, Melville had played the Victorian patriarch to the hilt. As he went off to do a "man's work," he split himself in two, obeying the dictates of his paternal head and ignoring the impulses of his maternal heart. Just as Malcolm Melville's obituaries were changed to report the cause of death as carelessness, not suicide, Billy's death is inaccurately reported by the fleet newspaper and memorialized in an incongruous sentimental ballad. Melville assured friends and relatives that Malcolm had never spoken an unfilial word to him, *but what could speak louder than a loaded gun?*

Melville started writing *Billy Budd* nearly two decades after Malcolm's death, when time and the promptings of his heart had eroded the wall of denial Melville had erected. The theme of an innocent young man victimized by an authority figure who lacked moral courage and compassion resonated with Melville's own experience in complex ways, from his emotionally unsatisfying relationship with his father and the sacrifice of hundreds of thousands of young men to the machinery of a war in which he had not fought, to his cold treatment of Malcolm on the day his son died.

As a small child, Melville had been the slow and backward child who didn't rock the boat, the family mascot who camouflaged himself by being amiable and agreeable. As a young sailor, he became a man of action according to a traditional definition of masculinity, and as a writer, he mutineed against civilization's institutionalization of violence and injustice, becoming the preeminent rocker of boats in nineteenth-century American literature. In middle age, he became the patriarch in a household that included growing sons, and at the moment he most needed wisdom and moral energy, he failed.

On the flyleaf of his English translation of *The Divine Comedy,* Melville copied Dante's poignant cry, *"tu asperges me,"* a plea for forgiveness traditionally answered by the *"te absolvo"* of the confessional. Guilty of the kind of moral privation, or failure of moral courage, which both St. Augustine and Dante defined as sin, Melville no longer saw himself either as a favored Isaac or an outcast Ishmael, but as an aged Abraham who had held a knife to his son's throat rather than saying "No! in thunder" to an unjust, angry God. In exorcising the authority who hides his "brass buttons" among the trappings of his role and sacrifices the Isaacs of this world to patriarchal power, Melville exorcised the authoritarian father he had become.

The manuscripts show that Melville composed *Billy Budd* in three stages. Creating an "inside narrative" of his own journey from boyhood to adulthood and then fatherhood, he wove a narrative as tangled as Dante's dark wood, then filtered the *Divine Comedy* through a kind of Hegelian dialectic, transforming it into a tragedy as searing as King Lear. The innocent Billy starts his voyage in the paradise of the *Rights of Man,* endures purgatorial persecution aboard the *Bellipotent,* and ends in an inferno of moral casuistry and legalistic expediency, where he suffers an undeserved early death.[38]

Being a man was dangerous in a family whose men were prone to bankruptcies and breakdowns unless they were at war. As William Butler Yeats once asked, "Why should we honor those who die on the field of battle, when a man may show as reckless a courage in entering into the abyss of himself?" Fortunately, despite his instability at times, Melville achieved great wisdom and enormous inner strength, some of it undoubt-edly the product of repression and denial, some of it the result of making peace with his Maker and himself. Cultivating the quietism of Schopenhauer and Buddha, he strove to integrate the polarities of his nature in a conscious, determined effort to achieve psychic balance and reconciliation. By writing *Billy Budd* and gathering bouquets of poems for Lizzie, Melville attempted to atone for the great sins of his life. After Lizzie's death, some-one found these words carved into the back panel of a hidden compartment in her desk: "To know all is to forgive all." Perhaps Melville succeeded in forgiving himself, and being forgiven, after all.[39]

Melville's vision of "authentic Edens in a pagan sea" blazed as brightly in his heart as the vision of "wise Solomon's hell" that had plunged him into blackness.

THIRTY

THE ROSE FARMER IN THE GARDEN OF TRUANT EVE

"Every man," Balzac wrote in his old age, "has only a certain amount of strength, of blood, of courage, of hope, and my store of all these is exhausted." As Melville entered his eighth decade, he could feel his "vigor sensibly declin[ing]" despite the "unobstructed leisure" he now enjoyed. For his seventieth birthday, Lizzie gave him a two-volume translation of Balzac's letters in which he underscored passages that expressed disenchantment with political ideas, exhaustion from overwork, and a desire to be released from both worldly cares and excessive preoccupation with the self. [1]

Melville's markings in Balzac's letters and novels show that he cared deeply about how later generations would view him, and in several of his poems he addresses the issue of literary reputation directly, though in very different voices. In "The American Aloe on Exhibition," for example, he takes the persona of the "Century-Plant" he had seen at the Philadelphia Exposition to prophesy that his literary reputation would be self-renewing and that his writings would be regarded by posterity as more than just "the bon-bons of an hour." [2]

In November 1889, Melville received a request from an "ardent admirer," Professor

Archibald MacMechan of Dalhousie University in Nova Scotia, for more information about his life than was available in printed sources such as Duyckinck's *Cyclopaedia*, and Melville replied with a thumbnail sketch of himself: "You do not know, perhaps, that I have entered my eighth decade. After twenty years nearly, as an outdoor Custom House officer, I have latterly come into possession of unobstructed leisure, but only just as, in the course of nature, my vigor sensibly declines. What little of it is left I husband for certain matters as yet incomplete, and which indeed may never be completed."[3]

One of the remarkable things about Melville was his ability to reinvent himself continually in his writings, right up to the end. In his late poems he displays a chameleon-like ability to enter into various personae. For "The Rusty Man," subtitled "by a soured man," he takes the persona of Sancho Panza observing that Don Quixote "rusts and musts" while every greengrocer "thriveth apace with the fulsome face / Of a fool serene." Although he speaks from the squire's point of view, Melville clearly identifies with the broken-down old tilter at windmills who "doteth and mopeth / In library fusty," his romantic dreams having all crumbled to dust amid the sad waste of years.[4]

Other uncollected persona poems speak to one another like ghosts in an attic. "Madam Mirror," for example, is "stranded with wrecks in a garret." Remembering the faces she has seen, and thinking back on the "truths unrevealed and unuttered," the "pangs after parties of pleasure," and the "tears of the hopeless unloved," she senses "old age drawing near" and breathes a sigh of relief: "Far from closet and parlor at strife / Content I escape from the anguish / Of the Real and the Seeming in life." Responding to her, the "Wise Virgins" of a companion poem toss their curls and answer flippantly, "Youth is immortal; / 'Tis the elderly only grow old," and they chirp, "Oh yes, we are giddy, we whirl in youth's waltz, / But a fig for *Reflections* when crookedly false!"[5]

Melville must have longed at times to dance out of his head, to escape from self-consciousness, from the endless analytical thinking about thinking that bedeviled him. A creative genius who found linear, rationalistic thought frustrating, he was drawn to philosophers such as Sir Thomas Browne and Robert Burton, both of whom were less interested in logical analysis than in the dynamism of the mind and its ability to explore new realms and imagine new ideas.

In the poem and prose preface called "Rammon," a mythical son of Solomon who is weary of life becomes interested in Buddhism, especially the transmigration of souls, as a release from his ennui. Following in the footsteps of Siddhartha, he goes on a spiritual journey and meets Tardi, a "suave and fluent" Tyrian importer and poet. Tardi, a lover of Buddha who avoids "entire segments of life and thought," tries to convince Rammon that he will find happiness in the "Enviable Isles," but the young prince decides he must live for the good that exists in his present life.[6]

"Bale out your individual boat, if you can, but the sea abides," the narrator of

"Rammon" had advised in his preface, and with old age and death closing in all around, this was probably the best Melville could do. Allan's widow, Jane, died in late March 1890, and shortly afterward, Melville suffered a second attack of erysipelas, which laid him low for several months. During this time he borrowed a number of books from the New York Society Library, including Douglas Jerrold's nautical drama *The Mutiny at the Nore*, and William Dean Howells's *A Hazard of New Fortunes*, a novel about class warfare and economic struggle in New York.[7]

Despite his illness, Melville kept writing and corresponding with a handful of British writers. Havelock Ellis wrote asking Melville his "race" for a study of the ancestries of famous English and American novelists and poets. A son and grandson of sea captains, Ellis had sailed around the world when he was sixteen; apparently the only book of Melville's he had read was *Moby-Dick*.[8]

By the late 1880s, many people assumed that Melville had been dead for decades. When Clark Russell was showing a friend who wrote adventure books for boys a copy of *John Marr*, he happened to ask if he had read "the noblest sea book ever written called *Moby Dick*," and his friend, flabbergasted, asked, "Is Herman Melville alive?" In a similar vein, the journalist Edward Bok opined, in his syndicated column "Literary Leaves": "There are more people to-day who believe Herman Melville dead than there are those who know he is living. And yet if one chose to walk along East Eighteenth Street, New York City, any morning about 9 o'clock, he would see the famous writer of sea stories— stories which have never been equalled perhaps in their special line. . . . Talk about literary fame? There's a sample of it!"[9]

Bok's column prompted a shocked rejoinder from a *Boston Post* columnist who found it hard to think of Melville as an old man because "there is an atmosphere of youth about his books." Taking New York to task for treating Melville as "really defunct," this writer argued that Boston would never treat an author whose "best work is unsurpassed in its way in English literature" so shabbily, and several New Yorkers wrote indignant letters saying they knew perfectly well that Melville was alive and living in Manhattan.[10]

Outside of a small, almost cultlike following on both sides of the Atlantic, few people read Melville, and only a few admirers knew his most recent work. When Edmund Clarence Stedman, a Wall Street broker turned writer and editor, asked him for a handwritten copy of one of his best-known shorter poems and an engraved portrait for his anthology *Poets of America*, Melville sent him the "Ditty of Aristippus," a lighthearted drinking song sung by the Cypriot in *Clarel*. It seems a curious choice, as it is certainly not one of Melville's finest poems. Even so, Stedman considered Melville "one of the strongest geniuses, & most impressive *personalities* that New York has ever harbored" and he tried to re-interest the Authors Club in making him an honorary member: "He is a sort of recluse now, but we might perhaps tempt him out," Stedman wrote to a fellow member. When he finally did arrange a dinner in Melville's honor, he worried right up to the last minute that Melville might not come.[11]

Stedman's son Arthur and several other admirers contemplated writing Melville's biography, but they were soon discouraged by both the lack of source material and the lack of interest in his work. Melville had very little interest in cooperating with would-be biographers and memoirists, as Hawthorne's son-in-law, George Parsons Lathrop, discovered when Melville met his request for permission to include several of his letters in his *Study of Hawthorne* "with a sort of gloomy reluctance." When Horace Scudder, the editor of *The Atlantic Monthly*, asked Lathrop to do a biography of Melville for a "miniature American Men of Letters" series, Lathrop demurred. "Melville, I believe, is alive still, clinging like a weary but tenacious barnacle to the N. Y. Custom House & very much averse to publicity. . . . I don't know of any unpublished material that I can get."[12]

To this, Scudder replied cold-bloodedly that "if Melville would only let go of life," it would be easier to write about him, as "so much more frankness of speech can be used when a fellow is apparently out of hearing . . . we had better wait for our shot at Melville, when his personality can be more freely handled." Had Melville seen the correspondence, he would not have been surprised by Scudder's attitude. As far as he was concerned, publishers were as cannibalistic as other capitalists. He had long ago become disgusted by the fickleness of readers, and he had no desire to submit himself to the flensing-knives of critics.[13]

He was profoundly disturbed by the tendency of moderns to value commodities mass-produced in factories over the noblest achievements of man's mind and spirit, philosophy, and the arts. In "The Age of the Antonines," one of the forty-two poems in *Timoleon*, he portrays the classical world as the "zenith of time / When a pagan gentleman reigned, / And the olive was nailed to the inn or the world / Nor the peace of the just was feigned. / Halcyon Age, afar it shines, / Solstice of Man and the Antonines." A striking indictment of Christianity, the poem implicitly contrasts the "inn" that had no room for the Christ Child to be born with the hospitable pagan inn that nails the "olive" to the door to welcome travelers, rather than nailing Jesus to the Cross. "We sham, we shuffle, while faith declines," the poet complains, wishing he might read "in America's signs / The Age restored of the Antonines."[14]

In his brilliant eight-line poem "The Ravaged Villa," he likens the decline of classical civilization to a ruined garden:

> In shards the sylvan vases lie,
> Their links of dance undone;
> And brambles wither by thy brim,
> Choked Fountain of the Sun!

The spider in the laurel spins,
The weed exiles the flower,
And, flung to kiln, Apollo's bust
Makes lime for Mammon's tower.

This poem, written by a poet who had been forced to agree to the pulping of 224 unsold copies of *Clarel* three years after its publication, links the fate of the artist to the fate of civilization as a whole.[15]

Though grouped together, the *Timoleon* poems do not move in a linear fashion from the individual to the cosmic, as do the poems in *John Marr and Other Sailors*; instead, they speak to one another polyphonically, interweaving themes, motifs, and imagery so that personal and cultural concerns blend seamlessly. While some are based on Melville's travels in Egypt, Greece, and Italy, other, more-personal poems reveal a great deal about Melville's inner life.[16]

The title poem, "Timoleon (394 B.C.)," is based on Plutarch's account of the rivalry between Timophanes and his younger brother, Timoleon, a Corinthian prince. Their mother lavishes all of her attention on "her pride, her pet," Timophanes, whom she favors because he is "what I would be were I a man" and because he can make her "an envied dame of power, a social queen." Although Timoleon has a "just heart and humane," Timophanes becomes king, and quite predictably turns out to be a tyrant. Eventually, Timoleon is forced to kill Timophanes to save the kingdom, and his mother banishes him. Oppressed by her "heavy ban," Timoleon hears "insidious tones" from Hades tempting him to end his sufferings, but instead of killing himself, he flees to Sicily and lives quite happily there. In time, the Corinthians invite him back, "Not [as] slayer of your brother, no, / But savior of the state." Unlike Melville, who returned to the "empire of the mother" to confront his demons instead of staying in a tropical paradise that might have sapped his creativity, Timoleon chooses to live out his life as "the Isle's loved guest" rather than return to Corinth.[17]

From his earliest days, Melville felt he was an exile, the outcast son of that absent parent who stands ready either to call the wanderer home or cast him into outer darkness on a whim. At times he saw God as an intrusive parent who demanded obedience, and he fled; at other times he saw God as an elusive parent who seemed to withhold love, and he ran after him hungrily. Finally he cut the umbilical cord, and like Ishmael floating up from the vortex, he was able to wrest hard-won recognition not from an indifferent universe, but from his wife, his family, his friends, and future generations of devoted readers.

In the extraordinary poem "After the Pleasure Party, Lines Traced under an Image of Amor Threatening," Melville adopts a female persona for a dramatic monologue exploring sexual identity and creativity. Inspired by both Plato's myth of the androgyne in the *Symposium* and Schopenhauer's "Metaphysics of the Love of the Sexes," and perhaps by his meeting with the Nantucket astronomer Maria Mitchell, the poem voices the anguish of a woman torn between her passion for science and her sexual desires. Her soul split in two with longing, the astronomer Urania has retreated to the terrace of a Mediterranean villa in a state of confused arousal after feeling sexually attracted to a man she observed walking arm in arm with a peasant girl at a picnic. She fears Amor "may wreak his boyish spite" on her "turbulent heart and rebel brain," and racked by "sensuous strife," she suspects that her devotion to the cold stars is barren "self-illusion self-sustained."[18]

Unable to reconcile the two sides of her nature, Urania moves to Rome intending to enter a convent, and on the way she stops before a picture of the Virgin Mary. Instead of praying to the Holy Mother, she invokes the "armed Virgin" Athena, asking the mighty "Helmeted woman" to arm her against the "sexual feud" that "clogs the aspirant life." Soon, however, Urania realizes that sexual energy, or *eros*, is the greatest source of creativity, and asking Athena to "raise me and arm me!" she decides to risk the "vengeance" of Amor.[19]

These poems expose the spiritual and sexual tensions that glide beneath the surface of Melville's art. "Buddha," for example, begins with a sensual image reminiscent of Tommo swimming with shoals of naked *whihinees*, and ends with the poem's speaker imagining Nirvana as a kind of cosmic orgasm leading to annihilation of the Self. In "Lamia's Song," sexual passion lures the traveler to come as "the cataracts come" from his "lonely Alp" to "the myrtles in valleys of May," and he yearns to succumb to the "downward way" where he can lose himself in sensual revelry. "In a Bye-Canal," by contrast, portrays a man drifting through the canals of Venice in "a swoon of noon, a trance of tide." As the "indolent gondolier" plies his languid oar, a mysterious woman clicks open her lattice and mesmerizes him with her "basilisk glance of conjuration!" Although the speaker of the poem has "swum . . . / Twixt the whale's black flukes and the white shark's fin," he is terrified of the woman's "latticed eye." Intellectualizing his anxiety by comparing his flight to the flight of "divine Ulysses" from those "waylayers in the sea," the Sirens, he orders the gondolier to go "shooting by." Obviously, deep fears and dark temptations lurk not only behind the latticed window, but also in the latticed depths of the poet's psyche.[20]

This mysterious encounter causes the poet to take refuge "In a Church of Padua," where, as he stands before the confessional, "an upright sombre box" with "a door, but fast, and lattice none," he hears an unidentified "murmurer" confessing his sins to an unseen priest, and he likens the confessional to a diving bell in which a person descends into the dark depths of the soul.[21]

Like the priest, the artist dives deep into the human soul, but the treasure he raises to the sunlit surface is the poem, as in the quatrain "In a Garret":

> Gems and jewels let them heap–
> Wax sumptuous as the Sophi:
> For me, to grapple from Art's deep
> One dripping trophy![22]

Only art can counteract the entropy of the universe and redeem history; only art allows man to transcend time and space and resolve the painful contradictions that threaten to engulf him.

In one of his finest poems, Melville likens the artist's struggle with his work to Jacob's struggle with the angel:

> In placid hours well-pleased we dream
> Of many a brave unbodied scheme.
> But form to lend, pulsed life create,
> What unlike things must meet and mate:
> A flame to melt–a wind to freeze;
> Sad patience–joyous energies;
> Humility–yet pride and scorn;
> Instinct and study; love and hate;
> Audacity–reverence. These must mate,
> And fuse with Jacob's mystic heart,
> To wrestle with the angel–Art.

Reading Arthur Schopenhauer's essays on genius and madness, art and suicide, in his multivolume set of the German philosopher's works, Melville must have been struck by the uncanny parallels between their lives. Schopenhauer was born in Danzig to a wealthy merchant family known for a streak of insanity on the paternal side. His father died when he was a child, an apparent suicide, and his mother, a novelist, moved to Weimar and created a celebrated literary salon. Resenting his mother's independence and blaming her for his father's death, young Arthur fought his mother bitterly, and after a fight in which she pushed him down a flight of stairs, he left home a confirmed misogynist and pessimist, though not a cynic.

Schopenhauer's philosophy appealed to Melville because he saw in it a way to transform pessimism into a positive force for the conditioning of the soul. Strongly influenced by Buddhism, Schopenhauer argued that man's will impels him to strive incessantly and that unhappiness comes from frustrated desire, as man rarely gets what he wants. On those rare occasions when a man does fulfill his desires, he immediately ceases to feel happy because the absence of striving leads to ennui and emptiness. Fulfillment is an illusory goal, but even so, man must not despair.

Suicide is no answer to this endless cycle of suffering, as it is an expression of the will; hence, the only meaningful response to suffering is to let go and renounce the will. According to Schopenhauer, art brings release from suffering because it allows a person to enter into a timeless world of contemplation that transcends willing. Schopenhauer's wise passivity had a profound appeal for Melville, who was as exhausted by his struggle to attain spiritual peace as Ahab was exhausted by his pursuit of the white whale.

In December 1890, Melville came down with a respiratory infection that settled into bronchitis after he had walked in "cold, bitter air." Lizzie tried to make him give up his habit of taking long walks in bad weather, but despite her admonitions and his persistent cough, he refused. After working inside for hours, he needed air and exercise, and he enjoyed strolling downtown and browsing in the bookshops, especially Albert L. Luyster's store on Fulton Street and Francis P. and Lathrop C. Harper's in the Astor House. Sometimes he quietly picked out books and prints and paid cash for them without ever identifying himself, and sometimes he struck up a "brief but pleasant friendship" with a shop's proprietor, as he did with John Anderson Jr., the owner of an antiquarian book and print shop at 99 Nassau Street. After his illness weakened him, Melville did business exclusively with Anderson, whose assistant would deliver purchases to him for a "modest but welcome tip."[23]

On December 14, Fanny's third daughter, Katherine Gansevoort Thomas, "a well formed and healthy baby . . . as 'plump as a partridge,'" was born, and Lizzie went to New Jersey to help Fanny with the new arrival. When Lizzie got home in the second week of January, she found Herman suffering from another attack of erysipelas, and she wrote Kate Lansing: "Herman has been pretty ill for the last week or so—when he had a turn of dizziness or vertigo in the night—which the Dr feared might eventuate in a serious way—but now I am glad to say that his strength which seemed to leave him in one night has gradually returned and he is improving every day—he has not been out yet or even down stairs, but the Dr says there seems to be no reason why he should not entirely recover and be as well as before. I have been so much absorbed with Herman who requires a good deal of attention."[24]

Before the year ended, the estate of Ellen Marett Gifford, who had died the previous year, was distributed. Melville received $8,000 and a paid share in the New York Society Library, which he used to borrow fifty-one books during the last year of his life. Lizzie received over twice that amount, and each of the children received several thousand dollars. Ironically, this bequest made the Melvilles almost wealthy, but it was quite apparent that money could not buy time, energy, good health, or happiness.[25]

Ellen Gifford's gift meant that Herman could afford to have all of his poems and his novella printed privately in fine editions, so he spent the winter sorting and arranging poems. Not long afterward, he delivered a fair copy of *Timoleon* to the Caxton Press. The volume was dedicated "To my countryman, Elihu Vedder," who had done the exquisite illustrations for an edition of *The Rubaiyat of Omar Khayyam* that Melville treasured.[26]

On June 13, 1891, Lizzie's birthday, he presented her with the first copy of *Timoleon*, inscribing it, "To Her—without whose assistance both manual and literary Timoleon &c could not have passed through the press—with her name I gratefully and affectionately inscribe this volume." They had been looking forward to vacationing with Fanny's family on Fire Island that summer, but Melville was not feeling well, and Fanny's children were all down with the measles, so the trip had to be postponed.[27]

In his last decade, Melville realized that the ideal mate of his youthful dreams had never existed, and that what he had longed for was a kind of intimacy with another person that could bring the warring masculine and feminine sides of his own personality into harmony. He knew he had failed to be the kind of husband he had intended to be when he presented Lizzie with a four-leaf clover on their wedding day, and every year, so he said, he reenacted this ritual on their anniversary. Coming to terms with his failure, he tried to make amends to the woman who had stuck by him for over forty years. The last poem in *Timoleon*, "L'Envoi: The Return of the Sire de Nesle," captures this autumnal passion in its portrayal of a knight-errant returning home to his castle after many years of roving. When he finds his wife waiting for him faithfully, he realizes that her "lasting love" is the "one lonely good" left in the world, and he embraces her and pledges to stay with her forever.[28]

By turning inward to achieve peace of mind, and by redirecting his energies from dealing with publishers to writing poetry for private publication, Melville grew mellower as he grew older. Although he and Lizzie were failing physically, in some ways their marriage became a deeper, more satisfying partnership than it had ever been in the days when they were raising children in a complicated, crowded household. Now that she was financially independent, Lizzie began to rely more on her own resources, making frequent trips away from home and spending more time with old friends such as Kate Lansing and Sarah Morewood's sister, Ellen Brittain. Perhaps as they gained psychological autonomy and strength, Lizzie and Herman posed less of a threat to each other. In these years they worked together on the preparation of each volume of Herman's poems, as they had on earlier manuscripts, but with less pressure and less tension. Herman read poems aloud to Lizzie and consulted her on word choices and phrasing, and she became his Muse. Like roses transplanted to roomier beds, they both put forth new blooms.[29]

"The most precious things I know of in this world," Melville had written in the dedicatory epistle to *John Marr and Other Sailors*, are "Health and Content." Although Melville had gained a certain measure of mental stability and contentment, his physical health was declining. He wanted to finish a volume of poetry for Lizzie before falling into what Balzac called "that long sleep where one rests from all things at last, and *especially from oneself.*"[30]

In early August of 1891, Lizzie made a fair copy of *Weeds and Wildings Chiefly: With a Rose or Two* for the printer. Symbolism that harks back to the flower language with which Herman and Lizzie flirted during their courtship links the "Weeds and Wildings" to the rose poems, making his last volume a bouquet of poetry for Lizzie. This collection expresses Melville's yearning for intimate union with a kindred soul and the tension he felt among art, domestic life, and sexuality. Channeling his ambivalent feelings about sexuality into the search for the second self within the Self that is the wellspring of his later poetry, he reaches toward a pagan vision of a world ruled by female deities–a world that is a projection of the inner Androgyne.[31]

According to a convention reminiscent of the troubadours and courtly love, he addresses Lizzie by a sobriquet. Initially he thought of calling the poems "roses without thorns, eternal ones, the roses of St. Elizabeth of Hungary," but instead of canonizing her as Saint Elizabeth, he decided to address her as "Winnefred," though it is not clear why. It seems to be an allusion either to "Winifreda," who represents happy marriage in Percy's *Reliques*, or to Saint Winifreda, the patron saint of bakers, as Lizzie enjoyed baking and was proud of her creations. She liked to tell the story of how a pie she had baked and taken to Boston for her brothers was "only a little flattened" when she took it from her trunk. At first her brothers were skeptical that any pie could rival one of their mother's, but once they tasted it, they pronounced it very nice.[32]

In the dedicatory epistle, the poet reminds "Winnefred" of their shared affection for the clover that grew in the fields at Arrowhead, especially the red clover. In a humorous vein, he explains that he loves the clover not because he and Winnefred were "living in clover" in those days, or even because clover reminds him of the "happy augury" of the four-leaf clover he found on their wedding day, but because "this little peasant of flowers" is hardy and beautiful, as well as accessible to all. Like Walt Whitman's grass, the "flag of democracy," the clover is a democratic flower. "No one can monopolise its charm," Melville writes, "we are communists here."[33]

Playing the courtier made Melville feel young again, and cemented Lizzie's devotion to the husband she had once wanted to divorce. He remembers coming in from a morning ramble "early in the bright summer mornings of old" with a handful of these "cheap little cheery roses" and placing them "on that bit of a maple-wood mantel—your altar somebody called it—in the familiar room facing your beloved South!" After a cryptic reference to the remodeling of the house that echoes "I and My Chimney," Melville pays tribute to the "Madonna of the Trefoil" and with a poignant acknowledgment that the end of his life is drawing near, the epistle ends.[34]

Melville considered several passages from Shakespeare, then chose this passage from Hawthorne's novel *The Dolliver Romance* as the headnote to the volume: "Youth, however eclipsed for a season is the proper, permanent, and genuine condition of man; and if we look closely into this dreary delusion of growing old, we shall find that it never absolutely succeeds in laying hold of our innermost convictions." Melville believed he and Hawthorne and Shakespeare were closely intertwined, and in "A Ground Vine Intercedes With the Queen of the Flowers for the Merited Recognition of Clover," Melville imagines Hawthorne, the Vine, asking Shakespeare, the Rose and Queen of Flowers, to admit Melville, the Clover, to the pantheon of great writers and poets. Identifying Shakespeare with a female deity was certainly not accidental, as Shakespeare's playful sexual mix-ups and reversals, and his recognition that great souls are genderless and self-engendered, lent support to Melville's openness to unconventional sexual expression.[35]

Some of the poems about life at Arrowhead may have been part of the volume Herman left with Lizzie and Allan before he sailed with Tom to California in 1860, but others seem to be new poems composed to re-create family life as Melville remembered it—or wanted to remember it. These poems evoke times gone by—from children playing peekaboo to Santa Claus driving "thro' the spooming of the snows" to deliver gifts to the poor and to a prisoner in jail, then filling the "Stockings in the Farm-House Chimney" for the "little ones." Others, such as "The Pauper in the Turnip-Field," deal with contrasts between rich and poor in ways that link them with the economic and social allegories of the 1850s.[36]

On first reading, many of the short lyrics in this collection appear to be cheerful pastoral poems celebrating spring ("The Loiterer"), birds ("The Blue-Bird" and "The Little Good Fellows"), flowers ("Field Asters" and "Clover"), little animals ("The Chipmunk"), and children ("Madcaps"). Below the surface, however, a dark diapason sounds, as every happy memory is tinged with grief, and every poem allegorizes a family tragedy: the crow haunts the pauper's field, the owl questions whether life is worth living, the robin hunting for worms finds an "unfriended man" lying "lifeless under forest-eaves" and tries to bury him, and the merry "chipmunk" who flits away to an unknown destination is Malcolm Melville.[37]

Weeds and Wildings offers an amazingly varied panoply of self-portraits, among them "Rip Van Winkle's Lilac," a portrait of the artist in his old age that turns Washington

Irving's story inside out. In this poem with a prose preface, Rip, an old man slightly befuddled with wine, returns after many years to the home he shared with his late wife, and discovers a painter and a hatchet-faced utilitarian standing before it, debating the picturesque. Recalling the idyllic early days of their marriage, he remembers wishing he could dally in the "nuptial bower" with his "winsome bride" forever, but she soon settles down to gardening and keeping house, expecting him to take care of the carpentry and painting. Although she nags her "good-hearted good-for-nothing" husband, she is a much more sympathetic character than Irving's shrewish Dame Van Winkle. Rip is a self-confessed "idler" who considers her telling him to work comparable to Adam's expulsion from the Garden, and he is jealous of his wife's thriving garden, so he plants a lilac seedling of his own.[38]

In the intervening years, the pink lilac has grown so tall that it usurps the space and crowds out the "immemorial willow" that once stood there, and the entire region has become known as "Lilac Land." The flowering lilac has proven that Nature will find a way to use even the seemingly useless, idle man. Children pick its blossoms, and its fragrance perfumes the surrounding air "till, lo, that region now is dowered / Like the first Paradise embowered / Thanks to the poor good-for-nothing Rip!" Rip realizes that long after he is gone, the lilac will bring pleasure to his "children's children." Despite the passage of years and myriad tragedies, Melville, like Rip, had created something lasting and beautiful for his descendants and for future generations of readers.[39]

In a related piece called "The Rose Farmer," Melville makes a clear bid for Oriental sensualism over Western rationality. The guiding spirit of the rose poems seems to be "that sublime old infidel" Omar Khayyam. The young protagonist has inherited a "farm in fee / Forever consecrate to roses" from a "corpulent grandee of the East / Whose kind good will to me began / When I against his Rhamadan / Prepared a *chowder* for his feast." Curiously, these lines evoke the opening of *Moby-Dick*, which suggests that the relationship between the young narrator and the grandee is also meant to recall the relationship between Ishmael and Queequeg, and, by association, Melville's relationship with Nathaniel Hawthorne.[40]

Just as the narrator is trying to decide whether to harvest "heaps of posies / Or some crystal drops of Attar?" he meets the rose-farmer who presides over a "seraglio" of roses. The rose-farmer, who has come to his roses late, savors the living flowers, not the distillation of the Attar. Like the "pleasure-ground" in Coleridge's "Kubla Khan," his garden is "Laved by streams that sacred are," and his "darlings cluster to caress" him. His neighbor, by contrast, is a lean Parsee, a "Headsman and Blue Beard of the flowers" who approaches the roses when they are "in virgin flush of efflorescence / When buds their blossoms just disclose" and "scimeters the living rose" while the flowers whom the blade spares sigh and quiver with relief.[41]

This violence persuades the young man not to put off sensual gratification for "transcendental essence hoarded / In hope of quintessential bliss," but to emulate the rose-farmer, who is wise enough to enjoy life while he can. Old men, writes Melville in the *envoi*, are "boys in gray wigs, young at core," and "come gray-beards to their roses late," they are "wiser in relish, if sedate." They relive their dreams in the rose garden, where "down in heart youth never dies."[42]

Women, according to the narrator of "Rip Van Winkle's Lilac," inherit "more of the instinct of Paradise." The goddess personified as a rebellious Eve appears in a number of the rose poems. In "The Devotion of the Flowers to their Lady," Eve is portrayed as a kind of pagan deity, and the flowers, who are "natives of Eden," sympathize with her reluctance to blame Adam for the Fall. They feel that God the Father is a manipulative and controlling patriarch, quick to anger, and they blame Him, not Man, for human sin and suffering. Yet, after an indignant angel has "Cast out the flowers wherewith Eve / decked her nuptials with man," the exiled flowers "Languish with the secret desire for the garden of God" before the Fall.[43]

The rose remains as a promise that Eve's banishment will end one day; it is the "voucher of Paradise, visible pledge . . . attesting in spite of the Worm." Before the Old Testament patriarchs twisted it into a symbol of sin and death as part of their campaign to destroy the worship of the Goddess, the snake was considered sacred because it was the creature who hugged the bosom of the Mother and heard her secrets. The inviolate Rose, a trope for the female genitals, embraces the phallic Worm, or serpent, who is demonized in the Scriptures. Thus the poem implies that violation and conquest are the direct legacy of a jealous God whose power is controlling and destructive, not generative and erotic.[44]

The butterflies in "The Butterfly Ditty" scold Man, who is "Eden's bad boy," for enslaving the beasts, raping the land, and laying Nature waste, and they long for harmony between Man and Nature to be restored. In "When Forth the Shepherd Leads His Flock," the poet proclaims that redemption will come not when Christ, the Good Shepherd, comes, but when an ordinary shepherd "leads the flock, / White lamb and dingy ewe, / And there's dibbling in the garden / And the world begins anew." Thus the sins of the world are taken away by the innocent coupling of sheep, not by the Lamb of God.[45]

In many of the rose poems, Melville uses Christian symbolism to attack Christianity. In "The New Rosicrucians," for example, "disciples of the Order / Whose rose-vine twines the Cross" have "drained the rose's chalice" only to find that "For all the preacher's din / There is no mortal sin—No, none to us but Malice!" In "Rose Window," a kind of Swedenborgian vision probably inspired by the poetry of William Blake as well as by Pre-Raphaelite paintings and stained-glass windows, the narrator falls asleep in a cathedral after hearing a "honied" homily on "Four words . . . with mystery rife—*The Rose of Sharon.*" In his dream, an angel advances toward him, carrying a rose as a crucifer carries the cross during a processional. The angel comes "out of Morning's garden-gate" and leads him through "a sepulchral Strait" to a place where the dead lie in shrouds of "plaids and chequered tartans red" as the rose casts its beams on them. When he wakes up, he notices that as the light from the rose window falls on the "dingy stains," dust motes dance on dusty pews. Nature's light dancing on the empty pews replaces the dim light of God, drawing the narrator outside the church to worship in the sun.[46]

Just as art endows Man with a love of beauty, love endows Man with a magical imagination that can transform the world. The poet in the eight-line poem "The Lover and the Syringa Bush" is waiting for "truant Eve" beside a flowering bush so brilliant that its branches seem to hold the sky and sea:

> Like a lit-up Christmas Tree,
>> Like a grotto pranked with spars,
> Like white corals in green sea,
>> Like night's sky of crowded stars—
> To me like these you show, Syringa
>> Such heightening power has love, believe,
> While here by Eden's gate I linger
>> Love's tryst to keep, with truant Eve.[47]

Like Picasso's late drawings of the Minotaur, Melville's rose poems express a resurgence of eroticism, marking his emergence from a boyhood Eden of male friendship and masturbatory bliss into the garden of the goddess, Eve's mother. The male narrators of the rose poems combine elements of Dionysus, Buddha, and the Gnostic Jesus, and Melville's Eve resembles the earth goddesses of pre-Olympian Greece. The unresolved contradictions of Melville's nature had warred in him for decades; now, in late life, by reaching deep inside himself, he was able to reconcile the masculine and feminine sides of his own nature, the pagan and the Puritan. With the rose poems and other late writings, Melville mastered the "midwifery" of the soul.[48]

～

At some point during his last illness, Melville marked in his copy of *The World as Will and Idea* Schopenhauer's statement that "to die willingly, to die joyfully, is the prerogative of the resigned, of him who surrenders and denies the will to live." Perhaps he had a premonition that, like Schopenhauer, he would die at age seventy-two. All his life he had pondered the mystery of death, and at times he was dangerously obsessed with the idea of suicide. Although he never found answers to the religious questions he had wrestled with all his life—at least not the conventional Christian answers—Melville kept asking the great questions, and that in itself took courage.

Unfortunately, Melville did not live to see a printed copy of *Weeds and Wildings*. By late summer of 1891, he was too weak to read the pale blue volumes of Schopenhauer comfortably, so he let Fanny make castles and bridges on the study floor while he read the old plays in the "Mermaid Series." One evening toward the end of September, Melville went to bed feeling unwell, and shortly after midnight he suffered a fatal heart attack.

The next morning, Dr. Everett S. Warner filled out the medical report, listing "Cardiac dilatation, Mitral regurgitation . . . Contributory Asthenia" as the cause of death. Melville's niece Maria Gansevoort Hoadley Mackintosh spoke for the family when she told Catherine Lansing, "The poor man is out of his suffering, and we can not but rejoice for him. Poor Aunt Lizzie must be about worn out with her long and constant care of him."[49]

Dr. Williams of All Souls' Church conducted a brief funeral service at the Melville home for a small group of mourners that included Lizzie and her daughters, Sam Shaw, Catherine Hoadley, Tom's widow Catherine, Allan's daughters Kate and Milie, Willie Morewood, and one of the Lathers girls, probably Julia. Also present were George Brewster, Titus Munson Coan, Arthur Stedman, George Dillaway, a partner in the Wall Street law firm of Dillaway, Davenport, and Leeds, and a neighbor of the Melvilles who was probably a friend of Allan's. According to Arthur Stedman, there were others in attendance, but he did not give their names. Titus Munson Coan delivered a eulogy in which he called Melville "the first and only man ever made captive in a valley full of Polynesian cannibals, who had the genius to describe the situation, and who got away alive to write his book," but as Stedman noted, his next comment—"*Typee* will be read when most of the Concord group are forgotten"—could not be repeated in Boston.[50]

Melville was buried next to Malcolm in Woodlawn Cemetery in the Bronx. From his rugged headstone, a thick granite slab, rough-edged and decorated with tendrils of ivy, a carved stone scroll unrolls down the face of the gravestone and curls upward slightly at the bottom. The scroll is blank. The following "unvarnished facts" are carved into the base of the stone:

HERMAN MELVILLE
Born August 1, 1819
Died September 28, 1891

The rest is silence.

"Your destiny is a secret between yourself and God," Balzac had written to a friend, and sometime during the last year of his life, Melville had underscored this line. He considered his writings the truest record of his life, and he did his best to foil biographers, so it seems fitting that the scroll bears no epitaph.[51]

When Melville died, more than one journalist expressed surprise, because most younger writers thought of Herman Melville as someone from another century, the days of innocence before the Civil War. The obituary writer for the *New York Times* called him "Henry," and another referred to him as "Hiram Melville." While Arthur Stedman in the *New-York Daily Tribune* and J. E. A. Smith in the Pittsfield *Evening Journal* both pointed out that Melville had been productive to the end of his life, *The Press* claimed that "he had done almost no literary work during the past sixteen years," stating as a fact that he had written nothing since *Clarel*. When Walt Whitman, "the good grey poet," died, however, he was well known, and even obituary writers who did not approve of some of his explicitly sexual themes and images acknowledged his contribution to the nation's literature.[52]

Joseph Smith, Arthur Stedman, Frank Jewett Mather Jr., and Henry S. Salt, a Fabian socialist who was a devotee of Thoreau and a biographer of James Thomson, all contemplated writing biographies of him, but they soon lost interest, claiming that there was little to say about Melville's life beyond what the writings themselves told. Richard Henry Stoddard called Melville "the prose poet of the strange islands and people of the South Seas," and a decade after Melville's death, Stoddard paid him this tribute: "Next to Emerson, he was the American mystic. He was more than that, however, he was one of our greatest unrecognized poets."[53]

As Arthur Stedman observed in his introduction to a new edition of *Typee* in 1892, Melville preserved an "entirely independent attitude" toward literary recognition, seeming content "to trust to the verdict of the future." His reputation was kept alive in his own time by a handful of readers who passed their love of his books down to others. In Britain he became something of a cult figure among socialists, freethinkers, and students at the major universities, especially young men and women intrigued by the sexual imagery of *Moby-Dick* and the early novels and by what they perceived to be Melville's homoeroticism. Although a generation and more of American readers remained largely oblivious of his existence, a small number of faithful fans kept his reputation alive until the "Melville Revival" in the 1920s.[54]

Lizzie outlived Herman by fifteen years, tending his literary estate as lovingly as he had tended his small garden on West Twenty-sixth Street. Referring to her husband's books as if they were children, she devoted much of her time to keeping Melville's reputation alive, exercising her role as his literary executor with care and diligence. She organized and preserved his unpublished manuscripts, kept accounts, negotiated copyrights, and corresponded with fans and potential biographers. She made "Memoranda" about her husband's life and writings that consist of fragmentary, almost random, factual notes, but nothing personal. Much remains unknown and always will. Perhaps it is better that way, because it is possible to imagine almost anything about a man as tormented and great-souled as Herman Melville. At some point, someone carved into the back panel of a hidden compartment in Lizzie's desk words that speak volumes: "To know all is to forgive all."[55]

At the conclusion of her memoir, Lizzie noted that her husband's death had come "after two years of failing health, induced partly by severe attacks of erysipelas terminating finally in enlargement of the heart." With that phrase, she may well have come closer than anyone else to capturing the secret of Melville's magnificent writing and his troubled life. All the doubting and daring, all the passion and ribald humor, all the pain and travail, the hunger for knowledge and the thirst for wisdom, and the restless, relentless quest for certainty had greatly enlarged Herman Melville's heart.

AFTERWORD:
MELVILLE'S SEXUALITY

With American popular culture tending to swing violently between puritanism and perversity, sex has become a peculiar American obsession, even in academia. The colonization of literary critical studies by French scholars who eroticize texts, then deconstruct them, has combined with the emergence of gay and lesbian studies to thrust sex and gender into the foreground of biographical studies. Sexuality has become the mask through which scholars—as mesmerized by Paul deMan, Jacques Derrida, Michel Foucault, Luce Irigaray, and Jacques Lacan as Ahab was by Fedallah and his crew of phantoms—feel compelled to strike. The pen is mightier than the sword *has become the weapon of choice in battles over academic turf, a hermeneutical harpoon to dart at literary leviathans like Herman Melville.*

The language of sex and gender has become hopelessly politicized, and current scholarship too often treats sex and gender as abstract entities that can be studied independently, rather than as organic components of complex, changeable human beings. The inevitable questions about Melville's relationship with Nathaniel Hawthorne frustrate me because I do not feel comfortable reducing human emotions and sexual diversity to sound bites.

In successive drafts of this biography, I have struggled to craft a language for talking about Melville's sexuality without force-fitting him into the Procrustean bed of theory. Gay critics claim Melville as a gay writer, but I feel it is restrictive to reduce Melville's writings to coy sexual disclosures, or his life to an elaborate lie. Individuals for whom intellect and sensuality form one strong erotic current may form passionate attachments to persons of both sexes that are not necessarily sexual. Although his writings reflect a deep longing for emotional intimacy with other men, Melville does not seem to have been actively homosexual, according to twentieth-century definitions of the term. He lived a very different life from Walt Whitman, Charles Warren Stoddard, or Oscar Wilde. Whereas Whitman openly proclaimed his preference for men and lived with a male lover, refusing to marry despite proposals from women admirers, Melville lived a heterosexual life, as far as we know. After escaping the forced homosexuality of the forecastle and the multiple seductions of the rover's life in the South Seas, he married and fathered four children. At the same time, because he had experienced a complete bouleversement of his assumptions about sex in the South Seas, sexuality became a more inclusive, multivalent expression of desire than anything his Calvinist Sunday-school teachers had envisioned, fueling the creative tensions that ignite his incandescent prose and poetry.[1]

Melville's relationship with his wife was obviously complex and contradictory, especially in the light of the late poetry, which hints at a resurgence of erotic feeling. As family tradition has it, Melville burned his love letters to Lizzie, so we have no Melville letters to compare with those of Calvin Stowe, for instance. Stowe not only wrote sexually suggestive love letters to his wife, Harriet, while she was away, describing his sexual frustration and imploring her to return to his bed as soon as possible; he also described sleeping with men during her absence. In one letter, Calvin told Harriet that a neighbor had come over to sleep with him while she was away and assured her that though the fellow's embraces were better than nothing, no male bedfellow could ever take her place. When a younger man developed a crush on Calvin Stowe and proclaimed that sleeping with him was "almost as good as being married," he wrote a tongue-in-cheek letter to Harriet making fun of the poor lad's ignorance of conjugal delights.

With birth control virtually nonexistent and childbirth extremely hazardous, married couples in the mid–nineteenth century often turned to same-sex friends for warmth and comfort in the absence of opposite-sex spouses or lovers. Men and women in Melville's America regularly employed erotic tropes when addressing intimate same-sex friends, perhaps because the language of passionate friendship was not construed as an invitation to sexual consummation, as it is today. As Harriet's biographer Joan Hedrick points out, although Calvin's letters demonstrate "the nineteenth century's easy acceptance of same-sex physical intimacy (later termed 'deviant' by sexologists)," it seems ludicrous to classify Calvin Stowe as "heterosexual," "homosexual," or "bisexual" on the basis of these references.[2]

In Melville's day, same-sex friends often shared beds when visiting each other's homes, partly because houses were small, furniture scarce, and central heating unknown. Men traveling alone slept with other men at roadside inns, as Ishmael and Queequeg do in *Moby-Dick*, and young men sowing their wild oats with whores in frontier towns regularly shared sleeping quarters and often slept in the same bed. In "Mark Twain and Homosexuality," Andrew J. Hoffman writes that Twain's relationship with one of his roommates was teasingly referred to as a "marriage" by a local tabloid. Even so, these relationships were not necessarily sexual. When Twain went west in the mid-1860s, Virginia City, Nevada, was wild and woolly, and bohemian San Francisco, then ninety percent male, was like the 1840s whale ship bound for the Marquesas. It had the reputation of being a paradise for bachelors in the sense that the men had access to both male camaraderie of all kinds and females who were sexually available.[3]

Compared with the material Hoffman presents about Mark Twain's relationships with Artemus Ward, Dan De Quille, and others, we have virtually no information about Melville's relationship with Eli James Murdock Fly, Richard Tobias Greene, Jack Chase, or Nathaniel Hawthorne. Melville and Fly may well have shared a bed during their trip west, Melville and "Toby" probably enjoyed polymorphous sexual experimentation in the Marquesas, but there is no evidence that they experimented with each other. Even Melville's passionate letters to Hawthorne, so often deemed homoerotic, are bursting more with self-discovery, psychological identification, intellectual excitement, and spiritual hunger than with sexual desire. More narcissistic than erotic, these passionate letters express Melville's infatuation with the new self-image and artistic self-confidence Hawthorne aroused in him.[4]

Focusing on Melville's sexual orientation deflects attention from the literary qualities of his extraordinary novels, stories, and poems. Many scholars argue that Melville must have had sexual contact with his shipmates *because all sailors did,* and as proof, they cite the sperm-squeezing scene in *Moby-Dick*. Literal interpretations notwithstanding, Melville transforms mutual masturbation into an iconoclastic image of brotherly love, and by thrusting shipboard sexuality into the foreground, he raises it above the quasi-pornographic underground novels and uses sperm-squeezing to dissolve constructions of masculinity that erect boundaries, not bridges, between man and man. A lifelong enemy of hierarchical oppression, Melville embraces homosociality as an alternative to masculinist cultural paradigms that were crippling men as well as women.[5]

Homophobia has led to the suppression of our "gay history," and current constructions of gender deny psychosexual multiplicity. Several generations of homosexual men and women have experienced a "shock of recognition" on encountering homoerotic tropes in *Typee* and *Moby-Dick*. While it's true that gay men in British universities made Melville a cult figure, or totem, as did members of the predominately bisexual Bloomsbury Group, it's equally true that sexual adverturism is only one of the many forms of adventure Melville celebrates and that men and women have been drawn to Melville for many reasons. In his provocative study of *Pierre,* James Creech argues convincingly that Melville's texts "wink" at homosexual readers and that incest is encrypted homosexuality. He is also quick to point out that calling Melville a "homosexual" clouds the issues more than it aids our understanding of either Melville or *Pierre*. Most useful, I think, is his comment that *Pierre* is Melville's response to "the oedipal family coming to flower in the nineteenth century," which, according to Creech, "was literally, an affair among men." It is no surprise that Melville's novel of incestuous love anticipates the intellectual climate that led to the formation of the Boston School of Psychiatry and later to Freudian psychoanalysis, as these movements were responses to the pathology of the bourgeois family.[6]

What Ishmael and Queequeg, Huck and Jim, and other same-sex interracial homosocial couples in American literature have in common is not necessarily overt, covert, or latent homosexuality, as Leslie Fiedler argued in *Love and Death in the American Novel,* but transgressive paradigms of homosocial brotherhood and male intimacy that challenge and seek to subvert the soulless, misogynistic competitive construction of masculinity dictated by the new market capitalism and industrialization.

Given human nature and the frequency with which previously unknown letters and manuscripts turn up in barns and attics, it's wise for a biographer to keep the territory open, the deepest seas uncharted, the most tantalizing mysteries unsolved. As Melville wrote in *Pierre,* "In their precise tracings-out and subtle causations, the strongest and fieriest emotions of life defy all analytical insight. We see the cloud, and feel its bolt, but meterology only idly essays a critical scrutiny as to how that cloud became charged, and how this bolt so stuns. The metaphysical writers confess, that the most impressive, sudden, and overwhelming event, as well as the minutest, is but the product of an infinite series of infinitely involved and untraceable foregoing occurrences. Just so with every motion of the heart." One never knows what "great gliding phantom" will emerge from the oceans of lost material about, or by, the elusive Herman Melville.

NOTES

AWH	Augusta Whipple Hunter	NH	Nathaniel Hawthorne
AM	Allan Melville (father)	PG	Peter Gansevoort
AMjr.	Allan Melville	RL	Richard Lathers
AuM	Augusta Melville	SAM	Sarah A. Morewood
CG/CGL	Kate Gansevoort/Catherine Gansevoort	SG	Stanwix Gansevoort
	Lansing	SH	Sophia Hawthorne
CMH	Catherine Melville Hoadley	SHS	Samuel Hay Savage
CMS	Catharine Maria Sedgwick	SM	Stanwix Melville
EAD	Evert A. Duyckinck	SSS	Samuel Savage Shaw
EMM	Eleanore Melville Metcalf	STM	Sophia Thurston Melville
EP	Elizabeth Peabody	TM	Thomas/Tom Melville
ESM	Elizabeth Shaw Melville	TMjr.	Major Thomas Melvill, Jr.
FM	Fanny Melville	WM	Willy Morewood
FPM	Frances Priscilla Melville		
GD	George Duyckinck	AIHA	Albany Institutes of History and Art
GG	Guert Gansevoort	BA	Berkshire Athenaeum
GM	Gansevoort Melville	BCHS	Berkshire County Historical Society
HelM or HMG	Helen Melville (Griggs)	GLA	Gansevoort-Lansing Collection, Augusta
HM	Herman Melville		Papers
HSG	Henry Sanford Gansevoort	GLC	Gansevoort-Lansing Collection
HSS	Hope Savage Shaw	HCL-MFP	Harvard College Library–Melville Family
JCH	John Chipman Hoadley		Papers
JEAS	Joseph E. A. Smith	HUA	Harvard University Archives
JMB	Julia M. Blatchford	LHS	Lansingburgh Historical Society
JMM	Julia Maria Melvill	NEMLA	Northeast Modern Language Association
JR	Julius Rockwell	NYHS	New-York Historical Society
JRM	John Rowland Morewood	MCNY	Museum of the City of New York
LS	Lemuel Shaw	MHS	Massachusetts Historical Society
LSjr.	Lemuel Shaw, Jr.	MHSS	Massachusetts Historical Society, Shaw Papers
MAG	Mary Anne Gansevoort	NYPL	New York Public Library
MB	Mary Blatchford	OCSWU	Osborne Collection of Melville Materials at
MD	Margaret Duyckinck		Southwestern University
MGM	Maria Gansevoort Melville	UCLA-JL	University of California at Los Angeles, Jay
MM	Malcolm Melville		Leyda Collection

PREFACE

1. When I began working on this book, I assumed that Hershel Parker, Jay Leyda's designated heir, would be releasing the *New Melville Log* in time for the centennial of Melville's death in 1991. As Julian Markels pointed out in "The *Moby-Dick* White Elephant," *American Literature* 66, no. 1 (March 1994), 105–22, the delay has been frustrating to Melville scholars.

2. Laurie Jean Lorant, *Herman Melville and Race: Themes and Imagery* (Ph.D. dissertation, New York University, 1972), a work that, in retrospect, anticipated New Historicism in many ways.

3. *sea-change* See, for example, Hennig Cohen and Donald Yannella, *Herman Melville's Malcolm Letter: "Man's Final Lore"* (New York: Fordham University Press and the New York Public Library, 1992); James Creech, *Closet Writing/Gay Reading: The Case of Melville's Pierre* (Chicago and London: University of Chicago Press, 1993); Caleb Crain, "Lovers of Human Flesh: Homosexuality and Cannibalism in Melville's Novels," *American Literature* 66, no. 1 (1964), 25–53; and Elizabeth Renker, "Herman Melville, Wife Beating, and the Written

Page," *American Literature* 66, no. 1 (1994), 123–50. Also, see my "Afterword" to this volume.

4. *"civilization"* Vernon Parrington, *Main Currents in American Thought: An Interpretation of American Literature from the Beginnings to 1920*, vol. 2 (New York: Harcourt, Brace & Company, 1930), 266. *"Doom!"* D. H. Lawrence, *Studies in Classic American Literature* (New York: Viking Press, 1954), 160.

5. Reading the Afterword to Carolyn L. Karcher's *The First Woman in the Republic: A Cultural Biography of Lydia Maria Child* (Durham and London: Duke University Press, 1994), 608–16, I was struck by how similar Child and Melville were in some ways, despite their obvious differences. *"earth"* *Moby-Dick, or The Whale*, with an introduction by Andrew Delbanco and notes and explanatory commentary by Tom Quirk (New York: Penguin Books, 1992),* 132.

6. *"begin"* EMM to Jay Leyda, 11/3/47, Leyda Collection, UCLA. Mrs. Metcalf, Melville's granddaughter and the author of *Herman Melville: Cycle and Epicycle* (Cambridge: Harvard University Press, 1953), was referring to Gansevoort, about whom she says in another letter: "Poor Gansevoort! It was in-

---

*Cited hereafter as "*PM-D.*"

deed ill health. If the family ever knew of the situation, no one could ever have divulged it to the next, or the next to the next, generation; for Gansevoort was always spoken of in the most glowing terms—indeed a good deal to Herman's disadvantage," EMM to JL, 11/19/47, Leyda Collection, UCLA.

1. LOFTY ORIGINS

1. *Melvill* The *e* was added after Allan's death in 1832.

2. *James Cargill* See the unpublished article by Eugene Taylor and Henry A. Murray, "Some Indian-Hating in the Melvill Family," Murray Papers, Harvard University Archives.

3. *"Aboriginals" and "daring chivalric deed"* AM's "Sketch of my Father's Life," 3/21/29, GLC, a document evidently written to persuade the Jackson administration not to relieve the old Major of his Custom House job. It's strange that the Bostonians styled themselves "Mohawks," as the Mohawk Indians were native to New York State. Perhaps calling themselves "Pequots" would have stirred guilty consciences, as whites in New England had slaughtered the Pequots. Many Bostonians kept the tea leaves that washed up on the beach the following day as souvenirs. In an interview published in the *New Bedford Standard-Times* on July 20, 1952, Mrs. Charles S. Hamlin of Albany reported meeting the elderly Herman Melville at the Lansing home in Albany when she was a little girl. According to Mrs. Hamlin, Herman Melville told her that his grandfather's *wife* had found the tea leaves in his boot, but Thomas Melvill did not marry Priscilla Scollay until the following year, so Herman probably meant to say "fiancée." The Green Dragon Tavern was the regular meeting place of the St. Andrew's Lodge of Freemasonry. The dragon that hung outside the tavern now resides in the Boston Masonic Temple, Grand Lodge of Massachusetts, 186 Tremont Street, Boston. Paul Revere and Dr. Joseph Warren, whose names (along with that of Samuel Adams) have been associated with the Tea Party, were Masons. Major Melvill was initiated into the Massachusetts Lodge on December 23, 1771 (see card files of memberships, Grand Masonic Lodge, Boston). See also Francis F. Drake, *Tea Leaves* (Boston: A. O. Crane, 1884)—a volume, incidentally, given to Herman Melville by his wife, Elizabeth Shaw Melville, in November 1886, according to Merton M. Sealts Jr., *Melville's Reading*, revised and enlarged edition (Columbia: University of South Carolina Press, 1988). I am grateful to Ward Williamson, Grand Librarian at Boston's Masonic Temple, for drawing my attention to *Tea Leaves* and for sharing with me his knowledge of Freemasonry. It is not known whether Major Melvill's sons Allan and Thomas Jr. were Masons, nor whether his grandsons were; Herman's writings contain numerous allusions to freemasonry, which deserve to be pursued.

4. *slaves* Sambo, and bill of sale for "a certain Negro wench Jude, and her two children," Francis Nicoll to Peter Gansevoort, June 28, 1804, BA. Among Leonard Gansevoort's papers in the Albany Institute are records of several transactions: On May 30, 1793, he bought a mulatto slave, Tom, from one Simon Ridder; in 1796 he sold a Negro man, Peter, about twenty-two years old, to Abraham A. Lansing and bought a Negro slave named Caesar; in 1812 he manumitted his faithful slave Chloe, a woman under fifty years of age, whom he deemed capable of caring for herself if freed. *family history* Alice P. Kenney, *The Gansevoorts of Albany* (Syracuse, N.Y.: Syracuse University Press, 1969).

5. *venison and later meeting* Isabel Thompson Kelsey, *Joseph Brant 1743–1807: Man of Two Worlds* (Syracuse, New York: Syracuse University Press, 1984), 267.

6. *Brant* From Leonard Gansevoort Jr.'s unpublished, undated "Reminiscence of a Revolutionary Officer," which can be found in the Gansevoort-Lansing Collection in the New York Public Library, GLC. Colonel Quackenboss appears to have been Melville's ancestor by marriage, perhaps through Herman Gansevoort's wife, Catherine Quackenboss. Gail Quackenbush, *The Quackenbush Family in America* (Wolfe City,

Texas: Henington Publishing Company, 1987), gives no corroboration of the relationship, but in any event, this memoir gives a glimpse of frontier life in New York State such as Melville might have heard about or seen it.

7. *blood* Leonard Gansevoort Jr., *Reminiscence.*

8. *Cincinnati* See Merton M. Sealts Jr., "The Melvilles, the Gansevoorts, and the Cincinnati Badge," *Melville Society Extracts* 70 (September 1987), 1, 4.

9. An older son named Peter Gansevoort died in 1788 at the age of two. *elector* Victor Paltsits to Marion Chitty, 3/14/1936, GLC. *"iniquity"* Kenney, *Gansevoorts*, 150.

10. J. C. Goldberg's bill for piano lessons, 8/27/07, GLC.

11. *"fiction"* Kenney, *Gansevoorts,* 173. Here and elsewhere, I am greatly indebted to Kenney's book as well as the Gansevoort-Lansing Collection in the New York Public Library for much of the information about Melville's family and Dutch society in the New World.

12. It's not certain when Allan and Maria first met, but they both could have attended Admiral Perry's ball.

13. AM copybook of 1793, Gansevoort-Lansing Collection, New York Public Library.

14. *real estate, mail* Numerous papers relating to real-estate transactions, and envelopes like those described here, may be found among the papers in the Gansevoort-Lansing Collection at the New York Public Library.

15. *Swan* "At this moment it would be difficult to effect sales of merchandize [*sic*]–people are completely panicstruck," Otis Swan to AM, 9/1/14, GLC.

16. *legal wrangles* AM to PG, 2/7/18, BA. *"love me more"* AM to PG, 3/26/18, BA.

17. *Edinburgh* AM to MGM, 5/17/18, GLC.

18. In 1821, Allan joined the Saint Andrew's Society, a Masonic society, whose register lists Scotland as his birthplace. It is impossible to tell from the listing whether Allan lied to boost his importance in the eyes of other members, or whether the Society's recorder mixed him up with his grandfather; either seems a possibility. The entry reads, "1821, Allan Melville [*sic*], b. Scotland, 1783; d. Albany, New York, Jan. 28, 1832. Dry goods." *The Register of Saint Andrew's Society of the State of New York* (organized 1756), second series, part 1, 1807–31, compiled by William M. MacBean (printed 1922).

19. *"Lover"* AM to MGM, 5/31/18, GLC. *"a sprig of myrtle," "brightness," etc.* AM to MGM, 6/7/18, BA. *style* For a discussion of British and Dutch letter-writing styles, see Alice P. Kenney, "Evidence of Regard: Three Generations of American Love Letters," *Bulletin of the New York Public Library* 76 (1978), 92–119.

20. See Henry A. Murray's introduction to *Pierre, or The Ambiguities* (New York: Hendricks House, 1949); Amy Puett Emmers, "Melville's Closet Skeleton: A New Letter about the Illegitimacy Incident in *Pierre*," *Studies in the American Renaissance* (Boston: Twayne, 1978), 339–42; Henry A. Murray, Harvey Myerson, and Eugene Taylor, "Allan Melvill's By-Blow," *Melville Society Extracts* 61 (February 1985), 1–6; and Philip Young, "Small World: Emerson, Longfellow, and Melville's Secret Sister," *New England Quarterly* 60, no. 3 (September 1987), 382–402. They base their speculations on a letter from Thomas Melvill Jr. in the Massachusetts Historical Society, which indicates that shortly after the deaths of both Thomas and Allan Melvill in 1832, two women, Mrs. Martha Bent and her foster daughter, Mrs. Ann Middleton Allen, came to the Melvill home at 20 Green Street and made a "claim" against the Melvill estate. The only family members who saw them were Allan's mother and her daughter Helen, and the only others who knew about the claim made by the two women were Thomas Melvill Jr. and Lemuel Shaw. It is by no means clear that the "obligation" alluded to was Allan's child rather than one of his many unpaid bills, as Martha Bent ran a business in the city, and either Allan or his father could have owed her money. One of Dr. Murray's researchers became convinced that if the "claim" referred to paternity, the girl might have been Thomas Melvill Sr.'s by-blow, not Allan's. "Thomas not only came home with tea in his boot but also on occasion had a wandering eye," Ina May Greer wrote to Dr. Murray, March 10, 1975, Murray Papers, Harvard University Archives.

21. *"shawl"* AM to MGM, 6/14/18, GLC. *"splendour," etc.,* and *"otherwise"* AM to TM, 6/27/18, GLC.

22. *Lafayette* AM to TMjr., 7/5/18, GLC. *Fleury* AM to TM, 9/19/18, GLC. *"avidity"* AM to MGM, 7/29/18, GLC.

23. *"fortitude"* AM to PG, 6/28/18, GLC. *"every possible situation"* AM to MGM, 7/29/18, GLC.

24. *"origin"* AM to MGM, 7/29/18, GLC.

25. *"love"* AM to MGM, 8/2/18, GLC.

26. *"miracle"* AM to TM, 8/31/18, BA.

27. *"delight"* *Democracy in America,* edited by J. P. Mayer (New York: Doubleday Anchor, 1969), 536.

28. *"happiness"* Ibid.

29. *Mrs. Margaret Bradish* See Roman Gilder's colorful anecdotal history, *The Battery, The story of the adventurers, artists, statesmen, grafters, songsters, mariners, pirates, guzzlers, Indians, thieves, stuffed-shirts, turn-coats, millionaires, inventors, poets, heroes, soldiers, harlots, bootlicks, nobles, nonentities, burghers, martyrs, and murderers who played their parts during full four centuries on Manhattan Island's tip* (Boston: Houghton Mifflin, 1936), 142. I have drawn on this delightful book, as well as on Blunt's *Stranger's Guide to New York* (1818), John A. Kouwenhoven's compendious *Columbia Historical Portrait of New York: An Essay in Graphic History* (New York: Harper & Row, 1972), the Dover *New York Walking Guides,* the Michelin Guide, and numerous other books about New York for flavor of the city.

30. *"Son & Daughter"* MGM to PG, 9/18/18, HCL.

31. *"inconvenient"* AM and MGM to PG, 9/12/18, BA. Elizabeth Blackmar, *Manhattan for Rent, 1785–1850* (Ithaca, New York: Cornell University Press, 1989), analyzes housing patterns in nineteenth-century New York. In her forthcoming *Melville's City: Urban and Literary Form in Nineteenth-Century New York* (New York: Cambridge University Press, 1996) Wyn Kelley points out ways in which Melville's awareness of the problems of urban space shapes his fiction.

32. *"a Healthy situation"* MGM to PG, 9/12/18, BA. I have added some punctuation for clarity.

33. *"mart"* Blunt, *Stranger's Guide,* 36.

34. *office* William H. Gilman, *Melville's Early Life and Redburn* (New York: New York University Press, 1951), 15. For a sobering account of the drinking habits of Allan Melvill's contemporaries, see William R. Rorabaugh, *The Alcoholic Republic: An American Tradition* (New York: Oxford University Press, 1979). There is no direct evidence that Allan Melvill drank heavily, and Gilman (p. 16) points out that Allan made notes for a lecture to his workers against smoking, gambling, lying, and drinking more than one glass of wine, although what he preached does not prove how he behaved. Even if he wasn't a heavy drinker, others in the family were. Mary Ann Gansevoort wrote her son Guert that Melville's uncle, Herman Gansevoort, "looks awfully–his nose is as red as a cherry, & several great purple pimples on it & all over his cheeks–Guert what does this mean? I cannot believe, that uncle Herman is *intemperate*–God forbid–& yet he looks like it–know he is threatened with a cancer on his cheek, & I think perhaps, it proceeds from that–& I pray it may; I would much rather he should die of cancer, than become a drunkard," MAG to GG, 5/11/48, GLC. Ironically, her sons Guert and Stanwix both had problems with alcohol.

35. *"insular city"* Herman Melville, *Moby-Dick, or The Whale* (Chicago and Evanston: Northwestern University Press and The Newberry Library, 1991).* *"forest of masts"* Washington Irving, *Knickerbocker's History of New York* (1809).

*Cited hereafter as "NN*M-D*."

36. *"Boot"* AM to MGM, 5/15/18, GLC. See Karen Halttunen, *Confidence Men and Painted Women: A Study of Middle-class Culture in America, 1830–1870* (New Haven: Yale University Press, 1982), for a detailed discussion of fashion and etiquette at midcentury. One can see in Allan Melvill's pretensions the seeds of the middle-class affectation that became widespread after his death. *Godey's Magazine and Lady's Book* later tried to provide a corrective to the trend. Numerous clippings of advertisements, shipping notes, etc., can be found among Melville Family papers in the New York Public Library, the Harvard College Library, and the Berkshire Athenaeum.

37. *"mortifications"* MGM to PG, 11/?/18, GLC.

38. *"Misanthrope"* MGM to PG, 11/?/18, GLC.

39. *sycamores* Blunt, *Stranger's Guide,* 140. In an unpublished draft of his biographical study of Melville through *Pierre,* Dr. Henry A. Murray, unaware that "delicate condition" was a stock euphemism for pregnancy in this era, wrongly interprets Allan's reference to Maria's "delicate condition" that February to mean that she nearly lost Herman through miscarriage. From this groundless and anachronistic supposition, Dr. Murray goes on to describe the hand of destiny holding the little embryo against the wall of his mother's womb so that the genius can come forth into the world. The passage is a notable example of the hysterical style popularly known as "purple prose" and often attributed to women writers, but not to men.

2. SNUG INVESTMENTS

1. *African burial ground* *The New York Times,* Sunday, 9 August 1992. Rose Butler *Fifth Avenue: Glances at the Vicissitudes and Romance of a World-Renowned Thoroughfare, Together with Many Rare Illustrations that Bring Back an Interesting Past* (New York: The Fifth Avenue Bank, 1915), 12.

2. *airiest places* AM to TM 8/13/19 in Jay Leyda, *The Melville Log: A Documentary Life of Herman Melville, 1819–1891,* 2 vols. (New York: Harcourt, Brace & Company, 1951).† Also Supplement to the *Log* (Gordian Press, 1969), 3. *molasses* AM to Thomas Melvill, 7/20/19, BA.

3. *"evils"* PG to CVSG, 7/2/19, GLC.

4. In his sketches, "The Broadway Hospital" (1862), Walt Whitman mentions Dr. Post. See also Gay Wilson Allen, *The Solitary Singer: A Critical Biography of Walt Whitman* (Chicago and London: University of Chicago Press, 1985), 278. In 1823, Dr. Post served on a special committee appointed to investigate the safety of the city's cemeteries, where so many hastily buried yellow fever victims were buried that people feared contagion from the grave. "An Account of the Proceedings of the Corporation of the City of New-York, in respect to the Existence of Cemeteries, 1823"; published by the *New-York Evening Post,* 3–5 June 1823.

5. *"Stranger"* AM to PG, 8/2/19, Leyda, *Log,* 3. *"brick-kiln"* HM to Nathaniel Hawthorne, 6/29/51, in Herman Melville, *Correspondence,* edited by Lynn Horth (Evanston and Chicago: Northwestern University Press and The Newberry Library, 1993),‡ 195.

6. *"chopping Boy"* AM to PG 8/2/19, Leyda, *Log,* 3. *"feeds kindly"* AM to PG 8/2/19, Leyda, *Log,* 3. In a memorandum for a memoir of Melville, his wife, Elizabeth Shaw Melville, jotted, "Distinguished men born in 1819–from Dr. Titus Coan who writes 'I think Mr. Melville's name will be remembered as long as any on the list.'" The list, written in column form, reads, "Herman Melville, James Russell Lowell, Walt Whitman, John Ruskin, Thomas Ball, Queen Victoria, Charles Kingsley, W. W. Story, T. W. Parsons, E. P. Whipple, C. A. Dana, J. G. Holland, H. P. Gray, Cyrus W. Field, Julia Ward Howe, Richard Storrs Willis." BA.

† Cited hereafter as "Leyda, *Log.*"
‡ Cited hereafter as "NN *Corr.*"

7. *"expected"* AM to TM, 8/13/19, BA, Leyda, *Log*, 3.

8. Receipt for liquor, CVSG, 8/18/19, GLC. For an account of Herman's baptism, I am indebted to T. Walter Herbert Jr., *Moby-Dick and Calvinism: A World Dismantled* (New Brunswick, N.J.: Rutgers University Press, 1977), 28–32.

9. *"escape the worst failures"* AM to TM, 8/13/19, Leyda, *Log*, 3.

10. *Pauperism* William Charvat, *The Profession of Authorship in America, 1800–1870,* in *The Papers of William Charvat,* edited by Matthew J. Bruccoli (Ohio State University Press, 1968), 51.

11. *"confidence will revive again," and "puppy"* AM to TM, 9/14/19, Leyda, *Log*, 4.

12. *"perseverance"* AM to TM, 9/14/19, Leyda, *Log*, 5.

13. *"rational wants"* AM to TM, 9/14/19, Leyda, *Log*, 5. In *Israel Potter* (1855), Melville satirizes Franklin's tendency to confuse material and spiritual gains.

14. *"very dirty"* PG to CVSG, 11/19/19, Leyda, *Log*, 5. *three tiny teeth* PG to CVSG, 11/19/19, Leyda, *Log*, 5. *brandy* See Rorabaugh, *The Alcoholic Republic. "investment"* Herman Melville, *Mardi and a Voyage Thither* (Evanston and Chicago: Northwestern University Press and The Newberry Library, 1970),* 206.

15. *Yates* From a later letter of MGM to CVSG, 5/24/66, Leyda, *Log*, 5–6.

16. See Robert G. Albion, *The Rise of the New York Port* (New York: Scribner's, 1970), 276–80. When Allan learned that the Massachusetts legislature had voted against an auction tax, he tried to console his father by saying the auction system would be less detrimental to commerce in Boston than to that in New York; it is "an evil which the nature of your commerce & local situation renders less formidable & pernicious," AM to TM, 3/28/20, BA.

17. *"reputation," "dispose of them forever"* AM to TM, 6/20/20, BA. He may even have joined those New York businessmen who, though publicly working against the auction system, were privately hedging their bets by investing in it just in case, though this is by no means clear.

18. *"rational expectations"* AM to TM, 8/15/20, BA.

19. According to Blunt (p. 253), "swine" were not to go at large without nose rings; a three-dollar fine was charged for each violation, though so many pigs roamed the streets at this time that it's hard to imagine how the law was enforced. The old Dutch system of garbage disposal was to load organize refuse in the gutter and turn the pigs loose to dispose of it.

20. Blunt, *Stranger's Guide,* 141–42, describes the public baths. Gilder (p. 109) writes that in George Washington's day, nude men of all ages disported themselves in the waters off Manhattan with such boyish abandon that in 1781 the *New-York Journal* complained that the sight of naked bathers was keeping married couples away from the Park, and the Corporation of the City of New York passed an ordinance banning the practice from six in the morning until eight at night.

21. *"uncomfortable"* AM to TM, 8/19/20, BA. *"ruin of our rising empire"* AM to LS, 8/8/20, Leyda, *Log*, 7.

22. *"entirely weaned"* AM to TM, 8/15/20, BA.

23. *a waiter named John* AM to PG, 9/26/20, Leyda, *Log*, 7. The name John is inferred from MGM to PG, 10/22/23, Leyda, 16. This site is now occupied by the World Trade Center. The house was so near the landing of the Hudson River Steamship Line that one day when Herman was about four years old, the Albany boat arrived ahead of schedule, and the captain walked to number 55 and escorted Allan Melvill back to the dock. Knowing Allan's character, it seems safe to say he probably used the incident to impress the family. In *Redburn,* Melville makes fun of his cabin-boy protagonist for expecting the captain to receive him in his cabin.

24. *"eruptions"* AM to PG, 1/10/21, in Jay Leyda, "From

the New *Log:* The Year 1821," *Melville Society Extracts* 62 (May 1985), 1–4.

25. *"anxiety" and "mortified"* AM to TMjr., 9/8/02, GLC.

26. *Fanny* Leyda, "New *Log,*" 2.

27. *snuff* TMjr. to AM, 5/12/21, MHS. *"silent envoy," "sensibilities"* TMjr. to AM, 7/7/21, MHS.

28. *"courage & resolution"* AM to TM, 3/11/22, Leyda, 10. *"a rational manner"* AM to TM, 4/16/22, GLC.

29. *"Bear"* AM to PG, 11/3/21, Leyda, *Log*, 9.

30. *lottery ticket* MGM to PG, 12/8/21, GLC.

31. *"evil," and "genius of Wisdom"* AM to PG, 4/23/22, BA.

32. *"risibility"* MGM to PG, 12/21/22, BA. In his undated *Journal of a Trip from Boston, Mass. to New York State to Canada and Back,* recently donated to the New York State Library in Albany, a John Aiken, traveling with his wife Mary, reports seeing the Melvills at the Chatham Garden Theatre's performance of *Damon and Pythias.* I'm grateful to Warren Broderick for calling my attention to it. The Melvills probably went out more frequently than surviving records show.

33. *"breadth"* MGM to PG, 5/1/23, GLC.

34. *Gansevoort* AM to PG, 4/8/23, Leyda, *Log*, 13. Gansevoort's question is inferred from his father's letter.

35. *Mrs. Plucknett's* MGM to PG, 1823 (no day or month), GLC. *"Man"* MGM to PG 10/22/23, Leyda, *Log*, 16.

36. *"gloom," etc.* MGM to PG, 3/11/24, HCL.

37. *"mine through Life"* MGM to PG, 3/11/24, HCL.

38. *"dejected … Hospital"* AM to PG, 4/1/24, Leyda, *Log,* 17. *"Rialto"* AM to PG, 4/1/24, Leyda, *Log*, 18.

39. *"throng"* Swedish visitor, Gustav Unonius, 1824, quoted in Charles Lockwood, *Manhattan Moves Uptown,* 24. "Shilling side" refers to the east side of Broadway, notorious for its vice and crime.

40. *house* MGM to PG, 3/11/24, HCL, and AM to PG, 4/1/24, Leyda, *Log*, 18.

41. *"dry"* AM to PG, 4/1/24, Leyda, *Log*, 17. *Coney Island* Notation for 7/23/24, Leyda, *Log*, 19. *"fits"* PG to CVSG, 8/9/24, Leyda, *Log*, 19.

42. It's not clear, even from the discussion of Lafayette's visit in Hennig Cohen and Donald Yannella, *Herman Melville's Malcolm Letter: "Man's Final Lore"* (New York: Fordham University Press and the New York Public Library, 1992), 76–77, 148–50, that Allan Melvill ever met Lafayette as he had hoped. Although Cohen and Yannella say his strategy of not meeting the marquis in a crowd proved effective, they do not establish the existence of a personal interview. Allan's letter to Peter Gansevoort, 9/28/24, GLC, is conveniently reprinted by Cohen and Yannella, 148–49.

43. *"Grandfather"* AM to GG, 10/27/24, GLC.

44. *"Fashionables"* MGM to PG, 12/29/24, HCL.

45. *"Health"* MGM to PG, 12/29/24, HCL.

46. *walks* MGM to PG, 12/29/24, HCL. *"Spirits"* MGM to PG, 12/29/24, HCL.

47. *"excellent health"* AM to PG, 2/14/25, Leyda, *Log*, 14. *"serious fears"* MGM to PG, 8/2/25, Leyda, 22. *"plagued"* MGM to PG, 12/29/24, HCL.

48. In her book *Melville's City: Urban and Literary Form in Nineteenth-Century New York* (New York: Cambridge University Press, 1996), Wyn Kelley demonstrates the ways in which Melville tried to reconstitute the town that lay buried in the heart of the rapidly growing city.

3. ELEGANT NEGLIGENCE

1. *July 1825* Gilder, *The Battery,* 153.

2. *"carousels"* AM to PG, 9/28/24, GLC. *canal* Gilder, 155.

3. *sacks or baskets* Henry A. Murray and Eugene Taylor, "The Lancaster System of Instruction," *Melville Society Extracts* 16 (February 1987), 5–6.

4. *Magazine of the Dutch Reformed Church* 4 (April 1829–March 1830), 349. Herbert, 42, n. 49. See Herbert, *Moby-Dick*

---

*Cited hereafter as "NN*Mardi.*"*

and *Calvinism*, 35–43, for a discussion of the Sabbath School Union.

5. *"genius"* MGM to PG, n.d., HCL; see also MGM to PG, 8/25/26, GLC, and AM to PG, 9/17/26, GLC. A modern student who showed such slow progress in reading and writing and a penchant for misspelling words would probably be referred for testing. Given his extraordinary but idiosyncratic creativity, Melville may have been dyslexic, like Albert Einstein, W. B. Yeats, and many other creative people. His mother was very anxious about his penmanship, which makes me wonder whether he was born left-handed and forced to change to his right. This might explain his initial slowness in reading and writing.

6. *boys* AM to PG, 9/17/27, Leyda, *Log*, 32. *"shipping"* Herman Melville, *Redburn: His First Voyage, Being the Sailor-boy Confessions and Reminiscences of the Son-of-a-Gentleman, in the Merchant Service* (Evanston and Chicago: Northwestern University Press and The Newberry Library, 1969),* 4–5.

7. NN*R*, 6. *books* As Emily Dickinson wrote, "There is no frigate like a book to take you lands away."

8. *"Sun & Heat"* AM to PG, 8/10/26, Leyda, *Log*, 5.

9. *"flattering terms"* AM to PG, 9/2/26, Leyda, *Log*, 26. *"attachment"* AM to PG, 9/26/26, BA.

10. *"disorder … I took one"* GM to MGM, 10/6/26, GLC.

11. *Crown* MGM to PG, 12/28/26, GLC. Henry A. Murray, "Another Triumph for Maria's Firstborn," *Melville Society Extracts* 58 (May 1984), 1–3.

12. *"Your little protégé"* AM to PG, 2/10/27, Leyda, *Log*, 29.

13. *"but money"* AM to PG, 2/10/27, Leyda, *Log*, 29.

14. *"fruits"* MGM to PG, 2/20/27, GLC.

15. *"another"* MGM to PG, 2/20/27, GLC.

16. *"disgrace"* AM to PG, 2/23/27, GLC.

17. *"sub rosa"* AM to PG, 2/27/27, GLC.

18. *"praise"* AM to PG, 3/2/27, GLC.

19. *"forfeited"* AM to PG, 3/27/27, GLC. *"utmost need"* AM to PG, 3/30/27, GLC.

20. *"engaging child"* LS to HS, 6/2/27, Metcalf, 30, Puett, 20; original in MHS-S.

21. *Elizabeth* LS to HS, 2/14/27, Leyda, 30. Shaw does say the poetry she was reading was "ordinary," however.

22. *letter to Aunt Lucy* HM to LM, 1828, Osborne Collection, NN*Corr.*, 3. *letter to his grandmother* HM to CVSG, 10/11/28, NN*Corr.*, 5.

23. Walt Whitman, "Crossing Brooklyn Ferry," *Leaves of Grass and Selected Prose*, edited with an introduction by Sculley Bradley (New York: Holt, Rinehart & Winston, 1949), 133ff. Mayor Philip Hone pronounced the Battery a "delightful scene" in 1825 as he watched children like Herman chasing balls and rolling hoops across the lawn while couples like Allan and Maria strolled arm in arm making note of what other couples were wearing.

24. *"incapable"* Mrs. Frances Trollope, *Domestic Manners of the Americans*, quoted in Gilder, *The Battery*, 160. *"swans"* Gilder, 148.

25. *"high spirits"* GM to MGM, 5/23/28, GLC.

26. Lydia Maria Child, *Letters from New-York*, second series (New York: C. S. Francis & Co., and Boston: J. H. Francis, 1845), 173. *"Bacchus"* Donald Smalley, ed. *Domestic Manners of the Americans* (New York: Alfred A. Knopf, 1949), 344–45.

27. "confidential *connexion*" AM to PG, 2/22/28, Leyda, 32. *house* AM to PG, 2/28/28, Leyda, 33. The irony would not have escaped Herman Melville, whose last full-length work of prose fiction was called *The Confidence-Man*. See also Michael Paul Rogin, *Subversive Genealogy: The Politics and Art of Herman Melville* (New York: Alfred A. Knopf, 1983), 249–54, and Herbert, *Moby-Dick and Calvinism*, 45ff.

28. *"grace," etc.* AM to PG, 2/23/29, Leyda, *Log*, 32, and MGM to PG, 2/28/28, Leyda, *Log*, 343.

---

*Cited hereafter as "NN*R.*"

29. *"indolent," "Sylph" "best Speaker,"* AM to PG, 2/23/28, Leyda, 32. It's not clear whether Helen Maria suffered from polio or a birth defect that caused her legs to grow unevenly, but both she and Gansevoort suffered leg ailments that may have inspired Tommo's psychosomatic leg affliction in *Typee*, as the three oldest Melvill children all had trouble finding "a leg to stand on."

30. *"yard"* MGM to PG, 2/28/28, Leyda, *Log*, 33.

31. *"maze of furniture"* AM to PG, 5/10/28, Leyda, *Log*, 34.

32. *John D'Wolf* See NN*R*, 35.

33. *"our Meal"* MGM to CVSG, 12/7/28, GLC.

34. *"Adams," etc.* AM to TM, 5/16/29, GLC.

35. *"ruin"* AM to TM, 5/16/29, GLC.

36. See John P. Runden, "Columbia Grammar School: An Overlooked Year in the Lives of Gansevoort and Herman Melville," *Melville Society Extracts* 46 (May 1981), 1–3, and "Old School Ties: Melville, the Columbia Grammar School, and the New Yorkers," *Extracts* 55 (September 1953), 1–5. Philip Hone's son was a student at the school while Melville was there, as was Cornelius Mathews, whom Melville saw frequently in the 1840s and early 1850s.

37. HelM to MGM, 5/23/29, GLC. *"ungovernable"* MGM to PG, 7/15/29, GLC.

38. *"unmanly"* MGM to PG, 7/15/29, GLC. *"favorite with us all"* TM quoted by AM to PG, 9/26/29, Leyda, *Log*, 39.

39. *"knowledge"* AM to TM, 5/20/30, Leyda, *Log*, 43.

40. *"friends"* AM to PG, 8/11/30, Leyda, *Log*, 44.

41. *"Tyrant,"* AM to PG, 9/4/30, Leyda, *Log*, 45.

42. The Luman Reed Gallery, New-York Historical Society, re-creates the original Gallery. The information in these paragraphs comes from the gallery's brochure.

43. *"neighborhood"* AM to JDW, 9/22/30, GLC. By an odd coincidence, when Melville bought a copy of Burton's *Anatomy of Melancholy* in a bookstore in Pittsfield, Massachusetts, in July 1851, he discovered that his father had owned the volume in 1816. Allan had probably given the book to his brother Thomas, who later sold it. See William H. Gilman, *Melville's Early Life and Redburn* (New York: New York University Press, 1951), 16. Both brothers had to sell personal effects from time to time to pay their debts.

44. William R. Rorabaugh, *The Alcoholic Republic, An American Tradition* (New York: Oxford University Press, 1979), 159–60, claims that Astor made his first substantial money at least as much through sales of liquor as through sales of furs. For a historical analysis of how Astor and other real-estate sharks made their fortunes by intensifying and exploiting the housing shortage in New York, see Elizabeth Blackmar, *Manhattan for Rent, 1785–1850* (Ithaca, N.Y.: Cornell University Press, 1989).

45. *James* Gay Wilson Allen, *William James: A Biography* (New York: Viking Press, 1967), 3–11.

46. See Ed Tick, "The Lost Boyhood of Herman Melville," *Capitol Region* (Albany), December 1986.

47. Their friendship ended years later when Stanwix, a naval officer, snubbed his cousin for being a common sailor, if not before, if *White-Jacket* reflects reality. See Wilson L. Heflin, "A Man-of-War Button Divides Two Brothers," *Boston Public Library Quarterly* 3 (January 1951), 51–60. Rogin also describes this episode fully in his *Subversive Genealogy*.

48. *Beck* See Gilman, *Early Life*.

49. *"Paley"* Ibid., 58. When he was in his late teens, Melville evidently courted girls in Lansingburgh with the volume, as at least three names are inscribed in the volume: Mary L. Day, Harriet M. Day, and Harriet Fly. See ibid., 149–50, and Leyda, *Log*, 86.

50. See David K. Titus, "Herman Melville at the Albany Academy," *Melville Society Extracts* 42 (May 1980), 1, 4–10.

51. From "Sketch of Major Thomas Melville, Jr. by a Nephew," GLC, reprinted in J. E. A. Smith's *History of Pittsfield* (1876).

52. *"intelligence"* MGM to PG, 8/17/31, Leyda, *Log*, 49.

The sparse records of Herman's schooling show that he attended the Albany Classical School for a few months in 1835, then re-enrolled in Albany Academy in the fall of 1836, as David Titus explained in "Herman Melville at the Albany Academy."

53. See Harold A. Larrabee, "Herman Melville's Early Years in Albany," *New York History* 15, no. 2 (April 1934), for a description of Albany in 1830.

54. Tick, "Lost Boyhood," 45, supplies the details.

55. *Psalm LV*, see Leyda, *Log,* 51. *"deranged man"* PG to TMjr., 1/10/32, Leyda, *Log,* 51.

56. *"Maniac"* Ibid.

57. *"misterious way"* MGM, Leyda, *Log,* 51.

58. The ambiguous chapter of *Moby-Dick* called "The Counterpane," in which Ishmael relates his half-waking boyhood dream of feeling a supernatural hand placed in his hand, has frequently been interpreted to allude to awakening sexuality, specifically masturbation, but it seems to me also to express a longing for physical contact with an aloof or unreachable parent of either sex, which easily leads to a longing for a God, or Goddess.

4. TORMENTED WITH AN ITCH OR THINGS REMOTE

1. See Ann Braude, *Radical Spirits: Spiritualism and Women's Rights in Nineteenth-Century America* (Boston: Beacon Press, 1989), 24–25, and Ann Douglas, *The Feminization of American Culture* (New York: Avon Books, 1977), esp. chapter 6, for an explanation of the "heavenly home" ideology.

2. *"forgive me these thoughts"* Augusta Whipple Hunter to Augusta Melville, 11/24/46, GLA. See Amanda Porterfield, *Feminine Spirituality in America from Sarah Edwards to Martha Graham* (Philadelphia: Temple University Press, 1980).

3. Just as men and women gravitated to separate spheres in matters of domesticity and finance, they often played different roles in the religious life of the family. Frances Trollope, mother of the novelist Anthony Trollope, said she "never saw a country where religion had so strong a hold upon the women, or a slighter hold upon the men." *Domestic Manners of the Americans,* edited by Donald Smalley (New York: Viking Press, 1949), 75.

4. Neal L. Tolchin, *Mourning, Gender, and Creativity in the Art of Herman Melville* (New Haven: Yale University Press, 1988), refers to Maria's needlework mourning tableau, which has never been found. Kathleen Tivnan of the Lansingburgh Historical Society says it may well have been among the household effects removed from the Lansingburgh house and taken to the dump several decades ago.

5. When the Albany Rural Cemetery was incorporated in 1841, the remains of Allan and other family members were moved from churchyards to the new establishment. For more on rural cemeteries, see both Halttunen, *Confidence Men,* and Ann Braude, *Radical Spirits,* 51–53.

6. From Cornelius Mathews, "Tickets for Greenwood," quoted in Tolchin, *Mourning,* 8.

7. *"Christian example"* MGM to Catherine Gansevoort Lansing, 1/17/66, quoted in Alice P. Kenney, *The Gansevoorts of Albany* (Syracuse, N.Y.: Syracuse University Press, 1984), 187.

8. *"said business"* Memorandum of MGM, 3/28/32, GLC. John Demos, *Past, Present, and Personal: The Family and the Life Course in American History* (New York: Oxford University Press, 1986), 99ff., makes the point that in this period, many young men juggled work and school, especially farm boys. Thus, interruptions in boys' educations were less unusual in Melville's time than in ours.

9. *"in Albany"* GM to PG 5/22/32, GLC, Leyda, *Log,* 54. *"$10,000 a year"* Memorandum of MGM, 9/24/32, Leyda, *Log,* 57.

10. Barbara Leslie Epstein, *The Politics of Domesticity: Women, Evangelism, and Temperance in Nineteenth-Century America* (Middletown, Conn.: Wesleyan University Press, 1981), 86–87;

Epstein compares the rights of colonial and Victorian women, 29–30, 79–80.

11. *"everything to me"* MGM to PG 7/14/32, GLC, Leyda, *Log,* 54.

12. *nap* Eleanor Melville Metcalf, *Herman Melville: Cycle and Epicycle* (Cambridge, Mass.: Harvard University Press, 1953). A curious story, if true. Perhaps she wanted to remind them how close we all are to death.

13. *"erase it"* NN*R,* 6.

14. Maria's bankbook for 1834 shows a deposit of $37.50 labeled "salary Herman, 22 April." I am grateful to John De Marco of the Lyrical Ballad Bookstore in Saratoga Springs, New York, for showing me this recently acquired item.

15. To Hamlet, who is stunned by his father's sudden death and his mother's hasty marriage to his uncle, Claudius says: "'Tis unmanly grief; / It shows a will most incorrect to heaven, / A heart unfortified, a mind impatient, / An understanding simple and unschooled" (Act I, scene ii). His mother's response is a hollow couplet: "Do not forever with thy vailed lids / Seek for thy noble father in the dust. / Thou know 'tis common all that lives must die, / Passing through nature to eternity."

16. *"strangles me"* NN*R,* 21. Tolchin, *Mourning,* analyzes in detail the effects of Maria's "blocked grieving" on her family, especially her two oldest sons, each of whom in different ways became "linking objects" to their dead father: Gansevoort in ways that evidently destroyed him; Herman in ways that strengthened him despite potentially crippling effects. Ironically, the "favored" son was, like Isaac, the sacrificial lamb who died young, while the outcast, like Ishmael, managed to survive, even though his writings attest to the painfulness of his struggle.

17. *"prudent"* MGM to PG, 8/7/32, GLC, Leyda, *Log,* 56.

18. *"controul them"* MGM to PG, 8/24/32, GLC.

19. *"writing to me"* and *"careful of himself"* MGM to PG 8/24/32, GLC.

20. *"daily"* MGM to PG 8/7/32. *"useful"* MGM with HelM to PG, Leyda, *Log,* 56.

21. The biographical information about Major Melvill is from Francis F. Drake, *Tea Leaves* (Boston: A. O. Crane, 1884), cxxix–cxxxv, card files and a handwritten ledger (Parker, Lodge records 1733–1804) in the Grand Masonic Temple, Boston, as well as from standard sources. Although to Newton Arvin, *Herman Melville* (Westport, Conn.: Greenwood Press, 1950), Major Melvill's wearing prerevolutionary garb and chasing after fires into his eightieth year strongly suggests mania or, to post-Freudians, senile dementia, there is no hint of pathology in contemporary descriptions of the man. But then, there is no dark side to contemporary descriptions of slaveowner and Indian fighter Peter Gansevoort, either, and we have plenty of evidence his grandson saw his maternal grandfather's dark side, and saw his dark side as an analogue of the nation's dark side, too.

22. *"desertion"* MGM to LS 6/20/33, Leyda, *Log,* 59. Maria apparently stayed at Melvill House with his in-laws in 1814, and Herman spent several summers on his Uncle Thomas's farm.

23. A vexed and vexing question. One researcher, Ina May Greer, believed old Major Melville was the girl's father, not Allan. See Ms. Greer's letter to Dr. Murray, March 10, 1975, Murray Papers, Harvard University Archives. I'm told Harrison Hayford is working on an article that will refute the "secret sister" theories. For more on the matter, see Henry A. Murray, ed., *Pierre: or The Ambiguities* (New York: Hendricks House, 1949); Amy Puett Emmers, "Melville's Closet Skeleton: A New Letter about the Illegitimacy Incident in *Pierre,*" *Studies in the American Renaissance* (1977), 339–42; Henry A. Murray, Joel Myerson, and Eugene Taylor, "Allan Melvill's By-Blow," *Melville Society Extracts* 61 (February 1985), 1–6; and Philip Young, "Small World: Emerson, Longfellow and Melville's Secret Sister," *New England Quarterly* (September

1987), corrected and included with additional material in Young's *The Private Melville* (University Park: The Pennsylvania State University Press, 1993). As E. L. Grant Watson pointed out long ago, if *Pierre* did not exist, no one would suspect that Melville had a "secret sister."

24. *"welfare of your children" and suggestion for guardian* LS to MGM 2/12/34, GLC.

25. "Sketch of Major Thomas Melvill Jr. By a Nephew," GLC, published in part by J. E. A. Smith in his *History of Pittsfield* (1876). See Merton M. Sealts Jr., *Pursuing Melville, 1940–1980* (Madison: University of Wisconsin Press, 1982).

26. *Thomas* Jeanne C. Howes, "Melville's Sensitive Years," *Melville and Hawthorne in the Berkshires: A Symposium, 1966*, edited by Howard P. Vincent. (Kent State University Press, 1968), 26–28.

27. *"very acceptable indeed"* JMM to Augusta Melvill, March, 1834, GLA. Educated young people were expected to know how to draw. Thomas Melvill Jr.'s copybooks (HCL), for example, contain quite a few handsome colored drawings.

28. *"Phoenicians"* JMM to AM, September 1834, GLA.

29. *"dreadfully"* JMM to AM, Saturday, n.d., 1836.

30. *"contact with it"* Leyda, *Journal* by GM, 1834, esp. 331, 333, 342. Maria's financial situation is difficult to pin down. During the summer of 1990, John DeMarco, owner of the Lyrical Ballad Bookstore in Saratoga Springs, New York, obtained a calfskin bank ledger belonging to Maria Melvill with transactions for 1834–35. It shows a balance of over twenty thousand dollars, which evidently includes nineteen thousand dollars invested by Peter Gansevoort to keep the business running.

31. Most of the information about the business comes from Jay Leyda, "An Albany Journal by Gansevoort Melville," *Boston Public Library Quarterly* 2 (1950), 327–47, reference to meeting Herman, 345. *"kangaroo skins"* GM 5/27/36, GLC.

32. *"Christian religion"* William H. Gilman, *Melville's Early Life and* Redburn (New York: New York University Press, 1951), 71.

33. *Horace Mann* See David E. Shi, *The Simple Life: Plain Living and High Thinking in American Culture* (New York: Oxford University Press, 1985), 121ff.

34. *"task"* Gillman, *Early Life,* 72.

35. *"care"* HMM to AM, 10/8/35, GLA.

36. *"pattern girl"* HMM to AM 10/8/35, GLA.

37. *Bryant* Arthur Schlesinger Jr., *The Age of Jackson* (Boston: Little, Brown, 1945), 217ff.

38. *"burned forever"* Henry Ward Beecher, *Seven Lectures,* in Halttunen, *Confidence-Men and Painted Women: A Study of Middle-Class Culture in America, 1830–1870* (New Haven: Yale University Press, 1982), 19.

39. *1837* William Charvat, "American Romanticism and the Depression of 1837, in *The Profession of Authorship in America, 1800–1870,* The Papers of William Charvat, edited by Matthew J. Bruccoli (Columbus, Ohio: Ohio State University Press, 1968), 49ff. Charvat makes the point that literature did not suffer a depression at this time, despite 250 bankruptcies in New York in the first two months of the panic, though it is not clear that the "literary boom" he talks about resulted in profits for the authors, despite their obvious productiveness.

40. *"family council"* Allan Melville's *Journal,* BA. $50,000 Again, assessing Maria Melville's financial situation is difficult given the sums mentioned in the available documents versus her feeling that she never had enough money, which could be a projection of the loss she felt after her husband's death, as sudden loss often leaves survivors with irrational fears that they might suddenly lose everything again.

41. *"savage"* JMM to AM 6/26/37, GLA.

42. *"village," "foxes"* HM to PG 12/31/37, GLC.

43. *"ascended," "compass"* HM to PG 12/30/37, NN *Corr.,* 8.

44. *"Common-Schools"* HM to PG, 12/30/37, GLC.

45. *"reading"* Ibid., 5. Whitman was teaching on Long Island at about the same time, 1836–41.

46. *dome* Kenney, *The Gansevoorts of Albany: Dutch Patricians in The Upper Hudson Valley* (Syracuse: Syracuse University Press, 1969), 200.

47. See Mark C. Carnes, *Secret Ritual and Manhood in Victorian America* (New Haven: Yale University Press, 1989), for provocative contextual material.

48. See Leyda, *Log,* 95, and Gilman, *Early Life,* 91–98.

49. For texts of the letters, see NN *Corr.,* 10–20 and 553–64.

50. *"broken"* Allan Melville's journal, BA. I'm indebted to Frances D. Broderick for her suggestions, corrections, and emendations to this section of the manuscript.

51. *"thronged city"* William Lamb, a newspaper editor, quoted in Warren F. Broderick, "Melville Attended Lansingburgh Academy," *The Record Newspapers, Troy, New York,* February 7, 1970. Two pamphlets are available from the Lansingburgh Historical Society, which occupies the house once rented by Maria Melville: *Lansingburgh, New York, 1771–1971,* edited by Jane S. Lord (The Lansingburgh Historical Society, 1971), and *Lansingburgh, New York, 1771–1971, 200th Anniversary,* a souvenir program. I am indebted to Kathleen Tivnan for a tour of the Melville house and much anecdotal information about the village.

52. Lord, *Lansingburgh,* 32.

53. *"furniture"* PG to MGM, 6/20/38, GLC.

54. The house was changed over the years. Frances D. Broderick writes that "there was no porch on the side of the building (such as exists at the present time). The original side Hall ran along inside this part of the building. You entered this Hall from the front door, and the large rooms opened off of this hall. There may not even have been a door on this north side (114th St side). As there is not room for a porch on what was the front of the house we believe there was only a landing and steps—when you entered the front door. Records indicate that the large porch on the north side of the dwelling (now the front) was built in the early 1870s and the Oak door installed at that date." FDB to LRL, 8/22/1990.

55. "The point is that the 72 traced are only a fraction of the ships built here ... would assume two or three times as many as I have proof of." FDB to LRL, 8/22/1990

56. Frances D. Broderick, "Lansingburgh as a Port" (unpublished material, Troy Public Library), which includes illustrations showing the shipping tunnels. Melville describes "wooden, one-masted, green-and-white painted sloops" gliding "up and down the river before our house on the bank" in Chapter 1 of *Redburn.*

57. Warren F. Broderick, "Lansingburgh Academy." Frances D. Broderick, "Talented Instructor Taught Melville," in *Pages from Lansingburgh's Past* (Troy Public Library). If the existence of a notebook dated 1796 containing diagrams, measurements, and geometrical notations is any indication, Allan Melvill Sr. evidently studied surveying too, and perhaps Maria showed Herman his father's neatly drawn and labeled notes. Melville's immediate source for the cetological chapters of *Moby-Dick* was the *Penny Cyclopaedia,* but Maltbie's class undoubtedly planted a seed.

58. *"education"* PG to Erie Canal Commissioner William Bouck, 4/4/39, Leyda, *Log,* 82–83.

59. *"DUMB AND DEAF!"* Fragment no. 2, Herman Melville, *The Piazza Tales and Other Prose Pieces, 1839–1860* (Evanston and Chicago: Northwestern University Press and the Newberry Library),* 204.

60. *Lynde Palmer* Lansingburgh, New York, 1771–1971 (see note 51, above). Alice P. Kenney, "Herman Melville and the Dutch Tradition," *Bulletin of the New York Public Library* 79 (1975–76), 386–99. I am grateful to Warren Broderick of Lansingburgh for drawing to my attention the five poems "signed

---

*Cited hereafter as "NN *PT.*"

'H.'" that appeared in the *Democratic Press and Lansingburgh Advertiser*, 15, 22 September 1838; 16, 23 March, 6 April 1839, two of which appear to have been written to Mary Parmelee. Most printed sources spell the name "Pelitiah," but "Pelatiah" is the way his name is spelled on his tombstone.

61. *"Your only Sister Maria"* MGM to PG, 5/23/39, GLC.

62. *"without success"* GM to AMjr., 5/24/39, GLC.

63. *"depravity"* MGM to AM, 10/17/38, GLA. It's interesting that few such letters to Herman have survived, perhaps because, unlike Allan and Augusta, he destroyed them.

64. *"gossiping"* Allan Melville's journal, BA. *"strange roof"* MGM to AMjr., 8/20/38, BA. *cult of domesticity* see Mary P. Ryan, *The Empire of the Mother: American Writing about Domesticity, 1830–1860* (New York: The Haworth Press, 1982).

65. *"acquaintance"* MGM to AM, 10/17/38, GLA.

66. Allan Melville's journal, BA.

67. *"introspections"* AM to AMjr., 8/12/39, GLC.

68. According to Dr. Jonathan Marlowe ("Developmental Issues in Adolescence," Stanley King Counseling Institute, 14 June 1990), if parents do not respond to the emotional needs of children and adolescents, their offspring may channel their feelings into physical ailments.

69. Allan Melville's journal, BA. Bradford's nickname is variously spelled "Ali," "Ally," or "Aly."

70. *insanity* Halttunen, *Confidence Men,* 222. John Demos, in his *Past, Present, and Personal* (p. 104), writes: "The common denominator in the experience of nineteenth-century youth—common to boys *and* girls—was dissonance."

71. *"instruction"* MGM to AMjr., 8/20/38, BA. *"temptations"* MGM to AMjr., 9/25/39, BA.

72. "Guert was here yesterday … he looks very much like Herman, we all noticed it, oh how he blames Herman for going to sea," AM to AMjr., 8/12/39, BA.

73. *"Norman"* Leyda, *Log,* 92. Melville may well have grown a few inches in the next few years.

74. *notice* The *New York-American.* *"low rates"* *Evening Post,* 2 June 1839.

75. *"bridle-bit"* NN*R,* 66. Melville's artful, teasing novel was taken by early critics such as Raymond Weaver to be an accurate account of his first voyage—a view that has been thoroughly discredited. However, its renderings of a young man's physical sensations on a fine day, its nautical terminology, and other factual material about shipboard life have the ring of truth.

5. A NATURALLY ROVING DISPOSITION

1. *"matter"* Richard Henry Dana, *Two Years before the Mast* (New York: Bantam Books, 1959), 24.

2. NN*R,* 120.

3. Ibid., 121.

4. *Liverpool* Kathleen E. Kier, *The Melville Encyclopaedia: The Novels* (Troy, N.Y.: The Whitston Publishing Company, 1990), 591–92. *"slave-trade"* Melville, *Redburn,* 155–56. In 1790 there were ninety-six slaves in Lansingburgh, and by 1814 this number declined to fifty-six. There were probably some slaves in the village when Melville was living there. Denunciations of slavery figure in *Redburn* and other of his writings. In her fine essay "The Riddle of the Sphinx: Melville's 'Benito Cereno' and the *Amistad* Case," *Critical Essays on Melville's "Benito Cereno,"* edited by Robert Burkholder (Boston: G. K. Hall, forthcoming), Carolyn Karcher points out that Melville mentions parliamentarian William Roscoe, a staunch foe of the slave trade whom Allan Melvill met in 1818, no fewer than four times. The *Amistad* trial concurred with Melville's return from Liverpool. Thanks to a masterly defense by John Quincy Adams, however, the mutineers were acquitted, and returned to Africa. Karcher's essay contextualizes references to slavery in *Redburn.* Melville's cousin Hun Gansevoort may have been a commissioned officer on the *Grampus* when the ship held the *Amistad* mutineers.

5. NN*R.*

6. *Moorish Arch* *Penny Magazine,* 30 April 1833, Leyda, *Log,* 93. He referred to the statue he had seen twenty years earlier in his 1856–57 journal, in *Journals* (Evanston and Chicago: Northwestern University Press and The Newberry Library, 1989),* 50 and n. 386.

7. Kier, *Encyclopedia, 591–2.*

8. Melville's *Redburn* borrows Adam Smith's *The Wealth of Nations* from the ship's library and studies it, observing disingenuously that although he worked to understand the book, he did not receive wages for his labor. That mercantile theories justify exploitation of workers by the wealthy managerial class and the exploitation of weak nations by strong is the common criticism of laissez-faire economics. In "Adam Smith Was No Gordon Gekko," *New York Times,* 23 January 1994, however, Sylvia Nasar argues that Smith has been misunderstood and misrepresented by his supporters and detractors alike. According to Nasar, Smith believed a free-market economy was the best means of achieving a balance between self-interest and the common good, by which he meant the eradication of poverty and fairer distribution of the wealth. A generation later, Darwin's theories would be similarly misappropriated and misused to produce "social Darwinism," which further justified economic and social inequality.

9. For various reasons, it seems possible that Melville began writing the first few chapters of an account of his voyage to Liverpool shortly after his return, but put it aside because he was ignorant of suitable models for the interweaving of social commentary with travelogue. He may also have found it hard to finish the book because he was grappling with the sexual undercurrents that would reappear in disguised form in *Redburn,* erupting in *Pierre.*

10. *"when necessary"* MGM to AMjr., 9/25/39, BA.

11. Biographers have identified Gansevoort's illness as tuberculosis and the disease that killed him as tubercular meningitis, but I suspect there was more to it than that. In a letter to Jay Leyda, dated 19 November 1947 (Leyda collection, University Research Library, UCLA), Eleanor Melville Metcalf exclaims, "Poor Gansevoort! It was indeed ill health. If the family ever knew of the situation, no one could ever have divulged it to the next, or the next to the next, generation; for Gansevoort was always spoken of in the most glowing terms—indeed a good deal to Herman's disadvantage." Early in my work on the present volume, I had a hunch that Gansevoort had contracted a venereal disease that affected his leg and aggravated his long-standing pulmonary weakness, and the tone of Mrs. Metcalf's cryptic remark appears to confirm this speculation.

12. Herman Melville, "The Death Craft," NN*PT,* 424–27.

13. Warren Broderick's "'Their Snowy Whiteness Dazzled my Eyes': 'The Death-Craft'—Melville's First Maritime Story," *The Hudson Valley Regional Review* 3, no. 1 (March 1986), argues convincingly in favor of the attribution on the basis of stylistic comparisons with "Benito Cereno." A number of scholars believe there are still newspaper sketches by Melville waiting to be discovered and identified.

14. *"from him"* MGM to AMjr., 12/7/39, BA.

15. *"Tawney"* HM to AMjr., 12/7/39, NN*Corr.,* 23.

16. *speaking voice* I'm indebted to Jack Putnam, manager of New York's South Street Seaport Bookshop, and a Melville look-alike who performs dramatic impersonations of Melville reading his work, for this speculative description of Melville's patrician accent. I added Gore Vidal to FDR and JFK because he adds a certain *je ne sais quoi* the others lack—a kind of sardonic, campy wit that characterized Melville in his middle years.

17. *"savage"* GM to MGM, 11/26/40, BA, calls his unshaven brother a "savage." *"anxiety," etc.* GM to AMjr., 11/26/40, BA.

18. *"conduct"* GM to AMjr., 1/21/40, Leyda, 103.

---

*Cited hereafter as "NN*J.*"

19. *"rent"* MGM to PG via AMjr., 5/16/40, Leyda, *Log,* 104.

20. *"what to do"* Ibid.

21. Rena Surprise, "Herman Melville Taught at the Brunswick School," *The Record Newspapers,* Troy, New York, 6 April 1968.

22. *"wealthy one"* NN*M-D,* 249.

23. Emily Dickinson, "I like to See It Lap the Miles" (no. 585, c. 1862); Henry David Thoreau, *Walden* (1854).

24. The Shaw Papers reside at the Massachusetts Historical Society, Boston. For a discussion of Shaw's contributions to American jurisprudence, see Frederic Hathaway Chase, *Lemuel Shaw: Chief Justice of the Supreme Judicial Court of Massachusetts 1830–1860* (Boston: Houghton Mifflin Company, 1918) and Leonard W. Levy, *The Law of the Commonwealth and Chief Justice Shaw* (Cambridge: Harvard University Press, 1957).

25. *"humped herds"* NN*M-D,* 460.

26. *Cherokees* See Michael Paul Rogin, *Fathers and Children: Andrew Jackson and the Subjugation of the American Indian,* (New York: Vintage Books, 1976), among others. *"knee-deep among Tiger-lilies"* Melville, *Moby-Dick,* ch. 1; Edgar Allan Poe, "To Science."

27. I'm indebted to Daniel J. Boorstin, *The Americans: The National Experience* (New York: Vintage Books, 1965), 127 and 141–48, for information about these frontier towns.

28. *"contrast"* "Sketch of Major Thomas Melvill, Jr., by a Nephew," edited by Merton M. Sealts from ms. in GLC; Leyda, *Log,* 106.

29. *"hard times"* Leon Howard, *Herman Melville: A Biography* (Berkeley: University of California Press, 1967), 36.

30. Herman Melville, *The Confidence-Man: His Masquerade* (Chicago and Evanston: Northwestern University Press and The Newberry Library, 1984),* 497. These phrases may be found in a fragment known as "The River," which Melville did not include in the published novel. The fragment is one among several in the collection of the Houghton Library, Harvard University.

31. Herman Melville, "Trophies of Peace: Illinois in 1840," *The Collected Poems of Herman Melville,* edited by Howard P. Vincent (Chicago: Hendricks House, 1947), 266–67.

32. *Nauvoo* Boorstin, *The Americans,* 62–64, and Alice Felt Tyler, *Freedom's Ferment: Phases of American Social History from the Colonial Period to the Outbreak of the Civil War* (New York: Harper & Row, 1944).

33. *debt, disgrace, etc.* Leyda, *Log,* 108, 110.

34. Melville's memory of these strong American frontier women might have influenced the later creation of Hunilla in "The Encantadas." Gansevoort had taken over the role of family caretaker.

"pestilence" GM to AMjr., 3/30/40, BA. When Allan expressed an interest in moving from Albany to New York, Gansevoort promised to help him get a job with his friend Alexander Bradford and advised him to "show yourself to be a businessman by being brief & to the point–Be careful not to suffer any illspelt words to appear–Commence with A. W. Bradford Esq.–Dear Sir–& close with Yours Truly–Allan Melville–that will be all sufficient. This last hint may appear trifling to you, as you probably are not aware of the difficulties which sometimes arise in meeting [*sic*] out due courtesies to our correspondents." He also asked Allan to take care of Helen during her visit to Albany because "in the present situation of society a lady is very much dependent [*sic*] upon the stronger sex for the power to pursue her own plans & render herself comfortable & at ease–Both duty and affection conspire to render you a good & assiduously attentive brother to Helen. My best love & a kiss to her," GM to AMjr., 11/26/40, BA.

35. *"tied to counters"* NN*M-D,* ch. 1. In his *Subversive Genealogy: The Politics and Art of Herman Melville* (New York: Alfred A. Knopf, 1983), 193–94, Michael Rogin suggests, as have

_____

*Cited hereafter as "NN*C-M.*"

others, that Fly was the model for Bartleby. *Cooper and Dana* Leyda, *Log,* 109.

36. *"watery part of the world,"* NN*M-D,* ch. 1.

37. *"unshored immensities"* NN*M-D,* ch. 1. After his sojourn in Polynesia, Melville called himself "Typee," or "lover of human flesh," for a while, then "Omoo," the Polynesian word for "rover." Robert K. Martin, *Hero, Captain, and Stranger: Male Friendship, Social Critique, Literary Form in the Sea Novels of Herman Melville* (Chapel Hill: University of North Carolina Press, 1986), points out that in sea lingo, *rover* had connotations of sexual promiscuity and homosexual dalliance. On the nicknames, see Charles R. Anderson, *Melville in the South Seas* (New York: Columbia University Press, 1939.)

6. THE WILD, THE WATERY, THE UNSHORED

1. *"ties and ballasts"* Walt Whitman, "Song of Myself," in *Leaves of Grass* (New York: Penguin Books, 1959), 57.

2. Mary Ellen Chase, *Sailing the Seven Seas* (Boston: Houghton Mifflin, 1958), 57ff., and Robert G. Albion, William A. Baker, Benjamin W. Labaree, and Marion V. Brewington, *New England and the Sea* (Middletown, Conn.: Wesleyan University Press, 1972), 110. Henry David Thoreau, observing the "Hyperborean" ice-cutters on Walden Pond, wrote, "It appears that the sweltering inhabitants of Charlestown and New Orleans, of Madras and Bombay and Calcutta, drink at my well," at the end of "The Pond in Winter," *Walden, or Life in the Woods.*

3. Thomas Melville's letters (GLA) home in the 1850s and 1860s give this impression, and some of his descriptions, especially of islands and pagodas near the Chinese mainland, are charming. *pets* Chase, *Seven Seas,* 111–113.

4. *Mary Russell* Linda Grant De Pauw, *Seafaring Women* (Boston: Houghton Mifflin, 1982), 106–7, and Augusta Penniman, *Journal of a Whaling Voyage, 1864 1868* (Eastham, Mass.: Eastern National Park and Monument Association, 1988). Russell and Penniman are only two of the many whalers' wives who went to sea. *laundry* De Pauw, 142ff. Ironing the clothes of the various family members took many hours and was impossible in heavy seas. *"sea captains"* Margaret Fuller, "Woman in the Nineteenth Century," in *The Woman and the Myth: Margaret Fuller's Life and Writings,* edited by Bell Gale Chevigny (Old Westbury, New York: The Feminist Press, 1976), 276. Mary Ellen Chase (see note 2, above) has written an engrossing story about her grandfather, Melatiah Chase, whose career typifies the seamen of his day who rose through the ranks, then took their families to sea. De Pauw makes the same point.

5. *"gratification"* GM to LS, 7/22/42, Leyda, *Log,* 119, and NN*Corr.,* 24–25.

6. *Stanwix* Mary Anne Gansevoort's letter of 3/22/44, GLC, leaves no doubt that alcoholism did him in. Her letters reveal her constant disappointment in him, and her anxiety about his taking up with a friend who "must stop & drink at every grog shop ... beware of him," 1849, GLC.

7. *Hun* Log of the USS *Constitution,* Leyda, *Log,* 109. Although Jay Leyda spells his name "Hunn," the manuscripts in the Gansevoort-Lansing Collection show that family members spelled it "Hun."

8. William Bolton Finch, the captain of the *Vincennes,* kept a journal, and both he and Charles S. Stewart, the ship's chaplain, published books about the cruise not long afterward. Melville drew on Finch's book and parodied Stewart's extreme prudishness in *Typee.* T. Walter Herbert Jr., *Marquesan Encounters: Melville and the Meaning of Civilization* (Cambridge, Mass.: Harvard University Press, 1980), provides an especially astute analysis of how Melville played off his observations against those of other whites in the South Seas.

9. *"paroxysms of passion"* Opinion of the court-martial, USS *Vincennes,* April 30, 1832; see Leyda, *Log,* 53. On 26 August 1844, Thomas Wilson Melvill's brother Robert wrote

Captain John D'Wolf that he thought Thomas had "left off his habit of drinking, and was an altered man" (Shaw Papers, Massachusetts Historical Society), but exactly one month later he was dead.

10. Daniel Henderson, *The Hidden Coasts: A Biography of Admiral Charles Wilkes* (New York: William Sloane Associates, 1953), discusses Wilkes's entire life and career. For a readable account of the expedition designed for youngsters, see William Bixby, *The Forgotten Voyage of Charles Wilkes* (New York: David McKay, 1966), written for young readers. Copies of Wilkes's *Narrative* itself are hard to come by.

11. *"world"* JMM to AM, 1842, GLA.

12. See Leyda, *Log*, 111–13. The *Acushnet*'s roster is on display at the New Bedford Whaling Museum. Melville, of course, would not be twenty-one until August 1, 1841. *height* According to John Demos, *Past, Present, and Personal: The Family and Life Course in American History* (New York: Oxford University Press, 1986), 95, "… there is reason to think that the attainment of full physical stature comes at a considerably earlier age now than in pre-modern times. According to one estimate, young men in early nineteenth-century America did not reach their final adult height until they were about twenty-five years old, whereas most of their contemporaries today do so by or before age twenty." In 1860, when he signed aboard the *Meteor* for a trip to California, Melville's height was listed as five feet nine and three-quarters inches, so despite his grandniece Charlotte Hoadley's recollection that he was six feet tall, I suspect he was about five feet ten or eleven at the most. Hoadley wrote librarian Victor Paltsits, "I should have described him as a tall man, quite six feet at least–a man changes as he grows older, of course but he was very erect as I always remember him–among people he was always agreeable, but kept much to himself in his study–among his [well bound?] books and old prints–when he did not feel in a social frame of mind, I fancy he stood by himself, taking the long walks in Central Park … I have so often thought he was not cut out for a family man but should have been able to travel to his heart's content–for that was where his great interest lay." CH to VP, 11/25/1935, GLC.

13. *"slop chest"* *Whale Fishery of New England: an account, with illustrations and some interesting and amusing anecdotes of the rise and fall of an industry which has made New England famous throughout the world,* pamphlet (Taunton, Mass.: State Street Bank and Trust Company, 1915; reprint, William S. Sullwold Publishing Company, 1968), 36. *"$200"* Paul Giambarba, *Whales, Whaling and Whalecraft* (Centerville, Mass.: The Scrimshaw Press), 87.

14. *"all was settled"* His mother wrote: "Last week I received a long letter from Herman, who has embarked on a long Voyage to the Pacific, under the most favorable auspices, and feeling perfectly happy. Gansevoort was with him to the last and assisted with his more matured judgement [*sic*] in supplying him with every comfort, Gansevoort says he never saw him so completely happy, as when he had determined upon a situation and all was settled," MGM to AM, 12/8/41, GLA. Unfortunately, Herman's "long letter" has not survived, either because his mother did not save it, or because it was discarded in one of the family's later moves.

15. *Teazer* According to a letter from Gansevoort to his brother Allan, 2/1/41, BA, Gansevoort was violently seasick early in his voyage to the West Indies.

16. Anderson, *Melville in the South Seas*, 25ff., identifies Edward Taylor of Boston as the model for Father Mapple. In *Moby-Dick*, Melville describes the Whaleman's Chapel in fantastic terms: it resembles the bow of a ship, with the fictitious Father Mapple–whose theatricality Melville modeled on the dynamic preaching of Boston's ex-sailor preacher, the Reverend Edward Taylor–climbing to the pulpit by a mock ship's ladder and pulling it up after him. *Whale Fishery of New England* (see note 13, above) provides a glimpse of Enoch Mudge and New Bedford as well as much useful background information on the history of the whaling trade, but it exemplifies the once

common error of taking the description of the Chapel and Father Mapple in *Moby-Dick* as fact.

17. *"Danger"* Mary Ellen Chase, *Seven Seas*, 74. *odds were two to one* De Pauw, *Seafaring Women*, 106. *"Better dead"* Giambarba, *Whales, Whaling*, 38. J. Ross Browne, in *Etchings of a Whaling Cruise, with Notes of a Sojourn on the Island of Zanzibar, to which is appended a brief History of the Whale Fishery, its past and present condition,* edited with an introduction by John Seelye (Cambridge, Mass.: Harvard University Press, 1968), 16, quotes a variation on this popular saying: "Ay, ay, better they never was weaned, than go driftin' round the world in a blubber-hunter."

18. According to the *Oxford English Dictionary*, "spermaceti" first appears in 1471, then in *Rates of Customs* (1545) and *Holinshed's Chronicles* (1577), one of the sources for Shakespeare's *Henry IV*, Part I.

19. *try-pots* Albion, et al., *New England and the Sea*, 118.

20. *1857* This was before the depression hit, of course. *line of ships* *Whale Fishery of New England*, 26.

21. Richard Henry Dana Jr. *Two Years Before the Mast* (New York: Bantam Books, 1969), 167. When the book was first published in 1840, Dana heard that some Nantucketers found this passage offensive, so he added a footnote to reassure them that he had the highest regard for their seamanship. The point about the short spars is made by William O. Stevens, *Nantucket: The Far-Away Island* (New York: Dodd, Mead & Company, 1966), 33–34.

22. *"Black Hole"* *Whale Fishery of New England*, 35.

23. *worms* De Pauw, 136. *food* *Whale Fishery of New England*, 36, Chase, *Seven Seas*, 108ff., and other sources describe the food. Elmo Paul Hohman, *The American Whaleman: A Study of Life and Labor in the Whaling Industry* (New York: Longmans, Green, 1928) also has a wealth of information on the whaling life. Descriptions of whaling from *Moby-Dick* are woven into the text.

24. Melville never describes the sometimes brutal initiation ceremony by which greenhorns were welcomed by King Neptune into the fraternity of seamen as they crossed the Line.

25. Melville's descriptions of the whale hunt and the processing, intermingled with his philosophical ruminations, are concentrated pretty much in chapters 60–78 of *Moby-Dick*, and it seems intrusive and unnecessary to break the narrative to cite the source of each and every phrase.

26. *toggle iron* Giambarba, *Whales, Whaling*, 53. A statue of Lewis Temple now stands in front of the New Bedford Free Public Library.

27. See Giambarba, *Whales, Whaling*, and John B. Putnam, *Whaling and Whalecraft: A Pictorial Account*, in W. W. Norton's paperback edition of *Moby-Dick*, 509–26. These are the main sources for this and the surrounding paragraphs.

28. Giambarba, *Whales, Whaling*, 35. *aphrodisiac* O. H. K. Spate, *Paradise Lost and Found*, in *The Pacific since Magellan*, vol. 3 (Minneapolis: University of Minnesota Press, 1988), 278. Spate gives Melville short shrift; he considers him a hopeless romantic and says that, although *Moby-Dick* is "a great work of art," it "has fatally distorted our perspective on the very hard-headed … trade of whaling."

29. *albatross/Coleridge* In a footnote to *Moby-Dick*, Melville writes about the effect seeing his first albatross had on him. *"glittering cold"* Herman Melville, *White-Jacket, or The World in a Man-of-War* (Evanston and Chicago: Northwestern University Press and The Newberry Library, 1970),* 116.

30. *"strange, congenial feelings"* HM to RHDjr., 5/1/50, NN *Corr.*, 160.

31. *"greasy luck"* See Leyda, *Log*, 119.

32. Wonderful collections of scrimshaw can be seen in the whaling museums of Nantucket and New Bedford, the Peabody Museum of Salem, and other institutions.

---

*Cited hereafter as "NN *W-J*."

33. NN*PT,* 125–73.

34. Leon Howard, *Herman Melville: A Biography* (Berkeley: University of California Press, 1951), 47, gives the delightful detail about the "oyster-trees."

35. *gamming* De Pauw, *Seafaring Women,* 117–21. *letters* Ibid., 111–12.

36. See Thomas Farel Heffernan, *Stove by a Whale: Owen Chase and the* Essex (Middletown, Conn.: Wesleyan University Press, 1981).

37. See David S. Reynolds, *Beneath the American Renaissance: The Subversive Imagination in the Age of Emerson and Melville* (Cambridge, Mass.: Harvard University Press, 1989), 195 ff.

38. Among the "Extracts of a Sub-Sub Librarian" prefatory to *Moby-Dick,* Melville includes quotations from this book and *The Life of Samuel Comstock.* Their presence suggests that Melville knew many more pulp novels than the documentary evidence would indicate.

7. THE FLOODGATES OF THE WONDER-WORLD

1. T. Walter Herbert, *Marquesan Encounters: Melville and the Meaning of Civilization* (Cambridge, Mass.: Harvard University Press, 1980), describes the Alexander mission.

2. Herman Melville, *Typee: A Peep at Polynesian Life* (Chicago and Evanston: Northwestern University Press and The Newberry Library, 1968),* 16. We may never be certain precisely which parts of Melville's later fictional account of his initial encounter with the natives are based on fact and which are pure invention, as Melville kept no journal during these years.

3. Although some have said bad weather would have prevented the women from swimming out that day, Mary Mallory in "'Bound to the Marquesas': Tommo Runs Away," *Melville Society Extracts* 82 (September 1990), 1, 3, has discovered in the log of the *Potomac* an account of the *Acushnet's* arrival that corroborates much of Melville's account.

4. As Herbert, *Marquesan Encounters,* points out, Melville acknowledged Porter, along with Captain James Cook, Edward Fanning, William Ellis, and Charles Stewart. Herbert's analysis of Melville's use of his sources is much more sophisticated than Charles Anderson's, though Anderson deserves credit for being the first to attempt to separate fact from fiction.

5. As Marvin Fisher, *Going Under: Melville's Short Fiction and the American 1850's* (Baton Rouge: Louisiana State University, 1977), points out in a marginal note, Henry David Thoreau, writing *A Week on the Concord and Merrimack Rivers* at Walden Pond, was similarly inverting the customary values of "wild" and "civilized."

6. Charles S. Stewart, *A Visit to the South Seas* (1831).

7. On Melville, transvestites, and homosexuality, see *Gay American History: Lesbians and Gay Men in the U.S.A.: A Documentary by Jonathan Katz* (New York: Thomas Y. Crowell, 1976), whose notes 467–80 contain pertinent information.

8. See Greg Dening, *Islands and Beaches: Discourse on a Silent Land: Marquesas, 1774–1880* (Melbourne University Press, 1980), 19; Donald Marshall, *Ra'ivavae: An Expedition to the Most Fascinating and Mysterious Island in Polynesia* (Garden City: Doubleday, 1961), 100, 114, 195, 199, 247, 289, 292ff.; Robert C. Suggs, *Marquesan Sexual Behavior* (New York: Harcourt, Brace & World, Inc., 1966) and *The Hidden World of Polynesia: The Chronicle of an Archaeological Expedition to Nuka Hiva in the Marquesas Islands* (New York: Harcourt, Brace & World, Inc., 1962); and David Howarth, *Tahiti: A Paradise Lost* (New York: Penguin Books, 1985), 167. *fire* See David Ketterer, "Censorship and Symbolism in *Typee* Revisited: The New Manuscript Evidence," *Melville Society Extracts* 69 (1987), 6–8; and J. Frank Stimson, *Songs and Tales of the Sea Kings: Oral Interpretations of the Oral Literature of Polynesia* (Salem, Mass.: The Peabody Museum, 1857).

9. *repressed Victorians* I am thinking of those who entered into heterosexual marriages, but lived an intense emotional

life centered around same-sex friendship: Hawthorne and Horatio Bridge, Emerson and Martin Gay, etc. See Katz, *Gay American History,* 467–80. His anthology of homoerotic passages from Melville's writings is a very useful reference, though a few statements about Melville in his commentary are based on outdated biographies.

10. Henry Adams to John Hay, 11/16/90, in *Henry Adams and His Friends: A Collection of His Unpublished Letters,* compiled, with a biographical introduction by Harold Dean Cater (Boston: Houghton Mifflin, 1947), 219. Paul Gauguin, *Noa Noa: The Tahitian Journal* (New York: Dover Publications, 1985), 19.

11. See Robert K. Martin, *Hero, Captain and Stranger: Male Friendship, Social Critique and Literary Form in the Sea Novels of Herman Melville* (Chapel Hill: University of North Carolina Press, 1986).

12. *priests* Marshall, *Ra'ivavae,* 17. See also Susan McClellan, "Transvestites as Actors and Translators," *Nexus* 2, no. 1 (Autumn 1981), 73–88; Carol E. Robertson, "The Mahu of Hawaii," *Feminist Studies* 15, no. 2 (1989), 313–21; and Pauline Paine, "Sex and Gender in Oceanic Societies," *Nexus* 2, no. 1 (Autumn 1981), 1–14.

13. *"mast"* Viktor Krupa, *The Polynesian Languages* (New York: Harcourt, Brace & World, 1962).

14. *gentlewomen* Emily Dickinson, poem no. 401, in *The Complete Poems of Emily Dickinson* (Cambridge, Mass.: Harvard University Press, 1955).

15. See Herbert, *Marquesan Encounters;* Dening, *Islands and Beaches;* and Suggs, *The Hidden World of Polynesia.*

16. *"noble"* Melville, *Typee,* 203. *"entertained"* Ibid., 125–26.

17. *"dream"* Herman Melville, *Omoo: A Narrative of Adventures in the South Seas* (Chicago and Evanston: Northwestern University Press and The Newberry Library, 1968),† 7.

18. *"bones"* Ibid., 12. See Historical Note to ibid., 319ff., also Harrison Hayford and Walter Blair, introduction to *Omoo* (Chicago: Hendricks House, 1969), 309–39.

19. *twenty-one-gun salute* From an undated letter (c. 1950?) from Wilson Heflin to Jay Leyda, Leyda collection, University Research Library, UCLA.

20. *"irons"* HM to George Lefevre, for Henry Smyth, 9/25/42, NN *Corr.,* 25.

21. *"ocean"* NN *Omoo,* 114. Charles R. Anderson, *Melville in the South Seas* (New York: Dover, 1966; originally published by New York: Columbia University Press, 1939), 216–17, quotes Stewart's description of the Broom Road. Portions of the accounts of both Porter and Stewart are accessible through Anderson's book, though often hard to obtain in libraries.

22. *"pinned"* NN *Omoo,* 116.

23. Joan D. Hedrick, *Harriet Beecher Stowe: A Life* (New York: Oxford University Press, 1994), 174–75, describes the use of mercury pills in allopathic therapies and their harmful side effects. More research needs to be done on the various medical complaints of the Melvilles, especially Herman and Lizzie, both of whom may have been affected by mercury poisoning in their later years.

24. *"hopeless"* NN *Omoo,* 192. In a footnote to chapter 49 of *Omoo,* Melville quotes the figures supplied by Cook and Wilkes.

25. *factory* NN *Omoo,* 190. Melville may have added the passage about the cotton factory to *Omoo* after consulting Ellis's *Polynesian Researches.*

26. Wilson L. Heflin, "Melville's Third Whaler," *Modern Language Notes* 64 (April 1949), 241–45.

27. See Linda Grant De Pauw, *Seafaring Women* (Boston: Houghton Mifflin, 1982), 116ff., and the journal of Augusta Penniman.

28. Both Anderson, *Melville in the South Seas,* 324–48, and Howard, *Herman Melville,* 65–71, reconstruct this period well despite having little evidence to go on.

---

*Cited hereafter as "NN *Typee.*"

†Cited hereafter as "NN *Omoo.*"

29. *"brutes"* NN *T*, 196.

30. *"Hawaiians"* NN *Omoo*, 188.

31. *Gerrit P. Judd and Laura Fish* Daniel Henderson, *The Hidden Coasts: A Biography of Admiral Charles Wilkes* (New York: William Sloane Associates, 1953), 166. Melville was relieved not to be apprehended when the *Acushnet* put into port in Honolulu on June 7, 1843, but he never knew when he might be discovered by her captain, or by the captain of the *Lucy Ann*, and sent to jail in Sydney.

32. See Leyda, *Log,* 171.

33. *whiskey* Anderson, *Melville in the South Seas,* 396.

34. Ships occasionally swapped whole libraries, according to Mary Ellen Chase, *Sailing the Seven Seas,* 153. On books: Anderson, *Melville in the South Seas,* 118, 358, and 375, also Merton M. Sealts, *Melville's Reading,* revised and enlarged edition (Columbia: University of South Carolina Press, 1988).

35. OR to HM, 2/4/59, Leyda, *Log,* 599–600. *Journal of a Cruise to the Pacific Ocean, 1842–1844, in the Frigate United States,* edited by Charles Robertson Anderson (Durham, N.C.: Duke University Press, 1937), author unknown, identifies Melville's shipmates.

36. For an excellent discussion of Melville's attitudes toward war and peace, see Joyce Sparer Adler, *War in Melville's Imagination* (New York: New York University Press, 1981).

37. Flogging was outlawed by an act of Congress in the summer of 1850, according to Anderson, *Melville in the South Seas,* 420–34. Hugh Hetherington, *Melville's Reviewers, British and American, 1846–1891* (Chapel Hill: University of North Carolina Press, 1961), 183–184, makes the point that because the novel appeared during the congressional hearings on flogging, it was not instrumental in correcting abuses in the navy; it certainly did not hurt the anti-flogging cause, however, and Melville transformed flogging into a symbol of injustice that implicitly relates to the slavery controversy, as Priscilla Allen Zirker, in her "Evidence of the Slavery Dilemma in White-Jacket," *American Quarterly* 18 (Fall 1966), 477–92, first pointed out.

38. See "Historical Note," NN *W-J,* 413ff.

39. See *Journal of a Cruise to the Pacific Ocean,* edited by Anderson.

40. These early impressions of inner decay resurface in *Timoleon.* Once again, Leon Howard vividly conjures these South American ports for the vicarious voyager.

41. See Samuel Eliot Morison, *"Old Bruin": Commodore Matthew C. Perry* (Boston: Atlantic–Little, Brown, 1967), in *Sailor Historian: The Best of Samuel Eliot Morison,* edited by Emily Morison Beck (Boston: Houghton Mifflin, 1977), 181–202.

42. Ibid.

43. Ibid. See also *The Somers Mutiny Affair,* edited by Harrison Hayford (Englewood Cliffs, N.J.: Prentice-Hall, 1959), and Harrison Hayford and Merton M. Sealts Jr., *Billy Budd, Sailor* (*An Inside Narrative*), (Chicago: Phoenix Books, 1962).

44. Morrison, *"Old Bruin,"* 189.

45. References to the *Somers* mutiny can be found in such disparate sources as Thurlow Weed's *Autobiography* (1883) and the *Boston Globe,* "Mexico Navy Joins US in bid to raise ship of war," 20 July 1990.

46. *Natchez,* "Abstract of a Cruise of the United States," Leyda, *Log,* 180–81.

47. The men had no shore leave for eight days, but Melville invented several escapades for his protagonist. In *The General in His Labyrinth,* Gabriel Garcia Marquez alludes to a young sailor named Herman Melville as one of the men with whom the longtime mistress of Simon Bolivar had a fling. Carmen Balcells, Mr. Marquez's agent in Barcelona, assures me this is *un jeu d'esprit,* as I had suspected, and not a Melville "find," though for Melville's sake, one might wish it were.

48. Michael Paul Rogin, *Subversive Genealogy: The Politics and Art of Herman Melville* (New York: Alfred A. Knopf, 1983), 89ff., makes much of this meeting–or non-meeting. We don't really know what passed between Herman and Stanwix in Rio, but we do know that these childhood friends were estranged after Herman got home. See also Wilson L. Heflin, "A Man-of-War Button Divides Two Brothers," *Boston Public Library Quarterly* 3 (January 1951), 51–60. The "anchor button" for which "Frank" feels such contempt prefigures the button on Captain Vere's uniform in *Billy Budd.*

49. In chapter 89 of *White-Jacket,* Melville declares that "the sins for which the cities of the plain were overthrown still linger" on these ships.

50. Margaret S. Creighton, "Fraternity in the American Forecastle, 1830–1870," *New England Quarterly* 63 (December 1990), 531–37, draws on sailor journals to give a sense of the shipboard culture Melville experienced. Creighton argues that "social worlds dominated by 'romantic' male friendships" predated "ones marked by heterosexual intimacy," and she is careful not to speculate and generalize about the specific sexual practices of this homosocial brotherhood.

51. *"slave breeder"* JQA's diary, quoted in Thomas Boylston Adams, "Adams, Slavery & Western Massachusetts," *Berkshire History* 2, no. 2 (Winter 1971), 13.

52. *aboard the Ohio* HelM to AuM, 11/27/43; GLA; *"officers"* HelM to AM, 1/24/42, GLA.

53. *Guert* Leyda, 185. *Guert's resemblance to Herman* Augusta to AMjr., 8/12/39, BA. *"days"* MAG to SG, 1/2/43, Leyda, *Log,* 159.

54. *"chills"* MAG to SG, 1/29/43, GLC.

55. HM to RHD, 5/1/50, *NNCorr.,* 160–61.

56. *"snivelization"* Mark Twain is often given credit for this clever play on words, but Melville first coined the term in *Redburn,* as William M. Gibson pointed out in "Snivelization," *American Speech* (1974), 303–4.

8. A LITTLE EXPERIENCE IN THE ART OF BOOK-CRAFT

1. *"earth"* NN *Typee,* 125.

2. *Robert Lucas* See Keith Huntress, "'Guinea' of *White-Jacket* and Chief Justice Shaw," *American Literature* 43 (1972), 639–41. Ironically, the South objected as much as the North to the federal government's diminution of states' rights, though for different reasons, and, ironically, the South would invoke the Declaration of Independence to justify its rebellion against northern tyranny. See also Stuart Frank, "Melville in the South Seas and *The Friend,"* *Melville Society Extracts* 82 (September 1990), 6.

3. *Shaw* Leonard W. Levy, *The Law of the Commonwealth and Chief Justice Shaw* (Cambridge, Mass.: Harvard University Press, 1957), 60. *Med and Latimer cases* Louis Filler, *The Crusade against Slavery, 1830–1860* (New York: Harper & Row, 1960), 169. Latimer gained his freedom through a deal worked out by abolitionists who bought him from his master.

4. *Creole* Carolyn L. Karcher, "The Riddle of the Sphinx: Melville's 'Benito Cereno' and the *Amistad* Case," *Critical Essays on Melville's "Benito Cereno,"* ed. by Robert Burkholder (Boston: G. K. Hall, forthcoming), 50, quotes Lydia Maria Child's editorial comment that the *Amistad* case had "prepared the way" for favorable public reaction to the *Creole* mutiny.

5. See Charles Sumner, "The Crime against Kansas," U.S. Senate, Washington, D.C., 19–20 May 1856. Adams was a hero to New Englanders for his vocal opposition to slavery and the war against the Seminoles. See Thomas Boylston Adams, "Adams, Slavery and Western Massachusetts," *Berkshire History* I, no. 2 (Winter 1971), 3–15. Amistad Jack Shepherd, *The Adams Chronicles: Four Generations of Greatness* (Boston: Little, Brown, 1975), 333.

6. *"frogs"* HelM to AM, 1/14/44. The new Melville letters ("Augusta Papers," GLA) give some lively glimpses of Helen's visit with Lizzie in Boston while Herman was away. I am also indebted to Amy Elizabeth Puett, *Melville's Wife: A Study of Elizabeth Shaw Melville* (unpublished doctoral dissertation,

Northwestern University, 1969), for much of my biographical information about Lizzie. Puett was the first scholar to focus on Elizabeth Shaw Melville after previous biographers either attacked or ignored her.

7. tableaux vivants, *theater*   HelM to AM, 3/7/42 and 11/27/42, GLA. When a dancer in another show appeared wearing shockingly short petticoats, however, Helen was very glad her brother wasn't there. She reported every detail of her Boston visits to Augusta, from Oakes Shaw's having a coat made of buffalo skins and trimmed with a squirrel collar and cuffs, and Kitty Sedgwick's becoming engaged to William Minot, to Aunt Helen's having an enormous rooster named "Bright Eye" at her house at Hingham, who, when called like a little spaniel by her eight-year-old cousin, would come and perch on her chair and eat right from her hand. During a side trip to see John Quincy Adams's homestead, her aunt reminisced about how the gallant ex-President had tried to save old Major Melvill's job in 1829. See HelM to AM, 1/24/42, 2/16/42, and 3/7/42, GLA.

8. *"Boz"*   HelM to AM, 1/24/42, 2/16/42, GLA.
9. *"knight"*   HelM to AM, 1/24/42, GLA.
10. See AMjr. to HM, 10/17/44, NN*Corr.*, 567–70.
11. Gansevoort's career in the 1840s is described by Hershel Parker, "Gansevoort Melville's Role in the Campaign of 1844," *New York Historical Society Quarterly* 49 (April 1965), 143–73.
12. *"blood"*   GM to AMjr., 9/4/44, BA. *"gas and glory"* *New-York Daily Tribune*, 12/12/44, Leyda, *Log*, 186.
13. *"eager crowds"*   GM to AMjr., 10/13/44, BA. *"Locofocoes" and "gander-brained"*   See Parker, "Campaign of 1844," 173. See David S. Reynolds, *Beneath the American Renaissance: The Subversive Imagination in the Age of Emerson and Melville* (Cambridge: Harvard University Press, 1988), 458. *"interests"*   TMjr. to LS, 4/18/44, Leyda, *Log*, 912.
14. *"clothing"*   MGM to AMjr., 8/7/42, BA.
15. *"world"*   MGM to AMjr., 5/1/41, BA.
16. *sticks*   MGM to AMjr., 8/7/42, BA.
17. "happier Lad"   MGM to AMjr., 5/1/41, BA.
18. Books that focus on Melville's religious attitudes include T. Walter Herbert, *Moby-Dick and Calvinism: A World Dismantled* (New Brunswick, N.J.: Rutgers University Press, 1977); William P. Braswell, *Melville's Religious Thought: An Essay in Interpretation* (Durham, N.C.: Duke University Press, 1943); Lawrance R. Thompson, *Melville's Quarrel with God* (Princeton, N.J.: Princeton University Press, 1952). The Rev. Walter Donald Kring, historian of Unitarianism and biographer of the Rev. Henry Whitney Bellows, is working on a new study of Melville and religion.
19. *"Mama's door"*   HelM to AM, 9/?/41, GLA.
20. This paragraph and the succeeding two are based on Helen's letters to Augusta, 1/24/42, 3/7/42, 1/28/43, 11/27/43, 1/14/44, GLA, which turned up in the new cache of family papers discovered in a barn in Saratoga County in 1983.
21. For this paragraph and the next, see AMjr. to AM, 10/13/41, 5/5/42, and 5/3/43, GLA. To soften the blow, he added to one of his letters: But dont [sic] get angry sister of mine I do not mean to offend you, but really this is my private opinion … (with all due deference to yours) and hoping you will take the hint, so let it rest." The "squiggly lines" scrawled on his letter can be seen at The New York Public Library.
22. *Waterford*   HelM to AM, 1/28/43, GLA. *"enthusiastic" movements*   Whitney R. Cross, *The Burned-Over District: The Social and Intellectual History of Enthusiastic Religion in Western New York* (Ithaca, N.Y.: Cornell University Press, 1950).
23. *"on the 22nd"*   L. Maria Child, *Letters from New York*, 2nd series (New York: C. S. Francis & Co., and Boston: J. H. Francis, 1845), Letter 26, 235ff.
24. *"unfolded"*   HM to NH, 6/1(?)/51, NN*Corr.*, 193.
25. *Grampus*   Leon Howard, *Herman Melville: A Biography* (Berkeley: University of California Press, 1951), *90*. The *Grampus* was the ship that took the *Amistad* rebels into custody.

Hun signed on 1/30/43 (see letter of Mary A. A. Gansevoort to Stanwix Gansevoort, 1/29/43, GLC), but he was on leave in August 1843, as he wrote in a letter to his cousin Stanwix from the Astor House. References to Hun are fleeting and imprecise. Item about Thomas Wilson Melvill, Leyda, *Log*, 183, and Supplement to Leyda, *Log*, 913. *Henry*   See Leyda, *Log*, 196.
26. See Julian Hawthorne, *Hawthorne and His Wife: A Biography in Two Volumes* (Boston: Houghton Mifflin, 1884), 407.
27. In a letter to his sister Kate, HM to CM, 1/20/45, NN*Corr.*, 27ff., Melville launches into a hyperbolic rhapsody on the name "Kate" for the benefit of his sister and the two other Kates in the household where she was staying: their mother's cousin Catherine Gansevoort Van Vechten, and her daughter Catherine Van Vechten. Melville later enjoyed a close correspondence with his cousin Catherine Gansevoort Lansing, another Kate.
28. *"manifest destiny"*   John L. O'Sullivan, *Democratic Review* 17 (July–August 1845 and October 1845); Albert K. Weinberg, *Manifest Destiny: A Study of Nationalist Expansionism in American History* (Baltimore, Md.: Johns Hopkins University Press, 1935), 112. *"more, more, more!"*   John L. O'Sullivan, *The New York Morning News*, 7 February 1845; Frederick Merk, *Manifest Destiny and Mission in American History: A Reinterpretation* (New York: Random House, 1966), 52. *Young America* Merk, ibid., 54, quotes the *United States Journal*, 3 May 1845. *spirit*   Boston Times, 11 December 1844. See also Leonard Engel, "Melville and the Young America Movement," *Connecticut Review* 4 (April 1971), 19–101.
29. Inferred from PG to EJMF, 1/28/43, Leyda, *Log*, 162.
30. Melville's sources are given in several places, notably the "Historical Note" to NN*Typee*, 291.
31. Ibid., 278, and Ezra Greenspan, "Evert Duyckinck and the History of Wiley and Putnam's Library of American Books, 1845–1847," *American Literature* 64, no. 4 (December 1992), 677–93. *Harper's*   Recollections of Frederick Saunders, Leyda, *Log*, 196. those *"stage-managers, the Fates"*   NNM-D, 7.
32. *contract with Murray*   Gansevoort Melville's 1846 London *Journal and Letters from England, 1845*, edited by Hershel Parker (New York Public Library, 1966), 19. *diplomatic uniform*   Ibid., 24. A reader for Murray named Henry Milton also spent 168½ hours getting the manuscript in shape. *"practised writer"* NN*Corr.*, headnote, 30.
33. John Bryant, in "reading Typee Historically" (paper presented at the American Literature Association, San Diego, June 1994) and other articles, has compared the various texts of *Typee* with the newly discovered manuscript draft to establish more clearly the nature of the alterations to the text.
34. *"see it"*   MVRT to AM, 2/22/45, GLA.
35. *"admirably"*   AW to AM, 1/14/46, GLA.
36. The dedication reads, "To Lemuel Shaw, Chief Justice of the Commonwealth of Massachusetts, this little work is affectionately inscribed by the author"–an alteration to Melville's "gratefully inscribed" that may have been made by Gansevoort, not Herman. In the copy he sent Judge Shaw 3/19/46, he wrote "Chief Justice Shaw, with the sincere respects of the author." *"fair chance"*   GM to MGM, 12/3/45. *"brilliant"*   MGM to AM, 2/28/46, GLA. Modern authors, who must wait a year or a year and a half to see completed books printed, bound, and distributed to bookstores, despite high-speed technology, might well envy the authors of Melville's days for the rapidity with which their books were published and reviewed.
37. "sacrifices"   NN*Typee*, 5.
38. *"temptation"*   Ibid., 15. Both Spate and De Pauw mention the sinking of the British line-of-battle ship *Royal George* in 1782 with three hundred women on board, but in chapter 54 of *White-Jacket*, Melville claims that "the custom of introducing women on board, in harbour, is now pretty much discontinued, both in the English and American Navy, unless a ship, commanded by some dissolute captain happens to lie in some far away, outlandish port, in the Pacific or Indian Ocean."

39. *"prevailed"* Ibid.

40. *"white man"* Ibid.

41. *"Happy Valley"* Ibid., 78.

42. *"spirits"* Ibid., 132.

43. "We were told that Fa-a-wa and a daughter of Melville's were still living, the former an old woman," according to "R.S." in *The Athenaeum*, reporting on a trip taken to "Melville's Marquesas" in late 1867, Leyda, *Log*, 694. When Melville was nearly seventy years old, a boy heard him bragging to the barber in Glens Falls, New York, that he had fathered a son in Polynesia. Melville was clearly being "Typee" or "Tommo" here, as he was only in the Typee Valley for a month, which was barely time enough for a "Fayaway" to know that she was pregnant.

44. *money* NN *Typee*, 126.

45. Augusta's friend Ellen Astor Oxenham to AM, 10/5/46, GLA, makes this provocative comment: "I present Typee with the fortunate words that rescued him from becoming too entirely one of his gentle savages–there is food for reflection in those two words." Melville evidently called himself "Typee"; he may have called his hero "Tommo" to please his little brother. Tom, who was everybody's darling, looked up to his sailor brother. The leg infection, though exaggerated for *Typee*, was real; Melville sought treatment for it from Dr. Johnstone once he reached Papeete. It was Gansevoort, of course, who had the more debilitating leg infection–an interesting coincidence.

46. NN *Typee*, 202–3.

47. Ibid., 125.

48. American reformers such as Horace Mann and Samuel Gridley Howe took pride in American penal reforms, but when Charles Dickens visited Philadelphia in 1842, he pronounced the system of "rigid, strict, and hopeless solitary confinement" to be "cruel and wrong." Dickens, in *American Notes* (Greenwich, Conn.: Fawcett Premier, 1961), 120–22, argued that "there is a depth of terrible endurance in it which none but the sufferers themselves can fathom, and which no man has a right to inflict upon his fellow creatures." The prisoner is "led to the cell, from which he never again comes forth until his whole term of imprisonment has expired. He never hears of his wife or children; home or friends; the life or death of any single creature. He sees the prison officers, but, with that exception, he never looks upon a human countenance, or hears a human voice. He is a man buried alive; to be dug out in the slow round of years; and in the meantime dead to everything but torturing anxieties and horrible despair."

"a *point d'appui*, below freshet and frost and fire, a place where you might find a wall or a state, or set a lamp-post safely, or perhaps a gauge, not a Nilometer, but a Realometer …" from Henry David Thoreau, *Walden, or Life in the Woods*.

49. *The Athenaeum*, 2/21/46 and 2/28/46, Leyda, 204; *Times*, 4/6/46, Leyda, 210; *John Bull*, 3/7/46, Leyda, *Log*, 205–6.

50. The first book in the series was the *Journal of an African Cruiser*, which Hawthorne edited for his close friend Horatio Bridge. *Greenwood* Willard Thorp, "'Grace Greenwood' Parodies *Typee*," *American Literature* 4, no. 9 (January 1938), 455–56.

51. *"perhaps"* ED to NH, 3/13/46, Leyda, *Log*, 206; *"life,"* Hawthorne, 3/25/46, Leyda, *Log*, 207–8.

52. *"glowing"* Longfellow's journal, 7/26/46, Leyda, *Log*, 223. *"charming"* Alcott's journal, 12/9/46. *Thoreau* Leyda, *Log*, 259.

53. *"easy, gossiping tone"* *The Knickerbocker*, May 1846, Leyda, *Log*, 216. *"animated style"* Charles Fenno Hoffman, *The Gazette and Times*, New York, 30 March 1846, Leyda, *Log*, 208. *"striking"* *Godey's Lady's Book*, 6 May 1846, Leyda, *Log*, 216. *"Typee"* *Harbinger*, 4 April 1846, quoted in Hugh W. Hetherington, *Melville's Reviewers, British and American, 1846–1891* (Chapel Hill, N.C.: University of North Carolina Press, 1961), 52–53. *"hit"* *New York Weekly News*, 21 March 1846, Leyda, *Log*, supplement, 914.

54. *"villages"* Fuller, *New-York Daily Tribune*, 4 April 1846, Leyda, *Log*, 209–10. *"day"* Whitman, *Brooklyn Eagle*, 14 April 1846, Leyda, *Log*, 211.

55. *"charming"* *National Antislavery Standard*, 2 April 1846, Leyda, *Log*, 208. *"scuffle"* Ibid., 52–53. *"next"* GD to Rosalie Baker, 4/14/46, Leyda, *Log*, 211.

56. NN *Typee*, 125–26. *"racily-written"* *New York Evangelist*, 17 April 1846, Leyda, *Log*, 211. *"traducer"* *Christian Parlor Magazine*, July 1846, Leyda, *Log*, 224–25.

57. *Albany Argus*, 21 April 1846, quoted in Merrel R. Davis, *Melville's Mardi: A Chartless Voyage* (New Haven, Conn.: Yale University Press, 1952), 18.

58. *Enquirer*, 17 April 1846, Leyda, *Log*, 211–12. *Bradford* AMjr. to HM, 10/17/44, NN *Corr.*, 570. *"to be"* HM to AB, 5/23/46, NN *Corr.*, 38.

59. *"breeches"* Gansevoort Melville, *London Journal*, 54. *"spirits"* GM to AMjr., 11/18/45, GLC. For a discussion of Gansevoort's conduct, see Parker's introduction to the *London Journal*, 13. In a funeral eulogy, Captain E. Knight told of visiting Cambridge with Gansevoort. At the sight of an immense globe, Gansevoort launched into a speech about America's role in the world. Ibid., 51.

60. *"breaking up"* GM to HM, 4/3/46, Leyda, *Log*, 208–9. *going blind* Louis McLane to James Buchanan, 5/4/46, Leyda, *Log*, 213. Unlike Leyda, the editor of NN *Corr.*, 575, finds no evidence that Gansevoort enclosed the passage in the letter he sent to Herman.

61. *"persons"* Henry Stevens to N. D. Hubbard, 5/19/46, Leyda, *Log*, supplement, 915.

62. *Texas* "Texas was a perfect example of how Manifest Destiny would work, a pattern to be copied by the remainder of the continent," Merk, *Manifest Destiny*, 46.

63. ST to AM, 12/9/46, GLA. John H. Schroeder, *Mr. Polk's War: American Opposition and Dissent, 1846–1848* (Madison: University of Wisconsin Press, 1974), refers to Polk's supporters ranting about enlarging "The Temple of Freedom"–a phrase that may have stuck in Melville's mind for the Great Temple of Vivenza in *Mardi*.

64. *"again"* HM to GM, 5/29/46, NN *Corr.*, 40–41.

65. AM to CVS, 6/23/46, Leyda, *Log*, supplement 925.

66. For letters of HM to Polk, et al., 6/6/46, see Leyda, *Log*, 217–18, and NN *Corr.*, 41ff.

67. *"spirits"* MGM to LS, 11/1/46, Leyda, *Log*, 228.

68. According to Eleanor Melville Metcalf, it was Agnes Morewood to whom Melville remarked that his mother "hated" him. One wonders if this statement was a projection of his own anger toward her. Melville may have had murderous impulses toward Gansevoort as a child, and pushed them down so deep that he became unaware of them himself. "Timoleon" depicts a troubled relationship between two brothers and their mother.

69. *"remains"* HM to PG, 6/22/46, NN *Corr.*, 47–48.

70. *"civil skepticism"* HM to ED, 7/3/46, NN *Corr.*, 50.

71. *Tetractys Club* See Perry Miller, *The Raven and the Whale: The War of Words and Wits in the Era of Poe and Melville* (New York: Harcourt, Brace, & World, 1956); Greenspan, "Evert Duyckinck," Donald Yannella, "Writing the 'Other Way': Melville, the Duyckinck Crowd, and Literature for the Masses," in *A Companion to Melville Studies*, edited by John Bryant (New York and Westport, Conn.: Greenwood Press, 1986), 63–81; and Daniel A. Wells, "Bartleby the Scrivener, Poe, and the Duyckinck Circle," *Emerson Society Quarterly* 21 (first quarter, 1975), 35–39. "Knights of the Round Table," Melville's term for the group, which included Horace Greeley, William Cullen Bryant, James Russell Lowell, Nathaniel Parker Willis, Charles Fenno Hoffman, possibly Washington Irving and Edgar Allan Poe, and, perhaps Margaret Fuller. The "Anecdotes," which appeared in several installments between July and September 1847, and an accompanying "Historical Note," are included in NN *PT*, 212–28.

72. Leyda, *Log*, 220.

73. For the full text of Toby's letter, see NN *Corr.*, 579–84. *"interest"* HM to ED, 7/3/46, NN *Corr.*, 50.

74. "alone" HM to JM, 7/15/46, NN *Corr.*, 54–58.

75. *"wonders"* Ibid., 57–58.

76. *"Odious word"* HM to ED, 7/30?/46, NN *Corr.*, 60.

77. *"evidences"* See headnote, JM to HM, 8/3/46, NN *Corr.*, 584. *"liberal . . . offer"* See HM to JM, 9/2/46, NN *Corr.*, 65. *"cabilistic"* HM to JM, 9/2/46, NN *Corr.*, 65.

78. "true" HM to JM, 9/2/46, NN *Corr.*, 66.

9. FIERCE CANNIBAL DELIGHT

1. *"book on the stocks"* HM to JM, 9/2/46, NN *Corr.*, 65. Melville's letters to Murray express his frustration with the public's perception of the writer's role. Like Shelley, Melville regarded poets as more worthy to be the legislators of their times than lawyers, and he had an exalted, romantic sense of the artist's power to shape the history and culture of his times. As F. O. Matthiessen said in *American Renaissance: Art and Expression in the Age of Emerson and Whitman* (New York: Oxford University Press, 1941), p. 377, *Mardi* is "A Source-Book for Plenitude." "belles" Even Augusta's New York friend Ellen Astor Oxenham could not refrain from gushing, "Typee, you dear creature, I want to see you so amazingly," EAO to Augusta Melville, 10/5/46, GLA.

2. *"particular lady"* HM to ED, 12/8/46, NN *Corr.*, 67–68; her identity remains a mystery.

3. *"natives"* HM to ED, 12/10/46, NN *Corr.*, 668–69. *"Tahiti"* ED to GD, Leyda, *Log*, 230.

4. *"agitating"* ED to GD, 12/15/46, Leyda, *Log*, 230. *sight unseen* Recollections of Frederick Saunders, Leyda, *Log*, 230. Saunders does not say whether the "Mr. Harper" in this anecdote was James or Fletcher.

5. See Amy Elizabeth Puett, *Melville's Wife: A Study of Elizabeth Shaw Melville*, for biographical material on Elizabeth Shaw (unpublished doctoral dissertation, Northwestern University, 1969).

6. Ibid., 22ff.; Hennig Cohen and Donald Yannella, *Herman Melville's Malcolm Letter: "Man's Final Lore"* (New York: Fordham University Press and the New York Public Library, 1992), 179–81. Founded as a coed school, Uxbridge reopened in 1831 as a girls' school. Lizzie's preceptor there was a man named Benjamin Parker, and she boarded with the Reverend Samuel Clarke.

7. *"good mothers"* Rita K. Gollin, "Subordinated Power: Mrs. and Mr. James T. Fields," in *Patrons and Protegees: Gender, Friendship, and Writing in Nineteenth-Century America*, edited by Shirley Marchalonis (New Brunswick: Rutgers University Press, 1988), 143, and Puett, *Melville's Wife*, 24–25.

8. Joyce Deveau Kennedy and Frederick James Kennedy, "Elizabeth and Herman" (part 2), *Melville Society Extracts* 34 (May 1978), pp. 3–8. In this series of articles the Kennedys have done an admirable job of helping to bring Lizzie into focus. Lizzie evidently saw Daniel McIlroy in Chicago during a visit with her father in 1845, and after her marriage, she asked Sam Savage to "tell Mr. McIlroy for yourself, *not from me,* that my marriage was very unexpected, and scarcely thought of until about two months before it actually took place. I have some reason for wishing him to know this fact but I want you to mention it casually on your own account." There is no evidence that Herman had serious flirtations between his return from the Pacific and his wedding day, though in February 1847, either his mother or one of his sisters mistakenly opened a letter, "quite a pretty one, from some fair lady in the village," and teased him about it. It is indicative of the number of fan notes he must have received from young women, all of whom apparently considered Typee quite a catch. MGM to AM, 2/15/47, GLA.

9. Puett, *Melville's Wife*, 28, quotes it in full; it begins: "1. And Lemuel said unto Hope, Come, let us go up into the house of Aunt Dow–and the number of them that went was three. 2. And Hope and Elizabeth took counsel together, say-

ing, What shall we wear? and wherewithal shall we array ourselves? And Hope said, ask thy cousin Jane concerning the matter, and whatsoever she says that shalt thou do." The parody continues for thirteen amusing verses.

10. *Literary World,* 6 March 1847. NN *PT*, 205–11. Browne was quite hurt by Melville's review and wrote a reply. See Leyda, *Log*, 239. As for Melville's plans for his next book, *Mardi* started out as a continuation of his first two novels, but Melville changed course twice in the process of writing it. The book that most fulfills Melville's original aim for *Mardi* is, of course, *Moby-Dick.*

11. HM to JRB, 3/31/47, also Leyda, *Log*, 237.

12. William Charvat, *The Profession of Authorship in America, 1800–1870,* in *The Papers of William Charvat,* edited by Matthew J. Bruccoli (Columbus: Ohio State University Press, 1968), 294, says that 60–75 percent of all male American writers who were professional or near-professional held or tried to hold public office, including James Kirke Paulding, Washington Irving, and Nathaniel Hawthorne.

13. *"Bond Street girls"* See Leyda, *Log*, 234–35.

14. *"Mother"* MGM to AM, 2/19/47, GLA, NN *Corr.*, headnote, 83. *Twitchell* Frances D. Broderick, "Local Artist Painted Melville's Portrait," *The* [Lansingburgh] *Voice,* 16 February 1973.

15. Somewhat conjectural. Reconstructing Melville's courtship of Lizzie is difficult, as written records of private matters are spotty, and in this section of the book, I have taken more liberties with speculation than elsewhere in an attempt to create a readable, plausible narrative based on solid inference.

16. *"Pacific"* HM to JM, 1/29/47, NN *Corr.*, 78.

17. "One week after it was issued the whole edition of 3,000, or 3,500, was disposed of and another was put in progress," according to Helen Melville, letter to Augustus van Schaick, 6/11/47, quoted in Davis, Merrell R. Davis, *Melville's Mardi: A Chartless Voyage* (New Haven: Yale University Press, 1952), 35.

18. *Godey's* Robert K. Wallace, *Melville and Turner: Spheres of Love and Fright* (Athens, Ga.: University of Georgia Press, 1993), 78. *Whitman Brooklyn Eagle,* 5 May 1857, Leyda, *Log,* 243. *Evening Mirror,* 21 May 1847, Leyda, *Log,* 244–45. (According to Leyda, the *Evening Mirror* review was possibly written by Evert Duyckinck, but the author seems more likely to have been Jedediah Auld, who later defended Melville against Peck's attack.)

19. *Peck The American Review,* see Leyda, *Log,* 249–50, and Perry Miller, *The Raven and the Whale. The War of Words and Wit in the Era of Poe and Melville* (New York: Harcourt, Brace & World, 1956), 216.

20. *Auld The Evening Mirror,* 21 July 1847, Leyda, *Log,* 251.

21. *"cloven foot"* 3/48, Leyda, *Log,* 275; *"grossly abusive"* ED's diary, 7/10/47; Leyda, *Log,* 250, cites the "Whig Review."

22. *Cramer Daily Wisconsin,* 1 July 1847; he seems to have been a big fan of Melville's, as he responded to several other papers that criticized the book.

23. See Leyda, *Log,* 227, and "Historical Note," Herman Melville, *A Peep at Polynesian Life* (Chicago and Evanston: Northwestern University Press and the Newberry Library, 1968), *Typee:* 296. See also Charvat, "Melville's Income," in *The Profession of Authorship,* 190–203; John Updike, "Melville's Withdrawal," in *Hugging the Shore: Essays and Criticism* (New York: Alfred A. Knopf, 1983), 90–106, also discusses Melville's income.

24. Figures from NN *Typee,* 298.

25. *Reed's gallery* see John M. J. Gretchko, "Melville at the New-York Gallery of the Fine Arts," *Melville Society Extracts* 82 (September 1990), 7–8 and Wallace, *Melville Turner,* 117.

26. "We have been particularly busy today in assisting him in embellishing the small front room as a library and study. The walls have been coloured (the bird stand removed), a new carpet, and curtains, the library has been removed and placed

before the door leading into the next room, and a great box & two trunks have been unpacked fill'd with books and handsomely displayed together with the ship and miniature anchor on his desk top together with three ancient mahogany chairs from the attic, he looks and his study looks ready to begin a new work, on the 'South Seas' of course." MGM to AM, 5/19/47, GLA.

27. *"steering oar"* Eleanor Melville Metcalf, *Herman Melville: Cycle and Epicycle* (Cambridge: Harvard University Press, 1953), 42. *"tomatoes" and "astounding truth"* HelM to AVS, 6/11/47, Leyda, *Log,* 247.

28. MGM to AM, 1847 (n.d.), GLA. In this letter, Melville's mother claims he and Lizzie will have been engaged eleven months in July, which appears to be an exaggeration. They may have been engaged in her mind while they were courting, but the official announcement would not be made until June 1847.

29. *"July"* MGM to AM, 6/15/47, GLA.

30. *"paper"* Leyda, *Log,* 253–54.

31. *"a peculiar choice"* Fanny Appleton Longfellow to Nathan Appleton, 8/3/47, Leyda, *Log,* supplement, 916. *"father"* Edmund Quincy to Caroline Weston, 7/2/47, from "Additions to Melville Log," *Melville Society Extracts* 31 (September 1977), 4–8. *"kindhearted"* MvRT to AM, 12/22/45?, GLA; AW to AM, 10/6/47, GLA.

32. Richard Henry Dana, Jr., *Journal,* edited by Robert F. Lucid, 3 vols. (Cambridge, Mass.: Harvard University Press, 1960), is a valuable source of information about reactions to Judge Shaw's decisions regarding escaped slaves; the entry about the dinner party, 8/23/47, is also quoted in Leyda, *Log,* 254.

33. See Luther S. Mansfield, "Melville's Comic Articles on Zachary Taylor," *American Literature* 9, no. 4 (January 1938), 411–18.

34. *Independent Democrat,* 12/17/46, quoted in Frederick Merk, *Manifest Destiny and Mission in American History: A Reinterpretation* (New York: Vintage Books, 1966), 100.

35. *The Piazza Tales and Other Prose Pieces* includes a number of unattributed pieces written for *Yankee Doodle;* they are *jeux d'esprits,* clearly written for pocket money. They include "On the Sea Serpent," "On the Chinese Junk," "A Short Patent Sermon," "The New Planet," and "View of the Barnum Property." The "Chinese Junk" piece was probably written after the outing with Evert Duyckinck described in Miller, *The Raven and the Whale,* 210.

36. *"mummies"* From "View of the Barnum Property," one of the *Yankee Doodle* pieces attributed to Melville by the editors of NN*PT,* 447–48. There are a number of references to Barnum in Melville's writings, usually intended as a bitter commentary on the debasement of popular taste and the ability of showmen in America to get rich by pandering to vulgar appetites. *Heth* See Neil Harris, *Humbug: The Art of P. T. Barnum* (Chicago: The University of Chicago Press, 1973).

37. *Barnum* Lydia Maria Child, *Letters from New York, 2d Series* (New York: C. S. Francis & Co. and Boston: J. H. Francis, 1845), 173.

38. *Haydon* See Neil Harris, *Humbug,* 229.

39. *"Irving"* ED's diary, 7/31/47, Leyda, *Log,* 253.

40. Descriptions of the ceremony are from ESM to her cousin Samuel Hay Savage, 47, from "Additions to the Melville Log," *Melville Society Extracts* 31 (September 1977).

41. *"cake"* Samuel Shaw to Lizzie, 8/4/56, Leyda, *Log,* 255.

42. *Boston Daily Evening Transcript,* 5 August 1847, Murray Papers, HUA. *"romantic"* ESM to HSS, 8/6/47, Leyda, *Log,* 255.

43. *breach of promise New-York Daily Tribune,* 7 August 1847, Leyda, *Log,* 256; ESM & HM to LS, 8/6/47, HCL.

44. *Montreal and Quebec* ESM to HSS, 8/21/47, HCL, Leyda, *Log,* 256–57, and Metcalf, *Herman Melville,* 45–46.

45. *canal boat* ESM to HSS, 8/28/47, HCL, Leyda, *Log,* 257–58, and Metcalf, 46–48.

46. *"crowd"* ESM to HSS, 8/28/47, HCL, Leyda, *Log,* 257–58.

47. *gown* STM to AM, 9/4/47. *vest* Davis, *Melville's* Mardi, 102.

48. *"ethereal"* AMPM to AM, 9/26/47, GLC, Leyda, *Log,* 260.

49. Sophia Thurston wrote Augusta, "You will never marry a man like either Herman or Allan, and if you are at all like me you have often looked at the husbands of your friends, and wondered at the choice they have made. No matter what kind of a man he may be, there is an indescribable something which you are certain would prevent you from ever being attached to him," ST to AM, 6/24/47, GLA. *"gods"* AMPM to AM, 9/26/47, GLC, Leyda, *Log,* 260. *Peebles* Lemuel Shaw Jr. to Samuel H. Savage, 8/13/47, quoted by Joyce Deveau Kennedy and Frederick J. Kennedy, "Elizabeth Shaw Melville and Samuel Hay Savage, 1847–1853," *Melville Society Extracts* 39 (September 1979), 1; and LSjr. to SHS, 3/11/48, MHS, "Additions to the Melville Log," *Melville Society Extracts* 31 (September 1977), 5. My hunch is that Augusta was more attracted to unattainable men such as Hawthorne than to attainable ones like Augustus Peebles. "Boston marriages" were common between women, as were "passionate friendships" between men. *"dame"* AWH to AM, 3/1/48, GLA.

50. *tracts* STM to AM, 1/27/47, GLA.

51. *Blackwood's* STM to AM, 6/24/47, GLA, and AM to Susan Lansing, 6/24/47, GLC.

52. *"old crooked Boston"* ESM to SHS, 9/12–18/47, Joyce and Frederick Kennedy, "Elizabeth and Herman" (part 1), *Melville Society Extracts* 33 (February 1978), 4–12.

53. ESM to SHS, ESM to SHS, 9/12–18/47, Joyce and Frederick Kennedy, "Elizabeth and Herman" (part 1), *Melville Society Extracts* 33 (February 1978), 4–12.

54. *103 Fourth Avenue* ESM to SHS, 4/3/48, HCL. The Thurstons had made a generous loan to Allan and his bride when they first got married.

55. *"Manahatta"* Walt Whitman, *Leaves of Grass and Selected Prose* (edited and with an Introduction by Sculley Bradley) (New York: Holt, Rinehart and Winston, 1949), 388.

56. Child, *Letters from New York,* 175.

57. *"voices"* ESM to HSS, 6/6/48, HCL. *"money-making rage"* Child, *Letters from New York,* 254.

58. Had Melville been living in New York in the early 1840s, he might have caught a glimpse of Walt Whitman, the young fellow who rode alongside the stagecoach drivers as they careened through the city and filled in for them when they were sick or needed a day off. See Gay Wilson Allen, *The Solitary Singer: A Critical Biography of Walt Whitman* (Chicago: University of Chicago Press, 1985), 41–66.

59. *"bo-beep"* Ibid., 167. *"birds"* Child, *Letters from New York,* 96–98.

60. *"beauty"* Ibid., 98.

61. *salt baths* "Allan is very well, he has fallen into the habit of taking a daily salt water bath—cold—Really a man might fall into a worse habit," GM to AM, 7/19/44, GLA. "took the salt waterbaths at the Battery—much benefit—very invigorating & refreshing during the exceedingly warm days we have here," AMjr. to AM, 8/6/44, GLA. *Croton water* Child, *Letters from New York,* 168.

62. *fountain* Child, *Letters from New York,* 96–97.

63. *"bouquets of flowers"* Ibid., 173.

64. *"raiment"* Ibid., 198.

65. *"importance"* Ibid., 254–55.

66. *"selfishness"* Ibid. *"obliging"* Ibid., 198.

67. *"Aladdin's lamp"* Ibid., 169. *"not a Sodom"* Ibid., 199.

68. ED's diary 10/6/47, Leyda, *Log,* 261. It's often difficult to ascertain whether social functions included married couples or only men; male diarists, listing names of guests at social functions, usually named husbands, taking the presence of their wives for granted. As a result, biographers have simply ignored or overlooked the pervasive role of women, just as the

role of the servants who made these elegant occasions possible has been ignored.

69. *"Ti"* ED to GD, 11/15/47, Leyda, *Log,* 264.

70. *"a late hour"* ESM to HSS, Leyda, *Log,* 264.

71. *drawers* ESM to HSS, 6/6/48, Leyda, *Log,* 277, writes: "tapes are *always* useful especially if one has a husband who is continually breaking strings off of drawers as mine is."

72. *"abomination"* ESM to HSS, 12/23/47, HCL, Leyda, *Log,* 267.

73. *"amusement"* Ibid.

74. See Susan K. Harris, "'But is it any good?' Evaluating Nineteenth-Century American Women's Fiction," *American Literature* 63, no. 1 (March 1991).

75. *"pecuniary value"* HM to JM, 10/29/47, NN *Corr.,* and Davis, *Melville's* Mardi, 212–13; JM to HM, 12/3/47, Leyda, *Log,* supplement, 917.

76. *"aim"* HM to JM, 1/1/48, NN *Corr.*

77. "wrapped up–without fire," ESM memoir of HM, BA, also Leyda, *Log,* 283, though her date is incorrect; reprinted in Puett, *Melville's Life,* 243–51.

1 0 . C R E A T I N G T H E C R E A T I V E

1. *"author-tribe"* Leyda, *Log,* 272.

2. *poem* Bayard Taylor to Mary Agnew, 2/23/48, Leyda, *Log,* 272. Robert K. Martin, "Knights-Errant and Gothic Seducers: The Representation of Male Friendship in Mid-Nineteenth Century America," in *Hidden from History: Reclaiming the Gay and Lesbian Past* (New York: Meridian, 1990), 171, calls Taylor "the most outspoken advocate of 'the other love' in mid-century America," but Caleb Crain, in "Lovers of Human Flesh: Homosexuality and Cannibalism in Melville's Novels, *American Literature* 66, no. 1 (March 1994), 25–53, argues that even though Taylor had called "manly loves … as tender and true as the love of woman," his work was genteel and tame, not subversive.

3. *"belle," "dissipated," "stay with me"* ESM to HSS, 2/4/48, HCL, Leyda, *Log,* 271. *revising their desires* Edith Wharton illustrates this phenomenon beautifully in her novel *Summer,* with the scene in the jewelry store.

4. *"Omoo"* EAD to GD, 3/8/49, Duyckinck Collection, NYPL, NN *Corr.,* 104.

5. Shortly after this he wrote, on the blank pages of a volume of Shakespeare, a sketch for a story whose subject was "Devil as a Quaker" (Leyda, *Log,* 97), an idea that anticipates the figure of Captain Ahab and may spring from an undocumented reading of Child's *Letters from New York,* where she alludes to a Quaker saying that the grass never grows where the Devil has planted his foot. Ahab, who asks where the green fields have gone, seems to spring from this reference in Child.

6. NN *Mardi,* 593–94.

7. *"creative"* NN *Mardi,* 595.

8. *"altogether"* HM to JM, 3/25/48, NN *Corr.,* 106.

9. *"too"* Ibid.

10. *"Omoo" and "must"* HM to JM, 3/25/48, NN *Corr.,* 106.

11. *Blatchford* MB to AM, 5/29/46, GLA. In a later letter, Blatchford mentions reading *The Blithedale Romance.*

12. In "'But is it any good?': Evaluating Nineteenth-Century American Women's Fiction," *American Literature* 1 (March 1991), 51, Susan K. Harris claims that few readers in the antebellum period recorded their responses to books they read, so absence of documentation proves nothing, as it would not today.

13. In her book *Correspondent Colorings: Melville in the Marketplace* (Amherst: University of Massachusetts Press, 1996), Sheila Post-Lauria recontextualizes Melville in the light of her painstaking study of contemporary periodicals and popular novels, offering new perspectives on reader response and popular culture in the antebellum period. See also James L. Machor, ed., "Historical Hermeneutics and Antebellum Fiction: Gender, Response, Theory and Interpretive Contexts," *Readers*

in History: Nineteenth Century American Literature and the Contexts of Response (Baltimore: John Hopkins University Press, 1993), and Ronald J. Zboray, *A Fictive People: Antebellum Economic Development and the American Reading Public* (New York: Oxford University Press, 1993), both of whom demonstrate that men and women in upper-middle-class homes were reading the same books.

14. *"the book!–the book"* ESM to SHS, 4/3/48, in Joyce Deveau Kennedy and Frederick J. Kennedy, "Elizabeth Shaw Melville and Samuel Hay Savage, 1847–1853," *Melville Society Extracts* 39 (September 1979), 4. Melville's fictional philosopher Babbalanja is possessed by Azzageddi, the visionary who inspires him to higher and higher flights of fancy and makes him talk wildly. Melville was clearly elated and euphoric at times, and at other times he was depressed and preoccupied with death. In modern clinical jargon, such mood swings might be termed "hypomanic," suggesting the kind of manic-depressive behavior exhibited by many creative people; it is probably closest to what psychiatrists describe as cyclothymia, a mild form of bipolar disorder. *Diagnostic and Statistical Manual of Mental Disorders* (3rd edition, revised) (Washington, D.C.: American Psychiatric Association, 1987), 213–28, esp. 225–28. Though Lizzie's moments of real worry about him at this point were fleeting, during the writing of *Mardi* she evidently experienced intimations of what, later on, when he was drinking heavily, became serious worries about his mental state. Allan Melvill certainly exhibited manic-depressive tendencies, with less creative results. Between writing and editing of this manuscript, Natalie Angier's "An Old Idea about Genius Wins New Scientific Support" appeared in the Science section of *The New York Times,* 12 December 1993. Angier draws explicit links between manic-depression, bipolar disorder, and artistic creativity.

15. *"colony"* ESM to SHS, 4/3/48, Kennedy and Kennedy, "Elizabeth Shaw Melville," 2.

16. *"beautiful"* AMPM to AM, 4/3/48, GLA.

17. *"before the flood"* ESM to SHS, 4/3/48, Kennedy, "Elizabeth Shaw Melville."

18. *"pet"* ESM to HSS, 5/5/48, HCL, Leyda, *Log,* 275.

19. *"without me"* ESM to HSS, 6/5/48, Leyda, *Log,* 277.

20. *"documents"* JM to HM, 5/20/48, inferred from HM to JM, 6/19/48, NN *Corr.,* 109.

21. *"Antarctic tenor"* HM to JM, 6/19/48, NN *Corr.,* 109.

22. *"dark wood"* Dante's *selva oscura,* or "gloomy wood" in Cary's translation. In "Melville's Copy of Dante: Evidence of New Connections between the *Commedia* and *Mardi,*" *Studies in the American Renaissance,* 1993, 305–38, Lea Bertani Vozar Newman establishes the influence of Cary's Dante on Melville's work-in-progress.

23. While she was in Italy, Fuller fell in love with the Marquese Giovanni Angelo Ossoli, an Italian count who fought with the revolutionaries. She became pregnant, and after much opposition from the Vatican, the couple married and chose Giuseppe Mazzini as their son's godfather. Many of Fuller's closest friends in New England were shocked and scandalized not only by her love affair but also by her choice of a husband who appeared to be her intellectual inferior. Tragically, Fuller never had the chance to test the loyalty and open-mindedness of her friends, as the ship bringing her to America with her family in 1849 ran aground off Fire Island in a storm. She chose to remain on board with her son Angelino rather than leave her husband alone, and when the ship sank, their bodies were lost, as was the trunk containing her history of the revolution. One of those who searched the beach for evidence of survivors was Henry David Thoreau. Their deaths saved the social arbiters from having to figure out how to receive Margaret and her irregular family. See Paula Blanchard, *Margaret Fuller: From Transcendentalism to Revolution* (New York: Delta/Seymour Lawrence, 1978) and Joseph Jay Deiss, *The Roman Years of Margaret Fuller* (New York: Thomas Y. Crowell, 1969).

24. *vacation* FM to TM, 7/6/48, GLA. In her letter from Black River, New Jersey, Fanny tells Tom she has been reading a book called *The Maneuvering Mother*.

25. *Dana* Leyda, *Log*, 278.

26. *Melvill House* Bernard Carman, "Names Made News at Stately Broadhall," n.d., BA. *"timid little wife"* Fanny Appleton Longfellow, 7/23/48, Leyda, *Log*, 279. Fanny Longfellow's characterization of Robert's wife as "timid" is tantalizing, especially in the light of Robert Melvill's reckless driving and the family history of alcoholism.

27. September and October are a fallow period as far as records go. In early November, Duyckinck sent Melville a review copy of Joseph C. Hart's *The Romance of Yachting*. Instead of reviewing it, Melville sent it back, denouncing it as "an abortion, the mere trunk of a book, minus head arm or leg" that should be "burnt in a fire of asafetida." Saying he bore "no malice" against the "hapless" author, he declined to review the book. "Why smite him?" he asked, and "as for glossing over his book with a few commonplaces, *that* I can not do." Melville was too sensitive to the criticism leveled at him to "publicly devour" a fellow writer. HM to ED, 11/14/48, Leyda, *Log*, 282–83.

28. *Malcolm* AM to ESM, 1/27/49, HCL. She downplayed the fact that "in our branch, not a single descendant has borne that noble name. During two hundred years, throughout the five generations, the name only occurs as many times." For a more complete discussion of the importance of the choice of name, see Hennig Cohen and Donald Yannella, *The Malcolm Letter: "Man's Final Lore"* (New York: Fordham University Press and the New York Public Library, 1992).

29. *"Oro's blessing"* AM to ESM, 1/27/49, HCL.

30. *title page* HM to JM, 1/28/49, NN*Corr.*, 114–15. *"moiety"* RB to HM, 3/3/49, Leyda, *Log*, 292.

31. *Emerson* HM to ED, 3/3/49, NN*Corr.*, 121.

32. *"thought-divers"* Ibid.

33. Kemble's *Journal of a Residence in America* was published in 1835; her *Journal of a Residence on a Georgia Plantation* was not published until 1863. When Harvard law student Wendell Phillips asked Judge Joseph Story how he reconciled his admiration for Fanny with his Puritanism, Story replied that it was not a problem: "I only thank God I'm alive in the same era with such a woman." Judge Story, quoted in Joseph Ward Lewis's column, "Berkshire Men of Worth," *Berkshire Evening Eagle*, 5 April 1939.

34. *Kemble* HM to ED, 2/24/49, NN*Corr.*, 119–20. Her tour helped make Shakespeare immensely popular in America.

35. HM to AMjr., 2/20/49, GLA, NN*Corr.*, 116–18. Cohen and Yannella, *The Malcolm Letter*, also print the entire text of the letter.

36. *"severe trial"* LS to PG, 2/26/49, Leyda, *Log*, 291.

37. Robert K. Wallace has contributed an exhaustive but very readable study of Melville's interest in the visual arts and his aesthetic philosophy in *Melville and Turner: Spheres of Love and Fright* (Athens, Ga.: University of Georgia Press, 1993).

38. *"Shakespeare's person"* HM to ED, 2/24/49, NN*Corr.*, 119; Leyda, *Log*, 287, includes Melville's marginalia; Bayle's *Dictionary*, HM to ED 4/5/49, NN*Corr.*, 128. Lawrence W. Levine's *Highbrow/Lowbrow: The Emergence of Cultural Hierarchy in America* (Cambridge, Mass.: Harvard University Press, 1988) is a wonderfully entertaining, solidly researched account of nineteenth-century theatrical and musical culture. His chapter describing performances of Shakespeare in America is especially lively.

39. *"Tammany Hall"* Leyda, *Log*, 290. See William Walker Cowan, "Melville's Marginalia" (Ph.D. dissertation, Harvard University, 1965 [Melville dissertation no. 134]).

40. *Shakespeare* HM to ED, 3/3/49, NN*Corr.*, 122.

41. *Parkman review* The Literary World, 3/31/49, Leyda, *Log*, 294–95; reprinted in NN*PT*, 230–34 and notes. *Cooper* NN*PT*, 235–36, and notes.

42. *"propositions"* HM to ED, 4/5/49, NN*Corr.*, 128.

43. Maxine Moore, *That Lonely Game: Melville,* Mardi, *and the Almanac* (Columbia: University of Missouri Press, 1975), gives a sense of Melville's interest in astrology and his prodigious erudition, but her analysis strikes me as too schemetic.

44. *"cliff"* NN*Mardi*, 37.

45. *"human homes"* Ibid., 191.

46. *"sun"* Ibid., 472–73.

47. Frederick Douglass, *The Narrative of the Life of Frederick Douglass, an American Slave, Written by Himself* (New York: Signet Books, 1968), 24.

48. *"collared menials"* NN*Mardi*, 515ff.

49. "Nulli," of course, refers to the nullification controversy. *wage slaves* By 1834, for example, the Dover girls were called "slaves" by their employers. Thomas C. Cochran and William Miller, *The Age of Enterprise: A Social History of Industrial America* (New York: Harper, 1961), 23. When Daniel Webster tried for the presidency in 1848, hoping that his opposition to the Mexican War would ensure his election, he was surprised to find that Abbot Lawrence and the entire business community of Boston supported Zachary Taylor because they resented Webster's uncompromising stand against slavery. See Hannah Josephson, *The Golden Threads: New England's Mill Girls and Magnates* (New York: Duell, Sloane & Pearce, 1949), 171, and Aileen Kraditor, *Means and Ends in American Abolitionism* (New York: Pantheon Books, 1969).

50. Yoomy resembles "The Poet" of Ralph Waldo Emerson, and it is no coincidence that Walt Whitman resembles Yoomy, as I believe Whitman read *Mardi* as well as Emerson's essays and was profoundly influenced by it, even though he evidently did not review it, as he had *Typee* and *Omoo*.

51. *"power"* NN*Mardi*, 627.

52. Even though Melville disavowed any connection with transcendentalism and mocked it occasionally, he had both sensuous and cerebral ways of apprehending the truth that lies beyond appearances. His "polysensuum" has affinities with Emerson's Oversoul, and he was, at least in some respects, a closet transcendentalist.

53. Apart from a thank-you letter from Melville to Gardner, and a few impersonal references in his 1849 journal to lodgings in Paris that Gardner recommended to him, there is no evidence of how Melville felt about Gardner or his theories.

54. For theories of sexuality published by Sylvester Graham and Augustus Kinsley Gardner, see G. J. Barker-Benfield, *The Horror of the Half-Known Life: Male Attitudes Toward Women and Sexuality in 19th-Century America* (New York: Harper and Row, 1976), 88. Gardner's theories sound suspiciously like the pornography served up by the penny press. See also Mary P. Ryan, *The Empire of the Mother: American Writing about Domesticity, 1830–1860* (New York: The Haworth Press, 1982), 28. It's hard to know how widely birth control was used in nineteenth-century America. The cervical cap was invented by a German in 1838, and a sheath, similar to the condom, was invented in 1843. The rubber diaphragm did not come into use until the 1880s. Carl H. Degler, "What Ought To Be and What Was: Women's Sexuality in the Nineteenth Century," *American Historical Review* 79, no. 5 (December 1974), offers a more pleasant picture than most commentators. He maintains that women enjoyed sex and experienced orgasm, and that many couples sought mutual sexual pleasure.

55. *"shades"* NN*Mardi*, 654.

56. Lea Newman, in her article "Melville's Copy of Dante," draws a parallel between Taji and Dante's Ulysses, on whom Tennyson modeled his Ulysses. *whist* EAD to GD, 3/8/49, Duyckinck Collection, NYPL, NN*Corr.*, 104.

57. *"puerility"* The Athenaeum, 3/24/49, Leyda, *Log*, 293. *"run mad"* 3/31/49, Leyda, *Log*, 295. *"talent"* 4/1/49, Leyda, *Log*, 295. *"trash"* 8/49, Leyda, *Log*, 311. For more on *Chorley* see Wallace, *Melville and Turner*, 316.

58. *"reflection"* Evert Duyckinck, *The Literary World*,

4/14/49, Leyda, *Log*, 298. *"obscurity"* George Ripley, *New-York Daily Tribune*, 10 May 1849, Leyda, *Log*, 303. *"defects"* Bayard Taylor(?), 6/49, Leyda, *Log*, 308.

59. *"Hebrew"* 7/49, Leyda, *Log*, 309. *"delights"* (N. P. Willis?), 4/21/49, Leyda, *Log*, 299. *"failure"* 5/49, Leyda, *Log*, 305. The family of the convicted blasphemer accused Judge Shaw of class prejudice, and Melville complained that he and Shaw had been "burnt by the common hangman." HM to LS, 4/23/47, Leyda, *Log*, 300.

60. *"curiosity"* ESM to HSS, 4/30/49, Leyda, *Log*, 301–2.

61. *"hair"* Henry Cood Watson, *Saroni's Musical Times*, quoted in Watson G. Branch, *The Critical Heritage* (New York and London: Routledge & Kegan Paul, 1974), 184. In *Mardi*, Melville was making what Emily Dickinson termed a "prognostic's push" toward nonlinear, Bakhtinian discourse. On this subject, see Leland S. Person Jr.'s *"Mardi* and the Reviewers: The Irony of (Mis)reading," *Melville Society Extracts* 72 (February 1988), 3–5.

62. *"Time"* HM to LS, 4/23/49, NN*Corr.*, 130.

11. THE MAN WHO LIVED AMONG THE CANNIBALS

1. *Astor Place Riot* John Van Buren, whom Melville had ridiculed in *Mardi*, tried to defend the rioters by arguing that audiences had the right to hiss actors off the stage. For further information, see *Account of the Terrific and Fatal Riot at the NY Astor Place Opera House on the Night of May 10, 1849* (New York: H.M. Ranney, 1849) and Peter George Buckley's *To the Opera House* (Stony Brook, N.Y.: State University of New York at Stony Brook, 1984).

2. *"broadside"* HM to RB, 6/5/49, NN*Corr.*, 131. *"matters"* Ibid.

3. *"miss"* Ibid.

4. *"if wreck I do"* NN*Mardi*, 557. According to William Charvat, *The Profession of Authorship in America, 1800–1870*, edited by Matthew J. Bruccoli (Columbus, Ohio: Ohio State University Press, 1968), 237, by the time *Redburn* appeared, Melville owed Harper's $832.

5. *"book"* RB to HM, 6/20/49, NN*Corr.*, 596–97. *number of copies printed* Charvat, *The Profession of Authorship*, 231.

6. *"Historical Note"* to NN*R*, 320, and "Historical Note" to NN*W-J*, 405.

7. *"drivelling absurdity"* RB to HM, 6/20/49, NN*Corr.*, 596.

8. *"home"* HM to RB, 6/5/49, NN*Corr.*, 132. In his paper "The Burden of Literary History in *Redburn*," Marvin Fisher argues persuasively that Melville is consciously rebelling against the old lords of American culture who ape British models by subtle parody and satire, making *Redburn* a "counter-*kunstlerroman*."

9. See RB to HM, 6/20/49, and HM to RB, 7/20/49, NN*Corr.*, 133–34.

10. Charvat, "The Condition of Authorship in 1820," in *The Profession of Authorship*, 29–48 and "James T. Fields and the Beginnings of Book Promotion," ibid., 168–89. A major flaw in the work of Charvat and other male scholars of his generation is their failure to treat women novelists with the same respect and seriousness they accord to men; hence their discussions of antebellum literature tend to be half-baked.

11. See Charvat, *The Profession of Authorship*, esp. "The Beginnings of Professionalism," 5–28, and "Cooper as Professional Author," 74. *Carey* Ibid., 43.

12. Michael T. Gilmore, in his *American Romanticism and the Marketplace* (Chicago: University of Chicago Press, 1985), 6, points out that there was a 300-percent population increase between 1820 and 1860, with an 800-percent rise in urban living.

13. *Cooper* Charvat, *The Profession of Authorship*, 20. *Irving* Ibid., 33.

14. *"markets"* Gilmore, *Marketplace*, 7. *"floods"* See Nina Baym's *Novels, Readers, and Reviewers: Responses to Fiction in An-*

tebellum America (Ithaca, N.Y.: Cornell University Press, 1984), which is crammed with information about publishing in the period and has none of the traditional biases against women writers.

15. For some of the sources and analogues of *Redburn*, see "Historical Note" to NN*R*, 327.

16. Marryat's *Peter Simple* and Briggs's *The Adventures of Harry Franco* are two known models for Redburn. *"nursery tale"* HM to RHDjr., 10/6/49, NN*Corr.*, 140–41.

17. See Charvat, *The Profession of Authorship*, 204. *"cannibals"* HM to NH, 6/51, NN*Corr.*, 193: "All Fame is patronage. Let me be infamous: there is no patronage in that. What 'reputation' H. M. has is horrible. Think of it! To go down to posterity as a 'man who lived among the cannibals'!"

18. ESM's memoranda for a memoir of her husband, HCL. "Helen is deeply engaged in copying for Herman," STM to AM, 7/1/49, GLA. *"style"* HM to RB, 7/20/49, NN*Corr.*, 134.

19. *"adversity"* NN*R*, 10.

20. *"remember"* NN*R*, 8. Melville's text can be read on several levels at once, like Shakespeare's. While this passage draws on archetypal images, it also exemplifies Melville's habit of occasionally amusing himself by weaving in little private jokes as he was writing.

21. *"countries"* Ibid., 5.

22. *"feelings"* Ibid., 13.

23. *"like fathers"* Ibid. This may be an allusion to Alexander Slidell Mackenzie's reputation for being exceptionally kind to young men who made their maiden voyages on ships he skippered. No irony was intended by those who praised his exceptional nurturing of young sailors.

24. *"double-shuffle"* NN*Mardi*, 460.

25. According to Robert K. Martin, *Hero, Captain and Stranger: Male Friendship, Social Critique and Literary Form in the Sea Novels of Herman Melville* (Chapel Hill: University of North Carolina Press, 1986), "Buttons" has a sexual meaning in shipboard slang, but he doesn't elaborate. I read it as a veiled invitation, or a threat, to undo his pants. James Creech, *Closet Writing/Gay Reading: The Case of Melville's Pierre* (Chicago: The University of Chicago Press, 1993) contextualizes homoeroticism in *Redburn* and *Pierre* in a particularly convincing way, although I feel that use of the word *homosexuality*—a distinctly modern term—confuses the issue of Melville's sexuality, which I see as more "bisexual" than "homosexual." Melville's ultimate attraction is his ambiguity, which taps our own ambivalence and reminds us of the insufficiency of normative terms from either homosexual or heterosexual culture to express human feelings and behavior fully more than a century later.

26. *"Jackson"* NN*R*, 202.

27. *"woman"* Ibid.

28. *"Independence"* Ibid.

29. *Adam Smith* Ibid., 87.

30. *"want"* Ibid., 181.

31. *"she desarves it"* Ibid., 182.

32. *"glistening"* Ibid., 184.

33. *roses* Ibid., 215.

34. *"bosom friend"* Ibid., 216.

35. *"slaves"* Ibid., 226.

36. For an illuminating discussion of the "wink" in *Redburn*, see Creech's *Closet Writing*.

37. *"visions"* NN*R*, 228–29. *"Bury blade"* NN*R*, 221; the phrase suggests both the dagger Harry fears he may use to kill himself, and a sexual pun. *"underneath"* Ibid., 230. *"Paris catacombs"* Ibid., 320. An allusion that suggests a variety of possible interpretations, none of them verifiable with the existing evidence; one might be that Melville is alluding to Augustus Kinsley's Gardner's *Old Wine in New Bottles*, or even "winking" at Gardner, to use Creech's useful idea; the other might be that the great secret of Allan Melvill's life was not an illegitimate daughter, as so many scholars have surmised, but an illicit homosexual liaison. Even though Melville on some level

celebrated his bisexuality as inclusive despite the guilt imposed by culture and religion, the discovery that his father was homosexual and that, in some sense, his own homoeroticism was a legacy from that father, would have made it problematic—another strand of a web he wanted to shake off.

38. Robert K. Martin, *Hero, Captain and Stranger,* decodes Melville's pictures as signifiers of London's homosexual men's clubs and bordellos. Creech, *Closet Writing,* demonstrates convincingly that Harry Bolton has been prostituting himself to other men. The pictures and wall hangings were identified by William H. Gilman, *Melville's Early Life and* Redburn (New York: New York University Press, 1951), 224 and n. 31, 355, and Martin, n. 16, 131.

39. *"still"* NN*R,* 233–34.

40. *"somnambulist"* Ibid., 236.

41. *"foliage"* Ibid., 247.

42. *"whaler"* Ibid., 312.

43. *"secret sharer"* Joseph Conrad's story of that name seems almost a dialogue with *Redburn,* almost an escape from Melville's pessimistic ending, in that, thanks to the captain who risks his ship and crew to set him free, Leggatt, the fugitive self, eludes detection and escapes.

44. *"graves"* NN*W-J,* 46.

45. Neal L. Tolchin, *Mourning, Gender and Creativity in the Art of Herman Melville* (New Haven: Yale University Press, 1988), 27, cites a Harvard bereavement study that concludes that men experience the loss of loved ones as dismemberment, while women experience it as abandonment.

46. *"shroud"* NN*W-J,* 3.

47. *"ship"* NN*W-J,* 27.

48. *"laws"* NN*W-J,* 138. See Collamer M. Abbott, " *White-Jacket* and the Campaign Against Flogging in the Navy," *Melville Society Extracts* 89 (June 1992) and Michael Crawford, " *White-Jacket* and the Navy in which Melville Served," *Melville Society Extracts* 94 (September 1993).

49. A number of critics have erroneously credited Jack Chase with sparing White-Jacket, but he does not. My suspicion is that this scene reflects the shipboard code that Melville occasionally evokes by hints and indirections.

50. *Exodus* I'm indebted to Neal Tolchin for this gloss.

51. *"Constitution"* NN*W-J,* 157.

52. *"sorrow"* NN*W-J,* 249. See John P. Runden, "A New Source for Surgeon Cuticle and His Horned Woman," *Melville Society Extracts* 71 (November 1987), 9–11.

53. *"touches it"* NN*W-J,* 257.

54. Marvin Fisher, "Melville's *White-Jacket* and the War Within," *Centennial Review* (Autumn 1993) draws illuminating parallels to modern history.

55. Ralph Ellison, *Invisible Man* (New York: Vintage Books, 1972), 17ff., and other black writers have depicted the battle royal as symbolic of how whites "divide and conquer" blacks by rounding them up and forcing them to kill each other off—an apt metaphor for the ghetto.

56. *sheared* GM to HM, 11/13/40, BA.

57. *"History"* NN*W-J,* 385.

58. *"more"* NN*W-J,* 396.

59. Melville "borrowed" this passage from Nathaniel Ames's *A Mariner's Sketches, Originally Published in the Manufacturers and Farmers Journal* (Providence, 1830), as Charles Anderson discovered, and the similarities between the two passages border on what we would call plagiarism. Melville, however, adds White-Jacket's recollection of family members during his fall, and there are other differences. See the "Historical Note" to NN*W-J,* 417. Sources for other passages of the novel include Samuel Leech's *Thirty Years from Home, or A Voice from the Main Deck* (Boston, 1843), *Life on Board a Man-of-War; including a Full Account of the Battle of Navarino, By a British Seaman* (Glasgow, 1829), *Life in a Man-of-War or Scene in "Old Ironsides" During her Cruise in the Pacific, By a Fore-Top-Man* (Philadelphia, 1841), *The Life and Adventures of John Nicol, Mariner* (Edinburgh, 1822), *The Penny Cyclopaedia of the Society*

for the Diffusion of Useful Knowledge, 27 vols., edited by Charles Knight (London, 1833–43), and several articles on flogging and impressment. Melville routinely "cannibalized" passages from other writers.

60. *"new book"* ED to GD, 9/12/49, Leyda, *Log,* 313. *guidebooks* Robert K. Wallace, *Melville & Turner: Sphere of Love and Fright* (Athens, Georgia: University of Georgia Press, 1992), 252, identifies two of these guidebooks as Cruchley's *Picture of London* and Murray's *Hand-Book for Travellers in Northern Italy.* Wallace says Melville may have taken Hazlitt's *Sketches of the Picture Galleries of England,* which Duyckinck is known to have taken on his own trip. I speculate that the other may have been Caroline Kirkland's *Holidays Abroad; or, Europe from the West,* which Melville mentions in his journal entry for Sunday, 10/14/49, NN*J,* 6, and which Wallace is evidently not counting because it is not strictly a "guidebook."

61. *"inconsolable"* AM to LS, 9/27/49, HCL.

62. Bellows succeeded Dr. Orville Dewey, who baptized the three younger Melville children in Pittsfield while the Melvilles were living at Arrowhead. The standard biography is Walter Donald Kring's *Henry Whitney Bellows* (Boston: Skinner House, 1979). Bellows, who spoke out forcefully against slavery after 1850, was president of the United States Sanitary Commission during the Civil War and one of the founders of Antioch College and the Union League. He also played a crucial role in the Melvilles' life in 1867. *"freinds"* HM to LS, 10/6/49, NN*Corr.,* 138.

63. *"mottoe"* Ibid.

64. *"nursery tale"* HM to RHDjr., 10/6/49, NN*Corr.,* 140–41.

65. *"dull" and* "jobs" HM to LS, 10/6/49, NN*Corr.,* 138–39.

66. *"egotism"* Ibid.

1 2 . THE PRINCE OF WHALES

1. *"gale"* *Journals,* eds. Howard Horsford and Lynn Horth. (Evanston and Chicago: Northwestern University Press and the Newberry Library, 1989). Eleanor Melville Metcalf, Melville's granddaughter, preserved and published Melville's journals as *Journal of a Visit to London and the Continent by Herman Melville, 1849–1850* (Cambridge, Mass.: Harvard University Press, 1948).

2. *"on board"* NN*J,* 4.

3. *"masthead"* Ibid.

4. *"almost crazy"* Ibid. After a later breakdown during which he suffered from paranoid delusions and had to be committed to Bloomingdale Asylum, Adler wrote a memoir called *Letters from a Lunatic, or, A Brief Exposition of my University Life During the Years 1853–1854.* Ibid., 251.

5. *"absolute"* Ibid., 4. *"jaunt"* Ibid., 7. Bayard Taylor had written a favorable review of *Mardi* for *Graham's Magazine.*

6. *"merry"* Ibid., 5.

7. *"to be had,"* etc. Ibid., 5. *"sea"* Ibid., 7.

8. *"foam"* Ibid., 9. *"sky,"* etc. Ibid., 6.

9. *"woman"* Ibid., 6 and 368. Melville probably had met Mrs. Kirkland at Anne Lynch's Valentine party in 1848.

10. *letter* EE to SR, 9/3/49, and others, see NN*J,* 611. Although Everett also wrote letters of introduction to Richard Monckton Milnes and Gustave de Beaumont, no evidence exists that Melville ever contacted either of them. According to Robert K. Wallace, *Melville and Turner: Spheres of Love and Fright* (Athens: University of Georgia Press, 1993), 286ff., Melville had probably read or leafed through Evert Duyckinck's copy of Rogers's *Italy* after reading *Modern Painters,* as John Ruskin had praised its illustrations, or "vignettes," by the controversial English painter J. M. W. Turner, several of whose paintings graced Rogers's walls. For more on the subject, see also Christopher Sten, ed., *The Savage Eye: Melville and the Visual Arts* (Kent, Ohio: The Kent State University Press, 1991). *"traveller"* NN*J,* 368.

11. *"dancing,"* etc. NN*J,* 6–7.

12. *pet names* Ibid., 7. Lizzie's sobriquet, which is derived from the medieval romance *Amadis de Gaul,* was one of the names bestowed on Queen Elizabeth by court poets. It was once assumed that the nickname "Barney" came from the *Acushnet*'s boatsteerer Wilson Barnard, who was known as "little Barney" because he was five feet tall, but we now know from Melville's extraordinary February 1849 letter to Allan that Melville had P. T. Barnum in mind. Orianna, or Oriana, was the mistress, later wife, of "The Knight with the Green Sword," or "The Green Knight," who was also known as "the Child of the Sea." Melville probably knew Tennyson's "The Ballad of Oriana," and perhaps also the thirteenth-century legend on which the poem was based. He also called Malcolm "Macky," or "Mackey," and he sometimes called Lizzie "Dolly," which was also the name of the whaleship in *Typee.* This has led some biographers to assume that Melville felt oppressed by marriage, when it could just as well have been a playful joke.

13. *"rainy"* NNJ, 8.

14. *"deal"* Ibid., 9.

15. *"advances"* Ibid., 11. On boarding the ship, Melville successfully warded off an attempt by a wealthy dry-goods merchant to persuade him to share the cabin with this hapless youth who was "bound for the Grand Tour," ibid., 3.

16. *"republic"* Ibid., 10.

17. *"Dover"* Ibid., 11.

18. *"coat," "books,"* etc. Ibid., 12.

19. *"affair,"* etc. Ibid., 13.

20. *"friends,"* coat Ibid.

21. *"trash,"* etc. Ibid.

22. *"laughable"* Ibid., 14.

23. According to Wallace, *Spheres of Love and Fright,* he would have seen *Venice–the Dogana,* the first Turner oil acquired by the National Gallery.

24. *"pomp," "waters"* NNJ, 14.

25. *"festivities"* NNJ, 15.

26. *"nobility"* Ibid. *"gilded dunces"* HM to Nathaniel Parker Willis, 12/14/49, ibid., 620. He told Willis that their degeneracy made him glad he wasn't rich. As pointed out by Lea Bertani Vozar Newman, *A Reader's Guide to the Short Stories of Herman Melville* (Boston: G. K. Hall, 1986) and others, the story based on this dinner also owes a debt to Catharine Maria Sedgwick's novel *The Poor Rich Man and the Rich Poor Man.*

27. *Templars* NNJ, 281–82.

28. *"gaffs"* Ibid., 288. *"afraid"* Ibid., 16.

29. *"advance"* Ibid.

30. *"unhappy"* Ibid., 17.

31. *the Mannings* Ibid., 287–88.

32. *"scene"* Ibid., 17.

33. *Dickens* Ibid., 288. Melville evidently did not meet Dickens, Thackeray, Trollope, or Thomas Carlyle while he was in England.

34. *"giraffes"* Ibid., 17.

35. *"mist,"* etc. Ibid., 18.

36. *"metaphysics"* Ibid., 19.

37. *"not be in his line"* Ibid.

38. *"no ales"* Ibid.

39. *"Champaigne,"* etc. Ibid., 26.

40. *Dulwich* Ibid., 19–20. Wallace, *Spheres of Love and Fright,* describes this gallery in a way that makes Melville's visit seem crucial to his artistic education, though Melville makes it sound as though Adler suggested going there. I suspect that Melville was less knowledgeable and less attentive to the visual arts during this visit than we might like to think. Judging from his journal, he seems to have been almost more interested in local color, light entertainment, conversation, and eating and drinking than in art. By the time Melville traveled in Europe again six years later, however, his knowledge of painting and statuary had deepened.

41. *"chop"* NNJ, 20.

42. *"gazing"* Ibid.

43. *"beat him"* Ibid., 24.

44. *"corpse"* HM to RHDjr., 5/1/50, NN *Corr.,* 161.

45. *Moxon* Interwoven from Melville's journal entry, NNJ, 23, and his letter to Dana, HM to RHDjr., 5/1/50.

46. *"to be sure,"* NNJ, 25–26.

47. *"bouncer"* Ibid., 21.

48. *"Negro,"* etc. Ibid., 23.

49. *"prince of whales"* Ibid., 24.

50. *Stevens* Wallace, *Spheres of Love and Fright,* 360 ff., describes their relationship more fully. *"rareities"* Ibid., 30. *signature* 1630 edition, no longer deemed authentic, Ibid., note, 328.

51. *"feeling"* and *"higher mysteries"* NNJ, 28. This strange but powerful allusion to the Greek mysteries suggests the depth of Melville's feelings. Perhaps Melville knew that the Greek dramatist Sophocles was a priest of the cult of Asklepios. Adhering to Aristotle's theory that the soul was most alive during sleep, when it was free to leave the body, these priests gave sufferers in mind and soul several draughts of wine, put them to sleep on goatskins, and discussed their dreams with them the following morning as a form of healing. Centuries later, Sigmund Freud substituted an upholstered horsehair couch and a notebook for the goatskin and wineskin, and it was called scientific progress.

52. *"tea"* Ibid.

53. pension See HM to AKG, 2/4(?)/50, Leyda, *Log,* 366. *"mystic circle"* NNJ, 31.

54. *Louvre* Ibid. Based on prints from Melville's collection in the Berkshire Athenaeum, Robert K. Wallace speculates that Melville was particularly taken with Rubens and Poussin.

55. *"fidelity to nature"* *The Literary World,* 10 November 1849. *"joy"* NNJ, 31.

56. *"closet,"* etc. NNJ, 31–32. *"jabbered"* Ibid., 32, suggests to me that Melville knew some French, but did not speak the language as fluently as he would have liked to speak it.

57. *"live,"* etc. Ibid., 32–33.

58. *"stay"* Adler to GD, Paris, 2/16/50.

59. *"foe,"* etc. NNJ, 35–36.

60. *"place"* Ibid., 36.

61. *"cheers"* Ibid., 37.

62. *"nightmare"* Ibid., 38.

63. *"New York"* Ibid., 39.

64. *"Indian's"* Ibid., 40.

65. *"pesky,"* Ibid., 40; *"money"* HM to Nathaniel Parker Willis, 12/14/49, NN *Corr.,* n. 151.

66. *"business here"* DD to GD, 12/24/49, GLC. Melville attended an evening of "coffee, music, dancing" at the home of Mrs. George Daniel, who had two "attractive" daughters. These "nymphs," as he called them (NN *Corr.,* 149), were the sisters of Mrs. Charles Welford, whose husband was co-owner of the bookshop Gansevoort frequented when he lived in the Astor House during his days as a young attorney. The world of the Anglo-American upper middle class was a small world indeed.

67. *Rev. Melvill* NNJ, 41.

68. *"Three weeks!"* Ibid., 42.

69. *"ninny,"* etc. Ibid., 42; and Wallace, *Spheres of Love and Fright,* 262–64.

70. *dinner* NNJ, 44. DD to GD, 12/24/49, GL, provides an odd sample of male dinner conversation: "We asked each other in the small smoking room–which we had to ourself with a fine fire–where–said he–where–said I–where–said we both together–where in America can you find such a place to dine and punch as this?" *"paintings"* NNJ, 368–69, and Wallace, *Spheres of Love and Fright,* 286.

71. *Knight* Ibid., 46. Melville consulted Knight's *Penny Cyclopaedia* while he was writing *Moby-Dick.* Knight, who believed in exposing the working classes to good literature, wrote a three-volume autobiography entitled *Passages of a Working Life.* *Tenniel* NNJ, 45.

72. *"beggar"* Ibid., 47.

73. *"home"* Ibid., 48.

74. *annotations* See Leyda, *Log,* 359ff.

75. *"cellar"* HM to EAD, 2/2/50, NN *Corr.,* 155. *gifts* See Leyda, *Log,* 364, 366, and 270, also notes to NN*J.*

76. *aloe* HM to ED, 2/2/50, NN *Corr.,* 155. Melville later wrote a short poem on "The American Aloe at the Exhibition," which implies that he believed *Mardi* would eventually attain the recognition it deserved.

77. *"darling"* AM to LS, 1/18/50, Leyda, *Log,* 361. Priscilla Melvill wrote Augusta from Pittsfield that she was sure Lizzie was "*secretly* glad" he had cut his trip short, "tho' he may not have accomplished all that he intended." Priscilla also said, "We have all been very interested in 'Redburn's' voyage—the incidents are very simple, but fascinating." PM to AM, 1/28/50, GLA.

78. *"stars"* HM to ED, 2/2/50, NN *Corr.,* 155.

79. *"revelation"* John Bull, Leyda, *Log,* 365–66.

80. *The Athenaeum,* 2 February 1850, Branch, 217–218. I'm indebted to Wallace, *Spheres of Love and Fright,* for pointing this out.

81. *Spectator,* 2 February 1850; Watson G. Branch, ed., *Melville: The Critical Heritage* (London: Routledge and Kegan Paul, 1974)., 222–24; *Atlas,* 9 February 1850, ibid., 224–26; *Britannia,* 2 February 1850, ibid., 218–19.

82. *Bentley's,* 1 March 1850, Leyda, *Log,* 367.

83. White-Jacket *sales* "Historical Note" to NN *W-J,* 437.

84. *Duyckinck* 3/16/50, quoted by Branch, *Melville: The Critical Heritage,* 226–29.

85. *Albion* 30 March 1850, Leyda, *Log,* 370–71; *Saroni's,* 30 March 1850, Branch, *The Critical Heritage,* 229–31.

86. *Boston Post* 10 April 1850, Branch, *Melville: The Critical Heritage,* 233–35; *U.S. Magazine,* April 1850, ibid., 231.

87. *religious press* The *Biblical Repository and Classical Review,* July 1850 (Leyda, *Log,* 381), after condemning Melville for his "characteristic faults," praised him for attacking "the whole system of war" in a book "well-manned, and armed to the teeth, fearlessly and proudly ploughing the deep broad sea of humanity, floating high the banner of Liberty, Reform, and Goodwill to the sailor." Ripley, *New-York Daily Tribune,* 9(?) April 1850, Leyda, *Log,* 371.

88. The House of Representatives debated flogging in the navy in its 1848–1849 session; the Senate ruled flogging illegal by a narrow margin on September 28, 1850. See Charles Robert Anderson, *Melville in the South Seas* (New York: Dover Publications, 1968), 430–31.

89. *Willis* 4/13/50, Leyda, *Log,* 372. *Selfridge* Ibid., 381–82, Anderson, 421ff., and Brook Thomas, *Cross-Examinations of Law and Literature: Cooper, Hawthorne, Stowe, and Melville* (New York: Cambridge University Press, 1987).

90. *Franklin* Anderson, 429. *"law"* HM to ED, NN *Corr.,* 171.

91. For a detailed discussion of American confidence men and their significance in Melville's works, see Helen P. Trimpi, *Melville's Confidence-Man and American Politics in the 1850s* (Connecticut Academy of Arts and Sciences, 1987).

92. Powell to ED, 10/2?/49, Leyda, *Log,* 315. *lying* Hershel Parker, "Historical Note" to *Moby-Dick* (Evanston and Chicago: Northwestern University Press and the Newberry Library, 1988),* 607. Powell had evidently forged some documents in England and in America, and he went on to commit libel several times.

93. See Parker's "Historical Note" to NN *M-D,* 607–9.

94. *copyright* British publishers apparently rationalized the practice of book piracy either by simply continuing to regard America as a colony, or by claiming British ancestry for America's established authors. Even John Murray talked himself into believing that Washington Irving's father was a British citizen, though naturally the august Murray was above piracy.

---

* Cited hereafter as "NN *M-D.*"

Thomas Delf inquired wryly, "As to Mr Herman Melville, what is his parentage birth and education? Had he a father or had he a mother, sister or brother?…We may require W. Irving's certificate of baptism and H. Melville's pedigree." TD to GD, 8/2/50, GLC; Leyda, 382. *"flippant"* See Parker, "Historical Note" to NN *M-D,* 609.

95. Briggs added that "much of their success is undoubtedly owing to the perfect carelessness with which they thrust themselves bodily before their countrymen," *Holden's,* February 1850. The magazine's editor, Charles Frederick Briggs, also wrote two novels often thought of as having influenced *Redburn: The Adventures of Harry Franco* and *The Trippings of Tom Pepper.* Joel T. Headley was the author of nonfiction books such as *Italy and the Italians* and *Washington and His Generals.*

96. "A Thought on Book-Binding," NN *PT,* 237–39.

13. THE ARDENT VIRGINIAN

1. *"weather"* ESM to HSS, 4/30/50, Leyda, *Log,* 373.

2. *"first love"* AMPM to AM, 4/3/48, GL. *"Banian Hall"* HM to EAD, 8/16/50, NN *Corr.,* 167.

3. *"blubber is blubber"* HM to RHDjr., 5/1/50, NN *Corr.,* 161–62.

4. *books* William Scoresby, Frederick Debell Bennett, Franklyn Allyn Olmsted, Captain James Colnett, Leyda, *Log,* 373, 377. He also borrowed Elizabeth Barrett Browning's *Poems,* Tennyson's *In Memoriam,* Carlyle's *German Romance,* Sylvester Judd's *Margaret,* and Henry David Thoreau's *A Week on the Concord and Merrimack Rivers* from Evert Duyckinck's library, and the following month he ordered Horace Greeley's *Hints Towards Reform* from Harper's. *sources* See NN *M-D* Note, 639–47. At least 160 sources are immediately discernible in *Moby-Dick,* and there are hundreds more.

5. *"harpooner"* HM to RB, 6/27/50, NN *Corr.,* 162–64.

6. *"upon me"* Thomas Farel Heffernan, *Stove by a Whale: Owen Chase and the* Essex (Middletown, Conn.: Wesleyan University Press), 191. Numerous articles have been written on the composition of *Moby-Dick,* many of them surprisingly ignorant of the organic nature of the writing process described by Melville in *Mardi.* See notes to NN *M-D,* also the important corrective by Julian Markels, "The *Moby-Dick* White Elephant," *American Literature* 66, no. 31 (March 1994), 105–22.

7. *"soul"* Leyda, *Log,* 377. *Turner* See Robert K. Wallace, *Melville and Turner: Spheres of Love and Fright* (Athens: University of Georgia Press, 1993).

8. See Leyda, *Log,* 378, 379.

9. Buford Jones conjectures that Melville interpreted Hawthorne's references to *Typee* as a covert signal of his [Hawthorne's] homosexuality.

10. *"plains"* From Melville's notes on the "rambling expedition" in the flyleaf of *A History of the County of Berkshire;* see Leyda, *Log,* 379.

11. *Report* NN *PT,* 449–51. Leyda, *Log,* 398.

12. According to Leyda, *Log,* 381, either Melville or the fellow from whom he purchased the volume underscored Mother Anne's identification of "the lustful gratifications of the flesh, *as the source and foundation of human corruption,*" and also marked a passage charging that associations fail when the "partial and often selfish relations of husbands, wives and children, and other kindred" give rise to jealousy and dissension.

13. *Ticknor & Fields* This venerable firm, unfortunately, was gobbled up by a conglomerate in 1994, another victim of the crass takeovers currently threatening small quality publishing houses and other small businesses in America.

14. The railroad also connected the Berkshires with the nation's capital, allowing Charles Sumner and Charles Sedgwick's protégé Julius Rockwell, a Massachusetts Representative and future United States senator and Berkshire County Superior Court judge, to keep a base in the Berkshires while serving in Washington. On September 9, 1850, the Pittsfield Cemetery was dedicated amid much fanfare, and Sarah Morewood read an ode she had composed for the occasion, as

did Dr. Oliver Wendell Holmes and John Chipman Hoadley. (Hoadley later married Melville's sister Catherine.) Several of Melville's cousins are buried in Pittsfield Cemetery, as are several members of the Morewood family, including Sarah.

15. Although it's not entirely clear whether the meeting with Field on the train was prearranged or coincidental, Duyckinck and Matthews had to wait for a Creole couple to check out of Melvill House Inn before they could have a room, so they were planning to spend their first night in a hotel when Field invited them to be his guests.

16. *"wonder"* EAD to Margaret Duyckinck, 8/4/50, Metcalf, *Herman Melville, Cycle and Epicycle* (Cambridge: Harvard University Press, 1953), 80.

17. *"features"* EAD to MD, 8/4/50, Leyda, *Log,* 383. Thomas Melvill Jr. and his family retained the original spelling of the name. The Melvill House, later known as "Broadhall," is the present site of the Pittsfield Country Club.

18. *"lilac"* Ibid.

19. *"sweeter," "lion lasso," and "blue mountains"* EAD to MD, 8/6/50, Duyckinck Collection, NYPL.

20. *"climb"* Cornelius Mathews, "Several Days in Berkshire," *Literary World,* 8/24/50, Leyda, *Log,* 383–84.

21. Sophia Hawthorne and Lizzie Melville presumably stayed home, taking care of children. Many accounts of this historic picnic erroneously list Annie Fields among the hikers; it was Eliza, his first wife. James T. Fields married Eliza Willard after her sister, whom he was courting, died suddenly. When Eliza died within two years of their wedding date, Fields then married her cousin Annie, who became a legendary figure in Boston literary circles.

22. *"cloud"* EAD to MD, 8/6/50, and EAD to GD, 8/7/50, Leyda, *Log,* 384; other details, Mathews, "Several Days"; James T. Fields, *Yesterdays with Authors* (Boston: James R. Osgood and Company, 1877), and Henry Dwight Sedgwick, "Reminiscences of Literary Berkshire," *Century Magazine,* August 1895, Leyda, *Log,* 383–85. *"rubber bag"* Sarah Higginson Begley points out that Dr. Holmes had one of the first rubber bags in America.

23. *outcropping* Variously identified as the "Devil's Pulpit" or another of the mountain's escarpments.

24. *"delectation"* James T. Fields, Leyda, *Log,* 384; *"Carbuncle"* EAD to MD, 8/6/50, Leyda, *Log,* 382.

25. *"turkeys and beeves"* EAD to GD, 8/7/50, Leyda, *Log,* 383; *"better spirits,"* etc. Fields, *Yesterdays.*

26. *"looked on"* EAD to MD, 8/6/50, Leyda, *Log,* 384. See Leyda, *Log,* 384, for the various accounts.

27. *"jagged"* Sophia Hawthorne to Elizabeth Peabody, 8/8/50, Leyda, *Log,* supplement, 923. *"merrymakers"* Fields, *Yesterdays,* 53.

28. Earlier biographers such as Leon Howard gave the impression that Miss Sedgwick came to sit at the feet of the "great ones," Hawthorne and Melville, but as Melville scholar Charlene Avallone points out (CA to LRL, 8/8/91), Sedgwick paved the way for Hawthorne, and Melville was "a pup." Furthermore, this was probably not the first time Melville and Sedgwick met, as she and the Melvilles had attended Anne Lynch's Valentine party in 1848, and the following year, Mrs. Melville became a pew-renter at All Soul's Unitarian Church, the parish Miss Sedgwick attended when she was in New York. She certainly knew Melville as that young sailor who had written *Typee,* at the very least.

29. *"a new book"* EAD to GD, 8/7/50, Leyda, *Log,* 384. "Talk and tea and a tall Miss Sedgwick and a cross examination which I did not stand very well on Hope Leslie and Magawisca," EAD to MD, 8/6/50, Leyda, *Log,* 385.

30. *Shakers* Ibid.

31. Now the site of Tanglewood, the Berkshire Music Center and summer home of the Boston Symphony. Nathaniel Hawthorne, who wrote *Tanglewood Tales* for his children, claimed to have given the Tappan property this name, but members of the John L. B. Brooke family of Lenox claim their

ancestor used the name long before Hawthorne gave it wider currency. *hospitality* CMS to her friend K.S. Minot, 10/13/49, Mary Dewey, ed., *The Life and Letters of Catharine Maria Sedgwick* (871), 315.

32. *"face"* SH to EP, 8/8/50, Leyda, *Log,* supplement, 923. *Thoreau* This essay is more commonly known as "Civil Disobedience," and while, once again, we have no direct evidence that Melville knew it, it's difficult to read the line about "passive resistance" in "Bartleby the Scrivener" (1853) without concluding that he did.

33. *"uncommonly well"* NH to EAD, 4/15/46, Leyda, *Log,* 211. *"liked Melville"* NH to HB, 8/17?/50, Leyda, *Log,* 389.

34. *"chamber," etc.* "Hawthorne and His Mosses," *NNPT,* 239. Exactly when Melville started writing the essay remains unknown, as does the degree of Duyckinck's involvement in its composition. See "Notes on 'Mosses,'" *NNPT,* 652–61. *costumes* Mathews, "Several Days," see Leyda, *Log,* 386.

35. *"capture"* William Allen Butler to George Duyckinck, 8/20/50, Leyda, *Log,* 386.

36. The information that Mathews was "a Yankee from the down-east jumping off place" and that she wore a black dress with a train, comes from a letter Sophia Melville wrote to her sister-in-law Augusta, 8/11/50, GLA, as does the information that the "Turk" was none other than Herman Melville. Augusta was away just then, and Helen's outfit is not described; perhaps she stayed home with the children.

37. *"toil of pleasure"* EAD to MD, 8/9?/50, Leyda, *Log,* 387. *"Cossacks"* Mathews, "Several Days," Leyda, *Log,* 387.

38. *accident* STM to AM, 8/11/50, GLA.

39. *"magically spread"* Mathews, "Several Days," Leyda, *Log,* 387.

40. *"spasms"* EAD to MD, 8/9/50, Leyda, *Log,* 387. *"elephant"* STM to AM, 8/11/50, GLA. There are minor discrepancies between these letters and the letter of MGM, 8/8/50, GLA. Either Mathews went or Robert Melvill went, or both. Dimensions of the barn are from a brochure by Eugene Merrick Dodd, "Melville and Hawthorne at Hancock" (Hancock, Mass., 1966).

41. *fair copy* Lizzie would leave a blank space and mark an "X" in the margin when she was not sure what word or words Melville intended, these marks, though erased, are still visible on the manuscript in the Houghton Library, Harvard University. When the essay was printed, Melville found "one or two ugly errors," either caused by his haste and/or by careless typesetting, he appears not to have put the blame on his copyist. See HM to EAD, 8/16/50, NN*Corr.,* 168.

42. *"grasshopper"* HM to EAD, 2/12/51, NN*Corr.,* 181.

43. *"dark characters"* From "Hawthorne and His Mosses," *NNPT,* 245.

44. *"blackness of darkness"* From "Hawthorne and His Mosses," *NNPT,* 243.

45. *sales* James D. Hart, *The Popular Book: A History of America's Literary Taste* (New York: Oxford University Press, 1950).

46. *women writers* See James D. Hart, *The Popular Book.* Several generations of misogynistic professors quoted this letter without telling their students that just two weeks later, Hawthorne finally read Grace Greenwood's *Pets* and Fanny Fern's *Ruth Hall* and told his sister-in-law, Elizabeth, that he admired them.

47. *Godey's* LAG to LS, 8/10/50, Leyda, *Log,* 387. *circulation* Baym, "Melodramas of Beset Manhood," *American Quarterly* 33, #2 (summer 1981), 144. By 1856 it reached 100,000, and during the Civil War, men carried it with them into battle in their rucksacks.

48. *"garrett-way"* HM to EAD, 8/16/50, NN*Corr.,* 167.

49. *"Abel"* Ibid.

50. *"twelve...babies"* Ibid. According to Amy Elizabeth Puett, *Melville's Wife: A Study of Elizabeth Shaw Melville,* unpublished doctoral dissertation (Evanston, Ill.: Northwestern University, 1970), 72, Mathews sent Lizzie an autographed copy of

Elizabeth Barrett Browning's "The Cry of the Human" in appreciation of her hospitality. *books for Hawthorne* Metcalf, *Herman Melville: Cycle and Epicycle*, 89, NN *Corr.*, 166.

51. *"barn"* SH to EP, 8/29?/50, Leyda, *Log*, supplement, 924. *"life"* NH to EAD, 8/29/50, Leyda, *Log*, 391.

52. *"secret mind," etc.* SH to EAD, 8/29/50, Metcalf, *Herman Melville: Cycle and Epicycle*, 90.

53. *"hidden," etc.* SH to EP, 8/29?/50, Leyda, *Log*, supplement, 924.

54. *"free"* "Hawthorne and His Mosses," NN *PT*, 243.

55. *"snatches," etc.* Ibid., 244. Just as the phrase "shock of recognition" appears to be an allusion to a Masonic rite, so the phrase "Great Art of Telling the Truth" seems to be an allusion to something known in Masonic and Deist circles as "the Theological Art of Lying."

56. *"dashed off"* SH to EP, 9/5–6/50, Leyda, *Log*, supplement, 924–25. "modest" SH to EP, 9/4/50, Leyda, *Log*, 393.

57. *"take you into himself"* SH to EP, Leyda, *Log*, 393. *"Spanish" eyes* N. P. Willis, *Hurry-Graphs, or Sketches of Scenery, Celebrities and Society taken from Life* (New York: Charles Scribner, 1851), 224.

58. *"spiritual life"* SH to EP, 9/5–6/50, Leyda, *Log*, supplement, 924.

59. *"treatment of him"* Ibid. Her words would prove eerily prophetic, as Melville's fair Apollo would later disappoint him by neglecting to review the book whose greatness he had in part inspired.

60. *"Handsomer than Lord Byron"* Elizabeth Peabody, quoted by Herbert, 263. On the images of impregnation and insemination, see Fisher, *Going Under*, 2, 11–12.

61. *"deck"* Randall Stewart, *Nathaniel Hawthorne: A Biography* (New Haven: Yale University Press, 1948), 3.

62. *incest* In *Hawthorne's Secret: An Un-Told Tale* (Boston: David R. Godine, 1984), Philip Young points out that Hawthorne's ancestor Nicholas Manning was convicted of incest with his sisters. James Mellow, in *Nathaniel Hawthorne In His Times* (Boston: Houghton Mifflin, 1980), raises the possibility that Robert Manning abused his nephew sexually in one way or another. David Leverenz, in *Manhood and the American Renaissance* (Cornell University Press, Ithaca, 1989), 244–48, claims that Hawthorne's texts reveal his fear of homosexual rape.

63. *Aunt Rawlins* EP to SH, 9/50, Leyda, *Log*, supplement, 924.

64. *"round"* Ibid., 249.

14. A SORT OF SEA-FEELING IN THE COUNTRY

1. *"happy hearts"* AM to Mary Blatchford, 8/29/50, GLA. While working on this book, I was pleased to read James C. Wilson's "Melville at Arrowhead: A Reevaluation of Melville's Relationship with Hawthorne and with His Family," *Emerson Society Quarterly* 30 (fourth quarter, 1984), 232–36, a revisionist view, similar to mine, which was dismissed as "naive" by *American Literary Scholarship*, a publication frequently inhospitable to new ways of looking at Melville's life and writings.

2. Both Arrowhead and Brewster's East Street house were rumored to be stations on the Underground Railroad, as was Melvill House, now Broadhall, but dates and details have remained obscure and it's almost impossible to find documentary evidence of what, so far, is oral lore. *"towered house"* SH to EP, 9/5–6/50, Metcalf, *Herman Melville: Cycle and Epicycle* (Cambridge: Harvard University Press, 1953), 92.

3. *"vegetables"* *Boston Daily Times*, 17 October 1850, Leyda, *Log*, 399.

4. *"glowing & Byzantine"* HM to EAD, 10/6/50, NN *Corr.*, 170–71. *"slope," etc.* AM to MB, 10/17/50, GLA.

5. "Jacquesizing," *"leaves," etc.* HM to EAD, 10/6/50, NN *Corr.*, 170–71. *"wild sublimity"* AM to MB, 10/17/50, GLA.

6. *"bureau"* HM to EAD, 10/6/50, NN *Corr.*, 170–71. *sages*

"I believe you go to Pittsfield every day," NH and SH to HM, 3/27/51, NN *Corr.*, 606–8.

7. *"chimney," "beauty," "locks* AM to MB, 10/17/50, GLA, reprinted in *Berkshire County Historical Society News & Notes* 25, no. 4 (September–October 1990). *casters* NN *M-D*, 624.

8. *"fortune"* Ebenezer R. Hoar to his wife, 10/26/50, Leyda, *Log*, supplement, 926.

9. *flogging* HM to EAD, 10/6/59, NN *Corr.*, 169–70, with commentary.

10. "No Union with Slaveholders" became the motto of Garrison's *Liberator*. *Sumner* Leonard W. Levy, *The Law of the Commonwealth and Chief Justice Shaw* (Cambridge: Harvard University Press, 1957), 86.

11. *Harrison* During the Civil War, he would serve as chaplain to the Massachusetts 54th Negro Regiment, commanded by Captain Robert Gould Shaw of Boston. One of the few survivors of the slaughter of that valiant regiment, Harrison returned home and served his parish until his death in 1900. See Edward Boltwood, *The History of Pittsfield, Mass. from the Year 1876 to the Year 1916* (City of Pittsfield, 1916). *"come what may,"* Julius Rockwell to Lucy Forbes Rockwell, 12/22/49, Rockwell Papers, Lenox Library.

12. *Vigilance Committee* Wilbur Siebert, *The Underground Railroad in Massachusetts* (Worcester: American Antiquarian Society, 1936).

13. *"dung-beetle"* I'm indebted to Marvin Fisher for reminding me of this line from Thoreau's essay "Slavery in Massachusetts."

14. *"do it"* AM to MB, 11/25/50, GLA.

15. *"steps flying"* AM to MB, 11/22/50, and 11/25/50, GLA.

16. *"too superior"* HS to SHS, 2/28/51, "Additions to The Melville Log," *Melville Society Extracts* 31 (September 1977), 8. *"bamdiddle"* AM to HelM, 12/5/50, GLA.

17. *"chimney"* HM to EAD, 12/13/50, NN *Corr.*, 173.

18. *"youths"* Ibid., 174.

19. *"sea-room"* "Hawthorne and His Mosses," NN *PT*, 246.

20. *"thing"* NN *M-D*, 370.

21. *Lee* AM to HelM, 12/21/50, GLA.

22. *"any longer"* AM to HelM, 1/6/51, GLA. *"devour," etc.* AM to HelM, 12/31/50, GLA. *"sparkling eyes"* AM to HS, 1/7/51, Leyda, *Log*, 402. *"pitch in"* STM to AM, 1/1/51, a slightly confusing letter, but when Sophia mentions her friend Tertullus Stewart's new baby, she writes: "I suppose he means the same thing as Herman does when he talks about pitching in to Malcolm. As the young gentleman is not three days old I think he has made a fair beginning in the way of play and frolic." The letter seems to imply that Melville spanked Malcolm.

23. *"unfavorable circumstances"* ESM, "Memoranda," Sealts, *Early Lives*, 169. *sewing circle* AM to HelM, 1/24/51, GLA. *"Blue-Beard"* AM to HelM, 1/14/51, GLA.

24. *"sorrowful"* AM to MB, 1/16/51, GLA. A few months later, Mary Blatchford read *David Copperfield* but couldn't finish it, preferring Ik Marvel's *Reveries* to Dickens's novel. MB to AM, 4/21/51, GLA.

25. *"one"* AM to MB, 1/16/51, GLA.

26. *"air"* AM to HelM, 1/14/51, GLA.

27. *"adventure"* MGM to AM, 12/29/51, GLA. From church records, it appears that Herman's family were active members of St. Stephen's parish in Pittsfield, the church his aunt and cousins also attended.

28. *"buried in snow," "vine"* HM to EAD, 2/12/51, NN *Corr.*, 179–81.

29. *"loveliest family"* AM to MB, 1/24/51, GLA. *"Universe"* HM to EAD, 2/12/51, NN *Corr.*, 179–81. *"powers of entertainment"* AM to HelM, 1/24/51, GLA.

30. *"please"* HM to NH, 1/29/51, NN *Corr.*, 175–78.

31. *Sedgwicks* AM to HelM, 1/24/51, GLA. The five hundred newly discovered letters in the New York Public Library show that Melville had a more active social life than biogra-

phers once believed. Catharine Maria Sedgwick lived with her brother Charles and his wife Elizabeth on Kemble Street from 1832 until they moved the house up the hill to a more open location, sometime in 1850. There the novelist enjoyed a bigger wing, a south-facing piazza, and a garden filled with fruits and vegetables. She liked to give strawberry breakfasts for her friends and neighbors.

32. *"phiz"* NH to EAD, 4/27/51, Metcalf, *Herman Melville: Cycle and Epicycle*, 102. *"oblivioned"* HM to EAD, 2/12/51, NN*Corr.*, 179–81. Melville's reply to Duyckinck's letter about the daguerreotype includes the retrospective on plans to have Hawthorne visit.

33. *"stiff"* MGM to AM, 3/12/51, GLA.

34. Melville's granddaughter Eleanor perpetuated the view that Lizzie was a poor housekeeper, perhaps because it was true to some extent, and perhaps because it was a way to excuse Melville for his rumored abuse of Lizzie. See Amy Elizabeth Puett, *Melville's Wife: A Study of Elizabeth Shaw Melville*, unpublished dissertation (Evanston, Ill.: Northwestern University, 1976), 76, 215.

35. "Stowing Down & Clearing Up," a whaleman's phrase for housekeeping, appears as the title of chapter 98 of *Moby-Dick*.

36. *piano* Inferred from various sources, especially HelM to AM, 4/11/54, GLA. In this letter, Helen criticizes Lizzie for complaining that she never can find time to play the piano, as she knows a woman "with three little children about the age of hers, a husband, three servants and a house to keep," who nonetheless finds time to play her piano.

37. *"speed"* MGM to AM, 3/10/51, GLA.

38. *"beau ideal"* MB to AM, 4/21/51, GLA.

39. *"smoking and talking metaphysics"* Theodore F. Wolfe, *Literary Shrines* (Philadelphia, 1895), Leyda, *Log*, 407. *"ontological heroics"* HM to NH, 6/29/51, NN*Corr.*, 196.

40. *The Mariner's Chronicle* by Archibald Duncan (Philadelphia, 1806), Leyda, *Log*, 408.

41. *infatuated* Oliver Wendell Holmes observed that trying to talk with Hawthorne was like "love-making" because Hawthorne's "shy, beautiful soul had to be wooed from its bashful prudery like an unschooled maiden." *The Atlantic Monthly* (July 1864), 98–101, quoted by Mellow, *Nathaniel Hawthorne*, 28. *"hates to be touched"* SH to JTF, 1/1/62, quoted by James R. Mellow, *Nathaniel Hawthorne in His Times* (Boston: Houghton Mifflin Company, 1980), 28. *hates to be touched* SH to JTF, 1/1/62, Mellow, 379. Edwin H. Miller in *Herman Melville: A Biography* (New York, George Braziller, 1975) claims that Hawthorne left the Berkshires because Melville made a sexual advance, a claim that cannot be proved one way or another. We have less direct evidence of Melville's sexual feelings than of Hawthorne's. As James Mellow points out, Hawthorne became impatient with "holy kisses" while courting Sophia, and during a brief separation from her in 1843, Hawthorne wrote her that "during my sleep, I seek thee throughout the empty vastitude of our couch; for I found myself, when I awoke, in a quite different region than I had occupied in the early part of the night," *Nathaniel Hawthorne*, 244. See also T. Walter Herbert, *Dearest Beloved: The Hawthornes and the Making of the Middle-Class Family* (Berkeley: The University of California Press, 1992).

42. *"plump sphericity"* HM to EAD, 2/12/51, NN*Corr.*, 178–80.

43. *"body"* CMS to K. S. Minot, New York, 3/24/50, Dewey, *Life and Letters*, 314.

44. *female friendships* See Carroll Smith-Rosenberg's analysis of female friendships, "The Female World of Love and Ritual: Between Women in Nineteenth-Century America," in *Disorderly Conduct: Visions of Gender in Victorian America*, (New York: Alfred A. Knopf, 1985), 53–76. Smith-Rosenberg concludes that Americans of the nineteenth century were more accepting of diverse sexual roles than are their twentieth-century counterparts.

45. *"youth," "soul," "wisdom," "god"* Ralph Waldo Emerson, "Love," *Selected Writings of Ralph Waldo Emerson*, edited by Brooks Atkinson (New York: Random House, 1950), 214, 220, 221. James R. Mellow, *Nathaniel Hawthorne in His Times* (Boston: Houghton Mifflin, 1980), 344–48, ably contextualizes these passionate friendships. See also Jonathan Katz, *Gay American History* (New York: W. W. Norton, 1971). The behavior of intimates, in any relationship, or combination of relationships, will always remain essentially mysterious to outsiders. Intimate relationships are sometimes mysterious to the participants themselves, and without documentation, commentators should exercise restraint.

46. *"jokes"* HM to NH, 1/29/51, NN*Corr.*, 175–78.

47. *"snug"* NH to EAD, 3/14/51, Leyda, *Log*, 408. *Brattleboro* HM to EAD, 3/26/51, NN*Corr.*, 183. Melville gave Fly a gift subscription to *The Literary World*, and his sisters sent him some guava jelly and his sister Harriet some handmade gifts for Christmas, according to AM to HelM, 12/21/50, GLA. When Melville broke off with Evert Duyckinck for a while in 1852, he canceled both his and Fly's subscriptions to *The Literary World*.

48. *eyes* HM to EAD, 3/26/51, NN*Corr.*, 183. *porch* "I suppose the Piazza is nearly finished by this time & the foundations of the new building being laid," MGM to AM, 3/10/51, GLA.

49. *clock and bedstead* NH and SH to HM, 3/27/51, NN*Corr.*, 606–8, a letter saved by Augusta. Hawthorne's letters to Melville in response to his own extraordinary epistles of 1850–51 were destroyed.

50. *"tragicalness"* HM to NH, 4/16?/51, NN*Corr.*, 186.

51. *"Custom House," etc.* Ibid.

52. *"Confessor," "silences," "witness"* SH to EP, 5/17/51, Leyda, *Log*, supplement, 926–27. NN*Corr.*, 184. Not everyone liked *The House of Seven Gables* as much as Melville did. Catharine Maria Sedgwick, for example, thought the book a failure despite the "marvelous beauty in the diction" and a "richness and originality of thought that give the stamp of unquestionable genius." The only character who engaged her sympathy or interest at all was little Phoebe, the book's "redemption." Otherwise the book was "an affliction" that affected Sedgwick "like a passage through the wards of an insane asylum, or a visit to specimens of morbid anatomy." She might have liked it better when she was younger, she admitted, "but as we go through the tragedy of life we need elixirs, cordials, and all the kindliest resources of the art of fiction." Older and wiser than Melville, she concluded that it was "as if a railroad should be built and a locomotive started to transport skeletons, specimens, and one bird of Paradise!" CMS to K. S. Minot, Lenox, 5/4/51, Mary E. Dewey, ed., *The Life and Letters of Catherine M. Sedgwick* (NYC: Harper, 1871), 328–29.

53. *Harper's and Stewart* Leyda, *Log*, 410. See also Patricia L. Barber, "Two New Melville Letters," *American Literature* 49 (November 1977).

54. *"tinkering," "jolting"* HM to NH, 6/1?/51, NN*Corr.*, 190, 191.

55. *"Gospels"* Ibid., 192.

56. *"concert"* Ibid., 191.

57. *"fame"* Ibid., 193.

58. *"live in the All"* Ibid., 194.

59. *"rose cold"* EMS to LS, 6/30/51, Leyda, *Log*, 415–16. *pregnant* ESM to HSS, 8/3/51, Metcalf, *Herman Melville*, 13.

60. *"brick-kiln"* HM to NH, 6/29/51, NN*Corr.*, 195.

61. *"make out the rest yourself"* Ibid., 196. *"hell-fired"* HM to Horatio Bridge, 2/3/50. Mellow, *Nathaniel Hawthorne*, 373, suggests that Melville may have known that Hawthorne considered *The Scarlet Letter* a "positively hell-fired story."

62. *"cooked"* HM to NH, 6/29/51, NN*Corr.*, 196. *"living ones"* HM to RB, 7/20/51, NN*Corr.*, 197–98.

63. *"mark," etc.* HM to NH, 7/22/51, NN*Corr.*, 199–200.

15. ONE GRAND HOODED PHANTOM

1. *"cavalier"* NH's *Journal*, Leyda, *Log*, 418–19; Julian Hawthorne, *Hawthorne and His Wife*, 2 vols. (Boston: Houghton Mifflin Company, 1884), 407. It would be interesting to know how much Spanish Melville knew; perhaps "Hola!" was the extent of his vocabulary. *Una* NH's *Journal*, Leyda, *Log*, 423.

2. *"room"* NH's *Journal*, Leyda, *Log*, 419.

3. *"Memnon"* From Smith's sketch of Melville, Merton M. Sealts Jr., *The Early Lives of Melville: Nineteenth Century Biographical Sketches and Their Authors* (Madison: The University of Wisconsin Press, 1974), 147. In the accounts of these parties that have come down to us, Lizzie is not mentioned, which either indicates that her presence was taken for granted, or that she was not feeling well as she approached her delivery time. *"ghastly"* ED to MD, 8/11/51, Leyda, *Log*, 423. *"filthy set"* NH's notebook, quoted by James Mellow, *Nathaniel Hawthorne in His Times* (Boston: Houghton Mifflin Company, 1980), 377. No one has really been able to determine dates of composition for various sections of *Moby-Dick*, so it's impossible to know whether or not Melville, to tease Hawthorne, actually added some passages to those chapters after this excursion.

4. *"grand excursion"* Sarah Morewood describes this incident in "That Excursion to Greylock," Leyda, *Log*, 424.

5. *"balls"* HM to SHS, 8/24/51, quoted by Joyce Deveau Kennedy and Frederick J. Kennedy in "Herman Melville and Samuel Hay Savage, 1847, 1851," *Melville Society Extracts* 35 (September 1978), 1ff.

6. *"wayward speculations"* HM to SHM, 9/12 or 9/19/51, NN *Corr.*, 205.

7. London's *Literary Gazette and Journal of Science and Art*, for example, objected that "Mr. Melville cannot do without savages, so he makes half of his *dramatis personae* wild Indians, Malays, and other untamed humanities," and called *Moby-Dick* "an odd book, professing to be a novel; wantonly eccentric, outrageously bombastic; in places charmingly and vividly descriptive," but impossible overall, as its narrator "appears to have been drowned with the rest," Hershel Parker and Harrison Hayford, eds., *Moby-Dick as Doubloon: Essays and Extracts (1851–1970)* (New York: W. W. Norton, 1970), 60–61.

8. *"literature"* *Morning Advertiser*, 10/24/51, Parker and Hayford, *Moby-Dick as Doubloon*, 7.

9. *"theme"* Herman Melville, P*M-D*, 497.

10. *"language"* Ibid., 82.

11. *"soul"* Ibid., 3. *"masthead"* Ibid., 5–6.

12. *"clasp"* Ibid., 30.

13. *"developed"* Ibid., 56. *"redeemed"* Ibid., 57.

14. *"pair"* Ibid., 58.

15. *"mask"* Ibid., 178.

16. "tail" Ibid., 148.

17. *"monster," "sounds," etc.* Ibid., 8

18. Melville mixes Metacomet up with "Annawon," Ibid., 223. *"divine retribution"* Cotton Mather, *Magnalia, Christi Americana*, the history of "God's chosen people in the Devil's Territories." See also Sacvan Bercovitch, *The American Jeremiad* (Madison: University of Wisconsin Press, 1978), and Michael T. Gilmore, *The Middle Way: Puritanism and Ideology in American Romantic Fiction* (New Brunswick, N.J.: Rutgers University Press, 1977). *"blasphemous leviathan"* Richard Slotkin, in his *Regeneration Through Violence: The Mythology of the American Frontier, 1600–1860* (Middletown, Conn.: Wesleyan University Press, 1974), suggests that Metacomet's fate may be the source for the *Pequod*'s "jawbone tiller."

19. *"the other way"* HM to NH, 6/1/51, NN *Corr.*, 190.

20. *"warrior hunters"* P*M-D*, 130. *"hisself"* Ibid., 324.

21. *"virtues," "fortress"* Ibid., 131. *"belly"* Ibid., 391–92.

22. *"mad"* Ibid., 453–54. *"look"* Ibid., 475.

23. Benjamin Roberts, an African-American, sued for the right to send his daughter to the closest public school, and Charles Sumner represented him and lost on appeal before Chief Justice Shaw. Dwight Lowell Dumond, in *Antislavery: The Crusade for Freedom in America* (New York: W. W. Norton, 1963), 323, argues that Sumner, rejecting the notion that the courts had the final say on constitutional issues, believed in Andrew Jackson's idea that "every public official has taken an oath to support the Constitution as he understands it." Leonard W. Levy, in *The Law of the Commonwealth and Chief Justice Shaw* (Cambridge: Harvard University Press, 1957), 109–17, says that Shaw's inability to foresee the long-term consequences of the decision was "an abdication of judicial responsibility." Leon F. Litwack, in *North of Slavery: the Negro in the Free States 1790–1860* (Chicago: The University of Chicago Press, 1961), 148, concludes that "Chief Justice Shaw's legal defense of segregated schools on the basis of the "separate but equal" doctrine established a controversial precedent in American law." Louis Ruchames, "The Pulitzer Prize Treatment of Charles Sumner," in *Black and White in American Culture: An Anthology from The Massachusetts Review*, edited by Jules Chametzky and Sidney Kaplan (New York: Viking, 1971), 148–71, claims that Sumner's arguments "on behalf of integration in the public schools of Boston anticipated the reasoning of the Supreme Court of the United States in 1854."

24. *"soul"* Longfellow, quoted in Levy, *Law of the Commonwealth*, 97.

25. *"slave pen"* Richard Henry Dana Jr., *The Journal of Richard Henry Dana Jr.*, edited by Robert F. Lucid, 3 vols. (Cambridge: The Belknap Press of Harvard University Press, 1968), vol. 2, 424. *"tyrannical statute" "weak judge"* Ibid., 633. *"Judges"* P*M-D*, 54. Longfellow's poem "The Building of the Ship" influenced Father Mapple's sermon; see Robert S. Ward, "Longfellow and Melville: The Ship and The Whale," *Emerson Society Quarterly* 22 (1961), 57–63.

26. *"black squall"* Dana, *Journal*, vol. 11, 412.

27. *slave* In the chapter on flogging in Richard Henry Dana's *Two Years Before the Mast* (New York: Bantam Books, 1963), 80, the captain tells the sailor he is flogging not to expect mercy from him because he is "a *slave-driver*–a *nigger-driver!*" Reformers concerned with the state of American democracy commonly drew a parallel between shipboard and plantation floggings.

28. "I have written a wicked book, and feel spotless as the lamb," HM to NH, 11/17/51, NN *Corr.*, 212.

29. *"Manifest Destiny"* G. J. Barker-Benfield, *The Horrors of the Half-Known Life: Male Attitudes toward Women and Sexuality in Nineteenth-Century America* (New York: Harper & Row, 1976), 267.

30. *spermatic economy* Ibid. In his *Lectures on Chastity*, Sylvester Graham, the creator of the graham cracker, counseled men to husband their sperm by refraining from intercourse more than once a month. Melville would surely have been amused by today's sperm banks. See Barker-Benfield for more on Todd and Gardner, who specialized in obstetrics and insanity (yes, obstetrics and insanity, which is an indication of what women were up against; the word *hysteria* comes from the Greek word for "womb"). Some have speculated that Gardner became the Melville family doctor when they moved back to New York–a frightening prospect, as Gardner treated almost all female complaints with the knife, and most of his theories sound like the grisly atrocities served up in dime novels. It's hard to know how widely birth control was used in nineteenth-century America, but Todd and Gardner and the other male experts on female reproduction opposed its use. The conjunction of phallic imagery and fire in the description of Captain Ahab may be a sly reference to the burning of the Reverend John Todd's church earlier that year, AM to HelM, 1/6/51, GLA.

31. *Gardner* See ibid., 297, and Leyda, *Log*, 82. Dr. Todd gave strict instructions to couples about when and how often to have intercourse. *nymphomania* Women's sexual desire was considered such a threat that toward the end of the nineteenth century, American doctors were routinely performing clitorec-

tomies to control it. In 1858, in an article on "The Lecture Season," the *Berkshire County Eagle* reported that "The Rev. Dr. Todd of this town...is one of the best and most attractive of the lecturers. Herman Melvill, Esq., of this town, the author, is also ready, as is reported, to receive applications to lecture," Leyda, *Log*, 596.

32. See Nancy Cott, "Passionlessness: An Interpretation of Victorian Sexual Ideology, 1790–1850," *Signs* 4 (Winter 1978), 219–36; T. Walter Herbert, *Dearest Beloved: The Hawthornes and the Making of the Middle Class Family* (Berkeley: The University of California Press, 1992); and John D. Hedrick, *Harriet Beecher Stowe: A Life* (New York: Oxford University Press, 1994), 122–23, 181–82.

33. *burlesque* See Joseph Flibbert, *Melville and the Art of Burlesque* (Amsterdam: Rodopi, 1974).

34. Words like *heterosexual, homosexual,* and *bisexual* are anachronistic. Melville envisioned male homosociality as a paradigm for democratic brotherhood that would subvert the oppressive patriarchy that devalued women and suppressed the feminine in man while glorifying slavery, war, greed, and competition.

35. *"language experiment"* Preface to the 1855 edition of *Leaves of Grass.*

36. *"archbishoprick"* PM-D, 459.

37. *"Polar wind"* HM to SM, 9/?/51, NN*Corr.*, 206.

38. *"rowing"* PM-D, 376.

39. *"nurseries," etc.* Ibid., 423–25.

40. *"killed and waifed," etc.* Ibid., 425–26.

41. Harrison Hayford, "Melville's Freudian Slip," *American Literature* 30 (1958), 366–68, has established that the error was a clerk's, not Melville's.

42. *"plump"* MGM to AM, 11/5/51, GLA. Maria's description of Lizzie's illness bears an uncanny resemblance to "The Yellow Wallpaper," Charlotte Perkins Gilman's masterful study of female hysteria brought on by male domination.

43. *copies* NN*M-D*, 686ff.

44. *party* MGM to AM, 11/5/51, GLA.

45. *"snuffs," etc.* Ibid. One wonders if James had started celebrating a bit too early and too enthusiastically.

46. *elephant* CMS to KSM, 11/2/51, Mary Dewey, ed., *The Life and Letters of Catharine Maria Sedgwick* (New York: Harper, 1871), 353, and MGM to AM, 11/2/51, GLA.

47. *"monster"* HM to EAD, 11/7/51, NN*Corr.*, 209. The reference to "fourteen years" is somewhat puzzling, as the editors of NN*Corr.* point out. Dr. Henry A. Murray claimed that it was a reference to the "sinking" he felt in the summer of 1837 when his Uncle Thomas told him of the existence of his illegitimate half sister, but there is absolutely no proof that the illegitimate sister existed, or that if she did, Melville had been told of his father's indiscretion in 1837. It may be that "fourteen" here is simply a random figure, or that Melville meant to write "months," not "years."

48. *"blubber"* Parker and Hayford, *Moby-Dick as Doubloon,* 9. *"originality," "vigour"* Ibid., 69, 72. *"humour"* 11/1/51, ibid., 18. *"park"* 11/8/51, ibid., 26. *"books"* *Morning Post,* 11/14/51, ibid., 28.

49. Greeley, *New-York Daily Tribune,* 11/22/51, Leyda, *Log,* supplement, 929. *"life"* *Harper's New Monthly Magazine,* 12/1/51, Parker and Hayford, *Moby-Dick as Doubloon,* 57; Leyda, *Log,* 438–39.

50. *"wit"* *National Intelligencer,* 12/16/51. *"profaneness"* *Traveller,* 11/12/51, Parker and Hayford, *Moby-Dick as Doubloon,* 32. *"affair"* *Boston Post,* 11/20/51, Parker and Hayford, 40. Judge Shaw was the last judge to send a man to jail for blasphemy, which he defined as "speaking evil of the Deity" in such a way as to alienate others from religion by lessening their reverence for God. Levy, *Law of the Commonwealth, Shaw,* 52.

51. *"manner"* *The Literary World,* 11/15/51, Parker and Hayford, *Moby-Dick as Doubloon,* 33–36.

52. In her revisionist article "'Philosophy in Whales ... Poetry in Blubber': Mixed Form in *Moby-Dick*," *Nineteenth-*

Century Literature (December 1990), Sheila Post-Lauria contextualizes the critical reception of *Moby-Dick* and clears up the distortions created by earlier scholars who viewed Melville ahistorically.

53. *"feeling," etc.* Ibid.

54. "One" Ibid. Hawthorne's letters, including the one about *Moby-Dick,* were among the papers Melville later claimed to have burned.

55. *orders* Harriette M. Plunkett, *Springfield Daily Republican,* July 1, 1900, writes that the advance orders of Hawthorne's book reached four thousand after the review appeared. *"delight"* HM to NH, 11/17?/51, NN*Corr.*, 211–14.

56. In his psychobiographical *Herman Melville: A Biography* (New York: George Braziller, 1975), Edwin Havilland Miller claimed that Hawthorne left Lenox abruptly because Melville made a sexual "advance" to him, but there is no evidence to support this notion. James Mellow, *Hawthorne in His Times,* 379–80, provides a more objective view of Hawthorne's departure.

57. Hawthorne gave a copy of his *A Wonder-Book for Boys and Girls* (Boston: Ticknor & Co., 1851) to Malcolm Melville on November 7. In "Biography and Responsible Uses of the Imagination: Three Episodes from Melville's Homecoming in 1844," *Resources for American Literary Study,* 21, no. 1 (1995), 16–42, Hershel Parker describes this meeting based on a report published in the Vermont *Journal* by a correspondent who evidently had little knowledge of Hawthorne, Melville, or Lenox.

58. *Boston* MGM to AM, 11/5/51, GLA, MGM to AM, 12/30/51, GLA, and Amos Nourse to Lemuel Shaw, 2/18/52, Leyda, *Log,* 47.

59. *The Literary World,* 11/15/51 and 11/22/51, Parker and Hayford, *Moby-Dick as Doubloon,* 49–52.

60. *"best points"* NH to EAD, 12/1/51, NN*Corr.* This is the only comment by Hawthorne on *Moby-Dick* that has come down to us; we have no idea what he wrote or said to Melville.

61. *"cords of wood"* HM to EAD, 11/7/51, NN*Corr.*, 210.

62. *"health"* SM to GD, 12/28/51, Leyda, *Log,* 441.

63. *wreath* MGM to AM, 12/30/51, GLA.

64. *"account"* SM to GD, 12/28/51, Leyda, *Log,* 441. *flirting* It's impossible to tell whether Melville did this in Lizzie's presence to annoy her, whether it was simple good fun and gallantry, enjoyed by all, or uncomfortable for Lizzie.

65. *"sell well"* Ibid.

66. *"religion"* 11/28/51, Parker and Hayford, *Moby-Dick as Doubloon,* 53. *"bore"* *Southern Quarterly Review,* 1/52, Parker and Hayford, *Moby Dick as Doubloon,* 80. *"licentiousness," etc.* U.S. *Magazine and Democratic Review,* 1/52, Parker and Hayford, *Moby-Dick as Doubloon,* 83.

67. "Historical Note," Herman Melville, *Moby-Dick, or The Whale* (Evanston and Chicago: Northwestern University Press and The Newberry Library, 1988), 688–89. According to William Charvat, *The Profession of Authorship in America, 1800–1870: The Papers of William Charvat,* edited by Matthew Bruccoli (Columbus: Ohio State University, 1968), 236, "success" would mean about five thousand copies sold within the year. *Moby-Dick* had a first printing of 2,915 copies, of which 2,500 were sold during the first five years, with a second printing of 2,965, which took the next twenty years to sell. *The Scarlet Letter,* according to Randall Stewart, *Nathaniel Hawthorne, A Biography* (New Haven: Yale University Press, 1949), 92, sold six thousand copies in its first two years. John Updike, "Melville's Withdrawal," in *Hugging the Shore: Essays and Criticism* (New York: Alfred A. Knopf, 1983), 89, claims that Melville made over eight thousand dollars on his first five books, or "an average annual earning, over five years, of sixteen hundred dollars," making him "one of the best-paid American authors of this era," which seems an erroneous conclusion.

68. *mediocrity* De Tocqueville observed that "Democratic literature is always infested with a tribe of writers who look upon letters as a mere trade; and for some few great authors who adorn it, you may reckon thousands of word-mongers."

16. KING OF THE CANNIBALS

1. *"bowl of milk"* HM to SH, 1/8/52, NN*Corr.*, 219.

2. *"nutcrackers"* HM to ED, 1/2?/52, NN*Corr.*, 217–18.

3. *terms* Hershel Parker and Brian Higgins, introduction to *Critical Essays on Herman Melville's* Pierre; or, the Ambiguities (Boston: G. K. Hall & Co., 1983), 11. According to Charvat, *The Profession of Authorship in America, 1800–1870: The Papers of William Charvat* (Columbus: Ohio State University Press, 1968), *Pierre* sold only 1,856 copies in thirty-five years. *"peanuts"* Herman Melville, *Pierre, or The Ambiguities* (Chicago and Evanston: Northwestern University Press and The Newberry Library, 1971),* 250.

4. *"nutmeg"* HM to NH, 6/1?/51, NN*Corr.*, 191.

5. *women writers* Merton M. Sealts, *Melville's Reading,* revised and enlarged edition (Columbia: University of South Carolina Press, 1988), 80–81. I am indebted to conversations with Sheila Post-Lauria and to her "Genre and Ideology: The French Sensational Romance and Melville's *Pierre,*" *Journal of American Culture* 15, no. 3, (Fall 1992), 1–8, for showing the relationship of this problematic novel to popular culture. David Reynolds, *Beneath the American Renaissance: The Subversive Imagination in the Age of Emerson and Melville* (Cambridge: Harvard University Press, 1988), links *Pierre* with the "dark subversive" novels of the period. For sources, see "Historical Note" to NN*Pierre,* 404, and Sealts, *Melville's Reading.* I am also indebted to Dr. Judith Ryan, Chair of the German Department, Harvard University, for information on *Ghost Tale* and *Elective Affinities.*

6. *homosexuality* James Creech, in his *Closet Writing/Gay Reading: The Case of Melville's Pierre* (Chicago: The University of Chicago Press, 1993), argues that incest stands for homosexuality, which was taboo in mainstream fiction. Although his analysis is provocative and plausible, I feel Melville's great accomplishment in *Pierre* was the intermingling and blurring of sexually transgressive and psychologically liminal themes. His great genius was in "reading himself" as a text expressive of the plight of American males, especially those who were in touch with their artistic or feminine sides in an era that demanded repression and workaholic competition. He speaks to readers regardless of their gender and sexual preferences because his psychosexual pain, pleasure, and perplexity illuminate cultural conflicts.

7. *"family matters"* According to Eleanor Melville Metcalf, Willie Morewood told Frances B. Thomas that *Pierre* dealt with "family matters." According to Eugene A. Taylor, a distant Melville relation named Eustace Corcoran told Henry Murray that *Pierre* was substantially true. These instances point up something remarkable and virtually unique to Melville scholarship: much of it is based on unsubstantiated rumor and innuendo. I can't think of any other writer of whom this is true, in part because Melville destroyed so many documents himself, probably to conceal secrets, although that is an assumption people have been quick to make because they already assume that there is some "hideous and intolerable" secret at the core of Melville's life. What would happen if for a moment we assumed there is not a secret? Which assumption gives us a better handle on Melville? I believe we gain more by keeping multiple possibilities in mind.

8. See Louise K. Barnett, "American Novelists and 'Portraits of Beatrice Cenci,'" *The New England Quarterly* (June 1980), 168–83.

9. *daughter* Eugene Taylor, who worked with Dr. Henry A. Murray on his unfinished biography, claims that a distant Melville relation named Eustace Corcoran said *Pierre* was substantially true. Ina May Greer, evidently a friend who was helping Henry Murray (see note 7, above) with research, believed that Major Thomas Melvill, not his son, was the father

---

*Cited hereafter as "NN*Pierre*."

of the illegitimate child. See the Murray Papers, Harvard University Archives.

10. Among studies that try to account for the inconsistencies and disjunctions of the text, and the additions to it, are Robert Milder, "Melville's 'Intentions' in Writing *Pierre,*" *Studies in the Novel* 6, no. 2 (Summer 1974), 186–99; Hershel Parker, "Why *Pierre* Went Wrong," *Studies in the Novel* 8 (Spring 1976), 7–23; and Hershel Parker and Brian Higgins, "The Flawed Grandeur of Melville's *Pierre,*" in *New Perspectives on Melville,* edited by Faith Pullin (Kent, Ohio: The Kent State University Press, 1978). For a fresh, contextually grounded, historically informed perspective on Melville's relationship to his materials and his use of popular forms in *Pierre,* see Sheila Post-Lauria's *Correspondent Colorings: Melville in the Marketplace* (Amherst: University of Massachusetts Press, 1996), ch. 5.

11. *"half profits"* and *"succession"* RB to HM, 3/4/52, NN*Corr.*, 618.

12. *"life,"* etc. HM to RB, 4/16/52, NN*Corr.*, 226–28. I'm indebted to Sheila Post-Lauria's research here.

13. *"necessary"* RB to HM, 5/5/52, NN*Corr.*, 620.

14. *"friends here say"* LSjr. to parents, 5/13/52. Melville also gave Lem Shaw a letter of introduction to John Murray, but no evidence exists that Melville offered them the book (NN*Corr.*, 223–24). I have my suspicions that Lem, who was the least sympathetic toward Melville's writings of anyone on either side of the family, at least partially prejudiced Bentley against *Pierre,* as Bentley seems to have backed off after Lem became involved.

15. *"Krakens"* HM to NH, 11/17/51, NN*Corr.*, 213.

16. *"hideous and intolerable"* In *Moby-Dick,* Ishmael says he does not want his story to be read as "a hideous and intolerable allegory," though of course, in some ways, that's exactly what it is.

17. *"inkstand"* PM-D, 497.

18. I'm indebted to Samuel Otter, "Landscape and Ideology in *Pierre:* The Eden of Saddle Meadows," a paper delivered at the Melville Centennial Conference on May 18, 1991, and published in *American Literature* 66, no. 1 (March 1994), 55–81, for some of these insights. *"plenty, virtue, and refinement"* Thomas Cole, "Essay on American Scenery" (1835), quoted by Otter, ibid.

19. *"library"* NN*Pierre,* 6. *"sires"* NN*Pierre,* 9. Melville's bachelors are men so blinded by power and privilege that they have no moral imagination and lack a tragic sense of life; Pierre is a precursor of Amasa Delano. See Mildred K. Travis, "Fact to Fiction in Pierre: The Arrowhead Ambience," *Melville Society Extracts* 15 (September 1973), 6–8; Thomas F. O'Donnell, "Where is Grand Old Pierre," *Melville Society Extracts* 28 (November 1976), 16–18; and Peter J. Bellis, *No Mysteries Out of Ourselves: Identity and Textual Form in the Novels of Herman Melville* (Philadelphia: University of Pennsylvania Press, 1990), an illuminating discussion of Melville's struggles with genealogical and textual authority.

20. *"plains"* NN*Pierre,* 6. *"heads"* NN*Pierre,* 30.

21. *"sharks"* Henry Christman, *Tin Horns and Calico: A Decisive Episode in the Emergence of Democracy* (New York: Henry Holt, 1945), 338. *"princes"* Ibid., 342–43. I am indebted to Nancy Fredericks, "Melville's 'Tinhorn' Rebellion: Melodrama and Class Culture in *Pierre*" (NEMLA paper, 7 April 1991), for drawing my attention to this book about New York's anti-rent wars.

22. *"run"* NN*Pierre,* 11. I am indebted to Otter, "Landscape and Ideology," for pointing out that this passage echoes the treaty with the Cherokees.

23. *"Revolution"* Ibid., 324–25. *"sweat"* Christman, *Tin Horns,* 332–33. *"Josh"* NN*Pierre,* 30–2.

24. *"fancy"* NN*Pierre,* 13.

25. *"sash"* NN*Pierre,* 7.

26. *naps* Raymond N. Weaver, *Herman Melville: Mariner and Mystic* (New York: George H. Doran Company, 1921), 60, from Eleanor Melville Metcalf.

27. *"romantic filial love"* NN*Pierre*, 18. *"command"* Ibid., 20.

28. *"dear park"* A pun intended to suggest a connection between the deer parks of Jonathan Swift's "A Modest Proposal" and Saddle Meadows. *"u daughter!!"* NN*Pierre*, 7.

29. *"Lady in Waiting"* NN*Pierre*, 13. *talking back* His sister probably admonished him for "unceremoniously" leaving their mother alone at the train station in Pittsfield, MGM to AM, 3/10/51, GLA.

30. *"tarn"* NN*Pierre*, 33. The love scenes between Pierre and Lucy resemble *tableaux vivants*, those "living pictures" created for after-dinner entertainment in genteel homes.

31. *"docile"* Ibid., 20. In her soliloquy she uses some form of the word *docile* ten times to describe Pierre, often coupled with the adjective *sweet*. *"paradise"* Ibid., 39.

32. *"gospel"* NN*Pierre*, 43. *"shriek"* NN*P*, 45. In psychoanalytic terms, Sleeping Beauty is a puberty myth. The blood, the prick, the drugged sleep, the arousal by the prince's kiss signify female sexual awakening.

33. *"thought"* Ibid., 51. *"phantoms"* Ibid., 49. *"inscrutableness"* Ibid., 49.

34. *"impious thing"* Ibid., 58.

35. *reverie* Both Robert K. Martin, *Hero, Captain and Stranger: Male Friendship, Social Critique and Literary Form in the Sea Novels of Herman Melville* (Chapel Hill: University of North Carolina Press, 1986), and James Creech, *Closet Writing*, point out that "reverie" was often associated with masturbation in Victorian advice books, but I question the idea that every time a character in a Victorian novel daydreams, it means that person is actually masturbating, not meditating. It seems more likely that writers like Melville wanted to exploit the ambiguity for its shock value and subversiveness, not to reduce such references to one-dimensional denotation. Creech argues that Pierre's reveries before the painting signify masturbation, as, in his view, Pierre suffers from a homosexual oedipal fixation on his father, which is displaced when he falls in love with Isabel, who resembles his father. While Creech's reading is very persuasive, it hinges on accepting the idea that incest in the novel is an understood signifier of homosexuality and *Pierre* is a "wink" at gay readers.

36. *portrait* I'm indebted to Creech, *Closet Writing*, for detailed analysis of the portrait. Evidently, Allan Melvill's provocative pose in 1810 was a conventional bachelor pose signifying sexual potency. Did it signify homosexuality as well? Who was the artist, and what was his relationship with Allan Melvill? Was the artist gay? Was Allan Melville gay? Was Gansevoort Melville gay, for that matter? It seems to me that these family relationships are so intricately entangled that one-to-one identifications of real people and fictional characters can be dangerously reductive. Melville was rumored to have said he did not like the portrait or think it portrayed the father he remembered. *"strong"* NN*Pierre*, 83. *"serene"* Ibid., 68.

37. *"seducer"* Ibid., 103.

38. *"Memnon Stone"* Ibid., 134.

39. *guitar* Tracing this scene to contemporary melodrama, a genre previously considered beneath scholarly notice, Nancy Fredericks writes in "Melodrama and Class Culture in *Pierre*," "In the secularized universe of melodrama, music is the messenger, like Hamlet's ghost, of a world beyond," 2, more evidence of Melville's responsiveness to popular culture. See also Nancy Fredericks, "The Valorization of Music in *Pierre's* Allegory of the Arts," *Melville Society Extracts* 396 (March 1994), 6–7.

40. *"a consecration of its own"* *The Scarlet Letter*, Norton Critical Edition (New York: W. W. Norton, 1978).

41. *Fuller* See also Henry Adams, "The Dynamo and the Virgin," in *The Education of Henry Adams* (New York: Random House, 1918), 379–409.

42. *"angels in the household"* Woman's "four cardinal virtues: piety, purity, submissiveness and domesticity" made her the guardian angel of hearth and home. See Barbara Welter, *Dimity Convictions: The American Woman in the Nineteenth Century* (Athens, Ohio: Ohio University Press, 1976), 21ff.; and Mary E. Ryan, *The Empire of the Mother: American Writing About Domesticity, 1830–1860* (New York: Haworth Press, 1982). The phrase "angel in the household" comes from a later poem, by Coventry Patmore, that articulates a concept formulated in the antebellum period.

43. *"soul"* Emerson, "Love," *Selected Writings of Ralph Waldo Emerson*, edited by Brooks Atkinson (New York: Random House, 1950), 234. See Wayne Koestenbaum, *Double Talk: The Erotics of Male Literary Collaboration* (New York: Routledge, 1989), for a provocative discussion of several artistic collaborations. See also Joseph A. Boone and Michael Cadden, eds., *Engendering Men: The Question of Male Feminist Criticism* (New York: Routledge, 1990).

44. Hennig Cohen and Donald Yannella, *Herman Melville's Malcolm Letter "Man's Final Lore"* (New York: Fordham University Press and the New York Library, 1992), call Pierre "an attack on patriarchy," and Henry A. Murray, in his "Introduction to *Pierre*," in *Endeavors in Psychology: Selections in the Personology of Henry A. Murray*, edited by Edwin S. Shneidman (New York: Harper & Row 1981), calls the novel Melville's "spiritual autobiography," a phrase that is much more appropriate to *Clarel*.

45. *"soul"* NN*Pierre*, 174.

46. *"masculineness"* Ibid., 180. *"vile boy"* Ibid., 193. *"no past"* Ibid., 199.

47. *"expediency"* Ibid., 214.

48. *"insanity"* Ibid., 239.

49. *"neglect"* Ibid., 280. Wyn Kelley, *Melville and the City* (New York: Cambridge University Press, 1996), contextualizes this section of the novel brilliantly. *"artists"* NN*Pierre*, 269–70. As Henry A. Murray points out in his "Introduction to *Pierre*," 419, the Church of the Apostles combines features of the South Baptist Church on Nassau Street and the Unitary Home on East 14th Street, a home for artists and enthusiasts of all kinds.

50. *"Captain Kidd Monthly"* NN*Pierre*, 253.

51. *"throbbings"* Ibid., 272. In his introduction to *Pierre, or the Ambiguities* (Hendricks House, 1949), Henry Murray offers a Jungian interpretation of the book that identifies Isabel as Pierre's *anima*, though he does not relate this to the artist's androgynous merging of male and female attributes. Isabel's initial appearance, almost in response to Pierre's intense longing for union with a female counterpart, enacts the Shelleyan belief that a man is not whole until he finds and joins with the feminine aspect of the self. *"intimations"* NN*P*, 282. Richard Dean Smith, *Melville's Complaint: Doctors and Medicine in the Art of Herman Melville* (New York and London: Garland Publishing, Inc., 1991), 111, points out that Isabel "resumes the role of a spiritual medium playing her mystical guitar." Citing Howard Kerr's *Mediums, and Spirit-Rappers, and Roaring Radicals* (Urbana, Ill.: University of Illinois Press, 1972), 3–21, Smith writes: "A few spiritual mediums claimed to be able to call on the creativity of dead poets for literary purposes." Smith also suggests references to mesmerism and phrenology. See also Gerard W. Shepherd, "Pierre's Psyche and Melville's Art," *Emerson Society Quarterly* 30, no. 2 (1984), 83–96.

52. *"a dry biscuit or two"* NN*Pierre*, 300–302.

53. *"ashes in his mouth"* Ibid., 289. *"Ass!"* Ibid., 293. Plinlimmon resembles Hawthorne's "Paul Pry" both in his aloofness and in his penetration of the human heart as his steely blue eyes peer into Pierre's soul, trying to divine his secret. Some commentators have contended that relation-ships between men in Hawthorne's novels of this period, especially Holgrave and Clifford in *The House of the Seven Gables* and Hollingsworth and Coverdale in *The Blithedale Romance*, reflect the tension Hawthorne felt between himself and Melville.

54. *"soul"* Ibid., 304.

55. *"sanity"* Ibid., 305. *"hell"* Ibid., 306.

56. No other American prose work achieved quite this quality until Toni Morrison's *Beloved,* with the possible exception of passages in William Faulkner's novella "The Bear."

57. Quotations from Dante's *Divina Commedia:* "Inferno," Canto I, from *The Vision: Hell, Purgatory and Paradise of Dante Alighieri,* translated by the Rev. H. F. Cary, A.M. (New York: The American News Company, 1883).

58. *"Good Angel," "Bad Angel"* NN*Pierre,* 329.

59. *"appetite for God"* Ibid., 345. *"incest"* Ibid., 347.

60. *"birthright"* Ibid.

61. *"soul"* Ibid., 351. "daughter... *sister"* Ibid., 353.

62. *"Voltaire"* Ibid., 356. *reviews* See Parker, "Why *Pierre* Went Wrong."

63. *"knew him not"* NN*Pierre,* 362.

64. *"soul of a man!"* NN*Pierre,* 285. Wyn Kelley's paper "Pierre in a Labyrinth: The Mysteries and Miseries of New York," delivered at the New-York Historical Society during the Melville Centennial gathering, September 26, 1991, inspired me to new ways of seeing in the novel Melville's relationship to the city. For a comprehensive look at Melville's urban imagination, see Kelley's *Melville's City: Urban and Literary Form in Nineteenth-Century New York.*

65. *"shaft"* NN*Pierre,* 289.

66. As Eugene Taylor will attempt to show in his forthcoming book on the development of psychiatry in America, the work of Boston psychotherapists in the 1880s influenced Sigmund Freud at a critical point in his career. E. L. Grant Watson, in his "Melville's *Pierre," New England Quarterly* 3 (April 1930), 195–234, impressed by Melville's interweaving of "thought and intuition," considered *Pierre* superior to *Moby-Dick.*

67. *existentialism* The resemblances of both "Billy Budd" and *Pierre,* Melville's psycho-philosophical novel, to Kierkegaard's psycho-novelistic philosophical work *Fear and Trembling* (1843) are astonishing. Kierkegaard was not available in America until much later, but both Melville and Kierkegaard identified Abraham's sacrifice of Isaac as the paradigm for relationships between Victorian fathers and their sons.

68. *profits* "Historical Note" to NN*Pierre,* 393. Recent scholarship takes a fresh look at Melville's relationship to the literary culture of the times. See Charlene Avallone, "Calculations for Popularity: Melville's *Pierre* and *Holden's Dollar Magazine," Melville Society Extracts* 72 (February 1988), 6–9, and Sheila Post-Lauria, *Correspondent Colorings: Melville in the Marketplace* (Amherst: University of Massachusetts, 1996).

69. *"mood"* NN*Pierre,* 347. For an insightful analysis of how women novelists managed to use sentimental conventions to subvert an oppressive patriarchal hegemony, see Jane Tompkins, *Sensational Designs: The Cultural Work of American Fiction 1790–1860* (New York: Oxford University Press, 1985).

17. COUNTER-FRICTION TO THE MACHINE

1. *excursions* See Merton M. Sealts Jr., "'An Utter Idler and a Savage': Melville in the Spring of 1852," *Melville Society Extracts* 79 (November 1989). Augusta's account of these outings, the "privately owned" document mentioned by Hershel Parker in "Herman Melville's *The Isle of the Cross," American Literature* 62, no. 1 (March 1990), 1–16, belongs to William Reese of New Haven, Connecticut. Augusta's notes end with the notation "No. 7," but there are no notes on a seventh excursion.

2. *"some of the gents"* LS to LSjr., 6/7/52, Leyda, *Log,* 451.

3. *curious* HM to NH, 8/13/52, NN*Corr.,* 232. Soon after, Clifford became the Whig governor of Massachusetts.

4. *"experience"* HM to NH, 8/13/52, NN*Corr.,* 232–33.

5. *"unaffected sympathy"* Ibid., 234.

6. *Pollard and Macy* Leyda, *Log,* 452. *"comets"* LS to LSjr., 7/20/52, Leyda, *Log,* 452.

7. Quakers were stricter and more doctrinaire in those days than today, as the film *A Dead Whale or a Stove Boat,* shown at the New Bedford Whaling Museum, shows. They wore plain, dark clothing, bonnets or hats, and dour expressions when they went to meeting, and men and women did not sit together as they do today. Modern Friends dress in casual, even colorful clothing, and enjoy music, dancing, and laughter, and they are often refugees from churches, seeking a more eclectic, incisive religious faith. For a description of "rating chronometers" written before Melville met Mitchell, see NN*Pierre,* 211. About Mitchell, see Alice Owen Albertson, *Maria Mitchell, 1818–1889,* a pamphlet reprinted by permission of *The Vassar Quarterly* (no date); Maria Karaganis, "The Sky Was Her Limit," *The Boston Globe Magazine,* 25 November 1984; and the *Dictionary of American Biography.* In *Night Watches: Inventions on the Life of Maria Mitchell* (Cambridge, Mass.: Alice James Books, 1985), Carole Oles brings Mitchell to life for contemporary readers.

8. *"Widows, 202"* Leyda, *Log,* 452.

9. *"glad to see"* LS to LSjr., 7/20/52, Leyda, *Log,* 453.

10. *"daydream"* HM to NH, 7/17/52, NN*Corr.,* 230. Hawthorne called his Brook Farm stay "essentially a daydream, and yet a fact," *Centenary* 3, no. 2, and James Mellow, *Nathaniel Hawthorne In His Times* (Boston: Houghton Mifflin, 1980), 392.

11. *"see how it is"* HM to NH, 8/13/52, NN*Corr.,* 234.

12. *"officiousness," "have it"* Ibid., 237. *intimacy* Wayne Koestenbaum, *Double Talk: The Erotics of Male Collaboration* (New York: Routledge, 1989), argues that male literary collaboration is sublimated sexual intercourse, with the text representing either a shared woman's body or the child produced by the two men. See James Mellow's account of the Agatha correspondence for Hawthorne's point of view.

13. For a whole new look at the reception of Melville's works by a broad spectrum of critics, see Sheila Post-Lauria, "Genre and Ideology: The French Sensational Romance and Melville's *Pierre," Journal of American Culture* 15, no. 3 (Fall 1982), 1–8. I am deeply indebted to her for sharing her research and discoveries with me as I was working on the present manuscript and she on hers. As she points out in her article on *Pierre* and the French sensational romance, several "cultivated" reviewers objected to the novel's affinity with French sensational romances, a genre whose influence on high culture they found deplorable.

14. *"dismal falsehood" The Literary World,* 2 August 1852, quoted by Watson G. Branch, ed. in *Melville: The Critical Heritage* (London and Boston: Routledge and Kegan Paul, 1974), 290.

15. *"trash" Boston Post,* 4 August 1852, unsigned review by Charles Gordon Greene, Branch, ibid., 294–96. *"failure"* Unsigned review by William Young, *The Albion,* 21 August 1852, Branch, ibid., 298–99. *"sad"* unsigned review by J. G. Holland(?), *Springfield Daily Republican,* 16 August 1852, Leyda, *Log,* supplement, 931–92. *crazy Day Book,* 7 September 1852, quoted in "Historical Note" to NN*Pierre,* 380. *"chops" Herald,* 18 September 1852, Branch, *The Critical Heritage,* 308–12.

16. *"agreeable visit"* LS to LSjr., 9/27/52, Leyda, *Log,* 459. *"potatoes"* HSS to LSjr., 10/4/52, Leyda, *Log,* 459. *"high faluting romance"* JOS to LSjr., 8/31/52, Leyda, *Log,* 459.

17. *"ocean" Godey's,* November 1852, in NN*Pierre,* 382–83.

18. *"Poe and Hawthorne" Graham's Magazine,* October 1852, Branch, *The Critical Heritage,* 382–83.

19. *"abortion" National Magazine,* January 1853, in Branch, *The Critical Heritage,* 385. See Nina Baym, *Novels, Novel Readers, and Reviewers: Responses to Fiction in Antebellum America* (Ithaca: Cornell University Press, 1984), for contemporary critiques of other writers, many of which were just as bad as Melville's.

20. *"society" American Whig Review,* November 1852, Branch, *The Critical Heritage,* 314–21. *"novelist" Southern Literary Messenger,* September 1852, Branch, 300–302. *rule* To convey "a pleasing moral" without "cold, didactic formality," as Baym phrases it in *Novels, Readers, and Reviewers,* 124–126.

21. *"recluse life"* ESM, quoted by Merton M. Sealts Jr., *Melville's Reading,* revised and enlarged edition (Columbia: University of South Carolina Press, 1988), 77.

22. *"Ambiguity"* PG to MGM, 10/9/52, Leyda, *Log,* 461.

23. *"pleasure"* HM to NH, between 12/3/52 and 12/13/52, NN*Corr.,* 242. Melville's working title for this adaptation of the Agatha story was "The Isle of the Cross," according to Hershel Parker, "Herman Melville's *The Isle of Cross:* A Survey and a Chronology," *American Literature* 62, no. 1 (March 1990), 1–16.

24. *"Pine"* Fitz James O'Brien, *Putnam's Magazine,* February 1853, Branch, *The Critical Heritage,* 323–29. Coincidentally, Koestenbaum, *Double Talk,* 12, regards the collaboration of Joseph Addison and Richard Steele, "whose sexualities are open to question, and who worked intimately on the *Tatler* and *Spectator,*" as illustrative of the erotics of male literary collaboration.

25. *"light as a wick"* SS to HS, 4/1/53, Joyce Deveau Kennedy and Frederick J. Kennedy, "Additions to *The Melville Log,*" *Melville Society Extracts* 31 (September 1977), 8.

26. *"consulship," etc.* MGM to PG, 4/20/53, GLC.

27. *"masters"* RHDjr. to AMjr., 5/10/53, Leyda, *Log,* 472–73. For a detailed discussion of Melville's various attempts to land a diplomatic job, see Harrison Hayford and Merrell Davis, "Herman Melville as Office-Seeker," *Modern Language Quarterly* 10 (May and September 1949), 68–183 and 377–88.

28. *"doctrines"* H. W. Bishop to William L. Marcy, 5/24/53, Leyda, *Log,* 473–74. *"citizens"* JVB to FP, 5/4/53, Leyda, *Log,* 472.

29. *"strain"* ESM's memoranda for a memoir of her husband, BA.

30. *"occasion"* LS to LSjr., 5/24/53, Leyda, *Log,* 473. *"notices"* PM to AM, 5/22/53, GLA. *"personage"* PM to AM, 6/12/53, GLA. No manuscript of "The Isle of the Cross" has survived.

31. *list* Leyda, *Log,* 475–76. *Hippodrome* STM to AM, 6/53, GLA.

32. *"politics"* *Reminiscences of Richard Lathers: Sixty Years of a Busy Life in South Carolina, Massachusetts, and New York,* edited by Alvah F. Sanborn (New York: Grafton Press, 1907).

33. *"instruction"* NN*Corr.,* 246, headnote. Holmes declined in a letter to Rockwell dated July 4, 1853, Rockwell Papers, Lenox Library.

34. *magazines* HM to RB, 7/20/51, NN*Corr.,* 198. For an encyclopedic but very readable compendium of information and interpretations of the short fiction, see Lea Bertani Vozar Newman, *A Reader's Guide to the Short Stories of Herman Melville* (Boston: G. K. Hall, 1986).

35. See Frank Luther Mott, *A History of American Magazines,* 5 vols. (Cambridge: Harvard University Press, 1938–57), and Perry Miller, *The Raven and the Whale: The War of Words and Wits in the Era of Poe and Melville* (New York: Harcourt, Brace and World, 1956).

36. *"best magazine"* William Makepeace Thackeray, quoted by Gordon Milne, *George William Curtis and the Genteel Tradition* (Bloomington: University of Indiana Press, 1956), 66. Also, George William Curtis quotes Thackeray to Joshua H. Dix, 9/7/55, Leyda, *Log,* 507.

37. *"admirably paid"* HSS to SHS, 7/27/53, Kennedy and Kennedy, "Additions to the *Melville Log,*" 8. Dates of writing, submissions, acceptance, etc. are conjectural; see notes to NN*PT,* 476–514, for a detailed discussion.

38. Jane Tompkins, *Sensational Designs: The Cultural Work of American Fiction, 1790–1860* (New York: Oxford University Press, 1985), points out that Hawthorne's contemporaries rarely praised the tales we consider Hawthorne's greatest. In "Hawthorne and His Mosses," although Melville praises several tales that are surprisingly weak by modern standards, he singles out "Young Goodman Brown" for special attention, which was unusual at the time.

39. *"Genessee," "black"* NN*PT,* 255. *"adders"* Ibid., 258. *"box"* Ibid., 259. *"happiness," "good old man"* Ibid., 260. *"failure"* Ibid., 261.

40. *"prodigy"* Ibid., 267.

41. *"murder"* Ibid., 270. *"highest"* Ibid., 271. *"plumage"* Ibid., 287.

42. Another valuable source of historical information for this story is Betsy Blackmar, *Manhattan for Rent, 1785–1850* (Ithaca: Cornell University Press, 1989).

43. *lawyer's self-characterization* See ibid., 13–14; *"bullion"* Ibid., 14. *"forlorn"* Ibid., 19.

44. *"high, blank walls"* NN*PT,* 15. See Newman, *Reader's Guide,* for a thorough discussion of possible sources. Sealts, in *Melville's Reading,* 90, writes that the idea for the character might have come from an advertisement in the *New York Times and Daily Tribune,* 18 February 1853, for a novel by James A. Maitland about a lawyer who hires an extra copying clerk. Some scholars have identified Bartleby with Melville's friend Eli James Murdock Fly, who worked as a copyist for a New York law firm. Bartleby has been associated with everyone from Jesus and Ralph Waldo Emerson to Melville himself, while identifications of the narrator have ranged from Melville's brother Allan and Judge Shaw to Evert Duyckinck. As Brook Thomas, *Cross-examinations of Law and Literature: Cooper, Hawthorne, Stowe, and Melville* (Cambridge: Cambridge University Press, 1987), and Robert Ferguson, *Law and Letters in American Culture* (Cambridge: Harvard University Press, 1984), point out, in a fluid society like America, laws and contracts took on immense significance.

45. *"crimpy hand"* NN*PT,* 20.

46. *"I would prefer not to"* NN*PT,* 20.

47. *"passive resistance"* NN*PT,* 23. Robert K. Wallace, *Melville and Turner: Spheres of Love and Fright* (Athens: University of Georgia Press, 1992), argues persuasively on the basis of internal evidence that Melville must have seen paintings by J. M. W. Turner at Queen Anne Street; similarly, it seems likely that Melville was acquainted with Thoreau's essay, though we have no documentary evidence.

48. *Cicero* Ferguson points out that Cicero was revered by the Founding Fathers as the codifier of republican laws. *"reasonable"* NN*PT,* 20.

49. *"loneliness"* Ibid., 26. *"disqualified"* Ibid., 29.

50. *"rockaway"* Ibid., 42.

51. *"dead men"* NN*PT,* 45. New York City Directories in the New-York Historical Society show that Allan Melville's law office was at 14 Wall Street before he moved to 17 Wall Street, then 37 Pine Street. Allan's residences are listed as 31st and Lexington, then 47 East 24th Street for those years.

52. *"dead letters"* Irving Adler, "Equity, Law, and Bartleby," *Science and Society* 51, no. 4 (winter 1987–88), identifies this as a reference to the Declaration of Independence, which proclaimed natural rights as the foundation of civil society. Antebellum readers were accustomed to looking for multiple subtextual signifiers, as Post-Lauria, *Correspondent Colorings;* James L. Machor, "Historical Hermeneutics and Antebellum Fiction: Gender, Response, Theory and Interpretive Contexts," *Readers in History: Nineteenth-Century American Literature and the Contents of Response* (Baltimore: John Hopkins University Press, 1993); and Ronald J. Zboray, *A Fictive People: Antebellum Economic Development and the American Reading Public* (New York: Oxford University Press, 1993), have pointed out. *"humanity"* NN*PT,* 45.

53. *"heart"* "Easter, 1916," in *The Collected Poems of W. B. Yeats* (New York: Macmillan, 1959), 179.

54. *Malcolm and Stanwix* ESM to LS, 8/10/53, Leyda, *Log,* 478–79. *"party of gentlemen"* Ibid. *"popular"* HS to LS, 8/26/53, Leyda, *Log,* 479. *"respect"* *Berkshire Evening Eagle,* 26 August 1853, Leyda, *Log,* 479.

55. *Hoadley* See HSS to SHS, 7/27/53, Kennedy and Kennedy, "Additions to the *Melville Log,*" 8, and entries of 9/15/53 and 1/6/54, Leyda, *Log,* 479–80, 483–84. Melville

added notes to Hoadley on the distinction between the words *friend* and *brother* that suggest he was pondering the meaning of the two ideas.

56. *"appetite"* George F. Adler to ED, 10/10/53, Leyda, *Log*, 480–81.

57. *"prevented"* Melville writes of being "prevented" from publishing a manuscript, HM to Harper Brothers, 11/24/53, NN *Corr.*, 250; Parker, "Melville's *Isle*," believes this refers to the lost "Isle of the Cross."

58. *"fortune"* MGM to HM, 2/10/54?, GLA.

59. *"market"* HM to Harper Brothers, 2/29/54, NN *Corr.*, 257.

60. Prudence L. Steiner, "Unreliable Guidebooks," *Harvard Magazine*, August 7, 1994, 13–18, compares Melville's islands with the real thing.

61. *"curse," "sky"* NN*PT*, 126. Melville had Darwin's *Voyage of the Beagle* in mind, as H. Bruce Franklin, "The Island Worlds of Darwin and Melville," *The Centennial Review* 11, (summer 1967), 353–70, and Mark Dunphy, "Melville's Turning of the Darwinian Tables in 'The Encantadas,'" *Melville Society Extracts* 79 (November 1989), 14, have shown.

62. *"world"* NN*PT*, 132. *"stews"* Ibid., 132–33.

63. *"third"* Ibid., 146.

64. *"cross," "calm"* Ibid., 157. James Russell Lowell admired the conclusion of this sketch so much that he told Charles Briggs he wished it longer; see "Historical Note" to NN*PT*, 509.

65. *"cruelty," "cannibals"* NN*PT*, 163. *"tyrants"* Ibid., 166. *"misanthrope"* Ibid., 169.

66. *"sea"* NN*PT*, 134. *"written"* *Berkshire County Eagle*, 10 March 1854, Leyda, *Log*, 485.

18. SHADOWS FORESHADOWING DEEPER SHADOWS

1. *winter* PM to LS, 3/27/54, Leyda, *Log*, 486. AM to FPM, 3/30/54, GLA.

2. I am indebted to Sheila Post-Lauria for the reference to McIntosh's stories.

3. I am indebted to Wyn Kelley's 1993 NEMLA paper "'I'm Housewife Here': Herman Melville and Domestic Economy," for this connection, *Melville Society Extracts* 98 (September 1994), 6–10. This article opens the house of Melville scholarship to much-needed fresh air.

4. *"snug cells"* NN*PT*, 319.

5. *"boys"* Emerson, "Self-Reliance," Brooks Atkinson, ed., *The Selected Writings of Ralph Waldo Emerson* (New York: Random House, 1950), 259.

6. *paper* NN*PT*, 328. *"fatal sentence"* Ibid., 330.

7. See Hannah Josephson, *The Golden Threads: New England's Mill Girls and Magnates* (New York: Duell, Sloan & Pearce, 1949). *"trampled upon"* George G. Foster, *New York by Gaslight and Other Sketches* (Berkeley: University of California at Berkeley, 1990). The old Carson's Mill is on the site now occupied by the Crane Paper Mill in Dalton, Massachusetts. The "Bellow's Pipe," or Notch Pass, on the southerly side of Mount Greylock, was where Melville hiked with Mrs. Morewood, the Duyckincks, and others in the summer of 1851.

8. *"seats," "scenes"* Edward Everett, quoted in Thomas Bender, *Toward an Urban Vision: Ideas and Institutions in Nineteenth-Century America* (Lexington: University of Kentucky Press, 1975), 44. See also Daniel Boorstin, *The Americans: The National Experience* (New York: Random House, 1965), 20–34.

9. *ease* As Joan D. Hedrick, *Harriet Beecher Stowe: A Life* (New York and Oxford: Oxford University Press, 1994), shows, Mrs. Stowe lost her dearest child and did not have an easy life by any measurement.

10. A memorial plaque on the wall of Grace Church's vestibule reads: "Wright Post, M.D., judicious, skilful, and industrious—in his deportment and in his religious principles a sincere, devout, & humble Christian. During many years he was vestryman of this church and at his decease its senior war-

den. He died June 14th A.D. 1828 aged 62 years 3 months & 26 days." See NN*PT*, 700–705, for other topical references.

11. *"public"* CFB to HM, 5/14/54, Leyda, *Log*, 487. *"sketch"* GPP to HM, 5/13/54, Leyda, *Log*, 488.

12. *"candy"* HMG to AM, 4/11/54, GLA.

13. *"adventure"* HM to GPP 6/7/54, NN *Corr.*, 265. As Sheila Post-Lauria points out, Melville started *Israel Potter* for *Harper's*, but switched to *Putnam's*.

14. *"beasts"* *Israel Potter: His Fifty Years of Exile* (Evanston and Chicago: Northwestern University Press and The Newberry Library, 1982),* 7. Continental currency: According to an untitled typescript in the New York Public Library's Gansevoort-Lansing Collection, Colonel Henry Quackenboss, who once loaned the government $60,000, kept a great chest of worthless money in his attic, and his descendants used to show it as evidence of their ancestor's patriotism. This "Reminiscence of a Revolutionary Officer" resides among miscellaneous Melville papers; it's not clear whether Colonel Quackenboss was related to Catherine Quackenboss and the Melville family or not, but it contains some vivid anecdotes of life in New York State as some of Melville's ancestors experienced it.

15. Robert A. Ferguson, *Law and Letters in American Culture* (Cambridge: Harvard University Press, 1984), 163, links Irving's description of America as an aggressive nation "insatiable of territory" in *A History of New York* with Melville's "bleak description of 1855." Ferguson's discussion of Diedrich Knickerbocker is a reminder of the extent of Melville's debt to Irving.

16. *"sarcasm"* *The National Magazine*, quoted in the "Historical Note," NN*IP*, 217.

17. *sales figures* "Historical Note," NN*PT*, 490–91, 494.

18. *"vat"* NN*Pierre*, 9.

19. In his cover letter to *Harper's* (HM to Harper Brothers, 9/18/54, NN *Corr.*, 269), Melville referred to "Jimmy Rose" and "The 'Gees" as a "brace of fowl—wild fowl."

20. *"rat"* NN*PT*, 342. *"survive"* Ibid., 344–45.

21. Although this story was published in *Harper's*, it seems more in keeping with the style of *Putnam's* pieces; it resembles a sarcastic piece called "On Niggers" that appeared in the same issue of *Putnam's* as Melville's "Benito Cereno." *"disdain"* NN*PT*, 350. Carolyn L. Karcher, in *Shadow Over the Promised Land: Slavery, Race, and Violence in Melville's America* (Baton Rouge: Louisiana State University Press, 1980), 128, points out that Melville's sketch was probably a response to a July 1854 review of Nott and Gliddon's *Types of Mankind* entitled "Is Man One, or Many?" in which a *Putnam's* reviewer endorsed the hierarchical classification of the races of mankind.

22. Benjamin Franklin, "On the Savages of North America," *The Norton Anthology of American Literature*, shorter edition (New York: W. W. Norton, 1979), 113–21.

23. *"credulity"* NN*PT*, 351.

24. See MGM to PG, 11/24/54 and 11/28/54, Leyda, *Log*, 493–94.

25. *Fanny* Amos Nourse to Lemuel Shaw, 3/8/55: "...another girl equalizes matters, which is very pleasant always–If it grows up to be as fine a child as the rest, she can have nothing more to desire," Leyda, *Log*, 499. *"helpless"* February 1855, ESM, memoranda for a Memoir of Melville, BA, reprinted in Merton M. Sealts Jr., *The Early Lives of Melville: Nineteenth Century Biographical Sketches and Their Authors* (Madison: University of Wisconsin Press, 1974), 169.

26. *"Diana"* HelM to AM, date uncertain (labeled "Lawrence, 1855?"), GLA. *Maria* The Hoadleys' baby was born May 30, 1855.

27. *"dogs"* NN*PT*, 84.

28. *stern-piece* The icon on the stern-piece reappears as Delano stands with his foot on the prostrate Babo, calling to mind Frederick Douglass's maxim that "if you want to keep your fellow man in a ditch, you have to stand there with your foot on his neck," or, as Abraham Lincoln put it, "As I would

---

* Cited hereafter as "NN*IP*."

not be a slave, so I would not be a master." Both master and slave are in bondage to slavery.

29. Sterling Stuckey's "'Follow Your Leader'": The Theme of Cannibalism in Melville's *Benito Cereno*," *Going Through the Storm: The Influence of African-American Art in History* (New York and Oxford: Oxford University Press, 1994), 171–86, elucidates the unspecified grisly details.

30. *rape* See Carolyn L. Karcher, "The Riddle of the Sphinx, Melville's 'Benito Cereno' and the Amistad Case," in *Critical Essays on Melville's* Benito Cereno, edited by Robert Burkholder (Boston: G. K. Hall, forthcoming), 56, n. 53. In defending Cinqué and the *Amistad* mutineers, John Quincy Adams successfully argued that the blacks were citizens of their own country and could not, therefore, be held as property in the United States or tried under U.S. statutes, with the result that the captives were extradited to Africa, where many of them established a missionary colony.

31. *"too hurriedly"* GWC to J. H. Dix, 4/20/55, Leyda, *Log*, 501. "Oh! dear, why can't Americans write good stories. They tell good lies enough, and plenty of 'em," GWC to JAD 7/31/55, Leyda, *Log*, 405. (Leyda mistakenly refers to Joshua A. Dix as "J. H. Dix.")

32. References to the Spanish Empire and the Inquisition suggest that Melville was drawing an analogy between the Holy Roman Empire, the Spanish empire in the New World, and the burgeoning American empire. See H. Bruce Franklin, "'Apparent Symbol of Despotic Command': Melville's 'Benito Cereno,'" *New England Quarterly* 34 (1961), 462–77, for a detailed elucidation of references to Charles V, Las Casas, etc. Karcher, in "The Riddle of the Sphinx," 29, points out that after the slave trade was outlawed by England and the United States, American slavers would run up a Spanish flag on the sight of patrol boats, but when Spain, too, outlawed the slave trade, Spanish slavers and pirates of all nations ran up the American flag because Americans would not search American vessels. See also Sandra Zagarell, "Reenvisioning America: Melville's *Benito Cereno*," ESQ 30, (fourth quarter, 1984), 245–57; Eric J. Sundquist, "*Benito Cereno* and New World Slavery," in *Reconstructing American Literary History*, edited by Sacvan Bercovitch (Cambridge: Harvard University Press, 1986), 93–122; and Sterling Stuckey, "The Death of Benito Cereno: A Reading of Herman Melville on Slavery," in *Going Through the Storm: The Influence of African-American Art in History* (New York: Oxford University Press, 1994).

33. For decades, scholars ignored the political implications of the story, analyzing it abstractly as an allegory of good and evil and generally assuming that Melville was using white and black in the conventional way, giving negative connotations to black and positive connotations to white. It took a nationwide civil rights movement to alert scholars to the story's historical context, and only recently have scholars appreciated Melville's genius in transforming Delano's original narrative into a multilayered text that deconstructs racism to reveal the bias behind all historical documents composed by conquerors. One of the earliest new historicist readings of this story appears in Laurie Jean Lorant, "Herman Melville and Race: Themes and Imagery" (unpublished dissertation, New York University, 1972).

34. Brook Thomas, in *Cross-Examinations of Law and Literature: Cooper, Hawthorne, Stowe, and Melville* (New York: Cambridge University Press, 1987), 97, points out that for Shaw, "preserving the Union was a moral imperative because the United States was not merely one government among many, but the hope of mankind. It, above all others, guaranteed the absolute and entire supremacy of law."

35. See Marvin Fisher's very fine analysis of the stories as reflective of political issues in *Going Under: Melville Short Fiction and the American 1850s* (Baton Rouge: Louisiana State University Press, 1977).

36. *"fascinating"* John Hoadley to Augusta Melville, 7/29/55, GLA.

37. *prescribed* ESM Memoranda, in Merton M. Sealts Jr., *The Early Lives of Melville: Nineteenth-Century Biographical Sketches and Their Authors* (Madison: University of Wisconsin Press, 1974), 169. Dr. Holmes's copy of George B. Wood, M.D., *A Treatise on the Practice of Medicine*, fourth edition, 2 vols. (Philadelphia: Lippincott, Grambo, and Co., 1855), is now in the Countway Library of the Harvard Medical School. The section on neuralgia and sciatica, which are related to rheumatism and gout, indicates that Melville's debilitating back pains as well as the eye trouble he suffered could have been aggravated by indulgence in strong coffee, tea, tobacco, and alcohol. Melville does not seem to have cut down his consumption of alcohol and tobacco; in fact, during these years he became more dependent on them for relief of both physical and emotional pain. The combination of these drugs with such contraindicated irritants as alcohol and tobacco probably affected his disposition.

Furthermore, neuralgia and sciatica were often "the immediate precursor, or rather the first obvious sign of Bright's Disease of the kidneys, and cirrhosis of the liver," with causes ranging from fatigue and cold to "strong mental emotion," overindulgence in food and drink, latent gout, rheumatism, or syphilis. Wood's comment, "Not infrequently a close examination will detect a syphilitic origin," is provocative given Melville's years as a sailor. It's quite possible that sailors had access to native remedies for venereal diseases, and that a man who had spent a relatively short period at sea could suffer slight residual effects of the disease, but this is merely unsupported surmise. Melville certainly spent enough time sitting at his writing desk, and suffered enough stress, to have sciatica without a venereal origin.

38. G. W. Curtis to J. H. Dix, 9/7/55, calls it "a capital, genial, humorous sketch by Melville, thoroughly magazinish," Leyda, *Log*, 507.

39. *tobacco* In his *Reminiscences*, Richard Lathers wrote: "the inscription painted over his capacious fireplace, 'I and my chimney smoke together' I have seen strikingly verified more than once when the atmosphere was heavy & the wind was east." Lathers observed that Melville always had on hand a supply of apple cider produced from his own orchard, and he was devoted to tobacco, "in the virtues of which he was a firm believer." In the late poem "Herba Santa," Melville extols the "Pacific herb" whose "sensuous plea" sways "the bristling clans of Adam/At least to fellowship in thee!" Though family and friends often gave Melville new pipes as gifts, he preferred the old clay pipe he kept beside his favorite chair. The inscription was carved over the fireplace by Allan Melville after he and his family moved into Arrowhead in 1863. *"surrender"* NN*PT*, 377.

40. The "slave room" was bricked up to make a family room in the basement in the 1940s. I am indebted to William Whittlesey of Holmes Road, Pittsfield, for sharing his memories of the "slave room" he saw as a child playing at Arrowhead. In Broadhall's cavernous basement, ancient dungeons can be seen, as well as ample space for harboring fugitives. See articles by Linda Carman, Joseph March, and Rosalie Wesley in *The Berkshire Hills*, Federal Writers' Project of the WPA (New York: Duell, Sloan & Pearce, 1939), for hints that Berkshire residents harbored fugitives.

41. The deletions occurred between the 1891 newspaper version of Smith's memoir and the 1897 "definitive" edition. For the original texts, see Sealts, *Early Lives*, 40, 253. "backbone" David Donald, *Charles Sumner and the Coming of the Civil War* (New York: Alfred A. Knopf, 1960), 188. Lizzie excised other references as well, including one to Fanny Kemble, whose scandalous divorce from a Georgia slaveowner and subsequent espousal of abolitionist causes struck her as a shocking violation of woman's role. See Sealts, *Early Lives*, 39–40 and 253, for the original texts.

42. According to *The Berkshire Hills* edited by Rosalie Wesley, 77, "Charles Sumner was a frequent visitor to Broad Hall,

and it was probably due to his influence that its ample cellar became one of the depots for the 'Underground Railroad' of the fleeing Negro slaves. Among its apple and potato bins there were vaults and passageways where trembling human flesh lay in concealment." Whether or not this legend had any basis in fact may never be known. I have tried to find additional references, but have so far been unsuccessful. Like many such bits of local lore that are inadmissible as documentary evidence, oral history should not be summarily discounted simply because no written proof exists; much information about the Underground Railroad has been lost because of the obvious need for secrecy about its activities. It seems that Melville did not read abolitionist newspapers or involve himself in political activities directly, but this cannot be proved conclusively, either. It's a tantalizing reference. *Roberts case* See Karcher's *Shadow over the Promised Land,* 31–32.

43. For evidence that Melville was opposed to school segregation, see *Omoo.* In 1827, Melville's Uncle Thomas served on a committee appointed by the Pittsfield School Committee to investigate the advisability of establishing separate schools for Negro pupils. They recommended dropping the idea. See J. E. A. Smith, *The History of Pittsfield, Mass. from 1800 to 1876,* vol. 2 (Springfield, Mass.: C. W. Bryan, 1876), 670. Sumner's father, a master mason who broke with the Lodge in 1829 over the issue of segregated schools and interracial marriage, said prophetically, "Our children's heads will some day be broken on a cannon-ball on this question"; see Edward L. Pierce, *Memoirs and Letters of Charles Sumner,* vol. 1 (Boston: Roberts Brothers, 1878–93), 24. Dwight Lowell Dumond, in *Antislavery: The Crusade for Freedom in America* (New York: W. W. Norton, 1963), 323, argues that Sumner rejected the notion that the courts had the final say on constitutional issues; he believed in Andrew Jackson's idea that "every public official has taken an oath to support the Constitution as he understands it." Leonard W. Levy, in *The Law of the Commonwealth and Chief Justice Shaw* (Cambridge: Harvard University Press, 1957), 109–17, says that Shaw's inability to foresee the long-term consequences of the decision was "an abdication of judicial responsibility." Leon F. Litwack, *North of Slavery: the Negro in the Free States 1790–1860* (Chicago: University of Chicago Press, 1961), 148, concludes that "Chief Justice Shaw's legal defense of segregated schools on the basis of 'separate but equal' doctrine established a controversial precedent in American law." Louis Ruchames, "The Pulitzer Prize Treatment of Charles Sumner," 148–71, in *Black and White in American Culture: An Anthology from* The Massachusetts Review, edited by Jules Chametzky and Sidney Kaplan (New York: Viking Press, 1971), claims that Sumner's arguments "on behalf of integration in the public schools of Boston anticipated the reasoning of the Supreme Court of the United States in 1854."

44. *"selfish hunkerism"* *The Journal of Richard Henry Dana Jr.,* vol. 2, edited by Robert Lucid (Cambridge: Harvard University Press, 1968), 413. There are also allusions to the Free Soil Movement, to Milton's *Paradise Lost,* to the Egyptian Pyramids, which were built by slaves, to the repairs on the Capitol Dome, to the Iroquois Indians, whose great councils inspired the Constitutional Convention, to the split between the Hunkers and the Barnburners, to the debate over internal improvements that raged in states like Melville's own New York, to Freemasonry, and to the trade in gold from Africa.

45. *"farm"* ESM, marginal notes, Melville Collection, Houghton Library, Harvard University (HCL).

46. *"Cuba"* Dana, *Journal,* vol. 2, 471. *Whitman* See Gay Wilson Allen, *The Solitary Singer: A Critical Biography of Walt Whitman* (Chicago and London: University of Chicago Press, 1985), 194–95.

47. *"sugar"* NN*PT,* 364–65. Stewart was the fellow who had loaned Melville $2,050; he may also have been a suitor of Helen's at one time.

48. *"savages," etc.* NN*PT,* 377. It is almost as though his paranoia conjures up workers rioting or slaves revolting; per-

haps Melville had in mind Gabriel Prosser, Denmark Vesey, and Nat Turner, the leaders of the South's three bloodiest slave revolts.

49. *"house divided"* Marvin Fisher, *Going Under: Melville's Short Fiction and the American 1850s* (Baton Rouge and London: Louisiana State University Press, 1977), 212, concludes that "Melville's tale of a house divided forecasts the moral paralysis, occasional flare-ups, and ultimate ruin of a domestic cold war." See also Lorant, "Herman Melville and Race," for a similar reading. *"reeked"* Henry Adams, *The Education of Henry Adams* (New York: Random House, 1918), 99.

50. Maunsell B. Field, *Memories of Many Men* (1874), Leyda, *Log,* 506.

51. The wife in "I and My Chimney" was described as having "an itch toward Swedenborgianism and the Spirit Rapping Philosophy," NN*PT,* 362. See Howard Kerr, *Mediums, Spirit-Rappers, and Roaring Radicals: Spiritualism in American Literature, 1850–1900* (Urbana: University of Illinois Press, 1972), and for more on spiritualism and its connection to the women's movement, see Ann Braude, *Radical Spirits: Spiritualism and Women's Rights in Nineteenth-Century America* (Boston: Beacon Press, 1989).

52. *Berkshire County Eagle,* 31 August 1855, Leyda, *Log,* 506.

53. *party* J. E. A. Smith(?), *Berkshire County Eagle,* 14 September 1855, Leyda, *Log,* 507. *"blot"* NN*C-M,* 133.

54. *"jaunt"* HM to P&SG, 9/18/55, NN*Corr.,* 280. *kite* HS to LSjr., 9/17/55, Leyda, *Log,* 508.

55. *embroidery* Advertisement in *The Pittsfield Sun,* 15 February 1855, and subsequent issues, Leyda, *Log,* 498. "I think they will *literally* have a great 'blow out,' as the Sailors say, for the winds are howling fiercely, & the air is full of Snow," PM to LS, 10/24/55, Leyda, *Log,* 509. In some places, the word *seamstress* was slang for "prostitute."

56. *"a good name"* GWC to JAD, mid-April(?) 1855, Leyda, *Log,* 500, and GWC to JAD, 1/2/56, Leyda, *Log,* 510.

57. *financial troubles* See HM to Shaw, 5/12/56 and 5/22/56, NN*Corr.,* 290–95, and Patricia Barber, "Two New Melville Letters," *American Literature* 49 (November 1977), 418–21.

58. *"imagination"* *United States Magazine and Democratic Review.* *"expression"* The New York *Daily Tribune;* see "Historical Note," NN*PT,* June 23, 1856, Leyda, *Log,* 516. *"reminiscences"* Richard Tobias Greene to HM, 6/16/56, Leyda, *Log,* 516.

59. *"monthlies"* I am indebted to Post-Lauria, *Correspondent Colorings: Melville in the Marketplace* (Amherst: University of Massachusetts Press, 1996), ch. 17, for this quotation.

60. *"productions"* LSjr. to SS, 7/15/56, Leyda, *Log,* 517–18.

19. WHAT SORT OF BAMBOO-ZLING STORY IS THIS?

1. Thompson: Johannes Dietrich Bergman, "The Original Confidence Man," *American Quarterly* 21 (Fall 1969), 560–77, first pointed out this contemporary analogue to Melville's elusive character. Bergman lists several types of confidence men, with urban criminals, Yankee sharpers and peddlers, clergy impostors, gamblers, forgers, thieves, humbugs, and counterfeiters among the most common frauds. The most convenient source of further information on real-life confidence men is the NN*C-M* "Historical Note," esp. 277–79, 283–85. An extensive bibliography of articles and books about this cryptic novel and its many sources may be found in the same volume, 350–57. *"No. 2"* James M. Hutchisson, "Confidence Men and Whales: Two *New York Tribune* Items from the Summer of 1849," *Melville Society Extracts* 71 (November 1987), 8. New York's *Merchants' Ledger, Literary World,* and *Herald* all carried the story, as did Albany's *Evening Journal* and Springfield's *Daily Republican.*

2. *"not the worst thing"* EAD, quoted by Tom Quirk, in *Melville's Confidence Man: From Knave to Knight* (Columbia: University of Missouri Press, 1982), 21.

3. Two notable full-length studies are Warwick Wadlington, *The Confidence-Game in American Literature* (Princeton: Princeton University Press, 1975), and Helen P. Trimpi, *Melville's Confidence Men and the Politics of the 1850's* (Hamden. Conn.: Archon Books, 1987), the fruit of prodigious research on visual materials such as political cartoons. Trimpi claims to be able to identify nearly all of *The Confidence-Man*'s characters as contemporary figures. Her argument is convincing, as she gives detailed descriptions of similarities in clothing, gesture, and appearance between, for example, Henry Ward Beecher and the Cosmopolitan. In the end, I feel topical identifications tell only part of the story and cannot be proven here.

4. *Weekly Times,* 22 November 1851, NN*C-M,* 284, n. 35.

5. For an annotated text of "The River" and a discussion of sources, see NN*C-M,* 511–18. For discussions of the debate over the picturesque in art, see, among others, Christopher Sten, ed., *The Savage Eye: Melville and the Visual Arts* (Kent, Ohio: Kent State University Press, 1991), which contains excellent material by many contributors, and James T. Callow, *Kindred Spirits: Knickerbocker Writers and American Artists, 1807–1855* (Chapel Hill: University of North Carolina Press, 1967), 127ff.

6. *"festival month"* NN*CM,* 9. For useful introductions to the novel, see the following: Elizabeth S. Foster, *The Confidence-Man: His Masquerade, by Herman Melville* (New York: Hendricks House, 1954), and H. Bruce Franklin, *The Confidence Man* (New York: Bobbs-Merrill, 1967).

7. *"hunters"* NN*C-M,* 9.

8. *"parcel," "East"* Ibid., 3. *"NO TRUST,"* etc. Ibid., 4–6.

9. *"massa"* NN*C-M,* 10.

10. *population figures* Eugene D. Genovese, *Roll, Jordan, Roll: The World the Slaves Made* (New York: Vintage Books, 1976), 400.

11. *slaves* See Francis Nicoll to Peter Gansevoort, June 28, 1804, BA. Among Leonard Gansevoort's papers in the Albany Institute are records of several such transactions.

12. *"destroyed"* Alexis de Tocqueville, *Democracy in America,* edited by J. P. Mayer, translated by George Lawrence (New York: Doubleday Anchor, 1969), 321.

13. See Robert F. Berkhofer Jr., *The White Man's Indian: Images of the American Indian from Columbus to the Present* (New York: Vintage Books, 1978), for a discussion of how psychological projections shaped white attitudes toward the people they encountered in the New World.

14. See Thomas Bender, *Toward an Urban Vision: Ideas and Institutions in Nineteenth-Century America* (Lexington: University of Kentucky Press, 1975), 132ff.

15. *reform schools* See Kenneth Stampp, *America in 1857: A Nation on the Brink* (New York: Oxford University Press, 1990).

16. See Hiram M. Chittenden, *The American Fur Trade of the Far West* (Lincoln: University of Nebraska Press, 1986).

17. William Cronon, *Changes in the Land: Indians, Colonists, and the Ecology of New England* (Boston: Charles E. Goodspeed, 1965), 42. Figures vary greatly, however. A publication of the U.S. Bureau of the Census called *Historical Statistics of the United States Colonial Times to 1970* (Washington, D.C.: Department of Commerce, 1975) states that the population of Massachusetts in 1765 was 216,700, including 5,000 blacks and only 1,681 Indians. The phrases "desolate and howling wilderness" and "vultures of hell" are from William Bradford's *Of Plimouth Plantation* and Cotton Mather's *Wonders of the Invisible World,* respectively. "The people of God settled in the Devil's territories" is also Mather's phrase.

18. *drum* PG presented the drum to the Albany Republican Artillery Company on the centennial of George Washington's birthday in 1832, according to the *Albany Daily Argus,* 28 February 1932. For this information I'm indebted to Michael P. Rogin, *Subversive Genealogy: The Politics and Art of Herman Melville* (New York: Alfred A. Knopf, 1983), 49, 55.

19. I am grateful to Eugene Taylor for alerting me to the unpublished article "Some Indian-Hating in the Melvill Family," which he wrote with Henry Murray (Murray Papers, Harvard University Archives).

20. A letter labeled "John Almy to Wise, Navy Yard March 21, 1862," states that "he had the command of her taken away from him on account of his habitual Drunkenness, and his habits are not over and above steady and correct now. Still, I wouldn't use this as an argument for my benefit and to his injury." See also Leyda, *Log,* 511, 522, 652, and 654n. *Seminoles and Cherokees* Howard Zinn, *A People's History of the United States* (New York: Harper and Row, 1990), 142–46. In 1976, Congress voted to pay reparations to their descendants in honor of the nation's Bicentennial.

21. I base the statement that Maria showed Herman his father's letters not on direct evidence, but on an educated guess. Allan Melvill's school copybooks and letters were carefully preserved, and it was common practice in Melville's day to use parental models for didactic purposes. If nothing else, she would have assumed Herman could profit from emulating his father's elegant penmanship.

22. I am indebted to David Sewell, "Mercantile Philosophy and the Dialectics of Confidence: Another Perspective on *The Confidence-Man,*" *Emerson Society Quarterly,* for information about periodicals and advice books.

23. The horned altar of the Israelites appears in I Kings, 1:50–53 and 2:28. Outcasts who grasped the horns were granted asylum. *"Masquerade"* NN*C-M,* 251.

24. Walt Whitman made Satan the fourth member of a quaternity in "Chanting the Square Deific," and Mark Twain probably modeled "The Mysterious Stranger" on Melville's Confidence-Man. Emily Dickinson's sardonic poem begins "I asked no other Thing."

25. *"Drummond light"* Ibid., 239. *"herself"* Ibid., 70. *"rara avis"* Ibid., 69.

26. *"quite an original,"* etc. See ibid., 239, etc.

27. See Richard H. Brodhead, "Sparing the Rod: Discipline and Fiction in Antebellum America," in *Cultures of Letters: Scenes of Reading and Writing in Nineteenth Century America* (Chicago: The University of Chicago Press, 1993), 13–47.

28. I once asked Melville's great-grandson, Paul Metcalf, whether he thought Melville was an alcoholic, and he seemed surprised. Then he said, "You know, that would explain why my mother and all the women in my family were so paranoid about liquor. They warned us never to touch the stuff. I think you have something there."

29. *royalty statement* Leyda, *Log,* 520.

30. *"excursion"* HG's remembrancer, Leyda, *Log,* 519. *"children"* PG to HM, 10/9/56, Leyda, *Log,* 524.

31. *"Lady of Paradise"* HM to SHM, 8/29/56, NN*Corr.,* 296. *Joseph E. A. Smith's report on the bull* Leyda, *Log,* 521–22.

32. *"remembrances"* Savage to LS and HSS, 8/27/56.

33. *"nervous affections"* LS to SS, 9/1/56, Leyda, *Log,* 521.

34. *"unknowable," "indecency"* EAD's diary, 10/1/56, Leyda, *Log,* 523.

35. *"up to her eyes"* Massachusetts Historical Society–Shaw; Eleanor Melville Metcalf, *Cycle and Epicycle* (Cambridge: Harvard University Press, 1953), 160.

36. *"ocean"* HM to PG, 10/7/56, NN*Corr.,* 298. *"friends"* PG to HM, 10/9/56, NN*Corr.,* 650.

37. *"distasteful"* MGM to PG, 11/28/56, Leyda, *Log,* 533.

38. *passport* Leyda, *Log,* 524.

39. *"wall"* NN*C-M,* 69.

20. CHILDE HERMAN'S PILGRIMAGE

1. *"hearty"* EAD Diary, 10/10/56, NN*J,* 183.

2. *Willard and Rankin* From HM to AMjr., 11/10/13,14/56, NN*Corr.,* 300–305. *"fate"* Notebook B, NN*J,* 144.

3. *"life"* HM to AMjr., 11/10,13,14/56, NN*Corr.,* 300–305.

4. *"pleased"* Ibid.

5. *"affectation"* NN*J,* 50. While most of the direct quotations from Melville's journal of the trip are consecutive, and page references seem almost redundant, there are places

where Melville fleshes out an earlier entry, and chronology becomes confusing. There are also places where I have compressed material describing a single place that has been gleaned from several entries. These are indicated. When phrases within a single paragraph are taken from different places, I indicate that, but when all quotations in a particular paragraph appear in the same entry or on the same page, I refer to one or two phrases by name. The reason I cite page numbers rather than journal dates is to avoid confusion, as from time to time Melville redates an entry, giving it, in effect, two dates.

6. *"20 years ago"* HM to AMjr., 11/10,13,14/56, NN *Corr.*, 300–305.

7. Entry 11/20/56, *The English Notebooks by Nathaniel Hawthorne*, edited by Randall Stewart (New York, 1941), 432–33, reprinted in NN*J*, 628ff.

8. *"linen"* NN*J*, 628.

9. *"most of us"* NN*J*, 628–29.

10. The quotations are from 11/12/56, NN*J*, 51.

11. Melville's passport, countersigned by Hawthorne, can be seen in the Berkshire Athenaeum, Pittsfield, Massachusetts.

12. *Chester* NH notebook, NN*J*, 629–33.

13. *"onward"* Ibid., 633.

14. *"than he"* Ibid., 633–34.

15. *"helped"* HM to AMjr., NN *Corr.*, 627. *"paradise"* NN*J*, 52.

16. *"piratical," etc.* NN*J*, 52.

17. *port* Ibid., 53–54, 71–72. See Ekaterini Georgioudaki, "Herman Melville's Trip to Syra in 1856–57," *Melville Society Extracts* 74 (September 1988), 1–8.

18. *"Tate"* NN*J*, 53. *"death"* Ibid., 65.

19. *"Five Points"* Ibid., 55. *"Olympus"* Ibid., 56. *arms story* Ibid., 56.

20. *Abbot* NN*J*, 56. See Ekaterina Georgioudaki's "Djékis Abbot of Thessaloniki and the Greek Merchant in Herman Melville's *Clarel*," *Melville Society Extracts* 64 (November 1985), 1–6.

21. *"sympathy"* NN*J*, 56.

22. *"harems"* Ibid., 57.

23. *fog lifting* Ibid., 58.

24. *"assassins," etc.* Ibid., 58.

25. *bazaar, etc.* Ibid., 59–60.

26. *"everything"* Ibid., 60. *"Bosporus"* Ibid., 65.

27. *mosque* Ibid., 60.

28. *"Sundays"* Ibid., 61.

29. *funeral* Ibid., 62–63. *"wheel"* Ibid., 63.

30. *"sapphire"* Ibid., 68.

31. *Lesbos* Ibid., 70.

32. *camel* Ibid., 69. I have bracketed "stilting" because the editors of NN*J* have amended it to "stalking." I prefer the older reading as more comically descriptive and original— hence, more Melvillean.

33. *"sunned Greek seas and skies"* From "Off Cape Colonna," in *Collected Poems of Herman Melville*, edited by Howard P. Vincent (Chicago: Packard & Co., Hendricks House, 1947),* 48.

34. *"dry," "disenchanting"* NN*J*, 71–72.

35. *"mad"* Henry Miller, *The Colossus of Maroussi* (New York: New Directions, 1941). *soul sickness* The Danish existentialist philosopher-theologian Sören Kierkegaard called it the "sickness unto death."

36. *"Golden Age"* NN*J*, 71.

37. *"champagne"* Ibid., 73. *"sucked"* Ibid., 77.

38. *Lockwood* See NN*J* note, 413. *poem* "A Rail Road Cutting in Alexandria in 1855," *CP*, 410.

39. NN*J*, 74. *elbows* Flaubert's letter from Cairo, 1850, *Flaubert in Egypt*, translated and edited by Francis Steegmuller (London: Bodley Head, 1972), 79–80; quoted by NN*J* note, 414.

40. *"ophthalmick"* Ibid.

_____

*Cited hereafter as *"CP."*

41. *"In the Desert,"* *CP*, 253. For information about the Shekhinah, I am indebted to the title note in Eleanor Wilner's *Shekhinah* (Chicago: University of Chicago Press, 1984), 105–6.

42. *"Alabaster," etc.* NN*J*, 74–75.

43. *"Ghost-Seer"* Ibid., 64.

44. *"more"* HM to NH, 4/1/6/51, NN *Corr.*, 186.

45. *"Hacks"* NN*J*, 72.

46. *"balloon"* Ibid., 75.

47. *"deliberately"* Ibid.

48. *"death"* Ibid.

49. *"assassination"* Ibid.

50. *"born here"* Ibid.

51. *"rock"* Ibid., 76.

52. *"wine"* Ibid., 77.

53. *"mould"* HM to NH, 6/1/51, NN *Corr.*, 193. *beings* In his *American Notebooks*, Hawthorne mentions a conversation to this effect with his friend Horatio Bridge, author of the *Journal of an African Cruiser*.

54. *"day"* NN*J*, 73.

55. *"Cairo"* Ibid.

56. *"Artisan"* From "The Great Pyramid," *CP*, 254. *"founded"* NN*J*, 78.

57. *hotel, "shadows," etc.* NN*J*, 70–80.

58. *"hills"* Ibid., 79.

59. *"arid," "bush"* Ibid., 82–83.

60. *"body"* Ibid., 83.

61. *"cells"* Ibid., 83–84.

62. *"rocks"* Ibid., 84.

63. *"devels"* Ibid.

64. *"cheat"* Ibid., 88.

65. *"twilight"* Ibid., 86.

66. *"Heaven"* Ibid., 91. *"tracts"* Ibid., 85. *"Christianized"* Ibid., 81. See ibid., 435, for notes on Melville's use of various people as characters in Clarel. Not long afterward, Dickson's wife and daughter were raped by Arab marauders and several of his family members killed, after which he and the surviving members of his family returned to their home in Groton, Mass., n. 93.3, ibid., 442. Deacon Dickson was the paternal great-grandfather of John Steinbeck, who read *Moby-Dick* aloud to his two sons and anyone else who would listen. JS to Elizabeth Otis, 2/19/66, Haifa, Israel, ibid., 93–94.

67. *"beach"* Ibid., 80–82.

68. *"water"* Ibid., 96.

69. *"bloom"* Ibid., 97.

70. *"ice," "strange"* Ibid., 98–99.

71. *"Archetype"* "Greek Architecture," *CP*, 248.

72. *"ball"* NN*J*, 104–5.

73. *"document"* Ibid., 102. See Gordon Poole, "A Note on Melville's Stay in Naples," *Melville Society Extracts* 68 (November 1986), 1–5.

74. *volcano, coat* NN*J*, 101.

75. *"light"* Ibid., 104.

76. *"barbarousness"* Ibid., 106.

77. *"poste restante"* Ibid. Dolly Sherwood, *Harriet Hosmer, American Sculptor 1830–1908* (St. Louis: University of Missouri Press, 1991), 54, bring this world to life.

78. *"Shelley"* NN*J*, 106–7.

79. *"Vatican"* Ibid., 108. Rome is intensely overstimulating to most travelers. In 1869, Henry James "went reeling and moaning through the streets in a fever of enjoyment." William B. Whitman, *Literary Cities of Italy* (Washington and Philadelphia: Starhill Press, 1990), 12, 13.

80. *"Rome"* NN*J*, 106–110.

81. He apparently did not see the work of Gibson's protégé Harriet Hosmer, who attended Mrs. Sedgwick's School as well as St. Louis Medical college. Hosmer was out of the country during Melville's visit because, ironically, she was accompanying her sculpture of Beatrice Cenci to the Royal Academy in London.

82. *"stout as usual"* NN*J*, note, 488.

83. *"mosaics"* Ibid., 114.

84. *"Sicilian"* Ibid., 115.

85. *Powers* NNJ, 116. Also see Jean Fagan Yellin's *Women & Sisters: The Antislavery Feminists in American Culture* (New Haven: Yale University Press, 1989), especially pages 99–124.

86. *"caffe"* NNJ, 117.

87. *"masque," etc.* Lord Byron, *Childe Harold's Pilgrimage,* Canto Fourth, stanza 3. *pinnacles* NNJ, 120.

88. *"sea Cybele"* Byron, "Childe Harold," Canto Fourth, stanza 2. *"Pan's might"* From "Venice," *CP,* 238–39.

89. *"Con. Man"* NNJ, 120.

90. *"brown"* Ibid., 119.

91. *"Tumblers," "one"* Ibid., 119–20.

92. *"lasting," etc.* Ibid., 120–21.

93. *"gods &c."* Ibid., 124.

94. Walt Whitman's article "One of the Lessons Bordering Broadway: The Egyptian Museum," in *New York Dissected,* edited by Emory Holloway (New York: Rufus Rockwell Wilson, 1936), 30–40, describes Abbott's collection and expresses his ideas about Egyptian history and religion, which Whitman called "vast and profound" because it respected the "principle of life in all things–even in animals. It respected truth and justice above all other attributes of men. It recognized immortality." Whitman points out that the sages of Greece, Rome, and western Europe learned everything they knew from the Egyptians, some of whom were Africans and some of whom were "red," though at that time there were not such strong categories. According to the volume's editors, in 1859 a number of "lovers of antiquity" began raising the money to buy the collection, then the New-York Historical Society took it over.

95. *Smythe* See n. 125.22, NNJ, 519, and see the two-part article by Harrison Hayford and Merrell R. Davis, "Herman Melville as Office-Seeker," *Modern Language Quarterly,* June 1949, 168–83, and September 1949, 377–88.

96. *Faust and Luther* NNJ, 126.

97. Bellows, "The Moral Significance of the Crystal Palace," pamphlet, N-YHS.

98. *Turner* NNJ, 128.

99. *"Packed"* Ibid., 129.

100. *"The Age of the Antonines"* CP, 235.

21. A CONVULSED AND HALF-DISSOLVED SOCIETY

1. *"country"* AM to PG, 4/7/57, Leyda, *Log,* 567.

2. Longer excerpts of these reviews can be found in Leyda, *Log,* 570ff., and in the "Historical Note" to NN *C-M.* *"entertaining"* The Athenaeum, 11 April 1857, Leyda, *Log,* 570. *"touches"* The Leader, 1 April 1857, ibid. *"humor"* The Critic 15 April 1857, ibid., 272. *"indeed"* Literary Gazette, 11 April 1857, ibid., 570. *"masquerade"* The Westminister and Foreign Quarterly Review, 1 July 1858, ibid., 581. *"age"* The Saturday Review, Leyda, *Log,* 579, and NN *C-M,* 327.

3. *"tendencies"* Putnam's Magazine, April 1857, quoted in NN *C-M,* 318–19.

4. The Boston *Puritan Recorder* prescribed reading the book as a cure for dyspepsia; conversely, the *Newark Daily Advertiser* accused Melville of suffering from dyspepsia when he wrote the book. *"story"* Philadelphia *North American,* 4 April 1857. *"successes," backward/forward quip* Mrs. Stephen's Illustrated New Monthly, June 1857, NN *C-M,* 320.

5. *"notions"* Worcester Palladium, 22 April 1857, NN *C-M,* 320. *"vagaries"* New York Daily Times, 11 April 1857, NN *C-M,* 319. *"distorted"* Berkshire County Eagle, 19 June 1857, NN *C-M,* 320. *"humorous"* LSjr. to SS, 4/21/57, Leyda *Log,* 574.

6. *"health"* ESM's memoir (BA), quoted in Leyda, *Log,* 578. *"life"* HSG, diary, Leyda, *Log,* 579. *"himself"* HSG, diary, Leyda, *Log,* 579.

7. *"Custom House"* LSjr. to SS, 6/2/57, Leyda, *Log,* 580. *Brooklyn house* See Patricia Barber, "Herman Melville's House in Brooklyn," *American Literature* 45 (November 1973), 433–34.

8. *advertisements,* 24 and 26 June 1857, Leyda, *Log,* 580. *down payment* See Barber, "Herman Melville's House," 434.

9. *The Atlantic Monthly* Phillips, Sampson & Co. to HM, 8/17?/57, NN *Corr.,* 654, and HM to Phillips, Sampson & Co., 8/19/57, NN *Corr.,* 310.

10. *"presume"* GWC to AMjr., 9/10/57, Leyda, *Log,* 582 and NN *Corr.* headnote, 311. *"5 Points"* HM to GWC, 9/15/57, NN *Corr.,* 313–14.

11. *"derangement"* Kenneth Stampp, *America in 1857: A Nation on the Brink* (New York: Oxford University Press, 1990), 225.

12. *"nothing"* Ibid.

13. *"bad practice"* Louis Auchincloss, ed., *The Hone & Stone Diaries of Old Manhattan* (New York: Abbeville Press, 1989), 168. *"corruption"* Ibid., 29. *"siege"* Stampp, 227–28. *"siege"* Ibid., 170.

14. *Walker* Stampp, *America in 1857,* 194.

15. *financiers* See Philip S. Foner, *Business and Slavery: The New York Merchants and The Irrepressible Conflict* (Chapel Hill: University of North Carolina Press, 1941).

16. *Webster* Stampp, *America in 1857,* 30; *"disgrace"* The Journals and Miscellaneous Notebooks of Ralph Waldo Emerson, edited by Susan Sutton Smith and Harrison Hayford, vol. 14 (Cambridge, Mass.: Harvard University Press, 1978), 170. *"pashas"* Ibid., 26. *"monster"* Stampp, *America in 1857,* 30.

17. *"Ye hypocrites," etc.* Ibid., 25. *"system"* John Hope Franklin, *From Slavery to Freedom: A History of Negro Americans* (New York: Vintage Books, 1969), 268.

18. *Lyceum Movement* See Daniel J. Boorstin, *The Americans: The National Experience* (New York: Vintage Books, 1965), 314–18. *"fixed institution"* Harper's Weekly, quoted by Boorstin, ibid., 315.

19. *"rejoice"* MAAM to LS, 10/31/57, Leyda, *Log,* 584. Stedman (New York *World,* 11 October 1891) credited Curtis with persuading Melville to lecture, Leyda, *Log,* 583. *"cadences"* Lawrence *Courier,* 15 November 1857, Leyda, *Log,* 584.

20. Merton M. Sealts, *Melville as Lecturer* (Cambridge, Mass.: Harvard University Press, 1957), is an indispensable starting place. Reconstructed texts of each lecture based on Sealts's research for this book can be found among the "other prose pieces," NN *PT,* 398–423. *"art"* NN *PT,* 408.

21. *"spectators"* NN *PT,* 404.

22. *"stone"* Ibid., 407.

23. *"horse"* Clarksville Daily Enquirer, 3 February 1858, Leyda, *Log,* 590. *"Apollo"* Bunker Hill Aurora, 13 February 1857, Leyda, *Log,* 592.

24. *"disquisitions"* HSG to PG, 11/23/57, Leyda, *Log,* 584. *"judgement"* HSG to PG, 12/9/57, Leyda, *Log,* 586.

25. *Reviews* See Sealts, *Melville as Lecturer,* and the "Historical Note" to NN *PT,* 518–22. *"child"* Auburn Daily Advertiser, Leyda, *Log,* supplement, 942, erroneously identified as "The South Seas," in Leyda, *Log,* 588.

26. *tour proceeds* Sealts, *Melville as Lecturer.*

27. *"severe crick"* ESM memoir, BA, Merton M. Sealts, Jr., *The Early Lives of Melville: Nineteenth-Century Biographical Sketches of Their Authors* (Madison: University of Wisconsin Press, 1974), 169. *"woods"* GD to ED, 8/24/58, Leyda, *Log,* 594–95. *"grace"* GD to RB, 7/7/58, Leyda, *Log,* 594. *"feet"* GD to ED, 9/12/58, Leyda, *Log,* 594.

28. *"conduct"* LS to LSjr., 9/19/58, Leyda, *Log,* 595. *"woman"* GD to Rosalie Baker, 10/4/58, Leyda, *Log,* 595.

29. *eyes* "cutting the leaves by way of pastime–as it wont do to read at present," HM to GD, 11/6/58, NN *Corr.,* 326–27. *"winter"* LS to HM, 11/8/58, NN *Corr.,* 662–63.

30. *"white man," "innocent"* NN *PT,* 415–16.

31. *"hospitals"* NN *PT,* 420. *"thoughts"* Berkshire County Eagle, 17 December 1858, Leyda, *Log,* 597. *"fee"* HM to GD, 12/20/58, NN *Corr.,* 332.

32. "literati" *Evening Express*(?), 8 February 1859, Leyda, *Log,* 601. *"attention"* HSG to CSG, 2/8/58, Leyda, *Log,* 600. *"himself"* HSG to CSG, 2/8/58, Leyda, *Log,* 601.

33. "*ease*," "*enchantment*"   Milwaukee *Daily Sentinel* (?), 26 February 1859, Leyda, *Log*, 603. "*infliction*"   Rockford *Republican*, 3 March 1859, Leyda, *Log*, 603.

34. *baby*   OR to HM, 2/4/59, NN*Corr*., 667. *snow*   MM to his cousin Maria Melville, 2/13/59, Leyda, *Log*, 602.

35. "*Fayaway*"   TMC to his mother, Leyda, *Log*, 605.

36. "*profane*"   Ibid.

37. "*nose*"   JTG, journal, Leyda, *Log*, 604–5.

38. "*complacency*"   Ibid., 605–6.

39. "*train*"   Ibid., 605.

40. "*doing nothing*"   ED to GD, 7/30/59, Leyda, *Log*, 607. "*Pieces*"   HM to Harper & Brothers, 5/18/59, NN*Corr*., 336. These "pieces" probably were poems.

41. *poem*   NN*Corr*., 336–39.

42. *grasshopper*   Leyda, *Log*, 607. *Willis*   Ibid. "*inheritance*"   LS to HM, 5/15/60, NN*Corr*., 673.

43. "*guides*"   NN*PT*, 422. *fleas*   Gansevoort-Lansing Collection, NPL.

44. "*travel*"   NN*PT*, 423.

45. "*ill*"   SM to GD, 11/21/59, Leyda, *Log*,, 609.

46. Gay Wilson Allen, "Emerson's Audience," *Ariel: A Review of International English Literature* 7, no. 3 (Calgary, Alberta: University of Calgary, 1 July 1976), 99. *Beecher*   Quote about voice is from Constance Mayfield Rourke, *Trumpets of Jubilee* (New York: Harcourt, Brace & Co., 1927), 171.

47. *Brown*   "The Portent," from *The Battle-Pieces of Herman Melville,* edited, with an introduction and notes, by Hennig Cohen (New York: Thomas Yoseloff, 1963), 35.

48. "*profound secret*"   ESM to ED, 6/23/60, Leyda, *Log*, 620.

49. *Lincoln*   Walter Donald Kring, *Henry Whitney Bellows* (Boston: Skinner House, 1979), 213, and Stefan Lorant, *Lincoln: A Picture Story of His Life* (New York: W. W. Norton, 1969), 169. "*house divided*"   See Marvin Fisher, *Going Under: Melville's Short Fiction and the American 1850's* (Baton Rouge and London: Louisiana State University Press, 1977), 179, and George B. Forgie, *House Divided: A Psychological Interpretation of Lincoln and His Age* (New York: W. W. Norton, 1979).

50. "*beneficial to you*"   LS to HM, 5/15/60, NN*Corr*., 672–73.

51. "*elements*"   HM to ED from Pittsfield, 5/21/60, NN*Corr*., 342. "*insignificant*"   HM to AM, 5/22/60, NN*Corr*., 344–46.

52. "*lazy latitudes*"   HM to ED, 5/28/60, NN*Corr*., 345–46.

53. "*aversion*"   ESM to ED, 6/1/60, Leyda, *Log*, 618. "*think*"   ESM to ED, 6/4/60, Leyda, *Log*, 618.

54. "*pay*"   CS to ED, 6/19/60, Leyda, *Log*, 619–20.

55. "*dull*"   ESM to ED, 6/23/60, Leyda, *Log*, 620.

56. "*sails*"   NN*J*, 132.

57. "*Doldrums*,"   Ibid., 132–33.

58. "*wild people*," *etc.*   Ibid., 133–34.

59. "*happen*"   Ibid., 134.

60. "*deck*"   Ibid., 134.

61. *happened*   HM to MM, 9/1, 16/60, NN*Corr*., 349.

62. "*acquaintance*"   Ibid.

63. "*Papa*"   HM to Bessie, 9/2/60, NN*Corr*., 350–54.

64. *sketch*   see NN*PT*, 638–44.

65. For Starr King's career and his talent for mimicry, see Kring, *Henry Whitney Bellows,* 216, and NN*J*, 201–2. In a letter to Julius Rockwell, Oliver Wendell Holmes praised King's oratorical talents over those of Ralph Waldo Emerson, "the prince of New England lecturers," Wendell Phillips, and Theodore Parker. OWH to JR, 12/3/52 (Rockwell Papers, Lenox Library).

66. *Aspinwall, Vanderbilt lines*   NN*J*, 204–6. "*worst place*"   Dana, Journal, III, 842, quoted in NN*J*, 205.

67. *letter*   Unlocated, see NN*Corr*., 355. "*health*"   MGM to PG, 11/5/60, Leyda, *Log*, 629. It's not known whether Melville tried to get back in time to vote once he made up his mind to cut his trip short; nor do we know how he would have voted, or how he felt about the election results. As Stanton Garner

points out in his study *The Civil War World of Herman Melville* (Lawrence: University Press of Kansas, 1993), most members of Melville's family were Democrats. Garner presumes Herman would have voted Democratic, too, but I feel there is room for doubt about this, if not in 1860, then certainly in 1864. In a note to his poem "The Victor of Antietam," Melville wrote: "Some there are whose votes aided in the reelection of Abraham Lincoln, who yet believed, and retain the belief, that General McClellan, to say the least, always proved himself a patriotic and honorable soldier, *The Battle-Pieces of Herman Melville* (see note 47, above), 233. This suggests that Melville may himself have voted for Lincoln the second time. Both John Hoadley and Dr. Amos Nourse were Republicans, and Melville had reservations about the ideology of the Democratic Party, which seemed neither Federalist nor Democratic-Republican in the Jeffersonian sense. His silence on the subject could be indicative of his avoidance of partisan politics, or it could indicate that he was still searching for an ideological home.

68. *New York*   Foner, *Business and Slavery,* 226ff.

69. "*limb of Satan*"   GTS, 10/13/60, Auchincloss, *Hone & Strong,* 197.

70. "*banquet*," *etc.*   HM and ESM to SM, 12/2/60, Leyda, *Log*, supplement, 944.

71. "*gallant Tom*"   "To the Master of the *Meteor,*" *CP*, 196. The two brothers, who were eleven years apart, had not spent an extended period of time together since their childhood, so spending 134 days at sea together as adults may have brought them closer than ever before.

72. Where possible, dates for these poems will be established when Robert Ryan's eagerly awaited edition of Melville's poetry is published. As of this writing, however, Ryan reports that he has found it difficult, if not impossible, to date the composition of most of them. At the moment, Howard P. Vincent's *Collected Poems of Herman Melville* (cited elsewhere herein as *CP*) remains the definitive edition.

22. FIERCE BATTLES AND CIVIL STRIFE

1. "*oath*"   RTG to HM, 1/4/61, NN*Corr*., 678–79.

2. *Pine Street meeting*   Philip S. Foner, *Business and Slavery: The New York Merchants, and the Irrepressible Conflict* (Chapel Hill: University of North Carolina Press, 1941). Lathers was a colonel in the 31st Regiment of the State of South Carolina during the Mexican War. See the *Reminiscences of Richard Lathers: Sixty Years of a Busy Life in South Carolina, Massachusetts and New York,* edited by Alvan F. Sanborn (New York: The Grafton Press, 1947), especially 91ff., also the volume entitled "(This Discursive) *Biographical Sketch 1841–1902 of Colonel Richard Lathers,* compiled as required for honorary members in Post 509, Grand Army of the Republic, embracing a Sixty Years' Residence in South Carolina, New York and Massachusetts: Devoted Actively to Commerce, Agriculture, Insurance, Banking, and Railroad Enterprise, *with these multifarious occupations in three of the most controversial if not the most distinguished States in the Union, he participated in all the discussions, rights, and duties of citizenship in perfect harmony and unobstructed by sectional or party prejudices*" (Philadelphia: J. B. Lippincott Co., 1902), 10.

3. *Star of the West   Harper's Weekly,* 10 January 1861.

4. "*honest face*"   *The Diary of George Templeton Strong,* vol. 3, *The Civil War, 1860–1865,* edited by Allan Nevins and Milton Halsey Thomas (New York: Macmillan, 1952). "*faces*"   Gay Wilson Allen, *The Solitary Singer* (Chicago: University of Chicago Press, 1985), 271.

5. Pseudoscientific racial theories abounded, viz. Josiah Clark Nott and George R. Gliddon, *Types of Mankind: or, Ethnological Researches, Based upon the Ancient Monuments, Paintings, Sculptures, and Crania of Races, and upon Their Natural, Geographical, Philological, and Biblical History* (1854). See Carolyn L. Karcher's analysis of racist ethnology in *Shadow Over the Promised Land: Slavery, Race and Violence in Melville's America*

(Baton Rouge: Louisiana State University Press, 1980); *"dwarf"* Strong, *Diary* vol. 3, 12; *"disgusting"* Stanton Garner, *The Civil War World of Herman Melville* (Lawrence: University Press of Kansas, 1993), 23.

6. *"knife"* Allen, *Solitary Singer*, 271.

7. *embankment* Strong, *Diary*, 102.

8. *"mind"* LS to AM, 2/2?/61, Leyda, *Log*, 634.

9. *petitions* JCH to CS, 3/11/61, Leyda, *Log*, 634. AWB to AL, before 3/20?/61, Leyda, *Log*, 635. JCH to AL, 3/19/61, Leyda, *Log*, 635.

10. *Weed* See Leyda, *Log*, 535ff. *Dana* HM to RHDjr., 3/20/61, NN *Corr.*, 362–63, and RHDjr. to CS, 3/21?/61, Leyda, *Log*, 636–37. *Rockwell* HM to JR, 3/20/61, NN *Corr.*, 363–64. JR to CS, 3/25/61 (National Archives of the State Department), Leyda, *Log*, 638.

11. *levee* HM to ESM, 3/22/61, Leyda, *Log*, 637. *beard* Lorant, *Lincoln/Picture Story*, 114.

12. *monument* HM to ESM, 3/24/61, NN *Corr.*, 364–67. The 555-foot-high shaft was designed by a neoclassical architect from South Carolina named Robert Mills. Lally Weymouth, *America in 1876: The Way We Were* (New York: Vintage Books, 1976), 104–5. See also Constance McLaughlin Green, *Washington: A History of the Capitol, 1800–1950* (Princeton, N.J.: Princeton University Press, 1976). In 1848, as two hundred men, escorted by fifes and drums, were hauling the ten-ton cornerstone to the site "on a great wagon with ropes," one of the wagon wheels broke through the rotted planks, and the stone had to be left until they could pry it loose and move it with blocks and rollers the next day, according to Julius Rockwell, writing to his son William Walker Rockwell, 6/7/48, Rockwell Papers, Lenox Library. Work on the monument came to a halt in 1854 because the funding ran out. In 1876, shortly before Congress appropriated money for its completion, Mark Twain described it as having "the aspect of a factory chimney with the top broken off" and a "skeleton of a decaying scaffolding [lingering] about its summit." *"Washington"* Strong, *Diary*, vol. 3, 164.

13. *dome* Constance McLaughlin Green, *Washington* (Princeton, New Jersey: Princeton University Press, 1962), 200. Michael Paul Rogin, *Subversive Genealogy: The Politics and Art of Herman Melville* (New York: Alfred A. Knopf, 1983), 71, calls Melville's "Iron Dome" a "prison," which distorts Melville's meaning.

14. *"Herman"* HM to ESM, 3/25/61, NN *Corr.*, 367.

15. *appointments* Harry J. Carman and Reinhard H. Luthin, *Lincoln and the Patronage* (New York: Columbia University Press, 1943), 104.

16. *Judge Shaw's death* HSS diary, 3/30/61, Leyda, *Log*, 639.

17. *"enemy"* Lathers, *Reminiscences*, 166–72.

18. *"newsboys"* Allen, *Solitary Singer*, 272. *Seventh Regiment*, Stanton Garner, "Melville and Sandford [sic] Gifford," *Melville Society Extracts* 48 (November 1981), 10–12, 23. Both men were on duty in Washington without seeing any fighting; after a month, the Seventh was given an early leave for having been first to serve. Gifford remained with the regiment, but Gansevoort asked for a commission and was reassigned.

19. *Allen Guard* Joseph Edward Allen Smith, *History of Pittsfield, 1800–1876*, 2 vols., 611ff and 626.

20. *patriotism* George M. Frederickson, *The Inner Civil War: Northern Intellectuals and the Crisis of the Union* (New York: Harper & Row, 1965), 65. *rally* John A. Kouwenhoven, *The Columbia Historical Portrait of New York: An Essay in Graphic History* (New York: Icon Editions, Harper and Row, 1972), 261. *Coan* Ernest A. McKay, *The Civil War and New York City* (Syracuse, N.Y.: Syracuse University Press, 1990), 126–27. *Thurston* Stanton Garner, *The Civil War World of Herman Melville* (Lawrence: University Press of Kansas, 1993), 93.

21. *"divine"* Iver Bernstein, *The New York City Draft Riots: Their Significance for American Society and Politics in the Age of the Civil War* (New York: Oxford University Press, 1990), 156. *Tiresias* I am thinking of the prophet's warning to the

tyrant Creon in *Antigone*, movingly delivered by John Gielgud.

22. *"Misgivings"* Looking through the Melville hymnal owned by the Berkshire Historical Society, I was struck by how many such nautical metaphors appear in Protestant hymns.

23. *Blackwell* McKay, *Civil War and New York City*, 66. *Raymond* Ibid., 85ff.

24. *Eliza Bellows* Walter Donald Kring, *Henry Whitney Bellows* (Boston: Skinner House, 1979), 227ff.

25. *Mrs. Fenn* Garner, *Civil War World*. *homelike* A point made in Glenna Matthews's excellent book *"Just a Housewife": The Rise and Fall of Domesticity in America* (New York: Oxford University Press, 1987). *"knitting"* CMS, quoted in Sarah Cabot Sedgwick and Christina Sedgwick Marquand, *Stockbridge 1739–1935: A Chronicle* (Great Barrington, Mass.: The Berkshire Courier, 1939), 235–36. *blackberry wine* Elizabeth Black to Frank Rockwell, 8/23/60, Rockwell Papers, Lenox Library.

26. *"stems"* SM to HSS, 7/11/61, HCL.

27. *Guert, Ward, and the "iniquity"* ED's diary, 7/3/61, Leyda, *Log*, 641. *ports The Dangers and Defenses of New York*, prepared for Secretary of War J. B. Floyd by Maj. John Gross Brainard, Corps of Engineers, U.S.A., by order of Chamber of Commerce (New York: D. Van Nostrand, 1859). *Opdyke* See McKay, *Civil War and New York City*, 87, 134–37.

28. *Lathers* Readers are advised to consult Hennig Cohen, "Melville and the Art Collection of Richard Lathers," *Melville Society Extracts* 99 (December 1994), 1–26, which includes illustrations and a detailed inventory, in the same issue, Eric Collum and Hershel Parker provide "Suggestions for Further Research" in their article "The Lost Lathers Collections," 26–28. *"high strawberry time"* RL to EAD, 6/28/61, Duyckinck Papers, NYPL. *"times" and "Bear"* ED's diary, 7/3/61, Leyda, *Log*, 641.

29. *drill* SM to HSS, 7/11/61, HCL; Stannie's letter to Hope Shaw summarizes The events of several weeks, perhaps because Aunt Augusta or Grandmother Melville made him sit down and write a letter that could be shared with the Boston relatives. *Pollock Guard* The Tenth Berkshire Regiment's Company D was called the Pollock Guard after a benefactor. J. E. A. Smith, *History of Pittsfield, 1800–1876*, vol. 2, 615–16.

30. *"poor"* SM to HSS, 7/11/61, HCL.

31. *place names* See Geoffrey C. Ward, et al., *The Civil War: An Illustrated History* (New York: Alfred A. Knopf, 1990), 69 and 267, for an explanation of the differences in the names by which North and South designated memorable battle sites. *"secessionists"* Strong, *Diary*, 169.

32. "The March into Virginia, ending in the First Manassas (July, 1861)," *The Battle-Pieces of Herman Melville*, edited, with an introduction and notes, by Hennig Cohen (New York: Thomas Yoseloff, 1963), 42–44.

33. *"sons"* LMC to Henrietta Sargent, 7/26/61, *The Letters of Lydia Maria Child* (Boston: 1884), 154.

34. "Lyon. Battle of Springfield, Missouri. (August, 1861)," *Battle-Pieces*, 44–46. Lyon was born in 1819. Evert Duyckinck included a full-page picture of him in his magazine *History of the Civil War* (1862), and in the copy of *Battle-Pieces* inscribed by Herman for Lizzie, someone has preserved a tiny newspaper clipping about Lyon; the item directly above mentions accusations about plagiarism against Paley's *Natural Theology*. A copy of the poem at Harvard's Houghton Library shows that Melville changed "pale" to "brave."

35. *"Stuff"* Leyda, *Log*, 642, as in the expression "stuff and nonsense."

36. *"eyes"* HM to PG, 8/15/61, NN *Corr.*, 371–72.

37. *Tom and John D'Wolf* Leyda, *Log*, 644ff.

38. *"rheumatism"* HM to ED, 2/1?/62, NN *Corr.*, 372–73.

39. *"Armida"* Underscored in Isaac Disraeli, *The Literary Character; or the History of Men of Genius, Drawn from their own Feelings and Confessions; Literary Miscellanies; and an Inquiry into*

the Character of James the first...A New Edition, Edited By His Son, the Right Hon. B. Disraeli (London: Routledge, 1859), Leyda, *Log*, 645–46, and Merton M. Sealts Jr., *Melville's Reading*, revised and enlarged edition (Charleston: University of South Carolina Press, 1988), 173. Thomas Hood, in "The Poet's Fate," *The Poetical Works*, 2 vols. (Boston: Little, Brown, 1860), Leyda, *Log*, 645–46 and Sealts, *Melville's Reading*, 186–87.

40. *bullets* Ward, *Civil War...Illustrated*, 265.

41. *Fredericksburg* Allen, *Solitary Singer*, 282–86. *fifty-thousand men* Green, *Washington*, 261. *"real war"* "The Wound-Dresser," in Walt Whitman, *Leaves of Grass*, edited and with an introduction by Sculley Bradley (New York: Holt, Rinehart and Winston, 1949), 258. Walt Whitman *Specimen Days* (New York: Signet Books, 1961), 111. Louisa May Alcott, *Hospital Sketches* (Chester, Conn.: Applewood Books, Globe Pequot Press, n.d.; orig. 1869).

42. *"guerdon"* *Harper's Weekly*, 6 September 1862, 570.

43. *"moment"* Whitman, *Specimen Days*, 59. Men also suffered chronic complaints. Lumped together under the fashionable label "neuraesthenia," they included a multitude of psychosomatic and psychogenic ills, perhaps even some of the Melvilles' ailments. For more information, see George Frederick Drinka, *The Birth of Neurosis: Myth, Malady and the Victorians* (New York: Simon & Schuster, 1984).

44. "The Stone Fleet. An Old Sailor's Lament. (December, 1861)," *Battle-Pieces*, 49–51, notes, 217–19. *Mallory* William M. Fowler Jr., *Under Two Flags: The American Navy in the Civil War* (New York: Avon Books, 1990), 45.

45. *ships* See *Harper's Weekly*, 19 February 1861, 92.

46. "The Cumberland (March, 1862)," *Battle-Pieces*, 63–65. *Monitor* Ward, *Civil War...Illustrated*, 99; *"glory"* "In the Turret (March, 1862)," *Battle-Pieces*, 67.

47. *"wings of war"* "The Temeraire," *Battle-Pieces*, 69. Melville owned an engraving of Turner's painting by James T. Willmore, as Cohen (224) points out.

48. "A Utilitarian View of the Monitor's Fight," *Battle-Pieces*, 69–70. The Rodman gun on the *Monitor*'s deck was manufactured not far from Pittsfield, at the Richmond Iron Works, accordinng to *The Berkshire Hills: A WPA Guide*, with a new foreword by Roger B. Linscott (Boston: Northeastern University Press, 1987 [orig. 1933]).

49. *Harper's Weekly*, 1 March 1862; it visually prefigures the monument erected at Iwo Jima after World War II. "Donelson (February, 1862)," *Battle-Pieces*, 51–63. According to Frank Moore, ed., *The Rebellion Record: A Diary of American Events, with Documents, Narratives, Illustrative Incident, Poetry, etc.*, vol. 9 (New York: D. Van Nostrand, 1985), Grant realized the fort's defenders would not stay because when he learned from a deserter that the men had been given a full six days' rations the previous day, he attacked soon afterward.

50. *"Bunker Hill"* *Battle-Pieces*, 58. *placard* "Donelson, II. 184–89, *Battle-Pieces*, 56.

51. "Shiloh. A Requiem. (April, 1862)," *Battle-Pieces*, 71–72.

52. *"cut in two"* Mary Chesnut's *Diary*, quoted in Ward, 127.

53. "The Battle for the Mississippi. (April, 1862)," *Battle-Pieces*, 72–74 and 230. Melville based his description on a report by the son of the commander of the legendary *Essex* in the Pacific during the World War of 1812, Commander David Porter, who served with Farragut.

54. *"letters of soldiers"* Caroline S. Whitmarsh, *Springfield Republican*, 21 October 1863; reprinted in the *Berkshire County Eagle*, 29 October 1863, as reported by Hershel Parker with Edward Daunais, "Sarah Morewood's last Drive, as told in Caroline S. Whitmarsh's 'A Representative Woman,'" *Melville Society Extracts* 93 (June, 1993), 3. *beef tea* FMT to EMM, 4/30/1925, Melville Family Papers, HCL. *Kitty* Katherine Gansevoort Melville to SM from New Rochelle, 3/25/62, GLA. *"socks"* MGM to CG, 1/6/62, Leyda, *Log*, 644.

55. *Twain, quartermaster* I'm indebted to Garner, *Civil War World*, 142–43 and 270, for this information.

56. See *Harper's Weekly*, 15 February 1862, 108.

57. *"prayers"* SM to AM, 4/24/62, GLA.

58. Several casual references in letters indicate that home tutoring was taken for granted: "Every day Aunt Fanny had school she had four scholars. Lucy was one of them," SM to HSS, 7/11/62, HCL; "We only have spelling lessons while Mama is so sick," Bessie to AM, 5/26/62, GLA.

59. *fire* Sam Shaw's diary, 3/1/62, MHS. *"topsy-turvy"* SM to AM, 4/30/62, GLA. *"all over"* SM to AM, 5/8/62, GLA. *horse* Names of Melville horses are confusing. Her letter refers to a five-year-old named Charley, which makes me think he was a successor to the old Charlie. *wages* Leyda, *Log*, 650.

60. "Mackey rides him almost every day," Bessie wrote Augusta, 5/26/62, GLA. *friends* SM to AM, 5/24/62, GLA. *Latin* HM to TM, 5/25/62, *NNCorr.*, 376–78.

61. *tools* EMM to FTM, 8/29/1919, HCL. Fanny claimed her father could not handle tools, but he seems to have been handy enough in his sailor days; perhaps he had some arthritis in his hands, which might also explain the slowdown in his phenomenal rate of production of manuscripts.

62. *"humanity"* HM to TM, 5/25/62, *NNCorr.*, 367–77.

63. *"admiration"* Ibid.

64. *"victory"* Ibid. *"abstinent"* Garner, *Civil War World*, 170.

65. *Madeira* Alice P. Kenney, *The Gansevoorts of Albany* (Syracuse, New York: Syracuse University Press, 1969), 248, and Leyda, *Log*, 654. In an article, Garner, *Civil War World*, 12, writes, "Flag Officer Samuel F. DuPont came to Guert Gansevoort's defense after the latter had wrecked his fine new ship, *Adirondack*, in the Caribbean, and Melville wrote 'Du Pont's Round Fight' for him."

66. "Malvern Hill (July, 1862)," *Battle-Pieces*, 74–76. Garner, "Melville/Gifford," 12, points out that Henry was at Malvern Hill as well as Antietam. *"heart," "enemy," "killed"* SM to WBM, 8/24/62 (Collection of the Berkshire County Historical Society at Arrowhead).

67. See SM to AM, 5/24/62 and 6/8/62, GLA.

68. *excursion* Sam's Shaw's diary, 8/25–26/62, MHS. *"ardent and indefatigable"* Joseph Edward Adams Smith, *Taghconic, the Romance and Beauty of the Hills* (Boston: Lee and Shepard; New York: Charles T. Dillingham; Pittsfield, Mass.: S.E. Nichols, 1879), 199.

69. *chestnuts* SM to AM, 10/8/62. *"heart"* HM's Emerson marginalia, Leyda, *Log*, 648.

70. *"blood"* Strong, *Diary*, 260–61.

71. *Brady* McKay, *Civil War and New York City*, 158.

72. *Antietam* William Gienapp, "Trying to Understand the Horror of America's Civil War," *Harvard Gazette*, 20 November, 1992, 6. "The Victor of Antietam. (1862)," *Battle-Pieces*, 76–79. "Only Antietam could atone."

73. J. E. A. Smith, "Biographical Sketch of Herman Melville, 1892," in *History of Pittsfield*. Oddly, the one account of the accident, Smith's own, does not specify which arm was injured, though Smith's comment about the interruption to Melville's work suggests it might have been his writing arm.

74. *walking vs. riding* "He has walked a great deal, which I think is better exercise for him than riding so much–he walked out to the farm the other day & back without injury," ESM to AM, 2/11/63, GLA. *drove fast* Melville later drove to Glens Falls to see the Curtises, for example.

75. *"value"* HM to SS, 12/10/62, *NNCorr.*, 381–82.

76. *"cares"* Ibid.

77. *gifts* SM to AM, 12/30/62, GLA.

78. *Malcolm* HMG to AM, 1/25/63, GLA: "Mackie has written that he's taking writing lessons and 'likes to live in the village first rate,'" GLA. *acting* HMG to AM, 3/6/63, GLA. *skating* SM to AM, 12/30/62. *"funny"* SM to AM, 3/3/63, GLA. Stannie's letters often appear quite a while after events

described in them, probably because, like most young people, he had to be prodded by grown-ups to write.

79. *minstrels* ST to AM, 3/3/63, GLA.

80. *"fig"* from doggerel verse addressed to Abraham Lincoln by an anonymous Berkshire poet: "Our mothers love their absent sons / Our wives their husbands true, / but no one cares a mouldy fig / For Cuffy or for you," quoted in Garner, *Civil War World*, 219. "Cuffy," like "Sambo," was a popular epithet for the Negro. *"glory"* Child quoted by Frederickson in *Inner Civil War*, 119.

81. *Douglass* "Free the Slaves, Then Leave Them Alone," an address to the Emancipation League in Boston, 1862, from "The Future of the Negro People of the Slave States," *Douglass' Monthly* (March 1862). *freed Negroes* *Harper's Weekly*, 21 February 1863, 116.

82. In a letter to Julius Rockwell, 7/1/63 (Rockwell Papers, Lenox Library), Davis admits that the Emancipation Proclamation had divided the West and that "the Southern people are increasing in hatred to us."

83. *drawing paper and pincushion* Bessie to AM, 2/10/63, GLA.

84. *"epoch"* HM to CG, 2/17/63, NN *Corr.*, 383.

85. *"grumbling"* ESM to AM, 2/11/63, GLA. *"faculties"* HMG to AM, 2/25/63?, GLA.

86. *"goings-on"* MESM to AM, 3/4/63, GLA. *correction* HGM to AM, 3/6/63, GLA. I have repunctuated this letter slightly to improve its clarity, as Helen wrote hurriedly and evidently did not read her letters over.

87. *fashions* HGM to FSM, 3/6/63, GLA.

88. *snowballs* HMG to AM, 3/22/63, GLA.

89. *"Miss Gusty"* ESM to AM, 4/10/63, GLA.

90. *bourbon* ESM to AM, 4/10/63, GLA. *"contraband"* MC to AM, 4/10/63, GLA—a current location for freed Negroes, as in *Harper's Weekly*, 24 January 1863, 68.

91. *legacy* ESM to AM, 10/16/63, GLA. *"beguiled"* MGM to AM, 5/11/63, GLA.

92. *Charlie and Kate and rabbits* SM to AM, 5/8/63, GLA. *catechism* SM to AM, 5/30/63, GLA.

93. *picnic* ESM to FM, 5/1?/63, GLA. *"Madam"* HMG to AM, 6/14/63, GLA. *shopping* ESM to FM, 6/14/63, GLA. Allan and Sophia had five children; Jane had none.

94. *cookstove, etc.* ESM to FM, 6/14/63, GLA. *"cold,"* *"dunce"* ESM to AM, 6/29/63, GLA.

95. *"new spirit"* DD to JR, 7/1/63, Rockwell Papers, Lenox Library. In his 8/19/63 letter, Davis also advises Rockwell not to let his son Will "command a Negro Regt I am in hopes that next winter we can get him placed in the regular army." When William Walker Rockwell was killed at Baton Rouge on December 4, 1863, Davis conveyed Lincoln's personal sympathies to Judge Rockwell. *pictures* See Thomas Nast's illustrations in *Harper's Weekly*, 31 January 1863 4 July 1863.

96. "Running the Batteries, As Observed from the Anchorage Above Vicksburgh. (April, 1863)," *Battle-Pieces*, 82–84, notes, 236–37. *Robert Melvill* Conjectured from HMG to AM, 2/25/63, GLA. *Toby* Inferred from RTG to HM, 10/20/63, NN *Corr.*, 693–94.

97. Henry got his position with the Guards with the help of Richard Lathers; see Fanny Melville to Augusta, 3/29/63, GLA. "Gettysburg. The Check," *Battle-Pieces,* 88.

98. *battle statistics* Ward, *Civil War...Illustrated*, 235–36. *"ended"* David Davis to Julius Rockwell, 8/19/63, Rockwell Papers, Lenox Library.

99. Alice P. Kenney, in "Sir Galahad and the Night of the Apron-String," *New York History* 51, no. 5 (October 1970), 501–522, says Henry Gansevoort's cavalry unit was called back to New York to put down the draft riots, but Henry was recuperating at the time. *poem* "The House-top: A Night Piece" (July 1863); see chapter 23 for a fuller discussion of both the riots and the poem.

100. *"popping, flashing"* JCH to AM, 7/10/63, GLA. *berries* FM to AM, 7/16/63, GLA.

101. *scenery* ESM to AM, 8/10/63, GLA. Melville may have written his short, nostalgic poems about Arrowhead retrospectively, after moving to New York, or he could have written them to read aloud to Lizzie and the family while they were there. As an earlier note indicates, it's impossible to tell, given the evidence we have.

102. Smith, *History of Pittsfield*, 620. *"fighting"* JRM to his son Willie (WBM), who was away at school in England, 8/26/63 (Morewood Papers, Berkshire County Historical Society).

103. See Leyda, *Log*, 662, and Warren Wilkinson, *Mother, May You Never See the Sights I Have Seen: The Fifty-Seventh Massachusetts Veteran Volunteers in the Army of the Potomac, 1864–65* (New York: Harper & Row, 1990), 20. *"Marches ... slow"* *Battle-Pieces*, 112–14. Bartlett's "Indian aloofness" may be picked up by Melville in his portrait of the Confederate soldier Ungar, in *Clarel*. The only parade Melville is known to have marched in was an academic procession celebrating the semicentennial anniversary of Albany Academy. On that occasion he sat on the dais to hear Alexander Bradford deliver an address extolling the virtues of the school founded by, among others, his uncle Peter.

104. *baptized* "September?" entry in Melville family Bible, Leyda, *Log*, 662. *schools* Fanny Melville Thomas contradicted Joseph Smith's contention that the Melvilles did not move back to the city because of the schools; according to Fanny, one of the main reasons for the move was so that the girls could go to school in New York City. Elizabeth Sedgwick died in 1864, but there were good schools in Berkshire County, i.e., the Pittsfield Female Academy.

105. *"How heavenly!"* ESM to AM, 10/16/63.

106. *wreath* ESM to AM, 10/28/63, GLA. *peaches* SM to AM, 9/30/63, GLA. *interment* JR to WMR, 1/1/63, Rockwell Papers, Lenox Library.

107. *carpets, etc.* ESM to AM, 10/28/63, GLA. *"botherations"* HM to Sophie Van Matre, 12/10/63, NN *Corr.*, 386.

108. *"vile habit"* HM to SVM, 12/10/63, NN *Corr.*, 386.

109. *"immense charred solitudes"* *Clarel: A Poem and Pilgrimage in the Holy Land*, IV, 5, II, 41–44 (Chicago and Evanston: Northwestern University Press and The Newberry Library, 1991), 401. These images could have come from *Harper's Weekly* or from photographs, and Melville most likely saw Brady's exhibit while in New York. Thus, despite the voluminous archival material available to scholars, Melville remains an enigma in many ways, his life a Gordian knot tossed to bemused biographers balanced at the edge of a volcano.

23. A TIME RICH IN CATAS-TROPHES

1. Information about the neighborhood can be found in Charles Neumeier and Donald Yannella, "The Melvilles' House on East 26th Street," *Melville Society Extracts* 47 (September 1981), 6–8; some of it comes from the priceless *Insurance Maps of the City of New York*, vol. 4, 1871, surveyed and published by Perris & Browne, 164 Fulton Street, preserved by the New-York Historical Society. My information about this neighborhood is based on research in old city guides at the New-York Historical Society.

2. For more information on the Union League Club, see George M. Frederickson's *The Inner Civil War: Northern Intellectuals and the Crisis of the Union* (New York: Harper & Row, 1965), 23, and Will Irwin, Earl Chapin May, and Joseph Hotchkiss, *A History of the Union League Club of New York City* (New York: Dodd, Mead, 1952).

3. I am indebted to Jean Ashton's Melville Centennial talk, September 26, 1991, for knowledge of this 1859 guide owned by the New-York Historical Society.

4. *"Trust in God"* Kenneth Silverman, *Edgar A. Poe, Mournful and Never-Ending Remembrance* (New York: HarperCollins, 1991), 233.

5. The number of the house was changed from 60 to 104 when Fourth Avenue was renumbered in 1868, but to avoid confusion, I refer to it consistently as number 104. Allan Melville's house number on Thirty-fifth Street also changed, as city directories in the New-York Historical Society and elsewhere show. *Restell* A social pariah despite her intimate relationships with the "best people" and the success of her business acumen had brought her, she longed, according to *Leslie's Illustrated,* "for the sympathy and respect that all her wealth cannot buy, even in this city, where we are told it can buy anything," Charles Lockwood, *Manhattan Moves Uptown: An Illustrated History* (Boston: Houghton-Mifflin, 1976), 95. Years later, when New York's one-man vice squad Anthony Comstock succeeded in sending her to the Tombs, she had the satisfaction of knowing the rich and powerful were trembling at the prospect of being named in court and featured in the tabloids. Released on bail, she returned home and–according to the newspaper reports–took her own life in 1878.

6. *sheds* Neumeier and Yannella, "Melvilles' House," 6.

7. Richard C. Doenges, "The Belle-Tower, or Diana's Polite Salute," *Melville Society Extracts* 52 (November 1982), 16. Powers's life-size statue of a nude female in chains eventually became a target of Anthony Comstock's fierce campaign against vice and pornography.

8. *dogs and boxers* Frederick Van Wyck, *Recollections of an Old New Yorker* (New York: Liveright, 1932), 113–14. Van Wyck was born in 1853; his paternal grandfather Stephen Van Wyck wore Revolutionary "small clothes" all his life, as Major Thomas Melvill did. Van Wyck's maternal grandfather, George W. Blunt, the author of *Blunt's Coast Pilot* and the editor of *Bowditch's Navigator,* was one of the first vice-presidents of the Union League Club, according to Van Wyck, and his wife was one of the signers of the "Presentation Address of the Ladies of the City of New York to the Officers and Men of the Twentieth United States Colored Troops," according to Irwin, May, and Hotichkiss, *History of the Union League Club,* 35. Van Wyck's charming anecdotal memoir gives a vivid picture of a boy's life in New York during the sixties, including the amusing pranks he and his friends played.

9. *milk* Ernest A. McKay, *The Civil War and New York City* (Syracuse, N.Y.: Syracuse University Press, 1990), 102. A prototype of Hearst's "yellow journalism," the *Herald* also ran personals columns that clergymen denounced as immoral, fit only for "gamblers, debauchees, profligate vagabonds."

10. *Tom Thumb* The wedding of Charles Stratton (a.k.a. General Tom Thumb) and Lavinia Warren was attended by everyone who was *anyone* in Manhattan, and even the President and Mrs. Lincoln sent the tiny couple gifts and invited them to tour the White House. Many parishioners, however, frowned on this "marriage of mountebanks" that displaced them from their own pews, according to Neil Harris, *Humbug: The Art of P. T. Barnum* (Chicago: University of Chicago Press, 1973), 163.

11. *"thereabouts"* Geoffrey C. Ward, et al., *The Civil War: An Illustrated History* (New York: Alfred A. Knopf, 1990), 242.

12. "The liberated Negroes, now working for wages, behave like Christians, bear no malice, and commit no outrages," George Templeton Strong observed. "Southern Cuffee seems of higher social grade than Northern Paddy," *The Diary of George Templeton Strong,* vol. 3, *The Civil War, 1860–1865,* edited by Allan Nevins and Milton Halsey Thomas (New York: Macmillan, 1952), 344–45.

13. Iver Bernstein's *The New York City Draft Riots: Their Significance for American Society and Politics in the Age of the Civil War* (New York: Oxford University Press, 1990) and Adrian Cook's *The Armies of the Streets: The New York City Draft Riots of 1863* (Lexington: University Press of Kentucky, 1974) put to rest George Templeton Strong's complaint that "Not half the history of this memorable week has been written. I could put down pages of incidents that the newspapers have omitted, any one of which would in ordinary times be the town's talk."

14. *Colored Orphan Asylum* Fortunately, most of the children escaped out a back door. See pictures, *Harper's Weekly,* 1 August 1863, 484–85. *"rebellion"* Strong, *Diary,* vol. 3, 336.

15. *"South"* Strong, *Diary,* vol. 3, 342. According to Mary P. Ryan, *Women in Public: Between Banners and Ballots, 1825–1880* (Baltimore: Johns Hopkins University Press, 1990), 149–150, white women chanted, "Go for the nigger, the sweet-scented nigger, the wool-headed nigger, and the whole abolitionist crew!" as they cut off body parts of black men for souvenirs.

16. *Treasury* Maunsell B. Field, *Memories of Many Men and of Some Women: Personal Recollections of Emperors, Kings, Queens, Princes, Presidents, Statesmen, Authors, and Artists, at Home and Broad, During the Last Thirty Years* (New York: Harper & Brothers, 1874), 260. Field, a diplomat who remembered Melville patting his trees at Arrowhead, was Assistant Secretary of the Treasury during the Lincoln administration. *Allan's address* New York City's Directory for 1863.

17. *"howitzers"* Strong, *Diary,* vol. 3, 340. *women* Ryan, *Women in Public,* 150–52.

18. *Dix* See Stanton Garner, The *Civil War World of Herman Melville* (Lawrence: University Press of Kansas, 1993), 277.

19. *"Devil's work!"* Gay Wilson Allen, *The Solitary Singer* (Chicago: University of Chicago Press, 1985), 307. *figures* McKay, *Civil War and New York City,* 209. *Jim Crow* Lydia Maria Child, *Selected Letters, 1877–1880,* edited by Milton Meltzer and Patricia G. Holland (Amherst: University of Massachusetts, 1982), 434; Charles Townsend Harris, *Memories of Manhattan in the Sixties and Seventies* (New York: Derrydale Press, 1928), 61.

20. *"mob"* DD to Julius Rockwell from Bloomington, Illinois, 7/28/63, Rockwell Papers, Lenox Library. The cover illustration of *Harper's Weekly,* September 5, 1863, depicted the drawing of the first name.

21. Bernstein points out that many of the signers of the Astor Place petition became members of the Union League. Melville, however, did not become a member.

22. "The House-top: A Night Piece," *The Battle-Pieces of Herman Melville,* edited, with an introduction and notes, by Hennig Cohen (New York: Thomas Yoseloff, 1963), 89.

23. Sirius is the "dog star." Although Thomas Nast is often credited with the first use of the tiger as a symbol of Tammany in cartoons exposing the corrupt machinations of the Tweed gang after the war, the tiger had been associated with Boss Tweed since 1851, when Joseph Johnson painted a red Bengal tiger on the Americus Club's powerful fire engine, "Big Six." See Andrew B. Callow, Jr., *The Tweed Ring* (New York: Oxford University Press, 1965), 13, and Leo Hershkowitz, *Tweed's New York: Another Look* (Garden City: Doubleday, 1977), 12. *"scourged"* "The House-top," *Battle-Pieces,* 89.

24. *"midst"* Olmstead, quoted by Bernstein, *Draft Riots,* 160. *Harper's Weekly,* 16 July 1863, 459.

25. *naval crews* William M. Fowler, Jr., *Under Two Flags: The American Navy in the Civil War* (New York: Avon Books, 1990), 164. *"Yes"* Quoted in Ward, *Civil War...Illustrated,* 249. *"freedom"* Thomas Wentworth Higginson, *Army Life in a Black Regiment* (New York: Collier Books, 1962), 251.

26. *"bungled"* Strong, *Diary,* vol. 3, 360. Wilkinson James, the younger brother of Alice, Henry, and William James, was wounded at Fort Wagner, but survived.

27. *"best culture"* Frederickson, *Inner Civil War,* 163.

28. See the poignant photograph by Alexander Gardner in *Harper's Weekly,* 24 November 1866, 740, for example.

29. *Toby* RTG to HM, 10/20/63, Leyda, *Log,* 663. *"unity"* Helen Melville Souther, 1863, from Hingham, GLA.

30. *"air"* "Look-out Mountain. The Night Fight. (November, 1863)," *Battle-Pieces,* 90–91.

31. *"night"* "Chattanooga. (November, 1863)," lines 55–64, *Battle-Pieces,* 93–94.

32. On Christmas Eve, Allan had invited Duyckinck to bring his boys over to see their Christmas tree, according to

AM to EAD, 12/24/63, Duyckinck Papers, NYPL. It's not always easy to tell whether or not wives were automatically included in such invitations, raising interesting questions for historians and biographers. *"go early"* HM to ED, 12/31/63, NN *Corr.*, 388–89. Garner, *Civil War World*, 279, speculates that other guests might have included members of the Thurston family and the young De Marinis, John D'Wolf's granddaughter Annie Downer and her husband, a Paris-born physician. John Hoadley, who had been in England assessing the British reactions to the war, returned in time for the holidays.

33. *appetite* AM to CG, 2/29/64, EMM, 202. *"old lady"* KC to CG, 2/13/64, Leyda, *Log*, 658.

34. *parade* Van Wyck, 109–10. May and Hotchkiss, *History of the Union League Club*, 35. The ladies' address is typical of the attitudes of patrician northerners toward the war.

35. *procession* Irwin, May, and Hotchkiss, *History of the Union League Club*, 34ff. Melville's name does not appear on lists of members of the Union League, though several close associates were members. According to the roster in *The Century, 1847–1946* (New York: The Century Association, 1947), Allan joined the Century Club in 1859, but Herman does not appear to have joined any of New York's many clubs for gentlemen. Henry Whitney Bellows was also a member of the Century Club.

36. *"niggers"* Irwin, May, and Hotchkiss, *History of the Union League Club*, 10.

37. *Melville and the Sanitary Fair* See Leyda, *Log*, 665. *"subserve"* HM to George McLaughlin, Cincinnati, 12/15/63, NN *Corr.*, 388. *Harper's Weekly* featured numerous illustrations of the fair throughout that month. Writer Caroline Kirkland, whom Melville had met in 1848, contracted paralysis as a result of her work for the Sanitary Fair. *"excitement," "population"* McKay, *Civil War and New York City*, 241. Dr. Bellows left the city on a trip with his wife on the opening day of the fair, according to Dr. Kring, 287.

38. *Brewster* Letter to Henry Sanford Gansevoort, 4/5/64, GLC. *Ebbitt House and theater* Stanton Garner, "Melville's Scout Toward Aldie," *Melville Society Extracts* 51 (September 1982), 5–16. I am heavily indebted to Garner's extensive research and this two-part article for information about Melville's Virginia trip, which he later incorporated into *The Civil War World of Herman Melville*.

39. Garner, "Melville's Scout," 8, and Leyda, *Log*, 666–67. Communications were slow at this point, and Henry, who was recovering from the flu, was also preoccupied with demands being put upon him by the mother of a new recruit. See Garner, "Scout," 9, and Alice P. Kenney's amusing article, "Sir Galahad and the Knight of the Apron-String," *New York History* 51, no. 5 (October, 1970), 501–22.

40. *Guert* I'm indebted to Garner, *Civil War World*, 303, for this information.

41. *Grant* JDM to HSG, 4/14/64, GLC. *"State Department"* Hawthorne, quoted by Ward, 276.

42. *"nice"* JDM to HSG, 4/13/64, GLC.

43. *"hill"* "The Scout Toward Aldie," lines 1–2, *Battle-Pieces*, 163.

44. *"gallop"* See Melville's note to the poem, *Battle-Pieces*, 289. *"Washington"* Garner, "Melville's Scout," 10–11; for a detailed history of the battalion, see Jeffry D. Wert, *Mosby's Rangers* (New York: Simon and Schuster, 1990).

45. *Lowell* Garner, "Melville's Scout," 10. As Martin Duberman points out in *James Russell Lowell* (Boston: Beacon Press, 1966), 168–69, it remains a mystery why nothing of Melville's ever appeared *The Atlantic Monthly*, even though the editors listed his name among potential contributors in 1857. Melville's state of mind at the time and Lowell's well-known dislike of "pessimistic" literature may have combined to prevent it. *"Effy"* Garner, "Melville's Scout," 9.

46. See Garner, "Scout/part 1," 12–13, and *Civil War World* for a more detailed account. The defector's name, "Ormsby,"

may have stuck in Melville's mind while he was writing his late poems and *Billy Budd*, as fragments show that Melville made notes on a character named "Orm" or "Daniel Orme." (He also knew a master seaman named William Budd); see Garner, *Civil War World*, 49ff.

47. *"antipodes"* HSG to GB, 3/11/64, see Garner, "Scout/part 1," 8. *horse, etc.* Stanton Garner, "Melville's Scout Toward Aldie, part 2: The Scout and the Poem," *Melville Society Extracts* 52 (November 1982), 3. *prison escapes* see *Harper's Weekly*, 17 October 1863, 669, and 5 March 1864, 151. Captain George Whitman also spent time in Libby Prison.

48. *Taylor* HM to HSG, 5/10/64, NN *Corr.*, 392.

49. *tingles* Garner, "The Scout Toward Aldie," lines 71–72. *"deep"* line 55, *Battle-Pieces*, 165. *"splashing"* *Battle-Pieces*, lines 106–7. *"sabres"* line 120, *Battle-Pieces*, 166. *"sophomores"* line 293, *Battle-Pieces*, 171.

50. *ranger wedding* Garner, "Scout," part 2, 6–7.

51. *Grant* See Garner, *Civil War World*, 326–27. After the war, the citizens of Galena gave Grant a mansion and put in a sidewalk, as he had complained about lack of sidewalks when he was there; they also wanted him to run for mayor, but settled for President of the United States instead. *Harper's Weekly*, 16 September 1965, 565.

52. *Mosby's postwar career* Wert, 294, is a wonderful example of the true political animal's infinite ability to shed his old skin and snake back into public life.

53. *"Capitol Dome"* "The Scout Toward Aldie," lines 29–35, *Battle-Pieces*, 164. *patients* lines 64–66, *Battle-pieces*, 165.

54. *orchards* "The Scout Toward Aldie," lines 246–52, *Battle-Pieces*, 170. *glide* lines 654–58, *Battle-Pieces*, 181. In "A Note on Melville's Concept of Mosby," *Melville Society Extracts* 62 (May 1985), 14–15, Joyce Sparer Adler points out that in the poem, Mosby personifies sudden death.

55. *"love"* "The Scout Toward Aldie," lines 36–40, *Battle-Pieces*, 164. *"ten"* lines 44–46, *Battle-Pieces*, 710–14, 785–91. Ibid., 165, 182, and 184–85.

56. *"ladies"* HM to ROT, 7/21/64, NN *Corr.*, 394.

57. *"eyes"* HM to HSG, 5/10/64, NN *Corr.*, 392.

58. *"salute"* Ibid. *conduct* Garner, "Scout/part 2," 7.

59. *contract* see Hennig Cohen and Donald Yannella, *Herman Melville's Malcolm Letter: "Man's Final Lore"* (New York: Fordham University Press and The New York Public Library, 1995), 154ff.

60. *"activity"* HSG to PG, 10/9/61, ibid. *"patriotism"* CG to HSG, 5/7/61, *Memoir of Henry Sanford Gansevoort*, privately printed.

61. *venereal infection* Suspected by me and confirmed by Garner's research in military archives, *Civil War World*, 244. *charges* Garner, "Melville's Scout," *Melville Society Extracts* 51, September 1982, 7.

62. *"Iris,"* *CP*, 276–77.

63. *Hawthorne and Ticknor* James R. Mellow, *Nathaniel Hawthorne in His Times* (Boston: Houghton Mifflin Company, 1980), 574–75.

64. *"loss"* MGM to PG, 5/24/64, Leyda, *Log*, 669. Tradition has it that out of his sorrow, Melville composed the poem "Monody," which remained unpublished until *Timoleon* was privately published by the Caxton Press in 1891; as Harrison Hayford points out, however, in "Melville's 'Monody,' Really for Hawthorne?" (Evanston: Northwestern University Press, 1990), the two stanzas of the poem (HCL) appear to have been written at different times and pasted together, and there is no evidence that Melville wrote the poem for Hawthorne.

65. *Mosses* Leyda, *Log*, 674.

66. *Greeley* quoted by Geoffrey A. Ward in *The Civil War: An Illustrated History* (New York: Alfred A. Knopf, 1990), 309.

67. *churches* Frederickson, *Inner Civil War*, 139.

68. *"prayers"* MGM to CG, 8/19/64, Eleanor Melville Metcalf, *Herman Melville: Cycle and Epicycle* (Cambridge, Mass.: Harvard University Press, 1953), 214.

69. *"grounds"* Ibid.

70. *"strangely"* CG to HSG, 10/19/64, GLC. *Guert's decision* MGM to CG, 10/4/64, Leyda, *Log,* 671.

71. *McClellan, platform, etc.* Garner, *Civil War World,* 360–61.

72. *epithets* Harper's Weekly, 24 September 1864, 612. *"majorities"* HW, 19 November 1864, 738. Emerson quoted in Stefan Lorant's *Lincoln, A Picture of His Life* (New York: Harper & Brothers, 1957), 234–35.

73. Joyce Sparer Adler, in her book *War in Melville's Imagination* (New York: New York University Press, 1981), 133–59, a pioneering study of Melville's attitude toward war, gives a sensitive and profound reading of *Battle-Pieces* as a "historic tragedy."

24. A SURVIVOR OF THE CIVIL WAR

1. *grandchildren* CG to HSG, 11/23/64, Leyda, *Log,* 671. *"United"* Harper's Weekly, 24 November 1864.

2. *beans and corn* reported by a former prisoner to George Strong, 8 June 1865. *Whitman and woman* Quoted by Geoffrey A. Ward in *The Civil War: An Illustrated History* (New York: Alfred A. Knopf, 1990), 336–38. The woman is not identified.

3. *Harper's Weekly,* 21 January 1865, 34, called "ridiculous" the *Richmond Dispatch*'s allegation that Sherman planned to take over slavery from the South, not end it.

4. *"over us"* Mary Chesnut's diary quoted by Ward, *Civil War...Illustrated,* 356.

5. *Bellows* Letter to Russell Bellows, 2/12/65, Ernest A. McKay, *The Civil War and New York City* (Syracuse, N.Y.: Syracuse University Press, 1990), 295.

6. *Travellers* Leyda, *Log,* 672. Descriptions of Bayard Taylor and Henry Bellows, as well as information about Allan Melville, from *The Century, 1847–1946,* various authors (New York: The Century Association, 1947), 9, 28, 40, etc. In addition to those listed by Taylor as members of the Authors Club, a whole host of other Melville acquaintances belonged to the Century, including Titus Munson Coan, Fitz Greene Halleck, Joel T. Headley, David Dudley Field, Elihu Vedder, Orville Dewey, George William Curtis, George Palmer Putnam, Parke Godwin, Fitz James O'Brien, Sanford Gifford, E. C. Stedman, R. H. Stoddard, and Wilson G. Hunt

7. See entries for March 1865, Leyda, *Log,* 672, and Piddledee Memorandum to Allan Melville, May 22, 1860. NN*Corr.* 343.

8. *dome* Featured on the cover of *Harper's Weekly,* 18 March 1865, 164–65, a lithograph from an Alexander Gardner photograph.

9. *"prophesy"* "The Conflict of Convictions (1860–61)," *The Battle-Pieces of Herman Melville,* edited, with an introduction and notes, by Hennig Cohen (New York: Thomas Yoseloff, 1963), 40–41.

10. *"grave"* "The Fall of Richmond. The tidings received in the Northern Metropolis. (April 1865)," *Battle-Pieces,* 125. *"Heaven"* JRL to Charles Eliot Norton, 4/17/65, quoted by Gardner, *Civil War World,* 380. *"wing"* "The Surrender at Appomattox. (April, 1865)," *Battle-Pieces,* 125–27.

11. *"mausoleum"* E. C. Stedman, *Life and Letters,* vol. 1, quoted in McKay, *Civil War/New York,* 305.

12. "The Martyr," *Battle-Pieces,* 130. *Lathers* I'm indebted to Stanton Garner, *The Civil War World of Herman Melville* (Lawrence: University Press of Kansas, 1993), 384, for this information.

13. "America," *Battle-Pieces,* 144–47.

14. *"lore"* " 'The Coming Storm,' a picture by S. R. Gifford, and owned by E. B. Included in the N. A. Exhibition, April 1865," ibid., 131–32.

15. "The Muster. Suggested by the Two Days' Review at Washington. (May, 1865)," ibid., 134. "Aurora-Borealis. Commemorative of the Dissolution of Armies at the Peace," ibid., 135.

16. *"rapidly"* CG to HSG, 5/3/65, Leyda, *Log,* 674.

17. *Sabbath schools* MGM to CG, 8/17/65, Leyda, *Log,* 675.

18. *"well"* AM to CG, 10/7/65. *gifts* Leyda, *Log,* 676.

19. *reading* MGM to CG, 12/21/65, Leyda, *Log,* 676. Yonge's novel *The Heir of Redclyffe,* which British officers in the Crimea read avidly, outsold Dickens and Thackeray among both male and female readers in England in 1854, according to Georgina Battiscombe's introduction to *The Clever Woman of the Family* (London: Penguin Books, Virago Modern Classics, 1985).

20. *Cary salon* Charles Hemstreet's *Literary New York* (New York, 1903), quoted in Leyda, *Log,* 676–77. These "fugitive" reports suggest that there were others that were unrecorded.

21. *"inspiring"* CG to HSG, 1/20/66, Leyda, *Log,* 678. *"splendid"* TM to CSG, 1/29/66, ibid. *"grand"* FPM to CG, 2/8/66, ibid. *payment* Note on a Harper's memo, Leyda, *Log,* 680. The four poems were "The March to the Sea," "The Cumberland," "Philip, Chattanooga," and "Gettysburg:-July, 1863."

22. *Tennyson, et al.* James D. Hart, *The Popular Book in America: A History of America's Literary Taste* (New York: Oxford University Press, 1950). *income* The Income Record, A List Giving the Taxable Income of Every Resident of New York, Leyda, *Log,* 677.

23. Prefatory Note, *Battle-Pieces,* 13: "With few exceptions, the Pieces in this volume originated in an impulse imparted by the fall of Richmond. They were composed without reference to collective arrangement, but, being brought together in review, naturally fall into the order assumed." The Aeolian-harp metaphor is self-consciously romantic, and designedly misleading.

24. Notes on proof sheets and binding of manuscript draft, HCL. *"miserable"* CG to HG, 7/23/66, Leyda, *Log,* 681. *croquet* AM to CG, 8/2/66, ibid.

25. *Battle-Pieces* salutes the vast military canvases of Salvator Rosa and Ambrose Louis Garneray, while "aspects" may be a nod at "S," whose quatrain "Painfully the people wait / For the news by flying car, / Eager for the battle's fate, / And the aspect of the war" appeared in the *Pittsfield Sun* in January 1863, according to Garner, *Civil War World.* This anonymous poet may well have been Sarah Morewood, who occasionally sent anonymous or pseudonymous verses to the *Sun.* *"Book World"* Leyda, *Log,* 682.

26. *"war"* From "The Armies of the Wilderness. (1863–1864)," *Battle-Pieces,* 95–101.

27. *"final good,"etc.* Ibid.

28. *"Prime"* lines 75–86, ibid., 97.

29. *"weeds"* lines 105–6 and 87–94, ibid., 97–98. *"kennel"* lines 103–105, ibid., 98.

30. *"skeleton"* lines 167–74, ibid., 100.

31. *"crutch"* See lines 179–83, 187–90, 197–202, 221–22, ibid., 100–101.

32. Joseph Bridgham Curtis was twenty-six. See letter of Orville Dewey to Mrs. David Lane, 12/19/62, in the *Autobiography and Letters of Orville Dewey, D.D.,* edited by his daughter Mary E. Dewey (Boston: Roberts Brothers, 1883), 262, and Gordon Milne, *George William Curtis and the Genteel Tradition* (Bloomington: Indiana University Press, 1956), 118.

33. *"sea"* "The March to the Sea. (December, 1864)," *Battle-Pieces,* 120–23.

34. *"rescind"* "The Frenzy in the Wake, Sherman's advance through the Carolinas," ibid., 123–24.

35. See notes to "The Conflict of Convictions" and "The Frenzy in the Wake," ibid., 207, 260–61.

36. "The Fall of Richmond. The tidings received in the Northern Metropolis," lines 222–24, ibid., 125.

37. "Lee in the Capitol," lines 71, 200, 145, ibid., 188–93. Lydia Maria Child, *Letters from New York,* 2d series (New York: C. S. Francis & Co. and Boston: J. H. Francis, 1845), 377, 452.

38. "A Meditation," lines 51–60, *Battle-Pieces,* 195.

39. *"Nation"* Supplement, *Battle-Pieces,* ibid., 195.

40. *art* Lathers, *Reminiscences,* 9.

41. *"manhood"* Supplement to *Battle-Pieces,* 199–200.

42. *"nutmeg"* Charles Gayarre to EAD, 3/29/67, and *"year"* 1/23/67, Duyckinck Collection, NYPL.

43. "The Swamp Angel," *Battle-Pieces,* 104–6 and 249–50, as well as George Templeton Strong's *The Diary of George Templeton Strong,* vol. 3, *The Civil War, 1860–1865,* edited by Allan Nevins and Milton Halsey Thomas (New York: Macmillan, 1952), 360.

44. "Formerly a Slave," *Battle-Pieces,* 139–40; Vedder knew Allan and Herman probably met the fun-loving painter at Allan's club. Even though Melville dedicated *Timoleon* to Vedder, Vedder's *Digressions of V.* omits any mention of Melville.

45. *war* lines 221–22, *Battle-Pieces,* 101.

46. *"broad"* Supplement, *Battle-Pieces,* 200. *"democracy"* Ibid., 201.

47. *"fearful"* *Gazette,* 1 September 1866, Leyda, *Log,* 682. *"poetry"* *The Nation,* 6 September 1866, Leyda, *Log,* 683.

48. *"war"* *Harper's,* 1 January 1867. *"words alone"* *The Atlantic Monthly,* 1 February 1867, Leyda, *Log,* 685.

49. *"too deep"* CG to HSG, 9/17/66, Leyda, *Log,* 683. *"beautiful"* HSG to PG, 9/1/66, Leyda, *Log,* 682.

50. *finances* See *Battle-Pieces,* 22–23. It would be a half-decade or more before he could liquidate the debt he had accumulated since he had last squared his accounts, in February 1864.

25. A TIME WHEN PEACE HAD HORRORS OF ITS OWN

1. *"Richmond"* Supplement, *Battle-Pieces,* 198. Obituary of Dr. Timothy Childs, *Boston Poet,* 11 September 1865, with other clippings and memorabilia in a folder labeled "Augusta and Malcolm," GLC.

2. *"enemies thereof"* *Battle-Pieces,* 295. *"stationery"* Stanton Garner, "Surviving the Gilded Age: Herman Melville in the Customs Service," *Essays in Arts and Sciences,* University of New Haven, vol. 15 (June 1986), 1–13. I'm much indebted to Garner for this essay and his "Melville in the Customhouse, 1881–1882: A Rustic Beauty among the Highborn Dames of Court," *Melville Society Extracts* 35 (September 1978), 12–14.

3. *"pittance"* JCH to George Boutwell, 1/9/73, Leyda, *Log,* 730–31. Henry Whitney Bellows earned $4,500 in 1858.

4. *"offending bullet"* Garner, "Surviving the Gilded Age," 5.

5. *duties* Ibid., 5–8.

6. *Whitman* Gay Wilson Allen, *The Solitary Singer* (Chicago: University of Chicago Press, 1985), 322.

7. See Willard Brown, *Civil-Service Reform in the New York Custom-House* (New York: G. P. Putnam's Sons, 1882), 16, and Robert Greenhalgh Albion, *The Rise of New York Port* (New York: Charles Scribner's Sons, 1970), 226–27. *statistics* Ari Hoogenboom, *Outlawing the Spoils: A History of the Civil Service Reform Movement, 1865–1883* (Urbana, Ill.: University of Illinois Press, 1968), 1. *"coercions"* George Templeton Strong, *The Diary of George Templeton Strong,* edited by Allan Nevins and Milton Halsey Thomas, 4 vols. (New York: Macmillan, 1952), December, 1868.

8. *"American life"* *Springfield Republican,* 24 June 1868. *"poets"* Richard Henry Stoddard, *Recollections: Personal and Literary* (New York: A. S. Barnes & Co., 1907), 142–43.

9. *"fogies"* Ibid., 137. See also Merton M. Sealts Jr., "Melville and Richard Henry Stoddard," *American Literature* 43, no. 3 (November 1971), 356–70. *"sensibilities"* Hawthorne, "The Custom-House," introduction to *The Scarlet Letter.* *"asylum"* Stoddard, *Recollections,* 137.

10. *"habits"* *Evening Post,* 4/17/66, quoted in Hoogenboom, *Outlawing the Spoils,* 35–36. *"ability"* *Harper's Weekly,* 12 May 1866, 300. *"schemer...Sundays"* Dorman B. Eaton, *The "Spoils" System and Civil-Service Reform in the Custom-House and Post-Office at New York* (New York: G. P. Putnam's Sons, 1882), 22.

11. *"disgrace"* Eaton, *"Spoils",* 2. *"rigid integrity"* *Harper's Weekly,* 12 May 1866, 300. *money on the side* Garner, "Surviving the Gilded Age," 6.

12. *"lifeblood of the nation"* Louis L. Stevenson *The Victorian Homefront: American Thought and Culture, 1860–1880* (New York: Twayne Publishers, 1991), 178.

13. *"Wail"* From "My Jacket Old," *CP,* 391.

14. *"less of a misanthrope"* CGL to HSG, 3/19/67, Leyda, *Log,* 686.

15. *coffee and oatmeal* Eleanor Melville Metcalf, *Herman Melville: Cycle and Epicycle* (Cambridge: Harvard University Press, 1953), 216.

16. *"challenging Lizzie"* Ibid., 259. In "Herman Melville, Wife Beating, and the Written Page," *American Literature* 66, no. 1 (March 1994), 123–50, Elizabeth Renker labels Melville a wife-beater.

17. *"redounds"* Metcalf, *Cycle and Epicycle,* 216, records this notation.

18. Charles Neumeier and Donald Yannella, "The Melvilles' House on East 26th Street," *Melville Society Extracts* 47 (September 1981), 6–8; see also Richard C. Doenges, "The Belle-Tower, or Diana's Polite Salute," *Melville Society Extracts* 52 (November 1982), 16. On the Melvilles' church, see Walter Donald Kring, *Henry Whitney Bellows* (Boston: Skinner House, 1979), 157ff. and 274.

19. *Bellows* His sermons and speeches are in the Massachusetts Historical Society. Bellows's young successor, Dr. Theodore Chickering Williams, who was known to his contemporaries primarily as a hymn writer, was a graduate of Harvard College and Harvard Divinity School and a minor poet. His *Poems of Belief* (Boston and New York: Houghton Mifflin Co., 1910) had a frontispiece by Elihu Vedder.

20. Walter Donald Kring and Jonathan S. Carey, "Two Discoveries Concerning Herman Melville," 11–15, reprinted from the *Proceedings of the Massachusetts Historical Society* 87 (1975), 137–41.

21. *"unauthorized by her"* SSS to HWB, 5/6/67, Bellows Papers, MHS. See also Carl L. Anderson, "The Minister's Advice to Elizabeth Melville," *Melville Society Extracts* 54 (May 1983), 10–12.

22. For the complete text of the two letters, commentary, and appendices, see Donald Yannella and Hershel Parker, *The Endless, Winding Way in Melville: New Charts by Kring and Carey,* (Glassboro, N.J.: The Melville Society, 1981), 14.

23. *Married Woman's Property Act* Norma Basch, *In the Eyes of the Law: Women, Marriage, and Property in Nineteenth-Century New York* (Ithaca: Cornell University Press, 1982), 94–95.

24. *Blackstones* Myra C. Glenn, "Wife-Beating: The Darker Side of Victorian Domesticity," *Canadian Review of American Studies* 5, no. 15 (Spring 1984), 18. *redress* Robert L. Griswold, "Law, Sex, Cruelty, and Divorce in Victorian America, 1840–1900" *American Quarterly* 38 (Winter 1986), 722–23.

25. *"legalized slavery"* Stanton, quoted in Glenn, "Wife-Beating," 22, 29–30. *"prochain ami"* Basch, *In the Eyes of the Law,* 99.

26. SSS to HWB, 5/6/67, MHS, Yannella and Parker, *The Endless, Winding Way,* 14.

27. *"lamentable state"* Ibid., 15.

28. *"perfect pattern of a wife"* Amos Nourse to Lemuel Shaw, 3/1/52, Leyda, *Log,* 448. Glenna Matthews, in *"Just a Housewife": The Rise and Fall of Domesticity in America* (New York: Oxford University Press, 1987), argues that reformers eventually won the vote for women not by arguing for women's rights, but by describing national politics in domestic terms so that allowing the fair sex to "put the national house in order" would come to be seen as natural and a moral good.

29. *"wife"* Phoebe Cary, quoted by Stevenson, *Victorian Homefront,* 12.

30. *"command"* ESM to HWB, 5/20/67, MHS, Yannella and Parker, *The Endless, Winding Way,* 15.

31. *Camoëns* 5/17/67, Leyda, *Log,* 686.

32. See Allan Stanley Horlick, *Country Boys and Merchant Princes: The Social Control of Young Men in New York* (Lewisburg, Pa.: Buckness University Press, 1975), for analysis and a complete bibliography. *"furnace"* William Howard Van Doren, *Mercantile Morals: or, Thoughts for Young Men Entering Mercantile Life* (New York, 1852), 167, quoted in ibid., 153. *"gaslight"* E. H. Chapin, *Humanity in the City* (New York, 1854), 17–20, quoted in ibid., 54. The Melville children may have been readers of *The Youth's Friend* from 1831 to 1838 (Merton M. Sealts, *Melville's Reading: Revised and Enlarged Edition* [Columbia University Press: University of South Carolina Press, 1988], 139), and Melville may have owned a copy of William Alcott's *The Young Man's Guide* (Boston, 1834). In *Redburn,* Melville mocks these advice books.

33. *Henry Clay* John G. Cawelti, *Apostles of the Self-Made Man* (Chicago: University of Chicago Press, 1965), 43–45. *"voyage of life"* Daniel Wise, *The Young Man's Counsellor: or, Sketches and Illustrations of the Duties and Dangers of Young Men* (New York, 1854), 17, quoted in Horlick, *Country Boys,* 161. *Alger* For information about his life and career, see Richard Fink, introduction to *Ragged Dick and Mark the Match Boy, Horatio Alger, Jr.* (New York: Collier Books, 1962), 5–31, and Milton Rugoff, *America's Gilded Age: Intimate Portraits from an Era of Extravagance and Change, 1850–1900* (New York: Henry Holt & Company, 1989), 7–12. *molesting boys* Ibid., 10–11; Fink omits this episode.

34. *"boy"* MGM to CG, 3/5/66, Leyda, *Log,* 678–79.

35. *gun* Stevenson reports this on page 43 of *Victorian Homefront,* but does not supply the date of this article. It appeared late in the war, or shortly afterward.

36. Metcalf, *Cycle and Epicycle,* 206.

37. *Niblo's "friends"* SSS to HSS, 9/12/67, Leyda, *Log,* 687. Hennig Cohen and Donald Yannella, *Herman Melville's Malcolm Letter: "Man's Final Lore"* (New York: Fordham University Press and The New York Public Library, 1992), 192 and 197, n. 38.

38. *"an end to his life"* CG to HSG, 9/16/67, Leyda, *Log,* 691.

39. *"late"* SS to HSS, ibid. "Valiant" is a conjectural reading; it could be "robust," "rational," etc.

40. *"ordeal"* SS to HSS, 9/12/67, Leyda, *Log,* 687.

41. *"vices"* Ibid.

42. *Melville's late arrival* Ibid. If he was much later than usual, was it because he stopped off at a tavern to fortify himself before confronting Malcolm, or did he stop off to see Evert Duyckinck, either to procrastinate, or to ask his old friend for advice about how to handle his rebellious son? Was he unconsciously mirroring his son's irresponsible behavior and causing Lizzie worry, or was he simply stuck at the office, having to work late?

43. *"composed"* CG to HSG, 9/16/67, quoting AM to MGM, 9/14?/67, Leyda, *Log,* 689.

44. *"pistols"* CG to HSG, 9/16/67; Stannie was at Arrowhead when Malcolm shot himself. *crime* Cohen and Yannella, *"Man's Final Lore,"* 208. Although this chapter was written before publication of Cohen and Yannella's book, the information the authors provide is invaluable, and I am grateful to Hennig Cohen for reading several chapters of my manuscript, as he was generous with both affirmation and correction of what I had written before his book appeared.

45. *"inefficient"* CG to HSG, 9/16/67, quoting AM to MGM, 9/14?/67, Leyda, *Log,* 689–90.

46. *"filialness"* HM to JCH, between 9/14 and 18/67, NN *Corr.,* 399–400.

47. *"regimental one"* HM to MGM2, 10/22/67, NN *Corr.,* 400–401. *"tear"* EB to ESM, 9/20/67, Leyda, *Log,* 691. The inscription does not, in fact, appear on the headstone.

48. *"suicide"* Excerpted in Leyda, *Log,* 690, these notices can be found *in toto* in a folder at the New York Public Library, GLC. *"despair"* Samuel Osgood, *New-York Evening Post,* 9/16/67, GLC.

49. *"evil thought"* JCH, GLC.

50. *"self-destruction"* JCH, GLC.

51. *"deeply"* TM to CG, 9/29/67, Leyda, *Log,* 692. *poem* In *"Man's Final Lore,"* Cohen and Yannella argue that the poem "The Chipmunk" refers to Malcolm. Melville may have written it during this visit; the date of the poem's composition is unknown.

52. *"grief"* CG to HSG, 11/24/67, Leyda, *Log,* 693.

53. *Harper's Weekly* described volcanic "convulsions" that upheaved green fields and mountains. "The Apparition (A Retrospect)," II. 11–15, *Battle-Pieces,* 140–41, *Harper's Weekly,* 24 August 1864, 542.

26. AGONIES THAT OPERATE UNSEEN

1. *"back"* MGM to CG, 12/23/67, Leyda, *Log,* 693.

2. Information from the Snug Harbor Cultural Center's "Tourscript," as well as Henry G. Steinmeyer, *Staten Island, 1524–1898* (Richmondtown: Staten Island Historical Society, 1987); Barnett Shepherd, *Sailor's Snug Harbor, 1801–1976* (Richmondtown: Staten Island Historical Society, 1979); and J. J. Boies, "Melville's Staten Island 'Paradise,'" *Staten Island Historian* 3, vol. 27 (July–September 1966), 24–28. The last two sources contain several errors, however.

3. *"winter months"* MGM to CG, 12/9/67, Leyda, *Log,* 693.

4. *Abby Lodge* Some details about the house come from an informal "History of Abbey [sic] Lodge" by Margaret T. Morewood, typescript, BCHS.

5. *wedding* CG, *Diary,* 6/6/68, Leyda, *Log,* 695.

6. See ESM, 3/5/68, Leyda, *Log,* 694, and aforementioned clippings, GLC. *death* See the chapter on "The Domestication of Death," in Ann Douglas, *The Feminization of American Culture* (New York: Avon Books, 1977), 240–72.

7. HM to CG, 8/16/68, NN *Corr.,* 405–6.

8. *"friends"* HSS fragment, 9/14/68, Leyda, *Log,* 698, and Amy Elizabeth Puett, *Melville's Wife: A Study of Elizabeth Shaw Melville* (Evanston: Northwestern University Press, 1969), note 53, 226.

9. *billiards, and Oakes Shaw* MGM to PG, 1/4/69, Leyda, *Log,* 699.

10. *backgammon* Titus Munson Coan's hitherto undiscovered penciled notes on an 1892 conversation with Mrs. Melville, Coan Papers, the New-York Historical Society Library.

11. *"fancy"* AM to CG, 3/13/69.

12. Lizzie's poem, 5/8/69, BA, and Leyda, *Log,* 701.

13. Melville underscored Wordsworth's lines; see Leyda, *Log,* 704.

14. *"eras"* Herman Melville, *Clarel: A Poem and Pilgrimage in the Holy Land,* edited by Harrison Hayford, Alma A. MacDougall, Hershel Parker, and G. Thomas Tanselle (Evanston and Chicago: Northwestern University Press and the Newberry Library, 1991),* IV, book v, lines 77–80. *"born"* Ticknor quoted by Geoffrey A. Ward, *The Civil War: An Illustrated History* (New York: Alfred A. Knopf, 1990), 400.

15. *Stanton* Mary P. Ryan, *Women in Public: Between Banners and Ballots, 1825–1880* (Baltimore: Johns Hopkins Press, 1990), 168.

16. *Sylvis* Alan Tractenberg, *The Incorporation of America: Culture and Society in the Gilded Age* (New York: Hill & Wang, 1982), 95–96.

17. I'm indebted to Tractenberg for much of the Gilded Age material.

18. *"disgrace"* George Templeton Strong, *The Diary of George Templeton Strong,* edited by Allan Nevins and Milton Halsey Thomas, 4 vols. (New York: Macmillan, 1952), 12/68.

19. *"persons"* Quoted by Ernest A. Mackay, *The Civil War and New York City* (Syracuse: Syracuse University Press, 1990), 216.

---

*Cited hereafter as "NN *Clarel.*"

20. *"lungs"* Bayrd Still, *Mirror for Gotham: New York as Seen by Contemporaries from Dutch Days to the Present* (New York: New York University Press, 1956), 225. *Central Park* See Elisabeth Blackmar and Roy Rosenzweig, *The Park and the People: A History of Central Park* (Ithaca, N.Y.: Cornell University Press, 1992). *"each"* Frederick Law Olmsted, "Public Parks and the Enlargement of Towns," 1870, quoted by Tractenberg, 110.

21. *"sad to him"* See Leyda, *Log,* 718.

22. *"absurdity," "made"* From Matthew Arnold; see Leyda, *Log,* 703–4.

23. *"weakness," "tell him"* ESM to SG, 10/28/69, Leyda, *Log,* 705. *Stanwix* Reported by AM to PG, 9/29/69, and MGM to CG, 10/8/69, Leyda, *Log,* 705.

24. *"duties of life"* CG to HSG, 2/1/70, Leyda, *Log,* 709–10.

25. *Pompeii* Puett, *Melville's Wife,* 138. According to Leyda, *Log,* 709 and 710, he acquired *Sinai and Palestine in Connection with Their History* (New York, 1863) by Arthur Penhyrn Stanley, and several other volumes on Sinai and Petra.

26. *"things"* HM to MGM, 5/5/70, Leyda, *Log,* 711.

27. *portrait* MGM to PG, 6/3/70, Leyda, *Log,* 712, and FPM to CG, 11/17/70, Leyda, *Log,* 714. *Fanny* Eleanor Melville Metcalf, *Herman Melville: Cycle and Epicycle* (Cambridge: Harvard University Press, 1953), 283.

28. *Maine* Puett, 140. *"machinery"* CG to HSG, 8/29/70, Leyda, *Log,* 713.

29. *books* Leyda, *Log,* 716.

30. *"art"* See Leyda, *Log,* 714–15.

31. *Kansas* ESM to CG, 5/17/71.

32. *Henry* See Leyda, *Log,* 719. *coat* See ESM to CG, 5/26/73, and CG to AL, 6/15/73, Leyda, *Log,* 733.

33. *Alger* Leyda, *Log,* 720.

34. *Beethoven* Leyda, *Log,* 721.

35. *"old lady," "empty still"* ESM to CG, 1/9/72, Leyda, *Log,* 722. *"hearts"* HM to PG, 12/26/71, Leyda, *Log,* 722. *food* Shepherd, *Sailors' Snug Harbor,* 22–23.

36. *"rudder," "spirits"* CG to PG/SG, 2/11/72, Leyda, *Log,* 723. *tulle cap* CG's diary, 4/3/72, Leyda, *Log,* 725. *"buried"* CG's diary, 4/4/72, Leyda, *Log,* 725.

37. *picture* ESM to CG, 5/6/72, Leyda, *Log,* 726.

38. Puett, *Melville's Wife,* 143, August 4, 1872, in Pittsfield, then Lizzie went to Boston, Herman back to work. *Una* Randall Stewart, *Nathaniel Hawthorne: A Biography* (New Haven: Yale University Press, 1961), 241.

39. *"losses"* ESM to CG, 12/29/72, Leyda, *Log,* 729.

40. *"self respect"* JCH to GB, 1/9/73, Leyda, *Log,* 730.

41. *account of Stanwix's travels* SM to HSS, 2/23/73, Leyda, *Log,* 731–32.

42. *"against me"* SM to HSS, 4/24/73, Leyda, *Log,* 733.

43. *"illness"* ESM to CG, 4/4/73, Leyda, *Log,* 732. *"demon"* ESM to CG, 5/26/73, Leyda, *Log,* 733. *"might"* Ibid.

44. *"hill-tops"* ESM to CG, 7/2/73, Leyda, *Log,* 734.

45. *"New York"* ESM to CG, 8/18/73, Leyda, *Log,* 735.

46. *"business"* ESM to CG, 11/23/73, Leyda, *Log,* 735.

47. *"women"* CGL to AL, 11/14/73, Leyda, *Log,* 735.

48. *Kate* See Alice P. Kenny, *The Gansevoorts of Albany: Dutch Patricians in the Upper Hudson Valley* (Syracuse, N.Y.: Syracuse University Press, 1969), and Hennig Cohen and Donald Yannella, *Herman Melville's Malcolm Letter "Man's Final Lore"* (New York: Fordham University Press and The New York Public Library, 1992).

49. *sheep ranch* ESM to HSS, 3/14/74, Leyda, *Log,* 736. *"defensive"* CGL to P&SG, 6/11/74, Leyda, *Log,* 737.

50. *dresses* CGL to AL, 11/18/74, Leyda, *Log,* 739. *ribbons* Frances Cuthbert Thomas Osborne, "Herman Melville Through a Child's Eyes," *Bulletin of the New York Public Library,* 69 (December 1965), reprinted in Merton M. Sealts Jr., *The Early Lives of Melville: Nineteenth-Century Biographical Sketches and Their Authors* (Madison: University of Wisconsin Press, 1974), 180.

51. *"world"* SM to HSS, 12/22/74, Leyda, *Log,* 739. *"left"* ESM to CGL, 6/7/75, Leyda, *Log,* 742.

52. *"spellbound"* AM to AL and CGL, 12/29/75, Metcalf, *Cycle and Epicycle,* 233–34.

53. *"duty"* AL to CGL, 4/6/76, ibid., 234. "hearts *of gold"* AM to AL and CGL, ibid. "Hearts-of-Gold," *CP,* 394.

54. *Dakota* Stephen Birmingham, *Life at the Dakota: New York's Most Unusual Address* (New York: Random House, 1979). There is very little information about their social life, which may have been scant, and even diaries and memoirs of the period that mention gatherings where friends and acquaintances of Melville's were present do not mention Melville himself; the voluminous diary of James Morse in the New-York Historical Society is a good example.

55. *"at all"* ESM to HSS, 3/9/75, Leyda, *Log,* 740.

56. *Fanny* Metcalf, *Cycle and Epicycle,* 66.

57. *"see you"* ESM to CGL, 2/2/76, Leyda, *Log,* 747.

58. *"strain"* ESM to CGL, 4/22/76, Leyda, *Log,* 748.

59. *"ensign"* NN *Clarel,* 540.

60. *kitten* ESM to CGL, 6/4/76, GLC. *"press"* HM to ESM, Leyda, *Log,* 749.

61. *"no traces"* HM to CWS, 12/?/67, Leyda, *Log,* 693.

62. *Twain,* 6/5/67, quoted by Still, *Mirror for Gotham,* 262.

27. DEVILISH TANTALIZATION OF THE GODS

1. References to Belzoni's excavations in "I and My Chimney" suggest that the narrator's conservatism is theological as well as political.

2. For a thorough and very readable analysis of how Saint Augustine's concept of the City of Man and the City of God figure in Melville writings, see Wyn Kelley's forthcoming book *Melville's City: Urban and Literary Form in Nineteenth-Century New York* (New York: Cambridge University Press, 1996)

3. See Richard Hofstadter, *Social Darwinism in American Thought* (Boston: Beacon Press, revised edition, 1955).

4. A copy of Evert Duyckinck's magazine-format history of the Civil War can be seen in the Berkshire Athenaeum; for information on Greeley and demobilized vets, see James D. Hart, *The Popular Book: A History of America's Literary Taste* (New York: Oxford University Press, 1950), 144.

5. *Clemenceau and "Negro question"* George M. Frederickson, *The Inner Civil War: Northern Intellectuals and the Crisis of the Union* (New York: Harper Torchbooks, 1965), 192. In his first address to Congress, Ulysses S. Grant had condemned "a system which looks to the extinction of a race [as] too horrible for a nation to adopt without entailing upon itself the wrath of all Christendom," Tractenberg, *The Incorporation of America,* 28.

6. Charles Gayarre's poignant letters may be found in a folder in the Duyckinck Collection, New York Public Library. His penmanship alone makes them worth reading. Allan Melville and Richard Lathers investigated ways to invest in rebuilding the economy of the South.

7. This excerpt of the "Catechism" is from Philip S. Foner, *Mark Twain, Social Critic* (New York: International Publishers, 1958), 90–91.

8. *"Darwin"* *The Education of Henry Adams* (New York: Modern Library, 1931), 266–67.

9. *"Damn fools!"* Quoted by Henry B. Thomas, Fanny's future husband. *"oratory"* Eleanor Melville Metcalf, *Herman Melville: Cycle and Epicycle* (Cambridge: Harvard University Press, 1953), 216.

10. *"storm"* Herman Melville, *Clarel: A Poem and Pilgrimage in the Holy Land,* edited by Walter E. Bezanson (New York: Hendricks House, Inc., 1960), I, book i, line 99.

11. *"stone"* Ibid., I, iii, 43–54.

12. *Nehemiah* Ibid., I, vii, 70–94, and NN *J,* 85.

13. *"town"* Ibid., I, x, 1–35.

14. *Celio* Ibid., I, xii, 101–4.

15. *"spell"* Ibid., I, xvi, 163–70.

16. *"heart"* Ibid., I, xviii, 51–56.

17. Walter Bezanson's exhaustive introduction to the Hendricks House edition of *Clarel* has been reprinted in the North-

western-Newberry edition of Melville's writings. Bezanson was the first to "prove" that Vine is modeled on Hawthorne.

18. *Vine   Clarel*, I, book xxviii, lines 131 to book xxix, line 58, and II, book xxvii, lines 1–142.

19. "*Indian mounds*" Ibid., I, xvii, 57–63.

20. "*first man*" Ibid., I, xvii, 139–43.

21. "*Holy Land*" Ibid., I, xvii, 259–64.

22. "*rod*" Ibid., I, xvii, 302–11.

23. Three other pilgrims drop out early in Book Two: the dour, unpleasant Scots-Presbyterian Elder who, armed with a gun, tape measure, and pruning knife, seems to be making a grim assault on the mysteries of Faith; the greedy, self-indulgent Levantine banker who fears death so much he cannot say the word aloud; and the banker's future son-in-law Glaucon, whose hedonism disgusts Clarel. Readers who wish to pursue connections between characters in the poem and actual people Melville met in 1856 should consult the extensive notes to the Northwestern-Newberry edition of *Clarel* as well as articles listed in the bibliography to that edition.

24. "*chivalry*" NN *Clarel*, III, book ix, lines 160–64.

25. "*Paraguay*" Ibid., II, i, 224–29. "*sway*" Ibid., II, xxii, 57.

26. "*Rama*" Ibid., I, xxxii, 1–20.

27. "*black slaver*" Ibid., II, xxxvi, 75–78.

28. "*Arcady*" Ibid., II, viii, 35–38.

29. *desert* Ibid., II, xi, 19–41.

30. *Cain* Ibid., II, x, 63–74. See Wyn Kelley, "Melville's Cain," *American Literature* 55, no. 1 (March 1983), 24–40.

31. "Science" NN *Clarel*, II, book xxxi, lines 99–100.

32. *ditty* Ibid., III, xi, 1–4.

33. *Agath* Ibid., III, xii, 31–35. Agath resembles Daniel Orme, an old sailor who has a Jerusalem cross tattooed on his chest. He is described as a pathetic old man with a shameful secret and a heart full of woe. A rather bathetic fragment, it remains unpublished. (See Melville Family Papers, HCL.) Some scholars have opined that Daniel Orme ("Or-Me") embodies Melvill's shameful awareness of his homosexuality. *palm tree* See NN *J*, 431. In 1892, the artist Peter Toft painted this tree in memory of Melville and presented it to Lizzie in memory of her husband.

34. *Ungar* NN *Clarel* IV, book i, lines 75–96.

35. *Civil War* Ibid., IV, v, 75–86. In addition to evoking the images of fratricide in *Battle-Pieces*, the term "Bridge of Sighs" refers to the bridge between the Doge's Palace in Venice and the bridge between the courtroom and the Tombs in New York City. I am indebted to Howard Zinn (Wellfleet Public Library lecture, August 11, 1994) for this insight about seizure of Indian lands. See Howard Zinn, *A People's History of the United States* (New York: Harper Perennial, 1980).

36. *democracy* NN *Clarel* IV, book xxi, lines 91–100.

37. "*Asia*" Ibid., xix, 36–46.

38. "*Hun*" Ibid., xxi, 19–25.

39. "*shore*" Ibid., xxviii, 12–13.

40. "*bowers*" Ibid., IV, xxvi, 301. The masochistic Syrian and the celibate monk Salvaterra appeal to Clarel's ascetic side, but their appeal is short-lived.

41. "*girls*" Ibid., IV, xxvii, 248–52. "*range*" Ibid., IV, xxvii, 302–10.

42. "*mind*" Ibid., IV, xxx.

43. "*universe*" Ibid., IV, xxx, 93–95.

44. "*face*" Ibid., IV, xxxii, 85–97.

45. "*prison*" Ibid., IV, xxxiii, 65. "*sea*" Ibid., IV, xxxiv, 51–53. See note, NN *Clarel*, 839.

46. "*God*" Ibid., IV, xxxv, 12–17. "*heaven*" IV, xxxv, 23–26.

47. "*victory*" Ibid., IV, xxxv, 27–34.

48. "*unpopularity*" Eleanor Melville Metcalf's phrase.

49. "*didactic*" London *Academy*. "*word*" *Westminster and Foreign Quarterly Review*, NN *Clarel*, 544–46.

50. *Sanborn   Springfield Daily Republican*, July 18, 1876, Leyda, *Log*, Supplement, 953. "*mediocrity*" *The World*, 26

June 1876, Leyda, *Log*, 750–51. For more reviews, see Leyda, *Log*.

51. "*extreme*" JCH to Abraham Lansing, 7/8/76, Leyda, *Log*, 751. "*happy!*" JCH to AL, 7/8/76, Leyda, *Log*, 751. "*Hermans Book*" TM to CGL, 6/30/76, Leyda, *Log*, 751. A number of Hoadley's poems are in the Gansevoort-Lansing Collection, New York Public Library.

52. *paper mill* NN *Clarel*, 659. Ironically, the most favorable comment on the poem is so insipid and inaccurate that it's obvious the reviewer never read it: "The verse is flowing and musical, the hero and his companions meet with the customary adventures, see the customary sights, and, during their journeyings, chance upon much that surprises and interests them and that furnishes abundant food for thought." The reviewer's comment that the poem's length might trouble a few readers is probably the greatest understatement in the history of literary criticism. *The Library Table*, August 1876, Leyda, *Log*, 753.

53. See HM to CGL, 7/25/76; HM to CGL, 8/2/76; HM to CGL, 9/13/76; NN *Corr.*, 437–44.

54. "*out of himself*" ESM to CGL, 6/21/76, Leyda, *Log*, 750.

55. "*Lizzie & the girls*" HM to CGL and AL, 8/27/76, NN *Corr.*, 440–41.

56. "*upside down*" Joel Munsell's *Annals of Albany*, quoted by Kenney in *The Gansevoorts of Albany* (Syracuse, N.Y.: Syracuse University Press, 1969), 200.

57. "*It is the thing*" HM to CGL and AL, 8/27/76, NN *Corr.*, 443.

58. Neil Harris, *Humbug: The Art of P. T. Barnum* (Chicago: University of Chicago Press, 1973), 21, 243. *whales* Several times, Barnum exhibited whales captured in the St. Lawrence River. The first whales exhibited in the American Museum died once they were put in fresh water, so Barnum filled his tanks with salt water. According to Joe Flibbert in *Melville and the Art of Burlesque* (Amsterdam: Rodopi, 1974), when critics accused Barnum of trying to pass off porpoises as whales, Professor Louis Agassiz of Harvard vouched for the authenticity of the whales. "*Vanity Fair*" HM to CGL, 10/12/76, NN *Corr.*, 446–47.

59. See Thomas J. Schlereth, *Victorian America: Transformation in Everyday Life, 1887–1915* (New York: HarperCollins, 1991).

60. *Howells* See Tractenberg, *The Incorporation of America*, 44. *Centennial Exposition* Lally Weymouth, *America in 1876* (New York: Vintage Books, 1976).

61. *Black Hills* SM to LSjr., 12/29/76, Leyda, *Log*, 756–57. "*iron & steel*" ESM to LSjr., 1/2/77, Leyda, *Log*, 758.

62. See Ari Hoogenboom, *Outlawing the Spoils: A History of the Civil Service Reform Movement, 1865–1883* (Urbana, Ill: University of Illinois Press, 1968), 130. "*nation*" GWC, quoted by Louise L. Stevenson, *The Victorian Homefront: American Thought and Culture, 1860–1880* (New York: Twayne Publishers, 1991), 178. *Bellows* Hoogenboom, *Outlawing the Spoils*, 187.

63. "*mention it*" ESM to CGL, 2/25/77, Leyda, *Log*, 759. "*dignity*" HM to CGL, 3/7/77, NN *Corr.*, 450–51.

64. *Compromise of 1877* See Geoffrey A. Ward, *The Civil War: An Illustrated History* (New York: Alfred A. Knopf, 1990), 400, and Tractenberg, *The Incorporation of America*, 76. *strikes* Ibid., 40.

65. *Hayes* HM to CGL, 3/7/77, NN *Corr.*, 450–51.

66. *Jews* ES to CGL, 3/25/77, Leyda, 760.

67. "*all-in-all*" HM to JCH, 3/31/77, NN *Corr.*, 452–54.

68. "*crazy*" Ibid.

69. "*relief*" ESM to CGL, 6/5/77, Leyda, *Log*, 762. "*pruning*" *New-York Daily Tribune*, 7 June 1877, Leyda, *Log*, 762.

70. "*conscience*" ESM to LSjr., 6/19/77, HCL. *library* CGL to AL, 6/17/77, Leyda, *Log*, 762–63. *sleeve buttons* HM to CGL, 7/12/77, NN *Corr.*, 458–59.

71. "*wicked*" HM to CGL, 9/5/77, NN *Corr.*, 463–64.

72. *Fanny* In her letter to Kate Gansevoort, 4/22/76,

GLC, Lizzie speaks of a great "desolation & change that has "come over Fanny," but the nature of the crisis is by no means clear. Lizzie thanks "heaven for Divine Help," as no one could "endure life without it." Fanny took her father's rousing her out of bed to proofread *Clarel* very hard, and she was also going through the throes of dating, having announced her intention to find a rich husband (ESM to CG, 4/28/78, GLC).

73. *Fanny* Metcalf, *Cycle and Epicycle,* 251. *Melville's height* Charlotte Hoadley to Victor Paltsits, 11/25/1935, GLC: "I should have described him as a tall man, quite six feet at least–a man changes as he grows older of course, but he was very erect as I always remember him."

74. *"gentlemanly"* FPM to CGL, 4/27/78, Metcalf, *Cycle and Epicycle,* 255.

75. *Harper's* 2/9/78, Leyda, *Log,* 767.

76. *"citadel"* ESM to CGL, 4/28/78, Metcalf, *Cycle and Epicycle,* 254. *dinners* Ibid., 259.

77. *carpet* ESEM to CGL, 11/6/78, Leyda, *Log,* 770.

78. *parlor* Ibid. I infer that he was "tickled" from the tone of his references to the pair in letters. *breakfast* Frances Thomas Osborne, "Herman Melville Through a Child's Eyes," *Bulletin of the New York Public Library* 69 (1865), 655–60. *"affair"* HM to CGL, 11/26/78, Leyda, *Log,* 770.

79. *"run down," "prostrated," and Bessie* FPM to CGL, 3/2/79, Leyda, *Log,* 771, and ESM to CGL, 3/7/79, Leyda, *Log,* 772. *Agnes Morewood* FPM to CGL, 6/2/79, Leyda, *Log,* 772.

80. *will* FPM to CGL, 9/13/78, Leyda, *Log,* 769. *wills* See Puett, *Melville's Wife: A Study of Elizabeth Shaw Melville* (Evanston, Illinois: Northwestern University, 1969), 161. *Hope Shaw* See Leyda, *Log,* 772, and *The Letters of Herman Melville,* edited by Merrell R. Davis and William H. Gilman (New Haven: Yale University Press, 1960), 279, n. 8.

81. *"sane"* NN *Clarel* III, xix, 97–98.

28. CONFRONTING SPHINX AND ANGEL

1. *Schiller* Eleanor Melville Metcalf, *Herman Melville: Cycle and Epicycle* (Cambridge: Harvard University Press, 1953), 284.

2. *"old fogy"* HM to AL, 12/8/80, NN *Corr.,* 475. *penmanship* HM to CMH, 12/28/81, NN *Corr.,* 477.

3. *"babby"* HM to CMH, 4/12/82, NN *Corr.,* 478. *Barnum* Ibid.

4. *Woodstock* HM to HMG and FPM, 8/26?/82, NN *Corr.,* 479. *constantly* ESM to CGL, 9/8/82, Leyda, *Log,* 781.

5. *"gathering"* Charles De Kay, reminiscences of the Authors Club, October(?), 1882, Leyda, *Log,* 781. *"elusive," "groups"* Brander Matthews, *These Many Years* (New York, 1917), quoted by Leyda, *Log,* 784; Matthews later taught at Columbia. Several such descriptions of Melville in his late years lead me to wonder whether he suffered from bone-conduction deafness, as a person with bone-conduction deafness hears well except when there is a lot of background noise. At a large party, a person with this condition may find that conversations across the room block out what the person next to him is saying.

6. From handwritten notes in the Coan Papers, New-York Historical Society. Several penciled notations on white paper are misfiled, including Coan's notes of an interview with Lizzie in 1892. Coan used such old-fashioned medical terms as "bilious," "sanguine," and "melancholic" to describe people whom he met, which undoubtedly amused Melville. This information and the anecdote about Bayard Taylor and the camel come from the Coan Papers in the New-York Historical Society. The importance of Coan's friendship is suggested by his article in the Boston *Literary World,* 19 December 1891 (Leyda, *Log,* 787), in which he says he visited Melville "frequently in New York, and had the most interesting talks with him," as well as by his being among the handful of mourners at Melville's funeral.

7. *"fled"* Leyda, *Log,* 781.

8. *"a certain time"* Titus Munson Coan, "Herman Melville," *Literary World* (Boston), 19 December 1891, reproduced in Merton M. Sealts, Jr., *The Early Lives of Melville: Nineteenth-Century Sketches and Their Authors* (Madison: University of Wisconsin Press, 1974), 116–19.

9. *"better"* See note to HM to JH, 8/10/83, NN *Corr.,* 480–81.

10. *"Melville"* Julian Hawthorne, *Nathaniel Hawthorne and His Wife,* 2 vols. (Boston: Houghton Mifflin Company, 1884).

11. *"sensitive nature"* MLP to AL, 7/7/85, Leyda, *Log,* 790.

12. *"Governor"* Catherine Lansing's Diary, 3/10–11/84, Leyda, *Log,* 785.

13. *"entertaining way"* ESM to CGL, 12/26/83, Metcalf, *Cycle and Epicycle,* 261. *Eleanor* Her aunt Frances Priscilla called her "a darling, sweet winning little thing," FPM to CGL, 11/13/83, ibid., 261.

14. *"solace"* Metcalf, *Cycle and Epicycle,* 215.

15. *"politics"* Balzac to Madame Carraud, 1834, Leyda, *Log,* 815. In this letter, which Melville marked, Balzac says it is better for an artist to struggle with his art than to run around in America and come back discouraged about the state of the world. *shantytown* John Kouwenhoven, *The Columbia Historical Portrait of New York: An Essay in Graphic History* (New York: Harper & Row, 1953), 392–93. In 1898, the Fifth Avenue Shantytown would be razed to make way for Andrew Carnegie's mansion. *Effy* George M. Frederickson, *The Inner Civil War: Northern Intellectuals and the Crisis of the Union* (New York: Harper Torchbooks, 1965), 212.

16. *"relaxation"* Herbert Spencer, 1876, quoted in Bayrd Still, *Mirror for Gotham: New York as Seen by Contemporaries from Dutch Days to the Present* (New York: New York University Press, 1956), 208.

17. *"Castoria"* Ibid., 209.

18. The figures appear in Alan Tractenberg, *The Incorporation of America: Culture and Society in the Gilded Age* (New York: Hill & Wang, 1982), 78.

19. Samuel R. Hole, *A Book of Roses* (New York, 1883), Leyda, *Log,* 785.

20. *"mate"* NN *Mardi,* 84. *"Constantinople"* Metcalf, *Cycle and Epicycle,* 217. *jumping on bed* Ibid., 258.

21. Melville knew Schopenhauer through a quotation he marked in the book by Sam Shaw's friend William Alger, and later in life he owned a set of the philosopher's major works. Although there is room in this book only to hint at the importance of eastern thought to Melville's development, fortunately a number of superb studies have been done, and more will surely follow. *church* According to Walter Donald Kring, *Henry Whitney Bellows* (Boston: Skinner House, 1979), 480. *"creeds"* NN *Clarel,* I, book 5, line 207. *Maurice* I'm indebted to Margaret Wiley Marshall's excellent article "Arichandra and *Billy Budd*," *Melville Society Extracts* 40 (November 1979), 7–10, for this information. Eloquently expressing Melville's perception of the universality and unity of religions and mythologies, Marshall furthers the work begun by James Baird in his *Ishmael: A Study of the Symbolic Mode in Primitivism* (Baltimore: Johns Hopkins University Press, 1956), by Dorothee M. Finkelstein in her *Melville Orienda* (New Haven: Yale University Press, 1961), and by H. Bruce Franklin in his *The Wake of the Gods: Melville's Mythology* (Stanford, Calif.: Stanford University Press, 1963).

22. *"rheumatism"* FPM to CGL, 11/25/84, Leyda, *Log,* 786. *"past"* FPM to CGL, 12/19/84, Metcalf, *Cycle and Epicycle,* 262.

23. *Bessie* HGM and FPM to CGL, 1/7/85, Leyda, *Log,* 788; CGL's Diary, 1/19/85, Leyda, *Log,* 788. *"hopeless"* HMG, 5/14/85, Leyda, *Log,* 789.

24. *dedication* Penciled note on the ms., Vincent, 486n. *Tribune* and *Herald,* 17 May 1885, Leyda, *Log,* 789.

25. "The Haglets," *CP,* 185–94.

26. *legacy*   Leyda, *Log,* 787.

27. *"desk"*   ESM to CGL, 7/29/85, Leyda, *Log,* 791.

28. *kitten*   *CP,* 381.

29. *"misfortunes"*   Balzac, Leyda, *Log,* 791.

30. *"enemy"*   ESM to CGL, 7/7/85, Leyda, *Log,* 790. *"spirit"*   Joseph Edward Adams Smith, "Biographical Sketch of Herman Melville," *Evening Journal* (1891). Sealts, *Early Lives,* 139.

31. *"trusted"*   HM to EMG, 10/5/85, NN *Corr.,* 490–91, with a postscript: "You see the rose-leaves have not yet given out. I shall always try and have a rose-leaf reserved for you, be the season what it may."

32. *"adored"*   Robert Buchanan, *The Academy,* 15 August 1885, Leyda, *Log,* 792. *"sleep"*   Robert Buchanan, "Socrates in Camden, With a Look Around," published in *The Academy* (of London), Leyda, *Log,* 792.

33. W. Clark Russell, *The Contemporary Review,* September 1884, Leyda, *Log,* 785–86. *"genius"*   See WCR to HM, 2/10/89, Leyda, *Log,* 813, and WCR to HM, 1/5/90 and 1/9/90, Leyda, *Log,* 820. *"writers"*   WCR to HM, 7/21/86, Leyda, *Log,* 801. Russell was a great fan, but he evidently did not save Melville's letters. His son told Dr. Henry A. Murray that it was his father's habit when he received a letter to say, "Hallo! Another letter from old Melville!" He would then read it and throw it away. Russell called *Redburn* "absolutely true to forecastle life," WCR to HM, 4/10/88, Leyda, *Log,* 806–7.

34. *"Sphinx and Angel"*   HM to JB, 12/31/88, NN *Corr.,* 514. *"quarters"*   HM to JB, 1/22/85, NN *Corr.,* 486. *"talents," "sort"*   HM to JB, 12/20/85, NN *Corr.,* 492–93. *Blake*   HM to JB, 4/2/86, NN *Corr.,* 498.

35. *Carroll*   See Leyda, *Log,* 796–97.

36. *"elderly"*   From an unidentified newspaper, Leyda, *Log,* 812. *"Literature"*   *The Literary World,* 28 November 1885, Leyda, *Log,* 794.

37. *"esteem"*   Quoted by Leyda, *Log,* 799.

38. *Simonson's*   See ESM Memorandum, BA.

39. *"over work"*   ESM to CGL, 1/10/86, Leyda, *Log,* 796.

40. Leyda, *Log,* 797. Melville had just written Stannie asking him to sign a power of attorney that would give him authority to collect his son's share of Frances Priscilla's estate, when he learned that Stannie was in the hospital. Leyda placed a torn-off signature from papers in the Berkshire Athenaeum that read: "Good bye & God bless you, Your affectionate Father H. Melville" beneath Melville's February 1886 letter to his son, but as the editors of NN *Corr.* point out (p. 537), there is no way of knowing when Melville wrote those words, and it is disconcerting to imagine him writing so casually to a son who was dying. Judging from his photograph, Stanwix was something of a dandy, sporting a long waxed mustache in his youth. He never married, and a male friend took care of him in his last days. When I told Paul Metcalf I had a hunch that Stanwix might have been homosexual, he said that could explain why Stanwix went so far away while the other Melville children stayed so close to home.

41. *"older"*   HGM to CGL, 3/16/86, Leyda, *Log,* 798. *"away"*   HGM to CGL, 5/5/86, Leyda, *Log,* 800.

42. *auction, etc.*   EMM notes, 265. *clock*   HMG to CGL, 5/6/86, Leyda, *Log,* 800.

43. *"vividly"*   Letter of Ferris Greenslet to Willard Thorp, 11/22/1946 (Melville Collection, Newberry Library), Sealts, *Early Lives,* 217, n. 75.

44. *"joie de vivre"*   Ferris Greenslet to Willard Thorp, 11/22/1946 (Murray Papers, Harvard University Archives). Despite Melville's claim to have had a child by Fayaway and Whitman's boast that he had fathered eight children in New Orleans, no one has ever stepped forth claiming to be the offspring of either of the two men.

45. See Paul Metcalf, *Genoa: A Telling of Wonders* (Penland, North Carolina: The Jargon Society, 1973), 73–79.

46. *"kiss to Grandpa"*   EMM to HM, 8/7/86, Leyda, *Log,* 801.

47. *"fires"*   Frances Cuthbert Thomas Osborne, "Herman Melville Through a Child's Eyes," *Bulletin of The New York Public Library* 69 (December 1965), reprinted in Sealts, *Early Lives,* 181.

48. *"blues"*   FCTO, Sealts, *Early Lives,* 184.

49. *"Mecca," "hat," "policeman"*   EMM, ibid., 178.

50. *"whisper"*   Ibid.

51. *"ships"*   FCTO, Sealts, *Early Lives,* 183. *Eden Musée* Ibid., 183.

52. *"upheavals"*   Ibid., 183.

53. *possessions*   EMM, ibid., 295, and FCTO, ibid., 183–84.

54. *desk, etc.*   From EMM to FCTO, ibid.

55. *"things"*   EMM, ibid., 283–84. The handsome edition of *Landseer's Dogs* that Melville gave Eleanor in 1891 for her ninth birthday can be seen in the Melville Room at the Berkshire Athenaeum.

56. Leyda, *Log,* quotes Hearn, 800; London, 803; Stevenson, 808–9; La Farge, 825; Adams, 832.

57. *statement*   Leyda, *Log,* 803.

29. THE HELLISH SOCIETY OF MEN

1. *cruise*   WCR to HM, 4/10/88, NN *Corr.,* 472–73, and Elizabeth Melville Metcalf, *Herman Melville: Cycle and Epicycle* (Cambridge: Harvard University Press, 1953), 273. *"heavy coat," etc.* Frances Cuthbert Thomas Osborne, "Herman Melville Through a Child's Eyes," *Bulletin of The New York Public Library* 69 (December 1965), reprinted in Merton M. Sealts Jr., *The Early Lives of Melville: Nineteenth-Century Sketches and Their Authors* (Madison: University of Wisconsin Press, 1974), 184. *cruise and blizzard*   I'm indebted to Richard C. Doenges, "The Blizzard and Tulips of '88: Clues for Dating Melville," *Melville Society Extracts* 56 (November 1983), 11–12, for clearing up some of the discrepancies in Leyda and Metcalf, but he raises almost as many questions as he answers. In the collection of Bradley H. Martin, Bob Ryan has seen an envelope postmarked Florida, with the date "1888" but no month and day, so the mystery remains.

2. *"thoughts"*   Sealts, *Early Lives,* 182.

3. *1887*   See Leyda, *Log,* 803–4. Jay Leyda dated Ferris Greenslet's recollections 1887, but Greenslet's account of Melville in the barbershop and the recollections of Melville's two oldest granddaughters have never been positively dated. *book rack*   Leyda, *Log,* 806, and Doenges, "Blizzard." *"entirety"* Wolfgang Iser, *The Implied Reader: Patterns of Communication in Prose Fiction from Bunyan to Beckett* (Baltimore: Johns Hopkins University Press, 1974), 280.

4. *sketches*   See Merton M. Sealts Jr., "Melville's Burgundy Club Sketches," a 1958 article reprinted in his *Pursuing Melville, 1940–1980* (Madison: University of Wisconsin Press, 1982), 77–90; also Sealts, "The Melvilles, the Gansevoorts, and the Cincinnati Badge," *Melville Society Extracts* 70 (September 1987), 1–4, Robert A. Sandberg, "'House of the Tragic Poet': Melville's Draft of a Preface to his Unfinished Burgundy Club Book," *Melville Society Extracts* 79 (November 1989), 1, 4–7, and Michael Paul Rogin, *Subversive Genealogy: The Politics and Art of Herman Melville* (New York: Alfred A. Knopf, 1983), 288–94. These sketches had a number of different titles; I use the most familiar of them. The maudlin, masochistic fragment "Daniel Orme," which Melville mercifully omitted from *Billy Budd,* can also be found among Melville's papers in Harvard's Houghton Library.

5. It is almost impossible to date the composition of individual poems, according to Robert C. Ryan, who is editing the Northwestern-Newberry edition of the poems.

6. Also known as *Billy Budd, Foretopman,* and *Billy Budd, Sailor (An Inside Narrative)* edited from the manuscript with an introduction and notes by Harrison Hayford and Merton M. Sealts Jr. (Chicago: Phoenix Books, 1962).* *Somers*   See

---

*The latter edition is cited hereafter as "HS*BB.*"

Leyda, *Log,* 807 and 814. The *Somers* capsized off Vera Cruz in 110 feet of water while on blockade duty, losing 32 of her 76 men. According to the *Boston Globe,* July 1, 1990, the brig was located by divers in June 1986, and arrangements are being made with Mexico for a joint Mexican-American undersea archaeological exploration.

7. *truth* *Poets & Writers Magazine,* vol. 24, issue 1 (January/February, 1996), 57.

8. *will* HM, 6/11/88 (witnessed by H. Minturn Smith, S. N. Robinson, and Henry B. Thomas), Leyda, *Log,* 807.

9. *dedication* See WCR to HM, 2/10/89, Leyda, *Log,* 813. "*wound*" "John Marr," *CP,* 159.

10. "*Asia*" *CP,* 163.

11. "*love-locks*" *CP,* 166.

12. "Tom Deadlight," ibid., 182–84.

13. "*fellow,*" etc. Ibid., 178. "*clan*" Ibid., 174.

14. "The Maldive Shark" and "The Berg," ibid., 200, 201. "*Edens,*" etc. "To Ned," ibid., 201. "The Aeolian Harp," ibid., 194–96.

15. "*glue*" *CP,* 198.

16. "*maritime*" WCR to HM, 9/18/88, Leyda, *Log,* 809. *Stoddard* Review of *John Marr,* 11/?/88, Leyda, *Log,* 811.

17. *Helen* SM to EMG, 1/4/89, Leyda, *Log,* 813. "*lips,*" "*chaplet*" From "Pontoosuce," *CP,* 396.

18. Melville's evasive, prevaricating narrator distorts the historical and military facts in ways most readers would not even notice, which may be part of Melville's point. Stanton Garner, "Fraud as Fact in Herman Melville's *Billy Budd,*" *San Jose Studies* 4, no. 2 (May 1978). Nelson, HS*BB,* 57–58.

19. *Hamilton article* *Cosmopolitan,* June 1889, Leyda, *Log,* 814–15.

20. "*guns*" HS*BB,* 59.

21. See Margaret Wiley Marshall, "Arichandra and *Billy Budd, Melville Society Extracts* 40 (November 1979), 7–10, on the influence of Hinduism. The unpublished poem and prose preface "Rammon" gives further evidence of Melville's interest in Buddhism.

22. "*urbane*" The word is associated with the serpent in HS*BB,* 52, as the serpent is later associated with Claggart, whose dead body is like the cold body of a snake. "*magnate*" HS*BB,* 203, Hershel Parker, *Reading Billy Budd* (Evanston, Ill.: Northwestern University Press, 1990), 104. I'm indebted to Parker's painstaking examination of the manuscripts of *Billy Budd,* especially his description and analysis of the genetic text, though I don't agree with him on some of his interpretations of the text, or on his characterizations of Melville's political attitudes, and I find the omission of any reference to Stanton Garner's "Fraud and Fact in Herman Melville's *Billy Budd,*" cited above, perplexing. "*citified man*" HS*BB,* 54, the stone with which Cain slew Abel being the foundation of the modern city; see HS*BB,* 143, n. 45.

23. "*worse*" HS*BB,* 74.

24. "*acerbity*" HS*BB,* 75. Garner, in "Fraud as Fact," documents Melville's intricate and clearly intentional errors of fact, establishing the unreliability of the narrator.

25. "*hang*" HS*BB,* 101. In the *Life of Nelson,* Melville underscored the passage in which Southey notes Sir William Hamilton's statement that the study of antiquities kept him "in constant thought *of the perpetual fluctuation of every thing.*"

26. "*nobility*" HS*BB,* 60–62.

27. "*buttons,*" etc. HS*BB,* 111. "*operate*" Ibid., 111.

28. "*embrace*" HS*BB,* 115. "Military justice is to justice as military music is to music," quipped French premier Georges Clemenceau.

29. "*not named*" HS*BB,* 117.

30. For more on the alleged sins of the Templars, see Beryl Rowland's article "Melville Bachelors and Maids: Interpretation through Symbol and Metaphor," in *On Melville: The Best from American Literature,* edited by Louis J. Budd and Edwin H. Cady (Durham, N.C.: Duke University Press, 1988), 155–71.

31. "*fleece*" HS*BB,* 124. Melville capitalizes on the double meaning of the word *fleece* to suggest that Billy has been "fleeced," or cheated and robbed, of justice.

32. "*euthanasia*" HS*BB,* 125. "*vindictively stabbed*" HS*BB,* 130.

33. "*Cross*" HS*BB,* 131.

34. In their bibliography, Hayford and Sealts list such works as E. L. Grant Watson, "Melville's Testament of Acceptance," *New England Quarterly* 6 (June 1933), 319–27, Richard Harter Fogle, "*Billy Budd*-Acceptance or Irony," *Tulane Studies in English* 8 (1958), 107–13, and Phil Withim, "Melville's Testament of Resistance," *Modern Language Quarterly* 20 (June 1959), 115–27, Barbara Johnson, "Melville's Fist: The Execution of Billy Budd," in *The Critical Difference: Essays on the Contemporary Rhetoric of Reading* (Baltimore: Johns Hopkins University Press, 1980), 79–109. *antimilitarism* For a thorough examination of Melville's attitudes toward war, see Joyce Sparer Adler, *War in Melville's Imagination* (New York: New York University Press, 1981).

35. For a description of this genetic text, see Parker, *Reading Billy Budd.* In such texts, as Wolfgang Iser puts it in *The Implied Reader,* pp. 284–85, "the very precision of the written details" causes the "imposed 'gestalt' of the text to disintegrate." In *Billy Budd,* Melville experiments with the creation of a voice which embodies the specious reasoning of a world in which innocence is guilt, and goodness is defined strictly by utility.

36. Marvin Fisher, in "The Question of Criminality in Melville's *Billy Budd,*" a paper presented at a forum titled "The Image of Crime in Literature, the Media, and Society," sponsored by the University of Southern Colorado and convened in Colorado Springs on March 8–9, 1991, likens Vere's arguments before the court to arguments rejected by the Nuremburg Tribunal after World War II. That Melville foresaw totalitarian regimes is not farfetched, or foreknowledge; Sophocles "foresaw" them in *Antigone,* and other great writers have been equally prescient.

37. "*Solomon's hell*" From "A Spirit Appeared to Me," *CP,* 390. "*oblivion*" HS*BB,* 115. *Epistemology of the Closet* (Berkeley: University of California Press, 1990). Eve Kosofsky Sedgwick infers Melville's homosexuality from his use of sodomy as a metaphor for unequal power relations between ruler and subject, man and man, a rather too literal reading, I believe. For further discussion of literary relationships between cannibalism and homosexuality, see David Bergman, *Gaiety Transfigured: Gay Self-Representation in American Literature* (Madison: University of Wisconsin Press, 1991) and Caleb Crain, "Lovers of Human Flesh: Homosexuality and Cannibalism in Melville's Novels," *American Literature* 66, no. 1 (March 1994), 25–53.

38. As Lea Bertani Vozar Newman has shown in "Marginalia as Revelation: Melville's 'Lost' Copy of Dante and a Private Purgatorial Note," *Melville Society Extracts* 92 (March 1993), 4, the line occurs in Canto XXXI of Purgatory, in *The Vision; or Hell, Purgatory, and Paradise, of Dante Alighieri,* translated by the Rev. Henry Francis Cary, a new edition, corrected (London, 1848), the edition Melville owned. Her paper and her article "Melville's Copy of Dante: Evidence of New Connections between the *Commedia* and *Mardi,*" *Studies in American Renaissance* (1993), 305–338, an exhaustive study of the markings and marginalia in Melville's copy of Dante, which documents both Melville's knowledge of Dante and the guilt he suffered over Malcolm's suicide.

39. "*all*" Amy Elizabeth Puett, *Melville's Wife: A Study of Elizabeth Shaw Melville* (Evanston, Ill.: Northwestern University Press, 1969), 167–89. The desk can be seen at the Berkshire Athenaeum in Pittsfield, Massachusetts.

30. THE ROSE FARMER IN THE GARDEN OF TRUANT EVE

1. "*exhausted*" Honoré de Balzac to Madame Hanska, 3/26/38, quoted in Leyda, *Log,* 815–16.

2. *aloe* *CP,* 278–79.

3. *MacMechan* See AMM to HM, 11/21/89, NN*Corr.*, 752; HM to AMM, 12/5/89, ibid., 518–19; and AMM to HM, 12/23/89, ibid., 753.

4. "*serene*" "The Rusty Man," *CP*, 377.

5. "*life*" "Madam Mirror," ibid., 371–73. "*false*" "The Wise Virgins to Madam Mirror," ibid., 373.

6. *Rammon* Ibid., 411–16.

7. *erysipelas* ESM Memoranda, Merton M. Sealts Jr., *The Early Lives of Melville: Nineteenth-Century Biographical Sketches and Their Authors* (Madison: University of Wisconsin Press, 1974), 171, and 247, n. 13. *Jerrold and Howells*, 5/31/90, Leyda, *Log*, 825.

8. Ellis was the author of a seven-volume study called *The Psychology of Sex* (1897–1928).

9. "*alive*" WCR to HM, 9/18/88, NN*Corr.*, 744–45. *Bok* Leyda, *Log*, 827.

10. "*literature*" *Boston Post*, 19 November 1890, Leyda, *Log*, 827.

11. "*Ditty*" Leyda, *Log*, 805. "*tempt him out*" E. C. Stedman to Charles Henry Phelps, 4/9/90, Leyda, *Log*, 823.

12. "*Men of Letters*" HES to GPL, 10/14/90, Leyda, *Log*, 826. "*barnacle*," etc. GPL to HES, 10/20/90, Leyda, *Log*, 826.

13. "*handled*" HES to GPL, 10/22/90, Leyda, *Log*, 826.

14. "The Age of the Antonines," *CP*, 235–36.

15. "The Ravaged Villa," ibid., 222. *pulping* HM to G. P. Putnam's Sons, 3/27/79, NN*Corr.*, 472.

16. One section of *Timoleon* is called "Fruits of Travel Long Ago," a series of short poems based on journal entries made during his 1857 travels through Europe and the Holy Land. As Leyda, *Log*, notes (p. 823), in the Harvard College Library there is a folder of poems labeled "Greece" with Melville's note, "Looked over March 23, '90."

17. "*queen*" "Timoleon," *CP*, 211–12. "*guest*" Ibid., 215. On the political implications of the Gansevoort-Melville clan and the impact on Melville as reflected in "Timoleon," see Vernon Shetley, "Melville's 'Timoleon,'" *Emerson Society Quarterly* 33, no. 2 (second quarter, 1987), 83–93.

18. One ms. version bears the title "A Boys Revenge, or After the Pleasure Party," alluding more directly to Cupid's mischief (HCL). "*brain*" *CP*, 220. "*self-sustained*" Ibid., 218.

19. "*life*" and "*arm me*" *CP*, 221.

20. "Buddha," ibid., 232. "Lamia's Song," ibid., 228. "*conjuration*" "In a Bye-Canal," ibid., 239. "*shooting by*" "In a Bye-Canal," ibid., 240.

21. "*none*" "In a Church of Padua," ibid., 241.

22. "*trophy*" Ibid., 228.

23. *booksellers* Sealts, *Early Lives*, 26, and Leyda, *Log*, 794. "*tip*" Oscar Wegelin, in *The Colophon* (Summer 1935), Leyda, *Log*, 826–27.

24. "*partridge*" ESM to CGL, 12/17/90, Leyda, *Log*, 828. "*attention*" ESM to CGL, 1/8/91, Leyda, *Log*, 831.

25. ESM received over $2,000 from Mrs. Martha Bird Marett. *books* Merton M. Sealts Jr., *Melville's Reading: A Checklist of Books Owned and Borrowed* (Madison: University of Wisconsin Press, 1966), 128–29.

26. *Vedder* Leyda, *Log*, 834. David Jaffe, "Sympathy with the Artist: Elizabeth Shaw Melville and Elihu Vedder," *Melville Society Extracts* 81 (May 1990). It's not certain how well Melville knew Vedder, as Vedder lived in Rome most of the time Melville was living in New York, but it's conceivable that he met Vedder at The Century Club with Allan. In *The Digressions of V*, his rambling, humorous, and disconcertingly superficial autobiography, Vedder does not mention Melville.

27. *Lizzie's birthday* Leyda, *Log*, 835.

28. "*lasting love*" "L'Envoi," *CP*, 256.

29. *Melville's consulting Lizzie* Robert Charles Ryan, ed., *Weeds and Wildings Chiefly: With a Rose or Two, by Herman Melville: Reading Text and Genetic Text, edited from the Manuscripts, with Introduction and Notes* (Evanston, Ill.: Northwestern University, 1967), 136.

30. "*Health and Content*" *CP*, 470. "*oneself*" Balzac to Mme. Hanska, 3/1/44, Leyda, *Log*, 816.

31. *collection* In his introduction and notes to the Northwestern edition of *Weeds and Wildings* (see note 29, above), esp. viiiff. and 169ff. Robert Charles Ryan gives as detailed an account as possible of the various groupings, arrangements, and revisions Melville made while preparing the last two volumes of poetry, including the proposed groupings "As They Fell" and "Meadows and Seas." *female deities* In *The Poetry of Melville's Later Years: Time, History, Myth and Religion* (Albany: State University of New York, 1970), William Bysshe Stein discusses the presence of the Triple Goddess in the poems. See also Laurie Robertson-Lorant, "Melville's Embrace of the Invisible Woman," *Centennial Review* 34, no. 3 (Summer 1990), 401–11.

32. *Winnefred* I am indebted to Ryan, ibid., ed., *Weeds and Wildings*, 60, for glosses of the name, but see Lyon Evans Jr., "Inaccuracies and Discrepancies in Herman Melville's 'To Winnifred,'" *Melville Society Extracts* 95, December 1993, 13–14, for a debunking view. *pie* EMM, 225.

33. "*here*" Ryan, ed., *Weeds and Wildings*, 5.

34. "*South*" Ibid., 6.

35. For quotes being considered by Melville, see Ryan, notes, 60.

36. "*snows*" *CP*, 272.

37. *crow* As Ryan, ibid., points out, the manuscripts show that Melville called the crow in "Always With Us" the "black preacher." The crow signifies the preacher with his cowl, a pest and a nuisance to the speaker of the poem, who longs for the return of the robin. Like Falsgrave, Melville's preachers are snobs and hypocrites; see Ryan, ibid., 10, 14. *Malcolm* I'm indebted to Hennig Cohen and Donald Yannella, *Herman Melville's Malcolm Letter: "Man's Final Lore"* (New York: Fordham University Press and The New York Public Library, 1992), for pointing out that "The Chipmunk" is about Malcolm; the phrase "self-slayer sad" appears in an early draft of the poem.

38. "Rip Van Winkle's Lilac," Ryan, ed., *Weeds and Wildings*, 26–34, and *CP*, 281–93. The poem bears traces of the old "Frescoes of Travel" idea, which seems to have been a debate among three brothers–a poet, a painter, and an idler (originally a scholar, but "idler" is a Hawthorne word). "*good-for-nothing*" Ryan, ed., *Weeds and Wildings*, 26–27.

39. "*willow*" Ryan, ed., *Weeds and Wildings*, 27. "*Rip*" *CP*, 293.

40. "*infidel*" HM to James Billson, 4/2/86, NN*Corr.*, 497. "*feast*" Ibid., 45.

41. "*caress*" Ryan, ed., *Weeds and Wildings*, 47. "*rose*" Ibid., 47.

42. "*dies*" Ibid., 47–48.

43. "*God*" Ibid., 42.

44. "*Worm*" Ibid., 42.

45. "*bad boy*" Ibid., 11. "*anew*" Ibid., 9.

46. "*Cross*" Ibid., 38. Rosicrucianism, as Ryan points out (p. 84), is a loosely mystical hedonistic philosophy, a kind of cousin of Freemasonry. "*stains*" Ibid., 40. Emerson, Swedenborg, etc. Ibid., 86–88.

47. "*Eve*" Ibid., 12.

48. "Midwifery should be taught in the same course with fencing and boxing, riding and rowing," says Ishmael, watching Queequeg deliver Tashtego from the whale's severed head, into which he had fallen and nearly drowned, NN*M-D*, 344.

49. "*Asthenia*" Leyda, *Log*, 836. "*care of him*" Leyda, *Log*, MGM2, 9/28/91, Leyda, *Log*, 836.

50. *funeral* Leyda, *Log*, 837. It's not known how many other people were present. George Dillaway first shows up in the city directories in 1870, and he lived a few blocks west of the Melvilles in 1889. According to notes made by Titus Munson Coan on the back of an envelope (Coan Papers, New-York Historical Society), Dillaway was ashamed of his father, who was a Boston teacher, and all he cared about was being fashionable. He was snobbish, even though he didn't know the

best people in Boston. When Dillaway broke his engagement, Coan called it a "good escape for the miss." Coan's comments at Melville's funeral, evidently from a eulogy, perhaps some from a conversation, were reported by Arthur Stedman and quoted in Sealts, *Early Lives,* 44, 100.

51. Based on a visit to the cemetery, whose main entrance is at Jerome Avenue and 233rd Street in the Bronx. Herman, Lizzie, Malcolm, Bessie, Eleanor, and Eleanor's husband are buried in this plot. "*God*" From Balzac's *Seraphita* (1889), Leyda, *Log,* 830.

52. *press notices* See Leyda, *Log,* 836–37.

53. Richard Henry Stoddard, *Recollections: Personal and Literary* (New York: A. S. Barnes & Company, 1903).

54. Stedman, quoted in Sealts, *Early Lives,* 166.

55. "*heart*" ESM Memoranda, Sealts, *Early Lives,* 171.

AFTERWORD: MELVILLE'S SEXUALITY

1. Margaret S. Creighton, "Fraternity in the American Forecastle, 1830–1870," *New England Quarterly* LXIII (December, 1990), 531–537, drawing on sailor journals to give a sense of the shipboard culture Melville experienced, argues that "social worlds dominated by 'romantic' male friendships" predated "ones marked by heterosexual intimacy," but she is careful not to speculate or generalize about the sexual practices of sailors. In *Hero, Captain and Stranger: Male Friendship, Social Critique and Literary Form in the Sea Novels of Herman Melville* (Chapel Hill: University of North Carolina Press, 1986), Robert K. Martin points out that "rover" was a code word for a gay male in Melville's day.

2. Joan D. Hedrick, *Harriet Beecher Stowe: A Life* (New York: Oxford University Press, 1994), 180–181.

3. Andrew J. Hoffman, "Mark Twain and Homosexuality," *American Literature* 67, no. 1 (March 1995), 23–49.

4. Caleb Crain, "Lovers of Human Flesh: Homosexuality and Cannibalism in Melville's Novels," *American Literature* 66, no. 1 (March 1994), 25–53, argues that the oral imagery of Melville's letters to Hawthorne is cannibalistic, and he links cannibalism with homosexuality on the grounds that both were "unspeakable." I find Melville's metaphors religious, not sexual, though; as Melville discovered in the Marquesas, the sacrament of the Christian Mass, which he invokes to describe his intellectual and spiritual intimacy with Hawthorne, has its origins in ancient fertility rites, which are often sexualized. See also David Bergman, *Gaiety Transfigured: Gay Self-Representation in American Literature* (Madison: University of Wisconsin Press, 1991).

5. Charles Haberstroh Jr. touches on this question in *Melville and Male Identity* (Cranbury, N.J.: Associated University Presses, 1980).

6. James Creech, *Closet Writing/Gay Reading: The Case of Melville's* Pierre (Chicago: University of Chicago Press, 1993). 151. *Psychiatry and psychoanalysis* I am indebted to Eugene Taylor for conversations about the connection between the Boston School of Psychiatry and Sigmund Freud.

SELECTED BIBLIOGRAPHY

ARCHIVAL MATERIAL

Albany Institutes of History and Art (AIHA)

Berkshire Athenaeum (BA)

Lansingburgh Historical Society (LHS)

Leyda Collection, University of California at Los Angeles (JL-UCLA)

Leyda, Jay. "An Albany Journal by Gansevoort Melville." *Boston Public Library Quarterly* II (1950): 327–47.

Melville Family Papers, Houghton Library, Harvard University (MFP-HCL)

Morewood Collection, Berkshire County Historical Society (BCHS)

Murray Papers, Harvard University Archives (HUA)

Museum of the City of New York (MCNY)

New-York Historical Society (N-YHS)

New York Public Library, Augusta Papers, Gansevoort-Lansing Collection (GLA)

New York Public Library, Gansevoort-Lansing Collection (GLC)

Osborne Collection of Melville Materials at Southwestern University (OCSWU)

Rockwell Papers, Lenox (Mass.) Library

Shaw Papers, Massachusetts Historical Society (MHS-Shaw)

EDITIONS OF MELVILLE'S WORKS

Melville, Herman. *The Battle-Pieces of Herman Melville,* ed. with introduction and notes by Hennig Cohen. New York: Thomas Yoseloff, 1964.

———. *Billy Budd, Sailor (An Inside Narrative): Reading Text and Genetic Text,* ed. Harrison Hayford and Merton Sealts Jr. Chicago: University of Chicago Press, 1962.

———. *Clarel: A Poem and Pilgrimage in the Holy Land,* eds. Harrison Hayford, Hershel Parker, and G. Thomas Tanselle. Evanston and Chicago: Northwestern University Press and the Newberry Library, 1991.

———. *Collected Poems of Herman Melville,* ed. Howard P. Vincent. Chicago: Packard and Co., Henricks House, 1947.

———. *The Confidence-Man: His Masquerade,* eds. Harrison Hayford, Hershel Parker, and G. Thomas Tanselle. Evanston and Chicago: Northwestern University Press and the Newberry Library, 1984.

———. *Correspondence,* ed. Lynn Horth. Evanston and Chicago: Northwestern University Press and the Newberry Library, 1993.

———. *Israel Potter: His Fifty Years in Exile,* eds. Harrison Hayford, Hershel Parker, and G. Thomas Tanselle. Evanston and Chicago: Northwestern University Press and the Newberry Library, 1982.

———. *Journals,* eds. Howard Horsford and Lynn Horth. Evanston and Chicago: Northwestern University Press and the Newberry Library, 1989.

———. *The Letters of Herman Melville,* eds. Merrell R. Davis and William H. Gilman. New Haven: Yale University Press, 1960.

———. *Mardi and the Voyage Thither,* eds. Harrison Hayford, Hershel Parker, and G. Thomas Tanselle. Evanston and Chicago: Northwestern University Press and the Newberry Library, 1970.

———. *Moby-Dick, or The Whale,* eds. Harrison Hayford, Hershel Parker, and G. Thomas Tanselle. Evanston and Chicago: Northwestern University Press and the Newberry Library, 1988.

———. *Moby-Dick, or The Whale,* The Northwestern-Newberry text, with introduction by Andrew Delbano, notes and explanatory by Tom Quirk. New York: Penguin Books, 1992.

———. *Omoo: A Narrative of Adventures in the South Seas,* eds. Harrison Hayford, Hershel Parker, and G. Thomas Tanselle. Evanston and Chicago: Northwestern University Press and the Newberry Library, 1968.

———. *Piazza Tales and Other Prose Pieces 1839–1860,* eds. Harrison Hayford, Alma MacDougall, and G. Thomas Tanselle. Evanston and Chicago: Northwestern University Press and the Newberry Library, 1987.

———. *Pierre, or the Ambiguities,* eds. Harrison Hayford, Hershel Parker, and G. Thomas Tanselle. Evanston and Chicago: Northwestern University Press and the Newberry Library, 1971.

———. *Redburn: His First Voyage, Being the Sailor-boy Confessions and Reminiscences of the Son-of-a-Gentleman, in the Merchant Service,* eds. Harrison Hayford, Hershel Parker, and G. Thomas Tanselle. Evanston and Chicago: Northwestern University Press and the Newberry Library, 1969.

———. *Typee: A Peep at Polynesian Life,* eds. Harrison Hayford, Hershel Parker, and G. Thomas Tanselle. Evanston and Chicago: Northwestern University Press and the Newberry Library, 1968.

———. *Weeds and Wildings Chiefly: with a Rose or Two, by Herman Melville: Reading Text and Genetic Text,* ed. with introduction by Robert Charles Ryan. Evanston, Ill.: Northwestern University Press, 1967.

———. *White-Jacket, or The World in a Man-of-War,* eds. Harrison Hayford, Hershel Parker, and G. Thomas Tanselle. Evanston and Chicago: Northwestern University Press and the Newberry Library, 1970.

BOOKS AND ARTICLES ABOUT MELVILLE

Adler, Joyce Sparer. *War in Melville's Imagination.* New York: New York University Press, 1981.

Anderson, Carl L. "The Minister's Advice to Elizabeth Shaw Melville." *Melville Society Extracts* 54 (1983): 10–12.

Anderson, Charles R. *Melville in the South Seas.* New York: Dover Publications, 1966.

Avallone, Charlene. "Calculations for Popularity: Melville's *Pierre* and *Holden's Dollar Magazine.*" *Melville Society Extracts* 72 (1988), 6–9.

Baird, James. *Ishmael: A Study of the Symbolic Mode in Primitivism.* Baltimore, Md.: Johns Hopkins University Press, 1956.

Barber, Patricia. "Herman Melville's House in Brooklyn." *American Literature* 45 (1993): 433–34.

———. "Two New Melville Letters." *American Literature* 49, no. 4 (1977): 418–21.

Bergmann, Hans, "'Turkey on His Back': 'Bartleby' and New York Words." *Melville Society Extracts* 90 (1992): 16–19.

Branch, Watson G., ed. *Melville: The Critical Heritage.* London and Boston: Routledge and Kegan Paul, 1974.

Brodhead, Richard H. "Sparing the Rod: Discipline and Fiction in Antebellum America." *Cultures of Letters: Scenes of Reading and Writing in Nineteenth-Century America.* Chicago: University of Chicago Press, 1993.

Bryant, John, ed. *A Companion to Melville Studies.* Westport, Conn.: Greenwood Press, 1986.

Charvat, William. *The Profession of Authorship in America, 1800–1870.* The Papers of William Charvat, ed. Matthew J. Bruccoli. Columbus: Ohio State University Press, 1968.

Cohen, Hennig and Donald Yannella. *Herman Melville's Malcolm Letter: "Man's Final Lore."* New York: Fordham University Press and The New York Public Library, 1992.

Crain, Caleb. "Lovers of Human Flesh: Homosexuality and

Cannibalism in Melville's Novels." *American Literature* 66, no. 1 (1964): 25–53.

Creech, James. *Closet Writing/Gay Reading: The Case of Melville's* Pierre. Chicago: University of Chicago Press, 1993.

Davis, Merrel R. *Melville's* Mardi: *A Chartless Voyage*. New Haven, Conn.: Yale University Press, 1952.

Doenges, Richard C. "The Blizzard and Tulips of '88: Clues for Dating Melville." *Melville Society Extracts* 56 (1983): 11–12.

Emmers, Amy Puett. "Melville's Closet Skeleton: A New Letter About the Illegitimacy Incident in *Pierre*." *Studies in American Renaissance, 1977.* Boston: Twayne Publishers, 1978. See also *Puett.*

Evans, Lyon Jr. "Inaccuracies and Discrepancies in Herman Melville's 'To Winnifred.'" *Melville Society Extracts* 95 (1993): 13–14.

Fisher, Marvin. *Going Under: Melville's Short Fiction and the American 1850s.* Baton Rouge: Louisiana State University Press, 1977.

Flibbert, Joseph. *Melville and the Art of Burlesque.* Amsterdam: Rodopi, 1974.

Franklin, H. Bruce. *The Wake of Gods: Melville's Mythology.* Stanford, Ca.: Stanford University Press, 1963.

Fredericks, Nancy. "Melville's 'Tinhorn' Rebellion: Melodrama and Class Culture in *Pierre*." A paper delivered at the Northeast Modern Language Association Conference, Hartford, Conn., April 7, 1991.

Garner, Stanton. *The Civil War: World of Herman Melville.* Lawrence: University Press of Kansas, 1993.

———. "Fraud and Fact in Herman Melville's *Billy Budd*." *San Jose Studies* 4, no. 4 (1978): 83–105.

———. "Melville in the Custom House, 1881–1882: A Rustic Beauty Among Highborn Dames of Court." *Melville Society Extracts* 35 (1978): 12–14.

———. "Melville and Sandford [*sic*] Gifford." *Melville Society Extracts* 48 (1981): 10–12.

———. "Melville's Scout Toward Aldie." *Melville Society Extracts* 51 (1982): 5–16.

———. "Melville's Scout Toward Aldie, Part 2: The Scout and the Poem." *Melville Society Extracts* 52 (1982): 1–14.

———. "Surviving the Gilded Age: Herman Melville in the Customs Service." *Essays in Arts and Sciences* 15 (1986): 1–13.

Gilman, William. *Melville's Early Life and* Redburn. New York: New York University Press, 1951.

Gilmore, Michael T. *American Romanticism and the Marketplace.* Chicago: University of Chicago Press, 1985.

Hart, James D. *The Popular Book: A History of America's Literary Taste.* New York: Oxford University Press, 1950.

Hayford, Harrison and Merrell Davis. "Herman Melville as Office-Seeker." *Modern Language Quarterly* 10, parts I and II (1949): 168–83, 377–88.

Hayford, Harrison. *"Melville's 'Monody,' Really for Hawthorne?"* Evanston, Ill.: Northwestern University Press, 1990.

Heffernan, Thomas Farel. *Stove by a Whale: Owen Chase and the Essex.* Middletown, Conn.: Wesleyan University Press, 1981.

———. "Melville's Third Whaler." *Modern Language Notes* 64 (1949): 145–50.

Herbert, T. Walter Jr. *Marquesan Encounters: Melville and the Meaning of Civilization.* Cambridge, Mass.: Harvard University Press, 1980.

———. Moby-Dick *and Calvinism: A World Dismantled.* New Brunswick, N.J.: Rutgers University Press, 1977.

Hetherington, Hugh. *Melville's Reviewers, British and American, 1846–1891.* Chapel Hill: University of North Carolina Press, 1961.

Higgins, Brian and Hershel Parker, eds. *Critical Essays on Herman Melville's* Moby-Dick. New York: G. K. Hall, 1992.

———. *Critical Essays on Herman Melville's* Pierre; *or the Ambiguities.* Boston: G. K. Hall and Company, 1983.

Howard, Leon. *Herman Melville: A Biography.* Berkeley: University of California Press, 1951.

Huntress, Keith. "'Guinea' of 'White-Jacket' and Chief Justice Shaw." *American Literature* 43 (1972): 639–41.

James, C. L. R. *Mariners, Renegades and Castaways: The Story of Herman Melville and the World We Live In.* New York: C. L. R. James, 1953.

Kaplan, Sidney. "Herman Melville and the American National Sin." *Images of the Negro in American Literature,* edited by Seymour L. Gross and John Edward Hardy. Chicago: University of Chicago Press, 1966.

Karcher, Carolyn. "The Riddle of the Sphinx, Melville's *Benito Cereno* and the Amistad Case." *Critical Essays on Melville's* Benito Cereno, ed. Robert Burkholder. Boston: G. K. Hall, 1996.

———. *Shadow Over the Promised Land: Slavery, Race and Violence in Melville's America.* Baton Rouge: Louisiana State University Press, 1980.

Kelley, Wyn. "Haunted Stone; Nature and City in *Clarel.*" *Essays in Arts and Sciences* 15 (1986): 15–29.

———. "'I'm Housewife Here': Herman Melville and Domestic Economy." *Melville Society Extracts* 98 (1994): 7–10.

———. "Melville's Cain." *American Literature* 55, no. 1 (1983): 24–40.

———. *Melville's City: Literary and Urban Form in Nineteenth-Century New York*. New York: Cambridge University Press, 1996.

———. "*Pierre* in a Labyrinth: The Mysteries and Misery of New York." *The Evermoving Dawn: Essays in Celebration of the Melville Centennial*, ed. John Bryant. Kent, Oh.: Kent State University Press, 1996.

Kennedy, Joyce Deveau and Frederick James Kennedy. "Additions to the Melville Log." *Melville Society Extracts* 3 (1977): 4–8.

———. "*Elizabeth and Herman*." *Melville Society Extracts* 33 and 34, parts I and II (1978): 4–12, 3–8.

———. "Elizabeth Shaw Melville and Samuel Hay Savage, 1847–1853." *Melville Society Extracts* 39 (1979): 1–7.

Kenney, Alice P. *The Gansevoorts of Albany: Dutch Patricians in the Upper Hudson Valley*. Syracuse, N.Y.: Syracuse University Press, 1969.

Kier, Kathleen E. *The Melville Encyclopedia: The Novels*. Troy, N.Y.: The Whitston Publishing Company, 1990.

Kring, Walter Donald. *Henry Whitney Bellows*. Boston: Skinner House, 1979.

Kring, Walter Donald and Jonathan S. Carey. "Two Discoveries Concerning Herman Melville." Reprinted from the *Proceedings of the Massachusetts Historical Society* 87 (1975): 11–15.

Leyda, Jay. *The Melville Log: A Documentary Life of Herman Melville, 1819–1891, 2 vols*. New York: Harcourt Brace and Company, 1951; reprinted with additional material, Fairfield, Conn.: Gordian Press, 1969.

Martin, Robert K. *Hero, Captain, and Stranger: Male Friendship, Social Critique, and Literary Form in the Sea Novels of Herman Melville*. Chapel Hill: University of North Carolina Press, 1986.

Mellow, James. *Nathaniel Hawthorne in His Times*. Boston: Houghton Mifflin Company, 1980.

Melvill, Jean F. "Melvill Genealogy." *Melville Society Extracts* 95 (1993): 10–13.

Metcalf, Eleanor Melville. *Herman Melville: Cycle and Epicycle*. Cambridge, Mass.: Harvard University Press, 1953.

Metcalf, Paul. *Genoa: A Telling of Wonders*. Highlands, N.C.: J. Williams, 1965.

Metcalf, Paul, ed. *Enter Isabel: The Herman Melville Correspondence of Clare Spark and Paul Metcalf*. Albuquerque: University of New Mexico Press, 1991.

Milder, Robert. "Melville's 'Intentions' in Writing *Pierre*." *Studies in the Novel* 6, no. 2 (1974): 186–99.

Miller, Edwin Havilland. *Melville.* New York: George Braziller, 1975.

Miller, Perry. *The Raven and the Whale: The War of Words and Wits in the Era of Poe and Melville.* New York: Harcourt, Brace and World, 1956.

Mumford, Lewis. *Herman Melville: A Study of His Life and Vision.* New York: Harcourt, Brace and World, 1929.

Murray, Henry A. "Another Triumph for Maria's Firstborn." *Melville Society Extracts* 58 (1984): 1–3.

———. Introduction and Explanatory Notes to *Pierre.* New York: Hendricks House, 1949.

———. "Some Indian Hating in the Melvill Family," unpublished article courtesy of Eugene Taylor.

Murray, Henry A., Harvey Myerson, and Eugene Taylor. "Allan Melvill's By-Blow." *Melville Society Extracts* 61 (1985): 1–6.

Murray, Henry A. and Eugene Taylor. "The Lancaster System of Instruction." *Melville Society Extracts* 16 (1987): 5–6.

Neumeier, Charles and Donald Yannella. "The Melvilles' House on East 26th Street." *Melville Society Extracts* 47 (1981): 6–8.

Newman, Lea Bertani Vozar. "Marginalia as Revelation: Melville's 'Lost' Copy of Dante and a Private Purgatorial Note." *Melville Society Extracts* 92 (1993): 4.

———. *A Reader's Guide to the Short Stories of Herman Melville.* Boston: G. K. Hall, 1986.

Parker, Hershel. "Biography and Responsible Uses of the Imagination: Three Episodes from Melville's Homecoming in 1844," *Resources for American Literary Study* 21, no. 1 (1995): 16–42.

———. "Gansevoort Melville's Role in the Campaign of 1844." *New-York Historical Society Quarterly* 49 (1965): 143–73.

———. "Herman Melville's *The Isle of the Cross.* A Survey and a Chronology." *American Literature* 62, no. 1 (1990): 1–16.

———. "Melville and Politics: A Scrutiny of the Political Milieu of Herman Melville's Life and Works." Diss. Northwestern University, 1963.

———. *Reading* Billy Budd. Evanston, Ill.: Northwestern University Press, 1990.

———. "Why *Pierre* Went Wrong." *Studies in the Novel* 8 (1976): 7–23.

Parker, Hershel and Edward Daunais. "Sarah Morewood's Last Drive, as Told in Caroline S. Whitmarsh's 'A Representative Woman.'" *Melville Society Extracts* 93 (1993): 1–4.

Parker, Hershel and Harrison Hayford, eds. Moby-Dick *as Doubloon: Essays and Extracts* (1851–1970). New York: W. W. Norton & Company, 1970.

Person, Leland S., Jr. "*Mardi* and the Reviewers: The Irony of (Mis)read-
ing." *Melville Society Extracts* 72 (1988): 3–5.

Post-Lauria, Sheila. "Canonical Text and Context: The Example of
Herman Melville's *Bartleby the Scrivener: A Story of Wall Street.*" *College
Literature* 20, no. 2 (1993): 196–205.

———. *Correspondent Colorings: Melville in the Marketplace.* Amherst: University
of Massachusetts Press, 1996.

———. "Genre and Ideology: The French Sensational Romance and
Melville's *Pierre.*" *Journal of American Culture* 15, no. 3 (1992): 1–8.

———. "Philosophy in Whales ... Poetry in Blubber: Mixed Form in *Moby-
Dick.*" *Nineteenth-Century Literature* 45, no. 3 (1990): 300–16.

Puett, Amy Elizabeth. *Melville's Wife: A Study of Elizabeth Shaw Melville.* Diss.
Northwestern University, 1969. See also *Emmers.*

Renker, Elizabeth. "Herman Melville, Wife Beating, and the Written Page."
American Literature 66, no. 1 (1994): 123–50.

Rogin, Michael Paul. *Subversive Genealogy: The Politics and Art of Herman
Melville.* New York: Alfred A. Knopf, 1983.

Runden, John P. "Columbia Grammar School: An Overlooked Year in the
Lives of Gansevoort and Herman Melville." *Melville Society Extracts* 46
(1981): 1–3.

———. "Old School Ties: Melville and the Columbia Grammar School, and
the New Yorkers." *Melville Society Extracts* 55 (1983): 1–5.

Sandberg, Robert A. "House of the Tragic Poet: Melville's Draft of a
Preface to His Unfinished Burgundy Club Book." *Melville Society
Extracts* 79 (1989): 4–7.

Sealts, Merton M., Jr. *The Early Lives of Melville: Nineteenth-Century
Biographical Sketches and Their Authors.* Madison: University of
Wisconsin Press, 1974.

———. *Melville as Lecturer.* Cambridge, Mass.: Harvard University Press, 1957.

———. "The Melvilles, the Gansevoorts, and the Cincinnati Badge." *Melville
Society Extracts* 70 (1987): 1–4.

———. *Melville's Reading.* Columbia: University of South Carolina Press, 1988.

———. "'An Utter Idler and a Savage': Melville in the Spring of 1852."
Melville Society Extracts 79 (1989): 4–7.

———. *Pursuing Melville, 1940–1980: Chapters and Essays.* Madison: University
of Wisconsin Press, 1982.

Shetley, Vernon. "Melville's 'Timoleon.'" *Emerson Society Quarterly* 33, no. 2
(1987): 82–93.

Stein, William Bysshe. *The Poetry of Melville's Later Years: Time, History, Myth, and Religion.* Albany: State University of New York, 1970.

Sten, Christopher, ed. *Savage Eye: Melville and the Visual Arts.* Kent, Oh.: Kent State University Press, 1991.

Stern, Milton R. *The Fine-Hammered Steel of Herman Melville.* Urbana: University of Illinois, 1957.

Stuckey, Sterling. "The Death of Benito Cereno: A Reading of Herman Melville on Slavery." *Journal of Negro History* 67, no. 4 (1982): 287–301.

Sundquist, Eric J. *"Benito Cereno* and New World Slavery." Reconstructing *American Literary History,* ed. Sacvan Bercovitch. Cambridge, Mass.: Harvard University Press, 1986.

Surprise, Rena. "Herman Melville Taught at the Brunswick School." *The Record Newspapers* (Troy, N.Y.), 1968.

Tanselle, G. Thomas. "Herman Melville's Visit to Galena in 1840." *Journal of the Illinois State Historical Society* 53 (1960): 376–88.

Titus, David K. "Herman Melville and the Albany Academy." *Melville Society Extracts* 42, no. 1 (1980): 4–10.

Tolchin, Neal L. *Mourning, Gender, and Creativity in the Art of Herman Melville.* New Haven: Yale University Press, 1988.

Travis, Mildred K. "Fact to Fiction in *Pierre:* The Arrowhead Ambience." *Melville Society Extracts* 15 (1973): 6–8.

Updike, John. "Melville's Withdrawal." *Hugging the Shore: Essays and Criticism.* New York: Alfred A. Knopf, 1983.

Vincent, Howard P. *The Tailoring of* White-Jacket. Evanston, Ill.: Northwestern University Press, 1970.

———. *The Trying-Out of* Moby-Dick. Boston: Houghton-Mifflin, 1949.

Wallace, Robert K. *Melville and Turner: Spheres of Love and Fright.* Athens: University of Georgia Press, 1992.

Weaver, Raymond. *Herman Melville: Mariner and Mystic.* New York: Pageant Books, 1961.

Wilson, James C. "Melville at Arrowhead: A Reevaluation of Melville's Relations With Hawthorne and With His Family." *Emerson Society Quarterly* 30, no. 4 (1984): 232–44.

Yannella, Donald and Hershel Parker. *The Endless, Winding Way in Melville: New Charts by Kring and Carey.* Glassboro, N.J.: The Melville Society, 1981.

Shortened from approximately four hundred titles, this list omits the many critical studies of Melville's writings and all of the tertiary material cited in the Notes.

ILLUSTRATION CREDITS

Courtesy of the author: page 194

Courtesy of the Berkshire Athenaeum: pages 72, 104, 126, 150, 216, 238, 256, 298, 340, 360, 374, 424, 456, 478, 498, 518, 538, and 582

Courtesy of the Bostonian Society, Old State House, Boston, Mass.: page 30

Courtesy of Frances D. Broderick, Lansingburgh, N.Y.: page 50

Courtesy of the J. Clarence Davies Collection, Museum of the City of New York: page xxvi

Courtesy of the Houghton Library, Harvard University, Boston, Mass.: page 564

Courtesy of the Metropolitan Museum of Art: page 16

Courtesy of the Naval Historical Foundation, Washington, D.C.: pages 274 and 596

Collection of The New York Historical Society: page 320

Courtesy of the Old Dartmouth Historical Society, New Bedford Whaling Museum (Mass.): page 86

Courtesy of Portrait File, Miriam and Ira D. Wallach Division of Art, Prints and Photographs, the New York Public Library, Astor, Lenox, and Tilden Foundations: page 174

Sketch (now missing) originally owned by Eleanor Melville Metcalf: page 400

INDEX

Abbot, Djékis, 379
Abbott, Henry, 397
Abby Lodge, 329, 516, 520
Abdallah, guide, 388
Abolitionists:
  and Dred Scott case, 406
  and emancipation, 448
  and Free Soil Party, 182
  and Fugitive Slave Law,
    128, 259, 282–83, 351
  and Gadsden Purchase, 332
  Garrisonians, 259, 260
  in New England, 128,
    259–60, 282–83, 351–52,
    448
  and safe havens, 353
  and Thirteenth Amend-
    ment, 480
  and Typee, 143
  World Anti-Slavery Con-
    vention, 181–82
  see also Slavery; Slaves
Acadia, 382, 383
Acushnet:
  gams with other ships,
    101–2
  HM jumping ship from,
    106–7
  HM's voyage on, 91,
    94–106
  in Marquesas, 103, 105–11
  in Rio de Janeiro, 99
  rounding the Horn, 99–100
  run aground, 106
Adams, Henry, 109, 355, 492,
    543, 581
Adams, John, 41, 43
Adams, John Quincy, 19, 90,
    124, 128, 130, 351, 429
Adams, Miss (nanny), 18, 27
Adams, Samuel, 2, 41
Adirondack, 444–45, 476
Adler, George J.:
  death of, 520–21
  and European trip, 218,
    220, 222–25, 228
  illness of, 337

Agassiz, Louis, 188
Agate, Alfred T., 90, 274, 598
Aguilar, Grace, 300
Albany, New York:
  culture in, 45
  Dutch in, 8, 34, 367
  economy of, 44, 46–47,
    367
  HM in, 34, 44, 45
  Melvills in, 7–8, 43–44
  suburbs of, 64–66
Albany Academy, 45
Albany Classical School, 60
Albany Female Academy, 45
Albany Microscope, The, 64
Albion, The, 234
Alcott, Bronson, 143, 310
Alcott, Louisa May, 438
Alcott, William, 70, 369
Alexander, William, 105, 107
Alger, Rev. Horatio Jr., 510
Alger, William Rounseville,
    528
Algonkians, in New York, 1
Allen, Anne Middleton, 57
Allen, Ethan, 345
All Souls' Church, 214, 504,
    572, 613
America, see United States
American Art-Union, 169
American Company of Book-
    sellers, 198–99
American Fur Company, 44
American Lyceum Move-
    ment, 407
American Museum, 160, 161,
    370, 426, 459
American Revolution:
  betrayal of, 345–46
  Fort Mackinac, 81
  P. Gansevoort and, 2, 3–4
  T. Melvill and, 2, 3, 7
  and Order of the Cincin-
    nati, 4
"American Scholar, The"
  (Emerson), 250
Amistad, 89, 128, 351

Anderson, John Jr., 606
Anthony, Susan B., 461, 556
Antonio, guide, 396
Appleton, Nathan, 159
Arcturus, 148
Armstrong, Capt. James, 117
Arnold, Matthew, 437, 525,
    526, 540
Arrowhead:
  Allan's purchase of, 451–52
  farming on, 258, 321
  HM's drawing of, 400, 420
  HM's purchase of, 257
  household of, 260, 266,
    371, 372, 422
  name of, 258
  offered for sale, 348, 403,
    444
  placed in trust, 371, 413
  poems about, 423, 585,
    609
  social life in, 264, 275–76
  spring in, 321, 452
  summer in, 445, 453
  visits to, 509, 516, 532
  winter in, 341, 450, 455
Arthur, Chester A., 460
Arthur, T. S., 510
Aspinwall, William Henry,
    405, 421
Astor, John Jacob, 44, 90,
    332–33
Astor, William B., 405, 459
Athenaeum, 142, 233, 277, 401
Atlantic Monthly, The, 198,
    404, 496
Audubon, John James, 38
Auld, Jedediah B., 157
Authors Club, 481, 566,
    601–2
Autograph Leaves of our Coun-
  try's Authors, 467

Baker, Abraham, 67
Balzac, Honoré de, 599, 608,
    613
Bancroft, George, 118

Barlow, Joel, 6, 22, 58
Barnum, P. T.:
 and American Museum,
  160, 161, 370, 426, 459
 and *Confidence-Man,* 160, 370
 and freakishness, 161–62,
  426, 460
 and Hippodrome, 555
 and illusion, 370
 and Jumbo, 459, 570
 and Tom Thumb, 161–62,
  460
Barrs, J. W., 575
Bartholomew, Edward, 394
Bartlett, Col. William Francis
 "Frank," 454, 479, 517
Bartley, Mr. and Mrs., 12
Batchelder, Eugene, 102
Battle-Pieces (HM), 471–72,
 484, 486–95
 money lost on, 497
 publication of, 488
 reactions to, 495, 496–97,
  569
 Supplement to, 492–95,
  496, 499
 and war as cannibalism, 490
Beale, Thomas, 241
Beck, T. Romeyn, 45
Beecher, Rev. Henry Ward,
 61, 414, 431–32
Beekman, Mary, 292
Bell, Alexander Graham, 556
Bellamy, Edward, 570
Bellows, Eliza, 433, 442
Bellows, Henry Whitney,
 398, 463, 467
 and All Souls' Church, 214,
  504
 and civic associations, 458,
  557
 and Civil War, 431,
  432–33, 464
 and Lizzie's "case," 505–8
 and materialism, 405, 480
 and Travellers, 481
Belmont, August, 405, 459
Bengal Tiger, 444, 476
"Benito Cereno" (HM), 77,
 141, 208, 595
 narrative of, 349–51
 publication of, 352
 and racism, 349–51, 426,
  448, 464
 writing of, 349
Bennett, Frederick Debell, 173
Bennett, James Gordon, 460

Bent, Martha, 10, 57
Bentley, Richard:
 and copyright laws, 198,
  272–73, 303
 hospitality of, 226
 and *Mardi,* 183, 197
 and *Moby-Dick,* 240–41, 272
 and *Pierre,* 302–3
 and *Redburn,* 201, 214, 223
 and *White-Jacket,* 213, 214,
  221, 222, 223, 230
Bentley's Miscellany, 234, 329
Benton, Thomas Hart, 420
Berkshire County Agricul-
 tural Society, 58, 241–42
Berkshires, 453–54; *see also*
 Pittsfield
Bernhardt, Sarah, 565
Bierstadt, Albert, 431, 481
Billson, James, 575
Billy Budd (HM), 587–93
 characters in, 592
 complexity of, 593–96
 early ideas for, 585
 interpretations of, 521, 594–96
 and *John Marr,* 586
 narrative of, 588–93
 publication of, 593
 serialization of, 588
 and *Somers* case, 122, 123,
  585
 writing of, 587–89, 596–97
*Billy Budd, Sailor (An Inside
 Narrative)* (Hayford and
 Sealts), 594
Bisexuality, 108, 109–10, 111,
 208, 268, 285, 311, 618–20
Blacks:
 and civil rights, 542,
  556–57
 free, 421, 447, 448, 449,
  452, 460, 461, 540
 and Ku Klux Klan, 542,
  558
 regiments of, 464–65,
  466–67
 rights of, 523
 and segregation, 354,
  460–61, 556, 558
 and Social Darwinism, 542
 and unions, 523–24
 and white supremacy,
  346–47
 see also Slavery; Slaves
Blackwell, Elizabeth, 432
*Blackwood's Edinburgh Maga-
 zine,* 165, 192, 221

Blake, William, 540, 575, 611
Blatchford, Mary, 178, 260,
 267
Bleecker, Harmanus, 5
Bliss, Pelatiah, 68
Blithedale Romance, The
 (Hawthorne), 310–12,
 323, 475
Blizzard of '88, 583
Bloomsbury Group, 620
Boccaccio, Giovanni, 342
Bok, Edward, 601
Book publishing, 197–200
 auction system in, 198–99
 audience for, 199, 200, 251,
  286–87, 295
 Boston vs. New York,
  143–44, 198, 243, 249
 as cannibalism, 313, 602
 and copyright, 197–98
 vs. magazine writing, 329,
  344, 358, 371, 486
 and piracy, 198
 poems, 416–17, 422, 486,
  497, 572–73
Booth, John Wilkes, 482
Boston:
 Negro regiment of, 464–65
 New York as rival to,
  143–44, 198, 243, 249
 Sims trial in, 272–83
 Thanksgivings in, 260–61,
  326, 348, 422, 485, 565
 see also New England
Boston Athenaeum, 183
Boston Latin School, 2
Boston Lyceum, 407
"Boston marriages," 268
Boston Post, 234–35, 290, 324,
 601
Boston Tea Party, 2–3, 306,
 368
Boston Vigilance Committee,
 259–60, 283, 352
Bouck, William, 67
Boutwell, George, 530
Brackenridge, Henry W., 12
Bradford, Alexander "Aly,"
 60, 62, 70, 71
 and HM's job, 428
 and *Typee,* 144
Bradford, William, 525
Bradish, Margaret, 12
Brady, Mathew, 446
Brant, Joseph, 3–4
Brewster, George, 467–68,
 470, 473, 613

Brewster, John, 257, 353
Bridge, Horatio, 247, 387
Briggs, Charles F., 200, 237, 344, 501
Brittain, Ellen, 356, 454, 607
Brodhead, Rev. Jacob, 32
Brodhead, John Romeyn:
    and *Omoo,* 152, 154, 155
    and *White-Jacket,* 214
Brook Farm, 142, 310, 323
Brown, John, 414
Brown, Oliver P., 71
Browne, J. Ross, 154, 240
Browne, Junius, 524
Browne, Sir Thomas, 173, 197, 240, 600
Browning, Elizabeth Barrett, 486
Browning, Robert, 491–92, 530
Brownson, Orestes, 449, 476
Bryant, William Cullen, 61, 169, 198, 415, 486, 504, 525
Buchanan, James, 146, 354–55
Buchanan, Robert, 574
Buffalo, New York, as frontier city, 80, 81
Buffalo Commercial Advertiser, 148, 149
Bull Run, Battle of, 435
Bulwer-Lytton, Edward, 277, 325
Bunker Hill Monument, 124, 345
Buntline, Ned, 196
Bunyan, John, 509
Burgoyne, Gen. John, 4
Burke, Edmund, 584, 588
Burns, Anthony, 351
Burns, Robert, 501
Burton, Robert, 173, 197, 240, 600
Burwell, Dudley, 70
Bush, Capt. David, 257
Butler, Pierce, 184
Butler, Rose, 18
Butler, William Allen, 248, 290
Byrne, Benbow, 112
Byron, Lord (George Gordon), 393, 395–96

California, gold discovered in, 94, 228
California and Oregon Trail, The (Parkman), 186

Calvinism, 252, 266, 356
Camoëns, Luis de, 509
Carey, Matthew, 198
Cargill, James, 2, 368
Cargill, Mary, 2
Carlyle, Thomas, 173
Carnbee, Malcolm, 11
Carnegie, Andrew, 460, 523, 542, 569
Carroll, J. W., 575
Cary, Alice and Phoebe, 485
Cary, Rev. Henry Francis, 181
Cat-o'-nine tails, 119
Caxton Press, 607
Cenci, Beatrice, 393, 416
Cenci, Count Francesco, 393
Century Club, 481, 529, 566
Cervantes, Miguel de, 240
Champollion, Jean François, 45
Charity Organization of New York, 569
Charles & Henry, 115
Chase, John J., 118, 619
Chase, Owen, 102, 241
Chase, William Henry, 102
Chatterton, Thomas, 336
Chaucer, Geoffrey, 501, 546
Chautauqua Assembly, 540
Cherokee Nation, 82, 306, 365
Cherry Valley massacre, 4
Chesnut, Mary, 441, 480
Chesterfield, Lord (Stanhope), 67–68
Child, Francis James, 412
Child, Lydia Maria, 39, 133, 161
    and Civil War, 435, 448–49, 492
    influence of, 247
    on New York, 166–69
    and slavery, 260
    success of, 250
Childs, Timothy, 499
China trade, 1–2, 8, 87
Choate, Rufus, 184
Chopin, Frédéric, 325
Chorley, Henry F., 142, 192, 193, 233–34, 277
Chris (slave), 8
Church, Capt. Benjamin, 280
Church, Frederic, 481
Ciceronian Debating Society, 63
City of Manchester, 398

Civilization:
    advancement of, 115–16, 135
    vs. ancient times, 398
    and colonialism, 114
    as confidence game, 368
    and disease, 113
    obliteration of, 385, 602–3
    and poverty, 113
    and "progress," 113–14
    vs. savages, 107, 109, 110–11, 114–16, 127, 134, 135, 141, 209, 351, 367–68, 463, 487, 493
Civil War, 425–55, 464–76, 479–84
    Appomattox, 482
    army camps visited in, 467–71
    battles of, 452–53, 465
    casualties of, 437–38, 445, 465
    commemorations of, 542
    death toll, 435–36, 440, 441, 446, 455, 465, 475
    desertions, 465
    draft riots, 453, 458, 460–64
    and economy, 451, 460, 480, 484, 542
    end of, 479–84
    events leading to, 421–22, 425–27, 430
    fall of Richmond, 482, 491–92
    first skirmishes, 435–36
    and free blacks, 447, 448, 452, 460
    and healing, 493
    HM's ambivalence on, 436
    Lincoln and, 427, 446
    Mosby's Raiders, 469–72
    Negro regiments in, 464–65, 466–67
    peace negotiations, 475
    and postwar corruption, 502, 542
    and Reconstruction, 491, 493, 494, 496, 542
    and religion, 475
    secession and, 421, 422, 423
    ships in, 433–34, 438–39
    state militias in, 431
    surrender, 482
    veterans of, 542, 554
    waste of, 492

Civil War (*cont'd*)
  as watershed, 523–25
  women's work in, 432–33,
    438, 460
Civil War poems (HM):
  "America," 483
  "Armies of the Wilderness,
    The," 488–89
  artistic influences on, 398
  "Battle for the Mississippi,
    The," 442
  "College Colonel, The," 454
  complexity of, 487, 488, 496
  "Conflict of Convictions,
    The," 434, 481–82
  "Cumberland," 439
  on death, 455, 466
  "Donelson," 440
  on draft riots, 453
  "Fall of Richmond, The,"
    491–92
  "Fighting *Temeraire*, The,"
    439
  "Formerly a Slave," 494–95
  "Frenzy in the Wake, The,"
    491
  "House-top, The: A Night
    Piece," 463–64
  "Inscription for the Slain at
    Fredericksburg," 467
  "In the Prison Pen," 470
  "Lee in the Capitol," 492,
    553
  literary influences on, 472,
    488, 489
  on Lookout Mountain, 465
  Lyon eulogized in, 436
  "March into Virginia, The,"
    435
  "March to the Sea, The,"
    486, 490–91, 496
  "Martyr, The," 482–83
  "Meditation," 492
  "Misgivings," 432, 492
  on naval warfare, 438,
    439–40
  "Portent, The," 488
  "Running the Batteries,"
    453
  "Scout Toward Aldie, The,"
    470, 471–72
  "Shiloh," 441
  "Swamp Angel, The," 494,
    495
  "Utilitarian View of the
    Monitor's Fight, A,"
    439–40

"Verses Inscriptive and
    Memorial," 490
"Victor of Antietam, The,"
    446–47
"Weird John Brown," 488
  see also Battle-Pieces
Claflin, Tennessee, 543
*Clarel: A Poem and Pilgrimage
    in the Holy Land* (HM),
    543–53
  caesura in, 553
  characters in, 379
  death, decay, and disillu-
    sionment in, 535, 539,
    545, 563
  dedication of, 536
  and Jerusalem, 388, 534
  language in, 553
  literary influences on,
    546–47, 548
  moral and spiritual ques-
    tions in, 521, 572
  publication of, 535–36
  pulped copies of, 554, 603
  reviews of, 553–54, 558
  tetrameter line in, 553
  writing of, 534–36
Clark, Justin, 46
Clark, Lewis Gaylord, 144,
    236–37
Clay, Henry, 130, 510
Clemenceau, Georges, 542
Cleveland, Grover, 460
Clifford, John, 321, 322,
    323
Clinton, DeWitt, 31
  and P. Gansevoort, 5, 27
Coan, Titus Munson, 411–12,
    431, 566–67, 613
Colburn, Henry, 224, 225
Cole, Thomas, 158, 169,
    304–5, 386
Coleman, Anne, 254
Coleman, Captain, 115
Coleridge, Samuel Taylor, 99,
    173
Colonialism:
  and enslavement, 116
  militaristic, 123
  and poverty, 113–14
  and rape, 139
  and religion, 368
  social damage of, 114,
    134–35
  and *Typee*, 144–45
Columbia Grammar School,
    42

Compromise of 1850, 259,
    260, 281
Compromise of 1877, 558
Confederacy, *see* South
Confidence man, as arche-
    type, 236, 361–62
Confidence-Man, The (HM),
    362–66
  and American frontier, 82
  balance sheets for, 403
  and Barnum, 160, 370
  characters in, 366
  complexity of, 365–66, 370,
    593
  contract for, 372–73, 378
  and disillusionment, 369
  and Hawthorne, 378
  and HM's western trip,
    362–63
  literary influences on,
    369–70
  narrative of, 369–70
  plates of, 403
  preliminary writings, 160
  publication of, 395, 402
  reviews of, 401–2
  sequel to, 376, 396, 486
  and skin color, 364–65
  writing of, 358–59
"Confidence Man, The"
    (play), 361
Constellation, 383
Constitution:
  Fourteenth Amendment,
    499–500
  Thirteenth Amendment,
    480
Cook, Capt. James, 113
Cooke, Robert Francis, 231,
    329
Cooper, James Fenimore:
  and P. Gansevoort, 5
  HM's reviews of, 186,
    237
  influence of, 237
  and *Putnam's*, 330
  on *Somers* case, 122
  success of, 296
  writings of, 9, 81, 84, 186,
    199, 237, 247
Copley, John Singleton, 2
Copperheads, 421–22, 431,
    476
Copyright:
  international, 197–98, 259,
    272–73
  and piracy, 198, 259

Copyright (*cont'd*)
and rejections, 223,
225–26, 303
Cortez, 421
Cosmopolitan, 588
Cotton trade:
and Liverpool, 75, 425
and New York, 182, 421,
425–26
and railroads, 332
and slavery, 405
and South, 421
Course of Empire, The (Cole),
158
Crane, Hart, 439
Crane Paper Company, 343
Crawford, Thomas, 483
Crédit Mobilier, 524
Creech, James, 620
Creole, 128
Cromwell, Samuel, 121
"Crossing Brooklyn Ferry"
(Whitman), 38
Cuba, and slave trade, 354–55
Cummins, Maria Susanna,
250
Currier, Nathaniel, 52
Curtis, George William, 469
and "Benito Cereno," 350
and civil-service reform,
502, 557
and Civil War, 490
and Dix & Edwards, 357,
403
as editor, 350, 357
and lecture tours, 404
and *Putnam's,* 350, 403
and travel writing, 376
Curtis, Joseph, 490
Curtis, Kate, 466
Curtis, Mary, 451
Curtis, Ned, 441, 442, 452
Customs Service, U.S.,
500–502; *see also* New
York Custom-House

Dana, Charles A., 330
Dana, James Dwight, 90
Dana, Richard Henry Jr., 84,
125, 328, 421
HM's acquaintance with,
160
and HM's job, 428
and HM's writings, 215,
240
and *Moby Dick* (ship), 352
and *Putnam's,* 330, 352

on sea voyages, 73–74, 99,
417
and slavery, 182, 259–60,
283, 352, 354
and *Somers* case, 121
Dante Alighieri, 395, 596
Divine Comedy of, 181, 300,
335, 488
influence of, 181, 240, 300,
338, 342, 488
and Tombs, 335
Darley, Felix, 355–56, 481
Darwin, Charles, 100, 118,
540, 541
Davidson, David, 225, 230
Davis, David, 452, 463
Davis, Jefferson, 425, 426
Davis, Theodore, 443
Death:
and cemeteries, 52–53
late poems about, 588
literature of, 520
mystery of, 612
and religion, 51–52, 377,
612–13
and social code, 51–52
"Death Craft" ("Harry the
Reefer"), 77
Decatur, Capt. Stephen, 12
Defoe, Daniel, 509
De Kay, Charles, 566
Dekker, Thomas, 437
Delano, Capt. Amasa, 349,
351, 496
Delf, Thomas, 225
Delmonico, Lorenzo, 459, 460
Democracy in America (Tocque-
ville), 12
*Democratic Press and Lansing-
burgh Advertiser,* 67, 77
Democratic Vigilant Associa-
tion, 405, 425–26
Denison Williams Company, 44
De Quille, Dan, 619
De Vinne, Theodore L., &
Company, 586
Dewey, Mary, 264
Dewey, Orville, 430
Dewey, Rodney H., portraits
by, 238, 424
DeWolf, Oscar C., 469
Dickens, Charles:
American impressions of,
141, 242, 366, 404
American tour of, 129–30
and Powell, 236–37
on public execution, 223

Dickinson, Emily, 80, 369,
553
Dillaway, Isaac, 613
Disraeli, Isaac, 437
District School, The (Taylor),
62, 63
Divine Comedy, The (Dante),
181, 300, 335, 488
Dix, Catherine, 155
Dix, Gen. John A., 155, 462,
464, 467
Dix, Joshua, 357
Dix, Rev. Morgan A., 462
Dix & Edwards, 357, 371,
372–73, 403
Dodge, Abigail R. (Hamil-
ton), 588
Doré, Gustave, 446
Douglas, Stephen A., 415,
426
Douglass, Frederick, 556
and abolitionists, 259, 406,
449, 494
and Boston Vigilante Com-
mittee, 259
and Dred Scott case, 406
as orator, 259
as vice-presidential candidate, 543
Dow, Jane, 129, 154, 233
Drake, Sir Francis, 420
Drew, Daniel, 542
Dumas, Alexandre, 325
DuPont, Samuel F., 445
Dutch:
in Albany, 8, 34, 367
art of, in Holland, 398
and economic control, 367
family connections of, 5
high standards of, 265–66
in Nieuw Amsterdam, 1
social gatherings of, 6
Dutch Church Academy, 5
Dutch Reformed Church, 32
Dutch West India Company,
34
Duyckinck, Evert, 174, 195,
263, 336
"cellar" of, 176, 566
and Civil War, 433, 493, 542
death of, 562
HM's estrangement from,
299–300, 326
HM's friendship with, 162,
169, 183, 191, 243, 269,
372, 436, 437, 521, 559
and HM's poems, 416–17

Duyckinck, Evert (cont'd)
and Holden's, 264–65
library of, 172, 437
and Literary World, 154,
249, 290, 293
and Mardi, 192
and Omoo, 152, 157
in Pittsfield, 243–44, 246,
248–49, 275–76
and Powell, 237–38
and Typee, 142, 147–48
Duyckinck, George, 143,
275–76, 295, 455
Duyckinck, Margaret, 243
D'Wolf, John, 40, 57, 437,
487, 529
D'Wolf, Mary Melvill (aunt),
40

Early, Jubal, 476
East India Trade, 87–88
Eastlake, Charles Lock, 185
Eaton, Joseph, portrait by, 527
Edison, Thomas Alva, 94, 570
Egyptian, 378–80
Ellis, Havelock, 601
Ellis, Sarah, 300
Ellis, William, 136
Ellison, Ralph, 369
Emancipation Proclamation,
448–49
Embargo Act (1807), 2
Emerson, George B., 153
Emerson, Ralph Waldo, 481
and Civil War, 431, 448,
469
and Eastern thought, 45
influence of, 173, 185, 187,
250, 342, 496
on love, 268, 311
ministry renounced by, 2
on politics, 406, 477
as speaker, 183–84, 407,
408
writings of, 413, 446, 510,
528, 556
Empress of China, 1–2, 87
Enceladus, 413
Engels, Friedrich, 76, 181
England, see Great Britain
Erie, 123
Erie Canal, 31, 44, 67, 80
Essex, 102, 241, 322
Etchings of a Whaling Cruise
(Browne), 154, 240
Europe:
HM in, 228–32, 391–98

New World colonized by,
367–68
preparations for trip to,
372–73
see also Great Britain
Everett, Edward, 219, 332,
343

Farragut, Adm. David, 441,
476
Fay, Theodore Sedgwick, 397
Fearon, Henry, 12
Fergusson, Robert, 437
Fern, Fanny (Parton),
250
Fiedler, Leslie, 620
Field, Cyrus, 481
Field, Rev. David Dudley,
241, 243
Field, David Dudley Jr., 243,
244, 245
and HM's job, 428
and Lincoln, 415
and New York City, 405,
462
and Tweed, 243, 524
Field, Maunsell, 355–56, 462
Fields, Eliza, 245
Fields, James T., 198, 244–46
Fillmore, Millard, 426
First Dutch Reformed
Church, 53
Fish, Laura, 116
Fisher, Macey, 418
Fisk, Jim, 524, 542
Fleury, Françoise Raymonde
Eulogie Marie des
Douleurs Lamé, see
Melvill, Françoise
Fleury family, 10
Florida, Seminoles of, 81
Fly, Eli James Murdock, 68,
84, 300, 619
illness of, 269
western trip of, 80, 82, 83
Fly, Harriet, 68
Folk art:
scrimshaw, 98, 100
from tortoise shells, 101
Forrest, Edwin, 195
Fort McHenry, 431
Fort Mackinac, 81
Fort Schuyler/Fort Stanwix,
3–4, 80, 288, 371
Fort Sumter, 430
Foster, George, 343
Fourierist communities, 142

Fowles, John, 369–70
France:
revolution in, 43, 181, 491
trade with, 2
see also Paris
Frankfurt, HM in, 397
Franklin, Benjamin, 20, 345,
347, 369, 510
Franklin, Adm. Samuel, 235
Fraser, Donald, 103
Freemasons, 385
Free School Society of New
York, 367
Free Soil Party, 182
Frémont, Col. John, 420,
476
Frémont, Jessie, 420
French and Indian Wars, 2,
368
Frost, Robert, 455
Fugitive Slave Law (1793),
128, 259, 282–83, 351
Fuller, Margaret, 88, 143, 181,
311
Fur trade, 44, 367

Gadsden Purchase, 332
Galápagos:
HM's story about, 337–38
Rock Rodondo, 101, 338
sea turtles of, 101
voyage to, 100–101
Gallatin, Albert, 145–46
Gansevoort, Catherine Van
Schaick (grandmother),
5, 8, 18
death of, 46, 53
family living with, 44
and HM's christening, 19
Gansevoort, Guert (cousin),
182, 484
and Adirondack, 444–45,
476
and Civil War, 442, 468
and Cumberland, 468
death of, 520, 521
and Decatur, 368, 433
and drinking, 368, 433, 445
and Navy, 27–28, 65, 70,
368, 445, 468, 476
and Ohio, 124
and Somers case, 121–22,
123, 124, 585
Gansevoort, Harme, 3, 53,
555
Gansevoort, Harmen Har-
mense Van, 3

Gansevoort, Henry Sanford
(cousin), 26, 484
and *Battle-Pieces,* 496
and Civil War, 431, 442,
445, 446, 449, 452, 453,
471, 472–74, 476
death of, 474, 528
and HM's lectures, 408, 410
and "lower orders," 463
Gansevoort, Herman
(cousin), 83–84
Gansevoort, Herman (great-
uncle), 4, 5
Gansevoort, Herman (uncle),
42, 77, 156, 357, 443, 521
Gansevoort, Hun (cousin), 89,
90, 134, 585
Gansevoort, John, 3
Gansevoort, Kate (cousin),
422, 478
and Barnum attractions, 426
and Civil War, 442
and fleas, 413
gifts from, 449, 530
and Henry, 473, 528
and HM's writings, 486,
496
and Lizzie, 526, 531
wedding of, 469, 532
see also Lansing, Kate Gansevoort
Gansevoort, Leendert, 3
Gansevoort, Leonard
(cousin), 70, 89, 476
Gansevoort, Leonard (uncle),
5, 24, 65, 89
Gansevoort, Leonard H. Jr.
(great-uncle), 4, 364
Gansevoort, Maria, *see*
Melville, Maria Ganse-
voort
Gansevoort, Mary Anne, 133
children of, 28, 89
as Leonard's widow, 24, 65
Gansevoort, Mary Sanford,
54, 89, 134
Gansevoort, New York:
Gansevoort family in, 5,
409, 436
Stanwix Hall in, 555
Gansevoort, Peter (great-
grandfather), 53
and Fort Stanwix, 3, 80,
288
and *Pierre,* 305
as Revolutionary hero, 2,
3–4

Gansevoort, Peter (uncle), 5,
538
death of, 54, 535
and economy, 62
European trip, 329
as head of family, 5–6, 24,
66, 296
health of, 485
as Henry's father, 473
HM's bequest from, 560
and HM's visits, 34, 326,
371, 466
and HM's writings, 533,
535, 536, 554
as Hun's father, 89, 134
and L. Shaw, 7
and Maria, 8, 26, 54,
65–66, 68, 77, 79, 83–84
marriages of, 54, 134
and A. Melvill, 36–37, 47
Gansevoort, Peter L. (cousin), 89
Gansevoort, Stanwix (cousin),
34, 45
at sea, 65, 89, 123
Gansevoort, Susan Lansing,
134, 329, 466, 485, 533
Gansevoort, Wessel (great-
uncle), 5, 455
Gardner, Augustus Kinsley,
228, 507
death of, 535
medical views of, 190–91,
284
Garrison, William Lloyd, 260,
351, 476
Garrisonians, 259, 260
Gates, Horatio Spofford, 65
Gauguin, Paul, 109
Gay, Martin, 268
Gayarre, Charles, 493, 494,
542
German, John, 112
Gibson, John, 394
Gifford, Ellen Marett, 563,
574, 606
Gifford, Sanford Robinson,
431, 483
Glasgow, 375
Gliddon, George R., 346
Godey, Louis Antoine, 251
Godey's Lady's Book (Hale,
ed.), 90, 156, 199, 251,
296, 325
Godkin, E. L., 502
Goethe, Johann Wolfgang
von, 300–301
Goldberg, J. C., 5

Gottschalk, Louis, 481
Gould, Jay, 524
G. P. Putnam & Company,
345, 535, 553
Graham, John, 12
Graham, Sylvester, 190
Graham's Magazine, 192, 325
Grampus, 89, 134
Grant, Ulysses S.:
and Civil War, 440,
465–66, 468, 482
HM's meeting with, 471
scandals in presidency of,
524, 543
Gray, Barry, 501
Great Britain:
and American Civil War,
425, 433
and American Revolution,
3–4
and Boston Tea Party, 2–3
Chartists in, 181
common law of, 128
and copyright, 197–98
Embargo Act of, 2
HM as cult figure in, 614,
620
New York occupied by, 1–2
and Oregon territory, 144
and Sandwich Islands,
115–16
trade with, 75, 425
see also Liverpool; London
Great Pyramid, 385
Great Western Insurance
Company, 494
Greek Slave, The (Powers), 395,
459
Greeley, Horace, 130, 330
and Civil War, 475, 542
as editor, 181, 542
and HM's writings, 290
and presidency, 476, 543
Greenbush & Schodack Academy, 78, 79, 80
Greene, Richard Tobias
"Toby," 104, 425, 619
and Civil War, 441, 442,
452, 453, 465
jumping ship, 106–7
in Marquesas, 111
and *Typee,* 148
Greenslet, Ferris, 577–78
Greenwood, Grace (Lippin-
cott), 142, 508
Griggs, George, 130, 337,
427, 476, 585

Griggs, Helen Melville, 560,
  577
  and childbirth, 348
  death of, 588
  and family visits, 450–51
  illness of, 585, 588
  marriage of, 337
  see also Melville, Helen Maria
Griggs, Willie, 450
Gulic, John Thomas, 411–12

Hale, Horatio, 90
Hale, Sarah Josepha, 90
Hall, James, 365
Hall, John, 102
Halyard, Harry, 102
Hamilton, Alexander, 385
Hamilton, Gail (Dodge), 588
Hamlin, Hannibal, 428
Hancock, John, 41
Harper, Francis P., 606
Harper, James, 458
Harper, Lathrop C., 606
Harper & Brothers:
  and Battle-Pieces, 488–95
  and book piracy, 198
  debts to, 271, 300, 319, 466,
    497
  income from, 561, 573, 581
  and "Isle," 329
  and Mardi, 196–97
  and Moby-Dick, 271, 276
  and Omoo, 152, 156
  and Pierre, 299, 318, 319
  and Typee, 136
  warehouse fire of, 337
  and White-Jacket, 213, 234
Harper's Family Library, on
  United States, 118
Harpers Ferry, raid on, 414
Harper's New Monthly Magazine:
  HM's poems in, 486
  HM's stories in, 329–36,
    341–42
  HM's work reviewed in,
    496
  income from, 330
  readers of, 330
Harper's Weekly:
  and Civil War, 438, 440,
    442–43, 449, 452, 464,
    479, 484
  guns advertised in, 511
  and Tweed, 524
Harrison, Samuel, 259
Harvard College Library,
  474, 579

Hatch, Agatha, 322, 323–24,
  326, 327
Hathorne, Daniel, 254
Hathorne, John, 255
Hathorne, Nathaniel, 254
Hathorne, William, 254
Hawaii, see Sandwich Islands
Hawthorne, Julian, 275, 455,
  567–68
Hawthorne, Nathaniel, 200,
  256, 264–65, 343, 481
  as consul, 327, 376, 378
  death of, 474–75
  forebears of, 254–55
  genius of, 246, 249–50,
    252, 255
  HM in journal of, 376–78
  HM's conversations with,
    245–46, 267, 272–73,
    275, 311, 326
  and HM's disillusionment,
    293, 294
  HM's feelings disclosed to,
    133, 267, 291, 619
  HM's friendship with, 247,
    253, 254, 257, 266–67,
    269–70, 273, 311, 312,
    610, 619
  and HM's writings, 251,
    290–92, 300, 310–11,
    378, 609
  income of, 250
  and Moby Dick, 244, 270,
    288, 290–92, 293,
    474–75
  outings with, 244–46
  paternal role of, 291, 292,
    294
  and Pierce, 324, 327, 427,
    474
  in Pittsfield, 247, 292
  and religion, 252, 254
  and repression, 267–68,
    269, 304, 311, 323
  at Salem Custom-House,
    500, 501–2
  and socializing, 263, 264,
    289
  and transcendentalists, 252,
    267
  Typee reviewed by, 142
  w added to name of,
    255
  and Wiley & Putnam,
    143–44, 243
  works by, see specific titles
  as writer, 296

Hawthorne, Sophia, 244, 268
  friendship with HM, 247,
    253, 263, 264, 269–70,
    270
  and "Hawthorne and His
    Mosses," 252–53
  husband's work bowdler-
    ized by, 255
  and Moby-Dick, 299
  and Typee, 253–54
Hawthorne, Una, 267, 530
Hawthorne and His Circle
  (J. Hawthorne), 567
"Hawthorne and His Mosses"
  (HM):
  and American culture,
    250
  copying of, 249, 251
  and Hawthornes, 252, 255
  HM's self-disclosures in,
    255, 269
  and Irving, 249
  and Mosses sales, 292
  and New York–Boston ri-
    valry, 249
  and Scarlet Letter, 252–53
  and Shakespeare, 249, 250,
    252
  and "Virginian," 249, 255
  writing of, 247, 248
Hay, John, 475
Haydon, Benjamin Robert,
  161–62
Hayes, Rutherford B., 558
Hayford, Harrison, 594
Hayward, George, 185,
  292–93, 451
Hazlitt, William, 185
Headley, Joel T., 237, 245
Hearn, Lafcadio, 581
Hedrick, Joan, 618
Heine, Heinrich, 446
Hemstreet, Charles, 485–86
Herbert, George, 412
Hercules, 89
Herrick, Robert, 412
Hicks, Edward, 169
Higginson, Col. Thomas
  Wentworth, 283, 351,
  464
Hine, Ephraim Curtis, 118
History of the United States
  (Bancroft), 118
Hoadley, Catherine Melvill
  "Kate," 560, 613
  children of, 348, 411, 453,
    485

marriage of, 336
see also Melvill, Catherine
Hoadley, Charlotte, 411, 453
Hoadley, Lt. Francis, 566
Hoadley, John Chipman, 326
  business of, 407, 527
  children of, 348, 411, 485
  death of, 578
  family visits of, 453, 487
  and HM's job, 427, 428,
    500, 530–31
  and HM's lectures, 407
  and HM's writings, 352,
    554, 559
  and Malcolm's death, 515–16
  marriage of, 336
  and politics, 476, 477
Hoadley, Maria Gansevoort
  "Minnie" (Mackintosh),
    348, 453, 613
Hoar, Ebenezer, 259
Hoffman, Andrew J., 619
Hoffman, Charles Fenno,
  160, 187
Holbrook, Josiah, 406–7
Holden's Dollar Magazine,
  264–65
Hole, Samuel, 571
Holland, Henry, 226
Holland, HM in, 398
Holmes, Oliver Wendell, 57,
  244–46, 257, 352, 355–56
Holmes, Oliver Wendell Jr.,
  446
Holy Land, *see* Mediterranean
Home and Colonial Library,
  and *Typee,* 136
Hone, Philip, 39, 43, 131
Hood, Thomas, 437
Hough, *Military Law* of, 118
House of the Seven Gables
  (Hawthorne), 263, 270,
  300
Houston, George, 362
Howe, Col. Frank E., 462
Howells, William Dean, 429,
  496, 556, 570, 601
Howland & Aspinwall, 71
Hudson, Hendrik, 1
Hunt, Freeman, 369
Hunter, Augusta Whipple,
  52, 137, 160, 164, 178
Hussey, Capt. Christopher, 93

Imperialism, *see* Colonialism
Increase, 89
Independence, 231, 232

Industrial Revolution, 284,
  541, 556
  and women's roles, 63,
    343–44, 460
International Centennial Exposition, 555–56, 599
Iroquois, Commissioner of, 4
Irving, Washington, 195
  and copyright, 198
  in Europe, 137
  and HM's review, 249
  influence of, 162
  success of, 199, 296
  and *Typee,* 137
  and *Weeds and Wildings,* 609–10
Iser, Wolfgang, 584
"Isle of the Cross, The" (HM),
  327, 328, 329, 337
Israel Potter, 344–46
  income from, 345–46, 348
  reprint of, 403, 481
  satire in, 345
  serialization of, 348
Italy:
  culture of, 393–96
  Florence, 394–95
  Milan, 396–97
  Naples, 391–92
  Rome, 392–94
  Venice, 395–96

Jackson, Andrew, 41, 61, 81,
  130, 501
Jackson, Jane, 494–95
Jackson, Robert, 73
Jackson, Gen. Stonewall, 452
James, G.P.R., 289
James, William, 44, 588
Jay, John, 462
Jefferson, Thomas, 41, 364, 541
Jerome, Jenny, 459
Jerrold, Douglas, 601
John Bull, 142, 233, 289–90
John Marr and Other Sailors
  (HM), 568
  and *Billy Budd,* 586
  dedication of, 572, 608
  publication of, 572–73,
    586–87
  stories in, 586–87, 603
Johnson, Samuel, 224
Johnstone, Francis, 112
Jones, John Paul, 345
Jones, Comm. Thomas ap
  Catesby, 122, 155
Judd, Gerrit P., 116
Jude (slave), 3, 364

Kafka, Franz, 332
Kamehameha, King, 115
Kansas-Nebraska Act (1854),
  405
Keats, John, 161, 252, 393
Kemble, Fanny, 38, 184
King, Thomas Starr, 420
King James Bible, 186, 240,
  304, 368, 391, 488, 489,
  509
King Philip's War, 280,
  368
Kirkland, Caroline, 219
Knickerbocker Magazine, 102,
  160–61, 236, 241
Knight, Charles, 231, 240
Knights of Labor, 523–24
Knights of the Round Table,
  172
Knights Templar, 222, 385,
  592
Kossuth, Lajos, 181
Krusenstern, A. J., 40

Ladies' Soldiers' Relief Asso-
  ciation, 442
La Farge, John, 581
Lafayette, Marquis de, 6, 10,
  22, 27, 31
LaFever, Minard, 519
Lamar, Gazaway Bugg, 421
Lamb, Charles, 173
Lamb, Mary, 153
Language:
  of flowers, 153, 171–72,
    188, 608
  French, 87
  and HM's style, 79, 553
  ideas and emotions merged
    in, 304
  of King James Bible, 186,
    304, 368
  Oceanic, 109
  of sailing vessels, 74, 87
  and sexual references, 111,
    285–86, 618
  of Shakespeare, 186, 304
Lansing, Abraham Jacob, 65,
  469–70, 532
Lansing, Edwin Y., 469
Lansing, Kate Gansevoort,
  577, 607
  eccentricities of, 532
  gifts from, 532, 533, 554,
    558, 562
  wedding of, 469, 532
  see also Gansevoort, Kate

Lansingburgh, New York, 50, 64–66, 158, 165
Lansingburgh Academy, 67
"Last Leaf, The" (Holmes), 57
Last Supper, The (da Vinci), 396–97
Lathers, Abby, 329, 426, 493
Lathers, Richard, 493, 510
  and Abby Lodge, 329, 516, 520
  and Civil War, 426, 430, 462, 468
  and Democratic Vigilante Association, 405, 425–26
  and Lincoln's death, 482
  slaves freed by, 260, 329, 425
  and Winyah Park, 329, 434
Lathrop, George Parsons, 602
Latimer, George, 128
Law, George, 501
Lawrence, Amos A., 404
Lawrence, Timothy Bigelow, 429
Lawrence Provident Association, 407
Leader, The, 290, 401–2
Leaves of Grass (Whitman), 166, 250, 286, 608
Lectures, 406–11
  fees from, 409, 411, 414
  first tour, 407–9
  HM's lack of interest in, 403, 411
  and lyceum movement, 407, 410
  Maria's encouragement of, 337, 403
  reading of, 408–9, 411
  reviews of, 407, 408, 409
  second tour, 409–11
  third tour, 413–14
  topics for, 404, 407, 409, 413
Lee, Mother Anne, 242
Lee, Gen. Robert E.:
  and Civil War, 435, 446, 452–53, 480, 482
  "Lee in the Capitol," 492, 553
Lenox, James, 227
Leonardo da Vinci, 396–97
Lewis, Edmonia, 556
Lincoln, Abraham, 146, 355
  and assassination, 426–27, 482
  and emancipation, 447, 448–49

inaugurations of, 426–27, 429, 481
  public appearances of, 415, 428
  renomination, 476–77
  and secession, 421
  and war, 427, 431, 446
Lincoln, Mary Todd, 426, 428
Linwoods, The (C. Sedgwick), 60, 178
Lippincott, Sara Jane (Greenwood), 142, 508
Literary World, The, 160, 200
  HM's reviews in, 154, 186, 240
  HM's work announced in, 201, 276
  HM's work excerpted in, 234
  HM's work reviewed in, 228, 290, 293, 295, 324
  and *Mosses*, 247, 248, 249–50, 251, 252, 255, 292
Liverpool:
  dry-goods business in, 20–21, 75, 425
  Hawthorne in, 327, 376–78
  HM's first voyage to, 70–71, 73–77, 89
  HM's second voyage to, 376–78
  A. Melvill in, 9–10
  poverty in, 75–76
Locke, John, 541
Lockwood, John Alexander, 226, 383, 385, 397
London:
  galleries in, 221, 225, 398
  Gansevoort in, 136, 137, 145, 227
  HM in, 221–27, 230–32, 398
  Moby-Dick published in, 277
  and *Omoo*, 154–55
  Piazza Tales in, 357
  public execution in, 223–24
  Typee published in, 136, 137–38
  and *White-Jacket*, 213–15, 222–26
London, Jack, 581
London Examiner, 142, 192
London Missionary Society, 113

London *Times*, 142
Longfellow, Fanny Appleton, 159, 182
Longfellow, Henry Wadsworth, 121, 182
  and poetry, 81, 414–15, 486, 554
  and *Putnam's*, 330
  and slavery, 283, 448
  and *Typee*, 142–43
Longman's, 395
Lowell, Abbott Lawrence, 61
Lowell, Carlotta, 476
Lowell, Col. Charles Russell, 469–71, 472, 476
Lowell, Effy, 569
Lowell, James Russell, 330, 469, 482, 486
Lowell, Josephine Shaw, 469
Lucas, Robert, 128–29
Lucy Ann, 111–14
Luyster, Albert L., 606
Lyell, Sir Charles, 540
Lynch, Anne Charlotte, 175, 422, 458
Lyon, Nathaniel, 435–36

Macaire, Cyrus, 347
McClellan, Gen. George B.:
  and Civil War, 435, 441, 445, 446
  and presidency, 476–77
McIlroy, Daniel, 154
Mackenzie, Alexander Slidell, 121–22, 124
Mackintosh, Maria Gansevoort Hoadley, 613
McLane, Louis, 137, 144–45
MacMechan, Archibald, 600
Macready, William Charles, 129, 195, 225
Macy, Obed, 322, 323
Macy, Thomas, 322
Mallory, Stephen, 439
Maltbie, Ebenezer, 67
Mangan, James Clarence, 437
Manhattan, *see* New York City
Mann, Horace, 60, 63, 407
Manning, Maria and George, 223–24, 232
Manning, Robert, 254
Marble Faun, The (Hawthorne), 301, 416, 474, 475
Marcy, William L., 146, 155, 354–55

Mardi and a Voyage Thyther
(HM), 118, 209
artistic influences on, 158,
173, 181, 183, 187
conventionality challenged
in, 240
dedication of, 182
and income, 183, 197
metaphysical aspect of, 173,
177, 181, 187, 196–97
narrative of, 188–90
publication of, 186–87, 197
reactions to, 192–93, 234,
277
sales of, 193, 196–97, 223
and slavery, 143
and truth, 200
uncut leaves of, 232
writing of, 171–73, 176–78,
179, 182–83, 186–87,
190, 191
Marett, Ellen (Gifford), 563,
574, 606
Marett, Martha Bird, 563
Marquesas, 598
Acushnet's voyage to, 103,
105–11
and civilization vs. savages,
107, 109, 110–11, 116,
134, 141
HM jumping ship in, 106–7
HM leaving, 111
and *Omoo*, 156
tribes of, 107, 274
and *Typee*, 106, 107–8, 110,
141
U.S. possession of, 107
Married Woman's Property
Act, 506
Marryat, Captain, 200
Marsh-Caldwell, Angela, 300
Martineau, Harriet, 277
Marvell, Andrew, 412, 414
Marx, Karl, 76, 181
Mason, John Y., 354–55
Massachusetts Lodge of
Freemasonry, 2–3
Masters, Edgar Lee, 490
Mather, Cotton, 280, 281,
356, 510
Mather, Increase, 280
Mathews, Cornelius, 53, 195
and *Arcturus*, 148
in Pittsfield, 243, 244, 248
and *Yankee Doodle*, 160
Mathews, Jeanie Lucinda, 245
Matthews, Brander, 566

Maurice, Thomas, 572
Mayflower, 92
Mayo, William Starbuck, 575
Med (fugitive), 128
Mediterranean:
archaeological finds in, 540
Cairo, 383–87
camels in, 382
Constantinople, 380–82
Dead Sea, 388
and Eastern thought,
384–85
and *Frescoes of Travel*, 423
Greek Islands, 382–83
HM's trip to, 375, 377,
378–99
Holy Land, 387–91, 399
Italy, *see* Italy
Jerusalem, 387–90
Parthenon, 399
Piraeus, 391
pyramids, 385–86, 387, 568
Scutari, 382
Smyrna, 382, 390
Syra (Syros), 378–79, 383
Thessaloniki, 379
Valley of the Kings, 385–87
Melvill, Allan (father), 16
in Albany, 44
alleged infidelities of, 10, 57
ambition of, 8, 9, 10, 11–12,
13, 20, 26
and brother Thomas, 46,
47–48
business of, 6–7, 8, 14,
19–21, 24, 28–29, 42–43,
47, 368–69
death of, 47–49, 52
debts of, 21, 22, 23, 24, 25,
26, 35–37, 39, 40, 44, 56,
57
education of, 6
failed investments of, 2, 21,
36–37, 39
as father, 512
and P. Gansevoort, 36–37,
47
and GOD, 11, 19, 369
in Liverpool, 9–10
and Maria, 6–7, 9–10
marriage of, 7–8
in New York, 18, 20–21
in Paris, 6–7, 10, 14
and real estate deals, 7, 9
and Scots nobility, 9, 11, 13
Melvill, Allan (great-
grandfather), 2

Melvill, Françoise (aunt):
death of, 23, 35
family of, 10
marriage of, 22–23
Melvill, Françoise "Fanny"
(cousin), 23
Melvill, Henry (cousin), 134
Melvill, Jean (great-
grandmother), 2
Melvill, John (cousin), 62, 455
Melvill, Julia Maria (cousin),
59, 91
Melvill, Mary Ann Hobart:
death of, 568
and farm, 62, 67
in Galena, 407
marriage to Thomas, 23
and Melvill House, 182
visits with, 260
Melvill, Nancy (aunt), 7
Melvill, Patricia Scollay
(grandmother), 3, 30
Melvill, Pierre François
Henry Thomas Wilson
(cousin), 90, 134
Melvill, Priscilla (aunt), 26,
409, 451, 455
Melvill, Priscilla (cousin), 35,
328
at Arrowhead, 337, 341
as seamstress, 337, 357
Melvill, Robert (cousin), 62,
67
and Civil War, 442, 453, 471
death of, 568
and HM's trip west, 80
in Pittsfield, 182, 241–42,
263
Melvill, Sir John, 6
Melvill, Sir Richard de, 6
Melvill, Susan Bates, 67
Melvill, Thomas (grandfa-
ther):
and Allan's debts, 56, 57
and Boston Tea Party, 2–3,
368
Custom-House job of, 23,
41, 501
death of, 57
home of, 30
marriage of, 3
as Revolutionary hero, 2, 3,
7, 57, 329
and Selfridge, 235
as shipowner, 2
and son Thomas, 23
and War of 1812, 3

Melvill, Thomas Jr. (uncle):
as "B.A.," 58–59
and brother Allan, 46, 47–48
debts of, 22, 23–24
and drawing, 59
in Illinois, 82, 83
marriages of, 22–23
in Paris, 6, 10, 58
in Pittsfield, 56, 58, 62
Melvill, Pierre Thomas Wilson (cousin), 90, 134
Melville, addition of *e* to name, 53
Melville, Allan Jr. (brother):
army camp visited by, 467–70
and Arrowhead, 451–52
and Augusta, 133
birth of, 25
childhood, 28, 42, 44
death of, 529
and excursions, 276
and Gansevoort, 131
and Great Western Insurance, 494
and HM's writings, 152, 165, 182, 373, 416, 529
investments of, 542
law career of, 62, 69, 70, 130
marriages of, 164, 415
money to mother from, 77, 79–80
and politics, 182, 335, 353
schooling of, 62
travel of, 487
Melville, Augusta (sister), 298, 485
and Allan, 133
birth of, 24
childhood, 28, 39, 40, 46, 59
and children's party, 533–34
death of, 535
and excursions, 276
and Hawthorne, 264, 267, 302
health of, 42
and HM's children, 132–33, 187, 443, 450, 451, 514–15, 522
HM's work copied by, 132, 183, 262, 272, 299
and marriage prospects, 69, 130, 164, 302
as teacher, 132, 179, 443
Melville, Catherine Bogart, 520, 522, 613
Melville, Catherine "Kate" (sister):
birth of, 28

childhood, 42
living at home, 132, 134
marriage of, 336
see also Hoadley, Catherine Melville
Melville, Elizabeth "Bessie" (daughter), 360, 526, 531, 577
and arthritis, 449, 528, 562, 563, 565–66, 568, 572, 578
birth of, 328
childhood of, 371, 449
HM's letter to, 420
schooling of, 450, 452
Melville, Elizabeth Shaw "Lizzie," 582
and alleged abuse, 372, 373, 504, 505–6
and bookkeeping, 346
and childbirth, 185, 288, 292–93, 294, 328, 344, 348
childhood of, *see* Shaw, Elizabeth Knapp
and child-rearing, 266, 512
and church, 504–5
and Civil War, 442
as grandmother, 568, 571
health of, 443, 519, 526, 530, 531, 563, 565, 568
and HM's literary reputation, 536, 614–15
and HM's moods, 371–72, 504, 509, 558
as HM's Muse, 607–8
HM's work copied by, 180, 262, 416, 486, 534, 608
household of, 169–70, 258, 260, 265–66, 325, 443, 447, 451, 503, 528, 559
and Malcolm's death, 513–16, 519, 529
and Maria, 159, 170, 180, 233, 265–66, 294
marriage of, 7, 150, 162–63, 165, 179, 531–32
money and property of, 159, 328, 371, 436, 506, 530, 531, 563, 573, 606
pregnancies of, 182, 183, 237, 271, 326, 346
"rose cold" of, 239, 272, 452, 522, 530, 554, 571, 574
and separation, 505–9
social life, 170–71, 175–76, 232–33, 244, 248,

356–57, 371, 454, 466, 534, 607
and Stanwix's death, 576–77
wedding trip of, 163–64
Melville, Frances "Fanny" (daughter), 360, 512, 526
birth of, 348
HM's work copied by, 534
at home, 528, 531
schooling of, 450
and Thomas, 561–63, 565
see also Thomas, Frances Melville
Melville, Frances Priscilla "Fanny" (sister), 182, 560, 583
birth of, 37
childhood of, 59
death of, 572
HM admired by, 134
and HM's poems, 486
living at home, 132, 170
Melville, Gansevoort (brother), 126
advice from, 84, 91–92
birth of, 8
and business, 53–54, 59–61, 62
childhood, 19, 25, 26, 35, 39, 40
death of, 145, 146–47, 521
as favorite, 25, 33
health of, 64, 69–70, 77, 91, 92, 131, 144–45
and HM, 25, 28, 33, 55, 227, 294
and law career, 62, 69, 130
in London, 136, 137, 145, 227
money needed by, 91
and politics, 130–31, 134–35, 144, 281
schooling of, 32, 42, 45, 46
and *Typee,* 136, 138, 144, 147
Melville, Helen Maria (sister), 8
in Boston, 129–30, 132
childhood, 19, 39, 40, 59
and Griggs, 130, 337
HM's work copied by, 201, 272
living at home, 132
schooling of, 60–61
see also Griggs, Helen Melville

Melville, Herman:
  and abolition, 430
  aging of, 447, 457, 523,
    527, 559, 561, 565,
    568–69, 571, 576,
    585–86, 607
  in Albany, 34, 44, 45
  appetite for the sea, 66–67,
    68, 70–71, 77, 84–85,
    87–89, 92
  army camp visit of, 467–71
  bank job of, 55, 60
  birth of, 1, 18–19
  and bisexuality, see Bisexu-
    ality
  childhood of, 25–26, 35,
    38–41, 45, 48
  complex identities of,
    423
  at Custom-House,
    500–503, 525, 530–31,
    557–58, 560–61, 573, 576
  dealing with pain, 267–68,
    269, 515
  death of, 593, 613–14, 615
  depression of, 294, 348,
    370, 390
  and disillusionment,
    293–94, 369, 388, 398,
    412, 497, 569, 571
  and drawing, 59, 400
  and drinking, 370–71, 504,
    509, 559, 569
  early writings of, 68, 77–78
  and engineering, 67
  as ex-celebrity, 457–58,
    481, 497, 575, 601
  eye problems of, 269, 393,
    409, 472, 530, 569
  family letters, 264
  family visits of, 34–35, 37,
    40–41, 42, 58, 62, 529,
    555
  and farming, 58, 62, 67, 82,
    83, 257–58, 321
  as father, 262, 370, 419–20,
    503–4, 509, 511–13, 515,
    516–17, 595–96
  and father's death, 48–49,
    55, 268, 303, 370, 573
  fortieth birthday of, 413
  and four-leaf clover, 162,
    607, 608
  and Gansevoort, 25, 28, 33,
    55, 146–47, 227, 294
  and genius, 297, 370, 525,
    576

  as grandfather, 562, 566,
    568, 578–81, 584
  as head of family, 146
  health of, 348, 352, 353,
    370, 372, 376, 414, 437,
    444, 447, 531, 561, 568,
    569, 601, 606, 615
  hiking and climbing, 63,
    245, 276, 336, 409, 446
  imagination of, 33–34,
    38–39, 40–41, 46, 48, 68,
    125, 171, 261, 269
  infancy, 19, 20
  injury of, 447
  and job-hunting, 67, 84,
    155, 328, 427–29, 497
  journal of, see Mediter-
    ranean
  and language, 79
  and lecturing, see Lectures
  letters burned by, 455
  literary influences on,
    33–34, 46, 84, 185
  and Lizzie, 7, 150, 151–53,
    155–56, 257, 258, 268,
    294, 504, 509, 530,
    531–32, 571, 607, 618; see
    also Melville, Elizabeth
    Shaw
  and madness, 509
  and Malcolm's death,
    513–17, 519, 527–28, 574,
    595–96
  and marriage, 158–59,
    171
  and men's clubs, 63–64,
    172, 385, 480–81, 566
  money needed by, 240–41,
    271, 348, 358, 371, 413
  moods of, 171, 265, 272,
    294, 295, 296, 370–71,
    504, 534, 558, 559
  and mortality, 447
  and mother, 265, 266, 294;
    see also Melville, Maria
    Gansevoort
  newer generations' discov-
    ery of, 574–76, 581, 601
  novels by, see Novels
  obituaries of, 614
  papers of, 593
  physical appearance of, 79,
    373, 412
  poems by, see Civil War
    poems; Poems
  and politics, 427–28, 430,
    543, 569

  portraits of, 72, 265, 424,
    518, 527
  pseudonyms of, 67, 77, 249
  reading as escape for, 84,
    525–26, 527, 572
  and religion, see Religion
  restlessness of, 166, 229,
    436
  reviews by, see Reviews
  schooling of, 32–33, 35, 38,
    39–40, 42, 45–46, 67
  at sea, see Sea voyages
  sexuality of, 617–20
  short pieces by, see Short
    pieces
  sixtieth birthday of, 563
  as slow child, 25–26, 28,
    32–34, 596
  in social situations, 295,
    355–56, 444, 485–86,
    559
  solitude sought by, 38–39,
    326, 437, 525–26, 528
  success sought by, 293–94,
    300, 302–3
  as teacher, 62–63, 78, 79,
    80
  tombstone of, 613
  twenty-fifth birthday of,
    122–23, 133
  and war, see Civil War
  wedding of, 162–63
  western travel of, 80–83,
    362–63
  will written by, 585–86
  writing routine of, 165,
    169–70, 176, 261, 262–63
  writings of, see specific works;
    Writing
Melville, Jane Louisa
    Dempsey, 415, 452, 487
  army camp visit, 467, 468
  death of, 601
Melville, Kitty (niece), 442
Melville, Malcolm (son), 360,
    449, 450, 510–17
  as actor, 448
  baptism of, 214
  birth of, 184–85
  childhood of, 201, 260–61,
    272, 326, 329, 348, 357
  and Civil War, 434, 511
  death of, 513–17, 519,
    527–28, 578
  and HM as father, 504,
    509, 511–13, 515
  HM's letters to, 418–19

Melville, Malcolm (son) (*cont'd*)
jobs of, 487–88, 509,
510–11
name of, 183
photograph of, 498,
529–30
schooling of, 411, 444, 445
Melville, Maria Gansevoort
"Milie" (niece), 452, 467,
468, 504, 563
birth of, 184
and Morewood, 532, 533
Melville, Maria Gansevoort
(mother), 216, 456
adolescence of, 5–6
aging of, 456, 466, 479, 520
and Allan (husband), 6–7,
9–10
and Allan (husband)'s
death, 48, 52–55
and Allan (son)'s death, 529
and brother Peter, 8, 26,
54, 65–66, 68, 77, 79,
83–84
and childbirth, 8, 18, 24,
25, 28, 37, 42
death of, 529
and depression, 26, 28, 43,
55, 132
duties of, 6, 132
and family visits, 19, 521,
522, 529
and fiction, 6
and Gansevoort's death,
146–47
health of, 27, 33, 132, 466,
487
and HM's careers, 78,
84–85, 91, 134, 135, 327,
337, 348, 403
HM's letters to, 56–57
and HM's marriage,
158–59, 162, 165, 265
and HM's writing, 57, 296,
327
household arrangements of,
8, 22, 26–27, 40, 54,
65–66, 77
and Lizzie, 159, 170, 180,
233, 265–66, 294
marriage of, 7–8
and money, 37, 54, 56, 57,
62, 65–66, 68, 77, 79,
83–84
as mother, 18–19, 48,
69–70, 84, 131–32, 212,
294

and name change, 53
and pregnancy, 24, 25, 28,
35, 37
and religion, 53
self-pity of, 77, 79, 84
social life of, 11, 14–15, 25,
26, 35, 36, 42–43, 54,
295
stoicism of, 48, 521
and womanly arts, 5–6
Melville, Sophia Thurston, 329
and Allan, 158
and childbirth, 184
death of, 409
and excursions, 276
and HM's writings, 165
pregnancies of, 182, 239,
248, 249
social life, 248
wedding of, 164
Melville, Stanwix (son), 360
birth of, 288, 344
childhood of, 336, 419–20,
434, 443, 450
and deafness, 519, 522, 531
death of, 576–77, 578
health of, 557, 562, 566, 573
as infant, 292–93, 326, 327
jobs of, 521, 522, 527, 528,
531, 533, 557
and Malcolm's death,
514–15, 519
schooling of, 444, 445
travels of, 522, 526, 528,
531, 533, 560
Melville, Thomas (brother):
and *Bengal Tiger,* 444, 476
birth of, 42
death of, 568
and HM's letters, 444–45
on merchant vessel, 180
and *Meteor,* 415–21
poem dedicated to, 572
and *Redburn,* 209
and Sailors' Snug Harbor,
88, 519–22, 529
visits with, 410, 487, 572
whaling and, 88, 134, 179
Men:
clothing for, 438
HM's attraction to, 108
and polyandry, 108
Polynesian, 108
privilege and power of, 523
rights of, 506, 556–57
and same-sex friendships,
268, 285, 311, 618–20

and self-improvement, 510
and separation or divorce,
184, 506–7
social lives of, 176
and spousal abuse, 505–8
as writers, 250–51, 296–97
Meteor, 415–21, 436
man overboard, 418–19
rounding the Horn, 417–18
trip curtailed, 420–21
Mexican War, 145–46, 332,
355
*Military Law Authorities and
Courts Martial* (Hough),
118
Miller, Henry, 382
Miller, William, 133
Milton, John, 240, 488, 489
Mitchell, Maria, 187, 322–23,
604
Mitchell, William, 322
Moby Dick (fugitive slave ship),
352
Moby-Dick (HM):
advance for, 241, 272
and American frontier, 82
artistic influences on, 398
dedication of, 288, 292
as epic journey, 262, 277
first-person narrative of,
318
and Hawthorne, 244, 270,
288, 290–92, 293, 474–75
HM's faith in, 271, 272,
284, 474
income from, 296, 561
life reflected in, 84, 276,
282–84
literary influences on, 237,
240, 241, 246–47,
277–78, 289, 304
metaphysical aspects of,
270, 279, 280, 284, 289,
290
moral vision of, 288, 493
narrative of, 278–80,
281–82
nature in, 287
and other whaling tales,
102–3, 262
and *Pierre,* 315, 316, 317–18
publication of, 272, 277,
288
religious subtext in, 286,
287, 293, 295–96, 317
reviews of, 277, 289–90,
293, 295–96, 575

Moby-Dick (HM) (*cont'd*)
  and "Rose Farmer," 610
  sales of, 296, 300
  sexual references in,
    285–86, 619–20
  volcanic language of, 304,
    594
  writing of, 251, 261–62, 266,
    269, 270–71, 272, 315
"Mocha Dick" (Reynolds),
  102, 241
Mohawks, 3–4, 367
Monitor, 439
Monroe, James, 22, 58
Montgomery, Isaac, 116
Monument Mountain, 244–45
Moore, Thomas, 437
More, Sir Thomas, 540
Moredock, Col. John, 365
Morewood, Agnes, 563
Morewood, John Rowland,
  243, 295, 336, 453
Morewood, Maria Melville
  "Milie," 533, 563; *see also*
  Melville, Maria Ganse-
  voort
Morewood, Sarah, 238, 321,
  414
  and Allan's marriage, 415
  and Civil War, 433, 442,
    445, 454
  death of, 454–55
  and HM's writings, 286,
    294–95
  parties planned by, 243,
    244, 247–49, 276, 295,
    356, 454
  poems by, 300, 326
Morewood, Willie, 532, 533,
  563
Morgan, J. P., 460, 542
Morning Advertiser, 277
Morning Post, 290
Morris, George P., 417
Mosby's Raiders, 469–72
Mosses from an Old Manse
  (Hawthorne), 241, 475
  HM's review of, *see*
    "Hawthorne and His
    Mosses"
  reissue of, 243
  sales of, 292
Mott, Lucretia, 182
Mount, William Sydney, 169
Moxon, Edward, 225–26
*Mrs. Stephens' Illustrated New
  Monthly,* 402

Mudge, Rev. Enoch, 92
Murray, John:
  hospitality of, 226
  and *Mardi,* 172, 177, 180,
    183
  and *Omoo,* 148–49, 151,
    152, 155, 156, 172
  and *Typee,* 136, 137, 145,
    148–49, 155, 180
  and *White-Jacket,* 221, 223,
    224

Nantucket, HM's trip to,
  321–23
Nast, Thomas, 443, 465
*National Antislavery Standard,
  The,* 143, 157
National Labor Union,
  523–24
National Museum of Natural
  History, 90
Native Americans:
  conquest of, 2, 4, 81–82,
    280, 306, 364–65,
    367–68
  and fur trade, 367
  in western U.S., 81
  see also specific tribes
*Natural History of the Sperm
  Whale, The* (Beale), 241
Nauvoo, Mormon settlement,
  83
Navy, U.S.:
  abuses of power in, 121
  and Articles of War, 119,
    133, 211
  executions without court-
    martial by, 120–22
  and flogging, 119–20, 194,
    210, 236, 259, 383
  frigates of, 117, 123
  HM discharged from, 129
  reforms in, 235–36, 259
  regulations of, 117, 119, 210
  and *Somers* case, 120–22,
    585
  as undemocratic, 123
  and *United States,* 117
  and *White-Jacket,* 123, 129,
    209, 215, 234, 235–36
Near East, *see* Mediterranean
Nelson, Lord Horatio, 588
New England:
  abolitionists in, 128,
    259–60, 282–83, 351–52,
    448
  King Philip's War, 280, 368

militias from, 431
  Personal Liberty Laws, 128,
    129
  settlers in, 367–68
  and war with Mexico, 145
  whaling industry in, 92–94,
    96
New Hampshire, Melvilles'
  wedding trip to, 163–64
New World:
  and Europe, 367–68
  settlement of, 2
  and utopia, 540–41
New York City:
  Astor Place Riot, 195–96
  Bleecker Street, 26–27
  Boston as rival to, 143–44,
    198, 243, 249
  British occupation of, 1–2
  Broadway, 26–27, 39, 40,
    41, 42, 167
  Brooklyn Bridge, 570
  Central Park, 525, 579
  and Civil War, 431, 453,
    460, 480
  corruption in, 406, 502,
    524–25
  and cotton trade, 182, 421,
    425–26
  Courtlandt Street, 22
  culture in, 158, 167–68,
    169, 171, 525, 560, 570
  disease in, 17, 19, 24, 239
  draft riots in, 453, 458,
    460–64
  economy of, 7, 480
  Eighteenth Street, 436
  ethnic groups in, 168–69,
    196, 460–61, 570
  excitement of, 166–71
  Fifth Avenue, 404, 459,
    569
  free blacks in, 421, 449, 461
  gold market, 524
  Hell's Kitchen, 459
  Hippodrome, 458, 555
  history of, 1
  HM's birth in, 1
  lodgings in, 12–13, 40
  Madison Square Garden,
    459
  Melvilles' moves to, 166,
    451, 455, 504
  A. Melvill's business in,
    20–21
  Melvills in, 18
  Metropolitan Fair, 467

New York City (*cont'd*)
  museums in, 525
  Pearl Street, 13, 18, 21–22, 33
  port of, 8–9, 10, 13–14, 21, 367, 421–22
  Potter's Field, 17
  public hangings in, 17–18
  public works in, 525
  segregation in, 460–61
  Seventh Regiment, 430–31
  southern sympathies of, 421–22
  Statue of Liberty, 570
  street gangs, 405
  street scenes, 167, 169, 458
  Tammany Hall, 524
  The Tombs in, 320, 334–35
  Twenty-sixth Street, 455, 457, 457–67
  Union League Club, 458, 464, 466–67
  war debt of, 437
  see also Nineteenth century
New York Custom-House, 397, 401, 427, 497
  HM's job with, 500–503, 521, 530–31, 557–58, 560–61, 573, 576
  other writers in similar jobs, 501–2
New-York Gallery of the Fine Arts, 43, 158
New-York Historical Society, 397, 410
New York House of Refuge, 367
New York Infirmary and College for Women, 432
New-York Male High School, 32, 367
New York Public Library, 413, 560
New York Society Library, 172, 240, 601, 606
New York State:
  Charities Aid Association, 524
  economy of, 484
  as frontier, 80, 367
  fur trade in, 8, 367
  Married Woman's Property Act, 506
  Negro regiments of, 464, 466–67
  public works in, 353
  rent wars in, 305–6

New York State Bank, 55, 83
Niebuhr, Barthold G., 390, 539–40
Nieuw Amsterdam, *see* New York City
Nightingale, Florence, 432
Nineteenth century:
  apprentice system, 70
  Blizzard of '88, 583
  childbirth in, 19, 182, 618
  civilization in, *see* Civilization
  clothing in, 438, 475–76
  commercialism in, 166–67, 369, 524, 539, 570
  divorce in, 184, 207–8
  economy in, 20–21, 41, 46, 61–62, 76, 82, 94, 135, 203, 404–6, 532
  factories in, 540–41
  familial patterns in, 301
  fiction in, 5–6, 240, 318–19, 326
  fraternal societies in, 63–64
  gap between rich and poor, 76, 167, 226, 404–5, 459, 541, 569
  guidebooks for life in, 510
  immigration in, 541, 569, 570
  Industrial Revolution in, 284, 541, 556
  letter-writing in, 6
  materialism in, 405, 523, 539
  matriarchy in, 306–7
  medical opinion in, 284–85
  men in, *see* Men
  minstrel shows, 448
  in New York, *see* New York City
  politics in, 405–6, 501–2, 523–25, 541, 557
  poverty in, 19, 46–47, 76, 366–67, 404, 524, 532, 541, 569
  publishing in, 197–200
  reading in, 178, 485, 486
  reform movement in, 366–67, 525
  religion in, *see* Religion
  revolutions in, 181
  same-sex friendships in, 268, 618–20
  schooling in, 46, 60, 443
  science in, 322–23, 346, 539, 540

separation and divorce in, 184, 505–9
sexuality in, 190–91, 284, 301–2, 311, 618–20
Social Darwinism in, 541–42, 569
social schizophrenia in, 70, 125, 301
Solitary System, 141
spermatic economy in, 284, 285
spoils system, 41, 130, 501, 557
spousal abuse in, 505–8
teaching in, 63
whaling in, 92–94
women in, *see* Women
Norris, Tommy, 459
North Star, 421
Norton, Charles Eliot, 330, 496
Nott, Josiah, 346
Nourse, Amos, 46, 428, 476, 477, 508, 560
Nourse, George, 533
Nourse, John, 153–54
Nourse, Lucy, 46, 562, 572
Novels (HM):
  Confidence-Man, 362–66, 369–70
  Mardi, 188–90
  Moby-Dick, 278–82
  Omoo, 156–57
  Pierre, 304–10, 312–17
  Redburn, 200–209
  Typee, 135–41
  White-Jacket, 209–14
  see also specific novels

O'Brien, Fitz-James, 326–27, 402
Odd Fellows, 63
Ōe, Kenzaburō, 585
Offenbach, Jacques, 570
Olmsted, Frederick Law, 244, 405, 458, 464, 525
Omoo (HM):
  advance for, 155
  dedication of, 156
  income from, 157, 172, 561
  life reflected in, 112, 137
  publication of, 156–57
  reviews of, 156–57
  sent to London, 154–55
  as sequel to *Typee,* 148–49, 151, 152, 156
  writing of, 151, 152

Opdyke, David, 434, 462
Order of the Cincinnati, 4,
    385
Oregon, 134
Orwell, George, 594
Osgood, Samuel, 514
O'Sullivan, John L., 135, 143
Our Young Friend, 511

Paddock, Ichabod, 93
Page, William, 394
Paine, Thomas, 584
Panama, Isthmus of, 421
Panic of 1837, 61–62, 135,
    332–33
Panic of 1857, 94
Paris:
    dry-goods business in,
        20–21
    and fur trade, 367
    HM in, 228–29
    A. Melvill in, 6–7, 10, 14
    T. Melvill in, 6, 10, 58
Parker, Theodore, 351
Parkman, Francis, 186
Parkman, George, 322
Parmelee, Mary Eleanor, 68
Parthenon, 399
Parton, Sarah (Fern), 250
Paulet, Lord George, 115–16
Peabody, Elizabeth, 247, 254
Peale, Titian Rembrandt, 90
Pease, Henry, 442
Pease, Capt. Valentine II, 94,
    100, 101, 106, 107
Peck, George Washington,
    157, 325
Peebles, Anthony Augustus,
    164, 568
Peebles, Maria Van Schaick,
    65, 164
Peebles, Mary Louisa, 68, 568
Penniman, Augusta, 88, 115
Pennsylvania, oil in, 94
Penny Cyclopaedia, 231, 240
Perry, Adm. Oliver Hazard, 6
Personal Liberty Laws, 128,
    129
Peterson, T.B. & Company,
    481
Phillibrown, T., engraving by,
    256
Phillips, Wendell, 128, 351,
    407, 476, 493–94, 574
Philo Logos Society, 63–64
Piazza Tales, The (HM),
    357–58, 371, 403

Pickering, Charles, 90
Pickett, Gen. George E., 453
Picture of Liverpool, The, 71
Pierce, Franklin, 324, 327,
    328, 355, 427, 474
Pierre, or The Ambiguities
    (HM):
    advance for, 302–3
    characters in, 123
    contract for, 299, 300
    dark ending of, 317
    dedication of, 304
    and incest, 57, 288, 301–2,
        314, 327, 620
    income from, 300, 319
    influences on, 304–6, 475
    initial ideas for, 277, 301
    interpretations of, 301,
        310–12
    and *Israel Potter,* 346
    lack of support for, 303,
        312, 318
    life reflected in, 10, 305–6,
        316, 336
    literary influences on, 247,
        253, 300–301
    and *Moby-Dick,* 315, 316,
        317–18
    narrative of, 304–10,
        312–17
    publication of, 317
    and *Redburn,* 206–7, 208
    reviews of, 317–19, 324,
        325–26, 327
    satire in, 302, 307
    self-flagellating in, 303, 312
    self-parody of, 302
    writing of, 303
Pinkerton, Allan, 427
Pittsfield:
    farm in, 56, 58, 62, 67, 240
    Homestead Inn, 574
    Melville family in, 56, 241,
        257–59, 260, 447
    Melvill House, 182, 353,
        355
    militia from, 431, 454
    Monument Mountain,
        244–45
    outings in, 242–49
    South Street house, 447,
        448
    see also Arrowhead
Plato, 604
Plutarch, 488, 603
Poe, Edgar Allan, 78, 82, 158,
    318, 481, 501

Poems (HM):
    "Admiral of the White,
        The," 572
    "After the Pleasure Party,
        Lines Traced under an
        Image of Amor Threat-
        ening," 603–4
    "Age of the Antonines,
        The," 398, 602
    allegories of family
        tragedies in, 609
    "American Aloe on Exhibi-
        tion, The," 599
    "Apparition, The," 517
    on Arrowhead life, 423,
        585, 609
    artistic influence on,
        393–98, 422–23
    "At the Hostelry," 584
    "Billy in the Darbies," 585,
        588
    "Buddha," 604
    "Burgundy Club sketches,"
        584
    "Butterfly Ditty, The," 611
    categories of, 585
    of Civil War, *see* Civil War
        poems
    Clarel, 388, 534–36, 539,
        543–53
    on Custom-House job, 503
    "Devotion of the Flowers to
        their Lady, The," 611
    "Ditty of Aristippus," 601
    "Falstaff's Lament over
        Prince Hal Become
        Henry V," 422
    "Field Asters," 423
    "Figure-Head, The," 587
    "Hearts-of-Gold," 534
    "In a Bye-Canal," 604
    "In a Church of Padua," 604
    "In a Garret," 605
    "In a Pauper's Turnip-
        Field," 423
    income from, 414–15, 486
    "In the Desert," 384
    invitation as, 412–13
    "Iris," 473
    on John Brown, 414
    John Marr, 568, 572–73,
        586–87
    "Lamia's Song," 604
    "L'Envoi: The Return of
        the Sire de Nesle," 607
    literary influence on, 412,
        414, 437, 604

Poems (HM) (*cont'd*)
  "Lover and the Syringa
    Bush, The," 612
  "Madam Mirror," 600
  "Montaigne and His Kit-
    ten," 573, 574
  "Naples in the Time of
    Bomba," 392, 584
  "New Ancient of Days,
    The," 564
  "New Rosicrucians, The,"
    611
  on Nile railroad, 383
  "Pontoosuce," 588
  for publication, 416–17,
    422, 486, 572–73, 585,
    586–87, 607
  on pyramids, 387
  "Rail Road Cutting near
    Alexandria in 1855, A,"
    422
  "Rammon," 600–601
  "Ravaged Villa, The,"
    602–3
  rejection of, 417, 421, 486
  "Rose Farmer, The,"
    610–11
  "Rose Window," 611
  "Rusty Man, The," 600
  Timoleon, 602–3, 607
  "Timoleon (394 B.C.)," 603
  "To the Master of the *Me-
    teor,*" 422
  turning inward in, 612
  Weeds and Wildings Chiefly,
    571, 608–12
  "When Forth the Shepherd
    Leads His Flock," 611
  "Wise Virgins," 600
"Poet, The" (Emerson), 250
Poets of America, 601–2
Polk, James K., 130, 135, 145–46
Pollard, Capt. George, 322
Polynesian islands:
  courtship behavior of, 108
  French warships and, 106
  gender boundaries blurred
    on, 109–11
  HM's writings on, *see Omoo;*
    Typee
  missionaries and, 105–6,
    107, 109, 114
  polyandry of, 108
  sexual freedom of, 109
  tribes of, 107, 110–11
  unspoiled, 135
  see also Marquesas

Pontiac, Chief, 81
"Poor Man's Pudding and
  Rich Man's Crumbs,"
  222, 247, 341–42, 485
Porter, Capt. David, 107, 136,
  339, 453
Post, Dr. Wright, 18
Potter, Col. Henry L., 500
Potter, Israel R., 215, 344
Pound, Ezra, 439
Powell, Thomas, 236–37
Powers, Hiram, 395, 459,
  483
Prosser, Gabriel, 351
Pullan, Mrs., cooking
  metaphors from, 342
Putnam, George Palmer, 137,
  344
Putnam, G. P., & Company:
  and *Clarel,* 535, 553
  and *Israel Potter,* 345
Putnam's Magazine, 327
  authors for, 330
  and Dana, 352
  HM's stories in, 330–36,
    337–39, 344, 348, 350,
    357–58
  income from, 330, 348
  readers of, 330, 344
  retrospective of HM's ca-
    reer in, 402
  sale of, 348, 358, 569

Quackenboss, Catherine, *see*
  Melvill, Catherine
  Quackenboss
Quackenboss, Henry, 4, 367
Quincy, Edmund, 159

Rabelais, François, 173, 240
Railroads:
  across Panama, 421
  along the Nile, 383, 422
  in Berkshire County, 243
  and cotton trade, 332
  and Crédit Mobilier, 524
  development of, 54, 80–81
  and eminent domain, 81,
    542
  HM's poem about, 383,
    422
  strikes and, 558
Randall, Robert, 519
Rankin, Col. George Camp-
  bell, 375
Ray, Benjamin, 418–19, 420
Raymond, Juliette, 432

Rebellion Record, The, 442–43,
  484, 486
Redburn (HM):
  advance for, 198
  characters in, 73
  dedication of, 209
  and HM's father's death,
    55
  and HM's first voyage, 76
  income from, 214, 223, 561
  life reflected in, 206, 208
  as literary joke, 208
  narrative of, 201–7
  reviews of, 221, 228
  sea life in, 74–75, 77
  and slave trade, 76, 203
  and trip to Liverpool, 73
  writing of, 200–201
Red Rover, The (Cooper), 84,
  237
Reed, Luman, 43–44, 158
Reeve, Tapping, 5
"Refugee, The" (*Israel Potter*),
  481
Religion:
  and archaeology, 540
  Buddhism, 600, 605–6
  Calvinism, 252, 266, 356
  vs. capitalism, 505
  and colonialism, 368
  communities of, 83, 242
  and death, 51–52, 612–13
  Eastern thought and, 356,
    384–85, 397, 572
  and fads, 133, 475, 541–42
  and God as parent, 603
  and Holy Land, 388–91,
    399, 540
  as insurance, 346
  and poetry, 45, 611
  and science, 346, 539, 540
  and sexuality, 284, 286
  Shakers, 242
  and skepticism, 32, 204,
    385, 388, 389
  and spirituality, 132, 356,
    542, 571–72
  state separated from, 541
  Unitarianism, 356
  and war, 475
Remington, Philo, 556
Renan, Joseph Ernest, 539
Reni, Guido, 393
Restell, Madame, 459
Reviews (HM):
  California and Oregon Trail,
    186

Reviews (HM) (*cont'd*)
  Etchings, 154, 240
  Mosses from an Old Manse,
    247, 248, 249–50, 251,
    252–53, 255, 269, 292
  Red Rover, 237
  Sailor's Life, 154
  Sea Lions, 186
Reynolds, Jeremiah N., 102,
  241
Reynolds, Joshua, 527
Rime of the Ancient Mariner,
  The (Coleridge), 99
Ringbolt, Captain, 154
Ripley, George, 143, 192, 235,
  290, 310, 330
Roberts, Benjamin, 353–54
Robertson, Eugene, 31
Robertson, James, 322
Rock, John, 480
Rockefeller, John D., 523
Rockwell, Julius, 259, 329,
  428, 452
Rogers, Samuel, 219, 230, 231
Roosevelt, Franklin D., 349
Roosevelt, Theodore, 459
Roscoe, William, 75
Rosetta stone, 45
Rousse, Anna, 394
Rousse, Peter, 393–94
Rousseau, Jean-Jacques, 109
Rubaiyat of Omar Khayyam,
  The, 607, 610
Ruffin, Edmund, 499
Ruskin, John, 221
Russ, Herman Melville, 411
Russ, Oliver, 118–19, 411
Russell, Ida, 160
Russell, Mary, 88
Russell, W. Clark, 576, 586,
  587, 601

Sailing vessels:
  beauty of, 87
  HM as cabin boy on, 73–74
  language of, 74, 87
  life aboard, 73–75
  replaced by steamships, 94
  trade and, 87–88
  as undemocratic, 71, 123
  see also Sea voyages
Sailors:
  scrimshaw carved by, 98,
    100
  superstitions of, 120
Sailor's Life and Sailor's Yarns
  (Ringbolt), 154

Sailors' Snug Harbor:
  family visits to, 521, 522,
    529, 533, 561, 562
  HM's visits to, 560, 568
  and T. Melville, 88, 519–22,
    529
Saint-Gaudens, Augustus, 459
St. Lawrence, HM as cabin
  boy on, 71, 73–75, 77
St. Leger, Barry, 4
Saladin, 384
Salt, Henry S., 575
Saltus, Edgar Evertson, 573
Sambo (slave), 3, 364
Sanborn, Franklyn G.,
  553–54
Sand, George, 325
Sandwich Islands:
  civilization vs. savages on,
    116, 134, 135
  consulate to, 328
  HM in, 115–16
  missionaries on, 115–16
  riots on, 116
  wood taken from, 332
Sanford, Edward, 558
San Francisco, HM's trip to,
  415–21
Saroni, 193, 234
Saturday Evening Post, Typee
  parodied in, 142
Saturday Review, The, 402
Saunders, Frederick, 152
Savage, Samuel Hay, 179,
  276, 327, 371–72
Savannah, 433–34
Scarlet Letter, The
  (Hawthorne):
  and "Hawthorne and His
    Mosses," 252–53
  influence of, 252–53, 310
  as romance, 240, 255, 300,
    310, 311
  success of, 243, 250
  tragedy of, 270
Schiller, Johann Christoph
  Friedrich von, 300, 385,
  565
Schirmer, Gustav, 534
Schopenhauer, Arthur,
  571–72, 604, 605–6
Schuyler, Louisa Lee, 524
Scott, Dred, 406
Scott, Sir Walter, 376
Scott, Gen. Winfield, 182
Scribner, Charles, 417
Scrimshaw, 98, 100

Scudder, Horace, 602
Seafaring, as career, 89
Sea Lions, The (Cooper), 186
Sealts, Merton M. Jr., 594
Seaman's Bethel, 92
Sea voyages:
  albatross sighted, 99
  corposants sighted, 219
  as escape, 88, 415
  and health, 372, 373, 415,
    421
  HM to Bermuda, 583
  HM to England and Eu-
    rope, 217–21
  HM to Europe and Near
    East, 375–99
  HM to Liverpool, 70–71,
    73–75
  HM to San Francisco,
    415–21
  HM to South Seas, 105–16
  and self-discovery, 127
  see also Sailing vessels
Sedgwick, Catharine Maria,
  121, 268, 289, 504
  as author, 60, 178
  influence of, 246–47
  success of, 60, 250
  and women's auxiliary, 433
Sedgwick, Charles, 246, 264,
  288–89, 446
Sedgwick, Elizabeth, 60, 246,
  289, 446
Sedgwick, Harry, 244, 245
Sedgwick, William Dwight,
  446
"Self-Reliance" (Emerson),
  187
Selfridge, Adm. Thomas O.
  Jr., 235
Selfridge, Thomas O. Sr., 235
Self Teacher, 62
Selkirk, Alexander, 100
Seminoles, 81, 365
Seneca, 185
Seneca Falls Convention, 523
Severn, Joseph, 393
Seward, William H., 260, 426
Sewell, Elizabeth, 300
Seymour, Horatio, 421, 462
Shaker settlements, visits to,
  242, 247, 249, 276, 321,
  452
Shakespeare, William,
  185–86, 240
  and American literary cul-
    ture, 249–50, 296

Shakespeare, William (*cont'd*)
  and Astor Place Riot,
    195–96
  Hawthorne compared with,
    246, 249–50, 252, 255
  influence of, 300, 304, 483,
    488, 590
  and King James Bible, 368
  language of, 186, 304
Shaw, Elizabeth Knapp,
    150–54
  birth of, 24
  childhood of, 38
  debut of, 129
  engagement of, 155–56,
    158–59, 162
  and Hope, 37, 153, 162,
    272, 325, 451, 521
  and Maria, 159
  and Nourse family, 46
  schooling of, 38, 153
  visiting with Melvilles,
    151–53
  see also Melville, Elizabeth
    Shaw
Shaw, Hope Savage, 443
  death of, 563
  and grandchildren, 357
  and Lizzie, 37, 153, 162,
    272, 325, 451, 521
  marriage of, 37, 153
Shaw, John, 153
Shaw, Lemuel, 340
  and Burns case, 351
  and eminent domain, 81,
    542
  and family visits, 260
  first wife of, 24
  as grandfather, 258–59, 357
  and HM's career, 327–28,
    427
  and HM's travel, 214, 372,
    415
  illness and death of, 429–30
  and Lizzie, 153, 155–56
  and Lizzie's finances, 159,
    328, 371, 436
  and Mass. Supreme Court,
    43, 80–81, 246
  and Melvill[e] family, 7, 23,
    57–58, 91, 155
  money lent by, 257, 296,
    372, 413
  on Nantucket, 321–23
  and public utility concept,
    81
  and real estate, 7

second marriage of, 37, 153
  and Selfridge, 235
  and Sims trial, 282–83
  and slavery, 22, 128–30,
    259, 260, 281, 282–83,
    351–52, 353–54
  Typee dedicated to, 137–38
Shaw, Lemuel Jr., 153, 554
  death of, 568, 573
  and HM's job, 403
  and HM's reputation, 303
  as youth, 162, 170–71
Shaw, Oakes, 325, 450, 521,
    531
Shaw, Col. Robert Gould,
    464–65, 469
Shaw, Samuel, 153, 162, 232
  and HM's funeral, 613
  and Lizzie's "case," 505–8
  and Malcolm's death, 513,
    514, 516
  visits with HM, 276, 394,
    413, 446
Shaw, Susannah, 24
Shelley, Mary, 300
Shepherd, Daniel, 371, 412
Sheridan, Gen. Philip, 476
Sherman, Gen. William
    Tecumseh, 479, 490–91
Sholes, Christopher B., 556
Short pieces (HM):
  agricultural report, 242
  "Apple-Tree Table, The,"
    356, 542
  "Authentic Anecdotes of
    'Old Zack'," 160–61
  "Bartleby the Scrivener: a
    Story of Wall Street,"
    330, 332–36, 357, 593
  "Bell-Tower, The," 352, 357
  "Benito Cereno," 349–52,
    357, 426, 464, 593, 595
  vs. books, 329
  "Burgundy Club sketches,"
    584
  "Cock-a-Doodle-Doo! or
    the Crowing of the No-
    ble Cock Beneventano,"
    330, 331–32
  collections of, 357–58
  "Death Craft, The," 77–78
  "Encantadas, The,"
    337–38, 339, 357
  "Fiddler, The," 330, 331
  "Fragments from a Writing
    Desk," 67–68, 78
  "'Gees, The," 346–47, 426

"Happy Failure: A Story of
    the River Hudson," 330,
    331
  for *Harper's,* 329–36
  "Hawthorne and His
    Mosses," 249–50, 251,
    252–53, 292
  heroes of, 336
  "Hood's Isle and the Her-
    mit Oberlus," 339
  "I and My Chimney,"
    352–55, 609
  income from, 78, 330, 358
  interpretations of, 330
  "Jimmy Rose," 346
  John Marr, 568, 572–73,
    586–87, 603
  "Lightning-Rod Man, The,"
    346, 357
  literary sources for, 342
  "New Planet," 322
  "Norfolk Isle and the Chola
    Widow," 338–39
  "Paradise of Bachelors and
    the Tartarus of Maids,"
    342–44
  "Piazza, The," 358
  Piazza Tales, 357–58
  "Poor Man's Pudding and
    Rich Man's Crumbs,"
    222, 247, 341–42, 485
  "Two Temples, The," 344
  for wider audiences, 251
Siddons, Sarah, 184
Simms, William Gilmore, 142
Sims, Thomas, 282–83
Slavery, 17, 22
  abolition of, 441, 468
  and "Bell-Tower," 352
  and "Benito Cereno,"
    350–51
  and civil disobedience, 351
  and *Confidence-Man,* 364
  and corruption, 462
  and cotton trade, 405
  and *Creole,* 128
  and Cuba, 354–55
  and emancipation, 447, 448
  and Founding Fathers, 364
  and Fourteenth Amend-
    ment, 499–500
  and free blacks, 421, 447,
    448
  and Fugitive Slave Law,
    128, 259, 282–83, 351
  and Great Compromise,
    259, 260, 281

Slavery, (cont'd)
  HM's views on, 493–94, 495
  and "I and My Chimney,"
    353
  and Kansas-Nebraska Act,
    405
  legal, marriage as, 506
  and Lincoln, 415
  and Mardi, 143
  and Moby-Dick, 282–84
  as moral issue, 260
  and patronage, 493–94
  as political issue, 181,
    259–60, 353
  and Redburn, 76, 203
  and Shaw, 22, 128–30, 259,
    260, 281, 282–83,
    351–52, 353–54
  and symbolism, 355
  and Thirteenth Amend-
    ment, 480
  wage, 332, 343–44
  see also Abolitionists
Slaves:
  and colonialism, 116
  factory workers, 332,
    343–44
  in HM's family, 3, 364
  in Potter's Field, 17
  as property, 128, 364
  rebellions by, 351
  Dred Scott, 406
Small, Elisha, 121
Smirne, 390
Smith, Adam, 76, 203, 368
Smith, Capt. Caleb, 242
Smith, David, 100
Smith, Lt. H. D., 585
Smith, Capt. John, 92
Smith, Joseph Edward
    Adams:
  as abolitionist, 260, 353
  and Civil War, 445–46
  as editor, 326
  HM's friendship with, 258,
    574
  and HM's writings, 339
Smith, Matthew Hale, 524–25
Smythe, Henry A., 397, 497,
    502
Snug Harbor, see Sailors'
    Snug Harbor
Social Darwinism, 541–42,
    569
Somers case, 120–22, 469
  and Billy Budd, 122, 123,
    585

and Guert, 121–22, 123,
    124, 585
Sons of Liberty, 2–3
Soulé, Pierre, 354–55
South:
  Confederacy, 425, 430, 431
  and cotton trade, 421
  economy of, 451, 480, 484,
    542
  Ku Klux Klan, 542, 558
  northern investments in,
    405, 421–22, 425
  prisons in, 479–80
  punitive measures against,
    499
  and Reconstruction, 491,
    493, 494, 496, 542
  secession of, 421, 423
  and slavery, see Slavery
Southampton, 217–21
Souther, Helen Melville, 465,
    466
Southey, Robert, 588
South Sea islands, see Polyne-
    sian islands
Spencer, Herbert, 541, 569
Spencer, Philip, 121, 585
Spenser, Edmund, 173
Spoon River Anthology (Mas-
    ters), 490
Stael, Madame de, 300
Stanhope, Philip Dormer,
    Lord Chesterfield, 67–68
Stanton, Edwin, 435, 468
Stanton, Elizabeth Cady:
  and draft riots, 461
  and lyceum movement, 407
  and women's rights, 182,
    506, 523, 556
Stanton, Henry, 461
Staten Island, Sailors' Snug
    Harbor, 519–20, 522
Steamships, 94
Stedman, Arthur, 353, 602,
    613
Stedman, Edmund Clarence,
    417, 460, 553, 601–2
Sterne, Laurence, 240
Stevens, Henry, 227
Stevenson, Robert Louis, 581
Stewart, Alexander, 43, 459
Stewart, Charles S., 107,
    135–36
Stewart, Tertullus D., 271,
    348, 355
Stoddard, Charles Warren,
    536, 581, 618

Stoddard, Richard Henry,
    501, 554, 587
Stone, Lucy, 407
Stowe, Calvin, 618, 619
Stowe, Harriet Beecher, 178,
    250, 319, 481
Strauss, David Friedrich,
    390–91, 539
Street, Alfred, 326
Strong, George Templeton:
  and Civil War, 435, 446,
    460
  and draft riots, 461–62
  on Lincoln, 426
  and secession, 422
  on Tweed, 524
  on Washington, D.C., 429
Stuart, Gilbert, 4
Sue, Eugène, 300, 325
Sullivan, Ellen, 187
Sully, Thomas, 38, 169
Sumner, Charles, 160, 182
  as abolitionist, 353, 428
  and HM's job, 468
  and Somers case, 121
  and Thirteenth Amend-
    ment, 480
Sumner, William Graham,
    541
Swan, Otis, 7
Swift, Jonathan, 173
Sykes District School, 62–63

Tahiti:
  British authorities in,
    112–13
  and civilization, 113, 116,
    135
  Lucy Ann in, 112–14
  United States in, 120
Taitt, Capt. Robert, 379
Tappan, Caroline Sturgis, 292
Tappan, William Aspinwall,
    247
Tarnmoor, Salvator R.
    (pseud.), 337
Taylor, Bayard:
  as author, 330, 376
  and camel, 566
  as lecturer, 407, 408, 413,
    414
  and Travellers, 480–81
Taylor, Benjamin Rush, 470
Taylor, Franklin, 218, 220
Taylor, Jeremy, 521–22
Taylor, John O., 62, 63
Taylor, Zachary, 160–61

Temple, Lewis, 97
Tenniel, John, 231
Tennyson, Alfred, 486, 554
Tetractys Club, 147–48
Texas, annexation of, 135, 145–46
Thackeray, William Make-peace, 329, 330
Thayer, Millie Van Rensselaer, 137, 159–60
Thayer, Nathaniel, 137
Theophilus Chase, 179
Thomas, Eleanor M.:
  birth of, 566
  and family papers, 579, 593
  HM as grandfather of, 562, 566, 568, 578–81
Thomas, Frances Cuthbert "Fanny," 583
  birth of, 568
  HM as grandfather of, 579–80, 584
  and HM's papers, 593
Thomas, Frances Melville "Fanny," 577
  children of, 566, 568, 578, 606
  wedding of, 565
  see also Melville, Frances
Thomas, Henry B., 561–63, 565, 566
Thomas, Katherine Gansevoort, 606
Thompson, William, 361–62
Thomson, James, 575
Thoreau, Henry David, 63, 80, 141, 267
  and John Brown, 414
  and Eastern thought, 45
  and *Putnam's,* 330
  and "Resistance to Civil Government," 247
  and slavery, 260
  and *Typee,* 143
  and *Walden,* 241, 356, 489
Thouars, Adm. Du Petit, 106
"Thought on Book-Binding, A" (HM), 237
Thumb, Tom, 161–62, 460
Thurston, Elizabeth, 455
Thurston, Henry, 431, 442
Ticknor, George, 523
Ticknor, William D., 198, 474
Ticknor & Fields, 198, 243, 323
Tilden, Samuel J., 558
Timoleon (HM), 602–3, 607

Tocqueville, Alexis de, 12, 364–65
Todd, Rev. John, 284
Toft, Peter, 576
Toussaint L'Ouverture, 351
Townsend, Samuel P., 459
Transcendentalists:
  and Brook Farm, 310
  and Eastern thought, 45
  and Emerson, 183
  and Hawthorne, 252, 267
  and spiritual friendships, 268
  and *Typee,* 143
"Travellers, The," 480–81
Trinidad, 583
Trollope, Frances, 14, 38, 39
Troy, John B., 112, 114, 115
Tuckerman, Henry T., 422
Tudor, Frederic, 88
Tupper, Martin Farquhar, 552
Turner, J.M.W., 221, 231, 234, 241, 398, 439
Turner, Nat, 351
Turner, Rachel, 473
Twain, Mark, 442
  and Civil War, 492
  and *Confidence-Man,* 369
  and New York City, 524, 537, 542–43
  and same-sex friends, 619
  writings of, 557, 570
Tweed, William Marcy "Boss," 243, 524, 542–43
Twice-Told Tales (Hawthorne), 263
Twitchell, Asa W., HM's portrait by, 72, 155
Two Years Before the Mast (Dana), 73–74, 84, 99
Tyler, John, 124
Tyler, Gen. Robert O., 472
Typee: A Peep at Polynesian Life (HM), 135–45
  bowdlerization of, 136, 138, 145, 149, 620
  and civilization vs. savages, 141
  and colonialism, 144–45
  dedication of, 137–38
  income from, 155, 157
  life reflected in, 107–8, 111
  and Marquesas, 106, 107–8, 110, 141
  and mutiny against injustice, 141–42
  mythic power of, 142

narrative of, 138–41
and paradise, 111
promotion of, 142
publication of, 136, 137–38
reviews of, 142–44, 147–49
sequel to, 148–49; *see also* *Omoo*
sources for, 136
as travel narrative, 135–36, 142
and truth, 143–44, 147–49, 180
writing of, 135–37

Uncle Tom's Cabin (Stowe), 75, 178
Union League Club, 458, 464, 466–67
United States:
  American dream, 43, 523
  Civil War, *see* Civil War
  Compromise of 1850, 259, 260, 281
  Compromise of 1877, 558
  expansion in, 20, 134–35
  French and Indian Wars, 2, 368
  Kansas-Nebraska Act, 405
  labor unions in, 523–24
  literary culture in, 243, 246, 249–51, 296
  and manifest destiny, 135, 145–46
  and Marquesas, 107
  Mexican War, 145–46, 332, 355
  moral anarchy in, 540
  newspapers in, 82
  nineteenth century in, *see* Nineteenth century
  Ostend Manifesto, 345, 355
  panic of 1837, 61–62, 135, 332–33
  panic of 1857, 94
  postwar corruption in, 542–43
  Revolution, 2, 3–4, 345–46
  slavery as issue in, 181
  spoils system in, 41, 130
  Thirteenth Amendment, 480
  and utopianism, 540–41
  War of 1812, 2, 3, 19, 23
  western states, 81, 405

United States, USS:
in Boston, 124
in Civil War, 438–39
daily drill of, 117
death on, 120
as floating hell, 123
HM discharged from, 129
HM's cruise on, 117–24
library of, 118
life on, 119–20
regulations of, 117
route of, 120, 122
and *White-Jacket,* 123,
124–25
see also Navy, U.S.

Van Buren, James, 328
Van Buren, Martin, 41, 82,
90, 130, 365
Vanderbilt, Cornelius, 501,
542, 570
Vanderbilt, Mrs. Cornelius,
570
Vanderbilt Steamship
Company, 421
Vanderlyn, John, 158
Van Loon, Charles, 64
Van Rensselaer, Kiliaen, 305
Van Rensselaer, Stephen, 130
Van Schaick, Augustus, 159
Vasari, Giorgio, 414
Vaux, Calvert, 525
Vedder, Elihu, 494–95, 607
Ventom, Captain, 112
Verrazano, Giovanni da, 1
Vesey, Denmark, 351
Viaud, Louis-Marie-Julien,
581
Victoria, Queen of England,
181, 227
Vincennes, 90, 107
Virginia, 439
"Virginian, The" (pseud.),
249, 255
von Langsdorff, Georg H.,
40, 136

Walden (Thoreau), 241, 356,
489
Walker, William, 362, 405
Walsh, Alexander, 65
Walsh, Mike, 131
Ward, Artemus, 619
Ward, Capt. James, 433
Warner, Everett S., 613
Warner, Susan Bogert, 250
War of 1812, 2, 3, 19, 23

Warrington, Lewis, 12
Washington, D.C.:
Capitol dome, 429, 446,
471, 481
Ford's Theatre, 482
Grand Review of the
Army, 483–84
HM in, 428–29
in wartime, 469, 470
Washington, George, 1, 2, 3,
4, 364, 385
Washington Monument,
428–29
Watson, Elkanah, 23, 355
Waud, Alfred, 443
Wealth of Nations, The (Smith),
76
Weber, Max, 542
Webster, Daniel, 31
and abolition, 260, 351
and Bank of the U.S., 406
and Boston Lyceum, 407
and Bunker Hill Monu-
ment, 124
and civil disobedience, 260
and T. Melvill, 23, 57
and L. Shaw, 23, 43
Webster, John, 321–22, 437
Weed, Thurlow, 428, 585
Weeds and Wildings Chiefly
(HM), 571, 608–12
West, Charles E., 60
Whale, The, see Moby-Dick
Whales:
ambergris from, 93, 99
baleen, 93
and Barnum, 555
blubber of, 92–93
diving, 96
harpooning of, 96–97
hunt for, 96
ivory from, 92
killing of, 97–98, 287–88
and *Moby-Dick,* 262, 279,
281, 284, 287–88
myths and fables about, 96,
102–3, 262
and Nantucket sleigh rides,
97
oil from, 92, 99
and pitchpoling, 97–98
processing of, 98–99
reality mirrored in, 280–82
and sharks, 98
ships rammed by, 102, 241,
289, 322
sperm, 92–93, 99, 102, 241

spermaceti from, 98
teeth of, 98, 100
whalebone products, 93
Whaling ships:
in Civil War, 438
as escape, 88–89
gams of, 101–2
golden age of, 93–94
hazards on, 92
and jumping ship, 95–96
lack of freedom on, 95
letters from, 102
life on, 88, 94–96
of New England, 92–94, 96
oil processed on, 93
profit-sharing on, 91
shipmates on, 89, 95
stamps of, 86
whaleboats on, 96
wives on, 88
White, Richard Grant, 501
White, Stanford, 459
White-Jacket (HM), 103
advance for, 213–14, 223,
241
characters in, 118, 123
and flogging, 120, 123, 210,
234, 235
HM's trip to London for,
213–15, 222–26
income from, 230, 561
life reflected in, 209
narrative of, 209–14
and navy, 123, 129, 209,
215, 234, 235–36
publication of, 233, 234
reviews of, 233–35, 240
and *United States* voyage,
123, 124–25
writing of, 209
Whitman, Walt, 567, 574
and Civil War, 430, 438,
467, 480
and Eastern thought, 45,
384, 397
HM's influence on, 187
HM's works reviewed by,
143, 156–57
and Indian Affairs, 501
language of, 285–86, 553
Leaves of Grass, 166, 250,
286, 608
on Lincoln, 426–27
male lover of, 618
on New York, 166, 459–60,
462–63
as nurse, 438, 467

Whitman, Walt, (cont'd)
  at Pfaff's, 236
  poems by, 38, 111, 487
  and slavery, 354
  style of, 339
  as teacher, 63
Whitten, Mary, 2, 368
Whittier, John Greenleaf,
  448, 554
Wilde, Oscar, 569, 618
Wiley, John, 149, 152
Wiley & Putnam:
  and Hawthorne, 143–44,
  243
  Library of America, 243
  Library of Choice Reading,
  147
  and Typee, 137, 142, 147,
  157
Wilkes, Charles, 90, 240
Wilkes Expedition, 90–91
Willard, Henry, 375
Williams, Theodore Chickering, 572, 613
Willis, George, 413
Willis, Nathaniel Parker, 142,
  192, 235, 237, 253, 397
Wilmot, David, 181
Wilmot Proviso, 181
Winthrop, John, 524, 540–41
Women:
  and antislavery issue,
  181–82
  and childbearing, 191
  Christian image of, 190
  clothing of, 438, 475–76
  and divorce, 184, 507–9
  and duty, 508–9
  as factory workers, 63,
  343–44, 460
  as hired wet nurses, 460
  as HM's audience, 137, 172,
  286–87, 295, 299
  in HM's writings, 68, 78,
  107, 588
  letter-writing as duty of, 6,
  132
  of Nantucket, 322
  and polyandry, 108
  Polynesian, 108, 115
  and property, 54, 506–7
  rights of, 182, 506–7, 523,
  556
  roles of, 5, 63, 69, 266, 285,
  306–7, 311, 508
  and same-sex friendships,
  268, 285, 619

  in Sandwich Islands, 115
  and science, 322–23
  social lives of, 196
  and spousal abuse, 505–8
  and spring cleaning, 266
  and war, 432–33, 438, 451,
  460
  whalebone corsets of, 93
  on whaling ships, 88
  and "widows' walks," 323
  and "womanly arts," 5–6
  as writers, 199, 250, 296,
  300, 344
Women's Central Relief Association, 432
Wonder-Book, A (Hawthorne),
  292
Wood, Fernando, 404–5,
  421–22, 431, 467
Woodhull, Victoria, 543
Woodlawn Cemetery, 613
Woolsey, Harriet, 467
Wordsworth, William, 523,
  548, 559
World Anti-Slavery Convention, 181–82
Writing:
  and anonymity, 329
  artistic influences on,
  225
  and burnout, 300
  and changing the world,
  134–35, 178–79, 486,
  492–95, 569
  and copyright, see Copyright
  as creation, 132, 179, 190,
  239, 261–62
  debt from, 197, 198, 371,
  403
  as duty, 132
  as escape, 125, 171, 237,
  294–95, 535
  exploration and, 296
  and fame, 271–72
  family's urging HM to quit,
  326, 327, 349, 401, 416
  as healing, 177, 312
  income from, 148, 149, 155,
  157–58, 172, 198, 199,
  239, 250
  ingathering that precedes,
  232, 357
  letdown after, 186–87,
  558
  and making a living, 199,
  250

  and marketplace, 149,
  296–97, 335, 344
  by men, 250–51, 296–97
  as misunderstood, 187, 192,
  303, 402
  for money, 215, 300, 302, 327
  and mutiny against injustice, 141–42, 282–84
  as necessity of spirit, 296,
  300, 327, 329, 528, 554
  of novels, 240, 300
  and political opinions, 134,
  348, 352, 354–55, 464,
  492–95
  and power, 132
  and publishing, 197–200,
  344
  reinvention of self in, 600
  relief from, 258, 271, 321
  and reputation, 303, 326,
  358, 599, 614
  self-disclosure in, 255, 270,
  604, 609–12
  and self-discovery, 171, 191,
  208, 248
  and sexual sublimation,
  191, 285, 311
  speed of, 158, 179, 200–201,
  214, 239, 251, 262, 300,
  302, 327, 569
  stress of, 371, 372, 534–35
  tales told in, 134
  traditional forms of, 240,
  250, 293, 296, 303, 318
  of travel narratives, 135–36,
  142, 148, 158, 200, 237,
  272, 481, 575
  and truth, 132, 143–44,
  147–49, 172, 178, 180,
  193, 200, 271–72
  and wildness, 187, 193
  by women, 199, 250, 296,
  300, 344
  see also specific works

Yankee Doodle, 160, 161, 329
Yates, Caroline, 20
Yeats, William Butler, 335,
  596
Yokohama, 522
Yonge, Charlotte Mary, 485
Young, Alexander, 162
Young Man's Own Book, The
  (W. Alcott), 70
Young Men's Association, 63

Zoological Science (Maltbie), 67